Contents

From the Editor — 3
Section Index — 4
Advertisers' Index — 352

Record Companies
International Hqs — 5
Record Companies & Labels — 5
DVD Companies — 51

Publishers
Publishers & Affiliates — 53
Sheet Music Suppliers — 85
Production Music — 86
Music Supervisors & Consultants — 90

Retail
Retailers — 93
Retail Services — 101
Mail Order Companies — 102

Digital
Music Portals & Online Magazines — 105
Download & Mail Order Websites — 109
Online Delivery & Distribution — 111
Mobile Delivery & Distribution — 113
Web Design & Digital Services — 116

Design, Pressing & Distribution
Pressers & Duplicators — 121
Mastering & Post Production — 125
Printers & Packaging — 129
Art & Creative Studios — 134
Merchandise Companies — 137
Distributors — 140

Business Services
Industry Organisations — 149
Accountants — 153
Legal — 158
Insurance — 165
Financial Advisors — 166
Artist Management — 166
Recruitment Agencies — 191
Event Management — 191
Conferences & Exhibitions — 193
Awards & Memorabilia — 194
Business Consultants — 194

Education
Computer Services — 202
Business Services & Miscellaneous — 202

Media
Print Media — 205
Radio — 212
Digital & Internet Radio — 226
Television — 227
Broadcast Services — 230
Advertising Agencies — 232
Video Production — 235
Video Production Services — 238
Choreography & Styling Services — 238
Media Miscellaneous — 239

Press & Promotion
Promoters & Pluggers — 241
PR Companies — 249
Photographers & Agencies — 264

Live
Booking Agents — 269
Concert Promoters — 275
Club Promoters — 278
Concert Hire — 278
Venues — 283
Festivals — 309
Ticketing Services — 310
Touring & Stage Services — 310
Travel & Transport Services — 313
Tour Miscellaneous — 315

Recording Studios & Services
Recording Studios — 317
Mobile Studios — 330
Producers & Producer Management — 331
Rehearsal Studios — 343
Session Fixers — 345
Studio Equipment Hire & Sales — 346
Studio Equipment Manufacture & Distribution — 347
Studio Design & Construction — 351
Studio Miscellaneous — 351

The Comprehensive Guide to The UK Music Industry and Associated Service Companies

Published annually: Number 42
ISSN: 0267-3290
ISBN: 9780862132040

Database, design and production

Fellows Media Ltd
The Gallery, Manor Farm,
Southam, Cheltenham,
Gloucestershire GL52 3PB
t 01242 259241
e media@fellowsmedia.com
w www.fellowsmedia.com

Editor: Paul Williams
Digital Content Manager: Tim Frost

Group Sales Manager: Steve Connolly
e sconnolly@cmpi.biz
Advertising Manager: Paul Reynolds

Music Week Website:
www.musicweek.com

Group Circulation/Marketing Manager:
David Pagendam
t 020 7921 8320
f 020 7921 8404
e dpagendam@cmpi.biz

Publishing Director: Joe Hosken

Published by Music Week
United Business Media
8th Floor
Ludgate House
245 Blackfriars Road
London SE1 9UR

**Additional copies are
available by contacting:**
Tower Publishing Services **t** 01858 438893
UK & Northern Ireland - **£40**
Europe & Eire - **£45**
Rest of World 1 - **£50** Rest of World 2 - **£60**
Cheques should be made payable to
UBM Information Ltd

All material copyright © Music Week 2010

From the Editor

Welcome to the latest Music Week Directory.

At first glance, what you have in your hands right now may simply be regarded as a series of A to Z listings of names, addresses, phone numbers and the like, neatly divided into different sections across more than 300 pages. But what this directory equally represents is a gateway into every corner of the UK music industry, an invaluable tool whether you have been in the business for years, have newly or recently arrived, are looking to get in or are simply a casual observer. It really is no exaggeration to say that this book can take you to some very exciting places.

During my time at Music Week – and that now takes in quite a high pile of MW Directories – I have had countless conversations with industry executives saying they used the directory to try to make their way into the business. It worked, for example, for Lucian Grainge whose diligent efforts to work his way through the entries in the directory three decades ago led him to a first industry job, an appointment that eventually took him to become chairman and CEO of Universal Music Group International.

This directory is also a handy barometer of where the UK music industry is and where it might be going. Twelve months in this business can feel like a decade these days, so since last year's directory there will be some company names and individuals that have departed these pages, but there have been others arriving, too. Some sectors become more prominent year after year, others less so, all reflected by the make-up of this book, which, as ever, covers everything from record companies, music publishers, retailers and venues to the likes of financial advisors and travel and transport services. If you want to know about the UK music industry, there really is something for everyone here.

Kind regards

Paul Williams
Editor, Music Week

Section Index

Accountants	153	Photographers & Agencies	264
Advertising Agencies	232	PR Companies	249
Art & Creative Studios	134	Pressers & Duplicators	121
Artist Management	166	Print Media	205
Awards & Memorabilia	194	Printers & Packaging	129
Booking Agents	269	Producers & Producer Management	331
Broadcast Services	230	Production Music	86
Business Consultants	194	Promoters & Pluggers	241
Business Services & Miscellaneous	202	Publishers & Affiliates	53
Choreography & Styling Services	238	Radio	212
Club Promoters	278	Record Companies & Labels	5
Computer Services	202	Recording Studios	317
Concert Hire	278	Recruitment Agencies	191
Concert Promoters	275	Rehearsal Studios	343
Conferences & Exhibitions	193	Retail Services	101
Digital & Internet Radio	226	Retailers	93
Distributors	140	Session Fixers	345
Download & Mail Order Websites	109	Sheet Music Suppliers	85
DVD Companies	51	Studio Design & Construction	351
Education	197	Studio Equipment Hire & Sales	346
Event Management	191	Studio Equipment Manufacture	
Festivals	309	& Distribution	347
Financial Advisors	166	Studio Miscellaneous	351
Industry Organisations	149	Television	227
Insurance	165	Ticketing Services	310
International Hqs	5	Tour Miscellaneous	315
Legal	158	Touring & Stage Services	310
Mail Order Companies	102	Travel & Transport Services	313
Mastering & Post Production	125	Venues	283
Media Miscellaneous	239	Video Production	235
Merchandise Companies	137	Video Production Services	238
Mobile Delivery & Distribution	113	Web Design & Digital Services	116
Mobile Studios	330		
Music Portals & Online Magazines	105		
Music Supervisors & Consultants	90		
Online Delivery & Distribution	111		

the music producers guild awards

The Music Producers Guild Awards take place on February 11th 2010 to celebrate the creative talent and technical ability of the UK's music producers, engineers, mixers and re-mixers.

Visit www.mpgawards.co.uk to find out more.

For information about sponsorship opportunities for the 2011 event please contact Natalie Besbrode: natalie@bubblesqueak.co.uk

For press releases, information and/or comments from the MPG board of directors, contact Sue Silitoe: sue@whitenoisepr.co.uk

headline sponsors

Contacts   Facebook  MySpace   Twitter   YouTube

Record Companies

International Hqs

DISNEY MUSIC GROUP

3 Queen Caroline St, Hammersmith, London, W6 9PE
t 020 8222 1000 **f** 020 8222 2283
e firstname.lastname@disney.com **w** disney.co.uk/music
 Executive Director, EMEA: Martin Morales.

EMI MUSIC

27 Wrights Lane, London, W8 5SW **t** 020 7795 7000
f 020 7795 7001 **e** firstname.lastname@emimusic.com
w emigroup.com Chief Executive of EMI Music &
President of New Music: Elio Leoni-Sceti. President of A&R -
UK & North America: Nick Gatfield. COO of New Music &
President of EMI Digital: Douglas Merrill. President of EMI
Catalogue: Ernesto Schmitt. President of EMI Music
Services: Ronn Werre.

SONY MUSIC ENTERTAINMENT INTERNATIONAL LTD

SONY MUSIC

9 Derry Street, London, W8 5HY **t** 020 7361 8000
f 020 7937 0188 **e** firstname.lastname@sonymusic.com
w sonymusic.com President, Europe & Africa: Kevin
Lawrie. EVP, Europe & Africa: Alan Newham. Snr Dir, Strategic
Business Development, Europe: Felix Von Waldthausen. SVP
Digital & Commercial, Europe & Africa: Ulrich Jaerkel. VP
Strategic & Catalogue Marketing, Europe & Africa: Tim
Fraser-Harding. SVP CFO, Europe & Africa: William Rowe. VP
HR, Europe & Africa: Toni Newcombe. Deputy Counsel,
International: Jonathan Sternberg. VP Global Digital
Operations: Matthew Hawn. VP International Marketing,
Europe & Africa: Ivan Malherbe.

UNIVERSAL MUSIC GROUP INTERNATIONAL

UNIVERSAL MUSIC GROUP INTERNATIONAL

364-366 Kensington High St, London, W14 8NS
t 020 7471 5000 **f** 020 7471 5001
e firstname.lastname@umusic.com **w** umusic.com
Chairman & CEO: Lucian Grainge . Executive Vice President /
CFO: Boyd Muir. Executive Vice President / President, Asia
Pacific Region: Max Hole. President, Mediterranean, South
America, Middle East / President, Universal Music
France: Pascal Negre. Senior Vice President, Human
Resources: Malcolm Swatton.

WARNER MUSIC INTERNATIONAL SERVICES LTD

WARNER MUSIC INTERNATIONAL

28 Kensington Church St, London, W8 4EP **t** 020 7368 2500
f 020 7368 2734 **e** firstname.lastname@warnermusic.com
w wmg.com CEO, Warner Music Europe & Vice-Chairman,
Warner Music International: John Reid. General Counsel: Chris
Ancliff. Chief Financial Officer: Mike Saunter. SVP,
International Marketing: Matthieu Lauriot-Prevost. SVP,
Human Resources: Maria Osherova. SVP, Commercial
Strategy - EMEA: Eric Daugan. SVP, Commercial Channels
and Consumer Marketing – EMEA: Isabel Garvey. VP,
Corporate Communications: Mel Fox.

Record Companies & Labels

2B3 Productions/Records t 020 7737 5334
f 020 7733 4449 **e** neville@2b3productions.com or
neville@2b3records.com **w** 2b3records.com
 facebook.com/neville.thomas2
 myspace.com/2b3productions
 twitter.com/2b3records youtube.com/2b3RecordsTv
 Producer: Neville Thomas.

2NV Records 1 Canada Sq,
29th Floor Canary Wharf Tower, London, E14 5DY
t 0870 220 0237 **f** 0870 220 0238 **e** info@2nvrecords.com
w 2nvrecords.com Co-MDs: Paul Boadi & Chris Nathaniel.

3 Bar Fire Arch 462, Kingsland Viaduct, 83 Rivington St,
London, EC2A 3AY **e** david@3barfire.com **w** 3barfire.com
 Label Manager: David Silverman.

Contacts Facebook MySpace Twitter YouTube

3 Beat Productions Limited 5 Slater St, Liverpool, Merseyside, L1 4BW **t** 0151 709 3355 **f** 0151 709 3707 **e** tim@3beat.co.uk **w** threebeatrecords.co.uk Label Mgr: Tim Condran.

3rd Stone Records (see Adasam Limited)

4AD 17-19 Alma Rd, London, SW18 1AA **t** 020 8870 9724 **f** 020 8877 9109 **e** 4ad@4ad.com **w** 4ad.com facebook.com/fourad myspace.com/4admusic twitter.com/4AD_Official youtube.com/user/4ADRecords MD: Simon Halliday.

4Real Records Myrtle Cottage, Rye Rd, Hawkhurst, Kent, TN18 5DW **t** 01580 754771 **f** 01580 754771 **e** scully4real@yahoo.co.uk **w** 4realrecords.com MD: Terry Scully.

4th Floor Records (see Defected Records Ltd)

7Hz Recordings 4 Margaret Street, London, W1W 8RF **t** 020 7462 1269 **f** 020 7436 5431 **e** barry@7hzrecordings.com **w** 7hzrecordings.com GM: Barry Campbell.

7Ts (see Cherry Red Records)

10 Kilo (see Tip World)

11c Recordings 1-2 St Albans Studio, South End Row, London, W8 5BT **t** 020 7993 5565 **e** office@pureuk.com **w** pureuk.com/11c CEO: Evros Stakis.

13th Hour Contact: Mute. (see Mute Records Ltd)

13th Moon Records PO Box 79, Bridgend, Mid Glamorgan, CF32 8ZR **t** 01656 872582 **f** 01656 872582 **e** liz@asf-13thmoon.demon.co.uk **w** asf-13thmoon.demon.co.uk Manager: Liz Howell.

14th Floor Records 12 Lancer Sq, London, W8 4EH **t** 020 7368 3500 **f** 020 7368 3760 **e** firstname.lastname@warnermusic.com **w** 14thfloorrecords.com MD: Christian Tattersfield.

21 SONGS LTD

TWENTY ONE SONES

5 St Johns Lane, Smithfield, London, EC1M 4BH **t** 020 7549 3568 **f** 020 7549 3569 **e** nshialsuk@21-songs.com **w** 21-songs.com CEO: Mr Norbert Shialsuk. Business Manager: Motunde Akiode. A&R Manager: Shialsuk Peter. Technical Director: Sawula Mbutakto. **21 Songs is an Independent Music Label aim at showcasing Nigerian Talent globally.**

21st Century Generation (see Plaza Records)

33 Jazz Records The Hat Factory, 65-67 Bute St, Luton, LU1 2EY **t** 01582 419584 **f** 01582 459401 **e** 33jazz@compuserve.com **w** 33jazz.com Director: Paul Jolly.

4 Zero Records 27 Arden Mhor, Pinner, Middlesex, HA5 2HR **t** 020 8868 5279 **e** dave@4zerorecords.co.uk **w** 4zerorecords.co.uk myspace.com/4zerorecords Founder: Dave Weller.

99 Degrees (see Higher State)

99 North (see Higher State)

100 Hits (see Demon Music Group)

500 Rekords PO Box 9499, London, E5 0UG **t** 020 8806 9500 **f** 020 8806 9500 **e** paul@500rekords.freeserve.co.uk w.myspace.com/500rekords MD: Paul C 07966 194346.

679 Electric Lighting Station, 46 Kensington Court, London, W8 5DA **t** 020 7938 5600 **f** 020 7368 4900 **w** blog.679artists.com MD: Nick Worthington.

852 Recordings 306 Smithfield Buildings, 44 Tib Street, Manchester, M4 1LA **t** 07790 909 896 **e** jonathan.waller@852records.com **w** 852recordings.com Director/A&R: Jonathan M Waller.

1-2-3-4 Records 27 Cowper St, London, EC2A 4AP **t** 020 7684 1126 **f** 020 7613 5917 **e** info@1234records.com **w** 1234records.com Dirs: Sean McLusky, James Mullord.

1965 RECORDS

9 Derry St, London, W8 5HY **t** 020 7361 8000 **e** info@1965records.com **w** 1965records.com Contact: James Endeacott.

The A Label (see Numinous Music Group)

A List Records Ltd 26-28 Hammersmith Grove, London, W6 7BA **t** 020 7117 6776 **f** 070 9221 6682 **e** mail@alistrecords.com **w** alistrecords.com Group Head of Music: Deon Sharma 0207 117 6776 ext 3.

A New Day Records 75 Wren Way, Farnborough, Hants, GU14 8TA **t** 01252 540 270 **f** 01252 372 001 **e** DAVIDREES1@compuserve.com **w** anewdayrecords.co.uk Editor: Dave Rees 07889 797 482.

Contacts   Facebook   MySpace   Twitter   YouTube

A&G RECORDS LTD

1st Floor, 5 Ching Court, 61-63 Monmouth Street, London, WC2H 9EY **t** 020 7845 9880 **f** 0207 845 9884 **e** rob@agrecords.co.uk **w** agrecords.co.uk 📇 Label Manager: Rob Hoile.

A&M 📇 (US SIGNED): Polydor (UK SIGNED) or Mercury. (see Polydor Records)

A3 Music PO Box 1345, Worthing, West Sussex, BN14 7FB **t** 01903 202426 **e** music@A3music.co.uk **w** A3music.co.uk 🎵 myspace.com/a3musicuk 🐦 twitter.com/a3music 📺 youtube.com/A3musicUK 📇 Secretary: Mike Pailthorpe.

Aardvark Records 65 The Terrace, Penryn, Cornwall, TR10 8RL **t** 01326 376013 **f** 01326 376707 **e** alex@aardvarkrecords.co.uk **w** aardvarkrecords.co.uk 📘 facebook.com/home.php?#/pages/Penryn-United-Kingdom/Aardvark-Records/61646399799?ref=ts 🎵 myspace.com/aardvarkrecordsuk 🐦 twitter.com/aardvarkrecords 📺 youtube.com/aardvarkrecords 📇 Managing Director: Alex di Savoia.

AB Entertainment Ltd Unit 11, 407-409 Hornsey Rd, London, N19 4DX **t** 020 7272 0358 **e** info@abentertainment.co.uk **w** abentertainment.co.uk 📇 Director: Alexander Balfour.

Abbey Records (SCS Music Ltd) PO Box 197, Beckley, Oxford, OX3 9YJ **t** 01865 358282 **e** info@scsmusic.co.uk 📇 MD: Steve C Smith.

Abeano Music (see XL Recordings)

Absolute Records Craig Gowan, Carrbridge, PH23 3AX **t** 01479 841257 **e** absolutemuse@hotmail.com **w** absoluterecords.co.uk 📘 theabsoluterecords 🎵 myspace.com/503910386 📇 absoluterecords 📺 youtube.com/theabsoluterecords 📇 MD: Sue Moss.

Absolution Records The Old Lamp Works, Rodney Pl, Merton, London, SW19 2LQ **t** 020 8540 4242 **f** 020 8540 6056 **e** simon@absolutemarketing.co.uk **w** absolutemarketing.co.uk 📇 MD: Simon Wills.

Absorb Music / Fruition PO Box 10896, Moseley, Birmingham, B13 0ZU **t** 07920 104 614 **f** 0121 247 6981 **e** rod@fruitionmusic.co.uk **w** absorbmusic.com 📇 MD: Rod Thomson.

Abstract Sounds LTD Buspace Studio, Unit 207, Conlan St, London, W10 5AP **t** 020 8968 3030 **f** 020 8968 3044 **e** abstractsounds@btclick.com **w** abstractsounds.co.uk 📇 MD: Edward Christie.

Accidental Records

Accidental Records, 2nd Floor, Hoy House, 11 Greenwich Quay, Clarence Rd, London, SE8 3EY **e** info@accidentalrecords.com **w** accidentalrecords.com 📇 Label Mgr: Joe Bentley.

Ace Eyed Records (see Blue Melon Records Ltd)

ACE RECORDS

42-50 Steele Rd, London, NW10 7AS **t** 020 8453 1311 **f** 020 8961 8725 **e** sales@acerecords.co.uk **w** acerecords.co.uk 📇 Sales & Marketing Dir: Phil Stoker.

Acid Jazz Records 146 Bethnal Green Rd, London, E2 6DG **t** 020 7613 1100 **e** info@acidjazz.co.uk **w** acidjazz.co.uk 🎵 myspace.com/acidjazzrecords 📇 Label Manager: Danny Corr.

ACL Records Studlands, Potters Bar, Hertfordshire, EN6 1LX **e** WMD644706@aol.com 📇 Contact: David Thomas.

Acorn Records 1 Tylney View, London Rd, Hook, Hants, RG27 9LJ **t** 07808 377 350 **e** acornrecords@hotmail.com **w** acorn-music.com 📇 MD: Mark Olrog.

Acoustics Records PO Box 350, Reading, Berkshire, RG6 7DQ **t** 0118 926 8615 **e** mail@AcousticsRecords.co.uk **w** AcousticsRecords.co.uk 📇 MD: HA Jones.

Acrobat Music Group LTD
3rd Floor, Monument House, 215 Marsh Road, Pinner, Middx, HA5 5NE **t** 020 8866 9900 **f** 020 8869 9847 **e** enquiries@acrobatmusic.net **w** acrobatmusic.net 📇 Contact: Warren Heal.

Action Records 46 Church St, Preston, Lancs, PR1 3DH **t** 01772 884 772 **f** 01772 252 255 **e** sales@actionrecords.co.uk **w** actionrecords.co.uk 📇 Manager: Gordon Gibson 01772 258809.

Activa (see 4Real Records)

AD Music 5 Albion Rd, Bungay, Suffolk, NR35 1LQ **t** 01986 894712 **e** admin@admusiconline.com **w** admusiconline.com 📇 Label Owner: Elaine Wright.

Adasam Limited PO Box 8, Corby, Northants, NN17 2XZ **t** 01536 202 295 **f** 01536 266 246 **e** steve@adasam.co.uk **w** adasam.co.uk 📇 Label Mgr: Steve Kalidoski.

Additive EMI House, 43 Brook Green, London, W6 7EF **t** 020 7795 7000 **f** 020 7605 5050 **e** firstname.lastname@emimusic.com **w** additiverecords.co.uk 📇 Director: Jason Ellis.

Adventure Records PO Box 261, Wallingford, Oxon, OX10 0XY **t** 01491 832 183 **e** info@adventuresin-music.com **w** adventure-records.com 📇 Label Manager: Katie Conroy.

📇 Contacts 🄵 Facebook 🄼 MySpace 🄱 Twitter 📺 YouTube

Afro Art Recordings 109 Dukes Avenue, Muswell Hill, London, N10 2QD **t** 020 8374 4412 **f** 020 8374 4410 **e** simonebeedle@afroartrecords.com **w** afroartrecords.com 📇 Director: Simone Beedle.

Afrocaribbean Asian and Pop Music Distribution Office 2, Stars Building, 10 Silverhill Close, Nottingham, Nottinghamshire, NG78 6QL **t** 01159 519 864 - 07766 945 663 **e** mgporductions@btconnect.com **w** mgmusicproductions.com 📇 07766945663: acts@african-caribbean-ents.com 01159519864.

Agency Global Enterprises Ltd 145-157 St John's Street, London, EC1V 4PY **t** 020 7043 3734 **f** 020 7043 3736 **e** info@agencyglobal.co.uk **w** agencyglobal.co.uk 📇 Dir: Nadeem Sham.

Agenda Music (see Peacefrog)

Ainm Music Unit C10, Wicklow Enterprise Pk, The Murrough, Wicklow Town, Co Wicklow, Ireland **t** +353 40 462 527 **f** +353 40 462 527 **e** fstubbs@ainm-music.com **w** ainm-music.com 📇 MD: Frank Stubbs.

Airplay Records The Sound Foundation, PO Box 4900, Earley, Berks, RG10 0GA **t** 0118 934 9600 **e** info@soundfoundation.co.uk **w** airplayrecords.co.uk 📇 Label Mgr: Hadyn Wood 07973 559 203.

Albert Productions Unit 29, Cygnus Business Centre, Dalmeyer Road, London, NW10 2XA **t** 020 8830 0330 **f** 020 8830 0220 **e** james@alberts.co.uk **w** albertmusic.co.uk 📇 Head of A&R: James Cassidy.

Alien Trax 2 Kingswood Road, London, SW2 4JF **t** 020 8671 5709 **f** 020 8671 5709 **e** info@alientrax.com **w** alientrax.com 📇 Contact: Max Alien Thing.

All Around The World 9-13 Penny St, Blackburn, Lancashire, BB1 6HJ **t** 01254 264120 **f** 01254 693768 **e** info@aatw.com **w** aatw.com 📇 GM: Matt Cadman.

Almighty Records PO Box 998, Wellesley House, Cheltenham, GL50 9FZ **t** 01242 224 444 **f** 01242 245 531 **e** info@almightyrecords.com **w** almightyrecords.com 📇 MD: Martyn Norris.

Alpha Engineering Records Ltd 6 Waterloo Park Industrial Est, Wellington Road, Bidford on Avon, Warwickshire, B50 4JG **e** alphaengine@hotmail.com **w** alphaengineeringrecords.co.uk 📇 Contact: Paul Townend.

Altarus Inc (UK Office) Warlow Farm House, Eaton Bishop, Hereford, HR2 9QF **t** 01225 852323 **f** 01225 852523 **e** sorabji-archive@lineone.net **w** altarusrecords.com 📇 UK Office Manager: Alistair Hinton.

Amalie (see Loose Tie Records)

Amazing Feet (see Rotator Studios / Interzone Management)

Amazon Records Ltd PO Box 5109, Hove, East Sussex, BN52 9EA **t** 01273 726414 **f** 01273 726414 **e** info@amazonrecords.co.uk **w** amazonrecords.co.uk 🄵 facebook.com/pages/Amazon-Records/41428516755 🄼 myspace.com/amazonrecords 🄱 twitter.com/amazonrecords 📇 MD: Frank Sansom.

Amber PO Box 1, Chipping Ongar, Essex, CM5 9HZ **t** 01277 362916 **e** management@amberartists.com **w** amberartists.com 📇 MD: Paul Tage 01277 365046.

Ambiguous Records UK London, UK **e** al@ambiguousrecords.com **w** ambiguousrecords.com 📇 Director/Label Manager: Al Mobbs 07929 742215.

Amethyst (see Rainbow Quartz Records)

Amphion (see Priory Records)

AMQ Records Ltd Utopia Village, 7 Chalcot Road, London, NW1 8LH **t** 020 7813 7964 **f** 020 7209 4092 **w** liveatthesuite.com 📇 Managing Director: Andrew.

Anagram (see Cherry Red Records)

Analogue Baroque (see Cherry Red Records)

Angel Air Records St Edmunds Offices, Broad Rd, Bacton, Stowmarket, Suffolk, IP14 4HP **t** 01449 782188 **f** 01449 782960 **e** sales@angelair.co.uk **w** angelair.co.uk 📇 MD: Peter Purnell.

Anjunabeats Fortress Studios, 34-38 Provost St, London, N1 7NG **t** 020 7608 1567 **f** 020 7253 9825 **e** info@anjunabeats.com **w** anjunabeats.com 📇 Label Manager: Soraya Sobh.

Ankst Musik Records The Old Police Station, The Square, Pentraeth, Anglesey, LL75 8AZ **t** 01248 450155 **f** 01248 450155 **e** emyr@ankst.co.uk **w** ankst.co.uk 🄼 myspace.com/ankstmusik 📇 MD: Emyr Glyn Williams.

Annie Records 39 Ivygreen Road, Chorlton, Manchester, M21 9AG **t** 0161 860 4133 **e** annie.records@ntlworld.com **w** annierecords.com 📇 CEO: Ann Louttit.

Antilles 📇 Contact: Island. (see Island Records Group)

Apace Music Ltd Unit LG3, Shepherds Building, Charecroft Way, London, W14 0EH **t** 020 7471 9270 **f** 020 7471 9383 **e** sales@apacemusic.co.uk **w** apacemusic.co.uk 📇 MD: Tim Millington.

Ape City (see Primaudial Recordings)

Apollo Sound 32 Ellerdale Rd, London, NW3 6BB **t** 020 7813 2253 **f** 020 7431 0621 **e** info@apollosound.com **w** apollosound.com 📇 MD: Toby Herschmann.

ARC Music Productions International Ltd PO Box 111, East Grinstead, West Sussex, RH19 4FZ **t** 0870 777 7272 **f** 0870 777 7273 **e** info@arcmusic.co.uk **w** arcmusic.co.uk 🄼 myspace.com/arcmusic 📇 Executive Director: Phil Collinson.

Archive Recordings Lower Grd Floor, 12 Thicket Rd, London, SE20 8DD **t** 07944 667 281 **e** archiverecordingspecial@yahoo.co.uk 📇 MD: Morris Christopher Wright.

Record Companies: Record Companies & Labels

Q Contacts   **f** Facebook   **M** MySpace   **t** Twitter   **▶** YouTube

Are We Mad? (see Ariwa Sounds Ltd)

Are We Mad? Studios 34 Whitehorse Lane, London, SE25 6RE **t** 020 8653 7744 **f** 020 8771 1911 **e** info@ariwa.com **w** ariwa.com **M** myspace.com/ariwamusic **Q** Studio Mgr: Kamal Fraser 020 8771 1470.

Arising Records 50-52 Paul St, London, EC2A 4LB **t** 020 7749 1994 **f** 020 7729 8951 **e** info@arisingartist.com **Q** Contact: Lisa DeLuca and Meredith Cork 020 749 1994.

Arista Q Contact: Arista. (see Sony Music Entertainment UK & Ireland)

Ariwa Sounds Ltd 34 Whitehorse Lane, London, SE25 6RE **t** 020 8653 7744 **f** 020 8771 1911 **e** ariwastudios@aol.com **w** ariwa.com **M** myspace.com/madprofessordub **Q** Label Manager: Holly Fraser.

Ark Records Fetcham Park House, Lower Rd, Leatherhead, Surrey, KT22 9HD **t** 01372 360300 **f** 01372 360878 **e** info@arkrecords.com **w** arkrecords.com **Q** MD: Greg Walsh.

Arlo and Betty Recordings Ltd Covetous Corner, Hudnall Common, LittLe Gaddesden, Hertfordshire, HP4 1QW **t** 01442 842 851 **e** christian.ulf@virgin.net **Q** Contact: Christian Ulf-Hansen.

Arriba Records 156-158 Gray's Inn Road, London, WC1X 8ED **t** 020 7713 0998 **f** 020 7713 1132 **e** info@arriba-records.com **w** arriba-records.com **Q** Dir: S-J Henry.

Arrivederci Baby! (see Cherry Red Records)

Artfield 5 Grosvenor Square, London, W1K 4AF **t** 020 7499 9941 **f** 020 7499 5519 **e** info@artfieldmusic.com **w** bbcooper.com **Q** MD: BB Cooper.

Arvee (see Everest Copyrights)

ASB Ltd (see Vanquish Music Group)

Ash International (see Touch)

Ash Records Hillside Farm, Hassocky Lane, Temple Normanton, Chesterfield, Derbyshire, S42 5DH **t** 01246 231762 **e** ash_music36@hotmail.com **Q** Head of A&R: Paul Townsend.

Associate (see Silverword Music Group)

ATG Records Kontakt Productions, 44b Whifflet Street, Coatbridge, ML5 4EL **t** 01236 434 083 **f** 01236 434 083 **e** fraser@kontaktproductions.com **w** kontaktproductions.com **Q** Label Manager: Fraser Grieve.

Athene (see Divine Art Record Company)

Atlantic Records UK The Electric Lighting Station, 46 Kensington Court, London, W8 5DA **t** 020 7938 5500 **f** 020 7368 4900 **e** firstname.lastname@atlanticrecords.co.uk **w** atlanticrecords.co.uk **Q** President: Max Lousada.

Authentic Media 9 Holdom Avenue, Bletchley, Milton Keynes, Buckinghamshire, MK1 1QR **t** 01908 364 200 **f** 01908 648 592 **e** info@authenticmedia.co.uk **w** authenticmedia.co.uk **Q** MD: David Withers.

Automatic Records Unit 5 Waldo Works, Waldo Rd, London, NW10 6AW **t** 020 8962 2208 **f** 020 8964 9090 **e** russel@digitalstores.co.uk **Q** MD: Russel Coultart.

Autonomy Music Group Suite 27, The Quadrant Centre, 135 Salusbury Road, Queens Park, London, NW6 6RJ **t** 020 7644 1450 **e** firstname@autonomymusicgroup.com

Aux Delux (see The Recoverworld Label Group (Supreme Music Ltd))

Avalon Records PO Box 929, Ferndown, Dorset, BH22 9YF **t** 01202 870 084 **e** band@galahadonline.com **w** galahadonline.com **Q** Mgrs: Stuart Nicholson, Lin Nicholson.

Avid Entertainment 15 Metro Centre, Dwight Rd, Tolpits Lane, Watford, Herts, WD18 9UL **t** 01923 281281 **f** 01923 281200 **e** info@avidgroup.co.uk **w** avidgroup.co.uk **Q** MD: Richard Lim.

Avie Records 1 Rose Alley, London, SE1 9AS **t** 020 7921 9233 **f** 020 7261 1058 **e** musicco@musicco.f9.co.uk **w** avierecords.com **Q** Executive Director: Simon Foster.

Axtone Records Ltd Viking House, 12 St Davids Close, Farnham, Surrey, GU9 9DR **t** 01252 330 894 **f** 01252 330 894 **e** james@axtone.com **w** axtone.com **Q** MD: James Sefton 07775 515025.

Azuli Records 25 D'Arblay Street, London, W1V 8ES **t** 020 7287 1932 **f** 020 7439 2490 **e** info@azuli.com **w** azuli.com **Q** Marketing: Sean Brosnan.

B-Unique Records 1A Cranbrook Rd, London, W4 2LH **t** 020 8987 0393 **f** 020 8995 9917 **e** info@b-uniquerecords.com **w** b-uniquerecords.com **Q** MDs: Mark Lewis, Martin Toher.

Back Alley Records (see Nikt Records)

BACK YARD RECORDINGS

150 Regents Park Road, London, NW1 8XN **t** 020 7722 7522 **f** 020 7722 7622 **e** info@back-yard.co.uk **w** back-yard.co.uk **M** myspace.com/backyardmyspace **Q** Managing Director: Gil Goldberg. Marketing Manager: Chris Kershaw. Business Affairs Manager: Julian Goodkind. A & R Manager: Anthony Specter.

Backbone (see Flair Records)

Backs Recording Company St Mary's Works, St Mary's Plain, Norwich, Norfolk, NR3 3AF **t** 01603 624290 **f** 01603 619999 **e** info@backsrecords.co.uk **Q** MD: Jonathan Appel 01603 626221.

Record Companies: Record Companies & Labels

Back2Basics Recordings Ltd PO Box 41, Tipton, West Midlands, DY4 7YT **t** 0121 520 1150 **f** 0121 520 1150 **e** info@back2basicsrecords.co.uk **w** back2basicsrecords.co.uk 📇 Directors: Jason Ball & Anamaria Gibbons.

Bad Sneakers Records 1-5 Springfield Mount, Leeds, LS2 9NG **t** 0113 243 1481 **e** info@badsneakers.co.uk **w** badsneakers.co.uk 📇 Dirs: Ash Kollakowski, Ed Mason.

Baktabak Records Network House, 29-39 Stirling Rd, London, W3 8DJ **t** 020 8993 5966 **f** 020 8992 0340 **e** chris@arab.co.uk **w** baktabak.com 📇 Dir: Chris Leaning.

Bandleader Recordings Unit 3, Faraday Way, St. Mary Cray, Kent, BR5 3QW **t** 01689 879090 **f** 01689 879091 **e** janice@modernpublicity.co.uk **w** bandleaderrecordings.co.uk 📇 GM: Janice Whybrow.

Bandwagon Records Studio 507 Enterprise House, 1-2 Hatfields, London, SE1 9PG **t** 020 7993 1221 **e** support@bandwagon.co.uk **w** bandwagon.co.uk 📇 Dirs: Owen Farrington, Huw Thomas.

Barely Breaking Even Records PO Box 25896, London, N5 1WE **t** 020 7607 0597 **f** 020 7607 4696 **e** leeb@bbemusic.demon.co.uk **w** bbemusic.com 📇 Co Sec: Lee Bright.

Baria Records 2 Kooringa Ave, Cleveland, Beisbane, Queensland 4163, Australia **t** +61 (0)408 76 00 22 **e** info@bariarecords.com **w** bariarecords.com 📇 MD: Ian Jones.

Baria Records 263 Warsash Rd, Locks Heath, Fareham, Hampshire, SO31 9NY **t** 07701 048582 or 01439 587149 **e** info@bariarecords.com **w** bariarecords.com 📇 Contact: Eugene Bari, Marcus Coles.

Barn Dance Publications Ltd 20 shirley Avenue, Old Coulsdon, Surrey, CR5 1QU **t** 020 8668 5714 **f** 020 8645 6923 **e** info@barndancepublications.co.uk **w** barndancepublications.co.uk 📇 MD: Derek Jones.

Bass of Bengal 34a Highgate Hill, London, N19 5NL **t** 07510 202 514 **e** bassofbengal@googlemail.com **w** bassofbengal.com 📇 Head of Operations: Dil Zaman.

BBC Audio Books St James House, Lower Bristol Rd, Bath, BA2 3BH **t** 01225 878 000 **f** 01225 878 001 **e** radio.collection@bbc.co.uk **w** bbcworldwide.com/spokenword 📇 MD: Paul Dempsey.

Bear Family (see Rollercoaster Records)

Bearcat (see Bearcat Records)

Bearcat Records PO Box 94, Derby, Derbyshire, DE22 1XA **t** 01332 332336 **f** 01332 332336 **e** chrishall@swampmusic.co.uk **w** swampmusic.co.uk 📇 Director: Chris Hall 07702 564804.

Beat Goes On Records (BGO) 7 St. Andrews St North, Bury St Edmunds, Suffolk, IP33 1TZ **t** 01284 724 406 **f** 01284 762 245 **e** andy@bgo-records.com **w** bgo-records.com 📇 MD: Andy Gray.

Beaten Track Records F114, Dam Park, Ayr, KA8 0EU **t** 01292 293 503 **e** beatentracks@aol.com **w** myspace.com/beatentrackrecords 📇 Contact: Yvonne McLellan.

Beathut 13 Greenwich Centre Business Park, Norman Road, Greenwich, London, SE10 9PY **t** 020 8858 7700 **e** info@beathutonline.com **w** beathutonline.com 📇 Manager: Caroline Hemingway.

Beautiful Jo Records PO Box 1039, Oxford, OX1 4UA **t** 01865 249 194 **f** 01865 792 765 **e** tim@bejo.co.uk **w** bejo.co.uk 📇 MD: Tim Healey.

Because Music 8 Kensington Park Rd, London, W113BU **t** 020 7229 3000 **e** Luc.Sarrabezolles@because.tv **w** because.tv 📇 GM: Luc Sarrabezolles.

Because Music Ltd 8 Kensington Park Rd, London, W11 3BU **t** 020 7229 3000 **f** 020 7221 8899 **e** jenny@adlington30.freeserve.co.uk **w** because.tv 📇 Label Manager: Jenny Adlington 07979 238142.

The Beggars Group 17-19 Alma Rd, London, SW18 1AA **t** 020 8870 9912 **f** 020 8871 1766 **e** postmaster@beggars.com **w** beggars.com

Bell Records (see Sony Music Entertainment UK & Ireland)

Bella Union 15-20 The Oval, London, E2 9DX **t** 020 7379 9700 **f** 020 7379 9007 **e** simon@bellaunion.com **w** bellaunion.com 🎵 myspace.com/bellaunion 🐦 twitter.com/bellaunion 📇 Owner: Simon Raymonde.

Berlin Records Caxton House, Caxton Avenue, Blackpool, Lancashire, FY2 9AP **t** 01253 591 169 **f** 01253 508 670 **e** info@berlinstudios.co.uk **w** berlinstudios.co.uk 📇 MD: Ron Sharples.

Better The Devil Records PO Box 292, Adversane, Billingshurst, West Sussex, RH14 9XY **t** 01403 784 920 **f** 01403 783 245 **e** info@btdrecords.com **w** betterthedevilrecords.com 📇 MD: Graham Stokes.

Beulah (see Priory Records)

Beyer (see Priory Records)

BGP (see Ace Records)

Biff Bang Pow Records (see Detour Records Ltd)

Big Bear Records PO Box 944, Birmingham, West Midlands, B16 8UT **t** 0121 454 7020 **f** 0121 454 9996 **e** records@bigbearmusic.com **w** bigbearmusic.com 📇 MD: Jim Simpson.

Big Beat (see Ace Records)

Big Brother Recordings 54 Linhope St, London, NW1 6HL **t** 020 7563 5070 **f** 020 7258 0962 **e** emmag@rkid.co.uk **w** oasisinet.com 📘 facebook.com/OasisOfficial 🎵 myspace.com/oasis 🐦 twitter.com/oasis ▶️ youtube.com/oasisinetofficial 📇 Label Head: Emma Greengrass.

Big Cat (UK) Records PO Box 34449, London, W6 0RT **t** 020 7751 0199 **f** 020 7751 0199 **e** info@bigcatrecords.com 📇 MD: Abbo.

Big Chill Recordings PO Box 52707, London, EC2P 2WE **t** 020 7684 1172 **f** 020 7684 2022 **e** eugenie@bigchill.net **w** bigchill.net 🔲 Label Mgr: Eugenie Arrowsmith.

Big City (see Candid Productions)

Big Dada PO Box 4296, London, SE11 4WW **t** 020 7820 3555 **f** 020 7820 3434 **w** bigdada.com 🔲 Lbl Mgr: Will Ashon. (see Ninja Tune)

Big Deal Records 83 Dartmouth Park Rd, London, NW5 1SL **t** 020 7681 0585 **f** 020 7681 0585 **e** Lew@Bigdealrecords.net 🔲 MD: Lew Wernick.

Big Moon Records PO Box 347, Weybridge, Surrey, KT13 9WZ **t** 01932 590169 **f** 01932 889802 **e** info@tzuke.com **w** tzuke.com 🔲 Label Head: Jamie Muggleton.

Binliner (see Detour Records Ltd)

Biondi Records 33 Lamb Court, 69 Narrow St, London, E14 8EJ **t** 020 7538 5749 **e** info@biondi.co.uk **w** biondi.co.uk 🔲 Label Manager: Marc Andrewes.

Birdland Records 39 Clitterhouse Crescent, Cricklewood, London, NW2 1DB **t** 020 8458 1020 **e** mike@mikecarr.co.uk **w** mikecarr.co.uk 🔲 MD: Mike Carr.

Bitch Records (see Automatic Records)

Bitzcore Wohlwillstr. 27, Hamburg, D-20359, Germany **t** +49 40 42 10 31 0 **f** +49 40 42 10 31 31 **e** chef@bitzcore.de **w** bitzcore.de 🔲 President: Juergen Goldschmitt.

BKO Productions c/o Haynes Orme, 3, Bolt Court, London, EC4A 3DQ **e** byron@bko-alarcon.co.uk 🔲 Director: Byron K. Orme.

Black (see Revolver Music Ltd)

Black Burst Records (see Rough Trade Records)

Black Eye Records 244 Fifth Avenue, #2686, New York, NY, 10001, United States **t** +1 212 592 4458 **f** +1 718 364 0721 **e** webmaster@Blackeyerecords.net **w** Blackeyerecords.net 🔲 VP, A&R Department: Arthur Armstrong.

Black Hole UK (see New State Entertainment)

Black Magic Records 296 Earls Court Rd, London, SW5 9BA **t** 020 7373 4083 **f** 020 7373 4083 **e** blackmagicrecords@talk21.com **w** blackmagicrecords.com 🔲 myspace.com/blackmagicrecords 🔲 MD: Mataya Clifford.

Black Market Records Holywell Cottage, Holywell Lane, Upchurch, Kent, UK, ME97HN **t** 0785 247 7144 **e** rene@blackmarket.co.uk 🔲 MD: Rene Gelston.

Black Mountain Records PO Box 89, Mumbles, Swansea, SA3 4XT **t** 01792 301 500 **f** 01792 301 500 **e** mike@choralworld.net **w** choralworld.net 🔲 MD: Michael Evans.

Blackend (see Plastic Head Records Ltd)

Blakamix International Records Garvey House, 42 Margetts Road, Bedford, MK42 8DS **t** 01234 856 164 **f** 01234 854 344 **e** info@blakamix.co.uk **w** blakamix.co.uk 🔲 MD: Dennis Bedeau.

Blast First 🔲 Contact: Mute. (see Mute Records Ltd)

Blix Street Records PO Box 5174, Hove, BN52 9HG **t** 01273 206509 **f** 01273 206579 **e** info@blixstreet.co.uk **w** blixstreet.co.uk 🔲 Director: Tom Norrell.

Blow Up Records Ltd PO Box 4961, London, W1A 7ZX **t** 020 7636 7744 **f** 020 7636 7755 **e** webmaster@blowup.co.uk **w** blowupclub.com 🔲 MD: Paul Tunkin.

Blu Bamboo Records Ltd 32 Ransomes Dock, 35-37 Parkgate Road, London, SW11 4NP **t** 020 7801 1919 **f** 020 7738 1819 **e** info@blu-bamboo.com **w** blu-bamboo.com 🔲 Dirs/A&R: Alister Jamieson, Stuart Muff.

Blue Apple Music PO Box 29, Ullapool, IV26 2WF **t** 01854 612388 **e** simon@blueapplemusic.co.uk **w** blueapplemusic.co.uk 🔲 MD: Simon Lawlor 07792 517508.

Blue Banana Records (see Blue Melon Records Ltd)

Blue Dot Music The White House, 68 Cranston Avenue, Bexhill, East Sussex, TN39 3NN **t** 01424 215617 **e** bluedot.music@virgin.net **w** bluedotmusic.net 🔲 youtube.com/BlueDotMusic 🔲 MD: Frank Rodgers.

Blue Juice Music Ltd Hobbs Barn, Wick End, Stagsden, Beds, MK43 8TS **t** 01234 824 390 **e** bluejuicemusic@aol.com **w** bluejuicemusic.co.uk 🔲 MD: Rob Butterfield.

Blue Melon Records Ltd 240A High Road, Harrow Weald, Middx, HA3 7BB **t** 020 8863 2520 **f** 020 8863 2520 **e** steve@bluemelon.co.uk 🔲 MD: Steven Glen.

Blue Planet Records (see Blue Melon Records Ltd)

Blue Pro Music Unit 11, 407-409 Hornsey Rd, London, N19 4DX **t** 020 7272 0358 **e** info@bluepromusic.com **w** bluepromusic.com 🔲 Director: Alexander Balfour.

Blue Thumb (see Decca Records)

Blueprint Recording Corporation PO Box 593, Woking, Surrey, GU23 7YF **t** 01483 715336 **f** 01483 757490 **e** blueprint@lineone.net **w** blueprint-records.net 🔲 MD: John Glover.

Bonaire Recordings (see Blue Melon Records Ltd)

Border Community Recordings PO Box 38846, London, W12 8YT **t** 020 8746 0407 **f** 020 8746 0407 **e** info@bordercommunity.com **w** bordercommunity.com 🔲 A&R: James Holden.

Born to Dance Records PO Box 50, Brighton, BN2 6YP **t** 01273 301555 **f** 01273 305266 **e** info@borntodance.com **w** borntodance.com 🔲 myspace.com/borntodancerecords 🔲 Label Managers: Natasha Brown / Dave Bonner.

Boss Sounds (see Cherry Red Records)

Contacts   **Facebook**   **MySpace**   **Twitter**   **YouTube**

Botchit & Scarper/eMotif Recordings 134-146 Curtain Road, London, EC2A 3AR **t** 020 7729 8030 **f** 020 7729 8121 **e** info@botchit.com **w** botchit.com Dir: Martin Love.

Boulevard (see Silverword Music Group)

Bowmans Capsule PO Box 30466, London, NW6 1GJ **t** 020 7431 3129 **f** 020 7431 3129 **e** sugar@bowmanscapsule.co.uk **w** bowmanscapsule.co.uk Director: Richard Burdett.

Box Out Records PO Box 697, Wembley, HA9 8WQ **t** 020 8904 6670 **f** 020 8681 1007 **e** info@boxoutrecords.com **w** boxoutrecords.com CEO: Harold Anthony 07956 583 221.

Boy Wonder Records 100 Highfield Road, Hall Green, Birmingham, B28 0HP **t** 01212 887 711 **e** boywonder@boywonderrecords.com **w** boywonderrecords.com MD: Anthony Herron.

Brainlove Records e john@brainloverecords.com **w** brainloverecords.com facebook.com/group.php?gid=2340098955 myspace.com/brainloverecords twitter.com/twitter youtube.com/brainlove Director: John Brainlove.

Breakin' Loose 32 Quadrant House, Burrell St, London, SE1 0UW **t** 020 7633 9576 **e** sjbbreakinloose@aol.com MD: Steve Bingham 07721 065618.

Brewhouse Music Breeds Farm, 57 High Street, Wicken, Ely, Cambridgeshire, CB7 5XR **t** 01353 720309 **f** 01353 723364 **e** info@brewhousemusic.co.uk **w** brewhousemusic.co.uk MD: Eric Cowell.

Brickyard (see Loose Records)

Bright Star Recordings Suite 5, Emerson House, 14b Ballynahinch Road, Carryduff, Belfast, BT8 8DN **t** 028 90 817111 **f** 028 90 817444 **e** brightstarrec@musicni.co.uk **w** brightstarrecordings.com MD: Johnny Davis.

Brightside Recordings 9 Derry Street, London, W8 5HY **t** 020 7361 8000

Brille Records Ltd. PO Box 65001, London, N5 9AJ **t** 020 7354 3494 **f** 020 7354 3494 **e** info@brillerecords.com **w** brillerecords.com Managing Director: Leo Silverman.

Bristol Archive (see Sugar Shack Records Ltd)

British Steel (see Cherry Red Records)

Bronze Records Ltd 17 Priory Road, London, NW6 4NN **t** 020 7209 2766 **f** 020 7813 2766 **e** gerrybron@bronzerecords.co.uk **w** bronzerecords.co.uk MD: Gerry Bron.

Brownswood Recordings 29a Brownswood Road, London, N4 2HP **t** 020 8802 4981 **e** info@brownswoodrecordings.com **w** brownswoodrecordings.com Directors: Simon Goffe & Gilles Peterson.

BTM (see Gotham Records)

Bugged Out! Recordings 15 Holywell Row, London, EC2A 4JB **t** 020 7684 5228 **f** 020 7684 5230 **e** paul@buggedout.net **w** buggedout.net Dirs: Paul Benney, John Burgess.

Burning Ice Records PO Box 48, Dorking, Surrey, RH4 1YE **t** 01306 877692 **e** info@objayda.co.uk **w** objayda.co.uk partner: Tim Howe.

Burning Petals Records The Studio, Homefield Court, Marston Magna, BA22 8DJ **t** 01935 851664 **e** enquiries@burning-petals.com **w** burning-petals.com Contact: Richard Jay.

Burning Shed c/o Windsor House, 74 Thorpe Rd, Norwich, Norfolk, NR1 1QH **t** 01603 767726 **f** 01603 767746 **e** info@burningshed.com **w** burningshed.com Production: Pete Morgan.

Bushranger Records Station Lodge, 196 Rayleigh Road, Hutton, Brentwood, Essex, CM13 1PN **t** 01277 222 095 **e** bushrangermusic@yahoo.co.uk Dir: Kathy Lister.

Buttercuts Limited PO BOX 150, Slough, SL1 1HD **t** 01753 759 701 **f** 01753 759 749 **e** contact@buttercutsrecords.com **w** buttercutsrecords.com MD: Andrew Oury 07957 420 492.

Butterfly Recordings 67-69 Chalton Street, London, NW1 1HY **t** 020 7554 2100 **f** 020 7554 2101 **e** ian@biglifemanagement.com **w** butterflyrecordings.com Label Manager: Ian Abraham.

Buzz To It Records PO Box 33849, London, UK, N8 9XJ **e** info@buzztoitrecords.co.uk **w** buzztoitrecords.co.uk MD: Michael Bukowski.

Buzz-erk Music Studio Two, Chocolate Factory 2, 4 Coburg Road, London, N22 6UJ **e** info@buzz-erk.com **w** buzz-erk.com Director: Niraj Chag.

Buzzin' Fly Records 31 Camden Lock Place, London, NW1 8AL **t** 020 7284 9940 **f** 020 7284 9941 **e** info@buzzinfly.com **w** buzzinfly.com Label Manager: Marianne Frederick.

BXR UK (see Media Records Ltd)

Cacophonous (see Visible Noise)

Cadence Recordings and Within Records (see Movementinsound)

Cafe de Soul 2nd Floor, 62 Belgrave Gate, Leicester, LE1 3GQ **t** 0116 299 0700 **f** 0116 299 0077 **e** cafedesoul@hotmail.com **w** cafedesoul.co.uk Label Managers: Nigel Bird, Vijay Mistry.

Cala Records 17 Shakespeare Gardens, London, N2 9LJ **t** 020 8883 7306 **f** 020 8365 3388 **e** music@calarecords.com **w** calarecords.com GM: Susi Kennedy.

Calig (see Priory Records)

Calliope-Muse-Ic Ltd The Fold, Waggon Lane, Upton, West Yorkshire, WF9 1JS **t** 0845 056 0238 **f** 01977 651391 **e** info@calliope-muse-ic.com **w** calliope-muse-ic.com MD: Andrea Meadows.

Contacts   **Facebook**   **MySpace**   **Twitter**   **YouTube**

Camino Records Crown Studios, 16-18 Crown Rd, Twickenham, Middlesex, TW1 3EE **t** 020 8891 4233 **f** 020 8891 2339 **e** mail@camino.co.uk **w** camino.co.uk Office Manager: Andrew Lodge.

Campion Records (see Disc Imports Ltd)

Candid Productions 16 Castelnau, Barnes, London, SW13 9RU **t** 020 8741 3608 **f** 020 8563 0013 **e** info@candidrecords.com **w** candidrecords.com MD: Alan Bates.

Candlelight Records Buspace Studio, Unit 207, Conlan St, London, W10 5AP **t** 020 8968 3030 **f** 020 8968 3044 **e** abstractsounds@btclick.com **w** candlelightrecords.co.uk MD: Edward Christie.

Candy Records (see PlayLouder Recordings)

Capri Music PO Box 150, Leeds, LS19 6YH **t** 07884 406 366 **f** 0113 250 1620 **e** glp@caprimusic.co.uk **w** glp.caprimusic.co.uk Label Manager: Chris Donnelly.

Caprio (see Silverword Music Group)

Captain Oi! PO Box 501, High Wycombe, Bucks, HP10 8QA **t** 01494 813 031 **f** 01494 816 712 **e** oi@captainoi.com **w** captainoi.com Owner: Mark Brennan.

Cara Music Ltd P.O. Box 28286, Winchmore Hill, London, N21 3WT **t** 020 8886 5743 **e** caramusicltd@dial.pipex.com Dir: Michael McDonagh.

Caragan Music Agency 5 The Meadows, Worlington, Suffolk, IP28 8SH **t** 01638 717 390 **e** daren@caragan.com **w** caragan.com Head of A&R: Daren Walder.

Care In The Community Recordings **e** info@careinthe.com Contact: Luis +44 20 8525 0301.

Cargo Records 17 Heathmans Road, London, SW6 4TJ **t** 020 7731 5125 **f** 020 7731 3866 **e** phil@cargorecords.co.uk **w** cargorecords.co.uk MD: Philip Hill.

Caritas Records Achmore, Moss Rd, Ullapool, Ross and Cromarty, IV26 2TF **t** 01854 612938 **f** 01854 612938 **e** caritas-records@caritas-music.co.uk **w** caritas-music.co.uk Professional Mgr: Katharine H Douglas.

Casa Nostra (see Wyze Recordings)

Casmara R.E.D. 16 West Pk, Mottingham, London, SE9 4RQ, United States **t** 07803 125742 **f** 020 8857 0731 Owner: Richard Hughes.

Casual Records Ltd 83 Rivington St, Shoreditch, London, EC2A 3AY **t** 020 7613 7746 **f** 020 7613 7740 **e** info@casuallondon.com **w** casuallondon.com Label Manager: William Baker.

Catskills Records PO Box 3365, Brighton, BN1 1WQ **t** 01273 626245 **f** 01273 626246 **e** info@catskillsrecords.com **w** catskillsrecords.com Directors: Khalid, Amr or Jonny.

Catskills:Projects (see Catskills Records)

Cavalcade Records Ltd 18 Pindock Mews, London, W9 2PY **t** 020 7289 7281 **f** 020 7289 2648 **e** songs@mindermusic.com **w** mindermusic.com MD: John Fogarty.

The CD Card Company 29-39 Stirling House, London, W3 8DJ **t** 020 8993 5966 **f** 020 8992 0340 **e** cdcard@arab.co.uk **w** cdcard.com Sales Mgr: Greg Warrington.

Celtic Heritage Series (see Ainm Music)

Cent Records Melbourne House, Chamberlain Street, Wells, BA5 2PJ **t** 01749 689 074 **f** 01749 670 315 **w** centrecords.com MD: Kevin Newton.

Centaur Discs 40-42 Brantwood Avenue, Dundee, DD3 6EW **t** 01382 776595 **f** 01382 776595 **e** centaur@cd-services.com **w** cd-services.com MD: Dave Shoesmith.

Centric Records c/o 9 Hayters Court, Grigg Lane, Brockenhurst, SO42 7PG **t** 01590 622 477 **f** 01590 622 481 **e** howard.lucas@tmp-uk.com **w** centricrecords.com Consultant: Howard Lucas.

Century Media Records 6 Water Lane, Camden, London, NW1 8NZ **t** 020 7482 0161 **f** 020 7482 3165 **e** andy@centurymedia.net **w** centurymedia.net Label Mgr: Andy Turner.

Champion Records Ltd 181 High St, Harlesden, London, NW10 4TE **t** 020 8961 5202 **f** 020 8961 6665 **e** mel@championrecords.co.uk; charmaine@championrecords.co.uk **w** championrecords.co.uk facebook.com/group.php?gid=91942328776 myspace.com/championrecordsuk twitter.com/championrecords Owner: Owner Mel Medalie A& R davide@championrecords.co.uk.

Chandos Records Chandos House, 1 Commerce Pk, Commerce Way, Colchester, Essex, CO2 8HX **t** 01206 225200 **f** 01206 225201 **e** blees@chandos.net **w** chandos.net Marketing Manager: Becky Lees.

Change of Weather Records Ltd 29 Gladwell Road, London, N8 9AA **t** 020 8245 2136 **e** pcarmichael@changeofweather.com **w** changeofweather.com MD: Paul Carmichael 07974 070 880.

Channel 4 Recordings 124 Horseferry Rd, London, SW1P 2TX **t** 020 7396 4444 **f** 020 7306 8044 **e** c4recordings@channel4.co.uk **w** channel4.com Music Manager: Liz Edmunds.

Chapter One Records Ltd Terwick Pl, Rogate, Petersfield, Hampshire, GU31 5BY **t** 01730 821644 **f** 01730 821597 **e** donna@lesreed.com **w** chapteronerecords.com Company Secretary: Donna Reed.

Charly (see Snapper Music)

Charly Acquisitions Ltd. The Old Station, The Avenue, Sark, via Guernsey, Channel Islands, GY9 0SB **t** 01481 832794 **f** 01481 832795 **e** firstname.lastname@Charly-acquisitions.com International Affairs: Jan Friedmann.

Record Companies: Record Companies & Labels

Charm Phoenix Music International, PO Box 46, Cromer, NR27 9WX **t** 0845 630 0710 **f** 0845 630 0720 **e** cindy.blackmore@phoenix-corp.co.uk **w** phoenixmusicinternational.com 📇 Accounts: Cindy Blackmore.

Chateau (see Silverword Music Group)

Cheeky 📇 Contact: BMG. (see Sony Music Entertainment UK & Ireland)

Chemikal Underground Room 2, 3rd Floor, 60 Brook St, Glasgow, G40 2AB **t** 0141 550 1919 **f** 0141 550 1918 **e** stewart@chemikal.co.uk **w** chemikal.co.uk 📇 myspace.com/chemikalunderground ▶ youtube.com/chemikal 📇 Director: Stewart Henderson.

Cherry Red Records 3a Long Island House, Warple Way, London, W3 0RG **t** 020 8740 4110 **f** 020 8740 4208 **e** infonet@cherryred.co.uk **w** cherryred.co.uk **f** facebook.com/people/Cherry-Red/1310740870 📇 myspace.com/cherryredgroup **t** twitter.com/cherryredgroup ▶ youtube.com/cherryredgroup 📇 Chairman: Iain McNay.

Choice (see Millennium Records Ltd)

Chunk Records 139 Whitfield St, London, W1T 5EN **t** 020 7380 1000 **e** info@chunkrecords.com **w** chunkrecords.com 📇 Label Mgr: Neil Stainton 07768 242 057.

Chute Records P.O. Box 211, Dundee, DD1 9PH **t** 07941 286555 **e** sparesnare@hotmail.com **w** wearethesnare.com 📇 myspace.com/sparesnare ▶ youtube.com/sparesnare 📇 Label Manager: Jan D Burnett.

Cinepop Records 61 Cedars Rd, Clockhouse, London, BR3 4JG **t** 07966 038615 **e** jc@cinepoprecords.com **w** cinepoprecords.com 📇 Label Director: JC Caddy.

Circulation Recordings 7C Lingfield Point, McMullen Road, Darlington, Co Durham, DL1 1RW **t** 01325 255 252 **f** 01325 255 252 **e** Graeme.circ@ntlworld.com **w** virtual-venue.net 📇 MD: Graeme Robinson 07917 690 223.

Ciwdod Unit 8, 24 Norbury Rd, Fairwater, Cardiff, CF5 3AU **t** 029 2083 8060 **f** 029 2056 6573 **e** gethin.evans@communitymusicwales.org.uk 📇 Co-ordinator: Gethin Evans.

Clan Stamp Records 6 The Square, Aspley Guise, Milton Keynes, Beds, MK17 8DF **t** 07943 880 933 **e** Stamp@clanstamprecords.co.uk **w** clanstamprecords.co.uk 📇 Head of A&R: Ross Henderson.

Claudio Records Ltd Studio 17, The Promenade, Peacehaven, East Sussex, BN10 8PU **t** 01273 580250 **f** 01273 580250 **e** Info@ClaudioRecords.com **w** ClaudioRecords.com 📇 MD: Colin Attwell.

Clay Records (see Universal Music (UK) Ltd)

Clean Up 📇 Contact: One Little Indian. (see One Little Indian Records)

Cleveland City Records 52A Clifton Street, Chapel Ash, Wolverhampton, West Midlands, WV3 0QT **t** 01902 838 500 **f** 01902 839 500 **e** info@clevelandcity.co.uk **w** clevelandcity.co.uk 📇 Contact: Mike Evans, Lee Glover.

Clovelly Recordings Ltd 1 The Old Cannery, Hengist Rd, Deal, Kent, CT14 6WY **t** 01304 382283 **f** 01304 382283 **e** clovellyrecordings@hotmail.com **w** clovellyrecordings.com 📇 MD: John Perkins.

Clown Records Suite 3, Rosden House, 372 Old Street, London, EC1V 9AU **t** 07986 359 568 **e** office@clownmagazine.co.uk **w** clownmagazine.co.uk 📇 Contact: Jack Dorrington.

Club AC30 Records 19 Daisy Road, South Woodford, London, E18 1EA **t** 020 85308381 **e** nick@clubac30.com **w** clubac30.com 📇 Label Manager: Nick Allport.

Clubscene 110 Clyde Street, Glasgow, G1 4LH **t** 07785 222 205 **e** mail@clubscene.co.uk **w** clubscene.co.uk 📇 Contact: Bill Grainger.

CMP (see Silva Screen)

Cohesion/Creature Music (see East Central One Ltd)

Cold Communications Ltd 6 Manor Fell, Runcorn, Cheshire, WA7 2UZ **t** 07950 685 822 **e** chris.oakley@coldcommunications.com **w** coldcommunications.com 📇 Managing Director: Chris Oakley.

Collecting Records LLP 314 Main Admin Building, Pinewood Studios, Pinewood Road, Iver Heath, Bucks, SL0 0NH **t** 01753 785500 **e** info@onemediapublishing.com **w** onemediapublishing.com 📇 CEO: Michael Infante.

Collective Music Ltd 5 Henchley Dene, Guildford, Surrey, GU4 7BH **t** 01483 431 803 **f** 01483 431 803 **e** info@collective.mu **w** collective.mu 📇 MD: Phil Hardy.

Collegium Records PO Box 172, Whittlesford, Cambridge, CB22 4QZ **t** 01223 832474 **f** 01223 836723 **e** info@collegium.co.uk **w** collegium.co.uk 📇 Sales & Marketing: John Harte/Emma Harrison.

COLUMBIA LABEL GROUP

9 Derry Street, London, W8 5HY **t** 020 7361 8000 **f** 020 7937 0188 **e** firstname.lastname@sonymusic.com **w** columbia.co.uk 📇 MD: Mike Smith. General Manager: Angie Somerside. Senior A&R Director: Phillippe Ascoli. Promotions Director: Joanne Burgess. VP Legal & Business Affairs: Simon Jenkins. Press: James Hopkins.

Comet Records 5 Cope St, Temple Bar, Dublin 2, Ireland **t** +353 87 2441 874 **f** +353 1 2891 074 **e** comet@indigo.ie **w** cometrecords.eu 📇 MD: Brian O'Kelly.

Commercial Recordings Ltd 12 Lisnagleer Rd, Dungannon, Co Tyrone, BT70 3LN **t** 028 8772 4621 **f** 028 8776 1995 **e** info@commercialrecordings.com **w** commercialrecordings.com ✉ MD: Raymond Stewart.

Complete Control Music Unit 8, 24 Norbury Road, Cardiff, CF5 3AU **t** 029 2083 8060 **f** 029 2056 6573 **e** touring@communitymusicwales.org.uk **w** completecontrolmusic.com ✉ Label Manager: Simon Dancey.

Composure Records (see Composure Records)

Composure Records 20 Churchward Drive, Frome, Somerset, BA11 2XL **t** 07816 285809 **e** composurerecords@btinternet.com **w** composurerecords.co.uk ✉ MD: Paul Davies.

Concept Music Shepherds Building, Charecroft Way, London, W14 0EE **t** 020 7751 1755 **f** 020 7751 1566 **e** info@conceptmusic.com **w** conceptmusic.com ✉ MD: Max Bloom 020 7751 1744.

Concrete Plastic Records PO Box 5019, Brighton, BN50 9JW **t** 01273 572 235 **e** info@concreteplastic.co.uk **w** concreteplastic.co.uk ✉ Label Manager: Steve Hyland 07949 266 495.

Concrete Recordings Ltd 35 Beech Rd, Chorlton, Manchester, M21 8BX **t** 0161 881 2332 **f** 0161 860 7283 **e** ms@concreterecordings.co.uk **w** concreterecordings.co.uk ✉ Director: Sarah Purcell.

Congo Music Ltd 17A Craven Park Road, Harlsden, London, NW10 8SE **t** 020 8961 5461 **f** 020 8961 5461 **e** byron@congomusic.freeserve.co.uk **w** congomusic.com ✉ A&R Director: Root Jackson.

Contra Music 13 Cotswold Mews, 30 Battersea Square, London, SW11 3RA **t** 020 7978 7888 **f** 020 7978 7808 **e** jerry.smith@automan.co.uk **w** genenet.co.uk ✉ MD: Jerry Smith.

Cookin' (see Good Looking Records)

Cooking Vinyl Ltd 10 Allied Way, London, W3 0RQ **t** 020 8600 9200 **f** 020 8743 7448 **e** info@cookingvinyl.com **w** cookingvinyl.com ✉ myspace.com/cookingvinyl ✉ twitter.com/CookingVinyl ▶ youtube.com/user/CookingVinylRecords ✉ MD: Martin Goldschmidt.

Cousins Records 57A North Woolwich Rd, via Dock Road, Silvertown, London, E16 2AA **t** 20 7055 8094 **f** 20 7055 8091 **e** cousinsrecords@aol.com **w** cousinsrecords.com ✉ Dir: Donville Davis.

Cowboy Records Ltd (see Amazon Records Ltd)

Cr2 Records PO Box 718, Richmond, Surrey, TW9 4XR **t** 020 8288 7438 **f** 020 8332 1171 **e** info@cr2records.co.uk **w** cr2records.co.uk ✉ MD: Mark Brown.

Cramer (see Priory Records)

Crapola Records PO Box 808, Hook, Hampshire, RG29 1UF **t** 01256 862865 **f** 01256 862182 **e** feedback@crapola.com **w** crapola.com ✉ facebook.com/dangerglobalwarming ✉ myspace.com/dangerglobalwarming ▶ youtube.com/dangerglobalwarming ✉ Head of A&R: Dan.

Creative World The Croft, Deanslade Farm, Claypit Lane, Lichfield, WS14 0AG **t** 01543 253576 **f** 01543 253576 **e** info@creative-world-entertainment.co.uk **w** creative-world-entertainment.co.uk ✉ MD: Mervyn Spence 07885 341745.

Crimson Productions Holden House, 57 Rathbone Place, London, W1T 1JU **t** 020 7396 8899 **f** 020 7470 6655 **e** info@demonmusicgroup.co.uk **w** vci.co.uk ✉ GM: Colin Auchterlonie. (see Demon Music Group)

Critical Mass (see Heat Recordings)

Crocodile Records 431 Linen Hall, 162-168 Regent St, London, W1B 5TE **t** 020 7580 0080 **f** 020 7637 0097 **e** music@crocodilemusic.com **w** crocodilemusic.com ✉ Contact: Malcolm Ironton, Ray Tattle.

Crossover Urban (see Heavenly Dance)

Crystal Wish Records 15/11 Caledonian Cres, Edinburgh, EH11 2AN **t** 0131 466 8296 **e** crystalwish@scotlandmail.com **w** myspace.com/crystalwishrecords ✉ A&R: Nick Munro.

Cube Records (see Fly Records)

Cube Soundtracks Onward House, 11 Uxbridge St, London, W8 7TQ **t** 020 7221 4275 **f** 020 7229 6893 **e** cube@bucksmusicgroup.co.uk **w** cubesoundtracks.co.uk ✉ MD: Simon Platz.

Culburnie (see Greentrax Recordings Ltd)

Cultural Foundation Rosedale, Pickering, North Yorkshire, YO18 8RL **t** 0845 458 4699 **e** info@cultfound.org **w** cultfound.org ▶ youtube.com/cultfound ✉ MD: Peter Bell 01751 417147.

Curb Records Ltd 45 Great Guildford Street, London, SE1 0ES **t** 020 7401 8877 **f** 020 7928 8590 **e** firstname@curb-uk.com **w** curb-records.co.uk ✉ MD: Phil Cokell.

Cyclops Records PO Box 834a, Surbiton, Surrey, KT1 9BZ **t** 020 8397 3990 **f** 020 8397 2998 **e** info@gft-cyclops.co.uk **w** gft-cyclops.co.uk ✉ MD: Malcolm Parker.

d Records 35 Brompton Rd, London, SW3 1DE **t** 020 7368 6311 **f** 020 7823 9553 **e** d@35bromptonroad.com **w** drecords.co.uk ✉ MD: Douglas Mew.

D-Mak Records 2A Downing Street, Ashton-under-Lyne, Lancashire, OL7 9LR **t** 0161 292 9493 **f** 0161 344 1673 **e** d.murphy@easynet.co.uk **w** pincermetal.com ✉ MD: Dale Murphy.

Record Companies: Record Companies & Labels

Record Companies: Record Companies & Labels

D.O.R. PO Box 1797, London, E1 4TX **t** 020 7702 7842
e info@dor.co.uk **w** dor.co.uk
ⓕ facebook.com/pages/DOR/8423761300
Ⓜ myspace.com/dorlabel ⓔ twitter.com/dorlabel
▶ youtube.com/user/DORfilm ✉ Contact: Martin Parker.

D6 Records PO Box 451, Macclesfield, Cheshire,
SK10 3FR **t** 07921 626 900 **e** darren@libertycity.biz
w libertycity.biz ✉ MD: Darren Eager.

Dad Records 10 rue du Hameau, Vaucresson, 92420,
France **t** +33 (0)1 47 952 440 **f** +33 (0)1 47 952 440
e dadinfo@dadrecords.com **w** dadrecords.com
ⓕ facebook.com/group.php?gid=27136816692&ref=ts
Ⓜ myspace.com/dadrecords ✉ Label Manager: David
Rousseau.

Daddy Records 1 Hulme Place, The Crescent, Salford,
Manchester, M5 4QA **t** 01613 515 507
e helen@daddyrecords.com **w** daddyrecords.com
✉ Commercial Manager: Helen Cantwell.

The Daisy Label Unit 2 Carriglea, Naas Rd, Dublin 12,
Ireland **t** +353 1 429 8600 **f** +353 1 429 8602
e daithi@daisydiscs.com **w** daisydiscs.com ✉ MD: John
Dunford.

Dance Paradise UK 207 Muirfield Rd, Watford, Herts,
WD19 6HZ **t** 020 8421 3817 **f** 020 8387 4299
e info@dance-paradise.co.uk **w** dance-paradise.co.uk
✉ MD: Andrei Riazanski.

Dance To The Radio Calls Landing, 36-38 The Calls,
Leeds, West Yorkshire, LS2 7EW **t** 0113 246 1200
f 0113 243 4849 **e** info@dancetotheradio.com
w dancetotheradio.com
Ⓜ myspace.com/dancetotheradiolabel
ⓔ twitter.com/dttrlabel ✉ A&R / Label Manager: Alistair
Tant.

Dancebeat (see Tema International)

Dangerous Records Sandwell Manor, Totnes, Devon,
TQ9 7LL **t** 01803 867 850 **f** 01803 867 850
e info@dangerousrecords.co.uk **w** dangerousrecords.co.uk
✉ Label Manager: Liam Smith 07738 543 746.

The Daniel Azure Music Group 72 New Bond St,
London, W1S 1RR **t** 07894 702 007 **f** 020 8240 8787
e info@jvpr.net **w** danielazure.com ✉ CEO: Daniel Azure.

Dara (see Dolphin Music)

Dark Beat (see Smexi Playaz Records)

Data 103 Gaunt St, London, SE1 6DP **t** 020 7740 8600
f 020 7403 5348 **e** initial+lastname@ministryofsound.com
w datarecords.co.uk ✉ Contact: Ben Cooke.

Datum (see Priory Records)

DB RECORDS

PO Box 19318, Bath, Somerset, BA1 6ZS **t** 01225 782322
f 01225 482013 **e** david@dbrecords.co.uk
w dbrecords.co.uk ✉ Contact: David Bates.
**The label was established in 1998 by David Bates,
former head of A&R for Mercury/Vertigo and head of
Fontana Records. During his time there he signed,
discovered and worked with Def Leppard, Teardrop
Explodes, Tears For Fears, Scott Walker, Tom Verlaine,
James, Texas, Pere Ubu, Wet Wet Wet, Was Not Was and
Oleta Adams.**

De Angelis Records Studio 5, Power Rd Studios,
114 Power Rd, London, W4 5PY **t** 020 8994 4600
f 020 8996 5743 **e** voices@de-angelisrecords.com **w** de-
angelisrecords.com ✉ Product Manager: Martine McLean.

de Wolfe Music Shropshire House, 11-20 Capper St,
London, WC1E 6JA **t** 020 7631 3600 **f** 020 7631 3700
e info@dewolfemusic.co.uk **w** dewolfemusic.co.uk
✉ MD: Warren De Wolfe.

Dead Happy Records 3B Castledown Avenue,
Hastings, East Sussex, TN34 3RJ **t** 01424 434778
e dave@deadhappyrecords.co.uk
w deadhappyrecords.co.uk ✉ Dir: Dave Arnold.

Dead Young Records 44-46 Canal Road, Leeds,
LS12 2PL **t** 0113 231 9326 **e** info@deadyoungrecords.co.uk
w deadyoungrecords.co.uk ✉ Head of A&R: Craig
Pennington.

Debonair Records & Tapes Ltd Eaton House,
39 Lower Richmond Road, Putney, London, SW15 1ET
t 020 8788 4557 **f** 020 8780 9711 **e** info@eatonmusic.com
w debonairrecords.co.uk ✉ MD: Terry Oates.

Decadent Records 6Q Atlas Business Centre,
Oxgate Lane, London, NW2 7HU **t** 020 8452 2255
f 020 8452 4242 **e** info@decadentrecords.co.uk
w decadentrecords.co.uk ✉ Label Manager: Nick Bennett.

The Decca Music Group 347-
353 Chiswick High Road, London, W4 4HS **t** 020 8742 5400
f 020 8742 5416 **e** firstname.lastname@umusic.com
w deccaclassics.com ✉ General Manager: Paul Moseley.

DECCA RECORDS

Beaumont House, Kensington Village, Avonmore Rd, London, W14 8TS **t** 020 7149 1010
e firstname.lastname@umusic.com **w** universalclassics.com 📇 MD: Dickon Stainer. General Manager: Mark Wilkinson. Finance Director: Andy Daymond. Head of Media Relations: Rebecca Allen. Head of A&R: Tom Lewis.

Deceptive Records PO Box 288, St Albans, Hertfordshire, AL4 9YU **t** 01727 834 130 📇 MD: Tony Smith.

Deeper Substance Records Flat 6, Evedon House, Philip Street, London, N1 5NS **t** 020 7245 3661
e lawrie@deepersubstance.com **w** deepersubstance.com 📇 MD: Lawrence Millar 07971 485 609.

Def Jam 📇 Contact: Mercury. (see Mercury Music Group)

Defected Records Ltd 8 Charterhouse Buildings, Goswell Road, London, EC1M 7AN **t** 020 7549 2970
f 020 7250 0449 **e** firstname@defected.com
w defected.com 📇 MD: Hector Dewar.

Delicious Records 78 Church Path, London, W4 5BJ **t** 020 8994 3142 **f** 020 8994 3142
e delicious@elenaonline.com **w** deliciousrecords.co.uk 📇 MD: Kris Gray.

Deltasonic Records 102 Rose Lane, Mossley Hill, Liverpool, L18 8AG **t** 0151 724 4760 **f** 0151 724 6286
e firstname@deltasonic.co.uk **w** deltasonic.co.uk 📇 Label Manager: Sean Atkins.

Demi Monde Records & Publishing
Demi Monde Records & Publishing, Foel Studio, Llanfair Caereinion, Powys, SY21 0DS **t** 01938 810758
f 01938 810758 **e** demimonde@dial.pipex.com
w demimonde.co.uk 📇 MD: Dave Anderson.

DEMON MUSIC GROUP

33 Foley St, London, W1W 7TL **t** 020 7612 3300
f 020 7612 3301
e firstname.lastname@demonmusicgroup.co.uk
w demonmusicgroup.co.uk 📇 Asst. to Directors: Alicia Hosking. Commercial Director: Adrian Sear. Sales & Marketing Director: Danny Keene. Catalogue & TV Director: Colin Auchterlonie.

Department of Sound Building 348a, Westcott Venture Park, Westcott, Aylesbury, Bucks, HP18 0XB **t** 01296 655 880
e enquiries@departmentofsound.com
w departmentofsound.com 📇 MD: Adrienne Aiken.

Destined Records (see Back Yard Recordings)

Destiny Music Iron Bridge House, 3 Bridge Approach, London, NW1 8BD **t** 020 7734 3251 **f** 020 7439 2391
e nick@destinymusic.co.uk **w** carlinmusic.co.uk 📇 MD: Nick Farries.

Detour Records Ltd PO Box 18, Midhurst, West Sussex. GU29 9YU **t** 01730 815 422 **f** 01730 815 422
e detour@btinternet.com **w** detour-records.co.uk
📇 Dirs: David Holmes & Tania Holmes.

Deutsche Grammophon 📇 Contact: PolyGram Classics. (see Decca Records)

Deviant Records Phoenix Music International, PO Box 46, Cromer, NR27 9WX **t** 0845 630 0710
f 0845 630 0720 **e** cindy.blackmore@phoenix-corp.co.uk
w phoenixmusicinternational.com 📇 Accounts: Cindy Blackmore.

Dew Process Records Unit 70, 3-6 Banister Rd, London, W10 4AR **t** 07896 163 003 **e** megan@dew-process.com **w** dew-process.com 📇 Publicity and Promotions Manager: Megan Reeder.

Dharma Records Ltd PO Box 50668, London, SW6 3UY **t** 020 7384 0938 **e** zen@dharmarecords.co.uk
w dharmarecords.co.uk 📇 Managing Director: Phil Knox-Roberts.

Digimix Records Ltd Sovereign House, 12 Trewartha Rd, Praa Sands, Penzance, Cornwall, TR20 9ST
t 01736 762826 **f** 01736 763328 **e** panamus@aol.com
w digimixrecords.com ⬛ myspace.com/digimixrecords
📇 CEO: Roderick Jones.

Digital Plastic Ltd 22 Rutland Gardens, Hove, East Sussex, BN3 5PB **t** 01273 779 793 **f** 01273 779 820
e enzo@plastic-music.co.uk **w** plastic-music.co.uk
📇 MD: Enzo (Vincent Amico).

Digital Soundboy Recording Co. **t** 07801 273351
e info@digitalsoundboy.com **w** digitalsoundboy.com
📘 facebook.com/digitalsoundboy
⬛ myspace.com/digitalsoundboy
🐦 twitter.com/digitalSoundBoy
▶️ youtube.com/digitalsoundboytv 📇 Label manager/A&R: Jon Bailey.

Dis-funktional Recordings (see 852 Recordings)

Disc Imports Ltd Magnus House, 8 Ashfield Rd, Cheadle, Cheshire, SK8 1BB **t** 0161 491 6655
f 0161 491 6688 **e** dimus@aol.com **w** dimusic.co.uk
📇 MD: Alan Wilson.

Discover (see The Recoverworld Label Group (Supreme Music Ltd))

Disky Communications Ltd Connaught House, 112-120 High Road, Loughton, Essex, IG10 4HJ **t** 020 8508 3723
f 020 8508 0432 **e** d.harrington@disky.nl 📇 MD: Alan Byron.

Record Companies: Record Companies & Labels

Disorient Recordings (see Mr Bongo)

Distile Records 13 rue du Roule, Paris, 75001, France **t** +33 6 63 69 14 63 **e** contact@distilerecords.com **w** distilerecords.com 📇 Contact: Jerome, Pierrick.

Distiller Records LLP Studio 11, 10 Acklam Rd, Ladbroke Gorve, London, W10 5QZ **t** 0208 968 8236 **f** 0208 9644706 **e** darrin@distiller-records.com **w** distiller-records.com 📇 Director of A&R: Darrin Woodford 020 8968 8236.

Distinct'ive Records 35 Drury Lane, Covent Garden, London, WC2B 5RH **t** 020 7689 0079 **e** richard@distinctiverecords.com **w** distinctiverecords.com 📇 Head of A&R: Richard Ford.

Distinct'ive Breaks 📇 Contact: Avex UK. (see Distinct'ive Records)

Disturbing London Records Ltd 1 Greenwich Quay, Clarence Rd, London, SE8 3EY **t** 0208 691 1579 **e** dumi@dlrecords.com 📇 Managing Director/Artist Manager: Dumi Oburota 07873137811.

Divine Art Record Company Castle Eden Studios, Stockton Rd, Castle Eden, Hartlepool, Co. Durham, TS27 4SD **t** 01609 882062 **e** toby@divine-art.co.uk **w** divine-art.co.uk 📇 UK Operations Director: Toby Horton.

DMI Arch 25, Kings Cross Freight Depot, York Way, London, N1 0EZ **t** 020 7713 8130 **f** 020 7713 8247 **e** info@dmirecords.com **w** dmirecords.com 📇 Directors: Massimo Bonaddio/Dan Carey.

Dolph Hamster Music 22 Dane Rd, Margate, Kent, CT9 2AA **t** 0560 366 0825 **e** label@dolphhamstermusic.com **w** dolphhamstermusic.com 📇 Director: Mark Loader.

Dolphin Music Unit 4, 3-4 Great Ship Street, Dublin 8, Ireland **t** +353 1 478 3455 **f** +353 1 478 2143 **e** irishmus@iol.ie **w** irelandcd.com 📇 Export Manager: Paul Heffernan.

Dome Records Ltd PO Box 3274, East Preston, W. Sussex, BN16 9BD **t** 01903 771 027 **f** 01903 779 565 **e** info@domerecords.co.uk **w** domerecords.co.uk 🅜 myspace.com/domerecords 🅣 domerecords 📇 Managing Director: Peter Robinson.

Domino Recording Company PO Box 47029, London, SW18 1WD **t** 020 8875 1390 **f** 020 8875 1391 **e** info@dominorecordco.com **w** dominorecordco.com 📇 Digital / online PR: Paul Sandell.

Dorian (see Priory Records)

Dovehouse Records Crabtree Cottage, Mill Lane, Kidmore End, Oxon, RG4 9HB **t** 0118 972 4356 **f** 0118 972 4809 **e** doverecords@btconnect.com **w** dovehouserecords.com 📇 President: Thomas Pemberton.

Down By Law Records PO Box 20242, London, NW1 7FL **t** 020 7485 1113 **e** info@proofsongs.co.uk

Dragonffli Records - Roc-I.T. Recording Studios Unit 21 North Pontypool Industrial Pk, Pontnewynydd, Pontypool, Gwent, NP4 6PB **t** 01495 740150 **e** dragonfflirecords@hotmail.co.uk - roc-i.t.recordingstudio@hotmail.co.uk 🅜 myspace.com/dragonfflirecords - http://www.myspace.com/rocitrecordingstudio 📇 MD: Nick Byrne 07891 767407.

Dragonfly Records 67-69 Chalton St, London, NW1 1HY **t** 020 7554 2100 **f** 020 7554 2154 **e** pathaan@pathaan.com **w** dragonflyrecords.com 📇 Label Mgr: Pathaan.

Dream Catcher Records Regent House, 1, Pratt Mews, Camden Town, London, NW1 0AD **t** 020 7554 4840 **f** 020 7388 8324 **e** info@dreamcatcher-records.com **w** dreamcatcher-records.com 📇 MD: Gem Howard-Kemp.

DreamWorks 📇 Contact: Polydor Associated. (see Polydor Records)

Drift Records 91 High Street, Totnes, Devon, TQ9 6ES **t** 01803 866 988 **e** info@driftrecords.co.uk **w** driftrecords.co.uk 📇 Label Manager: Rupert Morrison.

Drowned In Sound Recordings 1 Chilworth Mews, London, W2 3RG **t** 020 7087 8880 **f** 020 7087 8899 **e** info@disrecords.com **w** disrecords.com 📇 Label Mgr: Sean Adams.

Dtox Records Ltd 33 Alexander Road, Aylesbury, Bucks, HP20 2NR **t** 01296 434 731 **f** 01296 422 530 **e** joseph@dtox.co.uk **w** dtox.co.uk 📇 Label Manager: Joseph Stopps.

DTPM Recordings First floor, 40A Gt Eastern St, London, EC2A 3EP **t** 020 7749 1199 **f** 020 7749 1188 **e** guy@blue-cube.net **w** dtpmrecordings.net 📇 Label Mgr: Guy Williams.

Duffnote Ltd Vine Cottage, North Road, Bosham, W. Sussex, PO18 8NL **t** 01243 774606 or 575110 **e** info@duffnote.com **w** duffnote.com 📇 Dirs: Danny Jones, Richard Earnshaw.

Dulcima Records 39 Tadorne Rd, Tadworth, Surrey, KT20 5TF **t** 01737 812922 **f** 01737 812922 **e** info@dulcimarecords.com **w** dulcimarecords.com 📇 MD: Norma Camby.

Dune Records 1st Floor, 73 Canning Road, Harrow, Middx, HA3 7SP **t** 020 8424 2807 **f** 020 8861 5371 **e** info@dune-music.com **w** dune-music.com 📇 MD: Janine Irons.

Duophonic UHF PO Box 3787, London, SE22 9DZ **t** 020 8299 1650 **f** 020 8693 5514 **e** duophonic@btopenworld.com **w** duophonic.com 📇 Dir: Martin Pike.

Dusk Fire Whiteleaf Business Centre, Buckingham Ind. Pk, Buckingham, Bucks, MK18 1TF **t** 01296 715228 **e** info@duskfire.co.uk **w** duskfire.co.uk 📇 MD: Peter Muir.

Duty Free Recordings Courtsyard Office, 68-69 Chalk Farm Rd, London, NW1 8AN **t** 020 7424 0774 **f** 020 7424 9094 **e** info@dutyfreerecordings.co.uk **w** dutyfreerecordings.co.uk ✉ MD: Steffan Chandler.

Dynamic (see Priory Records)

Eagle Records Eagle House, 22 Armoury Way, London, SW18 1EZ **t** 020 8870 5670 **f** 020 8874 2333 **e** mail@eagle-rock.com **w** eagle-rock.com ✉ A&R Manager: Andy McIntyre 02088705670.

Earache Records Ltd Suite 1-3 Westminster Building, Theatre Square, Nottingham, NG1 6LG **t** 0115 950 6400 **f** 0115 950 8585 **e** mail@earache.com **w** earache.com ✉ MD: Digby Pearson.

Earthworks (see Stern's Records)

East Central One Ltd Creeting House, All Saints Rd, Creeting St Mary, Ipswich, Suffolk, IP6 8PR **t** 01449 723244 **f** 01449 726067 **e** enquiries@eastcentralone.com **w** eastcentralone.com ✉ Co-Dir: Steve Fernie.

East City Records 120-124 Curtain Rd, London, EC2A 3SQ **t** 020 7739 6903 **f** 020 7613 2715 **e** mark@eastcitymanagement.com ✉ A&R: Mark Sutton.

East West (see Atlantic Records UK)

Eastside Records Ltd Top Floor, Outset Building, 2 Grange Rd, London, E17 8AH **t** 020 8509 6070 **f** 020 8509 6021 **e** info@eastside-records.co.uk **w** eastside-records.co.uk ✉ Dir: Alexis Michaelides.

The Echo Label Ltd The Chrysalis Building, 13 Bramley Rd, London, W10 6SP **t** 020 7221 2213 **f** 020 7729 4498 **e** firstname.lastname@chrysalis.com ✉ CEO, Chrysalis Music Div: Jeremy Lascelles.

Edgy (see Metal Nation Records)

Edition (see Loose Records)

Edsel Records (see Demon Music Group)

EG Records PO Box 606, London, WC2E 7YT **t** 020 8540 9935 ✉ A&R: Chris Kettle.

Electric Minds Music 3B Beatty Rd, London, N16 8EA **t** 07958 614297 **e** info@electricminds.co.uk **w** electricminds.co.uk ✉ Label Manager: Dolan Bergin.

Electrix Records (see Tortured Records)

Electronic Alchemy Records Ltd PO Box 197, Bexhill on Sea, TN40 9BF **t** 01424 844 411 **f** 01424 844 466 **e** jenny@ea-records.com **w** ea-records.com ✉ Head of A&R: Jenny Strickson.

Elektra (see Atlantic Records UK)

Elemental ✉ Contact: One Little Indian. (see One Little Indian Records)

Emerald Music (Ireland) Ltd. 120A Coach Rd, Templepatrick, Ballyclare (Roughfort), Co Antrim, BT39 0HA, Ireland **t** 028 9443 2619 **f** 028 9446 2162 **e** info@emeraldmusic.co.uk **w** emeraldmusiconline.com ✉ MD: George Doherty.

The Emergency Broadcast System PO Box 6131, London, W3 8ZR **t** 020 8993 8436 **f** 020 8896 1778 **e** management@hawkwind.com **w** hawkwind.com ✉ Contact: Eve Carr.

EMI Catalogue/EMI Gold/EMI Liberty 27 Wrights Lane, London, W8 5SW **t** 020 7795 7000 **e** firstname.lastname@emimusic.com **w** emi.com ✉ SVP, Commercial Marketing & Catalogue: Steve Pritchard & Peter Duckworth.

EMI Classics International 27 Wrights Lane, London, W8 5SW **t** 020 7795 7000 **e** victor.orive-martin@emimusic.com **w** emiclassics.com ⚑ facebook.com/EMIVirginClassics ✉ International Marketing & Promotions Coordinator: Victor Orive-Martin 020 7752 5797.

EMI Classics UK 27 Wrights Lane, London, W8 5SW **t** 020 7795 7000 **e** firstname.lastname@emimusic.com **w** emiclassics.co.uk

EMI Music 27 Wrights Lane, London, W8 5SW **t** 020 7795 7000 **f** 020 7795 7001 **e** andria.vidler@emimusic.com **w** emi.com ▣ twitter.com/EMIWORLDWIDE ✉ President, EMI Music UK & Ireland: Andria Vidler.

EMI Music Commercial Marketing and Catalogue 27 Wrights Lane, Kensington, London, W8 5SW **t** 020 7795 7000 **e** firstname.lastname@emimusic.com **w** emimusic.co.uk

EMI Music Ireland EMI House, 1 Ailesbury Rd, Dublin 4, Ireland **t** +353 1 203 9900 **f** +353 1 269 6341 **e** firstname.lastname@emimusic.com **w** emirecords.ie ✉ Chairman: Willie Kavanagh.

EMI MUSIC UK & IRELAND EMI House, 43 Brook Green, London, W6 7EF **t** 020 7795 7000 **f** 020 7605 5050 **e** firstname.lastname@emimusic.com **w** emimusic.co.uk ✉ CFO UK&I & Interim Country Chair: Justin Morris.

Enable Music Ltd 54 Baldry Gardens, London, SW16 3DJ **t** 020 8144 0616 **e** mike@enablemusic.co.uk **w** enablemusic.co.uk ✉ MD: Mike Andrews 07775 737 281.

EPIC RECORDS

9 Derry Street, London, W8 5HY **t** 020 7361 8000 **f** 020 7937 0188 **e** firstname.lastname@sonymusic.com ✉ MD: Nick Raphael. Director Of A&R: Jo Charrington. Director Of A&R: Tris Penna. Marketing Manager: Murray Rose.

Erato (see Warner Classics & Jazz)

Erra Records Ltd 45 Kenwood Gardens, Gants Hill, Essex, IG2 6YQ **t** 07725 551746 **e** errarecords@googlemail.com **w** errarecords.com ✉ Director: Benji Olufowobi.

Record Companies: Record Companies & Labels

Essence Records 10 Trevelyan Gardens, London, NW10 3JY **t** 020 8930 4760 **f** 020 8451 3380 **e** info@essencerecords.co.uk **w** essencerecords.co.uk 📧 MD: Phil Cheeseman.

Estereo (see Skint Records)

Ether Music Broadway Studios, 28 Tooting High St, London, SW17 0RG **t** 020 8378 6956 **f** 020 8378 6959 **e** contact@etheruk.com **w** ethermusic.net 📧 Dir: Adrian Harley.

Ethereal Records 68 Seabrook Rd, Hythe, Kent, CT21 5QA **t** 01303 267509 **e** Robertmdrury@aol.com **w** etherealrecords.com 📧 MD: Bob Drury.

Euphoric (see Almighty Records)

Evangeline Recorded Works Ltd The Old School House, Knowstone, South Molton, Devon, EX36 4YW **t** 01398 341465 **f** 01398 341677 **e** evangelinemusic@aol.com **w** evangeline.co.uk 📧 Label Manager: Sarah Lock.

Evasive Music Unit 18-19 Croydon House, 1 Peall Rd, Croydon, Surrey, CR0 3EX **t** 020 8287 8585 **f** 020 8287 0220 **e** info@evasive.co.uk **w** evasive.co.uk ⬛ facebook.com/home.php?#/group.php?gid=20044773951 💠 myspace.com/evasiverecords 📧 MD: Rob Pearson.

Eve / Eve Nova (see The Recoverworld Label Group (Supreme Music Ltd))

Eventide Music (see Eventide Music)

Eventide Music PO Box 27, Baldock, Hertfordshire, SG7 6UH **t** 01462 893995 **f** 01462 893995 **e** eventide.music@ntlworld.com 📧 MD: Kevin Kendle.

Everest Copyrights Station House, Bucknell, Craven Arms, Shropshire, SY7.0AD. **t** 01547 530998 **e** austin.powell@ukonline.co.uk 📧 Contact: Austin Powell.

Evolve Records The Courtyard, 42 Colwith Road, London, W6 9EY **t** 020 8741 1419 **f** 020 8741 3289 **e** firstname@evolverecords.co.uk **w** evolverecords.co.uk 📧 Chairman: Oliver Smallman.

Excalibur Records (see Satellite Music Ltd)

Exceptional Records PO Box 16208, London, W4 1ZU **t** 020 8995 8738 **f** 020 8995 8738 **e** info@exceptionalrecords.co.uk **w** exceptionalrecords.co.uk 📧 MD: Bob Fisher.

Expansion Records Unit 2, Boeing Way, International Trading Estate, Brent Road, Southall, Middlesex, UB2 5LB **t** 020 8867 9361 **f** 020 8571 2624 **e** ralph@expansion-records.co.uk **w** expansionrecords.com 📧 MD: Ralph Tee.

Eyes Wide Shut Recordings 4-7 Forewoods Common, Holt, Wiltshire, BA14 6PJ **t** 0845 056 3834 **f** 0870 131 3701 **e** info@empspace.com **w** eyeswideshutrecordings.com 📧 Label Manager: George Allen 07909 995 011.

F Communications (UK) (see Wall of Sound)

F.I. (see Hot Lead Records)

Fabric 12 Greenhill Rents, London, EC1M 6BN **t** 020 7336 8898 **f** 020 7253 3932 **e** cds@fabriclondon.com **w** fabriclondon.com 📧 Label Manager: Geoff Muncey.

Face 2 Face (see Adasam Limited)

Face Value Records (see Matchbox Recordings Ltd)

Faculty Music Media Innovation Labs, Watford Road, Harrow, Middx, HA1 3TP **t** 020 7193 8036 **e** facultyoffice@facultymusic.com **w** facultymusic.com 📧 MD: Tony Martin.

Fairy Cake Universe **t** 020 8299 1645 **e** amanda@fairycakeuniverse.com **w** aquamanda.net 📧 MD: Amanda Greatorex.

Faith & Hope Records 23 New Mount St, Manchester, M4 4DE **t** 0161 839 4445 **f** 0161 839 1060 **e** email@faithandhope.co.uk **w** faithandhope.co.uk 📧 MD: Neil Claxton.

Fall Out (see Jungle Records)

Fantastic Plastic The Church, Archway Close, London, N19 3TD **t** 020 7263 2267 **f** 020 7263 2268 **e** enquire@fantasticplasticrecords.com **w** fantasticplasticrecords.com 📧 MD: Darrin Robson.

Fantasy (see Ace Records)

Far Out Recordings Unit 217, The Saga Centre, 326 Kensal Road, London, W10 5BZ **t** 020 8969 9545 **f** 020 8969 9544 **e** info@faroutrecordings.com **w** faroutrecordings.com 📧 MD: Joe Davis.

Fast Western Group Ltd Bank Top Cottage, Meadow Lane, Millers Dale, Derbyshire, SK17 8SN **t** 01298 872462 **e** fast.west@virgin.net 📧 MD: Ric Lee.

Fastforward Music Limited Sorrel Horse House, 1 Sorrel Horse Mews, Ipswich, Suffolk, IP4 1LN **t** 01473 210555 **f** 01473 210500 **e** sales@fastforwardmusic.co.uk **w** fastforwardmusic.co.uk 📧 Sales Director: Neil Read.

Fat Cat Records 11 Old Steine, Brighton, East Sussex, BN1 1EJ **t** 01273 699 020 **e** info@fat-cat.co.uk **w** fat-cat.co.uk 📧 Label Managers: Dave, Alex.

Fat City Recordings Third Floor, Habib House, 9 Stevenson Sq, Manchester, M1 1DB **t** 0161 228 7884 **f** 0161 228 7266 **e** matt@fatcity.co.uk **w** fatcity.co.uk 📧 Label Manager: Matt Triggs.

Fat! Records Unit 36, Battersea Business Centre, 99-109 Lavender Hill, London, SW11 5QL **t** 020 7924 1333 **f** 020 7924 1833 **e** info@thefatclub.com **w** thefatclub.com 📧 MD: Paul Arnold.

FDM Records 15 Woodcote Road, Leamington Spa, Warwickshire, CV32 4PX **t** 01926 833 460 **f** 01926 426 393 **e** info@fdmrecords.com 📧 Label Dir: Kieron Concannon.

Fellside Recordings Ltd PO Box 40, Workington, Cumbria, CA14 3GJ **t** 01900 61556 **e** info@fellside.com **w** fellside.com 📧 Director: Paul Adams.

Fenetik (see Soma Recordings Ltd)

Festivo (see Priory Records)

Ffin Records / Recordiau Ffin Chapter, Cardiff, CF5 1QE **t** 020 7043 2569 / 029 2022 0903 **e** studio@johnhardymusic.com **w** ffinrecords.co.uk / www.johnhardymusic.com ■ myspace.com/johnhardymusic ■ youtube.com/user/JohnHardyMusic?gl=GB&hl=en-GB ■ Director: John Hardy 029 2022 0903.

Fiasco London London **e** ed@fiascolondon.com **w** fiascolondon.com ■ myspace.com/fiascolondon ■ Contact: Ed Weidman 07966 438376.

Fierce Panda PO Box 43376, London, N5 2EA **t** 020 7704 6141 **e** ellie@fiercepanda.co.uk **w** fiercepanda.co.uk ■ Contact: Ellie Coden.

Finger Lickin' Records 2nd Floor Rear, 20 Great Portland St, London, W1W 8QR **t** 020 7255 2660 **f** 020 7637 2903 **e** info@fingerlickin.co.uk **w** fingerlickin.co.uk ■ MD: Justin Rushmore.

Fire Records & Fire Songs 21a Maury Rd, London, N16 7BP **t** 020 8806 9889 **f** 020 8806 9889 **e** james@firerecords.com **w** firerecords.com ■ myspace.com/firerecords ■ Director: James Nicholls.

First Night Records Ltd 3 Warren Mews, London, W1T 6AN **t** 020 7383 7767 **f** 020 7383 3020 **e** info@firstnightrecords.com **w** first-night-records.co.uk ■ MD: John Craig.

First Records 201-205 Hackney Road, London, E2 8JL **t** 020 7729 7593 **f** 020 7739 5600 **e** info@premises.demon.co.uk **w** premises.demon.co.uk ■ MD: Viv Broughton.

Flair Records 25 Commercial St, Brighouse, West Yorkshire, HD61AF **t** 01484 723557 **e** john@now-music.com **w** now-music.com ■ MD: John Wagstaff.

Flapper (see Pavilion Records Ltd)

Flatline Records Ltd 21 Hudson Avenue, Norwich, Norfolk, NR14 8GB **t** 0845 050 6276 **e** info@flatlinerecords.co.uk **w** flatlinerecords.co.uk ■ facebook.com/home.php?#/group.php?gid=199175650219&ref=ts ■ myspace.com/flatlinerecordsuk ■ MD: James Hildreth.

Flingdown (see Snapper Music)

Flo Records (see Nation Records Ltd)

FLOATING WORLD RECORDS LTD Executive Suite, Northway House, 1379 High Rd, London, N20 9LP **t** 020 8492 3355 **f** 020 8492 3356 **e** info@fwrecords.co.uk **w** fwrecords.co.uk ■ Director: Pete Macklin.

Flux Delux (see The Recoverworld Label Group (Supreme Music Ltd))

Fly Records Onward House, 11 Uxbridge St, London, W8 7TQ **t** 020 7221 4275 **f** 020 7229 6893 **e** info@flyrecords.co.uk **w** flyrecords.co.uk ■ MD: Simon Platz.

Flyfree Records - Sam Payne PO Box 336, Moortown, Leeds, LS17 1AE **t** 0113 2662112 **e** sales@sampayne.co.uk **w** sampayne.co.uk ■ Contact: Miss Sam Payne.

FM (see Revolver Music Ltd)

FM Dance (see Revolver Music Ltd)

FM Jazz (see Revolver Music Ltd)

Focus Music International Ltd 14 Fife Rd, London, SW14 7EL **t** 020 8876 7111 **f** 020 8878 0331 **e** info@focus-music.com **w** focus-music.com ■ MD: Don Reedman.

Fontana ■ Contact: Mercury. (see Mercury Music Group)

Food ■ Except Dubstar - EMI: Parlophone. (see Parlophone)

Formation Records PO Box 1401, Glen Parva, Leicester, LE2 8ZJ **t** 0116 277 9662 **f** 0116 277 3888 **e** info@formationrecords.com **w** formationrecords.com ■ Promotions Mgr: Melanie Small.

Formidable Management - Voluptuous Records 26 Top Rd, Five Crosses, Cheshire, WA6 6SW **t** 07939 140774 **e** carl@formidable-mgmt.com ■ Owner: Carl Marcantonio.

Formosa Music Ltd 3 Mills Studios, Three Mill Lane, London, E3 3DU **t** 0208 709 8700 **f** 0208 709 8701 **e** info@formosafilms.com ■ Director: Neil Thompson.

Formula One Records 71 Alan Moss Road, Loughborough, Leicestershire, LE11 5LR **t** 01509 213632 ■ MD: Ian Barker.

Fortune and Glory Osmond House, 78 Alcester Rd, Moseley, Birmingham, West Midlands, B13 8BB **t** 0121 256 1310 **f** 0121 256 1318 **e** hendricks@fortuneandglory.co.uk **w** fortuneandglory.co.uk ■ MD: Hendricks.

four:twenty (see Hope Music Group)

Fragile Records Unit 3, 1 St Mary Road, London, E17 9RG **t** 020 8520 4442 **f** 020 8520 2514 **e** info@fragilerecords.co.uk ■ MD: Dave Thompson.

Fred Label Ltd 45 Vyner St, London, E2 9DQ **t** 020 8981 2987 **f** 020 8981 9912 **e** info@fred-london.com **w** fred-label.com ■ myspace.com/fredlabellimited ■ Dir: Fred Mann.

free2air recordings The Blue Building, 8-10 Basing St, London, W11 1ET **t** 020 7229 1229 **f** 020 7243 8100 **e** info@free2airrecordings.com **w** free2airrecordings.com ■ Chairman: Clive Black.

Freemaison Records 36 Brunswick St West, Hove, East Sussex, BN3 1EL **t** 07979 757033 **f** 01273 325935 **e** info@freemaison.com **w** freemaison.com ■ Label Mgrs: Russell Small, James Wiltshire.

Freestyle Records 77 Fortess Rd, London, NW5 1AG **t** 020 7482 4555 **f** 020 7482 4551 **e** info@freestylerecords.co.uk **w** freestylerecords.co.uk

Frenetic Music PO Box 46360, London, SW17 0WT **e** info@freneticmusic.com **w** freneticmusic.com ■ youtube.com/freneticmusic ■ MD: Craig Dimech.

Contacts   **Facebook**   **MySpace**   **Twitter**   **YouTube**

Freshly Squeezed (Music Ltd)
116 Stanford Avenue, Brighton, BN1 6FE **t** 01273 563201
f 01273 563201 **e** info@freshlysqueezedmusic.com
w freshlysqueezedmusic.com   MD: Nick Perring.

Full Cycle Records Unit 23, Easton Business Centre,
Felix Road, Bristol, BS5 0HE **t** 0117 941 5824
f 0117 941 5823 **e** info@fullcycle.co.uk **w** fullcycle.co.uk
  Label Manager: Gerard Cantwell.

Full Fat Records (see Rumour Records Ltd)

Full Time Hobby 3rd Floor, 1A Adpar St, London,
W2 1DE **t** 020 7535 6740 **f** 020 7563 7283
e info@fulltimehobby.co.uk **w** fulltimehobby.co.uk
  ww.myspace.com/fulltimehobby
  ww.twitter.com/fulltimehobby   Director: Nigel Adams.

Fullfill LLC UK Ltd Unit 41, 249-251 Kensal Road,
London, W10 5DB **t** 020 8968 1231 **f** 020 8964 1181
e info@fullfill.co.uk **w** fullfill.co.uk   Office
Manager: Savanna Sparkes.

FUN (see Future Underground Nation)

Functional Breaks (see Future Underground Nation)

Furious? Records PO Box 40, Arundel, W Sussex,
BN18 0UQ **t** 01243 558 444 **f** 01243 558 455
e info@furiousrecords.co.uk **w** furiousrecords.co.uk
  Manager: Tony Patoto.

Furry Tongue Records (see Jackpot Records)

Fury Records PO Box 7187, Ringstead, Kettering,
NN16 6DJ **t** 01933 626945 **e** furyrecords@btconnect.com
w fury-records.com   Owner: Dell Richardson.

Future Earth Records 59 Fitzwilliam St,
Wath Upon Dearne, Rotherham, South Yorks, S63 7HG
t 01709 872 875 **e** records@future-earth.co.uk **w** future-
earth.co.uk   MD: David Moffitt.

Future Records Beaumont House, Kensington Village,
Avonmore Rd, London, W14 8TS **t** 020 7471 5400
f 020 7149 1090 **e** firstname.surname@umusic.com
w future-records.com   MD: Celia McCamley.

Future Underground Nation 80 Monks Rd, Exeter,
Devon, EX4 7BE **t** 01392 490064 **f** 01392 420580
e fun@fun-1.com **w** fun-1.com   Label Mgr: Colin Mitchell.

Futureproof Records Ltd 330 Westbourne Park Rd,
London, W11 1EQ **t** 020 7792 8597 **f** 020 7221 3694
e info@futureproofrecords.com **w** futureproofrecords.com
  MD: Phil Legg.

Gallic (see Silverword Music Group)

Gammer (see Annie Records)

Garry J Cape Ltd 17 Blenheim Road, Wakefield,
WF1 3JZ **t** 01924 299461 **e** garry@garryjcape.com
w garryjcape.com   MD: Garry J Cape.

GAS Records 10 St John's Square, Glastonbury,
Somerset, BA6 9LJ **t** 01458 833 040 **f** 01458 833 958
e info@planetgong.co.uk **w** planetgong.co.uk
  Contact: Johnny Greene.

GEFFEN

GEFFEN

Beaumont House, Kensington Village, Avonmore Rd, London,
W14 8TS   President: Colin Barlow 020 7149 1060.

Genepool Records 34 Windsor Rd, Teddington,
Middlesex, TW11 0SF **t** n/a **f** n/a
e contact@genepoolrecords.com **w** genepoolrecords.com
  Dir: Peter Ward-Edwards.

Genetic Records
A303.5 Tower Bridge Business Complex,
100 Clements Road, London, SE16 4DG **t** 020 8695 6999
e info@geneticrecords.co.uk **w** geneticrecords.co.uk
  Administrator: Lindsey Smith.

Genuine Recordings (see Wall of Sound)

Get Back (see Abstract Sounds LTD)

Giant Records Woking, Surrey, GU21 6NS
t 01483 859 849 **e** mark.studio@ntlworld.com   57
Kingsway: Mark Taylor.

Giants Of Jazz (see Hasmick Promotions)

Gig Records UK (see Wayward Records)

Gimell Records PO Box 197, Beckley, Oxford,
Oxfordshire, OX3 9YJ **t** 01865 358282 **e** info@gimell.com
w gimell.com   MD: Steve C Smith.

Glasgow Records Ltd Lovat House, Gavell Rd,
Glasgow, G65 9BS **t** 01236 826 555 **f** 01236 825 560
e info@glasgowrecords.com **w** glasgowrecords.com
  MD: Tessa Hartmann.

Gliss Records (see GAS Records)

Glitterhouse Records 123c Cadogan Terrace, London,
E9 5HP **t** 020 8533 3577 **e** tris@glitterhouserecords.co.uk
w glitterhouserecords.co.uk   MD: Tris Dickin 07958 564
624.

Global Journey Ltd Unit 3 Boston Court, Salford Quays,
Manchester, M50 2GN **t** 0870 264 7484 **f** 0870 264 6444
e psamuels@global-journey.com **w** global-journey.com
  Head of A&R: Peter Samuels.

Global Mania Entertainment Ltd
Victory House - 2nd floor, 99-101 Regent Street, London,
W1B 4EZ **t** 20 7494 3303 **f** 20 7494 3313
e info@globalmaniaentertainment.co.uk
w globalmaniaentertainment.co.uk   Office Manager: Laura
Fasser.

Global Music Development Ltd Global House,
7 Fernbank Drive, Bingley, West Yorkshire, BD16 4HB
t 0113 2256 707 **e** Kirk@globalmusicdevelopment.com
w globalmusicdevelopment.com   Label Director: Kirk
Worley 07887 852 393.

Contacts Facebook · MySpace · Twitter · YouTube

Global Underground 103 Gaunt St, London, SE1 6AD
t 0870 060 0010 **f** 020 7740 8654
e firstname@globalunderground.co.uk
w globalunderground.co.uk
facebook.com/group.php?gid=2211707653#/group.php
?gid=2211707653 myspace.com/globalundergrounduk
twitter.com/gu_music
youtube.com/user/globalundergroundtv

Globe Records (see Universal Music TV)

Go Beat (see Island Records Group)

Go Disc (see Island Records Group)

Go Entertain Broadley House, 48 Broadley Terrace,
London, NW1 6LG **t** 020 7569 2600 **f** 020 7569 2601
w goentertain.tv

Going for a Song Ltd Chiltern House, 184 High Street,
Berkhamsted, Hertfordshire, HP4 3AP **t** 01442 877417
f 01442 870944 **e** sales@goingforasong.com
w goingforasong.com Sales & Logistics C'tor: Luke White.

Gold Top Records (see Rumour Records Ltd)

Goldrush Records East Denbrae Cottage, Balbeggie,
Perth, PH2 6JD **t** 01821 650408 **f** 01821 650408
e sales@goldrushrecords.co.uk **w** goldrushrecords.co.uk
MD: John S. Thomson.

Goldtop Recordings (see Jungle Records)

Good Groove Recording Ltd 217 Buspace Studios,
Conlan St, London, W10 5AP **t** 020 7565 0050
f 020 7565 0049 **e** gary@goodgroove.co.uk
w goodgroove.co.uk Contact: Gary Davies.

Good Looking Records 54 Clarendon Rd, Watford,
Herts, WD17 2LA **t** 01923 431 614 **f** 01923 431 848
e info@goodlooking.org **w** goodlooking.org
Consultant: Tony Fordham.

Gorgeous Music Suite D, 67 Abbey Rd, London,
NW8 0AE **t** 020 7724 2635 **f** 020 7724 2635
e velliott@gorgeousmusic.net **w** gorgeousmusic.net
Label Manager: Victoria Elliott.

Gotham Records PO Box 6003, Birmingham,
West Midlands, B45 0AR **t** 0121 477 9553 **f** 0121 693 2954
e Barry@gotham-records.com **w** gotham-records.com
Proprietor: Barry Tomes.

Graduate Records PO Box 388, Holt Heath, Worcester,
Worcs, WR6 6WQ **t** 01905 620786
e davidrobertvirr@aol.com **w** graduaterecords.com
MD: Tina Virr.

Gramavision (see Palm Pictures)

Gramophone Records Unit X, 37 Hamilton Rd,
Twickenham, Middlesex, TW2 6SN **t** 020 8894 2169
e woo@attglobal.net Directors: Bruce Woolley, Andy
Visser.

Granada Ventures 48 Leicester Square, London,
WC2H 7FB **t** 020 7389 8555 **e** Mark.hurry@ITV.com
w granadaventures.tv Commercial Affairs Director: Mark
Hurry.

Grasmere Records - Patterdale Music Ltd
59 Marlpit Lane, Coulsdon, Surrey, CR5 2HF
t 020 8407 9440 **f** 01737 5553399
e grasmere1@blueyonder.co.uk **w** grasmeremusic.co.uk
Co-MDs: Jo Barratt, Annette Barratt.

Grateful Dead (see Ace Records)

Great Western Records (see Rollercoaster Records)

The Green Label Music Company Ltd
PO Box 133, Leatherhead, KT24 6WQ
t 01708 444282 and 01483 281300 **f** 01708 469100
e john@greenlabelmusic.co.uk Directors: Andrew
Humphries and John Boyden.

Greensleeves Records Unit 14 Metro Centre,
St John's Road, Isleworth, Middlesex, TW7 6NJ
t 020 8758 0564 **f** 020 8758 0811
e mail@greensleeves.net **w** greensleeves.net
facebook.com/group.php?gid=32135177167&ref=ts
myspace.com/greensleevesrecords
twitter.com/greensleevesrec
youtube.com/greensleevesvideos President: Olivier
Chastan.

Greentrax Recordings Ltd
Cockenzie Business Centre, Edinburgh Rd, Cockenzie,
East Lothian, EH32 0HL **t** 01875 814155 **f** 01875 813545
e greentrax@aol.com **w** greentrax.com MD: Ian D Green
01875 815888.

Gremlin Records **t** 01322 333137
e jason@gremlinproductions.co.uk
w gremlinproductions.com A&R: Jason Alloway.

Grey Mause Records 155 Regents Park Rd, London,
NW1 8BB **t** 0871 900 8410 **e** info@greymause.com
w GreyMause.com

Gridlockaz Records Unit S14,
Shakespeare Business Centre, 245a Coldharbour Lane,
London, SW9 8RR **t** 020 7501 9339 **f** 020 7501 9339
e info@gridlockaz.com **w** gridlockaz.com Label
Mgr: Victor Omosevwerha.

Griffin & Co 24 Church Lane, East Peckham, Tonbridge,
TN12 5JH **t** 01622 872226 **f** 01622 872229
e sales@griffinrecords.co.uk **w** griffinrecords.co.uk
Director: John Hawkings-Byass.

Gringo Records PO Box 7546, Nottingham, NG2 4WT
t 07747 389 696 **e** info@gringorecords.com
w gringorecords.com Boss: Matthew Newnham.

Gronland Records Unit 6 - Fleetwood Building,
2 Northwold Road, London, N16 7HG **t** 020 7553 9166
f 020 7553 9198 **e** thebear@groenland.com
w gronland.co.uk MD: Rene Renner.

Groovefinder Records 30, Havelock Rd, Southsea,
Portsmouth, PO5 1RU **t** 07831 450 241
e jeff@groovefinderproductions.com
w groovefinderproductions.com MD: Jeff Powell.

Groovin' Records PO Box 39, Hoylake, CH47 2HP
t 0845 458 0037 **e** info@groovinrecords.co.uk
w groovinrecords.co.uk Contact: AL Willard Peterson.

GRP Contact: a Universal label. (see Decca Records)

GTV Records Phoenix Music International, PO Box 46, Cromer, NR27 9WX **t** 08456 300 710 **f** 08456 300 720 **e** cindy.blackmore@phoenix-corp.co.uk **w** phoenixmusicinternational.com 🗃 Accounts: Cindy Blackmore.

G2 (see Greentrax Recordings Ltd)

Guess Records (see Duffnote Ltd)

Guild (see Priory Records)

Gutta (Sweden) (see Plankton Records)

GVC (see Highnote Ltd)

H&H Music Ltd. 15 Haslemere Rd, London, N21 3AB **t** 020 8886 4141 **e** info@handhmusic.eu **w** handhmusic.co.uk 🗃 Contact: Steve Brink.

The Hallowe'en Society (see Adasam Limited)

Halo UK Records 88 Church Lane, London, N2 0TB **t** 020 8444 0049 **e** halomanagement@hotmail.com **w** halo-uk.net 🗃 Dir: Mike Karl Maslen 07711 062 309.

Handspun Records 64 Harbour St, Whitstable, Kent, CT5 1AG **t** 07973 149 333 **e** handspun@haveaniceday.ws **w** haveaniceday.ws 🗃 Owner: Anthony Cooper.

Hannibal (see Palm Pictures)

Harbourtown Records PO Box 25, Ulverston, Cumbria, LA12 7UN **t** 01229 588290 **f** 01229 588290 **e** records@hartown.demon.co.uk **w** harbourtownrecords.com 🗃 MD: Gordon Jones.

Harkit Records PO Box 617, Bushey Heath, Herts., WD23 1SX **t** 020 8385 7771 **e** sales@harkitrecords.com **w** harkitrecords.com 🗃 C.E.O.: Michael Fishberg.

Harmless Recordings (see Demon Music Group)

Harper Collins Audio Books 77-85 Fulham Palace Road, Hammersmith, London, W6 8JB **t** 020 8741 7070 **f** 020 8307 4517 **e** rosalie.george@harpercollins.co.uk **w** fireandwater.com 🗃 Publishing Manager: Rosalie George 020 8307 4618.

Hasmick Promotions Unit 8, Forest Hill Trading Estate, London, SE23 2LX **t** 020 8291 6777 **f** 020 8291 0081 **e** jasmine@hasmick.co.uk **w** hasmick.co.uk 🗃 Contact: Carl Hazeldine.

Hassle Records 🗃 Contact: Eat Sleep Records. (see Full Time Hobby)

Haven Records St Mary's Works, St Mary's Plain, Norwich, Norfolk, NR3 3AF **t** 01603 624290 **f** 01603 619999 **e** derek@backsrecords.co.uk **w** havenrecords.co.uk 🗃 A&R: Derek Chapman/Boo Hewerdine 01603 626221.

Headscope Headrest, Broadoak, Heathfield, East Sussex, TN21 8TU **t** 01435 863994 **f** 01435 867027 **e** info@headscope.co.uk **w** headscope.co.uk 🗃 Partner: Ron Geesin.

Headstone Records 47 Fairfax Rd, Woking, Surrey, GU21 9HN **t** 01483 856 760 **e** colinspencer@ntlworld.com 🗃 MD: Colin Spencer 07811 387 220.

Hearmusic (see Mercury Music Group)

Heat Recordings 63 Hartland Rd, London, NW6 6BH **t** 020 7625 5552 **f** 020 7625 5553 **e** info@heatrecordings.com **w** heatrecordings.com 🗃 MD/A&R: Alex Payne.

Heavenly Dance PO Box 640, Bromley, BR1 4XZ **t** 07985 439 453 **f** 020 8290 4589 **e** Heavenlydance1@aol.com

Heavenly Recordings 219 Portobello Rd, London, W11 1LU **t** 020 7494 2998 **e** info@heavenlyrecordings.com **w** heavenlyrecordings.com ▪ myspace.com/heavenlyrecordings ▪ twitter.com/heavenlyrecs ▪ facebook.com/pages/HEAVENLY-RECORDINGS/21108820390 🗃 MD: Jeff Barrett.

Heavy Metal Records 152 Goldthorn Hill, Penn, Wolverhampton, West Midlands, WV2 3JA **t** 01902 345345 **f** 01902 345155 **e** Paul.Birch@revolverrecords.com **w** HeavyMetalRecords.com ▪ myspace.com/heavymetalrecords ▪ twitter.com/heavymetalrecs ▪ youtube.com/revolverrecords 🗃 MD: Paul Birch 0121 270 0877.

Hed Kandi 🗃 Contact: Ministry of Sound. (see Ministry Of Sound Recordings)

Helium Records 4th Floor Studio, 16 Abbey Churchyard, Bath, BA1 1LY **t** 01225 311661 **f** 01225 482013 **e** carole@heliumrecords.co.uk **w** heliumrecords.co.uk 🗃 Dirs: Chris Hughes, Carole Davies.

Hellsquad Records PO Box 54319, London, W2 7AZ **t** 020 77929494 **e** enquiries@hellsquadrecords.com **w** hellsquadrecords.com 🗃 MD: Thomas Dalton.

Hens Teeth Records Millham Lane, Dulverton, Somerset, TA22 9HQ **t** 01398 324 114 **f** 01398 324 114 🗃 MD: Andrew Quarrie.

HHO Ltd Suite 1, 1-13 Britannia Business Centre, Cricklewood Lane, London, NW2 1ET **t** 020 8830 8813 **f** 020 8830 8801 **e** info@hho.co.uk **w** hho.co.uk 🗃 MD: Henry Hadaway.

HHO Multimedia Suite 1, Brittania Business Centre, London, NW2 1EZ **t** 020 8830 8813 **f** 020 8830 8801 **e** info@hho.co.uk **w** hho.co.uk 🗃 MD: Henry Hadaway.

Hi-Fi (see Everest Copyrights)

Hidden Art Recordings PO Box 8, Corby, Nothants., NN17 2XZ **t** 01536 202 295 **f** 01536 266 246 **e** steve@adasam.co.uk **w** hiddenartrecordings.com 🗃 Label Manager: Steve Kalidoski.

High Barn Records The Bardfield Centre, Great Bardfield, Braintree, Essex, CM7 4SL **t** 01371 811 291 **e** info@high-barn.com **w** high-barn.com 🗃 MD: Chris Bullen.

High Voltage Sounds 61b Thomas St, Manchester, M4 1NA **t** 0161 839 2802 **f** 0161 839 2802 **e** rich@highvoltage.org.uk **w** highvoltage.org.uk 🗃 Head of A&R: Richard Cheetham.

Higher State 95-99 North Street, London, SW4 0HF **t** 020 7627 5656 **f** 020 7627 5757 **e** info@higherstate.co.uk **w** higherstate.co.uk 🔳 A&R Mgr: Jamie Pierce.

Highnote Ltd Studio 65, Shepperton Film Studio, Shepperton, Middx, TW17 0QD **t** 01932 592 949 **e** info08@highnote.co.uk **w** highnote.co.uk 🔳 Dir: Steve Waters.

Hip Bop (see Silva Screen)

The Hit Music Company Shepperton Film Studios, Studios Rd, Shepperton, Middx, TW17 0QD **t** 01932 593634 **e** chet@thehitmusiccompany.com **w** thehitmusiccompany.com 🔳 Chief: Chet Selwood.

HMV Classics 🔳 Contact: Premier. (see EMI Classics International)

HomeFront Productions Fir Tree Cottage, Churt, Surrey, GU10 2PY **t** 01252 790421 **e** roland@rolandchadwick.com **w** rolandchadwick.com 🔳 myspace.com/rolandchadwick 🔳 Director: Roland Chadwick 07980 822517.

Honchos Music (see NRK Sound Division Ltd)

Honey Records 85-89 Duke St, Liverpool, L1 5AP **t** 0151 708 7722 **e** info@honeyrecords.co.uk **w** honeyrecords.co.uk 🔳 Dirs: Mat Flynn, Keith Mullin.

Hope Records (see Music Fusion Ltd)

Hope Music Group Unit 4.16 The Paintworks, Bath Road, Bristol, BS4 3EH **t** 0117 971 2397 **f** 0117 972 8981 **e** caroline@hoperecordings.com **w** hoperecordings.com 🔳 MD: Leon Alexander.

Hope Recordings (see Hope Music Group)

Horatio Nelson PO Box 1123, London, SW1P 1HB **t** 020 7828 6533 **f** 020 7828 1271 🔳 MD: Derek Boulton.

Horus Music LCB Depot, 31 Rutland St, Leicester, LE1 1RE **t** 0116 253 3436 **e** nick.dunn@horusmusic.co.uk **w** horusmusic.co.uk 🔳 horusmusicgroup 🔳 horusmusicltd 🔳 MD: Nick Dunn.

Hospital Records 182-184 Dartmouth Rd, Sydenham, London, SE26 4QZ **t** 020 8613 0400 **f** 020 8613 0401 **e** info@hospitalrecords.com **w** hospitalrecords.com 🔳 Marketing & Promotions: Tom Kelsey.

Hot Dog (see The Store For Music)

Hot Lead Records 2, Laurel Bank, Lowestwood, Huddersfield, Yorkshire, HD7 4ER **t** 01484 846333 **f** 01484 846333 **e** HotLeadRecords@btopenworld.com **w** fimusic.co.uk 🔳 MD: Ian R. Smith.

Hours Beat Records (see Archive Recordings)

Housefly Records 3 Mill Row, Pontardawe, SA8 3AD **t** 07765 441 015 **e** info@houseflyrecords.com **w** houseflyrecords.com 🔳 Label Manager: Jules Hyland.

Household Name Records PO Box 12286, London, SW9 6FE **t** 020 7582 9972 **e** info@householdnamerecords.co.uk **w** householdnamerecords.co.uk 🔳 Label Manager: David Giles.

Housexy (see Ministry Of Sound Recordings)

Hungry Audio 7 Elwyn Rd, Norwich, NR1 2RX **t** 01603 632466 **e** contact@hungryaudio.co.uk **w** hungryaudio.co.uk 🔳 myspace.com/hungryaudiorecords 🔳 twitter.com/hungryaudio 🔳 MD: Adrian Cooke 07909 920574.

Hux Records PO Box 12647, London, SE18 8ZF **t** 07939 529772 **f** 01253 796 492 **e** info@huxrecords.com **w** huxrecords.com 🔳 Contact: Brian O'Reilly.

Hwyl (see Hwyl)

Hwyl 2 The Square, Yapham, York, North Yorkshire, YO42 1PJ **t** 01759 304514 **f** 01759 304514 **e** stevejparry@yahoo.co.uk **w** hwylnofio.com 🔳 Owner: Steve Parry.

Hydrogen Dukebox 89 Borough High Street, London, SE1 1NL **t** 020 7357 9799 **e** doug@hydrogendukebox.com **w** hydrogendukebox.com 🔳 Contact: Doug Hart.

Hyperion Records Ltd PO Box 25, London, SE9 1AX **t** 020 8318 1234 **f** 020 8463 1230 **e** info@hyperion-records.co.uk **w** hyperion-records.co.uk 🔳 Dir: Simon Perry.

I'll Call You Records Brooke Oast, Jarvis Lane, Goudhurst, Cranbrook, Kent, TN17 1LP **t** 01580 211 623 **e** rbickersteth@lookingforward.biz 🔳 Contact: E R Bickersteth.

I-Anka PO Box 917, London, W10 5FA **e** ianka.records@boltblue.com **w** bobandy.com 🔳 MD: J Punford.

Iconoclast Records Ltd 172 Fawe Park Rd, London, SW15 2EQ **t** 07900 241786 **f** 07092 109723 **e** al@iconoclastmedia.com 🔳 MD/A&R: Al Malik.

IDJ (see Incentive Music Ltd)

Iffy Biffa Records Welland House Farm, Spalding Marsh, Spalding, Linconshire, PE12 6HF **t** 07711 513791 **e** mark@iffybiffa.co.uk **w** iffybiffa.co.uk 🔳 MD: Mark Bunn.

IHT Records Unit 2D, Clapham North Arts Centre, 26-32 Voltaire Road, London, SW4 6DH **t** 020 7720 7411 **f** 020 7720 8095 **e** rob@ihtrecords.com **w** davidgray.com 🔳 Contact: Rob Holden.

Ikon (see Priory Records)

ill funk recordings 52 St Johns Rd, London, TW7 6NW **t** 020 8568 8914 **e** president@ill-funk.com **w** ill-funk.com 🔳 President: Gurdeep S Ubhie +44 7960257842.

Illicit Recordings PO Box 51871, London, NW2 9BR **t** 020 8830 7831 **f** 020 8830 7859 **e** ian@mumbojumbo.co.uk **w** illicitrecordings.com 🔳 MD: Ian Clifford.

Imagemaker Sound & Vision PO Box 69, Launceston, Cornwall, PL15 7YA **t** 01566 86308 **f** 01566 86308 **e** mail@timwheater.com **w** timwheater.com 🔳 MD: Olive Lister.

Imaginary Music 3 Cyril Wood Court, 89 West St, Bere Regis, Dorset, BH20 7HH **t** 01929 472 830 **e** gphall@tiscali.co.uk **w** gphall.com 🔳 Composer: GP Hall.

Record Companies: Record Companies & Labels

Immaterial Records PO Box 706, Ilford, Essex, IG2 6ED **t** 07973 676160 **f** 0870 705 1337 **e** bij@btinternet.com 🔲 Owner: Bijal Dodhia.

Immoral Recordings (see JPS Recordings)

Imprint (see D.O.R.)

In Stereo Arch 462 Kingsland Viaduct, 83 Rivington St, Shoreditch, London, EC2A 3AY **f** 0871 264 7065 **e** jan@in-stereo.net **w** in-stereo.net 🔲 Directors: Jan Sodderland, Jonathan Green.

Incentive Music Ltd Unit 21, Grand Union Centre, West Row, London, W10 5AS **t** 020 8964 2555 **f** 020 8964 8778 **e** incentive@incentivemusic.co.uk **w** incentivemusic.com 🔲 MD: Nick Halkes.

Independiente The Drill Hall, 3 Heathfield Terrace, Chiswick, London, W4 4JE **t** 020 8747 8111 **f** 020 8747 8113 **e** firstname@independiente.co.uk **w** independiente.co.uk

Indie 500 (see New Leaf Records)

Indigo Records (see Universal Music (UK) Ltd)

Indipop Records P.O.Box 369, Glastonbury, Somerset, BA6 8YN **t** 01749 831 674 **f** 01749 831 674 🔲 MD: Steve Coe.

Infectious t 020 7368 3500 🔲 Contact: Infectious.

Inferno Cool (see Inferno Records)

Inferno Records 32-36 Telford Way, London, W3 7XS **t** 020 8742 9300 **f** 020 8742 9097 **e** pat@infernorecords.co.uk **w** infernorecords.co.uk 🔲 Heaf of A&R: Pat Travers.

Infur (see Seriously Groovy Music)

INFX Records Buckinghamshire New University, High Wycombe Campus, Queen Alexandra Rd, High Wycombe, Buckinghamshire, HP11 2JZ **t** 01494 522141 ex 4020 **e** frazer.mackenzie@bucks.ac.uk **w** bucks.ac.uk 🔲 Head of Music, Entertainment & Moving Image: Frazer Mackenzie.

Inigo Recordings Label Group Suite 220, 241-251 Ferndale Rd, London, SW9 8BJ **t** 020 7168 9118 **f** 020 7168 9118 **e** info@inigorecordings.com **w** inigo-online.com 🔲 Contact: Label Manager.

Ink (see Distinct'ive Records)

Inner Rhythm (see Born to Dance Records)

Inner Sanctum Recordings (see Adasam Limited)

Innerground Records 8 Roland Mews, Stepney Green, London, E1 3JT **t** 020 7929 3333 **f** 020 7929 3222 **e** info@innergroundrecords.com **w** innergroundrecords.com 🔲 MD: Oliver J. Brown.

Instant Hit PO Box 34, Ventnor, Isle of Wight, PO38 1YQ **t** 01983 857 079 **e** jkt@diamondisle.co.uk **w** diamondisle.co.uk 🔲 MD: Jon Monks.

Instant Karma (see Dharma Records Ltd)

Institute Recordings Phoenix Music International, PO Box 46, Cromer, NR27 9WX **t** 08456 300 710 **f** 08456 300 720 **e** cindy.blackmore@phoenix-corp.co.uk **w** phoenixmusicinternational.com 🔲 Accounts: Cindy Blackmore.

Integrity Records Ltd 40 Mill Street, Bedford, MK40 3HD **t** 01234 267 459 **f** 01234 212 864 **e** david@integrityrecords.co.uk **w** integrityrecords.co.uk 🔲 Director: David R Twigden.

Interlude Records 30 Amity Street, Reading, Berks, RG1 3LP **t** 07879 894 593 **e** info@interluderecords.com **w** interluderecords.com 🔲 Label Manager: Tobias Andersson.

International Media rights Suite 111, The Broadway, Mill Hill, London, NW7 3LL **t** 0844 669 6943 **f** 0844 669 6945 **e** alan@internationalmediarights.com **w** internationalmediarights.com 🔲 GM: Alan Bellman 07768 065 661.

Interscope 🔲 Contact: Polydor Associated. (see Polydor Records)

Invicta Hi-Fi Records Limited 5th Floor, Gostin Building, 32-36 Hanover St, Liverpool, L1 4LN **t** 0151 709 5264 **f** 0151 709 8439 **e** admin@invictahifi.co.uk **w** invictahifi.co.uk 🔲 Contact: Jules Bennett.

Invisible Hands Music 15 Chalk Farm Rd, London, NW1 8AG **t** 020 7284 3322 **f** 020 7284 4455 **e** info@invisiblehands.co.uk **w** invisiblehands.co.uk 🔲 MD: Charles Kennedy.

Iodine Records (see Wayward Records)

Iona Records (see Lismor Recordings)

Iris Light Records 9 Station Walk, Highbridge, Somerset, TA9 3HQ **t** 01278 780904 **f** 01278 780904 **e** iLIGHT@irislight.co.uk **w** irislight.co.uk 🔲 MD: Adam Sykes.

IRL PO Box 30884, London, W12 9AZ **t** 020 8746 7461 **f** 020 8749 7441 **e** info@independentrecordsltd.com **w** independentrecordsltd.com 🔲 Dirs: David Jaymes & Tom Haxell.

Irma Records Srl Via Romagnoli 3/B, Bentivoglio, Bologna, 40010, Italy **t** +39 051 727 582 **f** +39 051 729 475 **e** corrado@irmagroup.com **w** irmagroup.com 🔳 myspace.com/irmarecords 🔲 Head Of Wolrdwide Licensing: Corrado Dierna +39 333 338 3835.

Iron Man Records Iron Man Records, PO Box 9121, Birmingham, West Midlands, B13 8AU **t** 08712 260910 **e** info@ironmanrecords.co.uk **w** ironmanrecords.co.uk 🔳 myspace.com/ironmanrecs 🅱 twitter.com/ironmanrecords 📺 youtube.com/ironmanrecords 🔲 Label Manager: Mark Badger 07974 746810

ISLAND RECORDS GROUP

Island Records Group

364-366 Kensington High St, London, W14 8NS
t 020 7471 5300 **f** 020 7471 5001
e firstname.lastname@umusic.com **w** islandrecords.co.uk
👤 Co-Presidents: Darcus Beese and Ted Cockle. Senior Vice
President: David Sharpe. Legal & Business Affairs
Director: Claire Sugrue. General Manager Island Label: Jon
Turner. Head of Press: Shane O'Neill. Marketing Director
Universal Records: Sarah Boorman.

Isobar Records 56 Gloucester Pl, London, W1U 8HJ
t 020 7486 3297 **f** 020 7486 3297
e info@isobarrecords.com **w** isobarrecords.com
👤 MD: Peter Morris 07956 493692.

ITN Corporation PO Box 1795, Sheffield, S3 7FF
t 0114 272 8726 **f** 0114 272 8726
e itn@itncorp.demon.co.uk **w** inthenursery.com
🔳 myspace.com/inthenursery 👤 Partner: Nigel
Humberstone.

J & S Construction (see Taste Media Ltd - Taste
Music)

Jackpot Records PO Box 2272, Rottingdean, Brighton,
BN2 8XD **t** 01273 304681 **f** 01273 308120
e steveb@a7music.com **w** a7music.com 👤 Label
Manager: Steve B.

Jagged Rock Music Ltd 111 Attingham Drive,
Sovereign Heights, Dudley, West Midlands, DY1 3HL
t 07876 774068 **e** peter.newton@jaggedrockmusic.com
w jaggedrockmusic.com 🔳 myspace.com/jaggedrockmusic
👤 Director: Peter Newton 0121 557 0467.

Jalapeno Records Unit 11, Impress House, Mansell Rd,
London, W3 7QH **t** 020 8743 5218 **f** 020 7681 3949
e info@jalapenorecords.com **w** jalapenorecords.com
👤 MD: Trevor McNamee.

Jam Central P.O. Box 230, Aylesbury, Buckinghamshire,
HP21 9WA **t** 07765 258225
e office@jamcentralrecords.co.uk
w jamcentralrecords.co.uk
🔳 myspace.com/jamcentralrecords
▶ youtube.com/jamcentralrecords 👤 Managing
Director: Stuart Robb.

Jamdown Music Ltd Stanley House Studios,
39 Stanley Gardens, London, W3 7SY **t** 020 8735 0280
f 07970 574924 **e** othman@jamdown-music.com
w jamdown-music.com 🔳 myspace.com/jamdownabood
👤 MD: Othman Mukhlis.

Jasmine Records (see Hasmick Promotions)

Jaygee Cassettes 5 Woodfield, Burnham on Sea,
Somerset, TA8 1QL **t** 01278 789 352 **f** 01278 789 352
e patricia@jaygeecassettes.co.uk **w** babysooth.com 👤 Snr
Partners: Roger & Patricia Wannell.

Jeepster Recordings Ltd Dedswell Suite, Surrey Pl,
Mill Lane, Godalming, Surrey, GU7 1EY **t** 01483 861000
f 01483 861888 **e** info@jeepster.co.uk **w** jeepster.co.uk
👤 Label Manager: Kay Heath.

Jessica Records Ltd 12 Parkside Gardens, Eastville,
Bristol, BS5 6TZ **e** jessicasongwriter@googlemail.com
w myspace.com/jessicaappla 👤 Label Manager: Jessica
Appla.

Jetstar Phoenix Music International, PO Box 46, Cromer,
NR27 9WX **t** 0845 630 0710 **f** 0845 630 0720
e cindy.blackmore@phoenix-corp.co.uk
w phoenixmusicinternational.com 👤 Accounts: Cindy
Blackmore.

Jewish Music Heritage Recordings PO Box 232,
Harrow, Middx, HA1 2NN **t** 020 8909 2445 **f** 020 8909 1030
e jewishmusic@jmi.org.uk **w** jmi.org.uk 👤 MD: Geraldine
Auerbach MBE.

JFM Records 11 Alexander House, Tiller Road, London,
E14 8PT **t** 020 7987 8596 **f** 020 7987 8596
e burdlawrence@btinternet.com 👤 MD: Julius Pemberton
Maynard.

JIVE

9 Derry Street, London, W8 5HY
e firstname.lastname@sonymusic.com 👤 Head Of Jive: Nick
Burgess 020 7361 8000.

JPS Recordings PO Box 2643, Reading, Berks, RG5 4GF
t 0118 969 9269 **f** 0118 969 9264 **e** johnjpsuk@aol.com
👤 MD: John Saunderson 07885 058 911.

JRC Records 113 Kitchener Road, Walthamstow, London,
E17 4LJ **t** 07737 540 075 **e** jayarcea@mac.com
w jayarcea.com 👤 Owner: John Clair.

Jumpin' & Pumpin' (see Passion Music)

Jungle (see Jungle Records)

Jungle Records Old Dairy Mews, 62 Chalk Farm Rd,
Camden, London, NW1 8AN **t** 020 7267 0171
f 020 7267 0912 **e** enquiries@jungle-records.com **w** jungle-
records.com 🔳 myspace.com/junglerecords
🔳 twitter.com/junglerecords ▶ youtube.com/junglerecords
👤 Directors: Alan Hauser, Graham Combi.

The Junk Label P.O. Box 308, Cobham, Surrey, KT11 2XH
t 01932 864016 **e** info@thejunklabel.com
w thejunklabel.com 🔳 myspace.com/thejunklabel
🔳 twitter.com/thejunklabel ▶ youtube.com/thejunklabel
👤 MD: Bob Gwilliam.

Jus Listen (see RF Records)

Just Music Hope House, 40 St Peters Rd, London, W6 9BD **t** 020 8741 6020 **e** justmusic@justmusic.co.uk **w** justmusic.co.uk **f** facebook.com/pages/Just-Music/24664117690 **M** myspace.com/justmusiclabel **t** twitter.com/justmusiclabel **Q** Directors: Serena & John Benedict.

K-Scope (see Snapper Music)

K-Tel Entertainment (UK) Unit 4 Northfield Industrial Estate, Beresford Avenue, Wembley, HA0 1NW **t** 020 8903 2052 **f** 020 8903 9527 **e** janie@k-tel-uk.com **w** kteluk.com **Q** GM: Janie Webber.

!K7 Records Heidestrasse 52, Berlin, 10557, Germany **t** +49 302 020 957 **f** +49 302 044 456 **e** nicky@k7.com **w** k7.com **f** facebook.com/K7Records **M** myspace.com/k7records **t** twitter.com/K7records **▶** youtube.com/user/K7rec#p/u **Q** !K7 Product Manager: Nicky Agunwa.

Kabuki 23 Weavers Way, Camden Town, London, NW1 0XF **t** 020 7916 2142 **e** email@kabuki.co.uk **w** kabuki.co.uk **Q** Manager: Sheila Naujoks.

Kamaflage Records (see Dragonfly Records)

Kamara Music Publishing PO Box 56, Boston, Lincolnshire, PE22 8JL **t** 07976 553624 **e** chris@kamaramusic.fsnet.co.uk **w** myspace.com/megahitrecordsuk **Q** MD: Chris Kamara.

Kamaric (see Fury Records)

Kamera Shy (see Gotham Records)

Kamikaze (see Superglider Records)

Kauris Entertainment International House, 226 Seven Sisters Rd, London, N4 3GG **e** kaurismusic@yahoo.com **w** kaurisentertainment.com **Q** CEO - General Manager: Didier Metelo 07909 927272.

Kennington Recordings 44 Norwood Park Road, London, SE27 9UA **t** 020 8670 4082 **e** corporatecommunications@kenningtonrecordings.com **w** kenningtonrecordings.com **Q** Contact: Mister L, Commissioner Gordon or The Chief.

Kent (see Ace Records)

Keswick (see Loose Records)

Kevin Mayhew (see Priory Records)

Kids Records London **t** 07739 840684 **e** wearedownwiththekids@gmail.com **w** kidsthelabel.co.uk **f** facebook.com/home.php?#/group.php?gid=129402293 582 **M** myspace.com/kidsrecords **Q** President: Dave Kids.

Kii Music 111 The Custard Factory, Gibb St, Birmingham, B9 4AA **t** 0121 693 0013 **e** geoff@saffamusic.co.uk **Q** MD: Geoff Pearce.

Kila Records & Distribution Charlemont House, 33 Charlemont St, Dublin 2 **t** +353 1 476 0627 **f** +353 1 476 0627 **e** info@kilarecords.com **w** kila.ie **f** facebook.com/kilaofficial **M** myspace.com/kilaofficial **Q** Manager: Sarah Glennane.

Kill the Lights (see The Recoverworld Label Group (Supreme Music Ltd))

Kingsize Records The Old Bakehouse, Hale St, Staines, Middx, TW18 4UW **t** 01784 458700 **f** 01784 458333 **e** info@kingsize.co.uk **w** kingsize.co.uk **Q** Lbl Mgr: Julian Shay.

Kingsway Music 26-28 Lottbridge Drove, Eastbourne, East Sussex, BN23 6NT **t** 01323 437700 **f** 01323 411970 **e** music@kingsway.co.uk **w** kingsway.co.uk **Q** A&R Mgr: Caroline Bonnett.

Kismet Records 91 Saffron Hill, London, EC1N 8PT **t** 020 7404 3333 **e** info@kismetrecords.com **w** kismetrecords.com **Q** Director: Gilly Da Silva.

Kitchenware 7 The Stables, Saint Thomas St, Newcastle upon Tyne, Tyne and Wear, NE1 4LE **t** 0191 230 1970 **f** 0191 232 0262 **e** info@kitchenwarerecords.com **w** kitchenwarerecords.com **Q** Administration: Nicki Turner.

Klone Records PO Box 54127, London, W5 9BE **t** 020 8997 7893 **f** 020 8997 7901 **e** post@rumour.demon.co.uk **w** klonerecords.com **Q** Managing Director: Anne Plaxton.

Kontakt Records (see ATG Records)

KRL - Bulk Music Ltd PO Box 5577, Newton Mearns, Glasgow, G77 9BH **t** 0141 616 0900 **f** 0141 639 6825 **e** krl@krl.co.uk **w** krl.co.uk **Q** MD: Isobel Waugh.

Krypton Records 31 Fife St, St James, Northampton, NN5 5BH **t** 01604 752800 **f** 01604 752800 **e** ray@thejets.co.uk **w** thejets.co.uk **Q** Contact: Ray Cotton.

Kudos Records Ltd 77 Fortess Road, Kentish Town, London, NW5 1AG **t** 020 7482 4555 **f** 020 7482 4551 **e** contact@kudos-digital.co.uk **w** kudos-digital.co.uk

L1ROPEWALK RECORDINGS

81 Gleneagles Drive, Ainsdale, Southport, Merseyside, PR8 3TH **t** 07982 529168 **e** publicservice2008@yahoo.com **w** l1ropewalkrecordings.co.uk **f** ropewalkrecordings **M** jacspublicservice **t** twitter.com/l1ropewalk **Q** owner/proprietor L1 Ropewalk Recordings: Mr Nigel Harrison 07982 529168.

Lager Records 10 Barley Rise, Baldock, Hertfordshire, SG7 6RT **t** 01462 636799 **f** 01462 636799 **e** dan@Lockupmusic.co.uk **Q** Dir: Steve Knight.

Lake (see Fellside Recordings Ltd)

Lammas Records 118 The Mount, York, YO24 1AS **t** 01904 624132 **f** 01904 624132 **e** enquiries@lammas.co.uk **w** lammas.co.uk **Q** Prop: Lance Andrews.

Contacts **f** Facebook **☒** MySpace **t** Twitter **▶** YouTube

LANDER RECORDS & MUSIC

Lander Music Group, Athene House, 86 The Broadway, London, NW7 3TD **t** 020 8906 2224 **e** judd@landerpr.com **w** landerpr.com **f** facebook.com/LanderPR **☒** myspace.com/landermusicpr **t** twitter.com/MusicPromotions **☒** Director: Judd Lander.

LAS Records UK LAS House, 10 Derby Hill Crescent, London, SE23 3YL **t** 020 8291 9236 **f** 020 8291 9236 **e** lasrecords@latinartsgroup.com **w** latinarts.com **☒** Director: Hector Rosquete 07956 446 342.

Last Suppa Records Limited The Coach House, 1a Putney Heath Lane, London, SW15 3JG **t** 020 7193 1325 **e** jon@lastsuppa.com **w** lastsuppa.com **☒** Managing Director: Jon Sexton.

Lazarus Marlinspike Hall, Walpole Halesworth, Suffolk, IP19 9AR **t** 01986 784664 **e** cally@thethe.com **w** thethe.com **☒** Soul Prop: Cally.

The Leaf Label PO Box 272, Leeds, LS19 9BP **t** 0113 216 1021 **f** 0700 6057821 **e** contact@theleaflabel.com **w** theleaflabel.com **☒** myspace.com/theleaflabel **☒** facebook.com/theleaflabel **▶** youtube.com/theleaflabel **☒** MD: Tony Morley.

Legend Music 5 Bream Close, Melksham, Wiltshire, SN12 7JX **t** 01225 790937 **e** davidrees55@aol.com **☒** MD: David Rees 07968 434570.

Legion Presents Records 7, 28a High St, Cardiff, CF10 1PU **t** 02920 399 383 **e** info@legionpresents.com **w** legionpresents.com **☒** Dirs: Dave or Kris Legion.

Leningrad Masters (see Priory Records)

Lewis Recordings PO Box 60201, London, EC1P 1QZ **t** 020 7713 0926 **f** 020 7833 2611 **e** info@LewisRecordings.com **w** LewisRecordings.com **☒** Director: Mike Lewis.

Lex (see Warp)

LHP Records / LHP Publishing 98 Wolseley Rd, Southampton, Hampshire, SO15 3ER **e** jayne.lhp@ntlworld.com **w** lhprecords.com **☒** Head of Management & Promotions (A&R): Jayne 07891165759.

Lick Records (see Automatic Records)

Lindenburg (see Priory Records)

Lineage Recordings P.O. Box 1034, Maidstone, Kent, ME15 0WZ **t** 07821 357 713 **e** lineage@toucansurf.com **☒** MD: CJ Jammer.

Linn Records Glasgow Rd, Waterfoot, Eaglesham, G76 0EQ **t** 0141 303 5026 **f** 0141 303 5007 **e** info@linnrecords.co.uk **w** linnrecords.com **☒** Business Manager: Caroline Dooley.

Liquid Sound (see Dragonfly Records)

LIR Classics (London Independent Records) **t** 020 3239 6855 **e** info@london-independent.co.uk **w** london-independent.co.uk **☒** Director: Jan Hart.

Lismor Recordings PO Box 7264, Glasgow, Strathclyde, G46 6YE **t** 0141 637 6010 **f** 0141 637 6010 **e** lismor@lismor.com **w** allcelticmusic.com **☒** MD: Ronnie Simpson.

Little Genius Recordings 91 Berwick Street, London, W1F 0NE **t** 020 7292 6462 **e** gene@littlegeniusrecordings.com **w** littlegeniusrecordings.com **☒** Contact: Michael Brown.

Little Piece of Jamaica (LPOJ) 55 Finsbury Park Rd, Highbury, London, N4 2JY **t** 020 7359 0788 **e** paulhuelpoj@yahoo.co.uk **☒** Dir: Paul Hue 07973 630729.

Live At The Suite Ltd Utopia Village, 7 Chalcot Road, London, NW1 8LH **t** 020 7813 7964 **f** 020 7209 4092 **e** ladyb@thesuite.sh **w** liveatthesuite.com **☒** Contact: Andrew, Lady B.

Livewire (see K-Tel Entertainment (UK))

LIXO SONIDO & DISCOS

Apartado Postal 54850, Medellin, 9995, Colombia **t** +57 4411 3878 **e** AlbertoArias@une.net.co **w** lixosonido.com **☒** myspace.com/lixosd **☒** Managing Director: Alberto Arias 57 4 4113878.

Lizard King Records UK The Unit, 2 Manor Gardens, London, N7 6ER **t** 020 7561 6700 **f** 020 7561 6701 **e** info@lizardkingrecords.co.uk **w** lizardkingrecords.co.uk **☒** myspace.com/lizardkingrecords **t** twitter.com/lizard_king_ **☒** CEO: Martin Heath.

Loaded (see Skint Records)

Lochshore (see KRL - Bulk Music Ltd)

Lock 2, The Old Parish Hall, The Square, Lenham, Maidstone, Kent, ME17 2PQ **t** 01622 858300 **f** 01622 858300 **e** info@eddielock.com **w** eddielock.co.uk **☒** myspace.com/eddielock **☒** Artist Manager: Eddie Lock.

Locked On Records 679 Holloway Road, London, N19 5SE **t** 020 7281 4877 **e** tas@puregroove.co.uk **w** puregroove.co.uk **☒** MD: Tarik Nashnush.

Lockjaw Records County House, St. Mary's St, Worcester, WR1 1HB **t** 01905 729149 **f** 01905 729149 **e** syd.emery@lockjawrecords.co.uk **w** lockjawrecords.co.uk **☒** myspace.com/lockjawrecords **t** twitter.com/lockjawrec **▶** youtube.com/lockjawuk **☒** Label Manager: Syd Emery.

LOE Records LOE House, 159 Broadhurst Gardens, London, NW6 3AU **t** 020 7328 6100 **f** 020 7624 6384 **e** watanabe@loe.uk.net **☒** Creative Mgr: Jonny Wilson.

| 📇 Contacts | 📘 Facebook | 🟦 MySpace | 🐦 Twitter | 📺 YouTube |

Lo-Five 22 Herbert Street, Glasgow, G20 6NB
t 0141 560 2748 or 0141 337 1199 **f** 0141 357 0655
e info@lo-fiverecords.com **w** lo-fiverecords.com 📇 Dir: Robin Morton.

Lojinx BCM Box 2676, London, WC1N 3XX
t 020 7193 9154 **f** 020 7691 9716 **e** hello@lojinx.com
w lojinx.com

London Records (see Warner Bros Records UK)

Long Island Records Long Island House, 1-4 Warple Way, London, W3 0RG **t** 020 8954 7144
e info@longislandstudios.com **w** longislandstudios.com 📇 Contact: Leanne Myers.

LongMan (see LongMan Records)

LongMan Records West House, Forthaven, Shoreham-by-Sea, W. Sussex, BN43 5HY **t** 01273 453422
f 01273 452914 **e** richard@longman-records.com
w longman-records.com 📇 Director: Richard Durrant.

Loog Records 364-366 Kensington High St, London, W14 8NS **t** 020 7471 5610 **e** loogrecords@umusic.com
w loogrecords.co.uk 📇 MD: James Oldham.

Loose Music Unit 205, 5-10 Eastman Road, London, W3 7YG **t** 020 8749 9330 **f** 020 8749 2230
e info@loosemusic.com **w** loosemusic.com 📇 MD/A&R: Tom Bridgewater.

Loose Records Pinery Building, Highmoor, Wigton, Cumbria, CA7 9LW **t** 016973 45422
e looserecords@gmail.com **w** looserecords.com
📘 facebook.com/pages/Loose-Records/139159737210
🟦 w.myspace.com/andrewjtitcombe
🐦 twitter.com/looserecords 📇 A&R: Tim Edwards.

Loose Tie Records 15 Stanhope Rd, London, N6 5NE
t 020 8340 7797 **f** 020 8340 6923
e paul@paulrodriguezmus.demon.co.uk 📇 MD: Paul Rodriguez.

Loriana Music PO Box 2731, Romford, RM7 1AD
t 01708 750185 **f** 01708 750185 **e** info@lorianamusic.com
w lorianamusic.com   www.biomusic-6in1.net
🟦 lorianamusic 📇 Owner: Jean-Louis Fargier 07748 343363.

Lost Highway (see Mercury Music Group)

LOT49 Records LGF 17 Whiteladies Rd, Bristol, BS8 1PB
t 01173 290108 **e** info@lot49.co.uk **w** lot49.co.uk
🟦 myspace.com/lot49records
📺 uk.youtube.com/LOT49ers 📇 Label Manager: James Fiddian.

LOVE DA MUSIC (S) PTE. LTD. 71B, Duku Rd, 429233, Singapore **t** +65 6348 9619 **f** +65 6348 9917
e james@ldm.com.sg **w** ldm.com.sg 📇 Director: James Chan +353 65 6348 9619.

Love Da Records Room 103, 1st floor Glory Rise, 128 Chun Yeung St, North Point, Hong Kong, Singapore, Malaysia **t** +852 2264 1025 **f** +852 2264 1211
e tommy@love-da-records.com **w** love-da-records.com 📇 C.E.O.: Tommy Chan.

Love Da Records Room 101, 1/F Glory Rise, 128 Chun Yeung St, North Point, Haddington **t** 852-22641025 **f** 852-22641211
e tommy@love-da-records.com **w** love-da-records.com 📇 Owner CEO: Tommy Chan.

Lovechild Records (see Big Cat (UK) Records)

Lovers Leap (see Ariwa Sounds Ltd)

Low Quality Accident 71 Lansdowne Rd, Purley, Surrey, CR8 2PD **t** 020 8645 0013
e flamingofleece@yahoo.com
w myspace.com/lowqualityaccident 📇 MD: Alvin LeDup.

Lowered Recordings Ltd The Dairy, Porters End, Kimpton, Hitchin, Herts, SG4 8ER **t** 01438 831 065
f 01438 833 500 **e** enquiries@loweredrecordings.com
w loweredrecordings.com 📇 MD: Jules Spinner.

LPMusic 14 Bellfield St, Edinburgh, EH15 2BP
t 0131 468 1716 **e** enquiries@lpmusic.org.uk
w lpmusic.org.uk 📇 MD: Lee Patterson.

LPW Records Ltd LPW House, 2 Cornflower Road, Abbeymead, Gloucester, GL4 4AJ **t** 07891 727 947
e info@lpwrecordsltd.biz 📇 A&R Director: Mike Longley.

Lucky 7's (see Tip World)

Lucky Number Music Ltd 158 Stapleton Hall Rd, Stroud Green, London, N4 4QJ **t** 07909 532723
e contact@luckynumbermusic.com
w luckynumbermusic.com
🟦 myspace.com/luckynumbermusic
🐦 twitter.com/luckynumbermus
📺 youtube.com/profile?user=LuckyNumberMusic
📇 Dirs: Stephen Richards, Michael Morley.

Luggage (see Silverword Music Group)

Lumenessence Recordings 103 Islingword Road, Brighton, E Sussex, BN2 9SG **t** 01273 701 997
f 01273 690 149 **e** people@lumenessence.co.uk
w lumenessence.co.uk 📇 MD: Mark Williams.

Luminous Records 92, Manor Rd, Deal, Kent, CT14 9DB
t 01304 369053 **e** luminousrecords@hotmail.com
w luminousrecords.co.uk 📇 MD: Howard Werth.

Lunar Records 5-6 Lombard Street, East, Dublin 2, Ireland **t** +353 1 677 4229 **f** +353 1 671 0421
e lunar@indigo.ie 📇 Gen Mgr: Judy Cardiff.

M60 Recordings 24 Derby St, Edgeley, Stockport, Cheshire, SK3 9HF **t** 0161 476 1172
e andylacallen@yahoo.co.uk **w** myspace.com/picnicarea
📇 A&R Director: Andy Callen 07950 119151.

Madam Music Ltd Studio 26, 24-28 St Leonards Rd, Windsor, Berkshire, SL4 3BB **t** 0870 7503755
f 0871 9941280 **e** mm@madammusic.com
w madammusicrecords.com 📇 MD: Deborah Collier.

Madfish (see Snapper Music)

Madrigal Records Guy Hall, Awre, Gloucestershire, GL14 1EL **t** 01594 510512 **f** 01594 510512
e artists@madrigalmusic.co.uk **w** madrigalmusic.co.uk
📇 MD: Nick Ford.

Contacts   Facebook   MySpace   Twitter   YouTube

Maelstrom (see New State Entertainment)

Maestro Records PO Box 2255, Mitcham, Surrey, CR4 3BG **t** 020 8687 2008 **f** 020 8687 1998 **e** music@maestrorecords.com **w** maestrorecords.com ☎ MD: Tommy Sanderson.

Magick Eye Records PO Box 3037, Wokingham, Berks, RG40 4GR **t** 0118 932 8320 **f** 0118 932 8320 **e** info@magickeye.com **w** magickeye.com ☎ MD: Chris Hillman.

Magik Muzik UK (see New State Entertainment)

Main Spring Recordings PO Box 38648, London, W13 9WJ **t** 020 8567 1376 **e** blair@main-spring.com **w** main-spring.com ☎ MD: Blair McDonald.

Make Some Noise Records PO Box 792, Maidstone, Kent, ME14 5LG **t** 01622 691 106 **f** 01622 691 106 **e** info@makesomenoiserecords.com **w** makesomenoiserecords.com ☎ Manager: Clive Austen.

Mango ☎ Contact: Island. (see Island Records Group)

MAPP Records LLC 1800 Camden Road, Suite 107, #16, Charlotte, NC 28203, United States **t** +1 704 965 5415 **e** theresa@mapprecords.com **w** mapprecords.com ▶ youtube.com/user/MappRecordsTV ☎ CEO: Theresa Patterson Majeed.

Marine Parade Records Unit 4.16 The Paintworks, Bath Road, Bristol, BS4 3EH **t** 0117 971 2397 **f** 0117 972 8981 **e** luke@marineparade.co.uk **w** marineparade.net ☎ Label Manager: Luke Allen.

Market Square Records Whiteleaf Business Centre, Buckingham Ind. Pk, Buckingham, Bucks, MK18 1TF **t** 01296 715228 **e** peter@marketsquarerecords.co.uk **w** marketsquarerecords.co.uk ☎ MD: Peter Muir.

Matador Records Ltd 17-19 Alma Rd, London, SW18 1AA **t** 020 8875 6200 **e** firstname@matadorrecords.com **w** matadorrecords.com ☎ Label Manager: Natalie Judge.

Matchbox Recordings Ltd Vine Cottage (A&R), Hailey, Middletown, OX29 9UB **t** 01993 834 743 **e** info@matchboxrecordings.co.uk **w** matchboxrecordings.co.uk ☎ Dir/Hd of A&R: Dale Olivier.

Maybe Records Ltd G17, Riverbank House, 1 Putney Bridge Approach, London, SW6 3JD **t** 020 7736 7611 **e** info@mayberecords.com **w** mayberecords.com ☎ Director: Duff Battye 020 736 7611.

Mazaruni (see Ariwa Sounds Ltd)

MCA ☎ Contact: MCA. (see Island Records Group)

MCI - Music Collection International (see Demon Music Group)

Media Records Ltd Units 1-2 Pepys Court, 84-86 The Chase, Clapham Common, London, SW4 0NF **t** 020 7720 7266 **f** 020 7720 7255 **e** info@nukleuz.co.uk **w** nukleuz.com ☎ MD: Peter Pritchard.

Mega Hit Records (UK) PO Box 56, Boston, Lincolnshire, PE22 8JL **t** 07976 553 624 **e** chriskamara@megahitrecordsuk.co.uk **w** megahitrecordsuk.co.uk ☎ MD: Chris Kamara.

Megafan Records London **t** 020 8133 3837 **e** stuart@megafanrecords.com **w** megafanrecords.com ☎ Contact: Stuart Muff.

Mellow Monkey Records 2 Stucley Place, Camden, London, NW1 8NS **t** 020 7482 6660 **f** 020 7482 6606 **e** art@mainartery.co.uk ☎ MD: Jo Mirowski.

Melodic 3rd Floor, 14 Tariff St, Manchester, M1 2FF **t** 0161 228 3070 **f** 0161 228 3070 **e** david@melodic.co.uk **w** melodic.co.uk ☎ myspace.com/melodicmanchester ▶ youtube.com/davidmelodic ☎ MD: David Cooper.

Memoir Records PO Box 66, Pinner, Middlesex, HA5 2SA **t** 020 8866 4865 **f** 020 8866 7804 **e** mor@memoir.demon.co.uk **w** memoir.demon.co.uk ☎ MD: Gordon Gray.

Memphis Industries 8 Ripplevale Grove, London, N1 1HU **t** 020 7607 2610 **e** info@memphis-industries.com **w** memphis-industries.com ☎ Co MDs: Ollie Jacob, Mattt Jacob.

MERCURY MUSIC GROUP

MERCURY MUSIC GROUP

364-366 Kensington High St, London, W14 8NS **t** 020 7471 5333 **f** 020 7471 5306 **e** firstname.lastname@umusic.com **w** mercuryrecords.com ☎ President: Jason Iley. GM: Joe Munns. Snr A&R Director: Paul Adam. Promotions Director: Bruno Morelli. Markeing Director: Duncan Scott.

Meridian Records PO Box 317, Eltham, London, SE9 4SF **t** 020 8857 3213 **f** 020 8857 0731 **e** mail@meridian-records.co.uk **w** meridian-records.co.uk ☎ Dir: Richard Hughes.

Messy Productions Ltd Studio 2, Soho Recording Studios, 22-24 Torrington Place, London, WC1E 7HJ **t** 020 7813 7202 **f** 020 7419 2333 **e** info@messypro.com **w** messypro.com ☎ MD: Zak Vracelli.

Metal Nation Records 2 Whitehouse Mews, The Green, Wallsend, Tyne & Wear, NE28 7EP **t** 07879812677 **e** metalnation1@hotmail.com **w** metalnationrecords.co.uk ☎ MD: Jess Cox.

Metalheadz Recordings Hollycroft, Vicrage Lane, Bovingdon, Hemel Hempstead, Hertfordshire, HP3 0LT **t** 01442 832256 **e** chris@metalheadz.co.uk **w** metalheadz.co.uk ☎ myspace.com/metalheadzltd ☎ twitter.com/metalheadzmusic ▶ youtube.com/user/TheMetalheadzTV ☎ Label Manager: Chris Ball.

Record Companies: Record Companies & Labels

Metalheadz Recordings Hollycroft, Vicrage Lane, Bovingdon, Hemel Hempstead, Hertfordshire, HP3 0LT **t** 07525 176 523 **e** chris@metalheadz.co.uk ⬛ Label Manager: Chris Ball 07525176523.

Metier (see Divine Art Record Company)

Mi5 Recordings UK
Houldsworth Mill Business & Arts Centre, Houldsworth Street, Reddish, Stockport, SK5 6DA **t** 07976 131 145 **f** 0871 433 8757 **e** info@mi5recordings.co.uk **w** mi5recordings.co.uk ⬛ Dir: Andrew Calvert.

MIA Video Emtertainment Ltd 4th Floor, 72-75 Marylebone High Street, London, W1U 5JW **t** 020 7935 9225 **f** 020 7935 9565 **e** miavid@aol.com ⬛ Gen Mgr: Vanessa Chinn.

Microphonic Limited 57A Railway Arches, North Woolwich Road, London, E16 2AA **t** 020 3039 2979 **e** info@microphonic.biz **w** microphonic.biz ⬛ Director: Colin Bird.

Microstar (see Rotator Studios / Interzone Management)

Midnight Rock (see Fury Records)

Mike Lewis Entertainment Ltd (see Lewis Recordings)

Milk n 2 Sugars 4-7 The Vineyard, London, SE1 1QL **t** 020 7378 7321 **e** jonathan@mn2s.com **w** mn2s.com
⬛ facebook.com/pages/Milk-n-2-Sugars/156770018254
⬛ myspace.com/mn2s ⬛ twitter.com/mn2s
⬛ youtube.com/user/mn2sofficial ⬛ PR Manager: Jonathan Chubb.

Millennium Records Ltd 6 Water Lane, Camden, London, NW1 8NZ **t** 020 7482 0272 **f** 020 7267 4908 **e** ben@millenniumrecords.com **w** millenniumrecords.com ⬛ MD: Ben Recknagel.

Mimashima Records PO Box 1083, Liverpool, L69 4WQ **t** 0151 222 5785 **f** 0151 222 5785 **e** mail@mimashimarecords.co.uk **w** mimashimarecords.co.uk ⬛ MD: Noel Fitzsimmons.

Mindlab Recordings PO Box 50045, London, London, SE6 2ZB **t** 07765 440 031 **f** 020 8695 2682 **e** info@mindlabrecordings.com **w** mindlabrecordings.com
⬛ facebook.com/mindlabrecordings
⬛ myspace.com/mindlabrecordings
⬛ twitter.com/harrymindgame
⬛ youtube.com/harrymindgame ⬛ Label Manager: Harry Pitters +447765440031 / +4420 8695 2682.

Ministry Of Sound Recordings 103 Gaunt St, London, SE1 6DP **t** 0870 060 0010 **f** 020 7403 5348 **w** ministryofsound.com ⬛ CEO: Lohan Presencer.

Mint (see Jungle Records)

Minta (see Plum Projects)

Mirabeau (see Silverword Music Group)

Miss Moneypenny's Music (see K-Tel Entertainment (UK))

Mission Recordings Ltd Fairlight Mews, 15 St Johns Rd, Kingston upon Thames, Surrey, KT1 4AN **t** 020 8977 0632 **f** 0870 770 8669 **e** info@missionlimited.com **w** missionlimited.com ⬛ MD: Harry Cowell 0208 977 0632.

Mo'Wax Labels Ltd 1 Codrington Mews, London, W11 2EH **t** 020 8870 7511 **f** 020 8871 4178 **e** mowax@almaroad.co.uk **w** mowax.com ⬛ Label Head: Toby Feltwell.

Mob (see New State Entertainment)

Mobb Rule Records PO Box 26335, London, N8 9ZA **t** 020 8340 8050 **e** info@mobbrule.com **w** mobbrule.com ⬛ MD: Stewart Pettey.

Mohican Records The Little House, Hatton Road, Bedfont, Middx, TW14 9QZ **t** 020 8751 2244 **e** David.hughes55@btinternet.com **w** mohicanrecords.co.uk ⬛ MD: David Hughes.

Moist Records Ltd PO Box 528, Enfield, Middx, EN3 7ZP **t** 070 107 107 24 **f** 0870 137 3787 **e** info@moistrecords.com **w** moistrecords.com ⬛ MD: Rodney Lewis.

Mona Records 144 Warren House, Beckford Close, Warwick Rd, London, W14 8TW **t** 020 7348 9161 **f** 020 7348 9165 **e** info@mona-records.co.uk **w** mona-records.co.uk ⬛ Label Co-ordinator: Kevin Clark 020 7348 9195.

Monarch (see KRL - Bulk Music Ltd)

Mook Records House of Mook Studios, Authorpe Rd, Leeds, West Yorkshire, LS6 4JB **t** 0113 230 4008 **e** mail@mookhouse.ndo.co.uk **w** mookhouse.ndo.co.uk ⬛ Label Manager/Producer: Phil Mayne.

Moon Records UK PO Box 2061, Ilford, Essex, IG1 9GU **t** 020 8551 1011 **f** 020 8553 4954 **e** moonrecordsuk@aol.com **w** moonrecords.co.uk ⬛ MD: Howard Berlin.

Mooncrest Records (see Universal Music (UK) Ltd)

Moshi Moshi Premises Studios, 201-209 Hackney Rd, London, E2 8JL **e** hello@moshimoshimusic.com **w** moshimoshimusic.com ⬛ GM: Michael McClatchey 07957 388389.

Mosquito Media 64a Warwick Avenue, Little Venice, London, W9 2PU **t** 07813 174 185 **e** mosquitomedia@aol.com **w** mosquito-media.co.uk ⬛ Contact: Richard Abbott.

Mother Should Know Records County House, St. Mary's St, Worcester, WR1 1HB **t** 01905 729149 **f** 01905 729149 **e** info@mothershouldknowrecords.com **w** mothershouldknowrecords.com ⬛ Label Manager: Jack Turner.

Motown ⬛ Contact: Universal/Island. (see Island Records Group)

Mottete Ursina (see Priory Records)

Move (see Divine Art Record Company)

Movementinsound 37 Ellacombe Rd, Torquay, Devon, TQ1 3AT **t** 07849 199613 **e** info@movementinsound.com **w** movementinsound.com
🔲 myspace.com/movementinsound 🔲 Dirs: Chris Clark, Stephen Gould.

Mr Bongo 2nd Floor, 24 Old Steine, Brighton, BN1 1EL **t** 01273 600 546 **f** 01273 600 578 **e** info@mrbongo.com **w** mrbongo.com 🔲 MD: Dave Buttle.

MRR 11 Gt George St, Bristol, BS1 5RR **t** 0117 929 2393 **f** 0117 929 2696 **e** craigg.williams@virgin.net 🔲 Label Manager: Craig Williams.

Multisonic (see Priory Records)

Mushroom (see Atlantic Records UK)

Music Club Deluxe (see Demon Music Group)

Music Factory Mastermix Hawthorne House, Fitzwilliam St, Parkgate, Rotherham, South Yorks, S62 6EP **t** 01709 710022 **f** 01709 523141 **e** info@mastermixdj.com **w** mastermixdj.com 🔲 MD: Rob Moore.

Music For Dreams Vesterbrogade 95 H, 1620 Copenhagen V, Denmark **t** 0045 3326 0046 **w** musicfordreams.net

Music For Nations (see Sony Music Entertainment UK & Ireland)

Music From Another Room Ltd The Penthouse, 20 Bulstrode Street, London, W1U 2JW **t** 020 7224 4442 **f** 020 7224 7226 **e** patrick@julianlennon.com **w** julianlennon.com 🔲 Manager: Patrick Cousins.

Music Fusion Ltd Shepperton Studios, Studio Rd, Shepperton, Middx, TW17 0QD **t** 01932 592016 **f** 01932 592046 **e** ben.williams@classicpictures.co.uk **w** rwcc.com 🔲 Mktg Mgr: Ben Williams.

Music Mercia (see Fortune and Glory)

Music Of Life Ltd Unit 9b, Wingbury Business Village, Upper Wingbury Farm, Wingrave, Bucks, HP22 4LW **t** 07770 364268 **e** musicofliferecords@gmail.com 🔲 MD: Chris France.

Music To Die For Recordings 10 Alexandra Park Road, London, N10 2AB **t** 07796 996 669 **e** info@musictodiefor.com **w** musictodiefor.com 🔲 Label Manager: Johnny Hudson.

Musketeer Records 56 Castle Bank, Stafford, Staffordshire, ST16 1DW **t** 01785 258746 **f** 01785 255367 **e** p.halliwell@tesco.net 🔲 MD: Paul Halliwell.

Must Destroy Music 7 Jeffreys Place, London, NW1 9PP **e** tremendousmike@mustdestroymusic.com **w** mustdestroymusic.com 🔲 Contact: Tremendous Mike.

Mutant Disc 36 Brunswick St West, Hove, East Sussex, BN3 1EL **t** 07979 757 033 **f** 01273 325 935 **e** info@phatsandsmall.com 🔲 Label Mgrs: Russell Small, Jason Hayward.

Mute Records Ltd 27 Wrights Lane, London, W8 5SW **t** 020 7752 5555 **e** info@mutehq.co.uk **w** mute.com 🔲 Chairman: Daniel Miller.

MVM Records 35 Alma Rd, Reigate, Surrey, RH2 0DN **t** 01737 224151 **f** 01737 241481 🔲 MD: Maryetta Midgley.

My Dad Recordings 39 Barnfield Rd, Hyde, Cheshire, SK14 4EL **t** 07967 732 616 **e** label@mydadrecordings.com **w** mydadrecordings.com 🔲 MD: Paul Vella.

My Kung Fu 68 Broad St, Canton, Cardiff, CF11 8BZ **e** john@my-kung-fu.com **w** my-kung-fu.com 🔲 Label Mgr: John Rostron.

N2 Records (see Evolve Records)

Nachural Records Unit 1, Chancel industrial estate, Darlington St, Wednesbury, West Midlands, Ws10 7SS **t** 0870 69 4401 **f** 0870 609 4401 **e** info@nachural.co.uk **w** nachural.co.uk 🔲 MD: Ninder Johal 07774 116545.

Narnack Records 8033 Sunset Blvd. #1052, Hollywood, California, 90046, United States **e** info@narnackrecords.com **w** narnackrecords.com 🔲 Info: Narnack.

Nascente (see Demon Music Group)

Nasha Records PO Box 42545, London, E1 6WZ **t** 07904 145 743 **f** 020 7709 0097 **e** music@nasha.co.uk **w** nasha.co.uk 🔲 Label Manager: Sobur Ahmed.

Natasha Lea Jones Honeypot Records 1 Victoria Bank, Robin Bank Rd, Darwen, Blackburn, BB3 0DF **e** natashahoneypot@hotmail.com **w** natashajones.org 🔲 artist and management: Natasha Lea Jones 07846123547.

Nation Records Ltd 19 All Saints Rd, Notting Hill, London, W11 1HE **t** 020 7792 8167 **e** akination@btopenworld.com **w** nationrecords.co.uk 🔲 MD: Aki Nawaz 07971 206144.

Natural Grooves 3 Tannsfeld Rd, Sydenham, London, SE26 5DQ **t** 020 8488 3677 **f** 020 8473 6539 **e** jon@naturalgrooves.co.uk **w** naturalgrooves.co.uk 🔲 MD: Jonathan Sharif.

Nebula Music (see New State Entertainment)

Nervous (see Nervous Records)

Nervous Records 5 Sussex Crescent, Northolt, Middlesex, UB5 4DL **t** 020 8423 7373 **f** 020 8423 7713 **e** info@nervous.co.uk **w** nervous.co.uk 🔲 MD: Roy Williams.

Nettwerk Music Group 59-65 Worship St, London, EC2A 2DU **t** 020 7456 9500 **f** 020 7456 9501 **e** rob@nettwerk.com **w** nettwerk.com
📘 facebook.com/nettwerkmusicgroup
🔲 myspace.com/nettwerkmusicgroup
🔳 twitter.com/nettwerkmusic
📺 youtube.com/nettwerkmusic 🔲 Dir: Gary Levermore.

Neuropa 60 Baronald Drive, Glasgow, G12 0HW **t** 0141 339 9894 **e** neuropa@talk21.com 🔲 Administrator: Alexander Macpherson.

New Christian Music (NCM Records) Meredale, The Dell, Reach Lane, Heath and Reach, Leighton Buzzard, Beds, LU7 0AL **t** 01525 237700 **f** 01525 237700 **e** enq@newmusicenterprises.com **w** newchristianmusic.co.uk 🔲 MD: Paul Davis.

📇 Contacts   📘 Facebook   🟦 MySpace   🐦 Twitter   ▶️ YouTube

New Dawn Records Box 1-2, 191 Greenhead Street, Glasgow, G40 1HX **t** 0141 554 6475 **f** 0141 554 6475 **e** newdawnrecords@talk21.com **w** belles.demon.co.uk 📇 Contact: Admin Dept.

New Head Records I Osborne Rd, Jesmond, Newcastle upon Tyne, Tyne & Wear, NE2 2AA **t** 07519 076255 **f** 0191 276 0736 **e** raymondsharp@newheadrecords.co.uk **w** newheadrecords.co.uk 🟦 myspace.com/thesynthdj39s 📇 Label Manager: Ray Sharp.

New Leaf Records 9 Church Road, Conington, Peterborough, Cambridgeshire, PE7 3QJ **t** 01487 830 778 **e** awclifton@btinternet.com **w** leavesmusic.co.uk 📇 Prop: Andrew Clifton.

New Music Records Meredale, The Dell, Reach Lane, Heath and Reach, Leighton Buzzard, Beds, LU7 0AL **t** 01525 237 700 **f** 01525 237 700 **e** enq@newmusicenterprises.com **w** newmusicenterprises.com 📇 Prop: Paul Davis.

New State Entertainment Unit 2A Queens Studios, 121 Salusbury Road, London, NW6 6RG **t** 020 7372 4474 **f** 020 7328 4447 **e** info@newstate.co.uk **w** newstate.co.uk 📇 MD: Tom Parkinson, Tim Binns.

NGM Records North Glasgow College, 110 Flemington Street, Glasgow, G21 4BX **t** 0141 558 6440 **f** 0141 558 9905 **e** cowens@north-gla.ac.uk **w** north-gla.ac.uk 📇 Senior Lecturer Music: Campell Owens 0141 558 9001 x 249.

Nice 'N' Ripe Records FX Promotions, Unit 30, Grenville Workshops, 502 Hornsey Rd, London, N19 4EF **t** 020 7281 8363 **f** 020 7281 7663 **e** nicenripe@fxpromotions.demon.co.uk **w** fxpromotions.demon.co.uk/nicenripe 📇 MD: George Power.

NiceTunes 111 Holden Rd, London, N12 7DF **t** 020 8445 8766 **e** Luke@ntunes.co.uk **w** ntunes.co.uk 📇 A&R Dir: Luke Simons.

Nikt Records Cadillac Ranch, Pencraig Uchaf. Cwm Bach, Whitland, Dyfed, SA34 0DT **t** 01994 484294 **f** 01994 484294 **e** cadillacranch@telco4u.net **w** nikturner.com 📇 Director: Nik Turner.

Ninja Records 97 Denmark Rd, London, SE25 5RE **e** info@ninjarecords.com 📇 Contact: Aubrey Whitfield.

Ninja Tune PO Box 4296, London, SE11 4WW **t** 020 7820 3535 **f** 020 7820 3434 **e** ninja@ninjatune.net **w** ninjatune.net 📇 MD: Peter Quicke.

NMC Recordings 3rd Floor, South Wing, Somerset House, Strand, London, WC2R 1LA **t** 020 7759 1827 **f** 020 7759 1829 **e** nmc@nmcrec.co.uk **w** nmcrec.co.uk 🟦 myspace.com/nmcrecordings 🟦 NMCRecordings ▶️ youtube.com/user/NMCRecordings 📇 Label Mgr: Hannah Vlcek.

No Dancing Records Oh Yeah @ The Outlet Building, 15-21 Gordon St, Belfast, BT1 2LG **t** 07887 915112 **e** info@nodancing.co.uk **w** nodancing.co.uk 📇 Label Manager: Jimmy Devlin.

Nocturnal Recordings (see 852 Recordings)

Nocturnal Groove 16A Walterton Rd, London, W9 3PN **t** 020 7289 1240 **e** info@nocturnalgroove.co.uk **w** nocturnalgroove.co.uk 🟦 myspace.com/nocturnalgroove 🟦 NocGrooveRecs ▶️ nocturnalgroove100 📇 Director: Lola Marlin.

Noise Music (see Innerground Records)

Nomadic Music Unit 18, Farm Lane Trading Estate, 101 Farm Lane, London, SW6 1QJ **t** 020 7386 6800 **f** 020 7386 2401 **e** info@nomadicmusic.net **w** nomadicmusic.net 📇 Label Head: Paul Flanagan 07779 257 577.

Nonesuch Records (Europe) The Electric Lighting Station, 46 Kensington Court, London, W8 5DA **t** 020 7938 5500 **f** 020 7368 4931 **e** firstname.lastname@nonesuch.com **w** nonesuch.com 📘 facebook.com/NonesuchRecords 🐦 twitter.com/NonesuchRecords 📇 Label Manager: Matthew Rankin.

North South (see Abstract Sounds LTD)

Not Now Music Ltd 19 Liddell Rd Estate, Maygrove Rd, West Hampstead, London, NW6 2EW **t** 020 7624 4335 **f** 020 7624 4866 **e** glenn@notnowmusic.co.uk **w** notnowmusic.co.uk 📇 Director: Glenn Gretlund.

Not On Your Radio PO Box 820, Portsmouth, PO1 9FG **t** 07811 469888 **e** dave@notonyourradio.com **w** notonyourradio.com 🟦 myspace.com/notonyourradio 🐦 twitter.com/davenoyr ▶️ youtube.com/notradio 📇 MD: Dave Robinson.

Nova Mute (see Mute Records Ltd)

NoWHere Records 30 Tweedholm Ave East, Walkerburn, Peeblesshire, EH43 6AR **t** 01896 870 284 **e** michaelwild@btopenworld.com 📇 MD: Michael Wild 07812 818 183.

NRK Sound Division Ltd Unit 5.3 Paintworks, Bath Rd, Bristol, BS4 3EH **t** 0117 300 5497 **f** 0117 300 5498 **e** info@nrkmusic.com **w** nrkmusic.com 📇 Dir: Nick Harris.

Ntone (see Ninja Tune)

Nude Records PO Box 59269, London, NW3 9HU **t** 020 7586 7895 **f** 020 7586 6484 **e** info@nuderecords.com **w** nuderecords.com 🟦 myspace.com/nuderecordlabel ▶️ youtube.com/nuderecordlabel 📇 MD: Saul Galpern.

Nukleuz (see Media Records Ltd)

NuLife (see Sony Music Entertainment UK & Ireland)

Numa Records 86 Staines Road, Wraybury, Middlesex, TW19 5AA **t** 01784 483589 **f** 01784 483211 **e** tonywebb@numan.co.uk **w** numan.co.uk 📇 MD: Tony Webb.

Numinous Music Group Figment House, Church St, Ware, Hertfordshire, SG12 9EN **t** 01273 680799 **f** 01920 463883 **e** jhbee@numinous.biz **w** numinous.biz 📇 Dir. A&R/Marketing/Promo: John Bee.

NYJO Records 11 Victor Road, Harrow, Middlesex, HA2 6PT **t** 020 8863 2717 **f** 020 8863 8685 **e** bill.ashton@virgin.net **w** NYJO.org.uk ⊠ Dir: Bill Ashton.

Obsessive (see Sony Music Entertainment UK & Ireland)

Ochre Records PO Box 155, Cheltenham, Gloucestershire, GL51 0YS **e** ochre@talbot.force9.co.uk **w** ochre.co.uk ⬚ myspace.com/ochrerecords ⊠ Proprietor: Talbot.

Offslip Productions 3 Lion Court, Studio Way, Borehamwood, WD6 5NJ **t** 07789 955 059 **e** danfeel@offslip.com **w** offslip.com ⊠ Dir: Daniel Roberts.

Ohmy Recordings PO Box 52284, London, SW16 5XR **t** 07005 98 18 38 **e** info@ohmyrecordings.com **w** ohmyrecordings.com ⊠ Directors: Sophie McAdam, Elliott J Brown.

Olympia (see Priory Records)

One 51 Records (see Duffnote Ltd)

One Little Indian Records 34 Trinity Crescent, London, SW17 7AE **t** 020 8772 7600 **f** 020 8772 7601 **e** info@indian.co.uk **w** indian.co.uk ⊠ GM: Paul Johannes.

Opal (see Pavilion Records Ltd)

Opera Rara 134-146 Curtain Rd, London, EC2A 3AR **t** 020 7613 2858 **f** 020 7613 2261 **e** info@opera-rara.com **w** opera-rara.com ⊠ MD: Stephen Revell.

Ophidian (see Rotator Studios / Interzone Management)

Optimum (see Silverword Music Group)

Or (see Touch)

Orbison Records Covetous Corner, Hudnall Common, Little Gaddesden, Herts, HP4 1QW **t** 01442 842 039 **f** 01442 842 039 **e** mhaynes@orbison.com **w** orbison.com ⊠ European Consultant: Mandy Haynes.

Org Records 19 Herbert Gardens, London, NW10 3BX **t** 020 8964 3066 **e** organ@organart.demon.co.uk **w** organart.com ⊠ MD: Sean Worrall.

Organ Grinder Records 29 Chelsea Crescent, Chelsea Harbour, London, SW10 0XB **t** 020 7351 9385 **f** 020 7351 9385 **e** info@organgrinderrecords.com **w** organgrinderrecords.com ⊠ Director: James Lesslie.

Oriental Star Agency 548-550 Moseley Road, Birmingham, West Midlands, B12 9AD **t** 0121 449 6437 **f** 0121 449 5404 **e** info@osa.co.uk **w** osa.co.uk ⊠ Director: Mohammed Farooq.

Ottavo (see Priory Records)

John Otway Records (see Rotator Studios / Interzone Management)

Outafocus Recordings 146 Bethnal Green Rd, London, E2 6DG **t** 020 7613 1100 **e** info@outafocus.co.uk **w** outafocus.co.uk ⊠ Label Manager: Danny Corr.

Outcaste Records Limited 27 Wrights Lane, London, W8 5SW **t** 020 7795 7000 **f** 020 7605 5188 **e** firstname@mvillage.co.uk **w** outcaste.com ⊠ Co-MDs: Paul Franklyn and Shabs Jobanputra.

Outdigo Records (see Shifty Disco Ltd)

Outer Recordings PO Box 18888, London, SW7 4FQ **t** 020 7373 1614 **f** 020 7373 8376 **e** danny@outer-recordings.co.uk **w** outer-recordings.co.uk ⊠ Label Mgr: Danny Jones.

Outstanding Records 7 Pelham Crescent, Hastings, East Sussex, TN34 3AF **t** 020 7871 4564 **e** outstanding.records@ntlworld.com **w** outstandingrecords.com ⊠ A&R Co-ordinator: Mark Randall.

Oval Records - Oval Music 326 Brixton Rd, London, SW9 7AA **t** 020 7622 0111 **e** charlie@ovalmusic.co.uk **w** ovalmusic.co.uk ⬚ myspace.com/ovalmusicuk ⊠ Dir: Charlie Gillett.

Ovation Recordings (see Adasam Limited)

Overground Records PO Box 1NW, Newcastle-upon-Tyne, NE99 1NW **t** 0191 266 3802 **f** 0191 266 6073 **e** john@overgroundrecords.co.uk **w** overgroundrecords.co.uk ⊠ MD: John Esplen.

Owl Records International Limited 7 Strand St, Youghal, Co. Cork, Ireland **t** +353 24 90702 **e** owl@eircom.net **w** owlrecords.com ⊠ MD: Reg Keating.

OxRecs Digital Maytree Cottage, 51 Eaton Rd, Appleton, Abingdon, Oxon, OX13 5JH **t** 01865 862310 **e** info@oxrecs.com **w** oxrecs.com ⊠ Dir: Bernard Martin.

Oyster Music Limited Oakwood Manor, Oakwood Hill, Ockley, Surrey, RH5 5PU **t** 01306 627277 **f** 01306 627277 **e** info@oystermusic.com **w** oystermusic.com ⊠ Dirs: Adrian Fitt.

P3 Music Ltd PO Box 6641, Blairgowrie, Perthshire, PH10 9AD **t** 01828 633790 **f** 0870 137 6738 **e** james@p3music.com **w** p3music.com ⨍ facebook.com/pages/P3-Music-Label/50374779811 ⬚ myspace.com/p3musiclabel ⓣ twitter.com/p3music ▶ youtube.com/P3MusicLabel ⊠ Director: James Taylor.

Pablo (see Ace Records)

Palawan Productions Ltd/JC Music 16 Waldeck Rd, Strand on the Green, London, W4 3NP **t** 07860 680022 or +1 310 577 2224 **f** +1 310 305 3763 **e** Palawan@me.com **w** palawanproductions.com ⊠ MD: John Campbell 07860 680022.

Pale Blue Records 26 King Street, London, WC2E 8JS **t** 020 7759 8554 **f** 020 7759 8549 **w** paleblue.com ⊠ Record Label Manager: Alison Butters.

Palm Pictures 8 Kensington Park Road, Notting Hill Gate, London, W11 3BU **t** 020 7229 3000 **f** 020 7229 0897 **e** firstname@palmpictures.co.uk **w** palmpictures.com ⊠ MD: Andy Childs.

Panton (see Prestige Elite Records Ltd)

Parachute Music (see Creative World)

Park Lane (see The Hit Music Company)

Park Records PO Box 651, Oxford, OX2 9AZ **t** 01865 241 717 **f** 01865 204 556 **e** info@parkrecords.com **w** parkrecords.com ⊠ MD: John Dagnell.

Contacts Facebook MySpace Twitter YouTube

Parlophone EMI, 27 Wrights Lane, London, W8 5SW
t 020 7795 7000 **e** firstname.lastname@emimusic.com
w parlophone.co.uk President A&R Labels: Miles Leonard.

Parlophone Rhythm Series (see Parlophone)

Partisan Recordings c/o Mute Song, 43 Brook Green,
London, W6 7EF **t** 020 8964 2001 **f** 020 8968 8437
e mamapimp@btopenworld.com **w** emusic.com
 MD: Caroline Butler.

**Pasadena Roof Orchestra - Pasadena
Records** Priors Hall, Tye Green, Elsenham,
Bishop Stortford, Hertfordshire, CM22 6DY **t** 01279 813240
f 01708 641625 **e** derek@pasadenaroof.f9.co.uk
w pasadena-roof-orchestra.com Director: Derek Jones
01708 227177.

Passion Music Unit 2, Boeing Way Inter Trading Est,
Brent Way, Southall, Middx, UB2 5LB **t** 020 8867 9361
f 020 8571 2624 **e** les@passionmusic.co.uk
w passionmusic.co.uk MD: Les McCutcheon.

Past Perfect Grange Mews, Station Rd, Launton,
OX26 5EE **t** 01869 325052 **f** 01869 325072
e info@pastperfect.com **w** pastperfect.com
 twitter.com/vintagemusic
 myspace.com/pastperfect_vintagemusic

Pavilion Records Ltd Sparrows Green, Wadhurst,
East Sussex, TN5 6SJ **t** 01892 783591 **f** 01892 784156
e pearl@pavilionrecords.com **w** pavilionrecords.com
 MD: John Waite.

Peacefrog PO Box 38171, London, W10 5WU
t 020 7575 3045 **f** 020 7575 3047 **e** info@peacefrog.com
w peacefrog.com Dir: Phil Vernol.

Peaceville Records PO Box 76, Heckmondwike,
West Yorkshire, WF16 9XN **e** paul@peaceville.co.uk
w peaceville.com A&R Manager: Paul Groundwell.

Pearl (see Pavilion Records Ltd)

Penguin Music Classics Contact: Decca.

People Music Adela Street Studio, The Saga Centre,
326 Kensal Road, London, W10 5BZ **t** 020 8968 9666
f 020 8969 9558 **e** info@goyamusic.com **w** goyamusic.com
 Director: Mike Slocombe.

Perfect Words & Music 31 Chester Rd, Poole, Dorset,
BH13 6DE **t** 01202 757 824
e philmurray.pac@btinternet.com A&R: Allison Longstaff.

Perry Road Records Ltd 75 Perry Rd, Buckden,
Cambs, PE19 5XG **t** 01480 819636 **f** 01480 819636
e enquiries@perryroadstudios.co.uk
w perryroadrecords.co.uk Chief Executive: Gill Lee.

Personal Records (see Baria Records)

PHAB Records High Notes, Sheerwater Avenue,
Woodham, Weybridge, Surrey, KT15 3DS **t** 019323 48174
f 019323 40921 MD: Philip HA Bailey.

Philips (see Decca Records)

Philips Classics Contact: PolyGram. (see Decca
Records)

Phoenix Music International PO Box 46, Cromer,
NR27 9WX **t** 08456 300 710 **f** 08456 300 720
e cindy.blackmore@phoenix-corp.co.uk
w phoenixmusicinternational.com Accounts: Cindy
Blackmore.

Phonetic Recordings Ltd PO Box 296, Twickenham,
Middx, TW1 9AS **t** 020 8241 7137 **f** 020 8241 7137
e info@phoneticrecordings.com **w** phoneticrecordings.com
 facebook.com/pages/Phonetic-
Recordings/122359249669?ref=mf
 myspace.com/phoneticrecordings
 youtube.com/user/PhoneticRecordings CEO: Rob Roar.

PHONOGENIC

9 Derry Street, London, W8 5HY **t** 020 7361 8000
f 020 7937 0188 **e** firstname.lastname@sonymusic.com
w phonogenic.net Directors: Paul Lisberg, Tops
Henderson.

Pickwick Group Ltd Suite 2, 2nd Floor, Merritt House,
Hill Avenue, Amersham, Bucks, HP6 5BQ **t** 01494 732800
f 01494 733498 **e** info@pickwickgroup.com
w pickwickgroup.com GM: Mark Lawton.

Picnic 22 Herbert St, Glasgow, G20 6NB
t 0141 560 2748 or 0141 337 1199 **f** 0141 357 0655
e info@picnicrecords.com **w** picnicrecords.com Dir: Robin
Morton.

Pier (see Wooden Hill Recordings Ltd)

Pilgrim's Star (see Divine Art Record Company)

Pinball Records (see Amazon Records Ltd)

Pinkpenny Records PO Box 244, Newton Abbot,
Devon, TQ12 1TH **t** 01626 201818
e sales@pinkpennyrecords.com **w** pinkpennyrecords.com
 myspace.com/pinkpennyrecords twitter.com/mrvinyl
 A&R: Matt Vinyl 07977 268306.

Planet Records 2nd Floor, 11 Newmarket Street, Colne,
Lancashire, BB8 9BJ **t** 01282 866 317 **f** 01282 866 317
e info@pendlehawkmusic.co.uk **w** pendlehawkmusic.co.uk
 MD: Adrian Melling.

Plankton Records PO Box 13533, London, E7 0SG
t 020 8534 8500 **e** plankton.records@virgin.net
 Partner: Keith Dixon.

Plastic Head Records Ltd Avtech House,
Hithercroft Rd, Wallingford, Oxon, OX10 9DA
t 01491 825 029 **f** 01491 826 320 **e** tom@plastichead.com
w plastichead.com Director: Tom Doherty.

Platipus Records PO BOX 49470, London, SE20 8WA
f 020 7806 8066 **e** richard@platipus.com **w** platipus.com
 Lbl Mgr: Richard Smith.

Playaville Records & Music Publishing
Woolwich Dockyard Ind Estate, Block1 Unit10, 2nd Floor, Woolwich Church St, London, SE18 5PQ **t** 0845 519 0067 **f** 0845 519 0076 **e** info@playaville.com **w** playaville.com 🟦 myspace.com/playavillerecords 🟦 twitter.com/playaville 📺 youtube.com/playaville 📇 Contact: Stevie Nash.

Player Records
Regents Park House, Regent St, Leeds, LS2 7QJ **t** 0113 223 7665 **f** 0113 223 7514 **e** info@playerrecords.com **w** playerrecords.com 📇 Label Manager: Sarah Flay.

PlayLouder Recordings
8-10 Rhoda St, London, E2 7EF **t** 020 7729 4797 **f** 020 7739 8571 **e** Jim.Gottlieb@playlouder.com 📇 Dir: Jim Gottlieb.

Plaza Records
PO Box 726, London, NW11 7XQ **t** 07790 905735 **f** 020 8458 6200 **e** roberto.danova@plazarecords.co.uk **w** plazarecords.co.uk 📇 MD: Roberto Danova.

Pleasuredome
PO Box 425, London, SW6 3TX **t** 020 7371 0784 **f** 020 7736 9212 **e** getdown@thepleasuredome.demon.co.uk **w** pleasuredome.co.uk 📘 facebook.com/thehollyjohnson 🟦 myspace.com/therealhollyjohnson 🟦 twitter.com/TheHolly Johnson 📺 youtube.com/user/thehollyjohnson 📇 Chairman: Holly Johnson.

Plum Projects
33 Rocks Lane, Barnes, London, SW13 0DB **t** 07985 298 371 **e** info@plumprojects.com **w** plumprojects.com 📇 Grand Wizard: Sl!m.

PM Muzik Publishing Ltd
226 Seven Sisters Rd, London, N4 3GG **t** 020 7372 6806 **f** 020 7372 0969 **e** info@pmmuzik.com **w** pmmuzik.com 📇 Dir: David Lindo.

Point Classics
(see Priory Records)

Pollytone
PO Box 124, Ruislip, Middlesex, HA4 9BB **t** 01895 638584 **e** info@pollytone.com **w** pollytone.com 🟦 myspace.com/pollytonerecords 🟦 twitter.com/Pollytone 📇 MD: Val Bird.

Polo Records
(see Champion Records Ltd)

POLYDOR RECORDS

364-366 Kensington High Street, London, W14 8NS **t** 020 7471 5400 **f** 020 7471 5401 **e** firstname.lastname@umusic.com **w** polydor.co.uk 📇 President: Ferdy Unger-Hamilton. Senior Dir, Legal & Business Affairs: James Radice. GM, Polydor UK: Orla Lee. GM, Marketing: Karen Simmonds. Senior Finance Director: Geoff Harris. Senior Dir of Promotions: Neil Hughes. Dir of Communications: Selina Webb. GM, Fascination: Peter Loraine. Head of Fiction: Jim Chancellor. Head of A&M: Simon Gavin. Head of Press: Susie Ember.

Polyphonic Reproductions - Studio Music Company
Cadence House, Eaton Green Rd, Luton, Beds, LU2 9LD **t** 01582 432139 **f** 01582 731989 **e** stan@studio-music.co.uk **w** studio-music.co.uk 📇 MD: Stan Kitchen.

Positiva
27 Wrights Lane, London, W8 5SW **t** 020 7795 7000 **f** 020 7605 5050 **e** firstname.lastname@emimusic.com **w** positivarecords.com 📇 Dir: Jason Ellis.

Positive Records
(see Evolve Records)

Possessed Records Ltd
PO Box 35064, London, NW1Y 9YX **t** 07890 877913 **e** info@possessedrecords.com **w** possessedrecords.com 📇 Contact: Abigail Hopkins.

Power Records
29 Riversdale Road, Thames Ditton, Surrey, KT7 0QN **t** 020 8398 5236 **f** 020 8398 7901 📇 MD: Barry Evans.

President Records Ltd
Units 6 & 7, 11 Wyfold Rd, Fulham, London, SW6 6SE **t** 020 7385 7700 **f** 020 7385 3402 **e** hits@president-records.co.uk **w** president-records.co.uk 📇 MD: David Kassner.

Prestige
(see Ace Records)

Prestige Elite Records Ltd
3 Faraday Way, St Mary Cray, Kent, BR53QW **t** 01689 826555 **f** 01689 823377 **e** info@prestige-elite.com **w** prestige-elite.com 📇 Chairman: Keith C Thomas.

Pretap Music
London, W12 8LR **t** 07533 438357 **e** ikeleo@btinternet.com **w** pretap.com 📺 youtube.com/ikeola 📇 A&R: Ike Leo.

Priestess Records
1A Edward road, St Leonards on Sea, E. Sussex, TN37 6ES **t** 01424 203 991 **e** kat.leeryan@btinternet.com **w** myspace.com/reddieselband 📇 MD: Kat Lee-Ryan 07814 659 729.

Primaudial Recordings
Flat 3, 157, Church Walk, Stoke Newington, London, N16 8QA **t** 020 7241 5283 **f** 07053 601309 **e** headhoncho@primaudialrecords.com **w** primaudialrecords.com 🟦 myspace.com/primaudialrecords 📇 Label Manager: Ski Oakenfull.

Prime Cut Music
PO Box 1309, High Wycombe, Bucks, HP11 9DZ **t** 07866 500910 **e** info@primecutmusic.co.uk **w** primecutmusic.co.uk 📇 Contact: Cassie James.

Priory Records
3 Eden Court, Eden Way, Leighton Buzzard, Bedfordshire, LU7 4FY **t** 01525 377566 **f** 01525 371477 **e** sales@priory.org.uk **w** priory.org.uk 📇 Managing Director: Neil Collier.

Profile
(see Silverword Music Group)

Prolific Recordings
PO Box 282, Tadworth, Surrey, KT20 5WA **t** 07770 874 282 **e** andy@prolificrecordings.co.uk **w** prolificrecordings.co.uk 📇 Label Manager: Andy Lewis.

Prolifica Records
Unit 101, Saga Land, 326 Kensal Rd, London, W10 5BZ **t** 020 8960 9562 **f** 020 8960 9971 **e** Gavino@btclick.com **w** Prolifica.net 🟦 myspace.com/prolificarecordings 📇 Label Manager: Gavino Prunas.

Record Companies: Record Companies & Labels

Proof Records (see Down By Law Records)

Proper Records Unit 1, Gateway Business Centre, Kangley Bridge Rd, London, SE26 5AN **t** 020 8676 5180 **f** 020 8676 5190 **e** malc@proper.uk.com **w** proper.uk.com MD: Malcolm Mills.

Prototype Recordings (see Virus Recordings)

Pucka (see Highnote Ltd)

Pulse Records & Productions Ltd
Cammell Lairds Waterfront Pk, Campbeltown Rd, Wirral, Merseyside, CH41 9HP **t** 0151 649 0427 **f** 0151 649 0894 **e** info@pulse-records.co.uk **w** pulse-records.co.uk youtube.com/pulsart7 MDs: Rob Fennah, Alan Fennah.

Pure Gold Records Sovereign House, 12 Trewartha Rd, Praa Sands, Penzance, Cornwall, TR20 9ST **t** 01736 762826 **f** 01736 763328 **e** panamus@aol.com **w** songwriters-guild.co.uk myspace.com/digimixrecords MD: Roderick Jones.

Pure Mint Recordings The Old Post Office, 31 Penrose St, London, SE17 3DW **t** 020 7703 1239 **f** 020 7703 1239 **e** info@pure-mint.com **w** pure-mint.com MD: Anthony Hall.

Pure Motion Muzik Ltd 226 Seven Sisters Rd, London, N4 3GG **t** 020 7372 6806 **f** 020 7372 0969 **e** info@pmmuzik.com **w** pmmuzik.com Dir: Plucky.

Pure Records PO Box 174, Penistone, Sheffield, S36 8XB **t** 0870 240 5058 **f** 0870 240 5058 **e** info@purerecords.net **w** purerecords.net

Pure Silk Music Broadley House, 48 Broadley Terrace, London, NW1 6LG **t** 020 7724 4500 **f** 020 7724 1300 **e** julian@puresilkmusic.com **w** puresilkmusic.corn myspace.com/puresilkmusic MD: Julian Goodkind.

PureUK Recordings (see Stirling Music Group)

Purple Records Aizlewood Mill, Nursery Street, Sheffield, South Yorkshire, S3 8GG **t** 0114 233 3024 **f** 0114 234 7326 **e** ann@darkerthanblue.fsnet.co.uk **w** purplerecords.net MD: Simon Robinson.

Purr Records 51 Claude Avenue, Oldfield Park, Bath, BA2 1AG **t** 01225 443 844 **e** info@purr.org.uk **w** purr.org.uk Contact: Dave Tinkham, Tim Orchard.

Q Music Recordings (see Suburban Soul (Music))

Qnote Records (see Cube Soundtracks)

Qritikal Records Pinsla Park Cottage, Cardinham, Nr Bodmin, PL30 4EH **t** 07802 584334 **e** david@qritikal.com **w** qritikal.com & www.qritikal.com myspace.com/qritikal Dirs: David Self, Stephen Wakeling.

Qton Records Studio One, Utopia Village, 7 Chalcot Road, London, NW1 8LH **t** 020 7586 9899 **e** enquiries@qtonrecords.com **w** qtonrecords.com Business Manager: Charlotte Hersh.

Quannum Projects (see Ninja Tune)

Racing Junior (see Glitterhouse Records)

Radio Geronimo Timperley House, 11 St.Albans Road, Skircoat Green, Halifax, W.Yorks, HX3 0ND **t** 01422 367 040 **e** bbyford@hotmail.co.uk **w** rhythmsisters.com MD: Bill Byford.

Radioactive Contact: MCA. (see Island Records Group)

Radiotone Records PO Box 43103, London, E17 8WD **t** 07989 301910 **e** info@radiotone.co.uk **w** radiotone.co.uk Dir: Steve Cooper.

Ragtag Music (see Fastforward Music Limited)

Rainbow Quartz Records 74 Riverside 3, Sir Thomas Longley Road, Rochester, Kent, ME2 4BH **t** +212 385 8000 **f** +212 385 7845 **e** rainbowqtz@aol.com **w** rainbowquartz.com Founder: Jim McGarry.

Rainy Day Records Sovereign House, 12 Trewartha Rd, Praa Sands, Penzance, Cornwall, TR20 9ST **t** 01736 762826 **f** 01736 763328 **e** panamus@aol.com **w** panamamusic.co.uk myspace.com/guildofsongwriters MD: Roderick Jones.

Raise the Roof (see Collecting Records LLP)

Ram Records Ltd PO Box 70, Hornchurch, Essex, RM11 3NR **t** 01708 445851 **f** 01708 441270 **e** info@ramrecords.com **w** ramrecords.com myspace.com/ramrecordsltd youtube.com/ramrecordstv Label Mgr: Scott Bourne.

Randan Basement, 52 Osborne St, Glasgow, G1 5QH **e** horse@randan.fsworld.co.uk **w** randan.org myspace.co/horserandan Business Affairs: Horse.

Rapster Records (see !K7 Records)

Raw Strings (see RF Records)

Rawkus Entertainment (see Island Records Group)

Rayman Recordings (see Adasam Limited)

RCA LABEL GROUP

9 Derry Street, London, W8 5HY **t** 020 7361 8000 **f** 020 7937 0188 **e** firstname.lastname@sonymusic.com **w** rca-records.co.uk MD: Craig Logan. VP Legal & Business Affairs: David Turnbull. Director Of Promotions: Nick Bray. A&R: Jonnie Blackburn.

RDL Records 132 Chase Way, London, N14 5DH **t** 020 8361 5002 **f** 0870 741 5252 **e** atlanticcrossingartists@yahoo.com **w** mkentertainments.8k.com Director: Colin Jacques 07050 055167.

Ready, Steady, Go! (see Graduate Records)

Real World Records Box Mill, Mill Lane, Box, Corsham, Wilts, SN13 8PL **t** 0845 146 1733 **f** 0845 146 1728 **e** records@realworld.co.uk **w** realworldrecords.com Label Mgr: Amanda Jones.

Really Free Music Ichthus House, 1 Northfield Rd, Aylesbury, Bucks, HP20 1PB **t** 01296 583700 **e** info@reallyfreemusic.co.uk **w** reallyfreemusic.co.uk 📇 Contact: Peter Wheeler.

The Really Useful Group 22 Tower St, London, WC2H 9TW **t** 020 7240 0880 **f** 020 7240 8977 **e** robinsond@reallyuseful.co.uk **w** reallyuseful.com 📇 Head Of Music Licensing: David Robinson.

Recharge (see The Recoverworld Label Group (Supreme Music Ltd))

Recoup Recordings Suite B, 2 Tunstall Rd, London, SW9 8DA **t** 020 7733 5400 **f** 020 7733 4449 **e** recouprecordings@westburymusic.net **w** westburymusic.net

Recover (see The Recoverworld Label Group (Supreme Music Ltd))

The Recoverworld Label Group (Supreme Music Ltd) PO Box 184, Hove, East Sussex, BN3 6UY **t** 01273 556321 **f** 01273 503333 **e** info@recoverworld.com **w** recoverworld.com 📘 facebook.com/group.php?gid=32921692062 ▦ myspace.com/recoverworld.com 🅣 twitter.com/recoverworld 📇 MD: Chris Hampshire.

RecPublica 1A The Bridge, Uxbridge Rd, London, W5 3LB **t** +48 694 424 057 **f** +48 683 529 923 **e** office@recpublica.com **w** recpublica.com 📇 Contact: Patrick Zukowski.

Red Admiral Records The Cedars, Elvington Lane, Hawkinge, Nr. Folkestone, Kent, CT18 7AD **t** 01303 893 472 **f** 01303 893 833 **e** info@redadmiralrecords.com **w** redadmiralrecords.com 📇 Exec: Chris Ashman.

Red Balloon (see 4Real Records)

Red Cat (see The Store For Music)

Red Chord (see Born to Dance Records)

Red Eye Music 76 Monthermer Road, Cathays, Cardiff, CF24 4QY **t** 02920 217 254 **e** info@redeyemusic.co.uk **w** redeyemusic.co.uk 📇 Director: Christopher Rees.

The Red Flag Recording Company 1 Star St, London, W2 1QD **t** 020 7258 0093 **f** 020 7402 9238 **e** info@redflagrecords.com **w** redflagrecords.com 📇 Contact: Tinca Leahy.

Red Grape Records Ltd 82 Chestnut Grove, New Malden, Surrey, KT3 3JS **t** 07976 272139 **f** 020 8942 4887 **e** info@redgraperecords.com **w** redgraperecords.com 📇 Director: Kerry Harvey-Piper.

Red Hot Records 105 Emlyn Rd, London, W12 9TG **t** 07985 467970 **e** redhotrecs@aol.com 📇 MD: Brian Leafe.

Red Ink (see Epic Records)

Red Lace Records c/o Trash, 9a Albion Street, Leeds, LS1 5ES **t** 0113 246 8899 **f** 0113 246 8899 **e** redlacerecords@googlemail.com **w** myspace.com/internationaltrust 📇 Label Managers: Jordan Franz, Neil Hanson.

Red Lightnin' The White House, 42, The St, North Lopham, Diss, Norfolk, IP22 2LU **t** 01379 687693 **f** 01379 687559 **e** peter@redlightnin.com **w** redlightnin.com 📇 Proprietor, Head Chef, Lackey & Oenophilist: Pete Shertser 01379 687 693.

Red Sky Records PO Box 27, Stroud, Gloucestershire, GL6 0YQ **t** 0845 644 1447 **f** 01453 836877 **e** info@redskyrecords.co.uk **w** redskyrecords.co.uk 📇 MD: Johnny Coppin.

Redemption Records PO Box 8045, Reading, RG30 9AZ **e** info@redemption-records.com **w** redemption-records.com 📇 MD: Phil Knox-Roberts.

Reel Track Records PO Box 1099, London, SE5 9HT **t** 020 7326 4824 **f** 020 7535 5901 **e** gamesmaster@chartmoves.com **w** chartmoves.com 📇 A&R Manager: Dave Mombasa.

Regal Recordings EMI, 27 Wrights Lane, London, W8 5SW **t** 020 7795 7000 **e** firstname.lastname@emimusic.com **w** regal.co.uk 📇 Head of Label: Miles Leonard.

Regent Records PO Box 528, Wolverhampton, West Midlands, WV3 9YW **t** 01902 424377 **f** 01902 717661 **e** regent.records@btinternet.com **w** regentrecords.com 📇 Contact: Gary Cole.

Regis Records Ltd Southover House, Tolpuddle, Dorset, DT2 7HF **t** 01305 848983 **f** 01305 848516 **e** info@regisrecords.co.uk **w** regisrecords.co.uk 📇 Contact: Michael Slocock 01305 848725.

Reiker Records PO Box 1851, Yate, BS37 6ZP **t** 0117 311 5052 **e** management@reiker.com **w** reikerrecords.com 📇 Manager: Elle Williams 07990 573 749.

Rekids Ltd PO Box 42769, London, N2 0YY **t** 020 8444 6074 **e** james@rekids.co.uk **w** rekids.com ▦ myspace.com/rekids ▶ youtube.com/rekids 📇 Owner: James Masters.

REL Records 86 Causewayside, Edinburgh, EH9 1PY **t** 0131 668 3366 **f** 0131 662 4463 **e** neil@holyroodproductions.com 📇 MD: Neil Ross.

Release Records Blenheim House, Henry Street, Bath, BA11 JR **t** 01225 428 284 **e** enquiries@acamusic.co.uk **w** acamusic.co.uk 📇 MD: Harry Finegold.

Religion Music 36 Fitzwilliam Sq, Dublin 1, Ireland **e** info@religionmusic.com **w** religionmusic.com 📇 CEO: Glenn Herlihy.

Renegade Hardware (see TOV Music Group Ltd (Trouble on Vinyl))

Renegade Recordings (see TOV Music Group Ltd (Trouble on Vinyl))

Rephlex PO Box 2676, London, N11 1AZ **t** 020 8368 5903 **f** 020 8361 2811 **e** info@rephlex.com **w** rephlex.com 📇 Press/Distrib: Marcus Scott.

Retek (see The Recoverworld Label Group (Supreme Music Ltd))

Rev-Ola (see Cherry Red Records)

Record Companies: Record Companies & Labels

Reveal Records 63 St Peters St, Derby, Derbyshire, DE1 2AB **t** 07779 017 236 **f** 01332 556 374 **e** tomreveal@mac.com **w** reveal-records.com 📇 MD: Tom Rose.

Reverb Records Ltd Reverb House, Bennett St, London, W4 2AH **t** 020 8747 0660 **f** 020 8747 0880 **e** records@reverbxl.com **w** reverbxl.com 📇 GM: Mark Lusty.

REVOLUTION RECORDS

9a Meadow Close, Hounslow, Middlesex, TW4 5LN **t** 020 8274 9712 **e** phil@revrecs.com **w** revrecs.com 📇 Director: Mr Phillip Marcombe. Director: Phillip Marcombe. Director: Dominic Norriss. Mastering Engineer: R Chaudhary.

Revolver (see Revolver Music Ltd)

Revolver Music Ltd 152 Goldthorn Hill, Penn, Wolverhampton, West Midlands, WV2 3JA **t** 01902 345345 **f** 01902 345155 **e** Paul.Birch@revolverrecords.com **w** revolverrecords.com 🆂 myspace.com/revolverrecords 🅱 twitter.com/revolverrecords ▶️ youtube.com/revolverrecords 📇 MD: Paul Birch 0121 270 0877.

Rex (see XL Recordings)

Rexx (see Highnote Ltd)

RF Records Room A30, City College, Chorlton St, Manchester, M1 3HB **t** 0161 279 7302 **f** 0161 279 7225 **e** pellis@ccm.ac.uk **w** rfrecords.com 📇 Label Mgr: Phil Ellis 07909 907 089.

Rhino UK The Warner Building, 28 Kensington Church St, London, W8 4EP **t** 020 7368 2500 **f** 020 7368 2773 **e** firstname.lastname@warnermusic.com **w** rhino.co.uk 🅱 twitter.com/rhinorecordsuk ▶️ youtube.com/rhinouk 📇 Vice President Rhino: Dan Chalmers.

Rhythmbank Records 8 Upper Grosvenor Street, London, W1K 2LY **t** 020 7495 8333 **f** 020 7495 7833 **w** rhythmbank.com 📇 Contact: Vicki Wickham.

Rich Mr Sax Ltd Box G016, Unit 7, Marshwood Close, Canterbury, Kent, CT1 1DX **t** 01227 500250 **e** enquiries@richmrsax.com **w** rmsrecords.co.uk 📇 Director: Mark Duggan.

Richmond (see Cherry Red Records)

Riddle (see Nikt Records)

Ridge Records 1 York Street, Aberdeen, AB11 5DL **t** 01224 573100 **f** 01224 572598 **e** office@ridge-records.com **w** ridge-records.com 📇 Manager: Mike Smith.

Right Recordings - Right Management - Right Music 177 High St, Harlesden, London, NW10 4TE **t** 020 8961 3889 **f** 020 8951 9955 **e** info@rightrecordings.com **w** rightrecordings.com 📇 Directors: David Landau, John Kaufman.

Rinseproof Records 140A Bell Hill Rd, St Georges, Bristol, BS5 7NF **t** 07864 714 695 **e** djskelm@hotmail.co.uk **w** rinseproofrecords.com 📇 Label Head: Skelm.

Rise & Shine (see Wyze Recordings)

Riverbank Media Limited 34 Meadowside, Cambridge Pk, Twickenham, TW1 2JQ **t** 020 8404 8307 **f** 020 8404 8307 **e** info@riverbankmedia.com 📇 MD: Nicholas Dicker.

Riviera Records 83 Dolphin Crescent, Paignton, Devon, TQ3 1JZ **t** 07071 226 078 **f** 0870 133 0100 **e** Info@rivieramusic.net **w** rivieramusic.net 📇 MD: Kevin Jarvis.

RMO/Chill-out Music & Film 5a Tonbridge Rd, Maidstone, Kent, ME16 8RL **t** 01622 768 668 **f** 01622 768 667 📇 Dir: Reg McLean.

Road Train Recordings (see Shout Out Records)

Roadrunner Records Ealing Studios, Ealing Green, London, W5 5EP **t** 020 8567 6762 **f** 020 8567 6793 **e** rrguest@roadrunnerrecords.co.uk **w** roadrunnerrecords.co.uk 📇 MD: Mark Palmer.

Rock Action Records PO Box 15107, Glasgow, G1 1US **e** info@rockactionrecords.co.uk **w** rock-action.co.uk 📇 Label Manager: Craig Hargrave.

Rocstar Recordings PO Box 113, Hove, BN32YQ **t** 01273 329528 **f** 01273 329528 **e** info@rocstar.com **w** rocstar.com 📇 MD: Marco Distefano.

Rogue Records Ltd PO Box 337, London, N4 1TW **t** 01252 615 210 **f** 020 8348 5626 **e** rogue@frootsmag.com **w** frootsmag.com/beatnik 📇 MD: Ian Anderson.

RokSolid Entertainment Ltd 1 The Village, North End Way, London, NW3 7HA **e** manny@rsg.me.uk **w** rsg.me.uk 📇 MD / Chairman: Manny Elias / Mo Siddiqui 07778 037396.

Rollercoaster Records Rock House, London Rd, St Mary's, Stroud, Gloucestershire, GL6 8PU **t** 01453 886 252 **f** 01453 885 361 **e** john@rollercoasterrecords.com **w** rollercoasterrecords.com 📇 Dir: John Beecher.

Ronco 107 Mortlake Street, London, SW14 8HQ **t** 020 8392 6876 **f** 020 8392 6829 **e** ray.levy@telstar.co.uk 📇 Label Manager: Ray Levy.

Ronnie Harris Records (see East Central One Ltd)

Roots Records PO Box 4549, Coventry, West Midlands, CV4 0DR **t** 02476 422 225 **f** 02476 462 398 **e** rootsrecs@btclick.com **w** rootsrecordsonline.co.uk 📇 MD: Graham Bradshaw.

Rosette Records 43-51 Wembley Hill Rd, Wembley, Middx, HA9 8AU **t** 020 8733 1440 **f** 020 8903 5859 **e** info@rosetterecords.com **w** rosetterecords.com 📇 MD: David Smith.

Ross Records (Turriff) Ltd 30 Main Street, Turriff, Aberdeenshire, AB53 4AB **t** 01888 568 899 **f** 01888 568 890 **e** gibson@rossrecords.com **w** rossrecords.com 📇 MD: Gibson Ross.

Rotator Studios / Interzone Management 74-77 Magdalen Road, Oxford, OX4 1RE **t** 01865 715705 **e** info@rotator.co.uk **w** rotator.co.uk ✉ MD: Richard Cotton.

Rough Trade Records 66 Golborne Rd, London, W10 5PS **t** 020 8960 9888 **f** 020 8968 6715 **e** jamiewoolgar@roughtraderecords.com **w** roughtrade.co.uk ✉ Contact: Jamie Woolgar.

RPM (see Cherry Red Records)

RPM Productions PO Box 158, Chipping Norton, Oxon, OX7 5ZL **t** 01608 643 738 **e** info@rpmrecords.co.uk **w** rpmrecords.co.uk ✉ MD: Mark Stratford.

RSK Entertainment Ltd Units 4&5, Home Farm, Welford, Newbury, Berkshire, RG20 8HR **t** 01488 608 900 **f** 01488 608 901 **e** info@rskentertainment.co.uk **w** rskentertainment.co.uk ✉ Joint MDs: Rashmi Patani and Simon Carver.

Rubber Road Records 4-10 Lamb Walk, London, SE1 3TT **t** 020 7921 8353 **e** rubber_road_records@yahoo.co.uk ✉ Head of A&R: Nick Lightowlers.

Rubicon Records 59 Park View Road, London, NW10 1AJ **t** 020 8450 5154 **f** 020 8452 0187 **e** rubiconrecords@btopenworld.com **w** rubiconrecords.co.uk ✉ Founder: Graham Le Fevre.

RubyRed Records 46 University St, Belfast, Northern Ireland, BT7 1HB **t** 07775 657234 **f** 08707 625672 **e** francotton@rubyredrec.com ✉ Contact: Fran Cotton.

Rubyworks Records 6 Park Rd, Dun Laoghaire, County Dublin, Ireland **t** +353 1 284 1747 **f** +353 1 284 1767 **e** info@rubyworks.com **w** rubyworks.com t twitter.com/rubyworks ✉ Dir: Niall Muckian.

Rumour Records Ltd PO BOX 54127, London, W5 9BE **t** 020 8997 7893 **f** 020 8997 7901 **e** post@rumour.demon.co.uk **w** rumourrecords.com ✉ MD: Anne Plaxton.

Rump Ltd PO Box 53512, London, SE19 2ZW **t** 07973 360 960 **e** rump.ltd@hotmail.com ✉ MD: Paul Eldon.

Running Man Records PO Box 32100, London, N4 1GR **f** 020 8374 5054 **e** runningman@oysterband.co.uk **w** oysterband.co.uk ✉ Label Manager: Colin Clowtt.

S Records (see Sony Music Entertainment UK & Ireland)

S.O.U.R. Recordings (see Tuff Street - SOSL Recordings)

S:Alt Records Ltd **e** info@saltrecords.com **w** saltrecords.com ✉ Label Manager: Roberto Concina.

Saddle Creek Records PO Box 8554, Omaha, Nebraska, 68108 0554, United States **e** info@saddle-creek.com **w** saddle-creek.com ✉ Contact: Robb Nansel, Jason Kulbel.

Safehouse Recordings The Blue Building, 8-10 Basing St, London, W11 1ET **t** 0207 229 1229 **f** 0207 243 8100 **e** info@safehouserecordings.com **w** safehouserecordings.com ✉ Chairman: Clive Black.

Sain Records Canolfan Sain, Llandwrog, Caernarfon, Gwynedd, LL54 5TG **t** 01286 831111 **f** 01286 831497 **e** sain@sainwales.com **w** sainwales.com ✉ CEO: Dafydd Roberts.

Sakay (see Rogue Records Ltd)

Salvia Recordings (see XL Recordings)

Sanctuary Classics (see Decca Records)

Sanctuary Records (see Universal Music (UK) Ltd)

Sangraal (see Science Friction)

Sargasso PO Box 221, Baldock, SG7 6WZ **t** 01462 892181 **e** info@sargasso.com **w** sargasso.com ✉ Director: John Hall.

Satellite Music Ltd 34 Salisbury St, London, NW8 8QE **t** 020 7402 9111 **f** 020 7723 3064 **e** satellite_artists@hotmail.com ✉ MD: Eliot Cohen.

Saturn Return Records PO Box 1083, Liverpool, L69 4WQ **t** 0151 222 5785 **f** 0151 222 5785 **e** mail@saturnreturnrecords.co.uk **w** saturnreturnrecords.co.uk ✉ MD: Noel Fitzsimmons.

Saucer (see Seriously Groovy Music)

SavageTrax Suite 147, 77 Beak Street, London, W1F 9BD **t** 020 7000 3146 **f** 020 7000 3146 **e** kevin@savagetrax.com **w** savagetrax.com ✉ Contact: Kevin Savage 07778 645 239.

RDL Music 132 Chase Way, London, N14 5DH **t** 07050 055 168 **f** 0870 741 5252 **e** atlanticcrossingartists@yahoo.com **w** mkentertainments.8k.com ✉ MD: Steven Hain.

Savoy Records PO Box 271, Coulsdon, Surrey, CR5 3YZ **t** 01737 554 739 **f** 01737 556 737 **e** admin@savoymusic.com **w** savoymusic.com ✉ MD: Wendy Smith.

Saydisc Records The Barton, Inglestone Common, Badminton, Gloucestershire, GL9 1BX **e** saydisc@aol.com **w** saydisc.com ✉ MD: Gef Lucena.

SBS Records PO Box 37, Blackwood, Gwent, NP12 2YQ **t** 01495 201116 **f** 01495 201190 **e** enquiry@sbsrecords.co.uk **w** sbsrecords.co.uk ✉ MD: Glenn Powell 07711 984651.

Scarlet Records Southview, 68 Siltside, Gosberton Risegate, Lincs, PE11 4ET **t** 01755 841750 **f** 01522 321166 **e** info@scarletrecording.co.uk **w** scarletmusicservices.co.uk ✉ MD: Liz Lenten.

Scatty Cat Records Unit 28, 502, Hornsey Rd, London, N19 4EF **t** 07813 966 818 **e** mail@scattycatrecords.com **w** scattycatrecords.com ✉ Dirs: Joe Carlo or Sophie Storr.

The Schizofreniks London
e niki@theschizofreniks.com w theschizofreniks.com
🔳 myspace.com/schizofreniksrecords
🔳 youtube.com/RecordLabel 🔲 Producer/Managing
Director: Niki Clarke.

Schnitzel Records Ltd. - Hamburger Publishing PO Box 64061, London, E1W 9AP
t 020 790 7915 f 020 790 7915 e info@schnitzel.co.uk
w schnitzel.co.uk 🔲 MD: Oliver Geywitz.

Science Friction 21 Stupton Rd, Sheffield, South Yorks,
S9 1BQ t 0114 261 1649 f 0114 261 1649
e dc@cprod.win-uk.net w royharper.co.uk 🔲 Label
Manager: Darren Crisp.

Scotdisc - BGS Productions Ltd Newtown St,
Kilsyth, Glasgow, Strathclyde, G65 0LY t 01236 821081
f 01236 826900 e info@scotdisc.co.uk w scotdisc.co.uk
🔲 MD: Dougie Stevenson.

Scratch (see The Store For Music)

Scribendum Ltd Burnt Oak Farm, Waldron, Heathfield,
East Sussex, TN21 0NL t 0560 171 6007
e mail@silveroak.biz w silveroakmusic.com
🔲 Contact: Giorgio Cuppini.

Sea Dream 🔲 Contact: Plankton. (see Plankton Records)

Seamless Recordings 192-194 Clapham High St,
London, SW4 7UD t 020 7498 5551 f 020 7498 2333
e simon@seamlessrecordings.com
w seamlessrecordings.com 🔲 Label Mgr: Simon Dawson.

Second Coming Records 6 Hesleyside Road,
South Wellfield, Whitley Bay, NE25 9HB t 07812 633 364
f 0191 253 5997 e james_climax@hotmail.com 🔲 Label
Manager: James Wilson.

Secret Records Regent House, 1 Pratt Mews, London,
NW1 0AD t 020 7554 4840 f 020 7388 8324
e partners@newman-and.co.uk 🔲 MD: Colin Newman.

Sedna Records London t 020 7467 0622
e jonathan@10management.com 🔲 Manager: Jonathan
Wild.

See Monkey Do Monkey Recordings
183a King's Rd, Pontcanna, Cardiff, CF11 9DF
t 02920 343244 e meg@seemonkeydomonkey.com
w seemonkeydomonkey.com 🔲 Contact: Megan Campbell.

Seeca Records 6, Ditton Hill Rd, Surbiton, Surrey.
KT6 5JD t 020 8398 2510 f 020 8398 1970
e info@seeca.co.uk w seeca.co.uk 🔲 Dir: Louise Blair.

Select Music & Video Distribution Ltd.
3 Wells Pl, Redhill, Surrey, RH1 3SL t 01737 645600 ext 211
f 01737 644065 e GBartholomew@selectmusic.co.uk
w naxos.com 🔲 Licensing Mgr: Graham Bartholomew 01635
871338.

Select Music and Video Ltd. 3 Wells Place, Redhill,
Surrey, RH1 3SL t 01737 645600 f 01737 644065
e BHolden@selectmusic.co.uk w naxos.com 🔲 Naxos Label
Mgr/Mktg Mgr: Barry Holden.

Selecta Records Ltd PO Box 357, Middlesbrough,
Cleveland, TS1 4WZ t 01642 806795 f 01642 351962
e info@millbrand.com w millbrand.com
📘 facebook.com/millbrand
🔳 myspace.com/selectarecords 🔲 MD: Paul Mooney.

Sense World Music 93, Belgrave Road, Leicester,
Leicestershire, LE4 6AS t 0116 266 7046 f 0116 261 0480
e alpesh@senseworldmusic.com w senseworldmusic.com
🔲 MD: Alpesh Patel.

Serengeti Records 43A Old Woking Rd, West Byfleet,
Surrey, KT14 6LG t 01932 351925 f 01932 336431
e info@serengeti-records.com 🔲 MD: Martin Howell.

Series 8 Records PO Box 5192, Hatfield Peverel,
Chelmsford, Essex, CM3 2QH t 07939 631390
e series8@supalife.com w series8records.co.uk
🔲 MD: Trevor Holden.

Seriously Groovy Music 3rd Floor, 28 D'Arblay St,
Soho, London, W1F 8EW t 020 7439 1947 f 020 7734 7540
e admin@seriouslygroovy.com w seriouslygroovy.com
🔲 Directors: Dave Holmes, Lorraine Snape.

Setanta Records 112 Manor Grove, Richmond, Surrey,
tw9 4qf t 020 8241 9807 e info@setantarecords.com
w setantarecords.com 🔲 MD: Keith Cullen.

Shade Factor Productions Limited
4 Cleveland Sq, London, W2 6DH t 020 7402 6477
f 020 7402 7144 e mail@shadefactor.com
w shadefactor.com 🔲 MD: Ann Symonds.

Shamtown Records 4/5 High Street, Galway, Ireland
t +353 91 521 309 f +353 91 526 341
e sawdoc@eircom.net w sawdoctors.com 🔲 MD: Ollie
Jennings.

Shellwood Productions (see Priory Records)

Shifty Disco Ltd OMC, 1st Floor, 9 Park End St, Oxford,
OX1 1HH t 01865 798791 e info@shiftydisco.co.uk
w shiftydisco.co.uk 🔲 MD: Dave Newton.

Shock Records PO Box 301, Torquay, Devon, TQ2 7TB
t 01803 614392 f 01803 616271
e info@shockrecords.co.uk w shockrecords.co.uk 🔲 A&R
Manager: Graham Eden.

Shoeshine Records PO Box 15193, Glasgow, G2 6LB
t 0141 204 5654 f 0141 204 5654 e info@shoeshine.co.uk
w shoeshine.co.uk 🔲 Proprietor: Francis Macdonald.

Shout Out Records 51 Clarkegrove Rd, Sheffield,
S10 2NH t 0114 268 5665 f 0114 268 4161
e entsuk@aol.com 🔲 MD: John Roddison.

Sidewalk 7 50A Kingsway Pl, London, EC1R 0LU
t 020 7253 7341 e info@sidewalk7.com w sidewalk7.com
🔲 MD: Rocco Gardner.

Silva Classics (see Silva Screen)

Silva Screen 3 Prowse Pl, London, NW1 9PH
t 020 7428 5500 f 020 7482 2385 e info@silvascreen.co.uk
w silvascreen.co.uk 🔲 MD: Reynold da Silva.

Silva Treasury (see Silva Screen)

📇 Contacts   📘 Facebook   🅜 MySpace   🅣 Twitter   ▶️ YouTube

Silverscope Music 53, Triq Ta Mellu, Mosta, MST3780, Malta **t** 00356 9989 6666 **e** silverscope@btconnect.com **w** myspace.com/silverscopemusic **t** w.silverscope 📇 MD: Richard Rogers.

Silverword Music Group 16 Limetrees, Llangattock, Crickhowell, Powys, NP8 1LB **t** 01873 810 142 **e** silvergb@aol.com **w** silverword.co.uk 📇 MD: Kevin Holland-King.

Simple Records First Floor, 75 Abbeville Rd, SW4 9JN **t** 020 8673 1818 **f** 020 8673 6751 **e** info@simplerecords.co.uk 📇 A&R Director: Will Saul.

Sinister Recordings 69a Mervan Rd, London, SW2 1DR **t** 07769 556 946 **e** info@sinister-recordings.com **w** sinister-recordings.com 📇 Label Manager: Paul Kiernan.

Sink and Stove Records Bristol **e** info@sinkandstove.co.uk **w** sinkandstove.co.uk 📘 facebook.com/pages/Sink-Stove-Records/47821954355?ref=ts 🅜 myspace.com/sinkandstove 📇 Label Mgr: Benjamin Shillabeer.

Sire (see Warner Bros Records UK)

Six Armed Man Records (see Dynamite Vision - Falling A Records)

Six Degrees Records (see Collective Music Ltd)

Skint Records PO Box 174, Brighton, East Sussex, BN1 4BA **t** 01273 738527 **f** 01273 208766 **e** mail@skint.net **w** skint.net 📇 Dir: Tim Jeffrey.

Skydog (see Jungle Records)

Skyline (see New State Entertainment)

SLAM Productions 3 Thesiger Rd, Abingdon, Oxon, OX14 2DX **t** 01235 529012 **e** slamprods@aol.com **w** slamproductions.net 📇 Proprietor: George Haslam.

Slave Records PO Box 200, South Shore, Blackpool, Lancs, FY1 6GR **t** 07816 926 944 **e** sploj3@yahoo.co.uk 📇 Contact: Rob Powell.

Sleeper Music Ltd Block 2, 6 Erskine Road, Primrose Hill, London, NW3 3AJ **t** 020 7580 3995 **f** 020 7900 6244 **e** info@sleepermusic.co.uk **w** guychambers.com 📇 Contact: Dylan Chambers, Louise Jeremy.

Smexi Playaz Records PO Box 2035, Blackpool, FY4 1WW **t** 01253 347329 **f** 01253 347329 **e** glenn@outlet-promotions.com **w** outlet-promotions.com 📇 MD: Glenn Wilson.

Smiled Records RGA Studio, 209 Goldhawk Road, London, W12 8EP **t** 020 8746 7000 **f** 020 8746 7700 **e** info@smiled.net **w** smiled.net 📇 MD: James Barton 07776 188 191.

Snapper Music 1 Star St, London, W2 1QD **t** 020 7563 5500 **f** 020 7563 5566 **e** sales@snappermusic.co.uk **w** snappermusic.co.uk 📇 Marketing Director: Johnny Wilks.

Sobriety Records (see Shout Out Records)

Soda (see Seriously Groovy Music)

Sofa (see Seriously Groovy Music)

Soldier Blue Records PO Box 56535, London, SW18 9DN **t** 07947 116 152 **f** 020 8408 3969 **e** info@soldierbluerecords.com **w** soldierbluerecords.com 📇 Label Relations and A&R Manager: Aishah Bilal.

Solent Records 68-70 Lugley St, Newport, Isle Of Wight, PO30 5ET **t** 01983 524110 **f** 0870 164 0388 **e** md@solentrecords.co.uk **w** solentrecords.co.uk 📇 Owner: John Waterman.

Soma Recordings Ltd 2nd Floor, 342 Argyle St, Glasgow, G2 8LY **t** 0141 229 6220 **f** 0141 226 4142 **e** info@somarecords.com **w** somarecords.com 📇 MD: Glenn Gibbons.

Sombrero 33 Riding House Street, London, W1W 7DZ **t** 020 7636 3939 **f** 020 7636 0033 **e** info@sonic360.com **w** sonic360.com 📇 Creative Director: Hana Miya.

Some Bizzare 10 Great Russell St, London, WC1B 3BQ **e** info@somebizarre.com **w** .myspace.com/somebizarrelabel 🅜 myspace.com/somebizarrerecords 📇 MD: Stevo.

Somerset Entertainment International Ltd 3D Moss Road, Witham, Essex, CM8 3UW **t** 01376 521 527 **f** 01376 521 528 **e** initial+surname@somersetent.com **w** somersetent.com 📇 Sales: Sarah Martin.

Something In Construction SIC/Wild Unit 2B, Westpoint, 39-40 Warple Way, London, W3 0RG **t** 020 8746 0666 **f** 020 8746 7676 **e** info@somethinginconstruction.com **w** somethinginconstruction.com 📘 apps.facebook.com/ilike/artist/something+in+construction 🅜 myspace.com/somethinginconstruction **t** @SICrecords 📇 MD: David Laurie.

Songphonic St Anns Court, St Anns Hill Rd, Chertsey, KT16 9NW **t** 01932 568969 **e** info@songphonic.com **w** songphonic.com 🅜 myspace.com/songphonic 📇 CEO: Osman Kent.

Sonic Cathedral Recordings PO Box 57718, London, NW11 1DR **t** 07929 037 366 **e** info@soniccathedral.co.uk **w** soniccathedral.co.uk

Sonic360 3 Wardour Castle, Tisbury, Wiltshire, SP3 6RH **t** 020 7636 3939 **f** 020 7636 0033 **e** info@sonic360.com **w** sonic360.com 🅜 myspace.com/sonic60 ▶️ youtube.com/s0nic360 📇 Label Manager: Zen Grisdale.

SonRise Records Western House, Richardson St, Swansea, SA1 3JF **t** 07815 770 001 **e** info@sonriserecords.co.uk **w** sonriserecords.co.uk 📇 Contact: Darren Pullin.

Sony Music Entertainment Ireland Ltd. Embassy House, Ballsbridge, Dublin 4, Ireland **t** +353 1 647 3400 **f** +353 1 647 3430 **e** firstname.lastname@sonymusic.com **w** sonymusic.ie 📘 facebook.com/pages/Sony-Music-Ireland/104560651373 🅑 bebo.com/Sony_Music_Ireland **t** twitter.com/SonyMusicIre ▶️ youtube.com/SonyMusicIrelandLtd 📇 MD: Annette Donnelly.

Record Companies: Record Companies & Labels

SONY MUSIC ENTERTAINMENT UK & IRELAND

SONY MUSIC

9 Derry Street, London, W8 5HY **t** 020 7361 8000
f 020 7937 0188 **e** firstname.lastname@sonymusic.com
w sonymusic.co.uk 🔲 Chairman and CEO: Ged Doherty.
C.O.O.: Paul Curran. SVP Legal & Business Affairs: Michael
Smith. SVP Commercial Sales: Nicola Tuer. VP
International: Dave Shack. VP Industry Affairs: Emma Pike.
MD Ireland: Annette Donnelly. MD Columbia Label
Group: Mike Smith. MD Epic: Nick Raphael. SVP Digital &
Strategic Partnerships: Graeme Ferguson. MD RCA Label
Group: Craig Logan. VP Human Resources: Simon Woolf. MD
Syco Music/Syco TV: Sonny Takhar.

Sorted Records t 0116 291 1580 **f** 0116 291 1580
e sortedrecords@Hotmail.com **w** sorted-records.org.uk
🔲 MD: Dave Dixey.

SOSL Recordings (see Tuff Street - SOSL Recordings)

Soul 2 Soul Recordings 45 Fouberts Place, London,
W1F 7QH **t** 020 7439 6060 **e** andy@soul2soul.co.uk
w soul2soul.co.uk 🔲 MD: Jazzie B.

Soul Brother (see Expansion Records)

Soul Jazz Records 7 Broadwick St, London, W1F 0DA
t 020 7734 3341 **f** 020 7494 1035
e info@soundsoftheuniverse.com **w** souljazzrecords.co.uk
🔲 Publicity & Production: Angela Scott.

Soundscape Music 4 Bridgefield, Farnham, Surrey,
GU9 8AN **t** 01252 721096 **e** bob@bobholroyd.com
w info@bobholroyd.com 🔲 Director: Bob Holroyd.

Southbound (see Ace Records)

Southern Fried Records Fulham Palace,
Bishops Avenue, London, SW6 6EA **t** 020 7384 7373
f 020 7384 7392 **e** nathan@southernfriedrecords.com
w southernfriedrecords.com 🔲 A&R Manager: Nathan
Thursting.

Southern Records/Studios 10 Myddleton Rd,
London, N22 8NS **t** 020 8888 8949 **f** 020 8889 6166
e firstname@southern.com **w** southern.com
📘 facebook.com/pages/Southern-Records/24964764156
🔳 myspace.com/southernrecords 🅱 southernrec
▶️ youtube.com/user/southernrecords 🔲 Managing
Director: Allison Schnackenberg.

Sovereign (see Hot Lead Records)

Space Age Recordings (see Adasam Limited)

Spaced Out Music 8 Southlands Close, Leek, Staffs,
ST13 8DF **t** 01782 772989 **e** nomed1@gmail.com **w** the-
demon.com 🔲 MD and Manager for Demon: Mike Stone.

Special Fried (see New State Entertainment)

Spit and Polish Records (see Shoeshine Records)

Splash Records Ltd 29 Manor House,
250 Marylebone Rd, London, NW1 5NP **t** 020 7723 7177
f 020 7262 0775 **e** splashrecords.uk@btconnect.com
w splashrecords.co.uk 🔲 Director: Chas Peate.

Split Records 13 Dagmar Terrace, London, N1 2BN
t 020 7226 8706 **f** 020 7226 8706
e max@splitrecords.co.uk **w** splitrecords.co.uk
🔳 myspace.com/splitrecordsmusic 🔲 Label Manager: Max
Odell 07813 893377.

Sprawl Imprint 63 Windmill Road, Brentford, Middx,
TW8 0QQ **t** 0208 568 3145 **e** sprawl@benfo.demon.co.uk
w sprawl.org.uk 🔲 MD: Douglas Benford.

Spring Records Dargan House, Bray, Co Wicklow, Ireland
f +353 12 861 514 **e** atrisk@iol.ie **w** mrspring.net
🔲 A&R: Springer.

Springthyme Records Balmalcolm House,
Balmalcolm, Cupar, Fife, KY15 7TJ **t** 01337 830 773
e admin@springthyme.myzen.co.uk **w** springthyme.co.uk
🔲 Director: Peter Shepheard.

Square Biz Records 65A Beresford Rd, London,
N5 2HR **t** 020 7503 6457 **e** sujiro.gray@btinternet.com
🔲 MD: Mr J Gray.

Squeaky Records Ltd. 37 Baldock Road, Royston,
Herts., SG8 5BJ **t** 01763 243 603 **f** 01763 243 603
e info@squeakyrecords.com **w** squeakyrecords.com
🔲 Director: Helen Gregorios-Pippas.

Squint Entertainment (see Collective Music Ltd)

Start Entertainments Ltd Fairways, Gorelands Lane,
Northwood, Chalfont St Giles, Buckinghamshire, HP8 4HQ
t 01494 876166 **f** 01494 876764
e info@startentertainments.com **w** nostalgiamusic.co.uk
🔲 GM: Nicholas Dicker.

state ART The Basement, 3 Eaton Pl, Brighton,
East Sussex, BN2 1EH **t** 01273 572090 **e** paul@stateart.org
w stateart.org 🔳 myspace.com/stateart 🔲 Co-
founder: Paul Mex.

State Records 67 Upper Berkeley St, London, W1H 7QX
t 020 7563 7028 **f** 020 7563 7029
e recordings@staterecords.co.uk **w** popmusic4synch.com
🔲 MD: Dr Wayne Bickerton.

Stax (see Ace Records)

Sterling (see Priory Records)

Stern's Records 74-75 Warren Street, London, W1T 5PF
t 020 7387 5550 **f** 020 7388 2756
e info@sternsmusic.com **w** sternsmusic.com 🔲 MD: Don
Bay 020 7388 5533.

Sticky Music PO Box 176, Glasgow, G11 5YJ
t 01698 207230 **f** 0141 576 8431
e info@stickymusic.co.uk **w** stickymusic.co.uk
🔲 Partner: Charlie Irvine.

Stiff Records (see ZTT Records Ltd)

Stirling Music Group 1-2 St Albans Studio,
South End Row, London, W8 5BT **t** 020 7993 5565
e office@pureuk.com **w** pureuk.com 🔲 CEO: Evros Stakis.

Stockholm 🖼 Contact: Polydor Associated. (see Polydor Records)

Stompatime (see Fury Records)

Stones Throw Records First Floor, 32 Clerkenwell Green, London, EC1R 0DU **t** 020 7253 6549 **e** alex@stonesthrow.com **w** stonesthrow.com 📘 facebook.com/stonesthrow 🅼 myspace.com/stonesthrow 🅱 twitter.com/stonesthrow ▶️ youtube.com/stonesthrow 🖼 Label Manager: Alex Robinson 07815 310246.

The Store For Music Hatch Farm Studios, Chertsey Rd, Addlestone, Surrey, KT15 2EH **t** 01932 828715 **f** 01932 828717 **e** brian.adams@dial.pipex.com **w** thestoreformusic.com 🖼 MD: Brian Adams.

Storm Music 2nd Floor, 1 Ridgefield, Manchester, M2 6EG **t** 0161 839 5111 **f** 0161 839 7898 **e** info@storm-music.com 🖼 MD: Mike Ball.

Stradivarius (see Priory Records)

Stray Cat Records 695 High Rd, Seven Kings, Ilford, Essex, IG3 8RH **t** 020 8590 0022 **f** 020 8599 2870 **e** jamie@straycatrecords.com **w** straycatrecords.com 🖼 Managing Director: Jamie Danan 07885 670294.

Stress Management - Quixotic Records Imex House, VIP Trading Estate, Anchor & Hope Lane, London, SE7 7TE **t** 020 8269 0352 **f** 020 8269 0353 **e** suzanne@quixoticrecords.com **w** quixoticrecords.com 🖼 Partner/Manager: Suzanne Hunt 07778 049706.

Strictly Rhythm (see Warner Bros Records UK)

Strike Records 7 Warren Mews, London, W1T 6AS **t** 020 7874 1704 **e** Info@bythepoolmusic.com 🖼 Contact: Lucille Jackson 0207 874 1704.

Sublime Music 211 Piccadilly, London, W1J 9HF **t** 020 7917 2948 **e** mw@sublime-music.co.uk **w** sublime-music.co.uk 🖼 Mgr: Nick Grant.

Sublime Recordings 77 Preston Drove, Brighton, East Sussex, BN1 6LD **t** 01273 236 300 or 07774 133 134 **e** info@sublimemusic.co.uk **w** sublimemusic.co.uk 🖼 MD: Patrick Spinks.

Subside Records SNC Via Vecchia Fiuggi 382, 03015-Fiuggi, FR, Italy **t** +39 0775 515122 **f** +39 0775 514218 **e** info@subsiderec.com **w** subsiderec.com 🖼 CEO: Vanni Giorgilli.

Sub-Urban Records (see Defected Records Ltd)

Suburban Soul (Music) PO Box 415, Bromley, Kent, BR1 2XR **t** 020 8402 1984 **f** 020 8325 0708 **e** urban_music@msn.com 🖼 Director: RT Brown 0798 406 1954.

Subversive Records Old House, 154 Prince Consort Road, Gateshead, NE8 4DU **t** 0191 469 0100 **f** 0191 469 0001 **e** info@subversiverecords.co.uk **w** subversiverecords.co.uk 🖼 Dir: Martin Jones.

Sugar Shack Records Ltd PO Box 73, Fishponds, Bristol, BS16 7EZ **t** 01179 855092 **f** 01179 855092 **e** info@sugarshackrecords.co.uk **w** sugarshackrecords.co.uk 🅼 myspace.com/sugarshackrecordsuk 🖼 Dir: Mike Darby.

Sugarstar Ltd IT Centre, York Science Park, York, YO10 5DG **t** 08456 448 424 **f** 0709 222 8681 **e** Info@sugarstar.com **w** sugarstar.com 🖼 MD: Mark Fordyce.

Summerhouse Records PO Box 34601, London, E17 6GA **t** 020 8521 3355 **e** office@summerhouserecords.co.uk **w** summerhouserecords.co.uk 🅼 myspace.com/summerhouserecords 🖼 MD: William Jones.

Sunday Best Recordings Studio 11, 25 Denmark St, London, WC2H 8NJ **t** 020 7379 3133 **f** 0870 420 4392 **e** info@sundaybest.net **w** sundaybest.net 🅼 myspace.com/sundaybestrecordings ▶️ youtube.com/sundaybestrecordings 🖼 Label Manager: Sarah Bolshi.

Sunny Records Ltd 29 Fife Road, East Sheen, London, SW14 7EJ **t** 020 8876 9871 **f** 020 8392 2371 **e** getcarter.sunny29@amserve.com 🖼 Contact: John Carter.

Sunrise Records Silverdene, Scaleby Hill, Carlisle, CA6 4LU **t** 01228 675822 **f** 01228 675822 **e** info@sunriserecords.co.uk **w** sunriserecords.co.uk 🖼 MD: Martin Smith.

SuperCharged Music 29 Kensington Gardens, Brighton, BN1 4AL **t** 01273 628 181 **f** 01273 670 444 **e** lloyd@superchargedmusic.com **w** superchargedmusic.com 🖼 Label Manager: Lloyd Seymour.

Superglider Records First Floor, 123 Old Christchurch Rd, Bournemouth, Dorset, BH1 1EP **t** 07968 345173 **e** mail@superglider.com **w** superglider.com 🖼 Contact: Griff.

Supersonic Records (see New State Entertainment)

Supertron Music 19-23 Fosse Way, London, W13 0BZ **t** 020 8998 6372 🖼 MD: Michael Rodriguez 020 8998 4372.

Supremo Recordings PO Box 8679, Dublin 7, Ireland **t** +353 1 671 7393 **f** +353 1 671 7393 **e** info@supremorecordings.com **w** supremorecordings.com 🖼 MD: Philip Cartin.

Surface2Air Ltd 28C Kilburn Lane, London, W10 4AH **t** 07960 957 939 **e** info@surface2air.net **w** surface2air.net 🖼 Head of A&R: Tom Nicolson.

Surfdog Records (see Collective Music Ltd)

Sursagar (see Sense World Music)

Survival Records PO Box 2502, Devizes, Wilts, SN10 3ZN **t** 01380 860500 **f** 01380 860596 **e** AnneMarie@survivalrecords.co.uk **w** survivalrecords.co.uk 🖼 Director: David Rome.

Record Companies: Record Companies & Labels

Suspect Records 58 Greenfell Mansions, Glaisher St, London, SE8 3EU **t** 07764 159175 **e** info@suspectrecords.com **w** suspectrecords.com 🔲 MD: Stephen Davison.

Susu (see Concept Music)

Sweet Nothing (see Cargo Records)

Swing Cafe 32 Willesden Lane, London, NW6 7ST **t** 020 7625 0231 **f** 020 372 5439 **e** lauriejay@btconnect.com 🔲 Head of A&R: Chas White.

Swing City (see Wyze Recordings)

Switchflicker 12 Hilton St, Northern Quarter, Manchester, M1 1JF **t** 07803 601885 **e** info@switchflicker.co.uk **w** switchflicker.com 🔲 myspace.com/switchflickerrecords 🔲 twitter.com/switchflicker 🔲 youtube.com/switchflicker 🔲 A&R: Jayne Compton.

SYCO MUSIC

SYCOmusic

9 Derry St, London, W8 5HY **t** 020 7361 8000 **f** 020 7937 0188 **e** firstname.lastname@sonymusic.com 🔲 Managing Director: Sonny Takhar. SVP International & Operations: Simon Jones. SVP US A&R: David Gray. Creative Director: Tim Byrne. Head of Media: Ann-Marie Thomson. Marketing: Laurence Boakes/ Anya Jones.

Sylvantone 11 Saunton Avenue, Redcar, North Yorkshire, TS10 2RL **t** 01642 479898 **f** 0709 235 9333 **e** sylvantone@hotmail.com **w** tonygoodacre.com 🔲 Prop: Tony Goodacre.

Symposium Records 110 Derwent Avenue, East Barnet, Herts, EN4 8LZ **t** 020 8368 8667 **f** 020 8368 8667 **e** symposium@cwcom.net **w** symposiumrecords.co.uk

Tahra (see Priory Records)

Talking Elephant 8 Martin Dene, Bexleyheath, Kent, DA6 8NA **t** 020 8301 2828 **f** 05602 056261 **e** info@talkingelephant.co.uk **w** talkingelephant.co.uk 🔲 Partner: Barry Riddington.

Tall Pop (see Adasam Limited)

TAPE Ltd 45-46 Charlotte Rd, London, EC2A 3PD **t** 0207 739 0939 **e** label@taperec.com **w** taperec.com 🔲 Manager: Daniel Cross.

Tara Music Company Basement, 18 Upper Mount St, Dublin 2, Ireland **t** +353 1 678 7871 **f** +353 1 678 7873 **e** info@taramusic.com **w** taramusic.com 🔲 MD: John Cook.

Taste Media Ltd - Taste Music 263 Putney Bridge Rd, London, SW15 2PU **t** 020 8780 3311 **f** 020 8785 9894 **e** info@tastemusic.com **w** tastemedia.com 🔲 Managing Director: Safta Jaffery.

TCM Music Ltd 26 School Lane, Herne, Kent, CT6 7AL **t** 01227 366 689 **e** info@tedcarfrae.com **w** tedcarfrae.com 🔲 Director: Ted Carfrae.

Teddington Media Limited 13 Hawkins Rd, Teddington, Middlesex, TW11 9ET **t** 020 8404 8307 **f** 020 8404 8307 **e** info@teddingtonmedia.com **w** teddingtonmedia.com 🔲 MD: Nicholas Dicker.

Teldec (see Warner Classics & Jazz)

Teleryngg (see RDL Music)

Telica Communications (see The Recoverworld Label Group (Supreme Music Ltd))

Tema International 151 Nork Way, Banstead, Surrey, SM7 1HR **t** 01737 219607 **f** 0871 715 1236 **e** music@tema-intl.demon.co.uk **w** temadance.com 🔲 Managing Director: Tony Evans.

Temple Records Shillinghill, Temple, Midlothian, EH23 4SH **t** 01875 830328 **f** 01875 830392 **e** robin@templerecords.co.uk **w** templerecords.co.uk 🔲 MD: Robin Morton.

Tenor Vossa Records Ltd PO Box 34803, London, W8 7OZ **t** 020 7221 0511 **f** 020 7221 0511 **e** tenor.vossa@virgin.net **w** tenorvossa.co.uk 🔲 tenorvossarecordsltd 🔲 MD: Ari Neufeld.

Terminus Records (see Collective Music Ltd)

Them's Good Records (see Adasam Limited)

Theobald Dickson Productions The Coach House, Swinhope Hall, Swinhope, Market Rasen, Lincs, LN8 6HT **t** 01472 399 011 **f** 01472 399 025 **e** tdproductions@lineone.net 🔲 MD: Bernard Theobald.

Thirty-Seven Records 28 St. Albans Gdns, Stranmillis Rd, Belfast, Co. Antrim, BT9 5DR **t** 07736 548 969 **e** sean@thirtysevenrecords.com **w** thirtysevenrecords.com 🔲 Label Mgr: Sean Douglas.

Three Black Feathers 61 Somers Rd, Malvern, Worcestershire, WR14 1JA **t** 01684 899457 **e** chris@threeblackfeathers.co.uk **w** threeblackfeathers.co.uk 🔲 Contact: Chris Heard 07793 152362.

Three Black Feathers Ltd 61 Somers Rd, Malvern, Worcestershire, WR14 1JA **t** 01684 899 457 **e** rachel@threeblackfeathers.co.uk **w** threeblackfeathers.co.uk 🔲 Co-owner: Rachel Heard 07834 450938.

Thunder (see Rollercoaster Records)

Thunderbird Records (see RPM Productions)

Thursday Club Recordings Ltd 310 King Street, London, W6 0RR **t** 020 8748 9480 **f** 020 8748 9489 **e** info@tcr.uk.com **w** tcr.uk.com 🔲 MD: Rennie Pilgrem.

Tiger Trax PO Box 204, Alton, Hampshire, GU34 1YA **t** 07838 111026 **e** info@tigertrax.co.uk **w** tigertrax.co.uk 🔲 myspace.com/tigertraxrecords 🔲 twitter.com/tigertrax 🔲 Business Affairs: Sam Radford.

Tiny Dog Records The Coach House, Churchill Road, Welton, Northamptonshire, NN11 2JH. **t** 01327 702 893 **f** 01327 702 893 **e** info@tinydog.co.uk **w** tinydog.co.uk 📇 MD: Pete Jennison.

Tip World PO Box 18157, London, NW6 7FF **t** 020 8537 2675 **f** 020 8537 2671 **e** info@tipworld.co.uk **w** tipworld.co.uk 📇 Label Manager: Richard Bloor.

Tomak Ltd (Slinky) PO Box 47002, London, SW18 5WS **t** 07717 722 929 **e** info@slinky.co.uk **w** slinky.co.uk 📇 Creative Director: Amadeus Mozart.

Tongue Master Records PO Box 38621, London, W13 8WG **f** 020 7371 4884 **e** info@tonguemaster.co.uk **w** tonguemaster.co.uk 📇 MD: Theodore Vlassopulos.

Too Pure 17-19 Alma Rd, London, SW18 1AA **t** 020 8875 6208 **f** 020 8875 1205 **e** toopure@toopure.co.uk **w** toopure.com 📇 Label Head: Jason White.

Too Young To Die Records Unit 14, Buspace Studios, Conlan St, London, W10 5AR **e** info@tooyoungtodierecords.com **w** tooyoungtodierecords.com 📇 MDs: Pete Hobbs, Jonathan Owen.

Top Cat Music Ltd Mill Side, Mill Lane, Box, Corsham, SN13 8PN **t** 01225 744413 **e** info@topcatmusic.co.uk **w** topcatmusic.co.uk 📱 myspace.com/thetopcatmusic 📇 Dir: Tim Oliver.

Topaz (see Pavilion Records Ltd)

Topic Records 50 Stroud Green Rd, London, N4 3ES **t** 020 7263 1240 **f** 020 7281 5671 **e** info@topicrecords.co.uk **w** topicrecords.co.uk 📇 MD: Tony Engle.

Tortured Records PO Box 32, Beckenham, BR3 6ZP **t** 01273 779 515 **e** billy@torturedrecords.co.uk **w** torturedrecords.co.uk 📇 MD: Billy Nasty.

Touch 13 Osward Road, London, SW17 7SS **t** 020 8355 9672 **f** 020 8355 9672 **e** info@touchmusic.org.uk **w** touchmusic.org.uk 📇 Directors: Jon Wozencroft, Michael Harding.

Tough Cookie Ltd part of Whizz Kid Entertainment Ltd, 4 Kingly Street, London, W1B 5PE **t** 020 7440 2550 **f** 020 7440 2599 **e** info@tough-cookie.co.uk **w** tough-cookie.co.uk 📇 Directors: Andy Wood, Neill Sullivan & Dave Castell 07977 248 646.

TOV Music Group Ltd (Trouble on Vinyl) 120 Wandsworth Rd, London, SW8 2LB **t** 020 7498 3888 **f** 020 7622 1030 **e** info@tovmusic.com **w** tovmusic.com 📇 MD: Clayton Hines.

Townsend Music Group 30 Queen St, Gt Harwood, Lancs, BB6 7QQ **t** 01254 885995 **f** 01254 887835 **e** bruce@townsend-records.co.uk **w** townsend-records.co.uk 📇 Sales Director: Bruce McKenzie.

Track Records PO Box 107, South Godstone, Redhill, Surrey, RH9 8YS **t** 01342 892074 **f** 01342 893411 **e** ian.grant@trackrecords.co.uk **w** trackrecords.co.uk 📱 myspace/trackrecordsuk 📇 MD: Ian Grant.

Trad Records 6 Queens Court, Wharfdale Road, Bournemouth, Dorset, BH4 9BS **t** 01202 757 494 **e** info@tradrecords.co.uk **w** tradrecords.co.uk 📇 Partner: Andy Burbidge.

Tradition 📇 Contact: Rykodisc. (see Palm Pictures)

Transgressive Records The Lexington, 96-98 Pentonville Rd, London, N1 9JB **e** lilas@transgressive.co.uk **w** transgressive.co.uk 📘 facebook.com/transgressiverecords 📱 myspace.com/transgressiverecords 🐦 twitter.com/transgressivehq 📇 Label Manager: Lilas Bourboulon.

Transient Records (see Automatic Records)

Transistor Records (see RPM Productions)

Transmission Recordings Ltd Bedford House, 8B Berkeley Gardens, London, W8 4AP **t** 020 7243 2921 **f** 020 7243 2894 **e** john@nottinghillmusic.com **w** nottinghillmusic.com 📇 Director: John Saunderson.

Transubstans Records Record Heaven, Landsvägen 20, Skivarp, 27450, Sweden **t** +46 40 466 644 **f** +46 40 466 647 **e** order@recordheaven.net **w** recordheaven.net 📇 Director: Johnny Christiansen.

Trial and Error Recordings 274 Caledonian Road, London, N1 1BA **t** 07867 552 931 **e** info@trialanderrorrecordings.com **w** trialanderrorrecordings.com 📇 Co-manager: JeanGa.

Trinity Records Company 72 New Bond St, London, W1S 1RR **t** 020 7499 4141 **e** info@trinitymediagroup.net **w** trinitymediagroup.net 📇 Business Affairs: Peter Murray.

Triple A Records Ltd 18 Redsells Close, Downswood, Kent, ME15 8SN **t** 01622 863778 **e** records@triple-a.uk.com **w** triple-a.uk.com 📇 CEO: Terry Armstrong.

TRL PO Box 20, Banbury, OX17 3YT **t** 01295 814995 **e** music@therecordlabel.co.uk **w** therecordlabel.co.uk 📇 Dirs: Steve Betts, Phil Knox-Roberts.

Tru Thoughts PO Box 2818, Brighton, East Sussex, BN1 4RL **t** 01273 694617 **f** 01273 694589 **e** info@tru-thoughts.co.uk **w** tru-thoughts.co.uk 📇 Label Mgr: Paul Jonas.

Truck Records Old Stable East, Church Lane, Steventon, OX13 6SW **t** 01235 821262 **e** paul@truckrecords.com **w** thisistruck.com 📇 Dirs: Paul Bonham, Robin Bennett.

Trust Me Records Dalsbergstien 7a, 0170 Oslo, Norway **t** +47 9324 9309 **e** info@trustmerecords.com **w** trustmerecords.com 📇 Director and A&R: Marit Karlsen.

TrustTheDJ Records White Horse Yard, 78 Liverpool Rd, London, N1 0QD **t** 020 7288 9814 **f** 020 7288 9817 **e** contact@trustthedj.com **w** trustthedj.com 📇 Label Managers: Matt Bullamore, Cam MacPhail.

Tuff Gong (see Island Records Group)

Tuff Street Recordings (see Tuff Street - SOSL Recordings)

Record Companies: Record Companies & Labels

Tuff Street - SOSL Recordings PO Box 7874, London, SW20 9XD **t** 07050 605219 **f** 07050 605239 **e** sam@pan-africa.org **w** umengroup.com 📇 CEO: Oscar Sam Carrol Jnr.

Tugboat Records (see Rough Trade Records)

Turn The Music Up Records 4 Wainwright Close, Swindon, Wiltshire, SN3 6JU **t** 07515 970592 **e** robert.gem@btinternet.com **w** turnthemusicuprecords.com 📇 Contact: Robert.

TV Records Ltd (see Tenor Vossa Records Ltd)

Tyrant 4a Scampston Mews, Cambridge Gardens, London, W10 6HX **t** 020 8968 6815 **f** 020 8969 1728 **e** info@tyrant.co.uk **w** tyrant.co.uk 📇 Dirs: Craig Richards/Amanda Eastwood.

Tyst Music UK Ltd 35 Albany Road, Chorlton, Manchester, M21 0BH **t** 0161 882 0058 **f** 0161 882 0058 **e** info@tsytdigital.com **w** tsytdigital.com 📇 Director: David Wheawill.

Udiscs Monk's Retreat, 33 Dumbreck Rd, Glasgow, G41 5LJ **t** 0141 427 3707 **f** 0141 427 3707 **e** info@udiscs.com **w** udiscs.com 📇 Label Mgr: Steve Bonellie.

U-Freqs 20 Athol Court, 13 Pine Grove, London, N4 3GU **t** 07831 770 394 **f** 0870 131 0432 **e** info@u-freqs.com **w** u-freqs.com 📇 Partner: Stevino.

UGR (see Urban Gospel Records)

Ultimate Dilemma (see Atlantic Records UK)

Umbrella Music (see East Central One Ltd)

Underground Music Movement (UMM) (see Media Records Ltd)

Underwater Records (see Southern Fried Records)

Union Square Music Unit 1.1 Shepherds Studios, Rockley Rd, London, W14 0DA **t** 020 7471 7940 **f** 020 7471 7941 **e** info@unionsquaremusic.co.uk **w** unionsquaremusic.co.uk 📇 MD: Peter Stack.

United Kingdom Christian Music Alliance PO Box 6207, Leighton Buzzard, Bedfordshire, LU7 0WQ **e** enq@newmusicenterprises.com 📇 Contact: Paul Davis 01525 237700.

United Nations Records (see Down By Law Records)

UNIVERSAL MUSIC (UK) LTD

UNIVERSAL MUSIC UK

364-366 Kensington High St, London, W14 8NS **t** 020 7471 5000 **f** 020 7471 5001 **e** firstname.lastname@umusic.com **w** umusic.com 📇 CEO & Chairman: David Joseph. Executive VP: Clive Fisher. CFO: David Bryant. MD, Commercial Division: Brian Rose. Dir of Programming & Business Development: Lesley Douglas. Head of Digital: Beth Appleton. Snr VP International Marketing: Hassan Choudhury. Director Of Communications: Selina Webb.

Universal Music Catalogue Beaumont House, Kensington Village, Avonmore Rd, London, W14 8TS **e** silvia.montello@umusic.com **w** umusic.co.uk 📇 Marketing Director: Silvia Montello.

Universal Music Ireland 9 Whitefriars, Aungier St, Dublin 2, Ireland **t** +353 1 402 2600 **f** +353 1 475 7860 **e** firstname.lastname@umusic.com **w** universalmusic.com

UNIVERSAL MUSIC TV

UNIVERSAL MUSIC TV

364-366 Kensington High St, London, W14 8NS **t** 020 7471 5000 **f** 020 7471 5001 **e** firstname.lastname@umusic.com 📇 PA to MD: Liz Clarke. MD: Brian Berg. Gen Manager: Paul Chisnall. Marketing Dir: Sharon Hardwick. Head of Legal: Oswin Brenner. Finance Dir: Keith Taylor.

Untalented Artist Inc. (see Low Quality Accident)

Upbeat Classics (see Upbeat Recordings)

Upbeat Jazz (see Upbeat Recordings)

Upbeat Recordings Larg House, Woodcote Grove, Coulsdon, Surrey, CR5 2QQ **t** 020 8668 3332 **f** 020 8668 3922 **e** liz@upbeat.co.uk **w** upbeat.co.uk 📇 Senior Partner, Exec Prod: Liz Biddle.

Upbeat Showbiz (see Upbeat Recordings)

Uplifted Music 125 Park Rd, Stretford, Manchester, M32 8ED **t** 07931 943226 **e** djsoundgarden@hotmail.com 📇 Label Manager: Mark Wheawill.

Uplifted Music 125 Park Rd, Stretford, Manchester, Lancashire, M32 8ED **t** 07931 943226 **e** djsoundgarden@hotmail.com 📇 General Manager: Mark Wheawill.

Upper 11 Records 4 Jupiter Court, 10-12 Tolworth Rise South, Surbiton, London, KT5 9NN **t** 020 8330 3434 **f** 020 8330 3447 **e** pmclean@upper11.com **w** upper11.com 🔲 Head of A&R: Patrick McLean.

Upside Records 14 Clarence Mews, Balham, London, SW12 9SR **t** 07786 066665 **e** simon@upsideuk.com **w** upsideuk.com 🔳 myspace.com/upsidemanagement 🔲 MD: Simon Jones.

Urban Angel Music Ltd 1st Floor, 126 Bloomfield Avenue, Belfast, BT5 5AE **t** 028 9046 0846 **e** info@urbanangelmusic.com **w** urbanangelmusic.co.uk 🔲 Artistic Director: Mark McAllister.

Urban Dubz Recordings PO Box 12275, Birmingham, B23 3AB **t** 07931 139 806 **e** info@urbandubz.com **w** urbandubz.com 🔲 Prop: Jeremy Sylvester.

Urban Gospel Records PO Box 178, Sutton, London, SM2 6XG **t** 020 8643 6403 **f** 020 8643 6403 **e** info@urbangospelrecords.com **w** urbangospelrecords.com 📘 facebook.com/home.php?#/profile.php?id=100000340794073&ref=profile 🔳 myspace.com/urbangrecords 📧 facebook.com/home.php?#/profile.php?id=100000340794073&ref=profile ▶️ youtube.com/user/Vibezkidtv 🔲 Head of A&R: P Mac 07904 255244.

Urban Influence UK Ltd 118 Caswell Close, Farnborough, Hants, GU14 8TF **t** 01252 521 892 or 07703 729 953 **f** 01252 404 043 **e** julianwhite@urban-influence.co.uk **w** myspace.com/urbaninfluence1 🔲 MD: Julian White.

URP (see Urban Gospel Records)

US Everest (see Everest Copyrights)

Usk Recordings 26 Caterham Road, London, SE13 5AR **t** 020 7274 5610 **f** 020 7737 0063 **e** info@uskrecordings.com **w** uskrecordings.com 🔲 Dir: Rosemary Lindsay 020 8318 2031.

V2 120-124 Curtain Road, London, EC2A 3SQ (see Mercury Music Group)

VA Recordings (see Finger Lickin' Records)

Vagabond (see Silverword Music Group)

Vagrant Records UK 3rd Floor, 1a Adpar St, London, W2 1DE **t** 020 7535 6738 **f** 020 7563 7283 **e** vagrantuk@vagrant.com **w** vagrant.com/uk 🔲 Label Manager: Dexter Hubbard.

Vanquish Music Group Suite F, 2 Doric Way, London, NW1 1LX **t** 020 7388 0446 **f** 08444 439 400 **e** info@vanquish-musicgroup.com **w** vanquish-musicgroup.com 🔲 Head of A&R: Adjei Amaning.

Venus Music & Records Ltd 13 Fernhurst Gardens, Edgware, Middlesex, HA8 7PQ **t** 020 8952 1924 **e** kamalmmalak@onetel.com 🔲 MD: Kamal M Malak 07507 193118.

Vertical Recordings Ltd 5-6 Road Farm, Ermine Way, Arrington, Herts, SG8 0AA **t** 01223 207 007 **f** 01223 207 007 **e** info@verticalrooms.com **w** verticalrooms.com 🔲 Dir: Pete Brazier.

Vertigo 🔲 Contact: Mercury. (see Mercury Music Group)

Verve (see Decca Records)

Vibe Entertainment (see Taste Media Ltd - Taste Music)

Vibezone (see Dead Happy Records)

Viktor Records The Saga Centre, 326 Kensal Road, London, W10 5BZ **t** 020 8969 3370 **f** 020 8969 3374 **e** info@streetfeat.demon.co.uk 🔲 MD: Colin Schaverien.

Vintage (see Collecting Records LLP)

Virgin Records 27 Wrights Lane, London, W8 5SW **t** 020 7795 7000 **f** 020 7795 7001 **e** Shabs.jobanputra@emimusic.com **w** virginrecords.com 🔲 President, Virgin Records: Shabs Jobanputra.

Virus Recordings Unit 125 Safestore, 5-10 Eastman Rd, Acton, London, W3 7YG

Visceral Thrill Recordings 8 Deronda Rd, London, SE24 9BG **t** 020 8674 7990 **f** 020 8671 5548 🔲 MD: Dave Massey 07775 806 288.

Visible Noise 231 Portobello Rd, London, W11 1LT **t** 020 7792 9791 **f** 020 7792 9871 **e** julie@visiblenoise.com **w** visiblenoise.com 📘 facebook.com/visiblenoise 🔳 myspace.com/visiblenoiserocks 📧 twitter.com/visiblenoise ▶️ youtube.com/visiblenoiserecords 🔲 MD: Julie Weir.

Visionquest (see Loose Tie Records)

Vixen Records Glenmundar House, Ballyman Rd, Bray   Co Wicklow, Ireland **t** +353 8 62 576 244 **f** +353 1 282 0508 **e** deke@adtrax.ie 🔲 CEO: Deke O Brien.

Vocaphone Records 64, Malvern Avenue, Rayners Lane, Harrow, Middx, Ha2 9EX **t** 07976 910382 **e** vocaphone@bigupjazz.com 🔲 Label Manager: Cole Parker.

Voltage (see New State Entertainment)

VP Records UK Ltd Unit 14 Metro Centre, St Johns Rd, Isleworth, Middlesex, TW7 6NL **t** 020 8758 0564 **f** 020 8758 0811 **e** joye@vprecords.com **w** vprecords.com 🔲 GM: Joy Ellington.

Wagram Music Unit 203, Westbourne Studios, 242 Acklam Rd, London, W10 5YG **t** 020 8968 8800 **f** 020 8968 8877 **e** wagrammusic@btclick.com 🔲 MD: Peter Walmsley.

Wah Wah 45s Flat 12, St. Luke's Church, 38 Mayfield Rd, London, N8 9LP **t** 07775 657 578 **e** info@wahwah45s.com **w** wahwah45s.com 🔲 Label Mgrs, A&R: Dom Servini & Simon Goss 07812 089 629.

Record Companies: Record Companies & Labels

Wall of Sound Unit 24 Farm Lane Trading Estate, 101 Farm Lane, London, SW6 1QJ **t** 020 7471 2786 **f** 020 7471 2774 **e** info@wallofsound.net **w** wallofsound.net
f facebook.com/wosound
Q myspace.com/wearewallofsound
E twitter.com/15wallofsound
YouTube youtube.com/user/WallofSoundRecording **Q** MD: Ami Yamauchi.

Wap Music Ltd Care Of Rockyourmobile LTD, 2nd Floor 145-147 St John St, London, EC1V 4PX **t** 07904 113034 **e** iaininm@aol.com **w** Rockyourmobile.co.uk **Q** MD: Iain MacDonald.

Warner Bros Records UK 12 Lancer Square, London, W8 4EH **t** 020 7368 3500 **f** 020 7368 3760 **w** warnerbrosrecords.com **Q** CEO, Warner Music UK and Chairman, Warner Bros Records UK: Christian Tattersfield.

Warner Classics & Jazz 3rd Floor, Griffin House, 161 Hammersmith Rd, London, W6 8BS **t** 020 8563 5100 **f** 020 8563 6226 **e** firstname.lastname@warnermusic.com **w** warnerclassicsandjazz.com **Q** GM: Stefan Bown.

WARNER MUSIC (UK) LTD
The Warner Building, 28 Kensington Church St, London, W8 4EP **t** 020 7368 2500 **f** 020 7368 2770 **e** firstname.lastname@warnermusic.com
w warnermusic.co.uk **Q** CEO, Warner Music UK and Chairman, Warner Bros Records UK: Christian Tattersfield. Chairman, Atlantic Records UK: Max Lousada. Vice-Chairman, Warner Bros Records UK: Jeremy Marsh. MD Rhino UK & International: Dan Chalmers. CFO: Simon Robson. SVP, Business Affairs: Rachel Evers. SVP, Artist Partnerships: Paul Craig. SVP, Commercial & Operations: Alan Young. A&R Director, sixseveunine: Nick Worthington. HR Director: Peter Wheeldon. Communications & Artist Relations Director: Jason Morais. Head of Press: Andy Prevezer.

Warner Music Ireland Ltd 2nd Floor, Skylab, 2 Exchange St Upper, Dublin 8, Ireland **t** +353 1 881 4500 **f** +353 1 881 4599
e firstname.lastname@warnermusic.com
w warnermusic.com **Q** General Manager: Pat Creed.

Warp Spectrum House, 32-34 Gordon House Rd, London, NW5 1LP **t** 020 7284 8350 **f** 020 7284 8360 **e** info@warprecords.com **w** warp.net **Q** GM: Kevin Fleming.

Wasted State Records 191/9 Easter Rd, Edinburgh, EH6 8LF **t** 0130 538 2660 **e** toni@wastedstate.com **w** wastedstate.com
Q myspace.com/wastedstateindustries **Q** Owner: Toni Martone.

Waterfall Records Inkognitogaten 5, Oslo, 0258, Norway **t** +47 23 08 50 80 **f** +47 23 08 50 81 **e** firstname@waterfall.no **w** myspace.com/waterfallrecords **Q** MD: Kai Robøle.

Wayward (see IRL)

Wayward Records PO Box 30884, London, W12 9AZ **t** 020 8746 7461 **f** 020 8749 7441 **e** wayward@spiritmm.com **Q** Label Manager: Tom Haxell.

Weekend Beatnik (see Rogue Records Ltd)

Weekender Records 1a Chalk Farm Parade, Adelaide Road, London, NW3 2BN **t** 020 7483 4248 **e** James@weekenderrecords.com **w** weekenderrecords.com **Q** Managing Director: James Amner 07974 224 004.

Welsh Gold (see Silverword Music Group)

What Records Ltd. 3 Belfry Villas, Belfry Ave, Harefield, Uxbridge, UB9 6HY **t** 01895 824674 **e** whatrecords@blueyonder.co.uk **Q** Contact: Mick Cater, David Harper.

Whirlie Records 14 Broughton Pl, Edinburgh, EH1 3RX **t** 0131 557 9099 **f** 0131 557 6519 **e** info@whirlierecords.co.uk **w** whirlierecords.co.uk **Q** MD: George Brown.

The White (see Jessica Records Ltd)

White Heat Records 96a Hanley Road, London, N4 3DW **t** 07971 907 143 **e** olly@whiteheatrecords.com **w** whiteheatrecords.com **Q** Dir: Olly Parker.

White Noise The Motor Museum, 1 Hesketh Street, Liverpool, L17 8XJ **t** 0151 222 2760 **e** office@whitenoiseuk.com **w** whitenoiseuk.com **Q** Label Manager: Eric Mackay.

Wichita Recordings 120 Curtain Rd, London, EC2A 3SQ **t** 020 7729 3371 **e** info@wichita-recordings.com **w** wichita-recordings.com
f facebook.com/home.php?#/group.php?gid=5566480479&ref=ts **Q** myspace.com/wichitarecordings
E twitter.com/wichitarecs
YouTube youtube.com/user/wichitarecordings **Q** Contact: Dick Green, Mark Bowen.

Wienerworld Ltd Unit 7 Freetrade House, Lowther Rd, Stanmore, Middlesex, HA7 1EP **t** 020 8206 1177 **f** 020 8206 2757 **e** anthony@wienerworld.com **w** wienerworld.com **Q** MD: Anthony Broza.

Wiiija (see 4AD)

Wild Card **Q** PolyGram: Polydor. (see Polydor Records)

Wizard Records PO Box 6779, Birmingham, B13 9RZ **t** 0121 778 2218 **f** 0121 778 1856 **e** pk.sharma@ukonline.co.uk **w** wizardrecords.co.uk **Q** MD: Mambo Sharma 07956 984 754.

Wonderland Media Ltd 23 London Road, Aston Clinton, Aylesbury, Bucks, HP22 5HG **t** 01296 631 003 **e** nick@wonderlandmedia.net **w** wonderlandmedia.net **Q** Contact: Nick Hindle.

Wooden Hill Recordings Ltd Lister House, 117 Milton Rd, Weston-super-Mare, Somerset, BS23 2UX **t** 01934 644126 **e** cliffdane@tiscali.co.uk **w** mediaresearchpublishing.com **Q** Chairman: Cliff Dane.

Working Class Records 22 Upper Brook St, Mayfair, London, W1K 7PZ **t** 020 7491 1060 **f** 020 7491 9996 **e** contact@workingclassrecords.co.uk **w** workingclassrecords.co.uk **Q** Contact: Matt Crossey, Lisa Barker.

Contacts Facebook MySpace Twitter YouTube

World Circuit 138 Kingsland Rd, London, E2 8DY
t 020 7749 3222 **f** 020 7749 3232
e post@worldcircuit.co.uk **w** worldcircuit.co.uk MD: Nick Gold.

World Music Network (UK) Ltd / Riverboat (UK) Music 6 Abbeville Mews, 88 Clapham Park Rd, London, SW4 7BX **t** 020 7498 5252 **f** 020 7498 5353
e post@worldmusic.net **w** worldmusic.net

Worst Case Scenario Records Global House, Bridge Street, Guildford, Surrey, GU1 4SB **t** 01483 501 210
f 01483 501 201 **e** info@wcsrecords.com
w wcsrecords.com Label Manager: Brendan Byrne.

Wrasse Records Wrasse House, The Drive, Tyrrells Wood, Leatherhead, KT22 8QW **t** 01372 376 266
f 01372 377 595 **e** jo.ashbridge@wrasserecords.com
w wrasserecords.com Joint MDs: Jo & Ian Ashbridge.

Wrench Records PO Box 52638, London, N7 8YD
f 020 7700 3855 **e** mail@wrench.org **w** wrench.org
myspace.com/wrenchrecs MD: Charlie Chainsaw.

Wundaland & Boogy Limited 65, Hazelwood Rd, Bush Hill Park, Middx., EN1 1JG **t** 020 8245 6573
f 020 8254 6573 **e** jemgant@yahoo.co.uk MD: Jem Gant.

Wyze Recordings PO Box 847, Camberley, Surrey, GU15 3ZZ **t** 01276 671441 **f** 01276 684460
e info@wyze.com **w** wyze.com MD: Kate Ross.

XL Recordings 1 Codrington Mews, London, W11 2EH
t 020 8870 7511 **f** 020 8871 4178 **w** xlrecordings.com

Xtra Mile Recordings 5-7 Vernon Yard, Off Portobello Rd, London, W11 2DX **t** 020 7792 9400
f 020 7243 2262 **e** charlie@xtramilerecordings.com / charlie@presscounsel.com **w** xtramilerecordings.com
myspace.com/xtramilerecordings
twitter.com/Xtra_Mile MD: Charlie Caplowe.

Yolk (see High Barn Records)

York Ambisonic PO Box 66, Lancaster, Lancs, LA2 6HS
t 01524 823020 **e** yorkambisonic@btinternet.com
MD: Brendan Hearne.

Young Turks (see XL Recordings)

Zane Records 162 Castle Hill, Reading, Berkshire, RG1 7RP **t** 0118 957 4567 **f** 0118 956 1261
e info@zanerecords.com **w** zanerecords.com
myspace.com/zanerecordsofficialsite MD: Peter Thompson.

Zebra (see Cherry Red Records)

Zebra 3 Records 27 Wotton Rd, Ashford, Kent, TN23 6JS **t** 07970 185443 **e** zebra3records@aol.com
w zebra3.co.uk facebook.com/zebra3records
myspace.com/zebra3 twitter.com/zebra3records
MD: Ben Watson.

Zebra Traffic (see Tru Thoughts)

Zeus Records Helions Farm, Sages End Rd, Helions Bumpstead, Suffolk, CB9 7AW **t** 01440 730 795
e info@zeusrecords.com **w** zeusrecords.com
Directors: Ash White, Darren King 07984 468 415.

Zoe Records 9 Campbell Road, Stratford, London, E15 1FL **t** 020 8534 2194 **e** Firstname@zoerecords.co.uk
Contact: Yemi Adeshina or Uzo Anyia.

ZTT Records Ltd The Blue Building, 8-10 Basing St, London, W11 1ET **t** 020 7229 1229 **f** 020 7221 9247
e firstname@spz.com **w** ztt.com Label & A&R Manager: Pete Gardiner.

Zuma Recordings (see Butterfly Recordings)

ZYX Records Ltd Unit 11, Cambridge Court, 210 Shepherds Bush Road, Hammersmith, London, W6 7NL
t 020 7371 6969 **f** 020 7371 6688 **e** sales@zyxmusic.co.uk
w zyxmusic.co.uk GM: Ralf Blasberg.

DVD Companies

10th Planet DVD and CD Duplication
10th Planet, 68-70 Wardour St, London, W1F 0TB
t 020 7434 2345 **f** 020 7287 2040 **e** sales@10pdm.com
w 10pdm.com Sales Director: Richard Lamb.

2 entertain Ltd 33 Foley St, London, W1W 7TL
t 020 7612 3000 **f** 020 7612 3003
e firstname.lastname@2entertain.co.uk **w** 2entertain.co.uk
Sales & Marketing Dir: Brian Hill.

Acorn Media UK 16, Welmar Mews, Ivy Works, 154, Clapham Park Rd, London, SW4 7DE **t** 020 7627 7200
f 020 7627 2501 **e** customerservices@acornmediauk.com
w acornmediauk.com MD: Paul Holland.

Artificial Eye Film Company Ltd 20-22 Stukeley St, London, WC2B 5LR **t** 020 7240 5353
f 020 7240 5242 **e** info@artificial-eye.com **w** artificial-eye.com DVD Mgr: Steve Lewis.

Classic Media Group Ltd
Shepperton Int'l Film Studios, Studios Rd, Shepperton, Middx, TW17 0QD **t** 01932 592016 **f** 01932 592046
e lyn.beardsall@classicpictures.co.uk
w classicpictures.co.uk Producer: Lyn Beardsall.

Clear Vision Mega Mail, PO Box 148, Enfield, Middx, EN3 4SA **t** 020 8292 4875 **f** 020 8805 9000
e info@clearvision.co.uk **w** silvervision.co.uk Contact: Ian Allan.

Contender Home Entertainment
48 Margaret Street, London, W1W 8SE **t** 020 7907 3773
f 020 7907 3777 **e** enquiries@contendergroup.com
w contendergroup.com Marketing Manager: Matt Brightwell.

Record Companies: Record Companies & Labels, DVD Companies

Record Companies: DVD Companies

EAGLE ROCK ENTERTAINMENT LTD.

eagle vision

Eagle House, 22 Armoury Way, London, SW18 1EZ
t 020 8870 5670 **f** 020 8874 2333 **e** mail@eagle-rock.com
w eagle-rock.com 📺 youtube/eaglerocktv 📇 Executive
Chairman: Terry Shand. Executive Chairman: Terry Shand.
Chief Operating Officer: Geoff Kempin. MD International
Operations: Lindsay Brown. MD Digital & Special
Interest: Peter Worsley. MD TV Sales and Music
Acquisition: Andrew Winter. Senior International Marketing
& Promotions Manag: Annick Barbaria. Head of
Royalties: Gareth Jenkins. UK Marketing Manager: Ian Rowe.
Group Finance Director: Simon Hosken. A&R Manager: Andy
McIntyre.

Eagle Vision Eagle House, 22 Armoury Way, London,
SW18 1EZ **t** 020 8870 5670 **f** 020 8874 2333
e mail@eagle-rock.com **w** eagle-rock.com 📇 COO: Geoff
Kempin 02088705670.

Eagle Vision (Broadcast) Eagle House,
22 Armoury Way, London, SW18 1EZ **t** 020 8870 5670
f 020 8874 2333 **e** mail@eagle-rock.com **w** eagle-rock.com
📇 MD of Digital Special Interest: Peter Worsley.

EMI Music UK & Ireland DVD Dept. EMI House,
27 Wright's Lane, London, W8 5SW **t** 020 7795 7000
f 020 7605 5050 **e** stefan.demetriou@emimusic.com 📇 VP
Visual A&R: Stefan Demetriou.

Fifth Avenue Films 14 South Avenue, Hullbridge,
Hockley, Essex, SS5 6HA **t** 01702 232396 **f** 01702 230944
e sales@fifthavenuefilms.com **w** fifthavenuefilms.co.uk
📇 Contact: Cheryl Harris.

Granada Ventures 48 Leicester Square, London,
WC2H 7FB **t** 020 7389 8555 **e** Mark.hurry@ITV.com
w granadaventures.tv 📇 Commercial Affairs Director: Mark
Hurry.

IQ Media (Bracknell) Ltd 2 Venture House,
Arlington Square, Bracknell, Berkshire, RG12 1WA
t 01344 422 551 **f** 01344 453 355 **e** information@iqmedia-
uk.com **w** iqmedia-uk.com 📇 MD: Tony Bellamy 07884 262
755.

[PIAS] DVD Unit 24 Farm Lane Trading Estate,
101 Farm Lane, London, SW6 1QJ **t** 020 7471 2700
f 020 7471 2706 **w** pias.com/uk 📇 Head of Audio
Visual: Andy Townsend.

Prism Leisure Corporation plc Unit 1,
1 Dundee Way, Enfield, Middlesex, EN3 7SX
t 020 8804 8100 **f** 020 8216 6645
e prism@prismleisure.com **w** prismleisure.com 📇 Head Of
Sales: Adrian Ball.

Screen Edge 102b St Annes House,
329 Clifton Drive South, Lytham St Annes, Lancashire,
FY8 1LP **t** 01253 781994 **e** johnb@outlaw23.com
w screenedge.com 📇 MD: John Bentham.

Sony DADC UK Ltd Kent House, 5th Floor, 14-
17 Market Pl, London, W1W 8AJ **t** 020 7307 9771
f 020 7307 9769 **e** sigi.obermayr@sonydadc.com
w sonydadc.com 📇 VP Sales & Customer Services: Siegfried
Obermayr.

Sony Pictures Home Entertainment
25 Golden Sq, London, W1R 6LU **t** 020 7533 1000
f 020 7533 1172 **e** firstname_lastname@fpe.sony.com
w sphe.co.uk

Universal Pictures UK Prospect House, 80-
110 New Oxford St, London, WC1A 1HB **t** 020 7079 6000
w universalstudios.com 📇 Managing Director Universal
Pictures UK: Ian Foster.

Universal Pictures Video Prospect House, 80-
110 New Oxford St, London, WC1A 1HB **t** 020 7079 6000
f 020 7079 6500 **e** firstname.lastname@nbcuni.com
w universalpictures.co.uk 📇 MDs: Johnny Fewings, Helen
Parker.

The Valentine Music Group 26 Litchfield Street,
London, WC2H 9TZ **t** 020 7240 1628 **f** 020 7497 9242
e pat@valentinemusic.co.uk 📇 MD: John Nice.

Warner Home DVD Warner House, 98 Theobald's Rd,
London, WC1X 8WB **t** 020 7984 6400 **f** 020 7984 5001
e firstname.lastname@warnerbros.com **w** warnerbros.com

Warner Music Entertainment
The Electric Lighting Station, 46 Kensington Court, London,
W8 5DA **t** 020 7938 5500 **f** 020 7368 4931
e firstname.lastname@warnermusic.com
📇 President: Conrad Withey.

Wienerworld Unit 7 Freetrade House, Lowther Rd,
Stanmore, Middlesex, HA7 1EP **t** 020 8206 1177
f 020 8206 2757 **e** anthony@wienerworld.com
w wienerworld.com 📇 MD: Anthony Broza.

Contacts  Facebook MySpace Twitter YouTube

Publishers

Publishers & Affiliates

2NV Publishing 1 Canada Sq, 29th Floor Canary Wharf Tower, London, E14 5DY **t** 0870 220 0237 **f** 0870 220 0238 **e** info@2nvpublishing.com **w** 2nvpublishing.com Co-MDs: Paul Boadi and Chris Nathaniel.

2Pointzero Music 79 Wensleydale Road, Hampton, TW12 2LP **t** 07855 353195 **e** info@2pointzero.tv **w** 2pointzero.tv A&R Director/Partner: Chris Bangs.

3rd Stone (see Heavy Truth Music Publishing Ltd)

4 Liberty Music (see Notting Hill Music (UK) Ltd)

4AD Music 17-19 Alma Rd, London, SW18 1AA **t** 020 8871 2121 **f** 020 8871 2745 **e** postmaster@almaroad.co.uk **w** 4AD.com facebook.com/fourad myspace.com/4admusic twitter.com/4ad_official youtube.com/user/4ADRecords MD: Andy Heath.

5HQ (see Paul Rodriguez Music Ltd)

7Hz Music 57b Riding House St, London, W1W 7EF **t** 020 7631 0576 **e** barry@7hz.co.uk **w** 7hz.co.uk MD: Barry Campbell.

7pm Music (see A7 Music)

9 Horses (see SGO Music Publishing)

23rd Precinct Ltd. 23 Bath St, Glasgow, G2 1HU **t** 0141 332 4806 **f** 0141 353 3039 **e** billy@23rdprecinct.co.uk **w** 23rdprecinct.co.uk facebook.com/23rdprecinct myspace.com/23rdprecinctmusic twitter.com/23rdprecinct MD: Billy Kiltie.

63 Songs (see Catalyst Music Publishing Ltd)

A List Music Ltd 500 Chiswick High Road, London, W4 5RG **t** 020 8956 2615 **f** 020 8956 2614 **e** mail@alistmusic.com **w** alistmusic.com Contact: Deon Sharma.

A Songs Publishing (see ASONGS / Anglo Plugging Music Ltd)

A Train Management (see Bucks Music Group Ltd)

A&C Black (Publishers) 36 Soho Sq, London, W1D 3QY **t** 020 7758 0200 **f** 020 7758 0222 **e** educationalsales@acblack.com **w** acblack.com Educational Music Ed: Sheena Hodge.

A&G SONGS LTD

1st Floor, 5 Ching Court, 61-63 Monmouth Street, London, WC2H 9EY **t** 020 7845 9880 **f** 020 7845 9884 **e** rob@agsongs.co.uk **w** agsongs.co.uk Manager: Rob Hoile. Managing Director: Roy Jackson.

Abacus (see Carlin Music Corporation)

Abigail London (see Warner/Chappell Music Ltd)

ABRSM 24 Portland Pl, London, W1B 1LU **t** 020 7636 5400 **f** 020 7637 0234 **e** publishing@abrsm.ac.uk **w** abrsmpublishing.co.uk Executive Director of Syllabus and Publishing: Leslie East.

ABRSM Publishing (see Oxford University Press)

Accolade Music 250 Earlsdon Avenue North, Coventry, West Midlands, CV5 6GX **t** 02476 711935 **f** 02476 711191 **e** rootsrecs@btclick.com MD: Graham Bradshaw.

Acorn Publishing 1, Tylney View, London Road, Hook, Hants, RG27 9LJ **t** 07808 377 350 **e** publishingacorn@hotmail.com **w** acorn-music.com MD: Mark Olrog.

Acton Green (see EMI Music Publishing)

Acuff-Rose Music (see Sony/ATV Music Publishing)

Ad-Chorel Music Ltd 86 Causewayside, Edinburgh, EH9 1PY **t** 0131 668 3366 **f** 0131 662 4463 **e** neil@ad-chorelmusic.com **w** ad-chorelmusic.com MD: Neil Ross.

Addington State (see The Valentine Music Group)

ADN Creation Music Library Sovereign House, 12 Trewartha Rd, Praa Sands, Penzance, Cornwall, TR20 9ST **t** 01736 762826 **f** 01736 763328 **e** panamus@aol.com **w** panamamusic.co.uk myspace.com/scampmusicpublishing MD: Roderick Jones 01736 762 826.

Adtrax Glenmundar House, Ballyman Rd, Bray Co Wicklow, Ireland **t** +353 1 282 0508 **f** +353 1 282 0508 **e** deke@adtrax.ie **w** adtrax.ie Ceo: Deke O'Brien +353862576244.

Adventures in Music 5 Mill Lane, Wallingford, Oxon, OX10 0DH **t** 01491 832 183 **f** 01491 824 020 **e** info@adventuresin-music.com **w** adventure-records.com MDs: Paul and Katie Conroy.

AE Copyrights (see Air-Edel Associates)

Afrikan Cowboy Music Publishing
35 Couthurst Rd, London, SE3 8TN **t** 07957 391418
e info@afrikancowboy.com **w** afrikancowboy.com
☒ Director: Dean Hart.

Agency Global Enterprises Ltd 145-
157 St John St, London, EC1V 4PY **t** 020 7043 3734
f 020 7043 3736 **e** info@agencyglobal.co.uk
w agencyglobal.co.uk **☒** Managing Director: Nadeem Sham.

Air (London) (see Chrysalis Music Ltd)

Air-Edel Associates 18 Rodmarton St, London,
W1U 8BJ **t** 020 7486 6466 **f** 020 7224 0344 **e** susan@air-
edel.co.uk **w** air-edel.co.uk **☒** Publishing Manager: Susan
Arnison.

Airdog Music (see Notting Hill Music (UK) Ltd)

Alan Price (see Carlin Music Corporation)

Alarcon Music Ltd c/o Haynes Orme, 3, Bolt Court,
London, EC4A 3DQ **e** byron@bko-alarcon.co.uk
☒ Director: Byron Orme.

Alaw 4 Tyfica Rd, Pontypridd, Rhondda Cynon Taf,
CF37 2DA **t** 01443 402 178 **f** 01443 402 178
e sales@alawmusic.com **w** alawmusic.com **☒** Dir: Brian
Raby.

J Albert & Son (UK) Ltd Unit 29,
Cygnus Business Centre, Dalmeyer Road, London,
NW10 2XA **t** 020 8830 0330 **f** 020 8830 0220
e james@alberts.co.uk **w** albertmusic.co.uk **☒** Head of
A&R: James Cassidy.

Alexscar (see Menace Music)

Alfred Publishing Co (UK) Ltd Burnt Mill,
Elizabeth Way, Harlow, Essex, CM20 2HX **t** 01279 828960
f 01279 828961 **e** music@alfreduk.com **w** alfreduk.com
☒ Markting Manager & General Manager: Andrew Higgins &
Gerard Mooney.

All Boys Music Ltd County Hall, Belvedere Rd, London,
SE1 7PB **t** 020 7902 8484 **f** 020 7902 8485 **e** helen@pwl-
studios.com **☒** Mgr: Helen Dann.

All Media Music (see Paul Rodriguez Music Ltd)

All Zakatek Music 3 Purley Hill, Purley, Surrey, CR8 1AP
t 020 8660 0861 **f** 020 8660 0861
e allzakatekmusic@aol.com **☒** MD: Lenny Zakatek 07831
521863.

Alola Music (see Westbury Music Ltd)

Alon Music (see Charly Publishing Ltd)

Alpadon Music Shenandoah, Manor Park, Chislehurst,
Kent, BR7 5QD **t** 020 8295 0310
e donpercival@freenet.co.uk **☒** MD: Don Percival.

Amazon Music Ltd PO Box 5109, Hove, East Sussex,
BN52 9EA **t** 01273 726 414 **f** 01273 726 414 (see
Peermusic (UK) Ltd)

Ambassador Music (see Hornall Brothers Music Ltd)

Amco Music Publishing 2 Gawsworth Rd,
Macclesfield, Cheshire, SK11 8UE **t** 01625 420163
f 01625 420168 **e** info@amcomusic.co.uk
w amcomusic.co.uk **☒** myspace.com/amcomusicpublishing
☒ youtube.com/amcomusic **☒** MD: Roger Boden.

Amigos De Musica (see Menace Music)

Amokshasong (see Tairona Songs Ltd)

Amos Barr Music (see Bucks Music Group Ltd)

Amphonic Music Ltd. 20 The Green, Warlingham,
Surrey, CR6 9NA **t** 01883 627 306 **f** 01883 623 594
e info@amphonic.co.uk **w** amphonic.co.uk **☒** MD: Ian Dale.

Anew Music (see Crashed Music)

Anglia Music Company 39 Tadorne Rd, Tadworth,
Surrey, KT20 5TF **t** 01737 812922 **f** 01737 812922
e angliamusic@ukgateway.net **☒** MD: Norma Camby.

Anglia TV (see Carlin Music Corporation)

Angus Publications 14 Graham Terrace, Belgravia,
London, SW1W 8JH **t** 07850 845280 **f** 020 7730 3368
e bill.puppetmartin@virgin.net **w** billmartinsongwriter.com
☒ Chairman: Bill Martin.

Anna (see Miriamusic)

Annie Reed Music Ltd Brow Cottage, 178a Top Lane,
Whitley, Wiltshire, SN12 8QU **t** 01225 707847
e annie@anniereedmusic.com **w** anniereedmusic.com
☒ Director: Annie Havard 07770 623110 or company tel.

Anorak Music Publishing Limited 79 Wardour St,
London, W1D 6QB **e** info@anorakmusic.tv **w** anorakmusic.tv
☒ twitter.com/anorakmusic **☒** Contact: Gary Downing /
Mike Sefton 07976 755949.

Anxious Music (see Universal Music Publishing Group)

Appertaining (see Catalyst Music Publishing Ltd)

Appleseed Music (see Bucks Music Group Ltd)

AppleTreeSongs Ltd 3940 Laurel Cyn Blvd, #408,
Studio City, California, CA 91604, United States
t 001 310 729 4708 **f** 0870 054 8130
e nigelrush@appletreesongs.com **w** pamsheyne.com
☒ Dir: Nigel Rush.

Applied Music (see Bucks Music Group Ltd)

Arcadia Production Music (UK) Greenlands,
Payhembury, Devon, EX14 3HY **t** 01404 841601
f 01404 841687 **e** admin@arcadiamusic.tv
w arcadiamusic.tv **☒** Prop: John Brett.

Ardmore & Beechwood (see EMI Music Publishing)

Arena Music Hatch Farm Studios, Chertsey Rd,
Addlestone, Surrey, KT15 2EH **t** 01932 828715
f 01932 828717 **e** brian.adams@dial.pipex.com
☒ MD: Brian Adams.

Ariel Music Malvern House, Sibford Ferris, Banbury, Oxon,
0X15 5RG **t** 01295 780 679 **f** 01295 788 630
e jane@arielmusic.co.uk **w** arielmusic.co.uk **☒** Managing
Partner: Jane Woolfenden.

Publishers: Publishers & Affiliates

Aristocrat Music Ltd Bournemouth Business Centre, 1052-54 Christchurch Rd, Bournemouth, Dorset, BH7 6DS **t** 020 8441 6996 **e** AristocratMusic@aol.com 🅑 MD: Terry King.

ARL (see TMR Publishing)

Arloco Music (see Bucks Music Group Ltd)

Arnakata Music Ltd (see Astwood Music Ltd)

Arnisongs Unit A, The Courtyard, 42 Colwith Rd, London, W6 9EY **t** 020 8846 3737 **f** 020 8846 3738 **e** susan@jmanagement.co.uk 🅑 MD: Susan Arnison.

Arpeggio Music Bell Farm House, Eton Wick, Windsor, Berkshire, SL4 6LH **t** 01753 864910 **f** 01753 884810 🅑 MD: Beverley Campion.

Art Music (see Paul Rodriguez Music Ltd)

Artfield 5 Grosvenor Square, London, W1K 4AF **t** 020 7499 9941 **f** 020 7499 5519 **e** info@artfieldmusic.com **w** bbcooper.com 🅑 MD: BB Cooper.

Arthur's Mother (see The Valentine Music Group)

Artwork (see Bucks Music Group Ltd)

Ascherberg, Hopwood & Crew (see Warner/Chappell Music Ltd)

Ascot Music (see Catalyst Music Publishing Ltd)

A7 Music PO Box 2272, Rottingdean, Brighton, BN2 8XD **t** 01273 304 681 **f** 01273 308 120 **e** info@a7music.com **w** a7music.com 🅑 Director: Seven Webster.

Ash Music (GB) Hillside Farm, Hassocky Lane, Temple Normanton, Chesterfield, Derbyshire, S42 5DH **t** 01246 231762 **e** ash_music36@hotmail.com 🅑 Head of A&R: Paul Townsend.

Ashley Mark Publishing Company 1 Vance Court, Trans Britannia Enterprise Pk, Blaydon on Tyne, Tyne & Wear, NE21 5NH **t** 0191 414 9000 **f** 0191 414 9001 **e** mail@ashleymark.co.uk **w** fretsonly.com 🅑 Division Manager: Andrew Curry.

ASONGS / Anglo Plugging Music Ltd Fulham Palace, Bishops Avenue, London, SW6 6EA **t** 020 7384 7373 **f** 020 7384 7375 **e** info@asongs.co.uk **w** asongs.co.uk 🅑 Business Affairs: Stephen Flannery.

Associated (see Music Sales Ltd)

Associated Music International Ltd Studio House, 34 Salisbury St, London, NW8 8QE **t** 020 7402 9111 **f** 020 7723 3064 **e** eliot@amimedia.co.uk **w** amimedia.co.uk ▶ youtube.com/amimedia 🅑 MD: Eliot Cohen.

Asterisk Music Rock House, London Rd, St Marys, Stroud, GL6 8PU **t** 01453 886 252 **f** 01453 885 361 **e** asterisk@rollercoasterrecords.com 🅑 MD: John Beecher.

Astwood Music Ltd Latimer Studios, West Kington, Wilts, SN14 7JQ **t** 01249 783 599 **f** 0870 169 8433 **e** Dolan@metro-associates.co.uk **w** media-print.co.uk 🅑 CEO: Mike Dolan.

Atlantic Seven Productions/Music Library Ltd 52 Lancaster Road, London, N4 4PR **t** 020 7263 4435 **f** 020 7436 9233 **e** musiclibrary@atlanticseven.com 🅑 MD: Patrick Shart.

Audio-Visual Media Music Library Sovereign House, 12 Trewartha Rd, Praa Sands, Penzance, Cornwall, TR20 9ST **t** 01736 762826 **f** 01736 763328 **e** panamus@aol.com **w** panamamusic.co.uk 🅜 myspace.com/digimixrecords 🅑 MD: Roderick Jones.

Autonomy Music Publishing (see Bucks Music Group Ltd)

AV Music (see The Valentine Music Group)

Avatar Music (see Notting Hill Music (UK) Ltd)

Aviation Music Ltd (see Maxwood Music)

Aviva (see Music Sales Ltd)

B Feldman & Co (see EMI Music Publishing)

B&C Music Publishing (see Maxwood Music)

Back Yard Music 150 Regents Park Rd, London, NW1 8XN **t** 020 7722 7522 **f** 020 7722 7622 **e** info@back-yard.co.uk **w** back-yard.co.uk 🅑 MD: Gil Goldberg.

Bad B Music (see Cheeky Music)

Bados Music (see Paul Rodriguez Music Ltd)

Bamaco Music 57 Kingsway, Woking, Surrey, GU21 6NS **t** 07876 222902 **e** mark.studio@ntlworld.com 🅑 Contact: Mark Taylor.

Bandleader Music Co. 7 Garrick St, London, WC2E 9AR **t** 020 7240 1628 **f** 020 7497 9242 **e** valentine@bandleader.co.uk 🅑 MD: John Nice.

Banks Music Publications The Granary, Wath Court, Hovingham, York, North Yorkshire, YO62 4NN **t** 01653 628545 **f** 01653 627214 **e** banksmusic@tiscali.co.uk **w** banksmusicpublications.co.uk 🅑 Proprietor: Margaret Silver.

Barbera Music Fulham Palace, Bishops Avenue, London, SW6 6EA **t** 020 7736 6905 **e** gwhite@barberamusic.co.uk **w** barberamusic.co.uk 🅜 myspace.com/barberahannah 🅑 Contact: Hugh Gadsdon, Gareth White, Mel Stephenson.

Bardell Smith (see EMI Music Publishing)

Bardic Edition 6 Fairfax Crescent, Aylesbury, Buckinghamshire, HP20 2ES **t** 01296 428609 **f** 01296 581185 **e** info@bardic-music.com **w** bardic-music.com 🅑 Proprietor: Barry Peter Ould.

Bardis Music Co.Ltd Suite 303 Q House, 76 Furze Rd, Sandyford, Dublin 18, Ireland **t** +353 1 206 3958 **f** +353 1 206 3965 **e** info@bardis.ie **w** bardis.ie 🅑 MD: Peter Bardon.

Barenreiter Ltd Burnt Mill, Elizabeth Way, Harlow, Essex, CM20 2HX **t** 01279 828930 **f** 01279 828931 **e** baerenreiter@dial.pipex.com **w** baerenreiter.com 🅑 MD: Christopher Jackson.

 Contacts   Facebook   MySpace   Twitter   YouTube

Publishers: Publishers & Affiliates

Barking Green Music Ltd 19 Ashford Carbonell, Ludlow, Shropshire, SY8 4DB **t** 01584 831475/4 **e** peterstretton@barkinggreenmusic.co.uk **Director:** Peter J. Stretton.

Barn Publishing (Slade) Ltd 1 Pratt Mews, London, NW1 0AD **t** 020 7554 4840 **f** 020 7388 8324 **e** partners@newman-and.co.uk **Pub:** Colin Newman.

Basement Music Ltd. 20 Cyprus Gardens, London, N3 1SP **t** 020 8346 3969 **f** 07075 024308 **e** info@basementmusic.co.uk **w** basementmusic.co.uk **Business Manager:** John Cefai.

Batoni (see Notting Hill Music (UK) Ltd)

BBC Music Publishing Media Centre, 201 Wood Lane, London, W12 0TT **t** 020 8433 1723 **f** 020 8433 2435 **e** victoria.watkins@bbc.com **w** bbcmusicpublishing.com **Catalogue Manager:** Victoria Watkins.

BDi Music Onward House, 11 Uxbridge St, London, W8 7TQ **t** 020 7243 4101 **f** 020 7229 6893 **e** sarah@bdimusic.com **w** bdimusic.com **MD:** Sarah Liversedge.

Beacon Music (see Paul Rodriguez Music Ltd)

Beamlink (see Paul Rodriguez Music Ltd)

Beat Music (see Paul Rodriguez Music Ltd)

Beat That Music Ltd (see Independent Music Group)

Beautiful (see Kassner Associated Publishers Ltd)

Beautiful Songs Ltd Wilden House, 36a Bromham Road, Biddenham, Beds, MK40 4AF **t** 01234 367 009 **f** 01234 346 175 **e** gordon@beautifulsongsmusic.com **w** abeautifulnoise.com **MD:** Gordon Charlton.

Bed & Breakfast Publishing 211 Piccadilly, London, W1J 9HF **t** 020 7917 2948 **e** mw@sublime-music.co.uk **w** sublime-music.co.uk **MD:** Nick Grant.

Beez (see Paul Rodriguez Music Ltd)

Beggars Group Publishing 17-19 Alma Rd, London, SW18 1AA **t** 020 8871 2121 **f** 020 8871 2745 **e** jenwillis@beggars.com **General Manager:** Jen Willis 020 8875 6260.

Beijing Publishing 105 Emlyn Rd, London, W12 9TG **t** 07985 467970 **e** brianleafe@aol.com **Owner:** Brian Leafe.

Belwin Mills (see EMI Music Publishing)

Berkley (see Bucks Music Group Ltd)

Best Sounds (see Paul Rodriguez Music Ltd)

Bicameral (see Menace Music)

Biffco Publishing **t** 01273 607 484 or +353 87 278 0233 **e** Ejbiffco@mac.com **w** biffco.net **Contact:** Emma Jane Lennon.

Big City Triumph Music 3 St Andrews St, Lincoln, Lincolnshire, LN5 7NE **t** 01522 539883 **f** 01522 528964 **e** steve.hawkins@easynet.co.uk **w** icegroup.co.uk **MD:** Steve Hawkins.

Big Fish Little Fish Music 14 Hanover Street, Brighton, BN2 9ST **t** 01273 691 879 **e** bigfish.littlefish@mac.com **w** bigfishlittlefishmusic.com **Contact:** Steve Burton.

Big Fish Songs Ltd PO Box 8922, Maldon, Essex, CM9 6ZW **e** john@music-village.com **w** music-village.com **Director:** John Carnell 07831 891610.

Big Life Music 67-69 Chalton Street, London, NW1 1HY **t** 020 7554 2100 **f** 020 7554 2154 **e** reception@biglifemanagement.com **w** biglifemanagement.com **MD:** Tim Parry.

Big Shot Music Ltd PO Box 14535, London, N17 0WG **t** 020 8376 1650 **f** 020 8376 8622 **e** Pingramc2@aol.com **Contact:** P Ingram.

Big Spliff (see Paul Rodriguez Music Ltd)

Big World Publishing PO Box 96, Midhurst, West Sussex, GU29 1AJ **t** 01730 817 995 **f** 01730 817 995 **e** songs@bigworldpublishing.com **w** bigworldpublishing.com **MD/A&R:** Patrick Meads.

Bigtime Music Publishing 86 Marlborough Road, Oxford, OX1 4LS **t** 01865 249 194 **f** 01865 792 765 **e** info@bejo.co.uk **w** bejo.co.uk **Administrator:** Tim Healey.

Billym (see Menace Music)

Billymac (see Paul Rodriguez Music Ltd)

Biswas Music Ltd 17 Tavistock Street, London, WC2E 7PA **t** 020 7379 9202 **f** 020 7379 9101 **e** guy@mgmaccountancy.co.uk **MD:** Guy Rippon MA FCCA ACIB.

Black Heat Music 13a Filey Avenue, London, N16 6JL **t** 020 8806 4193 **e** tmorgan@ntlworld.com **Director:** Tony Morgan.

Blow Up Songs Ltd PO Box 4961, London, W1A 7ZX **t** 020 7636 7744 **f** 020 7636 7755 **e** webmaster@blowup.co.uk **w** blowupclub.com **MD:** Paul Tunkin.

Blue Banana Music (see Blue Melon Publishing)

Blue Cat (see Asterisk Music)

Blue Dot Music The White House, 68 Cranston Avenue, Bexhill, East Sussex, TN39 3NN **t** 01424 215617 **e** bluedot.music@virgin.net **w** bluedotmusic.net youtube.com/BlueDotMusic **MD:** Frank Rodgers.

Blue Melon Publishing 240A High Road, Harrow Weald, Middx, HA3 7BB **t** 020 8863 2520 **f** 020 8863 2520 **e** steve@bluemelon.co.uk **MD:** Steven Glen.

Blue Mountain Music Ltd 8 Kensington Park Rd, London, W11 3BU **t** 020 7229 3000 **f** 020 7221 8899 **e** guymorris@bluemountainmusic.tv **w** bluemountainmusic.tv **MD:** Guy Morris.

Blue Planet Music (see Blue Melon Publishing)

Publishers: Publishers & Affiliates

Blue Ribbon Music Ltd (see Hornall Brothers Music Ltd)

BMG Rights Management (UK) Ltd. 1, Stephen Street, London, W1T 1AL **e** info@bmgrights.com 📇 MD: Tony Moss 020 7691 6111 / 6110.

BMP - Broken Music Publishing 9 Gleneldon Mews, London, SW16 2AZ **t** 07517 874384 **e** jurgen@bmpuk.co.uk **w** bmpuk.co.uk ▦ myspace.com/bmpuk 🅣 bmp39 📇 Director: Jurgen Dramm.

BobbySox (see Castle Hill Music)

Bobnal Music Inc (see Bucks Music Group Ltd)

Bocu Music Ltd 1 Wyndham Yard, Wyndham Place, London, W1H 1AR **t** 020 7402 7433 **f** 020 7402 2833 📇 Director: Carole Broughton.

Bolland & Bolland (see Menace Music)

Bollywood (see Notting Hill Music (UK) Ltd)

Bomber Music Ltd London, NW11 **t** 08715 089807 **e** music@bombermusic.com **w** bombermusic.com 📇 MD: Donagh O'Leary.

Boneless (see Menace Music)

Bonney Music Ltd (see Kassner Associated Publishers Ltd)

Boosey & Hawkes Music Publishers Ltd Aldwych House, 71-91 Aldwych, London, WC2B 4HN **t** 020 7054 7200 **f** 020 7054 7293 **e** marketing.uk@boosey.com **w** boosey.com 📇 Hd of Publicity & Mktg: David Allenby.

BOP Music (see The Valentine Music Group)

Boulevard Music Publishing (see Kevin King Music Publishing)

Bourne Music Ltd. 2nd Floor, 207-209 Regent St, London, W1B 4ND **t** 020 7734 3454 **f** 020 7734 3385 **e** bournemusic@supanet.com 📇 Office Manager: John Woodward.

Boy Wonder Publishing 100 Highfield Road, Hall Green, Birmingham, West Midlands, B28 0HP **t** 01212 887 711 **e** boywonder@boywonderpublishing.com **w** boywonderpublishing.com 📇 MD: Anthony Herron.

Bramsdene (see Music Sales Ltd)

Brandon Music Ltd. 171 Southgate Rd, London, N1 3LE **t** 020 7704 8542 **f** 020 7704 2028 **e** peterknightjr@btinternet.com **w** brandon-music.net 📇 Director: Peter Knight Jr..

Brass Wind Publications 4 St Mary's Rd, Manton, Oakham, Rutland, LE15 8SU **t** 01572 737409 **f** 01572 737409 **e** info@brasswindpublications.co.uk **w** brasswindpublications.co.uk

Breakloose (see Bucks Music Group Ltd)

Breezy Tunes (see Jonsongs Music)

Breitkopf & Hartel Main View Cottage, Main Rd, Terrington St. John, Norfolk, PE14 7RR **t** 01945 882221 **f** 01945 882222 **e** sales@breitkopf.com **w** breitkopf.com 📇 Sales Rep: Robin Winter.

Brentwood Benson Music (see Bucks Music Group Ltd)

Briar Music 5-6 Lombard Street, Dublin 2, Ireland **t** +353 1 677 4229 **f** +353 1 671 0421 **e** lunar@indigo.ie 📇 MD: Brian Molloy +353 1 677 9762.

Bright Music Ltd PO Box 62179, London, SW11 4YL **t** 020 7924 3417 **f** 020 7223 5919 **e** info@brightmusic.co.uk **w** brightmusic.co.uk 📇 MD: Martin Wyatt.

Brightly Music 11 Blaydon Close, London, N17 0TW **t** 020 7096 0490 **e** abrightly@yahoo.com 📇 MD: Anthony Brightly 07973 616 342.

Briter Music (see Asterisk Music)

Broadbent & Dunn Ltd 66 Nursery Lane, Dover, Kent, CT16 3EX **t** 01304 825604 **f** 0870 135 3567 **e** music@broadbent-dunn.com **w** broadbent-dunn.com 📇 Sales Manager: Pamela Withey.

Broadley Music (Int) Ltd Broadley House, 48 Broadley Terrace, London, NW1 6LG **t** 020 7258 0324 **f** 020 7724 2361 **e** admin@broadleystudios.com **w** broadleystudios.com 📇 MD: Ellis Elias.

Broadley Music Library (see Broadley Music (Int) Ltd)

Brookside (see Asterisk Music)

Broughton Park Music Kennedy House, 31 Stamford Street, Altrincham, Cheshire, WA14 1ES **f** 0161 980 7100 **e** harveylisberg@aol.com 📇 MD: Harvey Lisberg.

Bruco (see Menace Music)

Bryan Morrison Music 1 Star St, London, W2 1QD **t** 020 7706 7304 **f** 020 7706 8197 **e** bryanmorrisonmusic@btconnect.com 📇 GM: Cora Barnes.

Bryter Music Marlinspike Hall, Walpole Halesworth, Suffolk, IP19 9AR **t** 01986 784 664 **e** cally@brytermusic.com **w** brytermusic.com 📇 Proprietor: Cally.

Bs In Trees (see Menace Music)

Bill Buckley Music Saunders, Wood & Co, The White House, 140A Tatchbrook Street, London, SW1V 2NE **t** 020 7821 0455 **f** 020 7821 6196 **e** nigel@s-wood.dircon.co.uk 📇 Partner: Nigel J Wood.

Bucks Music Group Ltd Onward House, 11 Uxbridge St, London, W8 7TQ **t** 020 7221 4275 **f** 020 7229 6893 **e** info@bucksmusicgroup.co.uk **w** bucksmusicgroup.com 📇 Managing Director: Simon Platz.

Buffalo Music Ltd **f** 01923 261761 **e** info@buffalomusic.co.uk **w** buffalomusic.co.uk 📇 Office Manager: Janet LeSage 01923 266664.

Contacts Facebook MySpace ⓔ Twitter ▶ YouTube

Bug Music Ltd Long Island House, Unit GB, 1-4 Warple Way, London, W3 0RG **t** 020 8735 1868 **f** 020 8743 1551 **e** info@bugmusic.co.uk **w** bugmusic.com ✉ MD/VP International: Mark Anders.

Bugle Publishing Group Second Floor, 81 Rivington St, London, EC2A 3AY **t** 020 7012 1416 **f** 020 7012 1419 **e** tcgleg@aol.com **w** milescopeland.com

Bull-Sheet Music 18 The Bramblings, London, E4 6LU **t** 020 8529 5807 **f** 020 8529 5807 **e** irene.bull@btinternet.com **w** bull-sheetmusic.co.uk; bandmemberswanted.co.uk ✉ MD: Irene Bull.

Bullish Music Inc (see Bucks Music Group Ltd)

Burlington (see Warner/Chappell Music Ltd)

Burning Petals Music The Studio, Homefield Court, Marston Magna, Somerset, BA22 8DJ **t** 01935 851664 **e** enquiries@burning-petals.com **w** burning-petals.com ✉ MD: Richard Jay.

Burnt Puppy (see Bucks Music Group Ltd)

Burnt Toast Music Publishing 12 Denyer Court, Fradley, Nr Lichfield, Staffs, WS13 8TQ **t** 01543 444261 **f** 01543 444261 **e** phooper-keeley@softhome.net ✉ MD: Paul Hooper-Keeley.

Burton Way (see Universal Music Publishing Group)

Bushranger Music Station Lodge, 196 Rayleigh Road, Hutton, Brentwood, Essex, CM13 1PN **t** 01277 222 095 **e** bushrangermusic@yahoo.co.uk ✉ Dir: Kathy Lister.

Buzz-erk Music Studio Two, Chocolate Factory 2, 4 Coburg Road, London, N22 6UJ **e** info@buzz-erk.com **w** buzz-erk.com ✉ Director: Niraj Chag.

By The Pool Music 7 Warren Mews, London, W1T 6AS **t** 0207 874 1704 **e** Info@bythepoolmusic.com ✉ Contact: Carole Striker.

C.O.R.S. Ltd (see Conexion Music Ltd)

Cala Music Publishing 17 Shakespeare Gardens, London, N2 9LJ **t** 020 8883 7306 **f** 020 8365 3388 **e** music@calarecords.com **w** calarecords.com ✉ GM: Susi Kennedy.

California Phase (see Menace Music)

Campbell Connelly & Co (see Music Sales Ltd)

Candid Music 16 Castelnau, London, SW13 9RU **t** 020 8741 3608 **f** 020 8563 0013 **e** info@candidrecords.com **w** candidrecords.com ✉ MD: Alan Bates.

Candor Music (see TMR Publishing)

Cara Music P.O.B 28286, Winchmore Hill, London, N21 3WT **t** 020 8886 5743 **e** caramusicltd@dial.pipex.com ✉ Dir: Michael McDonagh.

Cardinal (see Carlin Music Corporation)

Cargo Music Publishing 39 Clitterhouse Crescent, Cricklewood, London, NW2 1DB **t** 020 8458 1020 **e** mike@mikecarr.co.uk **w** mikecarr.co.uk ✉ MD: Mike Carr.

Caribbean Music (see Paul Rodriguez Music Ltd)

Caribbean Music Library Sovereign House, 12 Trewartha Rd, Praa Sands, Penzance, Cornwall, TR20 9ST **t** 01736 762826 **f** 01736 763328 **e** panamus@aol.com **w** panamamusic.co.uk ☐ myspace.com/scampmusicpublishing ✉ MD: Roderick Jones.

Carlin Music Corporation Iron Bridge House, 3 Bridge Approach, London, NW1 8BD **t** 020 7734 3251 **f** 020 7916 8759 **e** davidjapp@carlinmusic.com **w** carlinmusic.com ✉ MD: David Japp.

Carnaby Music 78 Portland Rd, London, W11 4LQ **t** 020 7727 2063 **f** supplied on request **e** mail@negusfancey.com ✉ Dir: Charles Negus-Fancey.

Carte Blanche (see Fay Gibbs Music Services)

Castle Hill Music PO Box 7, Huddersfield, West Yorkshire, HD7 4YA **t** 01484 846333 **f** 01484 846333 **e** HotLeadRecords@btopenworld.com **w** fimusic.co.uk ✉ MD: Ian R Smith.

Cat's Eye Music (see Multiplay Music)

Catalyst Music Publishing Ltd 171 Southgate Rd, London, N1 3LE **t** 020 7704 8542 **f** 020 7704 2028 **e** peterknightjr@btinternet.com ✉ MD: Peter Knight Jr..

Cathedral Music King Charles Cottage, Racton, Chichester, West Sussex, PO18 9DT **t** 01243 379968 **f** 01243 379859 **e** enquiries@cathedral-music.co.uk **w** cathedral-music.co.uk ✉ MD: Richard Barnes.

Catskills Music Publishing PO Box 3365, Brighton, BN1 1WQ **t** 01273 626245 **f** 01273 626246 **e** info@catskillsrecords.com **w** catskillsrecords.com ✉ Directors: Khalid, Amr or Jonny.

Cauliflower (see Bucks Music Group Ltd)

Cavendish Music (see Boosey & Hawkes Music Publishers Ltd)

Cecil Lennox (see Kassner Associated Publishers Ltd)

Cee Cee (see Asterisk Music)

Celebrity Bulletin FENS House, 8-10 Wiseton Rd, London, SW17 7EE **t** 020 8672 3191 **f** 020 8672 2282 **e** enquiries@celebrity-bulletin.co.uk **w** celebrity-bulletin.co.uk ⓔ celebritybullet ✉ Managing Director: Neal Goddard.

Celtic Songs Unit 4, Great Ship Street, Dublin 8, Ireland **t** +353 1 478 3455 **f** +353 1 478 2143 **e** irishmus@iol.ie **w** irelandcd.com ✉ GM: Paul O'Reilly.

CF Kahnt (see Peters Edition)

Chain Music - Churchill Howells Associates Ltd 24 Cornwall Rd, Cheam, Surrey, SM2 6DT **t** 020 8643 3353 **f** 020 8643 9423 **e** gchurchill@c-h-a-ltd.demon.co.uk ✉ Chairman: Carole Howells.

Chain Of Love (see Sea Dream Music)

Chalumeau (see Paul Rodriguez Music Ltd)

Publishers: Publishers & Affiliates

Champion Music 181 High St, Harlesden, London, NW10 4TE **t** 020 8961 5202 **f** 020 8961 6665 **e** charmaine@championrecords.co.uk **w** championrecords.co.uk Label Manager: Charmaine Gray.

Chandos Music Supplies 21B Salisbury Ave, Colchester, Essex, CO3 3DW **t** 01206 520570 **f** 01206 520570 **e** s.hogger1@ntlworld.com Proprietor: Stephen Hogger.

Chantelle Music 3A Ashfield Parade, London, N14 5EH **t** 020 8886 6236 **e** info@chantellemusic.co.uk **w** chantellemusic.co.uk MD: Riss Chantelle.

Chapala Productions Rectory House, Church Lane, Warfield, Berks, RG12 6EE **t** 01344 890 001 **f** 01344 885 323 Contact: Alan Bown.

Chappell (see Warner/Chappell Music Ltd)

Chappell Morris (see Warner/Chappell Music Ltd)

Charisma Music Publishing (see EMI Music Publishing)

Charjan Music (see Paul Rodriguez Music Ltd)

Charlena (see Menace Music)

Charly Publishing Ltd Suite 379, 37 Store Street, London, WC1E 7BS **t** 07050 136143 **f** 07050 136144 Contact: Jan Friedmann.

Chart Music Company Ltd Island Cottage, Rod Eyot, Wargrave Road, Henley-on-Thames, Oxfordshire, RG9 3JD **t** 01491 412946 **e** mail@islandmusicjf.co.uk Dir: JW Farmer.

Chartel (see Bucks Music Group Ltd)

Chatwise Music (see Bucks Music Group Ltd)

Cheeky Music 181 High St, Harlesden, London, NW10 4TE **t** 020 8961 5202 **f** 020 8961 6665 **e** raj@championrecords.co.uk **w** championrecords.co.uk General Manager: Raj Porter.

Chelsea Music Publishing Co 125 Parkway, London, NW1 7PS **t** 020 7388 3370 **f** 020 7998 1612 **e** eddie@chelseamusicpublishing.com **w** chelseamusicpublishing.com MD: Eddie Levy.

Cherry Lane Music (see Catalyst Music Publishing Ltd)

Cherry Red Songs 3a Long Island House, Warple Way, London, W3 0RG **t** 020 8740 4110 **f** 020 8740 4208 **e** infonet@cherryred.co.uk **w** cherryred.co.uk facebook.com/people/Cherry-Red/1310740870 myspace.com/cherryredgroup twitter.com/cherryredgroup youtube.com/cherryredgroup Contact: Matt Bristow.

Chester Music - Novello & Co Ltd (Music Sales Group) 14-15 Berners St, London, W1T 3LJ **t** 020 7612 7400 **f** 020 7612 7549 **e** promotion@musicsales.co.uk **w** chesternovello.com MD: James Rushton.

Chick-A-Boom Music (see Asterisk Music)

China Music (see Catalyst Music Publishing Ltd)

Chipglow (see Asterisk Music)

Christabel Music 32 High Ash Drive, Alwoodley, Leeds, West Yorkshire, LS17 8RA **t** 0113 268 5528 **f** 0113 266 5954 MD: Jeff Christie.

Christian Music Ministries (see Sovereign Music UK)

Chrome Dreams PO Box 230, New Malden, Surrey, KT3 6YY **t** 020 8715 9781 **f** 020 8241 1426 **e** mail@chromedreams.co.uk **w** chromedreams.co.uk GM: Andy Walker.

Chrys-A-Lee (see Chrysalis Music Ltd)

CHRYSALIS MUSIC LTD

The Chrysalis Building, 13 Bramley Rd, London, W10 6SP **t** 020 7221 2213 **f** 020 7465 6339 **e** firstname.lastname@chrysalis.com **w** chrysalis.com A&R: Craig Michie. Managing Director: Alison Donald. CEO: Jeremy Lascelles. Chief Finance Officer: Andy Mollett. International Head of Royalties: Janet Andersen. Dir of Business Affairs: Simon Harvey. Head of Copyright Admin: Andy Godfrey. International Head of A&R: Ben Bodie. Creative Director: Kate Sweetsur. Head of Synchronistation: Gareth Smith.

CIC UK (see Universal Music Publishing Group)

Cicada (see Paul Rodriguez Music Ltd)

Cinephonie Co (see Music Sales Ltd)

Cinque Port Music (see The Valentine Music Group)

Citybeat (see 4AD Music)

Class 52 Music Ltd (see Paternoster Music)

Classic Editions (see Wilson Editions)

Classical Guitar Ashley Mark Publishing Co, 1 & 2 Vance Court, Trans Britannia Ent Pk, Blaydon On Tyne, NE21 5NH **t** 0191 414 9000 **f** 0191 414 9001 **e** david@ashleymark.co.uk **w** classicalguitarmagazine.com Sales Manager: David English.

Climax Music 6 Hesleyside Road, South Wellfield, Whitley Bay, NE25 9HB **t** 07812 633 364 **f** 0191 253 5997 **e** james_climax@hotmail.com Label Manager: James Wilson.

CLM 153 Vauxhall St, The Barbican, Plymouth, Devon, PL4 0DF **t** 01752 510710 **f** 01752 224281 **e** robhancock@lineone.net Partner: Rob Hancock.

Clouseau (see SGO Music Publishing)

CMA Publications Moving soon, Sufolk **e** cmapublications@btinternet.com **w** cma-publications.co.uk MD: Geraldine Price.

Coda (see Bucks Music Group Ltd)

Publishers: Publishers & Affiliates

Cold Harbour Recording Company Ltd
Creeting House, All Saints Rd, Creeting St Mary. Ipswich,
IP6 8PR **t** 01449 723244 **e** enquiries@eastcentralone.com
w eastcentralone.com 🔲 MD: Steve Fernie.

Collegium Music Publications PO Box 172,
Whittlesford, Cambridge, CB22 4QZ **t** 01223 832474
f 01223 836723 **e** info@collegium.co.uk **w** collegium.co.uk
🔲 Sales & Marketing: Emma Harrison/John Harte.

Collingwood O'Hare (see Bucks Music Group Ltd)

Columbia Publishing Wales Ltd Glen More,
6 Cwrt y Camden, Brecon, Powys, LD3 7RR **t** 01874 625270
f 01874 625270 **e** dng@columbiawales.fsnet.co.uk
w columbiapublishing.co.uk 🔲 MD: Dafydd Gittins.

Come Again Music (see Broadley Music (Int) Ltd)

Cometmarket (see Notting Hill Music (UK) Ltd)

Comma Music (see Paul Rodriguez Music Ltd)

Complete Music 3rd Floor, Bishops Park House, 25-
29 Fulham High Street, London, SW6 3JH **t** 020 7731 8595
f 020 7371 5665 **e** info@complete-music.co.uk
w complete-music.co.uk 🔲 A&R: Kareem Taylor.

Concord Music Hire Library (see Maecenas Music)

Conexion Media Group Plc 10 Heathfield Terrace,
London, W4 4JE **t** 020 8987 4150 **f** 020 8987 4160
e info@conexion-media.com **w** conexion-media.com
🔲 CEO: Justin Sherry.

Congo Music Ltd 17A Craven Park Road, Harlsden,
London, NW10 8SE **t** 020 8961 5461 **f** 020 8961 5461
e byron@congomusic.freeserve.co.uk **w** congomusic.com
🔲 A&R Director: Root Jackson.

Connoisseur Music (see Crashed Music)

Consentrated Music (see Bucks Music Group Ltd)

Constant In Opal Music Publishing
Sovereign House, 12 Trewartha Rd, Praa Sands, Penzance,
Cornwall, TR20 9ST **t** 01736 762826 **f** 01736 763328
e panamus@aol.com **w** panamamusic.co.uk
🔲 myspace.com/scampmusicpublishing 🔲 MD: Ian Collins.

Copeberg (see Bugle Publishing Group)

Copperplate Music (see Bardic Edition)

Copycare PO Box 77, Hailsham, East Sussex, BN27 3EF
t 01323 840 942 **f** 01323 849 555
e sandra@copycare.com **w** copycare.com
🔲 Contact: Sandra Coltman.

Cordella Music Alhambra, High St, Shirrell Heath,
Southampton, Hants, SO32 2JH **t** 08450 616 616
f 01329 833 433 **e** barry@cordellamusic.co.uk
w cordellamusic.co.uk 🔲 MD: Barry Upton.

Corelia Music Library Sovereign House,
12 Trewartha Rd, Praa Sands, Penzance, Cornwall, TR20 9ST
t 01736 762826 **f** 01736 763328 **e** panamus@aol.com
w panamamusic.co.uk
🔲 myspace.com/scampmusicpublishing 🔲 MD: Roderick
Jones.

Corner Stone (see The Valentine Music Group)

Cornerways Music Ty'r Craig, Longleat Avenue,
Craigside, Llandudno, LL30 3AE **t** 01492 549 759
f 01492 541 482 **e** gordon@gordonlorenz.com
w gordonlorenz.com 🔲 Contact: Gordon Lorenz.

Cot Valley Music Sovereign House, 12 Trewartha Rd,
Praa Sands, Penzance, Cornwall, TR20 9ST **t** 01736 762826
f 01736 763328 **e** panamus@aol.com
w panamamusic.co.uk 🔲 Administrator: Karen Williams.

CPP (see International Music Publications (IMP))

Cramer Music 23 Garrick St, London, WC2E 9RY
t 020 7240 1612 **f** 020 7240 2639
e enquiries@cramermusic.co.uk 🔲 MD: Peter Maxwell.

Crashed Music 162 Church Rd, East Wall, Dublin 3,
Ireland **t** +353 1 888 1188 **f** +353 1 856 1122
e shay@crashedmusic.com **w** crashedmusic.com
🔲 MD: Shay Hennessy.

CREATE YOUR OWN PUBLISHING COMPANY

🔒 **FirstMusicControl**
Your music. Your rights. Your future.

First Music Control, Central House, 1 Ballards Lane, London,
N3 1LQ **t** 0208 349 8025 **f** 0845 299 1592
e registrations@firstmusiccontrol.com
w firstmusiccontrol.com 🔲 Contact: 0208 348 6767.

Creative Minds (see Bucks Music Group Ltd)

Creole Music Ltd The Chilterns, France Hill Drive,
Camberley, Surrey, GU15 3QA **t** 01276 686077
f 01276 686055 **e** creole@clara.net 🔲 MD: Bruce White.

Crimson Flame (see Sea Dream Music)

Cringe Music (Publishing) The Cedars,
Elvington Lane, Hawkinge, Nr. Folkestone, Kent, CT18 7AD
t 01303 893472 **f** 01303 893833
e info@cringemusic.co.uk **w** cringemusic.co.uk 🔲 CEO: Chris
Ashman.

Cromwell Music (see The Essex Music Group)

Cross Music (see Music Sales Ltd)

Crumbs Music The Stable Lodge, Lime Ave, Kingwood,
Henley-on-Thames, Oxon, RG9 5WB **t** 01491 628 111
f 01491 629 668 **e** crumbsmusic@btopenworld.com
w raywilliamsmusic.com 🔲 MD: Ray Williams 07813 696
999.

Crystal City (see Sea Dream Music)

CSA Word 6a Archway Mews, 241a Putney Bridge Rd,
London, SW15 2PE **t** 020 8871 0220 **f** 020 8877 0712
e info@csaword.co.uk **w** csaword.co.uk 🔲 Audio
Manager: Victoria Williams.

CTV Music The Television Centre, St Helier, Jersey,
Channel Islands, JE1 3ZD **t** 01534 816816 **f** 01534 816778
e broadcast@channeltv.co.uk **w** channeltv.co.uk 🔲 Dir
Sales/Mktg: Gordon de Ste. Croix.

Contacts   Facebook   MySpace Twitter YouTube

David Cunningham Music 17 Kirkland Lane, Penkhull, Stoke on Trent, Staffordshire, ST4 5DJ **t** 01782 410237 **f** 01782 410237 **e** davidcunninghammusic@yahoo.co.uk **Contact:** David Cunningham 07754 170541.

Curious (see Bucks Music Group Ltd)

Cutting Edge Music Ltd Ground Floor, 36 King St, London, WC2E 8JS **t** 020 7759 8550 **f** 020 7759 8549 **e** philipm@cutting-edge.uk.com **w** cutting-edge.uk.com **MD:** Philip Moross.

Cutting Records Music (see Dejamus Ltd)

Cwmni Cyhoeddi Gwynn Cyf 28 Heol-y-Dwr, Penygroes, Caernarfon, Gwynedd, LL54 6LR **t** 01286 881797 **f** 01286 882634 **e** info@gwynn.co.uk **w** gwynn.co.uk **Administrator:** Wendy Jones.

Cyclo Music (see Bucks Music Group Ltd)

Cyhoeddiadau Sain Canolfan Sain, Llandwrog, Caernarfon, Gwynedd, LL54 5TG **t** 01286 831111 **f** 01286 831497 **e** rhian@sain.wales.com **w** sain.wales.com **Contact:** Rhian Eleri.

CYP Music Limited The Fairway, Bush Fair, Harlow, Essex, CM18 6LY **t** 01279 444707 **f** 01279 445570 **e** sales@cyp.co.uk **w** cyp.co.uk **Nat'l Accounts Mgr:** Gary Wilmot.

Cznin Music (see Menace Music)

d Music 35 Brompton Rd, London, SW3 1DE **t** 020 7368 6311 **f** 020 7823 9553 **e** d@35bromptonroad.com **w** drecords.co.uk **MD:** Douglas Mew.

D-Jon Music (see Menace Music)

D.O.R Encryption PO Box 1797, London, E1 4TX **t** 020 7702 7842 **e** Encryption@dor.co.uk **w** dor.co.uk/artists **MD:** Martin Parker.

DA Licensing Osmond House, 78 Alcester Road, Moseley Village, Birmingham, B13 8BB **t** 0121 449 3814 **e** rod@darecordings.com **w** emusu.com **Business Development Manager:** Rod Thompson.

Da Vinci Music Ltd (see Independent Music Group)

Dacara Music (see Menace Music)

Daisy Publishing Unit 2 Carriglea, Naas Rd, Dublin 12, Ireland **t** +353 1 429 8600 **f** +353 1 429 8602 **e** daithi@daisydiscs.com **w** daisydiscs.com **MD:** John Dunford.

Daisynook (see Notting Hill Music (UK) Ltd)

Publishers: Publishers & Affiliates

Contacts   Facebook   MySpace   Twitter YouTube

Dalmatian Music PO Box 49155, London, SW20 0YL
t 020 8946 7242 **f** 020 8946 7242
e w.stonebridge@btinternet.com Directors: Bill
Stonebridge.

The Daniel Azure Music Group 72 New Bond St,
London, W1S 1RR **t** 07894 702 007 **f** 020 8240 8787
e info@jvpr.net **w** danielazure.com CEO: Daniel Azure.

Danny Thompson Music (see SGO Music Publishing)

Dartsongs (see Asterisk Music)

Dash Music (see Music Sales Ltd)

Datsmaboy Music (see Menace Music)

David Paramor Publishing (see Kassner Associated
Publishers Ltd)

DCI Video (see International Music Publications (IMP))

De Haske Music (UK) Ltd PO Box 7482, Corby,
NN17 9FQ **t** 01536 260981 **e** music@dehaske.co.uk
w dehaske.com Sales & Marketing Mgr: Mark Coull.

De Sade Music (see Catalyst Music Publishing Ltd)

Death Or Glory Music ltd Woodcock Farm,
Woodcock Lane, Grafty Green, Maidstone, Kent, ME17 2AY
e ewan@deathorglorymusic.com **w** deathorglorymusic.com
 facebook.com/deathglorymusic
 myspace.com/deathorglorymusicltd Contact: Ewan
Grant.

Decentric Music PO Box 241, Harrow, Middlesex,
HA2 8YX **t** 020 8977 4616 **f** 020 8977 4616
e decentricjb@road.myzen.co.uk Dir: James Bedbrook.

Deceptive Music PO Box 288, St Albans, Hertfordshire,
AL4 9YU **t** 01727 834 130 MD: Tony Smith.

Deedle Dytle Music (see Dejamus Ltd)

Deekers (see Eaton Music Ltd)

Deep Blue Music (see Bucks Music Group Ltd)

Deep Blue Publishing (see Sovereign Music UK)

Dejamus Ltd Suite 11, Accurist House, 44 Baker St,
London, W1U 7AZ **t** 020 7486 5838 **f** 020 7487 2634
e firstnamelastname@dejamus.co.uk MD: Stephen
James.

Delerium Music Ltd PO Box 1288, Gerrards Cross,
Bucks, SL9 9YB **t** 01753 890635 **f** 01753 892289
e firstname.lastname@delerium.co.uk MD: Richard Allen.

Delfont Music (see Warner/Chappell Music Ltd)

Delicious Publishing Suite GB, 39-40 Warple Way,
Acton, London, W3 0RG **t** 020 8749 7272 **f** 020 8749 7474
e info@deliciousdigital.com **w** deliciousdigital.com
 MD: Ollie Raphael.

Design Music (see Carlin Music Corporation)

Destiny Destiny Towers, St Margaret's House,
21 Old Ford Road, London, E2 9PL **t** 020 8981 2746
e nick@destinytowers.com **w** destinytowers.com
 Contact: Nick Raymonde.

Deutscher Verlag Fur Musik, Leipzig (see
Breitkopf & Hartel)

Dharma Music PO Box 50668, London, SW6 3UY
e zen@instantkarma.co.uk Chairman: Rob Dickins 0207
384 0938.

Dick Music (see Tabitha Music Ltd)

Digger Music 17 Tavistock St, London, WC2E 7PA
t 020 7379 9202 **f** 020 7379 9101 **e** tills@globalnet.co.uk
 CEO: Tilly Rutherford.

Digimix Music Publishing Sovereign House,
12 Trewartha Rd, Praa Sands, Penzance, Cornwall, TR20 9ST
t 01736 762826 **f** 01736 763328 **e** panamus@aol.com
w panamamusic.co.uk myspace.com/guildofsongwriters
 MD: Roderick Jones.

Dinosaur Music Publishing 5 Heyburn Crescent,
Westport Gardens, Stoke On Trent, Staffordshire, ST6 4DL
t 01782 824 051 **f** 01782 761 752
e music@dinosaurmusic.co.uk **w** dinosaurmusic.co.uk
 MD: Alan Dutton.

Distiller Publishing LLP Studio 11, 10 Acklam Rd,
Ladbroke Gorve, London, W10 5QZ **t** 0208 968 8236
f 0208 964 4706 **e** darrin@distiller-records.com Director
of A&R: Darrin Woodford.

District 6 Unit 1F North Clapham Art Centre, 26-
32 Voltaire Rd, London, SW4 6DH
e firstname@district6.co.uk **w** district6.co.uk Dirs: Paul
Vials, Ed Ashcroft.

DJL Music (see Catalyst Music Publishing Ltd)

DL Songs (see Kassner Associated Publishers Ltd)

DMX Music Ltd Forest Lodge, Westerham Road, Keston,
Kent, BR2 6HE **t** 01689 882 200 **f** 01689 882 288
e vanessa.warren@dmxmusic.com **w** dmxmusic.co.uk
 Marketing Manager: Vanessa Warren.

Do It Yourself Music (see Bucks Music Group Ltd)

Domino Music (see Tabitha Music Ltd)

Domino Publishing Co Ltd Unit 3 Delta Park,
Smugglers Way, London, SW18 1EG **t** 020 8875 1390
f 020 8875 1391 **e** paull@dominorecordco.com
w dominopublishingco.com dominopublishingcompany
 GM: Paul Lambden.

Don't Call Me Music Brooke Oast, Jarvis Lane,
Goudhurst, Cranbrook, Kent, TN17 1LP **t** 01580 211 623
e rbickersteth@lookingforward.biz MD: E R Bickersteth.

Donna (see EMI Music Publishing)

Donogh Hennessy Music (see SGO Music
Publishing)

Dorsey Brothers Music (see Music Sales Ltd)

Douglas Music (see Anglia Music Company)

Douglas Sahm Music (see Menace Music)

Dr Watson Music (see Sherlock Holmes Music)

Dread Music (see Bucks Music Group Ltd)

Contacts   Facebook   MySpace   Twitter   YouTube

Dreambase Music PO Box 13383, London, NW3 5ZR **t** 020 7794 2540 **f** 020 7794 7393 **e** hitman@popstar.com ✉ A&R: Tony Strong.

Dreamscape Music Publishing Montrose Court, Finchley Road, London, NW11 **t** 07531 609789 **f** 01727 826308 **e** dreamscapemusicpublishing@hotmail.co.uk ✉ Owner/Head Of A&R/Creative Manager: Adam Charles Lamb.

Drumblade Music (see Bardic Edition)

Dub Plate Music (see Greensleeves Publishing Ltd)

Duffnote Publishing Ltd Vine Cottage, North Road, Bosham, W. Sussex, PO18 8NL **t** 01243 774606 or 575110 **e** info@duffnote.com **w** duffnote.com ✉ Dirs: Danny Jones, Richard Earnshaw.

Dune Music 1st Floor, 73 Canning Road, Harrow, Middx, HA3 7SP **t** 020 8424 2807 **f** 020 8861 5371 **e** info@dune-music.com **w** dune-music.com ✉ MD: Janine Irons.

Durham Music (see Bucks Music Group Ltd)

Earache Songs UK Ltd Suite 1-3 Westminster Building, Theatre Sq, Nottingham, NG1 6LG **t** 0115 950 6400 **f** 0115 950 8585 **e** mail@earache.com **w** earache.com ✉ MD: Digby Pearson.

Earlham Press (see De Haske Music (UK) Ltd)

Early Music Today Rhinegold Publishing, 241 Shaftesbury Avenue, London, WC2H 8TF **t** 020 7333 1744 **f** 020 7333 1769 **e** emt@rhinegold.co.uk **w** rhinegold.co.uk ✉ Ed: Jonathan Wikeley.

Earthsongs (see Bucks Music Group Ltd)

Eastside Music Publishing Ltd Unit 6, 53-55 Theobalds Rd, London, WC1X 8SP **t** 020 7685 8595 **e** paul@eastside-music.co.uk **w** eastside-publishing.co.uk ✉ Head Of A&R: Paul Kennedy.

Eaton Music Ltd Eaton House, 39 Lower Richmond Rd, Putney, London, SW15 1ET **t** 020 8788 4557 **f** 020 8780 9711 **e** info@eatonmusic.com **w** eatonmusic.com ✉ Dir: Mandy Oates.

Eclectic Dance Music (see Westbury Music Ltd)

Eddie Trevett Music (see Carlin Music Corporation)

Edition Kunzelmann (see Obelisk Music)

Edition Schwann (see Peters Edition)

Editions Jean Davoust (see Catalyst Music Publishing Ltd)

Editions Metropolitaines (see Catalyst Music Publishing Ltd)

Edward Kassner Music Co Ltd (see Kassner Associated Publishers Ltd)

Edwin Ashdown (see Music Sales Ltd)

EG Music Ltd PO Box 606, London, WC2E 7YT **t** 020 8540 9935 **e** ck@egmusic.demon.co.uk ✉ MD: Sam Alder.

Egleg Music (see Asterisk Music)

ELA Music Argentum, 2 Queen Caroline St, London, W6 9DX **t** 020 3178 7687 **f** 020 8323 8080 **e** ela@ela.co.uk **w** ela.co.uk ✉ MD: John Giacobbi.

Eleven East Music Inc. (see Bucks Music Group Ltd)

Embassy Music (see Music Sales Ltd)

Emerson Edition Ltd Windmill Farm, Ampleforth, North Yorkshire, YO62 4HF **t** 01439 788324 **f** 01439 788715 **e** JuneEmerson@compuserve.com ✉ MD: June Emerson.

EMI Film & Theatre Music (see EMI Music Publishing)

EMI MUSIC PUBLISHING 27 Wrights Lane, London, W8 5SW **t** 020 3059 3059 **e** firstinitial+lastname@emimusicpub.com **w** emimusicpub.com ✉ President: Guy Moot.

EMI Music Publishing Continental Europe 27 Wrights Lane, London, W8 5SW **t** 020 3059 3059 **e** firstinitial+lastname@emimusicpub.com **w** emimusicpub.com ✉ Contact: Claudia Palmer.

Encore Publications Juglans House, Brenchley Rd, Matfield, Kent, TN12 7DT **t** 01892 725 548 **f** 01892 725 568 **e** info@encorepublications.com **w** encorepublications.com ✉ Managing Editor: Tim Rogers.

Enterplanetary Koncepts (see Dejamus Ltd)

ERA Music (see Express Music (UK) Ltd)

Ernst Eulenburg (see Schott Music Limited)

Ernvik Musik (Sweden) (see Sea Dream Music)

Eschenbach Editions Achmore, Moss Rd, Ullapool, Ross and Cromarty, IV26 2TF **t** 01854 612 938 **f** 01854 612 938 **e** eschenbach@caritas-music.co.uk **w** caritas-music.co.uk ✉ Managing Director: James Douglas.

Esoterica Music Ltd 20 Station Road, Eckington Road, Sheffield, South Yorkshire, S21 4FX **t** 01246 432507 **f** 01246 432507 **e** richardcory@lineone.net ✉ MD: Richard Cory 07785 232176.

Esquire Music Company 185A Newmarket Road, Norwich, Norfolk, NR4 6AP **t** 01603 451139 ✉ MD: Peter Newbrook.

The Essex Music Group Suite 207, Plaza 535, Kings Road, London, SW10 0SZ **t** 020 7823 3773 **f** 020 7351 3615 **e** sx@essexmusic.co.uk ✉ MD: Frank D Richmond.

Euterpe Music (see Paul Rodriguez Music Ltd)

EV-Web (see Bucks Music Group Ltd)

Eventide Music Library Sovereign House, 12 Trewartha Rd, Praa Sands, Penzance, Cornwall, TR20 9ST **t** 01736 762826 **f** 01736 763328 **e** panamus@aol.com **w** panamamusic.co.uk ✉ myspace.com/scampmusicpublishing ✉ MD: Roderick Jones.

Evergreen Music (see Music Sales Ltd)

Evita Music (see Universal Music Publishing Group)

Contacts   Facebook MySpace Twitter YouTube

Evocative Music (see G2 Music)

Evolve Music Ltd The Courtyard, 42 Colwith Road, London, W6 9EY **t** 020 8741 1419 **f** 020 8741 3289 **e** firstname@evolverecords.co.uk **⊟** Co-MD: Oliver Smallman.

Ewan McColl Music (see Bucks Music Group Ltd)

Express Music (UK) Ltd Matlock, Brady Road, Lyminge, Kent, CT18 8HA **t** 01303 863 185 **f** 01303 863 185 **e** siggyjackson@onetel.net.uk **⊟** MD: Siggy Jackson.

Extra Slick Music (see Menace Music)

Faber Music Bloomsbury House, 74-77 Great Russell St, London, WC1B 3DA **t** 020 7908 5310 **f** 020 7908 5339 **e** information@fabermusic.com **w** fabermusic.com **⊟** Sales & Marketing Dir: Phillip Littlemore.

Faber Music Burnt Mill, Elizabeth Way, Harlow, Essex, CM20 2HX **t** 01279 828989 **f** 01279 828990 **e** sales@fabermusic.com **w** fabermusic.com **⊟** Sales & Mktg Dir: Phillip Littlemore 01279 828900.

Fabulous Music (see The Essex Music Group)

Fairwood Music (UK) Ltd 72 Marylebone Lane, London, W1U 2PL **t** 020 7487 5044 **f** 020 7935 2270 **e** betul@fairwoodmusic.com **w** fairwoodmusic.com **⊟** GM: Betul Al-Bassam.

Faith & Hope Publishing 23 New Mount St, Manchester, M4 4DE **t** 0161 839 4445 **f** 0161 839 1060 **e** email@faithandhope.co.uk **w** faithandhope.co.uk **⊟** MD: Neil Claxton.

Fall River Music (see Bucks Music Group Ltd)

Fanfare Music (see Chrysalis Music Ltd)

Far Out Music (see Westbury Music Ltd)

Fast Western Ltd. Bank Top Cottage, Meadow Lane, Millers Dale, Derbyshire, SK17 8SN **t** 01298 872462 **e** fast.west@virgin.net **⊟** MD: Ric Lee.

Favored Nations Music Publishing Ltd PO Box 31, Bushey, Herts, WD23 2PT **t** 01923 244 673 **f** 01923 244 693 **e** info@favorednationsmusic.com **w** favorednationsmusic.com **⊟** MD: Barry Blue.

Fellows Media Ltd The Gallery, Manor Farm, Southam, Cheltenham, Gloucestershire, GL52 3PB **t** 01242 259241 **e** media@fellowsmedia.com **w** fellowsmedia.com **⊟** Managing Director: Simon Fellows.

Fenette Music (see De Haske Music (UK) Ltd)

FI Music 2 Laurel Bank, Lowestwood, Huddersfield, West Yorkshire, HD7 4ER **t** 01484 846 333 **f** 01484 846 333 **e** HotLeadRecords@btopenworld.com **w** fimusic.co.uk **⊟** Co-Director: Ian R Smith.

John Fiddy Music Unit 3, Moorgate Business Centre, South Green, Dereham, NR19 1PT **t** 01362 697922 **f** 01362 697923 **e** info@johnfiddymusic.co.uk **w** johnfiddymusic.co.uk **⊟** Prop: John Fiddy.

Fintage Music Stationsweg 32, Leiden, 2312 AV, Netherlands **t** +31 71 565 9999 **f** +31 71 565 9924 **e** suzanne.plesman@fintagehouse.com **w** fintagemusic.com **⊟** EVP Fintage Talent: Suzanne Plesman.

Fireworks Music Ltd 28 Percy St, London, W1T 2DB **t** 020 7907 1511 **f** 020 7907 1512 **e** fwx@fireworksmusic.co.uk **w** fireworksmusic.co.uk

The First Composers Company (see Carlin Music Corporation)

First Resolution Publishing 1B Crieffe Rd, Kingston, Kingston, Kingston 6, Jamaica **t** 001 876 946 3718 **e** firstresolution@gmail.com **w** frp1.ne **⊟** Dir: Delma Pryce 876 946 3718.

First Time Music (Publishing) UK Sovereign House, 12 Trewartha Rd, Praa Sands, Penzance, Cornwall, TR20 9ST **t** 01736 762 826 **f** 01736 763 328 **e** panamus@aol.com **w** songwriters-guild.co.uk **⊟** myspace.com/scampmusicpublishing **⊟** MD: Roderick Jones 01736 762826.

Flip Flop Music (see Asterisk Music)

Flook Publishing (see SGO Music Publishing)

The Flying Music Company Ltd FM House, 110 Clarendon Road, London, W11 2HR **t** 020 7221 7799 **f** 020 7221 5016 **e** info@flyingmusic.com **w** flyingmusic.com **⊟** Directors: Paul Walden, Derek Nicol.

Focus Music (Publishing) Ltd 166 Haverstock Hill, London, NW3 2AT **t** 020 7722 3399 **e** info@focusmusic.com **w** focusmusic.com **⊟** MD: Paul Greedus.

Focus Music Library (see Focus Music (Publishing) Ltd)

FON Music (see Universal Music Publishing Group)

Fortissimo Music (see Carnaby Music)

Fortunes Fading Music Unit 1, Pepys Court, 84-86 The Chase, London, SW4 0NF **t** 020 7720 7266 **f** 020 7720 7255 **e** ffading@btinternet.com **⊟** MD: Peter Pritchard.

Fox Publishing (see EMI Music Publishing)

Francis Day & Hunter (see EMI Music Publishing)

Francis Dreyfus Music (see Catalyst Music Publishing Ltd)

Frank Chacksfield Music (see Music Sales Ltd)

Freak'n See Music Ltd 19c Heathmans Rd, London, SW6 4TJ **t** 020 7384 2429 **f** 020 7384 2429 **e** firstname@freaknsee.com **w** freaknsee.com **⊟** MD: Jimmy Mikaoui.

Freddy Bienstock Music (see Carlin Music Corporation)

Freedom Songs Ltd PO Box 272, London, N20 0BY **t** 020 8368 0340 **f** 020 8361 3370 **e** freedom@jt-management.demon.co.uk **⊟** MD: John Taylor.

Contacts   Facebook   MySpace   Twitter   YouTube

Friendly Overtures Walkers Cottage, Aston Lane, Henley-on-Thames, Oxfordshire, RG9 3EJ **t** 01491 574 457 **f** 01491 574 457 Creative Dir: Michael Batory.

Frontline Music (see Shanna Music Ltd)

Frooty Music (see No Known Cure Publishing)

Full Cycle Music (see Bucks Music Group Ltd)

Fungus (see Paul Rodriguez Music Ltd)

Funtastik Music 43 Seaforth Gardens, Stoneleigh, Surrey, KT19 0LR **t** 020 8393 1970 **f** 020 8393 2428 **e** info@funtastikmusic.com **w** funtastikmusic.com Contact: John Burns.

Future Stars Publishing Company (see Bucks Music Group Ltd)

FX Media Publishing (see Notting Hill Music (UK) Ltd)

G & M Brand Publications PO Box 650, Aylesbury, Buckinghamshire, HP22 4YY **t** 01494 775867 **e** michael@gmbrand.co.uk MD: Michael Brand.

G Whitty Music (see Bucks Music Group Ltd)

G2 Music 33 Bournehall Ave, Bushey, Herts, WD23 3AU **t** 020 8950 1485 **f** 020 8950 1294 **e** hitsongs@g2-music.com **w** g2-music.com CEO: Helen Gammons 07711 668121.

Gabsongs (see Arnisongs)

Gael Linn Music (see Crashed Music)

Garron Music Newtown Street, Kilsyth, Glasgow, Strathclyde, G65 0LY **t** 01236 821081 **f** 01236 826900 **e** info@scotdisc.co.uk **w** scotdisc.co.uk MD: Bill Garden.

Gazell Publishing International PO Box 370, Newquay, Cornwall, TR8 5YZ **t** 01637 831 011 **f** 01637 831 037 **e** emmapaterson1@aol.com Manager: Emma Paterson.

GDR Music Publishing Ltd 7C Lingfield Point, McMullen Road, Darlington, Co Durham, DL1 1RW **t** 01325 255 252 **f** 01325 255 252 **e** Graeme.circ@ntlworld.com **w** virtual-venue.net MD: Graeme Robinson 07917 690 223.

Mark Geary Songs (see SGO Music Publishing)

Gem And Son Music 4 Wainwright Close, Swindon, Wiltshire, SN3 6JU **t** 07515 970592 **e** robert.gem@btinternet.com **w** turnthemusicuprecords.com Contact: Robert.

Gerig, Cologne (see Breitkopf & Hartel)

Getaway Music (see Universal Music Publishing Group)

Ghost Music Ltd. (see Freedom Songs Ltd)

Fay Gibbs Music Services Warwick Lodge, 37 Telford Avenue, London, SW2 4XL **t** 020 8671 9699 **f** 020 8674 8558 **e** faygibbs@fgmusicservice.demon.co.uk **w** fgmusicservice.co.uk MD: Fay Gibbs.

Gill Music 40 Highfield Park Road, Bredbury, Stockport, Cheshire, SK6 2PG **t** 0161 494 2098 **e** a1.entertainment@btdigitaltv.com **w** a1entertainmentshowbiz.com Contact: Mrs Gill Cragen.

Glad Music (see Music Sales Ltd)

Glendale Music (see Music Sales Ltd)

Global Copyright Association (see Dejamus Ltd)

Global Music Ltd (see Chrysalis Music Ltd)

Global Talent Publishing 30 Leicester Sq, London, WC2H 7LA **t** 020 7766 6000 **f** 020 7288 4639 **e** firstname.lastname@thisisglobal.com **w** thisisglobal.com MD: Miller Williams.

GMW 50-52 Paul St, London, EC2A 4LB **t** 020 7749 1982 **f** 020 7729 8951 **e** williamhaighton@cs.com **w** gmwentertainment.com MD: William Haighton 07990 525982.

Go Ahead Music Ltd Kerchesters, Waterhouse Lane, Kingswood, Tadworth, Surrey, KT20 6HT **t** 01737 832 837 **f** 01737 833 812 **e** info@amphonic.co.uk MD: Ian Dale.

Gol-Don Publishing 3 Heronwood Rd, Aldershot, Hants., GU12 4AJ **t** 01252 312 382 **e** gol-don.music@ntlworld.com **w** goforit-promotions.com Partners: Golly Gallagher & Don Leach 07904 232 292.

Golden Apple Productions (see Music Sales Ltd)

Golden Cornflake Music (see Menace Music)

Golden Mountain Music (see Catalyst Music Publishing Ltd)

Good Groove Songs Ltd Unit 217 Buspace Studios, Conlan St, London, W10 5AP **t** 020 7565 0050 **f** 020 7565 0049 **e** gary@goodgroove.co.uk **w** goodgroove.co.uk Contact: Gary Davies.

Goodmusic Publishing PO Box 100, Tewkesbury, Gloucestershire, GL20 7YQ **t** 01684 773883 **f** 01684 773884 **e** sales@goodmusicpublishing.co.uk **w** goodmusicpublishing.co.uk

Grainger Society Edition (see Bardic Edition)

Grand Central Music Publishing Ltd Habib House, 3rd Floor, 9 Stevenson Sq, Piccadilly, Manchester, Greater Manchester, M1 1DB **t** 0161 238 8516 **f** 0161 236 6717 **e** grandcentral@btconnect.com **w** gcmusic.net Director: Rudi Kidd 07711 269 939.

Grapevine Music Ltd Creeting House, All Saints Rd, Creeting St Mary, Ipswich, IP6 8PR **t** 01449 723244 **e** enquiries@eastcentralone.com **w** eastcentralone.com MD: Steve Fernie.

Grass Roots Music Publishing 29 Love Lane, Rayleigh, Essex, SS6 7DL **t** 01268 747 077 MD: Gerald Mahlowe.

Greensleeves Publishing Ltd Unit 14, Metro Centre, St John's Rd, Isleworth, Middlesex, TW7 6NJ **t** 020 8758 0564 **f** 020 8758 0811 **e** clare@greensleeves.net **w** greensleeves.net Copyright Administrator: Gemma Lotfian 020 8380 4931.

GRG Music (see PXM Publishing)

Grin Music Hurston Mill, Pulborough, West Sussex, RH20 2EW **t** 01903 741502 **f** 01903 741502 Copyright Mgr: Patrick Davis.

Publishers: Publishers & Affiliates

Groove Consortium Studio 13,
The Old Truman Brewery, 91 Brick Lane, London, E1 6QL
t 020 7053 2091 **e** brian@thelemongroup.com
w thelemongroup.com 📇 MD: Brian Allen 07989 340 593.

Gwynn Publishing (see Cwmni Cyhoeddi Gwynn Cyf)

H&B Webman & Co (see Chelsea Music Publishing Co)

Habana Media Ltd The Offices, Colgreas Farm, Cubert,
Newquay, Cornwall, TR8 5YZ **t** 01637 831011
f 01637 831037 **e** rodbuckle@aol.com 📇 Manager: Rod
Buckle.

Habana Music Publishing (see Gazell Publishing
International)

Hal Leonard Corporation C/O 8 Whitehouse Lane,
Wooburn Moor, Bucks, HP10 0NR **t** 01494 730143
f 01494 730143 **e** mmumford@halleonard.com
w halleonard.com
📘 facebook.com/pages/GuitarInstructorcom/594773861
45 📇 Director - European Sales & Marketing: Mark Mumford.

Halcyon Music 233 Regents Park Road, Finchley,
London, N3 3LF **t** 07000 783633 **f** 07000 783634
📇 MD: Alan Williams.

Hallin Music Ltd 70A Totteridge Road, High Wycombe,
Bucks, HP13 6EX **t** 01494 528 665 **e** b.hallin@virgin.net
📇 MD: Brian Hallin.

Halo Publishing 88 Church Lane, London, N2 0TB
t 020 8444 0049 **e** halomanagement@hotmail.com
w halo-uk.net 📇 Dir: Mike Karl Maslen 07711 062 309.

Hamburger Publishing PO Box 64061, London,
E1W 9AP **t** 020 790 7915 **f** 020 790 7915
e info@schnitzel.co.uk **w** schnitzel.co.uk 📇 MD: Oliver
Geywitz.

Hammer Musik (see Bucks Music Group Ltd)

Hammerhead Music 14 Victoria Rd, Douglas,
Isle Of Man, IM2 4ER **t** 07973 129068
e hammer007@jerseymail.co.uk 📇 Director A&R: Bob Miller.

Harbrook Music (see Thames Music)

Hardmonic Music c/o MGR, 55 Loudoun Rd,
St. John's Wood, London, NW80DL **e** info@hardmonic.com
w hardmonic.com 📇 Director: Roberto Concina.

Harmony Music (see Bucks Music Group Ltd)

Harrison Music (see Music Sales Ltd)

Harvard Music (see Bucks Music Group Ltd)

Hatton & Rose Publishers 46 Northcourt Avenue,
Reading, Berkshire, RG2 7HQ **t** 0118 987 4938
f 0118 987 4938 📇 Contact: Graham Hatton.

Haynestorm (see Menace Music)

Hazell Dean Music (see Chelsea Music Publishing Co)

HBF Music (see Menace Music)

Heartsongs (see Bucks Music Group Ltd)

Heaven Music PO Box 92, Gloucester, GL4 8HW
t 01452 814321 **f** 01452 812106
e vic_coppersmith@hotmail.com 📇 MD: Vic Coppersmith-
Heaven.

Heavenly Music (see Paul Rodriguez Music Ltd)

Heavenly Songs 47 Frith Street, London, W1D 4SE
t 020 7494 2998 **f** 020 7437 3317
e info@heavenlyrecordings.com **w** heavenly100.com
📇 MDs: Jeff Barrett, Martin Kelly.

Heavy Harmony Music (see Menace Music)

Heavy Truth Music Publishing Ltd PO Box 8,
Corby, Northants, NN17 2XZ **t** 01536 202 295
f 01536 266 246 **e** info@heavytruth.com
w heavytruth.com 📇 Label Mgr: Steve Kalidoski.

Hedgecock Music (see Menace Music)

Heinrichshofen (see Peters Edition)

Hello Cutie/Heru Xuti Publishing Cadillac Ranch,
Pencraig Uchaf, Cwm Bach, Whitland, Carms., SA34 0DT
t 01994 484466 **f** 01994 484294
e cadillacranch@telco4u.net **w** nikturner.com 📇 Dir: Mendy
Menendes.

Hened Music (see Menace Music)

Heraldic Production Music Library
Sovereign House, 12 Trewartha Rd, Praa Sands, Penzance,
Cornwall, TR20 9ST **t** 01736 762826 **f** 01736 763328
e panamus@aol.com **w** panamamusic.co.uk
📇 MD: Roderick Jones.

Hibbert Ralph Entertainment Publishing Ltd
(see SGO Music Publishing)

High-Fye Music (see Music Sales Ltd)

Hilltop Publishing Ltd. PO Box 429, Aylesbury, Bucks,
HP18 9XY **t** 01844 238 692 **f** 01844 238 692
e info@hilltoppublishing.co.uk **w** brillsongs.com
📇 Director: David Croydon.

Hit & Run (see EMI Music Publishing)

HMP Publishing UK LAS House, 10 Derby Hill Crescent,
London, SE23 3YL **t** 020 8291 9236 **f** 020 8291 9236
e hmp@latinartsgroup.com **w** latinartsgroup.com
📇 Director: Hector Rosquete 07956 446 342.

Hoax Music Publishing - Hoax Records
PO Box 23604, London, E7 0YT **t** 020 8928 1900
e hoax@hoaxmusic.com **w** hoaxmusic.com 📇 MD: Ben
Angwin.

Honeyhill Music (see Bucks Music Group Ltd)

Hornall Brothers Music Ltd 1 Northfields Prospect,
Putney Bridge Rd, London, SW18 1PE **t** 020 8877 3366
f 020 8874 3131 **e** stuart@hobro.co.uk **w** hobro.co.uk
📇 MD: Stuart Hornall.

Hot Melt Music (see Universal Music Publishing Group)

HotHouse Music Publishing 1st Floor, 172a Arlington Rd, London, NW1 7HL **t** 020 7446 7446 **f** 020 7446 7448 **e** info@hot-house-music.com **w** hot-house-music.com ⬛ myspace.com/hothousemusicworldwide ⬛ Contact: Abbie Lister.

Hournew Music (see Music Sales Ltd)

Howard Beach Music Inc. (see Bucks Music Group Ltd)

Howlin' Music Ltd 114 Lower Park Rd, Loughton, Essex, IG10 4NE **t** 020 8508 4564 **e** djone@howardmarks.freeserve.co.uk **w** myspace.com/howlinmusic ⬛ Prop/A&R: Howard Marks 07831 430080.

Hub Music (see Universal Music Publishing Group)

Hubris Music (see BDi Music)

Hucks Productions (see Bucks Music Group Ltd)

Hummingbird Productions (see Bucks Music Group Ltd)

Humph Music (see Paul Rodriguez Music Ltd)

Huntley Music (see Bucks Music Group Ltd)

Hyde Park Music No. 8 Garden Flat, 15 Westbourne Terrace, London, W2 3UN **t** 020 7402 8419 **e** tony@tonyhiller.com **w** tonyhiller.com ⬛ Chairman: Tony Hiller.

Hydrogen Dukebox Music Publishing (see Reverb Music Ltd)

I.L.C Music Ltd The Old Props Building, Pinewood Studios, Pinewood Rd, Iver Heath, Bucks, SL0 0NH **t** 01753 785 631 **f** 01753 785 632 **e** Nigelwood@ilcgroup.co.uk ⬛ Directors: Nigel Wood & Ellis Elias.

i10Q Hurlingham Studios, Ranelagh Gardens, London, SW6 3PA **t** 020 7371 0051 **f** 020 7371 9004 **e** info@i10q.co.uk **w** i10q.co.uk ⬛ Creative Director: Sophie Sheen.

Ilona Sekacz Music (see Bucks Music Group Ltd)

Imagem Music Ltd The Matrix Building, 91 Peterborough Rd, London, SW6 3BU **t** 0207 384 6470 **f** 0207 384 6471 **w** imagemmusic.com ⬛ Contact: Lee Thomas.

Imma Play Jason Music (see Notting Hill Music (UK) Ltd)

Immortal Music Ltd (see Independent Music Group)

In The Frame Music 42 Winsford Gardens, Westcliff On Sea, Essex, SS0 0DP **t** 01702 390353 **f** 01702 390355 **e** will@willbirch.com **w** willbirch.com ⬛ Prop: Will Birch.

Incentive Music Ltd Unit 21, Grand Union Centre, West Row, London, W10 5AS **t** 020 8964 2555 **f** 020 8964 8778 **e** incentive@incentivemusic.co.uk **w** incentivemusic.com ⬛ MD: Nick Halkes.

Incredible Music (see Notting Hill Music (UK) Ltd)

Indian Hill Music (see Menace Music)

Indipop Music P.O.Box 369, Glastonbury, Somerset, BA6 8YN **t** 01749 831 674 **f** 01749 831 674 ⬛ MD: Steve Coe.

Industrial Music (see Bucks Music Group Ltd)

Infectious Music (see 4AD Music)

Infernal Music (see Notting Hill Music (UK) Ltd)

Inky Blackness Ltd PO Box 32089, Camden Town, London, NW1 0NX **t** 07958 520580 **e** inky@inkyblackness.co.uk **w** inkyblackness.co.uk ⬛ MD: Ian Tregoning.

International Music Network Ltd 3 York House, Langston Rd, Loughton, Essex, IG10 3TQ **t** 0845 371 1113 **f** 0845 371 1114 **e** erich@independentmusicgroup.com **w** independentmusicgroup.com ⬛ CEO: Ellis Rich. (see Independent Music Group)

Independent Music Group 3 York House, Langston Rd, Loughton, Essex, IG10 3TQ **t** 0845 371 1113 **f** 0845 371 1114 **e** erich@independentmusicgroup.com **w** independentmusicgroup.com ⬛ CEO: Ellis Rich.

International Music Publications (IMP) Griffin House, 161 Hammersmith Road, London, W6 8BS **t** 020 8222 9200 **f** 020 8222 9260 **e** imp.info@warnerchappell.com **w** wbpdealers.com ⬛ Sales Manager: Chris Statham.

International Songwriters' Music PO Box 46, Limerick City, Ireland **t** +353 61 228 837 **f** +353 61 228 8379 **e** jliddane@songwriter.iol.ie **w** songwriter.co.uk ⬛ MD: James D Liddane.

Intersate (see Paul Rodriguez Music Ltd)

IQ Music Limited Commercial House, 52 Perrymount Rd, Haywards Heath, West Sussex, RH16 3DT **t** 01444 452807 **f** 01444 451739 **e** kathie@iqmusic.co.uk ⬛ Dir: Kathie Iqbal.

IRS Music/IRS Songs (see Bugle Publishing Group)

Isobar Music 56 Gloucester Pl, London, W1U 8HJ **t** 020 7486 3297 **f** 020 7486 3297 **e** info@isobarrecords.com ⬛ MD: Peter Morris 07956 493692.

Ivy Music (see Music Sales Ltd)

Ixion (see Eaton Music Ltd)

J Curwen & Sons (see Music Sales Ltd)

J&H Publishing (see Dejamus Ltd)

J&M Music Publishing (see Paul Rodriguez Music Ltd)

Jack Good Music (see Carlin Music Corporation)

Jacobs Ladder Music Ltd 11 Claremont Crescent, Rickmansworth, Herts, WD3 3QP **t** 01923 220 628 **e** allen.jacobs@virgin.net ⬛ MD: Allen Jacobs.

Jacquinabox Music Ltd (see Independent Music Group)

Jap Songs (see Proof Songs)

Contacts Facebook MySpace Twitter YouTube

Publishers: Publishers & Affiliates

Jarb Publishing (see Charly Publishing Ltd)

Jay Nick Enterprises (see Menace Music)

Jayded Entertainment Ltd 2nd Floor, 9 Bourlet Close, London, W1W 7BP e billy@2point9.com w jaysean.com Managing Director: Billy Grant.

Jaykay Music (see Bucks Music Group Ltd)

Jazid Music (see Paul Rodriguez Music Ltd)

Jazz Art Music (see Bucks Music Group Ltd)

41GP Music Ltd 41 Great Portland Street, London, W1W 7LA t 020 7268 0124 f 020 7637 1997 e info@41gpmusic.com w 41gpmusic.com Dirs: Adrian Bullock, Richard Morris, Stephanie Hardwick.

Jenjo Music Publishing 68 Wharton Avenue, Sheffield, South Yorkshire, S26 3SA t 0114 287 9882 f 0114 287 9882 Contact: Mike Ward.

Jetstar Music Phoenix Music International, PO Box 46, Cromer, NR27 9WX t 08456 300 710 f 08456 300 720 e john.carnell@phoenix-corp.co.uk w phoenixmusicinternational.com Director: John Carnell.

Jewel Music Co (see Warner/Chappell Music Ltd)

Jewel Music Publishing Ltd (see Hornall Brothers Music Ltd)

Jiving Brothers (see G & M Brand Publications)

Joey Boy Music Publishing (see Dejamus Ltd)

JO Music Services (see SGO Music Publishing)

Jobete Music (UK) Ltd (see EMI Music Publishing)

Joe Gibb (see Westbury Music Ltd)

Johi Music (see Dejamus Ltd)

John Rubie (see Paul Rodriguez Music Ltd)

Johnsongs (see Universal Music Publishing Group)

Jonalco Music (see Halcyon Music)

Jonathan Music (see Catalyst Music Publishing Ltd)

Jonjo Music (see Bocu Music Ltd)

Jonsongs Music 3 Farrers Place, Croydon, Surrey, CR0 5HB t 020 8654 5829 f 020 8656 3313 e jonsongsuk@yahoo.co.uk GM: Patricia Bancroft.

Josef Weinberger Limited 12-14 Mortimer St, London, W1T 3JJ t 020 7580 2827 f 020 7436 9616 e promotion@jwmail.co.uk w josef-weinberger.com Promotion: Lewis Mitchell.

Joustwise Myrtle Cottage, Rye Road, Hawkhurst, Kent, TN18 5DW t 01580 754 771 f 01580 754 771 e scully4real@yahoo.co.uk w 4realrecords.com MD: Terry Scully.

JSE Music Publishing Ltd (see Independent Music Group)

Ju-Ju Bee Music (see Dejamus Ltd)

Jubilee Music Ltd (see IQ Music Limited)

David Julius Publishing 11 Alexander House, Tiller Road, London, E14 8PT t 020 7987 8596 f 020 7987 8596 e burdlawrence@btinternet.com MD: David Maynard.

June Songs (see Chelsea Music Publishing Co)

Jupiter 2000 (see Crumbs Music)

Just Isn't Music PO Box 4296, London, SE11 4WW t 020 7820 3535 f 020 7820 3434 e adrian@justisntmusic.com w justisntmusic.com Contact: Adrian Kemp.

Justice Music (see Bucks Music Group Ltd)

Kaleidoscope Music c/o Curzon Artificial Eye, 20-22 Stukeley St, London, WC2B 5LR t 020 7438 9567 f 020 7240 5242 e ross@kmmp.co.uk Director: Ross Fitzsimons.

Kalmann Music (see Carlin Music Corporation)

Karonsongs 20 Radstone Court, Hillview Rd, Woking, Surrey, GU22 7NB t 01483 755153 e ron.roker@ntlworld.com w ronroker.com MD: Ron Roker.

KASSNER ASSOCIATED PUBLISHERS LTD

Units 6 & 7, 11 Wyfold Rd, Fulham, London, SW6 6SE t 020 7385 7700 f 020 7385 3402 e songs@kassner-music.co.uk w kassnermusic.co.uk Managing Director: David Kassner. Finance Director: Veronique Kassner. Head of Legal and Business Affairs: Steven Fisher. Business Affairs / International: Alexander Kassner. Head of Copyright: Monika Weinmann. Copyright and Licensing Manager: Amanda King. Royalties Manager: Victoria Haslam. Online Development: Christopher Hall.

Katsback (see Menace Music)

Kaplan Kaye Music 95 Gloucester Rd, Hampton, Middlesex, TW12 2UW t 020 8783 0039 f 020 8979 6487 e kaplan222@aol.com Contact: Kaplan Kaye.

Kayenne Music (see The Valentine Music Group)

Kenny Lynch Music (see Carlin Music Corporation)

Kensington Music (see The Essex Music Group)

Kensongs (see Paul Rodriguez Music Ltd)

Kerroy Music Publishing 2 Queensmead, St John's Wood Park, London, NW8 6RE t 020 7722 9828 f 020 7722 9886 e kerroy@btinternet.com CEO: Iain Kerr.

Kevin King Music Publishing 16 Limetrees, Llangattock, Crickhowell, Powys, NP8 1LB t 01873 810 142 e kevinkinggb@aol.com w silverword.co.uk MD: Kevin King.

Key 23 Music Sovereign House, 12 Trewartha Rd, Praa Sands, Penzance, Cornwall, TR20 9ST **t** 01736 762826 **f** 01736 763328 **e** panamus@aol.com **w** panamamusic.co.uk 🅜 myspace.com/keytwentythree 🅐 Administrator: Karen Williams.

Key Music (see Bucks Music Group Ltd)

Kickstart Music 12 Port House, Square Rigger Row, Plantation Wharf, London, SW11 3TY **t** 020 7223 8666 **f** 020 7223 8777 **e** info@kickstart.uk.net 🅐 Director: Frank Clark.

Kid Gloves Music Ltd. PO Box 49155, London, SW20 0YL **t** 0208 946 7242 **f** 0208 946 7242 **e** w.stonebridge@btinternet.com 🅐 Director: Bill Stonebridge.

Kila Music Publishing Charlemont House, 33 Charlemont St, Dublin 2, Ireland **t** +353 1 476 0627 **f** +353 1 476 0627 **e** info@kilarecords.com **w** kila.ie 📘 facebook.com/kilaofficial 🅜 myspace.com/kilaofficial 🅐 Manager: Sarah Glennane +353 86 402 1179.

Killer Trax (see Universal Publishing Production Music)

King Jam Music (see Paul Rodriguez Music Ltd)

King Of Spades (see Paul Rodriguez Music Ltd)

Kingsway Music Lottbridge Drove, Eastbourne, East Sussex, BN23 6NT **t** 01323 437700 **f** 01323 411970 **e** music@kingsway.co.uk **w** kingsway.co.uk 🅐 Label Mgr: Stephen Doherty.

Kinsella Music 68 Schools Hill, Cheadle, Cheshire, SK8 1JD **t** 0161 491 5776 **f** 0161 491 6600 **e** kevkinsella@aol.com 🅐 MD: Kevin Kinsella Snr.

Kirklees Music 609, Bradford Rd, Bailiff Bridge, Brighouse, West Yorkshire, HD6 4DN **t** 01484 722855 **f** 01484 723591 **e** sales@kirkleesmusic.co.uk **w** kirkleesmusic.co.uk 🅐 MD: Graham Horsfield.

Kirschner-Warner Bros Music (see Warner/Chappell Music Ltd)

Kite Music Ltd Binny Estate, Ecclesmachan, Edinburgh, EH52 6NL **t** 01506 858885 **f** 01506 858155 **e** kitemusic@aol.com 🅐 MD: Billy Russell.

Knox Music (see Carlin Music Corporation)

Koala Publishing (see Music Exchange (Manchester) Ltd)

Kobalt Music Group 4 Valentine Place, London, SE1 8QH **t** 020 7401 5500 **f** 020 7401 5501 **w** kobaltmusic.com

Kojam Music (see Kobalt Music Group)

Koka Media (see Universal Publishing Production Music)

Kudos Film and TV (see BDi Music)

Kunzelmann (see Peters Edition)

Lady's Gold Mercedes (see Bucks Music Group Ltd)

Lakes Music Wakefield Place, Sandgate, Kendal, Cumbria, LA9 6HT **t** 01539 724 433 **f** 01539 724 499 **e** neil@ensign.uk.com 🅐 Director: Neil Clark.

Lakeview Music Pub Co (see The Essex Music Group)

LANDER RECORDS & MUSIC

Lander Music Group, Athene House, 86 The Broadway, London, NW7 3TD **t** 020 8906 2224 **e** judd@landerpr.com **w** landerpr.com 📘 facebook.com/LanderPR 🅜 myspace.com/landermusicpr 🅣 twitter.com/MusicPromotions 🅐 Director: Judd Lander.

Lantern Music 34 Batchelor St, London, N1 0EG **t** 020 7278 4288 **e** rgoldmff@aol.com 🅐 Contact: Rob Gold.

Lark Music (see Carlin Music Corporation)

Last Suppa Music Limited The Coach House, 1a Putney Heath Lane, London, SW15 3JG **t** 020 7193 1325 **e** jon@lastsuppa.com **w** lastsuppa.com 🅐 Managing Director: Jon Sexton.

Latino Buggerveil Music (see Notting Hill Music (UK) Ltd)

Laurel Music (see EMI Music Publishing)

Laurie Johnson Music (see Bucks Music Group Ltd)

Laws Of Motion Publishing (see Westbury Music Ltd)

Leaf Songs (see Reverb Music Ltd)

Leonard, Gould & Butler (see Music Exchange (Manchester) Ltd)

LEOPARD MUSIC PUBLISHING

LEOPARD music publishing

PO Box 77, Liversedge, West Yorkshire, WF15 7WT **t** 05601 480068, 07860 336569 or 07738 882264 **f** 01924 405 114 **e** info@leopardmusicgroup.com **w** leopardmusicgroup.com 🅜 myspace.com/leopardmusicpublishing 🅐 MD: Brian Williams.

Leosong Copyright Service Ltd (see Conexion Music Ltd)

Les Etoiles de la Musique (see Menace Music)

Leslie Veale Music Sovereign House, 12 Trewartha Road, Praa Sands, Penzance, Cornwall, TR20 9ST **t** 01736 762 826 **f** 01736 763 328 **e** panamus@aol.com **w** panamamusic.co.uk 🅐 MD: Roderick Jones.

Liberty Music (see Asterisk Music)

Publishers: Publishers & Affiliates

The Licensing Team Ltd 23 Capel Rd, Watford, WD19 4FE **t** 01923 234 021 **f** 020 8421 6590 **e** Info@TheLicensingTeam.com **w** thelicensingteam.com Director: Lucy Winch.

Lindsay Music 24 Royston St, Potton, Bedfordshire, SG19 2LP **t** 01767 260815 **f** 01767 261729 **e** office@lindsaymusic.co.uk **w** lindsaymusic.co.uk Publisher: Carole Lindsay-Douglas.

Linvoy Music (see Carlin Music Corporation)

Lionrich Music (see Menace Music)

Little Diva (see Menace Music)

Little Dragon Music (see Bucks Music Group Ltd)

Little Rox Music (see Celtic Songs)

Little Venice (see Bucks Music Group Ltd)

Little Victories 14 Spezia Rd, London, NW10 4QJ **t** 0794 099 240 **e** stuart@littlevictoriesltd.com **w** littlevictoriesltd.com Contact: Stuart.

Little Victory Music (see Menace Music)

Livingsting Music (see Greensleeves Publishing Ltd)

Lojinx Music Publishing BCM Box 2676, London, WC1N 3XX **t** 020 7193 9154 **f** 020 7691 9716 **e** hello@lojinx.com **w** lojinx.com

Lomond Music 32 Bankton Pk, Kingskettle, Fife, KY15 7PY **t** 01337 830 974 **e** admin@lomondmusic.com **w** lomondmusic.com Partners: Bruce & Pat Fraser.

Longstop Productions (see Bucks Music Group Ltd)

Loose Music (UK) Pinery Building, Highmoor, Wigton, Cumbria, CA7 9LW **t** 01697 345422 **f** 01697 345422 **e** looserecords@gmail.com **w** looserecords.com facebook.com/pages/Loose-Records/139159737210 w.myspace.com/andrewjtitcombe twitter.com/looserecords A&R: Tim Edwards.

Lorna Music (see EMI Music Publishing)

Los Angeles Post Music 165 Culver Blvd, Suite D, Playa Del Rey, California, 90293, United States **t** +1 818 501 8329 **f** +1 818 990 7661 **e** info@lapostmusic.com **w** lapostmusic.co.uk Sales: Tom Borton.

Louise Music (see Menace Music)

Love-Ly-N-Divine (see Menace Music)

Ludix Music (see Carlin Music Corporation)

Ludwig Van Music Ltd Hope House, 40 St Peters Rd, London, W6 9BD **t** 020 8741 6020 **e** info@spiritmm.com Director: David Jaymes.

Lupus Music 1 Star St, London, W2 1QD **t** 020 7706 7304 **f** 020 7706 8197 **e** lupusmusic@btconnect.com MD: Cora Barnes.

Lynton Muir Music Ltd 42 Lytton Road, Barnet, Middx, EN5 5BY **t** 020 8950 8732 **f** 020 8950 6648 **e** paul.lynton@btopenworld.com MD: Paul Lynton.

Lynwood Music 2 Church St, West Hagley, West Midlands, DY9 0NA **t** 01562 886625 **f** 01562 886625 **e** downlyn@globalnet.co.uk **w** users.globalnet.co.uk/~downlyn/index.html Mgr: Rosemary Cooper.

M2 Music (see Bucks Music Group Ltd)

Madena (see Eaton Music Ltd)

Madrigal Music Publishing Co Guy Hall, Awre, Gloucestershire, GL14 1EL **t** 01594 510512 **e** artists@madrigalmusic.co.uk **w** madrigalmusic.co.uk myspace.com/madrigalmusicmanagement MD: Nick Ford.

Canford Summer School of Music (see Maecenas Music)

Maecenas Music P.O.Box 629, Godstone, Godstone, Surrey, CR8 5AU **t** 01342 893963 **f** 01342 893977 **e** maecenasmusicltd@aol.com **w** maecenasmusic.co.uk Director: Malcolm Binney.

Maelstrom Music Publishing Ltd 23 Mariner Gardens, Richmond, Surrey, TW10 7UU **t** 0208 288 0155 **e** max@maelstromusic.com **w** maelstromusic.com Contact: Max Mackie.

Magic Frog Music (see Focus Music (Publishing) Ltd)

Magick Eye Publishing PO Box 3037, Wokingham, Berkshire, RG40 4GR **t** 0118 9328320 **e** info@magickeye.com **w** magickeye.com MD: Chris Hillman 0118 932 8320.

Magneil Publishing (see Bugle Publishing Group)

Magnet Music (see Warner/Chappell Music Ltd)

Main Spring Music PO Box 38648, London, W13 9WJ **t** 020 8567 1376 **e** blair@main-spring.com **w** main-spring.com MD: Blair McDonald.

Make Some Noise Publishing PO Box 792, Maidstone, Kent, ME14 5LG **t** 01622 691 106 **f** 01622 691 106 **e** info@makesomenoiserecords.com **w** makesomenoiserecords.com Manager: Clive Austen.

Malahat (see Menace Music)

MAM Music (see Chrysalis Music Ltd)

Man in the Street Publishing The Old Chapel, Hardwick, Aylesbury, Bucks, HP22 4DZ **t** 0845 644 1839 **e** manstreetpub@aol.com Proprietor: Derik Timms.

Mann Music Ltd (see Paternoster Music)

Manners McDade & McCleery Music Ltd 46 Copperfield St, London, SE1 0DY **t** 020 7928 9939 **e** info@mannersmcdade.co.uk **w** mannersmcdade.co.uk MD: Catherine Manners.

Mansem Music (see Wilson Editions)

Marlyn Music (see Carlin Music Corporation)

Marmalade Music (see Warner/Chappell Music Ltd)

Marquis Music (see Bocu Music Ltd)

George Martin Music c/o CA Management, Southpark Studios, 88 Peterborough Road, London, SW6 3HH **t** 020 7384 9575 **e** information@georgemartinmusic.com **w** georgemartinmusic.com 🔲 A&R: Adam Sharp.

Marzique Music (see Menace Music)

Match Production Music (see Universal Publishing Production Music)

Mattapan Music (see Bucks Music Group Ltd)

Mautoglade Music (see Hornall Brothers Music Ltd)

Max-Hill Music (see Notting Hill Music (UK) Ltd)

Maxwood Music Regent House, 1 Pratt Mews, London, NW1 0AD **t** 020 7554 4840 **f** 020 7388 8324 **e** partners@newman-and.co.uk **w** maxwoodmusic.com 🔲 MD: Colin Newman.

Mayhew Music (see Kassner Associated Publishers Ltd)

Mbop Publishing Mbop Publishing, 40 Bowling Green Lane, London, EC1R 0NE **t** 020 7415 7010 **f** 020 7415 7030 **e** paul.ballance@mbopglobal.co.uk **w** mbop.co.uk 🔲 MD: Paul Ballance.

Mcasso Music Publishing 32-34 Great Marlborough St, London, W1F 7JB **t** 020 7734 3664 **f** 020 7439 2375 **e** lisa@mcasso.com **w** mcasso.com 🔲 Contact: Lisa McCaffery.

McGuinness Whelan 30-32 Sir John Rogersons Quay, Dublin 2, Ireland **t** +353 1 677 7330 **f** +353 1 677 7276 🔲 MD: Paul McGuinness.

Mchoma Music (see Catalyst Music Publishing Ltd)

MCI Music Publishing Ltd 33 Foley St, London, W1W 7TL **t** 020 7612 3000 **f** 020 7612 3301 **e** firstname.lastname@demonmusicgroup.co.uk 🔲 Contact: James Bedbrook.

Mediant Music (see Kassner Associated Publishers Ltd)

Melody First Music Library Sovereign House, 12 Trewartha Rd, Praa Sands, Penzance, Cornwall, TR20 9ST **t** 01736 762826 **f** 01736 763328 **e** panamus@aol.com **w** panamamusic.co.uk 🔳 myspace.com/scampmusicpublishing 🔲 MD: Roderick Jones.

Melody Lauren Music Unit 7 Freetrade House, Lowther Rd, Stanmore, Middlesex, HA7 1EP **t** 020 8206 1177 **f** 020 8206 2757 **e** info@wienerworld.com **w** wienerworld.com 🔲 MD: Anthony Broza.

Menace Music 2 Park Rd, Radlett, Hertfordshire, WD7 8EQ **t** 01923 853 789 **f** 01923 853 318 **e** menacemusicmanagement@btopenworld.com 🔲 MD: Dennis Collopy.

Menace USA (see Menace Music)

Menlo Music (see International Songwriters' Music)

Mercury Music (see EMI Music Publishing)

Meringue Productions Ltd 37 Church St, Twickenham, Middx, TW1 3NR **t** 020 8744 2277 **f** 020 8744 9333 **e** meringue@meringue.co.uk **w** meringue.co.uk 🔲 Dir: Lynn Earnshaw.

Mesh Music 13 Sandys Rd, Worcester, WR1 3HE **t** 01905 613 023 **e** meshmusic@prison-records.com 🔲 MD: Chris Warren.

Mesmerizing Music 14 Church Crescent, London, N10 3ND **t** 07831 608644 **e** howard@mesmermusic.com 🔲 MD: Howard Berman.

Messer Music (see Bucks Music Group Ltd)

Metric Music (see Bugle Publishing Group)

Metro Music Library (see Amphonic Music Ltd.)

Metrophonic Tithebarns, Tithebarns Lane, Send, Surrey, GU23 7LE **t** 01483 225226 **f** 01483 479606 **e** mail@metrophonic.com 🔲 MD: Brian Rawling.

Michael Batory Music (see Friendly Overtures)

Middle Eight Music (see Cramer Music)

Miggins Music (UK) 33 Mandarin Place, Grove, Oxon, OX12 0QH **t** 01235 771577 **f** 01235 767171 **e** migginsmusic3@yahoo.com 🔲 Creative Director: Des Leyton.

Mighty Iron Music (see Asterisk Music)

Mikosa Music 9-10 Regent Square, London, WC1H 8HZ **t** 020 7837 9648 **f** 020 7837 9648 **e** mikosapanin@hotmail.com 🔲 MD: Mike Osapanin.

Millbrand Copyright Management Ltd PO Box 357, Middlesbrough, TS1 4WZ **t** 01642 806795 **f** 01642 351962 **e** info@millbrand.com **w** millbrand.com **f** facebook.com/millbrand 🔳 myspace.com/millbrand 🔲 Managing Director: Paul Mooney.

Millennium Songs 6 Water Lane, Camden, London, NW1 8NZ **t** 020 7482 0272 **f** 020 7267 4908 **e** mail@millenniumrecords.com 🔲 MD: Ben Recknagel.

Milstein Music (see Dejamus Ltd)

MINDER MUSIC LTD

18 Pindock Mews, London, W9 2PY **t** 020 7289 7281 **f** 020 7289 2648 **e** songs@mindermusic.com **w** mindermusic.com 🔲 MD: John Fogarty. Administration: Jenny Clough. Business Affairs: Roger Nickson. A&R: S Boy. Security: Jack Russell.

Minerva Vision Music (see Paul Rodriguez Music Ltd)

Mr & Mrs Music (see Dejamus Ltd)

Miracle Music (see Carlin Music Corporation)

Miriamusic 1 Glanleam Road, Stanmore, Middlesex, HA7 4NW **t** 020 8954 2025 🔲 MD: Zack Laurence.

Publishers: Publishers & Affiliates

Mission Publishing And Recordings
Fairlight Mews, 15 St. Johns Rd, Kingston upon Thames, Surrey, KT1 4AN **t** 0208 977 0632 **f** 0870 770 8669 **e** info@missionlimited.com **w** missionlimited.com 🔲 MD: Sir Harry +44 (0)208 977 0632.

Mistletoe Melodies (see Bocu Music Ltd)

Misty River Music (see Bucks Music Group Ltd)

Mizmo International (see Notting Hill Music (UK) Ltd)

MMV Music 4 Heathgate Place, 75-83 Agincourt Rd, London, NW3 2NU **t** 020 7424 8688 **f** 020 7424 8699 **e** info@mmvmusic.com 🔲 Contact: Björn Hall.

Moggie Music Ltd 41 Horsefair Green, Stony Stratford, Milton Keynes, MK11 1JP **t** 01908 567388 **e** artistes@halcarterorg.com **w** halcarterorg.com 🔲 Owner: Abbie Carter.

Moist Music Ltd PO Box 528, Enfield, Middx, EN3 7ZP **t** 070 107 107 24 **f** 0870 137 3787 **e** info@moistrecords.com **w** moistrecords.com 🔲 MD: Rodney Lewis.

Moncur Street Music Ltd PO Box 16114, London, SW3 4WG **t** 020 7349 9909 **e** mail@moncurstreet.com **w** moncurstreet.com 🔲 MD: Jonathan Simon.

MoonRock Music PO Box 883, Liverpool, L69 4RH **t** 0151 922 5657 **f** 0151 922 5657 **e** bstratt@mersinet.co.uk **w** mersinet.co.uk 🔲 Publishing Manager: Billy Stratton.

Moonsung Music PO Box 369, Glastonbury, Somerset, BA6 8YN **t** 01749 673173 **e** sheila@sheilachandra.com 🔲 Contact: Sheila Chandra.

Morgan Music Co Ltd (see Maxwood Music)

Moss Music 7 Dennis Rd, Corfe Mullen, Wimborne, Dorset, BH21 3NF **t** 01202 695 965 **f** 01202 695 965 **e** petermossmusic@onetel.com 🔲 MD: Peter Moss.

Mostyn Music 8 Milvil Court, Milvil Rd, Lee on the Solent, Hampshire, PO13 9LY **t** 023 9255 0566 **f** 023 9255 0566 **e** Maureen@mostynmusic.com **w** mostynmusic.com 🔲 Partner: Maureen Cresswell.

Mother Music (see McGuinness Whelan)

MP Belaieff (see Peters Edition)

Mr & Mrs Music Suite 11, Accurist House, 44 Baker St, London, W1U 7AZ **t** 020 7224 2280 **f** 020 7224 2290 **e** lesburgess45@aol.com 🔲 MD: Les Burgess.

Mr Sunshine (see Menace Music)

MRM Cedar House, Vine Lane, Hillingdon, Middlesex, UB10 0NF **t** 01895 251515 **f** 01895 251616 **e** mark@mrmltd.co.uk 🔲 Director: Mark Rowles.

MSM (see Music Exchange (Manchester) Ltd)

Muirhead Music 202 Fulham Rd, Chelsea, London, SW10 9PJ **t** 020 7460 4668 **e** dennis@muirheadmanagement.co.uk **w** muirheadmanagement.co.uk 🔲 CEO: Dennis Muirhead 07785 226542.

Mule UK Music PO Box 902, Suite 306, Bradford, BD1 9AH **t** 07971 874 942 **f** 01274 220 579 **e** katherine@full360ltd.com **w** full360ltd.com 🔲 MD: Katherine Canoville.

Multiplay Music PO Box 1323, Harrold, Bedford, MK43 7WT **t** 01234 720785 **f** 01234 720785 **e** kevin@multiplaymusic.com **w** multiplaymusic.com 🔲 MD: Kevin White 07971 885 375.

Mummer Music 38 Grovelands Rd, London, N13 4RH **t** 020 8882 3370 **f** 020 8350 0613 **e** jim@jcook21.freeserve.co.uk 🔲 Dir: Jim Cook.

Mummy Dust Music (see Catalyst Music Publishing Ltd)

Munka (see Paul Rodriguez Music Ltd)

Murfin Music International 1 Post Office Lane, Kempsey, Worcester, WR5 3NS **t** 01905 820659 **f** 01905 820015 **e** muffmurfin@btconnect.com 🔲 MD: Muff Murfin.

Murlyn Music Group Box 7013, Solna, 170 07, Sweden **t** +46 (0)8 444 99 50 **f** +46 (0)8 444 99 69 **e** mail@murlyn.se **w** murlyn.se

Music 1 Ltd. (see Independent Music Group)

Music Box Publications (see Paul Rodriguez Music Ltd)

Music By Design 5th Floor, Film House, 142 Wardour St, London, W1F 8ZU **t** 020 7434 3244 **f** 020 7434 1064 **e** rosa@musicbydesign.co.uk **w** musicbydesign.co.uk 🔲 Production Manager & Music Consultant: Rosa Martinez.

Music Exchange (Manchester) Ltd Claverton Rd, Wythenshawe, Greater Manchester, M23 9ZA **t** 0161 946 1234 **f** 0161 946 1195 **e** sales@music-exchange.co.uk **w** musicx.co.uk 🔲 Director: Gerald Burns.

The Music Factor (see Paul Rodriguez Music Ltd)

Music For Films (see Lantern Music)

Music Funtime (see G & M Brand Publications)

Music Like Dirt PO Box 96, Midhurst, West Sussex, GU29 1AJ **t** 01730 817995 **f** 01730 817995 **e** mld@bigworldpublishing.com **w** bigworldpublishing.com 🔲 MD/A&R: Patrick Meads.

Music Music (see Paul Rodriguez Music Ltd)

Music Partner (see Peters Edition)

Music Sales Ltd 14-15 Berners St, London, W1T 3LJ **t** 020 7612 7400 **f** 020 7612 7545 **e** firstname.lastname@musicsales.co.uk **w** musicsales.com 🔲 COO: Chris Butler.

Music To Picture (see The Valentine Music Group)

The Music Trunk Publishing Co. Ltd (see Broughton Park Music)

Musica Oscura (see Paul Rodriguez Music Ltd)

Musica Rara (see Breitkopf & Hartel)

Contacts   Facebook   MySpace Twitter YouTube

Musicare Ltd 60 Huntstown Wood, Clonsilla, Dublin 15, Ireland **t** +353 1 820 6483 **e** musicare@eircom.net
Dir: Brian Barker.

Musicland (see Peters Edition)

Musik'Image Music Library Sovereign House, 12 Trewartha Rd, Praa Sands, Penzance, Cornwall, TR20 9ST **t** 01736 762826 **f** 01736 763328 **e** panamus@aol.com **w** panamamusic.co.uk
myspace.com/scampmusicpublishing MD: Roderick Jones.

Musisca Publishing 34 Strand, Topsham, Exeter, Devon, EX3 0AY **t** 01392 874538 **f** 01453 751911 **e** info@musisca-publishing.co.uk **w** musisca-publishing.co.uk Prop: Philippe Oboussier.

Mustard Music Publishing Electroline House, 15 Lion Road, Twickenham, Middlesex, TW1 4JH **t** 020 8288 0155 **e** max@mustardmusic.co.uk **w** mustardmusic.co.uk Contact: Max Mackie.

Mute Song Ltd 1 Albion Pl, London, W6 0QT **t** 020 3300 0000 **f** 020 8563 2093 **e** info@mutesong.com **w** mutesong.com MD: Daniel Miller.

Myers Music (see Kassner Associated Publishers Ltd)

Myra Music (see Bucks Music Group Ltd)

N2 Music Ltd (see Evolve Music Ltd)

N2K Publishing Ltd The Studios, 8 Hornton Place, Kensington, London, W8 4LZ **t** 020 7937 0272 **f** 020 7368 6573 **e** marketing@n2kltd.com **w** n2k.ltd.uk Director: Marcus Shelton.

Native Songs Unit 32 Ransome's Dock, 35-37 Parkgate Rd, London, SW11 4NP **t** 020 7801 1919 **f** 020 7738 1819 **e** info@nativemanagement.com **w** nativemanagement.com Contact: Pete Evans.

Nervous Publishing 5 Sussex Crescent, Northolt, Middlesex, UB5 4DL **t** 020 8423 7373 **f** 020 8423 7713 **e** info@nervous.co.uk **w** nervous.co.uk MD: Roy Williams.

Nettwerk One Music 1st Floor, 59-65 Worship St, Shoreditch, London, EC2A 2DU **t** 020 7456 9500 **e** mark@nettwerk.com **w** nettwerkonemusic.com Co-MDs: Mark Jowett, Blair Macdonald.

New Ikon Music (see The Essex Music Group)

New Music Enterprises Meredale, The Dell, Reach Lane, Heath and Reach, Leighton Buzzard, Beds, LU7 0AL **t** 01525 237 700 **f** 01525 237 700 **e** enq@newmusicenterprises.com **w** newmusicenterprises.com Prop: Paul Davis.

New State Publishing Ltd Unit 2A Queens Studios, 121 Salusbury Road, London, NW6 6RG **t** 020 7372 4474 **f** 020 7328 4447 **e** info@newstate.co.uk **w** newstate.co.uk MD: Tom Parkinson, Tim Binns.

New Town Sound Ltd (see Maxwood Music)

Newquay Music (see Bucks Music Group Ltd)

Nice 'n' Ripe Music (see Westbury Music Ltd)

Nicklewhistle Music (see Menace Music)

NKS Publishing (see Westbury Music Ltd)

No Known Cure Publishing 162 Temple Avenue, Dagenham, Essex, RM8 1NB **t** 07760 427 306 **e** tomsong1@hotmail.com MD: TF McCarthy.

Noeland Productions (see Bucks Music Group Ltd)

Nomadic Music Unit 18, Farm Lane Trading Estate, 101 Farm Lane, London, SW6 1QJ **t** 020 7386 6800 **f** 020 7386 2401 **e** info@nomadicmusic.net **w** nomadicmusic.net Label Head: Paul Flanagan 07779 257 577.

Northern Light Music Noyna Lodge, Manor Road, Colne, Lancashire, BB8 7AS **t** 07970 728 210 **e** ajjh@freenetname.co.uk Director: Andrew Hall.

Not S'bad Music (see Crashed Music)

Notting Dale Songs (see Notting Hill Music (UK) Ltd)

NOTTING HILL MUSIC (UK) LTD

NOTTING HILL music

Bedford House, 8B Berkeley Gardens, London, W8 4AP **t** 020 7243 2921 **f** 020 7243 2894 **e** info@nottinghillmusic.com **w** nottinghillmusic.com
myspace.com/nottinghillmusic1 twitter.com/nhmusic MD: David Loader. Chair: Andy McQueen. Int Dir: Peter Chalcraft. Professional Manager: Leo Whiteley. Royalty Manager: Liz Davey. Head of Administration: Charles Garside.

Nowhere Publishing 30 Tweedholm Ave East, Walkerburn, Peeblesshire, EH43 6AR **t** 01896 870284 **e** michaelwild@btopenworld.com MD: Michael Wild.

Numinous Music Figment House, Church St, Ware, Hertfordshire, SG12 9EN **t** 01273 680799 **f** 01920 463883 **e** jhbee@numinous.biz **w** numinous.biz Dir. A&R/Marketing/Promo: John Bee.

Nuthouse Music (see Notting Hill Music (UK) Ltd)

Obelisk Music 32 Ellerdale Road, London, NW3 6BB **t** 020 7435 5255 **f** 020 7431 0621 MD: Mr H Herschmann.

Oblivion Music (see Accolade Music)

Ocean Music (see Express Music (UK) Ltd)

Off The Peg Songs (see In The Frame Music)

Old Bridge Music PO Box 7, Ilkley, LS29 9RY **t** 01943 602203 **f** 01943 435472 **e** mail@oldbridgemusic.com **w** oldbridgemusic.com Partner: Chris Newman.

Old Strains (see Paul Rodriguez Music Ltd)

Olin Music (see Asterisk Music)

Olrac Songs (see Asterisk Music)

One Note Music (see Asterisk Music)

Contacts   Facebook MySpace Twitter YouTube

One Step Music Ltd 3 York House, Langston Rd, Loughton, Essex, IG10 3TQ **t** 0845 371 1113 **f** 0845 371 1114 **e** erich@independentmusicgroup.com **w** independentmusicgroup.com CEO: Ellis Rich.

Online Music Unit 18, Croydon House, 1 Peall Road, Croydon, Surrey, CR0 3EX **t** 020 8287 8585 **f** 020 8287 0220 **e** publishing@onlinestudios.co.uk **w** onlinestudios.co.uk MD: Rob Pearson.

Onward Music (see Bucks Music Group Ltd)

Opal Music 4 Pembridge Mews, London, W11 1LU **t** 020 7221 4933 **f** 020 7727 5404 **e** opal@opaloffice.com Manager: Jane Geerts.

Open Times Music PO Box 5279, Hove, East Sussex, BN52 9QQ **t** 01273 774948 **e** pete@opentimesmusic.com **w** opentimesmusic.com ww.opentimesmusic@myspace.com Managing Director: Pete McGlinchey.

Orange Songs Ltd 4th Floor, 21 Denmark Street, London, WC2H 8NA **t** 020 7240 7696 **f** 020 7379 3398 **e** cliff.cooper@omec.com MD: Cliff Cooper.

Orbit22 Publishing & Entertainment Consultancy Churchill House, 12 Mosley St, Newcastle upon Tyne, NE1 1DE **t** 0191 230 8023 **e** orbit22media@gmail.com www.myspace.com/orbit22media CEO/Owner: Jacquiline Swinburne +44(0)7766115337.

Our Music (see Associated Music International Ltd)

Outcaste Music Publishing 27 Wrights Lane, London, W8 5SW **t** 020 7795 7000 **f** 020 7605 5188 **e** firstname@mvillage.co.uk **w** outcaste.com Co-MDs: Paul Franklyn and Shabs Jobanputra.

Oxford Film Co. (see Paul Rodriguez Music Ltd)

Oxford University Press Music Department, Great Clarendon St, Oxford, Oxfordshire, OX2 6DP **t** 01865 353349 **f** 01865 353749 **e** music.enquiry.uk@oup.com **w** oup.com/uk/music Music Sales & Mktng: Suzy Gooch.

P&P Songs Ltd Hope House, 40 St Peter's Rd, London, W6 9BD **t** 020 8237 8400 **f** 020 8741 0825 **e** firstname@pandpsongs.com **w** pandpsongs.com Contact: Peter McCamley, Paul Flynn.

P3 Music **t** 01828 633790 **f** 0870 137 6738 **e** james@p3music.com **w** p3music.com facebook.com/pages/P3-Music-Label/50374779811 twitter.com/p3music youtube.com/p3musiclabel MD: James Taylor.

Page One Music (see Kassner Associated Publishers Ltd)

Painted Desert Music Corp. (see Shapiro, Bernstein & Co Ltd)

Palace Music (see Warner/Chappell Music Ltd)

Pan Musik (see Kassner Associated Publishers Ltd)

Panache Music Ltd (see Maxwood Music)

Panama Music Library Sovereign House, 12 Trewartha Rd, Praa Sands, Penzance, Cornwall, TR20 9ST **t** 01736 762826 **f** 01736 763328 **e** panamus@aol.com **w** panamamusic.co.uk myspace.com/scampmusicpublishing MD: Roderick Jones.

Panganai Music 296 Earls Court Rd, London, SW5 9BA **t** 020 7373 4083 **f** 020 7373 4083 **e** blackmagicrecords@talk21.com **w** blackmagicrecords.com myspace.com/blackmagicrecords MD: Mataya Clifford.

Paper Publishing (see Westbury Music Ltd)

Par Entertainment (see Charly Publishing Ltd)

Paradise Line Music (see Blue Melon Publishing)

Parliament Music Ltd PO Box 6328, London, N2 0UN **t** 020 8444 9841 **f** 020 8442 1973 **e** info@parliament-management.com Director: David Woolfson.

Partisan Songs c/o Mute Song, 43 Brook Green, London, W6 7EF **t** 020 8964 2001 **f** 020 8968 8437 **e** mamapimp@btopenworld.com **w** emusic.com MD: Caroline Butler.

Pasadena Music (see Paul Rodriguez Music Ltd)

Patch Music (see SGO Music Publishing)

Paternoster Music 16 Thorpewood Avenue, London, SE26 4BX **t** 020 8699 1245 **f** 020 8291 5584 **e** peterfilleul@me.com MD: Peter Filleul, Sian Wynne.

Patricia Music (see Warner/Chappell Music Ltd)

Paul Cooke Music 6 Cheyne Walk, Hornsea, East Yorkshire, HU18 1BX **t** 01964 536 193 **e** paulcookemusic@btinternet.com **w** paulcookemusic.com MD: Paul Cooke.

Paul Rodriguez Music Ltd 15 Stanhope Rd, London, N6 5NE **t** 020 8340 7797 **f** 020 8340 6923 **e** paul@paulrodriguezmus.demon.co.uk **w** paulrodriguezmusic.co.uk MD: Paul Rodriguez.

Pearl Music (see Asterisk Music)

PEERMUSIC (UK) LTD

Greyhound House, 23/24 George Street, Richmond upon Thames, Surrey, London, TW9 1HY **t** 020 8939 1700 **f** 020 8605 3788 **e** peermusic@peermusic.com **w** peermusic.com MD: Nigel Elderton. Creative Director: Richard Holley. Head of Business Affairs: Allan Dann. Copyright Manager: Emma Bembridge. Synch Pomotions Manager: Diane Hayes.

Penkiln Burn (see Bryter Music)

Penny St Music (see Bucks Music Group Ltd)

Perfect Songs The Blue Building, 8-10 Basing St, London, W11 1ET **t** 020 7229 1229 **f** 020 7221 9247 **e** info@perfectsongs.com **w** perfectsongs.com MD: Stanley Banks.

Performance Music (see Kassner Associated Publishers Ltd)

Perpetuity Rights Management Office 341, 10 Great Russell St, London, WC1B 3BQ **t** 07765 661696 **e** info@perpetuity.tv **w** perpetuity.tv twitter.com/perpetuity MD: Michael Gordon.

Pete Allen Music (see Paul Rodriguez Music Ltd)

Peter Maurice (see EMI Music Publishing)

Peterman & Co (see Carlin Music Corporation)

Peters Edition 2-6 Baches St, London, N1 6DN **t** 020 7553 4000 **f** 020 7490 4921 **e** sales@editionpeters.com **w** editionpeters.com Marketing Manager: Linda Hawken 020 7553 4000 (Hire).

PHAB Music High Notes, Sheerwater Avenue, Woodham, Surrey, KT15 3DS **t** 019323 48174 **f** 019323 40921 MD: Philip HA Bailey.

Phillday (see Menace Music)

Phoenix Music Bryn Golau, Saron, Denbighshire, LL16 4TH **t** 01745 550317 **f** 01745 550560 **e** sales@phoenix-music.uk.com **w** phoenix-music.uk.com Proprietor: Kath Banks.

Phoenix Music International PO Box 46, Cromer, NR27 9WX **t** 08456 300 710 **f** 08456 300 720 **e** john.carnell@phoenix-corp.co.uk **w** phoenixmusicinternational.com Director: John Carnell.

Phonetic Music Publishing Ltd Viking House, 12 St Davids Close, Farnham, Surrey, GU9 9DR **t** 01252 330 894 **f** 01252 330 894 **e** james@phoneticmusic.com **w** phoneticmusic.com MD: James Sefton 07775 515 025.

PI34 Music (see Notting Hill Music (UK) Ltd)

Piano Bar Sovereign House, 12 Trewartha Road, Praa Sands, Penzance, Cornwall, TR20 9ST **t** 01736 762 826 **f** 01736 763 328 **e** panamus@aol.com **w** panamamusic.co.uk myspace.com/scampmusicpublishing MD: Roderick Jones 01736 762826.

Pinera Music (see Menace Music)

Pink Floyd Music Publishers Ltd 27 Noel St, London, W1F 8GZ **t** 020 7734 6892 **f** 020 7439 4613 **e** info@noelstreet.com MD: Peter Barnes.

Plan C Music Ltd Covetous Corner, Hudnall Common, Little Gaddesden, Herts, HP4 1QW **t** 01442 842851 **f** 01442 842082 **e** christian.ulf@virgin.net **w** plancmusic.com MD: Christian Ulf-Hansen.

Plangent Visions Music Ltd 27 Noel St, London, W1F 8GZ **t** 020 7734 6892 **f** 020 7439 4613 **e** info@noelstreet.com MD: Peter Barnes.

Plantation Music Pub (see Independent Music Group)

Platinum Sound Publishing Global House, Bridge Street, Guildford, Surrey, GU1 4SB **t** 01483 501 222 **f** 01483 501 201 **e** info@platinumsound.co.uk **w** platinumsound.co.uk Creative Assistant: Louise Sargeant.

Platinum Status (see Notting Hill Music (UK) Ltd)

Playwrite Music Limited 1 Star St, London, W2 1QD **t** 020 7258 0093 **f** 020 7402 9238 **e** nicky@playwrite.uk.com **w** playwrite.uk.com Manager: Nicky McDermott.

Plaza Music (see Express Music (UK) Ltd)

Plus 8 Music Europe (see Independent Music Group)

Pocket Rocket Music Ltd 5 Hanover Place, Bow, London, E3 4QD **t** 07855 121 787 **e** simon@pocketrocketmusic.com **w** pocketrocketmusic.com Dir: Simon Burke-Kennedy.

Point4 Music Unit 16 Talina Centre, Bagleys Lane, Fulham, London, SW6 2BW **e** info@point4music.com **w** point4music.com Dirs: Peter Day, Paul Newton.

Pollination Music 92 Camden Mews, Camden, London, NW1 9AG **t** 020 7424 8665 **f** 020 7482 2210 **e** info@pollinationmusic.co.uk **w** pollinationmusic.co.uk A&R Dir: Seamus Morley.

Polymath Music Publishing 103 Islingword Road, Brighton, E Sussex, BN2 9SG **t** 01273 701 997 **f** 01273 690 149 **e** publishing@polymathmusic.co.uk **w** polymathmusic.co.uk MD: Mark Williams.

Porpete Music (see Menace Music)

Portland Productions (see Cramer Music)

Poseidon Music 46a Woodbridge Road, Moseley, Birmingham, B13 8EJ **t** 0121 249 0598 **f** 0709 214 8920 **e** enquiries@poseidonmusic.com **w** poseidonmusic.com MD: Jon Cotton.

Possie Music (see Independent Music Group)

Post House Music Fairways, Benover Rd, Yalding, Kent, ME18 6ES **t** 01622 814154 **e** posthousemusic@btinternet.com A & R: Pauline Southcombe.

Powdermill Music Aka Ray Pillow Music (see Independent Music Group)

Power Music 29 Riversdale Road, Thames Ditton, Surrey, KT7 0QN **t** 020 8398 5236 **f** 020 8398 7901 MD: Barry Evans.

Power Music Company (see Music Sales Ltd)

Powis Music Limited Onward House, 11 Uxbridge St, Notting Hill, London, W8 7TQ **t** 020 7221 4275 **f** 020 7229 6893 **e** tmedcraft@powismusic.com Managing Director: Tim Medcraft.

Preshus Child Music (see Independent Music Group)

Prestige Music (see Bocu Music Ltd)

Prime Direction Inc (Avex) (see SGO Music Publishing)

Publishers: Publishers & Affiliates

Primo Music 39 Bettespol Meadows, Redbourn, Herts, AL3 7EN **t** 01582 626 015 **e** tony@primomusic.co.uk 🔲 MD: Tony Peters 07740 645 628.

Producer's Workshop Music (see Carlin Music Corporation)

Promo Sonor International (SARL) Sovereign House, 12 Trewartha Rd, Praa Sands, Penzance, Cornwall, TR20 9ST **t** 01736 762826 **f** 01736 763328 **e** panamus@aol.com **w** panamamusic.co.uk 🔲 myspace.com/scampmusicpublishing 🔲 MD: Roderick Jones.

Proof Songs PO Box 20242, London, NW1 7FL **t** 020 7485 1113 **e** info@proofsongs.co.uk **w** proofsongs.co.uk 🔲 myspace.com/proofsongs

Proper Music Publishing Ltd Unit 1, Gateway Business Centre, Kangley Bridge Rd, London, SE26 5AN **t** 020 8676 5180 **f** 020 8676 5190 **e** malc@proper.uk.com 🔲 MD: Malcolm Mills.

PS Songs (see Bucks Music Group Ltd)

PSI Music Library Sovereign House, 12 Trewartha Rd, Praa Sands, Penzance, Cornwall, TR20 9ST **t** 01736 762826 **f** 01736 763328 **e** panamus@aol.com **w** panamamusic.co.uk 🔲 myspace.com/scampmusicpublishing 🔲 MD: Roderick Jones.

Psychedelic Research Lab Songs (see Independent Music Group)

Psychotic Reaction Music Ltd PO Box 65001, London, N5 9AJ **t** 020 7354 3494 **e** info@brillemusic.com 🔲 Managing Director: Leo Silverman.

PUBLISHED BY PATRICK

18 Pindock Mews, London, W9 2PY **t** 020 7289 7281 **f** 020 7289 2648 **e** songs@mindermusic.com **w** mindermusic.com 🔲 MD: John Fogarty. Administration: Jenny Clough. Business Affairs: Roger Nickson. A&R: Patrick Fogarty. Security: Jack Russell.

Puppet Music (see Paul Rodriguez Music Ltd)

Pure Groove Music 679 Holloway Road, London, N19 5SE **t** 020 7281 1597 **e** mickshiner@puregroove.co.uk **w** puregroove.co.uk 🔲 Head of A&R: Mick Shiner.

Pure Silk Music Broadley House, 48 Broadley Terrace, London, NW1 6LG **t** 020 7724 4500 **f** 020 7724 1300 **e** julian@puresilkmusic.com **w** puresilkmusic.com 🔲 myspace.com/puresilkmusic 🔲 MD: Julian Goodkind.

Pushcart Music (see Independent Music Group)

PXM Publishing 68 Cranston Avenue, Bexhill, East Sussex, TN39 3NN **t** 01424 215617 **e** pxm.publishing@virgin.net **w** pxmpublishing.com 🔲 Director/Admin: Frank Rodgers.

QFM/SMAC Publishing c/o Nation Records Ltd, Notting Hill Gate, London, W11 1HE **t** 0207 792 8167 **e** akination@btopenworld.com 🔲 MD: Aki Nawaz 07971206144.

Quaives Music Ltd (see Bright Music Ltd)

Quick Step Music (see Lomond Music)

R&E Music (see Independent Music Group)

R37 Publishing PO Box 1083, Liverpool, L69 4WQ **t** 0151 222 5785 **f** 0151 222 5785 **e** mail@mimashimarecords.co.uk **w** mimashimarecords.co.uk 🔲 MD: Noel Fitzsimmons.

Raeworks (see Independent Music Group)

RAK Publishing Ltd 42-48 Charlbert St, London, NW8 7BU **t** 020 7586 2012 **f** 020 7722 5823 **e** rakpublishing@yahoo.com **w** rakpublishing.com 🔲 myspace.com/rakpublishing 🔲 GM, A&R Manager: Nathalie Hayes, Andy Leese.

Rakeway Music (see Kirklees Music)

Ralphie Dee Music (see Independent Music Group)

Randscape Music (see Menace Music)

Rapido Music (see Bucks Music Group Ltd)

RBT Publications PO Box 640, Bromley, BR1 4XZ **t** 07985 439 453 **f** 020 8290 4589 🔲 Mgr: Roy MacPepple.

Reach Global (UK) Ltd 4F Shirland Mews, London, W9 3DY **t** 020 7854 2836 **e** mcloster@reachglobal.com **w** reachglobal.com 🔲 President: Michael Closter.

Reach Global, Inc. (PRS/ASCAP) (see Reach Global (UK) Ltd)

Reach Global Songs (BMI) (see Reach Global (UK) Ltd)

Real Magic Publishing (see Bucks Music Group Ltd)

Real World Music Ltd Box Mill, Mill Lane, Box, Corsham, Wiltshire, SN13 8PL **t** 01225 743188 **f** 01225 744369 **e** publishing@realworld.co.uk **w** realworld.co.uk/publishing 🔲 Publishing Manager: Rob Bozas.

Rebecca Music Ltd Terwick Pl, Rogate, Petersfield, Hampshire, GU31 5BY **t** 01730 821644 **f** 01730 821597 **e** donna@lesreed.com **w** lesreed.com 🔲 Dir: Donna Reed.

Recent Future Music (see Universal Music Publishing Group)

Red House Music (see Bucks Music Group Ltd)

Red Songs (see Bucks Music Group Ltd)

Redemption Songs (see Chrysalis Music Ltd)

Redpoint Music (see Chrysalis Music Ltd)

Redwood Music (see Carlin Music Corporation)

Contacts   Facebook   MySpace   Twitter   YouTube

Reggae Giant Music (see Castle Hill Music)

Regina Music (see Music Exchange (Manchester) Ltd)

Reinforced Music (see Westbury Music Ltd)

Repetoire (see Bucks Music Group Ltd)

Respect Music Suite 2, 11 Sylvan Hill, London, SE19 2QB **t** 07919 533 244 **e** firstname@respectmusic.co.uk **w** respectmusic.co.uk **✉** Dir: Sharon Dean.

Restoration Music Ltd (see Sovereign Music UK)

Reveal Records 63 St Peters St, Derby, Derbyshire, DE1 2AB **t** 07779 017 236 **f** 01332 556 374 **e** tomreveal@mac.com **w** reveal-records.com **✉** MD: Tom Rose.

Reverb Music Ltd Reverb House, Bennett St, London, W4 2AH **t** 020 8747 0660 **f** 020 8747 0880 **e** publishing@reverbxl.com **w** reverbxl.com **✉** MD: Annette Barrett.

Revue Music (see Creole Music Ltd)

Reyshell Music (see Menace Music)

Richmond Music (see Paul Rodriguez Music Ltd)

Rickim Music Publishing Company Thatched Rest, Queen Hoo Lane, Tewin, Welwyn, Herts, AL6 0LT **t** 01438 798625 **f** 01438 798395 **e** joyce@bigmgroup.freeserve.co.uk **✉** MD: Joyce Wilde.

Riderwood Music (see Carlin Music Corporation)

Right Bank Music UK Home Park House, Hampton Court Road, Kingston upon Thames, Surrey, KT1 4AE **t** 020 8977 0666 **f** 020 8977 0660 **e** rightbankmusicuk@rightbankmusicuk.com **w** rightbankmusicuk.com **✉** Vice President: Ian Mack.

Right Key Music (see Independent Music Group)

Rights Worldwide Ltd (see Faber Music)

Rinsin Music (see Bucks Music Group Ltd)

Rita (Publishing) Ltd 12 Pound Court, The Marld, Ashtead, Surrey, KT21 1RN **t** 01372 276328 **e** thebestmusicis@ritapublishing.com **w** ritapublishing.com **✉** MD: Pat Norton.

Riverhorse Songs (see Conexion Music Ltd)

Rivers Music (see Independent Music Group)

Roba Music (see Independent Music Group)

Robbins Music Corp (see EMI Music Publishing)

Robert Forberg (see Peters Edition)

Robert Lienau (see Peters Edition)

Roberton Publications (see Goodmusic Publishing)

Robroy West Music (see Independent Music Group)

Rock And Roll Stew Music Limited 11 Church Green, Benington, Herts, SG2 7LH **t** 07786 084683 **e** info@rockandrollstewmusic.com **w** rockandrollstewmusic.com **✉** MD: Andy Spacey.

Rock Music Company Ltd 27 Noel St, London, W1F 8GZ **t** 020 7734 6892 **f** 020 7439 4613 **e** info@noelstreet.com **✉** MD: Peter Barnes.

RokSolid Entertainment Ltd 1 The Village, North End Way, London, NW3 7HA **e** manny@rsg.me.uk **w** rsg.me.uk **✉** MD / Chairman: Manny Elias / Mo Siddiqui 07778 037396.

Rokstone Music Ltd 21c Heathmans Road, Parsons Green, London, SW6 4TJ **t** 020 7736 1555 **f** 020 7736 1777 **e** mail@rokstone.net **w** rokstone.net

Roky Erickson (see Menace Music)

Roland Robinson Music (see Menace Music)

Rolf Baierle Music Limited (see Independent Music Group)

Rollercoaster Music (see Asterisk Music)

Romany Songs (see SGO Music Publishing)

Rondercrest (see Loose Music (UK))

Ronster Music (see Independent Music Group)

Rooster 117 Sinclair Rd, London, W14 0NP **t** 020 7602 2881 **e** roosteraud@aol.com **w** roosterstudios.com **✉** Proprietor: Nick Sykes.

Rose Rouge International AWS House, Trinity Square, St Peter Port, Guernsey, GY1 1LX **t** 01481 728 283 **f** 01481 714 118 **e** roserouge@cwgsy.net **✉** Director/Producer/Composer: Steve Free.

Rosette Music (see The Valentine Music Group)

The Rosewood Music Company PO Box 6754, Dublin 13, Ireland **t** +353 1 843 9713 **f** +353 1 843 9713 **e** rosewood@iol.ie **w** rosewoodmusic.ie **✉** Professional Mgr: Greg Rogers.

Rough Trade Publishing 81 Wallingford Rd, Goring, Reading, RG8 0HL **t** 01491 873612 **f** 0870 7301460 **e** info@rough-trade.com **w** rough-trade.com **🆇** myspace.com/roughtradepublishing **✉** MD: Cathi Gibson.

The Royalty Network (see Notting Hill Music (UK) Ltd)

RT Music (see Asterisk Music)

Rubber Road Music 4-10 Lamb Walk, London, SE1 3TT **t** 020 7921 8353 **f** 020 7579 4171 **e** rubber_road_records@yahoo.co.uk **w** rubberroadmusic.com **✉** Creative Manager: Nick Lightowlers.

RubyRed Publishing 46 University St, Belfast, Northern Ireland, BT7 1HB **t** 07775 657234 **f** 08707 625672 **e** francotton@rubyredpub.com **✉** Contact: Fran Cotton.

Rustomatic Music (see Menace Music)

Rybar Music (see Paul Rodriguez Music Ltd)

Rydim Music (see Blue Mountain Music Ltd)

S'Od Music (see Bucks Music Group Ltd)

Contacts | **Facebook** | **MySpace** | **Twitter** | **YouTube**

Publishers: Publishers & Affiliates

SA Rodger & SD Jones Publishing (see Westbury Music Ltd)

Sabre Music (see Eaton Music Ltd)

Safe (see Bucks Music Group Ltd)

Salsoul Music Publish (see Independent Music Group)

Salvo West Ltd t/a Union Square (see Bucks Music Group Ltd)

San Remo Music / Live Beaumont House, Kensington Village, Avonmore Rd, London, W14 8TS **t** 020 7471 5400 **f** 020 7149 1090 **e** info@sanremo-live.com **w** sanremo-live.com ✉ MD: Celia McCamley +44 (0) 20 7471 5400.

Sanctuary Music Publishing Ltd (see Universal Music Publishing Group)

Sands Music (see Independent Music Group)

Sanga Music (see Bucks Music Group Ltd)

Sarah Music Cherry Tree Lodge, Copmanthorpe, York, North Yorks, YO23 3SH **t** 01904 703764 **e** malspence@aol.com ✉ MD: Mal Spence 07913544417.

Satellite Music (see Associated Music International Ltd)

SATV Publishing Ltd Grant Way, Isleworth, Middlesex, TW7 5QD **t** 020 7805 8280 **f** 020 7805 8089 **e** sue.hepworth@bskyb.com ✉ Senior Licensing Executive: Sue Hepworth.

Scamp Music Publishing Sovereign House, 12 Trewartha Rd, Praa Sands, Penzance, Cornwall, TR20 9ST **t** 01736 762 826 **f** 01736 763 328 **e** panamus@aol.com **w** panamamusic.co.uk ✉ myspace.com/scampmusicpublishing ✉ MD: Roderick Jones 01736 762826.

Pauline Scanlon Music (see SGO Music Publishing)

Scaramanga Music (see Menace Music)

Scarf Music Publishing (see Sea Dream Music)

Schaeffers-Kassner Music (see Kassner Associated Publishers Ltd)

Schauer & May (see Boosey & Hawkes Music Publishers Ltd)

Schott Music Limited 48 Great Marlborough St, London, W1F 7BB **t** 020 7534 0700 **f** 020 7534 0749 **e** info@schott-music.com **w** schott-music.com ✉ Director: Sally Groves.

SCO Productions SCO Music 29 Oakroyd Ave, Potters Bar, Herts, EN6 2EL **t** 01707 651439 **e** steveconstantine@hotmail.co.uk ✉ MD: Steve Constantine.

Screen Gems-EMI Music (see EMI Music Publishing)

Screen Music Services (see Conexion Music Ltd)

Screwbox (see Menace Music)

Sea Dream Music Sandcastle Productions, PO Box 13533, London, E7 0SG **t** 020 8534 8500 **e** sea.dream@virgin.net ✉ Snr Partner: Simon Law.

Second Skin Music (see Reverb Music Ltd)

Seeca Music 6, Ditton Hill Rd, Surbiton, Surrey, KT6 5JD **t** 020 8398 2510 **f** 020 8398 1970 **e** info@seeca.co.uk **w** seeca.co.uk ✉ Dir: Louise Blair.

Semprini Music (see Carlin Music Corporation)

Sepia (see Bucks Music Group Ltd)

Seriously Groovy Music 3rd Floor, 28 D'Arblay St, Soho, London, W1F 8EW **t** 020 7439 1947 **f** 020 7734 7540 **e** admin@seriouslygroovy.com **w** seriouslygroovy.com ✉ Directors: Dave Holmes, Lorraine Snape.

Seriously Wonderful Music (see Bucks Music Group Ltd)

Sesame Love Music (see Dejamus Ltd)

Seven B Music (see Charly Publishing Ltd)

Seventh House Music (see Bucks Music Group Ltd)

SGO Music Publishing PO Box 2015, Salisbury, SP2 7WU **t** 01747 871563 **f** 01264 811172 **e** sgomusic@sgomusic.com **w** sgomusic.com ✉ myspace.com/sgomusic ✉ sgomusic ✉ sgoworld ✉ MD: Stuart Ongley.

Shadows Music (see Carlin Music Corporation)

Shaftesbury (see Chrysalis Music Ltd)

Shampeyne Songs Ltd 3940 Laurel Canyon Boulevard, # 408, Studio City, CA 91604, United States **t** 001 310 729 4708 **f** 0870 054 8130 **e** nigelrush@appletreesongs.com **w** pamsheyne.com ✉ Director: Nigel Rush.

Shapiro Bernstein & Company Inc (see Shapiro, Bernstein & Co Ltd)

Shapiro, Bernstein & Co Ltd 12th Floor, 488 Madison Avenue, New York, New York, 10022, United States **t** 020 7247 2001 **e** contactSB@shapirobernstein.com **w** shapiroberstein.com ✉ President: Michael Brettler.

Shaun Davey Music (see Bucks Music Group Ltd)

Shay Songs (see Crashed Music)

Sheila Music (see Creole Music Ltd)

Shepsongs Inc (see Independent Music Group)

Sherlock Holmes Music Unit 1 Chapel Road, Portslade, Brighton, BN1 1PF **t** 01273 424703 **f** 01273 418856 **e** mail@sherlockholmesmusic.co.uk **w** sherlockholmesmusic.co.uk ✉ MD: Vernon Rossiter.

Shipston Music (see Independent Music Group)

Shogun Music (see Eaton Music Ltd)

Shrub Music (see Menace Music)

Silence Music (see Independent Music Group)

Silk Music (see Independent Music Group)

Silktone Songs Inc (see Independent Music Group)

Silver Cradle Music (see Independent Music Group)

Alan Simmons Music PO Box 7, Scissett, Huddersfield, West Yorkshire, HD8 9YZ **t** 01924 848888 **f** 01924 849999 **e** mail@alansimmonsmusic.com **w** alansimmonsmusic.com 📇 MD: Alan Simmons.

Simon Rights Music (see Eaton Music Ltd)

Singletree Music (see Independent Music Group)

Sirens Music (see Catalyst Music Publishing Ltd)

Sixteen Stars Music (see Independent Music Group)

Size: Music PO Box 798, London, EN1 1ZP **t** 07977 181 121 **e** simon@size-music.com **w** size-music.com 📇 Contact: Simon Nicholls.

SJ Music 23 Leys Road, Cambridge, CB4 2AP **t** 01223 314771 **w** printed-music.com/sjmusic 📇 Principle: Judith Rattenbury.

Skidmore Music Co Ltd (see Shapiro, Bernstein & Co Ltd)

Slam Dunk Music (see Independent Music Group)

Slamina Music (see Carlin Music Corporation)

Sleeping Giant Music International (see St James Music)

SLI Music (see Asterisk Music)

Smackin' Music (see Universal Music Publishing Group)

Smirk (see Bucks Music Group Ltd)

SMK Publishing (see Independent Music Group)

Smooth Radio North West Manchester **e** andy.carter@gmgradio.com 📇 Contact: Andy Carter 0161 886 8700.

SMV Schacht Musikvalage (see Bucks Music Group Ltd)

Snappersongs (see Asterisk Music)

So Good Music (see Independent Music Group)

Solent Songs 68-70 Lugley St, Newport, Isle Of Wight, PO30 5ET **t** 01983 524110 **e** songs@solentrecords.co.uk **w** solentrecords.co.uk 📇 Owner: John Waterman.

Songs For Real (see Bucks Music Group Ltd)

Songs In The Key Of Knife Red Corner Door, 17 Barons Court Road, London, W14 9DP **t** 020 7386 8760 **f** 020 7381 8014 **e** info@hospitalrecords.com **w** hospitalrecords.com 📇 MD: Tony Colman.

Songstarr (Music Publishers) Ltd 23 Birkdale Close, Swindon, Wiltshire, SN25 2DH **t** 07713 80816 **e** mail@songstarr.com **w** songstarr.com 📇 Publisher: Stephen Kennedy 07713 804816.

Songstream Music Nestlingdown, Chapel Hill, Porthtowan, Truro, Cornwall, TR4 8AS **t** 01209 890606 📇 MD: Roger Bourne.

Songwriter Music (see International Songwriters' Music)

Songwriters' Showcase Sovereign House, 12 Trewartha Rd, Praa Sands, Penzance, Cornwall, TR20 9ST **t** 01736 762826 **f** 01736 763328 **e** panamus@aol.com **w** panamamusic.co.uk 🔲 myspace.com/guildofsongwriters 📇 MD: Roderick Jones.

Sonic Arts Network Jerwood Space, 171 Union Street, London, SE1 0LN **t** 020 7928 7337 **e** info@sonicartsnetwork.org **w** sonicartsnetwork.org 📇 Chief Exec: Phil Hallett.

Sonic Sheet (see Menace Music)

Sonic360 Music 3 Wardour Castle, Tisbury, Wiltshire, SP3 6RH **t** 020 7636 3939 **f** 020 7636 0033 **e** info@sonic360.com **w** sonic360.com 🔲 myspace.com/sonic360 ▶ youtube.com/s0nic360 📇 Publishing Mgr: Zen Grisdale.

SONY/ATV MUSIC PUBLISHING

30 Golden Sq, London, W1F 9LD **t** 020 3206 2501 **e** firstname.surname@sonyatv.com **w** sonyatv.com 📇 Managing Director: Rakesh Sanghvi. Senior Vice President, UK Operations: Janice Brock. Head of A&R: Ian Ramage. Head of Synchronisation & Marketing: Karina Masters. Head of Administration: Gary Bhupsingh. Finance Director: Will Downs. International Human Resources Manager: Ian Budhu.

The Sorabji Archive Warlow Farm House, Eaton Bishop, Hereford, HR2 9QF **t** 01225 852323 **f** 01225 852523 **e** sorabji-archive@lineone.net **w** sorabji-archive.co.uk 📇 Curator/Director: Alistair Hinton.

Souls Kitchens Music 7 The Stables, Saint Thomas St, Newcastle upon Tyne, Tyne and Wear, NE1 4LE **t** 0191 230 1970 **f** 0191 232 0262 **e** info@kitchenwarerecords.com **w** kitchenwarerecords.com 📇 Administration: Nicki Turner.

Soulstreet Music Publishing Inc (see Independent Music Group)

Sound Entertainment Ltd 11B Osiers Rd, London, SW18 1NL **t** 020 8874 8444 **f** 020 8874 0337 **e** info@soundentertainment.co.uk **w** ComedyCDs.co.uk 📇 Dir: Bob Nolan.

Sound Of Jupiter Music (see Carlin Music Corporation)

Sound Songs First Floor, 32 Brighton Road, Shoreham-By-Sea, West Sussex, BN43 6RG **t** 01273 248978 **e** info@thesoundgroup.com **w** thesoundgroup.com 📇 CEO: Paula Greenwood.

Soundslike Music (see Bucks Music Group Ltd)

Sovereign Lifestyle Music (see Sovereign Music UK)

📇 Contacts 📘 Facebook 🔲 MySpace 🇪 Twitter ▶️ YouTube

Publishers: Publishers & Affiliates

Sovereign Music UK PO Box 356, Leighton Buzzard, Beds, LU7 3WP **t** 01525 385578
e sovereignmusic@aol.com 📇 MD: Robert Lamont.

SP2 Music (USA & Canada) (see Perfect Songs)

Spadesongs (see Asterisk Music)

The Sparta Florida Music Group (see Music Sales Ltd)

Spazmo Music (see Catalyst Music Publishing Ltd)

Speegra 2 Stocks Meadow, Hemel Hempstead, Herts, HP2 7BZ **t** 07789 227 717 **e** richard@speegra.com **w** speegra.com 🔲 myspace.com/speegra 🇪 @speegra 📇 Director: Richard Jackson-Bass & Jane Henley 01442 896628.

Spielman Music (see Independent Music Group)

Spikey Music (see SGO Music Publishing)

Spirit Music Group The Penthouse, Highfield Court, Highfield Rd, London, NW11 9LT **t** 07870 648241
e anthonyc@spiritmusicgroup.com **w** spiritmusicgroup.com 📇 General Manager: Anthony Cavanagh.

Split Music (see Mesh Music)

Spoon Music (see Bucks Music Group Ltd)

Spring River Music (see Independent Music Group)

Squaw Peak Music (see Independent Music Group)

Squirrel (see Briar Music)

St James Music 3 Faraday Way, St Mary Cray, BR53QW
e info@prestige-elite.com **w** prestige-elite.com 📇 MD: Keith Thomas.

Stage Three Music 13a Hillgate St, London, W8 7SP
t 020 7792 6060 **f** 020 7792 6061
e info@stagethreemusic.com **w** stagethreemusic.com 📇 MD: Steve Lewis.

Stainer & Bell PO Box 110, Victoria House, 23 Gruneisen Rd, London, N3 1DZ **t** 020 8343 3303
f 020 8343 3024 **e** post@stainer.co.uk **w** stainer.co.uk 📇 Joint MD: Carol Wakefield.

Standard Music Library (see Bucks Music Group Ltd)

Star Street Music Ltd PO Box 375, Chorleywood, Herts, WD3 5ZZ **t** 01923 440608
e starstreet.uk@ntlworld.com **w** starstreetmusic.com 📇 MD: Nick Battle.

Stave & Nickelodeon (see Blue Melon Publishing)

Staves Music (see Kirklees Music)

Steelchest Music (see Menace Music)

Steelworks Songs 216 Buspace Studios, Conlan St, London, W10 5AP **t** 020 8960 4443 **f** 020 8960 9889
e freedom@frdm.co.uk 📇 MD: Martyn Barter.

Step by Step Music (see Independent Music Group)

Steve Dan Mills Music (see Independent Music Group)

Steve Glen Music (see Blue Melon Publishing)

Steve Marriott Licensing Ltd. Unit 9B, Wingbury Business Village, Upper Wingbury Farm, Wingrave, Bucks, HP22 4LW **t** 07770 364 268
e chris@stevemarriott.co.uk **w** stevemarriott.co.uk 📇 MD: Chris France.

Steve Warner Music (see Independent Music Group)

Stevensong Music (see Ash Music (GB))

Still Working Music Covetous Corner, Hudnall Common, Little Gaddesden, Herts, HP4 1QW
t 01442 842 039 **f** 01442 842 039
e mhaynes@orbison.com **w** orbison.com 📇 European Consultant: Mandy Haynes.

Stinkhorn Music (see Asterisk Music)

Stomp Off Music (see Paul Rodriguez Music Ltd)

Stop Drop & Roll Music Colbury Manor, Jacobs Gutter Lane, Eling, Southampton, SO40 9FY
t 0845 658 5006 **f** 0845 658 5009
e frontdesk@stopdroproll.com **w** stopdroproll.com 📇 Publishing Executive: Emma Curtis.

Storm Music Thornton-Cleveleys, Lancashire, FY5 3BG
t 01253 864598 **e** estelle@photo-stock.co.uk **w** photo-stock.co.uk/NearlyFamous.html 📇 Partner: Estelle Paulo.

Stormking Music (see Bucks Music Group Ltd)

Strada 2 Publishing 25 Heathmans Road, London, SW6 4TJ **t** 020 7371 5756 **f** 020 7371 7731
e office@pureuk.com **w** pureuk.com 📇 Creative Dir: Billy Royal.

Strange Art Music (see Miggins Music (UK))

Strathmere Music (see Independent Music Group)

Stratsong (see Carlin Music Corporation)

Strictly Confidential UK
Unit 1 , 3rd Floor, Front building,, 148-150 Curtain Road, London, EC2A 3AR **t** 0207 033 3673 **e** jo.hillier@strictly-confidential.net **w** strictly-confidential.net 📇 GM: Jo Hillier.

Structure Music PO Box 26273, London, W3 6FN
t 0870 207 7720 **f** 0870 208 8820
e sound@structure.co.uk **w** structure.co.uk 📇 Contact: Olly Groves.

Sublime Music Publishing 77 Preston Drove, Brighton, East Sussex, BN1 6LD
t 01273 236 300 or 07774 133 134
e info@sublimemusic.co.uk **w** sublimemusic.co.uk 📇 MD: Patrick Spinks.

Suburban Base Music (see Bryan Morrison Music)

Success Music (see Kassner Associated Publishers Ltd)

Sugar Bottom Publishing (see Independent Music Group)

Sugar Songs UK (see Chelsea Music Publishing Co)

Sugarfree Music (see Bucks Music Group Ltd)

Sugarmusic (see Universal Music Publishing Group)

Sugarstar Music Ltd IT Centre, York Science Park, York, YO10 5DG **t** 08456 448424 **f** 0709 222 8681 **e** info@sugarstar.com **w** sugarstar.com 📧 MD: Mark J. Fordyce.

Suggsongs (see Menace Music)

Suits You (see A7 Music)

Sun Star Songs (BMI) (see Independent Music Group)

Sun-Pacific Music (London) Ltd PO Box 5, Hastings, E. Sussex, TN34 lHR **t** 01424 721196 **e** aquarius.lib@clara.net 📧 MD: Gilbert Gibson.

Sunflower Music (see John Fiddy Music)

Supreme Songs Ltd (see Independent Music Group)

Survival Music PO Box 2502, Devizes, Wilts, SN10 3ZN **t** 01380 860500 **f** 01380 860596 **e** annemarie@survivalrecords.co.uk **w** survivalrecords.co.uk 📧 Dir: Anne-Marie Heighway.

Survivor Records (see Kingsway Music)

Susan May Music (see Paul Rodriguez Music Ltd)

Sutjujo Music (see Independent Music Group)

Suzuki (see International Music Publications (IMP))

Sweet 'n' Sour Songs 2-3 Fitzroy Mews, London, W1T 6DF **t** 020 7383 7767 **f** 020 7383 3020 📧 MD: John Craig.

Sweet City Ltd (see IQ Music Limited)

Sweet Glenn Music Inc (see Independent Music Group)

Sweet Karol Music Inc (see Independent Music Group)

Swiggeroux Music Ltd (see SGO Music Publishing)

Swivel Publishing (see Independent Music Group)

T H Music (see Chelsea Music Publishing Co)

Tabitha Music Ltd 39 Cordery Rd, Exeter, Devon, EX2 9DJ **t** 01392 279 914 **e** graham@tabithamusic.com **w** tabithamusic.com 📧 MD: Graham Sclater.

Tabraylah (see Menace Music)

Tafari Music (see Greensleeves Publishing Ltd)

Tairona Songs Ltd PO Box 102, London, E15 2HH **t** 020 8555 5423 **f** 020 8519 6834 **e** tairona@moksha.co.uk **w** moksha.co.uk 📧 MD: Charles Cosh.

Take It Quick Music (see Bucks Music Group Ltd)

Takes On Music (see Eaton Music Ltd)

Tales from Forever Publishing (see Independent Music Group)

Tancott Music (see Independent Music Group)

Tanspan Music (see Asterisk Music)

Tapadero Music (see Independent Music Group)

Tapestry Music (see Bucks Music Group Ltd)

Tapier Music (see Charly Publishing Ltd)

Tarantula Productions (see Bucks Music Group Ltd)

Tayborn Publishing (see Music Exchange (Manchester) Ltd)

TBM International (see Independent Music Group)

TCB Music (see Independent Music Group)

TCR Music (see Westbury Music Ltd)

Teleny Music (see Miriamusic)

Television Music (see EMI Music Publishing)

Tema International 151 Nork Way, Banstead, Surrey, SM7 1HR **t** 01737 219607 **f** 08717 151236 **e** music@tema-intl.demon.co.uk **w** temadance.com 📧 A&R Manager: Andrew James.

Terry Wayne Songs (see Asterisk Music)

Texas Red Songs (see Independent Music Group)

TGM Hammer (see Bucks Music Group Ltd)

Thames Music 445 Russell Court, Woburn Place, London, WC1H 0NJ **t** 020 7837 6240 **f** 020 7833 4043 📧 MD: C W Adams.

Thank You Music (see Kingsway Music)

Third Tier Music (see Catalyst Music Publishing Ltd)

Third World (see Paul Rodriguez Music Ltd)

Thomas & Taylor Music Works (see Independent Music Group)

Thompson Station Music (see Independent Music Group)

Three 4 Music (see Bucks Music Group Ltd)

Throat Music (see Warner/Chappell Music Ltd)

Thrust Magnum Inc (see Bucks Music Group Ltd)

Thumpin' Publishing (see Independent Music Group)

Tic-Toc Music (UK) Ltd 1 Wicklesham Farm Cottages, Faringdon, Oxon, SN7 7PJ **t** 01367 243895 **f** 01367 241858 **e** tictoc@nildram.co.uk **w** toallmylovedones.com 📧 Director of Administration: Ruth Stephens.

Tiger Trax Limited (see Independent Music Group)

Timbuk One Music (see Independent Music Group)

Timewarp (see Paul Rodriguez Music Ltd)

Tin Whistle Music (see Bucks Music Group Ltd)

Tinrib (see Paul Rodriguez Music Ltd)

Tiparm Music Publishers Inc (see Bucks Music Group Ltd)

TM Music (see Carlin Music Corporation)

TMC Publishing (see Triad Publishing)

TMR Publishing PO Box 3775, London, SE18 3QR **t** 020 8316 4690 **f** 020 8316 4690 **e** marc@wufog.freeserve.co.uk **w** Braindead-Studios.com 📧 MD: Marc Bell.

Contacts   Facebook   MySpace Twitter   YouTube

TNR Music 5B Oakleigh Mews, Whetstone, London, N20 9HQ **t** 020 8343 9971 **e** tnrmusic@thenextroom.com **w** thenextroom.com ☎ Co-MDs: Richard Burton, Bob Wainwright.

Todo Music (see Paul Rodriguez Music Ltd)

Tomake Music (see Independent Music Group)

Tomeja Music (see Independent Music Group)

Tomi Girl Music (see Independent Music Group)

Tomi Music Co (see Westbury Music Ltd)

Tonecolor Music (see Express Music (UK) Ltd)

Tony Carlisle Music (see Independent Music Group)

Tony Randolph (see Paul Rodriguez Music Ltd)

Too Hot Music Publishing Ltd (see Westbury Music Ltd)

Too Pure Music (see 4AD Music)

Torgrimson Music (see Independent Music Group)

Tosca Music (see Bucks Music Group Ltd)

Trace Elements (see Menace Music)

Trackdown Music Ickenham Manor, Ickenham, Uxbridge, Middlesex, UB10 8QT **t** 01895 672994 **e** mail@trackdownmusic.co.uk **w** trackdownmusic.co.uk ☎ Dir: Joanna Tizard.

Trailvine Publishing Ltd Unit 4C, Eggerton St, Nottingham, NG3 4GP **t** 0115 847 0899 **e** info@emitrecords.com **w** emitrecords.com ☎ MD: John Bagguley.

Trax On Wax Music Publishers Glenmundar House, Ballyman Rd, Bray, Co. Wicklow, Ireland **t** +353 86 257 6244 **e** picket@iol.ie ☎ Dir: Deke O'Brien.

Tree Music (see Sony/ATV Music Publishing)

Trekfarm Ltd 235 Regents Park Road, London, N3 3LF **t** 020 8343 1123 **e** jude@trekfarm.com **w** trekfarm.co.uk ☎ MD: Russell Spiro.

Trevor Fung (see Independent Music Group)

Treyball Music (see Notting Hill Music (UK) Ltd)

Triad Publishing PO Box 150, Chesterfield, S40 0YT **t** 0870 746 8478 **e** traid@themanagementcompany.biz **w** themanagementcompany.biz ☎ MD: Tony Hedley.

Trinity Music (see The Valentine Music Group)

Trinity Publishing Company 72 New Bond St, London, W1S 1RR **t** 020 7499 4141 **e** info@trinitymediagroup.net **w** trinitymediagroup.net ☎ Business Affairs: Peter Murray.

Triple A Publishing Ltd GMC Studio, Hollingbourne, Kent, ME17 1UQ **t** 01622 863778 **e** publishing@triple-a.uk.com **w** triple-a.uk.com ☎ CEO: Terry Armstrong.

Tristan Music Ltd (see Hornall Brothers Music Ltd)

TRO Essex Music (see The Essex Music Group)

Truck Publishing Old Stable East, Church Lane, Steventon, OX13 6SW **t** 01235 821262 **e** paul@truckrecords.com **w** thisistruck.com ☎ Dirs: Paul Bonham, Robin Bennett.

True Playaz Music Publishing (see Bucks Music Group Ltd)

Tsunami Sounds 54 Greek St, London, W1D 3DS **t** 020 7734 4488 **e** info@tsunamimusic.com **w** tsunamimusic.com ☎ Director: Ken Easter.

Tuesday Music 68 Cranston Avenue, Bexhill, East Sussex, TN39 3NN **t** 01424 215617 **e** tuesday.musicuk@virgin.net ☎ Director: Carolyne Rodgers.

Tuesday Productions (see Bucks Music Group Ltd)

Tumi Music (Editorial) Ltd 8-9 New Bond St. Place, Bath, Somerset, BA1 1BH **t** 01225 464736 **f** 01225 444870 **e** info@tumimusic.com **w** tumimusic.com ☎ MD: Mo Fini.

Tune Kel Publishing (see Charly Publishing Ltd)

TV4C Films Ltd (see SGO Music Publishing)

TVS Music (see Bucks Music Group Ltd)

Twangy Music (see Music Sales Ltd)

Two Guys Who Are Publishers (see Independent Music Group)

Two Song (see Menace Music)

Tyler Music (see The Essex Music Group)

Ubiquitunes (see Bucks Music Group Ltd)

UGR Publishing PO Box 178, Sutton, London, SM2 6XG **t** 020 8643 6403 **f** 020 8643 6403 **e** info@ugrpublishings.com **w** ugrpublishings.com ☎ Head of A&R: P Mac 07904 255244.

Ultimate Dilemma Music (see Westbury Music Ltd)

Ultramodern Music (see Bucks Music Group Ltd)

Under The Counter Music (see Westbury Music Ltd)

Unforgettable Songs (see Perfect Songs)

Unicorn Music Publishing 83 Duke Rd, Barkingside, Ilford, Essex, IG6 1NL **t** 020 8551 3624 **e** sharif@picturemusic.co.uk ☎ Contact: Sharif Ahmed Mobile: 0779 202 7146.

Union Square Music Publishing Ltd Unit 1.1, Shepherds Studios, Rockley Road, London, W14 0DA **t** 020 7471 7940 **f** 020 7471 7941 **e** info@usmpublishing.co.uk **w** usmpublishing.co.uk ☎ General Manager: Jonathan Kyte +44 (0) 20 7471 7940.

Unique Publishing (see Bucks Music Group Ltd)

Unit 11 Publishing Ltd (see Independent Music Group)

United Music GBMH (see Independent Music Group)

United Music Publishers Ltd 33 Lea Rd, Waltham Abbey, Essex, EN9 1ES **t** 01992 703110 **f** 01992 703189 **e** info@ump.co.uk **w** ump.co.uk ☎ MD: Shirley Ranger.

📇 Contacts   📘 Facebook   📹 MySpace   🇹 Twitter   ▶️ YouTube

United Songwriters Music (see International Songwriters' Music)

Universal Edition (London) 48 Gt Marlborough St, London, W1F 7BB **t** 020 7292 9166 **f** 020 7292 9173 **e** connell@universaledition.com **w** universaledition.com 📇 Sales/Mktng Mgr: Adrian Connell.

UNIVERSAL MUSIC PUBLISHING GROUP

UNIVERSAL MUSIC
PUBLISHING GROUP

20 Fulham Broadway, London, SW6 1AH **t** 020 7835 5200 **f** 020 7835 5375 **e** firstname.lastname@umusic.com **w** universalmusicpublishing.com 📇 President of Europe & UK: Paul Connolly. VP, Finance & Administration, Europe: Simon Baker. VP, International: Kim Frankiewicz. Deputy Managing Director: Mike McCormack. Director of Legal & Business Affairs, UK: Sarah Levin. UK Commercial Finance Director: Rob Morris. Head of UK Film, TV & Media: Barbara Zamoyska. Executive Vice President, International: Andrew Jenkins. Head of A&R: Caroline Elleray. Director of Legal & Business Affairs, International: Jackie Alway. VP Business Development, Europe: Simon Mortimer.

Universal Music Publishing Group Manchester First Floor, 62 Bridge St, Manchester, M3 3BW **t** 0161 838 9180 **f** 0161 838 9189 **e** caroline.elleray@umusic.com 📇 Contact: Caroline Elleray.

Universal Publishing Production Music 20 Fulham Broadway, London, SW6 1AH **t** 020 7835 5300 **f** 020 7835 5318 **e** firstname.lastname@umusic.com **w** unippm.co.uk 📇 General Manager and Head of Sales & Marketing: Duncan Schwier or Farah Hasan.

Uplifted Music Publishing 125 Park Rd, Stretford, Manchester, M32 8ED **t** 07931 943226 **e** djsoundgarden@hotmail.com 📇 General Manager: Mark Wheavill.

Upright Songs (see Independent Music Group)

Urban Angel Music Publishing Ltd 1st Floor, 126 Bloomfield Avenue, Belfast, BT5 5AE **t** 028 9046 0846 **e** info@urbanangelmusic.com **w** urbanangelmusic.co.uk 📇 Artistic Director: Mark McAllister.

Urban Influence UK Ltd 118 Caswell Close, Farnborough, Hants, GU14 8TF **t** 01252 521 892 or 07703 729 953 **f** 01252 404 043 **e** julianwhite@urban-influence.co.uk **w** myspace.com/urbaninfluence1 📇 MD: Julian White.

Utopia Publishing Utopia Village, 7 Chalcot Rd, London, NW1 8LH **t** 020 7586 3434 **f** 020 7586 3438 **e** utopiarec@aol.com 📇 MD: Phil Wainman.

The Valentine Music Group 26 Litchfield Street, London, WC2H 9TZ **t** 020 7240 1628 **f** 020 7497 9242 **e** pat@valentinemusic.co.uk 📇 MD: John Nice.

Valliant Publishing (see Charly Publishing Ltd)

Value Added Tunes (see Independent Music Group)

Van Steene Music Publishing 23 Anthony Rd, Borehamwood, Hertfordshire, WD6 4NF **t** 07956 211818 **e** guyvansteene@ntlworld.com 📇 MD: Guy Van Steene.

Vanderbeek & Imrie Ltd 15 Marvig, Lochs, Isle Of Lewis, Scotland, HS2 9QP **t** 01851 880216 **f** 01851 880216 **e** mapamundi@aol.com 📇 MD: M Imrie.

Vanessa Music Co 35 Tower Way, Dunkeswell, Devon, EX14 4XH **t** 01404 891598 📇 MD: Don Todd MBE.

Vanwarmer Music (see Independent Music Group)

Vaughan Williams Memorial Library (Sound Archive) Cecil Sharp House, 2 Regent's Park Rd, Camden, London, NW1 7AY **t** 020 7485 2206 **f** 020 7284 0534 **e** info@efdss.org **w** efdss.org 📇 Library Director: Malcolm Taylor 020 7241 8959.

Vector Music (see Independent Music Group)

Veltone Music (see Independent Music Group)

Verge Music (see Asterisk Music)

Veronica Music (see Music Sales Ltd)

Verulam Music (see Bocu Music Ltd)

Vicki Music (see Carlin Music Corporation)

Victoria Kay Music (see Independent Music Group)

Vidor Publications (see Independent Music Group)

Ville de Beest (see Asterisk Music)

Vince Barranco Music (see Independent Music Group)

VIP Music **e** rob@vip-24.com 📇 Contact: 0116 2771133.

Virgin Music (see EMI Music Publishing)

Visual Music Publishing West House, Forthaven, Shoreham-by-Sea, W. Sussex, BN43 5HY **t** 01273 453 422 **f** 01273 452 914 **e** richard@longman-records.com **w** richard-durrant.com 📇 Director: Richard Durrant.

Vitamin V Music 1 Sekforde St, London, EC1R OBE **t** 020 7075 6080 **f** 020 7075 6081 **e** firstname@vitaminv.tv 📇 Dir: Les Mear.

VLS Music Inc (see Independent Music Group)

W Bessel, London (see Breitkopf & Hartel)

W.A.M. Music Ltd. (see Broadley Music (Int) Ltd)

Walden Creek Music (see Independent Music Group)

Walk on the Wild Side 8 Deronda Road, London, SE24 9BG **t** 020 8674 7990 **f** 020 8671 5548 📇 MD: Dave Massey 07775 806288.

🔲 Contacts   📘 Facebook   💱 MySpace   📧 Twitter   ▶️ YouTube

Wall Of Sound Music
Unit 24 Farm Lane Trading Centre, 101 Farm Lane, London,
SW6 1QJ **t** 020 7471 2786 **f** 020 7471 2774
e info@wallofsound.net **w** wallofsound.net
📘 facebook.com/wosound
💱 myspace.com/wearewallofsound
📧 twitter.com/15wallofsound
▶️ youtube.com/user/WallofSoundRecording
🔲 Contact: Ami Yamauchi.

Walter Neal Music (see Asterisk Music)

Wardlaw Banks Ltd Park House, 111 Uxbridge Rd,
London, W5 5LB **t** 0845 299 0150 **f** 020 7117 3171
e info@wardlawbanks.com **w** wardlawbanks.com
💱 myspace.com/wardlawbanks 🔲 Director: Stanley Banks
07852 320736.

Wardo Music (see Bucks Music Group Ltd)

Wardour Music (see Express Music (UK) Ltd)

Warner/Chappell Music International (see
Warner/Chappell Music Ltd)

WARNER/CHAPPELL MUSIC LTD

The Warner Building, 28 Kensington Church St, London,
W8 4EP **t** 020 7938 0000 **f** 020 7368 2777
e firstname.surname@warnerchappell.com
w warnerchappell.com 🔲 MD: Richard Manners. Exc Asst to
MD: Rudo Shoniwa. SVP Intl Legal & Bus Affairs: Jane Dyball.
Regional Finance Director: Mike Lavin. Creative Director: Mike
Sault. Snr A&R Mgr: David Donald. A&R Mgr: Phil Christie.
A&R Mgr Standard Repetoire: Caroline Underwood. A&R Mgr
Writers & Producers: Jane Bell. A&R Scout: Ryan Farley.
Head of Film & TV (WEA/W/CM): Jim Reid. Mgr Film &
TV: Tom Foster. Mgr Film & TV: Pascale Khalaf. Head of
Business Affairs: Mark Waring. Financial Controller: Tom
Swayne. Worldwide Head of Administration: Steve Clark.
Head of UK Administration: Barry McKee. Worldwide
Copyright Mgr: Indi Chawla. Mgr Human Resources: Natalie
Longden. **Please note that Royalties and Copyright
Administration operate from Griffin House, 161
Hammersmith Road, London W6 8BS. t 020 8563 5800.
f 020 8563 5801.**

Water House Music (see Greensleeves Publishing Ltd)

Water Music Productions **t** 01962 760389
e splash@watermusic.co.uk 🔲 Producer: Tessa Lawlor.

Websongs The Troupe Studio, 106 Thetford Rd,
New Malden, Surrey, KT3 5DZ **t** 020 8949 0928
f 020 8605 0238 **e** kip@websongs.co.uk **w** websongs.co.uk
🔲 MD: Kip Trevor.

Westbury Music Ltd Suite B, 2 Tunstall Rd, London,
SW9 8DA **t** 020 7733 5400 **f** 020 7733 4449
e info@westburymusic.net **w** westburymusic.net 🔲 General
Manager: Paulette Long.

Westminster Music (see The Essex Music Group)

WGS Music (see Bardic Edition)

Whacker Music (see Independent Music Group)

Whispering Wings Music (see Independent Music
Group)

White Noise The Motor Museum, 1 Hesketh Street,
Liverpool, L17 8XJ **t** 0151 222 2760
e office@whitenoiseuk.com **w** whitenoiseuk.com 🔲 Label
Manager: Eric Mackay.

Whitman (see Eaton Music Ltd)

Whole Earth Music (see Independent Music Group)

Wiiija Music (see 4AD Music)

Wild Bouquet Music (see Independent Music Group)

Wildwood Music (see The Essex Music Group)

Willow Songs Ltd 39 High St, Harrold, Bedford,
MK43 7DA **t** 01234 720785 **f** 01234 720785
e kevin@willowsongs.com **w** willowsongs.com 🔲 Managing
Director: Kevin White.

Wilson Editions Magnus House, 8 Ashfield Rd, Cheadle,
Cheshire, SK8 1BB **t** 0161 491 6655 **f** 0161 491 6688
e dimus@aol.com **w** dimusic.co.uk 🔲 MD: Alan Wilson.

Windfall (see Bucks Music Group Ltd)

Window Music (see Independent Music Group)

Bug Music (London) (see P&P Songs Ltd)

Wintrup Songs Ltd 31 Buckingham St, Brighton,
East Sussex, BN1 3LT **t** 01273 880439
e allan@allanmcgowan.com 🔲 Contact: Allan McGowan.

Winwood Music Unit 7 Fieldside Farm, Quainton, Bucks,
HP22 4DQ **t** 01296 655777 **f** 01296 655778
e sales@winwoodmusic.com **w** winwoodmusic.com
🔲 MD: Eric Wilson.

Wipe Out Music PO Box 1NW, Newcastle-Upon-Tyne,
NE99 1NW **t** 0191 266 3802 **f** 0191 266 6073
e johnesplen@btconnect.com **w** wipeoutmusic.com
🔲 Manager: John Esplen.

The Wire 23 Jack's Pl, 6 Corbet Pl, London, E1 6NN
t 020 7422 5010 **f** 020 7422 5011 **e** listings@thewire.co.uk
w thewire.co.uk 📘 facebook.com/The.Wire.Magazine
📧 twitter.com/thewiremagazine 🔲 Publisher: Tony
Herrington.

WOMAD Music Ltd Box Mill, Mill Lane, Box, Wiltshire,
SN13 8PL **t** 01225 743188 **f** 01225 744369
e publishing@realworld.co.uk **w** realworld.co.uk/publishing
🔲 Publisher: Rob Bozas.

Wooden (see Bucks Music Group Ltd)

Woody Guthrie Publications (see Bucks Music
Group Ltd)

Work of Art Productions Ltd (see Independent
Music Group)

World Music Press (see Lindsay Music)

WW Music (see Paul Rodriguez Music Ltd)

WW Norton (see Peters Edition)

Wyze Music PO Box 847, Camberley, Surrey, GU15 3ZZ
t 01276 671441 f 01276 684460 e info@wyze.com
w wyze.com MD: Kate Ross.

Yancey Music (see Asterisk Music)

Yard Dog Music (see Independent Music Group)

Year Zero Music (see Bucks Music Group Ltd)

Yell Music PO Box 46301, London, W5 3UX
t 020 8579 8300 e jana.yell@yellmusic.com
w yellmusic.com MD: Jana Yell 07779 852 418.

Yergh Entertainment Group London
t 020 7193 0134 e antony@yergh.com w yergh.com
Contact: Antony Meola.

Yesterday's Music (see Multiplay Music)

Yok Music (see Bucks Music Group Ltd)

Young Beau Music (see Independent Music Group)

Young Man Moving (see Independent Music Group)

Zagora Editions (see Independent Music Group)

Zamalama Music (see Independent Music Group)

Zane Music 162 Castle Hill, Reading, Berkshire, RG1 7RP
t 0118 957 4567 f 0118 956 1261
e info@zaneproductions.demon.co.uk w zanerecords.com
Contact: Peter Thompson.

Zest Music - Zest Songs 91 Manor Rd South,
Hinchley Wood, Esher, KT10 0QB t 020 8398 4144
f 020 8398 4244 e steve@zestmusic.com
w zestmusic.com Chief Exec: Steve Weltman.

Zok Music (see Bucks Music Group Ltd)

Zonic Music (see Creole Music Ltd)

Zorch Music (see Nervous Publishing)

Sheet Music Suppliers

A&C Black Howard Road, Eaton Socon, Cambridgeshire,
PE19 8EZ t 01480 212666 f 01480 405014
e custser@acblack.com Educational Support Mgr: Hilary While.

Alker & Askem Arrangements and Transcriptions The Coach House, Market Sq, Bicester,
Oxon, OX26 6AG t 01869 250647 f 01869 321552
e aaa@groovecompany.co.uk w aaarrangements.co.uk
MD: Martin Alker.

Barnes Music Engraving Ltd Kinrara, Kintessack,
Forres, Moray, IV36 2TG t 01309 641 621 f 01309 641 622
e katie@barnes.co.uk Manager: Katie Johnston.

Chappell of Bond Street 152-160 Wardour Street,
London, W1F 8YA t 020 7432 4400 f 020 7432 4410
e enquiries@chappellofbondstreet.com
w chappellofbondstreet.co.uk Mgr: Mr N Hill.

Jazzwise 2B Gleneagle Mews, Ambleside Avenue,
London, SW16 6AE t 020 8769 7725 f 020 8677 7128
e admin@jazzwise.com w jazzwise.com MD: Charles Alexander.

Alfred A Kalmus/Universal Edition (London)
48 Gt Marlborough St, London, W1F 7BB t 020 7437 5203
f 020 7437 6115 e andrew.knowles@uemusic.co.uk
Sales Promo Mgr: Andrew Knowles.

London Orchestrations (c/o Jazzwise)

Mel Bay Music Ltd Office 512 Fortis House,
160 London Rd, Barking, Essex, IG11 8BB t 020 8214 1222
f 020 8214 1328 e salesUK@melbay.com w melbay.com
facebook.com/pages/Mel-Bay-Publications-Inc/60150101888 myspace.com/melbaypublicationsinc
twitter.com/MelBayMusic
youtube.com/melbaypublications Managing
Director: Chris Statham 020 8214 1022.

Meriden Music (Classical) The Studio Barn,
Silverwood House, Woolaston, Gloucestershire, GL15 6PJ
t 01594 529026 f 01594 529027
e info@meridenmusic.co.uk w meridenmusic.co.uk
Contact: The Secretary.

Music Exchange (Manchester) Ltd Claverton Rd,
Wythenshawe, Greater Manchester, M23 9ZA
t 0161 946 1234 f 0161 946 1195 e sales@music-exchange.co.uk w musicx.co.uk Director: Gerald Burns.

Music Exchange (Manchester) Ltd
Mail Order Dept., Claverton Rd, Wythenshawe, Manchester,
M23 9ZA t 0161 946 9301 f 0161 946 1195 e mail@music-exchange.co.uk w music-exchange.co.uk Mail Order
Department Manager: Martin Hutchinson.

Musicroom.com 14-15 Berners Street, London,
W1T 3LJ t 020 7612 7400 f 020 7836 4810
e info@musicroom.com w musicroom.com Dir, Internet
Operations: Tomas Wise.

Providence Music 1 St Georges Rd, Bristol, BS1 5UL
t 0117 927 6536 f 0117 927 6680
e shop@providencemusic.co.uk w providencemusic.co.uk
Manager: Ruth Cooper.

RSCM Music Direct c/o Norwich Books and Music,
St Mary's Works, St Mary's Plain, Norwich, NR3 3BH
t 0845 021 7726 f 0845 021 8826
e musicdirect@rscm.com w rscm.com Sales: Mr Matthew
Wright 01603 612914 ext 206.

sheetmusicdirect.com 14-15 Berners St, London,
W1T 3LJ t 020 7612 7400 f 020 7612 7545
e info@sheetmusicdirect.com w sheetmusicdirect.com
Dir. Internet Operations: Tomas Wise.

Stanza Music 11 Victor Rd, Harrow, Middlesex, HA2 6PT
t 020 8863 2717 f 020 8863 8685 e bill.ashton@virgin.net
w nyjo.org.uk Dir: Bill Ashton.

United Music Publishers 42 Rivington Street,
London, EC2A 3BN t 020 7729 4700 f 020 7739 6549
e info@ump.co.uk w ump.co.uk Mktng Mgr: James Perkins.

Publishers: Production Music

Production Music

2b Media Services Hill View, 93 Pointout Rd, Bassett, Southampton, Hampshire, SO16 7DL **t** 023 8070 1682 **e** info@2b-media.co.uk **w** 2b-media.co.uk ▣ myspace.com/colinwillshermusic ▣ twitter.com/2bMedia ▣ Composer & Creative Director: Colin Willsher.

Adage Music Keep Hill Lodge, Warren Wood Drive, High Wycombe, Bucks, HP11 1DY **t** 07973 295 113 **e** dobs@adagemusic.co.uk **w** adagemusic.com ▣ MD: Dobs Vye.

Adelphoi Music Ltd 26 Litchfield St, Covent Garden, London, WC2H 9TZ **t** 020 7240 7250 **f** 020 7240 7260 **e** info@adelphoimusic.com **w** adelphoimusic.com 🅕 facebook.com/home.php?#/pages/Adelphoi-Music-Ltd/84538267265?ref=ts ▣ twitter.com/AdelphoiMusic ▣ youtube.com/AdelphoiMusic ▣ Hd, Product'n & Bus. Dev.: Paul Reynolds.

J Albert & Son (UK) Ltd Unit 29, Cygnus Business Centre, Dalmeyer Road, London, NW10 2XA **t** 020 8830 0330 **f** 020 8830 0220 **e** james@alberts.co.uk **w** albertmusic.co.uk ▣ Head of A&R: James Cassidy.

Arcadia Production Music (UK) Greenlands, Payhembury, Devon, EX14 3HY **t** 01404 841601 **f** 01404 841687 **e** admin@arcadiamusic.tv **w** arcadiamusic.tv ▣ Prop: John Brett.

Arclite Studios The Grove Music Studios, Unit 10, Latimer Ind. Estate, Latimer Rd, London, W10 6RQ **t** 020 8964 9047 **e** Info@arcliteproductions.com **w** arcliteproductions.com ▣ Studio Mgrs: Alan Bleay, Laurie Jenkins.

Arketek Management Galway, Ireland **e** info@arketek.com **w** arketek.com ▣ myspace.com/arketek ▣ youtube.com/user/ArketekMusic ▣ Contact: Biggley.

David Arnold Music Ltd Unit 9, Dry Drayton Industries, Dry Drayton, Cambridge, CB3 8AT **t** 01954 212020 **f** 01954 212222 **e** alex@davidarnoldmusic.com **w** davidarnoldmusic.com

The Bar Chord 53 Ingelow Road, Clapham, London, SW8 3PZ **t** 020 7622 9010 **e** James@thebarchord.com **w** thebarchord.com ▣ Dir: James Mcilwraith.

Barefoot Communications 24 Coronet Street, London, N1 6HD **t** 020 7613 4697 **f** 020 7729 6613 **e** alex@barefootuk.co.uk **w** barefootuk.co.uk ▣ Dir: Alex Gover.

Beatsuite.com Music Library Suite 45, 7-15 Pink Lane, Newcastle, Tyne & Wear, NE1 5DW **t** 0845 094 1512 **e** info@beatsuite.com **w** beatsuite.com ▣ Marketing Manager: Mark Malekpour.

Beetroot Music Newlands House, 40 Berners St, London, W1T 3NA **t** 020 7255 2408 **e** tish@beetrootmusic.com **w** beetrootmusic.com ▣ Co MD: Tish Lord.

Big George and Sons PO Box 7094, Kiln Farm, MK11 1LL **t** 01908 566 453 **e** big.george@btinternet.com **w** biggeorge.co.uk ▣ Manager: Big George Webley.

Blossom Audiomedia Station Rd, Blaina, Gwent, NP13 3PW **t** 01495 290 960 **e** info@blossomstudio.co.uk **w** blossomstudio.co.uk ▣ Proprietor & Engineer: Noel Watson 07932 377 109.

BOB Ltd 29 Gloucester Place, London, W1U 8HX **t** 020 7580 9373 **f** 020 7580 9375 **e** boblimited@aol.com ▣ Dir: Alex White.

Boom! Music Ltd 16 Blackwood Close, West Byfleet, Surrey, KT14 6PP **t** 01932 336212 **e** Phil@boommusic.tv **w** boommusic.tv ▣ MD: Phil Binding.

Boosey Media Aldwych House, 71-91 Aldwych, London, WC2B 4HN **t** 020 7054 7200 **f** 020 7054 7293 **e** booseymedia@boosey.com **w** booseymedia.com ▣ Media Manager: Ann Dawson.

Br1 Productions 30 Highland Rd, Bromley, BR1 4AD **t** 07802 723124 **e** alan@br1productions.co.uk **w** br1productions.co.uk ▣ Producer: Alan Little 020 8249 9683.

Burning Petals Production Music The Studio, Homefield Court, Marston Magna, BA22 8DJ **t** 01935 851664 **e** enquiries@burning-petals.com **w** burning-petals.com ▣ Managing Director: Richard Jay.

Buzz-erk Music Studio Two, Chocolate Factory 2, 4 Coburg Road, London, N22 6UJ **e** info@buzz-erk.com **w** buzz-erk.com ▣ Director: Niraj Chag.

Caleche Studios 175 Roundhay Road, Leeds, LS8 5AN **t** 0113 219 4941 **f** 0113 249 4941 **e** calechestudios@ntlworld.com ▣ MD: Leslie Coleman.

Candle Music Ltd 44 Southern Row, London, W10 5AN **t** 020 8960 0111 **f** 020 8968 7008 **e** tony@candle.org.uk **w** candle.org.uk ▣ myspace.com/candlemusicuk ▣ twitter.com/CandleMusic ▣ youtube.com/CandleMusicLondon ▣ MD: Tony Satchell 07860 912 192.

Caritas Media Music (inc Caritas Music Library) Achmore, Moss Rd, Ullapool, Ross and Cromarty, IV26 2TF **t** 01854 612938 **f** 01854 612938 **e** media@caritas-music.co.uk **w** caritas-music.co.uk ▣ Publishing Manager: Katharine Douglas.

Century Media Corp **t** 07866 523691 **e** k@centurymediacorp.com **w** centurymediacorp.com ▣ Contact: KayCee.

Coda Recording C/O 41, Wren Wood, Welwyn Garden City, AL7 1QF **t** 01707 331771 **e** coda@coda-uk.co.uk **w** coda-uk.co.uk ▣ MD/Arranger, Composer, Keyboards: Colin Frechter.

Coolhunter Music 35 Steeds Rd, London, N10 1JB **t** 020 8883 8848 **e** jonathan@coolhunter.us or Raffaella@coolhunter.us **w** coolhunter.us ▣ Dir: Raffaella Golinucci or Jonathan Noyce.

📧 Contacts   📘 Facebook   🔲 MySpace   🐦 Twitter   ▶️ YouTube

Crocodile Music 431 Linen Hall, 162-168 Regent St, London, W1B 5TE **t** 020 7580 0080 **f** 020 7637 0097 **e** music@crocodilemusic.com **w** crocodilemusic.com 📧 Contact: Malcolm Ironton, Ray Tattle.

Cutting Edge Group 36 King Street, London, WC2E 8JS **t** 020 7759 8555 **f** 020 7759 8549 **w** cuttingedgegroup.com 📧 Managing Director: Phil Hope.

CYP The Fairway, Bush Fair, Harlow, Essex, CM18 6LY **t** 01279 444707 **f** 01279 445570 **e** sales@cypmusic.co.uk **w** kidsmusic.co.uk 📧 Sales & Marketing Director: John Bassett.

Dalishni Music 19 Market St, Castle Donington, Derby, DE74 2JB **t** 01332 810101 **f** 01332 850123 **e** Nira@Dalishni.com **w** Dalishni.com 🔲 myspace.com/Dalishni 🐦 twitter.com/Dalishni 📧 Senior Partner: Nira Amba.

David Beard Music Production 176 Sandbed Lane, Belper, Derbyshire, DE56 0SN **t** 01773 824340 **e** info@davidbeardmusic.com **w** davidbeardmusic.com 📧 MD: David Beard 07815 573121.

Deep East Music Ltd 4th Floor, 189 Wardour St, London, W1F 8ZD **t** 020 7734 6002 **e** ciaran@deepeastmusic.com **w** deepeastmusic.com 🐦 twitter.com/DeepEastMusic 📧 Music Director: Ciaran McNeaney 07810 365241.

delicious digital Suite GB, 39-40 Warple Way, Acton, London, W3 0RG **t** 020 8749 7272 **f** 020 8749 7474 **e** info@deliciousdigital.com **w** deliciousdigital.com 📧 Dirs: Ollie Raphael, Ed Moris.

Dreamscape Music 36 Eastcastle Street, London, W1W 8DP **t** 020 7631 1799 **f** 020 7631 1720 **e** lester@lesterbarnes.com **w** lesterbarnes.com 📧 Composer: Lester Barnes 07767 771 157.

ESIP Ltd P.O. Box 4702, Summerholme, Henley-on-Thames, RG9 9AA **t** 0118 940 6812 **f** 020 8181 7411 **e** info@esip.co.uk **w** esip.co.uk 📧 Dir: John Ellson.

Everyday Productions 33 Mandarin Place, Grove, Oxfordshire, OX12 0QH **t** 01235 767171 **e** smi_everyday_productions@yahoo.com 📧 VP Special Proj: David Wareham.

Fexx Cherry Tree St, Elsecar, South Yorkshire, RM6 6NL **t** 07931 752641 **e** adam.taylor@fexx.co.uk **w** fexx.co.uk 📧 MD: Adam Taylor.

Firebrand Management 12 Rickett St, West Brompton, London, SW6 1RU **t** 07885 282165 **e** vernfire@aol.com 📧 MD: Mark Vernon 07885 282 165.

flesh n' Blood PO Box 58238, London, N1 9GQ **t** 07712 583331 **f** 020 7837 9102 **e** colin@fleshnblood.co.uk **w** fleshnblood.co.uk 📘 facebook.com/colin.leggett 🔲 myspace.com/colinleggett 🐦 twitter.com/colindeanowise1 📧 Contact: Colin Leggett.

THE FUNKY JUNKIES MUSIC COMPANY

To Be Taken Aurally

18 Soho Sq, London, W1D 3QL **t** 020 7060 1234 **e** info@thefunkyjunkies.co.uk **w** thefunkyjunkies.co.uk 📘 facebook.com/pages/The-Funky-Junkies/73360617571 🔲 myspace.com/thefunkyjunkiesonmyspace 🐦 twitter.com/thefunkyjunkies ▶️ youtube.com/thefunkyjunkies 📧 Head Honcho: Tim Rushent 0207 060 1234. Musical Guru: Sophie Lovett. Marketing Whizz: Jackie Stuart. Deal Closer: Wendy Swinburne. A&R / Demo Geezer: Lee Bridges.

G3 Music 13 Hales Prior, Calshot Street, London, N1 9JW **t** 020 8361 2170 **f** 020 8361 2170 **e** g3music@g3music.com **w** g3music.com 📧 Creative Dir: Greg Heath.

Higher Ground Music Productions The Stables, Albury Lodge, Albury, Ware, Herts, SG11 2LH **t** 01279 776 019 **e** info@highergrounduk.com **w** highergrounduk.com 📧 Creative & Commercial Dir: Greg Newman.

HotHouse Music 1st Floor, 172a Arlington Rd, London, NW1 7HL **t** 020 7446 7446 **f** 020 7446 7448 **e** info@hot-house-music.com **w** hot-house-music.com 🔲 myspace.com/hothousemusicworldwide 📧 MDs: Becky Bentham/Karen Elliott.

HUM 31 Oval Road, London, NW1 7EA **t** 020 7482 2345 **f** 020 7482 6242 **e** firstname@hum.co.uk **w** hum.co.uk 📧 Prod: Daniel Simmons.

In Harmony Music Production 130 Cowley Road, Oxford, OX4 3TL **e** info@inharmonyproduction.com **w** inharmonyproduction.com 📧 Director: Chris Kennedy.

Instant Music 14 Moorend Crescent, Cheltenham, Gloucestershire, GL53 0EL **t** 01242 523 304 **f** 01242 523 304 **e** info@instantmusic.co.uk **w** instantmusic.co.uk 📧 MD: Martin Mitchell 07957 355 630.

Jingle Jangles The Strand, 156 Holywood Road, Belfast, Co Antrim, BT4 1NY **t** 028 9065 6769 **f** 028 9067 3771 **e** steve@jinglejangles.tv **w** jinglejangles.tv 📧 MD: Steve Martin.

Johnny Boy Records The Studio, 46 Chalk Hill, Watford, Herts, WD1 4BX **t** 01923 255389 **e** info@johnnyboyrecords.com **w** johnnyboyrecords.co.uk 📧 A&R/Production: John Ravenhall.

Carl Kingston 557 Street Lane, Leeds, West Yorkshire, LS17 6JA **t** 0113 268 7886 **f** 0113 266 0045 **e** carl@carlkingston.co.uk **w** carlkingston.co.uk 📧 Contact: Carl Kingston 07836 568888.

Publishers: Production Music

KPM Musichouse 27 Wrights Lane, London, W8 5SW
t 020 3059 3000 **f** 020 3059 2000
e elaine@kpmmusichouse.com **w** kpmmusichouse.com
✉ VP Production Music - Global Creative
Development: Elaine Van Der Schoot 020 3059 3010.

Larry Lush The Studio, 20 Holdenby Rd, Crofton Pk,
London, SE4 2DA **t** 07716 887576
e Laurence.e.p@gmail.com **w** larrylush.com
✉ Producer/Engineer/Arranger/Logic Pro
Progammer: Laurence Elliott-Potter.

Little Room Music Production 6 Crosby Rd,
West Bridgford, Nottingham, NG2 5GH
t 0115 981 6724 / 07947 173328 **e** steve@lrmp.co.uk
w lrmp.co.uk ✉ MD: Steve Phillips 07941 73328.

Living Productions 39 Tadorne Rd, Tadworth, Surrey,
KT20 5TF **t** 01737 812922 **f** 01737 812922
e Livingprods@ukgateway.net ✉ MD: Norma Camby.

London Arrangements 30 Maryland Square, London,
E15 1HE **t** 020 8221 2381
e enquiries@londonarrangements.co.uk
w londonarrangements.co.uk ✉ Prop: Stephen Robinson.

Los Angeles Post Music 165 Culver Blvd, Suite D,
Playa Del Rey, California, 90293, United States
t +1 818 501 8329 **f** +1 818 990 7661
e info@lapostmusic.com **w** lapostmusic.co.uk ✉ Sales: Tom
Borton.

Mad Hat Studios The Upper Hattons Media Centre,
The Upper Hattons, Pendeford Hall Lane,
Coven, Nr Wolverhampton, WV9 5BD **t** 01902 840440
f 01902 840448 **e** studio@madhat.co.uk **w** madhat.co.uk
✉ Dir: Claire Swan.

Made Up Music Giffords Oasthouse, Battle Rd,
Dallington, Heathfield, East Sussex, TN21 9LH
t 01323 449400 **e** info@madeupmusic.co.uk
w madeupmusic.co.uk ✉ Contact: Ray Russell, Rik Walton
+44 (0)1323 449400.

Pete Martin Productions 305 Canalot Studios,
222 Kensal Rd, London, W10 5BN **t** 020 8960 0700
f 020 8960 0762 **e** info@frontierrecordings.com
w frontierrecordings.com ✉ Dir: Pete Martin.

Mcasso Music Production 32-
34 Great Marlborough St, London, W1F 7JB
t 020 7734 3664 **f** 020 7439 2375 **e** dave@mcasso.com
w mcasso.com ✉ Producer: Mike Connaris.

Meringue Productions Ltd 37 Church St,
Twickenham, Middx, TW1 3NR **t** 020 8744 2277
f 020 8744 9333 **e** meringue@meringue.co.uk
w meringue.co.uk ✉ Dir: Lynn Earnshaw.

Metrophonic Tithebarns, Tithebarns Lane, Send, Surrey,
GU23 7LE **t** 01483 225226 **f** 01483 479606
e mail@metrophonic.com **w** metrophonic.com ✉ MD: Brian
Rawling.

Mews Productions The Hiltongrove Business Center,
Hatherley Mews, London, E17 4QP **t** 020 8520 3949
e nick@mewsproductions.com **w** mewsproductions.com
✉ Dir: Nick Michaels.

Mike Stevens Music Canalot Studios, 222 Kensal Rd,
London, W10 5BN **t** 020 8960 5069
e sue@msmusic.demon.co.uk ✉ MD: Mike Stevens.

Mix Media Productions Ltd. PO Box 4337,
Manchester, Manchester, Lancashire, M61 0BX
t 0844 561 0565 **e** kash@mixmediaproductions.com
w mixmediaproductions.com ✉ Contact: Kashief Ahmed
+44 (0) 772 9941 422.

Monster Music Management
28 Glen View Crescent, Heysham, Lancashire, LA3 2QW
t 01524 852037 **f** 01524 852037 **e** croftmc@aol.com
✉ Contact: Mike Croft.

MUMRA Ltd / Kentish Productions
71 Firs Avenue, Friern Barnet, London, N11 3NF
t 020 8361 9431 **e** aubrey@aubreynunn.com
w aubreynunn.com ✉ MD: Aubrey Nunn.

Music By Design 5th Floor, Film House, 142 Wardour St,
London, W1F 8ZU **t** 020 7434 3244 **f** 020 7434 1064
e rosa@musicbydesign.com **w** musicbydesign.com
✉ Production Manager & Music Consultant: Rosa Martinez.

Niles Productions Ltd. 34 Beaumont Rd, London,
W4 5AP **t** 020 8248 2157 **e** richard@richardniles.com
w richardniles.com ✉ Director: Richard Niles.

North Star Music Publishing Ltd PO Box 868,
West Wickham, Cambridge, CB21 4SJ **t** 01787 278256
e info@northstarmusic.co.uk **w** northstarmusic.co.uk
✉ MD: Grahame Maclean.

Offbeat Scotland 107 High St, Royal Mile, Edinburgh,
Midlothian, EH1 1SW **t** 0131 556 4882 **f** 0131 558 7019
e iain@offbeat.co.uk **w** offbeat.co.uk 📘 iain@offbeat.co.uk
🟦 myspace/offbeatscotland ▶ youtube/offbeatscotland
✉ Head Producer: Iain McKinna.

OMMusic 99 Penn Road, Hazlemere, High Wycombe,
Bucks, HP15 7NA **t** 01494 712 902 or 07960 564 568
f 01494 712 902 **e** ommusicinfo@aol.com **w** ommusic.info
✉ Dir: Liz Coffey.

Osceola Records - Attic Music 104 Devenport Rd,
London, W12 8NU **t** 020 8740 8898
e jimmythomas@btinternet.com **w** osceolarecords.com
✉ Proprietor: Jimmy Thomas.

Passport Approved 8383 Wilshire Blvd, Suite 100,
Beverly Hills, CA 90211, United States **t** 323.782.0770
f 323.782.9835 **e** brandon@passportapproved.com
w passportapproved.com ✉ Contact: Brandon Fuller.

Peacock Productions Ltd 34 Percy St, London,
W1T 2DG **t** 020 7580 8868 **f** 020 7323 9780
e mailus@peacockdesign.com **w** peacockdesign.com
✉ MD: Keith Peacock.

Pete Kirtley Medlars Cottage, 159 London Rd, Bagshot,
Surrey, GU19 5DH **t** 07767 607907 **e** pete@jiant.co.uk
🟦 myspace.com/petekirtley ✉ Director: Pete Kirtley.

Phatrax Productions
e phatraxproductions.googlemail.com
w phatraxproductions.googlepages.com ✉ Contact: Mark
Mills.

Pond-Life t 07973 759146 e cchesney@hotmail.com w chrischesney.co.uk ■ Dir: Chris Chesney.

Poportunity Highridge, Bath Rd, Farmborough, Nr Bath, BA2 0BG t 01761 471 089 e musicoflegend@aol.com w davidlegend.co.uk ■ Dir: David Rees 07968 434 570.

Primrose Music Publishing 1 Leitrim House, 36 Worple Rd, London, SW19 4EQ t 020 8946 7808 f 020 8946 3392 e primrose-uk@primrosemusic.com w primrosemusic.com ■ Director: R B Rogers.

Psi_Co_Acoustics The Land of Green Ginger, High Street, The Pludds, Ruardean, Gloucestershire, GL17 9TU e psi_co_acoustics@yahoo.co.uk ■ Proprietor: Rhys David 01594 861 484.

QritiKal Media Group Pinsla Park Cottage, Cardinham, Bodmin, PL30 4EH t 07802 584334 e david@qritikal.com w qritikal.co.uk ■ Dirs: David Self, Stephen Wakeling.

Radio Jingles Ltd 5 Victoria Parade, Torquay, Devon, TQ1 2BB t 01803 201 918 f 01803 400 406 e info@radiojingles.com w radiojingles.com ■ Commercial Prod: Julian Sharp.

RBM Composers Churchwood Studios, 1 Woodchurch Road, London, NW6 3PL t 020 7372 2229 f 020 7372 3339 e rbm@easynet.co.uk ■ MD: Ronnie Bond.

Really Useful Records 22 Tower St, London, WC2H 9TW t 020 7240 0880 f 020 7240 8922 e querymaster@reallyuseful.co.uk w reallyuseful.com ■ Senior Music Manager: Anna Brickles.

RELIABLE SOURCE MUSIC

67 Upper Berkeley St, London, W1H 7QX t 020 7563 7028 f 020 7563 7029 e library@reliable-source.co.uk w reliable-source.co.uk ■ myspace.com/reliablesourcemusic ■ twitter.com/ukmusiclibrary ■ MD: Dr Wayne Bickerton 0207-563-7028. MD and Chairman: Dr. Wayne Bickerton. General Manager: John Sweeney. Account Executive: Jeremy Crawford.

Repertoire Music Limited 5 Dean St, London, W1D 3RQ t 020 7287 6171 e info@repertoiremusic.com w repertoiremusic.com ■ SimonRepertoire ■ Director: Simon James.

Ricall Limited First Floor, 14 Buckingham Palace Road, London, SW1W 0QP t 020 7592 1710 f 020 7592 1713 e mail@ricall.com w ricall.com ■ Founder & CEO: Richard Corbett.

Savin Productions 19 Woodlea Drive, Solihull, Birmingham, West Midlands, B91 1PG t 0121 240 1100 f 0121 240 4042 e info@savinproductions.com w savinproductions.com ■ Prop: Brian Savin.

SBI Global Ltd 2 Norton Rd, Morecambe, Lancashire, LA3 1HA t 020 3239 8581 e keith@sbiglobal.com w sbiglobal.com ■ GM: Keith Page.

Shake Up Music Ickenham Manor, Ickenham, Uxbridge, Middlesex, UB10 8QT t 01895 672994 e mail@shakeupmusic.co.uk ■ Director: Joanna Tizard.

Signia Music - Signia Productions 44 Edith Rd, London, W14 9BB t 020 7371 2137 e dee@signiamusic.com w signiamusic.com ■ MD: Dee Harrington.

Slave Productions (UK) PO Box 200, South Shore, Blackpool, Lancs, FY1 6GR e sploj3@yahoo.co.uk ■ Creative Director: Rob Powell.

Solomon Productions 25a Chesterfield Road, Chiswick, London, W4 3HQ t 07949 507 018 e mail@solomonproductions.com ■ Dir: Sue Ballingall.

Somethin' Else Sound Direction Unit 1-4, 1A Old Nichol Street, London, E2 7HR t 020 7613 3211 f 020 7739 9799 e info@somethin-else.com w somethin-else.com ■ Dir: Steve Ackerman.

Soulem Productions The Cabin Studios, 24a Coleridge Rd, Crouch End, London, N8 8ED t 07906 172455 e soulemproductions@yahoo.co.uk w soulemproductions.com ■ soulem prods ■ myspace.com/soulemsongs ■ twitter.com/soulem ■ youtube.com/user/soulemprods ■ Music Producer, manager: Mathieu Karsenti 020 8340 9145.

Soundscape Music & Sounddesign Emmaweg 59, Kortenhoef, 1241 LH, Netherlands t +31 629 513 072 e tina@soundscape.nl w soundscape.nl ■ Producer: Tina Rutjes.

Space City Productions 77 Blythe Rd, London, W14 0HP t 020 7371 4000 f 020 7371 4001 e info@spacecity.co.uk w spacecity.co.uk ■ MD: Claire Rimmer.

Sticky Studios Great Oaks Granary, Kennel Lane, Windlesham, Surrey, GU20 6AA t 01276 479255 f 01276 479255 e admin@stickycompany.com w stickycompany.com ■ Jake Gosling ■ myspace.com/themusicproducer ■ jakegosling ■ jakegosling8 ■ MD: Jake Gosling.

Stickysongs 33 Trewince Rd, Wimbledon, London, SW20 8RD t 020 8739 0928 e stickysongs@hotmail.com w petergosling.com ■ myspace/petergosling ■ MD: Peter Gosling.

Street Level Management Ltd 1st Floor, 17 Bowater Road, Westminster Industrial Estate, Woolwich, London, SE18 5TF t 07886 260 686 e ceo@streetlevelenterprises.co.uk w streetlevelenterprises.com ■ MD: Sam Crawford.

Tom Dick and Debbie Productions 43a Botley Rd, Oxford, OX2 0BN t 01865 201564 f 01865 201935 e info@tomdickanddebbie.com w tomdickanddebbie.com ■ Director: Richard Lewis.

Tough Cookie Ltd part of Whizz Kid Entertainment Ltd, 4 Kingly Street, London, W1B 5PE **t** 020 7440 2550 **f** 020 7440 2599 **e** info@tough-cookie.co.uk **w** tough-cookie.co.uk 📇 Directors: Andy Wood, Neill Sullivan & Dave Castell 07977 248 646.

Tsunami Sounds Ltd. Muscott House, Meadrow, Godalming, Surrey, GU7 3HN **t** 01483 410100 **f** 01483 410100 **e** info@tsunami.co.uk **w** tsunami.co.uk 📇 Director: Ken Easter.

Ultimate Unit 6 Belfont Trading Estate, Mucklow Hill, Halesowen, West Midlands, B62 8DR **t** 0121 585 8001 **f** 0121 585 8003 **e** info@ultimate1.co.uk **w** ultimate1.co.uk 📇 Manager: Andy Tain.

V-The Production Library c/o Music 4 Ltd, 41-42 Berners Street, London, W1T 3NB **t** 020 7016 2010 **e** office@v-theproductionlibrary.com **w** v-theproductionlibrary.com

Visual Music West House, Forthaven, Shoreham-by-Sea, W. Sussex, BN43 5HY **t** 01273 453 422 **f** 01273 452 914 **e** richard@longman-records.com **w** richard-durrant.com 📇 Director: Richard Durrant.

Wavsub Music Penvose Cottage, Summers Street, Lostwithiel, Cornwall, PL22 0DH **t** 08700 702 265 **e** info@wavsub.com **w** wavsub.com 📇 Projects Manager: Lisa Baker.

Wesley Music Solace House, Sterling Court, Loddington, Kettering, Northants, NN14 1RZ **t** 01536 712266 **f** 01536 418211 **e** neil.heskins@wesleymusic.co.uk **w** wesleymusic.co.uk 📇 MD: Neil Heskins.

West One Music 28 Percy St, London, W1T 2DB **t** 020 7907 1500 **f** 020 7907 1510 **e** info@westonemusic.com **w** westonemusic.com 📇 GM: Edwin Cox.

Music Supervisors & Consultants

The 7 Stars 46 Charlotte Street, London, W1T 2GS **t** 020 7436 7275 **f** 020 7436 7276 **e** firstname.lastname@the7stars.co.uk **w** the7stars.co.uk 📇 Contact: Jenny Biggam.

Air-Edel Music Supervision 18 Rodmarton St, London, W1U 8BJ **t** 020 7486 6466 **f** 020 7224 0344 **e** air-edel@air-edel.co.uk 📇 Contact: Maggie Rodford & Matt Biffa.

The Alice Kendall Music Consultancy Address on request. **e** alice.kendall@mac.com **w** alicekendallmusic.com 📇 Music Supervisor: Alice Kendall.

AMI Music Library 34 Salisbury St, London, NW8 8QE **t** 020 7402 9111 **f** 020 7723 3064 **e** eliot@amimedia.co.uk **w** amimedia.co.uk 📇 MD: Eliot Cohen.

Anthem Ltd Long Ridge, Arrow Lane, Hartley Wintney, Hampshire, RG27 8LR **t** 07834 766 077 **e** info@anthemltd.co.uk **w** anthemltd.co.uk 📇 Creative Director: Jonathan Painter.

Bazza Productions 1 Chemin de la Sini, 66130 Ille-sur-Tet, France **t** +33(0)4 68 84 17 26 **e** bsguard@aol.com **w** barrieguard.com 📇 MD: Barrie Guard.

Beetroot Music Newlands House, 40 Berners St, London, W1T 3NA **t** 020 7255 2408 **e** tish@beetrootmusic.com **w** beetrootmusic.com 📇 Co MD: Tish Lord.

Belsize Music ltd 29 Manor House, 250 Marylebone Rd, London, NW1 5NP **t** 020 7723 7177 **f** 020 7262 0775 **e** belsizemusic@btconnect.com 📇 Dir: Chas Peate.

Bucks Music Group Ltd Onward House, 11 Uxbridge St, London, W8 7TQ **t** 020 7221 4275 **f** 020 7229 6893 **e** info@bucksmusicgroup.co.uk **w** bucksmusicgroup.com 📇 MD: Simon Platz.

Bulb ideas 27 Cedar House, Melliss Avenue, Richmond, TW9 4BG **t** 07810 186477 **e** bulb@bulbideas.com **w** bulbideas.com 📇 Creative Director: James Wilkinson.

Compact Collections Ltd Greenland Place, 115-123 Bayham Street, London, NW1 0AG **t** 020 7446 7420 **f** 020 7446 7424 **e** info@compactcollections.com **w** compactcollections.com 📇 Dirs: John O'Sullivan, James Sellar.

Curved Arrow 32-34 Great Marlborough St, London, W1F 7JB **t** 020 7734 3551/3664 **e** lisa@curvedarrow.co.uk **w** curvedarrow.co.uk 📇 Contact: Lisa McCaffery.

Cutting Edge Group 36 King Street, London, WC2E 8JS **t** 020 7759 8555 **f** 020 7759 8549 **w** cuttingedgegroup.com 📇 Managing Director: Phil Hope.

FKM PO Box 242, Haslemere, Surrey, GU26 6ZT **t** 01428 608 149 **e** fken10353@aol.com 📇 Chairman: Fraser Kennedy.

GMR Entertainment 1 Riverside, Manbre Road, London, W6 9WA **t** 020 8735 8336 **f** 08702 420 120 **e** davidw@gmrentertainment.com **w** gmrentertainment.com 📇 VP, Europe: David Wille.

Graphite 133 Kew Rd, Richmond, Surrey, TW9 2PN **t** 020 8948 5446 **e** info@graphitemedia.net **w** graphitemedia.net 📇 Director: Ben Turner.

Green Bandana Productions 7 Iron Bridge House, Bridge Approach, London, NW1 8BD **t** 020 7722 1081 **f** 020 7483 0028 **e** james@jameshyman.com **w** jlhmusic.com 📇 MD: James Hyman.

Hawk Media Monitoring DMS, 44-46 Scrutton Street, London, EC2A 4HH **t** 0845 055 0979 **f** 0845 055 0970 **e** amy.lecoz@dmsukltd.com **w** dmsukltd.com 📇 Dir: Amy Le Coz.

HotHouse Music 1st Floor, 172a Arlington Rd, London, NW1 7HL **t** 020 7446 7446 **f** 020 7446 7448 **e** info@hot-house-music.com **w** hot-house-music.com 📇 MDs: Becky Bentham, Karen Elliott.

Howling Monkey PO Box 60492, London, E8 9ER **t** 07917 086200 **e** ben.bleet@howlingmonkey.co.uk **w** howlingmonkey.co.uk 📇 Managing Director: Ben Bleet.

hushhush ATTACK! 8370 Wilshire Blvd, Suite 350, Beverly Hills, CA 90211, United States **t** 323 782 0770 **f** 323 782 9835 **e** joe@hushhushattack.com **w** hushhushattack.com 📇 Sr. Director of Broadcast Media & Marketing: Joe Arnold +1 323.782.0770.

Independent Media Pros 11400 Largo Dr, Savannah, Ga, 31419, USA **t** 912-659-7192 **e** jim@independentmediapros.com **w** independentmediapros.com 📇 Owner, Music-Supervisor: Jim Hughes.

Jeff Wayne Music Group The Media Village, 131-151 Great Titchfield St, London, W1W 5BB **t** 020 7724 2471 **f** 020 3178 7843 **e** info@jeffwaynemusic.com **w** jeffwaynemusic.com 📹 youtube.com/watch?v=_kDLAAmESVg 📇 Head of Search & Licensing: Paul Goodban.

Jester Song 78 Gladstone Rd, London, SW19 1QT **t** 020 8543 4056 **f** 020 8542 8225 **e** jestersong@msn.com 📇 MD: R B Rogers.

JG Consultancy 34 Burnmoor Drive, Eaglescliffe, Stockton-on-Tees, County Durham, TS16 0HZ **t** 01642 898822 **e** jgconsultantancy@gmail.com 📇 Music and Band Consultant: James Gair.

June Productions Ltd The White House, 6 Beechwood Lane, Warlingham, Surrey, CR6 9LT **t** 01883 622411 **f** 01883 622081 **e** david@mackay99.plus.com 📇 Producer: David Mackay.

JW Media Music Dolphyn Court, 10-11 Great Turnstile, London, WC1V 7JU **t** 0207 400 1460 **f** 0207 400 1470 **e** jenny@jwmediamusic.co.uk **w** jwmediamusic.com 🅜 myspace.com/jwmediamusic 📇 Production Music Manager / Music Consultant: Jenny Thornton 0207 400 1465.

Karen P Productions Ltd PO Box 52160, London, E9 7WR **t** 020 8986 8558 **e** karen@karenpproductions.com **w** karenp.co.uk 📇 Dir: Karen Pearson.

Killer Music Apartment 342, Rosden House, 372 Old St, London, EC1V 9AU **t** 07971 485609 **e** lawrence@killermusic.co.uk **w** killermusic.co.uk 📇 MD: Lawrence Millar.

Knifedge Knifedge Tower, 4 Margaret St, London, W1W 8RF **t** 020 7436 5434 **f** 020 7436 5431 **e** info@knifedge.net **w** knifedge.net 📇 Joint Managing Director: Jonathan Brigden.

Leap Music 5th Floor, 184-186 Regent St, London, W1B 5TW **t** 020 7453 4668 **f** 020 7453 4242 **e** info@leapmusic.com **w** leapmusic.com 🅜 myspace.com/leapmusicltd 🅣 twitter.com/leapmusic

Leland Music Ltd Ground floor, 60 Grafton Rd, London, NW5 3DY **t** 07961 369830 **e** abi@lelandmusic.co.uk **w** lelandmusic.co.uk 📇 MD: Abi Leland.

Liz Gallacher Music Supervision 18 Rodmarton St, London, W1U 8BJ **t** 020 7467 4488 **f** 020 7224 0344 **e** kay@cuttingedgegroup.com **w** lizg.com 📇 Music Supervisor: Liz Gallacher.

LOE Ltd LOE House, 159 Broadhurst Gardens, London, NW6 3AU **t** 020 7328 6100 **f** 020 7624 6384 **e** kato@loe.uk.net 📇 MD: Hiroshi Kato.

Dave McAleer- Music Consultant 38 Wharncliffe Gardens, London, SE25 6DQ **t** 020 8239 8464 **f** 020 8239 8464 **e** davemcaleer@blueyonder.co.uk 📇 Music Consultant: Dave McAleer.

Millbrand Media Licensing PO Box 357, Middlesbrough, TS1 4WZ **t** 01642 806795 **f** 01642 351962 **e** info@millbrand.com **w** millbrand.com 📘 facebook.com/millbrand 🅜 myspace.com/millbrand 📇 Director: Paul Mooney 07724 051117.

Musicalities Limited Snows Ride Farm, Snows Ride, Windlesham, Surrey, GU20 6LA **t** 01276 474 181 **f** 01276 452 227 **e** info@musicalities.co.uk **w** musicalities.co.uk 📇 Founder & CEO: Ivan Chandler.

Musicare 16 Thorpewood Avenue, London, SE26 4BX **t** 020 8699 1245 **f** 020 8291 5584 **e** peterfilleul@me.com 📇 MD: Peter Filleul & Sian Wynne.

Musicians Benevolent Fund 17-11 Britannia St, London, WC1X 9JS **t** 020 7239 9100 **f** 020 7713 8942 **e** info@mbf.org.uk **w** mbf.org.uk 📇 Chief Executive: David Sulkin.

NiceMan Productions (Licensing & Repertoire Mgmt) 111 Holden Rd, London, N12 7DF **t** 020 8445 8766 **e** scott@nicemanproductions.com **w** nicemanproductions.com 📇 Licensing Dir: Scott Simons.

Passport Approved 8383 Wilshire Blvd, Suite 100, Beverly Hills, CA 90211, United States **t** 323.782.0770 **f** 323.782.9835 **e** brandon@passportapproved.com **w** passportapproved.com 📇 Contact: Brandon Fuller.

Picture Music – Music Clearance & Licensing 83 Duke Rd, Barkingside, Essex, IG6 1NL **t** 020 8551 2820 **e** sharif@picturemusic.co.uk **w** picturemusic.co.uk 📇 Contact: Sharif Ahmed 07792 027146.

popmusic4synch.com 67 Upper Berkeley St, London, W1H 7QX **t** 020 7563 7028 **f** 020 7563 7029 **e** music@popmusic4synch.co.uk **w** popmusic4synch.com 📇 General Manager: John Sweeney 0207-563-7028.

The Product Exchange Ltd 68 Cranston Avenue, Bexhill On Sea, East Sussex, TN39 3NN **t** 01424 215617 **e** product.exchange@virgin.net **w** productexchange.co.uk 📇 MD: Frank Rodgers.

Real Time Information The Unit, 2 Manor Gardens, London, N7 6ER **t** 020 7561 6700 **f** 020 7561 6701 **e** hq@realtimeinfo.co.uk **w** realtimeinfo.co.uk 📇 GM: Dominic Louth.

Record Play Po Box 320, 372 Old Street, London, EC1V 9LT **t** 020 7739 0939 **f** 020 7117 3852 **e** daniel@record-play.net **w** record-play.net 📇 MD: Daniel Cross.

Record-Play Consultants Studio 203, 45-46 Charlotte Rd, London, EC2A 3PD **t** 020 7739 0939 or 07753 388 275 **e** info@record-play.net **w** record-play.net 📇 Prop: Daniel Cross.

Publishers: Music Supervisors & Consultants

RED-i Solutions Ltd e info@red-i.net w red-i.net
▣ Director: Matt Bullamore.

Ricall Limited First Floor, 14 Buckingham Palace Road,
London, SW1W 0QP t 020 7592 1710 f 020 7592 1713
e mail@ricall.com w ricall.com ▣ Founder & CEO: Richard
Corbett.

Right Music Limited Old Church Cottage, Wilby,
Suffolk, IP21 5LE t 01379 388365 f 01379 384731
e kirsten@rightmusic.co.uk w rightmusic.co.uk
▣ MD: Kirsten Lane.

Seeca Music 6, Ditton Hill Rd, Surbiton, Surrey, KT6 5JD
t 020 8398 2510 f 020 8398 1970 e info@seeca.co.uk
w seeca.co.uk ▣ Dir: Louise Blair.

SMA Talent The Cottage, Church St, Fressingfield,
Suffolk, IP21 5PA t 01379 586734 / 131 f 01379 586131
e info@smatalent.com w smatalent.com ▣ MDs: Carolynne
Wyper, Olav Wyper 01379 586734.

Spark Marketing Entertainment 16 Winton Ave,
London, N11 2AT t 0870 460 5439 e mbauss@spark-
me.com w spark-me.com ▣ Executive Director: Matthias
Bauss.

Squarepeg Studio 201, Westbourne Studios,
242 Acklam Rd, London, W10 5JJ t 020 7575 3325
e info@squarepeg-uk.com w squarepeg-uk.com
▣ MD: Matt Fisher.

Stream Music 80-82 Dean St, London, W1D 3HA
t 020 7573 6600 f 020 7573 6728
e dominic.caisley@stream-worldwide.com ▣ Managing
Partner, Music: Dominic Caisley 0207 573 6565.

Sync Music Unit 4, The Candlemakers, 112 York Road,
London, SW11 3RS t 020 7924 7636 w sync-music.com

Synchronicity 28 Howard House, 161 Cleveland St,
London, W1T 6QP t 020 7388 2099
e jp@synchronicity.uk.com w synchronicity.uk.com
▣ MD: Joanna Pearson 07976 743 081.

Tonic Music Ltd Noland House, 5th Floor, 12-
13 Poland St, London, W1F 8QB t 020 7287 1077
f 020 7692 4673 e hello@tonic.fm w tonic.fm
▣ @TonicMusic ▣ Owner/Creative Director: Susan Stone.

Torchlight Music 34 Wycombe Gardens, London,
NW11 8AL t 020 8731 9858 f 020 8731 9845
e tony@torchlightmusic.com ▣ Dir: Tony Orchudesch.

Townend Music 44 Eastwick Crescent, Rickmansworth,
Herts, WD3 8YJ t 01923 720083 f 01923 710587
e townendmus@aol.com ▣ MD: Mike Townend 07974
048955.

Upfront Promotions Ltd Unit 217 Buspace Studios,
Conlan Street, London, W10 5AP t 020 7565 0050
f 020 7565 0049 e richie@upfrontpromotions.com
w upfrontpromotions.com ▣ Music Project Manager: Richie
Deeney.

Ray Williams Music Consultant The Stable Lodge,
Lime Ave, Kingwood, Henley-on-Thames, Oxon, RG9 5WB
t 01491 628 111 f 01491 629 668
e crumbsmusic@btopenworld.com w raywilliamsmusic.com
▣ MD: Ray Williams 07813 696 999.

Yes Music Ltd Unit 212, The Saga Centre,
326 Kensal Road, London, W10 5BZ t 020 8968 0111
e simon@yesmusic.co.uk w yesmusic.co.uk ▣ Dirs: Simon
Goffe, Gilles Petterson.

YouLicense.com Ben Yehuda 32, Tel Aviv, Israel
t +972 777 033 116 e kaplan@youlicense.com
w youlicense.com ▣ VP Marketing: Tomer Kaplan.

Music**Week**

Creative Advertising Solutions

Contact the Music Week advertising sales team, and guarantee
you reach the right audience at the right time

Contact:
Becky Golland on 0207 921 8365
or Archie Carmichael on 0207 921 8372

www.musicweek.com

Contacts Facebook MySpace Twitter YouTube

Retail

Retailers

3 Beat Records 5 Slater St, Liverpool, L1 4BW
t 0151 709 3355 **f** 0151 709 3707 **e** info@3beat.co.uk
w 3beat.co.uk ⊠ Shop Mgr: Pezz.

8 Ball 18 Queen St, Southwell, Notts, NG25 0AA
t 01636 813040 **f** 01636 813141 **e** info@8ball.ltd.uk
w 8ball.ltd.uk ⊠ Prop: Tim Allsopp.

A&A Music 15 Bridge St, Congleton, Cheshire,
CW12 1AS **t** 01260 280778 **f** 01260 298311
e mail@aamusic.co.uk **w** aamusic.co.uk ⊠ Owner: Alan
Farrar.

Aardvark Music Compton House, 9 Totnes Rd,
Paignton, Devon, TQ2 5BY **t** 01803 664481
f 01803 664481 **e** cj@torrerecords.freeserve.co.uk ⊠ Co-
owner: Clive Jones.

Abergavenny Music 23 Cross St, Abergavenny,
Gwent, NP7 5EW **t** 01873 853 394
e service@abergavennymusic.com
w abergavennymusic.com ⊠ Owner: James Joseph.

Acorn Music 3 Glovers Walk, Yeovil, Somerset,
BA20 1LH **t** 01935 425 503 ⊠ Owner: Chris Lowe.

Action Records 46 Church St, Preston, Lancs,
PR1 3DH **t** 01772 884 772 **f** 01772 252 255
e sales@actionrecords.co.uk **w** actionrecords.co.uk
⊠ Manager: Gordon Gibson 01772 258809.

Action Replay 24 Lake Rd, Bowness-on-Windermere,
Cumbria, LA23 3AP **t** 01539 445089
e davidsnaith@actionreplay.wanadoo.co.uk
⊠ Owner: David Snaith.

Adrians 36-38 High Street, Wickford, Essex, SS12 9AZ
t 01268 733 318 **f** 01268 764 507 **e** sales@adrians.co.uk
w adrians.co.uk ⊠ Contact: Adrian Rondeau 01268 733
319.

AG Kemble Ltd 63 Leicester Rd, Wigston, Leics.,
LE18 1NR **t** 0116 288 1557 **f** 0116 288 3949 **e** kembles-
records@btconnect.com ⊠ Owners: Paul Watkins & Fiona
Nicholls.

All Ages Records 27a Pratt St, London, NW1 0BG
t 020 7267 0393 **e** shop@allagesrecords.com
w allagesrecords.com ⊠ GM: Nick Collins.

Amazon.co.uk Patriot Court, The Grove, Slough,
SL1 1QP **t** 020 8636 9200 **f** 020 8636 9400
e info@amazon.co.uk **w** amazon.co.uk ⊠ Contact: Music
Store.

Asda Southbank, Great Wilson St, Leeds, West Yorkshire,
LS11 5AD **t** 0113 241 8470 **f** 0113 241 8785
e andrew.powell@asda.co.uk **w** asda.co.uk ⊠ Buyer
Music: Andrew Powell 0113 241 2934.

Atomic Sounds PO Box 2074, Lancing, West Sussex,
BN15 8YA **t** 01903 754341 **e** atomic1@fastnet.co.uk
w atomicsounds.co.uk ⊠ Owner: Tony Grist.

Audio Relief 3rd Floor, 39 Hatton Garden, London,
EC1N 8EH **t** 020 7138 2922 **f** 020 7138 2922
e admin@audiorelief.co.uk **w** audiorelief.co.uk
⊠ Commercial Director: Chelone Wolf.

Avalanche Records (Head Office)
63 Cockburn Street, Edinburgh, EH1 1BS **t** 0131 225 3939
f 0131 225 3939 **e** avalanche634reps@btconnect.com
w avalancherecords.co.uk ⊠ Owner: Kevin Buckle.

Avid Records 32-33 The Triangle, Bournemouth,
BH2 5SE **t** 01202 295465 **f** 01202 295465
e paul@avidrecords-uk.com **w** avidrecords-uk.com
⊠ Owner: Martin Howes.

Badlands 11 St George's Pl, Cheltenham, Glos,
GL50 3LA **t** 01242 227724 **f** 01242 227393
e mike@badlands.co.uk **w** badlands.co.uk
⊠ Manager: Mike Ward 01242 246232.

Bailey's Records 40 Bull Ring Indoor Market,
Edgbaston Street, Birmingham, West Midlands, B5 4RQ
t 0121 622 6899 **f** 0121 622 6899
w birminghamindoormarket.co.uk ⊠ Manager: David Rock.

Banquet Records 52 Eden St, Kingston-upon-
Thames, KT1 1EE **t** 020 8549 5871
e shop@banquetrecords.com **w** banquetrecords.com
⊠ Owner: Jon Tolley.

Barneys 21A Cross Keys, Market Square, St Neots,
PE19 2AR **t** 01480 406270 **f** 01480 406270
e keith.barnes2@btinternet.com ⊠ Contact: Keith Barnes.

The Basement 7 North St, Carrickfergus, Co Antrim,
BT38 7AQ **t** 028 9332 9166 **e** phil@basementni.com
w basementni.com
🄵 facebook.com/home.php#/pages/The-
Basement/83982388255 ⊠ Owner: Phil Barnhill.

Bath Compact Discs 11 Broad St, Bath, BA1 5LJ
t 01225 464766 **f** 01225 482275
e Bathcds@btinternet.com **w** bathcds.btinternet.co.uk
⊠ Co-owner: Steve Macallister.

Beatin Rhythm Records 42 Tib St, Manchester,
M4 1LA **t** 0161 834 7783 **e** music@beatinrhythm.com
w beatinrhythm.com ⊠ Dir: Tom Smith.

The Beatmuseum Block 130, Unit 4,
Nasmyth Rd South, Hillington, Glasgow, G52 4RE
t 0141 882 4445 **f** 0141 882 8563
e james@beatmuseum.com **w** beatmuseum.com
⊠ Contact: James Rennie.

Bigshot Records 53a Harpur St, Bedford, Beds.,
MK40 2SR **t** 01234 355542 **f** 01234 355542
e info@bigshotrecords.com **w** bigshotrecords.com
⊠ Manager: Hayley Syratt.

Bim Bam Records Chalfont House, Botley Rd,
Horton Heath, Eastleigh, SO50 7DN **t** 02380 600329
f 02380 600329 **e** bob@bim-bam.com **w** bim-bam.com
⊠ Owner: Bob Thomas.

Retail: Retailers

Blackwell Music 23-25 Broad St, Oxford, OX1 3AX
t 01865 333580 **f** 01865 728020
e vanessa.williams@blackwell.co.uk **w** blackwell.co.uk
✉ Music Shop Manager: Vanessa Williams 01865 333576.

Bleep.com Unit L, Spectrum House, 32-
34 Gordon House Rd, London, NW5 1LP **t** 020 7284 8350
f 020 7284 8370 **e** info@bleep.com **w** bleep.com
f facebook.com/group.php?gid=99021031130
🐦 twitter.com/BleepBit ✉ General Manager: Dan
Minchom 020 7284 8171.

Boogietimes Records 3 Old Mill Parade, Victoria Rd,
Romford, Essex, RM1 2HU **t** 01708 727029
f 01708 740424 **e** info@boogietimes-records.co.uk
w boogietimes-records.co.uk ✉ Manager: Andy James.

Borders Books, Music & Video 4th Floor,
122 Charing Cross Rd, London, WC2 0JR **t** 020 7379 7313
f 020 7836 0373 **w** bordersstores.co.uk ✉ Head
Buyer: Tom Hancock.

Bridport Music 33A South St, Bridport, Dorset,
DT6 3NY **t** 01308 425707 **f** 01308 458271
e info@bridportmusic.co.uk **w** bridportmusic.co.uk
✉ Owners: Piers & Stephanie Garner.

Catapult 100% Vinyl 22 High Street Arcade,
Cardiff, CF10 1BB **t** 029 2022 8990 **f** 029 2023 1690
e enquiries@catapult.co.uk **w** catapult.co.uk ✉ MD: Lucy
Squire 029 2034 2322.

Chalkys.com 78 High St, Banbury, Oxon, OX16 5JG
t 01295 271190 **f** 01295 262221 **e** richard@chalkys.com
w chalkys.com ✉ MD: Richard White 01295 276944.

Citysounds Ltd 5 Kirby Street, London, EC1N 8TS
t 020 7405 5454 **f** 020 7242 1863 **e** sales@city-
sounds.co.uk **w** city-sounds.co.uk ✉ Owners: Tom & Dave.

ClassicLPs.co.uk 61 Somers Rd, Malvern,
Worcestershire, WR14 1JA **t** 01684 899457
e info@classiclps.co.uk **w** classiclps.co.uk
✉ Owner: Rachel Heard.

Clerkenwell Music 27 Exmouth Market, London,
EC1R 4QL **t** 020 7833 9757
e jeremy@clerkenwellmusic.co.uk ✉ Owner: Jeremy Brill.

CODA Music 12 Bank St, The Mound, Edinburgh,
Scotland, EH1 2LN **t** 0131 622 7246 **f** 0131 622 7245
e mail@moundmusic.co.uk **w** codamusic.co.uk
🟥 myspace.co.uk/codamusicedinburgh ✉ Contact: Music
Retail & Artist Distribution.

Compact Discounts 258-260 Lavender Hill,
Battersea, London, SW11 1LJ **t** 020 7978 5560
f 020 7978 5931 **e** info@compactdiscounts.co.uk
w compactdiscounts.co.uk ✉ Dir: Mark Canavan.

Concepts 4A Framwellgate Bridge, Durham, DH1 4SJ
t 0191 383 0745 **f** 0191 383 0112 **e** dave-
murray@lineone.net **w** concepts-durham.co.uk
✉ Owner: Dave Murray.

Connect Records 18 Badger Road, Coventry,
CV3 2PU **t** 024 7626 5400 **e** info@connect-records.co.uk
w connect-records.com ✉ Manager: Matt Green.

Coolwax Music Unit 13, The Craft Centre,
Orchard Sq Shopping Centre, Sheffield, S1 2FB
t 0114 279 5878 **e** staff@coolwax.co.uk **w** coolwax.co.uk
✉ Mgr: Corey Mahoney.

Counter Culture 130 Desborough Road,
High Wycombe, Bucks, HP11 2PU **t** 01494 463 366
f 01494 463 366 **e** counterculture1@btconnect.com
✉ Owner: Cheryl Evans.

Crash Records 35 The Headrow, Leeds,
West Yorkshire, LS1 6PU **t** 0113 243 6743
f 0113 234 0421 **e** store@crashrecords.co.uk
w crashrecords.co.uk ✉ Prop: Ian De-Whytell.

Crazy Beat Records 87 Corbets Tey Rd, Upminster,
Essex, RM14 2AH **t** 01708 228678
e sales@crazybeat.co.uk **w** crazybeat.co.uk
✉ Owner: Gary Dennis.

Crucial Music Pinery Buildings, Highmoor, Wigton,
Cumbria, CA7 9LW **t** 016973 45422 **f** 016973 45422
e crucialsales@crucialmusic.co.uk **w** crucialmusic.co.uk
✉ MD: Simon James.

Cruisin' Records 132 Welling High St, Welling, Kent,
DA16 1TJ **t** 020 8304 5853 **f** 020 8304 0429
e john@cruisin-records.fsnet.co.uk ✉ Owner: John
Setford.

Dance 2 Records 9 Woodbridge Road, Guildford,
Surrey, GU1 4PU **t** 01483 451002 **f** 01483 451006
e in2dance2@hotmail.com **w** dance2.co.uk ✉ MD: Hans
Vind.

Disc-N-Tape 17 Gloucester Road, Bishopston, Bristol,
BS7 8AA **t** 0117 942 2227 **f** 0117 942 2227
e graeme@disc-n-tape.co.uk **w** disc-n-tape.co.uk
✉ Owner: Graeme Cornish.

Discount Disc 21 Percy St, Hanley, Stoke-on-Trent,
Staffs, ST1 1NA **t** 01782 266888 **f** 01782 266888
e discountdisc@talk21.com **w** discountdisc.co.uk
✉ Manager: Ian Trigg.

Diskits 7 Outram St, Sutton-in-Ashfield, Notts,
NG17 4BA **t** 01623 441413 **f** 01623 441413
e shop@diskits.co.uk **w** diskits.co.uk ✉ Partner: Mel
Vickers 01623 466220.

Disky.com 3 York Street, St. Helier, Jersey,
Channel Islands, JE2 3RQ **t** 01534 509 687
e music.online@disky.com **w** disky.com ✉ Managing
Director: Robert Bisson.

Dixons Stores Group Maylands Avenue,
Hemel Hempstead, Hertfordshire, HP2 7TG
t 0844 800 2030 **f** 01442 233218
e dave.poulter@dsgiplc.com **w** dixons.co.uk ✉ Trading
Manager: Dave Poulter.

DJdownload.com Unit 1, 237 Queenstown Rd,
London, SW11 5RY **t** 020 8133 8844 **f** 020 7924 2329
e guy@djdownload.com, justin@djdownload.com
w djdownload.com
f facebook.com/pages/DJDOWNLOADCOM/117984641
79 🟥 myspace.com/djdownload
🐦 twitter.com/djdownload ✉ Managing Director, Sales &
Marketing Manager: Guy Osborne, Justin Pearse.

Dolphin Discs 56 Moore St, Dublin 1, Ireland
t +353 1 872 9364 **f** +353 1 872 0405 **e** irishmus@iol.ie
w irelandcd.com 🅑 GM: Paul Heffernan.

Dub Vendor Records 17 Davids Rd, London,
SE23 3EP **t** 020 8291 6253 **f** 020 8291 1097
e distribution@dubvendor.co.uk **w** dubvendor.co.uk
🅑 MD: John MacGillivray.

Earwaves Records 9/11 Paton St, Piccadilly,
Manchester, M1 2BA **t** 0161 236 4022 **f** 0161 237 5932
e info@earwavesrecords.co.uk **w** earwavesrecords.co.uk
🅑 Proprietor: Alan Lacy.

Eastern Bloc Records 5-6 Central Buildings,
Oldham Street, Manchester, M1 1JQ **t** 0161 228 6432
f 0161 228 6728 **e** info@easternblocrecords.co.uk
w easternblocrecords.co.uk 🅑 Mgr: John Berry.

Elkin Music 31 Exchange St, Norwich, NR2 1DP
t 01603 666332 **f** 01603 666332
e elkinmusic@hotmail.co.uk **w** elkinmusic.co.uk
🅑 Partner: Richard Elkin.

eMusic Europe 25-26 Poland St, London, W1F 8QN
t 020 7084 5358 **f** 020 7067 9731
e mmilne@emusic.com/ ksattar@emusic.com
w emusic.com 🅑 MD, Europe: Madeleine Milne.

The Energy 106 Store 63 High Street, Belfast,
Co Antrim, BT1 2JZ **t** 028 9033 3122 **f** 028 9033 3122
e cd.heaven@btclick.com 🅑 Mgr: Paul Chapman 028
9032 07780.

FAB Music 55 The Broadway, Crouch End, London,
N8 8DT **t** 020 8347 6767 **f** 020 8348 3270
e fab@fabmusic.co.uk 🅑 Directors: Mal Page, Kevin Payne.

Fat City Records Unit 22 Buspace Studios, Conlan St,
London, W10 5AP **t** 020 8960 8128 **f** 020 8964 9255
e shop@fatcity.co.uk **w** fatcity.co.uk 🅑 Director: Gerald
Short.

Fives 22 Broadway, Leigh-On-Sea, Essex, SS9 1AW
t 01702 711629 **f** 01702 712737 **e** peter@fives-
records.co.uk **w** fives-records.co.uk 🅑 Mgr: Pete Taylor.

Flashback 50 Essex Rd, Islington, London, N1 8LR
t 020 7354 9356 **f** 020 7354 9358
e mark@flashback.co.uk **w** flashback.co.uk
🅜 myspace.com/flashbackrecords
🅣 twitter.com/flashbacklondon 🅑 Owner: Mark Burgess.

Flip Records 2 Mardol, Shrewsbury, SY1 1PY
t 01743 244 469 **f** 01743 260 985
e sales@fliprecords.co.uk **w** fliprecords.co.uk
🅑 Owner: Duncan Morris.

Flying Records 94 Dean Street, London, W1D 3TA
t 020 7734 0172 **f** 020 7287 0766
e info@flyingrecords.com **w** flyingrecords.com
🅑 Manager: Anthony Cox.

Forest Records 7, Earley Court, High Street,
Lymington, Hampshire, SO41 9EP **t** 01590 676 588
f 01590 612 162 **e** forestrec@btconnect.com
🅑 Buyer: Neil Hutson.

Forsyth Brothers 126 Deansgate, Manchester,
M3 2GR **t** 0161 834 3281 **f** 0161 834 0630
e info@forsyths.co.uk **w** forsyths.co.uk 🅑 Dept. Mgr,
Recorded Music: Audrey Wilson.

45s Record Shop 64 Northgate Street, Gloucester,
GL1 1SL **t** 01452 309445 **f** 01452 309445
e chrismanna@onetel.net.uk 🅑 Contact: Chris Manna.

Gatefield Sounds 70 High Street, Whitstable, Kent,
CT5 1BB **t** 01227 263 337 🅑 MD: Mike Winch.

Gee CDs 5 Home Street, Tollcross, Edinburgh, EH3 9LZ
t 0131 228 2022 **e** sales@geecds.co.uk **w** gee-cds.co.uk

Golden Disc Group 11 Windsor Place, Pembroke St,
Dublin 2 **t** +353 1 676 8444 **f** +353 1 676 8565
e info@goldendiscs.ie **w** goldendiscs.ie

Good Vibrations Records 54 Howard Street,
Belfast, Co Antrim, BT1 6PG **t** 028 9058 2250
f 028 9058 2252 **w** goodvibrations.ie 🅑 MD: Terri Hooley.

Hits 10 The Arcade, Station Road, Redhill, Surrey,
RH1 1PA **t** 01737 773565 **f** 01737 773565
🅑 Contact: Brian Hawkins.

HMV UK Ltd Film House, 142 Wardour St, London,
W1F 8LN **t** 020 7432 2000 **f** 020 7432 2002
e firstname.lastname@hmv.co.uk **w** hmv.com 🅑 Head of
Press & PR: Gennaro Castaldo.

Honest Jon's Records 278 Portobello Rd, London,
W10 5TE **t** 020 8969 9822 **f** 020 8969 5395
e mail@honestjons.com **w** honestjons.com

HW Audio (Sound & Lighting) 180-
198 St Georges Rd, Bolton, Lancs, BL1 2PH
t 01204 385199 **f** 01204 364057 **e** sales@hwaudio.co.uk
w hwaudio.co.uk 🅑 Sales Dir: Richard Harfield.

iTunes Europe 1 Hanover St, London, W1S 1YZ
t 020 7184 1462 **f** 020 7184 1184 **w** itunes.com

J Sainsbury 33 Holborn, London, EC1N 2HT
t 020 7695 4295 **f** 020 7695 4295 **w** sainsbury.co.uk

Jibbering Records 136 Alcester Rd, Moseley,
Birmingham, B13 8EE **t** 0121 449 4551
e contact@jibberingrecords.com **w** jibberingrecords.com
🅑 Owner: Dan Raffety.

JMF Records 86 High Street, Invergordon, Ross-shire,
IV18 0DL **t** 01349 853369 **f** 01349 853369
e jmfrecords@hotmail.com **w** jmfrecords.co.uk
🅑 Manager: James Fraser.

Jumbo Records 5-6 St Johns Centre, Leeds,
West Yorkshire, LS2 8LQ **t** 0113 245 5570
f 0113 242 5019 **e** hunter@jumborecords.fsnet.co.uk
w jumborecords.co.uk 🅑 Partners: Hunter Smith, Lornette
Smith.

June Emerson Wind Music Windmill Farm,
Ampleforth, York, YO62 4HF **t** 01439 788324
f 01439 788715 **e** JuneEmerson@compuserve.com
🅑 Prop: June Emerson.

Kane's Records 14 Kendrick St, Stroud, Glocs., GL5 1AA **t** 01453 766 886 **f** 01453 755 377 **e** sales@kanesrecords.com **w** kanesrecords.com 🔲 Owner: Kane Jones.

Kingbee Records 519 Wilbraham Road, Chorlton-Cum-Hardy, Manchester, M21 0UF **t** 0161 860 4762 **f** 0161 860 4762 **e** kingbeerecords@lycos.co.uk 🔲 Contact: Les Hare.

Langland Records 2 Bell St, Wellington, Shropshire, TF1 1LS **t** 01952 244 845 🔲 Owner: Ian Bridgewater.

Lewks Music & Movies 3 Wales Court, Downham Market, Norfolk, PE38 9JZ **t** 01366 383762 **f** 01366 383544 **e** admin@lewks.co.uk **w** lewks.co.uk

Loco Records 5 Church Street, Chatham, Kent, ME4 4BS **t** 01634 818330 **f** 01634 880321 **e** info@locomusic.co.uk **w** locomusic.co.uk 🔲 Owner: Gary Turner.

Longplayer 3 Grosvenor Rd, Tunbridge Wells, Kent, TN1 2AH **t** 01892 539273 **f** 01892 516770 **e** shop@longplayer.fsnet.co.uk **w** longplayer.co.uk 🔲 Owner: Ali Furmidge.

Main Street Music 11 Smithfield Centre, Leek, Staffordshire, ST13 5JW **t** 01538 384 315 **e** mike@demon655.freeserve.co.uk

Malcolm's Musicland Baptist Chapel, Chapel St, Chorley, Lancashire, PR7 1BW **t** 01257 264 362 **e** sales@cdvideo.co.uk 🔲 Prop: Malcolm Allen.

MDC Classic Music Ltd 124 Camden High St, London, NW1 0LU **t** 020 7485 4777 **f** 020 7482 6888 **e** info@mdcmusic.co.uk **w** mdcmusic.co.uk 🔲 Dir: Alan Goulden.

Millenium Music 16-18 The Arcade, Oakhampton, Devon, EX20 1EX **t** 01837 659249 **e** milleniummusic@btopenworld.com **w** millenium-music.net 🔲 Owner: Richard Appleby.

Mixmaster Music & Entertainment Newport Road, Castlebar, Co Mayo, Ireland **t** +353 94 23732 **f** +353 94 23732 **e** mixmaster@eircom.net 🔲 Owner: Pat Concannon.

Morning After Music Llyfnant House Shop, 22 Penrallt Street, Machynlleth, Powys, SY20 8AJ **t** 01654 703767 🔲 Propietor: Malcolm Hume.

MSM Recordstore 1st Floor, 17 Chalk Farm Road, London, NW1 8AG **t** 020 7284 2527 **f** 020 7284 2504 **e** info@msmrecordstore.co.uk **w** msmrecordstore.co.uk 🔲 MD: Des Carr.

The Music Box 13 Market Place, Wallingford, Oxon, OX10 0AD **t** 01491 836269 **e** info@themusicbox.net 🔲 Owner: Richard Strange.

Music Magpie Entertainment Magpie limited T/A Music Magpie, 22 Castle Street, Macclesfield, Cheshire, SK11 6AF **t** 01625 427 774 **e** shop@musicmagpie.co.uk **w** musicmagpie.co.uk 🔲 Operations Manager: Craig Dawson.

The Music Room St. John's Pl, Cleckheaton, West Yorkshire, BD19 3RR **t** 01274 879 768 **f** 01274 852 280 **e** info@the-music-room.com **w** themusicroom-online.co.uk 🔲 Partner: John Turner.

Music Room 8 North Street, Sandwick, Isle of Lewis, Outer Hebrides, HS2 0AD **t** 07754 614498 **e** karen@celticmusicroom.com **w** celticmusicroom.com 🔲 Contact: John Clarke.

Music World The Old Armistice, 31 Hart St, Henley-On-Thames, Oxon, RG9 2AR **t** 01491 572700 **e** musicworldhenley@aol.com 🔲 Owner: Dave Smith.

Musicbank 5 Station Way, Cheam Village, Surrey, SM3 8SD **t** 020 8643 2869 **f** 020 8643 3092 🔲 Contact: Robert Bush.

Musisca (Music Stands & Accessories) Piccaddilly Mill, Lower St, Stroud, Gloucestershire, GL5 2HT **t** 01453 751911 **f** 01453 751911 **e** info@musisca.co.uk **w** musisca.co.uk 🔲 Director: Marc Oboussier.

Noise Annoys 53 Howard St, Sheffield, S1 2LW **t** 0114 276 9177 **f** 0114 276 9177 **e** sales@noise-annoys.co.uk **w** noise-annoys.co.uk 🔲 Mgr: Simon Baxter.

One Up 17 Belmont Street, Aberdeen, AB10 1JR **t** 01224 642 662 **f** 01224 646 560 **e** office@oneupmusic.com 🔲 Partner: Raymond Bird.

Pelicanneck Records 74-76 High St, Manchester, M4 1ES **t** 0161 834 2569 **f** 0161 236 3351 **e** mailboy@boomkat.com **w** boomkat.com 🔲 Owner: Shlom Sviri.

Pendulum Records 34 Market Place, Melton Mowbray, Leicestershire, LE13 1XD **t** 01664 565025 **f** 01664 560310 **e** mw@pendulum-records.co.uk **w** pendulum-records.co.uk 🔲 Owner: Mike Eden.

Phonica Records 51 Poland St, London, W1F 7LZ **t** 020 7025 6070 **e** simon@vinylfactory.co.uk **w** phonicarecords.co.uk 🔲 Manager: Simon Rigg.

Piccadilly Records 53 Oldham St, Manchester, Greater Manchester, M1 1JR **t** 0161 839 8008 **f** 0161 839 8008 **e** mail@piccadillyrecords.com **w** piccadillyrecords.com 🔲 myspace.com/piccadillyrecords 🔲 Directors: Philippa Jarman / Darryl Mottershead / Laura Kennedy 0161 834 8888.

Pied Piper Records 293 Wellingborough Rd, Northampton, NN1 4EW **t** 01604 624777 **f** 01604 624777 **e** piedpiperrecords@aol.com **w** pied-piper-records.co.uk 🔲 Prop: Nick Hamlyn.

Planet of Sound (Scotland) 236 High St, Ayr, South Ayrshire, KA7 1RN **t** 01292 265 913 **f** 01292 265 493 **e** planet-of-sound@btconnect.com 🔲 Manager: Ian Hollins.

Play.com Webworks, Sovereign House, Vision Park,, Chivers Way, Histon, Cambridge, CAMBS, CB24 9BY **t** 01223 484 000 **f** 01223 484 137 **w** play.com 🔲 facebook.com/Playcom 🔲 twitter.com/playcom

Popscene 97 High St, Cosham, Hants, PO6 3AZ
t 023 9242 8042 **f** 023 9279 2355
e enquiries@popsceneuk.com **w** popsceneuk.com
📇 Owner: Chris Lovett.

Prelude Records 25B Giles St, Norwich, NR2 1JN
t 01603 628319 **f** 01603 620170
e admin@preluderecords.co.uk **w** preluderecords.co.uk
📇 Partner: Andrew Cane.

Premier Record Stores 3-5 Smithfield Square,
Belfast, Co Antrim, BT1 1JE **t** 028 9024 0896
f 028 9027 8868 📇 Contact: Ciarna McBurney.

Probe Records 9 Slater St, Liverpool, Merseyside,
L1 4BW **t** 0151 708 8815 **f** 0151 709 7121 **e** probe-
records@btconnect.com **w** probe-records.com
📇 Owner: Anne Davies.

Providence Music 1 St Georges Road, Bristol,
BS1 5UL **t** 01179 276 536 **f** 01179 276 680
e shop@providencemusic.co.uk **w** providencemusic.co.uk
📇 Manager: Ruth Hopton.

Prozone Music 106a Bellingdon Road, Chesham,
Bucks, HP5 2HF **t** 01494 776 262
e info@prozonemusic.com **w** prozonemusic.com
📇 Contact: Tom Watson.

Pure Groove Records 649 Holloway Road, London,
N19 5SE **t** 020 7281 4877 **f** 020 7263 5590
e info@puregroove.co.uk **w** puregroove.co.uk
📇 Buyers: Ziad Nashnush, Simon Singleton, Tas Elias.

Range Records & Tapes 61 High St, Brownhills,
West Midlands, WS8 6HH **t** 01543 374299
f 01543 374299 **e** paul@rangerecords.com
w rangerecords.com 📇 Prop: Paul Whitehouse.

Rapture Entertainment Ltd
Unit 12 Woolgate Centre, Witney, Oxon, OX28 6AP
t 01993 700567 **f** 01993 862897 **e** info@rapture-
online.co.uk **w** rapture-online.co.uk 📇 Managing
Director: Gary Smith.

Rapture Records 37-38 St John's St, Colchester,
Essex, CO2 7AD **t** 01206 542541 **f** 01206 542546
e john@rapturerecords.com **w** rapturerecords.com
📇 Prop: John Parkhurst.

Rat Records 348 Camberwell New Rd, Camberwell,
London, SE5 0RW **t** 07795 424575
e ratrecords@btconnect.com **w** ratrecordsuk.net
📘 facebook.com/group.php?gid=113028440116
📇 Owner: Tom Fisher.

Ray's Jazz at Foyles 1st Floor, 113-
119 Charing Cross Rd, London, WC2H 0EB
t 020 7440 3205 **e** paul@foyles.co.uk **w** foyles.com
📇 Mgr: Paul Pace.

Record Corner Pound Lane, Godalming, Surrey,
GU7 1BX **t** 01483 422 006 **e** info@therecordcorner.co.uk
w therecordcorner.co.uk 📇 Prop: Tom Briggs.

**Records & Discs Ltd T/A Tower Records
Ireland** 6-8 Wicklow St, Dublin 2, Ireland
t +353 1 671 3250 **f** +353 1 671 3260
e cliveb@towerrecords.ie **w** towerrecords.ie
📘 facebook.com/towerrecords
🟦 myspace.com/tower_records
🅱 twitter.com/Tower_Records ▶ towerrecords.ie 📇 Store
Mgr: Clive Branagan.

Reflex 23 Nun Street, Newcastle upon Tyne, NE1 5AG
t 0191 260 3246 **f** 0191 260 3245 **e** info@reflexcd.co.uk
w reflexcd.co.uk 📇 Owner: Alan Jourdan.

Reform Ltd Easton Buildings, Little Castle St, Exeter,
Devon, EX4 3PX **t** 01392 435577 **f** 01392 435577
e enquiries@reform-records.co.uk **w** reform-records.co.uk

Release The Groove Records 20 Denman Street,
London, W1D 7HR **t** 020 7734 7712 **f** 020 7734 7713
e sales@easyvinyl.com **w** easyvinyl.com 📇 Managing
Directors: Gary Dillon, Dean Savonne.

Replay 73 Park Street, Bristol, BS1 5PF
t 0117 904 1134 **e** bristol@replay.co.uk **w** replay.co.uk
📇 Mgr: Bob Jones 0117 904 1135.

Replay Records Stall 18 Indoor Market, Tunstall,
Stoke On Trent, Staffs, ST6 5TP **t** 01782 823456
e mack937@btinternet.com 📇 Prop: Brian Mack.

Rhythm & Rhyme Records 9 High Street,
Launceston, Cornwall, PL15 8ER **t** 01566 772774
f 01566 775668 **e** chris@rrrecords.co.uk
w rrrecords.co.uk 📇 Owner: Chris Parsons.

Roadkill Records 89 Oldham St, Manchester, M4 1LW
t 0161 832 4444 **e** info@roadkill-records.com **w** roadkill-
records.com 📇 Mgr: Liam Stewart.

Rock Box 151 London Rd, Camberley, Surrey, GU15 3JY
t 01276 26628 **f** 01276 678776
e mailorder@rockbox.co.uk **w** rockbox.co.uk
📇 Owner: Alan Bush.

Rough Trade East Rough Trade East,
Old Truman Brewery, 91 Brick Lane, London, E1 6QL
t 020 7392 7788 **e** press@roughtrade.com
w roughtrade.com

Rough Trade Shops Old Truman Brewery,
91 Brick Lane, London, E1 6QL **t** 020 7392 7788
f 020 7392 7789 **e** pete@roughtrade.com
w roughtrade.com 📇 Contact: Peter Donne 020 7391
7780.

Rough Trade West 130 Talbot Rd, London, W11 1JA
t 020 7229 8541 or 020 7221 3066 **f** 020 7221 1146
e shop@roughtrade.com **w** roughtrade.com
📇 Contact: Nigel House.

Rounder Records 19 Brighton Sq, The Lanes,
Brighton, Sussex, BN1 1HD **t** 01273 325440
e philshop@btconnect.com **w** rounderbrighton.co.uk
📇 Manager: Johnny Hartford.

Rub A Dub 35 Howard St, Glasgow, Lanarkshire, G1 4BA
t 0141 221 9657 **f** 0141 221 9650 **e** info@rubadub.co.uk
w rubadub.co.uk 📇 Partner: Dan Lurinsky.

Runway UK Unit 2-B Orpin Road, Merstham, Redhill, Surrey, RH1 3EZ **t** 01737 306010 **e** info@runwayuk.com **w** runwayuk.com 🔲 Proprietor: Andy Wild 07941 241142.

Seaford Music 24 Pevensey Rd, Eastbourne, E. Sussex, BN21 3HP **t** 01323 732553 **f** 01323 417455 **e** mail@seaford-music.co.uk **w** seaford-music.co.uk

Seeds Records 7 Oxton Rd, Charing Cross, Birkenhead, CH41 2QQ **t** 0151 653 4224 **f** 0151 653 3223 **e** lee@seedsrecords.co.uk **w** seedsrecords.co.uk 🔲 Mgr: Lee Hessler.

Selectadisc 21 Market St, Nottingham, NG1 6HX **t** 0115 947 5420 **f** 0115 941 4261 **w** selectadisc.co.uk 🔲 Owner: Brian Selby.

Sellanby 245 Northolt Rd, South Harrow, Middx., HA2 8HR **t** 020 8864 2622 🔲 Owners: David & Peter Smith.

Sho'nuff...Beatz Workin' 86 Main St, Bangor, Co. Down, BT20 4AG **t** 028 9147 7926 **f** 028 9147 7927 **e** steve@shonuff.co.uk **w** shonuff.co.uk 🔲 Owner: Steve McDowell.

Silverback Records 40 Bloomsbury Way, London, WC1A 2SA **t** 020 7404 9456 **e** info@silverbackrecords.co.uk **w** silverbackrecords.co.uk 🔲 Owners: Ben Addison, Mike Oxley.

Sister Ray 34-35 Berwick St, London, W1F 8RP **t** 020 7734 3297 **e** sales@sisterray.co.uk **w** sisterray.co.uk 🔲 Owner: Phil Barton.

Slough Record Centre 241-243 Farnham Rd, Slough, Berks, SL2 1DE **t** 01753 528194 **f** 01753 692110 **e** sloughrecords@btconnect.com **w** sloughrecords.co.uk 🔲 Sales: Terry & Simon 01753 572272.

Smyths Musique 12 Railway St, Newcastle, Co Down, BT33 0AL **t** 028 4372 2831 **e** musique@smyths.biz **w** smyths.biz

Snv Music 8 Gammon Walk, Barnstaple, Devon, EX31 1DJ **t** 01271 323382 **f** 01271 327017 **e** snv@snv2000.com

Solo Music 22a Market Arcade, Guildhall Shopping Centre, Exeter, EX4 3HW **t** 01392 496564 **f** 01392 491785 **e** admin@solomusic.freeserve.co.uk **w** solomusic.co.uk 🔲 Co-Owner: Penny Keen, Maggie Garrett.

Soul Brother Records 1, Keswick Road, London, SW15 2HL **t** 020 8875 1018 **f** 020 8871 0180 **e** soulbrother@btinternet.com **w** soulbrother.com 🔲 Partner: Laurence Prangell.

Soundclash 28 St Benedicts Street, Norwich, Norfolk, NR2 4AQ **t** 01603 761004 **f** 01603 762248 **e** soundclash@btinternet.com **w** run.to/soundclash 🔲 MD: Paul Mills.

Sounds Good 7 Henrietta Street, Cheltenham, Gloucs, GL50 4AA **t** 01242 234 604 **f** 01242 253 030 **e** cds@soundsgoodonline.co.uk **w** soundsgoodonline.co.uk 🔲 MD: Robert Nichols.

Sounds of the Universe 7 Broadwick St, London, W1F 0DA **t** 020 7494 2004 **f** 020 7494 2004 **e** info@soundsoftheuniverse.com **w** souljazzrecords.co.uk 🔲 Contact: Karl Shale.

Sounds To Go 130 Holloway Rd, London, N7 8JE **t** 020 7609 3851 **f** 020 7609 3851 **e** sounds_to_go@hotmail.com **w** gem.co.uk 🔲 Owner: Alex Isaacs.

Speed Music PLC 195 Caerleon Road, Newport, NP19 7HA **t** 01633 215 577 **f** 01633 213 214 **e** info@speedmusic.co.uk **w** speedmusic.co.uk 🔲 Director: Nick Fowler.

Spillers Records 36, The Hayes, Cardiff, CF10 1AJ **t** 029 2022 4905 **f** 029 2034 0358 **e** info@spillersrecords.com **w** spillersrecords.com

Spin Compact Discs 8 High Bridge, Newcastle-upon-Tyne, NE1 1EN **t** 0191 261 4741 **f** 0191 261 4747 **e** info@spincds.com **w** spincds.com 🔲 Owner: Dave Dodds 0191 261 4742.

Spiral Classics Classical LPs 52 Herbert St, Loughborough, LE11 1NX **t** 01509 557 846 **f** 01509 557 847 **e** sophia@spiralclassics.co.uk **w** spiralclassics.co.uk 🔲 Owner: Sophia Singer.

Stagebeat Limited Unit 3, Riverside Industrial Pk, Dogflud Way, Farnham, Surrey, GU9 7UG **t** 01252 820388 **f** 01252 718656 **e** sales@stagebeat.com **w** stagebeat.com 🔲 Managing Director: Moss Hills 01252 719310.

Stand-Out Records Ltd 23 Fisherton Street, Salisbury, Wilts, SP2 7SU **t** 01722 411 344 **f** 01722 421 505 **e** stand-out@totalise.co.uk **w** myspace.com/standoutrecordsltd 🔲 MD: Andy Bennett.

Swordfish 14 Temple Street, Birmingham, B2 5BG **t** 0121 6334859 **f** n/a 🔲 Owner: Mike Caddick.

Tempest Records 83 Bull St, City Centre, Birmingham, West Midlands, B4 6AB **t** 0121 236 9170 **f** 0121 236 9270 **e** info@tempestrecords.co.uk **w** tempestrecords.co.uk 📘 facebook.com/tempestrecords 🔲 myspace.com/tempestrecords 🔲 Manager: Mark Thornton.

Tesco Stores Ltd PO Box 44, Cirrus Building C, Shire Park, Welwyn Garden City, Herts, AL7 1ZR **t** 01992 632222 **f** 01707 297690 **w** tesco.com 🔲 Commercial Manager - Music: Pete Selby.

Three Shades Records 16 Needless Alley, off New Street, Birmingham City Centre, West Midlands, B2 5AE **t** 0121 687 2772 **e** info@threeshades.com **w** threeshades.com 🔲 Shop Manager: Martin Banks.

Threshold Music & DVD 53 High St, Cobham, Surrey, KT11 3DP **t** 01932 865 678 **f** 01932 865 678 **e** sales@threshold-cd.co.uk 🔲 Mgr: Phil Pavling.

Time Life Music Brettenham House, Lancaster Place, London, WC2E 7TL **t** 020 7499 4080 **e** info@timelife.co.uk **w** timelife.co.uk

Contacts Facebook MySpace Twitter YouTube

Torre Records 240 Union St, Torquay, Devon, TQ2 5BY
t 01803 291506 **f** 01803 291506
e cj@torrerecords.freeserve.co.uk Co-owner: Lee Jones.

Townsend Records 30 Queen St, Gt Harwood,
Lancashire, BB6 7QQ **t** 01254 885995 **f** 01254 887835
e steve@townsend-records.co.uk **w** townsend-
records.co.uk MD: Steve Bamber.

Track Records 50 Goodramgate, York,
North Yorkshire, YO1 7LF **t** 01904 629 022
f 01904 610 637 **e** trackrecords@btinternet.com
w trackrecordsuk.com Owner: Keith Howe.

Tracks 14 Railway Street, Hertford, SG14 1BG
t 01992 589294 **f** 01992 587090
e enquiries@tracks.sonnet.co.uk **w** tracks.org.uk
 Buyer: Dennis Osborne.

Trading Post 23 Nelson St, Stroud, Glos
t 01453 759116 **f** 01453 756455
e simon@tradingpost.freeserve.co.uk **w** the-
tradingpost.co.uk

Tudor Tunes 7 Tudor Row, Lichfield, WS13 6HH
t 01543 257627 **f** 01543 257627
e tudortunes@williams3291.fsnet.co.uk Owners: Dave
& Janice Williams.

UDM Records 30 Southbury Rd, Enfield, Middx,
EN1 1SA **t** 020 8366 5422 **f** 020 8366 5422
e info@ultimatedancemusic.co.uk
w ultimatedancemusic.co.uk Owner: Neil Stamp.

Upbeat Trevelver, Belle Vue, Bude, Cornwall, EX23 8JL
t 01288 355763 **f** 01288 355763 Owner: Keith
Shepherd.

Uptown Records 3 D'Arblay Street, London, W1F 8DH
t 020 7434 3639 **f** 020 7434 3649
e izzy@uptownrecords.com **w** uptownrecords.com

Vinyl Addiction Record Shop 6 Inverness St,
Camden, London, NW1 7HJ **t** 020 7482 1114
f 020 7681 6039 **e** music@vinyladdiction.co.uk
w vinyladdiction.co.uk MD: Justin Rushmore.

Vox Pop 53-55 Thomas Street, Manchester, M4 1NA
t 0161 832 3233 **e** enquiries@voxpopmusic.com
w voxpopmusic.com Manager: Tim Giles.

Waterside Music 1 Waterside House, The Plains,
Totnes, Devon, TQ9 5DW **t** 01803 867947 Prop: John
Cooper.

Webworks powering Play.com Sovereign House,
Vision Park, Chivers Way, Histon, Cambridge, CB24 9BY
t 01223 484 000 **f** 01223 484 137 **w** play.com

WH Smith High Street Greenbridge Rd, Swindon,
Wilts, SN3 3LD **t** 01793 616161 **f** 01793 562570
e firstname.lastname@whsmith.co.uk
w whsmithgroup.com Music Product Manager: Graham
Pert.

What Records Shelford House Farm Barn,
Lutterworth Rd, Burton Hastings, CV11 6RD
t 01455 221189 **e** whatuk@aol.com **w** whatrecords.co.uk
 Director: Tim Ellis.

Whitelabel Records 4, Colomberie, St Helier, Jersey,
Channel Islands, JE2 4QB **t** 01534 725 256
f 01534 780 956 **e** info@whitelabelrecords.co.uk
w whitelabelrecords.co.uk Owner: Mal White.

WM Morrisons Supermarkets Plc
Hilmore House, Gain Lane, Bradford, West Yorkshire,
BD3 7DL **t** 0845 611 5000
e andrew.pleasance@morrisonsplc.co.uk
w morrisons.co.uk Home & Leisure Director: Andrew
Pleasance.

WS::Records 3 Mill Street, Bedford, Bedfordshire,
MK40 3EU **t** 01234 266244 **e** wsrcrds@aol.com
w wsrecords.com
 facebook.com/home.php#/group.php?gid=36171258
324&ref=ts Mgr: Paul Willsher.

www.mbopmegastore.com
40 Bowling Green Lane, Clerkenwell, London, EC1R 0NE
t 020 7415 7010 **f** 020 7415 7000
e paul.ballance@mbopglobal.co.uk
w mbopmegastore.com Director: Paul Ballance 07803
007707.

WyldPytch Records 51 Lexington St, London,
W1F 9HL **t** 020 7434 3472 **f** 020 7287 1403
e contact@wyldpytch.com **w** wyldpytch.com
 Owner: Digger Elias.

X-Records 44 Bridge St, Bolton, Lancs, BL1 2EG
t 01204 524018 **f** 01204 370214
e xrecords@xrecords.co.uk **w** xrecords.co.uk

Zhivago Sound And Vision 5-6 Shop Street,
Galway, Ireland **t** +353 91 564198 **f** +353 91 509951
e info@musicireland.com **w** musicireland.com Gen
Mgr: Des Hubbard.

The Zone PO Box 57, Radlett, Hertfordshire, WD7 8BU
t 01923 850650 **f** 01923 859903
e feedback@thezone.co.uk **w** thezone.co.uk MD: Carey
Budnick.

Retail Services

2Funky 62 Belgrave Gate, Leicester, LE1 3GQ
t 0116 299 0700 **f** 0116 299 0077 **e** shop@2-funky.co.uk
w 2-funky.co.uk Manager: Vijay Mistry.

Airplay The Manse, 39 Northenden Road, Sale, Cheshire,
M33 2DH **t** 0161 962 2002 **f** 0161 962 2112
e mailbox@airplay.co.uk **w** airplay.co.uk Head of
Music: Paul Maunder.

Blueprint Digital Unit 1, 73 Maygrove Road, London,
NW6 2EG **t** 020 7209 4224 **f** 020 7209 2334
e info@blueprint.net **w** blueprint.net SVP, Products &
Services: Mike Pears.

C-Burn Systems Ltd 33 Sekforde St, London,
EC1R 0HH **t** 020 7250 1133 **f** 020 7253 8553 **e** info@c-
burn.com **w** c-burn.com Sales & Marketing: Neil Phillips.

Retail: Retailers, Retail Services

📇 Contacts   📘 Facebook   🟦 MySpace   🐦 Twitter   ▶️ YouTube

Cardiff M Light & Sound
Units 9/10, Tarran Buildings, Freeschool Court, Bridgend, Mid Glamorgan, CF31 3AG **t** 01656 648170
f 01656 648412 **e** info@cardiffm.co.uk **w** cardiffm.co.uk
📇 MD: Philip Evans.

Colorset Graphics 2-3 Black Swan Yard, Bermondsey St, London, SE1 3XW **t** 020 7234 0300
f 020 7234 0118 **e** mail@colorsetgraphics.co.uk
w colorsetgraphics.co.uk 📇 Dir: Frank Baptiste.

Creative Retail Entertainment 2 Pincents Kiln, Calcot, Reading, Berkshire, RG31 7SD **t** 0118 930 5599
f 0118 930 3369 **e** lc@cre.co.uk **w** cre.co.uk 📇 Sales Co-Ordinator: Lesley Cooper.

Cube Music The Albany Boathouse, Lower Ham Rd, Kingston upon Thames, Surrey, KT2 6BB **t** 020 8547 1543
f 020 8547 1544 **e** info@cube-music.com **w** cube-music.com 📇 Music & Promotions Dir: Mick Hilton.

Digital DJ Ltd 22 The Ropery, Newcastle upon Tyne, NE6 1TY **t** 0191 276 2791 **f** 0191 224 0148
e info@digitaldjsystems.com **w** digitaldjsystems.com
📇 Dir: Paul Rogers.

Essanby Ltd Riverside Works, Amwell Lane, Ware, Herts, SG12 8EB **t** 01920 870596 **f** 01920 871553
e shatcher@essanby.co.uk **w** essanby.co.uk 📇 MD: Steve Hatcher.

HMV Group plc Shelley House, 2-4 York Rd, Maidenhead, Berkshire, SL6 1SR **t** 01628 818300
f 01628 818301 **e** firstname.lastname@hmvgroup.com
w hmvgroup.com 📇 Director of Corporate Communications: Paul Barker.

International Displays Stonehill, Stukeley Meadows Ind Estate, Huntingdon, Cambridgeshire, PE29 6ED **t** 01480 414204
f 01480 414205 **e** info@internationaldisplays.co.uk
w internationaldisplays.co.uk 📇 Sales & Marketing Dir.: Carl Jenkin.

Jacks Records Flat 1C, Backfields, Sheffield, S1 4HJ
t 0114 279 8937 **e** sales@jacksrecords.idps.co.uk
w jacksrecords.idps.co.uk 📇 Owner: Ian Gadsby 0114 2798937.

Kempner Distribution Ltd 498-500 Honeypot Lane, Stanmore, Middlesex, HA7 1JZ
t 020 8952 5262 **f** 020 8952 8061 **e** info@kempner.co.uk
w kempner.co.uk 📇 Mkting Mgr: Eddie Rollinson.

KPD London Ltd 297 Haydons Road, London, SW19 8TX **t** 020 8542 9535 **f** 020 8543 9406
e reception@kpd.co.uk **w** kpd.co.uk 📇 MD: Ivor Heller.

Masson Seeley & Co Ltd Howdale, Downham Market, Norfolk, PE38 9AL **t** 01366 388000
f 01366 385222 **e** admin@masson-seeley.co.uk
w masson-seeley.co.uk 📇 Contact: Martin Potten.

Micro Video Services 24 Cobham Rd, Ferndown Industrial Estate, Wimborne, Dorset, BH21 7NP
t 01202 861 696 **f** 01202 654 919
e av.sales@mvsav.co.uk **w** microvideoservices.com
📇 Contact: Sales Department.

Pentonville Rubber Products Ltd 104-106 Pentonville Road, London, N1 9JB **t** 020 7837 4582
f 020 7278 7392 **e** queries@pentonvillerubber.co.uk
w pentonvillerubber.co.uk

pre.vu The Cow Shed, Hyde Hall Farm, Buckland, Herts, SG9 0RU **t** 01763 276 007 **e** firstname.lastname@pre.vu
w pre.vu 📇 Commercial Dir: Andrew McGee.

Pro.Loc Europe Royal Albert House, Sheet Street, Windsor, Berks, SL4 1BE **t** 01753 705030
f 01753 831541 **e** proloc@proloc.co.uk **w** proloc-online.com 📇 GM: Mike Vickers.

Pro.Loc UK Ltd Northgate Business Centre, 38 Northgate, Newark on Trent, Nottinghamshire, NG24 1EZ **t** 01636 642827 **f** 01636 642865
e sales@proloc.co.uk **w** proloc-online.com 📇 Sales: Sam Jessop.

Retail Entertainment Displays Ltd (RED) 27-28 Stapledon Rd, Orton Southgate, Peterborough, Cambs, PE2 6TD **t** 01733 239001 **f** 01733 239002
e info@reddisplays.com **w** reddisplays.com 📇 MD: John Findlay.

Retail Management Solutions Bloxham Mill, Barford Rd, Bloxham, Banbury, OX15 4FF **t** 01295 724568
f 01295 722801 **e** info@rmsepos.com **w** rmsepos.com
📇 Contact: Robert Collier.

Sounds Wholesale Unit 2, Park St, Burton on Trent, Staffs, DE14 3SE **t** 01283 566823 **f** 01283 568631
e matpriest@aol.com **w** soundswholesaleltd.co.uk
📇 Dir: Matt Priest.

Mike Thorn Display & Design 30 Muswell Avenue, London, N10 2EG **t** 020 8442 0279 **f** 020 8442 0496
e info@bear-art.com 📇 MD: Mike Thorn.

Walsh & Jenkins plc Power House, Powerscroft Road, Sidcup, Kent, DA14 5EA
t 020 8308 6300 **f** 020 8308 6340 **e** sales@walsh-jenkins.co.uk **w** walsh-jenkins.co.uk 📇 Sales Office Co-ordiantor: Jackie Read.

West 4 Tapes And Records 105 Stocks Lane, Bracklesham Bay, West Sussex, PO20 8NU
t 01243 671238 📇 Sales Dir: Kenneth G Roe.

Wilton of London Stanhope House, 4-8 Highgate High Street, London, N6 5JL **t** 020 8341 7070
f 020 8341 1176 **w** wilton-of-london.co.uk
📇 Contact: The Managing Director.

Mail Order Companies

3 Beat Records 5 Slater St, Liverpool, L1 4BW
t 0151 709 3355 **f** 0151 709 3707 **e** info@3beat.co.uk
w 3beat.co.uk 📇 Shop Mgr: Pezz.

Alma Road Mail Order PO Box 3813, London, SW18 1XE **t** 020 8870 9912 **f** 020 8871 1766
e mailorder@almaroad.co.uk **w** beggars.com 📇 Mail Order Manager: Jo.

Contacts Facebook MySpace Twitter YouTube

Badlands Mail Order 11 St George's Place, Cheltenham, Gloucestershire, GL50 3LA **t** 01242 227724 **f** 01242 227393 **e** shop@badlands.co.uk **w** badlands.co.uk MD: Philip Jump.

Bus Stop Mail Order Ltd 42-50 Steele Road, London, NW10 7AS **t** 020 8453 1311 **f** 020 8961 8725 **e** info@busstop.co.uk **w** acerecords.co.uk Director: Yvette DeRoy.

Carbon Disks PO Box 28, Cromer, Norfolk, NR27 9RG **t** 01263 515963 **f** 01263 515963 **e** data@carbondisks.com **w** carbondisks.com Contact: Barry Fry.

CDX Music By Mail The Olde Coach House, Windsor Cresent, Radyr, South Glamorgan, CF4 8AG **t** 029 2084 3604 **f** 029 2084 2184 **e** sales@cdx.co.uk **w** cdx.co.uk MD: Paul Karamouzis 029 2084 2878.

CeeDee Mail Ltd PO Box 14, Stowmarket, Suffolk, IP14 1ED **t** 01449 770 138 **f** 01449 770 133 **e** CeeDeeMail@aol.com Sales Mgr: Peter.

City Sounds 5 Kirby Street, London, EC1N 8TS **t** 020 7404 1800 **f** 020 7242 1863 **e** sales@city-sounds.co.uk **w** city-sounds.co.uk Contact: Tom Henneby 020 7405 5454.

Compact Disc Services 40-42 Brantwood Avenue, Dundee, DD3 6EW **t** 01382 776595 **f** 01382 736702 **e** cdser@aol.com **w** cd-services.com Snr Partner: Dave Shoesmith.

Cooking Vinyl Mail Order PO Box 1845, London, W3 0BR **t** 020 8600 9200 **f** 020 8743 7534 **e** bob@cookingvinyl.com **w** cookingvinyl.com Direct Mktg Mgr: Bob Allan.

Copperplate Mail Order 68, Belleville Rd, London, SW11 6PP **t** 020 7585 0357 **f** 020 7585 0357 **e** copperplate2000@yahoo.com **w** copperplatemailorder.com MD: Alan O'Leary.

Corban Recordings (Folk/Jazz etc) PO Box 2, Glasgow, Netherlee, G44 3LB **t** 0141 637 5277 **f** 0141 637 5277 **e** alastair@corbanrecordings.com **w** corbanrecordings.co.uk Producer/Artiste: Alastair McDonald As Above.

Cyclops PO Box 834a, Surbiton, Surrey, KT1 9BZ **t** 020 8397 3990 **f** 020 8397 2988 **e** info@gft-cyclops.co.uk **w** gft-cyclops.co.uk MD: Malcolm Parker.

Didgeridoo PO Box 333, Brighton, East Sussex, BN1 2EH **t** 01403 740 289 **f** 01403 740 261 **e** ukorders@didgerecords.com **w** didgerecords.com Head of Mail Order: Sarah Clark.

Discurio - Military Recordings Specialist Unit 3, Faraday Way, St Mary Cray, Kent, BR5 3QW **t** 01689 879101 **f** 01689 879101 **e** discurio1@aol.com **w** discurio.com Manager: Jonathan Mitchell.

Esprit International Limited Esprit House, 5 Railway Sidings, Meopham, Kent, DA13 0YS **t** 01474 815010 **f** 01474 815030 **e** sales@eil.com **w** eil.com Managing Director: Robert Croydon 01474 815 007.

Fast Forward Units 9-10 Sutherland Court, Tolpits Lane, Watford, Hertfordshire, WD18 9SP **t** 01923 897080 **f** 01923 896263 **e** sales@fast-forward.co.uk MD: Ken Hill.

Freak Emporium Mail-Order PO Box 1288, Gerrards Cross, Bucks, SL9 9YB **t** 01753 893008 **f** 01753 892879 **e** sales@freakemporium.com **w** freakemporium.com MD: Richard Allen.

Global Groove Records Global House, 13 Bucknall New Rd, Hanley, Stoke-on-Trent, Staffordshire, ST1 2BA **t** 01782 215 554 **f** 01782 201 698 **e** mail@globalgroove.co.uk **w** globalgroove.co.uk Buyer: Pete 01782 207 234.

Greensleeves Mail Order Unit 14 Metro Centre, St John's Rd, Isleworth, Middlesex, TW7 6NJ **t** 020 8758 0564 **f** 020 8758 0811 **w** greensleeves.net Mail Order Manager: Chris O'Brien.

Hard To Find Record Vinyl House, 10 Upper Gough Street, Birmingham, West Midlands, B1 1JG **t** 0121 687 7777 **f** 0121 687 7774 **e** sales@htfr.com **w** htfr.com MD: Jason Kirby.

Jansmusic e jan@jansmusic.co.uk **w** jansmusic.co.uk Director: Jan Hart.

Jim Stewart, Motown, Soul & Sixties CD Specialist 37 Main Rd, Hextable, Swanley, Kent, BR8 7RA **t** 01322 613883 **f** 01322 613883 **e** jstew79431@aol.com **w** soulsearchingplus.co.uk Contact: Jim Stewart.

The Left Legged Pineapple PO BOX 8676, Loughborough, Leicestershire, LE11 9DY **t** 01509 210130 **e** pineapple@left-legged.com **w** left-legged.com Owner: Jason White.

Magpie Direct Music The Studio, 10 Kings Drive, Thames Ditton, Surrey, KT7 0TH **t** 020 8873 1090 **e** editor@highnote.co.uk **w** magpiedirect.com MD: Mark Rye.

Mostly Music 28 Carlisle Close, Mobberley, Knutsford, Cheshire, WA16 7HD **t** 01565 872650 **f** 01565 872650 **e** mostlymusic@btinternet.com **w** mostlymusic.co.uk Proprietor: Roger Wilkes.

Music Exchange (Manchester) Ltd Mail Order Dept., Claverton Rd, Wythenshawe, Manchester, M23 9ZA **t** 0161 946 9301 **f** 0161 946 1195 **e** mail@music-exchange.co.uk **w** music-exchange.co.uk Mail Order Department Manager: Martin Hutchinson.

New World Music Harmony House, Hillside Rd East, Bungay, Suffolk, NR35 1RX **t** 01986 891600 **f** 01986 891601 **e** info@newworldmusic.co.uk **w** newworldmusic.com MD: Jeff Stewart.

Nostalgia Direct 11 St Nicholas Chambers, Newcastle-upon-Tyne, NE1 1PE **t** 0191 233 1200 **f** 0191 233 1215 Contact: George Carr.

Open Ear Productions Ltd. Main Street, Oughterard, Co.Galway, Ireland **t** +353 91 552816 **f** +353 91 557967 **e** info@openear.ie **w** openear.ie MD: Bruno Staehelin.

Retail: Mail Order Companies

Red Lick Records P.O. Box 55, Cardiff, CF11 1JT
t 020 2049 6369 **f** 029 2049 4259 **e** sales@redlick.com
w redlick.com ✉ MD: Tony Chilcott.

Rocking Chair PO Box 296, Matlock, Derbyshire,
DE4 3XU **t** 01629 827013 **f** 01629 821874
e rc@mrscasey.co.uk **w** mrscasey.co.uk/rockingchair
✉ MD: Steve Heap.

Ross Record Distribution 30 Main St, Turriff,
Aberdeenshire, AB53 4AD **t** 01888 568 899
f 01888 568 890 **e** gibson@rossrecords.com
w rossrecords.com ✉ MD: Gibson Ross.

Rugby Songs Unlimited Whitwell, Colyford,
Colyton, Devon, EX24 6HS **t** 01297 553803
e very_funny@compuserve.com **w** rugby-songs.co.uk
✉ MD: Mike Williams.

Selections Dorchester, Dorset, DT2 7YG
t 01305 848725 **f** 01305 848516
e sales@selections.com **w** selections.com
✉ Contact: Michael Slocock.

Soul Brother Records 1 Keswick Road, London,
SW15 2HL **t** 020 8875 1018 **f** 020 8871 0180
e SoulBrother@btinternet.com **w** SoulBrother.com
✉ Partner: Laurence Prangell.

Soundtracks Direct 3 Prowse Place, London,
NW1 9PH **t** 020 7428 5500 **f** 020 7482 2385
e info@silvascreen.co.uk **w** soundtracksdirect.co.uk
✉ MD: Reynold D'Silva.

Stern's Music 74 Warren St, London, W1T 5PF
t 020 7387 5550 **f** 020 7388 2756
e info@sternsmusic.com **w** sternsmusic.com
✉ Contact: Robert Urbanus.

Sterns Postal 293 Euston Road, London, NW1 3AD
t 020 7387 5550 **f** 020 7388 2756
e info@sternsmusic.com **w** sternsmusic.com ✉ Retail
Mgr: Dominic Raymond Barker.

Tanty Records - The Dub Shop PO Box 557,
Harrow, Middlesex, HA2 6ZX **t** 07802 463 154
e store@tantyrecordshop.com **w** tantyrecordshop.com
✉ Owner: Kelvin Richard 07802 463154.

Thirdwave Music Direct PO Box 19, Orpington,
Kent, BR6 9ZF **t** 01689 609481 **f** 01689 609481
e info@thirdwavemusic.com **w** thirdwavemusic.com
✉ MD: Matt Gall.

Track Records 50 Goodramgate, York,
North Yorkshire, YO1 7LF **t** 01904 629 022
f 01904 610 637 **e** trackrecords@btinternet.com
w trackrecordsuk.com ✉ Owner: Keith Howe.

Tracks PO Box 117, Chorley, Lancashire, PR6 0UU
t 01257 269726 **f** 01257 231340 **e** sales@tracks.co.uk
w tracks.co.uk ✉ Contact: Paul Wane.

Upfront Direct Ltd 217 Buspace Studios, Conlan St,
London, W10 5AP **t** 020 7565 0050 **f** 020 7565 0049
e matthew@upfrontdirect.com ✉ Contact: Matthew
Taylor.

The Woods - The Compact Disc Club
Sussex House, 17a High St, Bognor Regis, West Sussex,
PO21 1RJ **t** 01243 827 712 **f** 01243 842 615
e sales@the-woods.co.uk **w** the-woods.co.uk
✉ Proprietor: Trevor Flack.

Contacts   Facebook   ◼ MySpace   ◼ Twitter   ▶ YouTube

Digital

Music Portals & Online Magazines

Band Family Tree 2 Oakfield Terrace,
Childer Thornton, Wirral, CH66 7NY **t** 0870 011 6289
e admin@bandfamilytree.com **w** bandfamilytree.com
◼ MD: Rob Cowley.

Base.ad PO Box 56374, London, SE1 3WF
t 0207 357 8066 **f** 0207 357 8166 **e** london@base.ad
w base.ad ◼ Editor: Tanya Mannar.

Blues & Soul 153 Praed St, London, W2 1RL
t 020 3174 8020 **f** 020 7224 8227
e editorial@bluesandsoul.com **w** bluesandsoul.com
◼ facebook/BluesandSoul
◼ ww.myspace.com/BluesandSoul
◼ twitter.com/BluesandSoul
▶ youtube.com/BluesandSoulMagazine
◼ Editor: Lee Tyler.

Chartwatch Magazine 34 Brybank Rd,
Hanchett Village, Haverhill, Suffolk, CB9 7WD
t 01440 713859 **e** ndr@sanger.ac.uk **w** chartwatch.co.uk
◼ Editors: Neil Rawlings, John Hancock.

Clickmusic Ltd 58-60 Fitzroy Street, London,
W1T 5BU **t** 020 7383 3038 **f** 0870 458 4183
e editor@clickmusic.co.uk **w** clickmusic.co.uk
◼ Editor: Stephen Ackroyd.

Cliff Chart Site 17, Podsmead Rd, Tuffley, Gloucester,
Gloucestershire, GL1 5PB **t** 01452 306104
f 01452 306104 **e** william@cliffchartsite.co.uk
◼ Contact: William Hooper.

Clown Magazine Suite 3, Rosden House,
372 Old Street, London, EC1V 9AU **t** 07986 359 568
e office@clownmagazine.co.uk **w** clownmagazine.co.uk
◼ Contact: Jack Dorrington.

CMU Daily Fl 3 Unicorn House, 221-
222 Shoreditch High St, London, E1 6PJ **t** 020 7099 9050
e cmu@unlimitedmedia.co.uk **w** theCMUwebsite.com
◼ facebook.com/cmuhq ◼ myspace.com/cmuhq
◼ twitter.com/cmu
◼ Editor/Publisher: Andy Malt/Chris Cooke.

Direct Drive TV 38 Twisaday House,
28 Colville Square, Notting Hill, London, W11 2BW
t 07916 277 272 **e** leroy@directdrive.tv **w** directdrive.tv
◼ CEO: Leroy Smith.

DMC Ltd PO Box 89, Slough, Berks, SL1 8NA
t 01628 667124 **f** 01628 605246 **e** info@dmcworld.com
w dmcworld.com ◼ Label Manager: Martin Madigan.

DMC Update DMC Update, 3 Progress Business Centre,
Whittle Parkway, Burnham, Buckinghamshire, SL16DQ
t 01628 667124 **f** 01628 605246 **e** info@dmcworld.com
w dmcupdate.com ◼ twitter.com/DMCUpdate
◼ Editor: Martin Madigan.

Drowned In Sound London
e firstname@drownedinsound.com
w drownedinsound.com
◼ facebook.com/DrownedinSound
◼ twitter.com/drownedinsound ◼ Editor: Sean Adams.

Drum & Bass Arena 2nd Floor, 36-
37 Featherstone Street, London, EC1Y 8QZ
t 020 7741 0050 **f** 020 7250 1726
e editorial@breakbeat.co.uk **w** breakbeat.co.uk
◼ MD: Del Dias.

**Electric Circus/Soviet Union
Records/Manchestemus** Musicdash, PO Box 1977,
Manchester, M26 2YB **t** 07771 958875
e jon@musicdash.co.uk **w** manchestermusic.co.uk
◼ facebook.com/manchestermusic
◼ myspace.com/manchestermusiccouk
◼ twitter.com/chairsmissing
▶ youtube.com/musicmanchester ◼ Director: Jon
Ashley.

EveryUrbanThing.com PO Box 48568, London,
NW4 9BF **t** 020 8922 0433 **e** ak@everyurbanthing.com
w everyurbanthing.com ◼ CEO: Akhil Suchak.

FirstForMusic.com 23 New Mount Street,
Manchester, M4 4DE **t** 0161 953 4081 **f** 0161 953 4091
e info@FirstForMusic.com **w** FirstForMusic.com
◼ Contact: Steven Oakes.

Fmagazine.com 9 Cambridge Court, Earlham Street,
Covent Garden, London, WC2H 9RZ **t** 020 7379 4466
e chrissie@fmagazine.com **w** fmagazine.com
◼ MD: Chrissie Adams 07979 905015.

G MaG Campro Entertainment, PO Box 18542, London,
E17 5UY **t** 020 8527 2720 **f** 020 8531 6050
e mel@campro.freeserve.co.uk **w** gmag.org.uk
◼ Editor/Publisher: Melissa Sinclair 07947 477628.

garageband.com United States
e artistmanager@garageband.com **w** garageband.com

GBOB International 21 Denmark Street, London,
WC2H 8NA **t** 020 7379 3777 **f** 020 7379 4888
e music@gbob.com **w** gbob.com ◼ Communications
Director: Matt Walker.

Get Ready to ROCK! 34 Coniston Rd, Neston,
Cheshire, CH64 0TD **t** 0151 3366199
e info@getreadytorock.com **w** getreadytorock.com
◼ Managing Editor: David Randall.

Give A Band A Chance
e admin@giveabandachance.com
w giveabandachance.com ◼ Contact: Sue O'Sullivan
07867522088.

God Is In The TV Zine 36 Loftus St, Canton, Cardiff,
CF5 1HL **t** 029 2019 1692 **e** bill@godisinthetvzine.co.uk
w godisinthetvzine.co.uk ◼ Editor: Bill Cummings.

Digital: Music Portals & Online Magazines

IHOUSEU.COM PO Box 1185, Tring, Hertfordshire, HP23 5WG **t** 08453 888903 **f** 08453 888904 **e** info@ihouseu.com **w** ihouseu.com 📘 facebook.com/adamgiddz 🐦 twitter.com/ihouseu 🖾 MD: Adam Giddens.

Jukebox 3 Gray Place, Wokingham Road, Bracknell, Berks, RG42 1QA **t** 01344 428 308 **f** 07043 018 674 **e** vikki@jukebo.cx **w** jukebo.cx 🖾 Editor: Vikki Roberts.

Jump Off TV e harry@jumpoff.tv **w** jumpoff.tv 📘 facebook.com/jumpofftv 🎵 myspace.com/jumpofftv 🐦 twitter.com/jumpofftv ▶️ youtube.com/jumpoff 🖾 CEO: Harold Anthony.

Kent & E Sussex Gig Guide The Cedars, Elvington Lane, Hawkinge, Nr. Folkestone, Kent, CT18 7AD **t** 01303 893472 **f** 01303 893833 **e** Chris@kentgigs.com **w** kentgigs.com 🎵 myspace.com/kentgigs 🖾 MD: Chris Ashman.

KinDups Ltd PO Box 711, Godalming, GU7 9BE **t** 07760 128 024 **e** info@kindups.com **w** kindups.com 🖾 Director: Dominic Graham-Hyde.

Let's Talk Music The Dog House, 32 Sullivan Crescent, Harefield, Middlesex, UB9 6NL **t** 01895 825 757 **e** Bill@letstalkmusic.com **w** letstalkmusic.com 🖾 Contact: Bill Smith.

livegigguide ltd The Windsor Centre, 15-29 Windsor Street, London, N1 8QG **t** 020 7359 2927 **f** 020 7359 7212 **e** info@livegigguide.com **w** livegigguide.com 🖾 Director of Operations: Olivier de Peretti Clark.

Liveroom.tv 407 Hornsey Road, London, N19 4DX **t** 07983 644 338 **e** Tamara@liveroom.tv **w** liveroom.tv 🖾 Dir, Business Dev't: Tamara Deike.

The Living Tradition PO Box 1026, Kilmarnock, Ayrshire, Scotland, KA2 0LG **t** 01563 571220 **f** 01563 544855 **e** admin@livingtradition.co.uk **w** folkmusic.net 🖾 Ed: Pete Heywood.

Luvu Luvu Music 6754 Pennywell Drive, Nashville, TN, 37205 3010, United States **t** +1 615 356 4585 **f** +1 615 356 4585 **e** luvuluvumusic@comcast.net **w** luvuluvumusic.com 🖾 Creative Director: Joyce Harrison.

Making Music (The Nat'l Fed. Of Music Societies) 2-4 Great Eastern St, London, EC2A 3NW **t** 020 7422 8280 **f** 020 7422 8299 **e** info@makingmusic.org.uk **w** makingmusic.org.uk 🖾 Chief Executive: Robin Osterley.

Music Hurts Ramp Industry, 3rd Floor, 20 Flaxman Terrace, London, WC1H 9AT **t** 020 7388 0709 **e** hello@musichurts.com **w** musichurts.com 🖾 Editorial Dir: Andy Crysell.

The Music Magazine PO Box 234, Washington, Tyne and Wear, NE37 9AE **t** 07860 945404 **e** scott.goodacre@themusicmagazine.co.uk **w** themusicmagazine.co.uk 📘 facebook.com/home.php#/pages/The-Music-Magazine/104047201449 🎵 myspace.com/themusicmagazinecouk 🐦 twitter.com/_musicmagazine 🖾 Editor: Scott Goodacre.

MUSIC WEEK

MusicWeek

8th Floor, Ludgate House, 245 Blackfriars Rd, London, SE1 9UY **t** 020 7921 5000 **f** 020 7921 8327 **e** firstname@musicweek.com **w** musicweek.com 🐦 twitter.com/MusicWeekNews 🖾 Editor: Paul Williams. Publishing Director: Joe Hosken. Associate Editor: Robert Ashton. Talent Editor: Stuart Clarke. Features Editor: Chris Barrett. News Editor: Ben Cardew. Contributing Editor, Live: Gordon Masson. Contributing Editor, Digital: Eamonn Forde. Contributing Editor, Publishing: Chas de Whalley. Chart consultant: Alan Jones. Chart & Data Controller: Isabelle Nesmon. Group Sales Manager: Steve Connolly. Advertising Manager: Becky Golland. Deputy Advertising Manager: Archie Carmichael. Features Sales Executive: Martin Bojtos. Digital Sales Executive: Yonas Blay Morkeh.

MUSIC WEEK DIRECTORY

MusicWeek
Directory

8th Floor, Ludgate House, 245 Blackfriars Rd, London, SE1 9UR **t** 020 7921 8357 **f** 020 7921 8327 **e** mwdirectory@cmpi.biz **w** musicweek.com 🖾 Digital Content Manager: Tim Frost. Publishing Director: Joe Hosken. Editor: Paul Williams. Group Sales Manager: Steve Connolly. Advertising Manager: Becky Golland. Deputy Advertising Manager: Archie Carmichael. Features Sales Executive: Martin Bojtos. Digital Sales Executive: Yonas Blay Morkeh.

Netsounds Music PO Box 3007, Church Stretton, SY6 7XH **t** 01694 723462 **e** enquiries@netsoundsmusic.com **w** netsoundsmusic.com

New CD Weekly 56 Manston Rd, Exeter, Devon, EX1 2QA **t** 01392 432 630 **f** 01392 432 630 **e** rod@newcdweekly.com **w** newcdweekly.com 🖾 MD: Rod Walsom.

Contacts   Facebook   MySpace   Twitter   YouTube

NME.com IPC Media, Blue Fin Building, 110 Southwark St, London, SE1 0SU **t** 020 3148 5000 **f** 020 3148 8107 **e** news@nme.com **w** nme.com Online Ed: David Moynihan.

Noise Festival Ltd PO Box 4106, Manchester, M60 1WW **t** 0161 237 9009 **e** info@noisefestival.com **w** noisefestival.com Executive Producer: Denise Proctor.

noizemakesenemies.co.uk // Online Music Magazine Top Floor Rear Studio, 2 Linacre RD, London, NW2 5BB **t** noizemakesenemies.co.uk **e** editor@noizemakesenemies.co.uk **w** noizemakesenemies.co.uk facebook.com/group.php?gid=2347448645 myspace.com/noizemakesenemies twitter.com/_noize youtube.com/noizemakesenemies Editor: Martin Kendrick.

Odyssey.fm PO Box 18888, London, SW7 4FQ **t** 020 7373 1614 **f** 020 7373 1614 **e** info@outer-media.co.uk **w** odyssey.fm Dir: Gregory Mihalcheon.

Online Classics Gnd & 1st Floors, 31 Eastcastle Street, London, W1W 8DL **t** 020 7636 1400 **f** 020 7637 1355 **e** team@onlineclassics.com **w** onlineclassics.com CEO: Christopher Hunt.

OnlineConcerts.com 2 Valentine Cottages, Petworth Rd, Witley, Godalming, Surrey, GU8 5LS **t** 01428 684537 **e** info@onlineconcerts.com **w** onlineconcerts.com Founder: John Doukas.

Oxfordmusic.net ltd 1st Floor, 9 Park End Street, Oxford, OX1 1HH **t** 01865 798 796 **f** 01865 798 792 **e** info@oxfordmusic.net **w** oxfordmusic.net MD: Andy Clyde.

Planet Loud 101 Elm Park, Reading, Berkshire, RG30 2HT **t** 07879 881 407 **e** graham@planet-loud.com **w** planet-loud.com Contact: Graham Finney.

Popjustice.com PO Box 64569, London, SW17 1BE **t** 020 3239 0258 **e** website.contact@popjustice.com **w** popjustice.com facebook.com/popjustice myspace.com/popjustice twitter.com/popjustice Editor: Peter Robinson.

Popworld Ltd. 14 Ransome's Dock, 35 Parkgate Road, London, SW11 4NP **t** 020 7350 5500 **f** 020 7350 5501 **e** firstname@popworld.com **w** popworld.com

Primal Sounds.com PO Box 5, Alton, Hants, GU34 2EN **t** 07967 155542 **e** mail@primalsounds.com **w** primalsounds.com Owner: Carl Saunders.

RedSpark Music PO Box 722, Oxford, Oxfordshire, OX1 9EQ **t** 01865 559281 **e** sales@redsparkmusic.com **w** redsparkmusic.com Director: Stephen McLeod.

Reminiscin' Craven House, 121 Kingsway, Holborn, London, WC2B 6PA **t** 020 7863 1787 **f** 020 7953 8009 **e** info@reminiscin.co.uk **w** reminiscin.co.uk Editor: Toni Williams.

Revolution 211 Western Road, London, SW19 2QD **t** 020 8646 7094 **f** 020 8646 7094 **e** info@revolutionsuk.com **w** revolutionsuk.com Ed: John Lonergan.

Rockarama Radio Network 2nd Floor, 145-157 St John Street, London, EC1V 4PY **t** 07732 213917 **e** news@rockaramaradionetwork.com **w** rockaramaradionetwork.com Managing Editor: Kevin Gover.

Rockfeedback.com The Lexington, 96-98 Pentonville Rd, London, N1 9JB **e** tom@rockfeedback.com **w** rockfeedback.com Editor: Tom Hannan.

Rocudo 216 Business & Innovation Centre, NUI Galway, Galway City, Ireland **t** +353 91 861 630 **e** info@rocudo.com **w** rocudo.com CEO: Culann mac Cabe.

Rokpool Caryatides House, 74 Blackfriars Rd, London, SE1 8HA **t** 08444 776 247 **e** robin@rokpool.com **w** rokpool.com Rokpoolmusic C.E.O: Robin Smith 07973623414.

Rokpool.com Caryatides House, 74 Blackfriars Rd, London, SE1 7HA **t** 0845 410 3511 **e** robin@rokpool.com **w** rokpool.com CEO: Robin Smith.

Roomthirteen.com 55 Cranleigh Dr, Cheadle, Cheshire, SK8 2DH **t** 07745 632 529 **f** 0845 280 7575 **e** guy.powell@roomthirteen.com **w** roomthirteen.com Editor: Guy Powell.

Sh-Boom Media Limited Suite 6, Ruxley House, 550B London Rd, Sutton, Surrey, SM3 9AA **t** 020 8641 8614 **e** shboommedia@btinternet.com MD: Brian Oliver.

Skrufff-E and Skrufff.com Available on request **e** jonty@skrufff.com **w** skrufff.com facebook.com/jontyskrufff myspace.com/djjontyskrufff twitter.com/jontyskrufff DJ/ producer/ journalist: Jonty Skrufff.

Sonic Network Ltd 74 Great Eastern St, London, EC2A 3JL **t** 020 7613 0555 **f** 020 7613 0708 **e** lawrence@sonicnetwork.net **w** sonicnetwork.net Director: Lawrence Cooke.

Supersweet Magazine PO Box 58240, London, N1 1PY **t** 020 7288 0965 **e** hello@supersweet.org **w** supersweet.org Editor: Choltida Pekanan.

thewhitelabel.com limited 1-3 Croft Lane, Henfield, W. Sussex, BN5 9TT **t** 01273 492620 **e** contact@thewhitelabel.com **w** thewhitelabel.com GM: Nic Vine.

This Day in Music.com Hazelhurst Barn, Valley Rd, Hayfield, Derbyshire, SK22 2JP **t** 01663 747970 **e** neil@thisdayinmusic.com **w** Thisdayinmusic.com myspace.com/neilcossar twitter.com/Thisdayinmusic Editor: Neil Cossar 07768 652 899.

You can subscribe at the Music Week

Student rate!

To subscribe at the Music Week **student rate**
call Gareth/Mark or Amy on 0207 921 8301/8318/8707 or email
musicweek@musicweek.com

www.**musicweek**.com

Tiscali UK 20 Broadwick St, London, W1F 8HT
t 020 7087 2000 **e** david.leonard@uk.tiscali.com
w tiscali.co.uk/music 🅱 Head of Music:
David Leonard 020 7087 2105.

TotalRock 1-6 Denmark Place, London, WC2H 8NL
t 020 7240 6665 **e** info@totalrock.com **w** totalrock.com
🅱 Head of Music: Tony Wilson.

Twistedear.com 8 Stirling Close, Ash Vale, Surrey,
GU12 5SD **t** 01252 890013 **e** beck@twistedear.com
w twistedear.com 🅱 Editor: Beck Kingsnorth.

UKMusic.com PO Box 53382, London, NW10 3XQ
t 07834 351 690 **e** management@ukmusic.com
w ukmusic.com 🅱 MD: Doug Cooper.

useyourears.com PO Box 52808, London, SW11 2YU
t 020 7223 7472 **e** nathalie@useyourears.com
w useyourears.com 🅱 Contact: Nathalie Plessis
& Virgilio Fino.

Virtual Festivals.com Valiant House, 4-
10 Heneage Lane, London, EC3A 5DQ **t** 020 7337 8839
e dan@virtualfestivals.com **w** virtualfestivals.com
ⓕ facebook.com/pages/Virtual-
Festivals/53861459663?ref=ts
Ⓜ profile.myspace.com/virtual_festivals
ⓔ twitter.com/vf 🅱 Editor: Daniel Fahey.

We Are Pop Slags 61 Earlsmead Rd, London,
NW10 5QD **t** 07906 359005 **e** info@wearepopslags.com
w wearepopslags.com ⓕ facebook.com/popslags
ⓔ twitter.com/popslags 🅱 Editor: Silvan Schreuder.

Web User IPC Inspire, Blue Fin Building,
110 Southwark Street, London, SE1 0SU **t** 020 3148 4327
f 020 3148 8122 **e** editor@web-user.co.uk **w** web-
user.co.uk 🅱 Editor: Richard Clark.

Yahoo! UK & Ireland 10 Ebury Bridge Rd, London,
WC2H 8AD **t** 020 7131 1000 **f** 020 7808 4203
e mccraw@uk.yahoo-inc.com **w** yahoo.co.uk
🅱 European Mktg Mgr, Mobile: Beth McCraw.

Download & Mail Order Websites

1 Off Wax PO Box 5139, Glasgow, G76 8WF
t 0141 585 7354 **f** 0141 585 7354
e sales@1offwax.co.uk **w** 1offwax.co.uk
🅱 Sales Director: Theresa Talbot.

101cd.com PO Box 103, Jersey, Channel Islands,
JEF 8QX **t** 020 8680 5282 **f** 01534 481 360
e service@101cd.com **w** 101cd.com
🅱 Commercial Dir: Hanif Virani.

991 The Nine Nine One Building, Railway Sidings,
Meopham, Gravesend, Kent, DA13 0LT **t** 01474 815010
f 01474 815030 **e** cathryn.draper@991.com **w** 991.com
🅱 Director: Cathryn Draper 01474 815007.

Action Records 46 Church St, Preston, Lancs,
PR1 3DH **t** 01772 884 772 **f** 01772 252 255
e sales@actionrecords.co.uk **w** actionrecords.co.uk
🅱 Manager: Gordon Gibson 01772 258809.

Arkade Fetcham Park House, Lower Road, Leatherhead,
Surrey, KT22 9HD **t** 01372 360 300 **f** 01372 360 878
e info@arkade.com **w** arkade.com

Audiojelly 80 Hadley Rd, Barnet, Herts, EN5 5QS
t 020 8440 0710 **f** 020 8441 8522
e ricky@audiojelly.com **w** audiojelly.com
ⓔ twitter.com/audiojelly
🅱 Managing Director: Ricky Simmonds.

Babymusic.com 17 Shakespeare Gardens, London,
N2 9LJ **t** 020 8883 7306 **f** 020 8365 3388
e music@babymusic.com **w** Babymusic.com
🅱 GM: Susi Kennedy.

Bandwagon Ltd Studio 507 Enterprise House, 1-
2 Hatfields, London, SE1 9PG **t** 020 7993 1221
e support@bandwagon.co.uk **w** bandwagon.co.uk
🅱 Dirs: Owen Farrington, Huw Thomas.

BBC Shop BBC Worldwide, 80 Wood Lane, London,
W12 0TT **t** 020 8433 1303 **f** 020 8225 7877
e bbcshop@bbc.co.uk **w** bbcshop.com
🅱 Executive Producer: Greg Jarvis.

Beathut.com PO Box 3365, Brighton, BN1 1WQ
t 01273 626245 **f** 01273 626246
e info@catskillsrecords.com **w** beathut.com
🅱 Dirs: Khalid, Amr or Jonny.

Beatport Schlesische Strasse 29/30, Aufgang B, Berlin,
10997, Germany **t** +49 30 611 035 1964
f +49 30 611 296 1966 **e** liz.miller@beatport.com
w beatport.com 🅱 Head of Label Management:
Elizabeth Miller.

Cargo Records (UK) Ltd 17 Heathmans Road,
Parsons Green, London, SW6 4TJ **t** 020 7731 5125
f 020 7731 3866 **e** info@cargorecords.co.uk
w cargorecords.co.uk 🅱 MD: Philip Hill.

CD Pool Devonshire House, 223 Upper Richmond Rd,
London, SW15 6SQ **t** 0845 458 8780 **f** 020 8789 8668
e admin@cdpool.co.uk **w** cdpool.com
ⓕ facebook.com/group.php?gid=7119824947&ref=searc
h&sid=277002272.4215512532..1
Ⓜ myspace.com/cdpool ⓔ twitter.com/cdpool
🅱 Contact: Steve Roberts 020 8780 0612.

CDJShop.com Unit 2, Crooks Industrial Estate,
Croft Street, Cheltenham, GL53 0ED **t** 01242 257 777
f 01242 257 774 **e** info@cdjshop.com **w** cdjshop.com
🅱 Director: Simon Brisk.

The All Celtic Music Store PO Box 7264, Glasgow,
G46 6YE **t** 0141 637 6010 **f** 0141 637 6010
e sales@allcelticmusic.com **w** allcelticmusic.com
🅱 MD: Ronnie Simpson.

Classical.com 18 Denbigh Road, London, W11 2SN
t 020 8816 8848 **e** conductor@classical.com
w classical.com 🅱 VP Content & Business: Roger Press.

Contacts Facebook MySpace Twitter YouTube

Crucial Music Pinery Buildings, Highmoor, Wigton, Cumbria, CA7 9LW **t** 016973 45422 **f** 016973 45422 **e** crucialsales@crucialmusic.co.uk **w** crucialmusic.co.uk **MD**: Simon James.

CYP Limited CYP Children's Audio, The Fairway, Bush Fair, Harlow, Essex, CM18 6LY **t** 01279 444707 **f** 01279 445570 **e** enquiries@CYP.co.uk **w** kidsmusic.co.uk Commercial Director: Paul Thorp.

Danceclick Via Bastione Mediceo n. 80, Pistoia, 51100, Italy **t** +39 (0) 573 358 837 **f** +39 (0) 573 508 456 **e** info@danceclick.com **w** danceclick.com Contact: Lorenzo Tiezzi.

Digital Animal Osmond House, 78 Alcester Rd, Birmingham, B13 8BB **t** 0121 449 3814 **e** info@digitalanimal.com **w** digitalanimal.com MD: Richard Powell.

Disky.com 3 York Street, St. Helier, Jersey, Channel Islands, JE2 3RQ **t** 01534 509 687 **e** music.online@disky.com **w** disky.com Managing Director: Robert Bisson.

Dub Vendor Mail Order Dub Vendor Records, 274 Lavender Hill, Clapham Junction, London, SE23 3EP **t** 020 7223 3757 **f** 020 7350 2688 **e** mailorder@dubvendor.co.uk **w** dubvendor.co.uk myspace.com/dubvendor MD: John MacGillivray.

EBTM Plc Unit A1, Riverside Business Centre, Haldane Place, London, SW18 4UQ **e** grant@EBTM.com **w** EBTM.com Director: Grant Calton 07713 404 101.

eil.com Esprit House, Railway Sidings, Meopham, Kent, DA13 0YS **t** 01474 815010 **f** 01474 815030 **e** sales@eil.com **w** eil.com Marketing Manager: Simon Wright.

Flip Records 2 Mardol, Shrewsbury, SY1 1PY **t** 01743 244 469 **f** 01743 260 985 **e** sales@fliprecords.co.uk **w** fliprecords.co.uk Owner: Duncan Morris.

Inspiration Sounds Suite 9A, 79 Lynch Lane, Weymouth, Dorset, DT4 9DW **t** 0845 094 3077 **e** support@producerloops.com **w** producerloops.com Managing Director: Jan Franklin.

Isa Music 260 St.Vincent St, Glasgow, G2 5RL **t** 0141 248 2266 **f** 0141 248 4333 **e** admin@isa-music.com **w** isa-music.com facebook.com/pages/Glasgow-United-Kingdom/Isa-Music twitter.com/allcelticmusic MD: Ronnie Simpson.

Lost Dog Recordings 1103 Argyle Street, Glasgow, G3 8ND **t** 0141 243 2439 **e** info@lostdogrecordings.com **w** lostdogrecordings.com A&R: Jonathan Stone.

THE MUSIC INDEX

THEmusicINDEX™
www.themusicindex.com

34 Coniston Rd, Neston, Cheshire, CH64 0TD **t** 0151 336 6199 **f** 0151 336 6199 **e** info@themusicindex.com **w** themusicindex.com Sales Director: Christine Randall. Sales Director: Christine Randall.

Music Magpie Entertainment Magpie limited T/A Music Magpie, 22 Castle Street, Macclesfield, Cheshire, SK11 6AF **t** 01625 427 774 **e** shop@musicmagpie.co.uk **w** musicmagpie.co.uk Operations Manager: Craig Dawson.

Musicroom.com 14-15 Berners Street, London, W1T 3LJ **t** 020 7612 7400 **f** 020 7836 4810 **e** info@musicroom.com **w** musicroom.com Dir, Internet Operations: Tomas Wise.

Musoswire PO Box 100, Gainsborough, Lincs, DN21 3XH **t** 01427 629184 **f** 01427 629184 **e** helpdesk@musoswire.com **w** musoswire.com Prop: Dan Nash.

Mute Bank c/o Recordstore.co.uk, Unit 5 Waldo Works, Waldo Rd, London, NW10 6AW **t** 020 8964 9020 **f** 020 8964 9090 **e** steve.wheeler@digitalstores.co.uk **w** mutebank.co.uk Manager: Recordstore.co.uk: Steve Wheeler.

Napster UK 57-61 Mortimer St, London, W1W 8HS **t** 020 7101 7275 **f** 020 7101 7120 **e** firstname.lastname@napster.co.uk **w** napster.co.uk Senior Marketing Manager: Dan Nash.

Oxfordmusic.net ltd 1st Floor, 9 Park End Street, Oxford, OX1 1HH **t** 01865 798 796 **f** 01865 798 792 **e** info@oxfordmusic.net **w** oxfordmusic.net MD: Andy Clyde.

Plastic Music Ltd 22 Rutland Gardens, Hove, East Sussex, BN3 5PB **t** 01273 779 793 **f** 01273 779 820 **e** enzo@plastic-music.co.uk **w** plastic-music.co.uk MD: Enzo (Vincent Amico).

PostEverything.com Suite 313, Bon Marché Centre, 241 Ferndale Road, London, SW9 8BJ **t** 020 7733 2344 **e** feedback@posteverything.com **w** posteverything.com GM: Des Berry.

Quaife Music Publishing Ltd 9 Carroll Hill, Loughton, Essex, IG10 1NL **t** 020 8508 3639 **e** quaife@talktalk.net **w** quaifemusic.co.uk MD: Alan Quaife.

Rap and Soul Ltd Box 60201, London, EC1R 1QZ **t** 020 7713 0926 **e** James@RapAndSoulMailOrder.com **w** RapAndSoulMailOrder.com Dir: Mike Lewis.

RawRip.com 130 Shaftsbury Avenue, London, W1D 5EU **t** 020 7031 4292 **f** 020 7031 4302 **e** info@rawrip.com **w** rawrip.com 📇 Business Development Mgr: Armond Mertikian.

Recordstore.co.uk Unit 5, Waldo Works, Waldo Rd, London, NW10 6AW **t** 020 8964 9020 **f** 020 8964 9090 **e** steve.wheeler@digitalstores.co.uk **w** recordstore.co.uk 🅣 twitter.com/recordstore 📇 Manager: Recordstore.co.uk: Steve Wheeler.

Resonance Music Store 3/2 Queens Gate, 35 Grant St, Glasgow, G3 6HJ **t** 0141 331 1455 **e** info@resonancemusicstore.com **w** resonancemusicstore.com 📇 Owner: Gordon 'Nobby' Nelson.

SANDBAG LTD

59/61 Milford Rd, Reading, RG1 8LG **t** 0118 9505812 **f** 0118 9505813 **e** mungo@sandbag.uk.com **w** sandbag.uk.com 📇 Contact: Christiaan Munro.

Secondsounds.com PO Box 570, Amersham, Bucks, HP6 5ZP **t** 01494 875759 **e** information@secondsounds.com **w** secondsounds.com 📇 Mkt Director: Kevin Rockett.

Smallfish Records Unit 3M, Leroy House, 436 Essex Road, London, N1 3QP **t** 020 7288 2900 **e** mike@smallfish.co.uk **w** smallfish.co.uk 📇 Manager: Mike Oliver.

Streetsonline.co.uk Overline House, Station Way, Crawley, West Sussex, RH10 1JA **t** 01293 402040 **f** 01293 402050 **e** nick.coquet@streetsonline.co.uk **w** streetsonline.co.uk 📇 Content Mgr: Nick Coquet.

Streetwise Music Ltd 20A High Street, Tuddenham, Suffolk, IP28 6SA **t** 0560 229 3247 **e** info@streetwisemusic.co.uk **w** streetwisemusic.co.uk 📇 Owner: Will L.

Tanty Records - The Dub Shop PO Box 557, Harrow, Middlesex, HA2 6ZX **t** 07802 463154 **e** kelvin.r@tantyrecord.com **w** tantyrecordshop.com 📇 Owner: Kelvin Richard.

Toughshed.com 72 Rosebank Road, Hanwell, London, W7 2EN **t** 07976 372 032 **f** 07092 272 032 **e** orders@toughshed.com **w** toughshed.com 📇 MD: Neato.

Tribal2Go.co.uk 11 Hillgate Place, London, SW12 9ER **t** 020 8673 4343 **f** 020 8675 8562 **e** sales@tribal2go.co.uk **w** tribal2go.co.uk 📇 Directors: Alison Wilson, Terry Woolner.

Tumi Music Ltd 8-9 New Bond Street Place, Bath, BA1 1BH **t** 01225 464736 **f** 01225 444870 **e** info@tumi.co.uk **w** tumimusic.com 📇 E Commerce: Damien Doherty.

TuneTribe 50-52 Paul St, London, EC2A 4LB **t** 020 7749 1980 **f** 020 7729 8951 **e** info@tunetribe.com **w** tunetribe.com 📇 CEO: William Haighton.

Tystdigital.com 35 Albany Road, Chorlton, Manchester, M21 0BH **t** 0161 882 0058 **f** 0161 882 0058 **e** info@tsytdigital.com **w** tsytdigital.com 📇 Director: David Wheawill.

Upbeat Recordings Larg House, Woodcote Grove, Coulsdon, Surrey, CR5 2QQ **t** 020 8668 3332 **f** 020 8668 3922 **e** liz@upbeat.co.uk **w** upbeat.co.uk 📇 Senior Partner, Exec Prod: Liz Biddle.

Vinyl Tap Old Chapel, 31 Chapel Hill, Linthwaite, Huddersfield, Yorkshire, HD7 5NJ **t** 01484 845999 **e** sales@vinyltap.demon.co.uk **w** vtmusic.co.uk 📇 Director: Tony Boothroyd.

Vinyl Tap Mail Order Music Old Chapel, 31 Chapel Hill, Linthwaite, Huddersfield, Yorkshire, HD7 5NJ **t** 01484 845999 **e** sales@vinyltap.demon.co.uk **w** vtmusic.co.uk 📇 manager: Tony Boothroyd.

Vivante Music Ltd Unit 6, Fontigarry Business Park, Reigate Road, Sidlow, Surrey, RG2 8QH **t** 01293 822 816 **f** 01293 821 965 **e** sales@vivante.co.uk **w** vivante.co.uk 📇 Managing Director: Steven Carr.

WeGotTickets.com 9 Park End St, Oxford, OX1 1HH **t** 01865 798797 **f** 01865 798792 **e** info@wegottickets.com **w** WeGotTickets.com 📇 Marketing Dir: Laura Kramer.

Online Delivery & Distribution

24-7 Entertainment Ltd. 15b Bergham Mews, Blythe Road, London, W14 0HN **t** 020 7602 9922 **f** 020 7602 9944 **e** info@247e.com **w** 247e.com 📇 VP UK: Jonathan Smith.

7digital GmbH Venloer Str. 241-245, Köln, 50823, Germany **t** +49 (221) 990 48 50 **e** alexander.maiwald+musicweek@7digital.com **w** 7digital.de 📇 Country Manager G/S/A: Alex Maiwald.

7digital Limited Unit 1G, Zetland House, 5-25 Scrutton St, London, EC2A 4HJ **t** 020 7099 7777 **f** 020 7504 8020 **e** info@7digital.com **w** 7digital.com 📇 CEO: Ben Drury.

Digital: Online Delivery & Distribution

ABSOLUTE DIGITAL

The Old Lamp Works, Rodney Pl, Wimbledon, London, SW19 2LQ **t** 020 8540 4242 **f** 020 8540 6056 **e** digital@absolutemarketing.co.uk **w** absolutemarketing.co.uk 🔲 Contact: Henry Semmence, Simon Wills, Richard Austen-Smith. **Digital distribution and marketing solutions.**

Art Empire Industries Ltd 2nd Floor. 36-37 Featherstone Street, London, EC1Y 8QZ **t** 020 7741 0050 **f** 020 7250 1726 **e** hello@artempireindustries.com **w** artempireindustries.com 🔲 MD: Del Dias.

AWAL (UK) Ltd (Sheffield) Sheffield Technology Park, Arundel St, Sheffield, S1 2NS **t** 0114 221 1906 **e** info@awal.co.uk **w** awal.co.uk 🔲 Label Manager: Paul Bower.

AWAL (UK) Ltd (London) 42-48 Charlbert St, London, NW8 7BU **t** 020 7449 6780 **e** marketing@awal.com **w** awal.com 🅣 twitter.com/AWALdotcom 🔲 Project Manager: Nick Rosenthal.

Blueprint Digital Unit 1, 73 Maygrove Road, London, NW6 2EG **t** 020 7209 4224 **f** 020 7209 2334 **e** info@blueprint.net **w** blueprint.net 🔲 SVP, Products & Services: Mike Pears.

Broad Street Digital 12-18 Paul Street, London, EC2A 4JH **t** 020 7338 0583 **f** 020 7375 1854 **w** broadstreetdigital.com

Cadiz Digital Ltd 2 Greenwich Quay, Clarence Rd, London, SE8 3EY **t** 020 8692 4691 **f** 020 8469 3300 **e** info@cadizdigital.net **w** cadizdigital.net 🔲 MD: Richard England.

Classical World Ltd. trading as Classical.com 18 Denbigh Road, London, W11 2SN **t** 020 8816 8848 **e** conductor@classical.com **w** classical.com 🔲 President: Roger Press.

Consolidated Independent 8-10 Rhoda St, London, E2 7EF **t** 020 7729 8493 **e** info@ci-info.com **w** ci-info.com 🔲 Sales and Business Development: Quentin Chambers.

Craze Productions 10 Great Russell St, London, WC1B 3BQ **t** 020 7993 8548 **e** Doctorofdance@gmail.com **w** crazedigital.com 🔲 Dir: Sam Kleinman 07877 691615.

DEA Records Via Valpolicella 3/C, San Pietro in Cariano, 37029 - VR, Italy **t** +39 045 620 0888 **f** +39 045 620 3091 **e** info@dearecords.it **w** dearecords.it 🔲 President: Salvatore Marletta.

Digital Stores Unit 5, Waldo Works, Waldo Rd, London, NW10 6AW **t** 020 8964 9020 **f** 020 8964 9090 **e** [firstname.surname]@digitalstores.co.uk **w** digitalstores.co.uk 🔲 Sales Director: Simon Moxon.

Ditto Music Branston Court, Branston St, Birmingham, B18 6BA **t** 0121 551 6624 **e** info@dittomusic.com **w** dittomusic.com 🔲 MD: Matt Parsons.

Doxmedia 29 Latimer Rd, London, E7 0LQ **t** 07713 510830 **e** info@doxmedia.co.uk **w** dowmedia.co.uk 🔲 Contact: Keith Dixon.

ePM Online PO Box 47264, London, W7 1WX **t** 020 8566 0200 **e** melle@epm-music.com **w** epm-music.com 🔲 Partner: Melle Boels.

FASTRAX

IMDFastrax
DEFINING MEDIA LOGISTICS

Allan House, 10 John Princes St, London, W1G 0JW **t** 020 7468 6888 **f** 020 7468 6889 **e** fastrax@imdplc.com **w** fastrax.co.uk 🔲 Contact: Rupak Rahman, Gareth Howells, Laurien Gloag, Lucy Dowland.

FATdrop - Digital music services PO Box 5107, Brighton, BN50 9RG **t** 0845 226 3726 **e** www.fatdrop.co.uk/contact.php **w** fatdrop.co.uk 🔲 Contact: Chris Gorsuch.

Fresh Digital PO Box 4075, Pangbourne, Berks, RG8 7FU **t** 0118 984 3468 **f** 0118 984 3463 **e** info@freshdigital.co.uk **w** freshdigital.co.uk 🔲 MD: Dave Morgan.

hmv.com Film House, 142 Wardour St, London, W1F 8LN **t** 020 7432 2000 **f** 020 7432 2002 **e** firstname.lastname@hmv.co.uk **w** hmv.co.uk

IMImobile 4th Floor, 7 Swallow Pl, London, W1B 2AG **t** 020 7053 6161 **e** info@dx3.net **w** imimobile.com 🔲 Director: Tim Newmarch.

Indian Music 4U 718 Kenton Rd, Harrow, Middlesex, HA3 9QX, United Arab Emirates **t** 020 8204 5000 **f** 020 8204 0120 **e** info@indianmusic4u.co.uk **w** indianmusic4u.co.uk 🔲 Proprietor: Jyotindra Patel.

Interactive Web Solutions 10 Parker Court, Dyson Way, Staffordshire Technology Park, Stafford, Staffs, ST18 0WP **t** 01785 279 920 **f** 01785 223 514 **e** services@iwebsolutions.co.uk **w** iwebsolutions.co.uk 🔲 Business Dev't Dir: Ian Gordon.

Interoute Walbrook Building, 195 Marsh Wall, London, E14 9SG **t** 020 7025 9000 **f** 020 7025 9858 **e** info@interoute.com **w** interoute.com 🅣 Interoute 🔲 Product Manager, Media Services: Simon Barlow.

IODA 10 Allied Way, London, W3 0RQ **t** 020 8600 9207 **e** info@iodalliance.com **w** iodalliance.com 🔲 MD: Pete Dodge.

Keynote Unsigned 6 Beckside, Norwich, Norfolk, NR10 3SY **t** 07828 594 232 **e** info@keynoteunsigned.co.uk **w** keynoteunsigned.co.uk 📇 Dir: Adem Genc.

Kudos Records (Digital) Ltd 77 Fortess Rd, Kentish Town, London, NW5 1AG **t** 020 7482 4555 **f** 020 7482 4551 **e** info@kudos-digital.co.uk **w** kudos-digital.co.uk 📇 Digital Co-ordinator: James Birchall.

Live At The Suite Ltd Utopia Village, 7 Chalcot Road, London, NW1 8LH **t** 020 7813 7964 **f** 020 7209 4092 **e** ladyb@thesuite.sh **w** liveatthesuite.com 📇 Contact: Andrew, Lady B.

Mbop iStores 40 Bowling Green Lane, Clerkenwell, London, EC1R 0NE **t** 020 7415 7010 **f** 020 7415 7030 **e** paul.ballance@mbopglobal.co.uk **w** mbop-promotions.co.uk/labels.html 📇 MD: Paul Ballance.

MbopGlobal Digital 40 Bowling Green Lane, Clerkenwell, London, EC1R 0NE **t** 020 7415 7010 **f** 020 7415 7030 **e** paul.ballance@mbopglobal.co.uk **w** mbop.co.uk f en-gb.facebook.com/people/Mbop-Megastore/1476618030 📇 Mbopmyspace.com/mbopglobal t twitter.com/Mbop ▶ ww.youtube.com/megaboprecords 📇 Director: Paul Ballance.

Mobiqa 111 George St, Edinburgh, EH2 4JN **t** 0131 225 3141 **f** 0131 220 5353 **e** info@mobiqa.com **w** mobiqa.com 📇 CEO: Iain McCready.

Musicpoint Andrews House, College Road, Guildford, Surrey, GU1 4QB **t** 01483 510 910 **f** 01483 510 911 **e** info@musicpointuk.com **w** musicpointuk.com 📇 Business Development Mgr: Richard Clark.

Musoswire PO Box 100, Gainsborough, Lincs, DN21 3XH **t** 01427 629184 **f** 01427 629184 **e** helpdesk@musoswire.com **w** musoswire.com 📇 Prop: Dan Nash.

NewState Digital Unit 2A Queens Studios, 121 Salusbury Rd, London, NW6 6RG **t** 020 7372 4474 **f** 020 7328 4447 **e** info@newstatedigital.com **w** newstatedigital.com 📇 Label Manager: Darren Latimer.

only Vinyl Unit 31-32, Atlas Business Centre, Oxgate Lane, London, NW2 7HU **t** 020 8452 5544 **f** 020 8452 4242 **e** info@only-vinyl.com **w** only-vinyl.com 📇 Contact: Dean Vincent.

[PIAS] Digital Unit 24 Farm Lane Trading Estate, 101 Farm Lane, London, SW6 1QJ **t** 020 7471 2700 **f** 020 7471 2706 **w** pias.com/digital 📇 Director of Digital and Business Development: Adrian Pope.

[PIAS] Ireland 5-6 Lombard St East, Dublin 2, Ireland **t** +353 1 677 9391 **f** +353 1 677 9449 **e** info@piasireland.com **w** piasireland.com 📇 General Manager: Alison Rogers.

RSK ENTERTAINMENT

Units 4&5, Home Farm, Welford, Newbury, Berkshire, RG20 8HR **t** 01488 608 900 **f** 01488 608 901 **e** info@rskentertainment.co.uk **w** rskentertainment.co.uk 📇 Joint MDs: Rashmi Patani & Simon Carver. Label Manager: Matt Groom. Label Manager: Gavin Harry. **RSK has a frontline global digital offer, incorporating mobile, with direct contracts with all the leading Digital Music Services and using CI for encoding and delivery.**

SoundCloud MOO Studios, Trans-World House, 100 City Rd, London, EC1Y 2BP **e** dave@soundcloud.com **w** http://soundcloud.com 📇 VP Business Development: Dave Haynes 0044 7786 136632.

Stream UK Ltd 1 Water Lane, London, NW1 8NZ **t** 020 7387 6090 **f** 020 7419 1819 **e** enquiries@streamuk.com **w** streamuk.com 📇 Contact: Danielle Philip.

Symbios Group 25 Barnes Wallis Rd, Segensworth East, Fareham, PO15 5TT **t** 0870 490 0000 **f** 0870 478 1530 **e** info@symbiosgroup.co.uk **w** symbiosgroup.co.uk 📇 Marketing Dir: Sarah Montague.

Tap It FAME, Inc. 207 N El Camino Real #172, San Clemente, California, 92672, United States **t** +1 949 369 5333 **f** +1 949 369 5336 **e** anu@tapitfame.com **w** tapitfame.com 📇 Marketing/PR: Anu Dhami.

Townsend Records 30 Queen St, Great Harwood, Lancashire, BB6 7QQ **t** 01254 885 995 **f** 01254 887 835 **e** bruce@townsend-records.co.uk **w** townsend-records.co.uk 📇 Sales Director: Bruce McKenzie.

Tribal2Go.co.uk 11 Hillgate Place, London, SW12 9ER **t** 020 8673 4343 **f** 020 8675 8562 **e** sales@tribal2go.co.uk **w** tribal2go.co.uk 📇 Directors: Alison Wilson, Terry Woolner.

Valuflik, Inc - Direct Choice TV Communications Ltd Suite 10, 3rd Floor, Macmillan House, 96 Kensington High Street, London, W8 4SG **t** 020 7082 3928 **f** 020 7082 0880 **e** jthomas@directchoicetv.com **w** valuflik.com 📇 Business Dev't Manager: Johanna Thomas 07884 268 082.

Mobile Delivery & Distribution

24-7 Entertainment Ltd. 15b Bergham Mews, Blythe Road, London, W14 0HN **t** 020 7602 9922 **f** 020 7602 9944 **e** info@247e.com **w** 247e.com 📇 VP UK: Jonathan Smith.

Only MusicWeek guarantees
you reach the right audience

www.musicweek.com

📧 Contacts　　📘 Facebook　　💬 MySpace　　💬 Twitter　　▶ YouTube

3 Star House, 20 Grenfell Rd, Maidenhead, Berks, SL6 1EH **t** 01628 765 000 **f** 01628 767 031
e firstname.lastname@three.co.uk **w** three.co.uk 📧 Hd of Music & Entertain't: Andrew Parker.

ABSOLUTE MOBILE

The Old Lamp Works, Rodney Pl, Wimbledon, London, SW19 2LQ **t** 020 8540 4242 **f** 020 8540 6056
e mobile@absolutemarketing.co.uk
w absolutemarketing.co.uk 📧 Contact: James McGuinness.
Direct mobile distribution and award winning marketing solutions.

Art Empire Industries Ltd 2nd Floor, 36-37 Featherstone Street, London, EC1Y 8QZ
t 020 7741 0050 **f** 020 7250 1726
e hello@artempireindustries.com
w artempireindustries.com 📧 MD: Del Dias.

Bandwagon Ltd Studio 507 Enterprise House, 1-2 Hatfields, London, SE1 9PG **t** 020 7993 1221
e support@bandwagon.co.uk **w** bandwagon.co.uk
📧 Dirs: Owen Farrington, Huw Thomas.

Blueprint Digital Unit 1, 73 Maygrove Road, London, NW6 2EG **t** 020 7209 4224 **f** 020 7209 2334
e info@blueprint.net **w** blueprint.net 📧 SVP, Products & Services: Mike Pears.

Broad Street Digital 12-18 Paul Street, London, EC2A 4JH **t** 020 7338 0583 **f** 020 7375 1854
w broadstreetdigital.com

Inventa Productions Buongiorno, 20 Orange Street, London, WC2H 7NN **t** 020 7766 4069 **f** 020 7437 3666
e theteam@inventa.co.uk **w** inventa.co.uk 📧 MD: Youssef Hammad.

Key Production Digital Services 7-8 Jeffrey's Pl, Camden, London, NW1 9PP **t** 020 7284 8800
f 020 7284 8844 **e** mail@keyproduction.co.uk
w keyproduction.co.uk
💬 myspace.com/keyproductionlondon 📧 Sales & Marketing: Wendy Wood.

Kodime 39 The Woodlands, Esher, Surrey, KT10 8DD
t 0870 787 4652 **f** 020 8224 0033 **e** info@kodime.com
w kodime.com 📧 MD: Nico Kopke.

Kudos Records (Digital) Ltd 77 Fortess Rd, Kentish Town, London, NW5 1AG **t** 020 7482 4555
f 020 7482 4551 **e** info@kudos-digital.co.uk **w** kudos-digital.co.uk 📧 Digital Co-ordinator: James Birchall.

Look Media Grove House, 27 Hammersmithe Grove, London, W6 0JL **t** 020 8600 2615 **f** 020 8600 2501
e info@lookmediauk.com **w** lookmediauk.com
📧 Managing Director: Jonathan Schultz.

M2Y-Siemens UK 90 Long Acre, London, WC2E 9RZ
t 07730 426 310 **e** leslie.golding@siemens.com
w siemens.com/m2y 📧 Hd of Content: Leslie Golding.

Masterpiece Unit 14 The Talina Centre, Bagleys Lane, London, SW6 2BW **t** 020 7731 5758 **f** 020 7384 1750
e leena.bhatti@masterpiece.net **w** masterpiece.net
📧 Business Development Manager: Leena Bhatti.

Melodi Three Spires House, Bird Street, Lichfield, Staffordshire, WS13 6PR **t** 0870 0622 900
e enquiries@melodimedia.co.uk **w** melodimedia.co.uk
📧 MD: Iain Kerr.

Mobiq Tech House, Reddicap Trading Estate, Coleshill Road, Sutton Coldfield, B75 7BU
t 0121 311 9980 **f** 0121 311 9981 **e** info@mobiq.tv
w mobiq.tv 📧 Commercial Dir: John Plant.

Mobiqa 111 George St, Edinburgh, EH2 4JN
t 0131 225 3141 **f** 0131 220 5353 **e** info@mobiqa.com
w mobiqa.com 📧 CEO: Iain McCready.

MonsterMob Group Plc 52 Berkeley Square, London, W1J 5BT **t** 020 7408 4732 **f** 020 7491 3794
e david.bloomfield@monstermob.com **w** mob.tv 📧 Head of Music: David Bloomfield.

MusiWave UK 77 Oxford St, London, W1D 2ES
t 020 7659 2053 **f** 020 7659 2100
e noel@musicwave.com **w** musiwave.com 📧 Business Dev't Mgr: Noel Penzer.

O2 O2 UK, 260 Bath Rd, Slough, Berks, SL1 4DX
t 01132 722000 **f** 01753 565010 **e** matt.ward@o2.com
w o2.co.uk/music 📘 facebook.com/o2ukofficial
💬 twitter.com/o2 ▶ youtube.com/o2ukofficial 📧 Music Specialist: Matt Ward.

Pocket Group Unit 62/63, Pall Mall Deposit, 124-128 Barlby Road, London, W10 6BL **t** 0870 241 1827
f 0870 241 1829 **e** info@pocketgroup.co.uk
w pocketgroup.co.uk 📧 MD: Andrew Hull.

pvNS - Alcatel Voyager Place, Shoppenhangers Road, Maidenhead, Berkshire, SL6 2PJ **t** 01633 413600
e firstname.lastname@alcatel.co.uk **w** alcatel.com
📧 Contact: Patrick Parodi.

Qpass Golden Cross House, 8 Duncannon St, London, WC2N 4JF **t** 020 7484 5031 **f** 020 7484 4958
e cpoepperl@qpass.com **w** qpass.com 📧 Marketing Dir: Claudia Poepperl.

Que Pasa Communications Ltd
Coppergate House, 16 Brune St, London, E1 7NJ
t 020 7953 7700 **f** 020 7953 7709
e hugh@quepasacomms.co.uk **w** que-pasa.co.uk
📧 Commercial Dir: Hugh Burrows.

ScreenFX Dudley House, 36-38 Southampton St, Covent Garden, London, WC1E 7HE **t** 020 7240 0123
f 020 7240 0611 **e** info@screenfx.com **w** screenfx.com
📧 Sales Dir: Billy Howard.

SMS MusicMaker P.O. Box 44197, Fulham, London, SW6 2XP **t** 07947 370 056 **e** info@smsmusicmaker.com
w smsmusicmaker.com 📧 Dir: Barney Cordell.

🔲 Contacts 🔲 Facebook 🔲 MySpace 🔲 Twitter 🔲 YouTube

Digital: Mobile Delivery & Distribution, Web Design & Digital Services

Valuflik, Inc - Direct Choice TV Communications Ltd Suite 10, 3rd Floor, Macmillan House, 96 Kensington High Street, London, W8 4SG **t** 020 7082 3928 **f** 020 7082 0880 **e** jthomas@directchoicetv.com **w** valuflik.com 🔲 Business Dev't Manager: Johanna Thomas 07884 268 082.

Victoria Real Ltd Shepherds Building Central, Charecroft Way, London, W14 0EE **t** 020 8222 4170 **f** 020 8222 4415 **e** susan.doherty@victoriareal.com **w** victoriareal.com 🔲 Hd of Business Dev't: Susan Doherty.

Vodafone Group Services 1 Kingdom St, Sheldon Square, London, W2D 1FA **t** 01635 666777 **e** morgan.donaghue@vodafone.com **w** vodafone.com 🔲 Vodafone Group 🔲 Head of Music: Morgan Donaghue.

WIN 1 Cliveden Office Village, Lancaster Road, High Wycombe, Bucks, HP12 3YZ **t** 01494 750500 **f** 01494 750800 **e** businessdevelopment@winplc.com **w** winplc.com 🔲 Marketing Manager: Ben King.

Xbox - Europe, Middle East & Africa Microsoft House, 10 Great Pulteney Street, London, W1F 9NB **t** 020 7434 6172 **f** 020 7434 6495 **e** markcad@microsoft.com 🔲 Hd, Strategic P'tnerships: Mark Cadogan.

Web Design & Digital Services

The 7 Stars 46 Charlotte Street, London, W1T 2GS **t** 020 7436 7275 **f** 020 7436 7276 **e** firstname.lastname@the7stars.co.uk **w** the7stars.co.uk 🔲 Contact: Jenny Biggam.

1000Greatest.com High Parsons, Lavenham, Suffolk, CO10 9SB **t** 07958 383063 **e** colin@colinlarkin.com **w** btoe.com 🔲 Ed-in-Chief: Colin Larkin.

Agitprop Design & Communications 19 Links Yard, 29a Spelman St, London, E1 5LX **t** 07989 586272 **e** musicweek@agitprop.co.uk **w** agitprop.co.uk 🔲 Creative Director: Jim Holt 07989 586 272.

Air MTM 27 The Quadrangle, 49 Atalanta St, London, SW6 6TU **t** 020 7386 1600 **f** 020 7386 1619 **e** info@airmtm.com **w** airmtm.com 🔲 twitter.com/airmtm 🔲 Contact: Jonny South.

All of Music Design PO Box 2361, Romford, Essex, RM2 6EZ **t** 01708 688 088 **f** 020 7691 9508 **e** michelle@allofmusic.co.uk **w** allofmusic.co.uk 🔲 MD: Danielle Barnett.

Amplifeye 5 Pendarves Road, Camborne, Cornwall, TR14 7QB **t** 0871 789 4219 **e** dan@amplifeye.com **w** amplifeye.net 🔲 Director: Daniel Mitchell 07886 923 821.

AOL 80 Hammersmith Road, London, W14 8UD **t** 020 7348 8000 **f** 020 7348 8002 **w** aol.com

ArtScience Limited 3-5 Hardwidge St, London, SE1 3SY **t** 020 7939 9500 **f** 020 7939 9499 **e** lab5@artscience.net **w** artscience.net 🔲 Dirs: Douglas Coates, Pete Rope.

Astream.com 2nd Floor, 36-37 Featherstone St, London, EC1Y 8QZ **t** 0845 230 8804 **f** 0845 230 8805 **e** Alex@Astream.com **w** Astream.com 🔲 Director: Alex Wolfe.

Atari Landmark House, Hammersmith Bridge Road, London, W6 9DP **t** 020 8222 9700 **e** firstname.lastname@atari.com **w** atari.com 🔲 UK Marketing Director: Richard Orr.

Bang On - Online PR 77 Leonard Street, London, EC2A 4QS **t** 020 7749 7826 **e** info@bangonpr.com **w** bangonpr.com 🔲 Online Publicists: Leanne Mison, Katie Riding.

Beatwax Communications 91 Berwick Street, London, W1F 0NE **t** 020 7734 1965 **f** 020 7292 8333 **e** michael@beatwax.com **w** beatwax.com 🔲 MD: Michael Brown.

Big Picture Interactive Ltd 9 Parade, Leamington Spa, Warwickshire, CV32 4DG **t** 01926 422002 **f** 01926 450945 **e** enquiries@bigpictureinteractive.co.uk **w** thebigpic.co.uk 🔲 PA: Sarah Pannell.

Bite Digital Ltd - SEO & web design Floor 1, Blackfriars House, Parsonage, Manchester, M3 2JA **t** 0845 688 4491 **f** 0870 490 2327 **e** sales@biteus.net **w** biteus.net 🔲 MD: Declan Cosgrove.

Bloc Media Ltd 61 Charlotte Rd, London, EC2A 3QT **t** 020 7739 1718 **f** 020 7739 9494 **e** contact@blocmedia.com **w** blocmedia.com 🔲 MD: Rick Palmer.

Blue Source Ltd. Lower Ground Floor, 49-51 Central St, London, EC1V 8AB **t** 020 7553 7950 **e** seb@bluesource.com **w** bluesource.com 🔲 Company Director: Seb Marling.

C-Burn Systems Ltd 33 Sekforde St, London, EC1R 0HH **t** 020 7250 1133 **f** 020 7253 8553 **e** info@c-burn.com **w** c-burn.com 🔲 Sales & Marketing: Neil Phillips.

Cake Group Ltd 10 Stephen Mews, London, W1T 1AG **t** 020 7307 3100 **f** 020 7307 3101 **e** andrea@cakegroup.com **w** cakegroup.com 🔲 Head of Marketing: Andrea Ledsham.

Clevercherry.com Victoria Works, Birmingham, B1 3PE **t** 0121 236 1060 **e** ineedhelp@clevercherry.com **w** clevercherry.com 🔲 MD: Ian Allen.

ColBrowne.co.uk St 4, Fl 4, The Old Truman Brewery, 91-95 Brick Lane, London, E1 6QL **t** 07802 824 001 **e** me@colbrowne.co.uk **w** colbrowne.co.uk 🔲 MD: Col Browne.

CopyMaster International Ltd Copymaster House, 14 Lombard Road, Merton, London, SW19 3TZ **t** 020 8543 9223 **f** 020 8543 3419 **e** firstname@copymaster.co.uk **w** copymaster.co.uk 🔲 CD & DVD Account Mgr: Ron Boucaud.

📇 Contacts   📘 Facebook   🟦 MySpace   🟦 Twitter   ▶️ YouTube

Digital: Web Design & Digital Services

THE CREATIVE CORPORATION

Magpie Studios, 2a Leconfield Rd, London, N5 2SN
t 020 7704 9234 **e** dave@thecreativecorporation.co.uk
w thecreativecorporation.co.uk 📇 Contact: Dave Stansbie
07779 615 217.

Creative Cultures 10 Alexandra Park Road, London,
N10 2AB **t** 020 7100 3254 **f** 0871 661 4578
e firstname.lastname@creativecultures.biz
w creativecultures.biz 📇 Managing Director: Johnny
Hudson.

Darling Social Services Ltd Unit 204/5,
Hatton Square Business Centre, 16-16A Baldwin Gardens,
London, EC1N 7RJ **t** 020 7061 6266
e info@darlingsocialservices.com
w darlingsocialservices.com
📘 facebook.com/darlingsocialservices
🟦 twitter.com/darlingsocial 📇 Directors: Patrick
Clifton/Ed Cartwright/Dan Stevens.

Design Lab Studio 336, Stratford Workshops,
Burford Road, London, E15 2SP **t** 020 8555 5540
f 0208 5555540 **e** info@design-lab.tv **w** design-lab.tv
📇 Art Director: Matthew James 07841 196 787.

Diverse Interactive 6 Gorleston Street, London,
W14 8XS **t** 020 7603 4567 **f** 020 7603 2148
e info@diverse.tv **w** diverse.co.uk 📇 Interactive Prod
Mgr: Nicola Wells.

Division 100 Unit Two, 34 Charlotte Rd, London,
EC2A 3PB **t** 020 7033 0000 **f** 020 7033 0001
e designers@division100.com **w** division100.com
📇 Dir: Terence Chisholm.

DMCC - Online Marketing and Search Engines
34 Hereford Road, London, W2 5AJ **t** 07092 047 348
f 07092 047 348 **e** SearchFindUse@DMCC.net
w dmcc.net 📇 Projects Director: Fiona Austin.

Dreamcatcher Studios Ltd 3, Merryman Drive,
Crowthorne, Berkshire, RG45 6TW **t** 07771 818 111
f 01344 779 677
e leeault@dreamcatcherstudiosltd.co.uk
w dreamcatcherstudios.co.uk 📇 Creative Director: Lee
Ault.

DS Emotion Ltd Chantry House, Victoria Road, Leeds,
West Yorkshire, LS5 3JB **t** 0113 225 7100
f 0113 225 7200 **e** info@dsemotion.com
w dsemotion.com

DVS Productions Ltd Prospect House,
Lower Caldecote, Biggleswade, Beds, SG18 9UH
t 01767 601398 **f** 0870 706 6257
e admin@dvsproductions.com **w** dvsproductions.com
📇 Director: David Smyth.

Effective Business Solutions P O Box 152,
Tewkesbury, Gloucestershire, GL20 9AU **t** 01242 620095
e nrb@ebsed.co.uk **w** ebsed.co.uk 📇 Proprietor: Nigel
Browning 07778 554190.

Elevate PR 3 Hurst Rd, Robbins, Sidcup, Kent,
DA15 9AE **t** 0845 355 0563 **f** 0870 881 0867
e info@elevatelondon.com **w** elevatelondon.com
📇 Dir: Penny Adaarewa.

Epic 52 Old Steine, Brighton, East Sussex, BN1 1NH
t 01273 728 686 **f** 01273 821 567
e marketing@epic.co.uk **w** epic.co.uk 📇 Marketing
Manager: Ericka Newton.

Eyetoeye Entertainment Tucketts Barn, Trusham,
Devon, TQ13 0NR **t** 01626 854 277
e brian@eyetoeye.com **w** eyetoeye.com 📇 Partner: Brian
Yates.

Fastchanges 15 Barlby Gardens, London, W10 5LW
t 020 7870 8159 **e** info@fastchanges.com
w fastchanges.com 📇 Design Director: Jude Samuel.

Fellows Media Ltd The Gallery, Manor Farm, Southam,
Cheltenham, Gloucestershire, GL52 3PB **t** 01242 259241
e media@fellowsmedia.com **w** fellowsmedia.com
📇 Managing Director: Simon Fellows.

Firebrand 3 Wish Rd, Eastbourne, East Sussex,
BN21 4NX **t** 01323 430700 **f** 01323 430223
e enq@firebrand.co.uk **w** firebrand.co.uk 📇 Creative
Director: Michael Dale.

TheFireFactory.com 3-5 High Pavement,
The Lace Market, Nottingham, NG1 1HF **t** 0115 989 7389
f 0870 131 4234 **e** info@thefirefactory.com
w thefirefactory.com 📇 Producer: Jake Shaw.

Fourmiles Media Services PO Box 5571,
Milton Keynes, MK3 5YN **t** 0709 222 3643
f 0705 069 8195 **e** enquiries@fourmiles.com
w fourmiles.com 📇 MD: David Wright.

Glasseye Unit 20A, Iliffe Yard, Crampton Street, London,
SE17 3QA **t** 020 7701 4300 **e** info@glasseyeltd.com
w glasseyeltd.com 📇 Director: James Jefferson.

Good Technology The Griffin Building,
83 Clerkenwell Road, London, EC1R 5AR **t** 020 7343 3700
f 020 7343 3701
e firstname.lastname@goodtechnology.com
w goodtechnology.com 📇 MD: Xanthe Arvanitakis.

Graphico Goldwell House, Old Bath Road, Newbury,
Berkshire, RG14 1JH **t** 01635 522 810 **f** 01635 580 621
e solutions@graphico.co.uk **w** graphico.co.uk 📇 Managing
Director: Graham Darracott.

Greenroom Digital 87A Worship St, London,
EC2A 2BE **t** 020 7426 5700 **f** 020 7377 8616
e emily@greenroom-digital.com **w** greenroom-digital.com
📇 Creative Assistant: Emily Eades.

Gwarsh Studio 79 Stanley St, Darlinghurst, Sydney,
2010 NSW, Australia **t** +61 2 9331 1113
e joel@gwarsh.com **w** gwarsh.com 📇 Creative
Director: Joel Wasserman +61 (0) 411 22 6467.

Contacts | **Facebook** | **MySpace** | **Twitter** | **YouTube**

Hotpot Digital First Floor, 62 Bridge St, Manchester, M3 3BW **t** 0161 838 9183 **f** 0161 838 9189 **e** hello@hotpotdigital.com **w** hotpotdigital.com Senior Designer: Steven Oakes.

House of Tears Design 522 Locust, Suite 104, Kansas City, MO, 64106, United States **t** +1 800 936 2170 **f** +1 800 936 2170 **e** vision@houseoftearsdesign.com **w** houseoftearsdesign.com
facebook.com/pages/House-of-Tears-Design/99356796999
myspace.com/houseoftearsdesign
twitter.com/houseoftears Principal: Curt Cuscino 800 936 2170.

Hutch Rose Cottage, South Dock Lock Office, Rope Street, London, SE16 7SZ **t** 020 7252 0147 **e** info@willhutchinson.co.uk **w** willhutchinson.co.uk MD: Will Hutchinson 07952 751614.

Hyperlaunch New Media Mardyke House, 16-22 Hotwell Rd, Bristol, BS8 4UD **t** 0117 914 0070 **f** 0117 914 0071 **e** don@hyperlaunch.com **w** hyperlaunch.com MD: Don Jenkins.

ID Interactive 5 Rolls Crescent, Manchester, M15 5JX **t** 0161 232 9314 **f** 0161 232 9514 **e** info@idinteractive.co.uk **w** idinteractive.net Manager: Azmat Mohammed.

Ignite Creative TV 90 Red Square, London, N16 9AG **t** 020 7502 2370 **e** info@ignitecreative.tv **w** ignitecreative.tv Multi Media Producer: Kary Stewart.

Interactive Web Solutions 10 Parker Court, Dyson Way, Staffordshire Technology Park, Stafford, Staffs, ST18 0WP **t** 01785 279 920 **f** 01785 223 514 **e** services@iwebsolutions.co.uk **w** iwebsolutions.co.uk Business Dev't Dir: Ian Gordon.

Interface New Media 20A Brownlow Mews, London, WC1N 2LA **t** 020 7416 0702 **f** 020 7416 0700 **e** info@interface-newmedia.com **w** interface-newmedia.com Dir: Neil Jones.

IntoMusic.co.uk Unit 8, 6 Bloom Grove, London, SE27 0HZ **t** 020 8676 4850 **e** info@intomusic.co.uk **w** intomusic.co.uk CEO: Gavin Moulton.

IQ Media (Bracknell) Ltd 2 Venture House, Arlington Square, Bracknell, Berkshire, RG12 1WA **t** 01344 422 551 **f** 01344 453 355 **e** information@iqmedia-uk.com **w** iqmedia-uk.com MD: Tony Bellamy 07884 262 755.

Kicking Digital 5 Parsonage Pl, Tring, Hertfordshire, HP23 5AT **t** 08453 888903 **f** 08453 888904 **e** adam@ihouseu.com **w** kickingdigital.com MD: Adam Giddens.

Lateral Net Ltd Charlotte House, 47-49 Charlotte Road, London, EC2A 3QT **t** 020 7613 4449 **f** 020 7613 4645 **e** studio@lateral.net **w** lateral.net New Business Manager: Jon Bains.

Legion Presents 7, 28a High St, Cardiff, CF10 1PU **t** 02920 399 383 **e** info@legionpresents.com **w** legionpresents.com Dirs: Dave or Kris Legion.

LoFly Web Technology Unit 2A Queens Studios, 121 Salusbury Road, London, NW6 6RG **t** 020 7372 4474 **f** 020 7328 4447 **e** info@lofly.co.uk **w** lofly.co.uk New Media Programmers: Peter Gill, Tom Parkinson.

Luna Internet Ltd 8 Triumph Way, Woburn Road Industrial Estate, Kempston, Bedford, MK42 7QB **t** 0845 345 0175 **f** 01234 299 009 **e** info@luna.co.uk **w** luna.co.uk Sales & Mktg Dir: Spencer Ecclestone.

Lynton Black Media 7 Ty Ddewi Court, Cardiff, CF11 9AW **t** 02920 195 300 **e** creativity@lyntonblack.net **w** lyntonblack.net Creative Director: Lynton Black 07921 903 943.

m3m 1 Church Lane, Rochdale, OL16 1NR **t** 0161 408 4300 **e** gus@modernmediamuse.com **w** modernmediamuse.com Founder: Gus Geraghty 0161 4084300.

Mackerel Design Ltd 15-17 Middle Street, Brighton, West Sussex, BN1 1AL **t** 01273 201313 **e** info@mackerel.co.uk **w** mackerel.co.uk Director: Mark Davis.

Mando Group Ltd 131 Mount Pleasant, Liverpool, L3 5TF **t** 0845 365 4040 **f** 0845 365 4041 **e** ian.finch@mandogroup.com **w** mandogroup.com MD: Ian Finch.

Martello Media Limited 4 Islington Avenue, Sandycove, Co Dublin, Ireland **t** +353 1 284 4668 **f** +353 1 280 3195 **e** info@martellomedia.com **w** martellomedia.com Project Manager: Iseult O'Siochain.

Mekon Ltd Mekon House, 31-35 St Nicholas Way, Sutton, Surrey, SM1 1JN **t** 020 8722 8400 **f** 020 8722 8500 **e** info@mekon.com **w** mekon.com Sales Dir: Julian Murfitt.

Microsoft - MSN Microsoft House, 10 Great Pulteney Street, London, W1R 3TG **t** 0870 60 10 100 **w** mircrosoft.com/uk/info

Moonfish Ltd 43 Hulme St, Manchester, M15 6AW **t** 08700 70 4321 **f** 08707 41 8931 **e** fish.market@moonfish.com **w** moonfish.com Creative Dir: Bill Croson.

Motion PR 1 Stucley Studios, Stucley Place, Camden, London, NW1 8NS **t** 020 7485 9773 **f** 020 7267 6638 **e** giovanna@motionpr.co.uk **w** motionpr.co.uk Head of PR and Marketing: Giovanna Ferin.

Musicalc/RoyaltyShare The Old Police Station, 6 Old London Road, Kingston-upon-Thames, Surrey, KT2 6QF **t** 020 8439 1518 **f** 020 8541 1885 **e** info@musicalc.com **w** musicalc.com General Manager: Asa Palmer.

Neuecom Web Solutions 9 Adam Street, London, WC2N 6AA **t** 020 8331 3646 **e** info@neuecom.com **w** neuecom.com MD: Chiduve Ameke.

Digital: Web Design & Digital Services

The New Black Beam End Cottage, Wooburn Green, Wash Hill, Buckinghamshire, HP10 0JA **t** 020 8123 0038 **e** info@newblack.me **w** newblack.me 📇 Managing Director: Ben Taub & Jim Tattersall 07779 794704.

Nile-On Online PR & Marketing 42a Charlotte Street, London, W1T 2NP **t** 020 7636 7322 **f** 020 7636 7325 **e** serena@nile-on.com **w** nile-on.com 📇 Online Press Director: Serena Wilson.

Opendisc® Medius House LG, 2 Sheraton Street, London, W1F 8BD **t** 020 7479 4839 **e** uk@opendisc.net **w** opendisc.net 📇 CEO: Guillaume Doret.

OR Multimedia Ltd Unit 5 Elm Court, 156-170 Bermondsey Street, London, SE1 3TQ **t** 020 7939 9540 **f** 020 7939 9541 **e** info@or-media.com **w** or-media.com 📇 Dir: Peter Gough.

Outpost Media Ltd Arch 462, Kingsland Viaduct, 83 Rivington Street, Shoreditch, London, EC2A 3AY **t** 020 7684 5634 **e** david@outpostmedia.co.uk **w** outpostmedia.co.uk 📇 Dir: David Silverman 07811 422 266.

Outside Line Butler House, 177-178 Tottenham Court Road, London, W1T 7NY **t** 020 7636 5511 **f** 020 7636 1155 **e** ant@outsideline.co.uk **w** outsideline.co.uk 📇 Director: Anthony Cauchi.

Oxfordmusic.net ltd 1st Floor, 9 Park End Street, Oxford, OX1 1HH **t** 01865 798 796 **f** 01865 798 792 **e** info@oxfordmusic.net **w** oxfordmusic.net 📇 MD: Andy Clyde.

Picaholic.com 160 Greentree Drive, Suite 101, Dover, Delaware, County of Kent, 19904, United States **t** +1 800 235 3698 **e** almira@picaholic.com **w** picaholic.com 📘 facebook.com/pages/Picaholiccom/42642290567?ref=mf 🅣 twitter.com/picaholic 📇 Marketing Director: Almira Pizovic.

Playniac t 020 7617 7516 **w** playniac.com 📘 facebook.com/playniac 🟦 myspace.com/playniac 🅣 twitter.com/playniac ▶️ youtube.com/playniac 📇 MD: Rob Davis.

Poptel Technology Ltd 35 Stukeley Street, London, WC2B 5LT **t** 0845 899 1001 **f** 0845 899 0160 **e** info@poptech.coop **w** poptech.coop 📇 Business Development: Paul Evans.

Prezence New Media and Mobile for Music 101 Colosseum, Century City, Cape Town, Western Cape, 7001, South Africa **t** +27 21 526 2080 **e** tim@prezence.co.za **w** prezence.co.za 📇 CEO: Tim Bishop.

Proactive PR Suite 201, Homelife House, 26 - 32 Oxford Road, Bournemouth, BH8 8EZ **t** 01202 315 333 **f** 01202 315 600 **e** info@proactivepr.org **w** proactivepr.org 📇 Dir: Cliff Lay.

Probe Media 2nd Floor, The Hogarth Centre, Hogarth Lane, London, W4 2QN **t** 020 8742 3636 **f** 020 8995 1350 **e** sanjay@probemedia.co.uk **w** probemedia.co.uk 📇 Account Director: Sanjay Vadher.

Real World Multimedia Box Mill, Millside, Mill Lane, Box, Wiltshire, SN13 8PL **t** 0845 146 1733 **f** 01225 744369 **e** york.tillyer@realworld.co.uk **w** realworld.co.uk 📇 Interactive Dir: York Tillyer.

RealNetworks Europe Ltd. 1st Floor, 233 High Holborn, London, WC1V 7DN **t** 020 7618 4000 **f** 020 7618 4001 **e** initial+lastname@real.com **w** realnetworks.com 📇 Sales Director: David Smith.

Rednet Ltd 6 Cliveden Office Village, Lancaster Road, High Wycombe, Buckinghamshire, HP12 3YZ **t** 01494 513 333 **f** 01494 443 374 **e** contactus@red.net **w** red.net 📇 Mktg Mgr: Zoe Marrett.

rehabstudio Ltd 1st Floor, 101 Redchurch St, London, E2 7DP **t** 020 3222 0080 **e** newbusiness@rehabstudio.com **w** rehabstudio.com 📇 Creative Director: Tim Rodgers.

Ricall Limited First Floor, 14 Buckingham Palace Road, London, SW1W 0QP **t** 020 7592 1710 **f** 020 7592 1713 **e** mail@ricall.com **w** ricall.com 📇 Founder & CEO: Richard Corbett.

Rootsmusic.com 22 Oregon Avenue, Manor Park, London, E12 5TD **t** 020 8553 1435 **f** 020 8553 1435 **e** info@rootsmusic.co.uk **w** rootsmusic.co.uk 📇 MD: Ayo Bamidele.

Sign-Up.to (E-Marketing) 60 Maltings Pl, London, SW6 2BX **t** 0845 644 4184 **e** solutions@sign-up.to **w** sign-up.to 📘 facebook.com/signupto 🅣 twitter.com/signupto ▶️ youtube.com/signuptech 📇 MD: Matt McNeill.

Simbiotic Mercat House, Argyle Court, 1103 Argyle St, Glasgow, G3 8ND **t** 0141 243 2439 **e** graham@simbiotic.co.uk **w** simbiotic.co.uk 📇 Dir: Graham Collins.

SimpleWeb Ltd First Floor, 64 Alma Road, Bristol, BS3 3EZ **t** 0117 923 8558 **e** mark@simpleweb-online.com **w** simpleweb-online.com 📇 Contact: Mark Panay.

Skinny Unit B, 53 Underhill Road, London, SE22 0QR **t** 020 8693 8798 **e** info@skinnycreative.com **w** skinnycreative.com 📇 Director: Sonya Skinner.

Slightly Sinister London **e** emma@slightlysinister.com **w** slightlysinister.com 📇 Business Development Director: Emma Peters 07871 265432.

Somethin' Else 20-26 Brunswick Place, London, N16DZ **t** 020 7250 5500 **f** 020 7250 0937 **e** steve.ackerman@somethinelse.com **w** somethinelse.com 📇 Managing Director: Steve Ackerman 020 7250 5617.

Sonic Arts The Shaftesbury Centre, 85 Barlby Road, London, W10 6BN **t** 020 8962 3000 **f** 020 8962 6200 **e** avi@sonic-arts.com **w** sonic-arts.com 📇 Contact: Miranda Webster.

Sony Psygnosis Ltd Napier Court, Wavertree Technology Park, Liverpool, Merseyside, L13 1HD **t** 0151 282 3000 **f** 0151 282 3001 **w** worldwidestudios.net/en/Homepage

Contacts   Facebook MySpace Twitter YouTube

Soundengineer.co.uk 49 Liddington Road, London, E15 3PL **t** 020 8536 0649 **f** 07092 022897 **e** ian@soundengineer.co.uk **w** soundengineer.co.uk Sound Engineer: Ian Hasell.

state51 8-10 Rhoda Street, London, E2 7EF **t** 020 7729 4343 **f** 020 7729 8494 **e** intouch@state51.co.uk **w** state51.co.uk Director: Paul Sanders.

Stream UK 1 Water Lane, London, NW1 8NZ **t** 020 7387 6090 **f** 020 7419 1819 **e** enquiries@streamuk.com **w** streamuk.com Sales Dir: Danielle Phillips.

Stylorouge 57/60 Charlotte Rd, London, EC2A 3QT **t** 020 7729 1005 **f** 020 7739 7124 **e** rob@stylorouge.co.uk **w** stylorouge.co.uk Creative Director: Rob O'Connor.

Telepathy Interactive Media Hardy House, High Street, Box, Wiltshire, SN13 8NF **t** 01225 744 225 **f** 01225 744 554 **e** info@telepathy.co.uk **w** telepathy.co.uk Dir: Nigel Milk.

Tomorrow Never Knows 15 Hopkin Close, Queen Elizabeth Park, Guildford, Surrey, GU2 9LS **t** 01483 234 428 **e** ritch@tomorrowneverknows.co.uk **w** tomorrownoverknows.co.uk MD: Ritch Ames.

Turnround Multi-Media Barn Studio, Chapel Farm, Over Old Road, Hartpury, Gloucestershire, GL19 3BJ **t** 01242 224 360 **e** studio@turnround.co.uk **w** turnround.co.uk MD: Ross Lammas.

UnLimited Digital Fl 3, Grampian House, Meridian Gate, London, E14 9YT **t** 0870 744 2643 **f** 070 9231 4982 **e** chris@unlimitedmedia.co.uk **w** unlimitedmedia.co.uk MD: Chris Cooke.

Version Industries Ltd 47 Lower End, Swaffham Prior, Cambridge, CB5 0HT **t** 07903 886 471 **f** 020 8374 4021 **e** team@versionindustries.com **w** versionindustries.com Lead Designer/Developer: Gavin Singleton.

Virgin Media 160 Gt Portland St, London, W1W 5QA **t** 020 7299 5000 **e** firstname.surname@virginmedia.co.uk **w** virginmedia.com Head of Publishing: Caroline Hugh.

Visualeyes Imaging Services 11 West Street, Covent Garden, London, WC2H 9NE **t** 020 7836 3004 **f** 020 7240 0079 **e** imaging@visphoto.co.uk **w** visphoto.co.uk Sales & Marketing Manager: Fergal O'Regan.

VocalTuning.com 9 Woodmancote Vale, Cheltenham, Glos, GL52 9RJ **t** 01242 676 672 **e** enquiries@vocaltuning.com **w** vocaltuning.com Sound engineer: James Kinnear.

Voodoo Ltd The Oast House, Mead Lane, Farnham, Surrey, GU9 7DY **t** 08700 278 444 **f** 07092 378 818 **e** sales@voodoo.co.uk **w** voodoo.co.uk Managing Director: James Puddicombe.

WayOutWebs.com PO Box 1345, Ilford, Essex, IG4 5FX **t** 07050 333 555 **e** info@wayoutwebs.com **w** wayoutwebs.com Business Dev't Director: Paul Booth.

WEB SHERIFF

Argentum, 2 Queen Caroline Street, London, W6 9DX **t** 020 8323 8013 **f** 020 8323 8080 **e** websheriff@websheriff.com **w** websheriff.com MD: John Giacobbi.

Yellocello Internet 49 Windmill Rd, London, W4 1RN **t** 020 8742 2001 **e** info@yellocello.com **w** yellocello.com MD: Charlie Carne.

YouLicense.com Ben Yehuda 32, Tel Aviv, Israel **t** +972 777 033 116 **e** kaplan@youlicense.com **w** youlicense.com VP Marketing: Tomer Kaplan.

ZDNet UK Ltd International House, 1 St Katharine's Way, London, E1W 1XQ **t** 020 7903 6800 **f** 020 7903 6000 **e** firstname.lastname@zdnet.co.uk **w** zdnet.co.uk Ops Dir: Jill Hourston.

Design, Pressing & Distribution

Pressers & Duplicators

10th Planet CD Duplication 68-70 Wardour St, London, W1F 0TB **t** 020 7434 2345 **f** 020 7287 2040 **e** sales@10pdm.com **w** 10pdm.com Sales Director: Richard Lamb.

Accurate Disc Duplication Queniborough Industrial Estate, Melton Road, Queniborough, Leicestershire, LE7 8FP **t** 0870 774 1112 **f** 0870 774 1113 **e** info@accuratedisc.com **w** accuratedisc.com

ACS Media Ltd 37 Bartholomew St, Newbury, Berkshire, RG14 5LL **t** 01635 552237 **f** 01635 34179 **e** sales@acsmedia.co.uk **w** acsmedia.co.uk MD: Wilber Craik 01635 580448.

AGR Manufacturing Ltd The Stables, 44 Stortford Rd, Great Dunmow, Essex, CM6 1DL **t** 01371 859 393 **f** 01371 859 375 **e** info@agrm.co.uk **w** agrm.co.uk Quotations and Prices: Martyn Hewitt.

Alfasound Duplication Old School House, 1 Green Lane, Ashton On Mersey, Sale, Cheshire, M33 5PN **t** 0161 905 1361 **f** 0161 282 1360 **e** garry.adl@btinternet.com MD: Garry Bowen.

AND Press (Manufacturing Agents) Westfield Cottage, Scragged Oak Rd, Maidstone, Kent, ME14 3HA **t** 01622 632 634 **f** 01622 632 634 **e** info@andpress.co.uk **w** andpress.co.uk MD: Andy Rutherford.

AWL Compact Disc Company 356 Scraptoft Lane, Leicester, LE5 1PB **t** 0116 241 3979 **f** 0116 243 3760 Dir: Andrew Lipinski.

BLUE PRO MEDIA

Unit 11, 407-409 Hornsey Rd, London, N19 4DX **t** +44 (0)207 272 0358 **e** info@bluepromedia.com **w** bluepromedia.com twitter.com/blueprogroup youtube.com/bluepromedia Director: Alexander Balfour.

C2 Productions Ltd **t** 01707 322600 **f** 01707 322800 **e** carlos@c2productions.co.uk **w** c2productions.co.uk Managing Director: Carlos Buhagiar.

Canon Video (UK) Ltd 15 Main Drive, East Lane Business Park, Wembley, Middlesex, HA9 7FF **t** 020 8385 4455 **f** 020 8385 0722 **e** snehal@canonvideo.co.uk **w** canonvideo.co.uk Sales Dir: Mr Saylash.

CD and Cassette Duplication Ltd. 77 Barlow Road, Stannington, Sheffield, South Yorkshire, S6 5HR **t** 0114 233 0033 **f** 0114 233 0033 MD: Ian Stead.

CD Industries Units 7-10, Sovereign Park, Coronation Road, London, NW10 7QP **t** 020 8961 8898 **f** 020 8961 8688 Production: Ms ME Tan.

CDA Disc Ltd Abbey House, 450 Bath Rd, Longford, Heathrow, UB7 0EB **t** 020 8757 8966 **f** 020 8757 8972 **e** sales@cdadisc.com **w** cdadisc.com Sales Manager: Ian Mackay.

Chameleon Developments Ltd 71 Rampton Drift, Longstanton, Cambridge, CB4 5EW **t** 0845 456 2144 **f** 01223 528449 **e** chameleon-d@btconnect.com **w** chameleon-developments.com MD: Tash Cox.

Design, Pressing & Distribution: Pressers & Duplicators

Cine Wessex Westway House, St Thomas Street, Winchester, Hampshire, SO23 9HJ **t** 01962 865 454 **f** 01962 842 017 **e** info@cinewessex.co.uk **w** cinewessex.co.uk ☒ Duplication Manager: Ema Branton.

Cinram Operations UK Ltd 2-6 Central Avenue, Ransomes Euro Park, Ipswich, Suffolk, IP3 9SL **t** 01473 271 010 **f** 01473 271 040 **e** uk.sales@cinram.com **w** cinram.com ☒ Senior Account Executive (Sales & Marketing): Ian Kerr.

Clear Sound And Vision Ltd CSV House, 51 Marlborough Rd, London, E18 1AR **t** 020 8989 8777 **f** 020 8989 9777 **e** sales@c-s-v.co.uk **w** clearsoundandvision.com ☒ Managing Director: Clive Robins.

CopyMaster International Ltd Copymaster House, 14 Lombard Road, Merton, London, SW19 3TZ **t** 020 8543 9223 **f** 020 8543 3419 **e** firstname@copymaster.co.uk **w** copymaster.co.uk ☒ CD & DVD Account Mgr: Ron Boucaud.

Copysound 3 Bowdens Business Centre, Hambridge, Somerset, TA10 0BP **t** 01458 259 280 **f** 01458 259 280 **e** sales@copysound.co.uk **w** copysound.co.uk ☒ Duplication Manager: Nigel Neill.

Cutgroove Ltd (Vinyl Pressing Agency) 101 Bashley Rd, Park Royal, London, NW10 6TE **t** 020 8838 8270 **f** 020 8838 2012 **e** nikki@cutgroove.com **w** intergroove.co.uk ☒ Manager: Nikki Howarth.

CVB Duplication 179A Bilton Road, Perivale, Middlesex, UB6 7HQ **t** 020 8991 2610 **f** 020 8997 0180 **e** sales@cvbduplication.co.uk **w** cvbduplication.co.uk ☒ Sales & Marketing: Phil Stringer.

dBm Ltd. The Loft, Mill Lane, Little Hallingbury, Bishop's Stortford, Hertfordshire, CM22 7QT **t** 01279 721434 **e** info@dbmltd.com **w** dbmltd.com ☒ Sales & Marketing Dirs.: Janice Glen, Richard Watts.

Diamond Black Ltd The Old Bancroft Buildings, Kingham Way, Luton, Beds, LU2 7RG **t** 01582 425555 **f** 01582 725900 **e** diamondblack@btconnect.com ☒ Director: Perri D'Cruz.

Digital Disc Duplication 105 Risbygate St, 1st Floor, Bury St Edmunds, Suffolk, IP33 3AA **t** 01284 700773 **e** sales@digitaldiscduplication.co.uk **w** digitaldiscduplication.co.uk ☒ Contact: Karl Adams.

Disc Manufacturing Services Ltd 48 Salisbury Rd, Plymouth, PL4 8QU **t** 01752 201275 **e** info@discmanufacturingservices.com **w** discmanufacturingservices.com ☒ MD: Dave Summers.

DOCdata UK Ltd Halesfield 14, Telford, Shropshire, TF7 4QR **t** 01952 680131 **f** 01952 583501 **e** uksales@docdata.com **w** docdata.co.uk ☒ Contact: Tina Buttery.

Downsoft Ltd Downsway House, Epsom Road, Ashtead, Surrey, KT21 1HA **t** 01372 272422 **f** 01372 276122 **e** work@downsoft.co.uk **w** downsoft.co.uk ☒ Mgr: Martin Dare.

Duplic8 Ltd Ashcroft, Wicken Bonhunt, Saffron Walden, Essex, CB11 3UL **t** 0845 873 3050 **f** 0845 873 3040 **e** ben@duplic8.co **w** duplic8.eu ☒ Director: Ben Bull.

Duplication.ie Morriscastle Village, Kilmuckridge, Wexford, Ireland. **t** +353 53 913 0968 **e** info@duplication.ie **w** duplication.ie ☒ Sales Mgr: Colin Turner.

EDC Blackburn Ltd Philips Road, Blackburn, Lancs, BB1 5RZ **t** 01254 505 300 **f** 01254 505 421 **e** firstname.lastname@edcllc.com **w** edc-blackburn.co.uk ☒ Sales: Bigsy & Angela Kaye.

EMS Audio Ltd Dir, 12 Balloo Avenue, Bangor, Co. Down, BT19 7QT **t** 028 9127 4411 **f** 028 9127 4412 **e** info@musicshop.to **w** musicshop.to ☒ William Thompson: EMS.

Eurodisc Manufacturing Ltd The Innovation Centre, Mewburn Rd, Banbury, OX16 9PA **t** 01295 817604 **e** info@euro-disc.co.uk **w** euro-disc.co.uk

Fairview Music Cavewood Grange Farm, Common Lane, North Cave, Brough, East Yorkshire, HU15 2PE **t** 01430 425546 **f** 01430 425547 **e** info@fairviewstudios.co.uk **w** fairviewstudios.co.uk ☒ Duplication Manager: Jackie Herd.

Filterbond Ltd 19 Sadlers Way, Hertford, Hertfordshire, SG14 2DZ **t** 01992 500101 **f** 01992 500101 **e** jbsrecords.filterbondltd@virgin.net ☒ MD: John B Schefel.

Finyl Tweek 7 Heathmans Rd, London, SW6 4TJ **t** 020 7371 0978 **e** natasha@finyltweek.com / dan@finyltweek.com **w** finyltweek.com ◻ facebook.com/pages/London-United-Kingdom/Finyl-Tweek/75923082714 ◻ twitter.com/FinylTweek ☒ Contact: Natasha Bicknell / Dan Smith.

First Choice Media Unit 1, Murray Business Centre, Murray Road, Orpington, Kent **t** 01689 828 182 **f** 01689 899 369 **e** dudley.perrin@firstchoiceltd.co.uk **w** firstchoiceltd.co.uk ☒ Head of Music: Dudley Perrin 07980 728 106.

GZ Digital Media UK 9 Bowmans Lea, Forest Hill, London, SE23 3WT **t** 020 8291 3175 **e** paul@gzcd.co.uk **w** gzdm.cz ☒ Sales Director (UK): Paul Bibby 4402082913175.

Heathmans 7 Heathmans Road, London, SW6 4TJ **t** 020 7371 0978 **f** 020 7371 9360 **e** susana@heathmans.co.uk **w** heathmans.co.uk

HHO Manufacturing Suite 1 Britannia Business Centre, Cricklewood Lane, London, NW2 1EZ **t** 020 8830 8813 **f** 020 8830 8801 **e** info@hhomanufacturing.com **w** hhomanufacturing.com ☒ Manager: Sami Chidiac.

Design, Pressing & Distribution: Pressers & Duplicators

HILTONGROVE MULTIMEDIA

3 Greenwich Quay, Clarence Rd, London, SE8 3EY
t 020 8521 2424 **f** 020 8691 3144
e info@hiltongrove.com **w** hiltongrove.com
Contact: Sales.

ICC Duplication Regency Mews, Silverdale Road,
Eastbourne, East Sussex, BN20 7AB **t** 01323 647 880
f 01323 643 095 **e** info@iccduplication.co.uk
w iccduplication.co.uk Operations Dir: Andy Thorpe.

Icon Marketing Ltd Park House, 27 South Avenue,
Thorpe St Andrew, Norwich, NR7 0EZ **t** 01603 708050
f 01603 708005 **e** Icon@dircon.co.uk **w** icon-
marketing.co.uk Production Manager: Sarah Neve.

Impress Music Ltd 5 Northfield Industrial Estate,
Beresford Avenue, Wembley, Middx, HA0 1NW
t 020 8795 0101 **f** 020 8795 0303
e firstname@impressmusic-uk.com **w** impressmusic-
uk.com Chairman: Alastair Bloom.

Isis Duplicating Co - Head Office
Unit 11 Shaftesbury Ind Centre, The Runnings,
Cheltenham, Gloucestershire, GL51 9NH **t** 01242 571 818
f 01242 571 315 **e** john@isis-uk.com **w** isis-uk.com
Divisional Mgr: John Fairclough.

ITD Cassettes Ltd 31 Angelvale,
Buckingham Industrial Park, Buckingham, Bucks,
MK18 1TH **t** 01280 821 177 **f** 01280 821 188
e ITDcassets@aol.com **w** ITDcassettes.com MD: Mike
McLoughlin.

KDG UK Ltd Unit 5 Triangle Business Park, Pentrebach,
Merthyr Tydfil, Mid Galmorgan, SF48 4TQ **t** 01685 354700
f 01685 354701 **e** sales@kdguk.com **w** kdg-mt.com
Sales Mgr: Ian Browning.

Key Production 8 Jeffreys Pl, London, NW1 9PP
t 020 7284 8800 **f** 020 7284 8844
e mail@keyproduction.co.uk **w** keyproduction.co.uk
MD: Karen Emanuel.

Keynote Audio Services Ltd Smoke Tree House,
Tilford Rd, Farnham, Surrey, GU10 2EN **t** 01252 794 253
f 01252 792 642 **e** admin@keynoteaudio.co.uk
w keynoteaudio.co.uk MD: Tim Wheatley.

Lemon Media Ltd The Hub, Warne Road, Weston-
super-Mare, Somerset, BS23 3UU **t** 01934 423 022
e Stuart@LemonMedia.co.uk **w** lemonmedia.co.uk
Sales Mgr: Stuart Timmis 07966 311 058.

Logicom Sound And Vision Portland House,
1 Portland Drive, Willen, Milton Keynes, Buckinghamshire,
MK15 9JW **t** 01908 663848 **f** 01908 666654
e grayham.amos@luk.net **w** luk.net Bus Dev
Mgr: Grayham Amos.

MacTrak Duplicating 3/2 Inveresk Industrial Estate,
Musselburgh, Edinburgh, EH21 7UL **t** 0131 665 5377
f 0131 653 6905 **e** mactrak@ednet.co.uk
w mactrak.co.uk Prop: MD MacGregor.

Meltones Media 3 King Edward Drive, Chessington,
Surrey, KT9 1DW **t** 020 8391 9406 **f** 020 8391 8924
e sales@meltones.com **w** meltones-media.co.uk
MD: Tony Fernandez.

Metro Broadcast Ltd 5-7 Great Chapel St, London,
W1F 8FF **t** 020 7434 7700 **f** 020 7434 7701
e info@metrobroadcast.com **w** metrobroadcast.com
Business Development Dir: Paul Beale.

MPO Ireland Ltd Blanchardstown Industrial Est,
Snugborough Road, Blanchardstown, Dublin 15, Ireland
t +353 1 822 1363 **f** +353 1 806 6064 **e** swalsh@mpo.ie
w mpo.fr Sales Director: Sharon Walsh.

MPO UK Ltd Centre 500, 500 Chiswick High Road,
London, W4 5RG **t** 0208 956 2727 **e** keith@mpo.co.uk
w MPO.fr UK Manager: Keith Young.

Multi Media Replication Ltd
Unit 4 Balksbury Estate, Upper Clatford, Andover, Hants,
SP11 7LW **t** 01264 336330 **f** 01264 336694
e info@replication.com **w** replication.com MD: Philip
Hall.

Music Ventures The Old Porch, 5-6 Vennington,
Westbury, Shrewsbury, Shropshire, SY5 9RG
t 01743 884567 **f** 01743 885123
e sales@musicventures.com **w** musicventures.com
Sales Manager: Andrew Smales.

Noisebox Digital Media Ltd Jonathan Scott Hall, Thorpe Rd, Norwich, NR1 1UH **t** 01603 767726 **f** 01603 767746 **e** info@noisebox.co.uk **w** noisebox.co.uk 🖾 MD: Pete Morgan.

Noon Media Solutions 4 Bessingby Road, Ruislip, Middx, HA4 9DA **t** 01895 472 882 **e** sales@noonmediasolutions.com **w** noonmediasolutions.com 🖾 MD: David Noonan.

ODPM Ltd Unit 19, Soho Mills, Wooburn Green, Buckinghamshire, HP10 0PF **t** 0870 288 5330 **f** 0870 522 5331 **e** duncan@odpm-ltd.com **w** odpm-ltd.com 🖾 myspace.com/odpm 📺 youtube.com/odpmltd 🖾 Director: Duncan Baldwin.

ODS Business Services The ODS Building (Spectrum), Mead Way, Westlea, Swindon, Wilts, SN5 7UT **t** 01793 421 300 **f** 01793 511 125 **e** sales@ods-businessservices.com **w** ods-businessservices.com

Open Ear Productions Ltd. Kinarva, Co. Galway, Ireland **t** +353 91 635810 **f** +353 87 58575588 **e** info@openear.ie **w** openear.ie 🖾 MD: Bruno Staehelin.

optimal media UK Ltd 16-18 Brushfield Street, London, E1 6AN **t** 020 7492 4880 **f** 020 7492 4886 **e** info@optimal-online.co.uk **w** optimal-online.co.uk 🖾 Contact: Rufus Kalex.

Orbis Digital Ltd Unit 52E, Sunnyside Road, Coatbridge, ML5 3DG **t** 0845 60 76 123 **e** alan@orbisdigital.co.uk **w** orbisdigital.co.uk 🖾 Optical Media Consultant: Alan Mann 01236 44 96 99.

Orlake Records (Vinyl Specialists) Sterling Industrial Estate, Rainham Road South, Dagenham, Essex, RM10 8HP **t** 020 8592 0242 **f** 020 8595 8182 **e** info@orlakerecords.com **w** orlakerecords.co.uk 🖾 Production Controller: Paula Pearl.

PR Records Hamilton House, Endeavour Way, London, SW19 8UH **t** 01423 541020 **f** 01423 540970 **e** pr@celtic-music.co.uk 🖾 Cust Liason: Ruth Bulmer.

Professional Magnetics Ltd Cassette House, 329 Hunslet Road, Leeds, West Yorkshire, LS10 1NJ **t** 0113 270 6066 **f** 0113 271 8106 **e** promags@aol.com **w** promags.freeserve.co.uk 🖾 Dir: Hilary Rhodes.

27 Lexington Street, Soho, London, W1F 9AQ **t** +44 (0)20 7287 7373 **e** craig@red-light.co.uk **w** red-light.co.uk 🖾 MD: Craig Dormer 07796 958 115. Finance: Wendy Meads. Studio Manager: Lindsey Dormer. Studio: Ben Bell.

Repeat Performance RPM 6, Grand Union Centre, West Row, London, W10 5AS **t** 020 8960 7222 **f** 020 8968 1378 **e** info@rpmuk.com **w** rpmuk.com 🖾 MD: Robin Springall.

Replica North Works, Hookstone Park, Harrogate, North Yorkshire, HG2 7DB **t** 01423 888979 **f** 01423 540970 **e** replica@northworks.co.uk 🖾 Dir: David Bulmer 01423 541020.

RMS Studios 43-45 Clifton Rd, London, SE25 6PX **t** 020 8653 4965 **e** rmsstudios@blueyonder.co.uk **w** rms-studios.co.uk 🖾 Bookings Mgr: Alan Jones.

SKM Europe Charlotte Cottage, 73 Leighton Rd, Wing, Leighton Buzzard, Bedfordshire, LU7 0NN **t** 01296 681 535 **f** 01296 689 428 **e** anita@skmeurope.co.uk **w** skm.co.kr 🖾 Sales Dir: Steve Castle.

Sound Discs CD DVD Mastering Duplication Design West Mount Farm, Woodmancote Lane, Chichester, West Sussex/Hampshire, PO18 8UL **t** 08453 707080 / 01243 572557 **e** info@sound-discs.co.uk **w** sound-discs.co.uk 🖾 ww.myspace.com/sounddiscscdduplication 🖾 Production Director: Peter Bullick 07721 624 868.

3 Greenwich Quay, Clarence Rd, London, SE8 3EY **t** 020 8691 2121 **f** 020 8691 3144 **e** sales@soundperformance.co.uk **w** soundperformance.co.uk 🖾 Contact: Sales.

Sound Recording Technology Audio House, Edison Road, St Ives, Cambs, PE27 3LF **t** 01480 461 880 **f** 01480 496 100 **e** sales@soundrecordingtechnology.co.uk **w** soundrecordingtechnology.co.uk 🖾 Dirs: Sarah Pownall, Karen Kenney.

Sounds Good Ltd 12 Chiltern Enterprise Centre, Station Rd, Theale, Reading, Berks, RG7 4AA **t** 0118 930 1700 **f** 0118 930 1709 **e** sales-info@sounds-good.co.uk **w** sounds-good.co.uk 🖾 Dir: Martin Maynard.

Sponge Multimedia Ltd Sponge Studios, Cross Chancellor Street, Leeds, West Yorkshire, LS6 2TG **t** 0113 234 0004 **f** 0113 242 4296 **e** damian@spongestudios.demon.co.uk **w** spongestudios.demon.co.uk 🖾 Director: Damian McLean-Brown.

Tapemaster (Europe) Ltd King George's Place, 764 Eastern Avenue, Newbury Park, Ilford, Essex, IG2 7HU **t** 020 8518 4202 **f** 020 8518 4203 **e** tapemaster@msn.com **w** tapemaster.co.uk 🖾 MD: Laji Lalli.

TC Video Wembley Commercial Centre, East Lane, Wembley, Middx, HA9 7UU **t** 020 8904 6271 **f** 020 8904 0172 **e** info@tcvideo.co.uk **w** tcvideo.co.uk ✉ Marketing Manager: Lissandra Xavier.

Technicolor Creative Services Perivale Park, Horsenden Lane South, Perivale, Middx, UB6 7RL **t** 020 8799 0555 **f** 020 8799 0579 **e** firstname.lastname@thomson.net **w** technicolor.com ✉ Sales Dir: Robert Dunne.

Thames Valley Video 660 Ajax Avenue, Slough, Berkshire, SL1 4BG **t** 01753 553131 **f** 01753 554505 **e** tvv@netcomuk.co.uk ✉ MD: Nigel Morris.

TRIBAL MANUFACTURING

11 Hillgate Pl, London, SW12 9ER **t** 020 8673 0610 **f** 020 8675 8562 **e** sales@tribal.co.uk **w** tribal.co.uk ✉ Directors: Alison Wilson, Terry Woolner. Production manager: Greg Bell.

UK Discs PO Box 1467, Oxford, OX3 3BH **t** 01865 741 802 **e** sales@ukdiscs.com **w** ukdiscs.com ✉ Dir: Dale Olivier.

VDC Group VDC House, Units 3 & 4, Nucleus Business Centre, Central Way, Wembley, NW10 7XT **t** 0208 963 3555 **f** 0208 965 9412 **e** enquiries@vdcgroup.com **w** vdcgroup.com ✉ Sales Executives: Alex Lytton, Mike Redfern, Mike Seamen.

The Vinyl Factory Manufacturing Ltd

Apollo House, 120 Blyth Rd, Hayes, Middlesex, UB3 1SY **t** 020 8756 0826 **f** 020 8756 0836 **e** robert.bailey@thevinylfactory.com **w** thevinylfactory.com ✉ Commercial Mgr: Bob Bailey.

Vinyl Factory Productions (One Stop Service)

Sterling Industrial Est, Rainham Rd South, Dagenham, Essex, RM10 8HP **t** 020 8526 8070 **e** paula.pearl@vinylfactory.co.uk **w** vinylfactory.co.uk ✉ Production Mgr: Paula Pearl.

Vinyl Pressing 308 High Street, London, E15 1AJ **t** 020 8519 4260 **f** 020 8519 5187 ✉ MD: Terence Murphy.

Mastering & Post Production

360 Mastering Ltd 18A Farm Lane Trading Centre, 101 Farm Lane, London, SW6 1QJ **t** 020 7385 6161 **f** 020 7386 0473 **e** studio@360mastering.co.uk **w** 360mastering.co.uk ✉ MD: Dick Beetham.

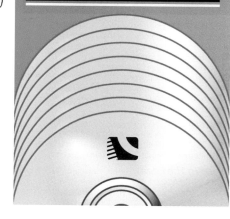
Design, Pressing & Distribution: Mastering & Post Production

Design, Pressing & Distribution: Mastering & Post Production

The 400 Company B3, The Workshops, 2A, Askew Crescent, London, W12 9DP **t** 020 8746 1400 **e** info@the400.co.uk **w** the400.co.uk 🖪 Production Manager: Christian Riou.

ABCD & DVD Ltd (All Branded CD & DVD) PO Box 53397, London, NW10 5QJ **t** 0845 257 3707 **e** sales@abcdanddvd.com **w** abcdanddvd.com 🖪 twitter.com/thatdisc 🖪 Director: Iliboku Martins.

Airtight Productions - DVD Authoring Unit 16, Albany Rd Trading Estate, Albany Rd, Chorlton, M21 0AZ **t** 0161 881 5157 **e** info@airtightproductions.co.uk **w** airtightproductions.co.uk 🖪 Dir: Anthony Davey.

Alchemy SoHo 12 Cock Lane, London, EC1A 9BU **t** 020 7248 2777 **e** mastering@alchemysoho.com **w** alchemysoho.com 🖪 Vinyl & CD Bookings: Phil Kinrade.

Arvato Digital Services (Sonopress) Wednesbury One Business Pk, Black Country New Rd, Wednesbury, West Midlands, WS10 7NY **t** 0121 502 7800 **f** 0121 502 7811 **e** sales@sonopress.co.uk **w** sonopress.co.uk 🖪 Sales Dir - Music: Anthony Daly.

Audio Sorcery Little Wold, Station Rd, Groombridge, East Sussex, TN3 9NE **t** 01892 862489 **e** info@tgas.co.uk **w** tgas.co.uk 🖪 Contact: Paul Midcalf.

AudiopleXus Mastering Studio 10 Manhattan, Fairfield Rd, London, E3 2UJ **t** 020 8980 8947 **f** 020 8980 8947 **e** info@audioplexus.com **w** audioplexus.co.uk 🖪 Founder/CEO: Chris Stilmant.

B&H Sound Services Ltd The Old School Studio, Crowland Road, Eye, Peterborough, PE6 7TN **t** 01733 223 535 **f** 01733 223 545 **e** sound@bhsound.co.uk **w** bhsound.co.uk 🖪 Recording Manager: Nicola Seager.

BLUE PRO MASTERING

BLUEPRO MASTERING

Unit 11, 407-409 Hornsey Rd, London, N19 4DX **t** 020 7272 0358 **e** info@bluepromastering.com **w** bluepromastering.com 🖪 facebook.com/bluepromastering 🖪 myspace.com/bluepromastering 🖪 twitter.com/blueprogroup 🖪 youtube.com/bluepromastering 🖪 Director: Alexander Balfour. Senior Mastering Engineer: John Webber. Mastering Engineer: Jerome Schmitt.

Chapel Media The Studios, 8 Hornton Place, Kensington, London, W8 4LZ **t** 020 7938 5329 **f** 020 7937 4326 **e** info@chapel-media.com **w** chapel-media.com 🖪 Technical Director: Alan Higgison.

Close To The Edge 2 The Embankment, Twickenham, Middlesex, TW1 3DU **t** 07785 755205 **e** Jon@CloseToTheEdge.biz **w** CloseToTheEdge.biz 🖪 Owner / Mastering Engineer: Jon Astley.

CopyMaster International Ltd Copymaster House, 14 Lombard Road, Merton, London, SW19 3TZ **t** 020 8543 9223 **f** 020 8543 3419 **e** firstname@copymaster.co.uk **w** copymaster.co.uk 🖪 CD & DVD Account Mgr: Ron Boucaud.

Cottage Media Mastering 2 Gawsworth Rd, Macclesfield, Cheshire, SK11 8UE **t** 01625 420163 **f** 01625 420168 **e** cmm@cottagegroup.co.uk **w** cottagegroup.co.uk 🖪 myspace.com/cottagestudios 🖪 MD: Roger Boden.

dB Entertainments Limited PO Box 147, Peterborough, Cambs., PE1 4XU **t** 01733 311755 **f** 01733 709449 **e** info@dbentertainments.com **w** dbentertainments.com 🖪 Director/Producer: Russell Dawson-Butterworth.

Digital Media Services UK Ltd DMS, 44-46 Scrutton Street, London, EC2A 4HH **t** 0845 055 0979 **f** 0845 055 0970 **e** amy.lecoz@dmsukltd.com **w** dmsukltd.com 🖪 Dir: Amy Le Coz.

Dolby Laboratories, Inc. Interface Business Pk, Wootton Bassett, Wiltshire, SN4 8QJ **t** 01793 842100 **f** 01793 842101 **e** info@dolby.co.uk **w** dolby.com 🖪 Manager, Business Development: Andrea Borgato.

Duplication.ie Morriscastle Village, Kilmuckridge, Wexford, Ireland. **t** +353 53 913 0968 **e** info@duplication.ie **w** duplication.ie 🖪 Sales Mgr: Colin Turner.

Electric Mastering 308 Westbourne Studios, 242 Acklam Rd, London, W10 5JJ **t** 020 7524 7557 **f** 020 7524 7558 **e** info@electricmastering.com **w** electricmastering.com 🖪 Studio Mgr: Phil Vernol.

The Exchange Mastering Studios 42 Bruges Pl, Randolph St, London, NW1 0TX **t** 020 7485 0530 **f** 020 7482 4588 **e** studio@exchangemastering.co.uk **w** exchangemastering.co.uk 🖪 MD: Graeme Durham.

Factory Studios Ltd 54-55 Margaret Street, London, W1W 8SH **t** 020 7580 5810 **f** 020 7580 5811 **e** info@factory.uk.com **w** factory.uk.com 🖪 Contact: Ingrid Armstrong.

Fat As Funk Mastering PO Box 5, Lydeard Saint Lawrence, Taunton, Somerset, TA4 4HA **t** 01984 618611 / 07779 527151 **e** loz@fatasfunk.com **w** fatasfunk.com 🖪 myspace.com/fatasfunkmusic 🖪 Mastering Engineer: Lawrence Gill 07779 527151.

Figment DVD 341-345 Old St, London, EC1V 9LL **t** 020 7729 1969 **f** 020 7739 1969 **e** mail@figment-media.com **w** figment-media.com 🖪 MD: Andrew Huffer.

Finesplice Ltd 1 Summerhouse Lane, Harmondsworth, West Drayton, Middlesex, UB7 0AT **t** 020 8564 7839 **f** 020 8759 9629 **e** info@finesplice.co.uk **w** finesplice.co.uk 🖪 MD: Ben Turner.

Finyl Tweek 7 Heathmans Rd, London, SW6 4TJ **t** 020 7371 0978 **e** natasha@finyltweek.com / dan@finyltweek.com **w** finyltweek.com 🖪 facebook.com/pages/London-United-Kingdom/Finyl-Tweek/75923082714 🖪 twitter.com/FinylTweek 🖪 Contact: Natasha Bicknell / Dan Smith.

Flare DVD Ingestre Court, Ingestre Place, London,
W1F 0JL **t** 020 7343 6565 **f** 020 7343 6555
e darrell@flare-dvd.com **w** flare-dvd.com
🖳 Designer: Darrell de Vries.

Fleetwood Post Denham Media Park,
North Orbital Road, Denham, Bucks, UB9 5HQ
t 08700 771 071 **f** 08700 771 068
e tim.s@fleetwoodmobiles.com **w** fleetwoodmobiles.com
🖳 Dir: Tim Summerhayes.

Flow Mastering 83 Brixton Water Lane, London,
SW2 1PH **t** 020 7733 8088 **f** 020 7326 4016
e brethes@mac.com **w** flowmastering.co.uk
🖳 myspace.com/flowmastering 🖳 Director: Dominique
Brethes.

Flying Ace Productions Walders, Oldbury Lane,
Ightham, Sevenoaks, TN15 9DD
t 01732 887056 or 07778 165931 **f** 01732 887056
e reiddick@toucansurf.com 🖳 Dir: Will Reid Dick 07778
165931.

Hafod Mastering Hafod, St Hilary, Cowbridge, Wales,
CF71 7DP **t** 01446 775512 **f** 01446 775512
e studio@hafodmastering.co.uk **w** hafodmastering.co.uk
🖳 Dir: Donal Whelan.

Hangman Studios 111 Frithville Gardens, London,
W12 7JQ **t** 020 8600 3440 **f** 020 8600 3401
e danielle@hangmanstudios.com **w** hangmanstudios.com
🖳 Studio Mgr: Danielle Edwards.

Hiltongrove Mastering Hiltongrove Business Centre,
Hatherley Mews, London, E17 4QP **t** 020 8509 2244
f 020 8509 1155 **e** theteam@hiltongrovemastering.com
w hiltongrovemastering.com 🖳 MD: David Blackman.

International Broadcast Facilities
15 Monmouth Street, London, WC2H 9DA
t 020 7497 1515 **f** 020 7379 8562 **e** post@ibf.co.uk
w ibf.co.uk 🖳 Head of Audio: Martin Reekie.

JRP Music Services Empire House, Hereford Rd,
Southsea, Hants, PO5 2DH **t** 023 9229 7839
e James.Perrett@soc.soton.ac.uk **w** jrpmusic.fsnet.co.uk
🖳 Senior Engineer: James Perrett.

JTS 73 Digby Road, London, E9 6HX **t** 020 8985 3000
f 020 8986 7688 **e** sales@jts-uk.com **w** jts-uk.com
🖳 Studio Mgr: Keith Jeffrey.

Keynote Audio Services Ltd Smoke Tree House,
Tilford Rd, Farnham, Surrey, GU10 2EN **t** 01252 794 253
f 01252 792 642 **e** admin@keynoteaudio.co.uk
w keynoteaudio.co.uk 🖳 MD: Tim Wheatley.

Lansdowne Studios Rickmansworth Road, Watford,
WD17 3JN **t** 020 8846 9444 **f** 05601 155 009
e info@cts-lansdowne.co.uk **w** cts-lansdowne.co.uk
🖳 Bookings Enquiries: Sharon Rose.

Liquid Mastering Unit 6Q, Atlas Business Centre,
Oxgate Lane, London, NW2 7HU **t** 020 8452 2255
f 020 8422 4242 **e** sales@liquidmastering.co.uk
w liquidmastering.co.uk 🖳 Contact: 0208 452 2255.

Locomotion 1-8 Bateman's Building, Soho Square,
London, W1D 3EN **t** 020 7304 4403 **f** 020 7304 4400
e info@locomotion.co.uk **w** locomotion.co.uk

Loud Mastering & Loud Independent 2-
3 Windsor Pl, Whitehall, Taunton, Somerset, TA1 1PG
t 01823 353123 **f** 01823 353055
e enquiries@loudmastering.com **w** loudmastering.com
🖳 Bookings Manager: John Wilkins.

The Machine Room 54-58 Wardour Street, London,
W1D 4JQ **t** 020 7734 3433 **f** 020 7287 3773
e paul.willey@themachineroom.co.uk
w themachineroom.co.uk 🖳 Contact: Paul Willey.

Master Blaster Music Unit 228, Canalot Studios,
222 Kensal Road, London, W10 5BN **t** 020 8969 9555
f 020 8969 9555 **e** info@masterblastermusic.net
w masterblastermusic.net 🖳 Mastering
Engineer: Matthew Denny.

MasteringWorld.com Hafod, St Hilary, Cowbridge,
CF71 7DP **t** 01446 771 789
e enquiries@masteringworld.com **w** masteringworld.com
🖳 Dir: Donal Whelan.

Masterpiece Media Unit 14 The Talina Centre,
Bagleys Lane, London, SW6 2BW **t** 020 7731 5758
f 020 7384 1750 **e** leena.bhatti@masterpiece.net
w masterpiece.net 🖳 Business Development
Manager: Leena Bhatti.

Masterworks Audio Unit 222, Canalot Studios,
222 Kensal Rd, London, W10 5BN **t** 07739 384688
e info@masterworksaudio.co.uk
w masterworksaudio.co.uk ☎ Contact: Milan Adamik.

Mediadisc Unit 4C, Farm Lane Trading Centre,
101 Farm Lane, Fulham, London, SW6 1QJ
t 020 7385 2299 **f** 020 7385 4888
e studio@mediadisc.co.uk **w** mediadisc.co.uk
☎ MD: Simon Payne.

Metropolis Digital Media The Power House,
70 Chiswick High Rd, London, W4 1SY **t** 020 8742 1111
f 020 8742 2626 **e** digitalmedia@metropolis-group.co.uk
w metropolis-group.co.uk
🅕 facebook.com/metropolisstudios
🅣 twitter.com/metropolisgroup
▶ youtube.com/user/MetropolisStudios ☎ Digital Media
Manager / Digital Media Sales Manager: Richard Osborn /
Sarah Page.

**Metropolis iMastering Online Mastering
Services** Metropolis Group, The Powerhouse,
70 Chiswick High Rd, London, W4 1SY **t** 020 8742 1111
f 020 8742 3777 **e** imaster@metropolis-group.co.uk
w imastering.co.uk 🅕 facebook.com/metropolisstudios
🅜 myspace.com/metroimaster
🅣 twitter.com/Metropolisgroup
▶ youtube.com/user/MetropolisStudios ☎ iMastering
Bookings: Dan Baldwin, Loretta Bogard, Michael Walsh.

Metropolis Mastering The Power House,
70 Chiswick High Rd, London, W4 1SY **t** 020 8742 1111
f 020 8742 3777 **e** mastering@metropolis-group.co.uk
w metropolis-group.co.uk
🅕 facebook.com/metropolisstudios
🅣 twitter.com/metropolisgroup
▶ youtube.com/user/MetropolisStudios ☎ Mastering
Bookings: Yvonne Zimmerling, Dan Baldwin, Loretta
Bogard, Michael Walsh.

Molinare 34 Fouberts Place, London, W1F 7PX
t 020 7478 7000 **f** 020 7478 7299
e bookings@molinare.co.uk **w** molinare.co.uk

ODPM Ltd Pinewood Studios, Block D Suite 49a,
Pinewood Rd, Iver Heath, Buckinghamshire, SL0 0NH
t 0870 288 5330 **f** 0870 288 5330 **e** info@odpm-ltd.com
w odpm-ltd.com 🅜 myspace.com/odpm
▶ youtube.com/odpmltd ☎ Director: Duncan Baldwin.

Optimum Mastering Ltd. Unit 5.4, The Paintworks,
Bath Rd, Bristol, BS4 3EH **t** 0117 971 6901
f 0117 971 0700 **e** info@optimum-mastering.com
w optimum-mastering.com
🅜 myspace.com/optimummastering
🅣 twitter.com/Optimast ☎ Engineer: Shawn Joseph.

PDRL PO Box 3, South Croydon, Surrey, CR2 0YW
t 0870 765 4334 **e** abjacobs@pdrl.net **w** pdrl.net
☎ Owner: A B Jacobs.

Phoenix Video Ltd Whyteleafe House,
31 Codmore Crescent, Chesham, Bucks, HP5 3LZ
t 0845 271 7300 **e** terry@phoenix-video.co.uk
w phoenix-video.co.uk ☎ MD: Terry Young.

The Pierce Rooms Mastering Pierce House,
London Apollo Complex, Queen Caroline St, London,
W6 9QH **t** 020 8563 1234 **f** 020 8563 1337
e gay@pierceroomsmastering.com **w** pierce-
entertainment.com ☎ Booking Manager: Gay Marshall.

Red Facilities 61 Timber Bush, Leith, Edinburgh,
EH6 6QH **t** 0131 555 2288 **f** 0131 555 0088
e doit@redfacilities.com **w** redfacilities.com
☎ Director: Max Howarth +44 (0)131 555 2288.

**RED LIGHT MASTERING, AUDIO POST &
DUPLICATION**

27 Lexington Street, Soho, London, W1F 9AQ
t +44 (0)20 7287 7373 **e** craig@red-light.co.uk **w** red-
light.co.uk ☎ MD: Craig Dormer 07796 958 115.
Finance: Wendy Meads. Studio Manager: Lindsey Dormer.
Studio Engineer: Ben Bell.

Redwood Studios Ltd 20 Great Chapel St, London,
W1F 8FW **t** 020 7287 3799 **e** andrestudios@yahoo.co.uk
w sound-design.net ☎ MD/Producer: Andre Jacquemin.

Repeat Performance RPM 6 Grand Union Centre,
West Row, London, W10 5AS **t** 020 8960 7222
f 020 8968 1378 **e** info@rpmuk.com **w** rpmuk.com
☎ MD: Robin Springall.

Revolution Digital 1st Floor, 34 Lexington St, London,
W1F 0LH **t** 020 7439 3332 **e** laura@rdigital.co.uk
w rdigital.co.uk ☎ MD: Laura Gate-Eastley.

Revolution Mastering 5 Falcon Pk, Neasden Lane,
London, NW10 1RX **t** 020 8965 5323
e studio@revolutionmastering.com
w revolutionmastering.com ☎ Director: Nick Bennett
07811 177355.

Reynolds Mastering PO Box 5092, Colchester, Essex,
CO1 1FN **e** info@reynoldsmastering.com
w reynoldsmastering.com ☎ MD: Peter Reynolds.

The Sanctuary (Soho) 53 Frith St, London, W1D 4SN
t 020 7734 4480 **f** 020 7439 7394
e info@thesanctuary.tv **w** thesanctuary.tv ☎ Joint
MDs: Maryan Kennedy, Daniel Stracey.

Silk Recordings 65 High Street, Kings Langley, Herts.,
WD4 9HU **t** 01923 270 852 **e** info@silkrecordings.com
w silkrecordings.com ☎ MD: Bob Whitney 07812 602 535.

Smoke & Mirrors 57-59 Beak St, London, W1F 9SJ
t 020 7468 1000 **f** 020 7468 1001 **e** production@smoke-
mirrors.co.uk **w** smoke-mirrors.com ☎ CEO: Penny Verbe.

Sonic Arts The Shaftesbury Centre, 85 Barlby Road,
London, W10 6BN **t** 020 8962 3000 **f** 020 8962 6200
e avi@sonic-arts.com **w** sonic-arts.com
☎ Contact: Miranda Webster.

Sound Discs Ltd. West Mount Farm, Woodmancote Lane, Chichester, West Sussex/Hampshire, PO18 8UL **t** 08453 707080 / 01243 572557 **e** info@sound-discs.co.uk **w** sound-discs.co.uk ww.myspace.com/sounddiscscdduplication **☎** Production Director: Peter Bullick 07721 624 868.

Sound Generation Unit 3, Clarence Road, Greenwich, London, SE8 3EY **t** 020 8691 2121 **f** 020 8691 3144 **e** at@soundperformance.co.uk **w** soundperformance.co.uk **☎** Studio Mgr: Andrew Thompson.

Sound Mastering 42-50 Steele Rd, Park Royal, London, NW10 7AS **t** 020 8961 1741 **e** info@soundmastering.com **w** soundmastering.com **☎** Contact: Duncan Cowell.

Sound Recording Technology Audio House, Edison Road, St Ives, Cambs, PE27 3LF **t** 01480 461 880 **f** 01480 496 100 **e** sales@soundrecordingtechnology.co.uk **w** soundrecordingtechnology.co.uk **☎** Dirs: Sarah Pownall, Karen Kenney.

The Soundmasters International Ltd The New Boathouse, 136-142 Bramley Road, London, W10 6SR **t** 020 7565 3020 **f** 020 7565 3021 **e** info@soundmasters.co.uk **w** soundmasters.co.uk **☎** Managing Director: Kevin Metcalfe.

Sounds Good Ltd 12 Chiltern Enterprise Centre, Station Rd, Theale, Reading, Berks, RG7 4AA **t** 0118 930 1700 **f** 0118 930 1709 **e** sales-info@sounds-good.co.uk **w** sounds-good.co.uk **☎** Dir: Martin Maynard.

South Union PO Box 357, Middlesbrough, TS1 4WZ **t** 01642 806795 **f** 01642 351962 **e** info@millbrand.com **w** millbrand.com **f** facebook.com/millbrand **☎** myspace.com/millbrand **☎** Director: Paul Mooney.

Stream Digital Media Ltd 61 Charlotte St, London, W1P 1LA **t** 020 7208 1567 **f** 020 7208 1555 **e** info@streamdm.co.uk **w** streamdm.co.uk **☎** Head of Stream: Paul Kind.

Super Audio Mastering Monks Withecombe, Chagford, Devon, TQ13 8JY **t** 01647 432858 **f** 01647 432308 **e** info@superaudiomastering.com **w** superaudiomastering.com **☎** MD: Simon Heyworth 07721 613145.

SVC 142 Wardour Street, London, W1F 8ZU **t** 020 7734 1600 **f** 020 7437 1854 **e** post@svc.co.uk **w** svc.co.uk **☎** Facilities Mgr: Jon Murray.

Tangerine Dreams Riverside Studios, Crisp Road, Hammersmith, London, W6 9RL **t** 0800 085 6732 **f** 020 8237 1220 **e** prodvd@tangerinedreams.co.uk **w** tangerinedreams.co.uk **☎** Contact: 01189 89 2306.

Tenth Egg Productions 47 Stanley Avenue, Beckenham, Kent, BR3 6PU **t** 020 7193 9603 **e** info@tenthegg.co.uk **w** tenthegg.co.uk **☎** Head Engineer: Nick Barron.

Transfermation Ltd 63 Lant Street, London, SE1 1QN **t** 020 7417 7021 **f** 020 7378 0516 **e** trace@transfermation.com **w** transfermation.com **☎** Co-ordinator: Tracey Roper.

Transition Mastering Studios Kemble House, Kemble Rd, London, SE23 2DJ **t** 020 8699 7888 **f** 020 8699 9441 **e** info@transition-studios.co.uk **w** transition-studios.com **☎** Manager: Jason Goz.

Trend A2 Canal Bank, Park West Industrial Park, Dublin 12, Ireland **t** +353 1 6060 600 **f** +353 1 6160 601 **e** muswk@trendstudios.com **w** trendstudios.com **☎** Tech Dir: Paul Waldron.

VDC Group VDC House, Units 3 & 4, Nucleus Business Centre, Central Way, Wembley, NW10 7XT **t** 0208 963 3555 **f** 0208 965 9412 **e** enquiries@vdcgroup.com **w** vdcgroup.com **☎** Sales Executives: Alex Lytton, Mike Redfern, Mike Seamen.

Videosonics 68a Delancey Street, London, NW1 7RY **t** 020 7209 0209 **f** 020 7419 4460 **e** info@videosonics.com **w** videosonics.com **☎** Studio Mgr: Peter Hoskins.

Printers & Packaging

ACS Media Ltd (Printers) 37 Bartholomew St, Newbury, Berks, RG14 5LL **t** 01635 552237 **f** 01635 34179 **e** sales@acsmedia.co.uk **☎** Contact: Wilber Craik 01635 580448.

After Dark Media Unit 29, Scott Business Park, Beacom Park Road, Plymouth, PL2 2PB **t** 01752 294130 **f** 01752 257320 **e** nigel@afterdarkmedia.net **w** afterdarkmedia.net **☎** Manager: Nigel Muntz.

AGI Berghem Mews, Blythe Rd, London, W14 0HN **t** 020 7605 1940 **e** AGI-EU-sales@eu.agimedia.com **w** agimedia.com **☎** Contact: Malcolm Swindell.

AGI Amaray Amaray House, Arkwright Road, Corby, NN17 5AE **t** 01536 274800 **f** 01536 274899 **e** amaraysales@uk.agimedia.com **w** agimedia.com **☎** Customer Services Manager: William Millen.

Airborne Packaging Pegasus House, Beatrice Rd, Leicester, Leics, LE3 9FH **t** 0116 253 6136 **f** 0116 251 4485 **e** sales@airbornebags.co.uk **w** airbornebags.co.uk **☎** Sales Manager: Gary Newby.

Audioprint Wolseley Court, Wolseley Rd Ind Estate, Kempston, Bedford, Beds, MK42 7AY **t** 01234 857566 **f** 01234 841700 **e** sales@audioprint.co.uk **w** audioprint.co.uk **☎** Director: Stephen Lawrence/Mark Craddock.

Bernard Kaymar Trout Street, Preston, Lancashire, PR1 4AL **t** 01772 562211 **f** 01772 257813 **e** sales@bernard-kaymar.co.uk **w** bernard-kaymar.co.uk **☎** MD: Mrs J Stead.

Design, Pressing & Distribution: Printers & Packaging

Blackgate Security Print & Promotions Ltd
PO Box 2696, Ascot, SL5 8ZQ **t** 01344 891 500
f 01344 891 500 **e** info@bspp.biz **w** bspp.biz ✉ Sales &
Marketing Director: Vicky Butcher.

THE BOX SET COMPANY

the box set co.
container ☑ contents ☑ complete ☑

3 Greenwich Quay, Clarence Rd, London, SE8 3EY
t 020 8469 4401 **f** 020 8691 3144 **w** boxsetco.com
✉ Contact: Sales 020 8469 4403.

Charitees 37 Barnfield Avenue, Kingston upon Thames,
Surrey, KT2 5RD **t** 020 8549 8653 **f** 020 8404 7368
e info@charitees.co.uk **w** charitees.co.uk
✉ Proprieter: Don Chetland.

CMCS Group Plc 1, Kennet Rd, Dartford, Kent,
DA1 4QN **t** 020 8308 5000 **f** 020 8308 5005
e sales@cmcs.co.uk **w** cmcs.co.uk ✉ MD: Adam Teskey.

CMJ Print Services (Poster Specialists)
t +353 87 232 1815 **e** jcomic@indigo.ie
w myspace.com/jimcomic ⬛ facebook.com/jim.morrish
⬛ myspace.com/jimcomic ✉ el Presidente: Jim Morrish.

Delga Group Seaplane House, Riverside Est.,
Sir Thomas Longley Rd, Medway City Estate, Rochester,
Kent, ME2 4BH **t** 01634 227 000 **e** info@delga.co.uk
w delga.co.uk ✉ Sales: Greg Barden.

Founders-Total Spectrum (UK) Ltd 11 Intec 2,
Wade Rd, Basingstoke, Hants, RG24 8NE **t** 01256 814114
f 01256 814115
e mark.norsworthy@totalspectrum.co.uk
w totalspectrum.co.uk ✉ MD: Mark Norsworthy.

GM Printing Ltd 7 Greenwich South St, Greenwich,
London, SE10 8NW **t** 0800 216 620
e accounts@gmprinting.co.uk **w** gmprinting.co.uk
✉ Owner: Graham Milton.

Go Digital Print Ltd 21 Wates Way, Mitcham, Surrey,
CR4 4HR **t** 020 8648 7060 **f** 020 8241 0989
e godigital@stjames.org.uk **w** godigitalprint.co.uk
✉ Production Manager: Steve Hill.

Jakebox AB Drottninggatan 104, Stockholm, SE-
111 60, Sweden **t** +46 8679 6050 **f** +46 8400 152 01
e info@jakebox.com **w** jakebox.com ✉ MD: Jakob Skarin.

Jourdans Kestral Way, Sowton Industrial Estate, Exeter,
Devon, EX2 7LA **t** 01392 445524 **f** 01392 445526
e rhino@jourdans.co.uk ✉ Mktg Dir: David Gargrave.

JTL Printed And Embroided Leisurewear
Unit 12, Worcester Rd Industrial Est, Chipping Norton,
Oxfordshire, OX7 5XW **t** 01608 645569 **f** 01608 645529
e sales@jtlembroidery.co.uk **w** jtlembroidery.co.uk
✉ Sales Director: Terry Kimble.

Keyprint (Printers) Research House, Fraser Rd,
Greenford, Middlesex, UB6 7AQ **t** 020 8566 7246
f 020 8566 7247 **e** sales@keyprinters.co.uk
w keyprinters.co.uk ✉ Managing Director: Mike Keyworth
01992 553193.

Lexon Group Park Road, Risca, Gwent, NP11 6YJ
t 01633 613444 **f** 01633 601333
e print@lexongroup.com **w** lexongroup.com
✉ Contact: Sales Dept.

Leyprint Leyland Lane, Leyland, Preston, Lancashire,
PR25 1UT **t** 01772 425000 **f** 01772 425001
e edward@leyprint.co.uk **w** leyprint.co.uk ✉ Sales & Mktg
Dir: Edward Mould.

Linards 16 Mead Business Centre, Mead Lane, Hertford,
Hertfordshire, SG13 7BJ **t** 01992 558820
f 01992 558831 **e** pat@linards.co.uk **w** linards.co.uk
✉ Contact: Patrick Leighton.

THE LONDON FANCY BOX Co Ltd.
Poulton Close, Dover, Kent CT17 0XB, UK
Tel: +44 (0)1304 242001 - Fax: +44 (0)1304 213570
www.londonfancybox.co.uk

With more than 100 years of experience, the London Fancy Box is one of Europe's leading suppliers to the Entertainment market.

From conception to production, our market focused Sales & Design team work closely with customers and key suppliers to provide innovative, cost effective packaging solutions. London Fancy Box has constantly invested in the latest equipment and technology giving us the largest, and most flexible box making facility in Europe.

We also operate in the following market areas: Beauty, Publishing, Imaging Media, Luxury Gifts and Premium Drinks.

For more information please contact:

Drew Dixon - Sales Director
d.dixon@londonfancybox.co.uk
Phone: 01304 242001
Mobile: 07768 210000

The market leading LFB was chosen to design and manufacture this year's ultimate Beatles Remastered Stereo boxset.

Design, Pressing & Distribution: Printers & Packaging

LONDON FANCY BOX CO LTD

Poulton Close, Dover, Kent, CT17 0XB **t** 01304 242 001 **f** 01304 213 570 **e** d.dixon@londonfancybox.co.uk **w** londonfancybox.com ✆ Sales Director: Drew Dixon 07768 210 000.

Modo Production Ltd 14 Regent Hill, Brighton, East Sussex, BN1 3ED **t** 01273 779030 **f** 01273 771900 **e** henry@modo.co.uk **w** modo.co.uk ✆ Creative Manager: Henry Lavelle.

Modo Production Ltd 14 Regent Hill, Brighton, East Sussex, BN1 3ED **t** 01273 779030 **f** 01273 771900 **e** mike@modo.co.uk **w** modo.co.uk ✆ Sales Manager: Mike Hicks 07917 422 474.

MPO UK Ltd Centre 500, 500 Chiswick High Road, London, W4 5RG **t** 0208 956 2727 **e** keith@mpo.co.uk **w** MPO.fr ✆ UK Manager: Keith Young.

Noon Media Solutions 4 Bessingby Road, Ruislip, Middx, HA4 9DA **t** 01895 472 882 **e** sales@noonmediasolutions.com **w** noonmediasolutions.com ✆ MD: David Noonan.

Nuleaf Graphics Ltd 49 - 51 Farringdon Rd, London, EC1M 3JP **t** 020 7242 5111 **e** peter@nuleaf-group.co.uk **w** nuleaf-group.co.uk ✆ Contact: Keith Morgan, Peter Moran.

ODS Business Services
The ODS Building (Spectrum), Mead Way, Westlea, Swindon, Wilts, SN5 7UT **t** 01793 421 300 **f** 01793 511 125 **e** sales@ods-businessservices.com **w** ods-businessservices.com

The Panda Group 1 The Hollands Centre, Hollands Road, Haverhill, Suffolk, CB9 8PR **t** 01440 762 011 **f** 01440 709 200 **e** sales@pandapress.co.uk **w** pandapress.co.uk ✆ Business Development Manager: Kim Williamson 07984 407 774.

Panmer Plastics (UK) Ltd. Unit 4-5, Delta Centre, Mount Pleasant, Wembley, london, HA0 1UX **t** 020 8903 7733 **f** 020 8903 3036 **e** info@panmer.com **w** panmer.com ✆ MD: Nimesh Shah 02089037733.

Pollard Boxes Ltd Feldspar Close, Enderby, Leicestershire, LE19 4SD **t** 0116 275 2666 **f** 0116 275 2567 **e** ian@pollardboxes.co.uk **w** pollardboxes.co.uk ✆ Sales Development Manager: Ian Bason.

Pozzoli Ltd 12 York Gate, Regent's Pk, London, NW1 4QS **t** 020 7384 3283 **f** 020 7384 3283 **e** mail@pozzolispa.com **w** pozzolispa.com ✆ Sales Dir UK: Tony Brooks 01628 580168.

Design, Pressing & Distribution: Printers & Packaging

MusicWeek
Creative Advertising Solutions

Contact the Music Week advertising sales team, and guarantee
you reach the right audience at the right time

Contact:
Becky Golland on 0207 921 8365
or Archie Carmichael on 0207 921 8372

www.musicweek.com

Proactive PR Suite 201, Homelife House,
26 - 32 Oxford Road, Bournemouth, BH8 8EZ
t 01202 315 333 **f** 01202 315 600
e info@proactivepr.org **w** proactivepr.org ✉ Dir: Cliff Lay.

RAD Printing Ltd Unit 10, Block F,
Northfleet Industrial Estate, Bluewater, Kent, DA11 9SW
t 01322 380775 **f** 01322 380647 **e** info@radprint.com
w radprint.com ✉ Production Manager: Emilie Bish.

Repeat Performance RPM 6 Grand Union Centre,
West Row, London, W10 5AS **t** 020 8960 7222
f 020 8968 1378 **e** info@rpmuk.com **w** rpmuk.com
✉ MD: Robin Springall.

Rowleys:London One Port Hill, Hertford, Hertfordshire,
SG14 1PJ **t** 01992 587350 **e** annie@rowleyslondon.co.uk
w rowleyslondon.co.uk ✉ MD: Anne Rowley.

Sarem Media Packaging **e** penny@media-
packaging.co.uk **w** media-packaging.co.uk
✉ Contact: Penny Coomber 01932 352535.

Senol Printing 6 Sandiford Rd,
Kimpton Road Trading Estate, Sutton, Surrey, SM3 9RD
t 020 8641 3890 **f** 020 8641 3486
e info@senolprinting.co.uk **w** senolprinting.co.uk
✉ Managing Director: Jacqui Gunn.

Shellway Press 42-44 Telford Way, Westway Estate,
London, W3 7XS **t** 020 8749 8191 **f** 020 8749 8721
e stuart@shellway.co.uk ✉ MD: Stuart Shelbourn.

SMP Group Plc 2 Swan Road, Woolwich, London,
SE18 5TT **t** 020 8855 5535 **f** 020 8855 5367
e John.Leahy@smpgroup.co.uk **w** smpgroup.co.uk
✉ MD: John Leahy 07808 909 292.

Sounds Good Ltd 12 Chiltern Enterprise Centre,
Station Rd, Theale, Reading, Berks, RG7 4AA
t 0118 930 1700 **f** 0118 930 1709 **e** sales-info@sounds-
good.co.uk **w** sounds-good.co.uk ✉ Dir: Martin Maynard.

St Ives Direct (Blackburn) Ltd
Greenbank Technology Pk, Challenge Way, Blackburn,
Lancashire, BB1 5QB **t** 01254 278800 **f** 01254 278811
e jamie.elson@st-ives.com **w** st-ives.com ✉ Sales
Director: Jamie Elson.

St Ives Print & Display Ltd Optima Park,
Thames Rd, Crayford, Kent, DA1 4QX **t** 01322 621 560
f 01322 625 060 **e** sales@stivespd.co.uk
w stivespd.co.uk ✉ Sales Director: Mark Vincent.

St James Litho 21 Wates Way, Mitcham, Surrey,
CR4 4HR **t** 020 8640 9438 **f** 020 8241 0989
e macroom@stjames.org.uk **w** stjames.org.uk
✉ Production Manager: Steve Hill.

Super Jewel Box (UK) Ltd Media House,
43A Old Woking Rd, West Byfleet, KT14 6LG
t 01932 343800 **f** 01932 336431
e martin@superjewelbox.co.uk **w** superjewelbox.co.uk
✉ Contact: Martin Howell.

T Shirt Printers Valley Farm Way, Wakefield Rd, Leeds,
LS10 1SE **t** 0113 276 0445 **e** sales@screen-
machine.co.uk **w** printwear.co.uk ✉ Works Manager: Tony
de Whytell.

Tapematic UK Hangar 3 Lodge Farm,
Nightingale Hall Rd, Earls Colne Airfield, Colchester, Essex,
CO6 2NR **t** 07836 626133 **f** 01787 224843
e uk@tapematic.com **w** tapematic.com ✉ MD: David Hill.

Target Transfers Ltd Anglia Way, Chapel Hill,
Braintree, Essex, CM7 3RG **t** 01376 326351
f 01376 345876 **e** info@targettransfers.com
w targettransfers.com ✉ MD: Robin Bull.

THINKTANK MEDIA

think TANK
your creative production partner

16 Highbridge Wharf, Greenwich, London, SE10 9PS
t 020 8858 0855 **f** 020 8858 1788
e info@thinktankmedia.co.uk **w** thinktankmedia.co.uk
✉ Sales Director: Dean Rose.
Creative packaging is our world! Extensive
knowledge and experience in this field. From ideas to
finished product visit www.thinktankmedia.co.uk for
inspiration.

VDC Group VDC House,
Units 3 & 4, Nucleus Business Centre, Central Way,
Wembley, NW10 7XT **t** 0208 963 3555 **f** 0208 965 9412
e enquiries@vdcgroup.com **w** vdcgroup.com ✉ Sales
Executives: Alex Lytton, Mike Redfern, Mike Seamen.

Vycon Products Ltd Units 1, Crathie Rd,
off Western Rd, Kilmarnock, Ayrshire, KA3 1NG
t 01563 574481 **f** 01563 533537 **e** sales@vycon.co.uk
w vycon.co.uk ✉ Sales Dir: Morag Belford..

Design, Pressing & Distribution: Printers & Packaging

Art & Creative Studios

After Dark Media Unit 29, Scott Business Park, Beacom Park Road, Plymouth, PL2 2PB **t** 01752 294130 **f** 01752 257320 **e** nigel@afterdarkmedia.net **w** afterdarkmedia.net 📇 Manager: Nigel Muntz.

Airside 339 Upper St, Islington, London, N1 0PB **t** 020 7354 9912 **e** studio@airside.co.uk **w** airside.co.uk 📇 PR and New Business: Anne Brassier.

Alchemy Carta Ltd The Alembic Hazel Drive, Narborough Rd South, Leicester, LE3 2JE **t** 0116 282 4824 **f** 0116 282 5202 **e** info@alchemygroup.com **w** alchemygroup.com 📇 Sales Dir: Sandra Philipson.

ArtScience Limited 3-5 Hardwidge St, London, SE1 3SY **t** 020 7939 9500 **f** 020 7939 9499 **e** lab5@artscience.net **w** artscience.net 📇 Dirs: Douglas Coates, Pete Rope.

Big Active Ltd (Art Direction & Design) Unit 6.01, The Tea Building, 56 Shoreditch High Street, London, E1 6JJ **t** 020 7739 5601 **f** 020 7739 7479 **e** contact@bigactive.com **w** bigactive.com 📇 Creative Dir: Gerard Saint.

Bijoux Graphics 10 L Peabody Bldgs, Clerkenwell Close, London, EC1R 0AY **t** 020 7608 1316 **f** 020 7608 0525 **e** davies@bijouxgraphics.co.uk **w** bijouxgraphics.co.uk 📇 Director: David Davies 07947 896 775.

Binary & The Brain 45-46 Charlotte Rd, Shoreditch, London, EC2A 3PD **t** 020 3157 4054 **e** simon@binaryandthebrain.com **w** binaryandthebrain.com 🐦 twitter.com/BinaryAndBrain 📇 Creative Director: Simon Dovar.

Blade Design Ltd Unit 4, 101 Pentonville Rd, Islington, London, N1 9LF **t** 020 3119 1022 **f** 020 3119 1033 **e** steve@bladeweb.co.uk **w** bladeweb.co.uk 📇 Director: Steve Knee.

Blag Magazine t 020 3286 0321 **e** blag@blagmagazine.com **w** weareblag.com 📘 facebook.com/pages/BLAG/84613854415 🎵 myspace.com/blagmag 🐦 twitter.com/blagmagazine ▶️ youtube.com/blagmagazine 📇 Directors: Sarah J Edwards & Sally A Edwards.

Blue Source Ltd. Lower Ground Floor, 49-51 Central St, London, EC1V 8AB **t** 020 7553 7950 **e** seb@bluesource.com **w** bluesource.com 📇 Company Director: Seb Marling.

Bravado International Group 12 Deer Park Rd, Wimbledon, London, SW19 3FB **t** 020 7471 5000 **f** 020 8542 1807 **e** alison.bramley@umusic.com **w** bravado.com 📇 Receptionist: Alison Bramley.

Brian Burrows Ind Illustration & Graphic Design Enterprise House, 133 Blyth Road, Hayes, Middlesex, UB3 1DD **t** 020 8573 8761 **f** 020 8561 9114 **e** bburrows@btinternet.com 📇 MD: Brian Burrows.

Century Displays 75-77 Park Road, Kingston Upon Thames, Surrey, KT2 6DE **t** 020 8974 8950 **f** 020 8546 3689 **e** info@centurydisplays.co.uk **w** centurydisplays.co.uk 📇 General Manager: Neil Wicks.

Colors The Clock House, Rowney Lane, Ware, Hertfordshire, SG12 0JY **t** 01920 438503 **e** chris@colors.co.uk **w** colors.co.uk 📇 Director: Chris Green.

Coloset Graphics 3 Black Swan Yard, Bermondsey St, London, SE1 3XW **t** 020 7234 0300 **f** 020 7234 0118 **e** info@colorsetgraphics.co.uk **w** colorsetgraphics.co.uk 📇 Dir: Frank Baptiste.

Crush Design & Art Direction 11 Vine St, Brighton, BN1 4AG **t** 01273 606058 **e** contact@crushed.co.uk **w** crushed.co.uk 📇 Director: Carl.

D-Face 6 Links View, London, N3 1RN **t** 020 8349 4973 **f** 020 8349 4973 **e** designone@d-face.co.uk **w** d-face.co.uk 📇 Creative Director: Donna Pickup.

D-Fuse 13-14 Great Sutton St, London, EC1V 0BX **t** 020 7253 3462 **e** info@dfuse.com **w** dfuse.com 📇 Dir: Michael Faulkner.

Darkwave Art 19 Birrell Rd, Nottingham, NG7 6LN **e** darkwaveart@hotmail.com **w** darkwaveart.co.uk 🎵 myspace.com/darkwaveart 📇 Designer: Matt Vickerstaff.

Delga Group Seaplane House, Riverside Est., Sir Thomas Longley Rd, Medway City Estate, Rochester, Kent, ME2 4BH **t** 01634 227 000 **e** info@delga.co.uk **w** delga.co.uk 📇 Sales: Greg Barden.

The Design & Advertising Resource 7 Kings Wharf, 301 Kingsland Road, Hoxton, London, E8 4DS **t** 020 7254 3191 **f** 0870 442 5297 **e** info@your-resource.co.uk **w** your-resource.co.uk 📇 Account Director: Richard Fearn.

Design Corporation (London) Ltd 7 Portland Mews, Soho, London, W1F 8JQ **t** 020 7734 5676 **e** us@designcorporation.co.uk **w** design4music.com 📇 MD: Nigel Pearce 07974 144830.

The Design Dell 13a Newnham St, Ely, Cambs, CB7 4PG **t** 01353 659 911 **f** 01353 650 011 **e** dan@design-dell.com **w** design-dell.com 📇 Creative Director: Dan Donovan.

Design Lab Studio 336, Stratford Workshops, Burford Road, London, E15 2SP **t** 020 8555 5540 **f** 0208 5555540 **e** info@design-lab.tv **w** design-lab.tv 📇 Art Director: Matthew James 07841 196 787.

The Designers Republic The Workstation, Unit 328, 15 Paternoster Row, Sheffield, South Yorkshire, S1 2BX **t** 0114 221 0220 **e** disinfo@thedesignersrepublic.com **w** thedesignersrepublic.com 📇 Creative Director: Ian Anderson 0770 957680.

Division 100 Unit Two, 34 Charlotte Rd, London, EC2A 3PB **t** 020 7033 0000 **f** 020 7033 0001 **e** designers@division100.com **w** division100.com 📇 Dir: Terence Chisholm.

DS Emotion Ltd Chantry House, Victoria Road, Leeds, West Yorkshire, LS5 3JB **t** 0113 225 7100 **f** 0113 225 7200 **e** info@dsemotion.com **w** dsemotion.com

Duke Creative Agency Second Floor, 17-18 Margaret St, London, W1W 8RP **t** 020 7580 7070 **f** 020 7636 8815 **e** marc@duke.tv **w** duke.tv ■ Head of Business Development: Marc Heal.

eject creative studios Omega Works, Fish Island, London, E3 2GZ **t** 020 8986 6320 **e** studio@eject.co.uk **w** eject.co.uk ■ Creative Director: Lee Murrell.

Eldamar Ltd 157 Oxford Rd, Cowley, Oxford, OX4 2ES **t** 01865 77 99 44 **e** ideas@eldamar.co.uk **w** eldamar.co.uk ■ Creative Director: Ayd Instone.

expdesign.co.uk 4-8 Rodney Street, London, N1 9JH **t** 020 7841 8737 **e** info@expdesign.co.uk **w** expdesign.co.uk ■ Creative Director: Mark Bailey.

Eyetoeye Entertainment Tucketts Barn, Trusham, Devon, TQ13 0NR **t** 01626 854 277 **e** brian@eyetoeye.com **w** eyetoeye.com ■ Partner: Brian Yates.

Farrow Design Ltd 23-24 Great James St, London, WC1N 3ES **t** 020 7404 4225 **f** 020 7404 4223 **e** studio@farrowdesign.com **w** farrowdesign.com ■ Contact: Mark Farrow 020 7831 4976 ISDN.

Fluid Graphic Design Ltd Fluid Studios, 12 Tenby St, Birmingham, B1 3AJ **t** 0121 212 0121 **f** 0121 212 0202 **e** james@fluidesign.co.uk **w** fluidesign.co.uk ■ Director: James Glover.

Form 47 Tabernacle St, London, EC2A 4AA **t** 020 7014 1430 **f** 020 7014 1431 **e** studio@form.uk.com **w** form.uk.com ■ facebook.com/home.php?#/group.php?gid=6319802502&ref=ts ■ Partners: Paula Benson, Paul West.

four23 Carver's Warehouse, 77 Dale St, Manchester, M1 2HG **t** 0161 236 3566 **f** 0161 833 9939 **e** warren@four23.net **w** four23.net ■ Director: Warren Bramley.

Framous Unit 12, Vale Grove, Acton, London, W3 7QP **t** 020 8735 0047 **f** 020 8735 0048 **e** lucy@framous.ltd.uk **w** framous.ltd.uk ■ Manager: Lucy Walker.

Glasseye Unit 20A, Iliffe Yard, Crampton Street, London, SE17 3QA **t** 020 7701 4300 **e** info@glasseyeltd.com **w** glasseyeltd.com ■ Director: James Jefferson.

Green Ink "Captains" Church Rd, Great Hallingbury, Bishop's Stortford, Herts, CM22 7TZ **t** 01279 718949 **e** info@green-ink.co.uk **w** green-ink.co.uk ■ MD: Bruce Gill.

Gwarsh Studio 79 Stanley St, Darlinghurst, Sydney, 2010 NSW, Australia **t** +61 2 9331 1113 **e** joel@gwarsh.com **w** gwarsh.com ■ Creative Director: Joel Wasserman +61 (0) 411 22 6467.

hng design Studio 7, 258 Cambridge Heath Rd, London, E2 9DA **t** 07956 967288 **e** hngdesign@gmail.com **w** hngdesign.com ■ Contact: Heidi Kayla.

Hold Link House, Link Place, Upper Hollingdean Rd, Brighton, East Sussex, Bn1 7DU **t** 01273 550066 **e** hello@wearehold.com **w** WeAreHold.com ■ Director: Anthony Oram 01273 55 00 66.

How Splendid 54-62 Regent St, London, W1B 5RE **t** 020 7287 4442 **f** 020 7287 5557 **e** dan@howsplendid.com **w** howsplendid.com ■ Account Dir: Dan Morris.

Hutch Rose Cottage, South Dock Lock Office, Rope Street, London, SE16 7SZ **t** 020 7252 0147 **e** will@willhutchinson.co.uk **w** willhutchinson.co.uk ■ MD: Will Hutchinson 07952 751614.

icoico creative 22 Jamaica St, 2nd Floor, Glasgow, G1 4QD **t** 0141 221 4171 **f** 0141 221 4172 **e** info@icoico.com **w** icoico.com ■ MD: Lee McLean.

ID Interactive 5 Rolls Crescent, Manchester, M15 5JX **t** 0161 232 9314 **f** 0161 232 9514 **e** info@idinteractive.co.uk **w** idinteractive.net ■ Manager: Azmat Mohammed.

Impac Associates Ltd Grafton House, 2-3 Golden Square, London, W1F 9HR **t** 020 7734 1134 **f** 020 7734 1135 **e** impac.tom@virgin.net ■ Contact: Tom Heron.

Intro 42 St John St, London, EC1M 4DL **t** 020 7324 3244 **f** 020 7324 3245 **e** intro@intro-uk.com **w** introwebsite.com ■ New Business Mgr: Jo Marsh.

Irrational Design 122 Hollydale Rd, Nunhead, London, SE15 2TQ **t** 07956 512509 **e** andy.knowles@irrational.info **w** irrational.info ■ Dir: Andy Knowles.

Jawa and Midwich 45-46 Charlotte Rd, London, EC2A 3PD **t** 020 3157 4054 **e** info@jawa-midwich.com **w** jawa-midwich.com ■ twitter.com/JawaAndMidwich ■ Designer (Partner): Simon Dovar.

Jeff Cummins Design 125, High Oak Rd, Ware, Herts, SG12 7PA **t** 07751 549098 **f** 01920 411434 **e** info@jeffcummins.com **w** jeffcummins.com ■ Art Director: Jeff Cummins 01920 411434.

Joel Harrison Design c/o Fresh, United House, North Rd, London, N7 9DP **t** 07968 773972 **f** 07968 773972 **e** info@joelharrisondesign.com **w** joelharrisondesign.com ■ Art Director: Joel Harrison.

JP3 Studio 3, 3A Brackenbury Road, London, W6 0BE **t** 020 8762 9153 **f** 020 8740 0200 **e** info@jp3.co.uk **w** jp3.co.uk ■ MD: Paul McGarvey.

Chris Kay (UK) Ltd 158 Station Road, Witham, Essex, CM8 3YS **t** 01376 500566 **f** 01376 500578 **e** sales@chriskay.com **w** chriskay.com ■ Contact: Eddie Clark.

LGD Ltd 180 Corporation St, Birmingham, B4 6UD **t** 0121 212 3450 **f** 0121 212 3455 **e** info@lgdgroup.co.uk **w** lgdgroup.co.uk ■ Partner: Phil Jolly.

Linards 16 Mead Business Centre, Mead Lane, Hertford, Hertfordshire, SG13 7BJ **t** 01992 558820 **f** 01992 558831 **e** Pat@linards.co.uk **w** linards.co.uk ■ Contact: Patrick Leighton.

Design, Pressing & Distribution: Art & Creative Studios

Design, Pressing & Distribution: Art & Creative Studios

Lust For Design P.O.Box 696, Felbridge, Surrey, RH19 2XS **t** 0845 370 9904 **f** 0845 370 9905 **e** deejay@lustfordesign.com **w** lustfordesign.com 🔲 Director: Deejay.

Lynton Black Media 7 Ty Ddewi Court, Cardiff, CF11 9AW **t** 02920 195 300 **e** creativity@lyntonblack.net **w** lyntonblack.net 🔲 Creative Director: Lynton Black 07921 903 943.

Mackerel Design Ltd 15-17 Middle Street, Brighton, West Sussex, BN1 1AL **t** 01273 201313 **e** info@mackerel.co.uk **w** mackerel.co.uk 🔲 Director: Mark Davis.

Mainartery Design 2 Stucley Place, London, NW1 8NS **t** 020 7482 6660 **f** 020 7482 6606 **e** art@mainartery.co.uk **w** mainartery.co.uk 🔲 Creative Dir: Jo Mirowski.

Me Company 14 Apollo Studios, Charlton Kings Rd, London, NW5 2SA **t** 020 7482 4262 **f** 020 7284 0402 **e** meco@mecompany.com **w** mecompany.com 🔲 Art Dir: Paul White.

Mental Block Chanctonbury Lodge, Washington Rd, Pulborough, West Sussex, RH20 4AF **t** 01903 743925 **e** johnathan@mentalblock.co.uk **w** mentalblock.co.uk 🔲 Contact: Johnathan Elliott.

The Mustard Laboratory Third Floor, 24 Denmark St, London, WC2H 8NJ **t** 020 8692 3555 **f** 020 8469 3300 **e** chris@mustardlab.co.uk **w** mustardlab.co.uk 🔲 Contact: Chris Musto 07970 069991.

Mystery Ltd 87a Worship St, London, EC2A 2BE **t** 020 7456 7833 **e** taya@mystery.co.uk **w** mystery.co.uk 🔲 Studio Manager: Taya Kajanus.

Navig8 Basement, 36 Charlotte Street, Fitzrovia, London, W1T 2NA **t** 020 7813 0373 **f** 020 7436 8996 **e** enquiries@navig8.co.uk **w** navig8.co.uk 🔲 Contact: Drew Corps.

Nu Urban Design Unit 9, Rivermead Industrial Estate, Pipersway, Thatcham, Berkshire, RG19 4EP **t** 01635 587900 **f** 01635 292314 **e** kevin@nu-urbanmusic.co.uk **w** nu-urbandesign.co.uk 🔲 Head of Design: Kevin Broome.

The Nuclear Family London **t** 01263 861159 **e** red@thenuclearfamily.co.uk **w** thenuclearfamily.co.uk 🔲 Creative Director: Red K Sanderson.

OR Multimedia Ltd Unit 5 Elm Court, 156-170 Bermondsey Street, London, SE1 3TQ **t** 020 7939 9540 **f** 020 7939 9541 **e** info@or-media.com **w** or-media.com 🔲 Dir: Peter Gough.

Plus Two Studio 153 Hagley Rd, Oldswinford, Stourbridge, West Midlands, DY8 2JB **t** 01384 393311 **f** 01384 393232 **e** andy@plustwo.co.uk **w** plustwo.co.uk 🔲 Art Director: Andrew Higginbotham.

Popular 117 Cleveland St, London, W1T 6PX **t** 07889 182808 **e** peter@popularuk.com **w** popularuk.com 🔲 Creative Director: Peter Chadwick.

Proactive PR Suite 201, Homelife House, 26 - 32 Oxford Road, Bournemouth, BH8 8EZ **t** 01202 315 333 **f** 01202 315 600 **e** info@proactivepr.org **w** proactivepr.org 🔲 Dir: Cliff Lay.

Raw-Paw Graphics 13-14 Great Sutton St, London, EC1 0BX **t** 020 7253 3462 **e** mike@dfuse.com **w** dfuse.com 🔲 MD: Michael Faulkner.

Real World Design Mill Lane, Box, Corsham, Wiltshire, SN13 8PN **t** 0845 146 1733 **f** 01225 744369 **e** york.tillyer@realworld.co.uk **w** realworld.co.uk 🔲 Interactive Director: York Tillyer.

Red James London, EC2 **t** 020 7628 7853 **e** red@redjam.com **w** redjam.com 🔲 Dir: Red James.

Red Sky Media 12 Austral Way, Althorne, Essex, CM3 6UP **t** 01621 743 979 **e** dan@redskymedia.co.uk **w** redskymedia.co.uk 🔲 Mgr: Daniel Raynham 07957 297 872.

The Reptile House 69-70 Long Lane, Smithfield, London, EC1A 9EJ **t** 020 7796 3545 **f** 020 7796 3561 **e** matt@the-reptile-house.co.uk **w** the-reptile-house.co.uk 🔲 Creative Director: Matt Hughes.

Robin Scott Ltd Kingstore Studio, The Green, Hampton Court, East Molsey, KT8 9BW **t** 07974 797711 **e** robin@robinscott.org **w** robinscott.org 🔲 Director: Robin Scott.

Ryan Art 48A Southern Row, London, W10 5AN **t** 020 8968 0966 **f** 020 8968 6418 **e** info@ryanart.com **w** ryanart.com 🔲 Contact: Simon Ryan.

Sane & Able 15a Bolingbroke Rd, Brook Green, London, W14 0AJ **t** 07515 657810 **e** studio@saneandable.co.uk **w** saneandable.co.uk 🔵 twitter.com/saneandable 🔲 Senior Designer: Alan Long.

Scott Parker Design Symington House, 14 School Lane, Market Harborough, Leicestershire, LE16 9DJ **t** 07817 956788 **e** scott@scottparkerdesign.co.uk **w** scottparkerdesign.co.uk 🔲 Creative Director, Photographer & Graphic Designer: Scott Parker.

Seed Software The Seed Warehouse, Maidenhead Yard, The Wash, Herts, SG14 1PX **t** 01992 558 881 **f** 01992 558 465 **e** info@seedsoftware.co.uk **w** seedsoftware.co.uk 🔲 MD: Andrew W Ellis.

Skinny Unit B, 53 Underhill Road, London, SE22 0QR **t** 020 8693 8798 **e** info@skinnycreative.com **w** skinnycreative.com 🔲 Director: Sonya Skinner.

Skinny Dip (Illustrators Agents) 6 Silver Place, London, W1F 0JS **t** 020 7287 9585 **e** info@skinnydip.co.uk **w** skinnydip.co.uk 🔲 Contact: Amy Foster, Jonny Wright.

Small Japanese Soldier 32-38 Saffron Hill, London, EC1N 8FH **t** 020 7421 9400 **f** 020 7421 9334 **e** Jungle@smallJapanesesoldier.com **w** smalljapanesesoldier.com 🔲 MD: Andy Hunns.

Sounds Good Ltd 12 Chiltern Enterprise Centre, Station Rd, Theale, Reading, Berks, RG7 4AA **t** 0118 930 1700 **f** 0118 930 1709 **e** sales-info@sounds-good.co.uk 🅱 Dir: Martin Maynard.

Studio Lobster & Design
e shorty@studiolobster.com **w** studiolobster.com 🅱 MD: Richard Short.

Studio Plum 39 Belgrade Road, London, N16 8DH **t** 0207 249 8198 **e** jonnie@studioplum.co.uk **w** studioplum.co.uk 🅱 Producer: Jonnie Pound.

StudioMix 3rd Floor, Mayfair House, 11 Lurke St, Bedford, MK40 3HZ **t** 01234 272347 **f** 01234 272327 **e** design@studiomix.co.uk **w** studiomix.co.uk 🅱 Senior Designer: Mick Lowe.

Stylorouge 57/60 Charlotte Rd, London, EC2A 3QT **t** 020 7729 1005 **f** 020 7739 7124 **e** rob@stylorouge.co.uk **w** stylorouge.co.uk ▶ youtube.com/stylorougelondon 🅱 Director: Rob O'Connor.

thelongdrop thelongdrop, Studio 2, 25 Halstead Rd, Earls Colne, Essex, CO6 2NG **t** 01787 224464 **e** studio@thelongdrop.com **w** thelongdrop.com 🅼 myspace.com/thelongdrop 🅴 twitter.com/thelongdrop 🅱 Creative Dir: Andy Carne.

Tom Hingston Studio 76 Brewer St, London, W1F 9TX **t** 020 7287 6044 **f** 020 7287 6048 **e** info@hingston.net **w** hingston.net 🅱 Contact: Tom Hingston.

Tourist 95a Rivington St, Shoreditch, London, EC2A 3AY **t** 020 7739 3011 **f** 020 7739 3033 **e** info@wearetourist.com **w** wearetourist.com 🅱 Directors: Rob Chenery, Keith White, Mark caylor, Errol Sidelsky.

Traffic 3 Astrop Mews, Hammersmith, London, W6 7HR **t** 020 8742 9559 **e** jeremy@traffic-design.com **w** traffic-design.com 🅱 Creative Director: Jeremy Plumb.

Traffic Design 3 Astrop Mews, Hammersmith, London, W6 7HR **t** 020 8742 9559 **e** jeremy@traffic-design.com **w** traffic-design.com 🅱 Creative Director: Jeremy Plumb.

Tumbling Dice Creative Management
PO Box 6234, Leighton Buzzard, LU7 2WX **t** 01525 217727 **e** enquiries@wearetumblingdice.com **w** wearetumblingdice.com 🅱 MD: Duncan Illing.

TWO:DESIGN Studio 45 - Hampstead House, 176 Finchley Rd, London, NW3 6BT **t** 020 8275 8594 **e** info@twodesign.net **w** twodesign.net 🅼 myspace.com/twodesign 🅴 twitter.com/twodesign 🅱 Creative Director: Graham Peake.

Undertow Design No7, 9-10 College Terrace, London, E3 5EP **t** 020 8983 4718 **f** 020 8983 4718 **e** info@undertow-design.co.uk **w** undertow-design.co.uk 🅱 Art Director: Steve Wilkins 07966170109.

UnLimited Creative Unicorn House, 221-222 Shoreditch High St, London, E1 6PJ **t** 020 7099 9050 **e** creative@unlimitedmedia.co.uk **w** unlimitedmedia.co.uk 🅱 Contact: Chris Cooke.

Version Industries Ltd 47 Lower End, Swaffham Prior, Cambridge, CB5 0HT **t** 07903 886 471 **f** 020 8374 4021 **e** team@versionindustries.com **w** versionindustries.com 🅱 Lead Designer/Developer: Gavin Singleton.

Vivid Design & Print Ltd 26 Sydney St, Brighton, East Sussex, BN1 4EP **t** 01273 604050 **e** info@vividbrighton.co.uk **w** vividbrighton.co.uk 🅱 Owner: Paul Jukes.

Wherefore Art? 8 Primrose Mews, Sharpleshall Street, London, NW1 8YW **t** 020 7586 8866 **f** 020 7586 8800 **e** info@whereforeart.com **w** whereforeart.com 🅱 Creative Director: David Costa.

White Label Productions Ltd 45-51 Whitfield St, London, W1T 4HB **t** 020 3031 6100 **f** 020 3031 6101 **e** c.grant@whitelabelproductions.co.uk **w** whitelabelproductions.co.uk 🅱 MD: Cheryl Grant.

Wolf Graphics - Exotica Records 49 Belvoir Rd, London, SE22 0QY **t** 020 8299 2342 **f** 020 8693 9006 **e** jim@exoticarecords.co.uk **w** exoticarecords.co.uk 🅼 myspace.com/exoticarecordings 🅱 MD: Jim Phelan.

ZiP Design Ltd Unit 2A Queens Studios, 121 Salusbury Rd, London, NW6 6RG **t** 020 7644 6581 **f** 020 7372 4484 **e** info@zipdesign.co.uk **w** zipdesign.co.uk 🅱 Head of Production & Business: Alex Cunningham.

Merchandise Companies

ABC Shirts Unit 16, Greenwich Centre Business Park, 53 Norman Road, London, SE10 9QF **t** 020 8853 1103 **f** 020 8293 1746 **e** sales@abcshirts.com **w** abcshirts.com 🅱 Contact: Jane Cheese.

Action Jacket Company PO Box 1180, Stourbridge, West Midlands, DY9 0ZF **t** 01562 887096 **f** 01562 882010 **e** info@actionjacket.co.uk **w** actionjacket.co.uk 🅱 Proprietor: Brian Smith.

Active Merchandising (T Shirts)
58, Overn Avenue, Buckingham, MK18 1LT **t** 01280 814510 **f** 01280 814519 **e** leonprice@lineone.net 🅱 MD: Leon Price.

Adrenalin Merchandising Unit 5, Church House, Church Street, London, E15 3JA **t** 020 8503 0634 **f** 020 8221 2528 **e** scott@adrenalin-merch.demon.co.uk **w** adrenalin-merch.demon.co.uk 🅱 Contact: Scott Cooper.

Alex Co 94 Guildford Road, Croydon, Surrey, CR0 2HJ **t** 020 8683 0546 **f** 020 8689 4749 **e** alexco@btinternet.com 🅱 MD: Stuart Alexander.

Alister Reid Ties 9 Applegate House, Applegate, Brentwood, Essex, CM14 5PL **t** 01277 375329 **f** 01277 375331 **e** colin@arties.fsbusiness.co.uk 🅱 Sales Manager: Colin Stoddart.

Contacts Facebook MySpace Twitter YouTube

Design, Pressing & Distribution: Merchandise Companies

Backstreet International Merchandise Ltd.
4th Floor, 10 Greenland St, Camden, London, NW1 0ND
t 020 7428 1105 **f** 020 7428 1101
e andy.allen@bsimerch.com **w** bsimerch.com
 CEO: Andy Allen 020 7428 1100.

Baskind Promotions Ltd 54 Otley Rd, Headingley,
Leeds, West Yorkshire, LS6 2AL **t** 0113 389 4100
f 0113 389 4101 **e** simon@baskind.com **w** baskind.com
 MD: Simon Baskind.

Blowfish U.V. 29 Granville St, Loughborough, Leics.,
LE11 3BL **t** 07900 262 052 **f** 01509 560 221
e anna@blowfishuv.co.uk **w** blowfishuv.co.uk MD: Anna
Sandiford.

Blue Apple Merchandise PO Box 29, Ullapool,
IV26 2WF **t** 01854 612388
e simon@blueapplemusic.co.uk
w blueapplemerchandise.co.uk Contact: Simon Lawlor.

Caterprint Ltd Unit 3, Chaseside Works,,
Chelmsford Rd, Southgate, London, N14 4JN
t 020 8886 1600 **f** 020 8886 1636
e info@caterprint.co.uk **w** caterprint.co.uk
 Contact: Leonard.

Century Displays 75-77 Park Road,
Kingston Upon Thames, Surrey, KT2 6DE **t** 020 8974 8950
f 020 8546 3689 **e** info@centurydisplays.co.uk
w centurydisplays.co.uk General Manager: Neil Wicks.

Chester Hopkins International PO Box 536,
Headington, Oxford, OX3 7LR **t** 01865 766 766
f 01865 769 736 **e** office@chesterhopkins.co.uk
w chesterhopkins.co.uk MDs: Adrian Hopkins, Jo
Chester 020 8441 1555.

EBTM Plc Unit A1, Riverside Business Centre,
Haldane Place, London, SW18 4UQ **e** grant@EBTM.com
w EBTM.com Director: Grant Calton 07713 404 101.

EMC Advertising Gifts Derwent House,
1064 High Road, Whetstone, London, N20 0YY
t 020 8492 2200 **f** 020 8445 9347
e sales@emcadgifts.co.uk **w** emcadgifts.co.uk Sales
Dir: John Kay.

Epona Fairtrade and Organic Cotton Clothing
Unit 216, Bon Marche Centre, 241-251 Ferndale Road,
London, SW9 8BJ **t** 020 7095 9888
e info@eponaclothing.com **w** eponaclothing.com
 Director: Tom Andrews.

Event Merchandising Unit 11, The Edge, Humber Rd,
London, NW2 6EW **t** 020 8208 1166 **f** 020 8208 4477
e event@eventmerch.com **w** eventmerchandising.com
 MD: Jeremy Goldsmith 0208 208 1166.

Fair Oaks Entertainments 7 Towers Street,
Ulverston, Cumbria, LA12 9AN **t** 01229 581 766
f 01229 581 766
e fairoaksorderline@roots2rockmusic.com
w roots2rockmusic.com Contact: JG Livingstone.

Fezborough Limited Manor Farm Studio, Cleveley,
Oxfordshire, OX7 4DY **t** 01608 677100 **f** 01608 677101
e kellogs@fezbro.com Top Promo Merch Guy: John
'Kellogs' Kalinowski 07889 787600.

Fifth Column T Shirt Design & Print
276 Kentish Town Road, London, NW5 2AA
t 020 7485 8599 **f** 020 7267 3718
e info@fifthcolumn.co.uk **w** fifthcolumn.co.uk
 MD: Rodney Adams.

Finally Fan-Fair PO Box 153, Stanmore, Middlesex,
HA7 2HF **t** 01923 896975 **f** 01923 896985 **e** hrano@fan-
fair.freeserve.co.uk MD: Mike Hrano.

Firebrand Live Ltd 41 Mitchell St, London, EC1V 3QD
t 020 7253 7185 **e** firstname@firebrandlive.com
w firebrandlive.com Dirs: Justin Smith.

Flag Standards Compass House, Waldron,
East Sussex, TN21 0RE **t** 01435 810080 **f** 01435 810082
e sales@flagstandards.co.uk **w** flagstandards.co.uk
 Owner: Tim Eustace.

GB Eye Ltd 1 Russell Street, Kelham Island, Sheffield,
S3 8RW **t** 0114 276 7454 **f** 0114 272 9599
e max@gbeye.com **w** gbeye.com Licensing
Manager: Max Arguile 0114 252 1614.

GMerch 2 Glenthorne Mews, London, W6 0LJ
t 020 8741 7100 **f** 020 8741 1170
e Paula.Campbell@gmerch.com **w** gmerch.com
 MD: Mark Stredwick.

Green Island Promotions Ltd Unit 31,
56 Gloucester Rd, Kensington, London, SW7 4UB
t 0870 789 3377 **f** 0870 789 3414
e greenisland@btinternet.com Dir: Steve Lucas.

IDD Enterprises Ltd The Old Boat House,
66 London Rd, Sheffield, South Yorkshire, S2 4LR
t 0114 273 9848 **f** 0114 278 7855 **e** ian@iddltd.co.uk
w iddltd.co.uk myspace.com/iddltd Sales
Director: Ian Bell.

Idle Eyes Printshop 81 Sheen Court, Richmond,
Surrey, TW10 5DF **t** 020 8876 0099 **f** 020 8876 0099
e IdleEyes@gmail.com **w** idleeyesprintshop.com
 Manager: Jonathan Rees.

Independent Posters PO Box 7259, Brentwood,
Essex, CM14 5ZA **t** 01277 372000 **f** 01277 375333
e info@independentposters.co.uk Publishing
Manager: Kim Miller.

Inkorporate 10A Lower Mall, Hammersmith, London,
W6 9DJ **t** 020 8748 3311 **f** 020 8563 7999
e sales@inkorporate.co.uk **w** inkorporate.co.uk Sales
Director: Melvyn de Villiers.

Iris Unit 8a, Southam St, London, W10 5PH
t 020 8969 4761 **e** info@irisprinting.co.uk
w irisprinting.co.uk Director: Tim.

JIGSAW DESIGNS East End, Fairy Hall Lane, Rayne,
Braintree, Essex, CM77 6SZ **t** 01376 347464
f 01376 347464 **e** jigsaw.designs@talk21.com
 Embroiderer/Screen Printer: Geoff Noble.

Keynote Unsigned 6 Beckside, Norwich, Norfolk,
NR10 3SY **t** 07828 594 232
e info@keynoteunsigned.co.uk **w** keynoteunsigned.co.uk
 Dir: Adem Genc.

Klobber Ltd 443 Streatham High Road, London, SW16 3PH **t** 020 8679 9289 **f** 020 679 9775 **e** info@fruitpiemusic.com **w** fruitpiemusic.com 🖪 Director: Kumar Kamalagharan.

Live Nation Merchandise Europe Zetland House, 5-25 Scrutton St, London, EC2A 4HJ **t** 020 7613 3555 **f** 020 7613 3550 **e** info@de-lux.net **w** livenation.com 🖪 MD: Jeremy Joseph.

LOGO Promotional Merchandise Ltd 10 Crescent Terrace, Ilkley, West Yorkshire, LS29 8DL **t** 01943 817238 **f** 01943 605259 **e** alan@logomerchandising.co.uk **w** logomerchandising.co.uk 🖪 Director: Alan Strachan.

Masons Music Dept. 260 Drury Lane, Ponswood Industrial Est, St Leonards On Sea, East Sussex, TN38 9BA **t** 01424 427562 **f** 01424 434362 **e** sales@masonsmusic.co.uk **w** masonsmusic.co.uk 🖪 Sales Admin: Alastair Sutton.

Metro Merchandising Ltd The Warehouse, 60 Queen Street, Desborough, Northamptonshire, NN14 2RE **t** 01536 763100 **f** 01536 763200 **e** mailbox@metro-ltd.co.uk **w** metro-ltd.co.uk 🖪 MD: Martin Stowe.

Mick Wright Merchandising 185 Weedon Road, Northampton, NN5 5DA **t** 07000 226397 **f** 08701 372735 **e** tshirts@mickwright.com **w** mickwright.com 🖪 CEO: Mick Wright 07802 500054.

Nymphs of Bacchus Apartment 17, The Tobacco Factory Phase 3, 2 Naples Street, Manchester, M4 4DH **t** 07742 462 574 **e** enquiries@nymphsofbacchus.co.uk **w** nymphsofbacchus.co.uk 🖪 Owner: Kelly Bucher.

PINK! Brand Solutions Ltd 565 24/28 St Leonards Road, Windsor, Berks, SL4 3BB **t** 01753 622555 **f** 01753 622557 **e** stuff@pink-brand.co.uk **w** pink-brand.co.uk 🖪 Dir: Stuart Bailey.

PKA Promotions 6 South Folds Road, Oakley Hay Industrial Estate, Corby, Northamptonshire, NN18 9EU **t** 01536 461122 **f** 01536 744668 **e** PKaPromotions@aol.com 🖪 MD: Mr D Dias.

Positive Branding Unit 17, Capitol Way, London, NW9 0EQ **t** 020 8912 1515 **f** 08708 681 467 **e** sales@positivebranding.co.uk **w** positivebranding.co.uk 🖪 Sales Manager: David Wilton.

Promotional Condom Co PO Box 111, Croydon, Surrey, CR9 6WS **t** 0033 29751 2950 **f** 0033 29739 3306 **e** promotionalcondoms@btopenworld.com 🖪 Dir: Andrew Kennedy.

Propaganda Symal House, 423 Edgware Road, London, NW9 0HU **t** 020 8200 1000 **f** 020 8200 4929 **e** sales@propa.net **w** propa.net 🖪 Sales Manager: Jason Stevens.

Pyramid Posters The Works, Park Rd, Blaby, Leicester, LE8 4EF **t** 0116 264 2642 **f** 0116 264 2640 **e** mordy.benaiah@pyramidinternational.com **w** pyramidinternational.com 🖪 Licensing Director: Mordy Benaiah.

Razamataz 4 Derby St, Colne, Lancashire, BB8 9AA **t** 01282 861099 **f** 01282 861327 **e** simon@razamataz.com **w** razamataz.com 🖪 Contact: Simon Hartley.

Rock-It! Promotions Old Employment Exchange, East Grove, (off Rectory Rd), Rushden, Northants, NN10 0AP **t** 0800 980 4660 **f** 01933 413279 **e** sales@rockitpromotions.com **w** onechordwonder.com 🖪 Sales Manager: Andy Campen.

Rowleys:London One Port Hill, Hertford, Hertfordshire, SG14 1PJ **t** 01992 587350 **e** annie@rowleyslondon.co.uk **w** rowleyslondon.co.uk 🖪 MD: Annie Rowley.

RTG Branded Apparel The Old Dispensary, 36 The Millfields, Plymouth, Devon, PL1 3JB **t** 01752 253888 **f** 01752 255663 **e** sales@rtg.co.uk **w** rtg.co.uk 🖪 Sales Dir: Andy Moulding.

Shirty Shirts 144 Algernon Road, London, SE13 7AW **t** 020 8690 7658 **f** 020 7692 9258 **e** justin@shirtyshirts.screaming.net 🖪 Ops Dir: Justin Simpson.

SMP Group Plc 2 Swan Road, Woolwich, London, SE18 5TT **t** 020 8855 5535 **f** 020 8855 5367 **e** John.Leahy@smpgroup.co.uk **w** smpgroup.co.uk 🖪 MD: John Leahy 07808 909 292.

SRL Group PO Box 74, Middlesbrough, TS7 0WX **t** 01642 318926 **f** 01642 318927 **e** sales@srlgroup.co.uk action@stashco.co.uk **w** srlgroup.co.uk www.stashco.co.uk 🖪 Contact: Roy Sunley.

STARWORLD

4A Stretton Distribution Centre, Grappenhall Lane, Appleton, Warrington, Cheshire, WA4 4QT **t** 01925 210018 **f** 01925 210028 **e** sales@starworlduk.com **w** starworldonline.com 🖪 Sales Manager: Chris Burrows. Sales Manager: Chris Burrows. **Starworld is a progressive corporate and promotional clothing brand that has supplied technically advanced, value-driven products to the European garment decoration industry since 1990.**

Sweet Concepts Symal House, 423 Edgware Road, London, NW9 0HU **t** 020 8200 5000 **f** 020 8200 4929 **e** sales@sweetconcepts.com **w** sweetconcepts.com 🖪 MD: Stephen Taylor.

T-Shirts 4 Less Ltd 1 Temple Parade, Netherlands Rd, Oakleigh Park, Hertfordshire, EN5 1DN **t** 020 8445 9955 **f** 020 8445 8700 **e** varn@t-shirts4less.co.uk **w** t-shirts4less.co.uk 🖪 Sales Director: Varn Lykourgos.

T.O.T. Shirts 14B Banksia Rd, Eley Estate, Edmonton, London, N18 3BH **t** 020 8807 8083 **f** 020 8345 6095 **e** sales@t-o-t-shirts.co.uk **w** t-o-t-shirts.co.uk 🖪 Snr Account Dir: Paul Whiskin.

Tabak Marketing Ltd Network House, 29-39 Stirling Road, London, W3 8DJ **t** 020 8993 5966 **f** 020 8992 0340 **e** tabak@arab.co.uk 🖂 Mgr: Chris Leaning.

TCB Merchandise Unit C1,, Mint Business Pk, 41, Butchers Rd, London, E16 1PH **t** 020 7511 5775 **e** guy@tcbinc.co.uk **w** tcbinc.co.uk 🖂 Managing Director: Guy Gillam.

TDC Neckwear 34 Chandlers Rd, St Albans, Hertfordshire, AL4 9RS **t** 01727 840548 **f** 01727 840552 **e** djt@tieman.co.uk **w** tieman.co.uk 🖂 MD: David Taylor.

Tie Rack Corporate Neckwear Capital Interchange Way, Brentford, Middlesex, TW8 0EX **t** 020 8230 2345 **f** 020 8230 2350 **e** corp.sales@tie-rack.co.uk **w** tierackcorporate.com 🖂 MD: Peter Hirsch.

The Tradewinds Merchandising Company Ltd The Courtyard, Lynton Road, Crouch End, London, N8 8SL **t** 0845 230 9005 **f** 0845 230 9006 **e** info@tradewinds.eu.com **w** tradewinds.eu.com 🖂 Sales Admin: Tammy Desouza.

Upfront Merchandising Ltd 217 Buspace Studios, Conlan St, London, W10 5AP **t** 020 7565 0050 **f** 020 7565 0049 **e** claire@upfrontpromotions.com **w** upfrontpromotions.com 🖂 Contact: Claire Gibson.

USB-FlashDrive.co.uk Nash House, Datchet Rd, Slough, Berkshire, SL3 7LR **t** 01753 491470 **f** 01753 539801 **e** neil@usb-flashdrive.com **w** USB-FlashDrive.co.uk 🖂 Marketing Manager: Neil Harris.

Vektor Clothing & Promotions Ground Floor Office, 36-38 Church Rd, Burgess Hill, RH15 9AE **t** 01444 253496 **e** chris@vektor.co.uk **w** vektor.co.uk 🖂 Contact: Chris Andrews 07810 633322.

West Country Marketing & Advertising Kyre Park, Kyre, Tenbury Wells, Worcestershire, WR15 8RP **t** 01885 410247 **f** 01885 410398 **e** info@wcma.co.uk **w** wcma.co.uk 🖂 Sales Director: Simon Adam.

Zephyr Flags And Banners Midland Road, Thrapston, Northants, NN14 4LX **t** 01832 734 484 **f** 01832 733 064 **e** sskey@zephyr-tvc.com **w** zephyr-tvc.com 🖂 Sales Mgr: Simon Skey.

Distributors

A.C. Entertainment Technologies Ltd (Equipment Supply) Centauri House, Hillbottom Rd, High Wycombe, Bucks, HP12 4HQ **t** 01494 446000 **f** 01494 461024 **e** sales@ac-et.com **w** ac-et.com

ABSOLUTE MARKETING & DISTRIBUTION LTD.

The Old Lamp Works, Rodney Pl, Wimbledon, London, SW19 2LQ **t** 020 8540 4242 **f** 020 8540 6056 **e** info@absolutemarketing.co.uk **w** absolutemarketing.co.uk 🖂 MD: Henry Semmence. Sales & Marketing Director: Simon Wills. Marketing & Label Manager: Mark Dowling. Production Manager: Rob Dwyer. Mobile Label Manager: James McGuinness. Online Label Manager: Richard Austin-Smith. Administration Manager: Fran O'Donnell. Marketing Consultant: John Waller. Administration Manager: Gina Deacon. **Absolute is a fully managed sales, marketing, administration, distribution and rights management company. Our business is taking care of a wide range of independent labels, from single artist labels where we'd look after all aspects of a release on their behalf, right through to your more traditional indies in which our role can be that of a more conventional distributor.**

ACTIVE MEDIA DISTRIBUTION LTD

Lower Farmhouse, Church Hill, East Ilsley, Newbury, Berkshire, RG20 7LP **t** 01635 281358 or 281377 **f** 01635 281607 **e** firstname@amdist.com **w** amdist.com 🖂 Directors: Nigel Reveler, Colin Jennings. **National Sales Representation, Export, Licensing, Project Management - fulfillment through Universal. Representing Runrig, Pete Shelley, Glenn Tilbrook, Gretchen Peters among others.**

ADA (US) 72 Spring Street (12th Fl), New York, NY 10012, United States **t** +1 212 991 5102 **f** +1 212 625 6404 **e** firstname.lastname@ada-music.com **w** ada-music.com 🖂 GM: Michael Black.

ADA UK

Electric Lighting Station, 46 Kensington Court, London, W8 5DA **t** 020 7938 5530 **f** 020 7938 4911 **e** info@ada-music.co.uk **w** ada-music.co.uk ✉ Contact: 0207 938 5530. Managing Director: Susan Rush. Business Manager: Ian Harmon. Label Manager: Nick Roden. Label Manager: Emma Camfield. Label Manager: Bek Cross. Label Co-Ordinator: Eddie Grant.

ADA Global Ltd First Floor, Electric Lighting Station, 46 Kensington Court, London, W8 5DA **t** 020 7938 5678 **f** 020 7368 4911 **e** info@ada-global.com **w** ada-global.com
🔲 facebook.com/search/?q=caroline+gerdolle&init=quick#/pages/ADA-Global/116224481761?ref=ts
🔲 twitter.com/adaglobal 🔲 youtube.com/adaglobal
✉ VP: Colleen Theis.

African Caribbean Asian Entertainment Agency
Stars Building, 10 Silverhill Close, Nottingham, NG8 6QL **t** 0115 951 9864 / 07944 432649 **f** 0870 830 0683 **e** acts@african-caribbean-ents.com **w** african-caribbean-ents.com ✉ MD: Mr Love Sackey 07766 945663.

Altered Ego 230 Centennial Park, Elstree Hill South, Elstree, Borehamwood, Herts., WD6 3SN **t** 020 8236 2310 **f** 020 8236 2312 **e** info@alteredegomusic.com **w** alteredegomusic.com ✉ GM: Mark Lawton.

alto / Musical Concepts UK Magnus House, 8 Ashfield Rd, Cheadle, Cheshire, SK81BB **t** 0161 491 6688 **e** musicalmerit@blueyonder.co.uk **w** musicalconcepts.net
✉ Sales/Distribution/Licensing: Robin Vaughan 01562 751330.

APEX Home Entertainment Ltd Unit 3 & 4, Albert St, Droylsden, Manchester, M43 7BA **t** 0161 370 6908 **f** 0161 371 8207 **e** sales@apexhomeentertainment.com **w** apexhomeentertainment.com ✉ MD: Bill White.

Arabesque Distribution Network House, 29-39 Stirling Road, London, W3 8DJ **t** 020 8992 7732 **f** 020 8992 0340 **e** sales@arab.co.uk **w** arab.co.uk ✉ MD: Brian Horn 020 8992 0098.

arvato scm ltd Chippenham Drive, Kingston, Milton Keynes, Bucks, MK10 0AT **t** 01908 452500 **f** 01908 452501 **e** firstname.lastname@arvatoentertainment.co.uk **w** arvatoscm.co.uk ✉ Head of Commercial Services: Neil Lander 01908 452690.

Authentic Media 9 Holdom Avenue, Bletchley, Milton Keynes, Buckinghamshire, MK1 1QR **t** 01908 364 200 **f** 01908 648 592 **e** info@authenticmedia.co.uk **w** authenticmedia.co.uk ✉ MD: David Withers.

Backs Distribution St Mary's Works, St Mary's Plain, Norwich, Norfolk, NR3 3AF **t** 01603 624290 **f** 01603 619999 **e** info@backsrecords.co.uk ✉ Distribution Manager: Derek Chapman 01603 626221.

Baked Goods Distribution Ducie House, 37 Ducie Street, Manchester, M1 2JW **t** 0161 236 3233 **f** 0161 236 3351 **e** simon@baked-goods.com **w** baked-goods.com ✉ Sales Director: Simon Tonkinson.

Beathut Distribution
13 Greenwich Centre Business Park, Norman Road, Greenwich, London, SE10 9PY **t** 020 8858 7700 **e** info@beathutonline.com **w** beathutonline.com ✉ Manager: Caroline Hemingway.

Beckmann Visual Publishing Milntown Lodge, Lezayre Rd, Ramsey, Isle of Man, IM8 2TG **t** 01624 816585 **f** 01624 816589 **e** videos@beckmanndirect.com **w** beckmanndirect.com ✉ MD: Jo White.

Black Arrow Distribution Ltd
57A North Woolwich Road, via Dock Road, Silvertown, London, E16 2AA **t** 020 7055 8094 **f** 020 7055 8091 **e** blackarrowltd@aol.com **w** cousinsrecords.com ✉ Dir: Donville Davis.

Cadiz Music Ltd 2 Greenwich Quay, Clarence Rd, London, SE8 3EY **t** 020 8692 4691 **f** 020 8469 3300 **e** richard@cadizmusic.co.uk **w** cadizmusic.co.uk ✉ MD: Richard England 020 8692 3555.

Candid Productions Ltd 16 Castelnau, London, SW13 9RU **t** 020 8741 3608 **f** 020 8563 0013 **e** info@candidrecords.com **w** candidrecords.com ✉ MD: Alan Bates.

Cargo Records (UK) Ltd 17 Heathmans Rd, Parsons Green, London, SW6 4TJ **t** 020 7731 5125 **f** 020 7731 3866 **e** info@cargorecords.co.uk **w** cargorecords.co.uk
🔲 facebook.com/group.php?gid=198143310172&ref=search&sid=100000185858194.3784478549..1
🔲 myspace.com/cargorecordsuk
🔲 twitter.com/CargoRecords ✉ MD: Philip Hill.

Changing World Distribution
Willow Croft, Wagg Drove, Huish Episcopi, Near Langport, Somerset, TA10 9ER **t** 01458 253 838 **f** 01458 250 317 **e** enquiries@changingworld.co.uk **w** changingworld.co.uk ✉ Manager: David Hatfield.

Cinram Logistics Rabans Lane, Aylesbury, Bucks, HP19 7TS **t** 01296 426151 **f** 01296 481009 **e** firstname.lastname@cinram.com **w** cinram.com/uklogistics ✉ MD: Alan McElroy.

Cisco Europe 144 Princes Avenue, London, W3 8LT **t** 020 8992 7351 **f** 020 8400 4931 **e** info@ciscoeurope.co.uk ✉ MD: Mimi Kobayashi.

Claddagh Records Dame House, Dame St, Dublin 2, Ireland **t** +353 1 677 8943 **f** +353 1 679 3664 **e** wholesale@crl.ie **w** claddaghrecords.com ◘ Co Mgr: Jane Bolton.

CM Distribution North Works, Hook Stone Park, Harrogate, North Yorkshire, HG2 7DB **t** 01423 888979 **e** info@northworks.co.uk ◘ MD: DR Bulmer.

CODE 7 MUSIC DISTRIBUTION

CODE 7

23 London Road, Aston Clinton, Aylesbury, Bucks, HP22 5HG **t** 01296 631 003 **e** info@code7music.com **w** code7music.com ◘ MD: Nick Hindle.

Contact (UK) Research House, Fraser Rd, Greenford, Middlesex, UB6 7AQ **t** 020 8997 5662 **f** 020 8997 5664 **e** contactukltd@btinternet.com **w** contactukmusic.com ◘ Director: Michael Lo Bianco.

Copperplate Distribution 68 Belleville Rd, London, SW11 6PP **t** 020 7585 0357 **f** 020 7585 0357 **e** copperplate2000@yahoo.com **w** copperplatedistribution.com ◙ myspace/copperplate ◘ CEO: Alan O'Leary.

Crucial Distribution Pinery Buildings, Highmoor, Wigton, Cumbria, CA7 9LW **t** 016973 45422 **f** 016973 45422 **e** crucialsales@crucialmusic.co.uk **w** crucialmusic.co.uk ◘ MD: Simon James.

CYP Children's Audio The Fairway, Bush Fair, Harlow, Essex, CM18 6LY **t** 01279 444707 **f** 01279 445570 **e** sales@cypmusic.co.uk **w** kidsmusic.co.uk ◘ Sales & Marketing Director: John Bassett.

DA Sales & Marketing 56 Castle Bank, Stafford, ST16 1DW **t** 01785 258746 **f** 01785 255367 **e** p.halliwell@tesco.net ◘ MD: Paul Halliwell.

Delta Leisure Group PLC 222 Cray Avenue, Orpington, Kent, BR5 3PZ **t** 01689 888 888 **f** 01689 888 800 **e** info@deltamusic.co.uk **w** deltamusic.co.uk ◘ MD: Laurie Adams.

Denis Tyler Ltd 59 High St, Great Missenden, Buckinghamshire, HP16 0AL **t** 01494 866262 **f** 01494 890321 **e** denistylerlimited@btinternet.com **w** denistyler.com ◘ MD: Elizabeth Tyler.

Digimix Worldwide Distribution Sovereign House, 12 Trewartha Rd, Praa Sands, Penzance, Cornwall, TR20 9ST **t** 01736 762826 **f** 01736 763328 **e** panamus@aol.com **w** digimixrecords.com ◙ myspace.com/digimixrecords ◘ CEO: Roderick Jones.

Digital Classics Distribution Ltd 31 Eastcastle St, London, W1W 8DL **t** 020 7636 1400 **f** 020 7299 8190 **e** nb@digitalclassics.co.uk **w** digitalclassics.co.uk ◘ Head of Sales: Rick Barker.

Discovery Records Nursteed Rd, Devizes, Wiltshire, SN10 3DY **t** 01380 728000 **f** 01380 722244 **e** info@discovery-records.com **w** discovery-records.com ◘ MD: Mike Cox.

Dynamic Distribution Unit 19c Coln Park, Andoversford Industrial Estate, Andoversford, Cheltenham, Gloucestershire, GL54 4HJ **t** 01242 820000 **f** 01242 820000 **e** info@dynamic-distribution.net **w** dynamic-distribution.net ◘ Director: Joanna Massive.

Dynamic Entertainment Unit 22 Acton Park Estate, The Vale, London, W3 7QE **t** 020 8746 9500 **f** 020 8746 9501 **e** info@dynamicentertainment.co.uk ◘ MD: Beverley King.

Elap UK Ltd 42 Keswick Close, Tilehurst, Reading, Berks, RG30 4SD **t** 01189 452999 **f** 01189 451313 **e** chris.wickens@elap.com **w** elap.com ◘ GM: Chris Wickens.

EMI Distribution Hermes Close, Tachbrook Park, Leamington Spa, Warwickshire, CV34 6RP **t** 01926 466300 **f** 01926 466392 **e** john.williams@emimusic.com ◘ Ops Dir: John Williams.

Empathy Records PO Box 3439, Brighton, BN50 9JG **t** 01273 623 117 **f** 01273 602 870 **e** info@empathyrecords.co.uk **w** empathyrecords.co.uk ◘ Director: Cat Gahan.

Entertainment UK Ltd 243 Blyth Road, Hayes, Middlesex, UB3 1DN **t** 020 8848 7511 **f** 020 8754 6600 **e** enquiries@entuk.co.uk **w** entuk.co.uk ◘ Retail Services Manager: Kevin Blee.

Ernie B's Reggae 74-75 Warren St, London, W1T 5PF **t** 020 7387 3344 **f** 020 7387 2756 **e** zep@sternsmusic.com **w** ebreggae.com ◘ Contact: Zep.

Essential Direct Ltd Brewmaster House, 91 Brick Lane, London, E1 6QL **t** 020 7375 2332 **f** 020 7375 2442 **e** info@essentialdirect.co.uk **w** essentialdirect.co.uk ◘ A&R/Dir: Gary Dedman.

Essential Exports Brewmaster House, 91 Brick Lane, London, E1 6QL **t** 020 7375 2332 **f** 020 7375 2442 **e** info@essentialdirect.co.uk **w** essentialdirect.co.uk ◘ A&R/Dir: Gary Dedman.

Essential Music & Marketing 10 Allied Way, London, W3 0RQ **t** 020 8749 7250 **f** 020 8740 0740 **e** essential@essential-music.com **w** essential-music.com ◘ MD: Mike Chadwick.

Euro Japan Trading Co PO Box 48515, London, NW4 3WE **t** 020 8202 6985 **f** 020 8202 6985 **e** myokoyama@eurojapantrading.com **w** eurojapantrading.com ◘ Dir: Masami Yokoyama.

Excel Marketing Services Ltd 151 Valley Rd, Rickmansworth, Herts, WD3 4BR **t** 01923 710629 **f** 01923 441127 **e** excelms@aol.com ◘ MD: Vinoth Kumar 07860 800808.

F Minor Ltd Unit 8, Commercial Mews North, 45A, Commercial Road, Eastbourne, East Sussex, BN21 3XF **t** 01323 736598 **f** 01323 738763 **e** sales@fminor.com **w** fminor.com ✉ MD: Paul Callaghan.

FAT CAT INTERNATIONAL LTD

19-20 Liddell Rd Estate, Maygrove Rd, London, NW6 2EW **t** 020 7624 4335 **f** 020 7624 4866 **e** info@fatcatint.co.uk ✉ MD: Trevor Reidy. Sales Director: Simon Checketts. Sales-Games & DVDs: James Taylor. Label Manager: Glenn Gretlund. Accounts Manager: Wendy Marchington. Buyer / Licensing: Trevor Reidy.

Fierce! Distribution PO Box 40, Arundel, West Sussex, BN18 0UQ **t** 01243 558444 **f** 01243 558455 **e** info@fiercedistribution.com **w** fiercedistribution.com ✉ Director: Jonathan Brown.

Forsyth Brothers Ltd 126 Deansgate, Manchester, M3 2GR **t** 0161 834 3281 **f** 0161 834 0630 **e** publishing@forsyths.co.uk **w** forsyths.co.uk ✉ Publishing Division Mgr: Michael Welton.

Forte Music Distribution Ltd Unit 5g, Ramsden Rd, Rotherwas Industrial Estate, Hereford, Herefordshire, HR2 6NP **t** 08707 622864 **f** 08707 626015 **e** info@fortedistribution.co.uk **w** fortedistribution.co.uk ✉ Sales and Label Manager: Chris Munton 01432 272777.

Fullfill Distribution LLC UK Ltd Unit 41, 249- 251 Kensal Road, London, W10 5DB **t** 020 8968 1231 **f** 020 8964 1181 **e** info@fullfill.co.uk **w** fullfill.co.uk ✉ Office Manager: Savanna Sparkes.

Futureproof Distribution 330 Westbourne Park Rd, London, W11 1EQ **t** 020 7792 8597 **f** 020 7221 3694 **e** info@futureproofrecords.com **w** futureproofrecords.com ✉ MD: Phil Legg.

Gordon Duncan Distributions 20 Newtown St, Kilsyth, Glasgow, Lanarkshire, G65 0LY **t** 01236 827550 **f** 01236 827560 **e** gordon-duncan@sol.co.uk ✉ Contact: Jack Scott, Senga Gregor.

Griffin & Co. Ltd Church House, 96 Church St, St Mary's Gate, Lancaster, LA1 1TD **t** 01524 844399 **f** 01524 844335 **e** sales@griffinrecords.co.uk **w** griffinrecords.co.uk ✉ GM: Ian Murray.

Handleman UK Ltd 27 Leacroft Rd, Birchwood, Warrington, Cheshire, WA3 6PJ **t** 0870 444 5844 **f** 0870 444 5944 **e** firstname.lastname@handleman.co.uk **w** handleman.co.uk ✉ Music Purchasing Mgr: John Misra.

Harmonia Mundi (UK) Ltd 45 Vyner St, London, E2 9DQ **t** 020 8709 9509 **f** 020 8709 9501 **e** info.uk@harmoniamundi.com **w** harmoniamundi.com ✉ Press Manager: Celia Ballantyne.

Hermanex Ltd Suite 11, The Chesnuts, Stortford Rd, Great Dunmow, Essex, CM6 1DA **t** 01371 879700 **f** 01371 879770 **e** d.harmer@hermanex.com **w** hermanex.com ✉ Director: Dave Harmer.

Horus Music Limited LCB Depot, 31 Rutland Street, Leciester, LE1 1RE **t** 0116 253 3436 **w** horusmusic.co.uk ✉ Contact: Nick Dunn.

Hot Records PO Box 333, Brighton, Sussex, BN1 2EH **t** 01403 740260 **f** 01403 740261 **e** info@hotrecords.uk.com **w** hotrecords.uk.com ✉ MD: Martin Jennings.

Impetus Distribution Ltd 10 High Street, Skigersta, Ness, Isle of Lewis, Outer Hebrides, HS2 0TS **t** 01851 810 808 **f** 01851 810 809 **e** mpetusrecs@aol.com ✉ MD: Paul Acott-Stephens.

IMS (Interactive Management Services)
Unit 4C, The Odyssey Centre, Corporation Rd, Birkenhead, Merseyside, CH41 1LB **t** 0845 644 1580 **f** 0845 644 1580 **e** daveims@compuserve.com **w** heritagevideo.co.uk ✉ MD: David MacWilliam.

Independent Thinking 4 Hall Farm Barns, Fornham All Saints, Bury St Edmunds, Suffolk, IP28 6JJ **t** 07795 516 065 **f** 01284 756 320 **e** jacqui@indie-thinking.co.uk **w** indie-thinking.co.uk ✉ MD: Jacqui Sinclair 020 7368 2596.

Interactive Music Ltd 2 Carriglea, Naas Rd, Dublin 12, Ireland **t** +353 1 419 5037 **f** +353 1 419 5409 **e** info@interactive-music.com **w** interactive-music.com ✉ MD: Oliver Walsh.

Jazz Music Glenview, Moylegrove, Cardigan, Dyfed, SA43 3BW **t** 01239 881278 **f** 01239 881296 **e** jazz.music@btinternet.com ✉ Sales Mgr: Jutta Greaves.

Jed-Eye Distribution Ltd Enterprise House, 113- 115 George Lane, London, E18 1AB **t** 020 8262 6277 **f** 020 8262 6361 **e** info@jed-eye.com **w** jed-eye.com ✉ MD: Adrian Smith.

Kelso Entertainment Ltd 592 London Rd, Isleworth, TW7 4EY **t** 020 8758 1635 **f** 020 8758 1635 **e** info@kelsoent.co.uk **w** kelsoent.co.uk ✉ MD: Oliver Comberti.

KRD 81-82 Stour St, Birmingham, B18 7AJ **t** 0121 248 2548 **f** 0121 248 2549 **e** krd1@supanet.com ✉ MD: Pat Ward.

Kudos Records Ltd 77 Fortess Road, Kentish Town, London, NW5 1AG **t** 020 7482 4555 **f** 020 7482 4551 **e** contact@kudos-digital.co.uk **w** kudos-digital.co.uk

Lasgo Chrysalis Ltd Units 2/3/4, Chapmans Pk Industrial Estate, 378- 388 High Rd, Willesden, London, NW10 2DY **t** 020 8459 8800 **f** 020 8451 5555 **e** info@lasgo.co.uk **w** lasgo.co.uk ✉ Account Manager: Paul Burrows.

Load Media Green Lane, Burghfield Bridge, Burghfield, Reading, RG30 3XN **t** 01189 599 944 **f** 01189 587 416 **e** info@load-media.co.uk **w** load-media.co.uk ✉ A&R & Production: Brillo.

Design, Pressing & Distribution: Distributors

Design, Pressing & Distribution: Distributors

absolute marketing & distribution — the successful solution, more than distribution — www.absolutemarketing.co.uk

Media UK Distribution Sovereign House, 12 Trewartha Rd, Praa Sands, Penzance, Cornwall, TR20 9ST **t** 01736 762826 **f** 01736 763328 **e** panamus@aol.com **w** songwriters-guild.co.uk 🖰 myspace.com/digimixrecords 🖴 MD: Roderick Jones.

Mental Music Management Email for address, London, E3 **e** mentalmusicmgt@yahoo.co.uk **w** myspace.com/mentalmusicmgt 🖴 Mgr: Gary Heath 07900 631883.

Metrodome Distribution 110 Park Street, London, W1K 6NX **t** 020 7408 2121 **f** 020 7409 1935 **e** video@metrodomegroup.com **w** metrodomegroup.com 🖴 Head Of Marketing: Jane Lawson.

Metronome Distribution Unit 3 Jubilee Wharf, Commercial Rd, Penryn, Cornwall, TR10 8FG **t** 01326 377738 **f** 01326 377738 **e** info@metronome.co.uk **w** metronomedistribution.co.uk 🖴 Managing Director: Tim Smithies.

Midland Records Chase Road, Brownhills, West Midlands, WS8 6JT **t** 01543 378222 **f** 01543 360988 🖴 Dir: Ms Wendy Creffield 01543 378225.

Multiple Sounds Distribution Units 1 - 2 Bay Close, Port of Heysham Ind Estate, Heysham, Lancs, LA3 2XS **t** 01524 851177 **f** 01524 851188 **e** info@multiplesounds.com **w** multiplesounds.com 🖴 MD: Mike Hargreaves.

Music Box Leisure Ltd Unit 9, Enterprise Court, Lancashire Enterprise Bus Park, Centurion Way, Leyland, PR26 6TZ **t** 01772 455000 **f** 01772 331199 **e** enquiries@musicboxleisure.com 🖴 Sales Director: Jan Beer.

Music Sales (Northern Ireland) 224B Shore Rd, Lower Greenisland, Carrickfergus, Co Antrim, BT38 8TX **t** 028 9086 5422 **f** 028 9086 2902 **e** musicsales@dnet.co.uk **w** musicsalesni.co.uk 🖴 Dir: Martin McCoubrey.

Musical Memories Ltd 11 Riverside, Wraysbury, Nr Staines, TW19 5JN **t** 01784 483217 **f** 01784 483210 **e** Info@musicalmemories.co.uk **w** musicalmemories.co.uk 🖴 MD: Jimmy Devlin.

Musonic (UK) 271B, Wenta Business Centre, Colne Way, Watford, Herts, WD24 7ND **t** 020 8950 5151 **f** 020 8950 5391 **e** sales@musonic.co.uk **w** musonic.co.uk 🖴 Dir: Stephen Blank.

NDN Distribution 7 St Nicholas Churchyard, Newcastle upon Tyne, NE1 1PF **t** 0191 300 0354 **e** info@ndndistribution.co.uk **w** ndndistribution.co.uk 🖴 Manager: Lisa McNab.

Nervous Records 5 Sussex Crescent, Northolt, Middlesex, UB5 4DL **t** 020 8423 7373 **f** 020 8423 7713 **e** info@nervous.co.uk **w** nervous.co.uk 🖴 MD: Roy Williams.

New Note Distribution Ltd Pinnacle Building, Teardrop Centre, London Road, Swanley, Kent, BR8 8TS **t** 01322 616 050 **f** 01322 615 658 **e** sales@newnote.com **w** newnote.com 🖴 Joint MDs: Graham Griffiths, Eddie Wilkinson.

Northern Record Supplies Ltd Star Works, Wham St, Heywood, Lancs, OL10 4QU **t** 01706 367 412 **e** nrs99@ukonline.co.uk 🖴 MD: Simon Jones.

Nova Sales and Distribution (UK) Ltd Isabel House, 46 Victoria Rd, Surbiton, Surrey, KT6 4JL **t** 020 8390 3322 **f** 020 8390 3338 **e** info@novadist.net **w** novadist.net 🖴 Managing Director: Wilf Mann 020 8390 6639 (Telesales).

Nu Urban Music Unit 9 Rivermead, Pipersway, Thatcham, Berks, RG19 4EP **t** 01635 587900 **f** 01635 292314 **e** kevin@nu-urbanmusic.co.uk **w** nu-urbanmusic.co.uk 🖴 Web/Art: Kevin Broome.

One Nation Vinyl Distribution Units G10/G11, Belgravia Workshops, 159-163 Marlborough Rd, London, N19 4NP **t** 020 7263 3100 **f** 020 7263 3002 **e** barry@onenation.co.uk **w** onenation.co.uk 🖴 MD: Barry Milligan.

One Shot Music (Wholesale Only) The Forge, Water Lane, Roydon, Essex, CM19 5DR **t** 01279 792 985 **e** vinylmo@btinternet.com 🖴 MD: Morris Cszechowicz.

Orange Music Electronic Company Ltd Omec House, 108 Ripon Way, Borehamwood, Herts, WD6 2JA **t** 020 8905 2828 **f** 020 8905 2868 **e** info@omec.com **w** orangeamps.com

The Orchard 23 East 4th St, 3rd Floor, New York, New York, 10003, United States **t** 212-201-9280 **f** 212-201-9203 **e** jvolpe@theorchard.com **w** theorchard.com 🖬 facebook.com/theorchard.com 🖴 twitter.com/orchtweets 🖴 Coordinator, Corporate Marketing & Communications: James Volpe 646-472-1857.

Pendle Hawk Music 2nd Floor, 11 Newmarket Street, Colne, Lancashire, BB8 9BJ **t** 01282 866 317 **f** 01282 866 317 **e** info@pendlehawkmusic.co.uk **w** pendlehawkmusic.co.uk 🖴 MD: Adrian Melling.

[PIAS] UK

[P I A S] U K

Unit 24 Farm Lane Trading Estate, 101 Farm Lane, London, SW6 1QJ **t** 020 7471 2700 **f** 020 7471 2706 **w** pias.com/uk ✆ UK Group CEO: Nick Hartley. Managing Director: Peter Thompson. Product Director: Ian Dutt. Director of Digital and Business Development: Adrian Pope. Sales Director: Richard Sefton. Director of International: Edwin Schroter. Head of Label Management: Craig Caukill.
The [PIAS] Entertainment Group is the definitive marketing, sales, distribution and licensing solution offering a highly professional and flexible service.

Plastic Head Music Distribution Ltd
Avtech House, Hithercroft Rd, Wallingford, Oxfordshire, OX10 9DA **t** 01491 825 029 **f** 01491 826 320 admin **e** info@plastichead.com **w** plastichead.com ✆ myspace.com/plasticheaddistribution ✆ Dir: Steve Beatty.

Play Right Distribution Crabtree Cottage, Mill Lane,
Kidmore End, Oxon, RG4 9HB **t** 0118 972 4356 **f** 0118 972 4809 **e** ppmusicint@aol.com **w** dovehouserecords.com ✆ Head of Sales: Lara Pavey.

Priory Records Ltd 3 Eden Court, Eden Way,
Leighton Buzzard, Bedfordshire, LU7 4FY **t** 01525 377566 **f** 01525 371477 **e** sales@priory.org.uk **w** priory.org.uk ✆ MD: Neil Collier.

Prism Leisure Corporation plc Unit 1,
1 Dundee Way, Enfield, Middlesex, EN3 7SX **t** 020 8804 8100 **f** 020 8216 6645 **e** prism@prismleisure.com **w** prismleisure.com ✆ Head Of Sales: Adrian Ball.

Proper Music Distribution Ltd Unit 1,
Gateway Business Centre, Kangley Bridge Rd, London, SE26 5AN **t** 0870 444 0800 **f** 0870 444 0801 **e** info@proper.uk.com **w** proper.uk.com ✆ MD: Malcolm Mills.

Rare Beatz Distribution PO Box 20176, London,
SE19 1DN **t** 020 8670 5338 **f** 0871 781 9364 **e** info@groovechronicles.net **w** groovechronicles.net ✆ Label Manager: Noodles.

Republic Of Music (Sales, Marketing & Distribution) PO Box 174, Brighton, BN1 4BA
t 01273 739 323 **f** 01273 208 766 **e** markmcquillan@mac.com **w** republicofmusic.net ✆ Dir: Mark McQuillan.

Right Track Records & Distribution 3rd Floor, 3-
4a Little Portland St, London, W1W 7JB **e** info@righttrackrecords.com **w** righttrackrecords.com ✆ Contact: Colin Peter, Neil Smith.

RMG Chart Entertainment Ltd. 2, Carriglea,
Naas Rd, Dublin 12 **t** +353 1 419 5000 **f** +353 1 419 5016 **e** info@rmgchart.ie **w** rmgchart.ie ✆ MD: Peter Kenny.

Roots Records PO Box 4549, Coventry, West Midlands,
CV4 0DR **t** 02476 422 225 **f** 02476 462 398 **e** rootsrecs@btclick.com **w** rootsrecordsonline.co.uk ✆ MD: Graham Bradshaw.

Route 1 Unit F34, Third Floor,
Park Hall Rd Trading Estate, 40 Martell Rd, London, SE21 8EN **t** 020 8670 9433 **f** 020 8670 8452 **e** steve@directdance.co.uk **w** route1direct.com ✆ MD: Steve Bradley.

RS Sound & Vision Unit C2, M4 Business Park,
Maynooth Road, Celbridge, Co.Kildare, Ireland **t** +353 1 627 4110 **f** +353 1 627 4107 **e** rsirl@indigo.ie **w** recordservices.biz ✆ MD: Brian Wynne.

RSK ENTERTAINMENT

Units 4&5, Home Farm, Welford, Newbury, Berkshire, RG20 8HR **t** 01488 608 900 **f** 01488 608 901 **e** info@rskentertainment.co.uk **w** rskentertainment.co.uk ✆ Joint MDs: Rashmi Patani & Simon Carver. Label Manager: Matt Groom. Label Manager: Gavin Harry.
RSK represents a label roster ranging from the best in rock, urban, and re-issue to award winning classical and popular TV brands.

The Sales Office Unit One, Georges Farm,
Hillesden Rd, Gawcott, Buckingham, MK18 4JF **t** 01280 823568 **f** 01280 822307 **e** nigel@thesalesoffice.co.uk **w** thesalesoffice.co.uk ✆ Managing Director: Nigel French.

Savoy Strict Tempo Distributors PO Box 271,
Coulsdon, Surrey, CR5 3TR **t** 01737 554 739 **f** 01737 556 717 **e** admin@savoymusic.com **w** savoymusic.com ✆ Dir: Wendy Smith.

Select Music & Video Distribution 3 Wells Place,
Merstham, Surrey, RH1 3SL **t** 01737 645600 **f** 01737 644065 **e** cds@selectmusic.co.uk **w** selectmusic.co.uk ✆ MD: Anthony Anderson.

Self Distribution 96a Hanley Road, London, N4 3DW
t 07971 907 143 **e** olly_parker@hotmail.com **w** whiteheatrecords.com ✆ Sales and Enquiries: Olly Parker.

Sharpe Music 9A Irish St, Dungannon, Co Tyrone,
BT70 3LN **t** 028 8772 4621 **f** 028 8775 2195 **e** info@sharpemusicireland.com **w** sharpemusicireland.com ✆ MD: Raymond Stewart.

Shellshock Distribution 23A Collingwood Rd, London, N15 4LD **t** 020 8800 8110 **f** 020 8800 8140 **e** info@shellshock.co.uk **w** shellshock.co.uk ✉ MD: Garreth Ryan.

Shop Genius Ltd Unit 7 Sutherland Court, Tolpits Lane, Watford, Hertfordshire, WD18 9SP **t** 01923 896688 **f** 01923 896633 **e** allan@shopgenius.biz **w** shopgenius.biz ✉ MD: Allan Nazareth.

Shure Distribution UK Unit 2, The IO Centre, Lea Road, Waltham Abbey, EN9 1AS **t** 01992 703058 **f** 01992 703057 **e** info@shuredistribution.co.uk **w** shuredistribution.co.uk ✉ Sales Manager: Mike Gibson.

SimplyVinyl.com LP Records 65 Duke Street, London, W1K 5AJ **e** info@simplyvinyl.com **w** simplyvinyl.com ✉ info@simplyvinyl.com: General Manager.

Soul Trader Unit 43, Imex-Spaces Business Centre, Ingate Place, London, SW8 3NS **t** 020 7498 0732 **f** 020 7498 0737 **e** soultrader@btconnect.com ✉ MD: Marc Lessner.

SRD (Southern Record Distribution) 70 Lawrence Road, London, N15 4EG **t** 020 8802 3000 **f** 020 8802 2222 **e** info@southern.com **w** southern.com ✉ MD: John Knight 020 8802 4444.

ST Holdings Ltd Unit 2 Old Forge Road, Ferndown Industrial Estate, Wimborne, Dorset, BH21 7RR **t** 01202 890 889 **f** 01202 890 886 **e** sales@stholdings.co.uk **w** stholdings.co.uk ✉ Dirs: Chris Parkinson, Andrew Parkinson.

Stern's Distribution 74 Warren St, London, W1T 5PF **t** 020 7388 5533 **f** 020 7388 2756 **e** sales@sternsmusic.com **w** sternsmusic.com ✉ Contact: 020 7387 5550.

Swift Record Distributors Units 8 & 9 Phoenix Works, R/O 93 Windsor Road, Bexhill-on-Sea, East Sussex, TN39 3PE **t** 01424 220028 **f** 01424 213440 **e** swiftrd@btinternet.com **w** swiftrd.btinternet.co.uk ✉ GM: Robin L Gosden.

Talking Books Ltd 11 Wigmore Street, London, W1U 1PE **t** 020 7491 4117 **f** 020 7629 1966 **e** support@talkingbooks.co.uk **w** talkingbooks.co.uk ✉ Dir: Stanley Simmonds.

Thames Distributors Ltd Unit 12, Mill Farm Business Pk, Millfield Rd, Hounslow, Middlesex, TW4 5PY **t** 020 8898 2227 **f** 020 8898 2228 **e** r.gibbon@thamesworldmusic.com ✉ Director: Roger Gibbon.

That's Entertainment (Yorkshire) Ltd 103 Heckmondwike Rd, Dewsbury, West Yorks, WF13 3PG **t** 01924 412856 **f** 01924 412882 **e** thatsent@btconnect.com ✉ Director: Andrew Knapton.

Tuned Distribution Unit 26 Acklam Workshops, 10 Acklam Road, London, W10 5QZ **t** 020 8964 1355 **f** 020 8969 1342 **e** info@tuned-distribution.co.uk **w** tuned-distribution.co.uk ✉ MD: Lee Muspratt.

Urban Gospel Records Distributions Sutton, London, SM2 6XG **t** 020 8643 6403 **f** 020 8643 6403 **e** ugrrecords@hotmail.com **w** urbangospelrecords.com ▣ myspace.com/urbangospelrecords ▣ twitter.com/urbangrecords ▣ youtube.com/user/Vibezkidtv ✉ Hd of Marketing & Sales: P. Mac 07904 255244.

VidZone The Limes, 123 Mortlake High St, London, SW14 8SN **t** 020 8487 5880 **f** 020 8487 9683 **e** adrian@vidzone.tv **w** vidzone.tv ✉ CEO: Adrian Workman.

Voiceprint PO Box 50, Houghton-le-Spring, Tyne & Wear, DH4 5YP **t** 0191 512 1103 **f** 0191 512 1104 **e** info@voiceprint.co.uk **w** voiceprint.co.uk ✉ MD: Rob Ayling.

White Light Ltd 20 Merton Industrial Pk, Jubilee Way, Wimbledon, London, SW19 3WL **t** 020 8254 4800 **f** 020 8254 4801 **e** info@WhiteLight.Ltd.uk **w** WhiteLight.Ltd.uk ✉ Managing Director: Bryan Raven.

Windsong International Heather Court, 6 Maidstone Rd, Sidcup, Kent, DA14 5HH **t** 020 8309 3857 **f** 020 8309 3905 **e** enquiries@windsong.co.uk **w** windsong.co.uk ✉ Hd Of International Sales: David Gadsby.

The Woods Sussex House, 17a High St, Bognor Regis, West Sussex, PO21 1RJ **t** 01243 864923 **f** 01243 842615 **e** twiddi@yahoo.co.uk **w** twiddi.co.uk ✉ Proprietor: Trevor Flack.

WRD Worldwide Music 282 Camden Rd, London, NW1 9AB **t** 020 7267 6762 **f** 020 7482 4029 **e** info@wrdmusic.com **w** wrdmusic.com ✉ MD: Steve Johanson.

Wwwatt CD Gregory House, Harlaxton Road, Grantham, Lincolnshire, NG31 7JX **t** 01476 577734 **f** 01476 579309 **e** malcolm@wwwatt.co.uk **w** wwwatt.com ✉ Ops Mgr: Malcolm Mclean.

Wyastone Estate Limited Wyastone Business Pk, Wyastone Leys, Monmouth, NP25 3SR **t** 01600 890007 **f** 01600 891052 **e** sales@wyastone.co.uk **w** wyastone.co.uk ▐ Nimbus Records ✉ Business Director: Antony Smith.

Z Audio Distribution 33 Atlas Business Centre, Oxgate Rd, London, NW2 7HJ **t** 020 8438 8877 **f** 020 8438 8914 **e** info@zaudio.co.uk **w** zaudio.co.uk ✉ MD: Zac Mendelsohn.

Design, Pressing & Distribution: Distributors

Design, Pressing & Distribution: Distributors

Zander Exports 34 Sapcote Trading Centre, 374 High Road, Willesden, London, NW10 2DJ
t 020 8451 5955 **f** 020 8451 4940
e zander@btinternet.com **w** zanderman.co.uk
▣ Dir: John Yorke.

Zeit Distribution PO Box 50, Houghton-le-Spring, Tyne & Wear, DH4 5YP **t** 0191 512 1103 **f** 0191 512 1104
e info@voiceprint.co.uk **w** voiceprint.co.uk
▣ MD: Rob Ayling.

ZYX Records Ltd Unit 11, Cambridge Court, 210 Shepherds Bush Road, Hammersmith, London, W6 7NL **t** 020 7371 6969 **f** 020 7371 6688
e sales@zyxmusic.co.uk **w** zyxmusic.co.uk
▣ GM: Ralf Blasberg.

Who You Gonna Call ™

WEB SHERIFF ®

www.websheriff.com
websheriff@websheriff.com
44-(0)208-3238013

Business Services

LICENSING RECORDED MUSIC ON BEHALF OF RECORD COMPANIES AND PERFORMERS.

STANDING UP FOR MUSIC RIGHTS.

Business Services

Industry Organisations

The Agents' Association (Great Britain)
54 Keyes House, Dolphin Square, London, SW1V 3NA
t 020 7834 0515 **f** 020 7821 0261
e association@agents-uk.com **w** agents-uk.com
📇 Administrator: Carol Richards.

AIM (The Association of Independent Music)
Lamb House, Church St, Chiswick, London, W4 2PD
t 020 8994 5599 **f** 020 8994 5222
e info@musicindie.com **w** musicindie.com 📇 Chief
Executive: Alison Wenham.

APRS (Assoc. of Professional Recording Services)
PO Box 22, Totnes, Devon, TQ9 7YZ
t 01803 868600 **f** 01803 868444 **e** info@aprs.co.uk
w aprs.co.uk 📇 Exec Director: Peter Filleul.

The Arts Council
70 Merrion Sq, Dublin 2, Ireland
t +353 1 618 0200 **f** +353 1 676 1302
e info@artscouncil.ie **w** artscouncil.ie 📇 Dir: Mary Cloake.

Arts Council England
143 Great Peter St, London, SW1P 3NQ **t** 0845 300 6200 **f** 020 7973 6590
e info@artscouncil.org.uk **w** artscouncil.org.uk 📇 Director of Music Strategy: Susanna Eastburn.

ASCAP (AMERICAN SOC. OF COMPOSERS AUTHORS & PUBL)

8 Cork St, London, W1S 3LJ **t** 020 7439 0909
f 020 7434 0073 **e** initial+lastname@ascap.com
w ascap.com 📇 Contact: Karen Hewson. Snr Vice
President, Int: Roger Greenaway. Vice President,
Membership: Seán Devine. Membership: Ross Gautreau.
Membership: Simon Greenaway.

The Association Of Blind Piano Tuners
31 Wyre Crescent, Lynwood, Darwen, Lancashire, BB3 0JG
t 0844 736 1976 **e** abpt@uk-piano.org **w** uk-piano.org
📇 Secretary: Barrie Heaton.

Association of British Jazz Musicians
First Floor, 132 Southwark St, London, SE1 0SW **t** 020 7928 9089
f 020 7401 6870 **e** info@jazzservices.org.uk
w jazzservices.org.uk 📇 Hon Sec: Chris Hodgkins.

Barclaycard Mercury Prize
202 Buspace Studios, Conlan St, London, W10 5AP **t** 020 8964 9964
f 020 8969 7249 **e** info@mercuryprize.co.uk
w mercuryprize.com

BASCA - British Academy of Songwriters, Composers and Authors
British Music House, 26 Berners St, London, W1T 3LR **t** 020 7636 2929
f 020 7636 2212 **e** info@basca.org.uk **w** basca.org.uk
📇 Membership Manager: Graham Jackson.

BM&A - Brasil Musica E Artes
Rua Fradique Coutinho 837, São Paulo, 05416 011, Brazil
t 00 5511 3031 7934 **f** 00 5511 3031 5346
e david@bma.org.br **w** redebma.ning.com
🅜 myspace.com/bmabrasilmusicaeartes
📇 Manager: David McLoughlin.

BMI (BROADCAST MUSIC INCORPORATED)

84 Harley House, Marylebone Rd, London, NW1 5HN
t 020 7486 2036 **f** 020 7224 1046 **e** London@bmi.com
w bmi.com 📇 Executive Director, Writer-Publisher
Relations, Europe & Asia: Brandon Bakshi.

BPI (THE BRITISH RECORDED MUSIC INDUSTRY)

The British Recorded Music Industry

Riverside Building, County Hall, Westminster Bridge Rd,
London, SE1 7JA **t** 020 7803 1300 **f** 020 7803 1310
e general@bpi.co.uk **w** bpi.co.uk 📇 Chief Executive: Geoff
Taylor. Chief Executive: Geoff Taylor. Director of
Communications: Adam Liversage. Director of
Membership and International Services: Julian Wall.
Director of Anti-Piracy: David Wood. Event and Charities
Director: Maggie Crowe.

Bristol Music Foundation
11 Great George St, Bristol, BS1 5RR **t** 01179 588849
e info@bristolmusicfoundation.com
w bristolmusicfoundation.com 📇 Dir: Matt Booth.

The BRIT Awards
c/o BPI, Riverside Building, County Hall, Westminster Bridge Rd, London, SE1 7JA
t 020 7803 1300 **f** 020 7803 1310 **e** brits@bpi.co.uk
w brits.co.uk 📇 Dir, Events & Charity: Maggie Crowe.

BRIT Trust
c/o BPI, Riverside Building, County Hall, Westminster Bridge Rd, London, SE1 7JA **t** 020 7803 1300
f 020 7803 1310 **e** brittrust@bpi.co.uk **w** brittrust.co.uk
📇 Dir, Events & Charity: Maggie Crowe.

📧 Contacts 📘 Facebook 🔲 MySpace 🐦 Twitter ▶️ YouTube

Business Services: Industry Organisations

British Federation Of Audio PO Box 365, Farnham, Surrey, GU10 2BD **t** 01428 714616 **f** 01428 717599 **e** chrisc@british-audio.org.uk **w** british-audio.org.uk 📧 Secretary: Chris Cowan.

British Interactive Media Association
The Lightwell, 12-16 Laystall St, Clerkenwell, London, EC1R 4PF **t** 020 7843 6797 **e** sharlenegerus@bima.co.uk **w** bima.co.uk 📧 Contact: Sharlene Gerus.

British Library Sound Archive 96 Euston Rd, London, NW1 2DB **t** 020 7412 7676 **e** sound-archive@bl.uk **w** bl.uk/soundarchive 📧 Contact: Director.

Broadcasting Commission of Ireland
2/5 Warrington Place, Dublin 2, Ireland **t** +353 1 644 1200 **f** +353 1 644 1299 **e** info@bci.ie **w** bci.ie 📧 CEO: Michael O'Keeffe.

BVA (British Video Association)
167 Great Portland St, London, W1W 5PE **t** 020 7436 0041 **f** 020 7436 0043 **e** general@bva.org.uk **w** bva.org.uk 📧 Dir Gen: Lavinia Carey.

Christian Copyright Licencing (Europe) Ltd
PO Box 1339, Eastbourne, East Sussex, BN21 4YF **t** 01323 417711 **f** 01323 417722 **e** info@ccli.co.uk **w** ccli.co.uk 📧 Sales Mgr: Chris Williams.

Community Media Association
15 Paternoster Row, Sheffield, South Yorkshire, S1 2BX **t** 0114 279 5219 **f** 0114 279 8976 **e** cma@commedia.org.uk **w** commedia.org.uk 📧 Dir: Diane Reid.

Contemporary Music Centre, Ireland
19 Fishamble St, Temple Bar, Dublin 8, Ireland **t** +353 16 731 922 **f** +353 16 489 100 **e** info@cmc.ie **w** cmc.ie 📘 facebook.com/CMCIreland 🔲 myspace.com/cmcireland 🐦 twitter.com/cmcireland ▶️ youtube.com/user/CMCIreland 📧 Director: Eve O'Kelly.

Copyright Advice and Anti-Piracy Hotline
t 0845 603 4567

Cornwall Music Industry Forum Krowji, West Pk, Redruth, Cornwall, TR15 3AJ **t** 01209 313200 **e** tim@metronome.co.uk **w** cornwallmusic.co.uk 📧 Chairman: Tim Smithies.

CPA (Concert Promoters Association)
6 St Mark's Rd, Henley-on-Thames, Oxfordshire, RG9 1LJ **t** 01491 575060 **e** carolesmith.cpa@virgin.net **w** concertpromotersassociation.co.uk 📧 Secretary: Carole Smith.

Department for Culture, Media and Sport 2-4 Cockspur St, London, SW1Y 5DH **t** 020 7211 6200 **e** enquiries@culture.gsi.gov.uk **w** culture.gov.uk 📧 Contact: Public Enquiries 0207 6211 6200.

EDiMA (European Digital Media Association)
Friars House, Office 118, 157-168 Blackfriars Road, London, SE1 8EZ **t** 020 7401 2661 **f** 020 7928 5850 **e** info@edima.org **w** edima.org 📧 Dir: Wes Himes.

English Folk Dance & Song Society
Cecil Sharp House, 2 Regent's Park Rd, Camden, London, NW1 7AY **t** 020 7485 2206 **f** 020 7284 0534 **e** marketing@efdss.org **w** efdss.org 📧 Marketing: Nick Hallam.

Enterprise Ireland 35-39 Shelbourne Road, Ballsbridge, Dublin 4, Ireland **t** +353 1 206 6000 **f** +353 1 206 6400 **e** client.service@enterprise-ireland.com **w** enterprise-ireland.com 📧 Development Advisor: Eileen Bell.

ERA (Entertainment Retailers Association)
1st Floor, Colonnade House, 2 Westover Rd, Bournemouth, Dorset, BH1 2BY **t** 01202 292 063 **f** 01202 292 067 **e** admin@eraltd.org **w** eraltd.org 📧 Director General: Kim Bayley.

FACT Europa House, Church St, Isleworth, Middlesex, TW7 6DA **t** 020 8568 6646 **f** 020 8560 6364 **e** eddy.leviten@fact-uk.org.uk **w** fact-uk.org.uk 📧 Head of Communications: Eddy Leviten.

Folk Arts Network PO BOx 296, Matlock, Derbyshire, DE4 3XU **t** 01629 827 014 **f** 01629 821 874 **w** folkarts-england.org.uk 📧 Administrator: Frances Watt.

French Music Bureau Institut Francais, 17 Queensberry Pl, London, SW7 2DT **t** 020 7073 1301 **f** 020 7073 1359 **e** london@french-music.org **w** french-music.org/uk 📘 tinyurl.com/lvesmj 🔲 myspace.com/frenchmusicbureau 🐦 twitter.com/frenchmusicuk 📧 Director: Patrice Hourbette 0207 073 1334.

Friends To The Stars 14 Carlisle Rd, London, NW6 6TS **t** 07989 609246 **e** kirsty@friendstothestars.com **w** friendstothestars.com 📧 Director: Kirsty Booth.

Gibson Guitar 3rd Floor, 29-35 Rathbone St, London, W1T 1NJ **t** 020 7167 2144 **f** 020 7167 2150 **e** jeremy.singer@gibson.com **w** gibson.com 📧 UK PR Mgr: Jeremy Singer.

GS1 UK Staple Court, 11 Staple Inn Buildings, London, WC1V 7QH **t** 020 7092 3500 **e** info@gs1uk.org **w** gs1uk.org 📧 Contact: Service Team.

GUILD OF INTERNATIONAL SONGWRITERS & COMPOSERS

Sovereign House, 12 Trewartha Rd, Praa Sands, Penzance, Cornwall, TR20 9ST **t** 01736 762826 **f** 01736 763328 **e** songmag@aol.com **w** songwriters-guild.co.uk 🔲 myspace.com/guildofsongwriters 📧 General Sec: Carole A Jones.

Business Services: Industry Organisations

IFPI (International Federation of the Phonographic Industry)
IFPI Secretariat, 10 Piccadilly, London, W1J 0DD **t** 020 7878 7900 **f** 020 7878 7950 **e** laura.childs@ifpi.org **w** ifpi.org Director of Communications: Adrian Strain 020 7878 7935.

IMRO (Irish Music Rights Organisation)
Copyright House, Pembroke Row, Lower Baggot St, Dublin 2, Ireland **t** +353 1 661 4844 **f** +353 1 676 3125 **e** keith.johnson@imro.ie **w** imro.ie Director of Marketing & Membership: Keith Johnson.

Intelligent Media
Clifton Works, 23 Grove Park Terrace, London, W4 3QE **t** 020 8995 0055 **f** 020 8995 9900 **e** jonm@intelligentmedia.com **w** intelligentmedia.com MD: Jon Mais 020 8996 6061.

Interactive Media in Retail Group
5 Dryden Street, London, WC2E 9BN **t** 07000 464674 **f** 07000 394674 **e** market@imrg.org **w** imrg.org MD: Jo Tucker.

International Music Managers Forum (IMMF)
1 York St, London, W1U 6PA **t** 020 7935 2446 **f** 020 7486 6045 **e** davids@immf.net **w** immf.net Exec Dir: David Stopps.

IRMA
IRMA House, 1 Corrig Avenue, Dun Laoghaire, Dublin, Ireland **t** +353 1 280 6571 **f** +353 1 280 6579 **e** irma_info@irma.ie **w** irma.ie Dir Gen: Dick Doyle.

ISA (INTERNATIONAL SONGWRITERS' ASSOCIATION)

PO Box 46, Limerick City, Limerick, Ireland **t** +353 61 228 837 **f** +353 61 228 8379 **e** jliddane@songwriter.iol.ie **w** songwriter.co.uk CEO: James D Liddane.

ISM (The Incorporated Society Of Musicians)
10 Stratford Place, London, W1C 1AA **t** 020 7629 4413 **f** 020 7408 1538 **e** membership@ism.org **w** ism.org Chief Exec: Neil Hoyle.

The Liverpool Institute For Performing Arts
Mount St, Liverpool, Merseyside, L1 9HF **t** 0151 330 3000 **f** 0151 330 3131 **e** marketing@lipa.ac.uk **w** lipa.ac.uk Director of Marketing: Corinne Lewis.

MCPS (Ireland)
Pembroke Row, Lower Baggot Street, Dublin 2, Ireland **t** +353 1 676 6940 **f** +353 1 661 1316 **e** victor.finn@mcps.ie **w** mcps.ie MD: Victor Finn.

Millward Brown UK
Olympus Avenue, Tachbrook Pk, Warwick, CV34 6RJ **t** 01926 826610 **f** 01926 826209 **e** bob.barnes@millwardbrown.com **w** millwardbrown.com Charts Dir: Bob Barnes.

MMF (Music Managers Forum)
British Music House, 26 Berners St, London, W1T 3LR **t** 020 7306 4885 **f** 0870 850 7801 **e** info@musicmanagersforum.co.uk **w** musicmanagersforum.co.uk Chief Executive: Jon Webster.

Mobile Entertainment Forum (MEF)
313 Westbourne Studios, 242 Acklam Rd, London, W10 5JJ **t** 020 7524 7878 **f** 020 7524 7879 **e** info@m-e-f.org **w** m-e-f.org Executive Director: Rimma Perelmuter.

Music Of Black Origin - Mobo Awards
22 Stephenson Way, London, NW1 2HD **t** 020 7419 1800 **f** 020 7419 1600 **e** info@mobo.com **w** mobo.com Founder: Kanya King MBE.

MPA (Music Publishers Association)
6th Floor, British Music House, 26 Berners St, London, W1T 3LR **t** 020 7580 0126 **f** 020 7637 3929 **e** info@mpaonline.org.uk **w** mpaonline.org.uk the_MPA Communications Officer: Will Lines.

MPG (The Music Producers Guild)
PO Box 38134, London, W10 6XL **t** 020 3239 7606 **e** mpg_info@mpg.org.uk **w** mpg.org.uk myspace.com/musicproducersguild youtube.com/mpg_uk Secretary: Paul Smith.

Music Industries Association
Ivy Cottage Offices, Finch's Yard, Eastwick Rd, Great Bookham, Surrey, KT23 4BA **t** 01372 750600 **f** 01372 750515 **e** paulmc@mia.org.uk **w** mia.org.uk Chief Executive: Paul McManus.

Music Preserved
Hillside Cottage, Hill Brow Road, Liss, Hants, GU33 7 **t** 01730 892148 **f** 01730 894264 **e** musicpreserved@dial.pipex.com **w** musicpreserved.org Chairman: Basil Tschaikov.

The Musicians Guide To World Domination
59 Nobles Close, Wantage, Oxford, Oxfordshire, OX12 0NR **t** 07928 282862 **e** marcus@starharbour.co.uk **w** www.themusiciansguide.co.uk Contact: Marcus 07928282862.

MUSICIANS' UNION

Musicians' Union

60-62 Clapham Rd, London, SW9 0JJ **t** 020 7582 5566 **f** 020 7582 9805 **e** info@musiciansunion.org.uk **w** musiciansunion.org.uk General Secretary: John Smith. General Secretary: John Smith. Asst Gen Sec - Industry: Horace Trubridge. Asst Gen Sec - Finance & Admin: David Ashley. Nat Organiser - Media: Nigel McCune. Nat Organiser - Live Performance & Teaching: Diane Widdison. Nat Organiser - Orchestras: Bill Kerr. In-house Solicitor: David Fenton. Comms Official: Keith Ames. Research & Press Official: Isabelle Gutierrez. Sessions Official: Peter Thoms.

Business Services: Industry Organisations

National Association of Youth Orchestras
Central Hall, West Tollcross, Edinburgh, EH3 9BP
t 0131 221 1927 **f** 0131 229 2921 **e** admin@nayo.org.uk
w nayo.org.uk

National Foundation for Youth Music (Youth Music) One America St, London, SE1 0NE
t 020 7902 1060 **f** 020 7902 1061
e info@youthmusic.org.uk **w** youthmusic.org.uk **a** Chief
Executive: Christina Coker.

National Ouddoor Events Association formerly National Entertainment Agents Council 23 Coral Avenue, Westward Ho!, Bideford,
Devon, EX39 1 UW **t** 01237 473113 **f** 01237 459661
e secretary@noea.org.uk **w** noea.org.uk **a** General
Secretary: John Barton.

NEMIS (New Music In Scotland) 2nd Floor,
22 Jamaica St, Glasgow, G1 4QD **t** 07803 752 913
e alec@nemis.org **w** nemis.org **a** Development
Officer: Alec Downie.

Nicolaou Solicitors The Barn Studios,
Burnt Farm Ride, Goffs Oak, Herts, EN7 5JA
t 01707 877707 **f** 01707 877708 **e** niclaw@tiscali.co.uk
a Solicitor: Constantina Nicolaou 07785 933377.

Nordoff-Robbins Music Therapy Studio A2,
1927 Building, 2 Michael Road, London, SW6 2AD
t 020 7371 8404 **f** 020 7371 8206 **e** lindamac@nrfr.co.uk
w silverclef.com **a** Appeals Manager: Linda McLean.

Ofcom Riverside House, 2a Southwark Bridge Rd,
London, SE1 9HA **t** 020 7981 3000 **f** 020 7981 3333
e contact@ofcom.org.uk **w** ofcom.org.uk

OFFICIAL CHARTS COMPANY

Riverside Building, County Hall, Westminster Bridge Rd,
London, SE1 7JA **t** 020 7620 7450 **f** 020 7620 7469
e info@theofficialcharts.com **w** theofficialcharts.com
a MD: Martin Talbot. Chart Director: Omar Maskatiya.
Finance & Commercial Director: Jonathan Woods. Head of
Charts Operations: Meriel Blackburn. Chart Operations
Assistant: Sarah Dalton.

The Patent Office Concept House, Cardiff Road,
Newport, Gwent, NP10 8QQ **t** 01633 814000
f 01633 813600 **e** enquiries@patent.gov.uk
w patent.gov.uk **a** Contact: 08459 500505.

PLASA (Professional Lighting & Sound Association) Redoubt House, 1 Edward Rd,
Eastbourne, East Sussex, BN23 8AS **t** 01323 524120
f 01323 524121 **e** info@plasa.org **w** plasa.org
a Executive Director: Ruth Rossington.

PPI (Phonographic Performance Ireland)
PPI House, 1 Corrig Avenue, Dun Laoghaire, Dublin, Ireland
t +353 1 280 5977 **f** +353 1 280 6579 **e** info@ppiltd.com
w ppiltd.com **a** CEO: Dick Doyle.

PPL (PHONOGRAPHIC PERFORMANCE LTD)

1 Upper James St, London, W1F 9DE **t** 020 7534 1000
f 020 7534 1111 **e** info@ppluk.com **w** ppluk.com **a**
Chairman & CEO: Fran Nevrkla. Executive Director: Peter
Leathem. Director of Licensing: Tony Clark. Director of HR
& Facilities: Janice Davies. Director of Performer
Affairs: Keith Harris. Director of IT: Frank Jaschinski.
Finance Director: Ben Lambert. Director of Government
Relations: Dominic McGonigal. Director of PR & Corporate
Communications: Jonathan Morrish. Head of Member
Services: Penny White.
**PPL, which does not retain any profit for itself, is the
music licensing company that, on behalf of 42,000
performers and 5,000 record companies in the UK,
and more internationally, licenses recorded music for
public performance, broadcast and new media use.**

PPL REPERTOIRE DATABASE (CATCO)

1 Upper James Street, London, W1F 9DE **t** 020 7534 1331
f 020 7534 1111 **e** repertoire@ppluk.com **w** ppluk.com
a Chairman & CEO: Fran Nevrkla. Executive Director: Peter
Leathem. Director of Licensing: Tony Clark. Director of HR
& Facilities: Janice Davies. Director of Performer
Affairs: Keith Harris. Director of IT: Frank Jaschinski.
Finance Director: Ben Lambert. Director of Government
Relations: Dominic McGonigal. Director of PR & Corporate
Communications: Jonathan Morrish. Repertoire Services
Manager: Simon Hutchinson.
**The Record Industry's track level sound recording
database, providing the 'one-stop-drop' for all sound
recording data needs.**

PRC (Performer Registration Centre)
1 Upper James Street, London, W1F 9DE **t** 020 7534 1234
f 020 7534 1383 **e** PRC.info@ppluk.com
w performersmoney.ppluk.com

The Prince's Trust 18 Park Sq East, London, NW1 4LH
t 020 7543 1234 **f** 020 7543 1200 **e** info@princes-
trust.org.uk **w** princes-trust.org.uk **a** Chief
Executive: Martina Milburn 0800 842 842.

Production Services Association PO Box 2709,
Bath, BA1 3YS **t** 01225 332 668 **f** 01225 332 701
e gm@psa.org.uk **w** psa.org.uk **a** GM: Andy Lenthall.

Royalty Auditing for the music industry   **T: 01372 840 280**   www.bevisandco.co.uk

PRS FOR MUSIC Copyright House, 29-33 Berners St, London, W1T 3AB **t** 020 7580 5544 **w** prsformusic.com
f facebook.com/PRSforMusic
myspace.com/prsformusic twitter.com/prsformusic
Contact: Switchboard. Chairman - PRS: Ellis Rich. Chairman - MCPS: Tom Bradley. Chief Executive (Acting): Jeremy Fabinyi. Managing Director Broadcast, Online & Recorded Media: Andrew Shaw. Managing Director, Membership: Jo Prowse. Managing Director, International: Karen Buse. Managing Director, Public Performance Sales: Keith Gilbert. Managing Director, Professional Services: Niall Stirling. Executive Director, Marketing & Communications: Emma Inston. General Counsel: Debbie Stones.
PRS for Music is the leading copyright and royalty collection society representing 60,000 songwriters, composers and music publishers.

RadioCentre 4th Floor, 5 Golden Sq, London, W1D 5DU **t** 020 7306 2603 **f** 020 7306 2505
e lucy@radiocentre.org **w** radiocentre.org
twitter.com/RadioCentre Contact: Lucy Forster.

Scottish Music Centre City Halls, Candleriggs, Glasgow, G1 1NQ **t** 0141 552 5222 **f** 0141 553 2789
e info@scottishmusiccentre.com
w scottishmusiccentre.com twitter.com/scottishmusic
MD: Gill Maxwell.

SESAC (SOCIETY OF EUROPEAN SONGWRITERS & COMPOSERS

67 Upper Berkeley St, London, W1H 7QX **t** 020 7616 9284 **f** 020 7563 7029 **e** rights@sesac.co.uk **w** sesac.com
Chairman, SESAC International: Wayne Bickerton. SESAC, UK Member Relations: John Sweeney.

UK Music Ltd British Music House, 26 Berners St, London, W1T 3LR **t** 020 7306 4446 **f** 020 7306 4449
e contact@ukmusic.org **w** ukmusic.org

Variety & Light Entertainment Council
54 Keyes House, Dolphin Square, London, SW1V 3NA **t** 020 7834 0515 **f** 020 7821 0261 Joint Secretary: Kenneth Earle.

Variety Club Children's Charity
93 Bayham Street, London, NW1 0AG **t** 020 7428 8100 **f** 020 7482 8123 **e** info@varietyclub.org.uk
w varietyclub.org.uk The Chief Barker: Norman Kaphan.

VPL

1 Upper James St, London, W1F 9DE **t** 020 7534 1400 **f** 020 7534 1367 **e** info@ppluk.com **w** ppluk.com
Chairman & CEO: Fran Nevrkla. Executive Director: Peter Leathem. Director of Licensing: Tony Clark. Director of HR & Facilities: Janice Davies. Director of Performer Affairs: Keith Harris. Director of IT: Frank Jaschinski. Finance Director: Ben Lambert. Director of Government Relations: Dominic McGonigal. Director of PR & Corporate Communications: Jonathan Morrish. Head of Member Services: Penny White.
VPL, which does not retain any profit for itself, is the music licensing company that, on behalf of approximately 1,400 record companies in the UK, licenses music videos for broadcast and public performance.

Welsh Music Foundation 33-35 West Bute St, Cardiff Bay, Cardiff, CF10 5LH **t** 0292 049 4110 **f** 0292 049 4210
e enquiries@welshmusicfoundation.com
w welshmusicfoundation.com
facebook.com/home.php?#/pages/Cardiff-United-Kingdom/Welsh-Music-Foundation-Sefydliad-Cerddoriaeth-Gymreig/10678344095 twitter.com/walesmusic
Acting Director: Lisa Matthews.

Women In Music 7 Lion Lane, Billericay, Essex, CM12 9DL **e** info@womeninmusic.org.uk
w womeninmusic.org.uk Honorary Secretary: Dr. Margaret Lucy Wilkins.

The Worshipful Company Of Musicians
6th Floor, 2 London Wall Buildings, London, EC2M 5PP **t** 020 7496 8980 **f** 020 7588 3633
e deputyclerk@wcom.org.uk **w** wcom.org.uk Dept Clerk: Margaret Alford.

Accountants

A & Co 36 Ferrymans Quay, William Morris Way, London, SW6 2UT **t** 020 3229 1229 **f** 020 7681 4487
e lesley.alexander@dugua .co.uk Principal: Lesley Alexander.

Addis & Co Emery House, 192 Heaton Moor Rd, Stockport, Cheshire, SK4 4DU **t** 0161 432 3307 **f** 0161 432 3376 **e** enquiries@a-addis.co.uk **w** a-addis.co.uk Partner: Anthony Addis.

Alan Boddy & Co Chartered Accountants
Damer House, Meadow Way, Wickford, Essex, SS12 9HA **t** 01268 571466 **f** 01268 570638
e alan@albodd.freeserve.co.uk **w** alanboddy.co.uk
Principal: Alan Boddy FCA.

Business Services: Accountants

Alan Heywood & Company 78 Mill Lane, London, NW6 1JZ **t** 020 7435 0101 **f** 020 7431 5410 **e** alan@alanheywood.co.uk **w** alanheywood.co.uk 🖂 Contact: Alan Heywood FCA.

Anthony Tiscoe & Company Brentmead House, Britannia Rd, London, N12 9RU **t** 020 8343 8749 **f** 020 8492 0159 **e** tony@tiscoe.fsnet.co.uk **w** tiscoeaccountants.com 🖂 Chartered Accountant: Anthony Tiscoe 07976 661217.

Baker Tilly 2 Bloomsbury St, London, WC1B 3ST **t** 020 7413 5100 **f** 020 7413 5101 **e** david.blacher@bakertilly.co.uk **w** bakertilly.co.uk 🖂 Head of Media Group: David Blacher.

BDO Stoy Hayward 55 Baker St, London, W1U 7EU **t** 020 7486 5888 **f** 020 7487 3686 **e** chris.maddock@bdo.co.uk **w** bdo.co.uk 🖂 Partner: Chris Maddock.

BERG KAPROW LEWIS LLP

Berg Kaprow Lewis

35 Ballards Lane, London, N3 1XW **t** 020 8922 9222 **f** 020 8922 9223 **e** firstname.lastname@bkl.co.uk **w** bkl.co.uk 🖂 Partner: Steven Hocking-Robinson.

Bettersounds Consultancy Little Orchards, Sandyhurst Lane, Ashford, Kent, TN25 4NT **t** 01233 643325 **e** Bettersounds@btconnect.com 🖂 Contact: Bernard Symonds.

BEVIS & CO

BEVIS&CO
Chartered Accountants
Royalty Auditing for the music industry

Apex House, 6 West St, Epsom, Surrey, KT18 7RG **t** 01372 840280 **f** 01372 840282 **e** chris@bevisandco.co.uk **w** bevisandco.co.uk 🖂 Partner: Chris Bevis. **Commercially experienced accountants with extensive music industry knowledge, royalty audits and catalogue valuations carried out, statutory audits, management accounts service.**

BKR Haines Watts Sterling House, 177-181 Farnham Road, Slough, Berkshire, SL1 4XP **t** 01753 530333 **f** 01753 576606 **e** slough@hwca.com **w** hwca.com 🖂 Partner: Michael Davidson.

Blackstone Franks LLP 26-34 Old St, London, EC1V 9QR **t** 020 7250 3300 **f** 020 7250 1402 **e** RMaas@blackstones.co.uk **w** blackstonefranks.com 🖂 Partner: Robert Maas.

Blinkhorns 27 Mortimer Street, London, W1T 3BL **t** 020 7636 3702 **f** 020 7636 0335 **e** Joel.Trott@blinkhorns.co.uk **w** blinkhorns.co.uk 🖂 Partner: Joel Trott.

Blue² 7 Bourne Court, Southend Rd, Woodford Green, Essex, IG8 8HD **t** 020 8418 2408 **f** 020 8550 6020 **e** info@bluesquaredfinance.co.uk **w** bluesquaredfinance.co.uk 🖂 Contact: Nick Lawrence.

Bowker Orford 15-19 Cavendish Pl, London, W1G 0DD **t** 020 7636 6391 **f** 020 7580 3909 **e** mail@bowkerorford.com **w** bowkerorford.com 🖂 Partner: Rashpal Parmar.

Brebner, Allen & Trapp The Quadrangle, 180 Wardour Street, London, W1F 8LB **t** 020 7734 2244 **f** 020 7287 5315 **e** partners@brebner.co.uk **w** brebner.co.uk 🖂 Partner: Jose Goumal.

Royalty Auditing for the music industry
T: 01372 840 280
www.bevisandco.co.uk

Breckman & Company 49 South Molton Street, London, W1K 5LH
e richardnelson@breckmanandcompany.co.uk
w breckmanandcompany.co.uk 🖂 Partner: Mr Richard Nelson 0207 499 2292.

Brett Adams-Chartered Accountants
25 Manchester Square, London, W1U 3PY
t 020 7486 8985 **f** 020 7486 8991
e Info@brettadams.co.uk 🖂 Music Partner: Steven Davidson.

Bright Grahame Murray Chartered Accountants 131 Edgware Rd, London, W2 2AP
t 020 7402 7444 **f** 020 7402 8444
e markcole@bgm.co.uk **w** bgm.co.uk 🖂 Managing Partner: Mark Cole.

Brighten Jeffrey James 421a Finchley Rd, Hampstead, London, NW3 6HJ **t** 020 7794 7373
f 020 7431 5566 **e** info@brightenjeffreyjames.co.uk
w brightenjeffreyjames.com 🖂 Partner: Roger Brighten.

Brown McLeod Ltd. 51 Clarkegrove Rd, Sheffield, South Yorkshire, S10 2NH **t** 0114 268 4747
f 0114 268 4161 **e** john@brownmcleod.co.uk
w brownmcleod.co.uk 🖂 MD: John Roddison.

Bullocks 41 Great Portland St, London, W1W 7LA
t 020 7268 0123 **f** 020 7637 1997
e enquiries@bullocks.co.uk **w** bullocks.co.uk
🖂 Contact: Adrian Bullock, Kash Khan.

CC YOUNG & CO

Chartered Accountants and Registered Auditors, 48 Poland Street, London, W1F 7ND **t** 020 7494 5680
e info@ccyoung.co.uk 🖂 Contact: Colin Young or Kate Dosanjh. Director: Colin Young. Office Manager: Kate Dosanjh.

Charlie Carne & Associates 33 Drayson Mews, London, W8 4LY **t** 020 8742 2001
e info@charliecarne.com 🖂 Chartered Accountant: Charlie Carne.

Conroy & Company 27 Beaumont Avenue, St. Albans, Herts, AL1 4TL **t** 01727 858 589
e conroyandcompany@btconnect.com 🖂 Snr Partner: A Conroy FCA, FSCA.

Cousins Brett 20 Bulstrode Street, London, W1U 2JW
t 020 7486 5791 **f** 020 7224 7226
e johncousins@cousinsbrett.com **w** cousinsbrett.com
🖂 Partner: John Cousins.

DALES EVANS & CO LTD CHARTERED ACCOUNTANTS

DALES EVANS
Chartered Accountants
88/90 Baker Street
London W1U 6TQ

88-90 Baker St, London, W1U 6TQ **t** 020 7298 1899
f 020 7298 1871 🖂 Directors: Lester Dales, Paul Makin.

dBM Ltd 8 The Glasshouse, 49A Goldhawk Rd, London, W12 8QP **t** 020 8222 6628 **f** 020 8222 6629
e david@dbmltd.co.uk 🖂 MD: David Hitchcock.

De La Haye Royalty Services 76 High St, Stony Stratford, Bucks, MK11 1AH **t** 01908 568800
f 01908 568890 **e** royalties@delahaye.co.uk
w delahaye.co.uk 🖂 MD: Roger La Haye.

Deloitte LLP 2 New Street Sq, London, EC4A 3BZ
t 020 7007 0833 **f** 020 7303 4786
e cbradbrook@deloitte.co.uk **w** deloitte.co.uk 🖂 Tax Partner, Music/Media: Charles Bradbrook.

DPC Media Holed Stone Barn, Stisted Cottage Fm, Hollies Rd, Bradwell, Braintree, Essex, CM77 8DZ **t** 01376 551426 **f** 01376 551787
e info@dpcmedia.demon.co.uk 🖂 Business Mgr: Dave Clark.

EMTACS-Entertainers & Musicians Tax & Accountancy 69 Loughborough Rd, West Bridgford, Nottingham, NG2 7LA **t** 0115 981 5001 **f** 0115 981 5005
e emtacs@aol.com **w** emtacs.com
🆕 facebook.com/home.php?#/group.php?gid=15589131 702&ref=ts 🖂 Partner: Geoff Challinger.

Entertainment Accounting International Limited Ground Floor Front, 9 Heathmans Rd, London, SW6 4TJ **t** 020 7384 9362 **f** 020 7731 1762
e contact@eai.uk.com 🖂 Dirs: Mike Donovan & Mark Howe.

Freedman Frankl & Taylor Reedham House, 31 King Street West, Manchester, M3 2PJ
t 0161 834 2574 **f** 0161 831 7608 **e** mail@fft.co.uk
w fft.co.uk

FSPG 21 Bedford Sq, London, WC1B 3HH
t 020 7637 4444 **f** 020 7323 2857 **e** jon@fspg.co.uk
🖂 Partner: Jon Glasner.

Grant Thornton UK LLP
Media & Entertainment Group, Grant Thornton House, Melton St, London, NW1 2EP **t** 020 7383 5100
f 020 7383 4715 **e** terry.a.back@gtuk.com **w** grant-thornton.co.uk 🖂 Head of Media & Entertainment: Terry Back.

Hardwick & Morris 41 Great Portland St, London, W1W 7LA **t** 020 7268 0100 **f** 0870 706 5204
e stephanie@hardwickandmorris.co.uk
w hardwickandmorris.co.uk 🖂 Partner: Stephanie Hardwick.

Harold Everett Wreford, Chartered Accountants 32 Wigmore St, London, W1U 2RP **t** 020 7535 5900 **f** 020 7535 5901 **e** jsloneem@hew.co.uk **w** hew.co.uk ✆ Partner, Entertainment: Jeffrey Sloneem 02075355945.

Harris & Trotter 65 New Cavendish St, London, W1G 7LS **t** 020 7467 6300 **f** 020 7467 6363 **e** mail@harrisandtrotter.co.uk **w** harrisandtrotter.co.uk ✆ Senior Partner: Ronnie Harris.

George Hay & Co 83 Cambridge Street, London, SW1V 4PS **t** 020 7630 0582 **f** 020 7630 1502 **e** info@georgehay.com **w** georgehay.com ✆ Contact: The Snr Partner.

HEMINGWAY LTD

HEMINGWAY LIMITED
Music and Media Accounting

Ground & Basement Studio, 485 Liverpool Rd, London, N7 8PG **t** 020 7609 5371
e samantha@hemingwayltd.com **w** hemingwayltd.com ✆ Owner / Director: Samantha Hemingway +44 7974 021 259.

HW Fisher & Company Acre House, 11-15 William Rd, London, NW1 3ER **t** 020 7388 7000 **f** 020 7380 4900 **e** info@hwfisher.co.uk **w** hwfisher.co.uk ✆ Partner: Martin Taylor.

Hyman Capital Services Ltd 25 Duke St, London, W1U 1LD **t** 020 7034 1974 **f** 070 9286 4010 **e** clive.hyman@hymancapital.com **w** hymancapital.com ✆ CEO: Clive Hyman 07802 634163.

Immediate Business Management
61 Birch Green, Hertford, Herts, SG14 2LR
t 01992 550573 **f** 01992 550573
e immediate@onetel.com ✆ Partner: Derek Jones.

Jeffrey James Chartered Accountants
421a Finchley Rd, Hampstead, London, NW3 6HJ
t 020 7794 7373 **f** 020 7431 5566
e info@jeffreyjames.co.uk ✆ Partner: Jeffrey Kaye.

JER 16 Cornerways, 1 Daylesford Avenue, London, SW15 5QP **t** 020 8878 3298 **f** 020 8878 3298 **e** julie@jeroyalties.com **w** jeroyalties.com ✆ Royalty Auditor: Julie Eyre.

John Gale Associates 415 Hillcross Avenue, Morden, Surrey, SM4 4BZ **t** 020 8542 7869 **f** 020 8715 3801 **e** john@jgacs.co.uk **w** jgacs.co.uk ✆ Principal: John Gale.

Johnsons Media 2nd Floor, 109 Uxbridge Rd, London, W5 5TL **t** 020 8567 3451 **f** 020 8840 6823 **e** mail@johnsonsca.com **w** johnsonsca.com ✆ Partner: David M Turner.

Jon Child & Co 107 Oldham St, Manchester, M4 1LW **t** 0161 834 8885 **f** 0161 834 9992 **e** jon@jonchild.com **w** jonchild.com ✆ Partner: Jon Child.

Kaizen Accounting Ltd 15 Blois Rd, Steeple Bumpstead, Essex, CB9 7BN **t** 01440 731984 **f** 01440 731984 **e** kentonm@hotmail.com **w** kaizenaccounting.co.uk ✆ KentonM ✆ Director: Kenton Mitchell 07969 056052.

Kingston Smith W1 141 Wardour St, London, W1F 0UT **t** 020 7304 4646 **f** 020 7304 4647 **e** ghowells@kingstonsmithW1.co.uk **w** kingstonsmithW1.co.uk ✆ Partner: Geraint Howells.

KPMG LLP Aquis Court, 31 Fishpool St, St Albans, AL3 4RF **t** 01727 733063 **f** 01727 733001 **e** charles.lestrangemeakin@kpmg.co.uk **w** kpmg.com ✆ Dir: Charles Le Strange Meakin.

Leigh Philip & Partners 1-6 Clay Street, London, W1U 6DA **t** 020 7486 4889 **f** 020 7486 4885 **e** mail@lpplondon.co.uk ✆ Snr Partner: Leigh Genis.

Lloyd Piggott Wellington House, 39/41 Piccadilly, Manchester, M1 1LQ **t** 0161 236 7677 **f** 0161 236 7678 **e** info@lloydpiggott.co.uk **w** lloydpiggott.co.uk ✆ Tax Director: Paula Abbott.

LUBBOCK FINE CHARTERED ACCOUNTANTS

LubbockFine
Chartered Accountants

Russell Bedford House, City Forum, 250 City Rd, London, EC1V 2QQ **t** 020 7490 7766 **f** 020 7490 5102 **e** enquiries@lubbockfine.co.uk **w** lubbockfine.co.uk ✆ Media Partners: Jeff Gitter & Russell Rich. Media Partner: Jeff Gitter. Media Partner: Russell Rich.

Mansfield & Co, Chartered Accountants 55 Kentish Town Rd, Camden Town, London, NW1 8NX **t** 020 7482 2022 **f** 020 7197 8016 **e** mco@mansfields.co.uk ✆ Senior Partner: David FL Mansfield.

MGM Accountancy Ltd 17 Tavistock Street, London, WC2E 7PA **t** 020 7379 9202 **f** 020 7379 9101 **e** guy@mgmaccountancy.co.uk ✆ MD: Guy Rippon MA FCCA ACIB.

MGR Media 55 Loudoun Road, St John's Wood, London, NW8 0DL **t** 020 7625 4545 **f** 020 7625 5265 **e** info@mgrmedia.com **w** atfgroup.com

Morris & Shah Lower Ground Floor, 28A York Street, London, W1U 6QA **t** 020 7486 9554 **f** 020 7486 9557 **e** morrisandshah@morrisandshah.co.uk ✆ Partners: Jonathan Morris, Kewal Shah.

MUSIC BUSINESS ASSOCIATES LTD

Apex House, 6 West St, Epsom, Surrey, KT18 7RG
t 01372 840281 **f** 01372 840282
e paulk@musicbusinessassociates.com
w musicbusinessassociates.com ✉ Royalties and
Accounts Manager: Paul Kerslake or Chris Bevis.

Music Royalties Ltd 26 Pavilion Way, Eastcote,
Middlesex, HA4 9JN **t** 07855 411 983
e david@musicroyalties.co.uk **w** musicroyalties.co.uk
✉ Dir: David Rayment.

MWM Chartered Accountants
11 Great George St, Bristol, BS1 5RR **t** 0117 929 2393
f 0117 929 2696 **e** office@mwmuk.com ✉ Dir: Craig
Williams.

Neill & Co 2a Forest Drive, Theydon Bois, Epping, Essex,
CM16 7EY **t** 01992 812211 **f** 01992 812299
e info@neill.co.uk **w** neill.co.uk ✉ Principal: Keith Neill.

Nieman Walters Niman 7 Bourne Court,
Southend Rd, Woodford Green, Essex, IG8 8HD
t 020 8550 3131 **f** 020 8550 6020
e info@nwnaccounts.com **w** nwnaccounts.com
✉ Partner: Edmund Niman.

Note for Note 15 Marroway, Weston Turville,
Aylesbury, Bucks, HP22 5TQ **t** 01296 614966
f 01296 614651 **e** Chris@note-for-note.co.uk
✉ Proprietor: Chris Turner.

Nyman Libson Paul Regina House, 124 Finchley Rd,
London, NW3 5JS **t** 020 7433 2400 **f** 020 7433 2401
e mail@nlpca.co.uk **w** nlpca.co.uk ✉ Partner: Amin Saleh.

Oasis Leisure Centre North Star Avenue, Swindon,
Wiltshire, SN2 1EP **t** 01793 445401 **f** 01793 465132
e mljones@swindon.gov.uk **w** swindon.gov.uk/oasis
✉ Bookings Mgr: Michelle Jones 01793 465173. Seated
Capacity: 1580 Standing capacity: 3000

OJK Ltd 6 Lansdowne Mews, London, W11 3BH
t 020 7792 9494 **f** 020 7792 1722
e initialsurname@ojk.co.uk **w** ojk.co.uk ✉ Contact: Patrick
Savage.

Pearson & Co 113 Smug Oak Business Centre,
Lye Lane, Bricket Wood, St Albans, Hertfordshire, AL2 3UG
t 01923 894404 **f** 01923 894990
e richard@stantonpearson.co.uk ✉ Partner: Richard
Pearson.

Pet Sounds One Alfred Pl, London, WC1E 7EB
t 07976 577773 **f** 0871 733 3401
e robin@petsoundsaccounts.co.uk ✉ Director: Robin Hill.

PKF (UK) LLP Farringdon Place, 20 Farringdon Road,
London, EC1M 3AP **t** 020 7065 0000 **f** 020 7065 0650
e info.london@uk.pkf.com **w** pkf.co.uk

PRAGER AND FENTON LLP

PRAGER AND FENTON
PRAGER AND FENTON LLP

8th Floor, Imperial House, 15-19 Kingsway, London,
WC2B 6UN **t** 020 7632 1400 **f** 020 7632 1401
e enquiries@pragerfenton.co.uk **w** pragerfenton.com
✉ Partner: Mark Boomla or Austin Jacobs. Partner: Mark
Boomla. Partner: Austin Jacobs.

PricewaterhouseCoopers 1 Embankment Place,
London, WC2N 6RH **t** 020 7583 5000 **f** 020 7822 4652
e firstname.lastname@uk.pwc.com **w** pwc.com ✉ Head
of UK E&M: Robert W Boyle.

RCO - Royalty Compliance Organisation
10a Sheen Gate Gardens, London, SW14 7NY
t 020 8878 2291 **e** ask@TheRCO.co.uk **w** rcoonline.com
✉ Partners: Mike Skeet, Gill Sharp.

Reeds Copperfields, Mount Pleasant, Crowborough,
East Sussex, TN6 2NF **t** 01892 668676 **f** 01892 668678
✉ Principle: Chris Reed.

ROSS BENNET-SMITH

ROSS BENNET-SMITH
CHARTERED ACCOUNTANTS

Ground Floor, Charles House, 5-11 Regent St, London,
SW1Y 4LR **t** 020 7930 6000 **f** 020 7930 7070
e info@rossbennetsmith.com **w** rossbennetsmith.com
✉ Partner: Daniel Ross.
**Representing many of the worlds' most prominent
recording artists, bands, producers, labels, industry
executives and new talent.**

RSM Robson Rhodes LLP 186 City Road, London,
EC1V 2NU **t** 020 7251 1644 **f** 020 7250 0801
e enquiries@rsmi.co.uk **w** rsmi.co.uk ✉ Contact: Dir of
Communications.

Ryan & Co 4F, Shirland Mews, London, W9 3DY
t 020 8960 0961 **f** 020 8960 0963
e ryan@ryanandco.com **w** ryanandco.com ✉ Chartered
Accountant: Cliff Ryan.

S.C. Song (Accountants) 50 Eaton Drive, Kingston-
Upon-Thames, Surrey, KT2 7QX **t** 07770 816015
f 020 8241 8309 **e** scsong403@msn.com
✉ Accountant: SC Song.

Saffery Champness Lion House, Red Lion St, London,
WC1R 4GB **t** 020 7841 4000 **f** 020 7841 4100
e nick.kelsey@saffery.com **w** saffery.com
✉ Partners: Nick Kelsey, Nick Gaskell.

SEDLEY RICHARD LAURENCE VOULTERS

Kendal House, 1 Conduit St, London, W1S 2XA
t 020 7287 9595 **f** 020 7287 9696 **e** general@srlv.co.uk
w srlv.co.uk ✉ Contact: Richard Rosenberg, Steve Jeffery,
Stephen Marks.

Neville Shulman CBE FCA 35A Huntsworth Mews,
Gloucester Place, London, NW1 6DB **t** 020 7616 0777
f 020 7724 8266 **e** 888@shulman.co.uk **w** shulman.co.uk
✉ Principal: Neville Shulman.

SLOANE & CO.

36-38 Westbourne Grove, Newton Rd, London, W2 5SH
t 020 7221 3292 **f** 020 7229 4810 **e** mail@sloane.co.uk
w sloane.co.uk ✉ Senior Partner: David Sloane.
Partner: Mark Allen. Office Manager: Annabel Fried.
Royalties: Dan Fethers. Head of Audit: Rishi Lokye.
Business Management: Vicky Santamaria.

Ivan Sopher & Company 5 Elstree Gate,
Elstree Way, Borehamwood, Herts, WD6 1JD
t 020 8207 0602 **f** 020 8207 6758
e accounts@ivansopher.co.uk **w** ivansopher.co.uk
✉ Proprietor: Ivan Sopher.

Synergy Business Management 143 Syon Lane,
Osterley, Isleworth, Middlesex, TW7 5PZ **t** 020 8568 0609
f 020 8568 6968 **e** eddie@synergybiz.co.uk
✉ Partner: Eddie Bull 07973 801169.

Tenon Media 66 Chiltern St, London, W1U 4JT
t 020 7535 1400 **f** 020 7535 1401
e julian.hedley@tenongroup.com **w** tenongroup.com
✉ Managing Director: Julian Hedley.

Thomas Harris Chartered Accountants
The 1929 Building, Merton Abbey Mills, Wimbledon,
London, SW19 2RD **t** 020 8542 4262 **f** 020 8545 0662
e ah@thomas-harris.com ✉ Partners: Chris Thomas/Andy
Harris.

Vantis plc 66 Wigmore St, London, W1U 2SB
t 020 7467 4000 **f** 020 7467 4040
e media@vantisplc.com **w** vantisplc.com ✉ Contact: Sarf
Malik.

W John Daniel FCCA The Beam House,
14 Winkfield Rd, Windsor, Berkshire, SL4 4BG
t 01753 852924 **f** 01753 852924
e johndaniel@btconnect.com ✉ Snr Partner: John Daniel.

Warley & Warley Chartered Accountants
76 Cambridge Road, Kingston-Upon-Thames, Surrey,
KT1 3NA **t** 020 8549 5137 **f** 020 8546 3022
e info@warleyandwarley.co.uk **w** warleyandwarley.co.uk
✉ Partner: Andrew Wordingham.

William Evans & Partners 20 Harcourt St, London,
W1H 4HG **t** 020 7563 8390 **f** 020 7569 8700
e wep@williamevans.co.uk ✉ Senior Partner: Stephen
Evans.

Wingrave Yeats Ltd (Chartered Accountants)
65 Duke St, London, W1K 5AJ **t** 020 7495 2244
f 020 7499 9442 **e** wyl@wingrave.co.uk **w** wingrave.co.uk
✉ Partner: Gerry Collins.

Winters 29 Ludgate Hill, London, EC4M 7JE
t 020 7919 9100 **f** 020 7919 9019 **e** info@winters.co.uk
w winters.co.uk ✉ Partner: Roy Bristow.

Wyndhams 177 High St, Harlesden, London, NW10 4TE
t 020 8951 9958 **f** 020 8951 9955
e dlandau@talk21.com ✉ Director: David Landau 020
8961 9952.

Yorke Edition Grove Cottage, Southgate Rd,
South Creake, Fakenham, Norfolk, NR21 9PA
t 01328 823501 **f** 01328 823502
e info@yorkedition.co.uk **w** yorkedition.co.uk
✉ Prop: Rodney Slatford OBE.

Legal

Iain Adam, Solicitor 2 Whitmore Gardens, London,
NW10 5HH **t** 020 8969 5243 **f** 020 8960 2128
✉ Contact: Iain Adam.

Addleshaw Goddard 150 Aldersgate Street, London,
EC1A 4EJ **t** 020 7606 8855 **f** 020 7606 4390
e paddy.graftongreen@addleshawgoddard.com
w addleshawgoddard.com ✉ Partner: Paddy Grafton
Green.

ADR Chambers - Mediators City Point,
1 Ropemaker St, London, EC2Y 9HT **t** 0845 072 0111
f 0845 072 0112 **e** duggan@adrchambers.co.uk
w adrchambers.co.uk ✉ Mediator: Dennis Muirhead
07785 226542.

Angel & Co 1 Green St, Mayfair, London, W1K 6RG
t 020 7495 0555 **f** 020 7495 7550 **e** mail@legalangel-
uk.com **w** legalangel-uk.com ✉ Principal: Nigel Angel.

Anthony Jayes LLP Solicitors, Universal House,
251 Tottenham Court Rd, London, W1T 7JY
t 020 7291 9110 **f** 020 7291 9120 **e** enquiries@ajllp.com
w ajllp.com ✉ Contact: Mary Collier.

Bandname.com 21 Market Pl, Blandford Forum,
Devon, DT11 7AF **e** information@bandname.com
w bandname.com ✉ Manager: Crystal Beaubien.

Baxter McKay Schoenfeld LLP
Suite 208 Panther House, 38 Mount Pleasant, London,
WC1X 0AN **t** 020 7833 9191 **f** 020 7833 9494
e gb@baxtermckay.com ✉ Partner: Gill Baxter.

"WITH US THERE'S NO NEED TO CHECK THE SMALL PRINT"

Amongst the small ads on these pages you'll find many firms and individuals offering you their "legal" services.

What you may not realise however, is that some of them are not even lawyers, let alone solicitors with music industry experience.

So, before you decide who to instruct to negotiate your record deal, publishing contract or management agreement make sure they really do have the necessary knowledge and expertise.

Alternatively, you need look no further than...

DWFM | DWFM BECKMAN SOLICITORS

33 WELBECK STREET, LONDON W1G 8LX
TEL: 020 7872 0023 FAX: 020 7872 0024/5
irving.david@dwfmbeckman.com
www.dwfmbeckman.com

**Contact:
Irving David**

WEB SHERIFF®
WWW.WEBSHERIFF.COM T: +44 (0)208 323 8013

Benedicts (Solicitors) LLP Hope House, 40 St Peters Road, London, W6 9BD **t** 020 8741 6020 **f** 020 8741 8362 **e** john@benedicts.biz **w** benedicts.biz 📧 Partner: John Benedict.

Brabners Chaffe Street 1 Dale St, Liverpool, L2 2ET **t** 0151 600 3000 **f** 0151 600 3009 **e** francis.mcentegart@brabnerscs.com **w** brabnerschaffestreet.com 📧 Solicitor, Media: Francis McEntegart.

Bray and Krais Solicitors
Suites 9 & 10, Fulham Business Exchange, The Boulevard, Imperial Wharf, London, SW6 2TL **t** 020 7384 3050 **f** 020 7384 3051 **e** bandk@brayandkrais.com 📧 Senior Partner: Richard Bray.

Briffa Business Design Centre, 52 Upper Street, Islington, London, N1 0QH **t** 020 7288 6003 **f** 020 7288 6004 **e** info@briffa.com **w** briffa.com 📧 Snr Partner: Margaret Briffa.

CALVERT SOLICITORS

77 Weston Street, London Bridge, London, SE1 3RS **t** 020 7234 0707 **f** 020 7234 0909 **e** nigel@calvertsolicitors.co.uk **w** calvertsolicitors.co.uk 📧 Senior Partner: Nigel Calvert.

Cambridge Civil Mediation Sheraton House, Castle Pk, Cambridge, CB3 0AX **t** 01223 370063 **f** 01223 307277 **e** john.byrne@ccmediation.co.uk 📧 Mediator: John Byrne.

Campbell Hooper Solicitors LLP
35 Old Queen Street, London, SW1H 9JD **t** 020 7222 9070 **f** 020 7222 5591 **e** paulrenney@campbellhooper.com **w** campbellhooper.com 📧 Contact: Paul Renney.

Charles Russell LLP, Solicitors 5 Fleet Pl, London, EC4M 7RD **t** 020 7203 5134 **f** 020 7203 5002 **e** michael.cover@charlesrussell.co.uk; mc@michaelcover.com **w** charlesrussell.co.uk 📧 Partner: Michael Cover.

Christopher Wilkins Chichester, West Sussex **t** 07921 789992 **e** chris@christopher-wilkins.com **w** christopher-wilkins.com 📧 Mediator: Christopher Wilkins.

Clintons 55 Drury Lane, London, WC2B 5RZ **t** 020 7379 6080 **f** 020 7240 9310 **e** amyers@clintons.co.uk **w** clintons.co.uk 📧 Contact: Andrew Myers, Peter Button, Nicky Stein.

Cobbetts LLP One Colmore Sq, Birmingham, B4 6AJ **t** 0845 404 2404 **f** 0845 166 6279 **e** frances.anderson@cobbetts.com **w** cobbetts.com 📧 Partner: Frances Anderson.

Collins Long Solicitors 24 Pepper St, London, SE1 0EB **t** 020 7401 9800 **f** 020 7401 9850 **e** info@collinslong.com **w** collinslong.com 📧 Partners: James Collins & Simon Long.

COLLYER BRISTOW LLP SOLICITORS

Collyer Bristow

4 Bedford Row, London, WC1R 4DF **t** 020 7242 7363 **f** 020 7405 0555 **e** howard.ricklow@collyerbristow.com **w** collyerbristow.com 📧 Partner: Howard Ricklow.

Davenport Lyons 30 Old Burlington St, London, W1S 3NL **t** 020 7468 2600 **f** 020 7437 8216 **e** mbrown@davenportlyons.com **w** davenportlyons.com 📧 Contact: Michelle Brown.

Dean Marsh & Co 73A Middle St, Brighton, BN1 1AL **t** 01273 823770 **f** 01273 208766 **e** dean@creativelaw.eu **w** creativelaw.eu 📧 MD: Dean Marsh.

Dennis Muirhead 202 Fulham Rd, Chelsea, London, SW10 9PJ **t** 07460 4668 **e** dennis@muirheadmanagement.co.uk **w** muirheadmanagement.co.uk 📧 Mediator: Dennis Muirhead 07785 226542.

DWFM Beckman Solicitors 33 Welbeck Street, London, W1G 8LX **t** 020 7872 0023 **f** 020 7872 0024 **e** irving.david@dwfmbeckman.com **w** dwfmbeckman.com 📧 Contact: Irving David.

DWFM BECKMAN

DWFM | D W F M   B E C K M A N
        | S O L I C I T O R S

33 Welbeck St, London, W1G 8LX **t** 020 7872 0023 **f** 020 7872 0024 **e** irving.david@dwfmbeckman.com **w** dwfmbeckman.com 📧 Contact: Irving David.

Effective Legal Services Waters Edge Frogmill, Frogmill, Hurley, Berks, SL6 5NL **t** 01628 820 000 **f** 01628 820 000 **e** henriette@effectivemusicservices.com **w** effectivemusicservices.com 📧 Solicitor: Henriette Amiel 07808 741 277.

WEB SHERIFF®
WWW.WEBSHERIFF.COM T: +44 (0)208 323 8013

ELA MUSIC - ENTERTAINMENT LAW ASSOCIATES

Argentum, 2 Queen Caroline St, London, W6 9DX
t 020 3178 7687 **f** 020 8323 8080 **e** ela@ela.co.uk
w ela.co.uk ⬛ MD: John Giacobbi.

Ent-Law Solicitors 3 Grange Farm Business Park, Shedfield, Southampton, Hampshire, SO32 2HD
t 01329 834100 **f** 01329 834448 **e** paul@ent-law.co.uk
⬛ Contact: Paul Lambeth LLB.

Entertainment Advice Ltd. 31 Penrose St, London, SE17 3DW **t** 020 7708 8822 **f** 020 7703 1239
e info@entertainmentadvice.co.uk
w entertainmentadvice.co.uk
⬛ Consultant/Lawyer: Anthony Hall.

Entertainment Industry Legal Services Ltd
37 Trinity Rd, E.Finchley, London, N2 8JJ **t** 020 8365 2962
f 020 8365 2484 **e** howard@hlivingstone.fsnet.co.uk
w musicattorney.co.uk ⬛ Music Lawyer (Retired Solicitor): Howard Livingstone.

ePM Online PO Box 47264, London, W7 1WX
t 020 8566 0200 **e** anne@epm-music.com **w** epm-music.com 🟥 myspace.com/epmonline ⬛ Contact: Anne Jenniskens LLM.

F C Cotton & Co 46 University St, Belfast, Northern Ireland, BT7 1HB **t** 07775 657234
f 08707 625672 **e** francotton@fccotton.com
w fccotton.com ⬛ Contact: Fran Cotton.

Finers Stephens Innocent 179 Great Portland St, London, W1W 5LF **t** 020 7323 4000 **f** 020 7580 7069
e marketing@fsilaw.co.uk **w** fsilaw.com ⬛ Partner: Robert Lands.

FORBES ANDERSON FREE

SOLICITORS
16-18 Berners St, London, W1T 3LN **t** 020 7291 3500
f 020 7291 3511 **e** info@forbesanderson.com
⬛ Partners: Andrew Forbes, Dominic Free & Martyn Bailey.

Forte Law The Cottage, Penmark, Vale of Glamorgan, CF62 3BP **t** 01446 713 599
e pamela.forte@fortelaw.co.uk **w** fortelaw.co.uk
⬛ Solicitor: Pamela Forte.

Fox Williams Ten Dominion Street, London, EC2M 2EE
t 020 7628 2000 **f** 020 7628 2100
e mail@foxwilliams.com **w** foxwilliams.com ⬛ Senior Associate: Jane Elliot.

GB Law 4B, Mascalls Lane, Brentwood, Essex, CM14 5LR
t 01277 231177 **f** 01277 226521
e info@gblawyers.co.uk ⬛ Senior Partner: Dale Beeson.

Goldkorn Mathias Gentle 6 Coptic Street, London, WC1A 1NW **t** 020 7631 1811 **f** 020 7631 0431
e davidgentle@gmglegal.com ⬛ Partner: David Gentle.

Gray & Co. Habib House, 3rd Floor, 9 Stevenson Sq, Piccadilly, Manchester, Greater Manchester, M1 1DB
t 0161 237 3360 **f** 0161 236 6717 **e** info@grayand.co.uk
w grayand.co.uk 🟥 myspace.com/grayandco
⬛ Principal: Rudi Kidd 07711 269 939.

GSC Solicitors 31-32 Ely Place, London, EC1N 6TD
t 020 7822 2222 **f** 020 7822 2211
e info@gscsolicitors.com **w** gscsolicitors.com ⬛ Senior Partner: Saleem Sheikh.

Hamlins Roxburghe House, 273-287 Regent St, London, W1B 2AD **t** 020 7355 6000 **f** 020 7518 9100
e w.farrow@hamlins.co.uk **w** hamlins.co.uk
⬛ Partner: Laurence Gilmore.

Harbottle and Lewis Hanover House, 14 Hanover Sq, London, W1S 1HP **t** 020 7667 5000 **f** 020 7667 5100
e hal@harbottle.com **w** harbottle.com ⬛ Head of Music Group: Paul Jones.

Harrisons Entertainment Law Ltd

8 The Glasshouse, 49a Goldhawk Rd, London, W12 8QP
t 020 8749 7377 **f** 020 8749 4643
e info@annharrison.co.uk **w** annharrison.co.uk
⬛ Principal: Ann Harrison.

Helen Searle - Legal & Business Adviser
End Cottage, Posingford Farm, Hartfield, East Sussex, TN7 4HA **t** 01892 770286 **e** helen@helensearle.com
⬛ Partner: Helen Searle 07973 663494.

Howell-Jones Partnership Flint House, 52 High St, Leatherhead, Surrey, KT22 8AJ **t** 01372 860 650
f 01372 860 659 **e** leatherhead@howell-jones.com
w howell-jones.com ⬛ Snr Partner: Peter Scott.

Independent Label Scheme 73A Middle Street, Brighton, BN1 1AL **t** 01273 823 770 **f** 01273 823 771
e dean@indielabelscheme.com **w** indielabelscheme.com
⬛ Principal: Dean Marsh.

Independent Music Law Advice 14 Vane Close, Hampstead, London, NW3 5UN **t** 07748 593758
f 020 7433 3266 **e** elliot@musiclawadvice.co.uk
w musiclawadvice.co.uk 📘 facebook.com/elliot.musiclaw
🟥 myspace.com/musiclawadvice
🟦 twitter.com/EllMusiclaw ⬛ Independent Music Law Adviser: Elliot Chalmers.

IPS Law LLP 2nd Floor, 5 Ridgefield, Manchester, M2 6EG **t** 0161 830 4710 **f** 0161 830 4711
e firstname.lastname@IPSLaw.co.uk **w** ipslaw.co.uk
⬛ Music Lawyer: Eleanor Brody.

Jane Clemetson 85 Charing Cross Rd, London, WC2H 0AA **t** 020 7287 1380 **f** 020 7734 3394
e jane.clemetson@clemetson.co.uk ⬛ Contact: Jane Clemetson.

Business Services: Legal

WEB SHERIFF®
WWW.WEBSHERIFF.COM T: +44 (0)208 323 8013

Jens Hills Solicitors LLP Northburgh House, 10 Northburgh St, London, EC1V 0AT **t** 020 7490 8160 **f** 020 7490 8140 **e** info@jenshills.com **w** jenshillssolicitors.com ✆ Senior Partner: Jens Hills.

Jim Cook 38 Grovelands Rd, London, N13 4RH **t** 020 8882 3370 **f** 020 8350 0613 **e** jim@jcook21.freeserve.co.uk ✆ Business Affairs / Legal Adviser: Jim Cook.

John Byrne & Co Sheraton House, Castle Pk, Cambridge, CB3 0AX **t** 01223 370063 **f** 01223 307277 **e** JB@johnbyrne.co.uk ✆ Principal: John Byrne.

John Ireland & Co - Unique & Natural Talent 57 Elgin Crescent, London, W11 2JU **t** 020 7792 1666 **f** 0870 051 6570 **e** john@johnirelandandco.net **w** johnirelandandco.net ✆ Contact: John Ireland.

Kirkpatrick & Lockhart Preston Gates Ellis LLP 110 Cannon St, London, EC4N 6AR **t** 020 7648 9000 **f** 020 7648 9001 **e** nigel.davies@klgates.com **w** klgates.com ✆ Partner: Nigel Davies.

Lawrence Harrison Limited 60 Redston Rd, London, N8 7HE **t** 020 8348 1616 **e** info@lawrenceharrison.co.uk **w** lawrenceharrison.co.uk ✆ Director: Lawrence Harrison.

Laytons Solicitors 22 St John St, Manchester, M3 4EB **t** 0161 834 2100 **f** 0161 834 6862 **e** music@laytons.com ✆ Music Law Department: Eleanor Brody or David Sefton.

Lazarus Media Cydale House, 249A West End Lane, London, NW6 1XN **t** 020 7794 1666 **f** 020 7794 1666 **e** info@lazarusmedia.co.uk **w** lazarusmedia.co.uk ✆ MD: Steve Lazarus 07976 239140.

Lea & Company Solicitors Bank Chambers, Market Pl, Stockport, Cheshire, SK1 1UN **t** 0161 480 6691 **f** 0161 480 0904 **e** mail@lealaw.com **w** lealaw.com ✆ Partner: Stephen Lea.

Lee & Thompson Greengarden House, 15-22 St Christopher's Pl, London, W1U 1NL **t** 020 7935 4665 **f** 020 7563 4949 **e** mail@leeandthompson.com **w** leeandthompson.com ✆ Partner: Andrew Thompson.

The Legal Side Limited 14 Birchlands Ave, London, SW12 8ND **t** 020 8675 5747 **f** 020 8675 9101 **e** sally@legalside.co.uk ✆ Principal: Sally Bevan.

LEONARD LOWY & CO

LEONARD LOWY & CO. Solicitors

85-87 Bayham St, London, NW1 0AG **t** 020 7788 4333 **f** 0870 880 9435 **e** lowy@leonardlowy.co.uk **w** leonardlowy.co.uk ✆ Principal: Leonard Lowy.

Lewis Davis Shapiro & Lewit see Smiths

Lewis Silkin LLP 5 Chancery Lane, Clifford's Inn, London, EC4A 1BL **t** 020 7074 8000 **f** 020 7864 1264 **e** becky.gillett@lewissilkin.com **w** lewissilkin.com ✆ Contact: Becky Gillett.

Lipkin Gorman 61 Grosvenor Street, Mayfair, London, W1K 3JE **t** 020 7493 4010 **f** 020 7409 1734 ✆ Partner: Charles Gorman.

Lovells Atlantic House, Holborn Viaduct, London, EC1A 2FG **t** 020 7296 2000 **f** 020 7296 2001 **e** penelope.thornton@lovells.com **w** lovells.com ✆ Senior Associate: Penelope Thornton.

Maclay Murray & Spens LLP 151 St Vincent St, Glasgow, G2 5NJ **t** 0141 248 5011 **f** 0141 248 5819 **e** andy.harris@mms.co.uk **w** mms.co.uk ✆ Contact: Andy Harris.

Magrath LLP 66/67 Newman St, London, W1T 3EQ **t** 020 7495 3003 **f** 020 7317 6738 **e** alexis.grower@magrath.co.uk **w** magrath.co.uk ✆ Consultant: Alexis Grower.

Manches Aldwych House, 81 Aldwych, London, WC2B 4RP **t** 020 7404 4433 **f** 020 7430 1133 **e** manches@manches.co.uk **w** manches.co.uk

Marriott Harrison Staple Inn, 11 Staple Inn Buildings, London, WC1V 7QH **t** 020 7209 2000 **f** 020 7209 2001 **e** tony.morris@marriottharrison.co.uk **w** marriottharrison.com ✆ Partner & Head of Media: Tony Morris 020 7209 2093.

Martine Alan 271 Regent St, London, W1B 2ES **t** 020 3089 4086 **e** martine@martinealan.co.uk ✆ myspace.com/martinealan ✆ twitter.com/martinealan ✆ Music Lawyer: Martine Alan 07944 558175.

MC Kirton & Co 83 St Albans Avenue, London, W4 5JS **t** 020 8987 8880 **f** 020 8181 4989 **e** michael@mckirton.com ✆ Snr Partner: Michael Kirton.

McClure Naismith 292 St Vincent St, Glasgow, Lanarkshire, G2 5TQ **t** 0141 204 2700 **f** 0141 248 3998 **e** eduncan@mcclurenaismith.com **w** mcclurenaismith.com ✆ IP Partner: Euan Duncan.

Metcalfes Solicitors 46-48 Queen Sq, Bristol, BS1 4LY **t** 0117 929 0451 **f** 0117 929 9551 **e** mburgess@metcalfes.co.uk **w** metcalfes.co.uk ✆ Entertainment Lawyer: Martino Burgess.

MICHAEL SIMKINS LLP

Michael Simkins LLP
SOLICITORS

Lynton House, 7-12 Tavistock Sq, London, WC1H 9LT **t** 020 7874 5600 **f** 020 7874 5601 **e** euan.lawson@simkins.com **w** simkins.com ✆ Partner: Euan Lawson.

Business Services: Legal

Miller Rosenfalck LLP Aylesbury House, 17-18 Aylesbury Street, London, EC1R 0DB **t** 020 7553 9932 **f** 020 7490 5060 **e** so@europeanbusinesslawyers.com **w** europeanbusinesslawyers.com ✉ Solicitor (England & Wales) & Avocat (France): Sebastien Oddos.

Robin Morton, Solicitor 22 Herbert Street, Glasgow, G20 6NB **t** 0141 560 2748 or 0141 337 1199 **f** 0141 357 0655 **e** robinmorto@aol.com ✉ Contact: Robin Morton 07870 590 909.

Murray Buchanan Associates 272 Bath St, Glasgow, G2 4JR **t** 0141 354 1660 **f** 0141 354 1661 **e** mail@mba-legal.com **w** mba-legal.com ✉ Contact: Murray Buchanan.

Music Royalty Investigations Ash House, 8 Second Cross Rd, Twickenham, TW2 8RF **t** 020 8894 3486 **e** david@musicroyaltyinvestigations.com **w** musicroyaltyinvestigations.com ✉ MD: David Morgan 07802 217064.

Nigel Dewar Gibb & Co Solicitors 43 St John St, London, EC1M 4AN **t** 020 7608 1091 **f** 020 7608 1092 **e** ndg@e-legaluk.co.uk **w** e-legaluk.co.uk ✉ Principal: Nigel Dewar Gibb.

Northrop McNaughtan Deller 18c Pindock Mews, Little Venice, London, W9 2PY **t** 020 7289 7300 **f** 020 7286 9555 **e** nmd@nmdsolicitors.com **w** nmdsolicitors.com ✉ Partners: Tim Northrop, Christy McNaughtan, Martin Deller.

Olswang 90 High Holborn, London, WC1V 6XX **t** 020 7067 3000 **f** 020 7067 3999 **e** olsmail@olswang.com **w** olswang.com ✉ Partner: John Enser.

P Ganz & Co Hawks Hill Studio, Hawks Hill Lane, Bredgar, Kent, ME9 8HE **t** 01795 830009 **f** 01795 830195 **e** penny.ganz@ganzlegal.com **w** www.ganzlegal ✉ Solicitor: Penny Ganz.

P Russell & Co, Solicitors Suite 61, London House, 271 King St, London, W6 9LZ **t** 020 8233 2943 **f** 020 8233 2944 **e** info@prcsolicitors.com ✉ Partner: Paul Russell.

Peter Last 75 Holland Rd, Kensington, London, W14 8HL **t** 020 7603 4245 ✉ Lawyer: Peter Last (LL.B, LL.M).

Pinsent Curtis Biddle 1 Gresham Street, London, EC2V 7BU **t** 020 7606 9301 **f** 020 7606 3305 **e** martin.lane@pinsents.com **w** pinsents.com ✉ Managing Ptnr: Martin Lane.

Business Services: Legal

Pitmans SK Sport and Entertainment LLP
I Crown Court, 66 Cheapside, London, EC2V 6LR
t 020 7634 4620 **f** 020 7634 4621
e ndewargibb@pitmans.com; jsummers@pitmans.com
w sk-se.com ☻ Solicitors: Nigel Dewar Gibb, Jeremy
Summers.

Quastels Midgen LLP 74 Wimpole St, London,
W1G 9RR **t** 020 7908 2525 **f** 020 7908 2626
e jspalter@quastels.com **w** quastels.com
☻ Partner: Julian Spalter 0207908 2543.

RafterMarsh Suite 404, Albany House, 324-
326 Regent St, London, W1B 3HH **t** 020 3371 7662
f 020 3031 1086 **e** terry@raftermarsh.com
☻ Solicitor: Terry Marsh.

Randall Harper – Solicitor Lawyers Direct,
53 Davies Street, London, W1K 5JH **t** 07713 258 767
f 08454 589398 **e** Randall.Harper@lawyers-direct.biz
w randall-harper-solicitor.com ☻ Consulting
Solicitor: Randall Harper.

Rohan & Co Solicitors Aviation House, 1-
7 Sussex Rd, Haywards Heath, West Sussex, RH16 4DZ
t 01444 450901 **f** 01444 440437
e partners@rohansolicitors.co.uk
w www.rohansolicitors.com ☻ Contact: Rupert Rohan.

Ross & Craig 12A Upper Berkeley Street, London,
W1H 7QE **t** 020 7262 3077 **f** 020 7724 6427
e david.leadercramer@rosscraig.com **w** rosscraig.com
☻ MD: David Leadercramer.

James Rubinstein & Co 149 Cholmley Gardens,
Mill Lane, London, NW6 1AB **t** 020 7431 5500
f 020 7431 5600 **e** help@jamesrubinstein.co.uk
w jamesrubinstein.co.uk ☻ Senior Partner: James
Rubinstein.

Russell-Cooke 8 Bedford Row, London, WC1R 4BX
t 020 7440 4843 **f** 020 7611 1721 **e** surname@russell-
cooke.co.uk **w** russell-cooke.co.uk ☻ Partner: Lawrence
Harrison.

Russells Regency House, 1-4 Warwick St, London,
W1B 5LJ **t** 020 7439 8692 **f** 020 7494 3582
e brianh@russells.co.uk **w** russellslaw.co.uk ☻ Snr
Partner: Brian Howard.

Sample 1 Ltd 10 Crystal Palace Rd, London, SE22 9HB
t 020 8637 9795 **f** 020 8516 5572 **e** info@sample1.co.uk
w sample1.co.uk ☻ MD: Mark Pearse.

Sample Clearance Services Ltd 28 Clifton Rd,
Brighton, East Sussex, BN1 3HN **t** 07540 97800
f 01273 381913 **e** saranne@sampleclearance.com
w sampleclearance.com ☻ Managing Director: Saranne
Reid 07976 662014.

Schillings 41 Bedford Sq, London, WC1B 3HX
t 020 7034 9000 **f** 020 7034 9200
e legal@schillings.co.uk **w** schillings.co.uk ☻ Partner: John
Kelly.

Seddons 5 Portman Square, London, W1H 6NT
t 020 7725 8000 **f** 020 7935 5049
e enquiries@seddons.co.uk **w** seddons.co.uk
☻ Partner: David Kent.

Sheridans Whittington House, Alfred Pl, London,
WC1E 7EA **t** 020 7079 0100 **f** 020 7079 0200
e sluckman@sheridans.co.uk **w** sheridans.co.uk
☻ twitter.com/sheridansuk ☻ Partner: Stephen Luckman.

Simons Muirhead & Burton 8 - 9 Frith St, London,
W1D 3JB **t** 020 3206 2700 **f** 020 3206 2800
e info@smab.co.uk **w** smab.co.uk ☻ Partner: Simon
Goldberg.

Smiths 17 Shorts Gardens, Covent Garden, London,
WC2H 9AT **t** 020 7395 8630 **f** 020 7395 8639
e lewis@smiths-law.com **w** smiths-law.com
☻ Partner: Andrew Lewis.

Sound Advice Music Services PO Box 567,
Durham, DH1 9GN, Durham, County Durham
e soundadvice@fsmail.net
w soundadvicemusicservices.co.uk ☻ Contact: Mick
Burgess 07861 023566.

SSB Solicitors Matrix Complex, 91 Peterborough Rd,
London, SW6 3BU **t** 020 7348 7630 **f** 020 7348 7631
e legal@ssb.co.uk **w** ssb.co.uk ☻ Partner: Paul Spraggon.

Statham Gill Davies 54 Welbeck St, London,
W1G 9XS **t** 020 7317 3210 **f** 020 7487 5925
e john.statham@sgdlaw.com ☻ Solicitor/Partner: John
Statham.

Steeles Law LLP Bedford House, 21A John Street,
London, WC1N 2BF **t** 020 7421 1720 **f** 020 7421 1749
e media@steeleslaw.co.uk **w** steeleslaw.co.uk
☻ Specialist Music Lawyers: Steven Fisher, Simon Conroy.

Swan Turton 68a Neal St, Covent Garden, London,
WC2H 9PA **t** 020 7520 9555 **f** 020 7520 9556
e info@swanturton.com **w** swanturton.com ☻ Head of
Music Group: Julian Turton.

Tarlo Lyons Watchmaker Court, 33 St John's Lane,
London, EC1M 4DB **t** 020 7405 2000 **f** 020 7814 9421
e info@tarlolyons.com **w** tarlolyons.com
☻ Partners: Stanley Munson, D Michael Rose.

Taylor Wessing 5 New Street Sq, London, EC4A 3TW
t 020 7300 7000 **f** 020 7300 7100
e london@taylorwessing.com **w** taylorwessing.com
☻ Partner: Paul Mitchell.

Teacher Stern LLP 37-41 Bedford Row, London,
WC1R 4JH **t** 020 7242 3191 **f** 020 7242 1156
e d.salisbury@teacherstern.com **w** teacherstern.com
☻ Snr Partner: David Salisbury.

Tods Murray LLP Edinburgh Quay, 133 Fountainbridge,
Edinburgh, EH3 9AG **t** 0131 656 2000 **f** 0131 656 2020
e firstname.lastname@todsmurray.com
w todsmurray.com ☻ Contact: Andy Harris or Richard
Findlay.

Tods Murray LLP (Glasgow) 33 Bothwell St,
Glasgow, G2 6NL **t** 0141 275 4771 **f** 0141 275 4781
e richard.findlay@todsmurray.com **w** todsmurray.com
☻ Entertainment Law Partner: Richard Findlay 0131 656
2276.

WEB SHERIFF®
WWW.WEBSHERIFF.COM T: +44 (0)208 323 8013

Turner Parkinson LLP Hollins Chambers, 64a Bridge St, Manchester, M3 3BA **t** 0161 833 1212 **f** 0161 834 9098 **e** andrew.booth@tp.co.uk **w** tp.co.uk Partner: Andy Booth.

Van Straten Solicitors RB Building, Portobello Dock, 557 Harrow Rd, London, W10 4RH **t** 020 8588 9660 **f** 020 8969 7285 **e** adam@vanstraten.co.uk **w** vanstraten.co.uk Contact: Adam Van Straten, Talya Shalson and Adam Brown.

The Waterfront Partnership 5 The Leathermarket, Weston Street, London, SE1 3ER **t** 020 7234 0200 **f** 020 7234 0600 **e** music@waterfrontpartnership.com **w** waterfrontpartnership.com Solicitor: Alison Berryman.

WEB SHERIFF

Argentum, 2 Queen Caroline Street, London, W6 9DX **t** 020 8323 8013 **f** 020 8323 8080 **e** websheriff@websheriff.com **w** websheriff.com MD: John Giacobbi.

WGS Solicitors 133 Praed St, London, W2 1RN **t** 020 7723 1656 **f** 020 7724 6936 **e** cl@wgs.co.uk **w** wgs.co.uk Partner: Charles Law.

Wiggin 10th Floor, The Met Building, 22 Percy St, London, W1T 2BU **t** 020 7612 9612 **f** 01242 224223 **e** alexander.ross@wiggin.co.uk **w** wiggin.co.uk Partner: Alexander Ross 07917 037204.

Zimmers Solicitors Rechtsanwaelte 5 Water Lane, London, NW1 8NZ **t** 020 7284 6970 **f** 020 7284 6980 **e** hanna.weber@zimmerslaw.com **w** zimmerslaw.com European Registered Lawyer: Hanna Weber.

Insurance

APEX Insurance Services Ltd Riverbank House, 1 Putney Bridge Approach, London, SW6 3JD **t** 020 7384 9222 **f** 020 7384 4411 **e** martin@apex-ins.co.uk **w** APEX-ins.co.uk Contact: Martin Goebbels, Pamela Choat.

NW Brown Insurance Brokers Ltd Richmond House, 16-20 Regent St, Cambridge, CB2 1DB **t** 01223 720310 **f** 01223 353705 **e** richard.rampley@nwbrown.co.uk **w** nwbrown.co.uk Account Exec: Richard Rampley.

Christie's Pop Memorabilia Auctions 85 Old Brompton Road, London, SW7 3LD **t** 020 7839 9060 **f** 020 7752 3183 **e** nroberts@christies.com **w** christies.com Head of Deptartment: Neil Roberts 020 7321 3281.

Doodson Albemarle 8 New Concordia Wharf, Mill Street, London, SE1 2BB **t** 020 7237 6809 **f** 020 7394 2154 **e** mark@albemarleinsurance.com **w** albemarleinsurance.com Contact: Mark Whayling.

Doodson Albemarle Unit 8 New Concordia Wharf, Mill St, London, SE1 2BB **t** 020 7237 6809 **f** 020 7394 2154 **e** mark@albemarleinsurance.com **w** albemarleinsurance.com Contact: Mark Whayling 020 7394 2153.

Doodson Entertainment Century House, Pepper Rd, Hazel Grove, SK7 5BW **t** 0161 419 3000 **f** 0161 419 3068 **e** rdoodson@doodsonbg.com **w** doodsonbg.com Dir: Richard Doodson.

Honour Point Limited 88 Hagley Rd, Edgbaston, Birmingham, West Midlands, B16 8LU **t** 0121 454 8388 **f** 0121 454 6685 **e** info@honour-point.co.uk **w** honour-point.co.uk Managing Director: Dominic Dolan.

La Playa The Stables, Manor Farm, Milton Road, Impington, Cambridge, CB4 9NF **t** 01223 522411 **f** 01223 237942 **e** media@laplaya.co.uk **w** laplaya.co.uk MD: Mark Boon.

Lark Insurance Ibex House, 42-47 Minories, London, EC3N 1DY **t** 020 8557 2410 **f** 020 7543 2801 **e** info@larkinsurance.co.uk **w** larkinsurance.co.uk/musical_instruments.html Musical Instrument Insurance Advisor: Clare Cromwell.

LongReach International Ltd 20-21 Took's Court, London, EC4A 1LB **t** 020 8421 7555 **f** 020 8421 7550 **e** ri@longreachint.com **w** longreachint.com Dir: Rick Inglessis.

Musicguard (Pavilion Insurance Management Ltd) Pavilion House, Mercia Business Village, Westwood Business Park, Coventry, CV4 8HX **t** 02476 851000 **f** 02476 851080 **e** sales@musicguard.co.uk **w** musicguard.co.uk Sales Dir: Sarah Gow.

Robertson Taylor Insurance Brokers Ltd 33 Harbour Exchange Square, London, E14 9GG **t** 020 7510 1234 **f** 020 7510 1134 **e** paul.twomey@rtib.co.uk **w** robertson-taylor.com myspace.com/robertsontaylorinsurance New Business Manager: Paul Twomey.

Stafford Knight Entertainment Insurance Brokers 55 Aldgate High Street, London, EC3N 1AL **t** 020 7481 6262 **f** 020 7481 7638 **e** tony.crawford@towergate.co.uk Divisional Dir: Tony Crawford.

Swinglehurst Ltd St Clare House, 30-33 Minories, London, EC3N 2DD **t** 020 7480 6969 **f** 020 7480 6996 **e** lastname@swinglehurst.co.uk **w** swinglehurst.co.uk Partner: Gordon Devlin.

Business Services: Legal, Insurance

WEB SHERIFF®
WWW.WEBSHERIFF.COM T: +44 (0)208 323 8013

Financial Advisors

Aaron Knight Saili Associates Ltd
27 Lynwood Avenue, Langley, Berkshire, SL3 7BJ
t 01753 676300 **f** 05601 162288 **e** arun@aksaili.com
w aksaili.com ☎ Director: Arun Saili.

Albemarle Insurance 7 Hodgkinson Farm, Boot Lane,
Heaton, Bolton, BL1 5ST **t** 01204 840444
f 01204 841411 ☎ Contact: Ruth Sandler.

Blacktower Financial Advisers Ltd
105 St Peter's St, St Albans, Hertfordshire, AL1 3EJ
t 01727 896 033 **f** 01727 896 001 **e** sta@bfa-uk.com
w bfa-uk.com ☎ Director: Derek Prentice.

Chelver Media Finance First Floor, Kendal House,
1 Conduit St, London, W1S 2XA **t** 020 7287 7087
f 020 7287 9696 **e** steve@ccdb.cc **w** ccdb.cc
☎ Contact: Steve Cherry.

Collins Financial Consultants Ltd
First Floor Building 1, Gateway 1000,
Whittle Way, Arlington Business Pk, Stevenage,
Hertfordshire, SG1 2FP **t** 01438 364439 **f** 01438 364500
e CFC@sjpp.co.uk **w** sjpp.co.uk/cfc ☎ Director: Paul
Collins.

Craig Ryle Financial Ltd 62 Lake Rise, Romford,
Essex, RM1 4EE **t** 01708 760 544 **f** 01708 760 563
e mail@craigryle.fsnet.co.uk ☎ Director: Linda Ryle.

HCF Partnership Devonshire House,
582 Honeypot Lane, Stanmore, Middlesex, HA7 1JS
t 020 8731 5151 **f** 020 8731 5178 **e** enquiries@hcf.co.uk
w hcfpartnership.co.uk ☎ Director: Kevin Simmonds.

Jelf Group plc 2 Palace Yard Mews, Bath, BA1 2NH
t 01225 822 036 **f** 01225 329 028
e tony.thorpe@jelfgroup.com **w** jelfgroup.com
☎ Associate Director: Tony Thorpe 07767 212 181.

LongReach International Ltd 20-21 Took's Court,
London, EC4A 1LB **t** 020 8421 7555 **f** 020 8421 7550
e ri@longreachint.com **w** longreachint.com ☎ Dir: Rick
Inglessis.

The Manor Partnership 9 Hayters Court, Grigg Lane,
Brockenhurst, Southampton, SO42 7PG **t** 01590 622 477
f 01590 622 481 **e** howard.lucas@tmp-uk.com
w themanorpartnership.com ☎ Dir: Howard Lucas.

MGR Media 55 Loudoun Road, St John's Wood, London,
NW8 0DL **t** 020 7625 4545 **f** 020 7625 5265
e info@mgrmedia.com **w** atfgroup.com

Music Media IFA Ltd Bright Cook House,
139 Upper Richmond Road, London, SW15 2TX
t 020 8780 0988 **f** 020 8780 1594
e post@musicmedia.co.uk **w** musicmedia.co.uk
☎ Planning Dir: Malcolm Lyons.

Smith & Williamson 30 Queen Square, Bristol,
BS1 4ND **t** 0117 925 7603 **f** 0117 922 5105
e tt1@smith.williamson.co.uk **w** smith.williamson.co.uk
☎ Senior Consultant: Tony Thorpe.

WTK Wealth Management Limited Regus House,
Manchester Business Park, 3000 Aviator Way, Manchester,
M22 5TG **t** 01625 599 944 **f** 01625 599 001
e info@wtkltd.com **w** wtkltd.com

Artist Management

1 2 One Entertainment Ltd. Unit 6, 53-
55 Theobalds Rd, London, WC1X 8SP **t** 020 7685 8595
e Paul@12one.net **w** 12one.net
☎ myspace.com/pk12one ☎ MD: Paul Kennedy.

1-2-hear management East London **e** clare@1-2-
hear.com **w** .1-2-hear.com ☎ myspace.com/claretucker1
☎ Director / artist manager: Clare Tucker 07900 452378.

10 Management London **t** 020 7467 0622
e jonathan@10management.com ☎ Manager: Jonathan
Wild.

140dB Artist Management Ltd The Chapel,
Everwood Court, Maybury Gardens, London, NW10 2AF
t 020 8208 5660 **f** 020 8459 3789 **e** first
name@140db.co.uk **w** 140db.co.uk
☎ http://www.140db.co.uk: Ros Earls or Justin Pritchard
0208 208 5660.

19 Management 33 Ransomes Dock, 35-
37 Parkgate Road, London, SW11 4NP **t** 020 7801 1919
f 020 7801 1920 **e** reception@19.co.uk **w** 19.co.uk
☎ MD: Simon Fuller.

**2-Tuff-Oscar Sam-Carrol Creative
Management** PO Box 7874, London, SW20 9XD
t 07050 605219 **f** 07050 605239 **e** sam@pan-africa.org
w umengroup.com ☎ CEO: Oscar Sam-Carrol Jnr.

21st Artists 1 Blythe Rd, London, W14 0HG
t 020 7348 4800 **f** 020 7348 4801 **e** info@wabbie.com
w eltonjohn.com ☎ Dir: Frank Presland, Clive Banks.

2Point9 Second Floor, 9 Bourlet Close, London,
W1W 7BP **t** 07801 033741 **e** office2@2point9.com
w 2point9.com ☎ myspace.com/2point9
☎ youtube.com/2point9Records ☎ Directors: Billy Grant,
Rob Stuart.

3cord Management 54 Portobello Road, London,
W11 3DL **t** 020 7229 9218 **e** simon@3cord.net
☎ Manager: Simon Hicks.

3rd Stone PO Box 8, Corby, Northants, NN17 2XZ
t 01536 202 295 **f** 01536 266 246
e steve@adasam.co.uk **w** adasam.co.uk ☎ Label
Mgr: Steve Kalidoski.

4 Tunes Management PO Box 36534, London,
W4 3XE **t** 020 8442 7560 **f** 020 8442 7561 **e** andy@4-
tunes.com **w** 4-tunes.com ☎ MD: Andy Murray.

7pm Management PO Box 2272, Rottingdean,
Brighton, BN2 8XD **t** 01273 304 681 **f** 01273 308 120
e seven@7pmmanagement.com
w 7pmmanagement.com ☎ Director: Seven Webster.

A Readman 6 Puslane, Wokingham, Berks, RG40 2DD
t 0118 978 2910 **e** annareadman@hotmail.com
w areadman.co.uk ☎ MD: Anna Readman.

WEB SHERIFF®
WWW.WEBSHERIFF.COM T: +44 (0)208 323 8013

A&S Management London **t** 020 7209 2586
f 020 8459 2759 **e** andy@aandsmanagement.com,
sue@aandsmanagement.com ✉ Contact: Andy Hart, Sue
Whitehouse.

Ablaze Management Unit 209,
Coborn Business House, 3 Coborn Road, London, E3 2DA
t 020 8980 9081 **e** nadia@ablazepr.com
✉ Director: Nadia Khan 07990 680 303.

Absorb Music / Fruition PO Box 10896, Moseley,
Birmingham, B13 0ZU **t** 07920 104 614 **f** 0121 247 6981
e rod@fruitionmusic.co.uk **w** absorbmusic.com ✉ MD: Rod
Thomson.

Abstrakt Management 55 Main Avenue, Sheffield,
South Yorkshire, S17 4FH
t 0114 262 0981 or 07801 028 809
e info@abstraktmanagement.com ✉ Sole Trader: Alf
Billingham.

ACA Music Management & Booking
Blenheim House, Henry St, Bath, Somerset, BA1 1JR
t 01225 428284 **e** enquiries@acamusic.co.uk
w acamusic.co.uk ✉ MD: Harry Finegold.

Acker's International Jazz Agency
53 Cambridge Mansions, Cambridge Rd, London,
SW11 4RX **t** 020 7978 5885 **f** 020 7978 5882
e pamela@ackersmusicagency.co.uk
w ackersmusicagency.co.uk ✉ Proprietor: Pamela F
Sutton.

Active Music Management (AMM) Suite 404,
324/326 Regent St, London, W1B 3HH **t** 0870 120 7668
f 0870 120 9880 **e** activemm@btinternet.com
w activemm.co.uk ✉ MD: Mark Winters.

Adastra The Stables, Westwood House, Main St,
North Dalton, Driffield, East Yorkshire, YO25 9XA
t 01377 217662 **f** 01377 217754 **e** chris.wade@adastra-
music.co.uk **w** adastra-music.co.uk
◼ facebook.com/pages/Driffield-United-
Kingdom/Adastra-Music/50710424147?ref=mf
◼ myspace.com/adastramusicbookings
◼ twitter.com/Adastra_Music ✉ Owner: Chris Wade.

Adventures in Music 5 Mill Lane, Wallingford, Oxon,
OX10 0DH **t** 01491 832 183 **f** 01491 824 020
e info@adventuresin-music.com **w** adventure-
records.com ✉ MDs: Paul and Katie Conroy.

Agency Global Enterprises Ltd 145-
157 St John's Street, London, EC1V 4PY **t** 020 7043 3734
f 020 7043 3736 **e** info@agencyglobal.co.uk
w agencyglobal.co.uk ✉ Dir: Nadeem Sham.

Air MTM 27 The Quadrangle, 49 Atalanta Street,
London, SW6 6TU **t** 020 7386 1600 **f** 020 7386 1619
e info@airmtm.com **w** airmtm.com ✉ Artist
Management: Marc Connor.

Air-Edel Associates 18 Rodmarton St, London,
W1U 8BJ **t** 020 7486 6466 **f** 020 7224 0344 **e** mlo@air-
edel.co.uk **w** air-edel.co.uk ✉ Business Manager: Mark Lo.

Albert Samuel Management
42 City Business Centre, Lower Road, London, SE16 2XB
t 020 7740 1600 **f** 020 7740 1700
e asm@missioncontrol.net **w** asmanagement.co.uk
✉ Director: Albert & David Samuel.

Alchemy Remix Management
33 Humberstone Ave, Manchester, M15 5EE
t 0161 232 1110 **f** 0161 232 1110 **e** info@alchemy-
remix.com **w** alchemy-remix.com
◼ facebook.com/alchemyremixmanagement
◼ myspace.com/alchemyremixmanagement
◼ alchemy_updates ✉ Owner: Howie Martinez
07855507179.

**Vern Allen Entertainments & Management
Agency** P.O Box 135, Exeter, Devon, EX2 9WA
t 01392 273305 **f** 01392 426421 **e** vern@vernallen.co.uk
w vernallen.co.uk ✉ Dir: Vernon Winteridge.

Ambush Management 32 Ransome's Dock, 35-
37 Parkgate Road, London, SW11 4NP **t** 020 7801 1919
f 020 7738 1819 **e** alambush.native@19.co.uk
w ambushgroup.co.uk ✉ MD: Alister Jamieson.

Amusico Limited Fides House, 10 Chertsey Rd,
Woking, Surrey, GU21 5AB **t** 07532 358514
e ralph@amusico.com **w** amusico.com ✉ Contact: Ralph
Lofting.

Nita Anderson Entertainments
165 Wolverhampton Road, Sedgley, Dudley,
West Midlands, DY3 1QR **t** 01902 882211
f 01902 883356 **e** nitaandersonagency@hotmail.com
w nitaanderson.co.uk ✉ Contact: Juanita Anderson.

Angel Artists Congreve House, London, N16 8LH
t 07908 984005 **e** info@angel-artists.com **w** angel-
artists.com
◼ facebook.com/people/Angel-Artists/1314711781
◼ myspace.com/angelartists ◼ twitter.com/AngelArtists
✉ CEO: M. Hague.

Bryter Music Marlinspike Hall, Walpole Halesworth,
Suffolk, IP19 9AR **t** 01986 784 664 **e** info@brytermusic.cc
w brytermusic.cc ✉ Soul Proprietor: Cally.

ArchangelUK 5A Invicta Parade, Sidcup High St,
Sidcup, DA16 5ER **t** 020 8300 0094
e info@archangeluk.co.uk **w** archangeluk.co.uk
✉ A&R: Bruce Elliott-Smith.

Archangelle **t** 07545 916362
e info@archangelle.co.uk **w** archangelle.co.uk
◼ archangelgreen ◼ archangelrecordings
◼ bru_earchangel ◼ archangelvideos ✉ CEO: Bruce
Elliott-Smith.

Archetype Management 91 Clarendon Rd, London,
W11 4JG **t** 07956 955 908 **f** 020 7691 7002
e jon@archetype.cc **w** archetype.cc ✉ MD: Jon Terry.

Arctic King Music Cambridge House, Card Hill,
Forest Row, East Sussex, RH18 5BA **t** 01342 822619
f 01342 822619 **e** mickeymodern@sky.com
w myspace.com/mickeymodern ✉ Partner: Mickey
Modern 07831 505883.

Business Services: Artist Management

WEB SHERIFF®
WWW.WEBSHERIFF.COM T: +44 (0)208 323 8013

Ardent Music PO Box 20078, London, NW2 3FA
t 020 7435 7706 **f** 020 7435 7712
e info@ardentmusic.co.uk **MD:** Ian Blackaby.

Armstrong Multimedia Arts Academy
18 Redsells Close, Downswood, Maidstone, Kent,
ME15 8SN **t** 01622 863778 **e** records@triple-a.uk.com
w triple-a.uk.com **CEO:** Terry Armstrong.

Artists & Media Ltd Devlin House,
36 St George Street, Mayfair, London, W1R 9FA
t 07951 406 938 **e** andrian@msn.com **MD:** Andrian
Adams.

Askonas Holt Ltd (classical artists only)
Lincoln House, 300 High Holborn, London, WC1V 7JH
t 020 7400 1700 **f** 020 7400 1799
e info@askonasholt.co.uk **w** askonasholt.co.uk **Joint**
Chief Executive: Robert Rattray.

Associated London Management PO Box 3787,
London, SE22 9DZ **t** 020 8299 1650 **f** 020 8693 5514
e duophonic@btopenworld.com **Contact:** Martin Pike.

Asylum Management Services PO Box 121, Hove,
Sussex, BN3 4YY **t** 020 8144 9064
e bob@AsylumGroup.com **w** bobjamesuk.com
 facebook.com/bobjamesuk
 myspace.com/bobjamesuk @bobjames
 Management Consultant: Bob James.

ATC Management 142 New Cavendish Street,
London, W1W 6YF **t** 020 7323 2430 **f** 020 7580 7776
e ollie@atcmanagement.com **Contact:** Ollie Slaney
07833 641 484.

Atomic Management & Music 8 Tavistock St,
Covent Garden, London, WC2E 7PP **t** 020 7379 3010
e info@atomic-london.com **w** atomic-london.com
 MD: Mick Newton.

Atrium Music PO Box 278, Wavertree, Liverpool,
L15 8WY **t** 0151 510 1410 **e** query@atrium-music.co.uk
w atrium-music.co.uk **MD:** Paula McCool 07786 537
866.

AuthorityMGMT 12 Cheviot Court, Luxborough St,
London, W1U 5BH **e** james@authoritymgmt.com
w authoritymgmt.com **Artist Manager / A&R:** James
Merritt 07958 419285.

Automatic Management 13 Cotswold Mews,
30 Battersea Square, London, SW11 3RA
t 020 7978 7888 **f** 020 7978 7808
e info@automaticmanagement.co.uk
w myspace.com/automaticmanagement **MD:** Jerry
Smith.

Autonomy Music Group
Suite 27, The Quadrant Centre, 135 Salusbury Road,
Queens Park, London, NW6 6RJ **t** 020 7644 1450
e firstname@autonomymusicgroup.com

Avalon Management Group Ltd 4a Exmoor St,
London, W10 6BD **t** 020 7598 8000 **f** 020 7598 7300
e enquiries@avalonuk.com **w** avalonuk.com

Axis Artist Management Limited 42 Ferry Road,
Barnes, London, SW13 9PW **t** 07768 852 216
f 020 8563 0290 **e** jeremy.pearce@axismanagement.net
 MD: Jeremy Pearce.

Bad Sneakers Management 1-
5 Springfield Mount, Leeds, LS2 9NG **t** 0113 243 1481
e info@badsneakers.co.uk **w** badsneakers.co.uk
 Dirs: Ash Kollakowski, Ed Mason.

Badger Management 4 Ormonde Gardens, Belfast,
BT6 9FL **t** 028 9079 1666 **e** steve@badger-
management.com **Contact:** Stephen Orr.

Bamonte Artist Management 6 Hawkshead Rd,
London, W4 1AD **t** 07768 332507 **e** daryl@bamonte.com
w bamonte.com **Owner:** Daryl Bamonte.

Banchory Management PO Box 25074, Glasgow,
G3 8TT **t** 0141 204 2269 **f** 0141 226 3181
e info@banchory.net **w** banchory.net **Managers:** John
Williamson, Fiona Morrison.

Bandana Management 100 Golborne Rd, London,
W10 5PS **t** 020 8969 0606 **f** 020 8969 0505
e info@banman.co.uk **w** banman.co.uk **MD:** Brian Lane.

Joe Bangay Enterprises River House, Riverwoods,
Marlow, Buckinghamshire, SL7 1QY **t** 01628 486 193
f 01628 890 239 **e** william.b@btclick.com
w joebangay.com **Managing Director:** Joe Bangay.

Barrington Pheloung Management Andrew's,
off Rand Rd, High Roding, Great Dunmow, CM6 1NQ
t 01371 874 022 **f** 01371 874 110 **e** info@pheloung.co.uk
 Composer: Barrington Pheloung.

Bastard Management Cefn Coch Gwyllt,
Cemmaes Rd, Machynlleth, Powys, SY20 8LU
t 01650 511574 **e** bastardmgt@hotmail.com **MD:** Alex
Holland.

Bedlam Management PO Box 34449, London,
W6 0RT **t** 07974 355 078
e info@bedlammanagement.com **MD:** Steven Abbott.

Beetroot Management Newlands House,
40 Berners St, London, W1T 3NA **t** 020 7255 2408
e info@beetrootmusic.com **w** beetrootmusic.com
 Assistant Manager: Annabel Burn.

Bermuda Management Matrix Complex,
91 Peterborough Road, London, SW6 3BU
t 020 7371 5444 **f** 020 7371 5454
e paul@crownmusic.co.uk **MD:** Paul Samuels.

**BH Productions Limited (Exclusive to Eddy
Grant)** 8 Hornton Place, Kensington, London, W8 4LZ
t 020 7937 9252 **Management:** Tony Calder 07525
614 389.

Big Blue Music Windy Ridge, 39-41 Buck Lane,
London, NW9 0AP **t** 020 8205 2990 **f** 020 8205 2990
e info@bigbluemusic.biz **w** bigbluemusic.biz
 Mgr/Producer: Steve Ancliffe.

Big Deal Management London
e info@bigdealmanagement.com
w bigdealmanagement.com **Managing Director:** Dhanny
Joshi 07590 664 784.

WEB SHERIFF®
WWW.WEBSHERIFF.COM T: +44 (0)208 323 8013

Big Dipper Productions 3rd Floor, 29-31 Cowper St, London, EC2A 4AT **t** 020 7608 4591 **f** 020 7608 4599 **e** john@bestest.co.uk **Dirs**: John Best, Dean O'Connor.

Big Fish Little Fish Music 14 Hanover Street, Brighton, BN2 9ST **t** 01273 691 879 **e** bigfish.littlefish@mac.com **w** bigfishlittlefishmusic.com **Contact**: Steve Burton.

Big Help Music Deppers Bridge Farm, Southam, Warwickshire, CV47 2SZ **t** 07782 172101 **e** dutch@bighelp.biz **w** bighelp.biz
myspace.com/bighelpcrew
twitter.com/BigHelpMGMT
youtube.com/user/bighelpmanagement Artist development: Dutch Van Spall.

Big K Music 3 Uplands, Ware, Hearts, SG12 7LB **t** 01920 464 406 **e** bigkmusic@btinternet.com **Contact**: Keith Hammond.

Big M Productions Thatched Rest, Queen Hoo Lane, Tewin, Welwyn, Herts, AL6 0LT **t** 01438 798625 **f** 01438 798395 **e** joyce@bigmgroup.freeserve.co.uk **Managing Director**: Joyce Wilde.

Big Out Ltd 27 Smithwood Close, Wimbledon, London, SW19 6JL **t** 020 8780 0085 **e** BigOutLtd@aol.com **w** bigoutltd.com myspace.com/bigoutltd MD: Louise Porter 07703 165 146.

Big Print Music 12 Cinnamon Row, Plantation Wharf, Battersea, London, SW11 3UX **e** andrew@bigprintmusic.com Contact: Andrew Gemmell +44 207 924 6428.

BIGBOY Management London **t** 020 7617 7226 **f** 020 7373 0600 **e** richard@thebigboy.com **w** thebigboy.com Managing Director: Richard Beck 07738 522474.

Bizarre Management Enfield, London **t** 020 8123 5221 **e** info@bizarremanagement.com MD: Matthias Siefert.

BK 40 Management 12 Cinnamon Row, Battersea, London, SW11 3UX **t** 020 7924 6428 **f** 020 7228 3447 **e** glynn@bk40.com **w** bk40.com Dirs: Glynn Smith, Barrie Knight 07843 500935.

Black Gold Management Limited 4 Heron's Place, Old Isleworth, Middlesex, TW7 7BE **t** 020 7193 5553 **f** 020 7900 3759 **e** artists@blackgoldmanagement.com **w** blackgoldmanagement.com Contact: John Black.

Black Lycett Fulham Palace, Bishop's Avenue, London, SW6 6EA **t** 020 7751 0175 **f** 020 7736 0606 **e** info@blacklycett.com **w** blacklistent.com Directors: Clive Black, Daniel Lycett.

Black Magic Management 296 Earls Court Rd, London, SW5 9BA **t** 020 7373 4083 **f** 020 7373 4083 **e** blackmagicrecords@talk21.com **w** blackmagicrecords.com
myspace.com/blackmagicrecords MD: Mataya Clifford.

Blacklist Entertainment - Blacklist Management The Blue Building, 8-10 Basing St, London, W11 1ET **t** 020 7229 1229 **f** 020 7243 8100 **e** firstname@blacklistent.com **w** blacklistent.com Chairman: Clive Black.

Blaim Media 5947 Great Oak Circle, Los Angeles, CA, 90042, United States **t** +1 323 206 3501 **e** stephen@blaim.me **w** blaim.me MD: Stephen Ewashkiw.

BlakPac Entertainment Limited 2nd Floor, 145-157 St John's St, London, EC1V 4PY **t** 020 8457 7633 **f** 020 8457 7633 **e** pcox@blakpacentertainment.com **w** blakpacentertainment.com
myspace.com/blakpacentertainment CEO: Phillip Cox 07961 767272.

Blast Artist Management **t** 07960 525 330 **e** Sam@bam.uk.com **w** myspace.com/blastartistmanagement Management: Sam Smith.

Blind Faith Management 1 Allevard, Blackrock Rd, Cork, Ireland **t** +353 87 226 9273 **f** +353 21 453 7478 **e** gerald@blindfaithmanagement.com **w** http//www.blindfaithmanagement.com MD: Gerald O'Leary.

Blue Sky Entertainment 41 Walters Workshop, 249 Kensal Road, London, W10 5DB **t** 07771 934 624 **e** firstname.lastname@blue-sky.uk.com Manager: Gordon Biggins.

Blueprint Management PO Box 593, Woking, Surrey, GU23 7YF **t** 01483 715336 **f** 01483 757490 **e** blueprint@lineone.net **w** blueprint-management.com Dirs: John Glover, Matt Glover.

Bodo Music Co Ashley Rd, Hale, Altrincham, Cheshire, WA15 9SF **t** 07939 521 465 **f** 0161 928 8136 **e** fgarcia777@hotmail.com(DO NOT PUBLISH) MD: FL Marshall.

BossMedia The New Building, 180 Kensington Church St, Notting Hill, London, W8 4DP **t** 020 7727 2727 or 07786 884867 **e** info@bossmedia.co.uk **w** bossmedia.co.uk
myspace.com/bossmedia Dir: Taharqa Daniel-Rashid.

Derek Boulton Management 76 Carlisle Mansions, Carlisle Place, London, SW1P 1HZ **t** 020 7828 6533 **f** 020 7828 1271 MD: Derek Boulton.

BPR Productions Ltd 27 Lewes Crescent, Brighton, East Sussex, BN2 1GB **t** 01273 684714 **f** 01273 622042 **e** info@bprmusic.com **w** info@bprmusic.com
myspace.com/bprproductionsltd MD: Ina Dittke.

Braw Management 31 Hartington Pl, Edinburgh, EH10 4LF **t** 0131 221 0011 **f** 0131 221 1313 **e** kenny@brawmusic.com **w** proclaimers.co.uk Manager: Kenny MacDonald.

Brenda Brooker Enterprises Suite 328, 162-168 Regent St, London, W1B 5TD **t** 020 7038 3722 **e** BrookerB@aol.com MD: Brenda Brooker.

WEB SHERIFF®
WWW.WEBSHERIFF.COM T: +44 (0)208 323 8013

Brian Gannon Management St James House, Kiln Lane, Milnrow, Rochdale, Lancs, OL16 3JF **t** 01706 374411 **f** 01706 377303 **e** brian@briangannon.co.uk **w** briangannon.co.uk ☎ Owner: Brian Gannon.

Brilliant Entertainment Management Ltd The Old Truman Brewery, 91-95 Brick Lane, London, E1 6QL **t** 07802 481630 **e** anita@brilliantmanagement.co.uk **w** brilliantmanagement.co.uk ☎ MD: Anita Heryet.

Brilliant! Castlett House, Guiting Power, Gloucestershire, GL54 5US **t** 01451 851101 **e** neilferris@me.com **w** brilpr.co.uk ☎ Contact: Neil Ferris and Jill Ferris 01451 851 101.

Brontone Limited 2nd Floor, 361-373 City Rd, Islington, London, EC1V 1PQ **t** 020 7278 7123 **f** 020 7837 1415 **e** alex@brontone.com ☎ Contact: Anthony Addis or Alex Wall.

Brotherhood Of Man Management Westfield, 75 Burkes Road, Beaconsfield, Buckinghamshire, HP9 1PP **t** 01494 673 073 **f** 01494 680 920 **e** agency@brotherhoodofman.co.uk **w** brotherhoodofman.co.uk

Bruised Fruit Marquis House, 89-91 Adelaide St, Belfast, BT2 8FE **t** 028 9023 9783 **e** admin@bruisedfruitpromotions.com **w** bruisedfruitpromotions.com ☎ Managing Director: Jennie McCullough 02890239783.

BTM PO Box 6003, Birmingham, West Midlands, B45 0AR **t** 0121 477 9553 **f** 0121 693 2954 **e** barry@barrytomes.com **w** gotham-records.com ☎ Proprietor: Barry Tomes.

Bulldozer Management 8 Roland Mews, Stepney Green, London, E1 3JT **t** 020 7929 3333 **f** 020 7929 3222 **e** oliver@bulldozermedia.com **w** bulldozermedia.com ☎ MD: Oliver J. Brown.

Bullitt Music Management Studio 11, 10 Acklam Rd, Ladbroke Gorve, London, W10 5QZ **t** 0208 968 8236 **f** 0208 964 4706 **e** darrin@bullittmusic.com ☎ Managing Director: Darrin Woodford.

Burning Candle Music 26 Marchants Road, Hurstpierpoint, BN6 9UU **t** 07767 388373 **e** chris.bradford@burningcandlemusic.co.uk **w** burningcandlemusic.co.uk ☎ Songwriter: Chris Bradford.

But! Management - But! Records Walsingham Cottage, 7 Sussex Sq, Brighton, East Sussex, BN2 1FJ **t** 01273 680 799 **e** jamesie@butgroup.com **w** butgroup.com ▶ youtube.com/user/TheBUTmusicgroup ☎ MD: Allan James.

Calder Artists Reps 8 Hornton Pl, Kensington, London, W8 4LZ **t** 020 7937 9252 **f** 020 7937 4326 **e** anthony.calder@caldereps.com **w** caldereps.com ☎ Artist Representation: Anthony Calder 07976 872343.

Calder Artists Reps 8 Hornton Pl, Kensington, London, W8 4LZ **t** 020 7937 9252 **f** 020 7937 4326 **e** anthony.calder@caldereps.com **w** caldereps.com ☎ Artist Representation: Anthony Calder 07976872343.

Cambrian Entertainments International 24 Titan Court, Laporte Way, Luton, LU4 8EF **t** 0870 200 5000 **f** 01582 488 877 **e** tim@cambrian.tv **w** cambrian.tv ☎ Managing Director Designate: Tim Savage 01582 544 793.

Magus Entertainment 158 West 23rd St, Suite 2, New York, 10011, United States **t** 00 121 2343 1577 **f** 00 121 2925 4007 **e** wendy@magusentertainment.com **w** magusentertainment.com ☎ CEO: Wendy Laister 0012123431577.

Carrot And Stick Management 28 Brooklyn Road, Bath, BA1 6TE **t** 01225 460 492 **e** info@carrotandstick.net **w** carrotandstick.net ☎ Dir: Adrian Feeney 07817 332 695.

CEC Management 65-69 White Lion St, London, N1 9PP **t** 020 7837 2517 **f** 020 7278 5915 **e** rebecca@cecmanagement.com ☎ MD: Peter Felstead.

CEC Producer Management 65-69 White Lion St, London, N1 9PP **t** 020 7837 2517 **f** 020 7278 5915 **e** jess@cecmanagement.com ☎ Managers: Jess Gerry or Claire Southwick.

Cent Management Melbourne House, Chamberlain Street, Wells, BA5 2PJ **t** 01749 689 074 **f** 01749 670 315 **w** centrecords.com ☎ MD: Kevin Newton.

Charles Gordon Entertainment A303.5 Tower Bridge Business Complex, 100 Clements Road, London, SE16 4DG **t** 020 7232 0800 **f** 020 8698 6600 **e** info@cgordon.co.uk **w** cgordon.co.uk ☎ MD: Berni Griffts.

Charmenko Email for details. **e** nick@charmenko.net **w** charmenko.net ☎ MD: Nick Hobbs.

Chris Griffin Management 17 Ledbury House, Portobello Court, Westborne Grove, London, W11 2DH **t** 07973 883159 **e** chris_griffin17@hotmail.com ☎ Contact: Chris Griffin.

Cigale Entertainment Ltd PO Box 38115, London, W10 6XG **t** 020 8932 2860 **e** info@cigale-ent.com **w** cigale-ent.com ☎ MD: Luc Vergier.

Civilian Music Group PO Box 80083, Stoneham, Massachusetts, MA 02180, United States **t** +1 617 379 0777 **f** +1 603 218 6126 **e** cjacobs@civilianmusicgroup.com **w** civilianmusicgroup.com ☎ Marketing/A&R: Chris Jacobs.

Clarion/Seven Muses (Classical Artist Management) 47 Whitehall Pk, London, N19 3TW **t** 020 7272 4413/5125/8448 **f** 020 7281 9687 **e** admin@c7m.co.uk **w** c7m.co.uk ☎ Partners: Caroline Oakes, Nicholas Curry.

WEB SHERIFF®
WWW.WEBSHERIFF.COM T: +44 (0)208 323 8013

CMO Management International Ltd Studio 2.6, Shepherds East, Richmond Way, London, W14 0DQ **t** 020 7316 6969 **f** 020 7316 6970 **e** reception@cmomanagement.co.uk **w** cmomanagement.co.uk ✉ MD: Chris Morrison.

Co Star Entertainment 24 Ashleigh Drive, Uttoxeter, Staffordshire, ST147RG **t** 07595 020629 **e** mail@craigbunting.co.uk ✉ Manager: Craig Bunting.

Coalition Management Studio 2, 3a Brackenbury Rd, London, W6 0BE **t** 020 8743 1000 **f** 020 8743 0500 **e** management@coalitiongroup.co.uk ✉ Office Manager: Faye Copeland.

Coalition Management Studio 2, 3a Brackenbury Rd, London, W6 0BE **t** 020 8743 1000 **f** 020 8743 0500 **e** management@coalitiongroup.co.uk ✉ Contact: Tim Vigon, Tony Perrin.

Raymond Coffer Management Ltd PO Box 595, Bushey, Herts, WD23 1PZ **t** 020 8420 4430 **f** 020 8950 7617 **e** raymond.coffer@btopenworld.com ✉ Contact: Raymond Coffer.

Collaboration 33 Montpellier St, Brighton, East Sussex, BN1 3DL **t** 01273 730744 **f** 01273 775134 **e** nikki@collaborationuk.com **w** collaborationuk.com ✉ MD: Nikki Neave.

Conception Artist Management 36 Percy St, London, W1T 2DH **t** 020 7580 4424 **f** 020 7323 1695 **e** info@conception.gb.com ✉ MD: Jean-Nicol Chelmiah.

Congo Music Ltd 17A Craven Park Road, Harlsden, London, NW10 8SE **t** 020 8961 5461 **f** 020 8961 5461 **e** byron@congomusic.freeserve.co.uk **w** congomusic.com ✉ A&R Director: Root Jackson.

Connected Artists 1-5 Exchange Court, Maiden Lane, London, WC2R 0JU **t** 020 7420 4300 **f** 020 7420 4398 **e** paulmcdonald@connectedlimited.com **w** connectedlimited.com ✉ Director: Paul McDonald.

Consigliari Ltd Langdale House, 11 Marshalsea Road, London, SE1 1EN **t** 020 7089 2608 **f** 020 7940 5656 **e** info@consigliari.com ✉ Contact: Mark Melton.

Coochie Hart 26 Harcourt St, London, W1H 4HW **t** 020 7724 9700 **f** 020 7724 2598 **e** info@coochie-hart.com **w** coochie-hart.com ✉ MD: Amanda G/Rosie H.

Cool Kids Music Management Ltd 93 Lavenham Road, London, SW18 5ER **t** 07748 321 266 or 07879 224 626 **e** info@coolkidsmusic.co.uk **w** coolkidsmusic.co.uk ✉ Directors: Sandra Skiba, Brijitte Dreyfus.

Cool Music Ltd 1a Fishers Lane, Chiswick, London, W4 1RX **t** 020 8995 7766 **f** 020 8987 8996 **e** enquiries@coolmusicltd.com **w** coolmusicltd.com ✉ Musicians Contractor: Gareth Griffiths.

Stewart Coxhead Munro House, High Close, Rawdon, Leeds, West Yorkshire, LS19 6HF **t** 0113 250 3338 **f** 0113 250 7343 **e** stewart@stewartcoxhead.com **w** acoustic-alchemy.net ✉ MD: Stewart Coxhead.

Craig Huxley Media 13 Christchurch Road, London, N8 9QL **t** 020 8374 9133 **f** 020 8292 1205 **e** craighuxleymedia@blueyonder.co.uk ✉ Proprietor: Craig Huxley.

Crashed Music 162 Church Rd, East Wall, Dublin 3, Ireland **t** +353 1 888 1188 **f** +353 1 856 1122 **e** info@crashedmusic.com **w** crashedmusic.com ✉ MD: Shay Hennessy.

Create Management Sollys Mill, Mill Lane, Godalming, Surrey, GU7 1EY **t** 01483 419 090 **f** 01483 419 504 **e** patrick@createmanagement.com **w** createmanagement.com ▣ @patrickhaveron 📺 youtube.com/createtv ✉ Director: Patrick Haveron 01483 419090.

Creative Music Management Unit 53, Simla House, Weston St, London, SE1 3RN **t** 020 7378 1642 **f** 020 7378 1642 **e** general@creativepruk.com ✉ CEO: Dave Norton.

Crisis Management 18 Reynard Road, Chorlton, Manchester, M21 8DD **t** 07771 934870 **f** 0161 882 0712 **e** firstname@crisismanagement.uk.com **w** crisismanagement.uk.com ✉ Director: Karen Boardman 07771 934 870.

Cromwell Management 20 Drayhorse Road, Ramsey, Cambs, PE26 1SD **t** 01487 815 063 **e** cromwellmanagement@hotmail.co.uk **w** paulleegan.com ✉ Managing Partner: Vic Gibbons.

Crown Music Management Services Matrix Complex, 91 Peterborough Rd, London, SW6 3BU **t** 020 7371 5444 **f** 020 7371 5454 **e** mark@crownmusic.co.uk **w** crownmusic.co.uk ✉ MD: Mark Hargreaves.

Crucial Music PO Box 425, Richmond, VIC, 3121, Australia **t** +613 9429 4848 **e** rae@crucialmusic.com.au **w** crucialmusic.com.au ✉ Manager: Rae Harvey 03 9429 4848.

Cruisin' Music Management Charlton Farm, Hemington, Bath, BA3 5XS **t** 01373 834161 **f** 01373 834164 **e** sil@cruisin.co.uk **w** cruisin.co.uk ✉ Chairman: Sil Willcox.

Daddy Management 15 Holywell Row, London, EC2A 4JB **t** 020 7684 5219 **f** 020 7684 5230 **e** paul@daddymanagement.net ✉ MD: Paul Benney.

Daisy Management Unit 2 Carriglea, Naas Rd, Dublin 12, Ireland **t** +353 1 429 8600 **f** +353 1 429 8602 **e** daithi@daisydiscs.com **w** daisydiscs.com ✉ MD: John Dunford.

The Daniel Azure Music Group 72 New Bond St, London, W1S 1RR **t** 07894 702 007 **f** 020 8240 8787 **e** info@jvpr.net **w** danielazure.com ✉ CEO: Daniel Azure.

Dara Management Unit 4, Great Ship Street, Dublin 8, Ireland **t** +353 1 478 3455 **f** +353 1 478 2143 **e** irishmus@iol.ie **w** irelandcd.com ✉ MD: Joe O'Reilly.

Business Services: Artist Management

Dark Blues Management Puddephats, Markyate, Herts, AL3 8AZ **t** 01582 842226 **f** 01582 840010 **e** info@darkblues.co.uk **w** darkblues.co.uk 📧 Office Mgr: Fiona Hewetson.

Darklight Entertainment 58 Speed House, Barbican, London, EC2Y 8AT **t** 020 7628 5180 **f** 020 7681 3588 **e** darklight_entertainment@yahoo.com 📧 Contact: James Little 07836 210 926.

Darling Artists 4th Floor, 19 Denmark Street, London, WC2H 8NA **t** 020 7379 8787 **f** 020 7379 5737 **e** david@darlinguk.com 📧 Manager: David Laub.

David Beard Artist Management 176 Sandbed Lane, Belper, Derbyshire, DE56 0SN **t** 01773 824 340 **e** info@davidbeardmusic.com **w** davidbeardmusic.com 📧 MD: David Beard 07815 573 121.

David Morgan Management Ash House, 8 Second Cross Rd, Twickenham, TW2 8RF **t** 020 8898 8183 **f** 020 8898 8185 **e** davidmanagement@aol.com **w** musicroyaltyinvestigations.com 📧 MD: David Morgan.

Lena Davis John Bishop Associates Cotton's Farmhouse, Whiston Road, Cogenhoe, Northamptonshire, NN7 1NL **t** 01604 891487 **f** 01604 890405 📧 Contact: Lena Davis.

DB MUSIC

4th Floor Studio, 16 Abbey Churchyard, Bath, BA1 1LY **t** 01225 311661 **f** 01225 482013 **e** david@dbmusic.co.uk **w** dbmusic.co.uk 📧 Contact: David Bates.
A new management company set up by David Bates, former head of A&R at Mercury / Vertigo, label head at Fontana and owner of db records. After a long, record breaking career in the industry and having signed numerous successful artists such as Def Leppard, Tears for Fears, Texas, Teardrop Explodes, Was Not Was, James, Scott Walker, Electric Soft Parade and Tom McRae, David is now available to offer his services and advice in a management capacity.

Death Or Glory Music Woodcock Farm, Woodcock Lane, Grafty Green, Kent, ME172AY **e** ewan@deathorglorymusic.com **w** deathorglorymusic.com 📘 facebook.com/deathorglorymusic 📧 Contact: Ewan Grant.

Deluxxe Management PO Box 373, Teddington, Middx, TW11 8ZQ **t** 020 8755 3630 **e** info@deluxxe.co.uk **w** deluxxe.co.uk 📧 MD: Diane Wagg 07771 861054.

Dennis Heaney Promotions Whitehall, 8 Ashgrove Rd, Newry, N. Ireland, BT34 1QN **t** 028 3026 8658 **f** 028 3026 6673 **e** dennis_heaney@hotmail.com **w** susanmccann.com 📧 Director: Dennis Heaney.

Destiny Destiny Towers, St Margaret's House, 21 Old Ford Rd, London, E2 9PL **t** 020 8981 2746 **e** carrie@destinytowers.com **w** destinytowers.com 📧 myspace.com/destinytowers 📧 Contact: Carrie Fade.

Deuce Management & Promotion PO Box 49454, London, SE20 7WS **t** 07875 245648 **e** rob@deucemp.com **w** deucemp.com 📧 myspace.com/deucesounds 📧 MD: Rob Saunders.

Deutsch-Englische Freundschaft 51 Lonsdale Rd, Queens Park, London, NW6 6RA **t** 020 7328 2922 **f** 020 7328 2322 **e** info@d-e-f.com 📧 Mgr: Eric Harle.

DGM Management PO Box 1533, Salisbury, Wiltshire, SP5 5ER **t** 01722 780187 **f** 01722 781042 **e** dgm@dgmhq.com **w** dgmlive.com 📧 MD: David Singleton.

Diamond Sounds Music Management The Fox and Punchbowl, Burfield Rd, Old Windsor, Berks, SL4 2RD **t** 01753 855420 **e** samueldsm@aol.com **w** loosecannonz.biz 📧 Director: Julie Samuel 07831 115223.

Direct Heat Management PO Box 1345, Worthing, West Sussex, BN14 7PY **t** 01903 202426 **e** mike@happyvibes.co.uk **w** happyvibes.co.uk 📧 Dir: Mike Pailthorpe.

Divine Management Top Floor, 9 Trinity Avenue, London, N2 0LX **t** 020 8922 9022 **e** info@divinemanagement.co.uk 📧 Manager: Natalie de Pace.

DJT Management Ltd PO Box 229, Sheffield, South Yorkshire, S1 1LY **t** 07778 400 512 **f** 0114 258 3164 **e** david@djtmanagement.co.uk 📧 Director: David Taylor.

DO-IT Management Ltd Suite 260, 63 Remuera Rd, Newmarket, Auckland, 1050, New Zealand **t** +64 27 437 8637 **e** paul@doitmanagement.com **w** doitmanagement.com 📧 myspace.com/doitmanagement 📧 Director: Paul Marshall.

David Dorrell Management 2nd Floor, Lyme Wharf, 191 Royal College St, London, NW1 0SG **t** 0870 420 5088 **f** 0870 420 5188 **e** Michelle@dorrellmanagement.com 📧 Contact: Michelle Beaver.

Doug Smith Associates Dalton House, 60 Windsor Avenue, London, SW19 2RR **t** 07802 338463 **e** mail@dougsmithassociates.com **w** dougsmithassociates.com 📧 Partners: Doug Smith, Eve Carr.

WEB SHERIFF®
WWW.WEBSHERIFF.COM T: +44 (0)208 323 8013

Dreamscape Management Limited Alsop Close, London Colney, St Albans, AL2 1BW **t** 07531 609789 **f** 01727 826308 **e** dreamscape25@hotmail.com
 facebook.com/home.php?#/group.php?gid=66790450 567 myspace.com/dreamscapemanagement
 Managing Director: Adam C. Lamb.

Dreem Teem Millmead Business Centre 86, Millmead Ind Estate, Millmead Rd, London, N17 9QU **t** 020 8801 8800 **f** 020 8801 4800
e viveka@urbanhousemusic.com
w urbanhousemusic.com Mgr: Viveka Nilsson.

The Dune Music Company 1st Floor, 73 Canning Road, Harrow, Middx, HA3 7SP **t** 020 8424 2807 **f** 020 8861 5371 **e** info@dune-music.com **w** dune-music.com MD: Janine Irons.

Duroc Media Limited Riverside House, 10-12 Victoria Rd, Uxbridge, Middx, UB8 2TW **t** 01895 810831 **f** 01895 231499
e info@durocmedia.com **w** durocmedia.com MD: Simon Porter.

Duty Free Artist Management 3rd Floor, 67 Farringdon Road, London, EC1M 3JB **t** 020 7831 9931 **f** 020 7831 9331 **e** info@dutyfreerecordings.co.uk
w dutyfreerecords.com Booking Agent: Sacha Hearn.

Barry Dye Entertainments PO Box 888, Ipswich, Suffolk, IP1 6BU **t** 01473 744287 **f** 01473 745442
e barrydye@aol.com Prop: Barry Dye.

Dyfel Management 19 Fontwell Drive, Bickley, Bromley, Kent, BR2 8AB **t** 020 8467 9605
f 020 8249 1972 **e** jean@dyfel.co.uk **w** dyfel.co.uk
 Dir: J Dyne.

Dynamik Music 22 Bittacy Rise, London, NW7 2HG **t** 020 7193 3272 **f** 020 7681 3699 **e** giles@dynamik-music.com **w** dynamik-music.com MD: Giles Goodman.

Eclipse-PJM PO Box 3059, South Croydon, Surrey, CR2 8TL **t** 020 8657 2627 **f** 020 8657 2627
e eclipsepjm@btinternet.com MD: Paul Johnson 07798 651691.

Eddie Lock Unit 2, The Old Parish Hall, The Square, Lenham, Kent, ME17 2PQ **t** 01622 858300
f 01622 858300 **e** info@eddielock.com **w** eddielock.co.uk
 metalheadz.co.uk myspace.com/goldie_art
 Exclusive Manager of Goldie: Eddie Lock 01622 858300 / 07710 772207.

EG Management Ltd PO Box 606, London, WC2E 7YT **t** 020 8540 9935 A&R: Chris Kettle.

Egg Management The Studio, 16 Station Road, Sevenoaks, Kent, TN13 2XA **t** 01732 462 554
f 01732 462 565 **e** info@egg-management.com **w** egg-management.com MD: Jonathan Rice.

ELA Management Contact: See Wild West Management.

Eleven Clements Yard, Iliffe St, London, SE17 3LJ **t** 020 7820 1262 **f** 020 7820 1846
e eleven@dsl.pipex.com Contact: Dave Bedford, Ruth Starns.

Elite Squad Management Valtony, Loxwood Road, Plaistow, W Sussex, RH14 0NY **t** 01403 871 200 **f** 01403 871 334 **e** tony@elitesquad.freeserve.co.uk
 MD: Tony Nunn.

Embargo Management (UK) Ltd
142 New Cavendish St, London, W1W 6YF
t 020 7323 2503 **e** enquiries@embargomanagement.com **w** embargomanagement.com MD: Sumit Bothra.

Embryonic Music
Unit 11 Network European Business Centre, 329-339 Putney Bridge Rd, London, SW15 5922
t 020 8788 5922 **e** david@embryonicmusic.com
w embryonicmusic.com myspace.com/embryonicmusic
 MD: David Steele.

Emperor Management 2 Brayburne Ave, London, SW4 6AA **t** 020 7720 0826 **f** 020 7720 1869
e john.empson@btopenworld.com
w myspace.com/emperormanagement MD: John Empson 07785 598472.

Empire Artist Management
Unit 4, Portobello Dock, 557 Harrow Rd, London, W10 4RH **t** 020 8968 5888 **f** 020 8968 5999 **e** info@empire-management.co.uk **w** empire-management.co.uk
 Dir: Neale Easterby, Richard Ramsey.

Enable Music Ltd 54 Baldry Gardens, London, SW16 3DJ **t** 020 8144 0616 **e** mike@enablemusic.co.uk
w enablemusic.co.uk MD: Mike Andrews 07775 737 281.

ePM PO Box 47264, London, W7 1WX **t** 020 8566 0200 **e** oliver@electronicpm.co.uk **w** electronicpm.co.uk
 Partner: Oliver Way.

Equator Music 17 Hereford Mansions, Hereford Road, London, W2 5BA **t** 020 7727 5858 **f** 020 7229 5934
e info@equatormusic.com **w** equatormusic.com
 Contact: Ralph Baker.

Eurock Distribution First Floor, 5 Cope Street, Temple Bar, Dublin 2, Ireland **t** +353 8 7244 1874
f +353 1 289 1074 **e** gforce@indigo.ie MD: Brian O'Kelly.

European Arts & Media 30 The Mall, Beacon Court, Sandyford, Dublin 18, Ireland **t** +353 1 293 4002
e Paul.Newman@euroartsmedia.ie **w** euroartsmedia.ie
 Director: Paul Newman.

Everlasting Music 71a Sutton Rd, London, N10 1HH **t** 020 8444 8190 **f** 020 8444 9656
e info@everlastingmusic.co.uk **w** everlastingmusic.co.uk
 MD: Danny Parnes 07958 208817.

Evolution Management 13 Haldane Close, London, N10 2PB **t** 020 8883 4486 **e** evomgt@aol.com
 MD: John Brice.

Extreme Music Productions - Eyes Wide Shut Recordings 4-7 Forewoods Common, Holt, Wiltshire, BA14 6PJ **t** 0845 056 3834 **f** 0870 131 3701
e george@empspace.com **w** empspace.com
 myspace.com/empspace1 MD: George D Allen.

WEB SHERIFF®
WWW.WEBSHERIFF.COM T: +44 (0)208 323 8013

Eyetoeye Entertainment Tucketts Barn, Trusham, Devon, TQ13 0NR **t** 01626 854 277
e brian@eyetoeye.com **w** eyetoeye.com ☏ Partner: Brian Yates.

Fanatic Management PO Box 153, Stanmore, Middlesex, HA7 2HF **t** 01923 896975 **f** 01923 896985
e hrano@fan-fair.freeserve.co.uk ☏ MD: Mike Hrano.

Fat and Frantic Management Brooke Oast, Jarvis Lane, Goudhurst, Cranbrook, Kent, TN17 1LP
t 01580 211 623 **e** rbickersteth@fatandfrantic.com
w fatandfrantic.com ☏ MD: E R Bickersteth.

Fat! Management Unit 36, Battersea Business Centre, 99-109 Lavender Hill, London, SW11 5QL **t** 020 7924 1333 **f** 020 7924 1833
e info@thefatclub.com **w** thefatclub.com ☏ MD: Paul Arnold.

FBI Routenburn House, Routenburn Road, Largs, Strathclyde, KA30 8SQ **t** 01475 673392 **f** 01475 674075
e wbrown8152@aol.com ☏ Owner: Willie Brown 0795 729 2054.

Feedback Communications The Court, Long Sutton, Hook, Hampshire, RG29 1TA
t 01256 862865 **f** 01256 862182
e feedback@crapola.com **w** crapola.com
🆕 facebook.com/dangerglobalwarming
🆕 myspace.com/dangerglobalwarming
🆕 youtube.com/dangerglobalwarming
☏ Management: Keir Jens-Smith.

First Column Management 60 Compton Rd, Brighton, East Sussex, BN1 5AN **t** 01273 501043
f 01273 388968 **e** fcm@firstcolumn.co.uk ☏ Dir: Phil Nelson.

First Time Management Sovereign House, 12 Trewartha Rd, Praa Sands, Penzance, Cornwall, TR20 9ST **t** 01736 762826 **f** 01736 763328
e panamus@aol.com **w** songwriters-guild.co.uk
🆕 myspace.com/scampmusicpublishing ☏ MD: Roderick Jones.

Flamecracker Management PO Box 394, Hemel Hempstead, HP3 9WL **t** 01442 403445
f 01442 403445 **e** kdavis@aol.com **w** frantik.org
☏ Manager: Karen Davis.

Flamencovision 54 Windsor Road, Finchley, London, N3 3SS **t** 020 8346 4500 **f** 020 8346 2488
e hvmartin@dircon.co.uk **w** flamencovision.com
☏ MD: Helen Martin.

Flamingo Record Management Thornhurst Place, Rowplatt Lane, Felbridge, East Grinstead, RH19 2PA
t 01342 317943 **f** 01342 317943
e ed@badgerflamingoanimation.co.uk
w badgerflamingoanimation.co.uk ☏ MD: Ed Palmieri.

Flat Cap Music 70 Codrington Hill, London, SE23 1ND
t 020 8690 2335 **f** 020 8690 2335
e mike@flatcapmusic.com **w** flatcapmusic.com
🆕 myspace.com/mrlonesome 🐦 twitter.com/mikeflatcap
☏ MD: Mike Watson 07887 660076.

The Flying Music Company Ltd FM House, 110 Clarendon Road, London, W11 2HR **t** 020 7221 7799
f 020 7221 5016 **e** info@flyingmusic.com
w flyingmusic.com ☏ Directors: Paul Walden, Derek Nicol.

Fools Paradise t 07973 297124 **e** julian@fools-paradise.co.uk ☏ Manager: Julian Nugent.

Four Seasons Management Mulliner House, Flanders Road, London, W4 1NN **t** 020 8987 2515
e 07841595647 **w** fsmc.co.uk ☏ MD: Daryl Costello 07841 595 647.

Four Seasons Music Ltd Killarney House, Killarney Rd, Bray, Co. Wicklow, Ireland **t** +353 1 286 9944
f +353 1 286 9945 **e** coulter@indigo.ie **w** philcoulter.com
☏ PA to MD: Moira Winget.

Fox Records Ltd (Management) 62 Lake Rise, Romford, Essex, RM1 4EE **t** 01708 760544
f 01708 760563 **e** foxrecords@talk21.com
w foxrecordsltd.co.uk ☏ Director: Colin Brewer.

Fox Records Ltd 62 Lake Rise, Romford, Essex, RM1 4EE **t** 01708 760544 **f** 01708 760563
e foxrecords@talk21.com ☏ myspace.com/foxrecordsltd
☏ partner: Colin Brewer/Linda Ryle.

Freak'n See Music Ltd 19c Heathmans Rd, London, SW6 4TJ **t** 020 7384 2429 **f** 020 7384 2429
e firstname@freaknsee.com **w** freaknsee.com
☏ MD: Jimmy Mikaoui.

Fredag Artist Management 53 George IV Bridge, Edinburgh, EH1 1EJ **t** 0131 225 5522
e David@Fredag.co.uk **w** Fredag.co.uk ☏ Managing Consultant: David Murray.

Freedom Management 216 Buspace Studios, Conlan St, London, W10 5AP **t** 020 8960 4443
f 020 8960 9889 **e** martyn@frdm.co.uk **w** frdm.co.uk
☏ MD: Martyn Barter.

Freshwater Hughes Management PO Box 54, Northaw, Herts, EN6 4PY **t** 01707 661431
f 01707 664141 **e** info@freshwaterhughes.com
w freshwaterhughes.com ☏ Contact: Jackie Hughes, Brian Freshwater 020 8360 0505.

Friars Management Ltd 33 Alexander Road, Aylesbury, Bucks, HP20 2NR **t** 01296 434 731
f 01296 422 530 **e** info@fmlmusic.com **w** fmlmusic.com
☏ Joint Managing Directors: Joseph Stopps and David Stopps.

Fruit Ground Floor, 37 Lonsdale Road, London, NW6 6RA
t 020 7328 0848 **f** 020 7328 8078
e fruitmanagement@btconnect.com ☏ Partner: Caroline Killoury.

Fruition Management PO Box 10896, Birmingham, B13 0ZU **t** 0121 247 6981 **f** 0121 247 6981
e rod@fruitionmusic.co.uk ☏ MD: Rod Thomson 07976 215 719.

Fruity Red Inc. PO Box 10349, London, NW1 9WJ
t 020 8889 3408 **e** Helen@fruityred.com **w** fruityred.com
☏ Dir: Helen Douglas.

WEB SHERIFF®
WWW.WEBSHERIFF.COM T: +44 (0)208 323 8013

Full 360 Ltd PO Box 902, Suite 306, Bradford, BD1 9AH
t 07971 874 942 **f** 01274 220 579
e katherine@full360ltd.com **w** full360ltd.com
✉ MD: Katherine Canoville.

Full Time Hobby Management 3rd Floor,
1a Adpar Street, London, W2 1DE **t** 020 7535 6740
f 020 7563 7283 **e** info@fulltimehobby.co.uk
w fulltimehobby.co.uk ✉ MD: Wez.

Fully Comprehensive Management
16C Highbury Grange, London, N5 2PX **t** 07939 724 143
e gavin@fullycomprehensive.com ✉ MD: Gavin Nugent.

Fun-Da-Mental C/O Nation Records Ltd,
19 All Saints Rd, Notting Hill Gate, London, W11 1HE
t 0207 792 9167 **e** akination@btopenworld.com
✉ Contact: Aki Nawaz 07971206144.

Fundamental Management Ltd Falkland House,
Falkland Road, London, N8 0QY **t** 020 8376 1876
f 020 8808 4413 **e** fundamentaluk@yahoo.co.uk
✉ Mgr: Maria James.

Furtive Mass Transit System 52-53 Margaret St,
London, W1W 8SQ **t** 020 7631 9205 **e** tankeelad@furtive-
mts.com **w** furtive-mts.com ✉ Contact: Tank.

Future Management PO Box 183, Chelmsford, Essex,
CM2 9XN **t** 01245 601910 **f** 01245 601048
e Futuremgt@aol.com **w** futuremanagement.co.uk
✉ MD: Joe Ferrari.

Fwinki Music London **t** 07976 851033
e amul@fwinki.com **w** fwinki.com ✉ MD: Amul Batra.

G Entertaining 16 Coney Green, Abbotts Barton,
Winchester, Hants, SO23 7JB **t** 0845 601 6285
e enquiries@g-entertaining.co.uk **w** g-entertaining.co.uk
✉ MD: Peter Nouwens.

Gailforce Management Matrix Complex,
91 Peterborough Rd, London, SW6 3BU **t** 020 7384 8989
f 020 7384 8988 **e** gail@gailforcemanagement.co.uk
✉ MD: Gail Colson.

Ganz Management 88 Calvert Rd, Greenwich,
London, SE10 0DF **t** 020 8333 9447 **f** 020 8355 9328
e sam.towers@ganzmanagement.com ✉ Manager: Sam
Towers.

Geronimo! Management 15 Canada Copse, Milford,
Surrey, GU8 5AL **t** 07960 187529
e barneyjeavons@supanet.com ✉ Owner: Barney
Jeavons.

Globeshine (UK) Ltd 70A Totteridge Road,
High Wycombe, Bucks, HP13 6EX **t** 01494 528 665
e b.hallin@virgin.net ✉ MD: Brian Hallin.

GM Promotions 17 The Athenaeum, 32 Salisbury Rd,
Hove, E. Sussex, BN3 3AA **t** 01273 774 469
e info@gmpromotions.co.uk **w** gmpromotions.co.uk
✉ Dir: Laura Ducceschi 07980 917 056.

Gol-Don Management 3 Heronwood Rd, Aldershot,
Hants., GU12 4AJ **t** 01252 312 382 **e** gol-
don.music@ntlworld.com **w** goforit-promotions.com
✉ Partners: Golly Gallagher & Don Leach 07904 232 292.

Gola Entertainment 7 Crofton Terrace,
Dun Laoghaire, Co.Dublin, Ireland **t** +353 1 230 4615
e gola@iol.ie **w** moyabrennan.com ✉ Manager: Tim Jarvis.

Good Groove Management 217 Buspace Studios,
Conlan St, London, W10 5AP **t** 020 7565 0050
f 020 7565 0050 **e** justine@goodgroove.co.uk
w goodgroove.co.uk ✉ Contact: Justine Young.

GR Management 974 Pollokshaws Rd, Shawlands,
Glasgow, Strathclyde, G41 2HA **t** 0141 632 1111
f 0141 649 0042 **e** info@grmanagement.co.uk
✉ MDs: Rab Andrew, Gerry McElhone.

Graham Peacock Management P.O.Box 84, Hove,
W. Sussex, BN3 6YP **t** 01273 777 409 **f** 01273 777 809
e Graha@GPManagement.net **w** gpmanagement.net
✉ MD: Graham Peacock.

Grand Union Management
Units 124 & 126 Buspace Studios, Conlan St, London,
W10 5AP **t** 020 8968 7788 **f** 020 8969 9888
e info@granduniongroup.com **w** granduniongroup.com
✉ Managers: David Bianchi, Nick Ember, Nick Yeatman.

Grant Management - G-Man Entertainment
Dalton House, 60 Windsor Avenue, London, SW19 2RR
t 0845 057 3739 **f** 020 7787 8788
e grant.music@btconnect.com ✉ MD: John Watson-
Grant.

Grapedime Music 28 Hurst Crescent, Barrowby,
Grantham, Lincolnshire, NG32 1TE **t** 01476 560241
e grapedime@pjbray.globalnet.co.uk ✉ Manager: Phil
Bray.

Graphite 133 Kew Rd, Richmond, Surrey, TW9 2PN
t 020 8948 5446 **e** info@graphitemedia.net
w graphitemedia.net ✉ Director: Ben Turner.

Gremlin Productions **t** 01322 333137
e jason@gremlinproductions.co.uk
w gremlinproductions.com ✉ A&R: Jason Alloway.

Grenade Artist Management London
e info@grenadeartists.com
🅜 myspace.com/grenadeartistmanagement
✉ Director: Lewis Frei 07793891174.

Grinning Rat Music Management Brays Cottage,
Bowden Hill, Chilcompton, Somerset, BA3 4EN
t 01761 233 555 **e** info@grinningrat.co.uk
w helenaonline.com ✉ MD: Ian Softley 07779 325 966.

Groovefinder Productions 30, Havelock Rd,
Southsea, Portsmouth, PO5 1RU **t** 07831 450 241
e jeff@groovefinderproductions.com
w groovefinderproductions.com ✉ MD: Jeff Powell.

Groover Management Ltd PO Box 357,
Middlesbrough, TS1 4WZ **t** 01628 636152
f 01642 351962 **e** info@grooverman.com
w grooverman.com ✉ Director: Steve Metcalfe.

Gulp! Marketing Studio 204, Westbourne Studios,
242 Acklam Road, London, W10 5JJ **t** 020 7575 3202
e richard@gulpmusic.co.uk/gareth@gulpmusic.co.uk
w gulpmusic.co.uk ✉ MD: Richard Marshall & Gareth Currie
07973 543 527.

WEB SHERIFF ®
WWW.WEBSHERIFF.COM T: +44 (0)208 323 8013

Hall Or Nothing Management 3rd Floor, 19 Denmark St, London, WC2H 8NA **t** 020 3119 2007 **f** 020 7240 5177 **e** firstname.lastname@hallornothing.co.uk **w** hallornothing.co.uk ☎ MD: Martin Hall.

Harmony Entertainment 23 Ruscombe Way, Feltham, Middx, TW14 9NY **t** 020 8751 6060 **f** 020 8751 6060 **e** harmonyents@hotmail.co.uk ☎ MD: Mike Dixon 07774 856 679.

Harvey Lisberg Associates Kennedy House, 31 Stamford St, Altrincham, Cheshire, WA14 1ES **f** 0161 980 7100 **e** harveylisberg@aol.com ☎ MD: Harvey Lisberg.

Hazard Chase - Classical Music Management 25 City Rd, Cambridge, CB1 1DP **t** 01223 312400 **f** 01223 460827 **e** info@hazardchase.co.uk **w** hazardchase.co.uk ☎ MD: James Brown.

Headstone Management 47 Fairfax Rd, Woking, Surrey, GU22 9HN **t** 01483 856 760 **e** colinspencer@ntlworld.com ☎ MD: Colin Spencer 07811 387 220.

Heavenly Management 47 Frith Street, London, W1D 4SE **t** 020 7494 2998 **f** 020 7437 3317 **e** lou@heavenlymanagement.com ☎ Dir: Martin Kelly.

Heavyweight Management Unit 212, The Saga Centre, 326 Kensal Rd, London, W10 5BN **t** 020 8968 0111 **f** 020 8968 0110 **e** heavyweight@dial.pipex.com **w** heavyweightman.com ☎ MD: Simon Goffe, Emily Moxon.

Hedgehog 9 Tavistock Court, Tavistock Square, London, WC1H 9HE **t** 020 7387 3220 **f** 020 7383 2832 **e** carol_hodge@hotmail.com ☎ Manager: Carol Hodge.

Henderson Management 51 Promenade North, Cleveleys, Blackpool, Lancashire, FY5 1LN **t** 01253 863386 **f** 01253 867799 **e** agents@henderson-management.co.uk **w** henderson-management.co.uk ☎ MD: John Henderson.

Herotech Management 24-25 Nutford Place, London, W1H 5YN **t** 020 7725 7064 **f** 020 7725 7066 **e** dylan@herotech.co.uk

Hope Management Unit 4.16 The Paintworks, Bath Road, Bristol, BS4 3EH **t** 0117 971 2397 **f** 0117 972 8981 **e** caroline@hoperecordings.com **w** hoperecordings.com ☎ MD: Steve Satterthwaite.

House of Clubs London **e** ed@houseofclubs.co.uk **w** houseofclubs.co.uk ☐ myspace.com/houseofclubs ☎ Contact: Ed Weidman 07966 438376.

Hyperactive Music Management PO Box 550, Brentford, TW8 0XZ **t** 020 8580 4912 **e** teresa@hyperactivemgt.com ☎ Contact: Teresa Sutterby.

Idle Eyes Management 81 Sheen Court, Richmond, Surrey, TW10 5DF **t** 07866 423 729 **e** Jon@IdleEyes.co.uk **w** idleeyes.co.uk ☎ Dir: Jonathan Rees 020 8876 0099.

IDMC Gospel Choir Suite 56, 56 Marden Crescent, Croydon, Surrey, CR0 3ER **t** 07971 766513 **e** john@idmcgospel.com **w** idmcgospel.com ☐ idmcsparetime ☐ myspace.com/idmcgospel ☐ John Fisher ☐ IDMC Gospel Choir ☎ MD: John Fisher.

IE Music Ltd 111 Frithville Gardens, London, W12 7JG **t** 020 8600 3400 **f** 020 8600 3401 **e** info@iemusic.co.uk **w** iemusic.co.uk ☎ MDs: David Enthoven, Tim Clark.

Ignition 54 Linhope St, London, NW1 6HL **t** 020 7298 6000 **f** 020 7258 0962 **e** mail@ignition-man.co.uk ☎ MD: Alec McKinlay.

IJT Management PO Box 696, Felbridge, Surrey, RH19 2XS **t** 0845 370 9904 **f** 0845 370 9905 **e** info@ijtmanagement.com ☎ Directors: Ian or Jo Titchener.

Immoral Management PO Box 2643, Reading, Berks, RG5 4GF **t** 0118 969 9269 **f** 0118 969 9264 **e** johnjpsuk@aol.com ☎ MD: John Saunderson.

Impatient Management The Ice House, The Bond, 180-182 Fazeley St, Birmingham, B5 5SE **t** 0121 687 1404 **f** 0121 475 7452 **e** rob@impatientmanagement.co.uk **w** bluehippomedia.com ☎ Director: Rob Taylor 07710 836471.

Impressive Celebrity Management 9 Jeffrys Pl, London, NW1 9PP **t** 0207 284 3444 **e** sacha@impressivepr.com **w** impressivepr.com ☎ Director: Sacha Taylor-Cox 07957 338 525.

Imprint Bookings & Management - DJ Agency Unit 13, Barley Shotts Business Park, 246 Acklam Rd, London, W10 5YG **t** 020 8964 1331 **f** 020 8960 9660 **e** gareth@imprintdjs.com **w** imprintdjs.com ☎ Contact: Gareth Rees.

Imprint Music Ltd. 17C Northwold Rd, London, N16 7DH **t** 020 7275 8682 **e** info@senser.co.uk **w** imprintmusic.co.uk ☐ facebook.com/pages/Senser/101518689505?ref=s ☐ myspace.com/senserband ☐ youtube.com/user/johnnysenser ☎ Managing Director: Paul West.

Impro Management The Coachhouse, Rockland All Saints, Attleborough, N17 1tu **t** 07775 934408 **e** firstname@impromanagement.com ☎ Dirs: Guy Trezise, Steve Baker.

In Phase Management 55A Ditton Rd, Surbiton, Surrey, KT6 6RF **t** 05601 759669 **e** mail@inphasemanagement.com **w** inphasemanagement.com ☎ Director: Fay Woolven.

In2music Flat 3, 1 Prince of Wales Rd, London, NW5 3LW **t** 020 7428 2604 **f** 020 7424 0183 **e** jessicain2music@aol.com ☎ Contact: Jessica Peel.

Incredible Management PO Box 28965, London, SW14 7WX **t** 020 8487 8868 **f** 020 8181 6487 **e** graham@incrediblemanagement.com **w** incrediblemanagement.com ☎ Director / Artist Manager: Graham Filmer.

WEB SHERIFF®
WWW.WEBSHERIFF.COM T: +44 (0)208 323 8013

Independent Sound Management (ISM)
3rd Floor, 39 Margaret St, London, W1G OJQ
t 020 7493 9200 **f** 020 7493 9111
e alexis@independentsound.net ✉ GM: Alexis Vokos.

Innocent Management 45 Sylvan Avenue, London,
N22 5JA **t** 07896 428 861
e info@innocentmanangement.com
w innocentmanangement.com ✉ Contact: Lise Regan.

Insanity Artists Agency Ltd Moray House, 23-
31 Great Titchfield Street, London, W1W 7PA
t 020 7927 6222 **f** 020 7927 6223
e info@insanitygroup.com **w** insanitygroup.com
✉ MD: Andy Varley.

Instinct Management 10 Nightingale Lane, London,
SW12 8TB **t** 020 8675 9233 **e** geoffsmith3@mac.com
✉ Manager: Geoff Smith.

Intelligent Music Management Ltd
42A Malden Road, London, NW5 3HG **t** 020 7284 1955
f 020 7424 9876 **e** verity.german@glatmanent.com
✉ MD: Daniel Glatman.

Interactive Music Management 2 Carriglea,
Naas Road, Dublin 12, Ireland **t** +353 1 419 5039
f +353 1 419 5409 **e** info@interactive-music.com
✉ MD: Oliver Walsh.

Interceptor Enterprises 11-14 Kensington St,
Brighton, BN1 4AJ **t** 01273 699777 **f** 01273 699555
e info@interceptor.co.uk ✉ Manager: Charlie Charlton.

International Artists** 4th Floor, Holborn Hall, 193-
197 High Holborn, London, WC1V 7BD **t** 020 7025 0600
f 020 7404 9865 **e** reception@intart.co.uk
w internationalartistes.com ✉ Dir: Phil Dale.

Intuition Music Limited 1 Devonport Mews, London,
W12 8NG **e** berni@intuitionmusic.com ✉ Contact: Berni
Griffiths 07771 743 077.

INXS Music Management (London)
PO Box 39464, London, N10 1WP **t** 07779 340 154
f 020 8883 4086 **e** info@inxs.com **w** inxs.com
✉ MD: Nathan Hull.

J Management Unit A, The Courtyard, 42 Colwith Rd,
London, W6 9EY **t** 020 8846 3737 **f** 020 8846 3738
e john.arnison@seginternational.com **w** johnarnison.com
✉ MD: John Arnison.

Jaba Music Management 57b Riding House St,
London, W1W 7EF **t** 020 7631 0576
e barry@jabamusic.co.uk **w** jabamusic.co.uk
✉ Contact: Barry Campbell.

Jack 'N' Jill Artiste Management
F3, 60 West End Lane, London, NW6 2NE **t** 07050 056 175
f 020 7372 3088 **e** JNJ@mgmt.fsbusiness.co.uk
w myspace.com/jnjmgmt ✉ MD: Joycelyn Phillips 07860
232 527.

Jackie Davidson Management
Network European Business Centre, 329-
339 Putney Bridge Rd, London, SW15 2PG
t 020 8788 5922 **f** 020 8785 2842
e firstname@jdmanagement.co.uk
w jdmanagement.co.uk ✉ MD: Jackie Davidson.

Jamdown Ltd Stanley House Studios,
39 Stanley Gardens, London, W3 7SY **t** 020 8735 0280
f 020 8930 1073 **e** othman@jamdown-music.com
w jamdown-music.com ✉ MD: Othman Mukhlis.

James Barnes Music The Basement, 6 Pond Rd,
London, SE3 9JL **t** 07710 373 235
e james@jamesbarnesmusic.com
w jamesbarnesmusic.com ✉ Contact: James Barnes
07710373235.

James Grant Music 94 Strand On The Green,
Chiswick, London, W4 3NN **t** 020 8742 4950
f 020 8742 4951 **e** enquiries@jamesgrant.co.uk
w jamesgrant.co.uk ✉ Co-MDs: Simon Hargreaves, Nick
Worsley.

Jax Management Ltd 45 Dalrymple Rd, London,
SE4 2BQ **t** 07939 131362 **e** ian@jaxmanagement.co.uk
✉ MD: Ian Mizen.

Jive Entertainment Services PO Box 9071, Gaulby,
Billesdon, Leicestershire, LE7 9YP **t** 01162 599095
e hojive@aol.com ✉ MD: Dave Bartram 07831 835635.

Jive Entertainments PO Box 9071, Gaulby, Billesdon,
Leicester, LE7 9YP **t** 01162 599225 **e** hojive@aol.com
✉ MD: Dave Bartram.

JJ Artist Management Studio Mews,
32 Milton Grove, London, N11 1AX **t** 07737 315 633
f 020 8351 9313 **e** info@jjartists.co.uk
w myspace.com/keishawhitemusic ✉ Creative
Director: Jennifer Dias.

John Miles Organisation Cadbury Camp Lane,
Clapton In Gordano, Bristol, BS20 7SB **t** 01275 854675
f 01275 810186 **e** john@johnmiles.org.uk
w johnmilesorganisation.org.uk ✉ MD: John Miles 01275
856770.

John Taylor Management PO Box 272, London,
N20 0BY **t** 020 8368 0340 **f** 020 8361 3370 **e** john@jt-
management.demon.co.uk ✉ MD: John Taylor.

**Jonathan Lipman Ltd - Talent Management &
PR** 7 Poland St, London, W1F 8PU **t** 0871 221 0011
e info@jonathanlipman.com **w** jonathanlipman.com
✉ Contact: Jonathan Lipman Ltd - Talent Management &
PR.

Jonny Paul Management 2 Downsbury Studios,
40 Steeles Rd, London, NW3 4SA **t** 020 7586 3005
f 020 7586 3005 **e** jonny@paul66.fsworld.co.uk
✉ MD: Jonny Paul.

JPR Management PO Box 3062, Brighton,
East Sussex, BN50 9EA **t** 01273 779944 **f** 01273 779967
e info@jprmanagement.co.uk **w** jprmanagement.co.uk
✉ MD: John Reid.

WEB SHERIFF®
WWW.WEBSHERIFF.COM T: +44 (0)208 323 8013

JPS Management PO Box 2643, Reading, Berks, RG5 4GF **t** 0118 969 9269 **f** 0118 969 9264 **e** johnjpsuk@aol.com ✉ MD: John Saunderson 07885 058 911.

Jukes Productions Ltd PO Box 13995, London, W9 2FL **t** 020 7286 9532 **e** jukes@easynet.co.uk **w** jukesproductions.co.uk ✉ MD: Geoff Jukes.

Just Another Management Co Hope House, 40 St Peters Road, London, W6 9BD **t** 020 8741 6020 **f** 020 8741 8362 **e** justmusic@justmusic.co.uk ✉ Director: Serena Benedict.

Just Noize PO Box 84, Bexley, Kent, DA5 9AP **t** 07972 243027 & 07816 958935 **e** info@justnoize.com **w** justnoize.com ✉ Directors: Laurie Moon & Daniel Millington.

Justin Perry Management PO Box 20242, London, NW1 7FL **t** 020 7485 1113 **e** info@proofsongs.co.uk

JW Management 380 Longbanks, Harlow, Essex, CM18 7PG **t** 01279 304 526 **f** 01279 304 526 **e** jpweston@ntlworld.com ✉ Manager/Consultant: John Weston ACCA.

Kabuki 23 Weavers Way, Camden Town, London, NW1 0XF **t** 020 7916 2142 **e** email@kabuki.co.uk **w** kabuki.co.uk ✉ Manager: Sheila Naujoks.

KAL Management 95 Gloucester Rd, Hampton, Middlesex, TW12 2UW **t** 020 8783 0039 **f** 020 8979 6487 **e** kaplan222@aol.com **w** kaplan-kaye.co.uk ✉ Dir: Kaplan Kaye.

Karma Entertainment Group Brentwood, Newby, Middlesbrough, TS8 0AQ **t** 07841 622 200 **e** info@karmaeg.com **w** karmaeg.com ✉ Dir: Kevin Parry.

Kartel 13 Milton House Mansions, Shacklewell Lane, London, E8 2EH **t** 020 8525 0055 **e** info@kartelcreative.co.uk **w** kartel.mu ✉ Artist Manager: Charles Kirby-Welch.

Katherine Howard Public Relations and Artist Management The Mill House, Bridge St, London, Norfolk, NR14 6NA **t** 01508 521800 **e** info@katherinehoward.co.uk **w** katherinehoward.co.uk ✉ MD: Katherine Howard.

Keith Aspden Management **e** keith@keithaspden.co.uk ✉ Contact: Keith Aspden 0754 383 1186.

Keith Harris Music PO Box 2290, Maidenhead, Berkshire, SL6 6WA **t** 01628 674422 **f** 01628 631379 **e** keith@keithharrismusic.co.uk ✉ MD: Keith Harris.

Key Management 20 Lower Stephens Street, Dublin 2, Ireland **t** +353 1 478 0191 **f** +353 1 475 1324 **e** info@thecube.ie ✉ A&R Director: Mark French.

Key Music Management 25 Bridge Lane, Bramhall, Cheshire, SK7 3AB **t** 0161 439 6238 **f** 0161 221 3682 **e** richard@kmmltd.com ✉ Managing Director: Richard Jones.

Kickstart Management 12 Port House, Square Rigger Row, Plantation Wharf, London, SW11 3TY **t** 020 7223 8666 **f** 020 7223 8777 **e** info@kickstart.uk.net ✉ Director: Ken Middleton.

Kim Glover Management The White House, 32 Thornton Hill, Wimbledon, London, SW19 4HS **t** 020 8947 5475 **f** 020 8947 5478 **e** info@bandandbrand.com **w** bandandbrand.com ✉ MD: Kim Glover.

Krack Music Management East Yorkshire **t** 01405 861124 **e** alan@krack.prestel.co.uk ✉ MD: Alan Lacey 07881 672 014.

KSO Management Consultancy PO Box 52,279, London, SW16 4YS **t** 07956 120837 **e** marcusanthony@ksorecords.com **w** ksorecords.com ⬛ KsorecordsConsultancy ⬛ myspace.com/ksorecords ⬛ twitter.com/ksorecords ⬛ youtube.com/user/ksorecords ✉ MD: Marcus Anthony.

Kudos Management Crown Studios, 16-18 Crown Rd, Twickenham, Middlesex, TW1 3EE **t** 020 8891 4233 **f** 020 8891 2339 **e** kudos@camino.co.uk ✉ MD: Billy Budis.

L25 Entertainment 16 Rowan Walk, London, N2 0QJ **t** 07973 624443 **e** info@L25entertainment.co.uk ✉ Directors: Darren Michaelson, Polly Comber 020 8455 2014.

Last Suppa Management The Coach House, 1a Putney Heath Lane, London, SW15 3JG **t** 020 71931325 **e** jon@lastsuppa.com **w** lastsuppa.com ✉ Managing Director: Jon Sexton.

Latin Arts Services LAS House, 10 Derby Hill Crescent, London, SE23 3YL **t** 020 8291 9236 **f** 020 8291 9236 **e** bookings@latinartsgroup.com **w** latinartsgroup.com ✉ Director: Hector Rosquete 07956 446 342.

Leafman 31 Belsize Park, London, NW3 4DX **t** 07767 405 056 **e** liam@leafsongs.com ✉ MD: Liam Teeling.

Lee & Co 3 Taylor Avenue, Silsden, Keighley, West Yorks, BO20 0DY **t** 01535 653 139 **e** erika@letstalkmusic.com ✉ Contact: Erika Lee 07969 697 660.

Lee Management Dean Street Studios, 59 Dean St, London, W1D 6AN **t** 020 7734 8009 **e** jazzlb@leemanagement.co.uk ✉ MD: Jasmin Lee.

The Lemon Group 1st Floor, 17 Bowater Road, Westminster Industrial Estate, Woolwich, London, SE18 5TF **t** 07989 340 593 **e** brian@thelemongroup.com **w** thelemongroup.com ✉ MD: Brian Allen.

Let It Rock Management - Let It Rock Promotions PO Box 3, Newport, NP20 3YB **t** 07973 715 875 **e** alanjones@cmcpromotions.co.uk ✉ Principal: Alan Jones.

Level 22 Management 111 Princess Rd, Manchester, M14 4RB **t** 0161 226 9156 **e** level22uk@yahoo.co.uk ✉ Director: Randolph Mike 07950 102 202.

WEB SHERIFF®
WWW.WEBSHERIFF.COM T: +44 (0)208 323 8013

Business Services: Artist Management

LH Management Studio 205, Westbourne Studios, 242 Acklam Road, London, W10 5JJ **t** 020 8968 0637 **e** info@lhmanagement.com 🔲 MD: Lisa Horan.

Liberation Management
The Shack at Walnut Cottage, Walden Road, Hadstock, Cambs, CB21 4NX **t** 01223 890 186
e jamie@liberationmanagement.com 🔲 Manager & Marketing Consultant: Jamie Spencer 07771 506 820.

Liberty City Music PO Box 451, Macclesfield, Cheshire, SK10 3FR **t** 07921 626 900
e darren@libertycity.biz **w** libertycity.biz 🔲 MD: Darren Eager.

Liquid Management Unit 101 Canalot Studios, 222 Kensal Rd, London, W10 5BN **f** 07092 389779
e info@Liquidmanagement.net
🔲 facebook.com/liquidmanagement
🔲 myspace.com/liquidmanagement
🔲 twitter.com/liquidmanagement 🔲 Management: David Manders.

Little Giant Music 2 Hermitage House, Gerrard Road, London, N1 8AT **t** 07779 616 552
e Liza@littlegiantmusic.com **w** littlegiantmusic.com
🔲 Dir: Liza Kumjian-Smith.

Little Victories 14 Spezia Rd, London, NW10 4QJ
t 0794 099 240 **e** stuart@littlevictoriesltd.com
w littlevictoriesltd.com 🔲 Contact: Stuart.

LM2 Entertainment PO Box 57619, London, NW7 1DE **t** 020 8349 1933 **f** 020 8349 1933
e brad.lazarus@LM2.co.uk 🔲 Director: Brad Lazarus.

LOE Music LOE Ltd, 159 Broadhurst Gardens, London, NW6 3AU **t** 020 7328 6100 **f** 020 7624 6384
e kato@loe.uk.net 🔲 MD: Hiroshi Kato.

The London Oratory School Schola
Foundation Seagrave Road, London, SW6 1RX
t 020 7381 7684 **f** 020 7381 7676 **e** schola@los.ac
w london-oratory.org/schola 🔲 Music Administrator: Sebastian Budner 020 7835 0102.

Louis Walsh Management 24 Courtney House, Appian Way, Dublin 6, Ireland **t** +353 1 668 0309
f +353 1 668 0721 **e** info@louiswalsh.net 🔲 MD: Louis Walsh +353 1 668 0982.

Low Fat Management
e darron@lowfatmanagement.com
w lowfatmanagement.com

LTM Innit Studios, 33a Wadeson Street, London, E2 9DR
t 020 8981 9210 **f** 020 8981 9210 **e** mail@lunchtm.co.uk
🔲 Contact: Ed Millett.

Lumin 50 Arne House, Worgan St, London, SE11 5EZ
t 020 7159 0289 **e** hello@lumin.org **w** lumin.org 🔲 Artistic Director: Joana Seguro.

M A C Services PO Box 121, Hove, East Sussex, BN3 4YY **t** 020 8144 9064 **e** sacha@macservices.org.uk
w macservices.org.uk 🔲 Directors: Sacha Taylor-Cox and Bob James.

M4 Management PO Box 605, Cardiff, CF24 3XU
t 02920 317 331 **e** m4management@btinternet.com
🔲 Dir: Jo Hunt 07770 988 503.

Machine Management 4th Floor, 10-16 Scrutton St, London, EC2A 4RU **t** 020 7247 4227 **f** 020 7247 4700
e iw@machinemanagement.co.uk
w machinemanagement.co.uk 🔲 Contact: Iain Watt (MD), Alexandra Popoff, Liz Pagett.

Mad Management 7a Knivet Close, Rayleigh, Essex, SS6 8PD **t** 01268 771113 **f** 01268 774192
e madmanagementltd@aol.com 🔲 MD: Alex Rose.

MaDa Music 25 Milton Court, Chesterton Close, Wandsworth, London, SW18 1ST **t** 07771 710234
e adamnicolmusic@gmail.com
w myspace.com/madamusicentertainment 🔲 MD: Adam Nicol.

Madison Management 6 Cinnamon Gardens, Guildford, Surrey, GU2 9YZ **t** 07810 540 990
e info@madisonmanagement.co.uk
w madisonmanagement.co.uk 🔲 Artist Manager: Paul Harvey.

MADRIGAL MUSIC artist management Guy Hall, Awre, Gloucestershire, GL14 1EL **t** 01594 510512
f 01594 510512 **e** artists@madrigalmusic.co.uk
w madrigalmusic.co.uk
🔲 myspace.com/madrigalmusicmanagement
🔲 MD/Head of A&R: Nick Ford.

magnoliamam Ltd - inc: the magnolia label
Bank View, Beeston Brook, Tarporley, CW6 9NH
t 01829 730733 **e** dave@magnoliamam.co.uk
w magnoliamam.co.uk 🔲 ww.
www.myspace.com/magnoliamamltd 🔲 davewibberley
🔲 youtube.com/magnoliaMAMLtd 🔲 MD: Dave Wibberley.

Mako Music 27 Waverton Rd, London, SW18 3BZ
t 020 8870 6790 **e** dombrownlow@tiscali.co.uk
🔲 MD: Dominic Brownlow.

Man's Best Friend The Big White House, Pett Level Rd, Pett Level, East Sussex, TN35 4EH
t 07830 294 522 **e** info@the-modern.co.uk **w** the-modern.co.uk 🔲 MD: Darron Sven Coppin.

Manager Bat for Lashes, Mechanical Bride
31 Mortimer Rd, London, NW10 5QR **t** 020 8962 0516
e dickodell@hotmail.com 🔲 Artist Manager: Dick O'Dell 07831 757156.

Manta Ray Music Ltd 145-157 St John St, London, EC1V 4PY **e** andre@mantaraymusic.co.uk
w mantaraymusic.co.uk 🔲 Contact: Andre do Valle +44 203 236 5358.

MAP Music Ltd 46 Grafton Rd, London, NW5 3DU
t 020 7916 0545 **f** 020 7284 4232 **e** info@mapmusic.net
w mapmusic.net 🔲 MD: Chris Townsend 020 7916 0544.

Marsupial Management Ltd 103 Camp Rd, Gerrards Cross, Bucks, SL9 7PF **t** 07774 982156
f +1 250 345 0316 **e** john@marsupialmanagement.com
🔲 MD: John Brand +1 250 345 0316.

WEB SHERIFF®
WWW.WEBSHERIFF.COM T: +44 (0)208 323 8013

Max Energy Limited The Old Steam House, Herstmonceux, E. Sussex, BN27 1RF
t 01323 731 727 or 07905 147709
e nelson@solarnavigator.net **w** solarnavigator.net
✉ Contact: Nelson Kruschandl.

MBL 1 Cowcross St, London, EC1M 6DR **t** 020 7253 7755 **f** 020 7251 8096 ✉ MD: Robert Linney.

MCM e mcmcork@aol.com ✉ Artist Manager / Music Consultant: Meredith Cork 07836 716333.

Mel Bush Organization Ltd
26 Albany Business Park, Cabot Lane, Poole, Dorset, BH17 7BX **t** 01202 691891 **f** 01202 691896
e info@melbush.com **w** davidessex.com ✉ MD: Mel Bush.

Memnon Entertainment Habib House, 3rd Floor, 9 Stevenson Sq, Piccadilly, Manchester, M1 1DB
t 0161 238 8516 **f** 0161 236 6717
e info@memnonentertainment.com
w memnonentertainment.com
✉ /memnonentertainment ✉ Director of Business Affairs: Rudi Kidd 07711 269939.

Menace Management Ltd. 2 Park Rd, Radlett, Herts, WD7 8EQ **t** 01923 853789 **f** 01923 853318
e menacemusicmanagement@btopenworld.com
✉ MD: Dennis Collopy 01923 854789.

Merlin Elite Ltd Hammersmith Studios, 55 Yeldham Road, London, W6 8JF **t** 020 8834 8900
f 020 8834 8901 **e** firstname.lastname@merlinelite.co.uk
w merlinelite.co.uk ✉ Contact: Richard Thompson, Giles Baxendale.

Metamorphosis Management Matrix Complex, 91 Peterborough Road, London, SW6 3BU
t 020 7751 2751 **f** 020 7371 5454
e mark@crownmusic.co.uk ✉ Manager: Mark Hargreaves.

Metro Associates Latimer Studios, West Kington, Wilts, SN14 7JQ **t** 01249 783 599 **f** 0870 169 8433
e Dolan@metro-associates.co.uk **w** media-print.co.uk
✉ CEO: Mike Dolan.

Michael McDonagh Management P.O.B 28286, Winchmore Hill, London, N21 3WT **t** 020 8886 5743
e caramusicltd@dial.pipex.com ✉ Director: Michael McDonagh.

Midi Management Ltd The Old Barn, Jenkins Lane, Great Hallingbury, Essex, CM22 7QL **t** 01279 759067
f 01279 504145 **e** midi-management@btconnect.com
✉ Manager/Director: Mike Champion.

Midnight To Six Management 4th Floor, 1 Cowcross St, London, EC1M 6DR **t** 020 7251 6226
e tony@midnighttosix.com ✉ Director: Tony Crean.

Mighty Music Management 2 Stucley Place, Camden, London, NW1 8NS **t** 020 7482 6660
f 020 7482 6606 **e** art@mainartery.co.uk ✉ Director: Jo Mirowski.

Mike Malley Entertainments
10 Holly Park Gardens, Finchley, London, N3 3NJ
t 020 8346 4109 **f** 020 8346 1104
e mikemalley@ukstars.co.uk **w** ukstars.co.uk ✉ MD: Mike Malley.

Mission Management Fairlight Mews, 15 St Johns Rd, Kingston upon Thames, KT1 4AN
t 0208 977 0632 **f** 0870 770 8669
e info@missionlimited.com **w** missionlimited.com
✉ MD: Sir Harry.

MK Music Ltd t 07939 080524 **e** debi@mickkarn.net
w mickkarn.net ✉ myspace.com/mickkarn
✉ Director: Debi Zornes.

Mobb Rule Management PO Box 26335, London, N8 9ZA **t** 020 8340 8050 **e** info@mobbrule.com
w mobbrule.com ✉ MD: Stewart Pettey.

Mockingbird Music PO Box 52, Marlow, Bucks, SL7 2YB **t** 01491 579214 **f** 01491 579214
e mockingbirdmusic@aol.com ✉ Artiste Management: Leon B Fisk.

Modal Management Prospect House, Lower Caldecote, Beds, SG18 9BA **t** 01767 601 398
e davidsamuel@modalmanagement.co.uk
w modalmanagement.co.uk ✉ MD: David Samuel 07976 254 651.

Modest! Management Studios 2-3, Matrix Complex, 91 Peterborough Rd, London, SW6 3BU **t** 020 7384 6410
f 020 7384 6411 **e** firstname@modestmanagement.com
w modestentertainment.com ✉ Partners: Richard Griffiths, Harry Magee.

Moksha Management Ltd PO Box 102, London, E15 2HH **t** 020 8555 5423 **f** 020 8519 6834
e info@moksha.co.uk **w** moksha.co.uk ✉ MD: Charles Cosh.

Mondo Management Unit 2D, Clapham North Arts Centre, 26-32 Voltaire Rd, London, SW4 6DH **t** 020 7720 7411 **f** 020 7720 8095
e rob@ihtrecords.com **w** davidgray.com ✉ Contact: Rob Holden.

Money Talks Management Cadillac Ranch, Pencraig Uchaf, Cwm Bach, Whitland, Dyfed, SA34 0DT
t 01994 484466 **f** 01994 484294
e cadillacranch@telco4u.net **w** nikturner.com ✉ Dir: Sid Money.

Moneypenny Management
The Stables, Westwood House, Main St, North Dalton, Driffield, East Yorks, YO25 9XA **t** 01377 217815
f 01377 217754 **e** nigel@adastey.demon.co.uk
w adastra-music.co.uk/moneypenny ✉ MD: Nigel Morton 07977 455882.

Monkeybiz Management Entertainment Agency 13 Homan House, Kings Avenue, London, SW4 8DB **t** 020 8683 9373
e info@monkeybizmanagement.com
w monkeybizmanagement.com ✉ Contact: Donlald Deans 07940 550 153.

WEB SHERIFF®
WWW.WEBSHERIFF.COM T: +44 (0)208 323 8013

Monumental Management Ltd 15 Chalk Farm Rd, Camden, London, NW1 8AG **t** 020 7428 2592 **e** info@monumentalmanagement.co.uk **w** MonumentalManagement.co.uk ✉ MD: Brett Leboff.

Morethan4 Music & Management PO Box 53847, London, SE27 7AD **t** 020 7043 6064 **e** info@morethan4.com **w** morethan4.com ✉ MD: Anthony Hamer-Hodges 07885 512 721.

Mothership Management Studio 3, 3a Brackenbury Rd, Hammersmith, London, W6 0BE **t** 020 8762 9159 **e** rebecca@mothershipmanagement.com **w** mothershipmanagement.com ▨ myspace.com/mothershipmanagement ◼ twitter.com/mothershipmgmt ✉ Contact: Rebecca Sichel-Coates.

Motive Music Management 93b Scrubs Lane, London, NW10 6QU **t** 07808 939 919 **e** nathan@motivemusic.co.uk ✉ Contact: Nathan Leeks.

MP Music Services Ltd 32 Ashley Close, Walton on Thames, Surrey, KT12 1BJ **t** 020 8123 6551 **e** info@mpmusicservices.co.uk **w** mpmusicservices.co.uk ✉ MD: Mark Plunkett.

MPC Entertainment MPC House, 15-16 Maple Mews, London, NW6 5UZ **t** 020 7624 1184 **f** 020 7624 4220 **e** mpc@mpce.com **w** mpce.com ✉ Chief Executive: Michael Cohen.

MSM Music Consultants PO Box 10036, Halesowen, B62 8WD **t** 07785 506637 **e** trevorlonguk@aol.com ✉ MD: Trevor Long.

Muirhead Management 202 Fulham Rd, Chelsea, London, SW10 9PJ **t** 020 7460 4668 **e** dennis@muirheadmanagement.co.uk **w** muirheadmanagement.co.uk ✉ CEO: Dennis Muirhead 07785 226542.

Music First PO Box 3418, Sheffield, S11 7WJ **t** 0114 268 5441 **e** info@musicfirst.info **w** musicfirst.info ✉ Dir: Barney Vernon.

Music Gets Me High (MGMH) D-72 Okhla Industrial Area Phase 1, New Delhi, 110020, India **t** +91 11 4652 5992 **e** mgmh@mgmh.net **w** mgmh.net ◼ facebook.com/group.php?gid=2247939086&ref=ts ▨ myspace.com/mgmhindia ✉ C.E.O.: Ritnika Nayan +91 98 1007 8890.

Music Management 65 Tierney Rd, London, SW2 4QH **t** 020 8678 0167 **e** paul@themusicmanagement.com **w** themusicmanagement.com ✉ Artist Manager: Paul Carey 07971 871481.

Musicians Incorporated Ltd PO Box 56907, London, N10 2WD **t** 020 8365 2976 **f** 020 8365 3748 **e** info@musiciansincorporated.com **w** musiciansincorporated.com ✉ Contact: Jason.

Musicmedia Artists **t** 08456 432678 **e** info@musicmediaartists.com **w** musicmediaartists.com ✉ Contact: Sean Quinn.

MWM Music Management Limited 11 Great George St, Bristol, BS1 5RR **t** 0117 929 2393 **f** 0117 929 2696 **e** craig@mwmuk.com ✉ Director: Craig Williams.

Native Management Unit 32, Ransomes Dock, 35-37 Parkgate Rd, London, SW11 4NP **t** 020 7801 1919 **f** 020 7738 1819 **e** marie.native@19.co.uk **w** nativemanagement.com ✉ MD: Peter Evans.

Negus-Fancey Company 78 Portland Rd, London, W11 4LQ **t** 020 7727 2063 **f** supplied on request **e** mail@negusfancey.com ✉ Contact: Charles Negus-Fancey.

NEM Productions (UK) Priory House, 55 Lawe Road, South Shields, Tyne and Wear, NE33 2AL **t** 0191 427 6207 **f** 0191 427 6323 **e** dave@nemproductions.com **w** nemproductions.com ✉ Contact: Dave Smith.

Nettwerk Management UK Clearwater Yard, 35 Inverness St, London, NW1 7HB **t** 020 7424 7500 **f** 020 7424 7501 **e** eleanor@nettwerk.com **w** nettwerk.com ✉ Contact: Sam Slattery.

Nigel Martin-Smith Management Nemesis House, 1 Oxford Court, Bishopsgate, Manchester, M2 3WQ **t** 0161 228 6465 **e** nigel@nmsmanagement.co.uk ✉ MD: Nigel Martin-Smith.

No Half Measures Ltd. 5 Eagle St, 1st Floor, Glasgow, G4 9XA **t** 0141 353 8822 **f** 0141 353 8823 **e** info@nohalfmeasures.com **w** nohalfmeasures.com ◼ facebook.com/nohalfmeasures ▨ myspace.com/nohalfmeasures ◼ twitter.com/nohalfmeasures ▨ youtube.com/nohalfmeasures ✉ MD: Dougie Souness.

Normal Management 30 Swinton St, London, WC1X 9NX **t** 07956 236041 / 07957 613167 **e** aliceharter@normal-management.com / mrpaulnoble@gmail.com ✉ MDs: Alice Harter, Paul Noble.

North & South PO Box 1099, London, SE5 9HT **t** 020 7326 4824 **f** 020 7535 5901 **e** gamesmaster@chartmoves.com ✉ MD: Dave Klein.

Northern Lights Mangement 74 Rosebery Road, London, N10 2LA **t** 07887 983 452 **f** 020 8342 8213 **e** jonathan@northernlightsmgt.co.uk **w** northernlightsmgt.co.uk ✉ Manager: Jonathan Morley.

Northern Music Company Cheapside Chambers, 43 Cheapside, Bradford, West Yorks, BD1 4HP **t** 01274 306361 **f** 01274 730097 **e** info@northernmusic.co.uk **w** northernmusic.co.uk ✉ MD: Andy Farrow.

NOW Music 25 Commercial St, Brighouse, West Yorkshire, HD61AF **t** 01484 723557 **e** john@now-music.com **w** now-music.com ✉ MD: John Wagstaff.

NoWHere Management 30 Tweedholm Ave East, Walkerburn, Peeblesshire, EH43 6AR **t** 01896 870284 **e** michaelwild@btopenworld.com ✉ Owner: Michael Wild 07812 818 183.

WEB SHERIFF®
WWW.WEBSHERIFF.COM T: +44 (0)208 323 8013

Nutty Tart Management Call for address.
t 07951 062 566 **e** nuttytartmanagement@hotmail.com
MD: Mandy Freedman.

NVA Management Canary Wharf Tower, 1 Canada Sq,
London, E14 5DY **t** 0844 335 3980 **f** 0844 335 3981
e info@nvamanagement.com **w** nvamanagement.com
myspace.com/nvamgt twitter.com/nvaent
youtube.com/nvatv **MD:** Chris Nathaniel.

O-Mix 18 Avonmore Rd, London, W14 8RR
t 020 7622 4176 **f** 020 7622 4176 **e** info@o-mix.co.uk
w o-mix.co.uk **Dir:** Alex Kerr-Wilson.

Octagon Music Octagon House, 81-
83 Fulham High St, London, SW6 3JW **t** 020 7862 0121
f 020 7862 0007 **e** firstname.lastname@octagon.com
w octagon-uk.com **MD:** Peter Rudge.

OMC Management 1st Floor, 9 Park End St, Oxford,
OX1 1HH **t** 01865 798791
e dave.newton@oxfordmusic.net **Mgr:** Dave Newton.

One Fifteen 1 Prince Of Orange Lane, Greenwich,
London, SE10 8JQ **t** 020 8293 0999 **f** 020 8293 9525
e enquiry@onefifteen.com **w** onefifteen.com **MD:** Paul
Loasby.

Onside Management Suite 4, Alexander House,
15 Ware Rd, Hertford, SG13 7DZ **t** 01992 535126
f 01992 535127 **e** mail@onside.co.uk **Managing
Director:** Nick Boyles.

Opal-Chant 4 Pembridge Mews, London, W11 1LU
t 020 7221 4933 **f** 020 7727 5404
e opal@opaloffice.com **Director:** Jane Geerts.

Open Top Music 20 Market Place,
Kingston upon Thames, KT1 1JP
e mail@opentopmusic.com **w** opentopmusic.com
Dir: Nick Turner.

Opium (Arts) Ltd 49 Portland Rd, London, W11 4LJ
t 020 7229 5080 **f** 020 7229 4841
e adrian@opiumarts.com **Contact:** Richard Chadwick,
Adrian Molloy.

OPL Management 4 The Limes, North End Way,
London, NW3 7HG **t** 020 8209 0025
e oplmanagement@aol.com **Director:** Miss Sabina Van
de Wattyne.

Ornadel Management Unit B, 11 Bell Yard Mews,
175 Bermondsey St, London, SE1 3TN **t** 020 7407 4466
e guy@ornadel.com **w** ornadel.com **Contact:** Guy
Ornadel.

Out There Management Strongroom, 120-
124 Curtain Rd, London, EC2A 3SQ **t** 020 7739 6903
f 020 7613 2715 **e** outthere@outthere.co.uk
Manager: Stephen Taverner.

Outerglobe (Global Fusion)
113 Cheesemans Terrace, London, W14 9XH
t 020 7385 5447 **f** 020 7385 5447
e debbie@outerglobe.com **w** outerglobe.com
MD: Debbie Golt.

Oxygen Management Ltd Floors 1-
3, 40a Old Compton St, Soho, London, W1D 4TU
t 020 7529 9753 **f** 020 7439 0794
e Giles.Cooper@oxygenmanagement.com
w oxygenmanagement.com **Directors:** Giles Cooper,
Mark Reid.

P&P Music International Crabtree Cottage,
Mill Lane, Kidmore End, Oxon, RG4 9HB **t** 0118 972 4356
f 0118 972 4809 **e** ppmusicint@aol.com
w dovehouserecords.com **President:** Thomas
Pemberton.

P. B. M. 16B Kingsgate Rd, London, NW6 4TB
t 020 7625 1082 **e** paul@paulbellmanagement.com
w paulbellmanagement.com **MD:** Paul Bell.

P3 Music Management Ltd. PO Box 6641,
Blairgowrie, PH10 9AD **t** 01828 633790 **f** 0870 137 6738
e james@p3music.com **w** p3music.com
facebook.com/pages/P3-Music-Label/50374779811
myspace.com/p3musiclabel twitter.com/p3music
youtube.com/P3MusicLabel **Director:** James Taylor.

P3M Music Management & Consultancy
126a Talbot Rd, London, W11 1JA **t** 07771 862401
e paulmoorep3m@aol.com **MD:** Paul Moore.

Parallel Universe Music 7 Eagle Court, 69 High St,
London, N8 7QG **t** 07788 545 112 **f** 020 8340 8031
e carmen@paralleluniversemusic.com **Artist
Manager:** Carmen Layton-Bennett.

Park Promotions PO Box 651, Oxford, OX2 9AZ
t 01865 241 717 **f** 01865 204 556
e info@parkrecords.com **w** parkrecords.com **MD:** John
Dagnell.

Parliament Management PO Box 6328, London,
N2 0UN **t** 020 8444 9841 **f** 020 8442 1973
e info@parliament-management.com **A&R:** Damian
Baetens.

Part Rock Management Ltd 1 Conduit St, London,
W1S 2XA **t** 01424 845815 **f** 020 7681 1817
e stewartyoung@mindspring.com **MD:** Stewart Young.

Patrick Garvey Management Ltd
40 North Parade, York, YO40 7AB **t** 01904 621222
f 08700 513884 **e** andrea@patrickgarvey.com
w patrickgarvey.com **Director:** Andrea McDermott.

Paul Barrett (Rock 'N' Roll Enterprises)
21 Grove Terrace, Penarth, South Glamorgan, CF64 2NG
t 029 2070 4279 **f** 029 2070 9989
e barrettrocknroll@ntlworld.com **Contact:** Paul Barrett.

Paul Crockford Management (PCM)
Latimer House, 272 Latimer Rd, London, W10 6QY
t 020 8962 8272 **f** 020 8962 8243
e pcm.assistant@virgin.net **MD:** Paul Crockford.

PCPR Ltd 65 Tierney Rd, London, SW2 4QH
t 07971 871481 **e** paul.carey@pcpr.co.uk
w themusicmanagement.com **Management/Personal
Representation:** Paul Carey.

Pegasus Management 8 Ashington Court, Westwood Hill, Sydenham, London, SE26 6BN **t** 020 8778 9918 **f** 020 8355 7708 **e** PegasusMgnt@hotmail.com ✉ Dir: James Doheny.

Personality Artistes Ltd PO Box 1, Blackpool, Lancashire, FY6 7WS **t** 01253 899 988 **f** 01253 899 333 **e** info@personalityartistes.com **w** personalityartistes.com ✉ MD: Mal Ford 07860 479 092.

Peter Haines Management Montfort, The Avenue, Kingston near Lewes, East Sussex, BN7 3LL **t** 07710 215441 **e** phaines@fsmail.net ✉ Artist Manager: Peter Haines.

PEZ Management 126 Clonmore Street, London, SW18 5HB **t** 020 8480 4445 **f** 020 8480 4446 **e** pezmanagement@aol.com ✉ Contact: Perry Morgan 07831 100 980.

PFB Management 9 Bowmans Lea, London, SE23 3TL **t** 020 8291 3175 **e** paulbibby@freenet.co.uk ✉ MD: Paul Bibby.

Phonetic Music Management Viking House, 12 St Davids Close, Farnham, Surrey, GU9 9DR **t** 01252 330 894 **f** 01252 330 894 **e** james@phoneticmusic.com **w** phoneticmusic.com ✉ MD: James Sefton 07775 515 025.

Pitch One Management Electroline House, Po Box 296, Twickenham, Middx, TW1 9AS **t** 020 8241 7137 **f** 020 8241 7137 **e** rob@pitch-one.net **w** pitch-one.net ✉ CEO: Rob Roar.

PJ Music 156A High St, London Colney, Herts, AL2 1QF **t** 01727 827017 **f** 01727 827017 **e** pjmusic@ukonline.co.uk **w** schmusicmusic.com ✉ Dir: Paul J Bowrey 07860 902 361.

Plan C Management Covetous Corner, Hudnall Common, Little Gaddesden, Herts, HP4 1QW **t** 01442 842851 **f** 01442 842082 **e** christian.ulf@virgin.net **w** plancmusic.com ✉ Manager: Christian Ulf-Hansen.

Playpen Management and Agency 1 Bank Street, Faversham, Kent, ME13 8PR **t** 01795 533 551 **e** terry@playpen.fsbusiness.co.uk **w** myspace.com/playpenagency ✉ Manager: Terry O'Brien 07932 720 058.

Plus Artist Management Plus Music Publishing 36 Follingham Court, Drysdale Pl, London, N1 6LZ **t** 020 7684 8594 **e** info@plusmusic.co.uk **w** plusmusic.co.uk ✉ Proprietor: Desmond Chisholm.

Popbox Management The Louisiana, Wapping Road, Bathurst Terrace, Bristol, BS1 6UA **t** 01179 663 615 **e** migstar007@hotmail.com **w** myspace.com/popboxmanagement ✉ Dir: Michael Schillace 07989 283 253.

PopWorks 1 Lopen Road, Silver Street, London, N18 1PN **t** 020 8807 6268 **f** 020 8351 1497 **e** popworks1@yahoo.com ✉ MD: Linda Duff.

Porcupine Management 33-45 Parr St, Liverpool, Merseyside, L1 4JN **t** 0151 707 1050 **f** 0151 709 4090 **e** oxygenmusic@btinternet.com ✉ Partners: Pete Byrne & Peasy.

Power Artist Management 29 Riversdale Road, Thames Ditton, Surrey, KT7 0QN **t** 020 8398 5236 **f** 020 8398 7901 **e** barry.l.evans@btinternet.com(DO NOT PUBLISH) ✉ MD: Barry Evans.

PR-ISM 2-14 Park Terrace, The Park, Nottingham, NG1 5DN **t** 0115 947 5440 **e** phil.long@virgin.net **w** pr-ism.co.uk ✉ MD: Phil Long 07971 780 821.

The Precious Organisation The Townhouse, 1 Park Gate, Glasgow, G3 6DL **t** 0141 353 2255 **f** 0141 353 3545 **e** elliot@precioustoo.com ✉ MD: Elliot Davis.

Prestige Management The Matrix, 91 Petersborough Rd, London, SW6 3BU **t** 020 7384 6477 **f** 020 7384 6477 **e** info@prestigeuk.com ✉ Partners: Richard Rashman, Matthew Fletcher, Darren Keating.

Previous Management PO Box 61, East Molesey, Surrey, KT8 6BA **t** 020 8224 7643 **e** info@previousmanagement.com **w** previousmanagement.com ✉ Manager: Janis Haves.

Principle Management 30-32 Sir John Rogersons Quay, Dublin 2, Ireland **t** +353 1 677 7330 **f** +353 1 677 7276 **e** Candida@numb.ie ✉ Dir: Paul McGuinness.

Pro-Rock Management Caxton House, Caxton Avenue, Blackpool, Lancashire, FY2 9AP **t** 01253 508670 **f** 01253 508670 **e** promidibfp@aol.com **w** members.aol.com/promidibfp ✉ MD: Ron Sharples.

Probation Management 1st Floor, Warwick Hall, Off Banastre Avenue, Cardiff, CF14 3NR **t** 029 2069 4450 **f** 029 2069 4455 **e** probmgt@btconnect.com **w** myspace.com/probationmanagement ✉ Dirs: Martin Bowen, Adam Stangroom.

Prohibition Management Fulham Palace, Bishops Avenue, London, SW6 6EA **t** 020 7384 7372 **f** 020 7371 7940 **e** Caroline@prohibitiondj.com **w** prohibitiondj.com ✉ MD: Caroline Prothero 07967 610 877.

Prolifica Management Unit 1, 32 Caxton Rd, London, W12 8AJ **t** 020 8740 9920 **f** 020 811 8170 **e** colin@prolifica.co.uk ✉ Dir: Colin Schaverien.

Pure Delinquent 134 Replingham Road, Southfields, London, SW18 5LL **t** 07972 701 243 **f** 020 8870 0790 **e** info@pure-delinquent.com **w** pure-delinquent.com ✉ Dir: Julie Pratt.

Pure DJs 2 Whiting St, Sheffield, S8 9QR **t** 01142 997707 **e** paul@puredjs.com **w** puredjs.com ✉ Director: Paul Grayson 07776 295329.

Pure Music Management 77 Beak St, No. 306, London, W1F 9DB **t** 07766 180 330 **f** 020 7439 3330 **e** puremusicmgmt@yahoo.com ✉ Contact: Michael Cox.

WEB SHERIFF®
WWW.WEBSHERIFF.COM T: +44 (0)208 323 8013

PVA Ltd 2 High Street, Westbury On Trym, Bristol, BS9 3DU **t** 0117 950 4504 **f** 0117 959 1786 **e** enquiries@pva.ltd.uk **w** pva.ltd.uk ✉ Sales Director: John Hutchinson.

PVA Management County House, St Mary's St, Worcester, WR1 1HB **t** 01905 616100 **f** 01905 610709 **e** maggie@pva.co.uk **w** pva.co.uk ✉ Marketing Manager: Maggie Pink.

Quest Management 36 Warple Way, Unit 1D, London, W3 0RG **t** 020 8749 0088 **f** 020 8749 0080 **e** info@quest-management.com ✉ Manager: Scott Rodger.

Quintessential Music PO Box 546, Bromley, Kent, BR2 0RS **t** 020 8402 1984 **f** 020 8325 0708 **e** urban_music@msn.com ✉ Senior Partner: Quincey 07956 389 840.

R2 Management PO Box 100, Moreton-in-Marsh, Gloucestershire, GL56 0ZX **t** 01608 651802 **f** 01608 652814 **e** editor@jacobsladder.org.uk **w** jacobsladder.org.uk ✉ MD: Robb Eden.

Radar Music and Management 31 Lingfield Crescent, Stratford-Upon-Avon, Warwickshire, CV37 9LX **t** 01789 268280 **e** joe@radarmusic.co.uk **w** radarmusic.co.uk ✉ Contact: Joe Cooper.

Radius Music Ltd PO Box 46375, London, SW17 9WJ **t** 020 8672 7030 **f** 020 8672 7030 **e** info@radiusmusic.co.uk **w** radiusmusic.co.uk ✉ Manager: Mark Wood.

Raf E 18 Coronation Court, London, W10 6AL **t** 020 8451 1352 **f** 020 8451 1352 **e** raf2raf@gmail.com ✉ Dir: Raf Edmonds.

Random London **t** 020 8459 1150 **e** steve.malins@btinternet.com **w** metamatic.com ✉ Manager: Steve Malins.

Raw Power Management Bridle House, 36 Bridle Lane, London, W1F 9BZ **t** 0845 331 3300 **f** 0845 331 3500 **e** info@rawpowermanagement.com **w** rawpowermanagement.com ✉ Contact: Craig Jennings.

Raygun Music Management Ltd 350 Portland Rd, Hove, East Sussex, BN3 5LF **t** 07930 376810 **e** julian.deane@raygunmusicmanagement.com **w** raygunmusicmanagement.com ⚑ myspace.com/raygunmusicmanagment ✉ Director: Julian Deane.

Razzamatazz Management 204 Holtye Rd, East Grinstead, West Sussex, RH19 3ES **t** 01342 301617 **e** razzamatazzmanagement@btconnect.com ✉ Dir: Jill Shirley 07836 268292.

Real Time Management PO Box 1275, High Wycombe, Bucks, HP12 3TQ **t** 07772 109 344 **e** chris.smith@real-time-management.co.uk **w** real-time-management.co.uk ✉ MD: Chris Smith.

Red Onion Productions 26-28 Hatherley Mews, Walthamstow, London, E17 4QP **t** 020 8520 3975 **f** 020 8521 6646 **e** info@redonion.uk.com **w** redonion.uk.com ✉ MD: Dee Curtis.

Redd Management The Courtyard, Unit A, 42 Colwith Rd, Hammersmith, London, W6 9EY **t** 020 8846 3737 **f** 020 8846 3738 **e** david@reddmanagement.com ✉ MD: David Moores.

Represents Artist Management Office 3, Bannon Court, 54-58 Micheal Road, London, SW6 2EF **t** 020 7384 2080 **f** 020 7384 2055 **e** ben@represents.co.uk **w** represents.co.uk ✉ MD: Ben King.

Richard Martin Management Fast Helicopter Building, Hangar 4, Shoreham Airport, West Sussex, BN43 5FF **t** 0845 460 0333 **f** 01273 446494 **e** ric@ricmartinagency.com **w** hot-chocolate.co.uk ✉ Manager: Richard Martin 07860 722255.

Richard Ogden Management Ltd Flat 6, 56 Cambridge Rd, Hove, BN3 1DF **t** 07775 942131 **e** thelma@richardogdenmanagement.com **w** richardogdenmanagement.com ✉ MD: Richard Ogden.

Richman Management Ltd 103 Southwood Lane, London, N6 5TB **t** 020 8374 2258 **e** richard@richmanmanagement.com ✉ MD: Richard Shipman.

Riot Management Limited 17 Clifford St, London, W1S 3RQ **e** Matt@Riot-Management.com ✉ Manager/Owner/Director: Matt Page.

Riverman Management Top Floor, George House, Brecon Rd, London, W6 8PY **t** 020 7381 4000 **f** 020 7381 9666 **e** info@riverman.co.uk **w** riverman.co.uk ✉ Dir: David McLean / Alex Weston.

Riviera Music Management 83 Dolphin Crescent, Paignton, Devon, TQ3 1JZ **t** 07071 226 078 **f** 0870 133 0100 **e** Info@rivieramusic.net **w** rivieramusic.net ✉ MD: Kevin Jarvis.

RLM (Richard Law Management) 58 Marylands Road, Maida Vale, London, W9 2DR **t** 020 7286 1706 **f** 020 7266 1293 **e** richard@rlmanagement.co.uk ✉ Manager: Richard Law.

Robert Miller Management Running Media Group Ltd., 14 Victoria Rd, Douglas, Isle of Man, IM2 4ER **t** 01624 677214 **e** info@runningmedia.com **w** runningmedia.com ✉ MD: Bob Miller 07973 129068.

Robin Morton Consultancy 22 Herbert Street, Glasgow, G20 6NB **t** 0141 560 2748 or 0141 337 1199 **f** 0141 357 0655 **e** robinmorto@aol.com ✉ Contact: Robin Morton 07870 590 909.

Roedean Music Ltd Suite 5, 52 Broadwick St, London, W1F 7AF **t** 020 7434 7286 **f** 020 7434 7288 **e** tonyhall@btconnect.com ✉ MD: Tony Hall.

Roger Boden Management 2 Gawsworth Rd, Macclesfield, Cheshire, SK11 8UE **t** 01625 420163 **f** 01625 420168 **e** rbm@cottagegroup.co.uk **w** cottagegroup.co.uk ✉ MD: Roger Boden.

WEB SHERIFF®
WWW.WEBSHERIFF.COM T: +44 (0)208 323 8013

Rose Rouge International AWS House, Trinity Square, St Peter Port, Guernsey, GY1 1LX **t** 01481 728 283 **f** 01481 714 118 **e** roserouge@cwgsy.net 📧 Director/Producer/Composer: Steve Free.

Rough Trade Management 66 Golborne Rd, London, W10 5PS **t** 020 8875 5194 **f** 020 8968 6715 **e** kellykiley@roughtraderecords.com **w** roughtradeproducers.com 📧 Artist Liason: Kelly Kiley.

Route One Management 24 Derby St, Edgeley, Stockport, Cheshire, SK3 9HF **t** 0161 476 1172 **e** andylacallen@yahoo.co.uk **w** spinning-fields.com 📧 Director: Andy Callen 07950 119 151.

RP Management - Urban Consultants 51A Wood Ville, The Heath, Surrey, CR7 8LN **t** 07956 368680 **e** R.Pascoe@RPMan.co.uk **w** RPMan.co.uk 📘 facebook.com/group.php?gid=10695920241 📷 myspace.com/RPManagement 🐦 twitter.com/RichardPascoe 📺 youtube.com/user/RichieDVIP 📧 CEO: Richard Pascoe.

RubyRed 46 University St, Belfast, Northern Ireland, BT7 1HB **t** 07775 657234 **f** 08707 625672 **e** francotton@rubyredmgmt.com **w** rubyredmanagement.com 📧 Contact: Fran Cotton.

Running Dog Management Whitecroft, Well Lane, Devauden, Monmouthshire, NP16 6NX **t** 07917 794801 **e** runningdogmanagement@yahoo.com **w** thyrdeye.com 📧 Managing Director: Les Modget 01291 650705.

Runrig Management 1 York St, Aberdeen, AB11 5DL **t** 01224 573100 **f** 01224 592320 **e** office@runrig.co.uk **w** runrig.co.uk 📧 Office Manager: Mike Smith.

Billy Russell Management Binny Estate, Ecclesmachan, Edinburgh, EH52 6NL **t** 01506 858885 **f** 01506 858155 **e** kitemusic@aol.com **w** kitemusic.com 📧 MD: Billy Russell.

Safe Management St Ann's House, Guildford Road, Lightwater, Surrey, GU18 5RA **t** 01276 476 676 **f** 01276 451 109 **e** firstname@safemanagement.co.uk **w** safemanagement.co.uk 📧 Manager: Chris Herbert or Tim Ferrone.

Safehouse Management PO Box 47200, London, W6 6DQ **t** 020 8743 4000 **f** 020 8743 4021 **e** info@safehousemanagement.com **w** safehousemanagement.com 📧 Director: Lynn Cosgrave.

Saphron Management 36 Belgrave Road, London, E17 8QE **t** 07973 415 167 **e** saph@btinternet.com 📧 Manager: Annette Bennett.

Satellite Artists Studio House, 34 Salisbury St, London, NW8 8QE **t** 020 7402 9111 **f** 020 7723 3064 **e** satellite_artists@hotmail.com 📧 MD: Eliot Cohen.

SB Management 2 Barb Mews, London, W6 7PA **t** 020 7078 9789 **f** 0871 253 1584 **e** info@sbman.co.uk **w** sbman.co.uk 📧 MD: Simon Banks.

Schoolhouse Management 42 York Pl, Edinburgh, EH1 3HU **t** 0131 557 4242 **e** bruce@schoolhousemanagement.co.uk **w** schoolhousemanagement.co.uk 📧 MD: Bruce Findlay.

Scruffy Bird Management 2nd Floor, 30-31 Shoreditch High Street, London, E1 6PG **t** 07725 651 199 **e** duncan@scruffybird.com **w** scruffybird.com 📧 Director: Duncan Ellis.

Dave Seamer Entertainments 46 Magdalen Road, Oxford, Oxon, OX4 1RB **t** 01865 240 054 **f** 01865 240 054 **e** dave@daveseamer.co.uk **w** daveseamer.co.uk 📧 MD: Dave Seamer.

Seaview Music 28 Mawson Rd, Cambridge, CB1 2EA **t** 01223 508431 **f** 01223 508449 **e** seaview@dial.pipex.com **w** seaview.dial.pipex.com 📧 Administrator: Alison Suter.

SEG Entertainment UK The Courtyard, Unit A, 42 Colwith Rd, Hammersmith, London, W6 9EY **t** 020 8846 3737 **f** 020 8846 3738 **e** info@seginternational.com **w** seginternational.com 📧 CEO/ MD: Marc Marot, John Arnison.

Alan Seifert Management 1 Winterton House, 24 Park Walk, London, SW10 0AQ **t** 020 7795 0321 **e** alanseifert@lineone.net 📧 MD: Alan Seifert 07958 241 733.

Sentinel Management 60 Sellons Avenue, London, NW10 4HH **t** 020 8961 6992 **e** sentinel7@hotmail.com 📧 Dirs: Sandra Scott 07932 737 547.

Jon Sexton Management (JSM) 9 Spedan Close, Branch Hill, London, NW3 7XF **t** 07855 551 024 **e** copasetik1@aol.com **w** copasetik.com 📧 MD: Jon Sexton.

SGO Music Management PO Box 2015, Salisbury, SP2 7WU **t** 01747 871563 **f** 01264 811172 **e** sgomusic@sgomusic.com **w** sgomusic.com 📧 MD: Stuart Ongley.

ShaftRoxy Management PO Box 39464, London, N10 1WP **t** 07779 340 154 **f** 020 8883 4086 **e** nathan@shaftroxy.com **w** shaftroxy.com 📧 MD: Nathan Hull.

Shalit Global Entertainment & Management 4th Floor, 34-35 Eastcastle St, London, W1W 8DW **t** 020 7462 9060 **e** info@shalitglobal.com **w** shalitglobal.com 📧 MD: Jonathan Shalit.

Shamrock Music Ltd 9, Thornton Pl, Marylebone, London, W1H 1FG **t** 020 7935 9719 **f** 020 7935 0241 **e** lindy@celtus.demon.co.uk 📧 Manager: Lindy McManus.

Shavian Enterprises 14 Devonshire Pl, London, W1G 6HX **t** 020 7935 6906 **f** 020 7224 6256 **e** info@sandieshaw.com **w** sandieshaw.com 📧 Director: Grace Banks.

Shaw Thing Management 20 Coverdale Rd, London, N11 3FG **t** 020 8361 6669 **f** 020 8361 9403 **e** hills@shawthingmanagement.com 📧 MD: Hillary Shaw.

WEB SHERIFF®
WWW.WEBSHERIFF.COM T: +44 (0)208 323 8013

Sheepfold 43 Broadleaf Avenue, Bishop's Stortford, Herts, CM23 4JY **t** 01279 835067 **f** 01920 461187 **e** pauljamesburrell@aol.com ⊠ Mgr: Paul Burrell.

Show Business Entertainment The Bungalow, Chatsworth Avenue, Long Eaton, Nottinghamshire, NG10 2FL **t** 0115 973 5445 **f** 0115 946 1831 **e** kimholmes@showbusinessagency.freeserve.co.uk ⊠ MD: Kim Holmes.

Shurwood Management Tote Hill Cottage, Stedham, Midhurst, West Sussex, GU29 0PY **t** 01730 817400 **f** 01730 815846 **e** shurley@shurwood.fsnet.co.uk ⊠ GM: Shurley Selwood.

Sidewinder Management Ltd
10 Cambridge Mews, Brighton & Hove, BN3 3EZ **t** 01273 774460 **e** sdw@SidewinderMgmt.com **w** SidewinderMgmt.com ⊠ MD: Simon Watson.

Silent Records Matrix Studios, 91 Peterborough Rd, London, SW6 3BU **t** 07957 165391 **e** julian.close@tubemanagement.com ⊠ myspace.com/tubemanagement ⊠ MD: Julian Close.

Silver Management London **e** silvermanagement@live.co.uk ⊠ Contact: Brian Smith 020 7502 0250.

Silverbird Ltd Amersham Common House, 133 White Lion Rd, Amersham Common, Bucks, HP7 9JY **t** 01494 766754 **f** 01494 766745 **e** donatella@silvrbird.demon.co.uk **w** leosayer.com ⊠ Mgr: Donatella Piccinetti.

Simple Management 36 Avenue Rd, Brentford, Middx, TW8 9NS **t** 020 8560 8402 **f** 020 8560 8402 **e** simonbentley@onetel.net ⊠ Manager: Simon Bentley.

Simply Entertainment Ltd Wilson's Corner, 1-5 Ingrave Road, Brentwood, Essex, CM15 8AP **t** 07900 262 486 **e** anthony@simplyentertainmentltd.com **w** simplyentertainmentltd.com ⊠ Dir: Anthony Campbell.

Sincere Management 35 Bravington Rd, London, W9 3AB **t** 020 8960 4438 **f** 020 8968 8458 **e** office@sinman.co.uk ⊠ Contact: Peter Jenner & Mushi Jenner.

Sleeper Music Block 2, 6 Erskine Road, Primrose Hill, London, NW3 3AJ **t** 020 7580 3995 **f** 020 7900 6244 **e** info@sleepermusic.co.uk **w** guychambers.com ⊠ Contact: Dylan Chambers, Louise Jeremy.

Slowburn Productions 18 Eastwick Lodge, 4 Village Road, Enfield, Middx, EN1 2DH **t** 020 8360 4670 **e** Harry@slowburnproductions.co.uk ⊠ MD: Harry Benjamin.

Small World 18A Farm Lane Trading Centre, 101 Farm Lane, London, SW6 1QJ **t** 020 7385 3233 **f** 020 7386 0473 **e** tina@smallworldmanagement.com ⊠ MD: Tina Matthews.

SMI/Everyday Productions 33 Mandarin Place, Grove, Oxon, OX12 0QH **t** 01235 771577 **e** smi_everyday_productions@yahoo.com ⊠ Contact: 01235 767171.

Soho Artists 1st Floor, 18 Broadwick St, London, W1F 8HS **t** 020 7434 0008 **f** 020 7434 0061 **e** paul@sohoartists.co.uk ⊠ myspace.com/sohoartists ⊠ CEO: Paul Burger.

Solar Management 13 Rosemont Rd, London, NW3 6NG **t** 020 7794 3388 **f** 020 7794 5588 **e** info@solarmanagement.co.uk **w** solarmanagement.co.uk ⊠ MD: Carol Crabtree.

Son Management 72 Marylebone Lane, London, W1U 2PL **t** 020 7486 7458 **f** 020 8467 6997 **e** sam@randm.co.uk ⊠ Mgr: Sam Eldridge.

Sonic Bang! Management 22B Upland Industrial Estate, Wyton, St Ives, Cambridgeshire, PE28 2DY **t** 07702 399 798 **e** info@sonicbang.co.uk **w** sonicbang.co.uk ⊠ MD: Adam J Mills.

Sound Artist Management 192 Portnall Road, London, W9 3BJ **t** 020 8960 9553 **e** info@soundartistmanagement.com **w** soundartistmanagement.com ⊠ Agents: Edward & Lucy Bigland.

The Sound Foundation The Sound Foundation, PO Box 4900, Earley, Berks, RG10 0GA **t** 0118 934 9600 **e** info@soundfoundation.co.uk **w** airplayrecords.co.uk ⊠ Label Mgr: Hadyn Wood 07973 559 203.

Sounds Like A Hit Ltd Matrix Complex, 91 Peterborough Rd, London, SW6 3BU **t** 020 7384 6464 **e** steve@soundslikeahit.com **w** soundslikeahit.com ⊠ Director: Steve Crosby.

Southside Management 20 Cromwell Mews, London, SW7 2JY **t** 020 7225 1919 **f** 020 7823 7091 **e** kate@southsidemanagement.co.uk ⊠ MD: Bob Johnson.

Sparklestreet HQ 18 Sparkle St, Manchester, M1 2NA **t** 0161 273 3435 **f** 0161 273 3695 **e** gary@pd-uk.com **w** sparklestreet.net ⊠ Dir: Gary McClarnan 07798 766 861.

Spirit Music & Media Hope House, 40 St Peters Rd, London, W6 9BD **t** 020 8741 6020 **e** info@spiritmm.com **w** irl.org.uk ⊠ myspace.com/spiritmusicmedia ⊠ MD: Tom Haxell & David Jaymes.

Split Music 13 Sandys Rd, Worcester, WR1 3HE **t** 01905 613 023 **e** meshmusic@prison-records.com ⊠ MD: Chris Warren.

Split Peach Management 15 Barley Hills, Bishops Stortford, Herts, CM23 4DS **t** 01279 865 070 **f** 0870 486 0812 **e** simon@splitpeach.co.uk ⊠ CEO: Simon Baker splitpeach.co.uk.

Starwood Management 33 Richmond Place, Brighton, E Sussex, BN2 9NA **t** 01273 675 444 **e** mark@illshows.fsnet.co.uk ⊠ Co-MD: Mark Nicholson.

Stevo Management 10 Great Russell St, London, WC1B 3BQ **e** info@somebizarre.com **w** somebizarre.com ⊠ MD: Stevo.

WEB SHERIFF®
WWW.WEBSHERIFF.COM T: +44 (0)208 323 8013

Stirling Music Limited 25 Heathmans Road, London, SW6 4TJ **t** 020 7371 5756 **f** 020 7371 7731 **e** office@pureuk.com **w** pureuk.com ⌨ Creative Dir: Billy Royal.

Streetfeat Management Ltd
Unit 105, The Saga Centre, 326 Kensal Rd, London, W10 5BZ **t** 020 8969 3370 **f** 020 8960 9971 **e** info@streetfeat.demon.co.uk ⌨ MD: Colin Schaverien.

Sublime Music 77 Preston Drove, Brighton, East Sussex, BN1 6LD **t** 01273 236 300 or 07774 133 134 **e** info@sublimemusic.co.uk **w** sublimemusic.co.uk ⌨ MD: Patrick Spinks.

Subside Records SNC Via Vecchia Fiuggi 382, 03015-Fiuggi, FR, Italy **t** +39 0775 515122 **f** +39 0775 514218 **e** info@subsiderec.com **w** subsiderec.com ⌨ CEO: Vanni Giorgilli.

Sugar Shack Management PO Box 73, Fishponds, Bristol, BS16 7EZ **t** 01179 855092 **f** 01179 855092 **e** mike@sugarshackrecords.co.uk **w** sugarshackrecords.co.uk ⌨ myspace.sugarshackrecordsuk ⌨ Dir: Mike Darby.

Sunrise UK Silverdene, Scaleby Hill, Carlisle, CA6 4LU **t** 01228 675822 **f** 01228 675822 **e** info@sunriseuk.co.uk **w** sunriseuk.co.uk ⌨ Proprietor: Martin Smith.

SuperVision Ankst Management LLP
104a Cowbridge Road East, Canton, Cardiff, CF11 9DX **t** 029 2039 4200 **f** 029 2037 2703 **e** alun@ankst.org ⌨ Contact: Alun Llwyd.

SuperVision Management 59-65 Worship St, London, EC2A 2DU **t** 020 7688 9000 **f** 020 7688 8999 **e** info@supervisionmgt.com ⌨ Dir: James Sandom.

SuperVision White Tiger LLP 55 Fawcett Close, London, SW16 2QJ **t** 020 8677 5199 **f** 020 8769 5795 **e** whitetiger@supervisionmgt.com ⌨ Partners: Paul & Corinne White.

Swing Cafe 26 Fox Lane, London, N13 4AH **t** 020 8882 7422 **e** lauriejay@swingcafemusic.com **w** swingcafemusic.com ⌨ MD: Laurie Jay.

T2 Management Dolphin Court, 42 Carleton Road, London, N7 0ER **t** 020 7607 6654 **e** hilltaryn@hotmail.com ⌨ Dir: Taryn Hill 07971 575810.

Talent Call 3 York House, Langston Rd, Loughton, Essex, IG10 3TQ **t** 0845 371 1113 **f** 0845 371 1114 **e** abailey@independentmusicgroup.com ⌨ Dir: Andrew Bailey.

TARGO Entertainment - There's A Riot Going On PO Box 1977, Salisbury, SP3 5ZW **t** 01722 716716 **e** targo.entscorps@virgin.net ⌨ Manager: Mathew Priest 07971 405874.

Teleryngg UK 132 Chase Way, London, N14 5DH **t** 07050 055 167 **f** 0870 741 5252 **e** atlanticcrossingartists@yahoo.com ⌨ MD: Richard Struple.

Terry Blamey Management PO Box 13196, London, SW6 4WF **t** 020 7371 7627 **f** 020 7731 7578 **e** info@TerryBlamey.com ⌨ Assistant Manager: Alli MacGregor.

The Animal Farm 4th Floor, Block A, Tower Bridge Business Complex, 100 Clements Rd, London, SE16 4DG **t** 020 7237 8768 **e** ville@theanimalfarm.co.uk **w** theanimalfarm.co.uk ⌨ theanimalfarm ⌨ MD: Ville Leppanen.

The Cardigan Suite PO Box 7438, New Bradwell, Milton Keynes, MK13 0WG **t** 07736 322731 **e** matt@thecardigansuite.com **w** thecardigansuite.com ⌨ MD: Matt Clark.

The Delicious Fox **t** 07588 234013 **e** latoya@velvetines.com / bianca@velvetines.com ⌨ Contact: Bianca Geldenhuys & Latoya Akisanya.

The ICE Group 3 St Andrews St, Lincoln, Lincolnshire, LN5 7NE **t** 01522 539883 **f** 01522 528964 **e** steve.hawkins@easynet.co.uk **w** icegroup.co.uk ⌨ MD: Steve Hawkins.

The Music & Media Partnership Grand Prix House, 126-129 Power Rd, London, W4 5PY **t** 020 8987 0818 **f** 020 8987 0828 **e** firstname@tmmp.co.uk ⌨ MD: Rick Blaskey.

The Music Partnership New Broad St House, New Broad St, London, EC2M 1NH **t** 020 7840 9590 **f** 0845 658 6915 **e** office@musicpartnership.co.uk **w** musicpartnership.co.uk ⌨ Artist Manager: Louise Badger.

The Screen Talent Agency Rich Mix Building, 35-47 Bethnal Green Rd, London, E1 6LA **t** 020 7729 7477 **f** 020 7681 3588 **e** info@screen-talent.com **w** screen-talent.com ⌨ m.d.: James Little.

The TCB Group 24 Kimberley Court, Kimberley Rd, Queens Pk, London, NW6 7SL **t** 020 7328 7272 **f** 020 7372 0844 **e** stevenhoward@tcbgroup.co.uk **w** tcbgroup.co.uk ⌨ CEO: Steven Howard.

The Umbrella Group **t** 07802 535696 **e** thomasmanzi@mac.com **w** umbrella-group.com ⌨ MD: Tommy Manzi +1 212 785 1133.

Theobald Dickson Productions The Coach House, Swinhope Hall, Swinhope, Market Rasen, Lincs, LN8 6HT **t** 01472 399 011 **f** 01472 399 025 **e** tdproductions@lineone.net ⌨ MD: Bernard Theobald.

Three Six Zero Group A14 Jacks Pl, 6 Corbet Pl, London, E1 6NN **t** 0203 0517 930 **f** 0203 0041 589 **e** duncan.murray@threesixzerogroup.com **w** threesixzerogroup.com ⌨ Remix Manager: Duncan Murray 0044 (0) 203 0517 930.

Thunderbird Management PO Box 60 396, Titirangi, Waitakere 0642, New Zealand **t** +64 9 826 3232 **f** +64 9 826 3232 **e** tom@thunderbirdmanagement.com **w** thunderbirdmanagement.com ⌨ Contact: Thomas Dalton +64 2140 6780.

Business Services: Artist Management

INSTALLATION EUROPE 09/10 — BUYER'S GUIDE

NEW Edition Now Out
Order yours today!

Brought to you by Installation Europe, Installation Europe Buyer's Guide 09/10 gives you up-to-date information on the products and the companies operating in the design of sound, vision and light in the built environment.

BUYER'S GUIDE TO PRODUCTS,
EQUIPMENT & SERVICES - OVER 100 PRODUCTS AND SERVICES

Whether you're buying or selling, this A-Z of products and services, complete with location and telephone numbers, allows you to pinpoint companies at a glance.

COMPANY DATA SECTION - OVER 2,200 COMPANIES AND 2,000 KEY CONTACTS

Full contact details as well as personnel and product information are given in this alphabetical guide to the companies serving sound, vision and light in the built environment.

ORDER YOUR COPIES TODAY FOR JUST £75 PER COPY

To ensure you have the most up-to-date information available on the products and the companies operating in this industry, email **Lianne Davey on Lianne.Davey@ubm.com**

WEB SHERIFF®
WWW.WEBSHERIFF.COM T: +44 (0)208 323 8013

Business Services: Artist Management

Tim Prior - Artist & Rights Management
The Old Lampworks, Rodney Place, London, SW19 2LQ
t 020 8542 4222 **f** 020 8540 6056 **e** tim@arm-eu.com
✉ MD: Tim Prior.

TK1 Management PO Box 38475, London, SE16 7XT
t 020 7481 1411 **f** 020 7481 1411
e info@tk1management.com **w** tk1management.com
✉ Dirs: Trina Torpey & Kathryn Nash.

Toni Medcalf Management
68 Upper Richmond Rd West, London, SW14 8DA
t 020 8876 2421 **e** ttmmanagement@aol.com **✉** Artist
Manager: Toni Medcalf 07767 832260.

Tony Hall Group of Companies Suite 5,
58 Broadwick St, London, W1F 7AJ **t** 020 7434 7286
f 020 7434 7288 **e** tonyhall@btconnect.com **✉** MD: Tony
Hall.

Top Banana Management Ltd Monomark House,
27 Old Gloucester St, London, WC1N 3XX
t 020 7419 5026 **e** info@topbananaman.com
w topbananaman.com **✉** Contact: Garry Kemp 07825
070330.

Top Draw Music Management The Media Centre,
Canada House, 272 Field End Rd, Eastcote, HA4 9NA
t 020 8582 0408 **e** james@tdmm.co.uk **w** tdmm.co.uk
▣ myspace.com/topdrawmusicmanagement
✉ Managing Director: James Hamilton.

Total Concept Management (TCM) PO Box 128,
Dewsbury, West Yorkshire, WF12 9XS **t** 01924 438295
f 0700 603 3898 **e** tcm@totalconceptmanagement.com
w totalconceptmanagement.com

Total Management Flat 2, 7 Milnthorpe Rd,
Meads Village, Eastbourne, East Sussex, BN20 7NS
t 07941 373897 **e** chris@totalmgt.biz
w myspace.com/catherinetran **✉** MD: Chris McGeever.

Touched Productions 4 Varley House, County St,
London, SE1 6AL **t** 020 7403 5451 **f** 020 7403 5446
e toucheduk@aol.com **w** touched.co.uk **✉** Dir: Armorel
Weston.

Transmission Management London
e sybil@transmissionmanagement.com **✉** Owner: Sybil
Bell.

TRC Management Ltd 10c Whitworth Court,
Manor Pk, Manor Farm Rd, Runcorn, Cheshire, WA7 1WA
t 01928 571111 **f** 0871 247 4923
e mail@trcmanagement.com **w** trcmanagement.com
✉ MD: Phil Chadwick.

Trinifold Management Third Floor, 12 Oval Rd,
London, NW1 7DH **t** 020 7419 4300 **f** 020 7419 4325
e trinuk@globalnet.co.uk **✉** MD: Robert Rosenberg.

Truelove Records - Tortured Artists
PO Box 63445, London, SE1P 5FL **t** 020 3239 2575
e business@truelove.co.uk **w** truelove.co.uk
✉ Contact: John Truelove, Brian Roach.

Twenty Four Seven Music Management
PO Box 2470, The Studio, Chobham, Surrey, GU24 8ZD
t 01276 855 247 **e** Jill@24-7musicmanagement.com
✉ MD: Craig Logan.

UKNY Music Ltd 55 Harrington Gardens, London,
SW7 4JZ **t** 020 7373 5890 **f** 020 7373 2525
e info@uknymusic.com **✉** Artist Manager: Zak Biddu.

Upbeat Classical Management PO Box 479,
Uxbridge, Middx, UB8 2ZH **t** 01895 259 441
f 01895 259 341 **e** info@upbeatclassical.co.uk
w upbeatclassical.co.uk **✉** Director: Maureen Phililps.

Upbeat Management Larg House, Woodcote Grove,
Coulsdon, Surrey, CR5 2QQ **t** 020 8668 3332
f 020 8668 3922 **e** liz@upbeat.co.uk **w** upbeat.co.uk
✉ Senior Partner, Exec Prod: Liz Biddle.

UPLIFTED MANAGEMENT 125 Park Rd, Stretford,
Manchester, Lancashire, M32 8ED **t** 07931 943226
e info@upliftedmanagement.org.uk
w upliftedmanagement.org.uk **✉** General Manager: Mark
Wheavill.

Upper 11 Group London **e** ameola@upper11.com
✉ A&R: Antony Meola 02072583360.

Upside Management 14 Clarence Mews, Balham,
London, SW12 9SR **t** 07786 066665
e simon@upsideuk.com **w** upsideuk.com
▣ myspace.com/upsidemanagement **✉** Co MDs: Simon
Jones & Denise Beighton.

Urban Influence UK Ltd 118 Caswell Close,
Farnborough, Hants, GU14 8TF
t 01252 521 892 or 07703 729 953 **f** 01252 404 043
e julianwhite@urban-influence.co.uk
w myspace.com/urbaninfluence1 **✉** MD: Julian White.

Valley Music Ltd. Unit 6 Upper Culham Farm Barns,
Upper Culham, Wargrave, Henley-on-Thames, Oxon,
RG10 8NR **t** 01491 845840 **f** 01491 413667
e info@valleymusicuk.com **w** tomjones.com **✉** MD: Mark
Woodward.

Value Added Talent Management (VAT)
1 Purley Pl, London, N1 1QA **t** 020 7704 9720
f 020 7226 6135 **e** vat@vathq.co.uk **w** vathq.co.uk
✉ MD: Dan Silver.

Vashti PO Box 2553, Maidenhead, Berkshire, SL6 1ZJ
t 01628 620082 **f** 01628 637066
e info@sheilaferguson.com **w** sheilaferguson.com
✉ MD: Sheila Ferguson.

Denis Vaughan Management PO Box 28286,
London, N21 3WT **t** 020 7486 5353 **f** 020 8224 0466
e dvaughanmusic@dial.pipex.com **✉** Director: Denis
Vaughan.

Vex Management 24 Caradoc St, Greenwich, London,
SE10 9AG **t** 020 8858 0800
e paul@vexmanagement.com **w** myspace.com/vex
✉ MD: Paul Ablett.

Violation Management 26 Mill Street, Gamlingay, Sandy, Bedfordshire, SG19 3JW **t** 01767 651552 **f** 01767 651228 **e** dicky_boy@msn.com 🔲 Manager: Dick Meredith 07768 667076.

Voicebox PO Box 82, Altrincham, Cheshire, WA15 0QD **t** 0161 928 3222 **f** 0161 928 7849 **e** vb@thevoicebox.co.uk **w** thevoicebox.co.uk 🔲 MD: Vicki Hope-Robinson.

W7 Management 69 Elgar Avenue, Surbiton, Surrey, KT5 9JP **t** 07949 023581 **e** wes@w7management.com **w** w7management.com 🔲 myspace.com/w7m 🔲 Artist and Business Consultant: Wes Jennison.

War Zones and Associates 33 Kersley Road, London, N16 0NT **t** 020 7249 2894 **f** 020 7254 3729 **e** wz33@aol.com 🔲 MD: Richard Hermitage 07831 857 011.

Watercress Management The Old Vicerage, Pickering, North Yorkshire, YO18 7AW **t** 01751 475502 **f** 01751 475502 **e** organised@ukonline.co.uk 🔲 Dir: Ian McDaid.

What Management 3 Belfry Villas, Belfry Ave, Harefield, Uxbridge, Middlesex, UB9 6HY **t** 01895 824674 **e** whatmanagement@blueyonder.co.uk 🔲 Contact: Mick Cater, David Harper.

Alan Whitehead Management
51 Chambers Grove, Welwyn Garden City, Herts, AL7 4FG **t** 07957 358 997 **e** alan_whitehead_uk@yahoo.com 🔲 MD: Alan Whitehead.

Whitehouse Management PO Box 50789, London, NW6 1BZ **t** 020 7209 2586 **f** 020 8459 2759 **e** sue@whitehousemanagement.com 🔲 MD: Sue Whitehouse.

Whitenoise Management PO Box 741, TW9 4WQ **t** 020 8878 8550 **e** chris@whitenoisemanagement.com **w** myspace.com/whitenoisemanagement 🔲 MD: Chris Butler.

Wild Honey Management 10 Lansdowne Road, Hove, East Sussex, BN3 3AU **t** 01273 738704 **f** 01273 732112 **e** jimtracey@aol.com **w** wildhoney.co.uk 🔲 Contact: Jim Tracey.

Wild West Management Argentum, 2 Queen Caroline Street, London, W6 9DX **t** 020 8323 8013 **f** 020 8323 8080 **e** ela@ela.co.uk **w** ela.co.uk 🔲 MD: John Giacobbi.

Wildlife Entertainment Ltd Unit F, 21 Heathmans Rd, London, SW6 4TJ **t** 020 7371 7008 **f** 020 7371 7708 **e** info@wildlife-entertainment.com 🔲 Managing Director: Ian McAndrew.

Allan Wilson Enterprises Queens House, Chapel Green Road, Hindley, Wigan, Lancashire, WN2 3LL **t** 01942 258565 **f** 01942 255158 **e** allan@allanwilson.co.uk 🔲 Owner: Allan Wilson 01942 255158.

Wise Buddah Talent 74 Great Titchfield St, London, W1W 7QP **t** 020 7307 1600 **f** 020 7307 1608 **e** chris.north@wisebuddah.com **w** wisebuddahtalent.com 🔲 Head of Wise Buddah Talent: Chris North.

Wiseblood Management 231 Portobello Rd, London, W11 1LT **t** 020 7792 9791 **f** 020 7792 9871 **e** julie@visiblenoise.com 🔲 Director: Julie Weir.

Wizard Artist Management PO Box 6779, Birmingham, B13 9RZ **t** 0121 778 2218 **f** 0121 778 1856 **e** pk.sharma@ukonline.co.uk **w** wizardrecords.co.uk 🔲 MD: Mambo Sharma 07956 984 754.

Wolfgang Kuhle Artist Management
P O Box 425, London, SW6 3TX **t** 020 7371 0397 **f** 020 7736 9212 **e** wolfgang@thepleasuredome.demon.co.uk **w** hollyjohnson.com 🔲 facebook.com/thehollyjohnson 🔲 myspace.com/therealhollyjohnson 🔲 twitter.com/TheHollyJohnson 🔲 youtube.com/user/thehollyjohnson 🔲 Manager: Wolfgang Kuhle.

Alan Wood Agency 346 Gleadless Road, Sheffield, South Yorkshire, S2 3AJ **t** 0114 258 0338 **f** 0114 258 0638 **e** celia@alanwoodagency.co.uk **w** alanwoodagency.co.uk 🔲 Contact: Alan Wood.

Working Class Music Management
22 Upper Brook St, Mayfair, London, W1K 7PZ **t** 020 7491 1060 **f** 020 7491 9996 **e** workingclassmusic@btinternet.com **w** workingclassmanagement.com 🔲 Contact: Matt Crossey, Lisa Barker.

World Famous Group 467 Fulham Rd, Fulham, London, SW6 1HL **t** 020 7385 6838 **f** 020 7385 0999 **e** info@worldfamousgroup.com **w** worldfamousgroup.com 🔲 Chairman: Alon Shulman.

XL Talent Reverb House, Bennett St, London, W4 2AH **t** 020 8747 0660 **f** 020 8747 0880 **e** management@reverbxl.com **w** reverbxl.com 🔲 Partners: Maggi Hickman, Mike Box, Julian Palmer.

Yergh Entertainment Group London **t** 020 7193 0134 **e** antony@yergh.com **w** yergh.com 🔲 MD: Antony Meola 02071930134.

Young Guns Ltd Unit 201, Shakespeare Business Centre, 245 Coldharbour Lane, London, SW9 8RR **t** 020 7733 6253 **e** enquiries@younggunsuk.com **w** younggunsuk.com 🔲 Artist Manager: Alexander Lyon 07980 222857.

Z Management The Palm House, PO Box 19734, London, SW15 2WU **t** 020 8874 3337 **f** 020 8874 3599 **e** office@zman.co.uk **w** zman.co.uk 🔲 MD: Zita Wadwa-McQ.

Zama Media Management 1400 Pacific Ave, Venice, Los Angeles, CA 90291, United States **t** +1 310 581 0200 **f** +1 310 581 1120 **e** info@zamamedia.com **w** zamamedia.com 🔲 CEO: Ray Cooper.

ZincSplash 71 Walerand Road, London, SE13 7PQ
t 07970 000 034 **e** theboss@zincsplash.com
w zincsplash.com 🅱 Manager: Craig Tarrant.

Zoot Management PO Box 3932, Birmingham,
B30 2EQ **t** 01527 578444 **e** jackie@zootmusic.net
w zootmusic.net 🅱 Artist Manager: Jackie Wade
07817204912.

Recruitment Agencies

Cat Entertainment Search Pinewood Studios,
Pinewood Road, Iver Heath, Buckinghamshire, SL0 0NH
t 01753 630040 **f** 01753 630830
e cat@catentertainmentsearch.com
w catentertainmentsearch.com 🅱 GM: Catherine Pianta-
McGill.

Grosvenor Bureau Secretarial Recruitment
22 South Molton St, London, W1K 5RB **t** 020 7491 0884
f 020 7409 1524 **e** gb@grosvenorbureau.co.uk
w grosvenorbureau.co.uk 🅱 MD: Jackie McGurrell.

HANDLE RECRUITMENT

handle
the brighter recruitment consultancy

4 Gees Court, London, W1U 1JD **t** 020 7569 9999
w handle.co.uk 🅱 Directors: Stella Walker and Peter Tafler.
**Handle is the leading recruitment consultancy to the
media and entertainment industry. Handle has six
specialist divisions - Office Support, Finance, Sales
and Marketing, Digital, HR and Legal.**

Matchstick Media 1st Floor, 10 Argyll Street, London,
W1F 7TQ **t** 020 7297 0030 **e** info@matchstickmedia.co.uk
w matchstickmedia.co.uk 🅱 Managing Partner: Tim
Palmer.

Media Moves First Floor, 1-2 Berners St, London,
W1T 3LA **t** 020 7908 7900 **f** 020 7908 7949
e richard.watson@careermovesgroup.co.uk
w careermovesgroup.co.uk 🅱 Contact: Richard Watson.

Media Recruitment 1 Parkway, London, NW1 7PG
t 020 7267 0555 **f** 020 7482 3666
e tanya@mediarecruitment.co.uk
w mediarecruitment.co.uk 🅱 Senior Consultant: Tanya
Ferris.

Positive Solutions Recruitment Ltd 1 The Mews,
Castle Street, Farnham, Surrey, GU9 7LP **t** 0871 300 4444
f 01252 891 720 **e** info@positivejobs.com
w positivejobs.com 🅱 Dir: Craig Chuter 07855 395 685.

Rose Inc 5th Floor, 133 Long Acre, London, WC2E 9DT
t 020 7836 2666 **f** 020 7836 2667 **e** tom@rose-inc.co.uk
w rose-inc.co.uk 🅱 Managing Partner: Tom Evans.

Event Management

A&R Worldwide 8383 Wilshire Blvd, Suite 100,
Beverly Hills, CA 90211, United States **t** 323.782.0770
f 323.782.9835 **e** brandon@anrworldwide.com
w anrworldwide.com 🅱 Contact: Brandon Fuller.

Ambush Management 32 Ransome's Dock, 35-
37 Parkgate Road, London, SW11 4NP **t** 020 7801 1919
f 020 7738 1819 **e** alambush.native@19.co.uk
w ambushgroup.co.uk 🅱 MD: Alister Jamieson.

B&H Sound Services Ltd Unit 3, Haddonbrook,
Fallodan Rd, Orton Southgate, Peterborough, PE2 6YX
t 01733 371250 **f** 01733 235016
e sound@bhsound.co.uk **w** bhsound.co.uk 🅱 General
Manager: Peter Lister.

B&H Sound Services Ltd Unit 3, Haddonbrook,
Fallodan Road, Orton Southgate, Peterborough,
Cambrigeshire, PE2 6YX **t** 01733 371250
f 01733 235016 **e** sound@bhsound.co.uk
w bhsound.co.uk 🅱 Production Manager: Julian Stanford.

Back Row Productions 71 Endell St, London,
WC2H 9AJ **t** 020 7836 4422 **f** 020 7836 4425
e firstname.lastname@backrow.co.uk **w** backrow.co.uk
🅱 Contact: Jacqui Garbett.

Ballistic Events Unit 13 Tay Building,
2A Wrentham Avenue, London, NW10 3HA
t 020 8968 7766 **f** 05602 046198
e louise@ballisticevents.com **w** ballisticevents.com
🅱 Director: Louise Stevens.

Big Bear Events 8 Thrush Rd, Poole, BH21 3AP
t 01202 684555 **f** 01202 684666 **e** ianw@fonix.co.uk
w bigbearevents.co.uk 🅱 Director: Ian Walker.

Big Cat Group Griffin House, 18-19 Ludgate House,
Birmingham, B3 1DW **t** 0121 200 0910 **f** 0121 236 1342
e info@bcguk.com **w** bcguk.com 🅱 Dir: Nick Morgan.

Big Fish Events Ltd Canal Building, Portobello Dock,
Kensal Road, London, W10 **t** 020 7524 7555
f 020 7524 7556 **e** robert@bigfishevents.co.uk
w bigfishevents.co.uk 🅱 MD: Robert Guterman.

Brickwerk Suite 33, Barley Mow Centre,
10 Barley Mow Passage, London, W4 4PH
t 020 8995 2258 **e** hello@brickwerk.co.uk
w brickwerk.co.uk 🅱 Dir: Jo Brooks-Nevin.

CA Event The Hollow, Peaslake Lane, Peaslake, Surrey,
GU5 9RJ **t** 0870 861 2123 **f** 0870 861 2124
e jcobb@caevent.com **w** caevent.co.uk
🅱 Contact: James Cobb.

Capitalize Specialist PR and Sponsorship Ltd
52 Thrale St, London, SE1 9HW **t** 020 7940 1700
e Info@capitalize.co.uk **w** capitalize.co.uk 🅱 MD: Richard
Moore.

Clockwork Entertainments Tudor House,
Llanvanor Road, London, NW2 2AR **t** 020 8731 8899
f 020 8455 9555 **e** sales@clockworkentertainment.com
w clockworkentertainment.com 🅱 Director: James Miller.

Contacts Facebook MySpace Twitter YouTube

Daytime Entertainments The Garden Studio, Willoughby Rd, Harpenden, Hertfordshire, AL5 4PF **e** diane@daytime-ent.com ☒ Director: Diane Young 01582 761041.

EnTEEtainment Ltd The Old Telephone Exchange, Long Lane, Hermitage, Berks, RG18 9QS **t** 01635 202618 **f** 01635 202628 **e** dick@dicktee.com **w** dicktee.com ☒ MD: Dick Tee.

Eventpro UK 43 Granby St, Loughborough, Leicestershire, LE11 3DU **t** 0845 838 5188 **f** 0845 299 4199 **e** anna@eventprouk.com **w** eventprouk.com ☒ Creative Events Coordinator: Anna Gabrielle Moss.

FM Productions 5 Homeside Farm, Bossingham, Kent, CT4 6AR **t** 01227 709790 **f** 01227 709730 **e** fmproductions@mac.com ☒ Tour & Prod Manager: Ken Watts.

Full 360 Ltd PO Box 902, Suite 306, Bradford, BD1 9AH **t** 07971 874 942 **f** 01274 220 579 **e** katherine@full360ltd.com **w** full360ltd.com ☒ MD: Katherine Canoville.

Fun Events Group 31 Lower Clapton Rd, London, E5 0NS **t** 020 8985 1054 **e** admin@funevents.com **w** funevents.com ☒ Director: Harv Sethi.

The Hope & Anchor 207 Upper St, London, N1 1BZ **t** 020 7700 0550 **e** info@bugbearbookings.com **w** bugbearbookings.com ☒ Promoters: Jim & Tony 07956 313239. Standing capacity: 80

Impact Ventures 51 Athlone Rd, London, SW2 2DT **t** 020 8671 2161 **e** info@impactventures.co.uk **w** impactventures.co.uk ☒ MD: Rachael Bee.

Juliette Slater 26 Middle Stoke, Limpley Stoke, Bath, BA2 7GF **t** 01225 722207 **f** 020 7681 1900 **e** julietteslater@mac.com **w** polararts.com ☒ Tour/Event & Producer Management: Juliette Slater.

Lee Charteris Associates 10 Marco Rd, London, W6 0PN **t** 020 8741 2500 **e** mail@LeeCharteris.com ☒ Production Mgr: Lee Charteris 07801 663 700.

LFX Consulting Venue & Event Solutions, Stockport, Cheshire **t** 0161 408 2220 **e** luke@lfxconsulting.co.uk **w** lfxconsulting.co.uk ☒ Owner: Luke Fitzmaurice 07545 042832.

LilyCo 21 Beckenham Place Park, Beckenham, Kent, BR3 5BP **t** 020 8663 4849 **f** 020 8663 4855 **e** info@lilyuk.com **w** lilyuk.com ☒ Dir: Paxton Talbot.

M&C Saatchi 36 Golden Square, London, W1F 9EE **t** 020 7543 4689 **f** 020 7543 4501 **e** firstnameinitialofsurname@mcsaatchi.com **w** mcsaatchi.com/sportandentertainment ☒ Sponsorship & Events: Georgia Terzis.

Mad As Toast, Events 60 Stamperland Drive, Clarkston, Glasgow, G76 8HF **t** 07717 437148 **e** info@madastoast.com ☒ Directors: George Watson, John Richardson. 07717 437148, 07834 158118..

Martin Coull Management Stoneyport Associates, Suite 10, Leith Business Centre, 130 Leith Walk, Edinburgh, EH6 5DT **e** martincoullmanagement@gmail.com ☒ Proprietor: Martin Coull 07803 137509.

Mi Live 6 Tower terrace, Kilmainham, Dublin 8, Ireland **t** + 353 87 9817535 **e** info@milive.net ☒ berniemcgrath@yahoo.com ☒ MD: Bernie McGrath.

Mrs Casey Music PO Box 296, Matlock, Derbyshire, DE4 3XU **t** 01629 827012 **f** 01629 821874 **e** info@mrscasey.co.uk **w** mrscasey.co.uk ☒ MD: Steve Heap.

MUSEXPO 8383 Wilshire Blvd, Suite 100, Beverly Hills, CA 90211, United States **t** 323.782.0770 **f** 323.782.9835 **e** brandon@anrworldwide.com **w** musexpo.net ☒ Contact: Brandon Fuller.

MUSEXPO Europe 8383 Wilshire Blvd, Suite 100, Beverly Hills, CA 90211, United States **t** 323.782.0770 **f** 323.782.9835 **e** brandon@anrworldwide.com **w** musexpo.net ☒ Contact: Brandon Fuller.

Musicmedia Events t 08456 432676 **e** info@musicmediaevents.com **w** musicmediaevents.com ☒ Contact: Sean Quinn.

MusicTalks 40 Palmeria Rd, Bexleyheath, Kent, DA7 4UX **t** 020 8301 6366 **e** pauline.slane@btinternet.com **w** musictalks.biz ☒ Party & Wedding Planning Consultant: Pauline Slane 07798 641400.

Octagon Octagon House, 81-83 Fulham High St, London, SW6 3JW **t** 020 7862 0000 **f** 020 7862 0001 **e** garry.dods@octagon.com **w** octagon-uk.com ☒ VP, Music: Garry Dods.

Oort PO Box 64079, London, E1W 9BL **t** 07871 265432 **e** emma@oortmedia.net **w** oortmedia.net ☒ Business Development: Emma Peters.

Remarkable Productions Ltd 54 Chalton Street, London, NW1 1HS **t** 020 7387 1203 **f** 08716 616 760 **e** julian@remarkableproductions.org **w** remarkableproductions.org ☒ Director: Julian Rudd.

Rowleys:Open One Port Hill, Hertford, Hertfordshire, SG14 1PJ **t** 01992 587 350 **e** jules@rowleysopen.com **w** rowleysopen.com ☒ Lead Player: Jules Woolley.

Saphron Management 36 Belgrave Road, London, E17 8QE **t** 07973 415 167 **e** saph@btinternet.com ☒ Manager: Annette Bennett. Standing capacity: 100

Sarm Live Events 8-10 Basing St, London, W11 1ET **f** 020 7221 9247 **e** matt@spz.com ☒ Director: Matt Ross +44 207 2291229.

Songmaker Ltd Suite 296, 2 Lansdowne Row, London, W1J 6HL **t** 0871 750 5555 **f** 0871 226 4256 **e** michelle@songmaker.co.uk **w** songmaker.co.uk ☒ PA to Director: Michelle Parsons.

Sound Advice 4b Ledbury Mews North, London, W11 2AF **t** 020 7229 2219 **f** 020 7229 9870 **e** info@soundadvice.uk.com **w** soundadvice.uk.com ☒ MD: Hugh Phillimore.

Sound And Light Productions PO Box 32295, London, W5 1WD **t** 0870 066 0272 **f** 0870 066 0273 **e** slp@soundandlightproductions.co.uk **w** soundandlightproductions.co.uk 🔲 Director: John Denby.

STN Music 6 Ashgrove Gardens, Whitchurch, Aylesbury, Bucks, HP22 4JL **t** 01296 640681 **f** 0871 504 8435 **e** info@stn-music.co.uk **w** myspace.com/stnmusicuk 🔲 myspace.com/stnmusicuk 🔲 Partner: John Bassil 07751 310983.

Supernova Entertainment London **t** 020 7617 7226 **f** 020 7373 0600 **e** richard@supernovaentertainment.org **w** supernovaentertainment.org 🔲 Managing Director: Richard Beck 07738 522474.

Tomak Ltd (Slinky) PO Box 47002, London, SW18 5WS **t** 07717 722 929 **e** info@slinky.co.uk **w** slinky.co.uk 🔲 Creative Director: Amadeus Mozart.

Traxx Connective 2nd floor, 342 Argyle St, Glasgow, G2 8LY **t** 0141 221 2495 **f** 0141 221 2495 **e** mark@wearetraxx.com **w** wearetraxx.com 🔲 Dir: Mark MacKechnie.

Turnround Multi-Media Barn Studio, Chapel Farm, Over Old Road, Hartpury, Gloucestershire, GL19 3BJ **t** 01242 224 360 **e** studio@turnround.co.uk **w** turnround.co.uk 🔲 MD: Ross Lammas.

UBM Events 7th Floor, Ludgate House, 245 Blackfriars Road, London, SE1 9UY **t** 020 7921 8605 **f** 020 7921 8505 **e** cjacksonlevy@cmpi.biz **w** cmpi.biz 🔲 Events Director: Caroline Jackson Levy.

Unique Events Ltd Gladstone House, 6A Mill Lane, Edinburgh, EH6 6TJ **t** 0315 613 380 **f** 0315 550 905 **e** verity@unique-events.co.uk **w** unique-events.co.uk 🔲 Contact: Verity Blanchard.

Upbeat Event Catering and Design Studio 4-5, Garnet Close, Watford, Herts, WD24 7GN **t** 01923 211702 **f** 01923 211704 **e** david.stringer@globalinfusiongroup.com **w** globalinfusiongroup.com 🔲 International Sales & Marketing Manager: David Stringer.

UZ Events 125-129 High St, Glasgow, G1 1PH **t** 0141 552 6027 **f** 0141 552 6048 **e** office@uzevents.com **w** uzevents.com 🔲 Dir: Neil Butler.

wildplum Live PO Box 999, Enfield, London, EN1 9AD **t** 020 7193 6783 **e** info@wildplum.co.uk **w** wildplum.co.uk 🔲 MySpace/wildplum 🔵 twitter.com/wildplumlive 🔲 Head of Music & Concept Development: AL Douglas.

Word Of Mouth Events PO Box 31348, London, SW11 5ZE **t** 020 8673 3782 **f** 020 8675 6816 **e** info@wordofmouthevents.co.uk **w** wordofmouthevents.co.uk 🔲 Events Organiser: AJ.

World Famous Group 467 Fulham Rd, Fulham, London, SW6 1HL **t** 020 7385 6838 **f** 020 7385 0999 **e** info@worldfamousgroup.com **w** worldfamousgroup.com 🔲 Chairman: Alon Shulman.

Worn Out Marketing 4th Floor, 52-53 Margaret Street, London, W1W 8SQ **t** 020 7631 9202 **e** tony@worn-out.net **w** worn-out.net 🔲 Manager: Tony Arthy.

XRL Events Ltd XRL House, Hatches Barn, Bradden Lane, Gaddesden Row, Hemel Hempstead, HP2 6JB **t** 0800 634 0900 **f** 0870 404 4101 **e** events@xrl.co.uk **w** xrl.co.uk 🔲 Contact: Renu Sen.

Zisys AVMN Ltd. 1 Alexander Pl, Irvine, Ayrshire, KA12 0UR **t** 01294 204213 **e** danny@zisysavmn.co.uk **w** zisysavmn.co.uk 🔲 Director: Danny Anderson.

Conferences & Exhibitions

Access Events International India House, 2nd Floor, 45 Curlew St, London, SE1 2ND **t** 020 7940 7070 **f** 020 7940 7071 **e** info@access-events.com **w** access-events.com 🔲 Marketing Dir: Paul Gilbertson.

Capricorn Events PO Box 15172, Redditch, Worcestershire, B97 9JW **t** 07821 909698 **e** groove@capricorn-events.co.uk **w** capricorn-events.co.uk 🔲 Professional DJ: Les Marshall.

Central Hall Westminster Storey's Gate, Westminster, London, SW1H 9NH **t** 020 7222 8010 **f** 020 7222 6883 **e** info@c-h-w.co.uk **w** c-h-w.co.uk 🔲 Managing Director: Michael Sharp. Seated Capacity: 2350

Cup Promotions Ltd Suite 14-16, Marlborough BC, 96 George Lane, South Woodford, London, E18 1AD **t** 020 8989 2204 **f** 020 8989 2219 **e** info@cup.uk.com **w** cup.uk.com 🔲 Dir: Mark Abery.

ESIP Ltd P.O. Box 4702, Summerholme, Henley-on-Thames, RG9 9AA **t** 01491 574 717 **f** 0870 122 4634 **e** info@esip.co.uk **w** esip.co.uk 🔲 Dir: John Ellson.

Event Management Systems (UK) Ltd Unit 100, Rockingham Street, London, SE1 6PD **t** 020 7407 2115 **f** 020 7407 2132 **e** support@ems-events.co.uk **w** ems-events.co.uk 🔲 Customer Liaison Mgr: Ms Taly Akiva.

Genesis Adoration Ltd Redwood House, Hurstwood Grange, Hurstwood Lane, Haywards Heath, W. Sussex, RH17 7QX **t** 01444 476 120 **f** 01444 476 101 **e** lorna.milner@genesisadoration.com **w** genesisadoration.com 🔲 Events Manager: Lorna Milner.

Hawksmere plc 7th Floor, Elizabeth House, York Road, London, SE1 7NQ **t** 020 7632 2300 **f** 0845 120 9612 **e** dominic.riley@hawksmere.co.uk **w** hawksmere.co.uk 🔲 MD: Dominic Riley.

IAAAM (Int Association Of African American Music) The Business Village, 3-9 Bromhill Road, London, SW18 4JQ **t** 020 8870 8744 **f** 020 8874 1578 **e** info@hardzone.co.uk **w** hardzone.co.uk 🔲 Co-Founder: Jackie Davidson.

Contacts   **f** Facebook   **MySpace**   **Twitter**   **YouTube**

IMS - International Music Summit 133 Kew Road, Richmond, Richmond, Surrey, TW9 2PN **t** 020 8948 5446
e ben@graphitemedia.net **w** graphitemedia.net
Director: Ben Turner.

In The City 8 Brewery Yard, Deva Centre, Trinity Way, Salford, M3 7BB **t** 0161 839 3930 **f** 0161 839 3940
e office@inthecity.co.uk **w** inthecity.co.uk
Director: Yvette Livesey.

International Live Music Conference (ILMC) 2-4 Prowse Pl, London, NW1 9PH **t** 020 7284 5868
f 020 7284 1870 **e** conference@ilmc.com **w** ilmc.com
Producer: Alia Dann Swift.

Intrak 6 Delaney Drive, Freckleton, Preston, Lancashire, PR4 1SJ **t** 01772 633697 **f** 01772 634875
e info@intrak.co.uk **w** intrak.co.uk **Prop: JA Foley.**

Jack Morton Worldwide 16-18 Acton Park Estate, Stanley Gardens, London, W3 7QE **t** 020 8735 2000
f 020 8735 2020
e Asitha_Ameresekere@jackmorton.co.uk
w jackmorton.com **Sales/Mkt Dir: Chris Morris.**

Lashed Worldwide Events Clearwater Yard, 35 Inverness St, London, NW1 7HB **t** 020 7424 7500
f 020 7424 7501 **e** roman@ornadel.com
Contact: Roman Trystram.

Midem (UK) Walmar House, 296 Regent St, London, W1B 3AB **t** 020 7528 0086 **f** 020 7895 0949
e javier.lopez@reedmidem.com **w** midem.com **Sales Mgr: Javier Lopez.**

Moonlite Productions 12 Chequers End, Winslow, Bucks, MK18 3HT **t** 07966 331000 **e** info@moonlite.co.uk
w moonlite.co.uk **MD: James Iyengar.**

MUSEXPO 8383 Wilshire Blvd, Suite 100, Beverly Hills, CA 90211, United States **t** 323.782.0770 **f** 323.782.9835
e brandon@anrworldwide.com **w** musexpo.net
Contact: Brandon Fuller.

MUSEXPO Europe 8383 Wilshire Blvd, Suite 100, Beverly Hills, CA 90211, United States **t** 323.782.0770
f 323.782.9835 **e** brandon@anrworldwide.com
w musexpo.net **Contact: Brandon Fuller.**

NUS Ents - Ents Convention 45 Underwood St, London, N1 7LG **t** 020 7490 0946 **f** 020 7490 1026
e steve@nus-ents.co.uk **w** nus-ents.co.uk **NUS Ents Co-ordinator: Steve Hoyland.**

onedotzero Unit 212c Curtain House, 136-146 Curtain Rd, London, EC2A 3AR **t** 020 7729 0072
f 020 7729 0057 **e** info@onedotzero.com
w onedotzero.com **Events Mgr: Anna Doyle.**

Sensible Events 2nd Floor, Regent Arcade House, 19-25 Argyll St, London, W1F 7TS **t** 020 7009 3470
e Andrew@sensibleevents.com **w** sensibleevents.com
MD: Andrew Zweck.

SMi Group Unit 122, Great Guildford Business Sq, 30 Great Guildford St, London, SE1 0HS **t** 020 7827 6000
f 020 7827 6001 **e** client_services@smi-online.co.uk
w smi-online.co.uk

Awards & Memorabilia

Award Framers International Ltd
The Framing Centre, By The Meadow Farm, Steventon, Oxon, OX13 6RP **t** 01235 821 469 **f** 01235 821 427
e info@awardframers.com **w** awardframers.com
Managing Director: Michael Selway.

Bonhams 2 Relay Rd, White City, London, W12 7SJ
t 08700 273620 **f** 08700 273626
e entertainment@bonhams.com **w** bonhams.com
Entertainment Dept: Stephanie Connell.

Century Displays 75-77 Park Road, Kingston Upon Thames, Surrey, KT2 6DE **t** 020 8974 8950
f 020 8546 3689 **e** info@centurydisplays.co.uk
w centurydisplays.co.uk **General Manager: Neil Wicks.**

The Gold Disc.com 12 Brampton Sidings, Hempstalls Lane, Newcastle-under-Lyme, Staffordshire, ST5 0SR **t** 01782 616165 **e** sales@thegolddisc.com
w thegolddisc.com **f** facebook.com/pages/The-Gold-Disccom/46615811600 **myspace.com/thegolddisc
twitter.com/thegolddisc **MD: Dave Breese.

ReprinT Records 9 The Causeway, Downend, Fareham, Hants, PO16 8RN **t** 07999 040621
e water.fall@virgin.net **Contact: Jo Womar.**

Business Consultants

The 7 Stars 46 Charlotte Street, London, W1T 2GS
t 020 7436 7275 **f** 020 7436 7276
e firstname.lastname@the7stars.co.uk **w** the7stars.co.uk
Contact: Jenny Biggam.

A&R Worldwide 8383 Wilshire Blvd, Suite 100, Beverly Hills, CA 90211, United States **t** 323.782.0770
f 323.782.9835 **e** brandon@anrworldwide.com
w anrworldwide.com **Contact: Brandon Fuller.**

A Minor Music Consultancy 101 High Street, Stetchworth, Newmarket, Suffolk, CB8 9TH
t 01638 508 582 **e** ed@oneservice.co.uk **MD: Edward Ashcroft 07711 088 972.**

ABSOLUTE CONSULTANCY

The Old Lamp Works, Rodney Pl, Wimbledon, London, SW19 2LQ **t** 020 8540 4242 **f** 020 8540 6056
e info@absolutemarketing.co.uk
w absolutemarketing.co.uk **Contact: Henry Semmence, Simon Wills.**

Arising Artist 50-52 Paul St, London, EC2A 4LB
t 020 7749 1980 **f** 020 7729 8951
e info@arisingartist.com **w** arisingartist.com
✉ Consultants: Lisa DeLuca and Meredith Cork.

Arrowsmith Communications 5 Norfolk Court,
Victoria Park Gardens, Worthing, BN11 4ED
t 01903 200 916 **e** eugeniearrowsmith@yahoo.co.uk
✉ Media Consultant: Eugenie Arrowsmith 07967 102 259.

Autonomy Music Group
Suite 27, The Quadrant Centre, 135 Salusbury Road,
Queens Park, London, NW6 6RJ **t** 020 7644 1450
e firstname@autonomymusicgroup.com

Blinkhorns 27 Mortimer Street, London, W1T 3BL
t 020 7636 3702 **f** 020 7636 0335
e Joel.Trott@blinkhorns.co.uk **w** blinkhorns.co.uk
✉ Partner: Joel Trott.

BossSound - Music Consultancy
4 The Candlemakers, 112 York Road, London, SW11 3RA
t 07812 349 798 **e** christian@bossSound.co.uk
✉ MD: Christian Siddell.

Box Music Ltd 2 Munro Terrace, Cheyne Walk, London,
SW10 0DL **t** 020 7376 8736 **f** 020 7376 3376
e sam@boxmusicltd.com ✉ GM: Sam Hilsdon.

Bravura - Life Coach 290 Old Rd, Chesterfield,
S40 3QN **t** 01246 231249 **e** lindsey@bravura-group.com
w bravura-group.com ✉ Music Career Coach: Lindsey
Benton.

Caragan Music Agency 5 The Meadows, Worlington,
Suffolk, IP28 8SH **t** 01638 717 390
e daren@caragan.com **w** caragan.com ✉ Head of
A&R: Daren Walder.

**Paul Chantler - Radio Programming
Consultant** 52 South Block, County Hall, Westminster,
London, SE1 7GB **t** 07788 584 888 **e** chantler@aol.com
w paulchantler.com ✉ MD: Paul Chantler.

Chris Merriman Media 91 Heathwood Gardens,
London, SE7 8ET **t** 07970 443262 **f** 07974 641139
e hello@chrismerrimanmedia.co.uk
w chrismerrimanmedia.co.uk t christhedj ✉ Music
Consultant, Journalist and Broadcaster: Chris Merriman.

Clear Focussed Minds 195 Micklefield Rd,
High Wycombe, Bucks, HP13 7HB **t** 01494 521 641
e kazlanglee@aol.com **w** clearfocussedminds.co.uk
✉ Consultant: Karen-Joy Langley (Bsc, BACP Reg.).

**Clearwater Special Projects Ltd (Threat
Management & Security)** Netley Hall, Shrewsbury,
Shropshire, SY5 7JZ **t** 01743 719 109 **f** 01743 719 170
e i.dewsnip@clearwaterprojects.com
w clearwaterprojects.com ✉ Operations Manager: Ian
Dewsnip.

Collective Music Ltd 5 Henchley Dene, Guildford,
Surrey, GU4 7BH **t** 01483 431 803 **f** 01483 431 803
e info@collective.mu **w** collective.mu ✉ MD: Phil Hardy.

Compact Collections Ltd Greenland Place, 115-
123 Bayham Street, London, NW1 0AG **t** 020 7446 7420
f 020 7446 7424 **e** info@compactcollections.com
w compactcollections.com ✉ Dirs: John O'Sullivan, James
Sellar.

Couchlife Devonshire House, 223 Upper Richmond Rd,
London, SW15 6SQ **t** 020 8780 0612 **f** 020 8789 8668
e rob@cdpool.com **w** couchlife.com ✉ Music Director: Rob
Sawyer.

Dave Newham Associates Windrush,
The Ridgeway, Enfield, Middlesex, EN2 8AN
t 020 8366 3311 **f** 020 8366 4443
e david.newham@firenet.uk.net **w** davidnewham.co.uk
✉ I P Consultant: David Newham.

Death Or Glory Marketing Consultancy
Woodcock Farm, Woodcock Lane, Maidstone, ME172AY
e ewan@deathorglorymusic.com
w deathorglorymusic.com ✉ Contact: Ewan Grant.

Discovery Media Ltd 39 Romney Court,
Shepherds Bush Green, London, W12 8PY
t 020 8740 7341 **e** lauren@discovery-media.biz
w discovery-media.biz ✉ Director: Lauren Lorenzo 07956
474379.

Enable Music Ltd 54 Baldry Gardens, London,
SW16 3DJ **t** 020 8144 0616 **e** mike@enablemusic.co.uk
w enablemusic.co.uk ✉ MD: Mike Andrews 07775 737
281.

**EP Music Licensing and Business
Affairs Consultants** 11 Richmond Way,
East Grinstead, W Sussex, RH19 4TG **t** 01342 313 035
f 01342 313 035 **e** clive@epmusic.f2s.com **w** epmusic.biz
✉ MD: Clive Wills.

GMR Entertainment 1 Riverside, Manbre Road,
London, W6 9WA **t** 020 8735 8336 **f** 08702 420 120
e davidw@gmrentertainment.com
w gmrentertainment.com ✉ VP, Europe: David Wille.

Graham Stokes Label Management
74 Great Titchfield St, London, W1W 7QP **t** 020 7636 7441
e graham@btdrecords.com **w** grahamstokes.com
✉ MD: Graham Stokes.

Green Consulting 17 Fairlawn Avenue, East Finchley,
London, N2 9PS **t** 020 8442 1730
e jonathan@jgreenconsulting.co.uk ✉ MD: Jonathan
Green 07831489488.

Gulp! Marketing Studio 204, Westbourne Studios,
242 Acklam Road, London, W10 5JJ **t** 020 7575 3202
e richard@gulpmusic.co.uk/gareth@gulpmusic.co.uk
w gulpmusic.co.uk ✉ MD: Richard Marshall & Gareth Currie
07973 543 527.

**Johnny Hudson – Music Consultant (Music To
Die For)** 10 Alexandra Park Road, London, N10 2AB
t 07796 996 669 **e** Johnny@musictodiefor.com
w musictodiefor.com ✉ Contact: Johnny Hudson.

ICP Group (Threat Management & Security)
2 Old Brompton Rd, London, SW1 3DQ **t** 020 7031 4440
e info@icpgroup.ltd.uk **w** icpgroup.ltd.uk ✉ MD: Will
Geddes.

Business Services: Business Consultants

Immediate Business Management
61 Birch Green, Hertford, Herts, SG14 2LR
t 01992 550573 **f** 01992 550573
e immediate@onetel.com **Q** Partner: Derek Jones.

Ingenious Media plc 15 Golden Sq, London, W1F 9JG
t 020 7319 4000 **f** 020 7319 4001
e enquiries@ingeniousmedia.co.uk
w ingeniousmedia.co.uk

**Innate Music - Project / PR & Marketing
Consultants** 58 Claremont Rd, Ealing, London,
W13 0DG **t** 020 8566 9824 **e** nathan@innate-music.com
w innate-music.com **Q** Director: Nathan Graves.

Inspiral 6 Cheyne Walk, Hornsea, East Yorkshire,
HU18 1BX **t** 01964 536 193
e paulcookemusic@btinternet.com
w paulcookemusic.com **Q** MD: Paul Cooke.

JN Promotions (Music Services) PO Box 6879,
Wellingborough, NN8 3YJ **t** 01933 228786
e jacqui@jnpromotions.biz **w** jnpromotions.biz
Q MD: Jacqui Norton.

John Waller Management & Marketing
The Old Truman Brewery, 91 Brick Lane, London, E1 6QL
t 020 7247 1057 **e** john@johnwaller.net
S myspace.com/johnwallermanagement **Q** MD: John
Waller.

Keith RD Lowde F.C.A. Minoru, Pharaoh's Island,
Shepperton, Middx, TW17 9LN **t** 01932 222 803
f 01932 222 803 **e** k.lowde@btconnect.com **Q** Contact:
0771 444 9765.

Lazarus Media Cydale House, 249A West End Lane,
London, NW6 1XN **t** 020 7794 1666 **f** 020 7794 1666
e info@lazarusmedia.co.uk **w** lazarusmedia.co.uk
Q MD: Steve Lazarus 07976 239140.

The Licensing Team Ltd 23 Capel Rd, Watford,
WD19 4FE **t** 01923 234 021 **f** 020 8421 6590
e Info@TheLicensingTeam.com **w** thelicensingteam.com
Q Director: Lucy Winch.

Lip Service 36 Redmore Rd, London, W6 0HZ
t 07764 166792 **e** patrick@lipserviceconsultants.com
w lipserviceconsultants.com **Q** Director: Patrick Clifton.

M A C Services PO Box 121, Hove, East Sussex,
BN3 4YY **t** 020 8144 9064 **e** sacha@macservices.org.uk
w macservices.org.uk **Q** Directors: Sacha Taylor-Cox and
Bob James.

Madrigal Consultancy Co Guy Hall, Awre,
Gloucestershire, GL14 1EL **t** 01594 510512
e artists@madrigalmusic.co.uk **w** madrigalmusic.co.uk
S myspace.com/madrigalmusicmanagement **Q** MD: Nick
Ford.

Mandy Haynes Consultancy Covetous Corner,
Hudnall Common, Little Gaddesden, Herts, HP4 1QW
t 01442 842039 **f** 01442 842082
e mandy@haynesco.fsnet.co.uk **Q** MD: Mandy Haynes.

**MECS (Music & Entertainment Consultancy
Services)** 14 Grasmere Ave, Kingston Vale, London,
SW15 3RB **t** 020 8974 5579 **f** 020 8974 5579 **e** tony@a-
b-u.demon.co.uk **Q** MD: Tony Watts.

Muirhead Management (Consultants)
202 Fulham Road, Chelsea, London, SW10 9PJ
t 07460 4668 **e** dennis@muirheadmanagement.co.uk
w muirheadmanagement.co.uk **Q** Music Industry
Consultant & Mediator: Dennis Muirhead 07785 226542.

Music & Merit Consultancy 9 Griffin Avenue,
Kidderminster, Worcs, DY10 1NA **t** 01562 751330
e musicalmerit@blueyonder.co.uk **w** musicalmerit.co.uk
Q Consultant (classical & nostalgia) / Owner / alto label
sales: Robin Vaughan 07774 117678.

Music & Arts Security Ltd 13 Grove Mews,
Hammersmith, London, W6 7HS **t** 020 8563 9444
f 020 8563 9555 **e** sales@musicartssecurity.co.uk
w music-and-arts-security.co.uk **Q** MD: Jerry Judge.

The Music Consultancy P.O.Box 696, Felbridge,
Surrey, RH19 2XS **t** 0845 370 9904 **f** 0845 370 9905
e ian@themusicconsultancy.com
w themusicconsultancy.com
S myspace.com/themusicconsultancy **Q** Director: Ian
Titchener.

The Music Label Agency Limited
33 Aldensley Rd, London, W6 0DH **t** 07718 893463
e judyneal@themusiclabelagency.com
w themusiclabelagency.com **Q** Contact: Judy Neal.

Music Village Ltd PO Box 8922, Maldon, Essex,
CM9 6ZW **e** info@music-village.com **w** music-village.com
Q Dir: John Carnell.

MusicBusinessCoach.com 39 Palmerston Place,
Edinburgh, EH12 5AU **t** 0131 202 6236 **f** 0131 202 6238
e coach@musicbusinesscoach.com
w musicbusinesscoach.com **Q** Managing
Consultant: David Murray.

MyRoyalties Unit 6 Spectrum House,
32 34 Gordon House Rd, London, NW5 1LP
t 07519 073336 **e** nick@carnmores.co.uk
w myroyalties.co.uk **Q** Partner: Nick Myles.

**NiceMan Productions (Licensing & Repertoire
Mgmt)** 111 Holden Rd, London, N12 7DF
t 020 8445 8766 **e** scott@nicemanproductions.com
w nicemanproductions.com **Q** Licensing Dir: Scott
Simons.

One Solution International Group
500 Chiswick High Rd, London, W4 5RG **t** 020 8956 2615
f 020 8956 2614 **e** info@onesolution-int.com
w onesolution-int.com **Q** Hd, Commercial Services: Alexis
Stanislaus.

Platinum Girls Media 1 Queens Walk,
Queens Walk House, London, W5 1TP
t 020 8740 7341 or 07956 474 379
e lorenzolauren@hotmail.com **Q** MD: Lauren Lorenzo.

📇 Contacts   📘 Facebook   📱 MySpace   🐦 Twitter   ▶️ YouTube

Pocket Rocket Music Ltd 5 Hanover Place, Bow, London, E3 4QD **t** 07855 121 787
e simon@pocketrocketmusic.com
w pocketrocketmusic.com 📇 Dir: Simon Burke-Kennedy.

Pure Delinquent 134 Replingham Road, Southfields, London, SW18 5LL **t** 07972 701 243 **f** 020 8870 0790
e info@pure-delinquent.com **w** pure-delinquent.com
📇 Dir: Julie Pratt.

PVA Ltd 2 High Street, Westbury On Trym, Bristol, BS9 3DU **t** 0117 950 4504 **f** 0117 959 1786
e enquiries@pva.ltd.uk **w** pva.ltd.uk 📇 Sales Director: John Hutchinson.

Quite Great Solutions Unit D, Magog Court, Shelford Bttm, Cambridge, CB2 4AD **t** 01223 410 000
e Harvey@quitegreat.co.uk **w** quitegreatsolutions.co.uk
📇 MD: Tony Lewis.

rainermusik.com 52 Meadow Lane, Slaithwaite, HD7 5EX **t** 01484 847097 **f** 01484 847097
e rainermusik@sky.com **w** rainermusik.com
📇 International Marketing Consultant: Rainer Focke.

Randall Harper – Solicitor Lawyers Direct, 53 Davies Street, London, W1K 5JH **t** 07713 258 767
f 08454 589398 **e** Randall.Harper@lawyers-direct.biz
w randall-harper-solicitor.com 📇 Consulting Solicitor: Randall Harper.

Record Play Po Box 320, 372 Old Street, London, EC1V 9LT **t** 020 7739 0939 **f** 020 7117 3852
e daniel@record-play.net **w** record-play.net 📇 MD: Daniel Cross.

RED TREE CONSULTANTS - LABEL AND PROJECT MANAGEMENT

The White House, 32 Thornton Hill, London, SW19 4HS
t 020 8947 5475 **w** redtreeconsultants.com
📇 Contact: Sam Forrest, Kim Glover.

Release Consulting Ltd (I.T.)
91 Peterborough Road, Parsons Green, London, SW6 3BU
t 0845 053 2975 **e** contact@releaseconsulting.co.uk
w releaseconsulting.co.uk 📇 MD: Will Lovegrove.

Richard Thomas - Consultant 42 Geraldine Rd, London, SW18 2NT **t** 020 8870 2701
e richtt123@yahoo.co.uk 📇 Contact: Richard Thomas.

Rightsman
The Rights Management and Marketing Group,
The Old Lamp Works, Rodney Pl, London, SW19 2LQ
t 020 8348 9179 / 020 8542 4222 **f** 020 8540 6056
e dick@rightsman.com **w** rightsman.com 📱 rightsman
📇 Consultants: Tim Prior, Dick Miller.

Rokkpool Consulting 11 Lawton Road, London, E10 6RR **t** 020 8558 6607 **e** research@rokkpool.com
w rokkpool.com 📇 Manager: Pippa Moye 07960 442 645.

Skullduggery Services 40a Love Lane, Pinner, Middlesex, HA5 3EX **t** 020 8429 0853
e xskullduggeryx@btinternet.com 📇 MD: Russell Aldrich.

The Sonic Services 41 route de la Corniche, Rouen, 76240 Bonsecours, France **t** + 33 (0) 663 330 488
e edouard@thesonicservices.com
w thesonicservices.com 📇 PDG: Edouard Lelievre-Brethiez.

Spark Marketing Entertainment 16 Winton Ave, London, N11 2AT **t** 0870 460 5439 **e** mbauss@spark-me.com **w** spark-me.com 📇 Executive Director: Matthias Bauss.

Stuart Batsford Ltd 5 Bolton Lodge, 19 Bolton Road, Chiswick, London, W4 3TG **t** 020 8995 3557
e stuart.batsford@btinternet.com 📇 Director: Stuart Batsford 07870 242 559.

Three Ones Music Ltd 111 The Custard Factory, Gibb St, Birmingham, B9 4AA **t** 0121 693 0013
e geoff@saffa.co.uk 📇 MD: Geoff Pearce.

Upfront Media Group Ltd 217 Buspace Studios, Conlan St, London, W10 5AP **t** 020 7565 0050
f 020 7565 0049 **e** simon@upfrontpromotions.com
w upfrontpromotions.com 📇 Contact: Simon Stanford.

Upside Productions (Music Consultancy)
14 Clarence Mews, Balham, London, SW12 9SR
t 07786 066665 **e** simon@upsideuk.com **w** upsideuk.com
📱 myspace.com/upsidemanagement 📇 Co MDs: Simon Jones & Denise Beighton.

Westbury Music Consultants Ltd
72 Marylebone Lane, London, W1U 2PL **t** 020 7487 5044
f 020 7935 2270 **e** pcornish@westburymusic.co.uk
📇 Director: Peter Cornish.

Yes Music Ltd Unit 212, The Saga Centre, 326 Kensal Road, London, W10 5BZ **t** 020 8968 0111
e simon@yesmusic.co.uk **w** yesmusic.co.uk 📇 Dirs: Simon Goffe, Gilles Petterson.

Education

3rd Precinct Ltd 26 South Hill Rd, Boxmoor, Hemel Hempstead, Hertfordshire, HP1 1JB
t 08451 309548 **f** 08451 309547
e charlotte@urbanprecinct.com **w** urbanprecinct.com
📘 facebook.com/urbanprecinct
📱 myspace.com/urbanprecinct
🐦 twitter.com/urbanprecinctuk
▶️ youtube.com/urbanprecinct 📇 CEO: Charlotte Roel 08451 309762.

Academy of Contemporary Music (ACM)
Rodboro Bld, Bridge St, Guildford, Surrey, GU1 4SB
t 01483 500800 **f** 01483 500801 **e** enquiries@acm.ac.uk
w acm.ac.uk

Access To Music Lionel House, 35 Millstone Lane, Leicester, LE1 5JN **t** 0800 281 842 **f** 0116 242 6868
e info@access-to-music.co.uk **w** accesstomusic.co.uk
📇 Head of Admissions: Alan Ramsay 0116 242 6888.

Alchemea College of Audio Engineering
The Windsor Centre, Windsor Street, London, N1 8QG
t 020 7359 4035 **e** info@alchemea.com **w** alchemea.com
🔲 Contact: Mike Sinnott.

Alternative Display Training 874 Pershore Road,
Selly Park, Birmingham, West Midlands, B29 7LS
t 0121 414 0436 **f** 0121 414 0436
e pauline@alternatedisplaytraining.com
w alternatedisplaytraining.com 🔲 MD: Pauline Carr.

Andy's Guitar Workshop 27 Denmark Street,
London, WC2H 8NJ **t** 020 7916 5080 **f** 020 7916 5714
e aguitar@btinternet.com 🔲 MD: Andy Preston.

**Associated Board of the Royal Schools of
Music** 24 Portland Place, London, W1B 1LU
t 020 7636 5400 **f** 020 7637 0234 **e** abrsm@abrsm.ac.uk
w abrsm.ac.uk 🔲 Fin Dir: Tim Leats.

The Helen Astrid Singing Academy
61 Bollo Bridge Road, London, W3 8AX **t** 07710 245 904
f 0870 774 0486
e helen@thehelenastridsingingacademy.com
w thehelenastridsingingacademy.com 🔲 Vocal
Coach: Helen Astrid (R.A.M.) plus associates.

Banana Row Drum School 47 Eyre Place,
Edinburgh, EH3 5EY **t** 0131 557 2088 **f** 0131 558 9848
e info@bananarow.com **w** bananarow.com 🔲 MD: Craig
Hunter.

Bass Guitar-X Bass School 76 Stanley Gardens,
London, W3 7SZ **t** 0208 749 3131 **f** 0208 740 8422
e info@guitar-x.co.uk **w** bassguitar-x.co.uk 🔲 Admissions
Advisor: Matt Hughes.

Bear Storm South Bank Technopark, 90 London Road,
London, SE1 6LN **t** 020 7815 7744 **f** 020 7815 7793
e greg@bearstorm.com Website: **w** bearstorm.com
🔲 MD: Greg Tallent.

**BIMM - Brighton & Bristol Institute Of Modern
Music** 38-42 Brunswick St West, Brighton, East Sussex,
BN3 1EL **t** 0844 2646 666 **f** 0844 2646 646
e info@bimm.co.uk **w** bimm.co.uk
🔳 youtube.com/bimmtv 🔲 Founding Directors: Kevin
Nixon, Sarah Clayman, Bruce Dickinson.

**The Brit School For Performing Arts &
Technology** 60 The Crescent, Croydon, Surrey,
CR0 2HN **t** 020 8665 5242 **f** 020 8665 8676
e admin@brit.croydon.sch.uk **w** brit.croydon.sch.uk 🔲 Arts
Industy Liason Mgr: Arthur Boulton.

Buckinghamshire New University
Queen Alexandra Rd, High Wycombe, Buckinghamshire,
HP11 2JZ **t** 0800 056 5660 **f** 01494 524392
e creative@bucks.ac.uk **w** bucks.ac.uk 🔲 Faculty
Marketing Manager: Nadine Bar.

Canford Summer School of Music P.O.Box 629,
Godstone, RH9 8WQ **t** 01342 893963 **f** 01342 893977
e canfordsummersch@btinternet.com
w canfordsummerschool.co.uk 🔲 Director of
Music: Malcolm Binney As above.

Centre For Voice The Tobacco Factory, Raleigh Rd,
Bristol, BS3 1TF **t** 0117 902 6606 **f** 0117 902 6607
e info@centreforvoice.idps.co.uk **w** centrecords.com
🔲 Principal: Andrew Hambly-Smith.

City University Music Department,
Northampton Square, London, EC1V 0HB
t 020 7040 8284 **f** 020 7040 8576 **e** music@city.ac.uk
w city.ac.uk/music 🔲 Administrator: Andrew Pearce.

Collage Arts Chocolate Factory 2, Coburg Rd, London,
N22 6JJ **t** 020 8365 7500 **f** 020 8365 8686
e info@collage-arts.org **w** collage-arts.org 🔲 Learning
Development Manager: Lance Williamson 020 8829 1318.

Community Music Wales Unit 8, 24 Norbury Rd,
Fairwater, Cardiff, CF5 3AU **t** 029 2083 8060
f 029 2056 6573 **e** admin@communitymusicwales.org.uk
w communitymusicwales.co.uk 🔲 Programme
Manager: Charlotte Little.

Cranford Summer School Of Music P.O.Box 629,
Godstone, RH9 8WQ **t** 01342 893963 **f** 01342 893977
e canfordsummersch@btinternet.com
w canfordsummerschool.co.uk

Dartington College of Arts Totnes, Devon, TQ9 6EJ
t 01803 861 650 **f** 01803 861 685
e enterprise@dartington.ac.uk
w dartington.ac.uk/enterprise 🔲 Director of
Enterprise: Adrian Bossey.

Deep Recording Trust 187 Freston Rd, London,
W10 6TH **t** 020 8206 5850 **f** Email only Please
e andy@deeprecordingstudios.co.uk,
enrol@deeprecordingstudios.co.uk,
w deeprecordingstudios.co.uk 🔲 Course Tutor: Andy
Paterson.

Dorset music forum 576 Christchurch Rd,
Boscombe, Dorset, BH1 4BH **t** 07866 489585
e suzy@dorsetmusic.com **w** dorsetmusic.com
🔳 facebook.com/dorsetmusicforum
🔳 myspace.com/dorsetmusic
🔳 twitter.com/dorsetmusic 🔲 CEO: Suzy Wheeler 07866
489 585.

Drumtech 76 Stanley Gardens, London, W3 7SZ
t 0208 749 3131 **f** 0208 740 8422 **e** info@drum-
tech.co.uk **w** drum-tech.co.uk
🔳 facebook.com/home.php?#/pages/London-United-
Kingdom/Tech-Music-Schools/31319252207?ref=ts
🔳 myspace.com/techmusicschools 🔲 Sales and
Marketing Supervisor: Darren Suckling.

Ebony and Ivory Vocal Tuition 11 Varley Parade,
Edgware Road, Colindale, Londno, NW9 6RR
t 020 8200 5510 **f** 020 8205 1907 **e** ajit123@aol.com
w ebonyivory.co.uk 🔲 MD: Ajit Sahajpal.

Education Group The Old Stables, 20 Bayes Street,
Kettering, NN16 8EH **t** 01536 411 334 **f** 01536 525 687
e dsmith@educationgroup.co.uk **w** educationgroup.co.uk
🔲 Contact: Darren Smith.

📇 Contacts   📘 Facebook   🔲 MySpace   🇪 Twitter   ▶️ YouTube

Faculty of the Arts Thames Valley University
Thames Valley University, St Mary's Rd, Ealing, London,
W5 5RF **t** 020 8579 5000 **f** 020 8231 2546
e ellie.wynn@tvu.ac.uk **w** tvu.ac.uk 📇 clearingguru
📇 Marketing Officer: Ellie Wynn 020 8231 2734.

Folk Music Journal 19 Bedford Rd, East Finchley,
London, N2 9DB **t** 020 8444 1137 **e** fmj@efdss.org
w efdss.org 📇 Ed: David Atkinson.

Gateway School of Recording 16 Bromells Rd,
London, SW4 0BG **t** 0870 770 8816 **e** info@gsr.org.uk
w gsr.org.uk 📇 Course Administrator: Hilary Cohen.

Global Entertainment Group Old House,
154 Prince Consort Road, Gateshead, NE8 4DU
t 0191 469 0100 **f** 0191 469 0001
e info@globalmusicbiz.co.uk **w** globalmusicbiz.co.uk
📇 Course Co-ordinator: Martin Jones.

**The Grove Music Studios - Bass & Drum
Tuition** 10 Latimer Industrial Estate, Latimer Road,
London, W10 6RQ **t** 020 8960 9601 **f** 020 8960 9606
e info@musicspace.co.uk **w** musicspace.co.uk
📇 Dir: Alistair R. Fincham.

Guildhall School of Music & Drama Silk Street,
Barbican, London, EC2Y 8DT **t** 020 7628 2571
f 020 7256 9438 **e** music@gsmd.ac.uk **w** gsmd.ac.uk
📇 Contact: Department of Music.

Guitar-X 76 Stanley Gardens, London, W3 7SZ
t 0208 749 3131 **f** 0208 740 8422 **e** info@guitar-x.co.uk
w guitar-x.co.uk
📘 facebook.com/home.php?#/pages/London-United-
Kingdom/Tech-Music-Schools/31319252207?ref=ts
🔲 myspace.com/techmusicschools 📇 Admissions
Advisor: Matt Hughes.

Hatchet Music Educational Resources
20 Intwood Rd, Norwich, Norfolk, NR4 6AA
t 01603 458 488 **e** mark@hatchetmusic.co.uk
📇 MD: Mark Narayn.

In The Music Biz 108 Oglander Road, London,
SE15 4DB **t** 07740 438537
e inthemusicbiz@btinternet.com **w** inthemusicbiz.com
📇 Course Manager: Amanda Hull.

**Institute of Contemporary Music
Performance** Foundation House, 1a Dyne Road,
London, NW6 7XG **t** 020 7328 0222 **f** 020 7372 4603
e enquiries@icmp.uk.com **w** icmp.uk.com 📇 MD: Paul
Kirkham.

Institute of Popular Music University of Liverpool,
Roxby Building, Chatham Street, Liverpool, L69 7ZT
t 0151 794 3101 **f** 0151 794 2566 **e** ipm@liverpool.ac.uk
w liv.ac.uk/ipm

**JAMES - Joint Audio media Education Sevices
- Industry education wing of MPG/APRS**
PO Box 915, Aylesbury, Buckinghamshire, HP20 9FT
e admin@jamesonline.org.uk,
contactus@jamesonline.org.uk **w** jamesonline.org.uk
📇 Secretary: Melvyn Toms Please email.

Jazzwise Direct 2B Gleneagle Mews,
Ambleside Avenue, London, SW16 6AE **t** 020 8769 7725
f 020 8677 7128 **e** admin@jazzwise.com **w** jazzwise.com
📇 Operations Mgr: Hugh Gledhill.

Jewel and Esk Valley College 24 Milton Road East,
Edinburgh, EH15 2PP **t** 0131 657 7321 **f** 0131 657 2276
e aduff@jevc.ac.uk **w** jevc.ac.uk 📇 Learning
Manager: Althea Duff.

Jewish Music Institute
School of Oriental & African Studies, University of London,
Thornhaugh St, Russell Sq, London, WC1H 0XG
t 020 8909 2445 **f** 020 8909 1030
e jewishmusic@jmi.org.uk **w** jmi.org.uk
📇 Director: Geraldine Auerbach MBE.

Keyboardtech Keyboard School
76 Stanley Gardens, London, W3 7SZ **t** 020 8749 3131
f 020 8740 8422 **e** info@vocal-tech.co.uk **w** keyboard-
tech.co.uk 📇 Admissions Advisor: Emma Marie Lea 0208
749 3131.

Leeds University BA Popular and World Musics,
School of Music, Leeds, LS2 9JT **t** 0113 343 2583
f 0113 343 2586 **e** s.r.warner@leeds.ac.uk
w leeds.ac.uk/music/ug/undergrad_ba_pwm.shtml
📇 Senior Teaching Fellow: Simon Warner.

London Music School 9-13 Osborn St, Brick Lane,
London, E1 6TD **t** 0845 299 0872
e music@londonmusicschool.com
w londonmusicschool.com 📇 Management Team: Lisa
Hedlund.

**The London Oratory School Schola
Foundation** Seagrave Road, London, SW6 1RX
t 020 7381 7684 **f** 020 7381 7676 **e** schola@los.ac
w london-oratory.org/schola 📇 Music
Administrator: Sebastian Budner 020 7835 0102.

Martin Belmont 101A Cricklewood Broadway, London,
NW2 3JG **t** 020 8450 2885 📇 Guitar Teacher: Martin
Belmont.

MMF Training PO Box 161, Romiley, Stockport,
SK6 3WQ **t** 0161 430 8324 **f** 0161 430 8333
e admin@mmf-training.com **w** mmf-training.com 📇 Head
of Training & Education: Stuart Worthington.

Music For Youth 102 Point Pleasant, London,
SW18 1PP **t** 020 8870 9624 **f** 020 8870 9935
e mfy@mfy.org.uk **w** mfy.org.uk 📇 Executive
Director: Larry Westland.

You can subscribe at the Music Week

Student rate!

Contacts   Facebook   MySpace   Twitter   YouTube

Business Services: Education

Music Teacher Rhinegold Publishing, 239-241 Shaftesbury Avenue, London, WC2H 8EH
t 020 7333 1747 **f** 020 7333 1765
e music.teacher@rhinegold.co.uk **w** rhinegold.co.uk
Ed: Clare Stevens.

Music, Arts & Culture Hiltongrove Business Centre, 25 Hatherley Mews, London, E17 4QP **t** 020 8520 3975
f 0208520 3975 **e** info@redonion-uk.com
Manager: Dee Curtis.

Newark College Friary Rd, Newark, Nottinghamshire, NG24 1PB **t** 01636 680680 **f** 01636 680681
e enquiries@lincolncollege.ac.uk **w** newark.ac.uk
Contact: Customer Services.

Nordoff-Robbins Music Therapy
2 Lissenden Gardens, London, NW5 1PQ **t** 020 7267 4496
f 020 7267 4369 **e** admin@nordoff-robbins.org.uk
w nordoff-robbins.org.uk Chief Executive
Officer: Pauline Etkin.

North Glasgow College 123 Flemington St, Glasgow, Lanarkshire, G21 4TD **t** 0141 558 9001
f 0141 558 9905 **e** hbrankin@north-gla.ac.uk
w northglasgowcollege.ac.uk Snr Lecturer: Hugh Brankin.

Point Blank Music College 23-28 Penn St, London, N1 5DL **t** 020 7729 4884 **f** 020 7729 8789
e david@pointblanklondon.com **w** pointblanklondon.com
facebook.com/pointblankcollege
myspace.com/pointblanklondon twitter.point_blank
youtube.com/pointblankonline Sales & Marketing
Mgr: David Reid.

Pulse Recording College 67 Pleasants Place, Dublin 8, Ireland **t** +353 1 478 4045 **f** +353 1 475 8730
e pulserecording@pulserecording.com
w pulserecording.com Dir: Tony Perrey.

The Recording Workshop Unit 10, Buspace Studios, Conlan St, London, W10 5AP **t** 020 8968 8222
f 020 7460 3164 **e** recordingworks@btconnect.com
w therecordingworkshop.co.uk Managing Director: Jose Gross.

The Royal Academy of Music
University of London, Marylebone Rd, London, NW1 5HT
t 020 7873 7373 **f** 020 7873 7374 **e** publicity@ram.ac.uk
w ram.ac.uk facebook.com/pages/Royal-Academy-of-Music/41083569097 Marketing Manager: Peter Craik
020 7873 7318.

The Royal College Of Music Prince Consort Rd, London, SW7 2BS **t** 020 7589 3643 **f** 020 7589 7740
e info@rcm.ac.uk **w** rcm.ac.uk Director of
Operations: Kevin Porter.

The Royal School of Church Music 19 The Close, Salisbury, Wiltshire, SP1 2EB **t** 01722 424 848
f 01722 424 849 **e** enquiries@rscm.com **w** rscm.com
Contact: Education Administrator.

The Royal School of Church Music (RSCM)
19 The Close, Salisbury, Wiltshire, SP1 2EB
t 01722 424848 **f** 01722 424849 **e** press@rscm.com
w rscm.com Mgr, Press/Music Direct: Tim Ruffer.

Royal Welsh College of Music & Drama
Castle Grounds, Cathays Pk, Cardiff, CF10 3ER
t 029 2039 1361 **f** 029 2039 1301
e music.admissions@rwcmd.ac.uk **w** rwcmd.ac.uk
facebook.com/profile.php?id=638118688&v=info&ref
=profile#/rwcmd twitter.com/RWCMD Music
Admissions: Aimee Bryett.

SAE Institute SAE House, 297 Kingsland Rd, London, E8 4DD **t** 020 7923 9159 **f** 020 7691 7653
e saelondon@sae.edu **w** sae.edu
facebook.com/pages/Oxford-United-Kingdom/SAE-Institute/106636269504?ref=ts
twitter.com/sae_london UK Marketing
Manager: James Bilios.

Safi Sounds Management 306 Vicarage Rd, Huddersfield, HD3 4HJ **t** 07929 868849
e info@safisounds.co.uk **w** safisounds.co.uk
myspace.com/safisez Contact: Sarah Hutton.

Sense of Sound Training Parr Street Studios, 33-45 Parr St, Liverpool, L1 4JN **t** 0151 707 1050
f 0151 709 8612 **e** info@senseofsound.net
w senseofsound.net Artistic Director: Jennifer John.

Show Me How to Play.com The Ironworks, 30 Cheapside, Brighton, E. Sussex, BN1 4GD
t 01273 670088 **f** 01273 626502
e info@showmehowtoplay.com **w** showmehowtoplay.com
MD: Mark Flannery.

SSR 65-69, Downing Street, Manchester, M1 7JE
t 0161 276 2100 **f** 0161 272 7242 **e** ian.hu@s-s-r.com
w s-s-r.com Principal: Ian Hu.

Streetlights Contemporary Music School
Tally House, Sheepdown Close, Petworth, GU28 0BP
t 01798 343388 **e** streetlights@btconnect.com
w streetlightsmusicschool.co.uk Principal: Chris Mountford.

Training in Sound Recording The Studio, Tower St, Hartlepool, TS24 7HQ **t** 01429 424440 **f** 01429 424441
e studiohartlepool@btconnect.com
w studiohartlepool.com Contact: Tony Rowsell.

Tribal Tree 66C Chalk Farm Road, London, NW1 8AN
t 020 7482 6945 **f** 020 7485 9244
e enquiries@tribaltreemusic.co.uk **w** tribaltreemusic.co.uk
Programme Mgr: Louise Nkosi.

University of Chester (Warrington Campus)
Commercial Music Production, Crab Lane, Fearnhead, Warrington, WA2 0DB **t** 01925 534308 **f** 01925 530001
e r.dyson@chester.ac.uk; j.mason@chester.ac.uk
w chester.ac.uk/undergraduate/commercial-music-production Module Leaders: Russell Dyson, Jim Mason.

University of St Andrews Music Centre
Younger Hall, North St, St Andrews, Fife, KY16 9AJ
t 01334 462226 **f** 01334 462228 **e** music@st-andrews.ac.uk **w** st-andrews.ac.uk/music Music Centre
Manager: Helen Gregory. Seated Capacity: 450 Standing
capacity: 1000

University of Surrey School of Performing Arts, Dept of Music, Guildford, Surrey, GU2 7XH
t 01483 686500 **f** 01483 686501 **e** spa@surrey.ac.uk **w** surrey.ac.uk/music

University Of Westminster
Centre for Commercial Music, Watford Rd, Harrow, Middlesex, HA1 3TP **t** 020 7911 5940 **f** 020 7911 5943 **e** k.hoji@westminster.ac.uk **w** westminster.ac.uk 🔲 Course Dir: Kienda Hoji.

Uplayon.com Chichester **e** nomismusic@gmail.com **w** uplayon.com 🔲 Singer-songwriter consultant: Simon Skinner 01243 573639.

Urban Precinct Limited 26 South Hill Rd, Boxmoor, Hemel Hempstead, Hertfordshire, HP1 1JB
t 08451 309548 **f** 08451 309547
e info@urbanprecinct.com **w** urbanprecinct.com
▶️ youtube.com/user/urbanprecinct 🔲 Co-Directors: Charlotte Roel & Floyd Adams III.

The Vocal Zone - Vocal Coach PO Box 25269, London, N12 9ZT **t** 07970 924 190
e info@thevocalzone.co.uk **w** thevocalzone.co.uk
🔲 Contact: Kenny Thomas.

Vocaltech Vocal School 76 Stanley Gardens, London, W3 7SZ **t** 0208 749 3131 **f** 0208 740 8422
e enquiries@vocal-tech.co.uk **w** vocal-tech.co.uk
📘 facebook.com/home.php?#/pages/London-United-Kingdom/Tech-Music-Schools/31319252207?ref=ts
🟦 myspace.com/techmusicschools 🔲 Admissions Advisor: Emma Marie Lea.

Computer Services

Barracuda Ltd Oatlands Chase, Weybridge, Surrey, KT13 9SD **t** 07050 678 205 **f** 07050 666 342
e support@zenassist.com **w** Zenassist.com 🔲 Technical Director: Baz Omidi.

Counterpoint Systems The Forum, 74-80 Camden St, London, NW1 0EG **t** 020 7543 7500
f 020 7543 7600 **e** info@counterp.com **w** counterp.com
🔲 CEO: Amos Biegun.

Effective Business Solutions P O Box 152, Tewkesbury, Gloucestershire, GL20 9AU **t** 01242 620095 **e** nrb@ebsed.co.uk **w** ebsed.co.uk 🔲 Proprietor: Nigel Browning 07778 554190.

Musicalc/RoyaltyShare The Old Police Station, 6 Old London Road, Kingston-upon-Thames, Surrey, KT2 6QF **t** 020 8439 1518 **f** 020 8541 1885
e info@musicalc.com **w** musicalc.com 🔲 General Manager: Asa Palmer.

Portech Systems Ltd 501 The Green House, Gibb Street, Birmingham, B9 4AA **t** 0121 624 2626
f 0121 624 0550 **e** s.naeem@portech.co.uk
w portech.co.uk 🔲 Sales Manager: S.Naeem.

Priam Software The Old Telephone Exchange, 32-42 Albert St, Rugby, CV21 2SA **t** 01788 558000
f 01788 558001 **e** office@priamsoftware.com
w priamsoftware.com 🔲 Commercial Manager: Neil Spektor.

Ranger Computers Ranger House, 2 Meeting Lane, Duston, Northamptonshire, NN5 6JG **t** 01604 589200 **f** 01604 589505 **e** enquiries@rangercom.com **w** ranger.demon.co.uk 🔲 Managing Director: David Viewing.

Spool Multi Media (UK) Unit 30, Deeside Industrial Park, Deeside, Flintshire, CH5 2NU
t 01244 280602 **f** 01244 288581 **e** rv@smmuk.co.uk **w** smmuk.co.uk 🔲 MD: Roy Varley.

Summit Services Rosebery Avenue, High Wycombe, Bucks, HP13 7YZ **t** 01494 447 562 **f** 01494 441 498 **e** summit@summit-services.co.uk **w** summit-services.co.uk 🔲 MD: Bob Street.

Worldspan Communications Ltd
Unit 19, Red Lion Business Centre, Red Lion Road, Surbiton, Surrey, KT6 7QD **t** 020 8288 8555
f 020 8288 8666 **e** sales@span.com **w** span.com
🔲 Sales: Rob Barth.

Zenassist Computer Services Oatlands Chase, Weybridge, KT13 **t** 08453 883 357 **f** 07050 666 342 **e** baron@zenassist.com **w** zenassist.com 🔲 Technical Director: Baz Omidi 07050 678 205.

Business Services & Miscellaneous

A&R Worldwide 8383 Wilshire Blvd, Suite 100, Beverly Hills, CA 90211, United States **t** 323.782.0770 **f** 323.782.9835 **e** brandon@anrworldwide.com **w** anrworldwide.com 🔲 Contact: Brandon Fuller.

A1 Reliable Discotheques 132 Chase Way, London, N14 5DH **t** 0800 298 2893 **f** 0208 361 3757
e a1disco@yahoo.co.uk **w** lastminutedjlondon.co.uk
🔲 Mgr: Colin Jacques.

Affinity Music 60 Kingly St, London, W1B 5DS
t 020 7453 4062 **f** 020 7436 3666
e info@affinitymusic.co.uk **w** affinitymusic.co.uk
🔲 MD: Simon Binns.

The Arts Clinic 14 Devonshire Place, London, W1G 6HX **t** 020 7935 1242 **f** 020 7224 6256
e mail@artsclinic.co.uk **w** artsclinic.co.uk
🔲 Director: Sandie Powell.

Assential Arts Coxeter House, 21-27 Ock Street, Abingdon, Oxfordshire, OX14 3ST **t** 01235 536008
f 01235 207070 **e** info@assentialarts.com
w assentialarts.com 🔲 MD: Mike Selway.

Bodyfixx - therapeutic bodywork for post-gig-recovery, injury prevention/repair, health & fitness 11 Lawton Rd, London, E10 6RR **t** 020 8558 6607 **e** bodyfixx@bodyfixx.co.uk **w** bodyfixx.co.uk ✉ Trainer/Therapist: Pippa Moye.

Caligraving Ltd Brunel Way, Thetford, Norfolk, IP24 1HP **t** 01842 752116 **f** 01842 755512 **e** info@caligraving.co.uk **w** caligraving.co.uk ✉ Sales Dir: Oliver Makings.

The Chain Music Services Ltd 30 Seby Rise, Uckfield, TN22 5EE **t** 01825 769829 **e** mail@chainmusic.com ✉ MD: Giorgio Cuppini.

Chart Moves-The Game 2 Move 2 PO Box 1099, London, SE5 9HT **t** 020 7326 4824 **f** 020 7535 5901 **e** gamesmaster@chartmoves.com **w** chartmoves.com ✉ MD: David Klein.

Christian Copyright Licensing (Europe) Ltd PO Box 1339, Eastbourne, East Sussex, BN21 4YF **t** 01323 417711 **f** 01323 417722 **e** executive@ccli.co.uk **w** ccli.co.uk ✉ Sales Mgr: Chris Williams.

Counterpoint Systems The Forum, 74-80 Camden St, London, NW1 0EG **t** 020 7543 7500 **f** 020 7543 7600 **e** info@counterp.com **w** counterp.com ✉ CEO: Amos Biegun.

DB Music Sales Ltd 5 O'Feld Terrace, Ferry Rd, Felixstowe, Suffolk, IP11 9NA **t** 01394 283712 **f** 01394 283712 **e** david@dbmusicsales.co.uk **w** dbloom.co.uk ✉ Dir: David Bloom.

Devolution London.com 30 Cambridge Gardens, Notting Hill, London, W10 5UD **t** 020 8960 2695 **e** Geremy@DevolutionLondon.com **w** DevolutionLondon.com ✉ MD: Geremy O'Mahony.

Esfor Limited PO Box 221, Hertfordshire, SG7 6WZ **t** 01462 892181 **e** info@esforlimited.com **w** s4cds.co.uk ✉ MD: John Hall.

Fonix L.E.D. 8 Thrush Rd, Poole, Dorset, BH12 4NP **t** 01202 684555 **f** 01202 684666 **e** ianw@fonix.co.uk **w** fonix.co.uk ✉ Director: Ian Walker.

Gas Music Tracking (GMT) OMC, 1st Floor, 9 Park End St, Oxford, OX1 1HH **t** 01865 798791 **e** gmt@oxfordmusic.net ✉ Master Tracker: Dave Newton.

Hamilton House Mailings Ltd Earlstrees Court, Earlstrees Rd, Corby, Northamptonshire, NN17 4HH **t** 01536 399000 **f** 01536 399012 **e** sales@hamilton-house.com **w** hamilton-house.com ✉ MD: Stephen Mister.

Hello Currency Ltd 2nd Floor, 145-157 St.John Street, London, EC1V 4PY **t** 020 7788 7765 **f** 0845 280 1549 **e** ngoddard@hellocurrency.com **w** hellocurrency.com ✉ MD: Noel Goddard.

I Like The Sound Of That London and Bath **e** sybil@ilikethesoundofthat.com ric@ilikethesoundofthat.com ✉ Director: Sybil Bell or Ric Yerbury.

International Security Ltd 55 Princes Gate, Exhibition Rd, London, SW7 2PN **t** 020 7158 0329 / 07707 297759 **f** 020 7158 0559 **e** liam.nammock@internationalsecurity.co.uk **w** internationalsecurity.co.uk ✉ Director: Liam Nammock.

Jazz Services 1st Floor, 132 Southwark St, London, SE1 0SW **t** 020 7928 9089 **f** 020 7401 6870 **e** info@jazzservices.org.uk **w** jazzservices.org.uk ✉ Director: Chris Hodgkins.

JBS Management UK Apartment 11, Dean Meadow, Newton-le-Willows, Lancs, WA12 9PX **e** xag84@jaybs.freeserve.co.uk

Madrigal Music Consultancy Co Guy Hall, Awre, Gloucestershire, GL14 1EL **t** 01594 510512 **e** artists@madrigalmusic.co.uk **w** madrigalmusic.co.uk 🅼 myspace.com/madrigalmusicmanagement ✉ MD: Nick Ford.

The Manor Partnership 9 Hayters Court, Grigg Lane, Brockenhurst, Southampton, SO42 7PG **t** 01590 622 477 **f** 01590 622 481 **e** howard.lucas@tmp-uk.com **w** themanorpartnership.com ✉ Dir: Howard Lucas.

Marken Time Critical Express Unit 2, Metro Centre, St Johns Road, Isleworth, Middlesex, TW7 6NJ **t** 020 8388 8555 **f** 020 8388 8666 **e** info@marken.com **w** marken.com ✉ Bus Devel Mgr: Rob Paterson.

Matinee Sound & Vision Ltd 132-134 Oxford Road, Reading, Berkshire, RG1 7NL **t** 0118 958 4934 **f** 0118 959 4936 **e** info@matinee.co.uk **w** matinee.co.uk ✉ Managing Director: Christopher Broderick.

Merseyside Music Development Agency (MMDA) Units 8-15, The Arts Village, Henry St, Liverpool, Merseyside, L1 5BS **t** 0151 707 4550 **e** info@mmda.org.uk **w** mmda.org.uk ✉ Administrative Assistant: Emma Kennedy.

Music Ally Ltd 1-5 Exchange Court, London, WC2R 0JU **t** 020 74204320 **f** 087 0160 6572 **e** paul.brindley@musically.com **w** musically.com ✉ CEO: Paul Brindley 020 7420 4321.

Music Village Ltd PO Box 8922, Maldon, Essex, CM9 6ZW **e** john@music-village.com **w** music-village.com ✉ Director: John Carnell 07831 891610.

Newman & Co Regent House, 1 Pratt Mews, London, NW1 0AD **t** 020 7554 4840 **f** 020 7388 8324 **e** partners@newman-and.co.uk **w** newman-and.co.uk ✉ Snr Partner: Colin Newman.

Portman Music Services Ltd Laurel House, Station Approach, Alresford, Hampshire, SO24 9GH **t** 01962 732033 **f** 01962 732032 **e** maria@portmanmusicservices.net **w** portmanmusicservices.co.uk ✉ Director: Maria Comiskey.

Rasheed Ogunlaru Life Coaching (for Singers and Performers), The Coaching Studio, 223a Mayall Rd, London, SE24 0PS **t** 020 7207 1082 **e** rasheed@rasaru.com **w** rasaru.com ✉ Life & Business Coach: Rasheed Ogunlaru.

Business Services: Business Services & Miscellaneous

RPM Research Suite 4, 17 Pepper St, London, E14 9RP
t 020 7537 3030 **f** 020 7537 0008
e info@rpmresearch.com **w** rpmresearch.com
🔲 Partners: Gary Trueman, David Lewis.

Sarahpilates Sunflower House, 68 Primrose Gardens,
Belsize Pk, London, NW3 4TP **t** 020 7722 4373
e srmgmt@aol.com **w** sarahpilates.com 🔲 Pilates
personal Trainer: Sarah Rosenfield.

Studio2 PA Services Studio 2, 25 Halstead Rd,
Earls Colne, Colchester, Essex, CO6 2NG **t** 01787 224464
f 01787 224464 **e** karen@studio2pa.com
w studio2pa.com 🔲 Personal Assistant: Karen Carne.

T&S Immigration Services Ltd 118 High St,
Kirkcudbright, DG6 4JQ **t** 01557 339123
e firstname@tandsimmigration.co.uk
w tandsimmigration.co.uk 🔲 Immigration
Specialists: Steve & Tina Richard.

**Terry McDonald - Music Licensing and
Royalties Consultant** 10 Tranquil Dale, Buckland,
Betchworth, Surrey, RH3 7EE **t** 01737 845434
e terry@terrymcdonald.co.uk **w** terrymcdonald.co.uk
🔲 Owner: Terry McDonald.

Contacts Facebook MySpace Twitter  YouTube

Media

Print Media

247 Magazine After Dark Media,
Unit 29, Scott Business Park, Beacon Park Road, Plymouth,
PL2 2PB **t** 01752 294 130 **f** 01752 564 010
e editorial@afterdarkmedia.com **w** 247mag.co.uk
🔲 Editor: Lucy Griffiths.

Access All Areas Ocean Media, One Canada Sq,
Canary Wharf, London, E14 5AP **t** 020 7772 8444
f 020 7772 8588 **e** nic.howden@oceanmedia.co.uk
w access-aa.co.uk 🔲 Editor: Nic Howden.

Artistes & Agents Richmond House Publishing Co, 70-
76 Bell St, Marylebone, London, NW1 6SP **t** 020 7224 9666
f 020 7224 9688 **e** sales@rhpco.co.uk **w** rhpco.co.uk
🔲 Manager: Spencer Block.

Attitude Trojan Publishing, Ground Floor, 211 Old Street,
London, EC1V 9PS **t** 020 7608 6461 **f** 020 7608 6380
e attitude@attitudemag.co.uk **w** attitudemag.co.uk
🔲 Ed: Adam Mattera.

Audience Media Ltd 26 Dorset St, London, W1U 8AP
t 020 7486 7007 **f** 020 7486 2002 **e** info@audience.uk.com
w audience.uk.com 🔲 Publisher/Managing Editor: Stephen
Parker.

Audio Media Magazine IMAS Publishing UK Ltd,
1 Cabot House, Compass Point Business Park, St Ives,
Cambs, PE27 5JL **t** 01480 461555 **f** 01480 461550
e p.mac@audiomedia.com **w** audiomedia.com
🔲 Editor: Paul Mac.

Audio Pro International Intent Media, Saxon House,
6a St Andrew Street, Hereford, SG14 1JA **t** 01992 535646
e Andy.Wood@intentmedia.co.uk
w audioprointernational.com 🔲 Editor: Andy Wood.

Bandit A&R Newsletter 68/70 Lugley St, Newport,
Isle Of Wight, PO30 5ET **t** 01983 524 110
e bandit@banditnewsletter.com **w** banditnewsletter.com
🔲 myspace.com/banditnewsletter 🔲 MD: John Waterman.

Base.ad PO Box 56374, London, SE1 3WF
t 0207 357 8066 **f** 0207 357 8166 **e** london@base.ad
w base.ad 🔲 Editor: Tanya Mannar.

BBC Music Magazine Origin Publishing,
14th Floor, Tower House, Fairfax St, Bristol, BS1 3BN
t 0117 927 9009 **f** 0117 934 9008
e music@bbcmagazines.com **w** bbcmusicmagazine.com
🔲 Editor: Oliver Condy.

The Beat 54 Canterbury Road, Penn, Wolverhampton,
West Midlands, WV4 4EH **t** 01902 652759 **f** 01902 652759
e steve-morris@blueyonder.co.uk **w** surf.to/thebeat
🔲 Ed: Steve Morris 07973 133416.

Between The Grooves 3 Tannsfeld Rd, London,
SE26 5DQ **t** 020 8488 3677 **f** 020 8333 2572
e info@betweenthegrooves.com
w betweenthegrooves.com 🔲 Editor: Jonathan Sharif.

The Big Issue 1-5 Wandsworth Rd, London, SW8 2LN
t 020 7526 3201 **f** 020 7526 3301
e matt.ford@bigissue.com **w** bigissue.com 🔲 Ed: Matt Ford.

Billboard Endeavour House, 5th floor,
189 Shaftesbury Avenue, London, WC2H 8TJ
t 020 7420 6003 **f** 020 7420 6014
e MSutherland@eu.billboard.com **w** billboard.com,
billboard.biz 🔲 Global Editor and London Bureau Chief: Mark
Sutherland.

Blues Matters! PO Box 18, Bridgend, CF33 6YW
t 01656 745628 **f** 01656 745028
e darren@bluesmatters.com **w** bluesmatters.com
🔲 facebook.com/group.php?gid=5350172405
🔲 myspace.com/bluesmatterspublication 🔲 Editor-in-
Chief: Darren Howells 02920399998.

borderevents.com Ltd 2 Heatherlie Park, Selkirk,
Selkirkshire, TD7 5AL **t** 01750 725 480
e info@borderevents.com **w** borderevents.com 🔲 Music
editor: Andrew Lang.

Brass Band World Impromptu Publishing, 4th Floor,
117-119 Portland Street, Manchester, M1 6FB
t 0161 236 9526 **f** 0161 247 7978
e advertising@brassbandworld.com **w** brassbandworld.com
🔲 Ad Mgr: Jerry Hall.

British & International Music Yearbook
Rhinegold Publishing Ltd, 241 Shaftesbury Avenue, London,
NW2 3DG **t** 020 7333 1761 **f** 020 7333 1766
e bmyb@rhinegold.co.uk **w** rhinegold.co.uk 🔲 Ed: Toby
Deller.

British Bandsman 66-78 Denington Rd,
Wellingborough, Northants, NN8 2QH **t** 01933 445 442
f 01933 445 435 **e** info@britishbandsman.com
w britishbandsman.com 🔲 Editor: Kenneth Crookston.

Broadcast Emap Media, 33-39 Bowling Green Lane,
London, EC1R 0DA **t** 020 7505 8000 **f** 020 7505 8050
e admin@broadcastnow.co.uk **w** broadcastnow.co.uk
🔲 Ed: Conor Dignam.

Campaign 22 Bute Gardens, London, W6 7HN
t 020 8267 4683 **f** 020 8267 4915
e campaign@haynet.com 🔲 Ed: Caroline Marshall.

City Life 164 Deansgate, Manchester, M3 3RN
t 0161 832 7200 **f** 0161 839 1488 **e** editor@citylife.co.uk
w citylife.co.uk 🔲 Editor: David Alan Lloyd.

City Living Magazine 1st Floor, Weaman St,
Birmingham, B4 6AT **t** 0121 234 5202 **f** 0121 234 5757
e jamie_perry@mrn.co.uk **w** icbirmingham.co.uk/cityliving
🔲 Product Mgr: Jamie Perry.

Contacts Facebook  MySpace Twitter YouTube

Clash Magazine/Clashmusic.com 29 D'Arblay St, Soho, London, UK, W1F 8EP **t** 0207 734 9351 **f** 01382 909909 **e** info@clashmusic.com **w** clashmusic.com facebook.com/clashmusic myspace.com/clashmagazine twitter.com/clashmusic youtube.com/ClashMagazine Editor: Simon Harper 0207 734 9351 London 01382 808808 Scotland.

Classic FM Magazine Haymarket Publishing, Teddington Studios, Broom Rd, Teddington, Middlesex, TW11 9BE **t** 020 8267 5180 **f** 020 8267 5150 **e** classicfm@haymarket.com **w** classicfm.com Editor: John Evans.

Classic Rock 2 Balcombe St, London, NW1 6NW **t** 020 7042 4000 **f** 020 7042 4419 **e** firstname.lastname@futurenet.com

Classical Music Rhinegold Publishing, 241 Shaftesbury Avenue, London, WC2H 8TF **t** 020 7333 1742 (Ed) **f** 020 7333 1769 (Ed) **e** classical.music@rhinegold.co.uk **w** rhinegold.co.uk Ed: Keith Clarke 020 7333 1733 (ads).

Cliff Chart Site.co.uk 17, Podsmead Rd, Tuffley, Glos, GL1 5PB **t** 01452 306104 **f** 01452 306104 **e** william@cliffchartsite.co.uk **w** cliffchartsite.co.uk Editor: William Hooper.

Clown Magazine Suite 3, Rosden House, 372 Old Street, London, EC1V 9AU **t** 07986 359 568 **e** office@clownmagazine.co.uk **w** clownmagazine.co.uk Contact: Jack Dorrington.

Computer Music Future Publishing, 30 Monmouth St, Bath, BA1 2BW **t** 01225 442244 **e** ronan.macdonald@futurenet.co.uk **w** computermusic.co.uk Ed: Ronan Macdonald.

Country Music People 1-3 Love Lane, London, SE18 6QT **t** 020 8854 7217 **f** 020 8855 6370 **e** info@countrymusicpeople.com **w** countrymusicpeople.com Ed: Craig Baguley.

Country Music Round Up PO Box 111, Waltham, Grimsby, NE Lincs, DN37 0YN **t** 01472 821808 **f** 01472 821808 **e** countrymusic_ru@hotmail.com **w** cmru.co.uk Publisher: John Emptage.

The Crack 1 Pink Lane, Newcastle upon Tyne, NE1 5DW **t** 0191 230 3038 **f** 0191 230 4484 **e** rob@thecrackmagazine.com **w** thecrackmagazine.com Ed: Robert Meddes.

Cuesheet Music Report 23 Belsize Crescent, London, NW3 5QY **t** 020 7794 2540 **f** 020 7794 7393 **e** cuesheet@songlink.com **w** cuesheet.net Editor/Publisher: David Stark.

Daily Mail Northcliffe House, 2 Derry Street, London, W8 5TT **t** 020 7938 6000 **f** 020 7937 3251 **e** editorial@dailymailonline.co.uk **w** dailymail.co.uk

Daily Record & Sunday Mail 1 Central Quay, GlasgowGlasgow, G3 8DA **t** 0141 309 3000 **f** 0141 309 3340 **e** reporters@dailyrecord.co.uk **w** dailyrecord.co.uk

Daily Telegraph 1 Canada Square, Canary Wharf, London, E14 5DT **t** 020 7538 5000 **f** 020 7538 7650 **w** telegraph.co.uk

Dazed & Confused 112-116 Old St, London, EC1V 9BG **t** 020 7336 0766 **f** 020 7336 0966 **e** tim@dazedgroup.com **w** dazeddigital.com facebook.com/DazedandConfusedMagazine myspace.com/dazedandconfusedmag twitter.com/DazedMagazine Music Editor: Tim Noakes 020 7549 6856.

Deuce Vision Publishing, 1 Trafalgar Mews, East Way, London, E9 5JG **t** 020 8533 9320 **f** 020 8533 9320 **e** editor@deucemag.com **w** deucemag.com Ed: Colin Steven.

Diplo Magazine 156-158 Gray's Inn Road, London, WC1X 8ED **t** 020 7833 9766 **f** 020 7833 9766 **e** charlesb@diplo-magazine.co.uk **w** diplo-magazine.co.uk Editor-in-Chief: Charles Baker.

Disorder Magazine Unit 4/5, First Floor, Universal House, 88-94 Wentworth St, London, E1 7SA **t** 020 7247 6504 **e** taylor@disordermagazine.com **w** disordermagazine.com Editor: Taylor Glasby.

DJ Magazine The Old Truman Berwery, London, E1 6QL **t** 020 7247 8855 **e** info@djmag.com **w** DJmag.com Deputy Editor: Tom Kihl.

Early Music Faculty of Music, University of Cambridge, 11 West Rd, Cambridge, CB3 9DP **t** 01223 335 178 **f** 01223 335 178 **e** earlymusic@oupjournals.org **w** em.oupjournals.org Editor: Dr Tess Knighton.

Echoes 3 Elsinore Rd, London, SE23 2SH **t** 020 8291 2870 **e** echoesmag@btconnect.com Editor: Chris Wells.

Essential Newcastle 5-11 Causey St, Newcastle-upon-Tyne, NE3 4DJ **t** 0191 284 9994 **f** 0191 284 9995 **e** richard.holmes@accentmagazines.co.uk Editor: Richard Holmes.

Evening Standard Northcliffe House, 2 Derry Street, London, W8 5TT **t** 020 7938 6000 **f** 020 7937 7392 **e** editor@thisislondon.co.uk **w** thisislondon.co.uk

Financial Times 1 Southwark Bridge, London, SE1 9HL **t** 020 7873 3000 **f** 020 7873 3062 **w** ft.com

The Fly 59-65 Worship St, London, EC2A 2DU **t** 020 7688 9000 **f** 020 7688 8999 **e** niall@channelfly.com **w** the-fly.co.uk Ed: Niall Doherty.

Foresight Bulletin/Planner Profile Group, Dragon Court, 27-29 Macklin St, London, WC2B 5LX **t** 020 7190 7829 **f** 020 7190 7858 **e** info@profilegroup.co.uk **w** foresightonline.co.uk Editor: Vicki Ormiston.

Fresh Direction Student Magazine Buliding D, Berkeley Works, Berkley Grove, London, NW1 8XY **t** 020 7449 0900 **f** 020 7449 0901 **e** paul.russell@fd-media.co.uk **w** fd-media.co.uk myspace.com/freshdirection Publisher: Paul Russell.

Media: Print Media

Contacts | Facebook | MySpace | Twitter | YouTube

fRoots c/o Southern Rag Ltd, PO Box 337, London, N4 1TW **t** 020 8340 9651 **f** 020 8348 5626 **e** froots@frootsmag.com **w** frootsmag.com
facebook.com/group.php?gid=6354678018
myspace.com/frootsmag Editor: Ian Anderson.

Fused Magazine Studio 315, The Greenhouse, Gibb St, Birmingham, B9 4AA **t** 0121 246 1946
e enquiries@fusedmagazine.com **w** fusedmagazine.com
facebook.com/group.php?gid=18350653872&ref=ts
myspace.com/fusedmagazine
twitter.com/fusedmagazine
youtube.com/fusedmagazine Editor: David O'Coy.

Future Music Future Publishing, 30 Monmouth Street, Bath, Somerset, BA1 2BW **t** 01225 442244
f 01225 732353 **e** andy.jones@futurenet.co.uk
w futuremusic.co.uk Snr Editor: Andy Jones.

The Gen Generator North East, Black Swan Court, 69 Westgate Rd, Newcastle, NE1 1SG **t** 0191 245 0099
f 0191 245 0144 **e** mail@generator.org.uk
w generator.org.uk Ed: David John Watton 07951 357 549.

GQ Vogue House, Hanover Sq, London, W1S 1JU
t 020 7152 3731 **f** 020 7495 1679
e andy.morris@condenast.co.uk **w** gqmagazine.co.uk
Commissioning Editor: Andy Morris.

Gramophone Haymarket Ltd, Teddington Studios, Broom Rd, Teddington, Middlesex, TW11 9BE
t 020 8267 5136 **f** 020 8267 5844
e gramophone@haymarket.com **w** gramophone.co.uk
Publishing Coordinator: Sue McWilliams.

The Grapevine 45 Underwood Street, London, N1 7LG
t 020 7490 0946 **f** 020 7490 1026 **e** nick@nus-ents.co.uk
w nusonline.co.uk Sales Manager: Nick Woodward.

The Guardian 119 Farringdon Road, London, EC1R 3ER
t 020 7278 2332 **f** 020 7713 4366
e arts.editor@guardianunlimited.co.uk **w** guardian.co.uk

The Guide The Guardian, 119 Farringdon Road, London, EC1R 3ER **t** 020 7713 4152 **f** 020 7713 4346 Contact: 020 7239 9980.

Guitar & Bass Magazine IPC Focus, Leon House, 233 High St, Croydon, Surrey, CR9 2TA **t** 020 8726 8000
f 020 8726 8397 **e** steven_bailey@ipcmedia.com
w guitarmagazine.co.uk Deputy Editor: Steven Bailey 020 8726 8306.

Guitarist Future Publishing, 30 Monmouth Street, Bath, Somerset, BA1 2BW **t** 01225 442244 **f** 01225 732285
e neville.martin@futurenet.co.uk Ed: Neville Marten.

Heat Endeavor House, 189 Shaftesbury Avenue, London, WC2H 8JG **t** 020 7295 5000 **f** 020 7859 8670
e heatmag@heatmag.com

The Herald 200 Renfield Street, Glasgow, G2 3QB
t 0141 302 7000 **f** 0141 302 7171 **e** arts@theherald.co.uk
w theherald.co.uk

Hi-Fi Choice Future Publishing, 99 Baker Street, London, W1U 6FP **t** 020 7317 2600 **f** 020 7317 0275
e tim.bowern@futurenet.co.uk **w** hifichoice.co.uk Dep Ed: Tim Bowern.

Hi-Fi News Leon House, 233 High St, Croydon, Surrey, CR9 1HZ **t** 020 8726 8310 **f** 020 8726 8397 **e** hifinews@ipcmedia.com **w** hifinews.co.uk; avexpo.co.uk
Ed: Steve Harris.

Hi-Fi World Audio Publishing, Unit G4, Imex House, Kilburn Park Road, London, W9 1EX **t** 020 7625 3134
e editorial@hi-fiworld.co.uk **w** hi-fiworld.co.uk
Editor: David Price.

Hip Hop Connection Infamous Ink Ltd, PO Box 392, Cambridge, CB1 3WH **t** 01223 210 536 **f** 01223 210 536
e hhc@hiphop.com **w** hhcmagazine.com Ed: Andy Cowan.

Hit Sheet 31 The Birches, London, N21 1NJ
t 020 8360 4088 **f** 020 8360 4088 **e** info@hitsheet.co.uk
w hitsheet.co.uk facebook.com/hitsheet
myspace.com/hitsheet twitter.com/paulhitsheet
Publisher: Paul Kramer 07932 034750.

Hokey Pokey Millham Lane, Dulverton, Somerset, TA22 9HQ **t** 01398 324 114 **f** 01398 324 114
e hokey.pokey@bigfoot.com Ed: Andrew Quarrie 07831 103 194.

The Hollywood Reporter Endeavour House, 189 Shaftesbury Avenue, London, WC2H 8TJ
t 020 7420 6000 **f** 020 7420 6014 **e** stuart.kemp@thr.com
w thr.com UK Bureau Chief: Stuart Kemp.

Honk Ty Cefn, Rectory Rd, Canton, Cardiff, South Glamorgan, CF5 1QL **t** 029 2066 8127
f 029 2034 1622 **e** honk@welshmusicfoundation.com
w welshmusicfoundation.com/honk Ed: James McLaren.

Hot Press Magazine 13 Trinity St, Dublin 2, Ireland
t +353 1 241 1500 **f** +353 1 241 1538 **e** info@hotpress.ie
w hotpress.com Ed: Niall Stokes.

i-D Magazine 124 Tabernacle St, London, EC2A 4SA
t 020 7490 9710 **f** 020 7251 2225 **e** reception@i-Dmagazine.co.uk **w** i-dmagazine.co.uk

The Independent On Sunday Northcliffe House, 2 Derry Street, London, W8 5TT **t** 020 7938 6000
f 020 7937 3251 **e** arts@independent.co.uk
w independent.co.uk

The Independent Northcliffe House, 2 Derry Street, London, W8 5TT **t** 020 7938 6000 **f** 020 7937 3251
e arts@independent.co.uk **w** independent.co.uk
Ed: Simon Kelner.

Installation Europe 8th Floor, Ludgate House, 245 Blackfriars Rd, London, SE1 9UR **t** 020 7921 8378
f 020 7921 8339 **e** ienews@ubm.com
w installationeurope.com Editor: Paddy Baker.

🔲 Contacts ⓕ Facebook 🔲 MySpace ⓔ Twitter ▶ YouTube

Media: Print Media

Installation Europe Buyer's Guide 8th Floor,
Ludgate House, 245 Blackfriars Rd, London, SE1 9UR
t 020 7921 8401 **f** 020 7921 8339
e lianne.davey@ubm.com
w installationeuropebuyersguide.com 🔲 Business Support
Manager: Lianne Davey.

International Broadcast Engineer
Business Media Ltd, 3rd Floor, Armstrong House,
38 Market Square, Uxbridge, Middlesex, UB8 1LH
t 01342 717 459 **e** info@bpl-business.com **w** ibeweb.com
🔲 Publisher: Clare Sturzaker.

IQ Magazine 2-4 Prowse Pl, London, NW1 9PH
t 020 7284 5867 **f** 020 7284 1870 **e** greg@iq-mag.net
w iq-mag.net 🔲 Editor: Greg Parmley.

Irish Music Magazine 11 Clare St, Dublin 2, Ireland
t +353 1 662 2266 **f** +353 1 662 4981
e info@selectmedialtd.com **w** irish-music.net
🔲 Publisher: Robert Heuston.

Irish Music Scene Bunbeg, Letterkenny, Co Donegal,
Ireland **t** +353 7495 31176 **e** donalkoboyle@eircom.net
🔲 Ed/Publisher: Donal K O'Boyle.

Irish Times 10-16 D'Olier Street, Dublin 2, Ireland
t +353 1 679 2022 **e** enquiries@irish-times.com
w ireland.com

Jazz Journal International Jazz Journal Ltd, 3-
3A Forest Road, Loughton, Essex, 1G10 1DR
t 020 8532 0456 **f** 020 8532 0440 🔲 Publisher/Ed: Eddie
Cook 020 8532 0678.

The Jazz Rag PO Box 944, Birmingham, West Midlands,
B16 8UT **t** 0121 454 7020 **f** 0121 454 9996
e jazzrag@bigbearmusic.com **w** bigbearmusic.com
🔲 Ed: Jim Simpson.

Jazzwise Magazine 2(B) Gleneagle Mews,
Ambleside Avenue, London, SW16 6AE **t** 020 8677 0012
f 020 8677 7128 **e** jon@jazzwise.com
w jazzwisemagazine.com 🔲 Editor & Publisher: Jon Newey.

Kerrang! Bauer Consumer Media, Mappin House,
4 Winsley St, London, W1R 7AR **t** 020 7436 1515
f 020 7312 8910 **e** feedback@kerrang.com **w** kerrang.com
🔲 Editor: Nichola Browne 020 7312 8957.

Keyboard Player 100 Birkbeck Rd, Enfield, Middlesex,
EN2 0ED **t** 020 8245 5840
e stevemillerkp@blueyonder.co.uk **w** keyboardplayer.com
🔲 Ed: Steve Miller.

Knowledge Magazine Vision Publishing,
1 Trafalgar Mews, Eastway, London, E9 5JG
t 020 8533 9300 **e** editor@knowledgemag.co.uk
w knowledgemag.co.uk 🔲 Ed: Colin Steven.

The Knowledge WLR Media & Entertainment, 6-
14 Underwood St, London, N1 6JQ **t** 020 7549 8666
f 020 7549 8668 **e** knowledge@wilmington.co.uk
w theknowledgeonline.com 🔲 Sales Manager: Sarah
Keegan.

Leeds Guide Ltd 30-34 Aire Street, Leeds,
West Yorkshire, LS1 4HT **t** 0113 244 1000 **f** 0113 244 1002
e editor@leedsguide.co.uk 🔲 Ed: Dan Jeffrey.

The List 14 High St, Edinburgh, EH1 1TE **t** 0131 550 3050
f 0131 557 8500 **e** editor@list.co.uk **w** thelist.co.uk
🔲 Ed: Nick Barley.

Loaded 26th Floor, Kings Reach Tower, Stamford Street,
London, SE1 9LS **t** 020 7261 5562 **f** 020 7261 5640
e firstname_lastname@ipcmedia.com **w** loaded.co.uk

Loud And Quiet Floor 1, 2 Loveridge Mews, Kilburn,
London, NW6 2DP **t** 07838 170 171
e info@loudandquiet.com **w** loudandquiet.com
🔲 Editor: Stuart Stubbs.

**M4 Media (music business contract
publishing)** 2-4 Prowse Place, London, NW1 9PH
t 020 7284 5869 **f** 020 7284 1870 **e** info@m-4media.com
w m-4media.com 🔲 Dir: Chris Prosser.

Mail On Sunday Northcliffe House, 2 Derry Street,
London, W8 5TT **t** 020 7938 6000 **f** 020 7937 3829
e editorial@dailymailonline.co.uk **w** mailonsunday.co.uk

Marketing 174 Hammersmith Road, London, W6 7JP
t 020 8267 4150 **e** Via website **w** marketing.haynet.com
🔲 Ed: Craig Smith.

Marketing Week 12-26 Lexington St, 50 Poland Street,
London, W1R 4 **t** 020 7970 4000 **f** 020 7970 6721
e stuart.smith@centaur.co.uk **w** marketing-week.co.uk
🔲 Ed: Stuart Smith.

Maverick Magazine 24 Bray Gardens, Maidstone, Kent,
ME15 9TR **t** 01622 744481 **e** editor@maverick-
country.com **w** maverick-country.com 🔲 MD: Alan Cackett.

Media Research Publishing Lister House,
117 Milton Rd, Weston-super-Mare, Somerset, BS23 2UX
t 01934 644126 **e** cliffdane@tiscali.com
w mediaresearchpublishing.com 🔲 Chairman: Cliff Dane.

M8 Magazine Trojan House, Phoenix Business Park,
Paisley, Renfrewshire, PA1 2BH **t** 0141 840 5980
f 0141 840 5995 **e** info@m8magazine.com
w m8magazine.co.uk 🔲 Ed: Kevin McFarlane.

Metal Hammer Future Publishing, 99 Baker St, London,
W1U 6FP **t** 01225 442244 **f** 020 7486 5678
e chris.ingham@futurenet.co.uk **w** metalhammer.co.uk
🔲 Ed: Chris Ingham.

Metro Scotland 20 Waterloo Street, Glasgow, G2 6DB
t 0141 225 3336 **f** 0141 225 3316
e scotlife@ukmetro.co.uk 🔲 Arts Editor: Rory Weller.

MI Pro Intent Media, Saxon House, 6a St Andrew St,
Hertford, Hertfordshire, SG14 1JA **t** 01992 535646
e mipro@intentmedia.co.uk **w** mi-pro.co.uk
ⓔ miprofessional 🔲 Managing Editor: Andy Barrett.

The Mirror 1 Canada Square, London, E14 5AP
t 020 7293 3000 **f** 020 7293 3405
e feedback@mirror.co.uk **w** mirror.co.uk

Mixmag Development Hell, 90-92 Pentonville Rd, London,
N1 9HS **t** 020 7078 8400 **e** mixmag@mixmag.net
w mixmag.net 🔲 Ed: Nick Decosemo 020 7078 8411.

📇 Contacts   ⓕ Facebook   🆂 MySpace   ⓣ Twitter   ▶️ YouTube

Mobile Entertainment Intent Media, St Andrew House, 46-48 St Andrew Street, Hertford, SG14 1JA **t** 01992 535 646 **e** stuart.obrien@intentmedia.co.uk **w** mobile-ent.biz 📇 Editor: Stuart O'Brien.

MOJO Bauer Media, Mappin House, 4 Winsley St, London, W1W 8HF **t** 020 7182 8616 **f** 020 7312 8296 **e** mojo@bauermedia.co.uk **w** mojo4music.com 📇 Editor: Phil Alexander.

Music Business Journal 3 Winsdown House, Three Gates Lane, Haslemere, Surrey, GU27 2LE **t** 01428 656 442 **e** info@musicjournal.org **w** musicjournal.org 📇 Managing Editors: JoJo Gould/ Jonathan Little.

Music Journal 10 Stratford Place, London, W1C 1AA **t** 020 7629 4413 **f** 020 7408 1538 **e** membership@ism.org **w** ism.org 📇 Ed: Neil Hoyle.

MUSIC WEEK

MusicWeek

8th Floor, Ludgate House, 245 Blackfriars Rd, London, SE1 9UY **t** 020 7921 5000 **f** 020 7921 8327 **e** firstname@musicweek.com **w** musicweek.com 🆃 twitter.com/MusicWeekNews 📇 Editor: Paul Williams. Publishing Director: Joe Hosken. Associate Editor: Robert Ashton. Talent Editor: Stuart Clarke. Features Editor: Chris Barrett. News Editor: Ben Cardew. Contributing Editor, Live: Gordon Masson. Contributing Editor, Digital: Eamonn Forde. Contributing Editor, Publishing: Chas de Whalley. Chart consultant: Alan Jones. Chart & Data Controller: Isabelle Nesmon. Group Sales Manager: Steve Connolly. Advertising Manager: Becky Golland. Deputy Advertising Manager: Archie Carmichael. Features Sales Executive: Martin Bojtos. Digital Sales Executive: Yonas Blay Morkeh.

MUSIC WEEK DIRECTORY

MusicWeek
Directory

8th Floor, Ludgate House, 245 Blackfriars Rd, London, SE1 9UR **t** 020 7921 8357 **f** 020 7921 8327 **e** mwdirectory@cmpi.biz **w** musicweek.com 📇 Digital Content Manager: Tim Frost. Publishing Director: Joe Hosken. Editor: Paul Williams. Group Sales Manager: Steve Connolly. Advertising Manager: Becky Golland. Deputy Advertising Manager: Archie Carmichael. Features Sales Executive: Martin Bojtos. Digital Sales Executive: Yonas Blay Morkeh. **The definitive contacts directory for the UK music industry.**

Music-Zine PO Box 9080, Bishops Stortford, Herts, CM23 4XW **t** 01279 865 070 **f** 0870 486 0812 **e** simon@music-zine.com **w** music-zine.com 📇 Publisher: Simon Eddie Baker 07941 142 779.

Musical Opinion 50 Collinstone Drive, St Leonards-on-Sea, E. Sussex, TN38 0NX **t** 01424 715 167 **f** 01424 712 214 **e** musicalopinion2@aol.com **w** musicalopinion.com 📇 Publisher: Denby Richards.

The Musical Times PO Box 464, Berkhamsted, Herts, HP4 2UR **t** 01442 879 097 **e** mustimes@aol.com **w** musicaltimes.co.uk 📇 Ed: Antony Bye.

Neon Buzz Magazine 1b Hepworth Road, Streatham, London, SW16 5DH **t** 07952 520 734 **e** thisisneonbuzz@googlemail.com **w** neonbuzz.net 📇 Editor: Claire Evans.

Nerve Talbot Campus, Fern Barrow, Poole, Dorset, BH12 5BB **t** 01202 965744 **f** 01202 535990 **e** suvpcomms@bournemouth.ac.uk **w** nervemedia.net 📇 Editor: Sarah Wiles.

A New Day - The Jethro Tull Magazine 75 Wren Way, Farnborough, Hants, GU14 8TA **t** 01252 540 270 **f** 01252 372 001 **e** DAVIDREES1@compuserve.com **w** anewdayrecords.co.uk 📇 Editor: Dave Rees 07889 797 482.

News Of The World News International, 1 Virginia Street, London, E1 9XR **t** 020 7782 7000 **f** 020 7583 9504 **e** Via website **w** newsoftheworld.co.uk

Night Magazine Mondiale Publishing Ltd, Waterloo Pl, Watson Sq, Stockport, Cheshire, SK1 3AZ **t** 0161 429 5580 **f** 0161 476 0456 **e** night@mondiale.co.uk **w** nightmagazine.co.uk 📇 Ed: Miss Rachel Esson.

Nightshift PO Box 312, Kidlington, Oxford, OX5 1ZU **t** 01865 372255 **e** nightshift@oxfordmusic.net **w** nightshift.oxfordmusic.net 📇 Editor: Ronan Munro.

NME IPC Music Magazines, Blue Fin Building, 110 Southwark St, London, SE1 0SU **t** 020 3148 5000 **f** 020 3148 8107 **e** editor@nme.com **w** nme.com 📇 Editor: Krissi Murison 020 3148 6864.

Northdown Publishing Ltd PO Box 49, Bordon, Hants, GU35 0AF **t** 07845 296 730 **e** enquiries@northdown.demon.co.uk **w** northdown.demon.co.uk 📇 Dir: Michael Heatley.

Notion Music HQ ltd., 4th Floor, 2 Plough Yard, London, EC2A 3LP **t** 0870 046 6622 **f** 0870 046 6611 **e** editorial@musichqmedia.com **w** notionmag.com 📇 Publisher: Bill Hussein.

The Observer 119 Farringdon Road, London, EC1R 3ER **t** 020 7278 2332 **f** 020 7713 4250 **e** firstname.lastname@observer.co.uk **w** observer.co.uk 📇 Contact: 020 7713 4286.

One To One 8th Floor, Ludgate House, 245 Blackfriars Road, London, SE1 9UR **t** 020 7921 8347 **f** 020 7921 8302 **e** etoppin@cmpi.biz **w** oto-online.com 📇 Editor: Elizabeth Toppin.

Contacts　　Facebook　　MySpace　　Twitter　　YouTube

Opera Now 241 Shaftesbury Avenue, London, WC2H 8EH **t** 020 7333 1733 **f** 020 7333 1736 **e** opera.now@rhinegold.co.uk **w** rhiegold.co.uk Ed: Ashutosh Khandekar 020 7333 1740.

Organ 19 Herbert Gardens, London, NW10 3BX **t** 020 8964 3066 **e** organ@organart.demon.co.uk **w** organart.com MD: Sean Worrall.

Original British Theatre Directory 70-76 Bell St, Marylebone, London, NW1 6SP **t** 020 7224 9666 **f** 020 7224 9688 **e** sales@rhpco.co.uk **w** rhpco.co.uk Manager: Spencer Block.

Orpheus Publications Ltd 3 Waterhouse Square, 138-142 Holborn, London, EC1N 2NY **t** 020 7882 1040 **f** 020 7882 1020 **w** thestrad.com Editor: Naomi Sadler.

Performing Musician Media House, Trafalgar Way, Bar Hill, Cambridge, CB23 8SQ **t** 01954 789888 **e** dave@performing-musician.com **w** performing-musician.com Editor: Dave Lockwood.

The Piano Rhinegold Publishing, 241 Shaftesbury Avenue, London, WC2H 8EH **t** 020 7333 1733 **f** 020 7333 1736 **e** piano@rhinegold.co.uk **w** rhinegold.co.uk Contact: 020 7333 1724.

Pipeline Instrumental Review 12 Thorkill Gardens, Thames Ditton, Surrey, KT7 0UP **e** editor@pipelinemag.co.uk **w** pipelinemag.co.uk Editor: Alan Taylor.

Popular Music Cambridge University Press, The Edinburgh Building, Shaftesbury Road, Cambridge, CB2 2RU **t** 01223 325757 **f** 01223 315052 **w** journals.cambridge.org/public/door Eds: Lucy Green, David Laing.

Press Association, Rock Listings 4th Floor, 292 Vauxhall Bridge Road, London, SW1V 1AE **t** 020 7963 7749 **f** 020 7963 7800 **e** gigs@pa.press.net Rock & Pop Editor: Delia Barnard.

Pro Sound News Europe CMP Information Ltd, 8th Floor, Ludgate House, 245 Blackfriars Rd, London, SE1 9UY **t** 020 7921 8319 **f** 020 7921 8302 **e** david.robinson@cmpi.biz **w** prosoundnewseurope.com Editor: David Robinson.

PSNLive 8th Floor, Ludgate House, 245 Blackfriars Rd, London, SE1 9UY **t** 020 7921 8319 **e** david.robinson@ubm.com **w** prosoundnewseurope.com Editor: David Robinson.

QSheet Markettiers4dc Ltd, 10a Northburgh House, Northburgh St, London, EC1V 0AT **t** 020 7253 8888 **f** 020 7253 8885 **e** editor@qsheet.com **w** qsheet.com Editor: Nik Harta.

The Radio Magazine Goldcrest Broadcasting, 21 West Saint Helen St, Abingdon, Oxfordshire, OX14 5BL **t** 07739 256260 **f** 01235 528121 **e** tony@theradiomagazine.co.uk **w** theradiomagazine.co.uk Contact: Tony Harbour.

Radio Times Woodlands, 80 Wood Lane, London, W12 0TT **t** 020 8576 2000 **e** radio.times@bbc.co.uk **w** radiotimes.com

Record Collector Room 101, 140 Wales Farm Rd, London, W3 6UG **t** 0870 732 8080 **f** 0870 732 6060 **e** firstname.lastname@metropolis.co.uk **w** recordcollectormag.com Editor: Alan Lewis 020 8752 8170.

Record of the Day PO Box 49554, London, E17 9WB **t** 020 8520 6646 **e** info@recordoftheday.com **w** recordoftheday.com Eds: Paul Scaife, Nicola Slade.

Revolutions 211 Western Road, London, SW19 2QD **t** 020 8646 7094 **f** 020 8646 7094 **e** john@revolutionsuk.com **w** revolutionsuk.com Editor: John Lonergan.

Rhythm Future Publishing, 30 Monmouth St, Bath, Somerset, BA1 2BW **t** 01225 442 244 **f** 01225 732 353 **e** phil.ascott@futurenet.co.uk **w** futurenet.co.uk Editor: Phil Ascott.

rock sound Unit 22 Jack's Pl, 6 Corbet Pl, Spitalfields, London, E1 6NN **t** 020 7877 8770 **f** 020 7377 0455 **e** info@rocksound.tv **w** rock-sound.net Publisher: Patrick Napier.

Roots And Branches 54 Canterbury Road, Penn, Wolverhampton, West Midlands, WV4 4EH **t** 07973 133 416 **e** steve-morris@blueyonder.co.uk **w** roots-and-branches.com Ed: Steve Morris.

Rough Guides Ltd 80 Strand, London, WC2R ORL **t** 020 7010 3701 **f** 020 7010 6767 **e** mail@roughguides.co.uk **w** roughguides.com Contact: Switchboard.

RTE Guide TV Building, Donnybrook, Dublin 4, Ireland **t** +353 1 208 2919 **f** +353 1 208 3085 **e** Aoife.Byrne@rte.ie Ed: Aoife Byrne.

RWD Aldwych House, 81 Aldwych, London, WC2B 4HN **t** 020 7492 6900 **f** 020 7492 6909 **e** hattiecollins@gmail.com or staff@rwdmag.com for general enquiries **w** rwdmag.com RWD Mag Myspace.com/rwdmag twitter.com/rwdmag youtube.com/rwdtv Editor: Hattie Collins 07932 636615.

Sandman Magazine PO Box 3720, Sheffield, S10 9AB **t** 0114 278 6727 **e** jan@sandmanmagazine.co.uk **w** sandmagazine.co.uk Ed: Jan Webster.

The Scotsman 108 Holyrood Road, Edinburgh, Midlothian, EH8 8AS **t** 0131 620 8620 **e** enquiries@scotsman.com **w** scotsman.com

Showcase Directory 6-14 Underwood Street, London, N1 7JQ **t** 020 7566 5763 **f** 020 7549 8668 **e** ecanavan@wilmington.co.uk **w** showcase-music.com Publishing Manager: Edward Canavan.

The Singer 241 Shaftesbury Avenue, London, WC2H 8TF **t** 020 7333 1746 **f** 020 7333 1769 **e** the.singer@rhinegold.co.uk **w** rhinegold.co.uk Ed: Antonia Couling.

Sky TV Guide & Digital TV Guide
The New Boathouse, 136-142 Bramley Rd, London,
W10 6SR **t** 020 7565 3000 **f** 020 7565 3056
e skymag@bcp.co.uk

Song And Media Promotions PO Box 218, Consett,
Co. Durham, DH8 1EP **t** 01207 500123 **f** 01736 763 328
e songandmedia@aol.com **w** songandmedia.com
📱 myspace.com/guildofsongwriters 📧 Editor: Colin Eade
01207 500825.

Songlines Unit F5, Shepherds Studios, Rockley Road,
London, W14 0DA **t** 020 7371 2777 **f** 020 7371 2220
e info@songlines.co.uk **w** songlines.co.uk 📧 Publisher: Paul
Geoghegan.

SongLink International 23 Belsize Crescent, London,
NW3 5QY **t** 020 7794 2540 **f** 020 7794 7393
e david@songlink.com **w** songlink.com
📱 myspace.com/songlink 🔳 twitter.com/songlink
📧 Ed/Publisher: David Stark 07956 270 592.

Songwriting & Composing Magazine
Sovereign House, 12 Trewartha Rd, Praa Sands, Penzance,
Cornwall, TR20 9ST **t** 01736 762826 **f** 01736 763328
e songmag@aol.com **w** songwriters-guild.co.uk
📱 myspace.com/guildofsongwriters 📧 Ed: Roderick Jones
01736 762 826.

Sound On Sound Media House, Trafalgar Way, Bar Hill,
Cambridge, Cambridgeshire, CB3 8SQ **t** 01954 789 888
f 01954 789 895 **e** sos@soundonsound.com
w soundonsound.com 📧 Publisher: Ian Gilby.

The Stage Stage House, 47 Bermondsey Street, London,
SE1 3XT **t** 020 7403 1818 **f** 020 7357 9287
e editor@thestage.co.uk **w** thestage.co.uk

Stage, Screen & Radio 373 -377 Clapham Rd,
London, SW9 9BT **t** 020 7346 0900 **f** 020 7346 0901
e info@bectu.org.uk **w** bectu.org.uk 📧 Ed: Janice Turner.

The Strad Newsquest Specialist Media Ltd,
30 Cannon St, London, EC4M 6YJ **t** 020 7618 3456
f 020 7618 3483 **e** ariane.todes@thestrad.com
w thestrad.com 📧 Ed: Ariane Todes.

Straight No Chaser 17D Ellingfort Rd, London, E8 3PA
t 020 8533 9999 **f** 020 8985 6447
e info@straightnochaser.co.uk **w** straightnochaser.co.uk
📧 Ed: Paul Bradshaw.

Sugar 64 North Row, London, W1K 7LL **t** 020 7150 7972
f 020 7150 7572 **e** lysannecurrie@hf-uk.com **w** hf-uk.com
📧 Editorial Dir: Lysanne Currie.

The Sun News International, 1 Virginia Street, London,
E1 9BD **t** 020 7782 4000 **f** 020 7782 4063
e talkback@the-sun.co.uk **w** thesun.co.uk

Sunday Mirror 1 Canada Square, London, E14 5AD
t 020 7510 3000 **f** 020 7293 3405 **e** Via website
w sundaymirror.co.uk

Sunday People 1 Canada Square, London, E14 5AP
t 020 7293 3000 **f** 020 7293 3810
e feedback@mirror.co.uk **w** people.co.uk

Sunday Telegraph 1 Canada Square, London, E14 5DT
t 020 7538 5000 **e** firstname.lastname@telegraph.co.uk
w telegraph.co.uk

Sunday Times News International, 1 Pennington Street,
London, E1 9XW **t** 020 7782 5000 **f** 020 7782 5658
e artsed@thetimes.co.uk **w** timesonline.co.uk

Swell Music Rocklyn, Trebarwith Strand, Tintagel,
Cornwall, PL34 0HB **t** 01840 779 054 **f** 01840 779 053
e info@swellmusic.co.uk **w** swellmusic.co.uk 📧 Dir: Andrew
Grainger.

Tempo (A Quarterly Review of Modern Music)
PO Box 171, Herne Bay, CT6 6WD **t** 020 7291 7224
e macval@compuserve.com **w** temporeview.com
📧 Ed: Calum MacDonald.

Time Out Universal House, 251 Tottenham Court Road,
London, W1T 7AB **t** 020 7813 3000 **f** 020 7813 6158
e music@timeout.com **w** timeout.com/london 📧 Music
Ed: Chris Salmon.

The Times Metro News International,
1 Pennington Street, London, E98 1TE **t** 020 7782 5000
f 020 7782 5525 **e** metro@the-times.co.uk 📧 Ed: Rupert
Mellor.

The Times 1 Pennington St, London, E98 1XY
t 020 7782 5000 **e** firstname.lastname@thetimes.co.uk
w timesonline.co.uk

TNT Magazine 14-15 Childs Place, London, SW5 9RX
t 020 7341 6685 **f** 0870 752 2717
e firstname.lastname@tntmagazine.com
w tntmagazine.com 📧 Entertainment Editor: Rebecca
Galton.

TV Times IPC Magazines, Kings Reach Tower,
Stamford Street, London, SE1 9LS **t** 020 7261 7740
e firstname_lastname@ipcmedia.com **w** ipc.co.uk

TVB Europe 8th Floor, Ludgate House,
245 Blackfriars Rd, London, SE1 9UR **t** 020 7921 8307
f 020 7921 8302 **e** tvbeurope@mediateam.ie
w tvbeurope.com 📧 Editor: Fergal Ringrose.

Uncut IPC Media 4th Floor, Blue Fin Building,
110 Southwark St, London, SE1 0SU **t** 020 3148 6985
e farah_ishaq@ipcmedia.com **w** uncut.net 📧 Editorial
Manager: Farah Ishaq.

Undercover Undercover Agents Ltd, Basement,
69 Kensington Gardens Sq, London, W2 4DG
t 020 7792 9392 **e** diagnostyx@hotmail.com 📧 Editor In
Chief: Nat Illumine.

Venue Magazine 4th Floor, Bristol News & Media,
Temple Way, Bristol, BS99 7HD **t** 0117 942 8491
f 0117 942 0369 **e** music@venue.co.uk **w** venue.co.uk
📧 Music Ed: Julian Owen.

Vice Magazine 77 Leonard St, London, EC2A 4QS
t 020 7749 7810 **e** info@viceuk.com **w** viceland.com
📧 Ed: Andy R. Capper.

The Voice 6th floor, Northern & Shell Tower,
4 Selsdon Way, London, E14 9GL **t** 020 7510 0386
f 020 7510 0341 **e** advertising@the-voice.co.uk **w** voice-
online.co.uk 📧 Recruitment Advertising: Tinu Fisher.

Media: Print Media, Radio

Volume10 Online Music Magazine
27 Trent Avenue, Liverpool, L31 9DE **t** 07779 793 555
e team@volume10.com **w** volume10.com 🔲 Editor: Tony
Mooney.

Web User IPC Inspire, Blue Fin Building,
110 Southwark Street, London, SE1 0SU **t** 020 3148 4327
f 020 3148 8122 **e** editor@web-user.co.uk **w** web-
user.co.uk 🔲 Editor: Richard Clark.

What Hi-Fi? Haymarket Magazines, 38-
42 Hampton Road, Teddington, Middlesex, TW11 0JE
t 020 8267 5000 **f** 020 8267 5019 **e** whathifi@haynet.com
w whathifi.com 🔲 Contact: Ed.

What's On - Birmingham & Central England
Weaman St, Birmingham, B4 6AT **t** 0121 234 5202
f 0121 234 5757 **e** jamie_perry@mrn.co.uk 🔲 Product
Mgr: Jamie Perry.

The White Book Inside Communications,
Bank House, 23 Warwick Rd, Coventry, West Midlands,
CV1 2EW **t** 024 7657 1171 **f** 024 7657 1172
e inside_events@mrn.co.uk **w** whitebook.co.uk 🔲 Business
Manager: Clair Whitecross..

Radio

3FM 45 Victoria Street, Douglas, Isle of Man, IM1 3RS
t 01624 616333 **f** 01624 614333
e moremusic@three.fm **w** three.fm 🔲 MD/Programme
Dir: Max Hailey.

3TR FM Riverside Studios, Warminster, Wilts., BA12 9HQ
t 01985 211 111 **f** 01985 211 110
e enquiries@3trfm.com **w** 3trfm.com 🔲 Programme
Controller: Jonathan Fido.

Absolute radio Great Titchfield St, London
e naturalvisibility@hotmail.com 🔲 Contact: Sarah Lee
0207 3997255.

Absolute Radio 1 Golden Square, London, W1F 9DJ
t 020 7434 1215
e firstname.surname@absoluteradio.co.uk
w absoluteradio.co.uk 🔲 Programme Manager: Mark
Bingham.

96.3 Radio Aire 51 Burley Rd, Leeds, West Yorkshire,
LS3 1LR **t** 0113 283 5500 **f** 0113 283 5501
e firstname.lastname@radioaire.com **w** radioaire.co.uk
🔲 Programme Director: Stuart Baldwin.

All Four Sides (radio production)
118 Petherton Rd, London, N5 2RT **t** 020 7683 2120
e rog@allfoursides.com **w** allfoursides.com
🔲 Director: Rog How 07595 538136.

Alpha 103.2 11 Woodland Road, Darlington,
Co Durham, DL3 7BJ **t** 01325 255 552 **f** 01325 255 551
e studio@alpha1032.com **w** alpha1032.com 🔲 Prog
Mgr/Head of Music: Dave Collins.

Argyll FM 27/29 Longrow, Campbeltown, Argyll,
PA28 6ER **t** 01586 551800 **e** studio@argyllfm.co.uk
w argyllfm.co.uk 🔲 Programme Director: Kenny Johnson.

The Arrow 1 The Square, 111 Broad Street,
Birmingham, B15 1AS **t** 0121 695 0000 **f** 0121 695 0055
e feedback@thearrow.co.uk **w** thearrow.co.uk
🔲 Programme Director: Alan Carruthers.

Arrow FM Priory Meadow Centre, Hastings, East Sussex,
TN34 1PJ **t** 01424 461177 **f** 01424 422662
e firstname.lastname@arrowfm.co.uk **w** arrowfm.co.uk
🔲 Programme Controller: Mike Buxton.

Asian Sound Radio Globe House, Southall St,
Manchester, M3 1LG **t** 0161 288 1000 **f** 0161 288 9000
e info@asiansoundradio.co.uk **w** asiansoundradio.co.uk
🔲 MD/Prog Cont: Shujat Ali.

107.9 Bath FM Station House, Ashley Avenue,
Lower Weston, Bath, North East Somerset, BA1 3DS
t 01225 471 571 **f** 01225 471 681
e studio@bathfm.co.uk **w** bathfm.co.uk 🔲 Head of
Programming: Paul Roberts.

The Bay PO Box 969, St Georges Quay, Lancaster,
LA1 3LD **t** 01524 848 747 **f** 01524 845 969
e firstname.lastname@cnradio.co.uk **w** thebay.fm
🔲 Station Manager: Jason Gill.

BBC 1Xtra Yalding House, 152-156 Gt Portland St,
London, W1W 6AJ **t** 020 7765 2413 **f** 020 7765 0759
e firstname.lastname@bbc.co.uk **w** bbc.co.uk/1Xtra
🔲 Deputy Controller: Ben Cooper.

BBC 6 Music 5th floor, Western House,
99 Great Portland St, London, W1A 1AA **t** 020 7580 4468
f 020 7765 4571 **e** firstname.lastname@bbc.co.uk
w bbc.co.uk/6music 🔲 Head Of Programmes: Lewis
Carnie.

BBC Asian Network 9 St Nicholas Pl, Leicester,
LE1 5YP **t** 0121 567 6767 **e** Asian.network@bbc.co.uk
w bbc.co.uk/asiannetwork 🔲 Head of Music: Mark
Strippel.

BBC Essex 198 New London Rd, Chelmsford, Essex,
CM2 9AB **t** 01245 616000 **f** 01245 616025
e gerald.main@bbc.co.uk **w** bbc.co.uk/essex
🔲 Editor: Gerald Main.

BBC Jersey 18-21 Parade Rd, St Helier,
Jersey, Channel Islands, JE2 3PL **t** 01534 870000
f 01534 732569 **e** radiojersey@bbc.co.uk
w bbc.co.uk/jersey 📘 BBC Radio Jersey
🟦 jerseyintroducing 🅱 bbcjersey or jsyintroducing
▶️ flickr.com/bbcjersey 🔲 Asst.
Editor/Programmes: Matthew Price 01534 837260.

BBC Leicester 9 St Nicholas Pl, Leicester, LE1 5LB
t 0116 251 6688 **f** 0116 251 1463
e patricia.dolman@bbc.co.uk **w** bbc.co.uk/leicester
🔲 Head of Music: Trish Dolman 0116 2516688.

BBC London 35 Marylebone High St, London, W1U 4QA
t 020 7224 2424 **e** yourlondon@bbc.co.uk
w bbc.co.uk/london 🔲 Managing Editor: David Robey.

BBC Nan Gaidheal 52 Church St, Stornoway,
Isle of Lewis, HS1 2LS **t** 01851 705000 **f** 01851 704633
e rapal@bbc.co.uk **w** bbc.co.uk/alba 🔲 Music
Producer: John Murray.

Media: Radio

BBC Radio 1 Yalding House, 152-156, Gt Portland St, London, W1N 6AJ **t** 020 7580 4468 **f** 020 7765 1439 **e** firstname.lastname@bbc.co.uk **w** bbc.co.uk/radio1 📇 Controller 1 & 1Xtra: Andy Parfitt.

BBC Radio 2 Western House, 99 Great Portland St, London, W1A 1AA **t** 020 7580 4468 **f** 020 7725 2578 **e** firstname.lastname@bbc.co.uk **w** bbc.co.uk/radio2 📇 Head of Programmes: Lewis Carnie.

BBC Radio 3 Room 4119, Broadcasting House, London, W1A 1AA **t** 020 7765 2512 **f** 020 7765 2511 **e** firstname.lastname@bbc.co.uk **w** bbc.co.uk/radio3 📇 Controller: Roger Wright.

BBC Radio 4 Broadcasting House, Portland Pl, London, W1A 1AA **t** 020 7580 4468 **f** 020 7765 3421 **e** firstname.lastname@bbc.co.uk **w** bbc.co.uk/radio4 📇 Controller: Mark Damazer.

BBC Radio 5 Live Room 6200, BBC TV Centre, London, W12 7RJ **t** 020 8743 8000 **f** 020 8624 9588 **e** firstname.lastname@bbc.co.uk **w** bbc.co.uk/radio5live 📇 Controller: Adrian Van Klaveren.

BBC Radio Lancashire 20-26 Darwen St, Blackburn, Lancashire, BB2 2EA **t** 01254 262411 **f** 01254 680821 **e** radio.lancashire@bbc.co.uk **w** bbc.co.uk/lancashire 📘 facebook.com/BBCLancashire 📇 Managing Editor: John Clayton 01254 841040.

BBC Radio Manchester PO Box 951, New Broadcasting House, Oxford Rd, Manchester, M60 1SD **t** 0161 200 2020 **f** 0161 236 5804 **e** radiomanchester@bbc.co.uk **w** bbc.co.uk/manchester 📇 Managing Editor: John Ryan.

BBC Radio Merseyside P.O.BOX 95.8, Liverpool, Merseyside, L49 1ZJ **t** 0151 708 5500 **f** 0151 794 0988 **e** radio.merseyside@bbc.co.uk **w** bbc.co.uk/liverpool 📇 Head of Music: Nickie Mackay.

BBC Radio Northampton Broadcasting House, Abington St, Northampton, NN1 2BH **t** 01604 239100 **f** 01604 230709 **e** ian.brown@bbc.co.uk **w** bbc.co.uk/northampton 📇 Head of Music: Ian Brown.

BBC Radio Suffolk Broadcasting House, St Matthews Str, Ipswich, Suffolk, IP1 3EP **t** 01473 250000 **f** 01473 340785 **e** foz@bbc.co.uk **w** bbc.co.uk/radiosuffolk 📇 Head of Music: Stephen Foster.

BBC Radio Ulster Broadcasting House, Ormeau Avenue, Belfast, Co Antrim, BT2 8HQ **t** 028 9033 8000 **f** 028 9033 8800 **e** firstname.lastname@bbc.co.uk **w** bbc.co.uk/northernireland/atl 📇 Senior Producer - Radio: Simon Taylor.

BBC Radio York 20 Bootham Row, York, North Yorkshire, YO30 7BR **t** 01904 641351 **e** radio.york@bbc.co.uk **w** bbc.co.uk/radioyork 📇 Station Sound: Neil Foster.

BBC Scotland 40 Pacific Sq, Glasgow, Strathclyde, G51 1BA **t** 0141 422 6000 **e** firstname.lastname@bbc.co.uk **w** bbc.co.uk/scotland 📇 Snr Prod Contemp. Music: Stewart Cruickshank.

BBC Southern Counties Radio Broadcasting Centre, Guildford, Surrey, GU6 7AP **t** 01483 306306 **f** 01483 304952 **e** surrey@bbc.co.uk **w** bbc.co.uk/surrey / bbc.co.uk/sussex 📇 Managing Editor: Nicci Holliday.

Beacon Radio 267 Tettenhall Rd, Wolverhampton, West Midlands, WV6 0DE **t** 01902 461 300 **f** 01902 461 299 **e** firstname.lastname@gcapmedia.com **w** beaconradiowestmids.co.uk 📇 Prog Cont: Darrell Woodman.

Beat 102-103 The Broadcast Centre, Ardkeen, Dunmore Rd, Waterford, Ireland **t** +353 51 849102 **f** +353 51 849103 **e** reception@beat102103.com **w** beat102103.com 📘 Beat 102-103 📇 CEO/Prog Dir: Gabrielle Cummins 00-353-51-846160.

107 The Bee 8 Dalton Court, Darwen, Lancashire, BB3 0DG **t** 01254 778000 **f** 01254 778001 **e** firstname.lastname@thebee.co.uk **w** thebee.co.uk 📇 Station Manager: Simon Brierley.

BBC Radio Berkshire PO Box 104.4, Reading, Berkshire, RG4 8FH **t** 0118 946 4200 **f** 0118 946 4555 **e** radio.berkshire@bbc.co.uk **w** bbc.co.uk/radioberkshire 📇 Managing Editor: Lizz Loxam.

Black Diamond FM Newbattle Community Learning Centre, 67 Gardiner Place, Newtongrange, EH22 4RT **t** 0131 663 4611 **e** admin@blackdiamondfm.com **w** blackdiamondfm.com 📇 Chairman: John Ritchie 0131 663 4488.

Radio Borders Tweedside Park, Galashiels, Selkirkshire, TD1 3TD **t** 01896 759 444 **f** 0845 345 7080 **e** info@radioborders.com **w** radioborders.com 📇 Station Director: Stuart McCulloch.

106.3 Bridge FM PO Box 1063, Bridgend, CF35 6wf **t** 0845 890 4000 **f** 0845 890 5000 **e** firstname.lastname@bridge.fm **w** bridge.fm 📇 MD: Martin Mumford.

Bright 106.4 11A Market Place Shopping Centre, Burgess Hill, West Sussex, RH15 9NP **t** 01444 248 127 **f** 01444 248 553 **e** mail@bright1064.com **w** bright1064.com 📇 Programme Controller: Andrew Dancey.

BBC Radio Bristol PO Box 194, Bristol, BS99 7QT **t** 0117 974 1111 **f** 0117 923 8223 **e** radio.bristol@bbc.co.uk **w** bbc.co.uk/radiobristol 📇 Managing Editor: Tim Pemberton.

British Forces Broadcasting Service Chalfont Grove, Narcot Lane, Chalfont St Peter, Gerrards Cross, Bucks, SL9 8TN **t** 01494 878 354 **f** 01494 870 552 **e** admin.officer@bfbs.com **w** ssvc.com 📇 General Manager: Kal Sutherland.

96.4 FM BRMB 9 Brindley Pl, 4 Oozells Sq, Birmingham, West Midlands, B1 2DJ **t** 0121 566 5200 **f** 0121 245 5900 **e** info@brmb.co.uk **w** brmb.co.uk 📇 Programme Director: Paul Kaye.

Media: Radio

Brunel FM The Lime Kiln Studios, Lime Kiln, Wootton Bassett, Swindon, SN4 7HF **t** 01793 853 777 **f** 01793 855 851 **e** enquiries@brunelfm.com **w** brunelfm.com ⊞ Programme Controller: Craig Rance.

BBC Radio Cambridgeshire PO Box 96, 104 Hills Road, Cambridge, CB2 1LD **t** 01223 259696 **f** 01223 460832 **e** Cambs@bbc.co.uk **w** bbc.co.uk/radiocambridgeshire ⊞ Music Librarian: Sophie Rowell.

95.8 Capital FM 30 Leicester Sq, London, WC2H 7LA **t** 020 7766 6958 **f** 020 7054 8399 **e** firstname.lastname@capitalfm.com **w** capitalfm.com ⊞ Group Programme Director: Paul Jackson.

Carillon Radio Loughborough General Hospital, Epinal Way, Loughborough, Leics, LE11 5JY **t** 01509 564 433 **f** 0870 751 8989 **e** info@carillonradio.com **w** carillonradio.com ⊞ Station Sec/Engineer: John Sketchley.

Radio Carmarthenshire PO Box 971, Llanelli, Carmarthenshire, SA15 1YH **t** 08458907000 **f** 08458905000 **e** enquiries@radiocarmarthenshire.com **w** radiocarmarthenshire.com ⊞ Programme Director: Andy Griffiths.

Central FM 201-203 High St, Falkirk, FK1 1DU **t** 01324 611164 **f** 01324 611168 **e** mail@centralfm.co.uk **w** centralfm.co.uk ⊟ @centralfm ⊞ Programme Controller: Gary Muircroft.

105.4 Century FM Laser House, Waterfront Quay, Salford Quays, Manchester, M50 3XW **t** 0161 662 4701 **f** 0161 662 4709 **e** firstname.lastname@centuryfm.co.uk **w** 1054centuryfm.com ⊞ Programme Director: Sarah Graham.

100.102 Century North East Century House, PO Box 100, Church St, Gateshead, Tyne and Wear, NE8 2YY **t** 0191 556 3000 **f** 0191 556 3109 **e** firstname.lastname@centuryfm.co.uk **w** 100centuryfm.co.uk ⊞ Programme Controller: Paul Smith.

Radio Ceredigion Yr Hen Ysgol Gymraeg, Heol Alecsandra, Aberystwyth, Ceredigion, SY23 1LF **t** 01970 627 999 **f** 01970 627 206 **e** admin@ceredigionfm.co.uk **w** ceredigionradio.co.uk ⊞ Head Of Music: Mark Simon.

CFM PO Box 964, Carlisle, Cumbria, CA1 3NG **t** 01228 818 964 **f** 01228 819 444 **e** reception@cfmradio.com **w** cfmradio.com ⊞ Prog Controller: David Bain.

Channel 103 FM 6 Tunnell St, St Helier, Jersey, Channel Islands, JE2 4LU **t** 01534 888 103 **f** 01534 887799/ 877177 **e** firstname.surname@channel103.com **w** channel103.com ⊞ Regional Programme Controller: Tim Manns.

Choice FM London 30 Leicester Sq, London, WC2H 7LA **t** 020 7766 6000 **f** 020 7766 6840 **e** robert.dovidio@thisisglobal.com **w** choicefm.com ⊞ Contact: Robert D'Ovidio 020 7054 8006.

Radio City 96.7 St. John's Beacon, 1 Houghton St, Liverpool, Merseyside, L1 1RL **t** 0151 472 6800 **f** 0151 472 6821 **e** firstname.lastname@radiocity.co.uk **w** radiocity.co.uk ⊞ Programme Director: Richard Maddock.

Belfast Citybeat 2nd Floor, Arena Building, 85 Ormeau Road, Belfast, Antrim, BT7 1SH **t** 028 9023 4967 **f** 028 9089 0100 **e** studio@citybeat967.co.uk **w** citybeat967.co.uk ⊞ Programme Controller: Bill Young.

Clare FM Abbeyfield Centre, Francis St, Ennis, Co. Clare, Ireland **t** +353 65 682 8888 **f** +353 65 682 9392 **e** info@clarefm.ie **w** clarefm.ie ⊞ Head of Music: Andrew Looby.

Classic FM 30 Leicester Square, London, WC2H 7LA **t** 020 7343 9000 **f** 020 7344 2789 **e** enquiries@classicfm.com **w** classicfm.com ⊞ MD: Darren Henley.

Classic VRN 1287 PO Box 1287, Kirkcaldy, KY2 5SX **t** 01592 654 828 **e** info@vrn1287.com **w** vrn1287.com ⊞ Group Programme Director: Colin Johnston.

BBC Radio Cleveland PO Box 95FM, Broadcasting House, Newport Road, Middlesborough, Cleveland, TS1 5DG **t** 01642 225 211 **f** 01642 211 356 **e** cleveland.studios@bbc.co.uk **w** bbc.co.uk/tees ⊞ Assistant Editor: Ben Thomas.

Club Asia 963 & 972 AM Asia House, 227-247 Gascoigne Rd, Barking, Essex, IG8 8LX **t** 020 8594 6662 **f** 020 8594 3523 **e** info@clubasiaonline.com **w** clubasiaonline.com ⊞ Programme Dir: Sumerah Ahmad.

Clyde 1 FM Clydebank Business Pk, Clydebank, Glasgow, G81 2RX **t** 0141 565 2200 **f** 0141 565 2265 **e** info@clyde1.com **w** clyde1.com ⊞ Programme Director: Paul Saunders.

Clyde 2 Clydebank Business Pk, Clydebank, Glasgow, G81 2RX **t** 0141 565 2200 **f** 0141 565 2265 **e** info@clyde2.com **w** clyde2.com ⊞ Programme Director: Paul Saunders.

Compass FM 96.4 26A Wellowgate, Grimsby, NE Lincs, DN32 0RA **t** 01472 346 666 **f** 01472 508 811 **e** enquiries@compassfm.co.uk **w** compassfm.co.uk ⊞ Station Manager: Richard Lyon.

Connect FM 2nd Floor, 5 Church Street, Peterborough, PE1 1XB **t** 0844 800 1769 **f** 01733 898 107 **e** info@connectfm.com **w** connectfm.com ⊞ Programme Controller: Russ Down.

Cool FM PO Box 974, Belfast, Co Antrim, BT1 1RT **t** 028 9181 7181 **f** 028 9181 4974 **e** music@coolfm.co.uk **w** coolfm.co.uk ⊞ Programme Director: Henry Owens.

Cork 96 FM Broadcasting House, Patrick's Pl, Wellington Rd, Cork, Ireland **t** +353 21 455 1596 **f** +353 21 455 1500 **e** info@96fm.ie **w** 96fm.ie ⊞ Prog Director/CEO: Kieran McGeary.

BBC Radio Cornwall Phoenix Wharf, Truro, Cornwall, TR1 1UA **t** 01872 275421 **f** 01872 240679 **e** radio.cornwall@bbc.co.uk **w** bbc.co.uk/radiocornwall ■ Music Librarian: Kath Peters.

Country Mix 106.8 - Dublin Radio Centre, Killarney Rd, Bray, Ireland **t** +353 1 272 4770 **f** +353 1 272 4753 **e** mail@countrymix.ie **w** countrymix.ie ■ facebook.com/countrymix ■ twitter.com/countrymix ■ Prog Director: Sean Ashmore.

County Sound Radio 1566 MW Dolphin House, North St, Guildford, Surrey, GU1 4AA **t** 01483 300964 **f** 01483 531612 **e** studio@countysound.co.uk **w** countysound.co.uk ■ Programme Controller: Dave Johns.

BBC Coventry & Warwickshire Priory Place, Coventry, West Midlands, CV1 5SQ **t** 024 7655 1000 **f** 024 7655 2000 **e** coventry@bbc.co.uk **w** bbc.co.uk/coventrywarwickshire ■ Assistant Editor: Duncan Jones.

CRMK Online 14 Vincent Avenue, Crownhill, Milton Keynes, Buckinghamshire, MK8 0AB **t** 01908 265266 **f** 01908 564893 **e** phil@crmk.co.uk **w** crmk.co.uk ■ Programme Controller: Phil Walsh.

Cuillin FM Stormyhill Rd, Portree, Isle of Skye, IV51 9DT **t** 01478 611797 **f** 01478 613341 **e** admin@cuillinfm.co.uk **w** cuillinfm.co.uk ■ Office Admin: Ruth Taylor.

BBC Radio Cumbria Annetwell Street, Carlisle, Cumbria, CA3 8BB **t** 01228 592444 **f** 01228 511195 **e** radio.cumbria@bbc.co.uk **w** bbc.co.uk/radiocumbria ■ SBJ/Programmes/Music: Liz Rhodes.

Dead Earnest PO Box 10170, Dundee, Tayside, DD4 8WW **e** deadearnest@btinternet.com **w** deadearnest.btinternet.co.uk ■ myspace.com/deadearnestdundee ■ Reviewer: Andy Garibaldi.

Dearne FM Unit 7, Network Centre, Zenith Park, Whaley Rd, Barnsley, S75 1HT **t** 01226 321733 **f** 01226 321755 **e** enquiries@dearnefm.co.uk **w** dearnefm.co.uk ■ Prog Mgr: Matt Jones.

Dee 106.3 2 Chantry Court, Chester, CH1 4QN **t** 01244 391000 **f** 01244 391010 **e** info@dee1063.com **w** dee1063.com ■ Prog Controller: Mike James.

Delta FM Tindle House, High Street, Bordon, Hants, GU35 0AY **t** 01420 473 473 **f** 01420 485 186 **e** firstname.surname@deltaradio.co.uk **w** deltaradio.co.uk ■ Station/ Progamme Manager: David Way.

BBC Radio Derby PO Box 104.5, Derby, DE1 3HL **t** 01332 361111 **f** 01332 290794 **e** radio.derby@bbc.co.uk **w** bbc.co.uk/derby ■ Managing Editor: Simon Cornes.

BBC Radio Devon Broadcasting House, Seymour Road, Plymouth, Devon, PL3 5YQ **t** 01752 260 323 **f** 01752 234 595 **e** radio.devon@bbc.co.uk **w** bbc.co.uk/radiodevon ■ Managing Editor: Robert Wallace.

Downtown Radio/DTR Newtownards, County Down, BT23 4ES **t** 028 9181 5555 **f** 028 9181 8913 **e** programmes@downtown.co.uk **w** downtown.co.uk ■ Programme Director: Henry Owens.

Dream 100 Northgate House, St Peter's St, Colchester, Essex, CO1 1HT **t** 01206 764 466 **f** 01206 715 102 **e** firstname.surname@dream100.com **w** dream100.com ■ Prog Mgr: Pete Bristow.

Dream 107.7FM 12 Bentalls Shopping Centre, Colchester Road, Heybridge, Maldon, Essex, CM9 4GD **t** 0845 365 1078 **f** 0845 365 1079 **e** firstname.lastname@dream107.com **w** dream107.com ■ Sales Manager: Annabel Smail.

Dublin's 98 The Malt House - South Block, Grand Canal Quay, Dublin 2, Ireland **t** +353 1 670 8970 **f** +353 1 670 8969 **e** andy.matthews@dublins98.ie **w** dublins98.ie ■ andymatthews98 ■ dublins98andy ■ Programme Director: Andy Matthews.

Dune 107.9 The Power Station, Victoria Way, Southport, Merseyside, PR8 1RR **t** 01704 502 500 **f** 01704 502 520 **e** phil.johnson@dune1079.co.uk **w** dune1079.co.uk ■ Programme Controller: Phil Johnson.

Durham FM 3 Framwell House, Framwelgate, Durham, Co Durham, DH1 5SU **t** 0191 374 0777 **f** 0191 384 7880 **e** enquiries@durhamfm.com **w** durhamfm.net ■ Station Manager: Peter Grant.

96.4 Eagle Radio Dolphin House, North St, Guildford, Surrey, GU1 4AA **t** 01483 300964 **f** 01483 531612 **e** peter.gordon@964eagle.co.uk **w** 964eagle.co.uk ■ Prog Director: Peter Gordon.

Easy Radio DAB Radio House, Merrick Rd, Southall, UB2 4AU **t** 020 8574 6666 **e** info@easy1035.com **w** easy1035.com ■ Programme Controller: Paul Owens.

Energy FM 100 Market Street, Douglas, Isle of Man, IM1 2PH **t** 01624 611 936 **f** 01624 664 699 **e** mail@energyfm.net **w** energyfm.net ■ Head of Music: Jason Quinn.

Fen Radio 107.5 5 Church Mews, Wisbech, Cambs, PE13 1HL **t** 01945 467 107 **f** 01945 467 464 **e** firstname.lastname@fenradio.co.uk **w** fenradio.co.uk ■ Prog Mgr: Richard Grant.

Fire 107.6 Quadrant Studios, Old Christchurch Rd, Bournemouth, Dorset, BH1 2AD **t** 01202 318 100 **f** 01202 318 110 **e** info@fireradio.co.uk **w** fireradio.co.uk ■ Programme Controller: Claire Edwards.

FM104 Hume House, Pembroke Road, Balls Bridge, Dublin 4, Ireland **t** +353 1 500 6600 **f** +353 1 668 9401 **e** Firstname+initial@fm104.ie **w** fm104.ie ■ Programme Director: Dave Kelly.

97.3 Forth One Forth House, Forth Street, Edinburgh, Lothian, EH1 3LE **t** 0131 556 9255 **f** 0131 558 3277 **e** info@forthone.com **w** forthone.com ■ Programme Director: Luke McCullough.

1548 Forth 2 Forth House, Forth Street, Edinburgh, Lothian, EH1 3LE **t** 0131 556 9255 **f** 0131 558 3277 **e** info@forth2.com **w** forth2.com 📇 Programme Director: Luke McCullough.

Fresh Radio The Watermill, Broughton Hall, Skipton, North Yorkshire, BD23 3AG **t** 0845 224 2052 **e** info@freshradio.co.uk **w** freshradio.co.uk ⨍ facebook.com/group.php?gid=2514832081&ref=ts 🅣 twitter.com/FreshSkipton 📇 Managing Director: Julian Hotchkiss.

Galaxy Birmingham 1 The Sq, 111 Broad St, Birmingham, B15 1AS **t** 0121 226 5700 **f** 0121 226 5779 **e** Neil.Greenslade@galaxybirmingham.co.uk **w** galaxybirmingham.co.uk 📇 Programme Controller: Neil Greenslade.

Galaxy Manchester Suite 1.1, 4 Exchange Quay, Salford, Manchester, M5 3EE **t** 0161 662 4700 **f** 0161 832 1102 **e** firstname.surname@galaxymanchester.co.uk **w** galaxy102.co.uk 📇 Programme Director: James Brownlow.

Galaxy North East Kingfisher Way, Silverlink Business Pk, Wallsend, Tyne & Wear, NE28 9NX **t** 0191 206 8000 **f** 0191 444 2509 **e** firstname.lastname@galaxyfm.co.uk **w** galaxynortheast.co.uk 📇 Programme Director: James Brownlow.

Galaxy Scotland Four Winds Pavilion, Pacific Quay, Glasgow, G51 1EB **t** 01415 666106 **e** firstname.lastname@thisisglobal.com **w** galaxyscotland.co.uk 📇 Programme Controller: Stuart Barrie.

Galaxy South Coast Segensworth West, Fareham, Hampshire, PO15 5SX **t** 01489 587600 **f** 01489 587659 **e** firstname.lastname@gcapmedia.com **w** galaxysouthcoast.co.uk 📇 Programme Controller: Jason Walkerden.

Galaxy Yorkshire Joseph's Well, Hanover Walk, Leeds, West Yorkshire, LS3 1AB **t** 0113 308 5100 **f** 0113 213 0109 **e** mail@galaxyyorkshire.co.uk **w** galaxyyorkshire.co.uk 📇 Programme Director: Brent Tobin.

Galway Bay FM Sandy Road, Galway City, Galway, Ireland **t** +353 91 770000 **f** +353 91 752689 **e** info@galwaybayfm.ie **w** galwaybayfm.ie 📇 CEO: Keith Finnegan.

BBC Radio Gloucestershire London Rd, Gloucester, GL1 1SW **t** 01452 308585 **f** 01452 306541 **e** radio.gloucestershire@bbc.co.uk **w** bbc.co.uk/radiogloucestershire 📇 Head of Music: Tom Lowe.

Gold Radio Network 30 Leicester Square, London, WC2H 7LA **t** 08452 318 888 **e** andy.turner@mygoldmusic.com **w** mygoldmusic.com 📇 Network Station Director: Andy Turner.

GTFM Pinewood Studios, Pinewood Avenue, Rhydyfelin, Pontypridd, CF37 5EA **t** 01443 406111 **f** 01443 492744 **e** andrew@gtfm.co.uk **w** gtfm.co.uk 📇 Station Mgr/Prog Dir: Andrew Jones.

BBC Radio Guernsey Bulwer Avenue, St Sampsons, Guernsey, Channel Islands, GY2 4LA **t** 01481 200600 **f** 01481 200361 **e** radio.guernsey@bbc.co.uk **w** bbc.co.uk/radioguernsey 📇 Editor: David Martin.

Hallam FM Radio House, 900 Herries Rd, Sheffield, South Yorks, S6 1RH **t** 0114 209 1000 **f** 0114 285 3159 **e** programmes@hallamfm.co.uk **w** hallamfm.co.uk ⨍ facebook.com/pages/Hallam-FM 📇 Programme Director: Simon Monk.

Heart (Anglesey & Gwynedd) Llys Y Dderwen, Parc Menai, Bangor, LL57 4BN **t** 01248 673400 **w** heartcymru.co.uk

Heart (Bedfordshire) 5 Abbey Court, Fraser Rd, Priory Business Pk, Bedford, Befordshire, MK44 3WH **t** 01234 235010 **f** 01234 235009 **e** firstname.lastname@heart.co.uk **w** heartbedford.co.uk 📇 Prog Cont: Tony Dibbin.

Heart (Beds, Bucks and Hertfordshire) Chiltern Rd, Dunstable, Bedfordshire, LU6 1HQ **t** 01582 676200 **w** heartdunstable.co.uk 📇 Programme Controller: Paul Holmes.

Heart (Berkshire and North Hampshire) The Chase, Calcot, Reading, RG31 7RB **t** 0118 945 4400 **w** heartberkshire.co.uk

Heart (Birmingham & The West Midlands) 1 The Square, 111 Broad St, Birmingham, West Midlands, B15 1AS **t** 0121 226 5700 **f** 0121 226 5779 **e** firstname.lastname@heart.co.uk **w** heartwestmids.co.uk

Heart (Bristol) One Passage St, Bristol, BS2 0JF **t** 0117 984 3200 **f** 0117 984 3202 **e** firstname.lastname@heart.co.uk **w** heartbristol.co.uk

Heart (Cambridge) Enterprise House, The Vision Park, Chivers Way, Histon, Cambs, CB24 9ZR **t** 01223 623800 **w** heartcambridge.co.uk

Heart (Cheshire and NE Wales) The Studios, Mold Rd, Wrexham, LL11 4AF **t** 01978 752202 **w** heartwrexham.co.uk

Heart (Colchester) Abbeygate Two, 9 Whitewell Rd, Colchester, Essex, CO2 7DE **t** 01206 577577 **w** heartcolchester.co.uk

Heart (Dorset and New Forest) 5 Southcote Rd, Bournemouth, Dorset, BH1 3LR **t** 01202 234900 **w** heartdorset.co.uk

Heart (Essex) Radio House, 31 Glebe Rd, Chelmsford, CM1 1QG **t** 01245 524500 **w** heartessex.co.uk

Heart (Exeter and East Devon) Hawthorn House, Exeter Business Pk, Exeter, Devon, EX1 3QS **t** 01392 444444 **f** 01392 354249 **e** firstname.lastname@heart.co.uk **w** heartexeter.co.uk

Heart (Gloucestershire) The Mall, Gloucester, GL1 1SS **t** 01452 572400 **w** heartgloucestershire.co.uk

Heart (Hampshire and West Sussex) Radio House, Apple Industrial Estate, Whittle Avenue, Segensworth West, Fareham, PO15 5SH **t** 01489 589911 **w** hearthampshire.co.uk

Heart (Kent) Radio House, John Wilson Business Pk, Whitstable, Kent, CT5 3QX **t** 01227 772004 **e** firstname.lastname@thisglobal.co.uk **w** heartkent.co.uk 📇 Programme Controller: Mike Osborne.

Heart (London) 30 Leicester Sq, London, WC2H 7LA **t** 020 7766 6222 **w** heartlondon.co.uk

Heart (Milton Keynes) 14 Vincent Avenue, Crownhill, Milton Keynes, Bucks, MK8 0AB **t** 01908 269111 **f** 01908 591619 **e** firstname.lastname@heart.co.uk **w** heartmk.co.uk 📘 facebook.com/thisisheart 🅜 myspace.com/heartmiltonkeynes 🅣 twitter.com/thisisheart ▶ youtube.com/thisisheart 📇 Programme Controller: Chris Gregg 01908 591600.

Heart (Norfolk and North Suffolk) 47-49 Colegate, Norwich, NR3 1DB **t** 01603 630621 **w** heartnorwich.co.uk

Heart (North Devon) Unit 2B, Lauder Lane, Roundswell, Barnstaple, North Devon, EX31 3TA **t** 01271 366 370 **f** 01271 366 359 **e** firstname.lastname@heart.co.uk **w** heart.co.uk 📇 Prog Cont: Paul Hopper.

Heart (North Wales Coast) PO Box 963, Bangor, LL57 4ZR **t** 01248 673401 **w** heartwalescoast.co.uk

Heart (Northamptonshire) 19-21 St Edmunds Rd, Northampton, NN1 5DY **t** 01604 795600 **w** heartnorthants.co.uk

Heart (Nottingham & The East Midlands) City Link, Nottingham, NG2 4NG **t** 0115 910 6100 **f** 0115 910 6107 **w** hearteastmids.co.uk

Heart (Oxfordshire) Radio House, Pony Rd, Cowley, Oxford, OX4 2XR **t** 01865 871000 **w** heartoxfordshire.co.uk

Heart (Peterborough) Queensgate Centre, Peterborough, PE1 1XJ **t** 01733 460460 **w** heartpeterborough.co.uk

Heart (Plymouth) Earls Acre, Alma Rd, Plymouth, Devon, PL3 4HX **t** 01752 275600 **w** heartplymouth.co.uk

Heart (Somerset) Haygrove House, Shoreditch Rd, Taunton, Somerset, TA3 7BT **t** 01823 338448 **f** 01823 368309 **e** firstname.lastname@heart.co.uk **w** heartsomerset.co.uk 📇 Programme Controller: Jon White.

Heart (South Devon) Unit 1G, South Hams Business Park, Churchstow, Kingsbridge, Devon, TQ7 3QR **t** 01548 854 595 **e** firstname.lastname@heart.co.uk **w** heartsouthdevon.co.uk 📇 Programme Controller: Richard Spencer.

Heart (Suffolk) Radio House, Alpha Business Park, 6-12 White House Rd, Ipswich, Suffolk, IP1 5LT **t** 01473 461000 **w** heartipswich.co.uk

Heart (Sussex) Radio House, Franklin Rd, Brighton, East Sussex, BN41 1AF **t** 01273 430111 **w** heartsussex.co.uk

Heart (Torbay and South Devon) Harbourpoint, Victoria Parade, Torquay, Devon, TQ1 2RA **t** 01803 201444 **w** hearttorbay.co.uk

Heart (Wiltshire) 1st Floor, Chiseldon House, Stonehill Green, Westlea, Swindon, SN5 7HB **t** 01793 842600 **w** heartwilts.co.uk

Heart (Wirral) Pacific Road Arts Centre, Birkenhead, CH41 1LJ **t** 0151 650 1700 **w** heartwirral.co.uk

Heartland FM 9 Alba Place, Pitlochry, Perthshire, PH16 5BH **t** 01796 474040 **f** 01796 474007 **e** mailbox@heartlandfm.co.uk **w** heartlandfm.co.uk 📇 Programme Controller: Pete Ramsden.

Heat Radio Bauer Media, Castle Quay, Castlefield, Manchester, M15 4PR **t** 0161 288 5000 **e** paul.mack@bauermedia.co.uk **w** heatradio.com 📇 Programmes Manager: Paul Mack.

BBC Hereford & Worcester Hylton Road, Worcester, WR2 5WW **t** 01905 748485 **f** 01905 337209 **e** worcester@bbc.co.uk **w** bbc.co.uk/herefordandworcester 📇 Managing Editor: James Coghill.

HertBeat FM The Pump House, Knebworth Park, Hertford, SG3 6HQ **t** 01438 810900 **f** 01438 815100 **e** info@hertbeat.com **w** hertbeat.com 📇 Programme Controller: Steve Folland.

HFM Innovation House, Welland Business Park, Valley Way, Market Harborough, LE16 7PS **t** 01858 464 666 **f** 01858 464 678 **e** info@harboroughfm.co.uk **w** harboroughfm.co.uk 📇 Programme Controller: Nick Shaw.

High Peak Radio PO Box 106, High Peak, Derbyshire, SK23 0DJ **t** 01298 813144 **f** 01298 813388 **e** info@highpeakradio.co.uk **w** highpeakradio.co.uk 📇 Director: Roger Price.

Highland Radio Pine Hill, Letterkenny, Co Donegal, Ireland **t** +353 74 912 5000 **f** +353 74 912 5344 **e** enquiries@highlandradio.com **w** highlandradio.com 📇 Head of Prog & Music: Linda McGroarty.

Hobo Partnership 7 Castlebar Rd, London, W5 2DL **t** 020 7434 2907 **e** deb@hobopartnership.com **w** hobopartnership.com 📇 MD: Debbie Wheeler.

Home 107.9 The Old Stableblock, Brewery Drive, Lockwood Park, Huddersfield, HD1 3UR **t** 01484 321 107 **f** 01484 311 107 **e** enquiries@homefm.co.uk **w** homefm.co.uk 📇 Station Manager: Ian Dickinson.

Hospital Broadcasting Association PO Box 341, Messingham, Scunthorpe, DN15 5EG **t** 0870 321 6019 **e** info@hbauk.com **w** hbauk.com

Media: Radio

BBC Radio Humberside Queens Court, Queens Gardens, Hull, East Yorkshire, HU1 3RH **t** 01482 323232 **f** 01482 226409 **e** radio.humberside@bbc.co.uk **w** bbc.co.uk/radiohumberside ◰ Head of Music: Richard James.

Imagine FM Regent House, Heaton Lane, Stockport, Cheshire, SK4 1BX **t** 0161 609 1400 **f** 0161 609 1401 **e** info@imaginefm.net **w** imaginefm.net ◰ Station Dir: Steve Howarth.

Independent Radio News Ltd 200 Gray's Inn Rd, London, WC1X 8XZ **t** 020 7430 4090 **f** 020 7430 4092 **e** news@irn.co.uk **w** irn.co.uk ◰ MD: John Perkins.

Inflight Productions 15 Stukeley Street, London, WC2B 5LT **t** 020 7400 0700 **f** 020 7400 0707 **e** firstname.lastname@inflightproductions.com **w** inflightproductions.com ◰ MD: Steve Harvey.

Island FM 12 Westerbrook, St Sampson, GY2 4QQ, Guernsey **t** 01481 242 000 **f** 01481 249 676 **e** firstname.lastname@islandfm.com **w** islandfm.com ◰ Regional Programme Controller: Tim Manns.

Isle Of Wight Radio Dodnor Pk, Newport, Isle Of Wight, PO30 5XE **t** 01983 822 557 **f** 01983 822 109 **e** claire.willis@iwradio.co.uk **w** iwradio.co.uk ◰ Station Director: Claire Willis 07761 549896.

Isles FM 103 PO Box 333, Stornoway, Isle Of Lewis, Western Isles, HS1 2PU **t** 01851 703333 **f** 01851 703322 **e** studio@isles.fm **w** isles.fm ◰ Managing Director: Ann Moqbel.

107.8 Radio Jackie, The Sound of South West London 110 Tolworth Broadway, Surbiton, Surrey, KT6 7JD **t** 020 8288 1300 **f** 020 8288 1312 **e** Dave.Owen@RadioJackie.com **w** radiojackie.com ◰ Programme Director: Dave Owen.

Brighton's Juice 107.2 170 North St, Brighton, East Sussex, BN1 1EA **t** 01273 386 107 **f** 01273 273 107 **e** info@juicebrighton.com **w** juicebrighton.com ◰ MD: Steve Stark.

Juice 107.6 FM Liverpool 27 Fleet St, Liverpool, L1 4AR **t** 0151 707 3107 **f** 0871 200 7001 **e** firstname.lastname@juiceliverpool.com **w** juice.fm.com ◰ Programme Manager: Gill Hall.

BBC Radio Kent The Great Hall, Mount Pleasant Rd, Royal Tunbridge Wells, Kent, TN1 1QQ **t** 01892 670 000 **f** 01892 675 644 **e** radio.kent@bbc.co.uk **w** bbc.co.uk/kent ◰ Managing Editor: Paul Leaper.

Kerrang! Radio 20 Lionel St, Kerrang! House, Birmingham, B3 1AQ **t** 0845 053 1052 **e** james.walshe@kerrangradio.co.uk **w** kerrangradio.co.uk ◰ Programme Director: James Walshe 0844 583 7955.

Radio Kerry Maine Street, Tralee, Kerry, Ireland **t** +353 66 712 3666 **f** +353 66 712 2282 **e** martin@radiokerry.ie **w** radiokerry.ie ◰ Group Head of Music: Martin Howard.

107.6 Kestrel FM 2nd Floor, Paddington House, The Walks Shopping Centre, Basingstoke, Hampshire, RG21 7LJ **t** 01256 694 000 **f** 01256 694 133 **e** studio@kestrelfm.com **w** kestrelfm.com ◰ Programme Manager: Mark Watson.

Key 103 Castle Quay, Castlefield, Manchester, M15 4PR **t** 0161 288 5000 **f** 0161 288 5071 **e** firstname.lastname@key103.co.uk **w** key103.co.uk ◰ Prog Director: Gary Stein.

KFM Radio M7 Business Park, Newhall, Naas, Co Kildare, Ireland **t** +353 45 898 999 **f** +353 45 898 993 **e** info@kfmradio.com **w** kfmradio.com ◰ GM/Exec Director: Clem Ryan.

Kick FM The Studios, 42 Bone Lane, Newbury, Berks, RG14 5SD **t** 01635 841 000 **f** 01635 841 010 **e** firstname@kickfm.com **w** kickfm.com ◰ Programme Mgr: James O'Neill.

Kingdom FM Haig House, Balgonie Road, Markinch, Fife, KY7 6AQ **t** 01592 753 753 **f** 01592 757 788 **e** office@kingdomfm.co.uk **w** kingdomfm.co.uk ◰ Station Mgr/Prog Ctrl: Kevin Brady.

Kiss 100 Bauer Media, Mappin House, 4 Winsley St, London, W1W 8HF **t** 020 7975 8000 **f** 020 7182 8489 **e** firstname.lastname@totalkiss.com **w** totalkiss.com ◰ Grp Programme Director: Andy Roberts.

Kiss 101 26 Baldwin St, Bristol, BS1 1SE **t** 0117 901 0101 **f** 0117 930 9149 **e** firstname.lastname@totalkiss.com **w** totalkiss.com/101 ▉ Kiss 101 ▣ Kiss 101 ◰ Marketing: Simone Traylen 01179309162.

Kiss 105-108 Reflection House, Olding Rd, Bury St Edmunds, Suffolk, IP33 3TA **t** 01284 715300 **f** 01284 715339 **e** kissconfidential@totalkiss.com **w** totalkiss.com ◰ Programme Mgr: Glen White.

KLFM 18 Blackfriars St, Kings Lynn, Norfolk, PE30 1NN **t** 01553 772 777 **f** 01553 766 453 **e** admin@klfm967.co.uk **w** klfm967.co.uk ◰ Station Mgr: Mark Pryke.

Kmfm (Ashford) Express House, 34-36 North Street, Ashford, Kent, TN24 8JR **t** 01233 623 232 **f** 01233 626 545 **e** initial+lastname@kmfm.co.uk **w** kmfm.co.uk/ashford ◰ Programme Controller: Steve Fountain.

Kmfm (Canterbury, Whitstable and Herne Bay) 9 St George's Place, Canterbury, Kent, CT1 1UU **t** 01227 786106 **f** 01227 785106 **e** initial+lastname@kmfm.co.uk **w** kmfm.co.uk/canterbury ◰ Programme Controller: Steve Fountain.

Kmfm (Medway) Medway House, Ginsbury Close, Sir Thomas Longley Rd, Medway City Estate, Rochester, Kent, ME2 4DU **t** 01634 841 111 **f** 01634 841 122 **e** initial+lastname@kmfm.co.uk **w** kentonline.co.uk/kmfm ◰ Programme Controller: Steve Fountain.

Kmfm (Thanet) Imperial House, 2-14 High St, Margate, Kent, CT9 1DH **t** 01843 220 222 **f** 01843 299 666 **e** tstewart@kmfm.co.uk **w** kmfm.co.uk/thanet 📇 Programme Controller: Steve Fountain.

Kmfm (West Kent) 1 East St, Tonbridge, Kent, TN9 1AR **t** 01732 369 200 **f** 01732 369 201 **e** initial+lastname@kmfm.co.uk **w** kmfm.co.uk/westkent 📇 Programme Controller: Steve Fountain.

Kmfm (Sheppway & Whitecliffs Country) 93-95 Sandgate Rd, Folkestone, Kent, CT20 2BQ **t** 01303 220 303 **f** 01303 246 659 **e** initial+lastname@kmfm.co.uk **w** kmfm.co.uk/shepway 📇 Programme Controller: Steve Fountain.

Kool AM PO Box 1072, Edmonton, London, N9 0WQ **t** 020 8373 1073 **f** 020 8373 1074 **e** info@c4trt.co.uk **w** koolam.co.uk 📇 Group Station Manager: Steve Saunders.

Lakeland Radio Lakeland Food Park, Plumgarths, Crook Rd, Kendal, Cumbria, LA8 8QJ **t** 01539 737 380 **f** 01539 737 390 **e** firstname.lastname@lakelandradio.co.uk **w** lakelandradio.co.uk 📇 Station Director: Bill Johnston.

Lanarkshire's L107 L107 House, 69 Bothwell Rd, Hamilton, Lanarkshire, ML3 0DW **t** 01698 303420 **f** 0871 661 5998 **e** radio@l107.com **w** l107.com 📇 Programme Director: Derek McIntyre.

LBC 97.3 30 Leicester Sq, London, WC2H 7LA **t** 020 7766 6000 **e** firstname.lastname@lbc.co.uk **w** lbc.co.uk

BBC Radio Leeds 2 St Peter's Square, Leeds, West Yorkshire, LS9 8AH **t** 0113 244 2131 **f** 0113 224 7316 **e** radio.leeds@bbc.co.uk **w** bbc.co.uk/leeds 📇 Managing Ed: Phil Roberts.

Leicester Sound 6 Dominus Way, Meridian Business Park, Leicester, Leicestershire, LE19 1RP **t** 0116 256 1300 **f** 0116 256 1303 **e** firstname.lastname@gcapmedia.com **w** leicestersound.co.uk 📇 Prog Cont/Head of Music: Simon Ritchie.

Leith FM 17 Academy Street, Leith, Edinburgh, EH6 7EE **t** 0131 555 0446 **f** 0131 555 0446 **e** studio@leithfm.co.uk **w** leithfm.co.uk 📇 PD/HoM: John Murray.

LifeFM 103.6 2nd Floor, 89-93 High Street, Harlesden, London, NW10 4NX **t** 020 8963 9560 **f** 020 8963 9561 **e** info@lifefm.org.uk **w** lifefm.org.uk

Limerick's Live 95FM Radio House, Richmond Court, Dock Rd, Limerick, Ireland **t** +353 61 400195 **f** +353 61 419595 **e** admin@live95fm.ie **w** live95fm.ie 📇 Programme Director: Gary Connor.

BBC Radio Lincolnshire PO Box 219, Newport, Lincoln, LN1 3XY **t** 01522 511 411 **f** 01522 511 058 **e** radio.lincolnshire@bbc.co.uk **w** bbc.co.uk/lincolnshire 📇 Managing Editor: Charlie Partridge.

Lincs FM 102.2 Witham Park, Waterside South, Lincoln, LN5 7JN **t** 01522 549900 **f** 01522 549911 **e** enquiries@lincsfm.co.uk **w** lincsfm.co.uk 📇 Chief Executive: Michael Betton.

Lite FM 2nd Floor, 5 Church St, Peterborough, PE1 1XB **t** 01733 898 106 **f** 01733 898 107 **e** info@Lite1068.com **w** lite1068.com 📇 Prog Dir/Head of Music: Russ Down.

LMFM Radio Broadcasting House, Rathmullen Rd, Drogheda, Co. Louth, Ireland **t** +353 41 983 2000 **f** +353 41 983 2957 **e** info@lmfm.ie **w** lmfm.ie 📇 Programme Director: Eamonn Doyle.

Lochbroom FM Radio House, Mill St, Ullapool, Ross-shire, IV26 2UN **t** 01854 613131 **f** 01854 613132 **e** Lochbroomfm@ecosse.net **w** lochbroomfm.co.uk

London Greek Radio LGR House, 437 High Rd, London, N12 0AP **t** 020 8349 6950 **f** 020 8349 6960 **e** sales@lgr.co.uk **w** lgr.co.uk 📇 Prog Contr/Head of Music: George Gregoriou.

London Turkish Radio (LTR) 185B High Road, London, N22 6BA **t** 020 8881 0606 **f** 020 8881 5151 **e** info@londonturkishradio.org **w** londonturkishradio.org 📇 MD: Erkhan Pastirmacioglu.

Magic 105.4 Bauer Media, Mappin House, 4 Winsley St, London, W1W 8HF **t** 020 7182 8000 **f** 020 7182 8165 **e** studio@magic.co.uk **w** magic.co.uk 📇 Programme Director: Pete Simmons.

Magic 1152 55 Degress North, Pilgrim St, Newcastle upon Tyne, Tyne and Wear, NE1 6BF **t** 0191 230 6100 **f** 0191 279 0288 **e** enquiries@metroandmagic.com **w** metroradio.co.uk 📇 Programme Director: Chris Pegg.

Magic 1152 (Manchester) Castle Quay, Castlefield, Manchester, M15 4PR **t** 0161 288 5000 **f** 0161 288 5151 **e** firstname.lastname@key103.co.uk **w** key103.co.uk 📇 Programme Director: Gary Stein.

Magic 1161 The Boathouse, Commercial Rd, Hull, East Yorkshire, HU1 2SG **t** 01482 325141 **f** 08454 580390 **e** firstname.lastname@vikingfm.co.uk **w** magic1161.co.uk 📇 Prog Director: Jono Symonds.

Magic 1170 Radio House, Yales Crescent, Thornaby, Stockton-on-Tees, TS17 6AA **t** 01642 888222 **f** 01642 868290 **e** tfm.reception@tfmradio.com **w** tfmradion.com 📇 Programme Director: Alex Roland.

Magic 1548 St.John's Beacon, 1 Houghton St, Merseyside, L1 1RL **t** 0151 472 6800 **f** 0151 472 6821 **e** firstname.lastname@radiocity.co.uk **w** magic1548.co.uk 📇 Programme Director: Richard Maddock.

Magic 828 51 Burley Rd, Leeds, West Yorkshire, LS3 1LR **t** 0113 283 5500 **f** 0113 283 5501 **e** firstname.lastname@radioaire.com **w** magic828.com 📇 Regional MD, Yorkshire: Tracy Eastwood.

Magic 999 St Paul's Square, Preston, Lancashire, PR1 1YE **t** 01772 477 700 **f** 01772 477 701 **e** firstname.lastname@magic999.com **w** magic999.com 📇 Programme Director: Dean O'Brien 01772 477000.

Media: Radio

Magic AM Radio House, 900 Herries Rd, Sheffield, South Yorks, S6 1RH **t** 0114 209 1000 **f** 0114 285 3159 **e** programmes@magicam.co.uk **w** magicam.co.uk 🔲 Programme Controller: Simon Monk.

Mansfield 103.2 Unit 4, Brunts Business Centre, Samuel Brunts Way, Mansfield, Nottinghamshire, NG18 2AH **t** 01623 646666 **f** 01623 660606 **e** info@mansfield103.co.uk **w** mansfield103.co.uk 🔲 Managing Director: Tony Delahunty.

Manx Radio PO Box 1368, Broadcasting House, Douglas, Isle Of Man, IM99 1SW **t** 01624 682 600 **f** 01624 682 604 **e** postbox@manxradio.com **w** manxradio.com 🔲 MD: Anthony Pugh.

Mercia Hertford Pl, Coventry, West Midlands, CV1 3TT **t** 024 7686 8200 **f** 024 7686 8209 **e** firstname.lastname@mercia.co.uk **w** mercia.co.uk 🔲 Programme Controller: Mike Newman.

Herts Mercury 96.6 Unit 5, The Metro Centre, Dwight Rd, Watford, WD18 9SS **t** 01923 205 470 **f** 01923 205 471 **e** firstname.lastname@hertsmercury.co.uk **w** hertsmercury.co.uk

102.7 Mercury FM 9 The Stanley Centre, Kelvin Way, Crawley, West Sussex, RH10 2SE **t** 01293 519 161 **f** 01293 565 663 **e** firstname.lastname@gcapmedia.com **w** mercuryfm.co.uk 🔲 Programme Controller: Chris Baughen.

Metro Radio 55 Degrees North, Pilgrim St, Newcastle upon Tyne, Tyne and Wear, NE1 6BF **t** 0191 230 6100 **f** 0191 279 0288 **e** enquiries@metroandmagic.com **w** metroradio.co.uk 🔲 Programme Director: Chris Pegg.

Marcher Sound The Studios, Mold Road, Gwersyllt, Wrexham, Clwyd, LL11 4AF **t** 01978 752 202 **f** 01978 722 209 **e** firstname.lastname@gcapmedia.com **w** marchersound.co.uk 🔲 Programme Controller: Lisa Marrey.

Mid West Radio Clare St, Ballyhaunis, Co. Mayo, Ireland **t** +353 94 963 0553 **f** +353 94 963 0285 **e** chris@mnwr.ie **w** mnwrfm.com 🔲 Station Mgr/Head of Music: Chris Carroll.

Midlands 103 The Mall, William St, Tullamore, Co Offaly, Ireland **t** +353 506 51333 **f** +353 506 52546 **e** goodcompany@midlandsradio.fm **w** midlandsradio.fm 🔲 GM Broadcasting: John McDonnell.

Ministry of Sound Radio 103 Gaunt St, London, SE1 6DP **t** 0870 060 0010 **f** 020 7403 5348 **e** soconnor@ministryofsound.com **w** ministryofsound.com/radio 🔲 Head of Radio: Steve O'Connor 020 7740 8862.

104.7 Minster FM Chessingham House, Dunnington, York, North Yorkshire, YO19 5SE **t** 01904 488 888 **f** 01904 488 811 **e** studio@minsterfm.com **w** ministerfm.com 🔲 Prog Cont: Mike Vitti.

Mix 107 PO Box 1107, High Wycombe, Buckinghamshire, HP13 6WQ **t** 01494 446 611 **f** 01494 445 400 **e** studio@mix107.co.uk **w** mix107.co.uk 🔲 Station Manager: Andy Muir.

MIX 96 Friars Sq Studios, Bourbon St, Aylesbury, Bucks, HP20 2PZ **t** 01296 399396 **f** 01296 398988 **e** danny.cox@mix96.co.uk **w** mix96.co.uk 🔲 Programme Controller: Danny Cox.

Moray Firth Radio PO Box 271, Inverness, IV3 8UJ **t** 01463 224433 **f** 01463 243224 **e** firstname.lastname@mfr.co.uk **w** mfr.co.uk 🔲 MD/PD: Danny Gallagher.

Raidio na Gaeltachta Casla, Conamara, County na Gaillimhe, Ireland **t** +353 91 506677 **f** +353 91 506666 **e** rnag@rte.ie **w** rnag.ie 🔲 Head of Sales: Mairin Mhic Dhonnchada.

NECR The Shed, School Road, Kintore, Inverurie, Aberdeenshire, AB51 0UX **t** 01467 632 878 **f** 01467 632 969 **e** enquiries@necrfm.co.uk **w** necrfm.co.uk 🔲 Prog Controller: John Dean.

Nevis Radio Ben Nevis Estate, Fort William, Inverness-shire, PH33 6PR **t** 01397 700007 **f** 01397 701007 **e** david@nevisradio.co.uk **w** nevisradio.co.uk 🔲 Station Manager: David Ogg.

BBC Radio Newcastle Broadcasting Centre, Barrack Road, Newcastle upon Tyne, Tyne and Wear, NE99 1RN **t** 0191 232 4141 **f** 0191 261 8907 **e** radionewcastle.news@bbc.co.uk **w** bbc.co.uk/radionewcastle 🔲 Senior Producer: Sarah Miller.

NME Radio B2 Blue Fin Building, 110 Southwark St, London, SE1 0SU **t** 020 7922 1991 **e** info@dx-media.co.uk **w** nmeradio.co.uk 🟦 facebook.com/nmeradio 🟥 myspace.com/nmeradio 🟦 twitter.com/nmeradio 🔲 Contact: Kylie Wallis.

NonStopPlay.com 1 Whitby Court, Reading, Berks, RG4 6SF **t** 020 3051 7571 **e** admin@nonstopplay.com **w** nonstopplay.com 🔲 Station Manager: James Pratt.

BBC Radio Norfolk The Forum, Millennium Plain, Norwich, Norfolk, NR2 1BH **t** 01603 617 411 **f** 01603 764 303 **e** radionorfolk@bbc.co.uk **w** bbc.co.uk/norfolk 🔲 Managing Editor: David Clayton.

North Norfolk Radio The Studio, Breck Farm, Stody, Holt, Norfolk, NR24 2ER **t** 01263 860 808 **f** 01263 860 809 **e** info@northnorfolkradio.com **w** northnorfolkradio.com 🔲 Contact: Jason Reynolds.

Northern Sound Radio Unit 1E, Mastertech Business Park, Athlone Rd, Longford, Ireland **t** +353 434 7777 **f** +353 434 9384 **e** info@northernsound.ie **w** northernsound.ie 🔲 CEO: Richard Devlin.

Northsound 1 Abbotswell Rd, West Tullos, Aberdeen, AB12 3AJ **t** 01224 337000 **f** 01224 400003 **e** firstname.lastname@northsound.co.uk **w** northsound1.com 🔲 Prog Director/HoM: Chris Thomson.

Contacts Facebook MySpace Twitter YouTube

Northsound 2 Abbotswell Rd, West Tullos, Aberdeen, AB12 3AJ **t** 01224 337 000 **f** 01224 400 222 **e** firstname.lastname@northsound.co.uk **w** northsound2.com Prog Director/HoM: Chris Thomson.

99.9 Radio Norwich Stanton House, 29 Yarmouth Rd, Norwich, NR7 0EE **t** 0845 365 6999 **f** 0845 365 7999 **e** firstname.lastname@999radionorwich.com **w** 999radionorwich.com Prog Mgr: Steve Bradley.

BBC Radio Nottingham London Road, Nottingham, NG2 4UU **t** 0115 955 0500 **f** 0115 902 1983 **e** radio.nottingham@bbc.co.uk **w** bbc.co.uk/nottingham Managing Editor: Mike Bettison.

Oak 107 Waldron Court, Prince William Rd, Loughborough, Leicestershire, LE11 5GD **t** 01509 211711 **f** 01509 246 107 **e** info@oak107fm.co.uk **w** oak107fm.co.uk Station Director: Eddie Startup.

Oak 107 & 107.9 FM Unit 3 Martins Court, Telford Way, Stephenson Industrial Estate, Coalville, Leicestershire, LE67 3HD **t** 01530 278200 **f** 01530 278201 **e** iison@oakfm.co.uk **w** oakfm.co.uk Programme Manager: Ian Ison.

Oban FM 132 George St, Oban, Argyll, PA34 5NT **t** 01631 570 057 **f** 01631 570 530 **e** obanfmradio@btconnect.com **w** obanfm.org Station Manager: Laura Johnston.

Ocean FM (Ireland) North West Business Park, Collooney, Co Sligo, Ireland **t** +353 71 911 8100 **f** +353 71 911 8101 **e** studio@oceanfm.ie **w** oceanfm.ie Station Mgr/Programme Dir: Niall Delaney.

Original 106 FM Roman Landing, Kingsway, Southampton, Hampshire, SO14 3HY **t** 023 8038 4100 **f** 023 8082 9844 **e** info@original106.com **w** original106.com

 Assistant Prog Dir: Martyn Lee.

BBC Radio Oxford 269 Banbury Rd, Summertown, Oxford, OX2 7DW **t** 08459 311 444 **f** 08459 311 555 **e** oxford@bbc.co.uk **w** bbc.co.uk/oxford Executive Editor: Steve Taschini.

Oxford 107.9FM 270 Woodstock Rd, Oxford, OX2 7NW **t** 01865 315 982 **f** 01865 553 355 **e** firstname.lastname@fm1079.co.uk **w** fm1079.com Station Mgr/Programme Dir: Ian Walker.

Palm 105.5 Marble Court, Lymington Road, Torquay, TQ1 4FB **t** 01803 321 055 **f** 01803 321 059 **e** info@palm.fm **w** palm.fm Station Manager: Mark Reason.

Peak FM Radio House, Foxwood Rd, Chesterfield, Derbyshire, S41 9RF **t** 01246 269 107 **f** 01246 269 933 **e** studio@peak107.com **w** peak107.com Prog Mgr: Chris Buckley.

Radio Pembrokeshire 14 Old School Estate, Narberth, SA67 7DU **t** 01834 869384 **f** 01834 861524 **e** firstname@radiopembrokeshire.com **w** radiopembrokeshire.com Group Prog Dir: Andy Griffiths.

Pirate FM Carn Brea Studios, Wilson Way, Redruth, Cornwall, TR15 3XX **t** 01209 314400 **f** 01209 315250 **e** firstname@piratefm.co.uk **w** piratefm.co.uk Programme Director: Bob McCreadie.

Premier Christian Radio 22 Chapter St, London, SW1P 4NP **t** 020 7316 1300 **f** 020 7233 6706 **e** premier@premier.org.uk **w** premier.org.uk Programme Controller: Dave Rose.

Pulse Classic Gold Pennine House, Forster Square, Bradford, West Yorkshire, BD1 5NE **t** 01274 203 040 **f** 01274 203 130 **e** firstname.lastname@pulseclassicgold.co.uk **w** pulseclassicgold.co.uk Head of Programming: Mark Brow.

The Pulse of West Yorkshire Pennine House, Forster Square, Bradford, West Yorkshire, BD1 5NE **t** 01274 203 040 **f** 01274 203 130 **e** firstname.lastname@pulse.co.uk **w** pulse.co.uk Programme Director: Mark Brow.

Q101.2FM 42A Market St, Omagh, Co. Tyrone, BT78 1EH **t** 028 6632 0777 **f** 028 8225 9517 **e** gm@qradionetwork.fm **w** q101west.fm MD: Padraig O'Dwyer.

Q102 Glenageary Office Park, Glenageary, Co. Dublin, Ireland **t** +353 1 662 1022 **f** +353 1 662 9974 **e** firstname.lastname@q102.ie **w** q102.ie CEO: Robert Walshe.

Q102.9 FM The Riverview Suite, 87 Rossdowney Rd, Waterside, Co Londonderry, BT47 5SU **t** 028 7134 4449 **f** 028 7131 1177 **e** reception@q102.fm **w** q102.fm Prog Dir: Robert Walshe.

Q97.2FM 24 Cloyfin Road, Coleraine, Co Londonderry, BT52 2NU **t** 028 7035 9100 **f** 028 7032 6666 **e** manager@q972.fm **w** q972.fm CEO: Robert Walshe.

107.4 The Quay PO Box 107.4, Portsmouth, Hampshire, PO2 8YG **t** 023 9236 4141 **f** 023 9236 4151 **e** firstname.lastname@quayradio.com **w** quayradio.com Programme Controller: Sam Matterface.

Quay West 107.4 PO Box 1074, Bridgwater, Somerset, TA6 4WE **t** 01278 727 701 **f** 01278 727 705 **e** info1074@quaywestfm.net **w** bcrfm.co.uk Station Manager: Dave Englefield.

Quay West 102.4/100.8 Harbour Studios, The Esplanade, Watchet, Somerset, TA23 0AJ **t** 01984 634 900 **f** 01984 634 811 **e** studio1024@quaywestfm.net **w** quay.fm Station Manager: Dave Englefield.

Radar Plugging Ltd 1A Codrington Mews, London, W11 2EH **t** 07718 731033 **e** brad@radarplugging.com **w** radarplugging.com MD: Brad Hunner.

Radio Maldwyn The Magic 756, The Studios, The Pk, Newtown, Powys, SY16 2NZ **t** 01686 623555 **f** 01686 623666 **e** radio.maldwyn@ukonline.co.uk **w** magic756.net MD/Prog Controller: Austin Powell.

Media: Radio

RNA FM Arbroath Infirmary, Rosemount Rd, Arbroath, Angus, DD11 2AT **t** 01241 879 660 **f** 01241 439 664 **e** info@radionorthangus.co.uk **w** radionorthangus.co.uk 📇 MD/Prog Dir: Malcolm J.B. Finlayson.

radio2XS Manor Farm Studios, Sheffield, South Yorkshire, S21 5RZ **t** 0870 321 1242 **e** studio@radio2xs.com **w** radio2XS.com 📇 Programme & Music Director: Jeff Cooper.

102.8 Ram FM 35-36 Irongate, Derby, DE1 3GA **t** 01332 324 000 **f** 01332 324 009 **e** firstname.lastname@gcapmedia.com **w** ramfm.co.uk 📇 Prog Cont: James Daniels.

Reading 107FM Radio House, Madejski Stadium, Reading, Berkshire, RG2 0FN **t** 0118 986 2555 **f** 0118 945 0809 **e** studio@reading107fm.com **w** reading107fm.com 📇 Prog Controller: Robert Kenny.

Real Radio Parkway Court, Glasgow Business Pk, Glasgow, G69 6GA **t** 0141 781 1011 **f** 0141 781 1112 **e** sandra.somers@realradio.co.uk **w** realradio.co.uk 📇 Station Co-ordinator: Sandra Somers 0141 781 2262.

Real Radio (Yorkshire) Sterling Court, Capitol Park, Leeds, WF3 1EL **t** 0113 238 1114 **f** 0113 238 1191 **e** firstname.lastname@realradiofm.com **w** realradiofm.com

Real Radio North West Manchester **e** andy.carter@gmgradio.com 📇 Contact: Andy Carter 0161 886 8800.

Real Radio Wales PO Box 6105, Ty-Nant Court, Morganstown, Cardiff, CF15 8YF **t** 02920 315100 **f** 02920 315150 **e** firstname.lastname@realradio.co.uk **w** realradio.co.uk 📇 Programme Controller: Gareth Setter 02920 315 100.

Red Dragon FM Atlantic Wharf, Cardiff Bay, South Glamorgan, CF10 4DJ **t** 029 2066 2066 **f** 029 2066 2060 **e** firstname.lastname@reddragonfm.com **w** reddragonfm.co.uk 📇 Prog Cont: Gavin Marshall.

Red FM 1, UTC, Bishopstown, Cork, Ireland **t** +353 21 486 5500 **f** +353 21 486 5501 **e** info@redfm.ie **w** redfm.ie 📇 Chief Executive: Carol O'Beirne.

Resonance Fm 144 Borough High Street, London, SE1 1LB **t** 020 7407 1210 **e** firstname@resonancefm.com **w** resonancefm.com 📇 MD/Programme Dir: Ed Baxter.

96.2 The Revolution PO Box 962, Oldham, Lancashire, OL1 3JF **t** 0161 621 6500 **f** 0161 621 6521 **e** studio@revolutiononline.co.uk **w** revolutiononline.co.uk 📇 Station Manager: Jacquie Sulkowski.

Ridings FM PO Box 333, Wakefield, West Yorkshire, WF2 7YQ **t** 01924 367 177 **f** 01924 367 133 **e** enquiries@ridingsfm.co.uk **w** ridingsfm.co.uk 📇 Programme Manager: John Tolson.

97.4 Rock FM St Paul's Square, Preston, Lancashire, PR1 1YE **t** 01772 477 700 **f** 01772 477 701 **e** firstname.lastname@rockfm.co.uk **w** rockfm.co.uk 📇 Station Director: Anthony Gay.

Rock Radio Manchester Laser House, Manchester **e** andy.carter@gmgradio.com 📇 Contact: Andy Carter 0161 886 8800.

96.3 Rock Radio Glasgow Business Pk, Glasgow, G69 6GA **t** 0141 781 1011 **f** 0141 781 1112 **e** firstname.lastname@realradiofm.com **w** gmgradio.co.uk ⓣ twitter.com/RockRadioEditor 📇 Station Manager: Ciaran O'Toole.

Rother FM PO Box 622, Aspen Court, Bessemer Way, Rotherham, S60 1FB **t** 01709 369 991 **f** 01709 369 993 **e** initial+lastname@rotherfm.co.uk **w** rotherfm.co.uk 📇 Admin Manager: Alison Brown.

RTE Radio 1 Radio Centre, Donnybrook, Dublin 4, Ireland **t** +353 1 208 3111 **f** +353 1 208 4523 **e** radio1@rte.ie **w** rte.ie 📇 Head of RTE Radio 1: Eithne Hand.

107.1 Rugby FM Suites 4-6, Dunsmore Business Centre, Spring St, Rugby, CV21 3HH **t** 01788 541 100 **f** 01788 541 070 **e** mail@rugbyfm.co.uk **w** rugbyfm.co.uk 📇 MD: Christine Arnold.

Rutland Radio 40 Melton Rd, Oakham, Rutland, LE15 6AY **t** 01572 757868 **f** 01572 757744 **e** enquiries@rutlandradio.co.uk **w** rutlandradio.co.uk 📇 Deputy Programme Manager: Rob Persani.

Sabras Radio Radio House, 63 Melton Rd, Leicester, LE3 6PN **t** 0116 261 0666 **f** 0116 266 7776 **e** firstname@sabrasradio.com **w** sabrasradio.com 📇 MD/Programme Controller: Don Kotak.

The Saint The Friends Provident, St Mary's Stadium, Brittania Rd, Southampton, Hampshire, SO14 5fp **t** 023 8033 0300 **f** 023 8020 6400 **e** thesaint@saintsfc.co.uk **w** saintsfc.co.uk 📇 Programme Controller: Stewart Dennis.

97.5 Scarlet FM Stebonheath Studios, The Foothold Centre, Stebonheath Terrace, Llanelli, SA15 1NE **t** 01834 869 384 **f** 01834 861 524 **e** firstname@Scarletfm.com **w** Scarletfm.com 📇 Group Prog Dir: Andy Griffiths.

Seven FM 1, Millenium Park, Woodside Industial Estate, Woodside Road, Ballymena, Co Antrim, BT42 4QJ **t** 028 256 48777 **f** 028 256 48778 **e** firstname.lastname@sevenfm.co.uk **w** sevenfm.co.uk 📇 Programme Director: Damien McGinley.

The Severn Abbey Studios, 13-14, Abbey Foregate, Shrewsbury, Shropshire, SY2 6AE **t** 01743 284 940 **e** initial+lastname@shropshirestar.com **w** thesevern.co.uk 📇 MD/Prog Controller: Pete Wagstaff.

Shannonside FM Unit 1E, Mastertech Business Park, Athlone Rd, Longford, Ireland **t** +353 43 47777 **f** +353 43 48384 **e** info@shannonside.ie **w** shannonside.ie 📇 CEO: Richard Devlin.

BBC Radio Sheffield 54 Shoreham St, Sheffield, South Yorkshire, S1 4RS **t** 0114 273 1177 **f** 0114 267 5454 **e** radio.sheffield@bbc.co.uk **w** bbc.co.uk/radiosheffield 📇 Head of Music: Jane Kitson.

Contacts   Facebook MySpace   Twitter YouTube

BBC Radio Shetland Pitt Lane, Lerwick, Shetland Isles, ZE1 0DW **t** 01595 694 747 **f** 01595 694 307 **e** radio.shetland@bbc.co.uk **w** bbc.co.uk/radioscotland ✉ Senior Producer: Caroline Moyes.

BBC Radio Shropshire 2-4 Boscobel Drive, Shrewsbury, Shropshire, SY1 3TT **t** 01743 248 484 **f** 01743 271 702 **e** radio.shropshire@bbc.co.uk **w** bbc.co.uk/england/radioshropshire ✉ Head of Music: Tim Page.

SIBC Market St, Lerwick, Shetland, ZE1 0JN **t** 01595 695299 **f** 01595 695696 **e** info@sibc.co.uk **w** sibc.co.uk ✉ MD/Prog Controller: Inga Walterson.

Signal 2 Stoke Road, Stoke-on-Trent, Staffordshire, ST4 2SR **t** 01782 441 300 **f** 01782 441 301 **e** reception@signalradio.com **w** signal2.co.uk ✉ Programme Controller: Kevin Howard.

Signal 1 Stoke Road, Stoke-on-Trent, Staffordshire, ST4 2SR **t** 01782 441 300 **f** 01782 441 301 **e** reception@signalradio.com **w** signal1.com ✉ Programme Controller: Kevin Howard.

106.9 Silk FM Radio House, Bridge Street, Macclesfield, Cheshire, SK11 6DJ **t** 01625 268 000 **f** 01625 269 010 **e** mail@silkfm.com **w** silkfm.com ✉ Programme Controller: Andy Bailey.

Six FM 2c Park Avenue, Burn Rd, Cookstown, Co. Tyrone, BT80 8AH **t** 028 8675 8696 **f** 028 8676 1550 **e** firstname.lastname@sixfm.co.uk **w** sixfm.co.uk ✉ Launch Director: Robert Walshe.

Smash! Hits Radio Castle Quay, Castlefield, Manchester, M15 4PR **t** 0161 288 5000 **e** paul.mack@bauermedia.co.uk ✉ Programmes Manager: Paul Mack.

Smooth Radio London 26-27 Castlereagh Street, London, W1H 5DL **t** 020 7706 4100 **f** 020 7723 9742 **e** firstname.lastname@smoothfm.com **w** smoothradio.co.uk ✉ Programme Director: Gavin McCoy.

Smooth Radio Scotland Glasgow Business Park, Glasgow, G69 6GA **t** 0141 781 1011 **f** 0141 781 1112 **e** firstname.lastname@realradiofm.com **w** gmgradio.co.uk ✉ Programme Director: Jay Crawford.

Smooth Radio East Midlands Alder Court, Riverside Business Pk, Nottingham, NG2 1RX **t** 0115 986 1066 **f** 0115 943 5000 **e** firstname.lastname@smoothradio.co.uk **w** smoothradio.com ⓕ facebook.com/smooth.radio ✉ Station Director, Midlands: Sam Fielding.

Smooth Radio North West Laser House, Waterfront Quay, Salford Quays, Manchester, M50 3XW **t** 0845 050 1004 **f** 0845 054 1005 **e** steve.collins@smoothradio.com **w** smoothradio.com ✉ Smooth Brand Programme Director: Steve Collins.

Smooth Radio West Midlands Crown House, 123 Hagley Rd, Edgbaston, Birmingham, B16 8LD **t** 0121 452 1057 **f** 0121 452 3222 **e** firstname.lastname@smoothradio.co.uk **w** smoothradio.co.uk ✉ Station Director: Jane Davies.

BBC Radio Solent Broadcasting House, Havelock Road, Southampton, Hampshire, SO14 7PW **t** 023 8063 1311 **f** 023 8033 9648 **e** radio.solent.news@bbc.co.uk **w** bbc.co.uk/england/radiosolent ✉ Managing Editor: Mia Costello.

BBC Somerset Sound Broadcasting House, Park St, Taunton, Somerset, TA1 4DA **t** 01823 323956 **f** 01823 332539 **e** somerset.sound@bbc.co.uk **w** bbc.co.uk/england/radiobristol/somerset ✉ Managing Ed: Simon Clifford.

South East Radio Custom House Quay, Wexford, Ireland **t** +353 53 914 5200 **f** +353 53 914 5295 **e** clive@southeastradio.ie **w** southeastradio.ie ✉ Prog Dir/Head of Music: Clive Roylance.

South West Sound Unit 40, The Loreburne Centre, High Street, Dunfries, DG1 2BD **t** 01387 250999 **f** 01387 265629 **e** firstname.lastname@southwestsound.co.uk **w** southwestsound.co.uk ✉ Programme Dir/Hd of Music: Alan Toomey.

107.5 Sovereign Radio 14 St Mary's Walk, Hailsham, East Sussex, BN27 1AF **t** 01323 442700 **f** 01323 442866 **e** info@1075sovereignradio.co.uk **w** 1075sovereignradio.co.uk ✉ Station Manager: Nigel Ansell.

Spectrum Radio 4 Ingate Place, London, SW8 3NS **t** 020 7627 4433 **f** 020 7627 3409 **e** enquiries@spectrumradio.net **w** spectrumradio.net ✉ MD: Toby Aldrich.

Spin 103.8 Level 3 South Block, The Malt House, Grand Canal Quay, Dublin 2, Ireland **t** +353 18 772 100 **f** +353 18 550 711 **e** info@spin1038.com **w** spin1038.com ✉ Programme Director: Andy Ashton.

Spire FM City Hall Studios, Salisbury, Wiltshire, SP2 7QQ **t** 01722 416644 **f** 01722 416688 **e** firstname.lastname@spirefm.co.uk **w** spirefm.co.uk ✉ Station Manager: Karen Bosley.

Spirit FM 9-10 Dukes Court, Bognor Rd, Chichester, West Sussex, PO19 8FX **t** 01243 773 600 **f** 01243 786 464 **e** info@spiritfm.net **w** spiritfm.net ✉ New Music Presenter: Milly Luxford.

Star 107 Radio House, Sturton Street, Cambridge, CB1 2QF **t** 01223 305 107 **f** 01223 577 686 **e** firstname.lastname@star107.co.uk **w** star107.co.uk ✉ Prog Controller: Mark Peters.

Star 107.5 1st Floor, West Suite, Cheltenham Film Studios, Hatherley Lane, Cheltenham, Gloucestershire, GL51 6PN **t** 01242 699 555 **f** 01242 699 666 **e** studio@star1075.co.uk **w** star1075.co.uk ✉ Programme Controller: Brody Swain.

Contacts | **Facebook** | **MySpace** | **Twitter** | **YouTube**

Star 107.7 11 Beaconsfield Rd, Weston-super-Mare, North Somerset, BS23 1YE **t** 01934 624 455 **f** 01934 629 922 **e** firstname.lastname@star1077.co.uk **w** star1077.co.uk **Station Mgr: Sue Brooks.**

Star 107.9 Brunel Mall, London Rd, Stroud, Gloucestershire, GL5 2BP **t** 01453 767 369 **f** 01453 757 107 **e** programming@star1079.co.uk **w** star1079.co.uk **Programme Manager: Brody Swain.**

Star Bristol Star Radio, County Gates, Ashton Rd, Bristol, BS3 2JH **t** 0117 966 1065 **f** 0117 953 1065 **e** firstname.lastname@starbristol.com **w** starbristol.com **Programme Controller: Matt Howells.**

BBC Radio Stoke Cheapside, Hanley, Stoke-on-Trent, Staffordshire, ST1 1JJ **t** 01782 208 080 **f** 01782 289 115 **e** radio.stoke@bbc.co.uk **w** bbc.co.uk/radiostoke **Managing Editor: Sue Owen.**

97.2 Stray FM The Hamlet, Hornbeam Park Ave, Harrogate, North Yorkshire, HG2 8RE **t** 01423 522 972 **f** 01423 522 922 **e** firstname.lastname@strayfm.com **w** strayfm.com **Programme Controller: Chris Bell.**

103.4 Sun FM PO Box 1034, Sunderland, Tyne and Wear, SR5 2YL **t** 0191 5481034 **f** 0191 5487171 **e** helen.edmondson@sun-fm.com **w** sun-fm.com **1034sunfm **Station Manager: Helen Edmondson.**

Sunrise FM Sunrise House, 30 Chapel St, Little Germany, Bradford, West Yorkshire, BD1 5DN **t** 01274 735 043 **f** 01274 728 534 **e** info@sunriseradio.fm **w** sunriseradio.fm **Chief Executive: Usha Parmar.**

Sunrise Radio Sunrise House, Merrick Rd, Southall, Middlesex, UB2 4AU **t** 020 8574 6666 **f** 020 8813 9800 **e** info@sunriseradio.com **w** sunriseradio.com **Operations Manager: Tony Patti.**

Sunshine 1530 (Worcester) PO Box 262, Worcester, WR6 5ZE **t** 01905 740 600 **f** 01905 740 608 **e** studio1530@sunshineradio.co.uk **w** sunshineradio.co.uk **Acting Station Manager: John Hyde.**

Sunshine 855 Unit 11, Burway Trading Estate, Bromfield Rd, Ludlow, Shropshire, SY8 1EN **t** 01584 873 795 **f** 01584 875 900 **e** firstname@sunshine855.com **w** sunshine855.com **Acting Station Manager: John Hyde.**

Sunshine 954 (Hereford) Otherton Lane, Cotheridge, Worcester, WR6 5ZE **t** 01905 740 600 **f** 01905 740 608 **e** studio954@sunshineradio.co.uk **w** sunshineradio.co.uk **Acting Station Manager: John Hyde.**

Swansea Bay Radio Newby House, Neath Abbey Business Park, Neath, SA10 7DR **t** 0845 890 4000 **f** 0845 890 5000 **e** firstname.lastname@swanseabayradio.com **w** swanseabayradio.com **Group MD: Martin Mumford.**

Swansea Sound 1170 MW Victoria Road, Gowerton, Swansea, SA4 3AB **t** 01792 511 964 **f** 01792 511 171 **e** info@swanseasound.co.uk **w** swanseasound.co.uk **Station Director: Carrie Mosley.**

talkSPORT 18 Hatfields, London, SE1 8DJ **t** 020 7959 7800 **f** 020 7959 7808 **e** firstname.lastname@talksport.co.uk **w** talksport.net **Programme Director: Moz Dree.**

Tay AM 6 North Isla St, Dundee, DD3 7JQ **t** 01382 200 800 **f** 01382 423 231 **e** firstname.lastname@tayam.co.uk **w** Tayam.co.uk **Head of Music: Graeme Waggott.**

Tay FM 6 North Isla St, Dundee, Tayside, DD3 7JQ **t** 01382 200 800 **f** 01382 423 252 **e** firstname.lastname@tayfm.co.uk **w** tayfm.co.uk **Head of Music: Graeme Waggott.**

107.4 Telford FM Shropshire Star Building, Waterloo Rd, Ketley, Telford, TF1 5UD **t** 01952 280 011 **f** 01952 280 010 **e** info@telfordfm.co.uk **w** telfordfm.co.uk **MD/Prog Controller: Pete Wagstaff.**

Ten-17 Latton Bush Business Centre, Southern Way, Harlow, Essex, CM18 7BU **t** 01279 431 017 **f** 01279 236 659 **e** firstname.lastname@gcapmedia.com **w** ten17.co.uk **Programme Controller: Freddie Scherer.**

TFM Yale Crescent, Thornaby, Stockton on Tees, Cleveland, TS17 6AA **t** 01642 888 222 **f** 01642 868 288 **e** tfm.reception@tfmradio.com **w** tfmradio.co.uk **Programme Director: Chris Rick.**

103.4 The Beach PO Box 103.4, Lowestoft, Suffolk, NR32 2TL **t** 0845 345 1035 **f** 0845 345 1036 **e** info@thebeach.co.uk **w** thebeach.co.uk **Prog Contr: Paul Carter.**

The Hits Radio Castle Quay, Castlefield, Manchester, M15 4PR **e** paul.mack@bauermedia.co.uk **w** thehitsradio.com **Programmes Manager: Paul Mack** 0161 288 5000.

The Radio Academy 5 Market Pl, London, W1W 8AE **t** 020 7927 9920 **f** 020 7636 8924 **e** info@radioacademy.org **w** radioacademy.org **@radioacademy **Chief Executive: Trevor Dann.**

BBC Three Counties Radio 1 Hastings St, Luton, Beds, LU1 5XL **t** 01582 637400 **f** 01582 401467 **e** bedfordshire@bbc.co.uk **w** bbc.co.uk/threecounties **Managing Editor: Angus Moorat.**

Time 106.6 FM The Observatory, Slough, Berkshire, SL1 1LH **t** 01753 551 066 **f** 01753 512 277 **e** firstname@timefm.com **w** timefm.com **Asst Programme Mgr: Mark Gale.**

Time 107.5 Lambourne House, 7 Western Rd, Romford, Essex, RM1 3LD **t** 01708 731643 **f** 01708 730383 **e** markdover@timefm.com **w** time1075.com **Programme Manager: Mark Dover.**

Time 106.8 2-6 Basildon Rd, London, SE2 0EW **t** 020 8311 3112 **f** 020 8312 1930 **e** gary@timefm.com **w** timefm.com **Grp Prog Cont: Gary Mulligan.**

Time 107.3 2-6 Basildon Rd, London, SE2 0EW **t** 020 8311 3112 **f** 020 8312 1930 **e** gary@timefm.com **w** timefm.com **Grp Prog Controller: Gary Mulligan.**

Media: Radio

Contacts Facebook MySpace Twitter YouTube

Tindle Radio First Floor, Radio House, Orion Court, Great Blakenham, Ipswich, Suffolk, IP6 0LW **t** 01473 836100 **f** 01473 836136 **e** info@town102.com **w** tindleradio.com Group Brand Director: David Rees.

Tipp FM Davis Road, Clonmel, Co Tipperary, Ireland **t** +353 522 5299 **f** +353 522 5447 **e** onair@tippfm.com **w** tippfm.com CEO: Ethel Power.

Tipperary Mid-West St Michael Street, Tipperary, Ireland **t** +353 62 52555 **f** +353 62 52671 **e** tippmidwest@radio.fm **w** tipperarymidwestradio.com Station Mgr: Anne Power.

100-102 Today FM Marconi House, Digges Lane, Dublin 2, Ireland **t** +353 1 804 9000 **f** +353 1 804 9099 **e** badams@todayfm.com **w** todayfm.com Head of Music: Brian Adams.

Touch 107.6 Unit 9, Manor Park, Banbury, Oxfordshire, OX16 3TB **t** 01295 661 076 **e** firstname.lastname@cnradio.co.uk **w** touchfm1076.co.uk Head of Presentation: Dale Collins 01295 661 070.

Touch FM East Staffs 5-6 Aldergate, Tamworth, Staffs, B79 7DJ **t** 01827 318 000 **f** 01827 318 002 **e** firstname.lastname@cnradio.co.uk **w** touchtbl.co.uk Programme Controller: Dave James.

Touch 102 The Guard House Studios, Banbury Rd, Stratford upon Avon, Warwickshire, CV37 7HX **t** 01789 262 636 **f** 01789 263 102 **e** firstname.lastname@cnradio.co.uk **w** touchfm102.co.uk Head of Presentation: Steve Hyden.

Touch 96.2 Watch Close, Spon Street, Coventry, West Midlands, CV1 3LN **t** 024 7652 5656 **f** 024 7655 1744 **e** firstname.lastname@cnradio.co.uk **w** touchfm962.co.uk Head of Presentation: Tom Newitt.

107.4 Tower FM The Mill, Brownlow Way, Bolton, BL1 2RA **t** 01204 387 000 **f** 01204 534 065 **e** firstname.lastname@towerfm.co.uk **w** towerfm.co.uk Station Dir: Dave Stankler.

Trax FM 5 Sidings Court, White Rose Way, Doncaster, South Yorkshire, DN4 5NU **t** 01302 341166 **f** 01302 326104 **e** enquiries@traxfm.co.uk **w** traxfm.co.uk Admin Manager: Michelle Hancock.

96 Trent FM Chapel Quarter, Maid Marian Way, Nottingham, NG1 6JR **t** 0115 873 1500 **f** 0115 873 1509 **e** firstname.lastname@gcapmedia.com **w** trentfm.co.uk Programme Director: Chris Pegg.

2BR (Two Boroughs Radio)
Lomeshaye Business Village, Nelson, Lancashire, BB9 7DR **t** 01282 690 000 **f** 01282 690 001 **e** enquiries@2br.co.uk **w** 2br.co.uk Programme Controller: Ricky Kirby.

U105 Ormeau Rd, Belfast, BT7 1EB **t** 028 9033 2105 **f** 028 9033 0105 **e** firstname.lastname@u105.com **w** u105.com Head of Music / Programme Controller: Maurice Jay.

Unique Production UBC Media Group PLC, 50 Lisson St, London, NW1 5DF **t** 020 7453 1600 **f** 020 7453 1665 **e** info1@ubcmedia.com **w** UBCMedia.com Commercial Dir: John Quinn.

Vale FM Longmead Studios, Shaftesbury, Dorset, SP7 8QQ **t** 01747 855 711 **f** 01747 855 722 **e** studio@valefm.co.uk **w** valefm.co.uk Programme Controller: Dave Webster.

Valleys Radio PO Box 1116, Ebbw Vale, NP23 8XW **t** 01495 301 116 **f** 01495 300 710 **e** firstname.lastname@valleysradio.co.uk **w** valleysradio.co.uk Programme Mgr: Tony Peters.

96.9 Viking FM The Boathouse, Commercial Rd, Hull, East Yorks, HU1 2SG **t** 01482 325 141 **f** 0845 4580 390 **e** programmes@vikingfm.co.uk **w** vikingfm.co.uk Programme Director: Craig Beck.

BBC Wales/Cymru Broadcasting House, Llantrisant Road, Llandaff, Cardiff, South Glamorgan, CF5 2YQ **t** 029 2032 2000 **f** 029 2032 3724 **e** radio.wales@bbc.co.uk **w** bbc.co.uk/wales Radio Wales Editor: Sali Collins.

96.4FM The Wave Victoria Road, Gowerton, Swansea, SA4 3AB **t** 01792 511 964 **f** 01792 511 965 **e** info@thewave.co.uk **w** thewave.co.uk Station Dir: Carrie Mosley.

Wave 105.2 FM 5 Manor Court, Barnes Wallis Rd, Segensworth East, Fareham, Hampshire, PO15 5TH **t** 01489 481 057 **f** 01489 481 100 **e** studio@wave105.com **w** wave105.com MD: Martin Ball.

Wave 96.5 965 Mowbray Drive, Blackpool, Lancashire, FY3 7JR **t** 01253 304 965 **f** 01253 301 965 **e** info@thewavefm.co.uk **w** wave965.com Station Director: Helen Bowden.

Wave 102 FM 8 South Tay St, Dundee, DD1 1PA **t** 01382 901 000 **f** 01382 900 999 **e** studio@wave102.co.uk **w** wave102.co.uk Programme Controller: Peter Mac.

Waves Radio 7 Blackhouse Circle, Blackhouse Industrial Estate, Peterhead, Aberdeenshire, AB42 1BN **t** 01779 491012 **f** 01779 490802 **e** waves@wavesfm.com **w** wavesfm.com MD: Norman Spence 01779 490333.

Wessex FM Radio House, Trinity St, Dorchester, Dorset, DT1 1DJ **t** 01305 250333 **f** 01305 266885 **e** firstname.lastname@wessexfm.com **w** wessexfm.com Station Manager: Steve Bulley 01305 250 333.

West FM Radio House, 54 Holmston Rd, Ayr, KA7 3BE **t** 01292 283662 **f** 01292 283665 **e** james.pllu@westfm.co.uk **w** westfm.co.uk Programme Controller: James Pllu.

Westsound AM Radio House, 54, Holmston Rd, Ayr, KA7 3BE **t** 01292 283 662 **f** 01292 283 665 **e** info@westsound.co.uk **w** west-sound.co.uk Prog Cont/Head of Music: Alan Toomey.

Media: Radio

Media: Radio, Digital & Internet Radio

BBC Radio Wiltshire Broadcasting House, Prospect Place, Swindon, Wiltshire, SN1 3RW **t** 01793 513626 **f** 01793 513650 **e** radio.wiltshire@bbc.co.uk **w** bbc.co.uk/radiowiltshire Head of Music: Mark Seaman.

107.2 Wire FM Warrington Business Park, Long Lane, Warrington, Cheshire, WA2 8TX **t** 01925 445 545 **f** 01925 657 705 **e** info@wirefm.com **w** wirefm.com MD: Chris Hurst.

Wired FM Mary Immaculate College, South Circular Road, Limerick, Ireland **t** +353 61 315773 **f** +353 61 315776 **e** wiredfm@mic.ul.ie **w** wiredfm.mic.ul.ie Station Manager: Kiaran Long.

102.4 Wish FM Orrell Lodge, Orrell Road, Orrell, Wigan, WN5 8HJ **t** 01942 761024 **f** 01942 777694 **e** firstname.lastname@wish-fm.com **w** wishfm.net MD: Chris Hurst.

WLR FM The Broadcast Centre, Ardkeen, Co Waterford, Ireland **t** +353 5187 2248 **f** +353 5184 6148 **e** studio@wlrfm.com **w** wlrfm.com Prog Controller: Billy McCarthy.

BBC WM The Mailbox, Birmingham, West Midlands, B1 1RF **t** 08453 00 99 56 **f** 0121 472 3174 **e** bbcwm@bbc.co.uk **w** bbc.co.uk/radiowm Managing Editor: Keith Beech.

107.7 FM The Wolf 2nd Floor, Mander House, Wolverhampton, West Midlands, WV1 3NB **t** 01902 571070 **f** 01902 571079 **e** firstname.lastname@thewolf.co.uk **w** thewolf.co.uk Programme Controller: Richard Dodd.

BBC World Service Room 101, Henry Wood House, 3/6 Portland Place, London, W1A 1AA **t** 020 7765 3938 **f** 020 7765 3945 **e** alan.rowett@bbc.co.uk **w** bbc.co.uk/worldservice Head of Music: Alan Rowett.

107.2 The Wyre Foley House, 123 Stourport Road, Kidderminster, Worcs., DY11 7BW **t** 01562 641 072 **f** 01562 641 073 **e** initial+lastname@shropshirestar.co.uk **w** thewyre.com Programme Director: Pete Wagstaff.

Wythenshawe FM 97.2 Suite A4, Alderman Gatley House, Hale Top, Manchester, M22 5RQ **t** 0161 499 7982 **f** 0161 499 7442 **e** info@wfmradio.org **w** wfmradio.org Programme Cont/Hd of Music: Jason Kenyon.

Wyvern FM First Floor, Kirkham House, John Comyn Drive, Worcester, WR3 7NS **t** 01905 545 500 **f** 01905 545 509 **e** firstname.lastname@gcapmedia.com **w** wyvernfm.co.uk Programme Cont/Hd of Music: Mark Watts.

Xfm London 30 Leicester Sq, London, WC2H 7LA **t** 020 7766 6600 **f** 020 7766 6601 **e** firstname.lastname@xfm.co.uk **w** xfm.co.uk Programme Director: Paul Jackson.

Xfm Manchester Suite 1.1, 4 Exchange Quay, Salford, Manchester, M5 3EE **t** 0161 662 4700 **f** 0161 662 4759 **w** xfm.co.uk Programme Controller: James Brown.

RadioXL KMS House, Bradford St, Birmingham, West Midlands, B12 0JD **t** 0121 753 5353 **f** 0121 753 3111 **e** info@radioxl.net **w** radioxl.net Head of Music/Sales: Sukhjinder Ghatoare.

Yorkshire Coast Radio PO Box 962, Scarborough, North Yorkshire, YO11 3ZP **t** 01723 581700 **f** 01723 588990 **e** chris.sigsworth@yorkshirecoastradio.com **w** yorkshirecoastradio.com Station Mgr/Prog Cont: Chris Sigsworth.

Yourradio FM Pioneer Park Studios, 80 Castlegreen St, Dumbarton, G82 1JB **t** 01389 734 422 **f** 08454 900 556 **e** initial+lastname@yourradiofm.com **w** yourradiofm.com Prog Controller: Dave Ross.

Digital & Internet Radio

Gaydar Radio PO Box 113, Twickenham, Middlesex, TW1 4WY **t** 020 8744 1287 **f** 020 8744 1089 **e** robin.crowley@gaydarradio.com **w** gaydarradio.com Programme Director: Robin Crowley.

Get Ready to ROCK! Radio 34 Coniston Rd, Neston, Cheshire, CH64 0TD **t** 0151 336 6199 **f** 0151 336 6199 **e** radio@getreadytorockradio.com **w** getreadytorockradio.com Programme Director: David Randall.

Music Choice Ltd (A member of the Music Choice Europe Ltd Group) The Old Truman Brewery, 91 Brick Lane, London, E1 6QL **t** 020 3107 0300 **f** 020 3107 0301 **e** contactus@musicchoice.co.uk **w** musicchoice.co.uk Finance Director: Jeff Clarkson.

Planet Rock 1 Golden Sq, London, W1F 9DJ **t** 020 7766 6810 **e** info@planetrock.com **w** planetrock.com facebook.com/pages/Planet-Rock/19992562080 myspace.com/officialplanetrock MD: Mark Lee.

Q Radio 20 Lionel St, Birmingham, West Midlands, B3 1AQ **t** 0121 600 7900 **e** firstname.surname@bauermedia.co.uk **w** qthemusic.com Programme Director: James Walshe.

Radio Magnetic 16 Argyle Court, 1103 Argyle St, Glasgow, G3 8ND **t** 0141 226 8808 **e** dougal@radiomagnetic.com **w** radiomagnetic.com facebook.com/pages/Radio-Magnetic/50173629578?v=wall&ref=search myspace.com/radiomagnetic twitter.com/radiomagnetic youtube.com/radiomagnetic Director: Dougal Perman.

RawRip.com 130 Shaftsbury Avenue, London, W1D 5EU **t** 020 7031 4292 **f** 020 7031 4302 **e** info@rawrip.com **w** rawrip.com Business Development Mgr: Armond Mertikian.

Score Digital Ltd 3 South Avenues, Clydebank Business Park, Glasgow, G81 2RX **t** 0141 565 2347 **f** 0141 565 2318 **e** firstname.lastname@emap.com **w** scoredigital.co.uk Managing Director: Steve Parkinson.

Contacts   Facebook   MySpace Twitter YouTube

The Storm PO Box 2000, 1, Passage St, Bristol, BS99 7SN **t** 020 7911 7300 **f** 020 7911 7369 **e** mail@stormradio.co.uk **w** stormradio.co.uk MD: Mark Lee.

TuneTribe Digital 50-52 Paul St, London, EC2A 4LB **t** 020 749 1994 **f** 020 7729 8951 **e** lisa.deluca@tunetribe.com **w** tunetribedigital.com Contact: Lisa DeLuca.

UCB Europe Hanchurch Christian Centre, PO Box 255, Stoke On Trent, Staffordshire, ST4 8YY **t** 01782 642 000 **f** 01782 641 121 **e** ucb@ucb.co.uk **w** ucb.co.uk Station Controller: Andrew Urquhart.

VIP Radio PO Box 909, Thorpe Salvin, Notts., S80 3YZ **t** 01909 774 111 **f** 01909-515171 **e** info@vipradio.net **w** vipradio.net Managing Director: Kev Roberts.

World Radio Network (WRN) PO Box 1212, London, SW8 2ZF **t** 020 7896 9000 **f** 020 7896 9007 **e** contactus@wrn.org **w** wrn.org Marketing Manager: Tim Ayris.

Television

The 3DD Group 5th Floor, 08-12 Camden High St, London, NW1 0JH **t** 020 7380 8100 **f** 020 7380 8118 **e** Sales@3DDgroup.com **w** 3DDgroup.com CEO: Dominic Saville.

3DD Group 5th Floor, 08-12 Camden High St, London, NW1 0JH **t** 020 7380 8100 **f** 020 7380 8118 **e** dominic.saville@3ddgroup.com **w** 3DDGroup.com CEO: Dominic Saville.

Anglia Anglia House, Norwich, Norfolk, NR1 3JG **t** 01603 615151 **f** 01603 631032 **e** duty.office@itv.com **w** itvregions.com/Anglia

At It Productions 68 Salusbury Road, Queens Park, London, NW6 6NU **t** 020 7644 0000 **f** 020 7644 0001 **e** enquiries@atitproductions.com **w** atitproductions.com MDs: Chris Fouracre, Martin Cunning.

BBC Midlands Today The Mailbox, Birmingham, West Midlands, B1 1AY **t** 0121 567 6130 **f** 0121 567 6005 **e** midlands.today@bbc.co.uk or ben.sidwell@bbc.co.uk or lindsay.doyle@bbc.co.uk **w** bbc.co.uk/midlandstoday Reporters: Ben Sidwell or Lindsay Doyle.

BBC Television Centre Wood Lane, Shepherd's Bush, London, W12 7RJ **t** 020 8743 8000 **e** info@bbc.co.uk **w** bbc.co.uk

Big Eye Film & Television Lock Keepers Cottage, Century Street, Whitworth Street West, Manchester, M3 4QL **t** 0161 832 6111 **f** 0161 834 8558 **e** eye@bigeye.u-net.com Contact: Steven Lock, Mary Richmond.

Blaze Television 2042-A Armacost Ave., Los Angeles, California, CA 90025, United States **t** +1 (310) 998-3366 **f** +1 (310) 998-3270 **e** firstname.lastname@blaze.tv **w** blaze.tv Writer / Producer / Director: Conor McAnally.

Blue Post Production 58 Old Compton St, London, W1D 4UF **t** 020 7437 2626 **f** 020 7439 2477 **e** info@primefocus2orld.com **w** primefocusworld.com twitter.com/prime_focus MD: Simon Briggs.

Border The Television Centre, Carlisle, Cumbria, CA1 3NT **t** 01228 525101 **f** 01228 541384 **w** border-tv.com

Box Television Mappin House, 4 Winsley St, London, W1W 8HF **t** 020 7436 1515 **f** 020 7376 1313 **e** ssadler@channel4.co.uk **w** 4music.com Dir of Music: Simon Sadler.

Brighter Pictures 10th Floor, Blue Star House, 234-244 Stockwell Road, London, SW9 9SP **t** 020 7733 7333 **f** 020 7733 6333 **e** info@brighter.co.uk **w** brighter.co.uk MD: Gavin Hay.

Carlton (Central) Carlton Studios, Television House, Nottingham, NG7 2NA **t** 0115 986 3322 **f** 0115 964 5552 **w** carlton.com/central

Carlton UK 101 St Martin's Lane, London, WC2N 4AZ **t** 020 7240 4000 **f** 020 7240 4171 **w** carlton.com

Carlton (Westcountry) Western Wood Way, Langage Science Park, Plymouth, Devon, PL7 5BG **t** 01752 333333 **f** 01752 333444 **w** carlton.com/westcountry

Chameleon TV Church House, 14 Town St, Horsforth, Leeds, LS18 4RJ **t** 0113 205 0045 **f** 0113 281 9454 **e** (firstname)@chameleontv.com **w** chameleontv.com MD: Allen Jewhurst.

Channel 4 124 Horseferry Rd, London, SW1P 2TX **t** 020 7396 4444 **f** 020 7306 8630 **e** Initial+lastname@channel4.co.uk **w** channel4.com Commissioning Editor, T4 & 4Music: Neil McCallum.

CHANNEL AKA

PO Box 64397, London, EC2P 2GU

Channel U PO Box 50239, London, EC1V 3YF **t** 020 7054 9010 **f** 020 7054 9011 **e** info@vitv.co.uk **w** channelu.tv CEO: Stewart Lund.

The Chart Show 37 Harwood Rd, London, SW6 4QP **t** 020 7371 5999 **f** 020 7384 2026 **e** info@chartshow.tv **w** chartshow.tv CEO: Gail Screene.

Chrome Productions 37 Lonsdale Road, Queens Park, London, NW6 6RA **t** 020 7644 1980 **f** 020 7624 4028 **e** info@chromeproductions.co.uk **w** chromeproductions.co.uk Production Manager: Hannah Chandler.

Different Ltd 10 Summerhill Terrace, Summerhill Square, Newcastle upon Tyne, NE4 6EB **t** 0191 261 0111 **f** 0191 221 1122 **e** dreid@different-uk.com **w** different-uk.com Producer: David Reid.

Media: Television

Direct Drive TV 38 Twisaday House, 28 Colville Square, Notting Hill, London, W11 2BW **t** 07916 277 272 **e** leroy@directdrive.tv **w** directdrive.tv 📇 CEO: Leroy Smith.

Eagle Eye Productions Eagle House, 22 Armoury Way, London, SW18 1EZ **t** 020 8870 5670 **f** 020 8874 2333 **e** mail@eagle-rock.com **w** eagle-rock.com 📇 Head of Production: Alan Ravenscroft 02088705670.

Eagle Vision (Video) Eagle House, 22 Armoury Way, London, SW18 1EZ **t** 020 8870 5670 **f** 020 8874 2333 **e** mail@eagle-rock.com **w** eagle-rock.com 📇 Managing Director of Eagle Media Production: Alan Ravenscroft.

BBC East St Catherine's Close, All Saints Green, Norwich, Norfolk, NR1 3ND **t** 01603 619331 **f** 01603 284455 **e** look.east@bbc.co.uk **w** bbc.co.uk/england/lookeast

Endemol UK Productions Shepherds Building Central, Charecroft Way, London, W14 0EE **t** 0870 333 1700 **f** 0870 333 1800 **e** info@endemoluk.com **w** endemoluk.com 📇 Music Supervisor: Amelia Hartley.

Five 1 Stephen St, London, W1T 1AL **t** 020 7550 5555 **f** 020 7550 5783 **e** martin.price@five.tv **w** five.tv 📇 Mgr, Music Services: Martin Price.

Fizz PO Box 50239, London, EC1V 3YF **t** 020 7054 9010 **f** 020 7054 9011 **e** info@vitv.co.uk **w** fizzmusic.com 📇 CEO: Stewart Lund.

GearBox 23 Shield Drive, West Cross Industrial Estate, Brentford, Middlesex, TW8 9EX **t** 020 8380 7400 **f** 020 8380 7410 **e** mail@gearbox.com **w** gearbox.com 📇 Contact: Michael Pearce.

GMTV London Television Centre, Upper Ground, London, SE1 9TT **t** 020 7827 7000 **f** 020 7827 7001 **e** talk2us@gmtv.co.uk **w** gmtv.co.uk 📇 Contact: Press Office.

Goldie 2, The Old Parish Hall, The Square, Lenham, Maidstone, kent, ME17 2PQ **t** 01622 858300 **f** 01622 858300 **e** info@eddielock.co.uk **w** eddielock.co.uk 🔲 myspace.com/goldie_art 📇 Contact: Eddie Lock.

Granada (Manchester) Granada Television, Quay Street, Manchester, M60 9EA **t** 0161 832 7211 **f** 0161 953 0298 **e** officers.duty@granadatv.co.uk **w** granadatv.co.uk 📇 Music & Fim Ent Dept: Louise Wilcockson.

Granada (News Centre) Albert Dock, Liverpool, Merseyside, L3 4BA **t** 0151 709 9393 **f** 0151 709 3389 **w** granada.co.uk 📇 Contact: 0161 832 7211.

Hamma & Glamma Productions Ltd 31 Vernon Street, London, W14 0RN **t** 020 7199 0020 **f** 020 7084 0377 **e** info@hammaglamma.com **w** hammaglamma.com 📇 Office Manager: Liz Orkney.

Influential Media 110 Ducie House, Ducie St, Manchester, M1 2JW **t** 07050 395708 **e** info@influential.tv **w** influential.tv 👍 /influentialmanchester 🐦 /influentialtv ▶️ /influentialfilms 📇 Creative Director: Mike Swindells.

Initial (An Endemol Company) Shepherds Building Central, Charecroft Way, London, W14 0EE **t** 0870 333 1700 **f** 0870 333 1800 **e** press@endemoluk.com **w** endemoluk.com 📇 Head of Music: Phil Mount.

ITV London The London Television Centre, Upper Ground, London, SE1 9LT **t** 020 7620 1620 **f** 020 7261 3307 **e** planning@itvlondon.com **w** itvregions.com/london

ITVWales Television Centre, Culverhouse Cross, Cardiff, CF5 6XJ **t** 029 2059 0590 **f** 029 2059 7183 **e** info@itvwales.com **w** itvwales.com

Kerrang! TV Mappin House, 4 Winsley St, London, W1W 8HF **t** 020 7182 8000 **w** kerrang.com

Kyng Films 14 Herbert St, Chalk Farm, London, NW5 4HD **t** 020 7267 3032 **f** 020 7267 3032 **e** mail@kyngfilms.com 📇 MD: GG Kyng.

Later With Jools Holland BBC TV Centre, Wood Lane, London, W12 7RJ **t** 020 8743 8000 **w** bbc.co.uk/later

Maguffin Ltd 10 Frith Street, London, W1V 5TZ **t** 020 7437 2526 **f** 020 7437 1516 **e** firstname@maguffin.co.uk **w** maguffin.co.uk 📇 MD / Prod: James Chads.

Maidstone Studios New Cut Rd, Vinters Park, Maidstone, Kent, ME14 5NZ **t** 01622 691 111 **f** 01622 684 411 **e** info@maidstonestudios.com **w** maidstonestudios.com 📇 Studio Rescources Manager: Helen Kristic.

Mike Mansfield Television Ltd 5th Floor, 41-42 Berners Street, London, W1T 3NB **t** 020 7580 2581 **f** 020 7580 2582 **e** mikemantv@aol.com **w** cyberconcerts.com 📇 MD: Mike Mansfield.

Meridian Television Centre, Northam, Southampton, Hampshire, SO14 0PZ **t** 023 8022 2555 **f** 023 8071 2012 **e** viewerliaison@meridiantv.com **w** meridiantv.co.uk

MTV UK & Ireland Hawley Crescent, London, NW1 0TT **t** 020 7284 7777 **f** 020 7284 6466 **e** lastname.firstname@mtvne.com **w** mtv.co.uk 📇 MD, MTV Networks UK & Ireland: David Lynn.

MTV2 17-29 Hawley Crescent, London, NW1 8TT **t** 020 7284 7777 **f** 020 7284 6466 **e** lastname.firstname@mtvne.com **w** mtv.co.uk 📇 Director Of Music Programming & Artist Relations: Matt Cook.

MusFlashTV Brycbox House, Cocks Crescent, New Malden, Surrey, KT3 4TA **t** 020 8336 2100 **f** 020 8605 0744 **e** enquires@musflashtv.com **w** musflashtv.com 📇 Chairman & MD: Barry Evans.

Music Box 30 Sackville Street, London, W1X 1DB **t** 020 7478 7300 **f** 020 7478 7403 **e** reception@sunsetvine.co.uk **w** music-bx.co.uk 📇 MD: John Leach.

NBC News Worldwide 200 Grays Inn Rd, London, WC1X 8XZ **t** 020 7843 8777 **e** london.newsdesk@nbc.com 📇 Contact: David Rudge/Cheryll Simpson.

BBC North BBC Broadcasting Centre, Woodhouse Lane, Leeds, West Yorkshire, LS2 9PX **t** 0113 244 1188 **f** 0113 243 9387 **e** look.north@bbc.co.uk **w** bbc.co.uk/england/looknorthyorkslincs

BBC North West New Broadcasting House, Oxford Road, Manchester, M60 1SJ **t** 0161 200 2020 **f** 0161 236 1005 **e** nwt@bbc.co.uk **w** bbc.co.uk/england/northwesttonight

BBC Northern Ireland Ormeau Avenue, Belfast, Co Antrim, BT2 8HQ **t** 028 9033 8000 **f** 028 9033 8800 **w** bbc.co.uk/northernireland

Oasis TV 6-7 Great Pulteney Street, London, W1R 3DF **t** 020 7434 4133 **f** 020 7494 2843 **e** sales@oasistv.co.uk **w** oasistv.co.uk 📇 Buisness Dev't Mgr: Matthew Lock.

Off the Radar TV Ltd 20-22 Rosebery Avenue, London, EC1R 4SX **t** 020 7520 8340 **e** Patrick@offtheradar.tv **w** OfftheRadar.tv 📇 Commercial Manager: Patrick Usmar.

Pearson Television Ltd 1 Stephen Street, London, W1P 1PJ **t** 020 7691 6000 **f** 020 7691 6100 **e** facilites.helpdesk@fremental.com **w** pearsontv.com

The Pop Factory / Avanti Television Welsh Hills Works, Jenkin St, Porth, CF39 9PP **t** 01443 688500 **f** 01443 688501 **e** info@thepopfactory.com **w** thepopfactory.com 📇 Contact: Emyr Afan Davies.

Remedy Productions Office 6, 9 Thorpe Close, London, W10 5XL **t** 020 8964 4408 **f** 020 8964 4421 **e** info@remedyproductions.tv **w** remedyproductions.tv 📇 MD: Toby Dormer.

Rogue 2-3 Bourlet Close, London, W1W 7BQ **t** 020 7907 1000 **f** 020 7907 1001 **e** charlie@roguefilms.co.uk **w** roguefilms.com 📇 MD: Charlie Crompton.

RTE (Radio-Telefis Eireann) Donnybrook, Dublin 4, Ireland **t** +353 1 208 3111 **f** +353 1 208 3080 **e** webmaster@rte.ie **w** rte.ie

RTE Network 2 Donnybrook, Dublin 4, Ireland **t** +353 1 208 3111 **f** +353 1 208 2511 **e** television@rte.ie **w** rte.ie

RTE TG4 Donnybrook, Dublin 4, Ireland **t** +353 1 208 3111 **f** +353 1 208 2511 **w** tg4.ie/tg4.htm

S4C (Sianel Pedwar Cymru) Parc Ty Glas, Llanishen, Cardiff, South Glamorgan, CF4 5DU **t** 029 2074 7444 **f** 029 2074 1457 **e** hotline@s4c.co.uk **w** s4c.co.uk

SixTV The Oxford Channel 270 Woodstock Rd, Oxford, OX2 7NW **t** 01865 557000 **f** 01865 553355 **e** ptv@oxfordchannel.com **w** sixtv.co.uk 📇 Producer: Tom Copeland.

Sky Box Office Skt Television, Unit 2, Grant Way, Isleworth, Middlesex, TW7 5QD **t** 020 7805 8126 **f** 020 7805 8130 **e** marc.conneely@bskyb.com **w** sky.com 📇 Hd of Pay-Per-View Events: Marc Conneely.

Sky Music Channels Unit 4, Grant Way, Isleworth, Middlesex, TW7 5QD **t** 020 7805 8526 **f** 020 7805 8522 **e** Ian.Greaves@bskyb.com 📇 Music Programming Manager: Ian Greaves.

BBC South Havelock Road, Southampton, Hampshire, SO1 0XQ **t** 023 8022 6201 **f** 023 8033 9931 **e** spotlight@bbc.co.uk **w** bbc.co.uk

BBC South West Broadcasting House, Seymour Road, Plymouth, Devon, PL3 5DB **t** 01752 229201 **f** 01752 234595 **e** spotlight@bbc.co.uk **w** bbc.co.uk/england/spotlight 📇 Press Office: Marlene Crawley 01752 234545.

Southampton Television Sir James Mathews Building, 157-187 Above Bar St, Southampton, SO14 7NN **t** 023 8023 2400 **f** 023 8038 6366 **e** James.Rostance@southamptontv.co.uk **w** southamptontv.co.uk 📇 Producer, Music & Ent.: James Rostance.

Sub.tv Music 140 Buckingham Palace Road, London, SW1W 9SA **t** 020 78812578 **e** music@sub.tv **w** sub.tv/music 📇 Contact: Matthew Baker 07886 193 070.

T4 At It Productions, Westbourne Studios, 242 Acklam Rd, London, W10 5YG **t** 020 88964 2122 **f** 020 8964 2133 **e** lindsey.brill@atitproductions.com 📇 Entertainment Booker: Lindsey Brill.

Tiscali TV 20 Broadwick St, London, W1F 8HT **t** 020 7087 2016 **f** 020 7087 2016 **e** lyall.sumner@uk.tiscali.com **w** tiscali.co.uk 📇 Head of Tiscali TV, Film & Music: Lyall Sumner 02070872016.

Tyne Tees Television Centre, City Road, Newcastle upon Tyne, Tyne and Wear, NE1 2AL **t** 0191 261 0181 **f** 0191 269 3770 **e** news@tynetees.tv **w** itvregions.com/Tyne_Tees

UTV (Ulster Television) Havelock House, Ormeau Road, Belfast, Co Antrim, BT7 1EB **t** 028 9032 8122 **f** 028 9024 6695 **w** utvlive.com 📇 Contact: 028 9026 2220.

Videotech 131-151 Great Titchfield St., London, W1W 5BB **t** 020 7665 8200 **f** 020 7665 8213 📇 Producer: Diana Smith.

BBC Wales Broadcasting House, Meirion Road, Bangor, LL57 3BY **t** 01248 370880 **f** 01248 352784 **e** feedback.wales@bbc.co.uk **w** bbc.co.uk/wales

WAM TV (Worldart Media Television Ltd) 1 High St, Lasswade, Midlothian, EH18 1NA **t** 0131 654 2372 **e** contact@wam.tv **w** wam.tv 📇 MD: Paul Blyth.

Whizz Kid Entertainment 4 Kingly St, London, W1B 5PE **t** 020 7440 2550 **f** 020 7440 2599 **e** info@whizzkid.tv **w** whizzkid.tv 📇 Chief Executive: Malcolm Gerrie.

Yorkshire Television Ltd Television Centre, Leeds, West Yorkshire, LS3 1JS **t** 0113 243 8283 **f** 0113 244 5107 **w** yorkshiretv.co.uk 📇 MD: David Croft.

Media: Broadcast Services

Broadcast Services

Aimimage Unit 5, St. Pancras Commercial Centre, 63 Pratt St, London, NW1 0BY **t** 020 7482 4340 **f** 020 7267 3972 **e** hire@aimimage.com **w** aimimage.com ✉ Production Manager: Atif Ghani.

Alice Unit 34D, Hobbs Ind Estate, Newchapel, Lingfield, Surrey, RH7 6HN **t** 01342 833500 **f** 01342 833350 **e** sales@alice.co.uk **w** alice.co.uk ✉ Sales Director: Garry Thompson.

Arcadia Production Music (UK) Greenlands, Payhembury, Devon, EX14 3HY **t** 01404 841601 **f** 01404 841687 **e** admin@arcadiamusic.tv **w** arcadiamusic.tv ✉ Prop: John Brett.

Audio Systems Components Ltd 1 Comet House, Calleva Park, Aldermaston, Berkshire, RG7 8JB **t** 0118 981 1000 **f** 0118 981 9813 **e** sales@ascuk.com **w** ascuk.com ✉ Contact: Iain Elliott 0118 981 9565.

Audionics 31 Jessops Riverside, Sheffield, South Yorkshire, S9 2RX **t** 0114 242 2333 **f** 0114 243 3913 **e** info@audionics.co.uk **w** audionics.co.uk ✉ Director: Phil Myers.

Audionics Ltd Petre Drive, Sheffield, S4 7PZ **t** 0114 242 2333 **f** 0114 243 3913 **e** online@audionics.co.uk **w** audionics.co.uk ✉ Production Director: Phil Myers.

Blur 1 Ltd 166 Regent's Pk Rd, Primrose Hill, London, NW1 8XN **t** 020 7483 1767 **e** info@blur1.com **w** blur1.com ⨍ Sarahjane Gabb ✉ Dir: Sarahjane Gabb 07958 629658.

British Forces Broadcasting Service Chalfont Grove, Narcot Lane, Chalfont St Peter, Gerrards Cross, Bucks, SL9 8TN **t** 01494 878 354 **f** 01494 870 552 **e** admin.officer@bfbs.com **w** ssvc.com ✉ General Manager: Kal Sutherland.

Calrec Audio Ltd Nutclough Mill, Hebden Bridge, West Yorkshire, HX7 8EZ **t** 01422 842159 **f** 01422 845244 **e** enquiries@calrec.com **w** calrec.com ✉ Sales & Mkting Dir: John Gluck.

Paul Chantler - Radio Programming Consultant 52 South Block, County Hall, Westminster, London, SE1 7GB **t** 07788 584 888 **e** chantler@aol.com **w** paulchantler.com ✉ MD: Paul Chantler.

Churches Media Council Box 6613, South Woodham Ferrers, Essex, CM3 5DY **t** 01245 322158 **f** 01245 321957 **e** office@churchesmediacouncil.org.uk **w** churchesmediacouncil.org.uk ✉ Dir: Peter Blackman.

Community Media Asociation The Workstation, 15 Paternoster Row, Sheffield, S1 2BX **t** 0114 279 5219 **f** 0114 279 8976 **e** cma@commedia.org.uk **w** commedia.org.uk ✉ Contact: Diane Reid.

Compact Collections Ltd Greenland Place, 115-123 Bayham Street, London, NW1 0AG **t** 020 7446 7420 **f** 020 7446 7424 **e** info@compactcollections.com **w** compactcollections.com ✉ Dirs: John O'Sullivan, James Sellar.

delicious digital Suite GB, 39-40 Warple Way, Acton, London, W3 0RG **t** 020 8749 7272 **f** 020 8749 7474 **e** info@deliciousdigital.com **w** deliciousdigital.com ✉ Dirs: Ollie Raphael, Ed Moris.

Digital One 33-34 Alfred Pl, London, WC1E 7DP **t** 020 7299 8670 **f** 020 7299 8671 **e** info@digitalone.co.uk **w** ukdigitalradio.com

DMX Music Ltd Forest Lodge, Westerham Road, Keston, Kent, BR2 6HE **t** 01689 882 200 **f** 01689 882 288 **e** vanessa.warren@dmxmusic.com **w** dmxmusic.co.uk ✉ Marketing Manager: Vanessa Warren.

Doctor Rock The Century, 2 A Newlands Rd, Waterlooville, Hampshire, PO7 5NF **t** 023 9225 4426 **e** bob.woodhead@hotmail.co.uk ✉ Producer/Presenter/Pop-Historian: Bob Woodhead.

Done and Dusted 2nd Floor, 151 Wardour Street, London, W1F 8WE **t** 020 7297 8060 **f** 020 7494 3067 **e** lou@doneanddusted.com **w** doneanddusted.com ✉ Producer: Louise Fox.

DT Productions Maygrove House, 67 Maygrove Rd, London, NW6 2SP **t** 020 7644 8888 **f** 020 7644 8889 **e** info@dtproductions.co.uk **w** dtproductions.co.uk ✉ Music Programming: Lee Taylor.

DTP Radio Production Studios 35 Tower Way, Dunkeswell, Devon, EX14 4XH **t** 01404 891598 ✉ MD: Don Todd MBE.

Eagle Media Productions Russell House, Ely Street, Stratford-upon-Avon, Warwickshire, CV37 6LW **t** 01789 415 187 **f** 01789 415 210 **e** amy@eaglemp.co.uk **w** eagle-rock.com ✉ MD: Alan Ravenscroft.

EAGLE ROCK ENTERTAINMENT LTD.

eagle vision

Eagle House, 22 Armoury Way, London, SW18 1EZ **t** 020 8870 5670 **f** 020 8874 2333 **e** mail@eagle-rock.com **w** eagle-rock.com 🎦 youtube/eaglerocktv ✉ Executive Chairman: Terry Shand.

Entertainment Media Research Studio One, Charter House, Crown Court, London, WC2B 5EX **t** 020 7240 1222 **f** 020 7240 8877 **e** patrick.johnston@entertainmentmediaresearch.com **w** entertainmentmediaresearch.com ✉ Dir of Business Devt.: Patrick Johnston.

Contacts Facebook MySpace Twitter  YouTube

FASTRAX

Allan House, 10 John Princes St, London, W1G 0JW
t 020 7468 6888 **f** 020 7468 6889 **e** fastrax@imdplc.com
w fastrax.co.uk ✉ Contact: Rupak Rahman, Gareth Howells,
Laurien Gloag, Lucy Dowland.

Feltwain 2000 42 Lytton Road, Barnet, Middx, EN5 5BY
t 020 8950 8732 **f** 020 8950 6648
e paul.lynton@btopenworld.com ✉ MD: Paul Lynton.

Festival Productions PO Box 107, Brighton,
East Sussex, BN1 1QG **t** 01273 669595 **f** 01273 669596
e post@festivalradio.com **w** festivalradio.com ✉ MD: Steve
Stark.

Freeway Press 20 Windmill Rd, Kirkcaldy, Fife, KY1 3AQ
t 01592 655309 **f** 01592 596177 **e** cronulla20@aol.com
w freewaypress.co.uk ✉ Dir: John Murray 07973 920 488.

Ignite Creative TV 90 Red Square, London, N16 9AG
t 020 7502 2370 **e** info@ignitecreative.tv
w ignitecreative.tv ✉ Multi Media Producer: Kary Stewart.

Immedia Broadcasting 7-9 The Broadway, Newbury,
Berks, RG14 1AS **t** 01635 572 800 **f** 01635 572 801
e customerservices@immediabroadcasting.com
w immediabroadcasting.com ✉ Office Mgr: Lesley Pye.

Independent Television News (ITN)
200 Grays Inn Road, London, WC1X 8XZ **t** 020 7833 3000
f 020 7430 4016 **e** press.office@itn.co.uk **w** itn.co.uk
✉ Contact: Press Office.

ITV Network Centre Ltd 200 Gray's Inn Road,
London, WC1X 8HF **t** 020 7843 8000 **f** 020 7843 8158
w itv.co.uk

Karen P Productions Ltd PO Box 52160, London,
E9 7WR **t** 020 8986 8558 **e** karen@karenpproductions.com
w karenp.co.uk ✉ Dir: Karen Pearson.

Medialane International The Old Garage, The Green,
Great Milton, Oxford, Oxfordshire, OX44 7NP
t 01844 278534 **f** 01844 278538 **e** stratton@medialane-
international.com **w** medialane-international.com
✉ Managing Director: Alan Stratton.

MetrobroadcastLtd 53 Great Suffolk Street, London,
SE1 0DB **t** 020 7202 2000 **f** 020 7202 2005
e info@metrobroadcast.com **w** metrobroadcast.com
✉ Director: Paul Braybrooke.

Musicpoint Andrews House, College Road, Guildford,
Surrey, GU1 4QB **t** 01483 510 910 **f** 01483 510 911
e info@musicpointuk.com **w** musicpointuk.com ✉ Business
Development Mgr: Richard Clark.

Neon - Rab Noakes Studio Two, 19 Marine Crescent,
Kinning Pk, Glasgow, G51 1HD **t** 0141 429 6366
f 0141 429 6377 **e** stephy@go2neon.com **w** go2neon.com
✉ Production Manager: Stephanie Pordage.

Nielsen Music Control 5th Floor, Endeavour House,
189 Shaftesbury Avenue, London, WC2H 8TJ
t 020 7420 9292 **f** 020 7420 9295
e info@nielsenmusiccontrol.com
w nielsenmusiccontrol.com ✉ Managing Director, Nielsen
Music Control: Jean Littolff.

Nielsen Music Control (Ireland) Top Floor,
6 Clare St, Dublin 2, Ireland **t** +353 1 605 0686
f +353 1 678 5343 **e** f.byrne@nielsenmusiccontrol.com
w myspace.com/musiccontrolireland ✉ GM: Feidhlim Byrne.

Outerglobe (ACL) Media London
e outerglobe@yahoo.co.uk ✉ Contact: DebbieOuterglobe
+447939564103.

Outerglobe African Caribbean Oriental London
e outerglobe@yahoo.co.uk ✉ Contact: DebbieOuterglobe
+447939564103.

Outerglobe Media London **e** outerglobe@yahoo.co.uk
✉ Contact: DebbieOuterglobe +447939564103.

Paul Sexton 117 Grove Rd, Sutton, Surrey, SM1 2DB
t 020 8661 2603 **f** 020 8661 2603
e psexton@blueyonder.co.uk ✉ Contact: Paul Sexton.

PPL VIDEO STORE (MUSIC MALL)

1 Upper James St, London, W1F 9DE **t** 020 7534 1444
f 020 7534 1367 **e** videostore@ppluk.com **w** ppluk.com ✉
Chairman & CEO: Fran Nevrkla. Executive Director: Peter
Leathem. Director of Licensing: Tony Clark. Director of HR &
Facilities: Janice Davies. Director of Performer Affairs: Keith
Harris. Director of IT: Frank Jaschinski. Finance Director: Ben
Lambert. Director of Government Relations: Dominic
McGonigal. Director of PR & Corporate
Communications: Jonathan Morrish. Production
Manager: Suzanne Willems.
**PPL Video Store (formerly Music Mall) provides copies
of music videos to major broadcasters, production
companies and businesses providing video jukeboxes,
music systems and video on demand services.**

Q Sheet Markettiers4dc, Northburgh House,
10a Northburgh St, London, EC1V 0AT **t** 020 7253 8888
f 020 7253 8885 **e** editor@qsheet.com **w** qsheet.com
✉ Music Editor: Nik Harta.

Radica Broadcast Systems Ltd
18 Bolney Grange Industrial Pk, Hickstead, Haywards Heath,
West Sussex, RH17 5PB **t** 01444 258285 **f** 01444 258288
e sales@radica.com **w** radica.com/radio ✉ Sales
Mgr: Graham Sloggett.

The Radio Advertising Bureau
77 Shaftesbury Avenue, London, W1D 5DU
t 020 3206 7800 **f** 020 7306 2505 **e** lucy@radiocentre.org
w radiocentre.org ✉ twitter.com/radiocentre ✉ Station
Liaison Officer: Lucy Forster.

RAJAR (Radio Joint Audience Research)
Paramount House, 162-170 Wardour St, London, W1F 8ZX
t 020 7292 9040 **f** 020 7292 9041 **e** info@rajar.co.uk
w rajar.co.uk 📧 MD: Sally de la Bedoyere.

Ricall Limited First Floor, 14 Buckingham Palace Road,
London, SW1W 0QP **t** 020 7592 1710 **f** 020 7592 1713
e mail@ricall.com **w** ricall.com 📧 Founder & CEO: Richard
Corbett.

RTÉ Lyric FM Cornmarket Sq, Limerick, Ireland
t +353 61 207300 **f** +353 61 207390 **e** lyric@rte.ie
w rte.ie/lyricfm 📧 Station Mgr/Prog Dir: Aodan O Dubhghaill.

Satellite Media Services Lawford Heath Teleport,
Lawford Heath Lane, Rugby, Warwickshire, CV23 9EU
t 01788 523000 **f** 01788 523001 **e** sales@sms-
internet.net **w** sms-internet.net 📧 MD: Tim Whittingham.

Straight TV Limited 4th Floor, 121 Princess Street,
Manchester, M1 7AG **t** 0161 200 6000 **f** 0161 228 0228
e info@straight.tv **w** straight.tv 📧 Contact: Clare Winnick.

Student Radio Association c/o The Radio Academy,
5 Market Pl, London, W1W 8AE **t** 07092 845935
f 020 7255 2029 **e** chair@studentradio.org.uk
w studentradio.org.uk
📘 facebook.com/home.php#/studentradio?ref=ts
📧 twitter.com/SRA 📧 Chair: Tim Dye.

Talk Of The Devil 5 Ripley Rd, Worthing, West Sussex,
BN11 5NQ **t** 01903 526515 **f** 01903 539634
e steve.power@talk-of-the-devil.com **w** talk-of-the-
devil.com 📧 MD: Steve Power.

TotalRock 1-6 Denmark Place, London, WC2H 8NL
t 020 7240 6665 **e** info@totalrock.com **w** totalrock.com
📧 Head of Music: Tony Wilson.

Transorbital Productions 557 Street Lane, Leeds,
West Yorkshire, LS17 6JA **t** 0113 268 7886
f 0113 266 0045 **e** carl@carlkingston.co.uk
w carlkingston.co.uk 📧 MD: Carl Kingston 07836 568 888.

**Unique Facilities (Location Broadcasting
Services)** 50 Lisson St, London, NW1 5DF
t 020 7723 0322 **f** 020 7453 1666
e info@uniquefacilities.com **w** uniquefacilities.com
📧 Facilities Mgr: Shane Wall.

Victoria Radio Network PO Box 1287, Kirkcaldy, Fife,
KY2 5ZX **t** 01592 268530 **e** info@vrn1287.com
w vrn1287.com 📧 Group Programme Director: Colin
Johnston.

The Video Pool 99A Linden Gardens, London, W2 4EX
t 020 7221 3803 **f** 020 7221 3280 **e** roz@videopool.com
w videopool.com 📧 MD: Roz Bea.

VIP Broadcasting 8 Bunbury Way, Epsom, Surrey,
KT17 4JP **t** 01372 721196 **e** cv@vipbroadcasting.co.uk
w vipbroadcasting.co.uk 📧 MD: Chris Vezey.

Vision Community Radio London **t** 07939 564 103
e visionradioltd@gmail.com 📧 Contact: Debbie Dunkwu
07939564103.

The Vocal Booth Toxteth TV, 37-45 Windsor St,
Liverpool, L8 1XE **t** 0151 707 2833 **f** 0151 707 2833
e mike.moran@thevocalbooth.com **w** thevocalbooth.com
📧 myspace.com/thevocalbooth 📧 Producer: Mike Moran
07800 993 192.

Advertising Agencies

A&GSYNC

1st Floor, 5 Ching Court, 61-63 Monmouth Street, London,
WC2H 9EY **t** 020 7845 9880 **f** 020 7845 9884
e roy@agsyncmusic.com **w** agsyncmusic.com 📧 Managing
Director: Roy Jackson.

Abbott Mead Vickers BBDO 151 Marylebone Road,
London, NW1 5QE **t** 020 7616 3500 **f** 020 7616 3580
e linseyf@amvbbdo.com **w** amvbbdo.com 📧 Hd of TV
Department: Francine Linsey.

ArtScience Limited 3-5 Hardwidge St, London,
SE1 3SY **t** 020 7939 9500 **f** 020 7939 9499
e lab5@artscience.net **w** artscience.net 📧 Dirs: Douglas
Coates, Pete Rope.

Bartle Bogle Hegarty 60 Kingly Street, London,
W1B 5DS **t** 020 7734 1677 **f** 020 7437 3666
e firstname.lastname@bbh.co.uk **w** bbh.co.uk

BBA Active Ltd Studio 3, 62 Muswell Hill Road, London,
N10 3JR **t** 020 8883 7635 **e** bba@bbagenius.com
w bbagenius.com 📧 MD: Stephen Benjamin.

BLM Group Eagle House, 50 Marshall St, London,
W1F 9BQ **t** 020 7437 1317 **f** 020 7437 1287
e info@blm.co.uk **w** blm.co.uk

Brotherhood Media 4th Floor, 52-53 Margaret St,
London, W1W 8SQ **t** 020 7631 9200 **e** info@brotherhood-
media.co.uk **w** brotherhood-media.co.uk 📧 Dirs: James
Heighway, Dom Murphy.

Leo Burnett Ltd Warwick Building, Kensington Village,
Avonmore Rd, London, W14 8HQ **t** 020 7751 1800
f 020 7348 3855 **e** firstname.lastname@leoburnett.co.uk
w leoburnett.com

CDP-Travis Sully 9 Lower John Street, London,
W1F 9DZ **t** 020 7437 4224 **f** 020 7437 5445
e melodyrichards@cdplondon.com **w** cdp-travissully.com
📧 Office Manager: Melody Richards.

The Clinic 32-38 Saffron Hill, London, EC1N 8FH
t 020 7421 9333 **f** 020 7421 9334
e firstname.lastname@clinic.co.uk **w** clinic.co.uk 📧 Creative
Dir: David Dragan.

Contacts Facebook MySpace Twitter YouTube

CMS MUSIC MEDIA LTD

CMS**MUSICMEDIA**Ltd

29 Central Parade, St Marks Hill, Surbiton, Surrey, KT6 4PJ
t 020 8390 6458 **f** 020 8390 6458 **e** info@cms-music.co.uk **w** cms-music.co.uk MD: Ian Compton.

Cranham Advertising Suite 1, Essex House, Station Road, Upminster, Essex, RM14 2SJ **t** 01708 641164 **f** 01708 220030 **e** cranham@globalnet.co.uk

Creative Marketing Services Hollinthorpe Hall, Swillington Lane, Leeds, LS26 8BZ **t** 0844 412 2688 **f** 0844 412 2699 **e** mail@cmsadvertising.co.uk **w** cmsadvertising.co.uk Contact: Andrew Batty FCIM.

Cunning 192 St John Street, London, EC1V 4JY **t** 020 7566 5300 **e** info@cunning.com **w** cunning.com MD: Anna Carloss.

Da Costa & Co 9 Gower Street, London, WC1E 6HA **t** 020 7916 3791 **f** 020 7916 3799 **e** nickdc@dacosta.co.uk **w** dacosta.co.uk

DDB London 12 Bishops Bridge Road, London, W2 6AA **t** 020 7258 3979 **f** 020 7402 4871 **e** firstname.lastname@ddblondon.com **w** ddblondon.com Business Development Manager: Philip Heimann.

Delaney Lund Knox Warren 25 Wellington Street, London, WC2E 7DA **t** 020 7836 3474 **f** 020 7240 8739 **e** info@dlkw.co.uk **w** dlkw.co.uk

The Design & Advertising Resource 7 Kings Wharf, 301 Kingsland Road, Hoxton, London, E8 4DS **t** 020 7254 3191 **f** 0870 442 5297 **e** info@your-resource.co.uk **w** your-resource.co.uk Account Director: Richard Fearn.

Dewynters 48 Leicester Square, London, WC2H 7QD **t** 020 7321 0488 **f** 020 7321 0104 **e** info@dewynters.com **w** dewynters.com Client Management: Richard Abba.

Diabolical Liberties 1 Bayham St, London, NW1 0ER **t** 020 7916 5483 **f** 020 7916 5482 **e** sales@diabolical.co.uk **w** diabolical.co.uk General Manager: Michael Chesters.

Different Ltd 10 Summerhill Terrace, Summerhill Square, Newcastle upon Tyne, NE4 6EB **t** 0191 261 0111 **f** 0191 221 1122 **e** dreid@different-uk.com **w** different-uk.com Producer: David Reid.

DKA 87 New Cavendish St, London171-177 Great Portland S, W1W 6XD **t** 020 7467 7300 **f** 020 7467 7380 **e** enquiries@dka.uk.com **w** dka.uk.com

Eat Your Greens - Brand Sponsorship Consultants 11 Cleves Way, Hampton, Middlesex, TW12 2PL **t** 020 8487 0394 **e** info@eatyourgreens.ltd.uk **w** eatyourgreens.ltd.uk MD: Denzil Thomas.

Euro RSCG London Cupola House, 15 Alfred Place, London, WC1E 7EB **t** 020 7467 9200 **f** 020 7467 9210 **e** infouk@eurorscg.com **w** eurorscglondon.co.uk

Lee Golding Advertising and Communications Ltd Edinburgh House, 40 Great Portland Street, London, W1W 7LZ **t** 020 7436 7910 **f** 020 7636 6091 **e** carol@leegolding.co.uk Contact: Carol Golding 020 7436 7978.

Grey London The Johnson Building, 77 Hatton Garden, London, EC1N 8JS **t** 020 3037 3000 **e** firstname.lastname@greyeu.com **w** grey.co.uk Contact: Sue Northcott.

Hive Associates Ltd Bewlay House, 2 Swallow Place, London, W1B 2AE **t** 020 7664 0480 **f** 020 7664 0481 **e** consult@hiveassociates.co.uk **w** hiveassociates.co.uk Account Director: Alex Moss.

JJ Stereo Unit 14, Barley Shotts Business Park, 246 Acklam Road, London, W10 5YG **t** 020 8969 5444 **f** 020 8969 5544 **e** info@jjstereo.com **w** jjstereo.com Directors: Ruth Paveley and John Paveley.

John Boddy Agency LLP 10 Southfield Gardens, Twickenham, Middlesex, TW1 4SZ **t** 020 8892 0133 **f** 020 8892 4283 **e** jba@johnboddyagency.co.uk **w** johnboddyagency.co.uk Partner: John Boddy 020 8891 3809.

Lavery Rowe 69-71 Newington Causeway, London, SE1 6BD **t** 020 7378 1780 **f** 020 7407 4612 **e** sales@laveryrowe.co.uk

Leagas Delaney 1 Alfred Place, London, WC1E 7EB **t** 020 7758 1758 **f** 020 7758 1760 **e** infouk@leagasdelaney.com **w** leagasdelaney.com

The Leith Agency 37 The Shore, Leith, Edinburgh, EH6 6QU **t** 0131 561 8600 **f** 0131 561 8601 **e** p.adams@leith.co.uk **w** leith.co.uk MD: Phil Adams.

The London Advertising Partnership 61-63 Portobello Road, london, W11 3DB **t** 020 7229 9755 **f** 020 7229 6720 **e** london_ad@btinternet.com MD: Simon Dodds.

Lowe & Partners Bowater House, 3rd Floor, 68-114 Knightsbridge, London, SW1X 7LT **t** 020 7584 5033 **f** 020 7581 9027 **e** info@loweworldwide.com **w** loweworldwide.com

M&C Saatchi 36 Golden Square, London, W1F 9EE **t** 020 7543 4689 **f** 020 7543 4501 **e** firstnameinitialofsurname@mcsaatchi.com **w** mcsaatchi.com/sportandentertainment Sponsorship & Events: Georgia Terzis.

Matters Media Ltd 1st Floor, 146 Marylebone Rd, London, NW1 5PH **t** 020 7224 6030 **f** 020 7224 6010 **e** mark@mattersmedia.co.uk Contact: Mark Riley.

McCann-Erickson 7-11 Herbrand St, London, WC1N 1EX **t** 020 7837 3737 **f** 020 7837 3773 **e** firstname.lastname@europe.mccann.com **w** mccann.com

McConnells McConnell House, Charlemont Place, Dublin, Ireland **t** +353 1 478 1544 **f** +353 1 478 0224 **e** firstname.lastname@mcconnells.ie **w** mcconnells.ie Contact: John Fanning.

Media: Advertising Agencies

Mearns & Gill Advertising Ltd 7 Carden Place, Aberdeen, Grampian, AB10 1PP **t** 01224 646311 **f** 01224 631882 **e** alan@mearns-gill.com **w** mearns-gill.net

Media Campaign Services - MCS
20 Orange Street, London, WC2H 7EW **t** 020 7389 0800 **f** 020 7839 6997 **e** dwoods@mediacampaign.co.uk **w** mediacampaign.co.uk Contact: David Woods.

Media Junction 40a Old Compton St, Soho, London, W1D 4TU **t** 020 7434 9919 **f** 020 7439 0794 **e** mailbox@mediajunction.co.uk **w** mediajunction.co.uk MD: Giles Cooper.

Mediacom TED The Entertainment Division, 124 Theobalds Rd, London, WC1X 8RX **t** 020 7874 5500 **f** 020 7874 5999 **e** jane.ratcliffe@mediacom.com **w** mediacomuk.com Chief Executive Officer: Jane Ratcliffe.

Mediamix - Media planning, buying & consultancy 107 Mortlake High St, London, SW14 8HQ **t** 020 8392 6885 **f** 020 8392 6803 **e** info@themediamix.co.uk MD: David Collins.

MJ Media 97 Charlotte Street, London, W1T 4QA **t** 020 7467 9700 **f** 020 7467 9701 **e** reception@mjmedia.co.uk **w** mjmedia.co.uk Account Director: Matt Fuller.

Nick Pease Jingles and Copywriting Services
290 Elgin Avenue, Maida Vale, London, W9 1JS **t** 020 7286 8181 **f** 020 7286 8181 **e** nickpease@btconnect.com **w** misterdojingles.co.uk MD: Nick Pease.

Ogilvy Primary Contact 5 Theobald's Rd, London, WC1X 8SH **t** 020 7468 6900 **f** 020 7468 6950 **e** firstname.lastname@primary.co.uk **w** primary.co.uk MD: Gareth Richards.

Pawson Media 207 High Holborn, London, WC1V 7BW **t** 020 7405 9080 **f** 020 7831 7391 **e** mail@pawson-media.co.uk Media Director: David Cecil.

PD Communications The Business Village, Broomhill Road, London, SW18 4JQ **t** 020 8871 5033 **f** 020 8871 5034 **e** sales@pdcom.net **w** pdcom.net Creative Dir: Peter Saag.

Probe Media 2nd Floor, The Hogarth Centre, Hogarth Lane, London, W4 2QN **t** 020 8742 3636 **f** 020 8995 1350 **e** sanjay@probemedia.co.uk **w** probemedia.co.uk Account Director: Sanjay Vadher.

Profound Media & Management Ltd
PO Box 4222, Coventry, CV4 0BH **t** 024 7667 7712 **e** info@profoundmedia.co.uk **w** profoundmedia.co.uk Dir: Paul Flower.

Publicis Ltd 82 Baker Street, London, W1M 2AE **t** 020 7935 4426 **f** 020 7487 5351 **e** re-fresh@publicis.co.uk **w** publicis.co.uk

Purple Frog The Threshing Barn, North Weston, Thame, Oxon, OX9 2HA **t** 01844 295170 **f** 01844 260696 **e** more@purplefrog.co.uk **w** purplefrog.co.uk purple frog purplefroguk Managing Director: David Finch.

QRBT Ltd Great Guildford Business Sq, 30 Great Guildford St, London, SE1 0HS **t** 020 7921 9292 **f** 020 7921 9342 **e** qrbt@qrbt.com **w** qrbt.com

Rainey, Kelly, Camppbell, Rolfe/Y&R
Greater London House, Hampstead Road, London, NW1 7QP **t** 020 7387 9366 **f** 020 7611 6570 **e** firstname_lastname@uk.yr.com **w** rkcryr.com

Ramp Industry Studio 242, Bon Marche Centre, 241-251 Ferndale Rd, London, SW9 8BJ **t** 020 7326 0345 **e** andy@rampindustry.com **w** rampindustry.com Managing Partner: Andy Crysell.

Robertson Saxby Associates Standard House, 107-115 Eastmoor Street, London, SE7 8LX **t** 020 8858 3202 **f** 020 8853 2103 **e** dresource@aol.com Contact: Dick Saxby.

Rowleys:London One Port Hill, Hertford, Hertfordshire, SG14 1PJ **t** 01992 587 350 **e** annie@rowleyslondon.co.uk **w** rowleyslondon.co.uk MD: Annie Rowley.

Saatchi & Saatchi plc 80 Charlotte St, London, W1A 1AQ **t** 020 7636 5060 **f** 020 7637 8489 **e** firstname.surname@saatchi.co.uk **w** saatchi-saatchi.com

Sarsaparilla Ltd 1 Lyric Square, London, W6 0NB **t** 020 7147 9960 **e** info@sarsaparillamarketing.com Contact: Kimberly Davis 0207 147 9960.

Skinny Unit B, 53 Underhill Road, London, SE22 0QR **t** 020 8693 8798 **e** info@skinnycreative.com **w** skinnycreative.com Director: Sonya Skinner.

Sold Out The Windsor Centre, 16-29 Windsor Street, London, N1 8QG **t** 020 7704 0409 **f** 020 7226 8249 **e** michelle@soldout.co.uk

St Luke's Communications Ltd 18 Dukes Rd, London, WC1H 9PY **t** 020 7380 8888 **f** 020 7380 8899 **e** initial+lastname@stlukes.co.uk **w** stlukes.co.uk

Target Media Fitzroy House, 11 Chenies Street, London, WC1E 7EY **t** 020 7907 1777 **f** 020 7907 1751 **e** info@target-media.co.uk **w** target-media.co.uk MD: Robert Wilkerson.

TCS Media 35 Garway Rd, London, W2 4QF **t** 020 7221 7292 **f** 020 7221 0460 **e** information@tcsmedia.co.uk **w** tcsmedia.com Dir: Mike Ashby.

J Walter Thompson Co Ltd 1 Knightsbridge Green, London, SW1X 7NW **t** 020 7656 7000 **f** 020 7656 7010 **e** firstname.lastname@jwt.com **w** jwtworld.com

TMD Carat 43-49 Parker St, London, WC2B 5PS **t** 020 7430 6000 **f** 020 7430 6299 **e** firstname_lastname@carat.co.uk **w** carat.com MD: Colin Mills.

TMP Worldwide Chancery House, 53-64 Chancery Lane, London, WC2A 1QS **t** 020 7406 5000 **f** 020 7406 5001 **e** firstname.lastname@tmp.com **w** tmpw.co.uk

Waxmans Ltd 56 St John St, London, EC1M 4HG **t** 020 7253 5500 **f** 020 7490 2387 **e** info@waxman.co.uk **w** waxman.co.uk Account Manager: Lorraine Wells.

Contacts   Facebook   MySpace   Twitter   YouTube

Wood Brigdale Nisbet & Robinson
Granville House, 132-135 Sloane Street, London, SW1X 9AX
t 020 7591 4800 **f** 020 7591 4801

Wunderman Greater London House, Hampstead Road,
London, NW1 7QP **t** 020 7611 6666 **f** 020 7611 6668
e firstname_lastname@uk.wunderman.com
w wunderman.com

Young Euro RSCG 64 Lower Leeson Street, Dublin 2,
Ireland **t** +353 1 614 5300 **f** +353 1 661 1992
e info@young-ad.ie **w** youngeurorscg.ie

Video Production

The 400 Company B3, The Workshops,
2A, Askew Crescent, London, W12 9DP **t** 020 8746 1400
e info@the400.co.uk **w** the400.co.uk ✉ Production
Manager: Christian Riou.

Abbey Road Studios 3 Abbey Rd, London, NW8 9AY
t 020 7266 7366 **f** 020 7266 7367
e videoservices@abbeyroad.com **w** abbeyroad.com
✉ Video Services Manager: Lucy Launder.

Agile Films Unit 1, 68-72 Redchurch Street, London,
E2 7DP **t** 020 7689 2373 **f** 020 7689 2374
e info@agilefilms.com **w** agilefilms.com ✉ Head of Music
Videos: Jo Rudolphy.

Angelic Films Ltd Block A, Commercial Square,
Leigh Street, High Wycombe, Bucks, HP11 2RH
t 0845 094 1138 **e** info@angelicfilms.co.uk
w angelicfilms.co.uk ✉ Producer: Adam Coop.

Autopsy Red Bus Studios, 34 Salisbury St, London,
NW8 8QE **t** 020 7724 2243 **f** 020 7724 2871
e info@crimson.globalnet.co.uk ✉ MD: Simon Crawley.

Banana Split Productions 11 Carlisle Road, London,
NW9 0HD **t** 020 8200 1234 **f** 020 8200 1121
e accounts@bananasplitprods.com **w** banana-split.com
✉ MD: Steve Kemsley.

The Big Yellow Feet Production Co. Ltd.
Dunley Hill Farm, Dorking, Surrey, RH5 6SX **t** 01483 285928
e greg@bigyellowfeet.com **w** bigyellowfeet.com
✉ Director: Gregory Mandry.

Black Dog Films Ltd 42-44 Beak St, London, W1F 9RH
t 020 7434 0787 **f** 020 7734 4978
e initial+surname@rsafilms.co.uk **w** blackdogfilms.com
✉ Rep: Svana Gisla.

Black Shark Media 11 Mascotte Road, London,
SW15 1NN **t** 020 8785 1557 **e** jk@blacksharkmedia.com
w blacksharkmedia.com ✉ Director: James Kibbey.

Blue Planet 96 York Street, London, W1H 1DP
t 020 7724 2267 **e** base@blueplanet.co.uk
✉ Contact: Bruce Robertson.

Bomdigi Productions 2 Duke's Rd, London, WC1H 9AD
t 07949 617863 **e** jo@bomdigi.com **w** bomdigi.com
✉ Multimedia Producer & Director: Jo Roach.

Box 5th floor, 121 Princess Street, Manchester, M1 7AD
t 0161 228 2399 **e** info@the-box.co.uk **w** the-box.co.uk
✉ Director: Mike Kirwin.

Camberwell Studios **t** 020 7737 0007
e andy.woodruff@camberwellstudios.co.uk
w camberwellstudios.co.uk

CC-Lab 5-6 Newman Passage, London, W1T 1EH
t 020 7580 8055 **f** 020 7637 8350 **e** info@cc-lab.com
w cc-lab.com ✉ Executive Producer: Jason Hocking & Justin
Rees.

CC-Lab 5-6 Newman Passage, London, W1T 1EH
t 020 7580 8055 **f** 020 7637 8350 **e** info@cc-lab.com
w cc-lab.com

Channel 20-20 20-20 House, 26-28 Talbot Lane,
Leicester, LE1 4LR **t** 0116 233 2220 **f** 0116 222 1113
e rob.potter@channel2020.co.uk **w** channel2020.co.uk
✉ CEO: Rob Potter.

Chrome Productions 37 Lonsdale Road, Queens Park,
London, NW6 6RA **t** 020 7644 1980 **f** 020 7624 4028
e info@chromeproductions.co.uk
w chromeproductions.co.uk ✉ Production Manager: Hannah
Chandler.

Cowboy Films 11-29 Smiths Court,
Great Windmill Street, London, W1D 7DP **t** 020 7287 3808
f 020 7287 3785 **e** info@cowboyfilms.co.uk
w cowboyfilms.co.uk ✉ Dir: Robert Bray.

Davey Inc. 20 Denmark St, London, WC2H 8NA
t 020 7209 0385 **f** 020 7209 0385 **e** gail@daveyinc.com
w daveyinc.com 📘 facebook.com/daveyinc
📷 myspace.com/daveyinc 🐦 twitter.com/daveyinc
📺 youtube.com/daveyinc ✉ Producer: Gail Davey 07795
220145.

Document Productions Ltd. 43 High St,
Market Harborough, Leics, LE16 7AQ **t** 01858 463758
f 0870 458 1686 **e** karen.craig@documentuk.com
w documentuk.com ✉ Production Manager: Karen Craig
07941 197937.

Done and Dusted 2nd Floor, 151 Wardour Street,
London, W1F 8WE **t** 020 7297 8060 **f** 020 7494 3067
e lou@doneanddusted.com **w** doneanddusted.com
✉ Producer: Louise Fox.

El Nino 32 Rue Des Jeûneurs, Paris, 75002
t +33 (0) 1 44 889 575 **e** jules@75.tv **w** elnino.tv ✉ Music
Video Producer: Jules Dieng.

Exceeda Films 110-116 Elmore Street, London, N1 3AH
t 020 7288 0433 **f** 020 7288 0735
e contact@exceeda.co.uk **w** exceeda.co.uk
✉ Producer: Sarah Davenport.

Factory Films 30 Bloomsbury St, London, WC1B 3QJ
t 020 7291 6130 **f** 020 7291 6140
e toby@factoryfilms.net **w** factoryfilms.net
📘 facebook.com/pages/London-United-Kingdom/Factory-
Films/138553609750?ref=ts ✉ Managing Director: Toby
Hyde.

Filmmaster Clip The Old Lampworks, Rodney Place,
London, SW19 2LQ **t** 07870 818 004
e luca.legnani@filmmaster.com **w** filmmaster.com ✉ UK
Representative: Luca Legnani.

Contacts   **Facebook**   **MySpace**   **Twitter**   **YouTube**

Fire House Productions 42 Glasshouse Street, London, W1B 5DW **t** 020 7439 2220 **f** 020 7439 2210 **e** postie@firehouse.biz **w** firehouse.biz **✉** MD: Julie-Anne Edwards.

Formosa Films Bridge House, 3 Mills Studios, Three Mill Lane, London, E3 3DU **t** 020 8709 8700 **f** 020 8709 8701 **e** info@formosafilms.com **w** formosafilms.com **✉** Producer: Neil Thompson 07973 165 942.

FreeAgent UK 1, Westbourne Studios, 242 Acklam Road, London, W10 5JJ **t** 020 7524 7577 **e** alexa@freeagent.uk.com **✉** MD: Alexa Haywood.

Gas & Electric Ltd 5B Camden Road, London, NW1 9LG **t** 020 7284 4800 **f** 020 7424 7277 **e** info@gasandelectric.co.uk **w** gasandelectric.co.uk **✉** MD: Jon Stephenson.

Glassworks 33-34 Great Poulteney Street, London, W1F 9NP **t** 020 7434 1182 **f** 020 7434 1183 **e** amanda@glassworks.co.uk **w** glassworks.co.uk **✉** Joint MD: Amanda Ryan.

Gorgeous Enterprises 11 Portland Mews, London, W1F 8JL **t** 020 7287 4060 **f** 020 7287 4994 **e** gorgeous@gorgeous.co.uk **w** gorgeous.co.uk **✉** MD: Paul Rothwell.

Great Guns Ltd 43-45 Camden Road, London, NW1 9LR **t** 020 7692 4444 **f** 020 7692 4422 **e** sheridan@greatguns.com **w** greatguns.com **✉** Prod Mgr: Sheridan Thomas.

Groovy Badger 284a Lee High Rd, London, SE13 5PJ **t** 07831 431 019 **f** 0870 124 5135 **e** info@groovybadger.com **w** groovybadger.com **✉** Dir: Sebastian Smith 07956 273 883.

Habana Productions PO Box 370, Newquay, TR8 5YZ **t** 01637 831 011 **f** 01637 831 037 **e** emmapaterson1@aol.com **✉** Manager: Emma Paterson.

Hangman Studios 111 Frithville Gardens, London, W12 7JQ **t** 020 8600 3440 **f** 020 8600 3401 **e** danielle@hangmanstudios.com **w** hangmanstudios.com **✉** Studio Mgr: Danielle Edwards.

High Barn Productions The Bardfield Centre, Great Bardfield, Braintree, Essex, CM7 4SL **t** 01371 811 291 **e** info@high-barn.com **w** high-barn.com **✉** MD: Chris Bullen.

HLA 35 Adam and Eve Mews, London, W8 6UG **t** 020 7299 1000 **f** 020 7299 1001 **e** mike@hla.net **w** hla.net **✉** Managing Director: Mike Wells.

The Hold 20 Craigs Park, Edinburgh, EH12 8UL **t** 0131 339 0164 **e** kris@thehold.co.uk **w** thehold.co.uk **✉** Director: Kris Bird.

Icast UK Ltd Film House, Top Floor, 142 Wardour St London, London, W1F 8ZU **t** 020 7434 2100 **e** gill@icast.uk.com **w** icast.uk.com **▣** myspace.com/icast **🅣** bestofmyspace **▶** /icast **✉** Director: Gill Mills 07970 488 179.

Ideas Redding House, Redding, Falkirk, FK2 9TR **t** 01324 716827 **f** 01324 716827 **e** inquiries@ideas.co.uk **w** ideas.co.uk **f** facebook.com/home.php#/DonJack?ref=profile **▣** profile.myspace.com/index.cfm?fuseaction=user.viewprofile&friendid=311602833 **▶** youtube.com/user/dodosticks **✉** Creative Director: Don Jack.

IMS Interactive Management Services Ltd Unit 19, Price St Business Centre, Birkenhead, Merseyside, CH41 4JQ **t** 0151 651 0100 **f** 0151 652 0077 **e** daveims@compuserve.com **w** heritagevideo.co.uk **✉** MD: David McWilliam.

Independent Films 3rd Floor, 7A Langley Street, London, WC2H 9JA **t** 020 7845 7474 **f** 020 7845 7475 **e** mail@independ.net **✉** Head of Music Video: Richard Weager.

IQ Media (Bracknell) Ltd 2 Venture House, Arlington Square, Bracknell, Berkshire, RG12 1WA **t** 01344 422 551 **f** 01344 453 355 **e** information@iqmedia-uk.com **w** iqmedia-uk.com **✉** MD: Tony Bellamy 07884 262 755.

JamDVD London **t** 07976 820 774 **f** 07092 003 937 **e** jamdvd@macunlimited.net **w** jamdvd.com **✉** Producer: Julie Gardner.

Juxtapose Films 31 Glengall Rd, London, NW6 7EL **t** 020 8728 3148 **e** info@juxtaposefilms.com **w** juxtaposefilms.com **✉** Executive Producer: Tom Norton.

Legion Presents 7, 28a High St, Cardiff, CF10 1PU **t** 02920 399 383 **e** info@legionpresents.com **w** legionpresents.com **✉** Dirs: Dave or Kris Legion.

Liveroom.tv 407 Hornsey Road, London, N19 4DX **t** 07983 644 338 **e** Tamara@liveroom.tv **w** liveroom.tv **✉** Dir, Business Dev't: Tamara Deike.

Mad Cow Productions 75 Amberley Rd, London, W9 2JL **t** 020 7289 0001 **f** 020 7289 0003 **e** info@madcowfilms.co.uk **w** madcowfilms.co.uk **✉** Head of Production: Anwen Rees-Myers.

Maguffin Ltd 10 Frith Street, London, W1V 5TZ **t** 020 7437 2526 **f** 020 7437 1516 **e** firstname@maguffin.co.uk **w** maguffin.co.uk **✉** MD / Prod: James Chads.

Masterpiece Unit 14 The Talina Centre, Bagleys Lane, London, SW6 2BW **t** 020 7731 5758 **f** 020 7384 1750 **e** leena.bhatti@masterpiece.net **w** masterpiece.net **✉** Business Development Manager: Leena Bhatti.

Melling White Productions West Hill Dairy, Avington, Winchester, Hants, SO21 1DE **t** 01962 779 002 **f** 01962 779 002 **e** info@mellingwhite.co.uk **✉** Head Prod: Carol White.

📇 Contacts 📘 Facebook 🟪 MySpace 🐦 Twitter ▶️ YouTube

Metropolis Digital Media The Power House, 70 Chiswick High Rd, London, W4 1SY **t** 020 8742 1111 **f** 020 8742 2626 **e** digitalmedia@metropolis-group.co.uk **w** metropolis-group.co.uk 📘 facebook.com/metropolisstudios 🐦 twitter.com/metropolisgroup ▶️ youtube.com/user/MetropolisStudios 📇 Digital Media Manager / Digital Media Sales Manager: Richard Osborn / Sarah Page.

Midas Media 11 Ashley Pk South, Aberdeen, AB10 6RP **t** 0845 680 0028 **e** info@midasmedia.tv **w** midasmedia.tv 📇 Director: Scott Brown.

The Moving Picture Company 127 Wardour Street, London, W1F 0NL **t** 020 7434 3100 **f** 020 7287 5187 **e** mailbox@moving-picture.co.uk **w** moving-picture.co.uk 📇 Snr Prod: Simon Gosling.

Nexus 113-114 Shoreditch High St, London, E1 6JN **t** 020 7749 7500 **f** 020 7749 7501 **e** info@nexusproductions.com **w** nexusproductions.com

One Small Step 30D Great Sutton St, London, EC1V 0DU **t** 020 7490 2001 **f** 020 7490 2010 **e** dan@onesmallstep.tv **w** onesmallstep.tv 📇 Managing Partner: Dan Kreeger.

Original Concept Studio 2, Fusion Arts, Kingston, London, KT1 1BW **t** 020 8123 5823 **e** hello@originalconcept.tv **w** originalconcept.tv 📇 Creative & Director: Colin Melville.

OVC Media Ltd 88 Berkeley Court, Baker St, London, NW1 5ND **t** 020 7402 9111 **f** 020 7723 3064 **e** joanne.ovc@virgin.net **w** ovcmedia.com 📇 MD: Joanne Cohen.

Partizan 40-42 Lexington St, London, W1F 0LN **t** 020 7851 0200 **f** 020 7851 0249 **e** firstname.surname@partizan.com **w** partizan.com 📇 Office Manager: Elizabeth Harrison.

Passion Pictures 33-34 Rathbone Place, London, W1T 1JN **t** 020 7323 9933 **f** 020 7323 9030 **e** info@passion-pictures.com 📇 Producer: Spencer Friend.

Picture Production Company 19-20 Poland St, London, W1F 8QF **t** 020 7439 4944 **f** 020 7434 9140 **e** steve@theppc.com **w** theppc.co.uk 📇 Sales & Marketing Dir: Steve O'Pray.

Pinball 6 Eton Garages, Lambolle Place, London, NW3 4PE **t** 07941 474 721 **e** paula@pinballonline.net **w** pinballonline.net 📇 Producer: Paula Alvarez Vaccaro.

Poisson Rouge Pictures Ltd 140 Battersea Park Road, London, SW11 4NB **t** 020 7720 5666 **f** 020 7720 5757 **e** info@poissonrougepictures.com **w** poissonrougepictures.com 📇 Producer: Christopher Granier-Deferre.

POP @ Paul Weiland Film Co Ltd 14 Newburgh Street, London, W1V 1LF **t** 020 7494 9600 **f** 020 7434 0146 **e** eatpop@aol.com 📇 Producer: Alex Johnson.

PTE Media 123 Regents Park Rd, London, NW1 8BE **t** 020 7722 5566 **f** 020 7586 4133 **e** info@ptemedia.com **w** ptemedia.com 📇 Contact: Simon Poon Tip.

Pulse Films 1 Book Mews,, Flitcroft St, London, WC2H 8DJ **t** 020 7240 2414 **f** 020 7240 3244 **e** marisa@pulsefilms.co.uk **w** pulsefilms.co.uk 📇 Head of Production: Marisa Clifford.

Ring-pull Records 241A East Barnet Rd, East Barnet, Hertfordshire, EN4 8SS **t** 07932 653196 **e** info@ringpullrecords.com **w** ringpullrecords.com 📇 Label Mgr: Angelique Ekart.

Scopitone Ltd HMS President, Victoria Embankment, London, EC4Y 0HJ **t** 020 7353 3496 **e** chris@scopitone.co.uk **w** scopitone.co.uk 📇 Production Manager: Chris Burton.

The Showreel Company Ltd. 28 Cleveland Avenue, London, W4 1SN **t** 020 8525 0058 **e** the.showreelcompany@virgin.net **w** theshowreelcompany.co.uk 📇 Director: John Gugolka.

Silvertip Films 31 Smithbrook Kilns, Cranleigh, Surrey, GU6 8JJ **t** 01483 268 578 **e** info@silvertipfilms.co.uk **w** silvertipfilms.co.uk 📇 Dir: Geoff Cockwill.

Sounds Good Ltd 12 Chiltern Enterprise Centre, Station Rd, Theale, Reading, Berks, RG7 4AA **t** 0118 930 1700 **f** 0118 930 1709 **e** sales-info@sounds-good.co.uk **w** sounds-good.co.uk 📇 Dir: Martin Maynard.

South Manchester Studios Studio House, Battersea Rd, Heaton Mersey, Stockport, SK4 3EA **t** 0161 432 9000 **f** 0161 443 1325 **e** info@southmanchesterstudios.co.uk **w** southmanchesterstudios.co.uk 📇 MD: Robert Topliss.

Spectre Vision 48 Beak Street, London, W1F 9RL **t** 020 7851 2000 **e** spectre@spectrevision.com 📇 Contact: Janie Balcomb.

Splinter Films Studio 34, Clink St Studios, 1 Clink St, London, SE1 9DG **t** 020 7378 9378 **f** 020 7378 9388 **e** splinter@splinterfilms.com **w** splinterfilms.com 📇 Producer: Emer Patten.

Stink Ltd 87 Lancaster Road, London, W11 1QQ **t** 020 7908 9400 **f** 020 7908 9400 **e** info@stink.tv **w** stink.tv 📇 Head of Promos: Alexa Hayward.

Storm Film Productions Ltd 32 Great Marlborough Street, London, W1F 7JB **t** 020 7439 1616 **f** 020 7439 4477 **e** sophie.storm@btclick.com 📇 Prod Mgr: Sophie Inman.

Straightwire 10 Cranbrook Court, Fleet, Hants, GU15 4QA **t** 01252 665873 **f** 01252 665873 **e** rob@straightwire.co.uk **w** straightwire.co.uk 📇 Producer: Rob Weston 07940 032286.

Studio Plum 39 Belgrade Road, London, N16 8DH **t** 0207 249 8198 **e** jonnie@studioplum.co.uk **w** studioplum.co.uk 📇 Producer: Jonnie Pound.

Tom Dick and Debbie Ltd 43A Botley Road, Oxford, OX2 0BN **t** 01865 201564 **f** 01865 201935 **e** info@tomdickanddebbie.com **w** tomdickanddebbie.com 📇 Director: Richard Lewis.

Media: Video Production

Media: Video Production, Video Production Services, Choreography & Styling Services

Tomato Films 29-35 Lexington Street, London, W1R 3HQ **t** 020 7434 0955 **f** 020 7434 0255 **e** films@tomato.co.uk **w** tomato.co.uk [contact] MD: Jeremy Barrett.

Tough Cookie Ltd part of Whizz Kid Entertainment Ltd, 4 Kingly Street, London, W1B 5PE **t** 020 7440 2550 **f** 020 7440 2599 **e** info@tough-cookie.co.uk **w** tough-cookie.co.uk [contact] Directors: Andy Wood, Neill Sullivan & Dave Castell 07977 248 646.

tracking-shot Abingdon, Oxfordshire **t** 07590 504352 **e** music@tracking-shot.com **w** tracking-shot.com [Facebook] facebook.com/trackingshot [MySpace] myspace.com/tracking_shot [Twitter] twitter.com/tracking_shot [YouTube] youtube.com/trackingshot [contact] Contact: Nick Addison.

TSI Video 10 Grape St, London, WC2H 8TG **t** 020 7379 3435 **f** 020 7379 4589 **e** rwillcocks@tsi.co.uk [contact] Bkings Co-ord: Rebecca Willcocks.

UAV Productions 1st Floor, 126 Bloomfield Avenue, Belfast, BT5 5AE **t** 028 9046 0846 **e** hush62@mac.com **w** uavproductions.com [contact] Creative Director: Ed Hunsdale.

Yawning Dog Productions 70A Uxbridge Road, London, W12 8LP **t** 020 8742 9067 **f** 020 8742 9118 **e** nina@yawningdog.fsnet.co.uk [contact] Prod: Nina Beck.

Video Production Services

Agency Global Enterprises Ltd 145-157 St John's Street, London, EC1V 4PY **t** 020 7043 3734 **f** 020 7043 3736 **e** info@agencyglobal.co.uk **w** agencyglobal.co.uk [contact] Dir: Nadeem Sham.

Audio Motion Ltd Osney Mead House, Osney Mead, Oxford, Oxon, OX2 0ES **t** 08701 600 504 **f** 01865 728 319 **e** info@audiomotion.com **w** audiomotion.com [contact] Audio Mgr: Des Tong.

Bill Charles London Ltd Unit 3E1 Zetland House, 5-25 Scrutton Street, London, EC2A 4HJ **t** 020 7033 9284 **f** 020 7033 9285 **e** dan@billcharles.com **w** billcharles.com [contact] Contact: Daniel Worthington or Olivia Gideon Thomson.

BLACK & BLONDE VIDEO COMMISSIONING SERVICES

The Primrose Hill Business Centre, 110 Gloucester Avenue, London, NW1 8HX **t** 020 7209 3760 **f** 020 7209 3761 **e** hermione@blackandblonde.co.uk **w** blackandblonde.co.uk [contact] Directors: Hermione Ross, Jo Hart 07703 201 111 or 07968 499 037.

Broadley Productions Broadley House, 48 Broadley Terrace, London, NW1 6LG **t** 020 7725 5858 **f** 020 7725 5859 **e** info@broadley.tv **w** broadley.tv [contact] Managing Directors: Richard Landy, Mark French.

Classlane Media The Coach House, Newport Grange, Main Road Newport, East Yorkshire, HU15 2PR **t** 01430 472055 **e** dave_l@classlane.co.uk **w** classlane.co.uk [contact] Dir: David Lee.

Flynn Productions Ltd Top Floor, Pitfield House, 31 - 35 Pitfield St, London, N1 6HB **t** 020 7251 6197 **e** mary@flynnproductions.com **w** flynnproductions.com [contact] Managing Director: Mary Calderwood.

Freehand Limited Unit 52, Dunsfold Pk, Cranleigh, Surrey, GU6 8TB **t** 01483 200111 **f** 01483 200101 **e** phil.kerby@freehand.co.uk **w** freehand.co.uk [contact] Contact: Phil Kerby.

GALA Productions Ltd 25 Stamford Brook Rd, London, W6 0XJ **t** 020 8741 4200 **f** 020 8741 2323 **e** beata@galaproductions.co.uk **w** galaproductions.co.uk [contact] Executive Producer: Beata Romanowski 07768 078864.

Illumina Digital 8 Canham Mews, Canham Rd, London, W3 7SR **t** 020 8600 9300 **f** 020 8600 9333 **e** matt.jones@illumina.co.uk **w** illumina.co.uk [contact] Head of Production: Matt Jones.

Mothcatcher Films 20 Craigs Pk, Edinburgh, Scotland, EH12 8UL **t** 01387 613005 **e** info@mothcatcher.co.uk **w** mothcatcher.co.uk/music-videos [contact] Dirs: Kerry Mullaney & Kris Bird.

New Stream Media Ltd First Floor, 29 Great Guildford St, London, SE1 9EZ **t** 020 7536 1614 **f** 020 7620 0595 **e** info@newstreammedia.co.uk **w** newstreammedia.co.uk [contact] Contact: Abigail Hemingway.

Shagreen Motion Picture Co Ltd 6 Billberry Close, Bradford, West Yorkshire, BD14 6ND **e** info@shagreen.org **w** shagreen.org [contact] Contact: Harvinder Singh +447590493060.

Urban Music Entertainment Network (U-Men) Group PO Box 7874, London, SW20 9XD **t** 07050 605219 **f** 07050 605239 **e** sam@pan-africa.org **w** umengroup.com [contact] CEO: Oscar Sam Carrol Jnr.

Vanderquest 7 Latimer Rd, Teddington, Middlesex, TW11 8QA **t** 020 8977 1743 **f** 020 8943 2818 **e** info@vanderquest.co.uk **w** vanderquest.co.uk [contact] MD: Nick Maingay.

Choreography & Styling Services

Bill Charles London Ltd Unit 3E1 Zetland House, 5-25 Scrutton Street, London, EC2A 4HJ **t** 020 7033 9284 **f** 020 7033 9285 **e** dan@billcharles.com **w** billcharles.com [contact] Contact: Daniel Worthington or Olivia Gideon Thomson.

Carol Hayes Management Ltd 5-6 Underhill Street, London, NW1 7HS **t** 020 7482 3666 **e** ian@carolhayesmanagement.co.uk **w** carolhayesmanagement.co.uk ✉ Head Booker: Ian Loughran.

JK Dance
South Manchester Film & TV Studios, Studio House, Battersea Road, Heaton Mersey, Stockport, SK4 3EA **t** 0161 4325222 **f** 0161 4326800 **e** info@jkdance.co.uk **w** jkdance.co.uk ✉ MD: Julie Kavanagh.

Fay Leith - Makeup Artist 6 Silver Place, London, W1F 0JS **t** 020 7287 9585 **e** info@skinnydip.co.uk **w** skinnydip.co.uk ✉ Contact: Amy Foster, Jonny Wright.

Terri Manduca Ltd The Basement, 11 Elvaston Place, London, SW7 5QG **t** 020 7581 5844 **f** 020 7581 5822 **e** sally@terrimanduca.co.uk **w** terrimanduca.co.uk ✉ MD: Terri Manduca.

A United Production (U.P) 6 Shaftesbury Mews, London, SW4 9BP **t** 020 7498 6563 **f** 020 7498 6563 **e** info@unitedproductions.biz **w** unitedproductions.biz ✉ Choreographer: Lyndon Lloyd.

Media Miscellaneous

Ascent Media Ltd. Ascent Media, 1 Stephen St, London, W1T 1AL **t** 020 7878 0000 **f** 020 7878 7870 **e** firstname.lastname@ascentmedia.co.uk **w** ascentmedia.com ✉ SVP of Marketing EMEA: Sally Reid.

Bearsongs PO Box 944, Birmingham, West Midlands, B16 8UT **t** 0121 454 7020 **f** 0121 454 9996 **e** bigbearsong@compuserve.com **w** bigbearmusic.com ✉ MD: Jim Simpson.

Big Blue Star Ltd Gatehouse, Kippen, Stirling, FK8 3EL **t** 01786 870910 **e** paulgoodwin@bigbluestar.co.uk **w** bigbluestar.co.uk ✉ MD: Paul Goodwin.

Broadchart International Limited 31 Vernon St, London, W14 0RN **t** 020 7637 8800 **e** andy.hill@broadchart.com **w** broadchart.com ✉ CEO: Andy Hill.

Celebrities Worldwide 39-41 New Oxford St, London, WC1A 1BN **t** 020 7836 7702/3 **f** 020 7836 7701 **e** info@celebritiesworldwide.com **w** celebritiesworldwide.com ✉ Co-MDs: Claire Nye, Richard Brecker.

Classic Rock (UK) Ltd - Classic Rock Society
PO Box 7487, Daventry, Northants, NN11 1EG **t** 01327 310088 **e** miles@classicrocksociety.co.uk **w** classicrocksociety.co.uk ✉ MD: Miles Bartaby.

Cuesheet Film/TV Tipsheet 23 Belsize Crescent, London, NW3 5QY **t** 020 7792 2540 **f** 020 7794 7393 **e** cuesheet@songlink.com **w** cuesheet.net ✉ Editor/Publisher: David Stark 07956 270592.

Electric Banana **e** andy@electric-banana.co.uk **w** electric-banana.co.uk ✉ Group Editor in Chief: Andy Parker.

Entertainment Press Cuttings Agency Unit 7, Lloyds Wharf, Mill Street, London, SE1 2BD **t** 020 7237 1717 **f** 020 7237 3388 **e** epca@ukonline.co.uk ✉ Manager: Sally Miller.

Fony Records & Modern Leopard Media
Cambridge House, Card Hill, Forest Row, East Sussex, RH18 5BA **t** 01342 822619 **f** 01342 822619 **e** mickeymodern@sky.com ✉ Partner: Mickey Modern 07831 505883.

Giant Mobile 57 Kingsway, Woking, Surrey, GU21 6NS **t** 01483 859 849 **e** mark.studio@ntlworld.com ✉ Contact: Mark Taylor.

Graff of Newark Ltd Wood Hill Rd, Collingham, Newark, Notts, NG23 7NR **t** 01636 893036 **f** 01636 893317 **e** sales@graffofnewark.co.uk **w** graffofnewark.co.uk ✉ Sales Co-ordinator: Maureen Baumber.

Green Island Promotions Unit 31, 56 Gloucester Road, London, SW7 4UB **t** 0870 789 3377 **f** 0870 789 3414 **e** greenisland@btinternet.com **w** greenislandpromotions.com ✉ Dir: Steve Lucas.

Gym Screen Media South Manchester Studios, Battersea Rd, Heaton Mersey, Stockport, SK4 3EA **t** 0161 442 4205 **f** 0161 442 2677 **e** info@gymscreenmedia.com **w** gymscreenmedia.com ✉ COO: Simon Archibald.

Hanspeter Kuenzler Journalistic Services
25 Plympton Avenue, London, NW6 7TL **t** 020 7328 0052 **e** hpduesi@aol.com **w** hanspeterkuenzler.com ✉ Contact: Hanspeter Kuenzler 07879 855126.

Hot New Music Review Salisbury, Wiltshire **e** hotnewmusicreview@yahoo.co.uk ✉ Editor: Robbie Romero 07545 695989.

JN Associates 8 Broxash Rd, London, SW11 6AB **t** 020 7223 5280 **f** 020 7223 9493 **e** jonnewey@btinternet.com ✉ Research & Archivist Dir: Jon Newey.

Klipjoint - Photo archive service.
25 Plympton Ave, London, NW6 7TL **t** 020 8357 3499 **f** 020 7372 2572 **e** mail@klipjoint.info **w** klipjoint.info ✉ MD: Duncan Brown.

LDNstudio Box 10293, CM16 4DD **t** 0844 567 9720 **f** 07623 192021 **e** info@LDNstudio.com **w** LDNstudio.com 🔲 myspace.com/LDNstudio 🔳 twitter.com/LDNstudio ✉ Dir: Ralph Watson.

The Life Alchemist Ltd PO Box 111, London, W13 0ZH **t** 08448 843 108 **f** 0208 566 7215 **e** info@johnrushton.com **w** thelifealchemist.com 📘 facebook.com/johnrushton 🔳 twitter.com/johnrushton ▶ youtube.com/watch?v=qaV8DKoz9hA ✉ Dir: John S Rushton 02085667215.

M4 Media (music business contract publishing) 2-4 Prowse Place, London, NW1 9PH **t** 020 7284 5869 **f** 020 7284 1870 **e** info@m-4media.com **w** m-4media.com ✉ Dir: Chris Prosser.

Media: Media Miscellaneous

MediaPack 8th Floor, Ludgate House, 245 Blackfriars Rd, London, SE1 9UR **t** 020 7921 8347 **f** 020 7921 8339 **e** etoppin@cmpi.biz **w** mediapack-online.com
⬛ Editor: Elizabeth Toppin.

Mike Music Freshwater House, Outdowns, Effingham, Surrey, KT24 5QR **t** 01483 281500 **f** 01483 281502 **e** yellowbal@aol.com ⬛ MD: Mike Smith.

Music & Media Law Services Ltd Wychwood, Kencot, Oxon, GL7 3QT **t** 01367 860256 **f** 01367 860116 **e** anicholas@btinternet.com ⬛ MD: Alastair Nicholas.

Nearly Famous Blackpool, FY5 3BG **t** 01253 864598 **e** wayne@waynepaulo.com
w waynepaulo.com/NearlyFamous.html ⬛ Author - Owner: Wayne Paulo.

Openplay Limited Suite 106, Hiltongrove Business Centre, Hatherley Mews, London, E17 4QP **t** 020 8520 6644 **f** 020 8520 7755 **e** info@openplay.co.uk **w** openplay.co.uk ⬛ Director: David Hoskins.

Passport Approved 8383 Wilshire Blvd, Suite 100, Beverly Hills, CA 90211, United States **t** 323.782.0770 **f** 323.782.9835 **e** brandon@passportapproved.com **w** passportapproved.com ⬛ Contact: Brandon Fuller.

The Pavement 1 Lexington St, London, W1F 9AF **t** 020 7220 2990 **f** 020 7437 5402 **e** info@thepavement.com **w** thepavement.com
📘 facebook.com/pages/London-United-Kingdom/The-Pavement/95830624268 📧 twitter.com/thepavement
⬛ Manging Director: Andy Evans.

Pro-Motion 33 Kendal Rd, Hove, East Sussex, BN3 5HZ **t** 01273 327175 **e** info@martinjames.demon.co.uk
⬛ Executive Producer: Martin James.

RockBox (A Division of Clear Channel Outdoor) 33 Golden Sq, London, W1F 9JT **t** 020 7478 2200 **f** 020 7287 8129 **e** aimee.mckay@clearchannel.co.uk **w** clearchannel.co.uk ⬛ Group Head: Aimee McKay.

Rovi Europe Malvern House, 14-18 Bell St, Maidenhead, Berkshire, SL6 1BR **t** 020 7324 2330 **f** 020 7566 8259 **e** scott.winchester@rovicorp.com **w** rovicorp.com ⬛ Head of Business Development, Europe: Scott Winchester.

Sarem Media Packaging 43A Old Woking Rd, West Byfleet, Surrey, KT14 6LG **t** 01932 352535 **f** 01932 336431 **e** penny@media-packaging.co.uk **w** media-packaging.co.uk ⬛ Contact: Penny Coomber.

Shazam Entertainment 4th Floor, Block F, 375 Kensington High St, London, W14 8QH **t** 020 7471 3440 **f** 020 7471 3477 **e** tim.porter@shazamteam.com **w** shazamentertainment.com ⬛ Marketing Dir: Tim Porter.

Sound Stage Production Music Kerchesters, Waterhouse Lane, Kingswood, Surrey, KT20 6HT **t** 01737 832837 **f** 01737 833812 **e** info@amphonic.co.uk **w** amphonic.com ⬛ MD: Ian Dale.

St Pierre Publicity - R&B Music Consultants The Hoods, High St, Wethersfield, Nr Braintree, Essex, CM7 4BY **t** 01371 850238 **e** stpierre.roger@gmail.com ⬛ MD: Roger St Pierre.

Upfront Promotions Ltd 217 Buspace Studios, Conlan St, London, W10 5AP **t** 020 7565 0050 **f** 020 7565 0049 **e** simon@upfrontpromotions.com **w** upfrontpromotions.com ⬛ Managing Director: Simon Stanford.

MUSIC HOUSE GROUP
THE UK'S LEADING RADIO, TV, CLUB AND STUDENT PROMOTIONS COMPANY

EUROSOLUTION
COMMERCIAL,
UNDER 18, GAY AND
URBAN
CLUB PROMOTION.

SOULFOOD MUSIC
URBAN
PROMOTION - RADIO,
CLUB & STREET TEAM

SIZE NINE
NATIONAL AND
REGIONAL
RADIO PROMOTION.

A GUIDE TO **PROMOTION**

MRW
REMIXERS &
PRODUCTION/
ARTIST
MANAGEMENT

RENEGADE
INDIE / ALTERNATIVE / ROCK CLUB
& COLLEGE PROMOTION.
STUDENT PRESS & RADIO. BARS / CAFES /
RETAIL PROMOTION.

HYPERACTIVE
TOP SPECIALIST
DANCE & MAINSTREAM
CLUB PROMOTION SERVICES.

MUSIC HOUSE GROUP
40 ST. PETER'S ROAD
LONDON
W6 9BD

TEL: 020 8563 7788
FAX: 020 8741 9431
www.music-house.co.uk

For further information please contact
Simon Walsh
simon.walsh@music-house.co.uk.

▶ the music producers guild awards

The Music Producers Guild Awards take place on February 11th 2010 to celebrate the creative talent and technical ability of the UK's music producers, engineers, mixers and re-mixers.

Visit www.mpgawards.co.uk to find out more.

For information about sponsorship opportunities for the 2011 event please contact Natalie Besbrode: natalie@bubblesqueak.co.uk

For press releases, information and/or comments from the MPG board of directors, contact Sue Silitoe: sue@whitenoisepr.co.uk

headline sponsors

Contacts   Facebook   MySpace   Twitter   YouTube

Press & Promotion

Promoters & Pluggers

1-2-hear East London **e** clare@1-2-hear.com **w** 1-2-hear.com myspace.com/claretucker1 Director: Clare Tucker 07900 452 378.

Absolute PR Hazlehurst Barn, Valley Rd, Hayfield, Derbyshire, SK22 2JP **t** 01663 747970 **f** 01663 747970 **e** neil@thisdayinmusic.com **w** myspace.com/absolutepr myspace.com/absolutepr Contact: Neil Cossar 07768 652899.

Aiken Promotions Ltd 418 Lisburn Rd, Belfast, BT9 6GN, Northern Ireland **t** 028 9068 9090 **f** 028 9068 2091 **e** office@aikenpromotions.com **w** aikenpromotions.com MD: Peter Aiken.

Airplayer Ltd Studio 3, 3a Brackenbury Road, London, W6 0BE **t** 020 8762 9155 **f** 020 8740 0200 **e** firstname@airplayer.co.uk **w** airplayer.co.uk Contact: Rob Lynch 07795 462 661.

Alan James PR Ground Floor, 60 Weston St, London, SE1 3QJ **t** 020 7403 9999 **e** promo@ajpr.co.uk **w** ajpr.co.uk MD: Alan James.

Alchemy Radio Gable House, 18-24 Turnham Green Terrace, London, W4 1QP **t** 020 8996 4811 **e** chris@alchemyradio.com **w** alchemyradio.com Dir: Chris Slade.

All About Promotions 27a Kings Gardens, West End Lane, London, NW6 4PX **t** 020 7328 4836 **f** 020 7372 3331 **e** info@allaboutpromo.com **w** allaboutpromo.com Contacts: Amanda Beel.

Anglo Plugging Fulham Palace, Bishops Avenue, London, SW6 6EA **t** 020 7384 7373 **f** 020 7371 9490 **e** firstname@angloplugging.co.uk **w** angloplugging.co.uk Promotions Co-ordinator: Anne Reid.

ASK ME PR

e liam@askmepr.com **w** askmepr.com MD: Liam Walsh 07976258577.

Avalon Public Relations 4A Exmoor Street, London, W10 6BD **t** 020 7598 8000 **f** 020 7598 7223 **e** danl@avalonuk.com **w** avalonuk.com Head of PR: Dan Lloyd.

BarBands e ross@barbands.co.uk

Beatwax Communications 91 Berwick Street, London, W1F 0NE **t** 020 7734 1965 **f** 020 7292 8333 **e** michael@beatwax.com **w** beatwax.com MD: Michael Brown.

Big Sister Promotions Studio 3, 3A Brackenbury Road, London, W6 0BE **t** 020 8740 0100 **f** 020 8740 0200 **e** karen@bigsisteruk.com MD: Karen Williams.

Bigger Things Records 33 Montagu Gardens, Edmonton, London, Middlesex, N18 2HB **t** 020 8807 6059 **f** 020 8807 6059 **e** anthonystrn@aol.com **w** stringbeanrecords.com stringbeanrecords.com stringbeanrecords.com stringbeanrecords.com Managing Director: Anthony Campbell 07963 900576.

BR-Asian Media Consulting 45 Circus Rd, St Johns Wood, London, NW8 9JH **t** 020 8550 9898 **f** 020 7289 9892 **e** moizvas@brasian.com **w** brasian.com MD: Moiz Vas.

Brotherhood Media 4th Floor, 52-53 Margaret St, London, W1W 8SQ **t** 020 7631 9200 **e** info@brotherhood-media.co.uk **w** brotherhood-media.co.uk Dirs: James Heighway, Dom Murphy.

Chapple Davies 53 Great Portland St, London, W1W 7LG **t** 020 7299 7979 **f** 020 7299 7978 **e** firstname@chapdav.com **w** chapdav.com Partners: Gareth Davies & James Chapple Gill.

Content Studio 204, Latimer Rd, London, W10 6QY **t** 020 8960 1384 **e** gideon@contentunlimited.com **w** independent-music.co.uk MD: Gideon Palmer 07976 279 716.

Content PR 223d Canalot Studios, 222 Kensal Rd, London, W10 5BN **t** 020 8960 4660 **e** joggs@contentpr.co.uk Director: Joggs Camfield 07799 882 333.

Cool Badge Cabin R, Clarendon Building, 25 Horsell Road, London, N5 1XL **t** 020 7609 5115 **e** music@coolbadge.com **w** coolbadge.com MD: Russell Yates 07766 233 368.

Crashed Music 162 Church Rd, East Wall, Dublin 3, Ireland **t** +353 1 888 1188 **f** +353 1 856 1122 **e** info@crashedmusic.com **w** crashedmusic.com MD: Shay Hennessy.

Creative Cultures – Digital Promotions & Marketing 10 Alexandra Park Road, London, N10 2AB **t** 020 7100 3254 **f** 0871 661 4578 **e** firstname.lastname@creativecultures.biz **w** creativecultures.biz Managing Director: Johnny Hudson.

Crunk! Promotions Unit 11 Impress House, Mansell Road, London, W3 7QH **t** 020 8932 3030 **f** 020 8932 3031 **e** duncan.2710@power.co.uk **w** power.co.uk/crunk Promotions Mgr: Duncan Stump.

Destiny Destiny Towers, St Margaret's House, 21 Old Ford Road, London, E2 9PL **t** 020 8981 2746 **e** john@destinytowers.com **w** destinytowers.com Contact: John Brogan.

Press & Promotion: Promoters & Pluggers

Dylan White National Radio and TV promotion Studio 3, 3a Brackenbury Rd, London, W6 0BE **t** 07768 791479 **e** dylan@dylanwhite.co.uk **w** dylanwhite.co.uk 📘 facebook.com/dylanwhite 📧 myspace.com/dylanwhitepromotion 📧 twitter.com/DylanGWhite 📧 Contact: Dylan White.

EUROSOLUTION

Music House Group, 40 St. Peter's Road, London, W6 9BD **t** 020 8563 7788 **f** 020 8748 9431 **e** craig@music-house.co.uk **w** music-house.co.uk 📧 Head Of Promotions: Craig Jones 020 8563 3923. **Euro Solution provides a full range of crossover pop & r&b club promotion, targeting Commercial/High Street clubs & bars, Under 18 venues, and Gay venues.**

Fake Media National and Digital Radio Plugging May Villas, 50 Main Road, Naphill, Buckinghamshire, HP14 4QB **t** 07966 233275 **e** adam.fisher@fakemedia.com 📧 myspace.com/fakemedia 📧 fakeboy 📧 MD: Adam Fisher.

FFR UK 2 Hastings Terrace, Conway Road, London, N15 3BE **t** 020 8826 5900 **f** 020 8826 5902 **e** fullfrontalrecords@hotmail.com **w** ffruk.com 📧 Dir: Tara Rez.

Fiend TV Arch 462, Kingsland Viaduct, 83 Rivington Street, London, EC2A 3AY **t** 020 7684 5634 **f** 020 7117 4527 **e** info@fiendtv.co.uk **w** fiendtv.co.uk 📧 Dir: David Silverman.

FLEMING ASSOCIATES PR

FLEMING　ASSOCIATES

1st Floor, 74 Great Titchfield St, London, W1W 7QP **t** 020 7636 7441 **f** 020 7636 9523 **e** firstname@fclpr.com **w** flemingassociatespr.com 📧 Chairman: Nick Fleming. Radio & TV promotion: Sean Cooney. Radio Promotion: Neil Ashby. Radio & TV Promotions Co-Ordinator: Jo Menzies Smith.

Futureproof Promotions 330 Westbourne Park Rd, London, W11 1EQ **t** 020 7792 8597 **f** 020 7221 3694 **e** info@futureproofrecords.com **w** futureproofrecords.com 📧 MD: Phil Legg.

Gorgeous Promotions Suite D, 67 Abbey Rd, St John's Wood, London, NW8 0AE **t** 020 7724 2635 **f** 020 7724 2635 **e** promotion@gorgeousmusic.net **w** gorgeousmusic.net 📧 TV/Radio Consultants: David Ross & Victoria Elliott.

Groovefinder Productions 30, Havelock Rd, Southsea, Portsmouth, PO5 1RU **t** 07831 450 241 **e** jeff@groovefinderproductions.com **w** groovefinderproductions.com 📧 MD: Jeff Powell.

HART MEDIA LTD.

The Primrose Hill Business Centre, 110 Gloucester Avenue, London, NW1 8HX **t** 020 7209 3760 **f** 020 7209 3761 **e** info@hartmedia.co.uk **w** hartmedia.co.uk 📧 MD: Jo Hart.

HESSO MEDIA LTD

e chris@hessomedia.com / Natalie@hessomedia.com 📧 Contact: Chris Hession / Natalie Peyton 07793 630426 / 07960 215268.

Holier Than Thou Records Ltd 46 Rother St, Stratford on Avon, Warwickshire, CV37 6LT **t** 01789 268661 **e** david@httmusic.co.uk **w** holierthanthou.co.uk 📧 Managing Director: David Begg.

HorizonVUMusic 2 Villa Monceau, Paris, 75017, France **t** +33 6 2269 9665 **e** phillip.cartwright@horizonvumusic.cim **w** horizonvumusic.com 📧 CEO: Phillip A. Cartwright +33622699665.

The Howlin' Promotion Company 114 Lower Park Rd, Loughton, Essex, IG10 4NE **t** 020 8508 4564 / 07831 430080 **e** djone@howardmarks.freeserve.co.uk 📘 HowardMarks 📧 HowardMarks 📧 Prop: Howard Marks 07831 430080.

Hungry Media Ltd 3 Berkley Grove, London, NW1 8XY **t** 020 7722 6992 **e** woolfie@hungrylikethewoolf.com 📧 MD: Woolfie.

THE UK'S LEADING RADIO AND TELEVISION PROMOTIONS COMPANY

National Radio, National Television, Regional Radio, Regional Television, Media Training

Clients past and present include; Peter Andre, Aled Jones, Backstreet Boys, Blink 182, Britney Spears, Bryan Adams, BWO, Celine Dion, Cerys Matthews, David Bowie, Ella Chi, Eva Cassidy, Fugative, Glen Campbell, High School Musical, Janet Jackson, Jools Holland, Justin Timberlake, Katie Melua, Keith Urban, LeAnn Rimes, Martha Wainwright, Mary J Blige, Michael Jackson, Miley Cyrus, Nelly, Paul Carrack, Pearl Jam, Peter Gabriel, Queen, R Kelly, Radiohead, Rhydian Roberts, Sharon Corr, Shena, Sheryl Crow, Status Quo, Stereophonics, Sting, TLC, Ultravox, Van Morrison…

fleming associates

For further information
contact
NICK FLEMING nick@fclpr.com
SEAN COONEY sean@fclpr.com
NEIL ASHBY battashby@mac.com

Fleming Associates Pr
74, Great Titchfield Street,
London, W1W 7QP
Tel. 020 7636 7441
Fax. 020 7636 9523

www.flemingassociatespr.com

 Contacts   Facebook MySpace Twitter YouTube

HYPER ACTIVE

Music House Group, 40 St. Peter's Road, Hammersmith, London, W6 9BD **t** 020 8563 7788 **e** markb@music-house.co.uk **w** music-house.co.uk/hyperactive ✉ Head of Promotions: Mark Bowden 020 8563 3924.
The leading club promotions company in the UK for specialist and mainstream dance.

ish-media 2, Devonport Mews, Devonport Rd, London, W12 8NG **t** 020 8742 9191 **f** 020 8742 9102 **e** info@ish-media.com **w** ish-media.com ✉ Director: Eden Blackman.

James Grant Music 94 Strand On The Green, Chiswick, London, W4 3NN **t** 020 8742 4950 **f** 020 8742 4951 **e** enquiries@jamesgrant.co.uk **w** jamesgrant.co.uk ✉ Co-MDs: Simon Hargreaves, Nick Worsley.

JBMusicMedia 2, The Bush, Newtown Road, Awbridge, Romsey, Hampshire, SO51 0GG **t** 01794 342426 **f** 01794 432426 **e** jacqui@kwinstanley.free-online.co.uk ✉ GM: Jacqui Bateson.

Jeff Chegwin National TV & Radio PR Suite 139, 2 Lansdowne Row, Berkeley Sq, London, W1H 6JL **e** jeffchegwin@hotmail.com **w** jeffchegwin.com ✉ Dir: Jeff Chegwin 07957 939072.

Jon Turner & Julian Spear 56 Cole Park Rd, Twickenham, TW1 1HS **t** 020 8891 3333 **f** 020 8891 3222 **e** jon@turnerspear.com; julian@turnerspear.com ✉ Partners: Jon Turner & Julian Spear Jon=07950 413259; Julian=07939 118015.

LANDER PR LTD

Lander Music Group, Athene House, 86 The Broadway, London, NW7 3TD **t** 020 8906 2224 **e** judd@landerpr.com **w** landerpr.com ❋ facebook.com/LanderPR ❋ myspace.com/landermusicpr ❋ twitter.com/MusicPromotions ✉ Director: Judd Lander. Radio: Sean Denny. TV: Carlien van Heerden.
One of the best-known names in the music business and one of the UK's leading independent promotion companies. Covering the wide arena of media - National TV & National Radio - On line TV / Radio, we can also arrange Regional PR & National & Regional Press PR - plus UK distribution and visibility on most major download sites.

Large PR Ltd 1 Brickfield Cottages, High Rd, Epping, Essex, CM16 6TH **t** 01992 570461 **f** 0870 051 8459 **e** info@largepr.com **w** largepr.com ✉ Contact: Stuart Emery.

LES MOLLOY GROUP

lmg music

Box 27, Hindon Court, 104 Wilton Rd, London, SW1V LDU **t** 07860 389598 **f** 020 7976 5029 **e** molloymolloy@hotmail.co.uk **w** lesmolloy.co.uk ✉ Artist and Media Consultant: Les Molloy 07860 389 598.

Lisa Davies Promotions Caravela House, Waterhouse Lane, Kingswood, Surrey, KT20 6DT **t** 01737 362444 **f** 01737 362555 **e** lisa@lisadaviespromotions.co.uk **w** lisadaviespromotions.co.uk ✉ MD: Lisa Davies.

Lisa MacDonald Promotions 4 Norse Rd, Scotstoun, Glasgow, G14 9HP **e** lisamacdonald666@yahoo.com ✉ Dir: Lisa MacDonald 07836 211012.

LPW PLuggers LPW House, 2 Cornflower Road, Abbeymead, Gloucester, GL4 4AJ **t** 07891 727 947 **e** info@lpwrecordsltd.biz ✉ Contact: Mike Longley.

Lucid PR 2nd Floor, Kenilworth House, 79/80 Margaret St, London, W1W 8TA **t** 020 7307 7449 **e** hi@lucidpr.co.uk **w** lucidpr.co.uk ✉ Dirs: Charlie Lycett.

M P Promotions Hollywood House, Billesley Lane, Portway, Birmingham, B48 7HG **t** 01564 829 214 **e** mikeperry@btinternet.com ✉ Dir: Mike Perry.

Mainstream Promotions The Music Village, 11B Osiers Road, London, SW18 1NL **t** 07000 4 77666 **f** 020 8870 2101 **e** mainstream@rush-release.co.uk ✉ MD: Jo Underwood 020 8870 0011.

Making Waves 40 Underwood Street, London, N1 7JQ **t** 020 7490 0944 **f** 020 7490 1026 **e** info@makingwaves.co.uk or scotty@makingwaves.co.uk **w** makingwaves.co.uk ✉ MD: Matt Williams.

Media2Radio Worldwide **e** eddie@media2radio.com **w** media2radio.com ❋ myspace.com/media2radiocom ❋ media2radio ✉ MD: Eddie Gordon.

Mixmedia Productions Manchester, Manchester, Lancashire, PO BOX 43370 **t** 0844 561 0565 **e** kash@mixmediaproductions.com **w** mixmediaproductions.com ✉ Contact: Kashief Ahmed +44 (0) 772 994 1422.

Mocking Bird Music PO Box 52, Marlow, Bucks, SL7 2YB **t** 01491 579214 **f** 01491 579214 **e** mockingbirdmusic@aol.com ✉ Artiste Management: Leon B Fisk.

Press & Promotion: Promoters & Pluggers

Press & Promotion: Promoters & Pluggers

Mosquito Media 64a Warwick Avenue, Little Venice, London, W9 2PU **t** 07813 174 185
e mosquitomedia@aol.com **w** mosquito-media.co.uk
🔲 Contact: Richard Abbott.

MP Promotions (MPP) 13 Greave, Romiley, Stockport, Cheshire, SK6 4PU
t 0161 494 7934 / 07801 191784
e maria@mppromotions.co.uk 🔲 Director: Maria Philippou.

The Music Elevator PO Box 23474, Edinburgh, EH6 8YY **t** 07941 815059 **e** mail@themusicelevator.com
w themusicelevator.com 🔲 Manager: Ewan McKenzie.

Music House Group Music House, 40 St Peter's Road, Hammersmith, London, W6 9BD **t** 020 8563 7788
f 020 8748 9431 **e** simon.walsh@music-house.co.uk
w music-house.co.uk 🔲 Director: Simon Walsh 020 8653 7788.

Neon Street Marketing 6 Homerton House, Homerton Street, Cambridge, CB2 8NZ
t 01223 246 744 or 07817 794 342
e phil@neonstreet.co.uk **w** neonstreet.co.uk 🔲 Managing Director: Phil Pethybridge.

NoBul Promotions 59 New River Crescent, Palmers Green, London, N13 5RD **t** 020 8882 3677
f 020 8882 3688 **e** info@nobulmusic.co.uk
w nobulmusic.co.uk 🔲 MD: Alex Alexandrou.

NONSTOP PROMOTIONS

Studio 8, Cliveden House, 19-22 Victoria Villas, Richmond, London, TW9 2JX **t** 020 8334 9994 **f** 020 8334 9995
e info@nonstop1.co.uk 🔲 Contact: Niki Sanderson & Stuart Kenning.

Out Promotion 4th Floor, 33 Newman St, London, W1T 1PY **t** 020 7434 4525 **e** caroline@out-london.co.uk
w out-london.co.uk 🔲 Head of Radio & TV: Caroline Poulton.

Outpost Media Ltd Arch 462, Kingsland Viaduct, 83 Rivington Street, Shoreditch, London, EC2A 3AY
t 020 7684 5634 **e** david@outpostmedia.co.uk
w outpostmedia.co.uk 🔲 Dir: David Silverman 07811 422 266.

Overground Radio Promotions PO Box 1NW, Newcastle upon Tyne, NE99 1NW **t** 0191 232 6700
f 0191 232 6701 **e** has@overground.co.uk 🔲 MD: Hasan Gaylani.

Peafish Promotions 30 Mildmay Grove South, Islington, London, N1 4RL **t** 07772 405 545
e info@peafish.com **w** myspace.com/peafish
🔲 Contact: Sarah Pink.

Pepper Music Promotions Ltd 2 Ball Rd, Pewsey, SN9 5BN **t** 07788 926616
e jamie@peppermusicpromotions.com
w peppermusicpromotions.com 🔲 Dir: Jamie Watherston.

Don Percival Artists' Promotion Shenandoah, Manor Park, Chislehurst, Kent, BR7 5QD **t** 020 8295 0310
f 020 8295 0311 **e** donpercival@freenet.co.uk 🔲 MD: Don Percival.

Pioneer Promotions 5 Emerson House, 14B Ballynahinch Rd, Belfast, BT8 8DN **t** 028 9081 7111
f 028 9081 7444 **e** ppromo@musicni.co.uk 🔲 MD: Johnny Davis.

Pivotal PR 4 Heathgate Pl, 75-83 Agincourt Rd, London, NW3 2NU **t** 020 7424 8688 **f** 020 7424 8699
e bjorn@pivotalpr.co.uk **w** pivotalpr.co.uk
🔲 Contact: Björn Hall.

Planetlovemusic 2 Gregg St, Lisburn, Co Antrim, BT27 5AN **t** 02892 667 000 **f** 02892 668 000
e eddie@planetlovemusic.com **w** planetlovemusic.com
🔲 Dir: Eddie Wray.

The Play Centre Marketing Ltd.
Unit 2 Devonport Mews, Shepherd's Bush, London, W12 8NG **t** 020 8749 1651 **f** 07970 642974
e info@theplaycentre.com **w** ww.theplaycentre.com
🔲 MD: Shaun "STuCKee" Willoughby 07973 115328.

Poparazzi Unit 11, Impress House, Mansell Rd, London, W3 7QH **t** 020 8932 3030 **f** 020 8932 3031
e Tracey@power.co.uk **w** power.co.uk 🔲 Promotions Director: Tracey Webb.

Power Plugging Power Promotions, Unit 11 Impress Hse, Mansell Rd, London, W3 7QH
t 020 8932 3030 **e** Luke@power.co.uk **w** power.co.uk
🔲 Contact: Luke Neville.

Prohibition Ltd Fulham Palace, Bishops Avenue, London, SW6 6EA **t** 020 7384 7372 **f** 020 7371 7940
e Caroline@prohibitiondj.com **w** prohibitiondj.com
🔲 MD: Caroline Prothero 07967 610 877.

Public City PR 31 Twelve Acres, Welwyn Garden City, Hertfordshire, AL7 4TG **e** hayley@publiccitypr.com
w publiccitypr.com 🔲 Radio & TV Promotions: Hayley Codd 07967 303857.

Radical PR Suite 134, Southbank House, Black Prince Rd, London, SE1 7SJ **t** 07980 297759
f 020 7463 0670 **e** radical@radicalpr.com **w** radicalpr.com
🔲 Director: Paul Ruiz.

RADIO PROMOTIONS

PO Box 20, Banbury, Oxon, OX17 3YT **t** 01295 814995
e music@radiopromotions.co.uk **w** radiopromotions.co.uk
🔲 Contact: Steve Betts.

NATIONAL TV, RADIO and PRESS

Hayley Codd – National TV and Radio Promotion
hayley@publiccitypr.com | 07967 303857

TV and Radio Roster Includes:
Enter Shikari, Escape The Fate, Exit Avenue, Flood Of Red, Japanese Voyeurs, Laruso,
Saving Aimee, The Mission District, Twin Atlantic, You Me At Six, Young Guns

Em Van Duyts – National Press
em@publiccitypr.com | 07949 554666

Press Roster Includes:
Audra Mae, Buck 65, Deftones, Disturbed, Filter, Head Automatica
Henry Rollins, Mastodon, Static-X, Skindred, Story Of The Year, The Gaslight Anthem,
The Used, The Mission District, Parkway Drive, The Worldonfire, The Eyes Of A Traitor

www.publiccitypr.com

THE OLD HOUSE, 39a North Road, London, N7 9DP

STAY TUNED
With Matt Connolly
TV PROMOTION

Email: matt@staytuned.me • www.staytuned.me

020 7700 4682
m:07801 231255

Red Shadow - Blue Sky Radio Wisteria House,
56 Cole Park Rd, Twickenham, Middlesex, TW1 1HS
t 020 8891 3333 **f** 020 8891 3222
e julian@redshadow.co.uk 🔲 Director: Julian Spear.

RENEGADE

Music House Group, 40 St. Peter's Road, Hammersmith,
London, W6 9BD **t** 020 8563 7788 **f** 020 8748 9431
e chris@renegademusic.co.uk **w** music-
house.co.uk/renegade 🔲 Head Of Promotions: Chris
Smith 020 8563 3929.
**Full range of indie/alternative/rock club & college
promotion. Student press & radio. Bars/cafes & retail
promotion. Renegade offers the ultimate music
marketing and promotion service to the 18-40
demographic.**

Rocket St Matthews Church, Brixton Hill, London,
SW2 1JF **t** 020 7326 1234 **e** radio@rocketpr.co.uk
w rocketpr.co.uk 🔲 myspace.com/rocketpr
🔲 MD: Prudence.

Rocketscience Media 1st Floor, The Griffin,
93 Leonard St, London, EC2A 4RD **t** 020 7033 4000
e office@rocketsciencemedia.com
w rocketsciencemedia.com 🔲 rempr 🔲 Contact: Lou
Wilson, Simon Busby and Glenn Herweijer 020 70334000.

Rush Release Promotions PO Box 696, Felbridge,
Surrey, RH19 2XS **t** 0845 370 9904 **f** 0845 370 9905
e jo@rushrelease.com **w** rushrelease.com
🔲 myspace.com/rushrelease 🔲 MD: Jo Titchener.

Scene Not Herd 28 Main St, Newbigging,
South Lanarkshire, ML11 8LZ **t** 07986 527947
e lesley@scenenotherd.co.uk **w** scenenotherd.co.uk
🔲 Sales & Marketing: Lesley Woodall.

SCREAM PROMOTIONS

PROMOTIONS

4th Floor, 57 Poland St, London, W1F 7NW
t 020 7434 3446 **f** 020 7434 3449
e firstname@screampromotions.co.uk
w screampromotions.co.uk 🔲 Contact: Tony Cooke, Claire
Jarvis, Scott Bartlett 07971 859 947.

Scruffy Bird The Nest, 2nd Floor, 61-63 Brick Lane,
London, E1 6QL **t** 020 7650 7840
e emily@scruffybird.com **w** scruffybird.com 🔲 Head of
Radio & TV: Emily Cooper.

Sedgemoor Contemporary Music Group
11 Bath Rd, Ashcott, Bridgwater, TA7 9QS
t 07779 723061 **e** matt@midnightmango.co.uk
w midnightmango.co.uk f facebook.com/MidnightMango
🔲 myspace.com/midnightmango
🔲 twitter.com/MidnightMango 🔲 MD: Matt Bartlett.

Seesaw PR Ltd First Floor, 50 Great Portland St,
London, W1W 7ND **t** 07831 171353 **e** sam@seesawpr.net
w seesawpr.net 🔲 Managing Director: Sam Wright 020
7631 4645.

Sharp End PR 14-15 Bentinck Mansions, Bentinck St,
London, W1U 2ER **t** 020 7487 2865
e ronmccreight@btinternet.com 🔲 Contact: Ron
McCreight 0777 566 3537.

Shoot Promotion Limited 4th Floor, 52-
53 Margaret St, London, W1W 8SQ **t** 020 7631 9208
e info@shootmusic.co.uk **w** shootmusic.co.uk
🔲 twitter.com/shootmusic 🔲 Dir: Tom Roberts.

Showcase Live 127 Kennington Park Rd, London,
SE11 4JJ **t** 07981 967135 **e** showcaselive@yahoo.co.uk
w myspace.com/showcaseliveevents 🔲 Event
organiser: George Eason.

Single Minded Promotions 1 Lyric Sq, London,
W6 0DB **t** 020 7460 3410 **e** tony@singleminded.com
w singleminded.com ▶ singlemindedTV 🔲 MD: Tony
Byrne 07860 391902.

FIFTH ELEMENT
Public Relations & Artist Management

5 Public Relations
Pr

TEL: 020 7722 0000
info@fifthelement.biz
www.fifthelement.biz

SIZE 9

Music House Group, 40 St. Peter's Rd, Hammersmith, London, W6 9BD **t** 020 8563 7788 **f** 020 8748 9431 **e** craigm@music-house.co.uk **w** music-house.co.uk/size9 **⊠** Head Of Radio Promotions: Craig McClintock. **Size 9 offer a full range of national & specialist radio promotion, and music events.**

Skullduggery Services
40a Love Lane, Pinner, Middlesex, HA5 3EX **t** 020 8429 0853 **e** xskullduggeryx@btinternet.com **⊠** MD: Russell Aldrich.

SongandMedia.com
PO Box 218, Consett, County Durham, DH8 1EP **t** 01207 500123 **f** 01736 763328 **e** songandmedia@aol.com **w** songandmedia.com **☉** myspace.com/songandmedia **⊠** MD: Colin Eade.

SOULFOOD MUSIC

Music House, 40 St. Peter's Rd, Hammersmith, London, W6 9BD **t** 020 8563 7788 **f** 020 8748 9431 **e** steve@soulfoodmusic.org **w** music-house.co.uk/soulfood **☉** myspace.com/stevesoulfoodmusic **☉** twitter.com/soulfoodmusic **⊠** Head Of Promotions: Steve Ripley 07702 161290. **Urban Promotion - Club, Radio and Street Teams.**

Special D (SDDP)
29 St Barnabas Street, Belgravia, London, SW1W 8QB **t** 020 7730 7697 **f** 020 7730 7697 **e** steve.stimpy@btinternet.com **w** special-d.com **⊠** MD: Stimpy 0790 427 2668.

STAY TUNED

STAY TUNED
TV Promotion

152B Haverstock Hill, London, NW3 2AY **t** 020 7700 4682 **f** 020 7609 1921 **e** matt@staytuned.me **w** staytuned.me **☉** myspace.com/staytunedpr **⊠** Director: Matt Connolly 07801 231 255.

Steve Osborne Promotions
6 Lincoln Way, Daventry, Northants., NN11 4SX **t** 0845 250 8860 **e** steveosbornepr@yahoo.co.uk **w** steveosborne.tk **⊠** Proprietor: Steve Osborne.

Stringbean International Records Limited
33 Montagu Gardens, Edmonton, London, Middlesex, N18 2HB **t** 020 8807 6059 **f** 020 8807 6059 **e** sales@stringbeanrecords.com **w** stringbeanrecords.com **◘** stringbeanrecords.com **☉** stringbeanrecords.com **⊠** Managing Director: Donovan Campbell 07758 669161.

Swell Music Marketing
Rocklyn, Trebarwith Strand, Tintagel, Cornwall, PL34 0HB **t** 01840 779 054 **f** 01840 779 053 **e** info@swellmusic.co.uk **w** swellmusic.co.uk **⊠** Dir: Andrew Grainger.

Terrie Doherty Promotions
40 Princess St, Manchester, M1 6DE **t** 0161 234 0044 **e** terriedoherty@zoo.co.uk **⊠** Director: Terrie Doherty.

Tomkins PRomotions Ltd (Regional Radio and TV Promotion)
The Old Lampworks, Rodney Place, London, SW19 2LQ **t** 020 8540 8166 **f** 020 8540 6056 **e** susie@tomkinspr.com **w** tomkinspr.com **⊠** Managing Director: Susie Tomkins 07710 867676.

Videopops
Power Promotions, Unit 11 Impress Hse, Mansell Rd, London, W3 7QH **t** 020 8932 3030 **e** Tracey@power.co.uk **w** power.co.uk **⊠** Contact: Tracey Webb.

Vigilante Music Ltd
138 Sinclair Rd, London, W14 0NL **t** 020 7371 6244 **e** vigilante@peroxidemusic.com **w** peroxidemusic.com/vigilante **⊠** Contact: Rupert Withers.

Vision
22 Upper Grosvenor St, London, W1K 7PE **t** 020 7499 8024 **f** 020 7499 8032 **e** vision@visionmusic.co.uk **w** visionmusic.co.uk **☉** myspace.com/visionpromotions **⊠** Head Of Promotions: Rob Dallison 0207 199 0109.

White Dolphin Films
t 020 7993 5944 **e** chris@whitedolphinfilms.co.uk **⊠** Contact: 020 7993 5944 - 07545 092504.

Whitenoise Promotions
PO Box 991, St Albans, AL1 9LG **t** 07880 540598 **e** colin@whitenoisepromo.com **w** whitenoisepromo.com **⊠** MD: Colin Hobbs.

Wild
2B Westpoint, 39-40 Warple Way, London, W3 0RG **t** 020 8746 0666 **f** 020 8746 7676 **e** info@wild-uk.com **w** wild-uk.com **⊠** MD: Dave Roberts.

Worn Out Marketing
4th Floor, 52-53 Margaret Street, London, W1W 8SQ **t** 020 7631 9202 **e** tony@worn-out.net **w** worn-out.net **⊠** Manager: Tony Arthy.

PR Companies

1-2-hear PR
East London **e** clare@1-2-hear.com **w** 1-2-hear.com **☉** myspace.com/claretucker1 **⊠** Director: Clare Tucker 07900 452 378.

9PR
65-69 White Lion St, 2nd Floor, London, N1 9PR **t** 020 7833 9303 **f** 020 7833 9322 **e** jo@9pr.co.uk **w** 9pr.co.uk **⊠** MD: Jo Donnelly.

A Star PR is a dynamic creative arts company, at the forefront of innovations within the music and entertainment industry.

The exceptional quality of our past PR, marketing and creative consultancy campaigns speak for themselves, with coverage in all major print, online, digital and broadcast media outlets. From Broadsheets to Tabloids; Social Networking to Mobile Platforms – A Star PR have it covered.

The A Star team is knowledgeable, passionate and creative, all with unrivalled expertise in particular fields. Be it Print Press, Digital, Fashion or Marketing, A Star are able to offer effective bespoke campaigns to all clients, thus priding ourselves by never using 'off the shelf' campaigns.

If you're looking to sell records, raise awareness of yourselves or your client and are ready to become a star, get in touch!

Contact:
Ian Roberts, Managing Director ian.roberts@astarpr.com
Ben Allen, Client and Digital Manager ben.allen@astarpr.com
+44 (0)20 7836 11 22
www.astarpr.com

FIFTH ELEMENT
Public Relations & Artist Management

TEL: 020 7722 0000
info@fifthelement.biz
www.fifthelement.biz

A STAR PR

6 Mercer St, Covent Garden, London, WC2H 9QA
t 020 7836 1122 **f** 0207 836 1144
e ian.roberts@astarpr.com **w** astarpr.com
 myspace/weareastar @astarpr Managing
Director: Ian Roberts 07971 191582.

Ablaze PR Unit 209, Coborn Business House,
3 Coborn Road, London, E3 2DA **t** 020 8980 9081
e nadia@ablazepr.com Director: Nadia Khan 07990 680
303.

Abstrakt Publicity 21d Gloucester St, Pimlico,
London, SW1V 2DB **t** 020 7834 0440
e abstrakt@abstraktpublicity.co.uk MD: Anna Goodman
07976 247026.

Air MTM 27 The Quadrangle, 49 Atalanta Street,
London, SW6 6TU **t** 020 7386 1600 **f** 020 7386 1619
e info@airmtm.com **w** airmtm.com Contact: Sheela
Bates.

ALCHEMY PR

Gable House, 18-24 Turnham Green Terrace, Chiswick,
London, W4 1QP **t** 020 8996 4810
e matt@alchemypr.com **w** alchemypr.com Managing
Director: Matt Learmouth 0208 996 4810. Alchemy
Content: Tom Kihl. Alchemy Radio: Chris Slade. PR
Assistant: Madeleine Smith.
**The Alchemy PR Group's campaigns cover print, radio
and digital media for clients ranging from music
artists to lifestyle products.**

All Press The Cottage, 85 St Charles Sq, London,
W10 6EB **t** 020 8969 3636 **e** nienke.klop@all-press.co.uk
w myspace.com/all_press MD: Nienke Klop 07931 557
970.

Anorak London The Hood, 2nd Floor, 61-
63 Brick Lane, London, E1 6QL **t** 020 7650 7840
e info@anoraklondon.com **w** www.anoraklondon.com
 myspace.com/anoraklondon
 twitter.com/anoraklondon Director: Emily Cooper,
Laura Martin.

APB Studio 18, Westbourne Studios, 242 Acklam Road,
London, W10 5JJ **t** 020 8968 9000 **f** 020 8968 8500
e apb.press@which.net MD: Gordon Duncan.

Archipelago PR 22 Stonecroft Rd,
Northumberland Heath, Erith, Kent, DA8 1HP
t 01322 405961 **e** info@archipelagopr.co.uk
w archipelagopr.co.uk ARCHIPELAGOPR Company
Director: Charlie O'Connor.

Ark PR The Office, 79 De Montfort Rd, Lewes,
East Sussex, BN7 1ST **t** 01273 476 921 **e** del@arkpr.co.uk
w arkpr.co.uk myspace.com/arkpr
 twitter.com/TheArkster MD: Derek Day 07759 528
006.

Arrowsmith Communications 5 Norfolk Court,
Victoria Park Gardens, Worthing, BN11 4ED
t 01903 200 916 **e** eugeniearrowsmith@yahoo.co.uk
 Media Consultant: Eugenie Arrowsmith 07967 102 259.

ASAP Communications Ltd. Suite One,
2 Tunstall Rd, London, SW9 8DA **t** 020 7978 9488
f 020 7978 9490 **e** info@asapcomms.co.uk
w asapcomms.com MD: Yvonne Thompson.

The Associates UK Monticello House, 45 Russell Sq,
London, WC1B 4JP **t** 020 7907 4770 **f** 020 7907 4771
e info@the-associates.co.uk **w** the-associates.co.uk
 Exec Dir: Lisa Richards.

Avalon Public Relations 4A Exmoor Street, London,
W10 6BD **t** 020 7598 8000 **f** 020 7598 7223
e danl@avalonuk.com **w** avalonuk.com Head of PR: Dan
Lloyd.

Backdrop Promotions The Summit,
40 Highgate West Hill, Highgate, London, N6 6LS
t +44 (0)208 3472792 **e** info@backdrop-promotions.com
w backdrop-promotions.com twitter.com/backdroppr
 Director: Adam Savage.

Background Noise 221-222 Shoreditch High St,
London, E1 6PJ **t** 020 7099 9060
e sam@backgroundnoise.co.uk **w** backgroundnoise.co.uk
 Director: Sam Taylor 07724 526 500.

Bad Moon Publicity Ltd 8 Jeffrey's Pl, Camden,
London, NW1 9PP **t** 020 7284 8921
e firstname@badmoon.co.uk
 myspace.com/badmoonpublicity BadMoonPR
 MD: Anton Brookes.

Badger Promotions PO Box 9121, Birmingham,
B13 8AU **t** 08712 260 910
e info@badgerpromotions.co.uk
w badgerpromotions.co.uk Promoter: Mark Badger.

Band & Brand The White House, 32 Thornton Hill,
Wimbledon, London, SW19 4HS **t** 020 8947 5475
f 020 8947 5478 **e** info@bandandbrand.com
w bandandbrand.com MD: Kim Glover.

Bang On - Online PR 77 Leonard Street, London,
EC2A 4QS **t** 020 7749 7826 **e** info@bangonpr.com
w bangonpr.com Online Publicists: Leanne Mison, Katie
Riding.

Bang PR 28 Sebastian House, Hoxton Street, London,
N1 6QH **t** 020 7739 2269 **e** info@bangpr.co.uk
w bangpr.co.uk Press Officer: Krista Booker.

FIFTH ELEMENT
Public Relations & Artist Management

TEL: 020 7722 0000
info@fifthelement.biz
www.fifthelement.biz

Barrington Harvey Troopers Yard, Bancroft, Hitchin, Hertfordshire, SG5 1JW **t** 01462 456780 **f** 01462 456781 **e** simon@bhpr.co.uk **w** barringtonharvey.co.uk
Dir: Simon Harvey.

Beatwax Communications 91 Berwick Street, London, W1F 0NE **t** 020 7734 1965 **f** 020 7292 8333 **e** michael@beatwax.com **w** beatwax.com MD: Michael Brown.

Beyond Publicity 2nd Floor, 16 - 18 Hollen St, London, W1F 8BQ **t** 020 7851 0075 **f** 020 7494 0995 **e** Natasha@beyondpublicity.net
w myspace.com/beyondpublicity Contact: Angela Robertson & Natasha Mann.

Big Cat Group Griffin House, 18-19 Ludgate House, Birmingham, B3 1DW **t** 0121 200 0910 **f** 0121 236 1342 **e** info@bcguk.com **w** bcguk.com Dir: Nick Morgan.

Big Group Ltd 91 Princedale Road, Holland Park, London, W11 4NS **t** 020 7229 8827 **f** 020 7243 1462 **e** info@biggroup.co.uk **w** biggroup.co.uk Account Director: Simon Broyd.

Big Machine Media 48 Charlotte Street, London, W1T 2NS **t** 020 3178 2441
e erika@bigmachinemedia.com **w** bigmachinemedia.com National Press Director: Erika Thomas.

Big Mouth Publicity Hope House, 40 St Peters Rd, London, W6 9BD **t** 020 8748 7276
e info@bigmouthpublicity.co.uk
w bigmouthpublicity.co.uk Contact: Steve Phillips and Jakub Blackman.

Black Arts PR - The Regional Press Specialist
Apartment 21, Number One The Parade, Cowes, Isle of Wight, PO31 7QJ **t** 01983 281567
e simonblackmore@blackartspr.com Proprietor: Simon Blackmore 07973 374 423.

Blag Promotions **t** 07966 140644 or 07812 167973
e firstname.lastname@Blagpromotions.com
w blagpromotions.com Directors: Ali Davidson & Michelle Barrett.

Blurb PR 8 West Heath Yard, 174 Miil Lane, West Hampstead, London, NW6 ITB **t** 020 7419 1221
e hello@blurbpr.com **w** blurbpr.com
myspace.com/BlurbPR BlurbMusicPR MD: Mike Plumley 0207 419 1221.

Borkowski PR 65 Clerkenwell Rd, London, EC1R 5BL
t 020 7404 3000 **e** larry@borkowski.co.uk
w borkowski.co.uk MD: Larry Franks.

BR-Asian Media Consulting 45 Circus Rd, St Johns Wood, London, NW8 9JH **t** 020 8550 9898 **f** 020 7289 9892 **e** moizvas@brasian.com **w** brasian.com MD: Moiz Vas.

Brassneck Publicity 170 Southgate Rd, London, N1 3HX **t** 020 7254 1112 **e** brassneckpr@aol.com MD: Mick Houghton.

Burt Greener Communications 6th Floor, 41 St Vincent Pl, Glasgow, G1 2ER **t** 0141 248 6007 **f** 0141 248 3322 **e** firstname@burtgreener.co.uk Dirs: Lorna Burt, Janine Greener.

Cake Group Ltd 10 Stephen Mews, London, W1T 1AG **t** 020 7307 3100 **f** 020 7307 3101
e andrea@cakegroup.com **w** cakegroup.com Head of Marketing: Andrea Ledsham.

Cannonball PR 695 High Rd, Seven Kings, Ilford, Essex, IG3 8RH **t** 020 8590 0022 **f** 020 8599 2870
e jamie@cannonballpr.com **w** cannonballpr.com
twitter.com/kevcannonballpr
ww.youtube.com/Cannonballpr MD: Jamie Danan 07885 670294.

Capitalize Ltd 52 Thrale Street, London, SE1 9HW
t 020 7940 1700 **f** 020 7940 1739
e Info@capitalize.co.uk **w** capitalize.co.uk MD: Richard Moore.

Caroline Moss PR Ltd 50 Marine Parade, Brighton, BN2 1PH **t** 020 8968 5597 **e** pr@carolinemoss.co.uk
w carolinemoss.co.uk Director: Caroline Moss.

Casablanca PR 26 Porchester Sq, London, W2 6AN
t 020 7221 2287 **f** 020 7221 2287
e fozia@casablancapr.co.uk MD: Fozia Shah 07887 610 027.

Celebration PR Ltd 8 Ashington Court, Westwood Hill, Sydenham, London, SE26 6BN
t 020 8778 9918 **f** 020 8355 7708
e celebration@dial.pipex.com Dir: James Doheny.

Ian Cheek Press Suite 5, 51D New Briggate, Leeds, West Yorkshire, LS2 8JD **t** 0113 246 9940
f 0113 246 9960 **e** iancheek@talk21.com Head of Press: Ian Cheek.

Chilli PR 21 Ferdinand St, Camden, London, NW1 8EU
t 020 7428 7505 / 7506 **e** firstname@chillipr.com
w chillipr.com Directors: Helen Jones & Jenni Page.

Chris Hewlett PR & Artist Management
127 North View Rd, London, N8 7LR
t 020 8348 6767 or 07966 491786
e info@chrishewlett.com **w** chrishewlett.com
Contact: Chris Hewlett.

CHUFFMEDIA

The Yard, 2a Oakford Rd, Tufnell Pk, London, NW5 1AH
t 020 7485 5726 **e** warren@chuffmedia.com
w chuffmedia.com myspace.com/chuffmedia
twitter.com/chuffmedia MD: Warren Higgins 0207485726. Press Officer: Holly Wild. Press Officer: Jenn Nemmo-Smith.

FIFTH ELEMENT
Public Relations & Artist Management

Pr   5 Public Relations

TEL: 020 7722 0000
info@fifthelement.biz
www.fifthelement.biz

Circus PR Argo House, Kilburn Park Rd., Maida Vale, London, NW6 5LF **t** 020 7644 0267 **f** 020 7644 0698 **e** bernard@circusrecords.net **w** circusrecords.net **MD:** Bernard MacMahon.

Max Clifford Associates 49-50 New Bond Street, London, W1Y 9HA **t** 020 7408 2350 **f** 020 7409 2294 **e** max@mcapr.co.uk **MD:** Max Clifford.

CNC Associates 95 Tantallon Rd, London, SW12 8DQ **t** 020 8673 0048 **f** 020 8673 0048 **e** office@cnclimited.co.uk **w** cnclimited.co.uk **MD:** Conor Nolan.

Complete Control PR 178 Seaforth Avenue, Motspur Pk, Merton, Surrey, KT3 6JN **t** 020 8942 9978 **e** polly@completecontrolpr.co.uk **MD:** Polly Birkbeck 07958 380353.

Complete PR PO Box 34126, London, NW10 5BZ **t** 020 8830 3300 **f** 020 8830 0033 **e** alison@completepr.co.uk **w** completepr.co.uk **MD:** Alison McNichol.

Connie Filippello Publicity 49 Portland Rd, London, W11 4LJ **t** 020 7229 5400 **f** 020 7229 4804 **e** cfpublicity@aol.com **w** cfpublicity.co.uk **MD:** Connie Filippello.

Cool Kids Music Ltd 93 Lavenham Road, London, SW18 5ER **t** 07748 321 266 or 07879 224 626 **e** info@coolkidsmusic.co.uk **w** coolkidsmusic.co.uk **Directors:** Sandra Skiba, Brijitte Dreyfus.

Copperplate Consultants 68 Belleville Rd, London, SW11 6PP **t** 020 7585 0357 **f** 020 7585 0357 **e** copperplate2000@yahoo.com **w** copperplateconsultants.com myspace/copperplate **MD:** Alan O'Leary.

Creative Cultures – Digital PR & Marketing 10 Alexandra Park Road, London, N10 2AB **t** 020 7100 3254 **f** 0871 661 4578 **e** firstname.lastname@creativecultures.biz **w** creativecultures.biz **Managing Director:** Johnny Hudson.

Cunning 192 St John Street, London, EC1V 4JY **t** 020 7566 5300 **e** info@cunning.com **w** cunning.com **MD:** Anna Carloss.

Cypher PR Newstate Ents, Unit 2A Queens Studios, 121 Salusbury Rd, London, NW6 6RG **t** 020 7372 4474 **f** 020 7328 4447 **e** info@cypherpr.com **w** cypherpr.com **Contact:** Rupert Cogan / Lou Page.

Darkhorse Publicity Studio 401, Westbourne Studios, 242 Acklam Rd, London, W10 5JJ **t** 07595 899054 **e** jd@darkhorsepublicity.co.uk **w** darkhorsepublicity.co.uk myspace.com/darkhorsepublicity james_davies **MD:** James Davies.

Darling Promotions Unit 204, 16-16A Baldwin Gardens, London, EC1N 7RJ **t** 020 7379 8787 **f** 020 7379 5737 **e** info@darlinguk.com **w** darlingdepartment.com

DawBell Office 417, 8 Duncannon Street, London, WC2N 4JF **t** 020 7484 5012 **e** info@dawbell.com **w** dawbell.com facebook.com/group.php?gid=127572234650 twitter.com/DawBell **Managing Directors:** Richard Dawes & Stuart Bell.

Delta PR PO Box 25285, London, N12 0XD **t** 0845 680 1857 **e** mal@delta-pr.com **w** delta-pr.com **Owner:** Mal Smith.

Destiny Destiny Towers, St Margaret's House, 21 Old Ford Rd, London, E2 9PL **t** 020 8981 2746 **e** martin@destinytowers.com **w** destinytowers.com myspace.com/destinytowers **Contact:** Martin Evans.

Diffusion PR PO Box 2610, Mitcham, Surrey, CR4 2YH **t** 020 7384 3200 **f** 0871 277 3055 **e** jodie@diffusionpr.co.uk **w** diffusionpr.co.uk **MD:** Jodie Stewart.

Division Media Ltd Studio 7 Acklam Workspace, 10 Acklam Rd, London, W10 5QZ **t** 020 8962 8282 **e** zac@divisionpromotions.com **w** divisionpromotions.com **Dirs:** Zac Leeks, James Sherry.

DNA Publicity Unit 4, Wellington Close, London, W11 2AN **t** 020 7792 5100 **e** odaniaud@aol.com **Director:** Olly Daniaud 020 7792 5200.

Dog Day Press Finsbury Business Centre, 40 Bowling Green Lane, London, EC1R 0NE **t** 020 7415 7108 or 7164 **e** info@dogdaypress.com **w** dogdaypress.com **Contact:** Nathan Beazer, Anna Mears 07811 159623.

Dorothy Howe Press & Publicity 41 Hartington Court, Hartington Rd, Chiswick, London, W4 3TT **t** 020 8995 3920 **e** press@dorothyhowe.co.uk **MD:** Dorothy Howe.

Duff Press G17, Riverbank House, 1, Putney Bridge Approach, London, SW6 3JD **t** 020 7736 7611 **f** 020 7371 9949 **e** info@duffpress.co.uk **w** duffpress.com myspace.com/duffpress **Director:** Duff Battye 07904 385308.

DWL (Dave Woolf Ltd) 53 Goodge St, London, W1T 1TG **t** 020 7436 5529 **f** 020 7637 8776 **e** dave@dwl.uk.net **w** dwl.uk.net **MD:** Dave Woolf.

Electric PR 24A, Bartholomew Villas, London, NW5 2LL **t** 020 7424 0405 **f** 020 7424 0305 **e** electric_pr@hotmail.com **MD:** Laurence Verfaillie.

Emms Publicity 215 Aberdeen House, 22-24 Highbury Grove, London, N5 2EA **t** 020 7226 0990 **e** info@emmspublicity.com **w** emmspublicity.com **MD:** Stephen Emms.

Emmsix: Unit A, The Courtyard, 42 Colwith Rd, London, W6 9EY **t** 020 8846 3737 **f** 020 8846 3738 **e** christianne@emmsix.co.uk **MD:** Christianne Lambert.

EPM PO Box 47264, London, W7 1WX **t** 020 8566 0200 **e** jonas@epm-music.com **w** epm-music.com myspace.com/epmonline **Partner:** Jonas Stone.

FIFTH ELEMENT
Public Relations & Artist Management

5
Public Relations
Pr

TEL: 020 7722 0000
info@fifthelement.biz
www.fifthelement.biz

Never subscribed to
MusicWeek before?

Visit musicweek.com
and sign up for your free trial

www.musicweek.com

Excess Press The Metway, 55 Canning St, Brighton, BN2 OEF **t** 01273 667991 **e** info@excesspress.co.uk **w** excesspress.co.uk ✉ Dirs: Jayne Houghton, Fiona Clarke, Jack Thunder..

FerraraPR 18 Fitzgerald House, 169 East India Dock Rd, London, E14 0HH **t** 07946 523007 **e** rosalia@ferrarapr.com **w** ferrarapr.com
f facebook.com/ferraraPR
myspace.com/rosaliaferrara twitter.com/FerraraPR
✉ MD: Rosalia Ferrara 020 7515 3643.

FFR UK 2 Hastings Terrace, Conway Road, London, N15 3BE **t** 020 8826 5900 **f** 020 8826 5902 **e** fullfrontalrecords@hotmail.com **w** ffruk.com ✉ Dir: Tara Rez.

Fifth Avenue PR 37 Fifth Avenue, London, W10 4DL **t** 020 8960 5802 **e** fifthavenuepr@googlemail.com ✉ Director: Sarah Lowe.

FIFTH ELEMENT PR

125 Parkway, London, NW1 7PS **t** 020 7722 0000 **e** info@fifthelement.biz **w** fifthelement.biz ✉ Director: Catherine Hockley 07976 758491.
Launched in 2000 Fifth Element is one of the UK's leading independent PR agencies, covering national, regional and online press.

Fistral PR 114 The Royal, Wilton Pl, Salford, Manchester, M3 6FT **t** 0161 835 4142 **e** info@fistralpr.co.uk **w** fistralpr.co.uk fistral fistralpr ✉ MD: Peggy Manning.

Focus Marketing Communications
Suite 6, Ruxley House, 550B London Rd, Sutton, Surrey, SM3 9AA **t** 020 8641 8614 **e** info@focusmarketingcommunications.com **w** focusmarketingcommunications.com ✉ MD: Brian Oliver.

Free Associates
Unit S17 - Shakespeare Business Centre, 245 A Coldharbour Lane, London, SW9 8RR **t** 020 7095 8188 **e** jody@freeassociates.org ✉ Dir: Jody Gillett 07818 453 650.

Freeman PR Room 236, The Bon Marche Centre, 241-251 Ferndale Rd, London, SW9 8BJ **t** 020 7738 3754 **f** 020 7738 6739 **e** info@freemanpr.net **w** freemanpr.net ✉ Dir: Amanda Freeman.

Freewheelin' PR Freewheelin Media, 2 Sutton Lane, London, EC1M 5PU **t** 020 7490 5675 **f** 020 7253 6281 **e** info@freewheelinmedia.com **w** freewheelinmedia.com ✉ Dir: Vikas Malik.

Frequency Media (FMG UK Ltd) Suite 115 The Greenhouse, Custard Factory 2, Gibb Street, Birmingham, West Midlands, B9 4AA **t** 0121 224 7450 or 0121 224 7452 **f** 0121 224 7451 **e** gerard@fmguk.com **w** fmguk.com ✉ PR Directors: Gerard Franklin & Margaret Murray 07866 422109.

Frontier Promotions The Grange, Cockley Cley Rd, Hilborough, Thetford, Norfolk, IP26 5BT **t** 01760 756 394 **f** 01760 756 398 **e** frontieruk@btconnect.com ✉ MD: Sue Williams.

G Promo PR 2 Streatley Mews, Corve St, Ludlow, Shropshire, SY8 2PN **t** 01584 873211 **e** GPromo@btinternet.com **w** gpromopr.com ✉ Contact: Geraint Jones.

Garrett Axford Ltd Studio 12, The Triangle Centre, 1 Commerce Way, Lancing Business Park, Lancing, W. Sussex, BN15 8UP **t** 01903 854 900 **f** 01903 854 901 **e** mail@garrett-axford.co.uk **w** garrett-axford.co.uk ✉ Partners: Georgina Garrett, Simon Axford Jones.

Gerry Lyseight PR Unit S17, Shakespeare Business Centre, 245a, Coldharbour Lane, London, SW9 8RR **t** 020 7095 8146 **e** gerry@mambo.eclipse.co.uk **w** gerrylyseight.co.uk ✉ MD: Gerry Lyseight.

Get Involved Communications Ltd The Studio, 131C Salusbury Rd, London, NW6 6RG **t** 020 7604 2944 **f** 0870 420 4392 **e** jamiestockwood@getinvolvedltd.com **w** getinvolvedltd.com ✉ Head Of PR & Music: Jamie Stockwood.

GFI Promotions t 07904 232292 **e** gfi-promotions@ntlworld.com **w** gfi-promotions.com ✉ Master of Promotion: Golly Gallagher.

Glass Ceiling PR 50 Stroud Green Rd, London, N4 3ES **t** 020 7263 1240 **f** 020 7281 5671 **e** promo@glassceilingpr.com ✉ MD: Harriet Simms.

Global Guest List PR Suite 42, Pall Mall Deposits, 124-128 Barlby Road, London, W10 6BL **t** 020 8962 0601 **f** 020 8962 0575 **e** info@globalguestlist.net **w** globalguestlist.net ✉ MD: Babs Epega.

Global Publicity 60, Maltings Pl, London, SW6 2BX **t** 07957 434517 **e** nikki@globalpublicity.co.uk **w** globalpublicity.co.uk myspace.com/globalpublicity twitter.com/globalpr ✉ MD: Nikki Wright-McNeill.

Gold Star Agency PO Box 130, Ross on Wye, Herefordshire, HR9 6WY **t** 01989 770105 **e** info@goldstarpr.com **w** goldstarpr.com ✉ MD: Nita Keeler.

Gorgeous PR Inc. 7551 Melrose Avenue, Suite 7, Los Angeles, CA 90046, United States **t** +1-323-782-9000 **f** +1-323-658-6189 **e** versa@gorgeouspr.com **w** gorgeouspr.com ✉ President: Versa Manos.

Greendesk Publicity 29a Waller Road, London, SE14 5LE **t** 07986 235 855 **e** helen@greendesk.demon.co.uk ✉ MD: Helen Maleed.

FIFTH ELEMENT
Public Relations & Artist Management

Pr

TEL: 020 7722 0000
info@fifthelement.biz
www.fifthelement.biz

GreenGab-PR LTD 85 Clifton Hill, London, London, NW8 0JN **t** 020 7625 7951 **e** gaby@greengabpr.co.uk 🖴 Director: Gaby Green 07968 199617.

Hackford Jones PR Third Floor, 16 Manette St, London, W1D 4AR **t** 020 7287 9788 **f** 020 7287 9731 **e** info@hackfordjonespr.co.uk **w** hackfordjonespr.com 🖴 Co-MDs: Simon Jones, Jonathan Hackford.

Hall Or Nothing Unit 4A, Ransomes Dock, 35-37 Parkgate Rd, Battersea, London, SW11 4NP **t** 020 7228 3390 **f** 020 7350 2472 **e** press@hallornothing.com **w** hallornothing.com 🖴 MD: Terri Hall.

HardZone Marketing & PR
Network European Business Centre, 329-339 Putney Bridge Rd, 3-9 Broomhill Rd, London, SW15 2PG **t** 020 8788 5922 **f** 020 8785 2842 **e** firstname@hardzone.co.uk **w** hardzone.co.uk 🖴 MD: Jackie Davidson.

Hartmann Media Lovat House, Gavell Rd, Kilsyth, Glasgow, G65 9BS **t** 01236 826666 **f** 01236 825560 **e** tessa@hartmannmedia.co.uk 🖴 MD: Tessa Hartmann.

Hawk Media Monitoring DMS, 44-46 Scrutton Street, London, EC2A 4HH **t** 0845 055 0979 **f** 0845 055 0970 **e** amy.lecoz@dmsukltd.com **w** dmsukltd.com 🖴 Dir: Amy Le Coz.

Henry's House PR 108 Gt. Russell Street, London, WC1B 3NA **t** 020 7291 3000 **f** 020 7291 3001 **e** jane@henryshouse.com **w** henryshouse.com 🖴 Dir: Jane Shaw.

Hermana PR 44 Church Rd, London, SE19 2ET **t** 020 8771 8800 **e** firstname@hermana.co.uk 🖪 myspace.com/hermanapress 🖪 twitter.com/hermanapr 🖴 Dir: Ken Lower.

Hero PR 3 Tennyson Rd, Thatcham, Berkshire, RG18 3FR **t** 01635 868385 **f** 01635 868385 **e** owen@heropr.com **w** heropr.com 🖴 MD: Owen Packard.

Hill & Knowlton (UK) 20 Soho Sq, London, W1A 1PR **t** 020 7413 3000 **f** 020 7413 3111 **e** wfick@hillandknowlton.com **w** hillandknowlton.co.uk 🖴 Brand Mgr: Wayne Fick.

hush-hush Suite 14-15, Old Truman Brewery, 91 Brick Lane, London, E1 6QL **t** 020 8989 1726 **e** danielle@hush-hush.org.uk 🖴 Press Officer: Danielle Richards 020 7223 7456.

Hyperactive Publicity Ltd 47 Riverview Gardens, Barnes, London, SW13 8QZ **t** 020 8741 7343 **e** info@hyperactive-publicity.com 🖴 Contact: Caroline Turner.

Hyperlaunch New Media Mardyke House, 16-22 Hotwell Rd, Bristol, BS8 4UD **t** 0117 914 0070 **f** 0117 914 0071 **e** don@hyperlaunch.com **w** hyperlaunch.com 🖴 MD: Don Jenkins.

Ice-Pr Ltd Unit 5, 10 Acklam Road, London, W10 5QZ **t** 020 8968 2222 **f** 020 8968 2220 **e** info@ice-pr.com **w** ice-pr.com 🖴 Contact: Jason Price.

ID Publicity 25 Britannia Row, London, N1 8QH **t** 020 7359 4455 **f** 020 7704 1616 **e** info@idpublicity.com 🖴 MD: Lisa Moskaluk.

Idea Generation 11 Chance St, London, E2 7JB **t** 020 7749 6850 **f** 020 7428 4948 **e** info@ideageneration.co.uk **w** ideageneration.co.uk 🖪 twitter.com/igmusic 🖴 Associate Director: Kate Statham 02077496854.

IMPRESSIVE

9 Jeffrey's Place, Camden, London, NW1 9PP **t** 020 7284 3444 **f** 020 7284 1840 **e** mel@impressivepr.com **w** impressivepr.com 🖴 MD: Mel Brown.
National, Regional, Student and On-line PR. Visual advice and photoshoots. Experienced, dedicated, enthusiastic, creative... The future is Impressive. Music, Tours, Comedy, Celebrities & events.

In House Press 3rd Floor, 14 Tariff St, Manchester, M1 2FF **t** 0161 228 2070 **f** 0161 228 3070 **e** info@inhousepress.com **w** inhousepress.com 🖪 myspace.com/inhousepress 🖴 MD: David Cooper.

INCUBATOR CREATIVE MEDIA

19 Catherine Place, London, SW1E 6DX **t** 020 7802 0160 **e** info@incubator-uk.com **w** incubator-uk.com 🖪 twitter.com/incubatoruk 🖴 Founder & Creative/Strategic Diretcor: Dan Walsh.

Indiscreet PR 30 The Crescent, Whitley Bay, Tyne & Wear, NE26 2JG **t** 07813 290474 **e** alan@indiscreetpr.com **w** indiscreetpr.com 🖴 Dirs: Alan Robinson, Lesley Shone 07930 810751.

Infected 29 Castle Rd, Causewayhead, Stirling, FK9 5JB **t** 01786 471133 **e** mike.infected000@btclick.com 🖴 MD: Mike Gourlay 07782 269750.

Infinite Top Floor, 126 New Bond St, London, W1S 1DZ **t** 020 7290 9590 **e** murray@infinitepr.co.uk 🖴 MD: Murray Chalmers.

inform@tion communication ltd
6 Hornsey Lane Gardens, London, N6 5PB **t** 020 8374 6040 **e** infocom@dial.pipex.com 🖴 MD: Michael Thorne.

FIFTH ELEMENT
Public Relations & Artist Management

TEL: 020 7722 0000
info@fifthelement.biz
www.fifthelement.biz

Interactive M Ltd Bridge House, St Marys Rd, West Hythe, Kent, CT21 4NU **t** 01303 261893 **e** info@interactivem.co.uk **w** interactivem.co.uk ✉ MD: Jo Cerrone.

J2PR 131C Salusbury Rd, London, NW6 6DG **t** 07866 435876 **e** j2pr@thesundayclub.com ✉ Owner: Jamie Stockwood.

Jackie Gill Promotions 3 Warren Mews, London, W1T 6AN **t** 020 7383 5550 **f** 020 7383 3020 **e** jackie@jackiegill.co.uk ✉ MD: Jackie Gill.

James Grant Music 94 Strand On The Green, Chiswick, London, W4 3NN **t** 020 8742 4950 **f** 020 8742 4951 **e** enquiries@jamesgrant.co.uk **w** jamesgrant.co.uk ✉ Co-MDs: Simon Hargreaves, Nick Worsley.

Jennie Halsall Consultants PO Box 22467, London, W6 0SG **t** 020 8741 0003 **f** 020 8846 9652 **e** jhc@dircon.co.uk ✉ MD: Jennie Halsall.

Joanna Burns PR Athene House, 86 The Broadway, London, NW7 3TD **t** 020 8906 3444 **e** info@JoannaBurnsPR.com **w** JoannaBurnsPR.com ⦿ Facebook.com/MusicPR ⬛ Twitter.com/MusicPR ✉ MD: Joanna Burns.

John Crosby Music Publicity/PR PO Box 230, Hastings, E Sussex, TN34 3XZ **t** 0845 108 7811 **f** 0870 041 0577 **e** john@johncrosby.plus.com **w** johncrosby.plus.com ⦿ facebook.com/johncrosbyPR ⬛ myspace.com/johncrosbypr ⬛ twitter.com/johncrosby1950 ✉ MD: John Crosby 07920 260 824.

Judy Totton Publicity EBC House, Ranelagh Gardens, London, SW6 3PA **t** 020 7371 8158 / 8159 **f** 020 7371 7862 **e** judy@judytotton.com **w** judytotton.com ✉ MD: Judy Totton.

Karenstringer.pr 60 Shirley Drive, Hove, East Sussex, BN3 6UF **t** 01273 240246 **e** karenstringer.pr@ntlworld.com ✉ Contact: Karen Stringer 07808 404 242.

Kelly Pike Publicity Suite 120, Park Royal Business Centre, 9-17 Park Royal Road, London, NW10 7LQ **t** 020 8621 2345 **f** 020 8621 2344 **e** kpikepr@globalnet.co.uk ✉ MD: Kelly Pike.

Kish Communications 6 Creasy Estate, Aberdour St, London, SE1 4SL **t** 07931 423646 **e** kate@kishcommunications.com **w** kishcommunications.com ✉ Managing Director: Kate Matheou 0044 7931423646.

LA DIGIT - ONLINE PR

Hope House, 40 St Peter's Road, London, W6 9BD **t** 02085633926 **e** Info@LaDigit.co.uk **w** LaDigit.co.uk ✉ Director: Paul Piggott 020 8563 3926.

LANDER PR LTD

Lander Music Group, Athene House, 86 The Broadway, London, NW7 3TD **t** 020 8906 2224 **e** judd@landerpr.com **w** landerpr.com ⦿ facebook.com/LanderPR ⬛ myspace.com/landermusicpr ⬛ twitter.com/MusicPromotions ✉ Director: Judd Lander.

Laura Norton PR 37 Longcroft Gardens, Welwyn Garden City, Herts, AL8 6TR **t** 07908 575 359 **e** Laura@lauranortonpr.com **w** lauranortonpr.com ✉ Director / Publicist: Laura Norton.

LD Communications 58-59 Gt. Marlborough St, London, W1F 7JY **t** 020 7439 7222 **f** 020 7734 2933 **e** info@ldcommunications.co.uk **w** ldcommunications.co.uk ✉ CEO: Bernard Doherty.

Leslie Gilotti - Music & New Media Promotions 79 Northcote Rd, London, E17 7DT **t** 07867 785 070 **e** info@gilotti.net **w** gilotti.net ✉ Dir: Leslie Gilotti.

Leyline Publicity Studio 24, Westbourne Studios, 242 Acklam Rd, London, W10 5JJ **t** 020 7575 3285 **f** 020 7575 3286 **e** firstname@leylinepromotions.com **w** leylinepublicity.com ⬛ myspace.com/leylinepublicity ✉ MD: Adrian Leigh, Ben Mercer, Nick Bateson.

Lucid PR 2nd Floor, Kenilworth House, 79/80 Margaret St, London, W1W 8TA **t** 020 7307 7449 **e** hi@lucidpr.co.uk **w** lucidpr.co.uk ✉ Dirs: Charlie Lycett.

LVPR 23 Ashfield Rd, London, W3 7JE **t** 020 8743 6137 **e** linda@lindavalentine.biz ✉ MD: Linda Valentine 07949 174811.

MaDa Music Entertainment 25 Milton Court, Chesterton Close, Wandsworth, London, SW18 1ST **t** 07771 710234 **e** adamnicolmusic@gmail.com ⬛ myspace.com/madamusicentertainment ✉ MD: Adam Nicol.

Magnum PR 41 Halcyon Wharf, 5 Wapping High St, London, E1W 1LH **t** 020 7709 0914 **e** Tammy@magnumpr.co.uk ✉ MD: Tammy Arthur 07956 241542.

FIFTH ELEMENT
Public Relations & Artist Management

Making Waves 40 Underwood Street, London, N1 7JQ **t** 020 7490 0944 **f** 020 7490 1026 **e** info@makingwaves.co.uk or scotty@makingwaves.co.uk **w** makingwaves.co.uk 🖂 PR Manager: Dan Minty.

The Management A108 The Oak, Grange Hall, Brehon Field Rd, Rathfarnham, Dublin 16, Ireland **t** +353 1 443 3111 **e** kathryn@themanagement.ie **w** themanagement.ie 🖂 Owner: Kathryn Mason +353 (0) 87 262 7977.

Manilla PR Ltd Evans Business Centre, Stephenson Court, Skippers Lane Industrial Estate, Middlesbrough, TS6 6UT **t** 01642 453425 **e** info@manillapr.com **w** manillapr.com 🖂 MD: Tony McDonagh 07792 647760.

Material Marketing & Communications Riverside House, 260 Clyde St, Glasgow, G1 4JH **t** 0141 204 7970 **f** 0141 221 8643 **e** spence@materialmc.co.uk **w** materialmc.co.uk 🖂 myspace.com/wearematerial 🖂 youtube.com/materialblog 🖂 Directors: Colin Spence & Sera Miller.

MBC PR Wellington Building, 28-32 Wellington Rd, London, NW8 9SP **t** 020 7483 9205 **f** 020 7483 9206 🖂 Co-MDs: Barbara Charone, Moira Bellas.

Mbop Promotions 40 Bowling Green Lane, Clerkenwell, London, EC1R 0NE **t** 020 7415 7010 **f** 020 7415 7030 **e** paul.ballance@mbopglobal.co.uk **w** mbop.co.uk 🖂 Head of Promotions: Paul Ballance +44(0)2074157010.

Mercenary Publicity Unit 17, Saga Centre, 326 Kensal Rd, London, W10 5BZ **t** 020 8354 4111 **e** kas@mercenarypublicity.com **w** mercenarypublicity.com 🖂 myspace.com/mercenarypublicity 🖂 Dir: Kas Mercer 07904 157 720.

Midas Public Relations 10-14 Old Court Pl, London, W8 4PL **t** 020 7361 7860 **e** charlie.harris@midaspr.co.uk **w** midaspr.co.uk 🖂 twitter.com/midaspr 🖂 Senior Account Manager: Charlie Harris.

Midnight Communications 3 Lloyds Wharf, Mill St, London, SE1 2BA **t** 020 7232 4517 **f** 020 7232 4540 **e** enquiries@midnight.co.uk **w** midnight.co.uk 🖂 Director: Vicki Hughes.

Million PR London **e** gillian@millionpr.com **w** millionpr.com 🖂 Director: Gillian Pittaway 07947 174246.

Mingo PR Flat 3/1, 19 Duke St, Glasgow, G4 0UL **t** 0141 552 3623 **e** mingo@easynet.co.uk **w** mingopr.co.uk 🖂 MD: Jill Mingo 0780 372 8469.

Momentum PR Omnibus Workspace, 39-41 North Rd, London, N7 9DP **t** 020 7700 0275 **e** mandy@momentumpr.co.uk **w** momentumpr.co.uk 🖂 MD: Mandy Crompton.

Moore Publicity 187 Mackenzie Rd, Beckenham, BR3 4SE **t** 07809 642044 or 020 8676 9540 **e** nik@moorepublicity.co.uk **w** moorepublicity.co.uk 🖂 Proprietor: Nik Moore.

Mosquito Media 64a Warwick Avenue, Little Venice, London, W9 2PU **t** 07813 174 185 **e** mosquitomedia@aol.com **w** mosquito-media.co.uk 🖂 Contact: Richard Abbott.

Motion PR 1 Stucley Studios, Stucley Place, Camden, London, NW1 8NS **t** 020 7485 9773 **f** 020 7267 6638 **e** giovanna@motionpr.co.uk **w** motionpr.co.uk 🖂 Head of PR and Marketing: Giovanna Ferin.

MP Promotions 13 Greave, Romiley, Stockport, Cheshire, SK6 4PU **t** 0161 494 7934 / 07801 191784 **e** maria@mppromotions.co.uk 🖂 Director: Maria Philippou.

Music & Media Consulting Ltd 3 Cypress Close, Doddington, Cambs, PE15 0LE **t** 07774 426966 **f** 01354 740847 **e** john@musicandmediaconsulting.com **w** musicandmediaconsulting.com 🖂 Director: John S. Cronin 01354 740847.

Music Company (London) Ltd. 1 Rose Alley, London, SE1 9AS **t** 020 7921 9233 **f** 020 7261 1058 **e** musicco@musicco.f9.co.uk 🖂 MD: Melanne Mueller.

MusicPress PR 16 The Green, Wolviston, Co. Durham, TS22 5LN **t** 01740-644453 **e** allan@musicpresspr.com 🖂 MD: Allan Glen.

Mutante Inc First Floor, 3 - 9 Belfast Rd, London, N16 6UN **t** 07947 609867 **e** sean@mutante.co.uk **w** mutante.co.uk 🖂 Director: Sean Newsham.

Name Music Innovation Labs, Watford Rd, Harrow, Middlesex, HA1 3TP **t** 020 8357 7305 **e** sam@namemusic.co.uk **w** namemusic.co.uk 🔳 tinyurl.com/namefacebook 🖂 twitter.com/namemusic 🖂 MD: Sam Shemtob.

Nelson Bostock Communications
Compass House, 22 Redan Pl, London, W2 4SA **t** 020 7229 4400 **f** 020 7727 2025 **e** info@nelsonbostock.com **w** nelsonbostock.com 🔳 facebook.com/group.php?gid=2505616690&ref=searc h&sid=575590108.3927833083..1 🖂 Assistant Director: Bruce McLachlan.

New Crime Press 1 Soneyford, Uttoxeter, Staffordshire, ST14 8BW **e** newcrimepress@googlemail.com 🖂 Press Agents: James Brighouse / Craig Bunting.

Noble PR 2 Prospero Rd, London, N19 3RF **t** 020 7272 7772 **e** peter@noblepr.co.uk **w** noblepr.co.uk 🖂 MD: Peter Noble 0794 908 9762.

Norwich Artistes Bryden, 115 Holt Rd, Hellesdon, Norwich, NR6 6UA **t** 01603 407101 **f** 01603 405314 **e** brian@norwichartistes.co.uk **w** norwichartistes.co.uk 🖂 MD: Brian Russell.

O PR PO Box 34002, London, N21 3WX **t** 020 8351 2542 **f** 020 8482 9270 **e** info@o-pr.com **w** o-pr.com 🖂 MD: Olga Hadjilambri.

OceanFall International Media Marketing & PR e info@oceanfall.com **w** oceanfall.com oceanfall.co.uk 🖂 Marketing Director: Leon Mitchell.

FIFTH ELEMENT
Public Relations & Artist Management

5 Public Relations
Pr

TEL: 020 7722 0000
info@fifthelement.biz
www.fifthelement.biz

Orbit PR Unit 206, 2nd Floor, Curtain House, 134-146 Curtain Rd, London, EC2A 3AR **t** 020 7033 4667 **f** 020 7033 4668 **e** karen@orbitpr.net
myspace.com/orbitpr Director: Karen Johnson 07930 391607.

Orbit22 Media & Entertainment Churchill House, 12 Mosley St, Newcastle upon Tyne, NE1 1DE **t** 0191 230 8023 **e** orbit22media@gmail.com www.myspace.com/orbit22media CEO/Owner: Jacquiline Swinburne +44(0)7766115337.

Outerglobe 113 Cheeseman's, London, W14 9XH **t** 07939564103 **e** debbie@outerglobe.com **w** outerglobe.com outerglobe myspace.com/outerglobe MD: Debbie Golt.

Outpost Media Ltd Arch 462, Kingsland Viaduct, 83 Rivington Street, Shoreditch, London, EC2A 3AY **t** 020 7684 5634 **e** david@outpostmedia.co.uk **w** outpostmedia.co.uk Dir: David Silverman 07811 422 266.

Outside Management Butler House, 177-178 Tottenham Court Rd, London, W1T 7NY **t** 020 7436 3633 **f** 020 7436 3632 **e** info@outside-org.co.uk **w** outside-org.co.uk Director: Alan Edwards.

The Outside Organisation Ltd. Butler House, 177-178 Tottenham Court Rd, London, W1T 7NY **t** 020 7436 3633 **f** 020 7436 3632 **e** info@outside-org.co.uk **w** outside-org.co.uk @outsideorg Chairman: Alan Edwards.

P&M (Public Relations & Marketing)
3rd Floor, Winchester House, 259-269 Old Marylebone Rd, London, NW1 5RA **t** 020 7170 4189 **f** 020 7170 4001 **e** info@pmltd.co.uk **w** pmltd.co.uk Head of PR: Phyllisia Adjei.

Pad Communications 11 Junction Works, Paradise Wharf, 40 Ducie St, Manchester, M1 2DF **t** 0845 458 8662 **f** 0845 458 8663 **e** info@padcom.co.uk **w** padcom.co.uk MD: Simon Morrison.

Paddy Forwood PR The Studio, Manor Farmhouse, Stubhampton, Blandford, Dorset, DT11 8JS **t** 01258 830014 **f** 01258 830014 **e** pad.forwood@virgin.net Dir: Paddy Forwood 07779 606 533.

Palmer Evans Associates 5 Landseer Rd, Hove, East Sussex, BN3 7AF **t** 01273 775801 **e** jimevans@talk21.com MD: Jim Evans.

Parallel PR Tewkesbury, Gloucestershire, GL20 6AZ **e** steve@parallelpr.co.uk **w** parallelpr.co.uk Media Consultant: Steve Benton 01684 833132.

Peafish Promotions 30 Mildmay Grove South, Islington, London, N1 4RL **t** 07772 405 545 **e** info@peafish.com **w** myspace.com/peafish Contact: Sarah Pink.

Peter Thompson Associates
Flat 1, 12 Bourchier St., London, W1D 4HZ **t** 020 7439 1210 **f** 020 7439 1202 **e** info@ptassociates.co.uk MD: Peter Thompson.

Phill Savidge PR 8 Denton Rd, London, N8 9NS **t** 020 8348 0373 **f** 020 8348 0373 **e** phill@savagepr.com **w** savagepr.com MD: Phill Savidge.

Phuture Trax Press & Events PR PO Box 48527, London, NW4 4ZB **t** 020 8959 9131 **f** 020 8959 9131 **e** nicky@phuturetrax.co.uk **w** phuturetrax.co.uk myspace.com/phuturetrax MD: Nicky Trax 07951 128001.

Piranha PR Flat 7, 51 The Gardens, London, SE22 9QQ **t** 020 8299 1928 **e** rosie@piranha-pr.co.uk **w** piranha-pr.co.uk myspace.com/piranhapr MD: Rosie Wilby 07956 460372.

Planet Earth Publicity 49 Rylstone Way, Saffron Walden, Essex, CB11 3BL **t** 01799 501347 **f** 01799 501347 **e** info@planetearthpublicity.com **w** planetearthpublicity.com MD: Dave Clarke 07966 557 774.

Plug Two Cardiff **t** 07972 537440 **e** paul@plugtwo.com **w** plugtwo.com Plugger, Writer, Editor of Swn Magazine: Paul Barnett.

Poker PR Creative Media 8 Foundry St, Brighton, East Sussex, BN1 4AT **t** 0845 871 8011 **e** dave@pokerpr.co.uk **w** pokerpr.co.uk pokerpr.co.uk/pokerprcreativemedia myspace.com/poker_pr twitter.com/poker_pr Creative Director: David Mitchell.

Pomona Suite 4, Bridge House, 13 Devonshire Street, Keighley, West Yorkshire, BD21 2BH **t** 01422 846900 **e** Mark@pomonauk.co.uk **w** pomonapr.com Owner: Mark Hodkinson.

Porter Frith Panther House, 38 Mount Pleasant, London, WC1X 0AN **t** 020 7833 8444 **e** porterfrith@hotmail.com MD: Liz Frith.

Power Promotions Unit 11, Impress House, Mansell Rd, London, W3 7QH **t** 020 8932 3030 **f** 020 8932 3031 **e** mark@power.co.uk **w** power.co.uk Promotions Manager: Mark Loverush.

PPR Rylett Studios, 77 Rylett Crescent, London, W12 9RP **t** 020 8746 4600 **f** 020 8746 4618 **e** peteflatt@pprpublicity.com **w** pprpublicity.com MD: Pete Flatt 020 8746 4601.

Precious PR 3 Eliot Place, Blackheath, London, SE3 0QL **t** 020 8318 0368 **e** jack@preciouspr.plus.com **w** myspace.com/preciouspr MD: Jacqueline McKillion 07958 495 199.

Prescription PR 102a Pentonville Rd, London, N1 9JB **e** james@prescriptionpr.com **w** prescriptionpr.co.uk MD: James Parrish 07758216559.

Press Counsel PR 5-7 Vernon Yard, Off Portobello Rd, London, W11 2DX **t** 020 7792 9400 **f** 020 7243 2262 **e** info@presscounsel.com **w** presscounsel.com myspace.com/presscounsel MD: Charlie Caplowe.

PresStop Creatives 4E Oakdale Road, London, SW16 2HW **t** 020 8677 0193 **e** shazia@presstopcreatives.com **w** presstopcreatives.com MD: Shazia Nizam.

FIFTH ELEMENT
Public Relations & Artist Management

5
Public Relations
Pr

TEL: 020 7722 0000
info@fifthelement.biz
www.fifthelement.biz

Progressive Publicity County House, St Mary's St, Worcester, WR1 1HB **t** 01905 729149 **f** 01905 729149 **e** kate.brookes@progressivepublicity.com **w** progressivepublicity.com 🖪 myspace.com/progressivepublicity 🖪 Contact: Kate Brookes.

Psycho Media 111 Clarence Rd, Wimbledon, London, SW19 8QB **t** 020 8540 8122 **f** 020 8715 2827 **e** john@psycho.co.uk **w** psycho.co.uk 🖪 Director: John Mabley.

Public City PR 3 Nicholls Yard, Crow Lane, Reed, Royston, SG8 8BJ **e** em@publiccitypr.com **w** publiccitypr.com 🖪 Publicity: Em Van Duyts 07949 554666.

Public Eye Communications Ltd Plaza Suite 318, 535 Kings Road, London, SW10 0SZ **t** 020 7351 1555 **f** 020 7351 1010 **e** ciara@publiceye.co.uk 🖪 Chairman: Ciara Parkes.

The Publicity Connection 3 Haversham Lodge, 2-4 Melrose Avenue, London, NW2 4JS **t** 020 8450 8882 **f** 020 8208 4219 **e** sharon@thepublicityconnection.com **w** thepublicityconnection.com 🖪 MD: Sharon Chevin.

Pure Press e alison@purepress.co.uk **w** purepress.co.uk 🖪 MD: Alison Edwards.

Pure Publicity 31 Mapesbury Rd, London, NW2 4HS **t** 020 8208 1279 **e** kim.machray@purepublicity.co.uk **w** purepublicity.co.uk 🖪 MD: Kim Machray 07720 941 391.

Purple PR (Entertainment) 28 Savile Row, London, W1S 2EU **t** 020 7434 7092 **e** firstname@purplepr.com **w** purplepr.com 🖪 Dirs: William Rice, Carl Fysh.

Queen of the Crop™ C/O Reception, The Custard Factory, Gibb Street, Birmingham, West Midlands, B9 4AA **t** 0121 753 7700 **e** info@queenofthecrop.co.uk **w** queenofthecrop.co.uk 🖪 Contact: Miss Nzinga Graham-Smith aka Naz +44 (0)7858 444 913.

Quite Great Design Unit D, Magog Court, Shelford Bttm, Cambridge, CB2 4AD **t** 01223 410000 **e** Harvey@quitegreat.co.uk **w** quitegreat.co.uk 🖪 myspace.com/quitegreat 🖪 twitter.com/QuiteGreat 🖪 MD: Pete Bassett.

Quite Great Publicity Unit D, Magog Court, Shelford Bttm, Cambridge, CB2 4AD **t** 01223 410 000 **e** Harvey@quitegreat.co.uk **w** quitegreat.co.uk 🖪 MD: Pete Bassett.

Raised On Radio 23 Handley Court, Aigburth, Liverpool, L19 3QS **t** 0151 427 9884 **f** 0151 427 9884 **e** steve.raisedonradio@tinyworld.co.uk 🖪 Director of Promotion: Steve Dinwoodie.

Random PR 41 Walters Workshop, 249 Kensal Road, London, W10 5DB **t** 020 8968 1545 **f** 020 8964 1181 **e** danni@randompr.co.uk **w** randompr.co.uk 🖪 Office Manager: Danni Chambers.

Rare Communications 144 Gloucester Avenue, Primrose Hill, London, NW1 8JA **t** 020 7483 2500 **f** 020 7483 3700 **e** louise@rarecommunications.co.uk **w** rarecommunications.co.uk 🖪 Director: Louise Drabwell 07979 241 458.

Razzle PR 66 Red Lion Street, Holborn, London, WC1R 4NA **t** 020 7430 0444 **e** karen@razzlepr.com 🖪 Head of Press: Karen Childs.

The Red Consultancy 41-44 Great Windmill St, London, W1D 7NF **t** 020 7465 7700 **f** 020 7025 6500 **e** red@redconsultancy.com **w** redconsultancy.com 🖪 CEO: Mike Morgan.

Relatively Entertainment PO Box 1034, Maidstone, ME15 0WZ **t** 07821 357 713 **e** lineage@toucansurf.com 🖪 MD: Paul Aaaron.

Republic Media Ltd Studio 202, Westbourne Studios, 242 Acklam Rd, London, W10 5JJ **t** 020 8960 7449 **f** 020 8960 7524 **e** info@republicmedia.net **w** republicmedia.net 🖪 Director: Sue Harris.

Richard Wootton Publicity 572 Kingston Rd, Raynes Park, London, SW20 8DR **t** 020 8545 9299 **f** 020 8417 8470 **e** richard@rwpublicity.com 🖪 MD: Richard Wootton 07774 111 692.

RKM Public Relations Suite 201, Erico House, 93-99 Upper Richmond Rd, London, SW15 2TG **t** 020 8785 5640 **f** 020 8785 5641 **e** info@rkmpr.com **w** rkmpr.com 🖪 Dir: Rob Montague.

RMP 2C Woodstock Studios, Woodstock Grove, London, W12 8LE **t** 020 8749 7999 **f** 020 8811 8162 **e** firstname@rmplondon.co.uk 🖪 MD: Regine Moylett.

Rock Solid PR 11 Downton Avenue, Streatham Hill, London, SW2 3TU **t** 020 8674 2224 **f** 020 8674 2224 **w** rocksolidsounds.co.uk 🖪 MD: John Welsh 07968 817 359.

Rokkpool PR 11 Lawton Road, London, E10 6RR **t** 020 8558 6607 **e** exposure@rokkpool.com **w** rokkpool.com 🖪 Manager: Pippa Moye 07960 442 645.

Rollingpress Studio 11, 10 Acklam Rd, Ladbroke Grove, London, W10 5QZ **t** 020 8969 6699 **f** 020 8964 4706 **e** lee@rollingpress.co.uk **w** rollingpress.co.uk 🖪 Contact: Lee Haynes 07971 292154.

Rood Media PO Box 21469, Highgate, London, N6 4ZG **t** 07973 366301 **e** roo@roodmedia.com **w** roodmedia.com 🖪 myspace.com/roodmedialtd 🖪 Director: Roo Farndon.

RRR Management 96 Wentworth Rd, Birmingham, B17 9SY **t** 0121 426 6820 **f** 0121 426 5700 **e** enquiries@rrrmanagement.com **w** rrrmanagement.com 🖪 MD: Ruby Ryan.

Run Music 68a Rochester Pl, London, NW1 9JX
t 020 7485 1141 **e** ben@runmusic.co.uk
w runmusic.co.uk ✉ Contact: Ben Harris.

Sainted PR Office 17, Shaftesbury Centre,
85 Barlby Rd, London, W10 6BN **t** 020 8962 5700
f 020 8962 5701 **e** heatherfinlay@saintedpr.com
w saintedpr.com ✉ MD: Heather Finlay.

Sally Reeves PR 81 Green End, Landbeach,
Cambridge, CB25 9FD **t** 01223 864710
e sallyreeves@btinternet.com ✉ MD: Sally Reeves 07790
518 756.

Sarah J. Edwards PR PO Box 2423, London,
WC2E 9PG **t** 0870 138 9430 **f** 0870 138 9430
e blag@blagmagazine.com **w** blagmagazine.com
✉ Dir: Sarah J. Edwards.

Sarsaparilla Ltd 1 Lyric Sq, London, W6 0NB
t 020 7147 9960 **w** sarsparillamarketing.com
✉ Dir: Kimberly Davis.

Seb & Fiona 3rd Floor, 61-63 Brushfield St,
Old Spitalfields Market, London, E1 6AA **t** 020 7377 9868
f 0870 094 1950 **e** firstname@sebandfiona.com
w sebandfiona.com ✉ Dirs: Fiona Wootton, Seb Emina.

Serious Press and PR 30 West Street, Stoke-sub-
Hamdon, Somerset, TA14 6PZ **t** 01935 823719
f 01935 823719 **e** janehamdon@yahoo.co.uk ✉ MD: Jane
Osborne.

Silver PR 41 Lavers Rd, London, N16 0DU
t 020 7502 0240 **f** 020 7502 0240
e rachel.silver@silverpr.co.uk **w** silverpr.co.uk ✉ Dir: Rachel
Silver.

Singsong Entertainment Publicity
Whiteleaf Business Centre, Buckingham Ind. Pk, Bucks,
MK18 3AF **t** 01296 715228 **e** peter@singsongpr.biz
w singsongpr.biz ✉ MD: Peter Muir.

Siren Music Ltd PO Box 166, Hartlepool, Cleveland,
TS26 9JA **t** 01429 424603 **e** daveianhill@yahoo.co.uk
w tenacitymusicpr.co.uk ✉ Dir: Dave Hill 07951 679666.

Sister 1st Floor, 46a Carnaby St, London, W1F 9PS
t 020 7287 9601 **f** 020 7287 9602 **e** rufus@sister-pr.com
w sister-pr.com ✉ Director: Rufus Stone 020 287 9601.

Six07 Press 21 Ferdinand Street, London, NW1 8EU
t 020 7428 0911 **f** 020 7428 0919 **e** ritu@six07press.com
w six07press.com ✉ Director: Ritu Morton.

Skullduggery Services 40a Love Lane, Pinner,
Middlesex, HA5 3EX **t** 020 8429 0853
e xskullduggeryx@btinternet.com ✉ MD: Russell Aldrich.

Slice The Engine Group, 60 Great Portland St, London,
W1W 7RT **t** 020 7309 5700 **f** 020 7309 5701
e firstname@slice.co.uk **w** slice.co.uk ✉ MD: Nadia Gabbie
0207 309 5700.

SLIDING DOORS PUBLICITY

The Media Centre, Canada House, 272 Field End Rd,
Eastcote, HA4 9NA **t** 020 8582 0404
e james@slidingdoors.biz **w** slidingdoors.biz ✉ MD: James
Hamilton.

Smash Press London, SE23 1DL **t** 07721 662933
e nick@smashpr.co.uk ✉ MD: Nick White 07721 662 933.

SMC Europe 14 Bowling Green Lane, London, EC1R 0BD
t 0207 251 8770 **f** 0207 251 8557
e info@smceurope.com **w** thesmc-group.com
✉ Contact: Leon Hamilton.

Sofa PR 15 Haynes Lane, London, SE19 3AN
t 07970 551283 **e** sofapr@mac.com ✉ MD: Simon Ward
020 8771 5354.

Some Friendly 93 Leonard St, London, EC2A 4RD
t 020 7729 3999 **e** samantha@somefriendly.co.uk
w somefriendly.co.uk ✉ Dirs: Sophie Williams & Andy
Fraser 07961 436736.

SONIC PR

● **sonic pr**

5 The Hedgerows, Whitworth, Rochdale, Lancashire,
OL12 8AW **t** 01706 853 554 or 07882 882 314
e rob@sonicpr.co.uk **w** sonicpr.co.uk
✉ myspace.com/sonicpr ✆ twitter.com/robsonicpr
✉ MD: Rob Kerford 07882 882 314. MD: Rob Kerford.
Press Officer: James McArdle.

Southern PR 6 Stuceley Place, Camden, London,
NW1 8NT **t** 020 7267 3466 **e** lisa@southernpr.co.uk
✉ MD: Lisa Southern 020 7267 3498.

Spring PR and Marketing 301 b/c Aberdeen House,
Aberdeen Centre, 22-24 Highbury Grove, London, N5 2EA
t 020 7704 0999 **f** 020 7704 6999 **e** rhiannon@spring-
pr.com **w** spring-pr.com ✉ Dir: Rhiannon Sheehy.

Starling Publicity Flat F,
13 Stoke Newington Church St, Stoke Newington, London,
N16 0NX **e** firstname@starlingpublicity.com
w starlingpublicity.com ✉ Director: Alix Wenmouth 07760
105469.

Stay Gold Press Brighton Media Centre,
15 - 17 Middle Street, Brighton, BN1 1AL
t 01273 201 327 **e** mel@staygold.co.uk **w** staygold.co.uk
✉ 07768 865 737: Mel Thomas.

20 YEARS IN ROCK!

Previous clients have included:

BRUCE DICKINSON	BLACK DAHLIA MURDER
ROB HALFORD	GOOD CHARLOTTE
THUNDER	THE STARTING LINE
JET LAG GEMINI	APOLLYON SUN
ONEIDA	FINCH
BRAINIAC	DR JOHN
THE WRENS	FALLOUT BOY
BRAND NEW	ESCAPE ACT
UNEARTH	BAILTERSPACE
AS I LAY DYING	THE MOVIELIFE
SLOW BURN	METAL BLADE RECORDS
LET OUR ENEMIES BEWARE	SMALLTOWN AMERICA
DRIVE THRU RECORDS	TURNBUCKLE RECORDS

STEPHEN ANDERSON PUBLICITY

Tel: 028 9031 0949
Email: stephen@stephenandersonpublicity.com
Website: www.stephenandersonpublicity.com

FIFTH ELEMENT
Public Relations & Artist Management

5 Public Relations **Pr**

TEL: 020 7722 0000
info@fifthelement.biz
www.fifthelement.biz

STEPHEN ANDERSON PUBLICITY

Cathedral Buildings, 64 Donegall St, Belfast, Co Antrim, BT1 2GT, Northern Ireland **t** 028 9031 0949 **f** 028 9031 5905 **e** stephen_anderson@btconnect.com **w** stephenandersonpublicty.com 🖂 MD: Stephen Anderson.

Stoked PR 1 Hardwick St, London, EC1R 4RB **t** 020 7841 7085 **e** info@stokedpr.com **w** stokedpr.com 🖂 Director: Kate Head.

Stone Immaculate Press Music Room, 12 Alderton Rd, London, SE24 0HS **t** 020 7737 6359 **f** 020 7274 8921 **e** stone@stoneimmaculate.co.uk **w** stoneimmaculate.co.uk 🖂 MD: Chris Stone.

Strategix Mobile App 9 Elle Court, 96 Nether St, London, N12 8ET **t** 0845 680 1857 **e** mal@strategix-mobile.com **w** strategix-mobile.com 🖂 Owner: Mal Smith.

Street Press PR 20 Dulse Craig, Eyemouth, Berwickshire, TD14 5EJ **t** 07801 313 225 **e** heather@streetpress.co.uk **w** myspace.com/streetpress 🖂 MD: Heather Moul.

Supersonic PR 2nd Floor, 64 Great Eastern St, London, EC2A 3QR **t** 020 7033 7992 **e** info@supersonicpr.com **w** supersonicpr.com 🖂 MD: Sundraj Sreenivasan.

Sure Shot PR - Online PR and Digital Marketing The Premises Studios, 207 Hackney Rd, London, E2 8JL **t** 020 7729 5256 **e** info@sureshotpr.co.uk **w** ww.sureshotpr.co.uk 🖂 Director: Giovanna Ferin.

Tara Tomes PR PO Box 6003, Birmingham, B45 0AR **t** 0121 477 9553 **f** 0121 693 2954 **e** tara@taratomes.com **w** taratomespr.com 🖂 MD: Tara Tomes 07966 174 319.

Technique Publicity One Codrington Mews, London, W11 2EH **t** 020 8870 7511 **e** jon@technique-pr.com **w** technique-pr.com 🖂 MD: Jon Wilkinson 020 8875 6257.

Tenacity Po Box 166, Hartlepool, Cleveland, TS26 9JA **t** 01429 424 603 **e** info@tenacitymusicpr.co.uk **w** tenacitymusicpr.co.uk 🖂 Proprietor: Dave Hill 07951 679 666.

Terrie Doherty Promotions 40, Princess St, Manchester, M1 6DE **t** 0161 234 0044 **e** terriedoherty@zoo.co.uk 🖂 Director, Regional Rad/TV: Terrie Doherty.

Toast Press Room 209, Bon Marche Building, 241-251 Ferndale Rd, Brixton, London, SW9 8BJ **t** 020 7326 1200 **e** info@toastpress.com **w** toastpress.com 📘 toastpress 🐦 toastpress 🖂 MD: Ruth Drake or Beth Drake.

Tomorrow Never Knows 15 Hopkin Close, Queen Elizabeth Park, Guildford, Surrey, GU2 9LS **t** 01483 234 428 **e** ritch@tomorrowneverknows.co.uk **w** tomorrowneverknows.co.uk 🖂 MD: Ritch Ames.

Tora! Company Clearwater Yard, 35 Inverness St, London, NW1 7HB **t** 020 7424 7500 **f** 020 7424 7501 **e** gary@tora-co.demon.co.uk 🖂 Dir: Gary Levermore.

Traffic Marketing 6 Stuceley Place, London, NW1 8NS **t** 020 7485 7400 **f** 020 7485 5151 **e** info@trafficmarketing.co.uk **w** trafficmarketing.co.uk 🖂 MD: Lisa Paulon.

Trailer Media Suite 36, 99-109 Lavender Hill, London, SW11 5QL **t** 020 7924 6443 **f** 020 7733 9966 **e** anton@trailermedia.com **w** trailermedia.com 🖂 MD: Anton Hiscock.

Triad Publicity 27D Lady Somerset Rd, London, NW5 1TX **t** 020 7267 5121 **e** firstname.lastname@triadpublicity.co.uk 🖂 Director: Vanessa Cotton / Johnny Hopkins 07803 500818 / 07711 654772.

Trinity Media Group 72 New Bond St, London, W1S 1RR **t** 020 7499 4141 **e** info@trinitymediagroup.net **w** trinitymediagroup.net 🖂 Business Affairs: Peter Murray.

Uproar Communications The Old Dairy, 35 Little Russell Street, London, WC1A 2HH **t** 020 7580 1852 **f** 020 7580 1855 **e** julian@uproaruk.com **w** uproaruk.com 🖂 Chief Urbanaire: Julian Davis.

VELOCITY COMMUNICATIONS

25 Waverley Rd, St Albans, Hertfordshire, AL3 5PH **t** 0207 060 9111 **f** 0207 060 9112 **e** andy@velocitypr.co.uk **w** velocitypr.co.uk 🖂 Managing Director: Andy Saunders.

Wasted Youth 21-22 Great Castle Street, London, W1G 0HZ **t** 020 7493 5873 **e** sarah@wastedyouthpr.com **w** wastedyouthpr.com 🖂 MD: Sarah Pearson.

We R Pr Unit 7, Bridgecourt, 12 Cook St, Glasgow, G5 8JN **t** 07870 974 750 **e** werprglasgow@gmail.com 🖂 MD: Maco.

WildKat PR 36 Bruton St, London, W1J 6QZ **t** 020 7499 9334 **e** info@wildkatpr.com **w** wildkatpr.com 🖂 MD: Kathleen Alder.

Work Hard PR 35 Farm Avenue, London, SW16 2UT **t** 020 8677 8466 **e** roland@workhardpr.com **w** workhardpr.com 🖂 MD: Roland Hyams.

The Works PR 11 Marshalsea Road, London, SE1 1EN **t** 020 7940 4686 **f** 020 7940 5656 **e** info@theworkspr.com **w** theworkspr.com 🖂 Press: Judy Lipsey.

Press & Promotion: Photographers & Agencies

FIFTH ELEMENT
Public Relations & Artist Management

5
Public Relations
Pr

TEL: 020 7722 0000
info@fifthelement.biz
www.fifthelement.biz

Writing Services 20 Rockfield Rd, Monmouth, NP25 5BA **t** 01600 713758 **e** anita@writing-services.co.uk **w** writing-services.co.uk ✉ Owner/manager: Anita Holford.

Xtaster – Music, Lifestyle & Brand Marketing 1 Stucley Studios, Stucley Place, Camden, London, NW1 8NS **t** 020 7482 7000 **f** 020 7267 6638 **e** info@xtaster.co.uk **w** xtaster.co.uk ✉ MDs: Stuart Knight, Nick Dryden.

Ya Basta! PR Tithe Barn, Tithe Court, Langley, SL3 8AS **t** 07764 575 600 **e** ash@yabastapr.co.uk **w** yabastapr.co.uk ✉ Director: Ash Eaton.

Yes Please PR 29 Harford House, 35 Tavistock Crescent, London, W11 1AY **t** 020 7792 2843 **e** yespleasepr@btinternet.com ✉ MD: Ginny Luckhurst.

Photographers & Agencies

3D Media Services Seton Lodge, 26 Sutton Avenue, Seaford, East Sussex, BN25 4U **t** 01323 892 303 **e** talk2us@3dmediaservices.com **w** 3dmediaservices.com ✉ MDs: Anthony Duke, Kim Duke.

aandr Photographic 16a Crane Grove, Islington, London, N7 8LE **t** 020 7607 3030 **f** 020 7607 2190 **e** info@aandrphotographic.co.uk **w** aandrphotographic.co.uk ✉ Photographers Agents: Anita Grossman, Rosie Harrison.

Adam Gasson Photography 25 Rhymney St, Cathays, Cardiff, CF24 4DF **t** 07720 053 526 **e** adam@adamgasson.com **w** adamgasson.com ✉ Photographer: Adam Gasson.

All Action Digital 32 Great Sutton St, London, EC1V 0NB **t** 020 7608 2988 **f** 020 7336 0491 **e** mo@allaction.co.uk **w** allactiondigital.com ✉ GM: Isabelle Vialle.

Mark Allan 30 Barry Road, London, SE22 0HU **t** 020 8693 6625 or 07836 385 352 **e** mark@markallan-photographer.com **w** markallan-photographer.com

Ami Barwell - Music Photographer Suite 6, 344 Old St, London, EC1V 9DR **t** 07787 188 452 **e** ami@musicphotographer.co.uk **w** musicphotographer.co.uk ▣ myspace.com/musicphotographer ✉ Photographer: Ami Barwell.

Amit & Naroop Photography Studio 1B, 39 - 40 Westpoint, Warple Way, London, W3 0RG **t** 020 8743 4646 **e** info@amitandnaroop.com **w** amitandnaroop.com ✉ Partners: Amit Amin & Naroop Jhooti.

Christian Ammann Contact: ERA Management Ltd

Andy Fallon Photography London **t** 07956 303122 **e** andy@andyfallon.co.uk **w** andyfallon.co.uk ✉ Music, PR and Advertising Photographer: Andy Fallon.

Arcangel Images Ltd Calle Las Mimosas 85, Campo Mijas, Malaga, 29649, Spain **t** 0871 218 1023 **e** sales@arcangel-images.com **w** arcangel-images.com ✉ Studio Manager: Gloria Mejuto.

Peter Ashworth 107 South Hill Park, London, NW3 2SP **t** 020 7435 4142 **e** peter@ashworth-photos.com **w** ashworth-photos.com ✉ Photographer: Peter Ashworth.

Balcony Jump Management 61 Bayham Pl, Camden, London, NW1 0ET **t** 0207 121 6380 **f** 0207 121 6382 **e** info@balconyjump.co.uk **w** balconyjump.co.uk ✉ MD: Tim Paton.

Kingsley Barker Contact: Inspired Reflection Ltd

Sam Barker Contact: Inspired Reflection Ltd

Oly Barnsley Contact: Darling Creative

Bartolomy 28 Royal Close, Manor Road, London, N16 5SE **t** 07870 137 373 **f** 020 8211 8909 **e** Bartolomy@gmail.com **w** bartolomy.com ✉ Photographer: Bartolomy.

Frank Bauer Contact: Skinny Dip

Bijoux Graphics 10 L Peabody Bldgs, Clerkenwell Close, London, EC1R 0AY **t** 020 7608 1316 **f** 020 7608 0525 **e** davies@bijouxgraphics.co.uk **w** bijouxgraphics.co.uk ✉ Director: David Davies 07947 896 775.

Bill Charles London Ltd Unit 3E1 Zetland House, 5-25 Scrutton Street, London, EC2A 4HJ **t** 020 7033 9284 **f** 020 7033 9285 **e** dan@billcharles.com **w** billcharles.com ✉ Contact: Daniel Worthington or Olivia Gideon Thomson.

George Bodnar Churchill House, 137 Brent St, London, NW4 4DJ **t** 020 8248 1004 **f** 020 8457 2602 **e** george@gbimages.com **w** GBimages.com ▣ twitter.com/GBphoto ✉ Photographer: George Bodnar.

Jay Brooks Contact: PC.P

Ken Browar Contact: Serlin Associates

Bruce Fleming Photography 60 Wimpole Street, London, W1G 8AG **t** 020 7486 4001 or 07778 020 978 **e** mail@brucefleming.com **w** brucefleming.com ✉ Production: Kim Fleming.

Ray Burmiston Contact: Shoot Production Ltd

Willy Camden Contact: Shoot Production Ltd

Matt Canon Contact: Shoot Production Ltd

Capital Pictures 85 Randolph Avenue, London, W9 1DL **t** 020 7286 2212 **e** sales@capitalpictures.com **w** capitalpictures.com ✉ Dir: Phil Loftus.

Carlos Cicchelli Photography & Film 320 W 37th St., New York, 10018, United States **t** +1 917 297 5093 **e** mail@carloscicchelli.com **w** carloscicchelli.com ✉ Photographer: Carlos Cicchelli.

Contacts Facebook MySpace Twitter YouTube

Andy Carne thelongdrop, Studio 2, 25 Halstead Rd, Earls Colne, Essex, CO6 2NG **t** 01787 224464 **e** studio@andycarne.com **w** andycarne.com ◼ myspace.com/andycarne ◼ twitter.com/andycarne ◼ Photographer: Andy Carne.

CCPHOTOART.biz 11 Chiltern Pl, 96 Harestone Valley Rd, Caterham,, Surrey, CR3 6HZ **t** 07799 174199 **e** patrick@ccphotoart.biz **w** christiegoodwin.com ◼ Manager: Patrick Cusse.

Dean Chalkley Contact: Shoot Production Ltd

Chiaki Nozu Photography 79 Consfield Avenue, Motspur Park, Surrey, KT3 6HD **t** 07973 167 754 **f** 020 8942 3834 **e** info@chiakinozu.com **w** chiakinozu.com ◼ Contact: Chiaki Nozu.

Claire Grogan Photography 18 Calverley Grove, Archway, London, N19 3LG **t** 020 7272 1845 **e** claire@clairegrogan.co.uk **w** clairegrogan.co.uk ◼ Contact: Claire Grogan 07932 635381.

Neil Cooper Contact: Eminent Management & Production Ltd

Tom Corbett Contact: Darling Creative

Sarah Cresswell Contact: ERA Management Ltd

Pete Cronin 14 Lakes Rd, Keston, Kent, BR2 6BN **t** 01689 858719 **e** pete@petecronin.com **w** petecronin.com ◼ Contact: 07860 391985.

Dan Griffiths - Music Photography 4 Osborne House, St. Mary's Terrace, London, W2 1SG **t** 07734 188328 **e** dan@dangriffiths.com **w** dangriffiths.com ◼ Music Photographer: Dan Griffiths.

Jack Daniels Plot 2, The Plantation, Swanage, Dorset, BH19 2TD **t** 07831 356719 **f** 01929 427471 **e** musicweek@jackdaniels.me.uk **w** jackdaniels.me.uk ◼ Contact: Jack Daniels 01929 427429.

Darling Creative Unit 227 Worlds End Studios, 132 - 134 Lots Rd, London, SW10 0RJ **t** 020 7349 7033 **f** 020 7351 5044 **e** studio@darling-creative.com **w** darling-creative.com ◼ Director: Kitty Wengraf.

Davix Management Suite D, 67 Abbey Rd, St John's Wood, London, NW8 0AE **t** 07956 302894 **e** davixuk@hotmail.com **w** davixmedia.com ◼ Photographer: David Ross.

Corinne Day Contact: Susie Babchick Agency

Bruno Dayan Contact: Serlin Associates

Ian Derry Contact: ERA Management Ltd

Digital Pyrotechnics - Photography & Design 5c Crystal Palace Park Rd, London, SE26 6EG **t** 07738 415711 **e** james@digitalpyrotechnics.net **w** digitalpyrotechnics.net ◼ MD: James Sellar.

Tom Dunkley Contact: Shoot Production Ltd

Frederic Duval 6 Dorset Court, Hertford Road, London, N1 4SD **t** 020 7503 6870 **e** jenny_duval@hotmail.com ◼ Contact: 07876 481 279.

Andy Earl 29 Curlew Street, London, SE1 2ND **t** 020 7403 1156 **f** 020 7403 1157 **e** mail@andyearl.com **w** andyearl.com

East Photographic 8 Iron Bridge House, 3 Bridge Approach, London, NW1 8BD **t** 020 7722 3444 **f** 020 7722 3544 **e** roger@eastphotographic.com **w** eastphotographic.com ◼ Contact: Roger Silveira or Sue Ireland.

David Ellis Contact: Terri Manduca Ltd

Eminent Management & Production Ltd The Old Truman Brewery, 91 Brick Lane, London, E1 6QL **t** 020 7247 4750 **f** 020 7247 4712 **e** anita@eminentmanagement.co.uk **w** eminentmanagement.co.uk ◼ MD: Anita Heryet.

Nicky Emmerson Contact: Darling Creative

ERA Management Ltd 120 The Beaux Arts Building, 10-18 Manor Gardens, London, N7 6JT **t** 020 7281 5996 **f** 020 7281 6202 **e** info@eramanagement.com **w** eramanagement.com ◼ Dir: Eva Dijkstra.

Famous Pictures & Features Agency 13 Harwood Rd, London, SW6 4QP **t** 020 7731 9333 **f** 020 7731 9330 **e** info@famous.uk.com **w** famous.uk.com ◼ Library Manager: Rob Howard.

Daniela Federici Contact: Darling Creative

Freelance Directory NUJ, Acorn House, 314-320 Gray's Inn Road, London, WC1X 8DP **t** 020 7843 3703 **f** 020 7278 1812 **e** pamelam@nuj.org.uk **w** gn.apc.org/media ◼ Contact: Pamela Morton.

Dean Freeman Contact: Terri Manduca Ltd

Eric Frideen Contact: Serlin Associates

Future Earth 59 Fitzwilliam St, Wath Upon Dearne, Rotherham, South Yorks, S63 7HG **t** 01709 872875 **e** david@future-earth.co.uk **w** future-earth.co.uk ◼ MD: David Moffitt.

George Chin Photography **t** 01707 646420 **e** george@georgechin.com **w** georgechin.com ◼ Photographer: George Chin 07876 745943.

Louis Girardi Contact: Inspired Reflection Ltd

Bob Glanville 77 Shelley House, Churchill Gardens, Pimlico, London, SW1V 3JE **t** 07957 363 472 **e** info@bobglanville.com **w** bobglanville.com ◼ Photographer: Bob Glanville.

Christie Goodwin 11 Chiltern Place, 96 Harestone Valley Rd, Caterham, Surrey, CR3 6HZ **t** 07799 174199 **e** patrick@ccphotoart.biz **w** christiegoodwin.com ◼ Manager: Patrick Cusse 07799174199.

Graham Smith Photography **e** info@grahamsmithphotography.com **w** grahamsmithphotography.com ◼ Photographer/Film Maker: Graham Smith.

Adrian Green Contact: Shoot Production Ltd

Steve Gullick Contact: Eminent Management & Production Ltd

Press & Promotion: Photographers & Agencies

Guy Dixon Photography 5 Tremblant Close, Prestbury, Cheltenham, Gloucestershire, GL52 5FL **t** 07971 195310 **e** guydixonphotography@mac.com **w** guydixon.com 📇 Director: Guy Dixon.

Halo Event Photography 49 Hopton Rd, Streatham, London, SW16 2EL **t** 020 7993 4693 or 07886 757501 **e** contact@haloep.co.uk **w** haloep.co.uk 📇 Director of Photography: Andrew Paine.

Cary Hammond Contact: Eminent Management & Production Ltd

Damon Heath Contact: Six Seven Photographic Ltd

Hugo Morris Photography 134 Renfrew St, Glasgow, G3 6ST **t** 07929 194 571 **e** info@XTmedia.co.uk **w** hugomorris.com 📇 Contact: Hugo Morris.

Ian Gavan Photography
1a Lovelace Villas Basement, Portsmouth Road, Surbiton, KT7 0XS **t** 07956 682 021 **e** iangavan@hotmail.com **w** iangavan.com 📇 Photographer: Ian Gavan.

Thomas Ibsen Contact: Six Seven Photographic Ltd

Idols Licensing And Publicity Image House, Station Rd, London, N17 9LR **t** 020 7385 5121 **e** james@idols.co.uk **w** idols.co.uk 📇 CEO: James Claydon - james@idols.co.uk.

Inoya Photography **t** 07888 723197 **e** web@inoya.co.uk **w** inoya.co.uk 📇 Photographer: Zen Inoya.

Inspired Reflection Ltd 28 Dayton Grove, Peckham, London, SE15 2NX **t** 0870 919 3587 **f** 0870 919 3588 **e** deborah@inspiredreflection.com **w** inspiredreflection.com 📇 MD: Deborah Williams.

Russell James Contact: Serlin Associates

Drew Jarrett Contact: Skinny Dip

J.C.Mac 5 Lawnwood Court, Catteshall Lane, Godalming, Surrey, GU7 1XS **t** 07768 475 622 **e** jcmac@blissmedia.co.uk **w** blissmedia.co.uk 📇 Photographer: J.C. Mac.

Mitch Jenkins Contact: Shoot Production Ltd

Joe Bangay Photography River House, Riverwoods, Marlow, Bucks, SL7 1QY **t** 01628 486 193 **f** 01628 890 239 **e** william.b@btclick.com **w** JoeBangay.com 📇 MD: William Bangay 07860 812 529.

John Beecher Photo Library Rock House, London Rd, St Mary's, Stroud, Gloucs, GL6 8PU **t** 01453 886 252 **f** 01453 885 361 **e** photo@rollercoasterrecords.com **w** rollercoasterrecords.com 📇 Owner: John Beecher 0845 456 9759.

Jon Stone Performance Photography
143 Liverpool Road, Southport, Merseyside, PR8 4NT **t** 01704 563 195 or 07785 913 400 **e** jon-stone@excite.com 📇 Contact: Jon Stone.

Jonathan Rea Photography 49 Josephine Avenue, London, SW2 2JZ **t** 020 8674 7828 or 07799 673 383 **e** jonathanrea@mac.com **w** jonathanrea.net 📇 Proprietor: Jonathan Rea.

Joseph Kaler Photography 3 Maude Terrace, London, E17 7DG **t** 07957 561217 **e** info@josephkaler.com **w** josephkaler.com ⬛ facebook.com/pages/Joseph-Kaler/217386895573 🟦 myspace.com/joseph_kaler 📇 Dir: Joseph Kaler.

Junction10 Photography 292- 294 Wolverhampton Rd West, Walsall, West Midlands, WS2 0DS **t** 07973 618503 **e** jason@junction10.net **w** junction10.net ⬛ facebook.com/junction10 🟦 myspace.com/junction10 🟦 twitter.com/junction10 📇 Freelance Photographer: Jason Sheldon.

Katie Kaars Contact: Six Seven Photographic Ltd

Kochi Photography 33/37 Hatherley Mews, Walthamstow, London, E17 4QP **t** 020 8521 9227 **f** 020 8520 5553 **e** xplosive@supanet.com 📇 Director: Terry McLeod.

Charlotte Krag Contact: Inspired Reflection Ltd

Kristine Skovli Photography 22a Morval Road, London, SW2 1DQ **t** 07947 332 514 **e** kristine@kskovli.com **w** kskovli.com 📇 photographer: Kristine Skovli.

Laura Hart Contact: PC.P

Laurie Lewis 176 Camden Road, London, NW1 9HG **t** 020 7267 0315 📇 Dir: Topsy Corian.

Rebecca Lewis Contact: Skinny Dip

Link Photographers 41A The Downs, London, SW20 8HG **t** 020 8944 6933 **e** office@linkphotographers.com **w** linkphotographers.com 📇 Proprietor: Orde Eliason.

London Features International Ltd 3 Boscobel St, London, NW8 8PS **t** 020 7723 4204 **f** 020 7723 9201 **e** john@lfi.co.uk **w** lfi.co.uk 📇 Editorial Dir: John Halsall.

Loud Pixels Photography
391a Upper Richmond Rd, London, SW15 5QL **t** 07738 920225 **e** marc@loudpixels.net **w** loudpixels.net ⬛ facebook.com/pages/Marc-Broussely-Photographer/42761718244 🟦 myspace.com/sonicmoo 🟦 twitter.com/Loudpixels 📇 Contact: Marc Broussely.

Andrew Macpherson Contact: Six Seven Photographic Ltd

Sarah Maingot Contact: Serlin Associates

Gered Mankowitz Contact: PC.P

Mark Latham - Music Photographer 267 Park Rd, Barnsley, South Yorkshire, S70 1QJ **t** 07900 802858 **e** mark@marklatham.co.uk **w** marklatham.co.uk 📇 Contact: Mark Latham.

Mark McNulty 8E Sunnyside, Princes Park, Liverpool, L8 3TD **t** 0151 727 2012 **e** mark@mcnulty.co.uk **w** mcnulty.co.uk 📇 Contact: 07885 847806.

Marta Stoyanova Photography Bullen Street, Battersea, London, SW11 3HG **t** 07946380581 **e** info@martegallery.com **w** martegallery.com 🖂 Music, Portrait and Fashion photographer: Marta Stoyanova.

Sean McMenomy Contact: Six Seven Photographic Ltd

John McMurtrie t 07976 961188 **e** jmc@picturedesk.co.uk **w** picturedesk.co.uk 🖂 Contact: John McMurtrie.

Anne Menke Contact: Serlin Associates

Michael Taylor Photography Belfast **t** 028 9065 4450 **w** mtphoto.co.uk 🖂 Contact: Michael Taylor.

Mission Photographic Ground Floor, 10 St Johns Crescent, Canton, Cardiff, CF5 1NX **t** 07816 857 450 **e** mei@missionphotographic.com **w** missionphotographic.com 🖂 Contact: Mei Lewis.

Stephen Morgan Contact: Skinny Dip

Nick Tansley Pictures 1 Lopen Rd, London, N18 1PN **t** 020 8807 6268 **f** 020 8351 1497 **e** popworks1@yahoo.com 🖂 Contact: Nick Tansley.

One Photographic 4th Floor, 48 Poland St, London, W1F 7ND **t** 020 7287 2311 **f** 020 7287 2313 **e** harriet@onephotographic.com **w** onephotographic.com 🖂 Agents: Belinda Taylor, Harriet Essex.

Scarlet Page Contact: PC.P

Ellis Parrinder Contact: PC.P

Paul Harries Photography 95 Waldegrave Rd, Teddington, Middlesex, TW11 8LA **t** 020 8977 1958 **e** paul@paulharries.co.uk **w** paulharries.co.uk 🖂 Contact: Paul Harries 07889 767 179.

PC.P 5-7 Vernon Yard, off Portobello Rd, London, W11 2DX **t** 020 7313 9100 **f** 020 7313 9109 **e** penny@presscounsel.com **w** pcp-agency.com 🖂 Dir: Penny Caplowe.

Rena Pearl 8A The Drive, London, NW11 9SR **t** 020 8455 7661 **f** 020 8381 4050 **e** rena@renapearl.com **w** renapearl.com 🖂 Freelance Photographer: Rena Pearl 07798 693756.

Antonio Petronzio Contact: Eminent Management & Production Ltd

Soulla Petrou Contact: Shoot Production Ltd

Photo-Stock Library International 14 Neville Avenue, Anchorsholme, Blackpool, Lancashire, FY5 3BG **t** 01253 864598 **f** 01253 864598 **e** wayne@waynepaulo.com **w** photo-stock.co.uk 🖂 WaynePaulo 🅜 WaynePaulo 🅣 twitter.com/WaynePaulo ▶ WaynePaulo 🖂 Partner: Wayne Paulo.

Pictorial Press Ltd Unit 1 Market Yard Mews, 194 Bermondsey Street, London, SE1 3TQ **t** 020 7378 7211 **f** 020 7378 7194 **e** info@pictorialpress.co.uk **w** pictorialpress.com 🖂 Director: Tony Gale.

Phil Poynter Contact: Serlin Associates

Ralf Pulmanns Contact: ERA Management Ltd

Rebecca Valentine Agency 37 Foley St, London, W1W 7TN **t** 07968 190 411 **e** rebecca@rebeccavalentine.com **w** rebeccavalentine.com 🖂 MD: Rebecca Valentine.

Red represents Ltd Unit 2, 98 De Beauvoir Rd, London, N1 4EN **t** 020 7275 2722 **f** 070 0580 0027 **e** ginny@redrepresents.com **w** redrepresents.com 🖂 Contact: Ginny Mettrick.

Redferns Music Picture Library 21-31 Woodfield Rd, London, W9 2BA **t** 020 3227 2720 **f** 020 7266 2414 **e** info@redferns.com **w** gettyimages.com/redferns 🖂 Library Mgr: Jon Wilton.

John Rensten Contact: Rebecca Valentine Agency

Repfoto 108 Sutton Court, Fauconberg Rd, London, W4 3EE **t** 020 8995 3632 **e** repfoto@btinternet.com **w** repfoto.com 🖂 Partner: Robert Ellis.

Retrograph Nostalgia Archive Ltd 10 Hanover Crescent, Brighton, E. Sussex, BN2 9SB **t** 01273 687554 **e** retropix1@aol.com **w** Retrograph.com 🖂 MD: Jilliana Ranicar-Breese.

Rex Features 18 Vine Hill, London, EC1R 5DZ **t** 020 7278 7294 **f** 020 7837 4812 **e** editorial@rexfeatures.com **w** rexfeatures.com 🖂 News Editor: John Melhuish 020 7278 5789.

Paul Rider Contact: Shoot Production Ltd

Rip Contact: Ripley & Ripley Ltd (London)

Ripley & Ripley Ltd (London) Fairwinds, Hindon, SP3 6EG **t** 07739 745 495 **f** 01747 820 336 **e** studio@ripleyandripley.com **w** ripleyandripley.com 🖂 Contact: Rip & Colette.

Rock Lens Photography 6 West of St. Laurence, Old Warwick Rd, Rowington, Warcs, CV35 7AB **t** 07786 261 950 **e** info@rocklens.com **w** rocklens.com 🖂 Owner / Photographer: Steve Thorne.

Sheila Rock Contact: Terri Manduca Ltd

Martyn Rose Contact: Rebecca Valentine Agency

Russ Tannen Photography 4c, Coldharbour Lane, Camberwell, London, SE5 9PR **t** 07855 679 499 **e** info@russtannen.com **w** russtannen.com 🖂 Photographer: Russ Tannen.

Contacts   Facebook   MySpace   Twitter   YouTube

Press & Promotion: Photographers & Agencies

Sarahphotogirl The Studio, 9 Belmont Rd, Scarborough, North Yorkshire, YO11 2AA **t** 07803 108884 **e** info@sarahphotogirl.com **w** sarahphotogirl.com
facebook.com/sarahphotogirl
myspace.com/sarahphotogirl
flickr.com/photos/sarahphotogirl
ww.youtube.com/sarahphotogirl
Photographer: Sarahphotogirl.

Thomas Schenk Contact: Serlin Associates

Diana Scheunemann Contact: Terri Manduca Ltd

Kristian Schuller Contact: Darling Creative

Serlin Associates Unit 445 Highgate Studios, 53-79 Highgate Rd, London, NW5 1TL **t** 020 7424 8888 **f** 020 7424 8889 **e** lisa@serlinassociates.com **w** serlinassociates.com Contact: Lisa Davies.

Jon Shard Contact: Eminent Management & Production Ltd

Shoot Production Ltd Unit 2.08, Tea Building, Shoreditch High St, London, E1 6JJ **t** 020 7324 7500 **f** 020 7324 7514 **e** production@shootgroup.com **w** shootproduction.com MD: Adele Rider.

Morgan Silk Contact: Rebecca Valentine Agency

Six Seven Photographic Ltd 307 Lillie Road, London, SW6 7LL **t** 020 7386 3232 **f** 020 7386 3233 **e** info@sixsevenphotographic.com **w** sixsevenphotographic.com Dir: Laura Carlile.

Skinny Dip 6 Silver Place, London, W1F 0JS **t** 020 7287 9585 **e** info@skinnydip.co.uk **w** skinnydip.co.uk Contact: Amy Foster, Jonny Wright.

Steve Smith Contact: ERA Management Ltd

Soren Solkaer Starbird Contact: PC.P

Paul Spencer Contact: Rebecca Valentine Agency

Stem Agency 102 Barnet Grove, London, E2 7BJ **t** 07790 026628 **e** info@stemagency.com **w** stemagency.com Contact: Will Robinson 07790 026 628.

Stewart Birch Photography 30 Kenilworth Rd, Bognor Regis, West Sussex, PO21 5NF **t** 07789 648 646 **e** info@stewartbirch.co.uk **w** stewartbirch.co.uk Contact: Stewart Birch.

The Street Studios 2 Dunston St, London, E8 4EB **t** 020 7923 9430 **f** 020 7923 9429 **e** mail@streetstudios.co.uk **w** streetstudios.co.uk Studio Manager: Chris Purnell.

Susie Babchick Agency Top Floor, 6 Brewer St, London, W1F 0SD **t** 020 7287 1497 **f** 020 7439 6030 **e** susie@susiebabchick.com **w** susiebabchickagency.com Dir: Susie Babchick.

Syndicated International Network 89a North View Road, London, N8 7LR **t** 020 8348 8061 **f** 020 8340 8517 **e** sales@sin-photo.co.uk **w** sin-photo.co.uk Contact: Marianne Lassen.

Terri Manduca Ltd The Basement, 11 Elvaston Place, London, SW7 5QG **t** 020 7581 5844 **f** 020 7581 5822 **e** sally@terrimanduca.co.uk **w** terrimanduca.co.uk MD: Terri Manduca.

Terri Berg Photographic PO Box 20072, London, NW2 3ZU **t** 020 8450 6378 **f** 020 8450 7058 **e** tnb@dircon.co.uk **w** tbphoto.co.uk Contact: Terri N Berg.

Timothy Cochrane Photography 8 Colgrove, Welwyn Garden City, Herts, AL8 6HU **t** 07919 411662 **e** tim@timothycochrane.com **w** timothycochrane.com Photographer: Timothy Cochrane.

David Titlow Contact: Six Seven Photographic Ltd

Visualeyes Imaging Services 11 West Street, Covent Garden, London, WC2H 9NE **t** 020 7836 3004 **f** 020 7240 0079 **e** imaging@visphoto.co.uk **w** visphoto.co.uk Sales & Marketing Manager: Fergal O'Regan.

Lawrence Watson Contact: Skinny Dip

Uli Weber Contact: Terri Manduca Ltd

WildeHague Ltd Unit 9, The Coach Works, 80 Parsons Green Lane, London, SW6 4HU **t** 020 7384 3444 **f** 020 7384 3449 **e** info@wildehague.com **w** wildehague.com Dirs: Janice Hague, Dilys Wilde.

Contacts   Facebook    MySpace   Twitter   YouTube

Live

Booking Agents

13 Artists 11-14 Kensington St, Brighton, BN1 4AJ
t 01273 601355 **f** 01273 626854
e postmaster@13artists.com **w** 13artists.com
MD: Charlie Myatt.

ABS Agency 2 Elgin Avenue, London, W9 3QP
t 020 7289 1160 **f** 020 7289 1162 **e** nigel@absagency.u-net.com MD: Nigel Kerr.

Acker's International Jazz Agency
53 Cambridge Mansions, Cambridge Rd, London, SW11 4RX
t 020 7978 5885 **f** 020 7978 5882
e pamela@ackersmusicagency.co.uk
w ackersmusicagency.co.uk Prop: Pamela Frances Sutton.

Active 60 Love St, Paisley, PA3 2EQ **t** 0141 561 0271
f 0141 561 0272 **e** active.events@virgin.net
w activeevents.org.uk MD: Lisa Whytock.

The Agency Group Ltd 361-373 City Rd, Islington,
London, EC1V 1PQ **t** 020 7278 3331 **f** 020 7837 4672
w theagencygroup.com Chief Executive Officer: Neil Warnock.

AIR (Artistes International Representation Ltd) AIR House, Spennymoor, Co Durham, DL16 7SE
t 01388 814632 **f** 01388 812445 **e** info@airagency.com
w airagency.com Directors: Colin Pearson, John Wray.

Air Artist Agency 27 The Quadrangle, 49 Atalanta St,
London, SW6 6TU **t** 020 7386 1600 **f** 020 7386 1619
e info@airmtm.com **w** airmtm.com
facebook.com/pages/Air-MTM/7986276834
myspace.com/airmtm twitter.com/airmtm
youtube.com/user/Airmtm Booking Agent: Bethan Hay.

Aire International 27 The Quadrangle, 49 Atalanta St,
London, SW6 6TU **t** 020 7386 1600 **f** 020 7386 1619
e bethan@airmtm.com **w** airartistagency.com
Contact: Bethan Hay.

Alan Cottam Agency 19 Charles St, Wigan, WN1 2BP
t 01254 668471 **f** 01254 697599
e alan7000uk@yahoo.com **w** alancottamagency.co.uk
MD: Alan Cottam.

Asgard Promotions 125 Parkway, London, NW1 7PS
t 020 7387 5090 **f** 020 7387 8740 **e** info@asgard-uk.com
w asgard-uk.com Jnt MDs: Paul Fenn, Paul Charles.

Avenue Artistes PO Box 1573, Southampton, Hants,
SO16 3ET **t** 02380 760930 **f** 02380 760930
e info@avenueartistes.com **w** avenueartistes.com
Dir: Terence A Rolph.

Austin Baptiste Entertainments Agency
29 Courthouse Gardens, London, N3 1PU **t** 020 8346 3984
f 020 8922 3770 **e** steelbands@aol.com
w steelbands.uk.com MD: Austin Baptiste.

Barn Dance and Line Dance Agency
62 Beechwood Road, South Croydon, Surrey, CR2 0AA
t 020 8668 5714 **f** 020 8645 6923
e barndanceagency@btinternet.com **w** barn-dance.co.uk
Dir: Derek Jones.

Barry Collings Entertainments PO Box 2112,
Hockley, Essex, SS5 4WD **t** 01702 201880 **e** Barry-Collings@btconnect.com **w** barrycollings.co.uk
Proprietor: Barry Collings.

The Bechhofer Agency 51 Barnton Pk View,
Edinburgh, EH4 6HH **t** 0131 339 4083 **f** 0131 339 9261
e agency@bechhofer.demon.co.uk
w bechhoferagency.com Contact: Frank Bechhofer.

John Bedford Enterprises 40 Stubbington Avenue,
North End, Portsmouth, Hampshire, PO2 0HY
t 023 9266 1339 **f** 023 9264 3993
e agency@johnbedford.co.uk **w** johnbedford.co.uk
Dir: John Bedford.

Big Bear Music PO Box 944, Birmingham,
West Midlands, B16 8UT **t** 0121 454 7020 **f** 0121 454 9996
e agency@bigbearmusic.com **w** bigbearmusic.com
Dirs: Jim Simpson, Tim Jennings.

The Bob Paterson Agency (BPA) PO Box 670,
Ipswich, Suffolk, IP9 9AU **t** 01473 749 556 **f** 01473 749 556
e bp@bobpatersonagency.com **w** bobpatersonagency.com
MD: Bob Paterson 07946 038 634.

Garry Brown Associates (International)
27 Downs Side, Cheam, Surrey, SM2 7EH **t** 020 8643 3991
f 020 8770 7241 **e** GBALTD@btconnect.com
Chairman: Garry Brown 020 8643 8375.

Carol & Associates 57 Meadowbank, Bushy Park Rd,
Dublin 6, Ireland **t** +353 1 490 9339 **f** +353 1 492 1100
e info@carolandassociates.com **w** carolandassociates.com
MD: Carol Hanna.

Castaway Suite 3, 15 Broad Court, London, WC2B 5QN
t 020 7240 2345 **f** 020 7240 2772 **e** info@castaway.org.uk
w castaway.org.uk MD: Sheila Britten.

CEE Worldwide Entertainment Agency
9 Coltsfoot Square, Oxford, Oxfordshire, OX4 7YN
t 0845 833 3232 **e** enquiries@cee-worldwide.com **w** cee-worldwide.com
facebook.com/pages/manage/#/pages/CEE-Worldwide-Entertainment-Agency/152427577342
twitter.com/CEEWorld
youtube.com/user/CEEWorldwide CEO: Paul Sims.

Central Music Agency Flat 1, Viewfield, Como Rd,
Great Malvern, Worcs, WR14 4HD **e** cmamalvern@aol.com
Agent/Promoter: Suzi Glantz.

CNL PO Box 518, Nottingham, NG3 6BF **t** 01636 831434
f 01636 831433 **e** info@cnltouring.co.uk **w** cnltouring.co.uk
Agent: Jon Barry.

CODA Music Agency LLP 229 Shoreditch High St, London, E1 6PJ **t** 020 7456 8888 **f** 020 7456 8800 **e** maryann@codaagency.com **w** codaagency.com 🖂 Office Manager: Maryann Spencer.

Complete Entertainment Services PO Box 112, Seaford, East Sussex, BN25 2DQ **t** 0870 755 7610 **f** 0870 755 7613 **e** info@completeentertainment.co.uk **w** completeentertainment.co.uk 🖂 Events Mgr: Emalee Welsh.

Consolidated PO Box 87, Tarporley, CW6 9FN **t** 01829 730488 **f** 01829 730499 **e** alecconsol@aol.com 🖂 Agent: Alec Leslie.

Continental Drifts Hilton Grove, Hatherley Mews, London, E17 4QP **t** 020 8509 3353 **f** 020 8509 9531 **e** Chris@continentaldrifts.co.uk **w** continentaldrifts.uk.com 🖂 Director: Chris Meikan.

Creative Artists Agency UK Ltd 4th Floor, Space One, 1 Beadon Rd, London, W6 0EA **t** 020 8846 3000 **f** 020 8846 3090 **e** ebanks@caa.com **w** caatouring.com 🖂 Agent: Emma Banks.

Creeme Entertainments East Lynne, Harper Green Road, Doe Hey, Farnworth, Bolton, Lancashire, BL4 7HT **t** 01204 793441 **f** 01204 792655 **e** info@creeme.co.uk **w** creeme.co.uk 🖂 MD: Tom Ivers 01204 793018.

Crisp Productions PO Box 979, Sheffield, South Yorkshire, S8 8YW **t** 0114 261 1649 **f** 0114 261 1649 **e** dc@cprod.win-uk.net 🖂 MD: Darren Crisp.

Crown Entertainments 103 Bromley Common, Bromley, Kent, BR2 9RN **t** 020 8464 0454 **f** 020 8290 4038 **e** info@crownentertainments.co.uk **w** crownentertainments.co.uk 🖂 MD: David Nash.

Dave Seamer Entertainments 46 Magdalen Road, Oxford, Oxon, OX4 1RB **t** 01865 240 054 **f** 01865 240 054 **e** dave@daveseamer.co.uk **w** daveseamer.co.uk 🖂 MD: Dave Seamer.

David Hull Promotions 46 University St, Belfast, BT7 1HB **t** 028 9024 0360 **f** 028 9024 7919 **e** info@dhpromotions.com **w** davidhullpromotions.com 🖂 MD: David Hull.

Dawson Breed Music Ltd Matrix Studios, 91 Peterborough Rd, London, SW6 3BU **t** 020 7733 0508 **e** debra@dawsonbreedmusic.com **w** dawsonbreedmusic.com 🔗 facebook.com/people/Debra-Downes/1404316499 🔗 myspace.com/dawson_breed 🔗 twitter.com/DawsonBreed 🖂 Director: Debra Downes 07977 555770.

The Day Job 122 London Rd, Twickenham, Middlesex, TW1 1HD **t** 020 8607 9282 **e** nina@thedayjob.com **w** thedayjob.com 🔗 \thedayjob 🖂 Director: Nina Jackson.

DCM International Suite 3, 294-296 Nether St, Finchley, London, N3 1RJ **t** 020 8343 0848 **f** 020 8343 0747 **e** dancecm@aol.com **w** dancecrazy.co.uk 🖂 MD: Kelly Isaacs.

Denis Vaughan Promotions PO Box 28286, London, N21 3WT **t** 020 7486 5353 **f** 020 8224 0466 **e** dvaughanmusic@dial.pipex.com 🖂 Director: Denis Vaughan.

Dexnfx Agency & Management London, N19 5DN **t** 020 7272 2323 **f** 0700 603 8753 **e** jill@dexnfx.com **w** dexnfx.com 🔗 facebook.com/dexnfx 🖂 Dir: Jill Thompson 07773376450.

Dinosaur Promotions/Pulse (The Agency) 5 Heyburn Crescent, Westport Gardens, Stoke On Trent, Staffordshire, ST6 4DL **t** 01782 824 051 **f** 01782 761 752 **e** agency@dinoprom.com **w** dinoprom.com 🖂 MD: Alan Dutton.

The Dixon Agency 58 Hedley Street, Gosforth, Newcastle upon Tyne, Tyne and Wear, NE3 1DL **t** 0191 213 1333 **f** 0191 213 1313 **e** bill@dixon-agency.com **w** dixon-agency.com 🖂 Owner: Bill Dixon.

Steve Draper Entertainments 2 The Coppice, Beardwood Manor, Blackburn, Lancashire, BB2 7BQ **t** 01254 679 005 **f** 01254 679 005 **e** steve@stevedraperents.fsbusiness.co.uk **w** stevedraper.co.uk 🖂 Proprietor: Steve Draper.

Barry Dye Entertainments PO Box 888, Ipswich, Suffolk, IP1 6BU **t** 01473 744287 **f** 01473 745442 **e** barrydye@aol.com 🖂 Prop: Barry Dye.

Dyfel Management 19 Fontwell Drive, Bickley, Bromley, Kent, BR2 8AB **t** 020 8467 9605 **f** 020 8249 1972 **e** jean@dyfel.co.uk **w** dyfel.co.uk 🖂 Dir: J Dyne.

EC1 Music Agency 1 Cowcross St, London, EC1M 6DR **t** 020 7490 8990 **f** 020 7490 8987 **e** jack@ec1music.com 🖂 MD: Alex Nightingale.

Elastic Artists Agency Ltd 101 Micawber Wharf, 17 Micawber St, London, N1 7TB **t** 020 7336 8340 **f** 020 7608 1471 **e** agents@elasticartists.net **w** elasticartists.net 🖂 Managing Director: Jon Slade.

Elite Music Management PO Box 3261, Brighton, BN2 4WA **t** 01273 554022 **f** 01273 566123 **e** hq@elitemm.co.uk **w** elitemm.co.uk 🔗 www.myspace.com/elitemusicmanagement 🔗 twitter.com/elitemm 🖂 Contact: Paul Wells.

ePM PO Box 47264, London, W7 1WX **t** 020 8566 0200 **e** oliver@electronicpm.co.uk **w** electronicpm.co.uk 🖂 Partner: Oliver Way.

Excession: The Agency Ltd 242 Acklam Rd, London, W10 5JJ **t** 020 7524 7676 **f** 020 7524 7677 **e** bookings@excession.co.uk **w** excession.co.uk 🖂 MD: Tara Morgan.

Fat! Agency Unit 36, Battersea Business Centre, 99-109 Lavender Hill, London, SW11 5QL **t** 020 7924 1333 **f** 020 7924 1833 **e** info@thefatclub.com **w** thefatclub.com 🖂 MD: Paul Arnold.

Faze 2 - International DJ Agency PO Box 430, Manchester, M14 0BB **t** 0161 445 6531 **f** 0161 953 4038 **e** iain@faze2agency.com **w** faze2agency.com 🖂 Mgr: Iain Taylor.

Contacts   Facebook  MySpace Twitter YouTube

First Contact Agency Ltd
206 Chalk Farm Road (Top Floor), Camden Town, London, NW1 8AB **t** 020 7485 0999 **f** 020 7485 1112 **e** info@firstcontactagency.com **w** firstcontactagency.com Agent: Adam Elfin.

Free Trade Agency
20-22 Chapel Pl, London, EC2A 3NF **t** 020 7655 6900 **f** 020 7655 6909 **e** enquiries@freetradeagency.co.uk **MD**: Paul Boswell.

Fruit Pie Music Agency
The Shop, 443 Streatham High Road, London, SW16 3PH **t** 020 8679 9289 **f** 020 8679 9775 **e** info@fruitpiemusic.com **w** fruitpiemusic.com **MD**: Kumar Kamalagharan.

Frusion
1 Holme Road, Matlock Bath, Derbyshire, DE4 3NU **t** 07791 699 889 **f** 01629 57082 **e** frusion@mac.com **w** frusion.co.uk Contact: Ian Smith.

G Entertainment
16 Coney Green, Abbotts Barton, Winchester, Hants, SO23 7JB **t** 0845 601 6285 **e** enquiries@g-entertaining.co.uk **w** g-entertaining.co.uk **MD**: Peter Nouwens.

Gordon Poole Agency Ltd
The Limes, Brockley, Bristol, Somerset, BS48 3BB **t** 01275 463222 **f** 01275 462252 **e** agents@gordonpoole.com **w** gordonpoole.com **MD**: Gordon Poole.

The Groove Company
The Coach House, Market Sq, Bicester, Oxon, OX26 6AG **t** 01869 250647 **f** 01869 321552 **e** tracey@groovecompany.co.uk Manager: Tracey Askem.

Hal Carter Organisation
41 Horsefair Green, Stony Stratford, Milton Keynes, Bucks, MK11 1JP **t** 01908 567388 **e** artistes@halcarterorg.com **w** halcarterorg.com Managing Director: Abbie Carter 07958 252 906.

Hartbeat Entertainments Ltd
PO Box 348, Brixton, Plymouth, Devon, PL8 2ZW **t** 01752 881 155 **f** 01752 880 133 **e** hartbeat@lineone.net **w** hartbeat.co.uk **MD**: Mr RJ Hart.

The Headline Agency
39 Churchfields, Milltown, Dublin 14, Ireland **t** +353 1 260 2560 **f** +353 1 260 2560 **e** info@theheadlineagency.com **w** theheadlineagency **MD**: Madeleine Seiler +353 8 72 475 791.

Helter Skelter
Bond House, 347-353 Chiswick High Rd, London, W4 4HS **t** 020 8742 5500 **f** 020 8742 5611 **e** info@helterskelter.co.uk **w** helterskelter.co.uk Snr Agent: Nigel Hassler.

John Howe Entertainment Agency
2 Meadow Way, Ferring, Worthing, BN12 5LD **t** 01903 249 912 **f** 01903 507 698 **e** johnhowe@btconnect.com Dir: John Howe.

IMD
29 Westminster Palace Gardens, 1-7 Artillery Row, London, SW1P 1RL **t** 020 7222 3095 **f** 020 7222 0898 **e** rachel@imd.dj **w** imd.dj myspace.com/imddjs twitter.com/IMDDJ CEO: Rachel Birchwood.

Imprint Bookings & Management
110 Willow Vale, London, W12 0PB **t** 020 8746 0400 **f** 020 8929 8097 **e** gareth.rees@imprintdjs.com **w** imprintdjs.com Director: Gareth Rees.

IN DEMAND AGENCY LTD

35 Jackson Court, Rose Avenue, Hazlemere, Buckinghamshire, HP15 7TZ **t** +44 (0) 844 357 35 82 **e** info@indemandagency.com **w** indemandagency.com facebook.com/InDemandAgency myspace.com/indemanduk twitter.com/INDEMANDAGENCY youtube.com/InDemandAgency Director: Ms Simone Craig +44(0) 7957 996 724. Account Manager: Ryan Forbes. Account Manager: Serena Thorn. Financial Accountant: Roy Forbes. Promotions Coordinator: Sally Webb.

Insanity Artists Agency Ltd
Moray House, 23-31 Great Titchfield Street, London, W1W 7PA **t** 020 7927 6222 **f** 020 7927 6223 **e** info@insanitygroup.com **w** insanitygroup.com **MD**: Andy Varley.

International Talent Booking
Ariel House, 74A Charlotte St, London, W1T 4QJ **t** 020 7637 6979 **f** 020 7637 6978 **e** mail@itb.co.uk **w** itb.co.uk **MD**: Barry Dickins.

Jade-Inc
Cameo House, 11 Bear St, London, WC2H 7AS **t** 020 7930 6996 **e** Jade@jade-inc.net **w** jade-inc.net Music Management: Jade Richardson.

K2 Agency
4 Courtyard House, Lensbury Avenue, Imperial Wharf, London, SW6 2TR **t** 020 7736 4948 **f** 020 7471 4949 **e** info@k2ours.com **MD**: John Jackson.

King's Lynn Arts Centre
27-29 King St, King's Lynn, Norfolk, PE30 1HA **t** 01553 765565 **f** 01553 762141 **e** entertainment_admin@west-norfolk.gov.uk **w** west-norfolk.gov.uk **GM**: Les Miller. Seated Capacity: 349

The Leighton-Pope Organisation
8 Glenthorne Mews, 115a Glenthorne Rd, London, W6 0LJ **t** 020 8741 4453 **f** 020 8741 4289 **e** info@l-po.com **w** l-po.com **MD**: Carl Leighton-Pope.

Les Hart (Southampton Entertainments)
6 Crookhorn Lane, Purbrook, Waterlooville, Hants, PO7 5QE **t** 02392 258373 **f** 02392 258369 **e** rod@leshart.co.uk **w** leshart.co.uk Proprietor: Rod Watts 02380 456149.

Limelight Entertainment
23 Westbury Avenue, Droitwich Spa, Worcs, WR9 0RT **t** 01905 796 816 **e** limelight.ent@googlemail.com **w** limelight-ent.co.uk Partners: John and Lisa Nash.

Mainstage Artists
Unit B, 11 Bell Yard Mews, 175 Bermondsey St, London, SE1 3TN **t** 020 7407 4466 **f** 020 7407 9719 **e** simon@mainstageartists.com **w** mainstageartists.com **MD**: Simon Clarkson.

MusicWeek

Creative Advertising Solutions

Contact the Music Week advertising sales team, and guarantee
you reach the right audience at the right time

Contact:
Becky Golland on 0207 921 8365
or Archie Carmichael on 0207 921 8372

www.musicweek.com

Live: Booking Agents

Malcolm Feld Agency Malina House, Sandforth Rd, Liverpool, L12 1JY **t** 0151 259 6565 **f** 0151 259 5006 **e** Malcolm@malcolmfeld.co.uk **w** malcolmfeld.co.uk ✉ Agent: Malcolm Feld.

MassiveUK 36-40 Edge Street, Northern Quarter, Manchester, M4 1HN **t** 0161 833 4982 **f** 0161 833 4982 **e** info@massiveuk.org.uk **w** massiveuk.org.uk ✉ Director: Jo Fidler.

McLeod Agency Ltd Priory House, 1133 Hessle High Rd, Hull, East Yorkshire, HU4 6SB **t** 01482 565444 **f** 01482 353635 **e** alex@mcleodagency.co.uk **w** mcleodagency.co.uk ✉ Director: Alex Temperton.

Mezonbeam Music 1 Cedars Drive, Hilingdon, Middlesex, UB10 0JT **t** 07760114814 **e** Mezonbeam@googlemail.com **w** myspace.com/mezonbeam3000 ✉ Dirs: Merryn Phillips 07760 114814.

Mi Live 55 St Albans Road, S.C.R., Dublin 8, Ireland **t** +353 1 416 9418 **f** +353 1 416 9418 **e** info@milive.net ✉ MD: Bernie McGrath +353 (0) 87 9817535.

Miracle Artists 26 Dorset St, London, W1U 8AP **t** 020 7935 9222 **f** 020 7935 6222 **e** info@miracle-artists.com ✉ Agency Dir: Steve Parker.

Mission Control Artist Agency 2-3 City Business Centre, Lower Rd, London, SE16 2XB **t** 020 7252 3001 **f** 020 7252 2225 **e** info@missioncontrol.net **w** missioncontrol.net ✉ MD: Craig D'Souza.

Money Talks Agency Cadillac Ranch, Pencraig Uchaf, Cwm Bach, Whitland, Carms., SA34 0DT **t** 01994 484466 **f** 01994 484294 **e** cadillacranch@telco4u.net **w** nikturner.com ✉ Dir: Chick Augustino.

Moneypenny Agency The Stables, Westwood House, Main St, North Dalton, Driffield, East Yorks, YO25 9XA **t** 01377 217815 **f** 01377 217754 **e** nigel@adastey.demon.co.uk **w** adastra-music.co.uk/moneypenny ✉ MD: Nigel Morton 07977 455882.

Monkeybiz Management Entertainment Agency 13 Homan House, Kings Avenue, London, SW4 8DB **t** 020 8683 9373 **e** info@monkeybizmanagement.com **w** monkeybizmanagement.com ✉ Contact: Donlald Deans 07940 550 153.

Musicians Inc. 4 Solar Court, 22 Chambers Street, London, SE16 4XL **t** 0845 450 1962 **e** enquiries@musiciansinc.co.uk **w** musiciansinc.co.uk/musicians.htm ✉ MD: Sarah Ings.

Neil O'Brien Entertainment 14 Thirsk Rd, Battersea, London, SW11 5SX **t** 020 7978 6475 **e** neil@neilobrienentertainment.com **w** neilobrienentertainment.com ✉ MD: Neil O'Brien 07944 225459.

NMP Live Limited 8 Blenheim Court, Brook Way, Leatherhead, Surrey, KT22 7NA **t** 020 8669 3128 **f** 020 8404 2621 **e** live@nmp.co.uk **w** nmplive.co.uk ✉ Director: Neil Martin.

NVB Entertainments 80 Holywell Road, Studham, Dunstable, Bedfordshire, LU6 2PD **t** 01582 873623 **f** 01582 873618 **e** NVBEnts@aol.com ✉ Bookers: H Harrison, Frances Harrison.

Orange Promotions 3 Charter Court, Linden Grove, New Malden, Surrey, KT3 3BL **t** 020 8942 7722 **e** livegigs@mail.com **w** orangepromotions.com ✱ myspace.com/orangepromotions ✉ Bookings Manager: Phil Brydon 07958 967666.

Peller Artistes Ltd. 39 Princes Ave, London, N3 2DA **t** 020 8343 4264 **f** 07092 808 252 **e** agent@pellerartistes.com **w** pellerartistes.com ✉ MD: Barry Peller 0114 247 2365.

Plug Artists 49 East Court Yard, Tullyvale, Cherrywood, Co. Dublin, Ireland **t** +353 87 938 2754 **e** plugartists@gmail.com **w** myspace.com/plugartists ✉ MD: Eoin Banahan.

Positive Nuisance 180 Muswell Hill Broadway, London, N10 3SA **t** 020 8444 9944 **e** chrissie@positivenuisance.com **w** positivenuisance.com ✉ MD: Chrissie Yiannou.

Primary Talent International The Primary Building, 10-11 Jockey's Fields, London, WC1R 4BN **t** 020 7400 4500 **f** 020 7400 4501 **e** mail@primary.uk.com **w** primary.uk.com ✉ MD: Peter Elliott.

Prodmix International 98 Edith Grove, Chelsea, London, SW10 0NH **t** 020 7565 0324 **f** 0870 051 3581 **e** karen@prodmix.com **w** prodmix ✉ MD: Karen Goldie Sauve 07768 877426.

Profile Artists Agency ✉ Contact: See Primary Talent Int..

Psycho Management 111 Clarence Rd, Wimbledon, London, SW19 8QB **t** 020 8540 8122 **f** 020 8715 2827 **e** agents@psycho.co.uk **w** psycho.co.uk t @circusofhorrors ▶ youtube.com/psychomanagement ✉ MD: John Mabley 01483 419429.

Reveal Records 63 St Peters St, Derby, Derbyshire, DE1 2AB **t** 07779 017 236 **f** 01332 556 374 **e** tomreveal@mac.com **w** reveal-records.com ✉ MD: Tom Rose.

Roots Around the World The Barn, Fordwater Lane, Chichester, West Sussex, PO19 6PT **t** 01243 789786 **e** rootsaroundtheworld@btopenworld.com **w** rootsaroundtheworld.info ✉ Dir: Mark Ringwood 07802 500050.

RRR Management 96 Wentworth Road, Birmingham, B17 9SY **t** 0121 426 6820 **f** 0121 426 5700 **e** enquiries@rrrmanagement.com **w** rrrmanagement.com ✉ MD: Ruby Ryan.

📇 Contacts 📘 Facebook 🔲 MySpace 🇹 Twitter ▶️ YouTube

Sasa Music 309, Aberdeen House, 22-24 Highbury Grove, London, N5 2EA **t** 020 7359 9232 **f** 020 7359 9233 **e** postroom@sasa.demon.co.uk **w** sasamusic.com 📇 MD: David Flower.

Sensible Events 2nd Floor, Regent Arcade House, 19-25 Argyll St, London, W1F 7TS **t** 020 7009 3470 **e** Andrew@sensiblevents.com **w** sensiblevents.com 📇 MD: Andrew Zweck.

Snogadog Agency 53, Triq Ta Mellu, Mosta, MST3780, Malta **t** 00356 2143 3303 **e** maltamusic@live.com **w** myspace.com/snogadogmusicpromotions 🔲 myspace.com/snogadogmusicpromotions 📇 Contact: Richard Rogers/Tanweer Rayasat 00356 9989 6666.

Solo Agency & Promotions 2nd Floor, 53-55 Fulham High St, London, SW6 3JJ **t** 020 7384 6644 **f** 020 3266 1076 **e** soloreception@solo.uk.com **w** solo.uk.com 📇 MD: John Giddings.

Sounds Fair Promotions 9 Park Place, Ashton Keynes, Nr Swindon, Wiltshire, SN6 6NT **t** 01285 861486 **f** 01285 862302 **e** info@soundsfair.freeserve.co.uk **w** soundsfair.freeserve.co.uk 📇 Agent: Dave Beckley.

Spun Out 2A Southam St, London, W10 5PH **t** 020 8960 3253 **f** 020 8968 5111 **e** caroline@mumbojumbo.co.uk 📇 MD: Caroline Hayes.

Steve Allen Entertainments 60 Broadway, Peterborough, Cambs, PE1 1SU **t** 01733 569589 **f** 01733 561854 **e** steve@sallenent.co.uk **w** sallenent.co.uk 📇 Principal: Steve Allen.

Stoneyport Associates Suite 10, 130 Leith Walk, Edinburgh, EH6 5DT **t** 07968 131737 **f** 08700 510557 **e** jb@stoneyport.demon.co.uk **w** stoneyport.co.uk 📇 MD: John Barrow 0131-443 4784.

Swamp Music PO Box 94, Derby, DE22 1XA **t** 01332 332336 **f** 01332 332336 **e** chrishall@swampmusic.co.uk **w** swampmusic.co.uk 📇 MD: Chris Hall 07702 564804.

Talking Heads (Voice Agency) 2-4 Noel St, London, W1F 8GB **t** 020 7292 7575 **f** 020 7292 7576 **e** voices@talkingheadsvoices.com **w** talkingheadsvoices.com 📇 Principal: John Sachs.

Time And Talent Agency PO Box 51146, London, SE13 7WD **t** 07986 420811 **e** clive@timeandtalentagency.co.uk **w** timeandtalentagency.co.uk 📇 Director: Clive Johnson.

Time And Talent Agency Ltd PO Box 51146, London, SE13 7WD **t** 07986 420811 **e** clive@timeandtalentagency.co.uk **w** timeandtalentagency.co.uk 📇 Director: Clive Johnson.

Tony Bennell Entertainments 10 Manor Way, Kidlington, Oxford, Oxfordshire, OX5 2BD **t** 01865 372645 **f** 01865 372645 **e** tonybennell@hotmail.com **w** tonybennell.co.uk 📇 MD: Tony Bennell 07885 204274.

Tony Denton Promotions Ltd 19 South Molton Lane, Mayfair, London, W1K 5LE **t** 020 7629 4666 **f** 020 7629 4777 **e** peter@tdpromo.com **w** tdpromo.com www.here-and-now.info 📘 facebook.com/group.php?gid=6292867505 📇 Director: Tony Denton.

Top Talent Agency Yester Road, Chiselhurst, Kent, BR7 5HN **t** 020 8467 0808 **f** 020 8467 0808 **e** top.talent.agency@virgin.net 📇 MD: John Day.

Tribute Entertainment Limited 2 Unity Pl, Westgate, Rotherham, South Yorkshire, S60 1AR **t** 01709 820379 **e** tributebands@btconnect.com **w** tributebandreviews.co.uk 🇹 twitter.com/bandreviews ▶️ youtube.com/tributebandreviews 📇 Dir: Anthony French.

UK Booking Agency Box 1, 404 Footscray Rd, London, SE9 3TU **t** 020 8857 8787 **f** 020 8857 8775 **e** stevecanbefound@hotmail.co.uk 📇 Owner: Steve Goddard 07740 351163.

Upfront Television 39-41 New Oxford St, London, WC1A 1BN **t** 020 7836 7702/3 **f** 020 7836 7701 **e** info@upfronttv.com **w** celebritiesworldwide.com 📇 Co-MDs: Claire Nye, Richard Brecker.

Vagabond Artists Floor 2, Building B, Tower Bridge Business Complex, 100 Clements Road, London, SE16 1ED **t** 020 7921 8353 **e** rubber_road_records@yahoo.com 📇 MD: Dexter Charles.

Value Added Talent 1 Purley Pl, Islington, London, N1 1QA **t** 020 7704 9720 **f** 020 7226 6135 **e** vat@vathq.co.uk **w** vathq.co.uk 📇 MD: Dan Silver.

Vibe Promotions 91-95 Brick Lane, London, E1 6QL **t** 020 7426 0491 **f** 020 7426 0491 **e** info@vibe-bar.co.uk **w** vibe-bar.co.uk 📇 Event & Bookings: Adelle Stripe.

Victor Hugo Salsa Show 10 Derby Hill Crescent, London, SE23 3YL **t** 020 8291 5838 **f** 020 8291 9236 **e** vhs@victorhugosalsa.com **w** victorhugosalsa.com 📇 MD: Victor Hugo 07956 446 342.

The Village Agency 13-14 Dean Street, London, W1D 3RS **t** 020 7734 5566 **f** 020 7605 5188 **e** firstname@mvillage.co.uk **w** thevillageagency.net 📇 Live Agent: Francesca T Davies and Paul Franklyn.

Vital Edge Artist Agency PO Box 25965, London, N18 1YT **t** 0870 350 1045 **f** 0870 350 1046 **e** info@vitaledgeagency.com **w** vitaledgeagency.com 📇 Prop: Nicky Jackson.

Jason West Agency Gables House, Saddle Bow, Kings Lynn, Norfolk, PE34 3AR **t** 01553 617586 **f** 01553 617734 **e** info@jasonwest.com **w** jasonwest.com 📇 MD: Jason West.

William Morris Endeavor Entertainment Centrepoint Tower, 103 New Oxford St, London, WC1A 1DD **t** 020 7534 6800 **f** 020 7534 6900 **e** ldnmusiccentral@wmeentertainment.com **w** wmeentertainment.com 📇 London Music Central: Music Central 020 7534 6941.

📧 Contacts   📘 Facebook   📱 MySpace   🇹 Twitter   ▶️ YouTube

X-ray Touring Suite A, Nena House, 77-79 Great Eastern St, London, EC2A 3HU **t** 020 7749 3500 **f** 020 7749 3501 **e** info@xraytouring.com **w** xraytouring.com 📧 Office Manager: Lucy Henrit.

Concert Promoters

3A Entertainment Ltd 4 Princeton Court, 53-55 Felsham Rd, London, SW15 1AZ **t** 020 8789 6111 **f** 020 8789 6222 **e** aaaents@aol.com 📧 Dirs: Peter Wilson, Martyn Stanger, Dennis Arnold.

A.M.P. Level 3, 13-14 Margaret St, London, W1W 8RN **t** 020 7224 1992 **f** 020 7224 0111 **e** mail@harveygoldsmith.com **w** harveygoldsmith.com 📧 Contact: Serena Emden.

Active Sandycroft, Hillbrow, Bromley, Kent, BR1 2PQ **t** 020 8325 2222 **f** 020 8325 2226 **e** info@active-group.co.uk **w** active-group.co.uk 📧 MD: Matthew Lewis.

AEG Live 25 Canada Sq, Canary Wharf, London, E14 5LQ **t** 020 7536 2600 **f** 020 7536 2603 **e** info@aegworldwide.co.uk **w** aeglive.co.uk 📧 President International: Rob Hallett.

Aiken Promotions Ltd 24 Holles St, Dublin 2, Ireland **t** +353 17 755 800 **f** +353 17 755 888 **e** office@aikenpromotions.com **w** aikenpromotions.com 📧 Office Mgrs: Mary Kelly / Sorcha.

Anonymous Groove 186 Town Street, Armley, Leeds, LS12 3RF **t** 0113 368 9912 **e** info@anonymous-groove.com **w** anonymous-groove.com 📧 MD: Chris Shipton 0793 044 3048.

Badger Promotions PO Box 9121, Birmingham, B13 8AU **t** 08712 260 910 **e** info@badgerpromotions.co.uk **w** badgerpromotions.co.uk 📧 Promoter: Mark Badger.

Barrucci Leisure Enterprises Ltd 45-47 Cheval Place, London, SW7 1EW **t** 020 7225 2255 **f** 020 7581 2509 **e** barrucci@barrucci.com 📧 MD: Bryan Miller.

BB Promotions 3 Roberts Road, Pokesdown, Bournemouth, BH7 6LN **t** 07749 768 904 **e** info@bb-promotions.co.uk **w** bb-promotions.co.uk 📧 Contact: Bert Burnell.

BDA 32 Chiltern Road, Culcheth, Warrington, Cheshire, WA3 4LL **t** 01925 766 655 **f** 01925 765 577 **e** briandurkin@btconnect.com **w** bdaltd.co.uk 📧 MD: Brian Durkin.

Big Wheel Promotions 43 Brook Green, London, W6 7EF **t** 020 7795 7000 **f** 020 7605 5188 **e** clare@mvillage.co.uk **w** bigwheelpromotions.com 📧 Promoter: Clare O'Bree.

BKO Productions Ltd c/o Haynes Orme, 3, Bolt Court, London, EC4A 3DQ **t** 07872 954 828 **e** byron@bko-alarcon.co.uk 📧 Director: Byron Orme.

Blow Up PO Box 4961, London, W1A 7ZX **t** 020 7636 7744 **f** 020 7636 7755 **e** webmaster@blowup.co.uk **w** blowupclub.com 📧 MD: Paul Tunkin.

Brian Yeates Associates Home Farm House, Canwell, Sutton Coldfield, West Midlands, B75 5SH **t** 0121 323 2200 **e** info@brianyeates.co.uk **w** brianyeates.co.uk 📧 Partner: Ashley Yeates.

Bugbear Promotions 40 Dunford Rd, London, n7 6el **t** 020 7700 0550 / 020 7700 0880 **e** info@bugbearbookings.com **w** bugbearbookings.com 📱 myspace.com/bugbearpromotions 📧 Contact: Jim Mattison, Tony Gleed.

CMC PO Box 3, Newport, NP20 3YB **t** 07973 715 875 **e** alanjones@cmcpromotions.co.uk 📧 Principal: Alan Jones.

CMP Entertainment - Music & Sport 08 Place, 36-38 Whitechapel, Liverpool, L1 6DZ **t** 0151 708 6050 **f** 0151 707 0400 **e** info@cmplive.com **w** cmplive.com 📧 MD: Chas Cole.

Cream Group Cream Office, 1 - 3 Parr St, Wolstenholme Sq, Liverpool, L1 4JJ **t** 0151 707 1309 **f** 0151 707 1761 **e** gill@cream.co.uk **w** cream.co.uk 📧 Head of PR & Communications: Gill Nightingale.

Curious Generation Brassmore House, 151-153 Curtain Rd, London, EC2A 3QL **e** info@curiousgeneration.com **w** curiousgeneration.com 📧 Head of Music: Alex Martin.

Dangerfield Promotions 49 East Court Yard, Tullyvale, Cherrywood, Co. Dublin, Ireland **t** +353 87 650 7481 **e** dangerfieldpromotions@gmail.com **w** myspace.com/dangerfieldpromotions 📧 MD: Marcus Lester.

David Hull Promotions 46 University St, Belfast, County Antrim, BT38 8RG, Northern Ireland **t** 028 9024 0360 **f** 028 9024 7919 **e** info@dhpromotions.com **w** davidhullpromotions.com 📧 Director: David Hull.

DCB Promotions 30 A College Green, Bristol, BS1 5TB **t** 0117 9834503 **f** 0117 9042269 **e** dave@dcbpromotions.com **w** dcbpromotions.com 📧 MD: Dave Brayley.

Dead Or Alive PO Box 34204, London, NW5 1FS **t** 020 7482 3908 **e** gigs@deadoralive.org.uk **w** deadoralive.org.uk 📱 myspace.com/deadoralivepromotions 📧 MD: Nicholas Barnett.

Denis Vaughan Promotions PO Box 28286, London, N21 3WT **t** 020 7486 5353 **f** 020 8224 0466 **e** dvaughanmusic@dial.pipex.com 📧 Director: Denis Vaughan.

Derek Block Artistes Agency Ltd 70-76 Bell St, Marylebone, London, NW1 6SP **t** 020 7724 2101 **f** 020 7724 2102 **e** dbaa@derekblock.co.uk 📧 MD: Derek Block.

DF Concerts 272 St Vincent St, Glasgow, G2 5RL **t** 0141 566 4999 **f** 0141 566 4998 **e** admin@dfconcerts.co.uk **w** gigsinscotland.com 📧 Contact: Wendy Sams.

Live: Concert Promoters

Electric Broom Cupboard 2 Lauder Court, Coldharbour, Milborne Port, Dorset, DT9 5EL **t** 01963 251407 **e** simon@evolver.org.uk **w** evolver.org.uk 📇 MD: Simon Barber.

Eurobiketours Corner House, Pullham Lane, Wetwang, Yorkshire, YO25 8XD **t** 01904 431360 **f** 01904 623660 **e** music@eurobiketours.com **w** eurobiketours.com 📇 MD: Phillip Sash.

Festival Republic 35 Bow St, London, WC2E 7AU **t** 020 7009 3000 **e** info@festivalrepublic.com **w** festivalrepublic.com 📇 MD: Melvyn Benn.

Flick Productions PO Box 888, Penzance, Cornwall, TR20 8ZP **t** 01736 788798 **f** 01736 787898 **e** Flickprouk@aol.com 📇 MD: Mark Shaw.

The Flying Music Company Ltd FM House, 110 Clarendon Road, London, W11 2HR **t** 020 7221 7799 **f** 020 7221 5016 **e** info@flyingmusic.com **w** flyingmusic.com 📇 Directors: Paul Walden, Derek Nicol.

Futuresound Music Ltd Calls Landing, 36 - 38 The Calls, Leeds, LS2 7EW **t** 0113 244 3446 **f** 0113 243 4849 **e** info@thecockpit.co.uk **w** thecockpit.co.uk 📇 Dir: Richard Todd.

Geronimo! 15 Canada Copse, Milford, Surrey, GU8 5AL **t** 07960 187529 **e** barneyjeavons@supanet.com 📇 Promoter: Barney Jeavons.

GM Promotions 17 The Athenaeum, 32 Salisbury Rd, Hove, E. Sussex, BN3 3AA **t** 01273 774 469 **e** info@gmpromotions.co.uk **w** gmpromotions.co.uk 📇 Dir: Laura Ducceschi 07980 917 056.

Goldenvoice UK 29 Great Guildford St, London, SE1 9LS **t** 020 7536 2626 **f** 020 7620 0595 **e** rupert@goldenvoice.co.uk **w** goldenvoice.co.uk 📇 Promoter: Rupert Dell.

Hallogen Ltd The Bridgewater Hall, Manchester, M2 3WS **t** 0161 950 0000 **f** 0161 950 0001 **e** admin@bridgewater-hall.co.uk **w** bridgewater-hall.co.uk 📇 Programming Manager: Sara Unwin.

Handshake Ltd 2 Holly House, Mill St, Uppermill, Saddleworth, Lancs, OL3 6LZ **t** 01457 819350 **f** 01457 810052 **e** info@handshakegroup.com **w** handshakegroup.com 📇 Director: Stuart Littlewood.

Chester Hopkins Int Ltd PO Box 536, Headington, Oxford, OX3 7LR **t** 01865 766 766 **f** 01865 769 736 **e** office@chesterhopkins.co.uk **w** chesterhopkins.co.uk 📇 MDs: Adrian Hopkins, Jo Chester 020 8441 1555.

IMG Arts & Entertainment Pier House, Strand on the Green, London, W4 3NN **t** 020 8233 5000 **f** 020 8233 5001 **e** concerts@imgworld.com **w** imgworld.com 📇 Managing Director: Stephen Flint Wood.

Infinite Events Ltd 2 Dickson Road, Blackpool, Lancashire, FY1 2AA **t** 01253 299 606 **f** 01253 299 454 **e** infinite@mct-online.com 📇 Contact: Julian Murray.

Insanity Artists Agency Ltd Moray House, 23-31 Great Titchfield Street, London, W1W 7PA **t** 020 7927 6222 **f** 020 7927 6223 **e** info@insanitygroup.com **w** insanitygroup.com 📇 MD: Andy Varley.

Jay Taylor Flat 114, India House, 75 Whitworth St, Manchester, M1 6HB **t** 0161 278 6087 **e** jaytaylor@cwcom.net **w** bone-box.com 📇 Promoter: Jay Taylor 07931 797 982.

Kennedy Street Enterprises Ltd Kennedy House, 31 Stamford St, Altrincham, Cheshire, WA14 1ES **t** 0161 941 5151 **f** 0161 928 9491 **e** kse@kennedystreet.com 📇 Dir: Danny Betesh.

King Georges Hall BLACKBURN Northgate, Blackburn, Lancashire, BB2 1AA **t** 01254 582579 **f** 01254 667277 **e** geoff.peake@blackburn.gov.uk **w** kinggeorgeshall.com 📇 Events/Promo Mgr: Geoff Peake 01254 503225. Seated Capacity: 1853 Standing capacity: 2000

Laughing Stock Productions. 38/40 Eastcastle St, E, London, W1W 8DT **t** 020 7631 4290 **e** mike@laughingstock.co.uk **w** laughingstock.co.uk 📇 Director: Mike O'Brien.

Line-Up PMC Inc On-Line Records 10 Matthew Close, Newcastle-upon-Tyne, Tyne and Wear, NE6 1XD **t** 0191 275 9745 **e** chrismurtagh@line-up.co.uk **w** line-up.co.uk 📇 Owner: Christopher Murtagh.

Live Nation 1st Floor, Regent Arcade House, 19-25 Argyll St, London, W1F 7TS **t** 020 7009 3333 **f** 0870 749 0560 **e** firstname.lastname@livenation.co.uk **w** livenation.co.uk 📇 Chief Operating Officer, International Music: Paul Latham.

Liverpool Philharmonic Hall & Events Ltd Liverpool Philharmonic Hall, Hope St, Liverpool, Merseyside, L1 9BP **t** 0151 709 3789 **f** 0151 210 2902 **e** simon.glinn@liverpoolphil.com **w** liverpoolphil.com 📇 Executive Director: Simon Glinn 0151 210 2895.

Scott Mackenzie Associates The Gatehouse, Porlock, Mine, Somerset, TA24 8ES **t** 01643 863 330 **f** 01643 863 341 **e** enquiries@scottmackenzie.co.uk **w** scottmackenzie.co.uk 📇 MD: Scott Mackenzie.

The Marquee Club 21a Maury Road, London, N16 7BP **t** 020 8815 4747 **e** info@plummusic.com **w** plummusic.com 📇 Independant Promoter: Allan North 020 7734 5467.

Marshall Arts Ltd Unit 6, Utopia Village, 7 Chalcot Rd, London, NW1 8LH **t** 020 7586 3831 **f** 020 7586 1422 **e** info@marshall-arts.co.uk **w** marshall-arts.com 📇 MD: Barrie Marshall.

Matpro Ltd Cary Point, Babbacombe Downs, Torquay, Devon, TQ1 3LU **t** 01803 322 233 **f** 01803 322 244 **e** mail@matpro-show.biz **w** babbacombe-theatre.com 📇 MD: Colin Matthews.

Phil McIntyre Promotions 2nd Floor, 35 Soho Square, London, W1D 3QX **t** 020 7439 2270 **f** 020 7439 2280 **e** reception@mcintyre-ents.com 📇 Promoter: Paul Roberts.

Live: Concert Promoters

Mean Fiddler 59-65 Worship St, London, EC2A 2DU
t 020 7688 9000 **f** 020 7688 8999
e editor@meanfiddler.co.uk **w** meanfiddler.com
🅃 twitter.com/meanfiddlerlive ✉ MD: Steve Forster.

Metropolis Music 69 Caversham Rd, London, NW5 2DR
t 020 7424 6800 **f** 020 7424 6849
e reception@metropolismusic.com **w** gigsandtours.com
✉ MD: Bob Angus.

Monto 328 Grays Inn Rd, Kings Cross, London, WC1X 8BZ
t 020 7837 4412 **e** info@themonto.com **w** themonto.com
🅵 facebook.com/profile.php?id=1380221404&ref=ts
🅼 myspace.com/montolondonlive ✉ Director: Terry Kirby.
Standing capacity: 100

Music First PO Box 3418, Sheffield, S11 7WJ
t 0114 268 5441 **e** info@musicfirst.info **w** musicfirst.info
✉ Dir: Barney Vernon.

Partners In Crime 18 Chenies St, London, WC1E 7PA
t 020 8521 7764 **e** saphron@msn.com
✉ Promoter: Annette Bennett 07973 415 167.

Performing Arts Management
Canal 7, Clarence Mill, Bollington, Macclesfield, Cheshire,
SK10 5JZ **t** 01625 575681 **f** 01625 572839
e info@performingarts.co.uk **w** performingarts.co.uk
✉ Marketing Manager: Fifi Butler.

Planet Of Sound - Live (Scotland) 236 High St,
Ayr, South Ayrshire, KA7 1RN **t** 01292 265 913
f 01292 265 493 **e** planet-of-sound@btconnect.com
✉ Manager: Ian Hollins.

Platform Music Bedford Chambers, The Piazza,
Covent Garden, London, WC2E 8HA **t** 07779 582 927
f 020 7379 4793 **e** info@platformmusic.net
w platformmusic.net ✉ Promoter: Lisa Cowan.

Plum Music 56b Farringdon Rd, London, EC1R 3BL
t 020 7336 7326 **f** 020 7336 7326 **e** info@plummusic.com
w plummusic.com ✉ Dirs: Allan North, Sarah Thirtle,
Matthew Grundy.

Plymouth Music Collective Ltd 21-
24 St Johns Road, Plymouth, PL4 0PA **t** 01752 201275
e info@pmc.uk.net **w** pmc.uk.net ✉ Dir: Oli James.

Gordon Poole Agency The Limes, Brockley, Bristol,
Somerset, BS48 3BB **t** 01275 463222 **f** 01275 462252
e agents@gordonpoole.com **w** gordonpoole.com
✉ Consultant: James Poole.

Psychic Pig Promotions 13a British Row, Trowbridge,
Wiltshire, BA14 8PB **t** 07973 314237
e alloutmgmt@hotmail.com ✉ Promotions: George
Johnston.

PVC 51 Bath Rd, Southsea, Hants, PO4 0HX
t 023 9275 2782 **f** 023 9234 6799 **e** ianbpvc@hotmail.com
✉ Promoter: Ian Binnington.

Regular Music 42 York Pl, Edinburgh, EH1 3HU
t 0131 525 6700 **f** 0131 525 6701
e mark@regularmusic.co.uk **w** regularmusic.co.uk
✉ MD: Mark Mackie..

Rooti-Tooti Music - Festival Planning
6 Princess Cottages, Coffinswell, Newton Abbot, TQ12 4SR
t 01803 875 527 **f** 01803 875 527
e graham@tooti.freeserve.co.uk ✉ Venue
Programmer: Graham Radley.

Serious Ltd 51 Kingsway Pl, Sans Walk, Clerkenwell,
London, EC1R 0LU **t** 020 7324 1880 **f** 020 7324 1881
e david@serious.org.uk **w** serious.org.uk
🅵 facebook.com/serious.live 🅼 myspace.com/seriouslive
🅃 twitter.com/serious_live
▶ youtube.com/seriouspresents ✉ Dir: David Jones.

Sink And Stove Top Floor Office, 53 Coronation Rd,
Southville, Bristol, BS3 1AR **t** 0117 907 6931
f 0117 907 6931 **e** info@sinkandstove.co.uk
w sinkandstove.co.uk ✉ Promoter: Benjamin Shillabeer.

SJM Concerts St Matthews, Liverpool Rd, Manchester,
M3 4NQ **t** 0161 907 3443 **f** 0161 907 3446
e vicky@sjmconcerts.com **w** gigsandtours.com ✉ Office
Manager: Vicky Potts.

Sonic Arts Network Jerwood Space,
171 Union Street, London, SE1 0LN **t** 020 7928 7337
e info@sonicartsnetwork.org **w** sonicartsnetwork.org
✉ Chief Exec: Phil Hallett.

Sound Bites Promotions The Abbey Tavern,
124 Kentish Town Road, London, NW1 9QB
t 020 7267 9449 **e** radha@abbey-tavern.com
w myspace.com/soundbitesmusic ✉ Promotion
Manager: Radha Kothari 07757 870 568.

South West Artist Network 3 Westend Terrace,
Millbrook, Torpoint, Cornwall, PL10 1AL **t** 01752 829 138
e chrisfunkymonkey@hotmail.com ✉ MD: Christian Murison.

SPC Live Unit 6, Utopia Village, 7 Chalcot Rd, London,
NW1 8LH **t** 020 7483 5736 **e** info@spclive.co.uk
w spclive.co.uk ✉ Director: Matt Jones 02074 83 57 36.

Straight Music Ltd 2 Munro Terrace, London,
SW10 0DL **t** 020 7376 4456 **f** 020 7351 5569
e shelley@straightmusic.com ✉ MD: John Curd.

Surface Unsigned Festival 20 Pool St, Walsall,
WS1 2EN **t** 01922 629140 **e** info@surfaceunsigned.co.uk
w surfaceunsigned.co.uk ✉ Events Manager: Jay Mitchell.

T.T.S. Promotions PO Box 10349, London, NW1 9WJ
t 020 8889 3408 **e** info@thetalentscout.co.uk
w thetalentscout.co.uk
🅼 myspace.com/thetalentscoutlondon ✉ Dir: Helen
Douglas.

Tidal Concerts 174 Camden High St, London, NW1 0NE
t 020 7267 3939 **f** 020 7482 1955
e contact@theunderworldcamden.co.uk ✉ Promoter: Jon
Vyner.

Trailer Park Trash PO Box 2679, Bath, BA2 3XS
t 07976 152 694 **e** trailparktrash@hotmail.com
w trailerparktrash.org.uk ✉ MD: Lee Cotterell.

Traxx Connective 2nd floor, 342 Argyle St, Glasgow,
G2 8LY **t** 0141 221 2495 **f** 0141 221 2495
e mark@wearetraxx.com **w** wearetraxx.com ✉ Dir: Mark
MacKechnie.

| 🖂 Contacts | 📘 Facebook | 🟦 MySpace | 🇹 Twitter | ▶ YouTube |

Truck Old Stable East, Church Lane, Steventon, OX13 6SW
t 01235 821262 **e** paul@truckrecords.com
w thisistruck.com 🖂 Dirs: Paul Bonham, Robin Bennett.

Underworld 174 Camden High St, London, NW1 0NE
e contact@theunderworldcamden.co.uk
w theunderworldcamden.co.uk
🟦 myspace.com/thecamdenunderworld

Up All Night Music 20 Denmark St, London,
WC2H 8NA **t** 020 7419 4696 **e** info@upallnightmusic.com
w upallnightmusic.com 🖂 MD: Phil Taylor.

Weekender Promotions PO Box 571, Taunton,
Somerset, TA1 3WZ **t** 07799 416 276
e weekenderlive@btopenworld.com 🖂 Artist Roster and
Booking: Paul Dimond.

WOM@ TT WOM@ TT c/o The Tabernacle, Powis Sq,
London, W11 2AY **e** womaatt@gmail.com
w worldofmusicatt.org.uk 🖂 Contact: Debbie Golt, Fred K,
Wala Danga, Wil Joseph 07939564103.

World Unlimited 34, Rothesay Croft, Kitwell,
Birmingham, West Midlands, B32 4JG **t** 01803 875 527
f 01803 875 527 **e** graham@tooti.freeserve.co.uk
w worldunlimited.freeuk.com 🖂 Music Programmer: Graham
Radley.

Zoe Gospel Promotions 9 Campbell Road, Stratford,
London, E15 1FL **t** 020 8534 2194
e firstname@zoegospelpromo.co.uk 🖂 Contact: Yemi
Adeshina or Uzo Anyia.

Club Promoters

The Arches 253 Argyle St, Glasgow, G2 8DL
t 0141 565 1009 **f** 0141 565 1001
e brian@thearches.co.uk **w** thearches.co.uk 🖂 Music
Programmer: Brian Reynolds. Seated Capacity: 330 Standing
capacity: 800

Attitude is Everything 54 Chalton St, London,
NW1 1HS **t** 0207 383 7979
e graham@attitudeiseverything.org.uk
w attitudeiseverything.org.uk 🖂 Business Manager: Graham
Griffiths.

Back To The Wood 15 Hamburg St, London, E1 6QL
e backtothewood@mac.com **w** backtothewood.com
🖂 Contact: Nick Smith 07795127373.

Cambridge University Students Union
Old Examination Hall, Free School Lane, Cambridge, CB2 3RF
t 01223 333313 **f** 01223 333179 **e** ents-
manager@cusu.cam.ac.uk **w** cusuents.com
📘 facebook.com/group.php?gid=26673214811&ref=ts
🖂 Entertainments Mgr: Mathew Morgan.

**Exposure (Nation-wide flyer distribution
services)** 1st floor Beehive Mill, Jersey St, Manchester,
M4 6JG **t** 0161 950 4241 **f** 0161 950 4240
e keith@exposureuk.com 🖂 MD: Keith Patterson.

King Tut's Wah Wah Hut/DF Concerts
272A St Vincent St, Glasgow, G2 5RL **t** 0141 248 5158
f 0141 248 5202 **e** kingtuts@dfconcerts.co.uk
w kingtuts.co.uk 🟦 myspace.com/kingtuts
🇹 twitter.com/kingtuts 🖂 Promoter/Venue Manager: Dave
McGeachan.

The Marquee Club 21a Maury Road, London, N16 7BP
t 020 8815 4747 **e** info@plummusic.com **w** plummusic.com
🖂 Independant Promoter: Allan North 020 7734 5467.

Movement London Bar Rumba,
36 Shaftesbury Avenue, London, W1D 7EP **t** 07813 198 066
e jordan@movement.co.uk **w** movement.co.uk 🖂 Head of
Promotions: Jordan V.

New Years Eve Manchester Churton Villa,
7 Churton Rd, Chester, Cheshire, CH3 5EB **t** 01244 329718
e ralph@new-years-eve-manchester.co.uk **w** new-years-
eve-manchester.co.uk 🖂 Director: Ralph Thornton.

Plastic Music Ltd 22 Rutland Gardens, Hove,
East Sussex, BN3 5PB **t** 01273 779 793 **f** 01273 779 820
e enzo@plastic-music.co.uk **w** plastic-music.co.uk
🖂 MD: Enzo (Vincent Amico).

Up All Night Music 20 Denmark St, London,
WC2H 8NA **t** 020 7419 4696 **e** info@upallnightmusic.com
w upallnightmusic.com 🖂 MD: Phil Taylor.

XK8 Organisation 16-24 Underwood St, London,
N1 7JQ **t** 020 7490 0666 **e** info@xk8organisation.com
w xk8organisation.com 🟦 myspace.com/xk8organisation
🖂 Director: Jeff Davy.

Concert Hire

A-C Technology Ltd 30 Grove Road, Pinner, Middlesex,
HA5 5HW **t** 020 8429 3111 **f** 020 8429 4240
e actech@btclick.com 🖂 MD: George Ashley-Cound.

Adlib Audio Ltd Adlib House, Fleming Rd, Speke,
Liverpool, L24 9LS **t** 0151 486 2216 **f** 0151 448 1454
e hire@adlibaudio.co.uk **w** adlibsolutions.co.uk 🖂 MDs: Andy
Dockerty, Dave Kay, Mark Roberts 0151 486 2214.

Analogue Unit 8, Bridge Court, 12 Cook St, Glasgow,
G5 8JN **t** 0141 418 2500 **e** hire@analoguelive.com
w analoguelive.com 🖂 Dirs: Dave Town, Iain Mackie.

Aquarius Acoustics Unit 1, Stanley St, Colne,
Lancashire, BB8 9DD **t** 01282 859797 **f** 01282 863250
e dave@aquariusacoustics.com **w** aquariusacoustics.com
🖂 MD: Dave Pickering.

Atlantic Hire 4 The Limes, North End Way, London,
NW3 7HG **t** 020 8209 0025 **e** info@atlantichire.com
w atlantichire.com 🖂 Partner: Jez Strode.

Audile Unit 1 Clayton Court, The Cityworks, Welcomb St,
Manchester, M11 2NB **t** 0161 223 0014 **f** 0161 223 7948
e rob@audile.co.uk **w** audile.co.uk 🖂 Director: Rob
Ashworth.

Audio & Acoustics United House, North Rd, London,
N7 9DP **t** 020 7700 2900 **f** 020 7700 6900
e aaaco@aol.com 🖂 Dir: Nick Kantoch.

Contacts   Facebook   MySpace   Twitter   YouTube

Audioforum Ltd Unit 20, Dixon Business Centre, Dixon Rd, Brislington, Bristol, BS4 5QW **t** 0870 240 6444 **f** 0117 972 3926 **e** sales@audioforum.co.uk **w** audioforum.co.uk MD: Mike Reeves.

Avolites Ltd 184 Park Avenue, Park Royal, London, NW10 7XL **t** 020 8965 8522 **f** 020 8965 0290 **e** hire@avolites.com **w** avolites.com Sales Manager: May Lee.

Banana Row Backline Hire 47 Eyre Place, Edinburgh, EH3 5EY **t** 0131 557 2088 **f** 0131 558 9848 **e** info@bananarow.com **w** bananarow.com MD: Craig Hunter.

Bandit Lites Ltd 235 Ampthill Rd, Bedford, MK42 9QH **t** 01234 363 820 **f** 01234 365 382 **e** bandituk@banditlites.com **w** banditlites.com Chief Executive: Lester Cobrin.

Barrowlands Ballroom 244 Gallowgate, Glasgow, G4 0TT **t** 0141 552 4601 **e** tom.joyes@glasgow-barrowland.com Manager: Tom Joyes. Standing capacity: 1900

Bennett Audio 41 Sherriff Rd, London, NW6 2AS **t** 07748 705 067 **e** bennettaudio1@f2s.com **w** bennettaudio.co.uk Dir. and Audio Engineer: Clem Bennett 020 7372 1077.

Bonza Sound Services Ltd Alfriston House, Guildford Road, Normandy, Surrey, GU3 2AR **t** 01483 235313 **f** 01483 236015 **e** ray@bonza.co.uk **w** bonza.co.uk MD: Ray Bradman.

Borough Hall Middlegate, Headland, Hartlepool, TS24 0JD **t** 01429 266522 **f** 01429 523005 **e** firstname.lastname@hartlepool.gov.uk GM: Ernie Merrilees 01429 523409.

The Bridgewater Hall Lower Mosley St, Manchester, M2 3WS **t** 0161 950 0000 **f** 0161 950 0001 **e** concerts@bridgewater-hall.co.uk **w** bridgewater-hall.co.uk Programming Manager: Becky Dibben. Seated Capacity: 2341

Canegreen Unit 2, 12-48 Northumberland Park, London, N17 0TX **t** 020 8801 8133 **f** 020 8801 8139 **e** yan@canegreen.com **w** canegreen.co.uk MD: Yan Stile.

Capital Productions - Capital Sound Hire Abacus House, 60 Weir Rd, London, SW19 8UG **t** 020 8944 6777 **f** 020 8944 9477 **e** firstname@capital-productions.co.uk **w** capital-productions.co.uk Managing Director: Keith Davis.

CAV Unit F2, Bath Road Trading Estate, Stroud, Gloucestershire, GL5 3QF **t** 01453 751865 **f** 01453 751866 **e** sales@cav.co.uk **w** cav.co.uk Prop: Hans Beier.

Celco Midas House, Willow Way, London, SE26 4QP **t** 020 8699 6788 **f** 020 8699 5056 **e** sales@celco.co.uk **w** celco.co.uk Sales: Mark Buss.

Chaps Production Co 4 Fairdene Road, Coulsdon, Surrey, CR5 1RA **t** 01737 551144 **f** 01737 552244 **e** hires@chapsproduction.com Dir: Steve Ludlam.

Cheltenham Stage Services ltd Unit 31, Ullenwood Court, Ullenwood, Cheltenham, Gloucestershire, GL53 9QS **t** 01242 244978 **f** 01242 250618 **e** enquiries@ullenwood.co.uk **w** ullenwood.co.uk/css Business Manager: Chris Davey.

Choir Connexion & London Community Gospel Choir Brookdale House, 75 Brookdale Rd, Walthamstow, London, E17 6QH **t** 020 8509 7288 **f** 020 8509 7299 **e** info@choirconnexion.co.uk **w** lcgc.org.uk Principal: Bazil Meade.

The Cloud One Group of Companies 24 Proctor St, Birmingham, B7 4EE **t** 0121 333 7711 **f** 0121 333 7799 **e** admin@cloudone.net **w** cloudone.net MD: Paul Stratford.

Coast To Coast 3 Lane Top Cottages, Whalley Lane, Denholme, Bradford, W. Yorkshire, BD13 4LE **t** 01274 835 558 **f** 01274 835 558 **e** gerardrolfe@orange.net Dir: Gerard Rolfe.

Concept Entertainment Bay Hill, Battledown Drive, Cheltenham, Gloucestershire, GL52 6RX **t** 0845 055 9789 **f** 01242 228730 **e** info@concept-ents.com **w** concept-ents.com Director: Adam Elliott 01242 228730.

Concert Lights (UK) Ltd Undershore Works, Brookside Rd, Bolton, Lancs, BL2 2SE **t** 01204 391343 **f** 01204 363238 **e** clightuk@aol.com **w** concertlights.com Hire Manager: Chris Sinnott.

Concert Sound Unit C, Park Avenue Ind Estate, Sundon Park Road, Luton, Bedfordshire, LU3 3BP **t** 01582 565855 **f** 01582 565856 **e** davec@concert-sound.co.uk **w** concert-sound.co.uk GM: David Catlin 07768 418413.

Concert Systems Unit 4D, Stag Industrial Est, Atlantic Street, Altrincham, Cheshire, WA14 5DW **t** 0161 927 7700 **f** 0161 927 7722 **e** hire@concert-systems.com **w** concert-systems.com Prop: Paul Tandy.

Conway Hall South Place Ethical Society, 25 Red Lion Sq, London, WC1R 4RL **t** 020 7242 8032 **f** 020 7242 8036 **e** conwayhall@ethicalsoc.org.uk **w** conwayhall.org.uk Lettings Manager: Carina Dvorak. Seated Capacity: 300 Standing capacity: 500

Corporate Events UK Ltd Gratitude, Foxley Lane, Binfield, Berkshire, RG42 4EE **t** 01344 649549 **f** 01344 649549 **e** info@corporateeventsuk.co.uk **w** corporateeventsuk.co.uk Dir: Paul Donnelly.

CPL Cottar House, Chapel of Seggat, Auchterless, Aberdeenshire, AB53 8DH **t** 01888 511262 **f** 0700 6006792 **e** cyrus@cpl-electrical.co.uk **w** cpl-electrical.co.uk Director: Cyrus Shroff 07860 419728.

Creative Lighting And Sound Unit 6, Spires Business Units, Mugiemoss Road, Bucksburn, Aberdeen, AB21 9NY **t** 01224 683111 **f** 01224 686611 **e** clsabdn@aol.com Owner: Mr Flett.

DHA Lighting 284-302 Waterloo Rd, London, SE1 8RQ **t** 020 7771 2900 **f** 020 7771 2901 **e** sales@dhalighting.co.uk **w** dhalighting.co.uk MD: Diane Grant.

Live: Concert Hire

Die Hard Productions The Fishergate Centre, 4 Fishergate, York, YO10 4FB **t** 0845 226 1923 **f** 0870 705 2958 **e** info@diehardproductions.co.uk **w** diehardproductions.co.uk 📇 Director: John McLean.

Dimension Audio Unit E2, Sussex Manor Business Park, Gatwick Road, Crawley, RH10 9NH **t** 01293 582 005 **f** 01293 582 006 **e** info@dimension.co.uk **w** dimension.co.uk 📇 MD: Colin Duncan.

DM Audio Block 4, Unit 2, Peffermill Industrial Estate, Edinburgh, EH16 5UY **t** 0131 661 3097 **f** 0845 833 9189 **e** info@dmaudio.co.uk **w** dmaudio.co.uk 📇 Hire Manager: Scott Moncrieff.

DPL Production Lighting Units 2 & 3 Dodds Farm, Hatfield Broad Oak, Bishop's Stortford, Herts, CM22 7JX **t** 0870 1610 141 **f** 0870 1610 151 **e** darren@dplighting.com **w** dplighting.com 📇 Contact: Darren Parker.

Electric Ballroom 184 Camden High Street, London, NW1 8QP **t** 020 7485 9006 **f** 020 7284 0745 **e** info@electricballroom.co.uk **w** electricballroom.co.uk 📇 DIRECTOR: MARGARET GIBSON 020 7485 9007. Standing capacity: 1100

Empire Mobile Services 15 Hildens Drive, Tilehurst, Berkshire, RG31 5HW **t** 0118 942 7062 **f** 0118 942 7062 **e** geoffwemp@aol.com 📇 Prop: Geoff West.

Entec Sound And Light 517 Yeading Lane, Northolt, Middlesex, UB5 6LN **t** 020 8842 4004 **f** 020 8842 3310 **e** dick@entec-soundandlight.com **w** entec-soundandlight.com 📇 Sound Dept Mgr: Dick Hayes.

ESE Audio Great Job's Cross Farm, Hastings Road, Rolvenden, Kent, TN17 4PL **t** 01580 243330 **f** 01580 243216 **e** janewinterese@hotmail.com 📇 Partner: Jane Winter.

ESS Unit 2 Maun Close, Hermitage Lane, Nottinghamshire, NG18 5GY **t** 01623 647291 **f** 01623 622500 **e** richardmjohn@me.com 📇 Partner: Richard John.

Eurosound (UK) Unit 12, Station Court, Clayton West, Huddersfield, West Yorkshire, HD8 9XJ **t** 01484 866066 **f** 01484 866299 **e** sales@eurosound.co.uk **w** eurosound.co.uk 📇 Prod Mgr: Tony Bottomley.

Fexx Live Sound Cherry Tree St, Elsecar, South Yorkshire, S74 8DG **t** 07931 752641 **e** adam.taylor@fexx.co.uk **w** fexx.co.uk 📇 MD: Adam Taylor.

FX Music 525 Yeading Lane, Northolt, Middlesex, UB5 6LN **t** 020 8841 7666 **f** 020 8841 1333 **e** sales@fx-music.co.uk **w** fx-music.co.uk 📇 Hire Mgr: Dave Beck.

FX Rentals 38-40 Telford Way, London, W3 7XS **t** 020 8746 2121 **f** 020 8746 4100 **e** info@fxrentals.co.uk **w** fxgroup.net 📇 Operations Director: Peter Brooks.

Hand Held Audio Unit 2, 12-48 Northumberland Park, London, N17 0TX **t** 020 8880 3243 **f** 020 8365 1131 **e** info@handheldaudio.co.uk **w** handheldaudio.co.uk 📇 Dir: Mick Shepherd.

HSL Group Holdings Ltd Unit O, Ribble Business Pk, Challenge Way, Blackburn, BB1 5RB **t** 01254 698808 **f** 01254 698835 **e** simon@hslgroup.com **w** hslgroup.com 📇 Managing Director: Simon Stuart.

IllumiNation **t** 07976 244489 **e** andrewliddle@mac.com **w** concertlightingdesign.com 📇 Concert Lighting Designer: Andy Liddle +44 7976 244489.

Intasound PA (NO THIRD PARTY USE) Unit 15, Highgrove Farm Ind Estate, Pinvin, Pershore, Worcestershire, WR10 2LF **t** 01905 841591 **f** 01905 841590 **e** sales@intasoundpa.co.uk **w** intasoundpa.co.uk 📇 Lighting Manager: Chris Dale.

John Henry's 16-24 Brewery Road, London, N7 9NH **t** 020 7609 9181 **f** 020 7700 7040 **e** johnh@johnhenrys.com **w** johnhenrys.com 📇 MD: John Henry.

Juice Lighting & Sound 9-10 Gresley Close, Drayton Fields, Daventry, Northants, NN11 5RZ **t** 01327 876883 **f** 01327 310094 **e** sales@juicesound.co.uk **w** juicesound.co.uk 📇 Prop: John Silk.

Lancelyn Theatre Supplies Poulton Road, Bebington, Wirral, Cheshire, CH63 9LN **t** 0151 334 8991 **f** 0151 334 4047 **e** sales@lancelyn.co.uk **w** lancelyn.co.uk 📇 Mgr: Bob Baxter 0151 334 3000.

Light & Sound Design 201 Coventry Road, Birmingham, B10 0RA **t** 0121 766 6400 **f** 0121 766 6150 **e** uksales@lsdicon.com **w** fourthphase.com 📇 Ops Mgr: Kevin Forbes.

Lighting Design Services Ltd Crede Barn, Crede Lane, Old Bosham, Chichester, West Sussex, PO18 8NX **t** 01243 575373 **f** 01243 572076 **e** jon@light-design.co.uk **w** light-design.co.uk 📇 MD: Jon Pope.

Lite Alternative Unit 4, Shadsworth Business Pk, Duttons Way, Blackburn, Lancashire, BB1 2QR **t** 01254 279654 **f** 01254 278539 **e** anyone@lite-alternative.com **w** lite-alternative.com 📇 Hire Mgr: Jon Greaves.

Martin Bradley Sound & Light 69A Broad Lane, Hampton, Middlesex, TW12 3AX **t** 020 8979 0672 **e** mslbradley@aol.com 📇 Contact: Martin Bradley 07973 331451.

MCL 18 Lord Byron Square, Stowell Technical Park, Salford Quays, Manchester, M50 2XH **t** 0161 745 9933 **f** 0161 745 9975 **e** jleah@mcl-manchester.com **w** mclwebsite.com 📇 Marketing Manager: John Leah.

Media Control (UK) Ltd 69 Dartmouth Middleway, Birmingham, West Midlands, B7 4UA **t** 0121 333 3333 **f** 0121 333 3347 **e** hire@mcl-birmingham.com **w** mcl-europe.com 📇 MD: Tony Cant.

Midnight Electronics Off Quay Building, Foundry Lane, Newcastle upon Tyne, Tyne and Wear, NE6 1LH **t** 0191 224 0088 **f** 0191 224 0080 **e** info@midnightelectronics.co.uk **w** midnightelectronics.co.uk 📇 Manager: Dave Cross.

Mikam Sound (Ireland) Ltd
38 Parkwest Enterprise Centre, Park West, Dublin 12, Ireland
t 00 353 1 623 7277 **f** 00 353 1 623 7350 **e** mikam@iol.ie
📇 Contact: Paul Aungier.

Multiplex Productions 239 Clarendon Park Road,
Leicester, LE2 3AN **t** 0116 270 4007 **f** 0116 270 4007
e dave.davies1@virgin.net 📇 Mgr: Teri Wyncoll.

Mushroom Event Services Ltd 3 Encon Court,
Owl Close, Moulton Park Industrial Estate, Northampton,
NN3 6HZ **t** 01604 790900 **f** 01604 491118
e info@mushroomevents.co.uk **w** mushroomevents.co.uk
📇 Business Manager: David Goldman.

Music Bank (Hire) Ltd Buildings C & D,
Tower Bridge Business Complex, 100 Clement's Road,
London, SE16 4DG **t** 020 7252 0001 **f** 020 7231 3002
e nunu@musicbank.org **w** musicbank.org 📇 Dir: Nunu
Whiting.

Music Room The Old Library, 116-118 New Cross Rd,
London, SE14 5BA **t** 020 7252 8271 **f** 020 7252 8252
e sales@musicroom.web.com **w** musicroom.web.com
📇 MD: Gordon Gapper.

Nightair Productions Unit 1, Eastfield Side,
Sutton In Ashfield, Notts, NG17 4JW **t** 01623 557 040
f 01623 555 586 **e** sales@nightair.co.uk **w** nightair.co.uk
📇 Prop: Andrew Monk 01623 455 051.

Nitelites Unit 3E, Howdon Green Ind Est, Norman Terrace,
Wallsend, Tyne and Wear, NE28 6SX **t** 0191 295 0009
f 0191 295 0009 **e** nitelites@onyxnet.co.uk
📇 Partner: Gordon Reay.

Northern Light 35-41 Assembly Street, Leith,
Edinburgh, Lothian, EH6 7RG **t** 0131 553 2383
f 0131 553 3296 **e** enquiries@northernlight.co.uk
w northernlight.co.uk 📇 Hire Mgr: Gordon Blackburn 0131
440 1771.

O2 Academy Glasgow 121 Eglinton St, Glasgow,
G5 9NT **t** 0141 418 3000 **f** 0141 418 3001
e mail@o2academyglasgow.co.uk
w o2academyglasgow.co.uk
f facebook.com/profile.php?id=516097956&ref=hpbday#
/o2academyglasgow?ref=ts
🎵 myspace.com/o2academyglasgow
t twitter.com/O2AcademyGgow 📇 General Manager: Joe
Splain. Standing capacity: 2500

OPTI 38 Cromwell Rd, Luton, Bedfordshire, LU3 1DN
t 01582 411413 **f** 01582 400613
e optiuk@optikinetics.com **w** optikinetics.com 📇 Sales
Dir: Neil Rice.

The PA Company Ltd Unit 7, Ashway Centre,
Elm Crescent, Kingston-Upon-Thames, Surrey, KT2 6HH
t 020 8546 6640 **f** 020 8547 1469
e thepacompany@aol.com **w** thepaco.com 📇 MD: Doug
Beveridge 07836 600 081.

Pandora Productions Unit 38 Hallmark Trading Ctr,
Fourth Way, Wembley, Middlesex, HA9 0LB **t** 020 8795 2432
f 020 8795 2431 **e** pandoraprods@btconnect.com
📇 Prop: John Montier.

Pearce Hire Unit 27, Second Drove,
Industrial Estate, Fengate, Peterborough, Cambridgeshire,
PE1 5XA **t** 01733 554950 **f** 01733 892807
e info@pearcehire.co.uk **w** pearcehire.co.uk 📇 Prop: Shaun
Pearce 07850 363543.

Pegasus Sound & Light 23-25 Canongate,
The Royal Mile, Edinburgh, Lothian, EH8 8BX
t 0131 556 1300 **f** 0131 557 6466 **e** pegasussl@aol.com
w pegasussl.co.uk 📇 Sales Mgr: David Hunter.

PSL Concert Touring The Heights,
Cranborne Industrial Estate, Potters Bar, Herts, EN6 3JN
t 01707 648 120 **f** 01707 648 123
e pod.bluman@presservgroup.com **w** presservgroup.com
📇 Dir: Pod Bluman.

Pure Energy Production Services Suite 91,
2 Lansdowne Crescent, Bournemouth, Dorset, BH1 1SA
t 01202 579673 **f** 01202 579679 **e** sales@pepuk.com
w pepuk.com 📇 Dir: Ian Walker.

Remote Live 36 Shrewsbury Rd, Carshalton, Surrey,
SM5 1LZ **t** 07968 100 557
e info@remoteliverecordings.co.uk
w remoteliverecordings.co.uk 📇 Proprietor: Mike Knight.

RG Jones Sound Engineering 16 Endeavour Way,
London, SW19 8UH **t** 020 8971 3100 **f** 020 8971 3101
e info@rgjones.co.uk **w** rgjones.co.uk 📇 Hire Dept Mgr: John
Carroll.

Rhythm Audio Rhythm House, King Street, Carlisle,
Cumbria, CA1 1SJ **t** 01228 515141 **f** 01228 515161
e hire@rhythmaudio.co.uk **w** rhythmaudio.co.uk 📇 Head of
Prod: Ian Howe.

SAV Ltd Party House, Mowbray Drive, Blackpool, FY3 7JR
t 01253 302602 **f** 01253 301000 **e** sales@stardream.co.uk
📇 Technical Director: Steve Salisbury.

Sheffield Arena Broughton Lane, Sheffield,
South Yorkshire, S9 2DF **t** 0114 256 2002 **f** 0114 256 5520
e sheffieldhospitality@livenation.co.uk
w sheffieldarena.co.uk 📇 GM: Rob O'Shea. Seated Capacity:
12500

Silent Concerts care of Value Added Talent,
1, Purley Pl, London, N1 1QA **t** 020 7704 9720
f 020 7226 6135 **e** dan@vathq.co.uk **w** vathq.co.uk
📇 Managing Agent: Dan Silver.

Silent Disco 1 Purley Pl, London, N1 1QA
t 0207 704 0024 **f** 0207 226 6135 **e** dan@vathq.co.uk
w silentdisco.com 📇 Agent: Dan Silver 0207 704 9720.

Silent Disco C/O Value Added Talent, 1 Purley Pl,
London, N1 1QA **t** 020 7704 9720 **f** 020 7226 6135
e dan@vathq.co.uk **w** ww.silentdisco.com 📇 Managing
Agent: Dan Silver 020 7704 9720.

The Small PA Company 49 Liddington Rd, London,
E15 3PL **t** 020 8536 0649 **f** 07092 022 897
e ian@soundengineer.co.uk **w** soundengineer.co.uk
📇 MD: Ian Hasell 07785 584 273.

Live: Concert Hire

Live: Concert Hire

Sound Hire Unit 7, Kimpton Trade Business Centre, Minden Road, Sutton, Surrey, SM3 9PF **t** 020 8644 1248 **f** 020 8644 6642 **e** richard@sound-hire.com **w** sound-hire.com 👤 MD: Richard Lienard.

Sound & Light Guys Unit 1 Warkworth Close, Banbury, Oxon, OX16 1BD **t** 01295 720 825 **f** 01295 720 825 **e** hire@soundandlightguys.co.uk **w** soundandlightguys.co.uk 👤 Dir: Freddie Fitzpatrick 07718 796 276.

Sound of Music 14 Runswick Drive, Wollaton, Nottingham, NG8 1JD **t** 0845 644 8550 **f** 0845 644 8551 **e** info@pahire.com **w** pahire.com 👤 Director: Sash Pochibko 07946 739384.

SouthWestern Management 13 Portland Road, Street, Somerset, BA16 9PX **t** 01458 445186 **f** 01458 841186 **e** info@sw-management.co.uk **w** sw-management.co.uk 👤 Dir: Chris Hannam 07831 437062.

SRS (Norwich) 59 Darrell Place, Norwich, Norfolk, NR5 8QN **t** 01603 250486 **f** 01603 250486 **e** srs@deafgeoff.co.uk 👤 Owner: Geoff Lowther 07850 235161.

Stage Audio Services Unit 2, Bridge St, Wordsley, Stourbridge, DY8 5YU **t** 01384 263629 **f** 01384 263620 **e** kevinmobers@aol.com 👤 Dir: Kevin Mobberley.

Stage Electrics Third Way, Avonmouth, Bristol, BS11 9HB **t** 0117 938 4000 **f** 0117 916 2828 **e** sales@stage-electrics.co.uk **w** stage-electrics.co.uk 👤 Hire Mgr: Adrian Searle.

Stage Two Hire Services
Unit J, Penfold Trading Estate, Imperial Way, Watford, Hertfordshire, WD24 4YY **t** 01923 230789 **f** 01923 255048 **e** richard.ford@stage-two.co.uk **w** stagetwo.co.uk 👤 Hire Mgr: Richard Ford 01923 244822.

Star Events Group Milton Road, Thurleigh, Bedfordshire, MK44 2DG **t** 01234 772233 **f** 01234 772272 **e** firstname.lastname@stareventsgroup.com **w** StarEventsGroup.com 👤 Dir: Mark Armstrong.

Stratford Acoustics 24 Procter Street, Birmingham, B7 4EE **t** 0121 333 7711 **f** 0121 333 7799 **e** admin@cloudone.net **w** cloudone.net 👤 MD: Paul Stratford.

STS Touring Productions Ltd
Unit 104 Cariocca Business Park, 2 Hellidon Close, Ardwick, Manchester, M12 4AH **t** 0161 273 5984 **f** 0161 272 7772 **e** firstname.lastname@ststouring.co.uk **w** ststouring.co.uk 👤 Director: Peter Dutton.

Tega (Hull) Limited 58 Stockholm Road, Sutton Fields Ind. Est, Hull, East Yorkshire, HU7 0XW **t** 01482 831 031 **f** 01482 831 331 **e** hire@tega.co.uk **w** tega.co.uk 👤 Business Development: Richard Moorhouse 07900 215 024.

Terminal Studios Hire 4-10 Lamb Walk, London, SE1 3TT **t** 020 7403 3050 **f** 020 7407 6123 **e** info@terminal.co.uk **w** terminal.co.uk 👤 MD: Charlie Barrett.

TMC Hillam Road, off Canal Road, Bradford, West Yorkshire, BD2 1QN **t** 01274 370966 **f** 01274 308706 **e** sales@tmc.ltd.uk **w** tmc.ltd.uk 👤 Sales Mgr: Nick Bolton.

TMS Show Services Chichester Road, Sidlesham Common, Sidlesham, Chichester, PO20 7PY **t** 01243 641166 **f** 01243 641888 **e** info@tms1.co.uk 👤 Partner: Dick Edney.

Tourtech 3 Quarry Park Close, Moulton Park Industrial Estate, Northampton, NN3 6QB **t** 01604 494846 **f** 01604 642454 **e** tourtecuk@aol.com **w** tourtech.co.uk 👤 MD: Dick Rabel.

Travelling Light (Birmingham) Ltd Unit 34, Boulton Industrial Centre, Icknield Street, Birmingham, West Midlands, B18 5AU **t** 0121 523 3297 **f** 0121 551 2360 👤 Dir: Chris Osborn.

Roy Truman Sound Services Unit 23, Atlas Business Centre, Oxgate Lane, London, NW2 7HJ **t** 020 8208 2468 **f** 020 8208 3320 **e** rtss@london.com 👤 Mgr: Elisabeth Wirrer.

TSProfessional SOUND + LIGHT
Unit 6, Avocet Trading Estate, Burgess Hill, West Sussex, RH15 9NH **t** 01444 233030 **f** 01444 233159 **e** sales@tsprofessional.co.uk **w** tsprofessional.co.uk 👤 MD: Keith Upton.

Utopium Lighting Unit A, Diamonite Ind Pk, Goodneston Rd, Fishponds, Bristol, BS16 3JX **t** 0845 026 0919 **f** 0870 950 3355 **e** info@utopium.co.uk **w** utopium.co.uk 👤 Production Manager: Ian Evans.

Wackiki Unit 73, Dunmurry Industrial Estate, Dunmurry, Belfast, BT17 9HU **t** 02890 623 177 **f** 02890 624 945 **e** joe@wackiki.com **w** wackiki.com 👤 Dir: Joe Brush 07709 855 112.

Wigmore Hall 36 Wigmore St, London, W1U 2BP **t** 020 7258 8200 **f** 020 7258 8201 **e** info@wigmore-hall.org.uk **w** wigmore-hall.org.uk f facebook.com/wigmore.hall 🅱 ww.twitter.com/wigmore_hall 👤 Contact: Management Office. Seated Capacity: 540

Wigwam Unit 6, Junction 19 Ind Est, Green Lane, Haywood, Lancashire, OL10 1NB **t** 01706 363400 **f** 01706 363410 **e** events@wigwam.co.uk **w** wigwam.co.uk 👤 MD: Mike Spratt 01706 363800.

Younger Hall University of St Andrews, North Street, St Andrews, KY16 9AJ **t** 01334 462226 **f** 01334 462228 **e** music@st-andrews.ac.uk **w** st-andrews.ac.uk/music Seated Capacity: 900

Zig Zag Lighting (South) 68 Morton Gardens, Wallington, Surrey, SM6 8EX **t** 020 8647 1968 **f** 020 8401 2216 **e** kev@zigzag-lighting.com 👤 Prop: Kevin Ludlam.

Zique Audio Highfield Works, John Street, Hinkley, Leicestershire, LE10 1UY **t** 01455 610364 **f** 01455 610164 **e** garry@msn.com (DO NOT PUBLISH) 👤 Prop: Gary Hargraves 07831 342355.

Venues

3 B's Bar and Cafe Reading Town Hall, Blagrave Street, Reading, Berkshire, RG1 1QH **t** 0118 939 9815 **f** 0118 956 6719 **e** andrew.hefferan@reading.gov.uk ✉ Bookings Mgr: Andy Hefferan. Seated Capacity: 95 Standing capacity: 150

12 Bar Club 26, Denmark St, London, WC2H 8NL **t** 020 7240 2120 **e** 12barclub@btconnect.com **w** 12barclub.com ✉ Bookings Mgr: Andy Lowe. Standing capacity: 150

42nd Street Nightclub 2 Bootle St, off Deansgate, Manchester, M2 5GU **t** 0161 831 7108 **f** 0161 831 7108 **e** simon@42ndstreetnightclub.com **w** 42ndstreetnightclub.com ✉ Manager: Simon Jackson. Standing capacity: 920

53 Degrees Brook St, Preston, Lancashire, PR1 2TQ **t** 07812 347680 **f** 01772 894970 **e** devans@53degrees.net **w** 53degrees.net ✉ Ents Mgr: David Evans. Standing capacity: 1900

100 Club 100 Oxford St, London, W1D 1LL **t** 020 7636 0933 **f** 020 7436 1958 **e** jenny@the100club.co.uk **w** the100club.co.uk ✉ Events Manager: Jeff Horton / Jenny Angus. Seated Capacity: 290 Standing capacity: 290

229 – The Venue 229 Great Portland Street, London, W1W 5PN **t** 020 7323 7229 **e** info@229thevenue.co.uk **w** 229thevenue.co.uk ✉ Entertainments Manager: Stuart Ellerker. Standing capacity: 760

606 Club 90 Lots Road, London, SW10 0QD **t** 020 7352 5953 **f** 020 7349 0655 **e** jazz@606club.co.uk **w** 606club.co.uk ✉ Owner: Steve Rubie. Seated Capacity: 130 Standing capacity: 165

The Abbey Tavern 124 Kentish Town Road, London, NW1 9QB **t** 020 7267 9449 **e** radha@abbey-tavern.com **w** abbey-tavern.com ✉ Bookings: Radha Kothari 07757 870 568. Standing capacity: 200

Aberdeen Exhibition and Conference Centre Bridge of Don, Aberdeen, AB23 8BL **t** 01224 824824 **f** 01224 825276 **e** llonie@aecc.co.uk **w** aecc.co.uk ✉ Concert Bookings: Louise Lonie. Seated Capacity: 4700 Standing capacity: 8000

Aberdeen Music Hall Union Street, Aberdeen, AB10 1QS **t** 01224 632 080 **f** 01224 632 400 **e** musichallinfo@aberdeenperformingarts.com **w** musichallaberdeen.com ✉ Venue Manager: Julie Sinclair. Seated Capacity: 1282 Standing capacity: 1500

Aberdeen University Union Union Bar, 10 Littlejohn Street, Aberdeen, AB10 1BA **t** 01224 638 369 **f** 01224 638 369 **e** adg155@abdn.ac.uk **w** abdn.ac.uk\union ✉ Ents Mgr: Duncan Stuart. Seated Capacity: 500 Standing capacity: 600

Aberystwyth Arts Centre Penglais, Aberystwyth, Ceredigion, SY23 3DE **t** 01970 622882 **f** 01970 622883 **e** lla@aber.ac.uk **w** aber.ac.uk/artscentre ✉ Dir: Alan Hewson. Seated Capacity: 1000 Standing capacity: 1200

The Academy Cleveland Road, Uxbridge, Middlesex, UB8 3PH **t** 01895 267 447 **f** 01895 462 300 **e** firstname.lastname@brunel.ac.uk **w** brunelstudents.com ✉ Promoter: Stephen Dedman. Seated Capacity: 450 Standing capacity: 600

Accrington Town Hall Blackburn Road, Accrington, Lancashire, BB5 1LA **t** 01254 380297 **f** 01254 380291 **e** leisure@hyndburnbc.gov.uk **w** leisureinhyndburn.co.uk ✉ Mrktng & Events Officer: Nigel Green. Seated Capacity: 400 Standing capacity: 360

AK Bell Library York Place, Perth, PH2 8EP **t** 01738 444949 **f** 01738 477010 **e** kmcwilliam@pkc.gov.uk **w** pkc.gov.uk ✉ Theatre Mgr: Kenny McWilliam. Seated Capacity: 125

The Alban Arena Civic Centre, St Albans, Hertfordshire, AL1 3LD **t** 01727 861078 **f** 01727 865755 **e** info@alban-arena.co.uk **w** alban-arena.co.uk ✉ GM: Paul McMullen. Seated Capacity: 856 Standing capacity: 1132

The Albany Douglas Way, London, SE8 4AG **t** 020 8692 0231 **f** 020 8469 2253 **e** reception@thealbany.org.uk **w** thealbany.org.uk ✉ Programmer: Gavin Barlow. Seated Capacity: 300 Standing capacity: 425

Albert Halls Dumbarton Rd, Stirling, FK8 2QL **t** 01786 473544 **f** 01786 448933 **e** brownj@stirling.gov.uk **w** stirling.gov.uk/alberthalls ✉ Venues Mgr: Jess Brown. Seated Capacity: 893 Standing capacity: 1200

Alexandra Palace Alexandra Palace Way, Wood Green, London, N22 7AY **t** 020 8365 2121 **f** 020 8365 2662 **e** sales@alexandrapalace.com **w** alexandrapalace.com ✉ Sales Manager: Debbie Dudley. Seated Capacity: 10200 Standing capacity: 10200

Alexandra Theatre Station Street, Birmingham, West Midlands, B5 4DS **t** 0121 643 5536 **f** 0121 632 6841 **e** firstname.lastname@livenation.co.uk **w** livenation.co.uk ✉ Gen Mgr: Andrew Lister. Seated Capacity: 1365

Alloa Town Hall 6 Mars Hill, Alloa, Clackmannan, FK10 1AB **t** 01259 222345 **f** 01259 222341 **e** leisure@clacks.gov.uk **w** clacks.gov.uk Seated Capacity: 500

Anglia Polytechnic University Students Union, East Road, Cambridge, CB1 1PT **t** 01223 460008 **f** 01223 417718 **e** a.tadjrishi@apusu.com **w** apusu.com ✉ Ents Mgr: Ash Tadjrishi. Seated Capacity: 230 Standing capacity: 300

The Anvil Churchill Way, Basingstoke, Hampshire, RG21 7QR **t** 01256 819797 **f** 01256 331733 **e** Ann.Dickson@theanvil.org.uk **w** theanvil.org.uk ✉ Prog Mgr: Ann Dickson. Seated Capacity: 1400

Apollo Theatre Shaftesbury Avenue, London, W1D 7EZ ✉ Concerts & Hirings Mgr: Mike Townsend. Seated Capacity: 775

Apollo Victoria 17 Wilton Road, London, SW1V 1LG **t** 020 7834 6318 **f** 08707 492 351 **e** firstname.lastname@livenation.co.uk **w** getlive.co.uk ✉ GM: Richard Brown. Seated Capacity: 1564

Area Gade House, 46 The Parade, High St, Watford, Herts, WD17 1AY **t** 01923 281100 **f** 01923 281101 **e** chris@areaclub.com **w** areaclub.com ☎ Events & PR Manager: Neil Campbell 01923 281500. Seated Capacity: 1500 Standing Capacity: 1500

The Arena 208 Newport Road, Middlesbrough, TS1 5PS **t** 01642 503128 **f** 01642 503128 **e** info@thearena.co.uk **w** thearena.co.uk ☎ Bookings Mgrs: Edzy. Standing capacity: 600

Artslink Theatre Knoll Road, Camberley, Surrey, GU15 3SY **t** 01276 707612 **f** 01276 707644 ☎ Contact: Pat Pembridge. Seated Capacity: 400 Standing capacity: 600

Ashcroft Theatre Park Lane, Croydon, Surrey, CR9 1DG **t** 020 8681 0821 **f** 020 8760 0835 **e** info@fairfield.co.uk **w** fairfield.co.uk Seated Capacity: 749

The Assembly Spencer Street, Leamington Spa, Warcs, CV31 3NS **t** 01926 888 666 **e** firstname.lastname@leamingtonassembly.com **w** leamingtonassembly.com ☎ Production Manager: Dutch Van Spall. Standing capacity: 1000

Assembly Hall Stoke Abbott Rd, Worthing, West Sussex, BN11 1HQ **t** 01903 231799 **f** 01903 215337 **e** theatres@worthing.gov.uk **w** worthingtheatres.co.uk ☎ Theatres Manager: Peter Bailey. Seated Capacity: 940 Standing capacity: 1100

Assembly Hall Theatre Crescent Road, Royal Tunbridge Wells, Kent, TN1 2LU **t** 01892 530 613 **f** 01892 525 203 **e** theatreadmin@tunbridgewells.gov.uk **w** assemblyhalltheatre.co.uk ☎ Marketing Mgr: Sheila Ryall 01892 532 072. Seated Capacity: 930 Standing capacity: 1000

Assembly Rooms Market Pl, Derby, DE1 3AH **t** 01332 255443 **f** 01332 255788 **e** assemblyrooms@derby.gov.uk **w** assemblyrooms-derby.co.uk ☎ Gen Mgr: Peter Ireson. Seated Capacity: 1500 Standing capacity: 2000

Assembly Rooms 54 George Street, Edinburgh, Midlothian, EH2 2LR **t** 0131 624 2442 **f** 0131 624 7131 **e** info@assemblyrooms.com **w** assemblyrooms.com ☎ GM: Kath M Mainland. Seated Capacity: 700 Standing capacity: 750

Aston University Students Guild The Triangle, Birmingham, B4 7ES **t** 0121 359 6531 **f** 0121 333 4218 **e** l.b.cook@aston.ac.uk **w** astonguild.org.uk ☎ Venues Mgr: Larry Cook. Seated Capacity: 400 Standing capacity: 942

Aylesbury Civic Centre Market Square, Aylesbury, Bucks, HP20 1UF **t** 01296 585 541 **f** 01296 392 091 **e** rheason@aylesburyvaledc.gov.uk **w** aylesburycivic.co.uk ☎ Manager: Richard Heason. Seated Capacity: 640 Standing capacity: 1000

Babbacombe Theatre Babbacombe Downs, Torquay, Devon, TQ1 3LU **t** 01803 322233 **f** 01803 322244 **e** colin@matpro-show.biz **w** babbacombe-theatre.com ☎ Resident Dir: Colin Matthews. Seated Capacity: 600

Barbican Centre Silk St, Barbican, London, EC2Y 8DS **t** 020 7382 7308 **f** 020 7382 7241 **e** press@barbican.org.uk **w** barbican.org.uk ☎ Head of Music: Robert Van Leer 020 7382 7038. Seated Capacity: 1989

Barfly Camden 49 Chalk Farm Rd, London, NW1 8AN **t** 020 7424 0800 **f** 020 7691 4243 **e** adam.ryan@Barflyclub.com **w** barflyclub.com ☷ myspace.com/barflyclublondon ☎ Promoter: Adam Ryan 020 7688 9000. Standing capacity: 200

Barfly Cardiff Kingsway, Cardiff, CF10 3FD **t** 02920 396589 **e** Ben.potter@barflyclub.com **w** barflyclub.com ☷ myspace.com/cardiffbarfly ☷ twitter.com/cardiffbarfly ☎ Promoter: Ben Potter. Standing capacity: 200

Bartok 78-79 Chalk Farm Rd, London, NW1 8AR **t** 020 7916 0595

The Basement 4-8 Fisher Street, Carlisle, Cumbria, CA3 8RN **t** 01228 510444 **e** Jnightclub@aol.com **w** Jnightclub.co.uk ☎ Promoter/Owner: David Jackson. Standing capacity: 600

Bath and West Trading Co. Ltd The Bath & West Trading Company, Royal Bath & West Showground, Shepton Mallet, Somerset, BA4 6QN **t** 01749 822 219 **f** 01749 823 169 **e** jo.perry@bathandwest.co.uk **w** bathandwest.co.uk ☎ Gen Mgr: Jo Perry. Seated Capacity: 4000 Standing capacity: 5250

Bath Pavilion North Parade Road, Bath, BA2 4EU **t** 01225 486902 **f** 01225 486976 **e** bath.pavilion@aquaterra.org **w** aquaterra.org ☎ GM: Jenny Jacob. Seated Capacity: 1000 Standing capacity: 1675

Bath Spa University College Students Union, Newton Park, Bath, BA2 9BN **t** 01225 875588 **f** 01225 874765 **e** bathspasu@bathspa.ac.uk **w** bathspasu.co.uk ☎ Events: Diane Starling. Standing capacity: 250

Bath Theatre Royal St John's Place, Sawclose, Bath, BA1 1ET **t** 01225 448815 **f** 01225 444080 **e** firstname.lastname@theatreroyal.org.uk **w** theatreroyal.org.uk ☎ TRB Productions: Nicky Palmer. Seated Capacity: 978

Beach Ballroom Beach Leisure Centre, Beach Promenade, Aberdeen, AB2 1NR **t** 01224 647647 **f** 01224 648693 Seated Capacity: 1200

Beau Sejour Centre Amherst, St Peter Port, Guernsey, GY1 2DL **t** 01481 747215 **f** 01481 747298 **e** firstname.lastname@cultureleisure.gov.gg **w** freedomzone.gg ☎ Events Mgr: Penny Weaver. Seated Capacity: 1500 Standing capacity: 2000

Beck Theatre, Hayes Grange Road, Hayes, Middlesex, UB3 2UE **t** 020 8561 7506 **f** 020 8569 1072 **e** firstname.lastname@livenation.co.uk **w** getlive.co.uk ☎ GM: Louise Clifford. Seated Capacity: 600

Bedford Corn Exchange St Paul's Square, Bedford, MK40 1SL **t** 01234 344813 **f** 01234 325358 **e** cornexch-bedford@btinternet.com **w** bedfordcornexchange.co.uk ✉ Manager: Carl Amos. Seated Capacity: 830 Standing capacity: 1000

The Bedford 77 Bedford Hill, Balham, London, SW12 9HD **t** 020 8682 8940 **e** info@thebedford.co.uk **w** thebedford.co.uk ✉ Dir, Music, Art & Dev't: Tony Moore. Seated Capacity: 250

Belgrade Theatre Belgrade Square, Coventry, CV1 1GS **t** 024 7625 6431 **f** 024 7655 0680 **e** admin@belgrade.co.uk **w** belgrade.co.uk ✉ Artistic Dir: Hamish Glen. Seated Capacity: 865

The Betsey Trotwood 56 Farringdon Rd, London, EC1R 3BL **t** 020 7253 4285 **e** info@plummusic.com **w** thebetsey.com ✉ Manager: Scott Baker. Standing capacity: 60

The Bierkeller All Saints St, Bristol, BS1 2NA **t** 0117 926 8514 **f** 0117 925 1347 **e** bs1bierkeller@aol.com **w** bristolbierkeller.co.uk ✉ Promoter: Dave Hebson. Standing capacity: 750

The Big Chill House 257-259 Pentonville Rd, King's Cross, London, N1 9NL **t** 020 7427 2540 **f** 020 7684 2021 **e** info@bigchill.net **w** bigchill.net f facebook.com/pages/London-United-Kingdom/The-Big-Chill-House/98380903602 ◙ myspace.com/bigchillhouse ◘ twitter.com/Bigchillfest ✉ General Manager: Grace West. Seated Capacity: 550

Birkbeck College Student Union, Malet Street, London, WC1E 7HX **t** 020 7631 6335 **f** 020 7631 6270 **e** administrator@bcsu.bbk.ac.uk **w** bbk.ac.uk/su ✉ Contact: Phil Ross. Seated Capacity: 100

Bivouac® 3 St Andrews St, Lincoln, Lincolnshire, LN5 7NE **t** 01522 539883 **f** 01522 528964 **e** steve.hawkins@easynet.co.uk ✉ Booker: Steve Hawkins. Standing capacity: 200

Blackheath Halls 23 Lee Rd, London, SE3 9RQ **t** 020 8318 9758 **f** 020 8852 5154 **e** programming@blackheathhalls.com **w** blackheathhalls.com Seated Capacity: 700 Standing capacity: 1000

Blackpool Grand Theatre - National Variety Theatre 33 Church Street, Blackpool, Lancashire, FY1 1HT **t** 01253 290111 **f** 01253 751767 **e** geninfo@blackpoolgrand.co.uk **w** blackpoolgrand.co.uk ✉ GM: Paul Isles. Seated Capacity: 1192

Blackpool Winter Gardens 97 Church St, Blackpool, Lancashire, FY1 1HL **t** 01253 625252 **e** events@leisure-parcs.co.uk **w** wintergardensblackpool.co.uk ✉ General Manager: Peter Walter. Seated Capacity: 3250 Standing capacity: 4000

Bletchley Leisure Centre Princes Way, Bletchley, Milton Keynes, Buckinghamshire, MK2 2HQ **t** 01908 377251 **f** 01908 374094 **e** bletchley@leisureconnection.co.uk **w** bletchleyleisurecentre.co.uk ✉ Manager: David Taylor. Seated Capacity: 1300 Standing capacity: 1500

Bloomsbury Theatre 15 Gordon St, London, WC1H 0AH **t** 020 7679 2777 **f** 020 7383 4080 **e** blooms.theatre@ucl.ac.uk **w** thebloomsbury.com ✉ Administrator: Shalini Simpson 020 7388 8822. Seated Capacity: 550 Standing capacity: 550

Bluecoat Arts Centre Bluecoat Chambers, School Lane, Liverpool, Merseyside, L1 3BX **t** 0151 709 5297 **f** 0151 709 0048 **e** admin@bluecoatartscentre.com **w** bluecoatartscentre.com

The Boileroom 13 Stokefields, Guildford, Surrey, GU1 4LS **t** 01483 440022 **f** 01483 440020 **e** ross@theboileroom.net **w** theboileroom.net f facebook.com/theboileroom ◙ myspace.com/boileroomgu1 ◘ twitter.com/boileroom ▣ youtube.com/user/boileroomgu1 ✉ Promotions Manager: Ross Allmark. Standing capacity: 200

The Borderline 5 Goslett Yard, London, WC2H 0EA **t** 020 7734 5547 **e** james.gall@meanfiddler.co.uk **w** meanfiddler.com f facebook.com/borderline.london ◙ myspace.com/borderlinevenue ◘ twitter.com/the_borderline ✉ General Business Manager: James Gall as above.

The Boston 178 Junction Road, London, N19 5QQ **t** 020 7272 8153 **f** 020 7281 2651 **e** Patrick.Fahey@btworld.com **w** bostonlivemusicvenue.co.uk ✉ Manager: PJ Fahey. Standing capacity: 600

Bournemouth International Centre Exeter Rd, Bournemouth, Dorset, BH2 5BH **t** 01202 456400 **f** 01202 456500 **e** steve.turner.bic@bournemouth.gov.uk **w** bic.co.uk ✉ Entertainment Programming Manager: Steve Turner. Seated Capacity: 3500 Standing capacity: 4100

Bournemouth Pavilion Theatre Westover Road, Bournemouth, Dorset, BH1 2BU **t** 01202 456 400 **f** 01202 451 024 **w** bic.co.uk ✉ Entertainment & Events Manager: Steve Turner. Seated Capacity: 1512

Bournemouth University The Old Fire Station, 36 Holdenhurst Road, Bournemouth, Dorset, BH8 8AD **t** 01202 503888 **f** 01202 503913 **e** info@oldfirestation.co.uk **w** oldfirestation.co.uk ✉ Events & Marketing Mgr.: Angus Carter. Seated Capacity: 300 Standing capacity: 600

Bradford University Commmunal Building Students Union, Richmond Road, Bradford, West Yorkshire, BD7 1DP **t** 01274 233245 **f** 01274 235530 **e** ubu-ents@bradford.ac.uk **w** ubuonline.co.uk Standing capacity: 1300

Braehead Arena Glasgow Braehead, Kings Inch Rd, Glasgow, G51 4BN **t** 0141 886 8300 **f** 0141 885 4620 **e** scott-martin@capshop.co.uk **w** braehead-arena.co.uk ✉ Arena Manager: Scott Martin. Seated Capacity: 5100

Brangwyn Hall The Guildhall, Swansea, SA1 4PE **t** 01792 635 432 **f** 01792 635 447 **e** brangwyn.hall@swansea.gov.uk **w** swansea.gov.uk/brangwynhall ✉ Manager: Tracy Ellicott. Seated Capacity: 1070 Standing capacity: 1286

Brel 39 Ashton Lane, Glasgow, G12 8SJ
t 0141 560 2748 or 0141 337 1199 **f** 0141 357 0655
e contact@brelbarrestaurant.com **w** brelbarrestaurant.com
🔲 Booker: Robin Morton. Standing capacity: 100

Brentford Fountain Leisure Centre
658 Chiswick High Road, Brentford, Middlesex, TW8 0HJ
t 020 8994 9596 **f** 020 8994 4956 🔲 Contact: Alan
Boulden. Seated Capacity: 1200 Standing capacity: 1500

Brentwood Centre Doddinghurst Road, Brentwood,
Essex, CM15 9NN **t** 01277 261111 x 381 **f** 01277 200152
🔲 Concerts & Promotions Mgr: Steve Allen. Seated
Capacity: 1900 Standing capacity: 1900

Brewery Arts Centre Highgate, Kendal, Cumbria,
LA9 4HE **t** 01539 725133 **f** 01539 730257
e hannah.flynn@breweryarts.co.uk **w** breweryarts.co.uk
🔲 Marketing Officer: Hannah Flynn. Seated Capacity: 300
Standing capacity: 450

The Brickmakers 496 Sprowston Rd, Norwich, Norfolk,
NR3 4DY **t** 01603 441 118 **e** info@thebrickmakers.com
w thebrickmakers.com 🔲 Bookings Mgr: Charley South.
Standing capacity: 300

Bridge Lane Theatre Bridge Lane, London, SW11 3AD
t 020 7228 5185 **f** 020 7262 0090 🔲 Artistic Dir: Terry
Adams 020 7228 8828. Seated Capacity: 200

Bridgwater Arts Centre 11-13 Castle Street,
Bridgwater, Somerset, TA6 3DD **t** 01278 422700
f 01278 447402 🔲 Contact: Charlie Dearden 01278
422701. Seated Capacity: 196 Standing capacity: 186

Bridlington Spa Theatre And Royal Hall
South Marine Drive, Bridlington, East Yorkshire, YO15 3JH
t 01262 678255 **f** 01262 604625 🔲 Contact: Rob
Clutterham. Seated Capacity: 1800 Standing capacity:
3200

Brighton Centre Kings Rd, Brighton, Sussex, BN1 2GR
t 01273 290131 **f** 01273 779980
e brightoncentre@brighton-hove.gov.uk
w brightoncentre.co.uk 🔲 Managing Director: Steve Piper
0844 847 1515. Seated Capacity: 4273 Standing capacity:
5127

Brighton Dome & Festival Ltd Church St, Brighton,
East Sussex, BN1 1UE **t** 01273 700747 **f** 01273 705705
e m.hort@brightondome.org **w** brightondome.org.uk
🔲 Director of Operations: Maxine Hort 01273 261515.
Seated Capacity: 1800 Standing capacity: 1800

Bristol Hippodrome St Augustine's Parade, Bristol,
BS1 4UZ **t** 0117 926 5524 **f** 0117 925 1661 🔲 Gen
Mgr: John Wood. Seated Capacity: 1981

Bristol University, Anson Rooms
University of Bristol Union, Queens Road, Clifton, Bristol,
BS8 1LN **t** 0117 954 5810 **f** 0117 954 5817 **e** ents-
ubu@bristol.ac.uk **w** ubu.org.uk 🔲 Ents Mgr: Kay Lowrie.
Seated Capacity: 600 Standing capacity: 900

Broadstairs Pavilion Harbour Street, Broadstairs,
Kent, CT9 1EY **t** 01843 865726 Seated Capacity: 260
Standing capacity: 340

Broadway Theatre Rushey Green, Catford, London,
SE6 4RU **t** 020 8690 2317 **f** 020 8314 3144
e firstname@broadwaytheatre.org.uk
w broadwaytheatre.org.uk 🔲 GM: Martin Costello 020 8690
1000. Seated Capacity: 855 Standing capacity: 1000

The Broadway Theatre 46 Broadway, Peterborough,
PE1 1RT **t** 01733 316109 **f** 01733 316101
e admin@thebroadwaytheatre.co.uk
w thebroadwaytheatre.co.uk 🔲 GM: Dave King. Seated
Capacity: 1168

Brunel University Student Union, Runnymede Campus,
Coopers Hill Lane, Egham, Surrey, TW20 0JZ
t 01784 435508 Standing capacity: 320

Brunton Theatre Ladywell Way, Musselburgh,
Edinburgh, EH21 6AA **t** 0131 665 9900 **f** 0131 665 7495
🔲 Contact: Lesley Smith. Seated Capacity: 302

Buckinghamshire College Newland Park Campus,
Gorelands Lane, Chalfont St Giles, Buckinghamshire,
HP8 4AD **t** 01494 871225 **f** 01494 871954

Buffalo Bar 259 Upper St, London, N1 1RU
t 020 7359 6191 **e** buffalobars@aol.com
w buffalobar.co.uk
📘 facebook.com/group.php?gid=89089362193&ref=ts
🔲 Bookings: Michael, Stacey. Standing capacity: 150

Bull & Gate Promotions 389 Kentish Town Rd,
London, NW5 2TJ **t** 020 8826 5000
e info@bullandgate.co.uk **w** bullandgate.co.uk
🔲 Booker: Phil Avey 020 7485 5358. Standing capacity: 150

The Bullingdon Arms 162 Cowley Road, Oxford,
OX4 1UE **t** 01865 244516 **f** 01865 202457
e info@thebullingdon.com 🔲 Manager: Arron Whan. Seated
Capacity: 200 Standing capacity: 280

Burnley Mechanics Manchester Road, Burnley,
Lancashire, BB11 1HH **t** 01282 664411 Seated Capacity:
495 Standing capacity: 600

Café de Paris 3-4 Coventry Street, London, W1D 6BL
t 020 7395 5807 **f** 020 7395 5816
e Patrick@cafedeparis.com **w** cafedeparis.com
🔲 Contact: Patrick Tustian. Seated Capacity: 220 Standing
capacity: 715

Cambridge Arts Theatre 6 St Edward's Passage,
Cambridge, CB2 3PJ **t** 01223 578933 **f** 01223 578997
e smarsh@cambridgeartstheatre.com
w cambridgeartstheatre.com 🔲 Contact: Ian Ross. Seated
Capacity: 660

Cambridge Corn Exchange 3 Parsons Court,
Wheeler St, Cambridge, CB2 3QE **t** 01223 457555
f 01223 457559 **e** admin.cornex@cambridge.gov.uk
w cornex.co.uk 🔲 Asst Head - Arts & Ents: Graham Saxby.
Seated Capacity: 1200 Standing capacity: 1837

Cambridge Guildhall Cambridge City Council,
Market Square, Cambridge, CB2 3QJ **t** 01223 457000
f 01223 463364 Seated Capacity: 699 Standing capacity:
400

Camden Bars C/O The Monarch, 40-42 Chalk Farm Rd, London, NW1 8BG **e** jeremy.ledlin@monarchbar.com **w** camdenbars.com ✉ Contact: Jeremy Ledlin 020 7482 2054.

The Camden Head 100 Camden High St, London, NW1 0LU **e** info@camdenhead.com **w** camdenhead.com ✉ Contact: Adie Nunn, Jeremy Ledlin 020 7485 4019.

Canterbury Christ Church University College Student Union, North Holmes Rd, Canterbury, Kent, CT1 1QU **t** 01227 782080 **f** 01227 458287 **e** ents@cant.ac.uk **w** c4online.net ✉ Ents & Marketing Mgr: Matt Wynter. Standing capacity: 450

Cardiff International Arena Mary Ann Street, Cardiff, CF10 2EQ **t** 029 2023 4500 **f** 029 2023 4501 **w** sfx-europe.com/cia ✉ GM: Graham Walters 029 2023 4600. Seated Capacity: 4994 Standing capacity: 6700

Cardiff University Students Union, Park Place, Cardiff, CF10 3QN **t** 029 2078 1400 **f** 029 2078 1407 **e** westawayj@cardiff.ac.uk **w** cardiffstudents.com ✉ Ents Mgr: Josh Westaway 029 2078 1456. Seated Capacity: 100 Standing capacity: 300

Cargo Kingsland Viaduct, 83 Rivington St, Shoreditch, London, EC2A 3AY **t** 020 7613 7743 **f** 020 7613 7740 **e** james.p@cargo-london.com **w** cargo-london.com ⓕ facebook.com/group.php?gid=6988021258 ⓢ myspace.com/cargolondon ⓣ twitter.com/cargo_london ✉ Press, Online & Ticketing manager: James Park 07595947728. Seated Capacity: 500

Carnegie Hall East Port, Dunfermline, Fife, Scotland, KY12 7JA **t** 01383 602301 **e** firstname.lastname@attfife.org.uk **w** carnegiehall.co.uk ✉ Artistic Dir: Evan Henderson 08451 555555 x 493368. Seated Capacity: 590

Carnegie Theatre Finkle St, Workington, Cumbria, CA14 2BD **t** 01900 602122 **e** paul.sherwin@allerdale.gov.uk **w** carnegietheatre.co.uk ✉ Mgr: Paul Sherwin. Seated Capacity: 354

The Cathouse 15 Union Street, Glasgow, G1 3RB **t** 0141 248 6606 **f** 0141 248 6741 **e** enquiries@cplweb.com **w** cplweb.com ✉ MD: Donald Macleod. Standing capacity: 400

The Cavern Club 8-10 Mathew St, Liverpool, Merseyside, L2 6RE **t** 0151 236 1965 **f** 0151 236 8081 **e** jon@thecavernliverpool.com **w** caverncitytours.com ✉ Director: Dave Jones 0151 236 9091. Standing capacity: 500

The Cavern Club 83-84 Queen St, Exeter, Devon, EX4 3RP **t** 01392 495370 **e** exetercavern@hotmail.com **w** cavernclub.co.uk ⓢ myspace.com/exetercavern ⓣ twitter.com/ExeterCavern ✉ Promoters: Pippa, David. Standing capacity: 250

Cecil Sharp House 2 Regents Park Road, London, NW1 7AY **t** 020 7485 2206 **f** 020 7284 0534 **e** hire@efdss.org **w** efdss.org ✉ Office Mgr: Verity Flecknell. Seated Capacity: 400 Standing capacity: 450

University of Central England Student Union, Franchise Street, Perry Barr, Birmingham, B42 2SU **t** 0121 331 6801 **f** 0121 331 6802 **w** uce.ac.uk Standing capacity: 350

Central Station 15 - 17 Hill St, Wrexham, LL11 1SN **t** 01978 358 780 **f** 01978 311 884 **e** contact@centralstationvenue.com **w** centralstationvenue.com ✉ Promoter: Aled Owens. Seated Capacity: 225 Standing capacity: 500

The Central Theatre 170 High Street, Chatham, Kent, ME4 4AS **t** 01634 848584 **f** 01634 827711 **e** theatres@medway.gov.uk ✉ Contact: Tony Hill 01634 338338. Seated Capacity: 945

Charter Hall Colchester Leisure World, Cowdray Avenue, Colchester, Essex, CO1 1YH **t** 01206 282946 **f** 01206 282916 **e** claire.jackson@colchester.gov.uk **w** colchesterleisureworld.co.uk ✉ Event Co-ordinator: Claire Jackson 01206 282020. Seated Capacity: 1216 Standing capacity: 1216

Cheese & Grain Market Yard, Frome, Somerset, BA11 1BE **t** 01373 455768 **f** 01373 455765 **e** office@cheeseandgrain.co.uk **w** cheeseandgrain.co.uk ✉ Programme Manager: Martin Dimery. Standing capacity: 800

Cheltenham Town Hall Imperial Square, Cheltenham, Gloucestershire, GL50 1QA **t** 01242 521621 **f** 01242 573902 **e** townhall@cheltenham.gov.uk **w** cheltenhamfestivals.co.uk ✉ Ents & Mktg Mgr: Tim Hulse 01242 227979. Seated Capacity: 1008 Standing capacity: 1008

Chequer Mead Theatre & Arts Centre De La Warr Road, East Grinstead, W Sussex, RH19 3BS **t** 01342 325 577 **f** 01342 301 416 **e** info@chequermead.org.uk **w** chequermead.org.uk ✉ Administration: Sally Norris. Seated Capacity: 320

Chesterfield Arts Centre Chesterfield College, Sheffield Road, Chesterfield, Derbyshire, S41 7LL **t** 01246 500578 **e** littlewj@chesterfield.ac.uk **w** chesterfield.ac.uk ✉ Co-ordinator: Joe Littlewood. Seated Capacity: 250

Chingford Assembly Hall Station Road, Chingford, London, E4 8NU **t** 020 8521 7111 **w** walthamforest.gov.uk ✉ Contact: Halls Mgr.

The Citadel Arts Centre Waterloo Street, St Helens, Merseyside, WA10 1PX **t** 01744 735436 **e** info@citadel.org.uk **w** citadel.org.uk Seated Capacity: 161 Standing capacity: 300

City Halls and Old Fruitmarket Candleriggs, Glasgow, G1 1NQ **t** 0141 353 8080 **f** 0141 353 8006 **e** laurasweeten@glasgowconcerthalls.com **w** glasgowconcerthalls.com ✉ Senior Conference and Events Co-ordinator: Laura Sweeten.

City Varieties Music Hall Swan St, Leeds, LS1 6LW **t** 0113 391 7777 **f** 0113 234 1800 **e** info@cityvarieties.co.uk **w** Cityvarieties.co.uk ✉ GM: Peter Sandeman. Seated Capacity: 531

Live: Venues

You now have two options...

Print or Digital

you choose

Clair Hall Perrymount Rd, Haywards Heath, West Sussex, RH19 3DN **t** 01444 455440 **f** 01444 440041 **e** ClairHall@midsussex.gov.uk

Clickimin Leisure Complex Lochside, Lerwick, Mainland, Shetland Islands, ZE1 0PJ **t** 01595 741000 **f** 01595 741001 **e** mail@srt.org.uk **w** force10.co.uk/srt/pages/clickimin.htm 📧 Contact: Mrs Shona Nisbet. Seated Capacity: 1200 Standing capacity: 1500

Cliffs Pavilion Station Rd, Southend-on-Sea, Essex, SS0 7RA **t** 01702 390 657 **f** 01702 391 573 **e** info@southendtheatres.org.uk **w** thecliffspavilion.co.uk 📧 Theatre Director: Ellen McPhillips. Seated Capacity: 1630 Standing capacity: 2000

The Cockpit Swinegate, Leeds, LS1 4AG **t** 0113 2443 446 **f** 0113 2434 849 **e** info@thecockpit.co.uk **w** thecockpit.co.uk 📧 Dir: Richard Todd. Standing capacity: 750

Colchester Arts Centre Church Street, Colchester, Essex, CO1 1NF **t** 01206 500900 **f** 01206 500187 **e** info@colchesterartscentre.com **w** colchesterartscentre.com 📧 Dir: Anthony Roberts. Seated Capacity: 300 Standing capacity: 400

Colne Municipal Hall Bank House, 61 Albert Road, Colne, Lancashire, BB8 0PB **t** 01282 661220 **f** 01282 661221 **e** info@pendleleisuretrust.co.uk **w** pendleleisuretrust.co.uk 📧 Devel / Mkt Mgr: Gary Hood. Seated Capacity: 600 Standing capacity: 700

Colston Hall Colston St, Bristol, BS1 5AR **t** 0117 922 3693 **f** 0117 922 3681 **e** info@colstonhall.org **w** colstonhall.org 📧 Business Development Dir: Graeme Howell. Seated Capacity: 1840 Standing capacity: 1940

The Comedy 7 Oxendon St, London, SW1Y 4EE **t** 020 7482 3908 **e** n_barnett@madasafish.com **w** deadoralive.org.uk 📧 Promoter: Nicholas Barnett. Standing capacity: 100

The Complex 1-5 Parkfield Street, London, N1 6NU **t** 020 8961 5490 **f** 020 8961 9238 📧 Contact: David Green 020 7288 1986. Standing capacity: 800

Concordia Leisure Centre Forum Way, Cramlington, Northumberland, NE23 6YB **t** 01670 717421 **f** 01670 590648 **e** rcalvert@blythvalley.gov.uk **w** blythvalley.gov.uk 📧 Centre Mgr: Richard Calvert. Seated Capacity: 920

The Congress Theatre Carlisle Road, Eastbourne, East Sussex, BN21 4BP **t** 01323 415500 **f** 01323 727369 **e** theatres@eastbourne.gov.uk **w** eastbourne.org 📧 Gen Mgr: Chris Jordan. Seated Capacity: 1689

King's Lynn Corn Exchange Tuseday Market Place, King's Lynn, Norfolk, PE30 1JW **t** 01553 765 565 **f** 01553 762 141 **e** entertainment_admin@west-norfolk.gov.uk **w** kingslynncornexchange.co.uk 📧 GM: Ellen McPhillips. Seated Capacity: 738

The Corn Exchange Market Place, Newbury, Berks, RG14 5BD **t** 01635 582 666 **f** 01635 582 223 **e** admin@cornexchangenew.co.uk **w** cornexchangenew.com 📧 Dir: Martin Sutherland. Seated Capacity: 400

The Coronet Theatre 28 New Kent Rd, London, SE1 6TJ **t** 020 7701 1500 **f** 020 7701 1300 **e** bookings@coronettheatre.co.uk **w** coronettheatre.co.uk 📧 facebook.com/group.php?gid=17994095305&ref=ts 📧 profile.myspace.com/index.cfm?fuseaction=user.viewpro file&friendID=308880606 📧 twitter.com/CoronetLondon 📧 Bookings: Mike Weller. Seated Capacity: 550 Standing capacity: 1650

Corporation Milton St, Sheffield, S Yorks, S1 4JU **t** 0114 276 0262 **f** 0114 252 7606 **e** mrkeef@corporation.org.uk **w** corporation.org.uk 📧 Contact: Mr M Hobson. Seated Capacity: 700 Standing capacity: 700

Coventry University Students Union, Priory Street, Coventry, West Midlands, CV1 5FJ **t** 024 7679 5200 **f** 024 7679 5239 **e** suexec@coventry.ac.uk **w** cusu.org 📧 Gen Mgr: William Blake. Seated Capacity: 1000

Crawley Leisure Centre Haslett Avenue, Crawley, West Sussex, RH10 1TS **t** 01293 537431 **f** 01293 523750 **e** enquiries@crawleyleisurecentre.co.uk **w** crawleyleisurecentre.co.uk 📧 Promotions & Ents Mgr: David Watmore. Seated Capacity: 1550 Standing capacity: 2400

The Crypt 53 Robertson Street, Hastings, East Sussex, TN34 1HY **t** 01424 444675 **f** 01424 722847 **e** pete@the-crypt.co.uk **w** the-crypt.co.uk 📧 Contact: 01424 424458. Seated Capacity: 350

Cumbernauld Theatre Kildrum, Cumbernauld, Glasgow, Lanarkshire, G67 2BN **t** 01236 737235 **f** 01236 738408 **e** info@cumbernauldtheatre.co.uk **w** cumbernauldtheatre.co.uk 📧 Administrator: Debra Jaffray. Seated Capacity: 258 Standing capacity: 300

Dancehouse Theatre 10 Oxford Road, Manchester, M1 5QA **t** 0161 237 9753 **f** 0161 237 1408 **e** admin@thedancehouse.co.uk **w** thedancehouse.co.uk 📧 Mgr: Chrispin Radcliffe. Seated Capacity: 433

Darlaston Town Hall Victoria Road, Wednesbury, West Midlands, WS10 8AA **t** 01922 650303 **f** 01922 720885 **e** bookings@walsall.gov.uk Seated Capacity: 300

Darlington Arts Centre Vane Terrace, Darlington, Co Durham, DL3 7AX **t** 01325 486 555 **f** 01325 365 794 **e** info@darlingtonarts.co.uk **w** darlingtonarts.co.uk 📧 Music Programmer: Lynda Winstanley. Seated Capacity: 320

Darlington Civic Theatre Parkgate, Darlington, Co Durham, DL1 1RR **t** 01325 468 555 **f** 01325 368 278 **e** info@darlingtonarts.co.uk **w** darlingtonarts.co.uk 📧 Programming Officer: Lynda Winstanley. Seated Capacity: 909

De La Warr Pavilion Marina, Bexhill-on-Sea, East Sussex, TN40 1DP **t** 01424 787900 **f** 01424 787940 **e** Ben.Osborne@dlwp.com **w** dlwp.com 🖳 Head of Live Music: Ben Osborne. Seated Capacity: 1004 Standing capacity: 800

De Montfort Hall Granville Rd, Leicester, LE1 7RU **t** 0116 233 3111 **f** 0116 233 3183 **e** richard.haswell@leicester.gov.uk **w** demontforthall.co.uk 🖳 twitter.com/demontforthall 🖳 Mgr: Richard Haswell 0116 233 3113. Seated Capacity: 1973 Standing capacity: 2300

De Montfort Student Union First Floor, Campus Centre Building, Mill Lane, Leicester, LE2 7DR **t** 0116 255 5576 **f** 0116 257 6309 **e** initial+surname@dmu.ac.uk **w** mydsu.com Standing capacity: 1200

De Montfort University, Bedford Students Union, Pole Hill Avenue, Bedford, MK41 9EA **t** 01234 793155 **f** 01234 217738 **e** rhurll@dmu.ac.uk **w** mydsu.com 🖳 Bar & Ents Mgr: Robert Hurll. Standing capacity: 200

Debates Chamber, Glasgow University Glasgow University, 32 University Avenue, Glasgow, G12 8LX **t** 0141 339 8697 **f** 0141 341 1124 **e** info@guu.co.uk **w** guu.co.uk 🖳 Marketing & Promotions Manager: Heather McMaster. Standing capacity: 900

Deeside Leisure Centre Chester Road West, Queensferry, Deeside, Clwyd, CH5 1SA **t** 01244 812311 **f** 01244 836287 **e** deeside_leisure_centre@flintshire.gov.uk **w** flintshire.gov.uk Seated Capacity: 3500

University of Derby UDSU, Kedleston Rd, Derby, DE22 1GB **t** 01332 622238 **f** 01332 348846 **e** m.j.shepherd@derby.ac.uk **w** derby.ac.uk/udsu 🖳 Ents Mgr: Matt Shepherd. Seated Capacity: 700

Derngate Theatre 19-21 Guildhall Road, Northampton, NN1 1DP **t** 01604 626222 **f** 01604 250901 **e** info@royalandderngate.com **w** royalandderngate.com 🖳 Contact: Rosemary Jones. Seated Capacity: 1500 Standing capacity: 1550

Dingwalls Middle Yard, Camden Lock, Chalk Farm Rd, London, NW1 8AB **t** 020 7428 5929 **e** david@dmpuk.com **w** dingwalls.com 🖳 In-House Booker/Promoter: David Messer 01920 823098. Standing capacity: 487

Dominion Theatre 269 Tottenham Court Rd, London, W1P 0AQ **t** 020 7580 1889 **f** 020 7580 0246 **e** firstname.lastname@clerchannel.co.uk **w** getlive.co.uk 🖳 GM: Stephen Murtath. Seated Capacity: 2101

Doncaster Dome Doncaster Leisure Park, Bawtry Road, Doncaster, South Yorkshire, DN4 7PD **t** 01302 370777 **f** 01302 379135 **e** info@the-dome.co.uk **w** the-dome.co.uk Seated Capacity: 1850 Standing capacity: 3264

Dover Town Hall Biggin Street, Dover, Kent, CT16 1DL **t** 01304 201200 **f** 01304 201200 **e** townhall@dover.gov.uk **w** dover.gov.uk/townhall 🖳 Contact: Gen Mgr. Seated Capacity: 500 Standing capacity: 600

Dublin Castle 94 Parkway, London, NW1 7AN **t** 020 7700 0550 **e** info@bugbearbookings.com **w** bugbearbookings.com 🖪 facebook.com/bugbearpromotions 🖳 myspace.com/bugbearpromotions 🖳 Promoters: Jim & Tony. Standing capacity: 134

Dudley Town Hall St James's Road, Dudley, West Midlands, DY1 1HF **t** 01384 815544 **f** 01384 815534 **e** dudley.townhall@dudley.gov.uk **w** dudley.gov.uk 🖳 Production Mgr: Tim Jones. Seated Capacity: 1060 Standing capacity: 1000

Caird Hall City Sq, Dundee, Tayside, DD1 3BB **t** 01382 434030 **f** 01382 434451 **e** cairdhall@dundeecity.gov.uk **w** cairdhall.co.uk 🖳 Caird Hall Manager: Susan Gillan. Seated Capacity: 2400 Standing capacity: 2300

Dundee University Student Association, Airlie Pl, Dundee, Tayside, DD1 4HP **t** 01382 384021 **f** 01382 227124 **w** dusa.co.uk 🖳 Ents & Publicity Mgr: Trevor San. Seated Capacity: 600 Standing capacity: 600

Durham University Student Union, Dunelm House, New Elvet, Co Durham, DH1 3AN **t** 0191 374 3331 **f** 0191 374 3328 **e** dsu.ents@dur.ac.uk **w** dsu.org.uk 🖳 Venue Mgr: Jez Light. Seated Capacity: 550 Standing capacity: 800

Ealing Town Hall Halls & Events, Ground Floor, Perceval House, London, W5 2HL **t** 020 8758 5624 **f** 020 8566 5088 **e** HandM@Ealing.Gov.uk **w** Ealing.Gov.uk/HE&M 🖳 Head of Halls & Events: M Hand 020 8758 8079. Seated Capacity: 500 Standing capacity: 500

Earls Court & Olympia Earls Court Exhibition Centre, Warwick Rd, London, SW5 9TA **t** 020 7370 8839 **f** 020 7370 8144 **e** firstname.lastname@eco.co.uk **w** eco.co.uk 🖳 Live Event Manager: Suzie Pollock. Seated Capacity: 18000 Standing capacity: 22000

East Kilbride Civic Centre Andrew Street, East Kilbride, Lanarkshire, G74 1AB **t** 01355 806000

East London University Romford Road, London, E15 4LZ **t** 020 8223 3000 **f** 020 8223 3000

University of East London Union Building, Longbridge Road, Dagenham, Essex, RM8 2AS **t** 020 8590 6017 **f** 020 8597 6987

Eastbourne Theatres - Winter Garden Compton Street, Eastbourne, East Sussex, BN21 4BP **t** 01323 415500 **f** 01323 727369 **e** theatres@eastbourne.gov.uk **w** eastbourne.org 🖳 Gen Mgr: Chris Jordan. Seated Capacity: 1100 Standing capacity: 1200

Live: Venues

Eden Court Theatre and Cinema Bishops Rd, Inverness, IV3 5SA **t** 01463 239841 **f** 01463 713810 **e** marketing@eden-court.co.uk **w** eden-court.co.uk **f** facebook.com/edencourttheatre **t** twitter.com/EdenCourt youtube.com/user/EdenCourt1 Head of Marketing: Laurie Piper 01463 234234. Seated Capacity: 810

Edinburgh International Conference Centre The Exchange, Morrison Street, Edinburgh, EH3 8EE **t** 0131 300 3000 **f** 0131 300 3030 **e** sales@eicc.co.uk **w** eicc.co.uk Snr Sales Team Leader: Lesley Stephen. Seated Capacity: 1200 Standing capacity: 1200

Edinburgh Playhouse 18-22 Greenside Pl, Edinburgh, EH1 3AA **t** 0131 524 3333 **f** 0131 524 3355 **w** edinburghplayhouse.org.uk **f** facebook.com/EdinburghPlayhouse ww.youtube.com/EdinburghPlayhouse Gen Mgr: James Haworth. Seated Capacity: 3056

Edinburgh University Students Association, Mandela Centre, 5/2 Bristo Square, Edinburgh, EH8 9AL **t** 0131 650 2656 **f** 0131 668 4177 **e** ian.evans@eusa.ed.ac.uk **w** eusa.ed.ac.uk Entertainments Manager: Ian Evans 0131 650 2649. Standing capacity: 120

Elements Bath University, Students Union, Claverton Down, Bath, BA2 7AY **t** 01225 386612 **f** 01225 444061 **e** union@bath.ac.uk **w** bathstudent.com Bars & Ents Co-ordinator: Mike Dalton. Seated Capacity: 250 Standing capacity: 500

Elgin Town Hall 5 Trinity Place, Elgin, IV30 1VL **t** 01343 543451 **f** 01343 563410 Contact: Eric McGilvery. Seated Capacity: 723

Ellesmere Port Civic Hall Civic Way, Ellesmere Port, South Wirral, Cheshire, CH65 0BE **t** 0151 356 6780 **f** 0151 355 0508 Contact: Miles Veitch 0151 356 6890. Seated Capacity: 636

Embassy Centre Grand Parade, Skegness, Lincolnshire, PE25 2UN **t** 01754 768444 **f** 01754 761737 Head of Leisure & Tourism: Bob Suich 01507 329411. Seated Capacity: 1158 Standing capacity: 1158

Empire Theatre High Street West, Sunderland, Tyne and Wear, SR1 3EX **t** 0191 566 1040 **f** 0191 566 1065 **e** Sarah.b.Clarke@clearchannel.co.uk **w** getlive.co.uk/sunderland GM: Paul Ryan. Seated Capacity: 1875 Standing capacity: 1875

The Empire Milton Keynes Leisure Plaza, 1 South Row, Charles Way, Milton Keynes, Buckinghamshire, MK9 1BL **t** 01908 394 074 **f** 01908 696 768 **e** info@empire-mk.co.uk **w** empire-mk.co.uk Promotions Manager: Nicky Harris. Standing capacity: 2000

The English Folk Dance and Song Society Cecil Sharp House, 2 Regent's Park Road, London, NW1 7AY **t** 020 7485 2206 **f** 020 7284 0534 **e** info@efdss.org **w** efdss.org Publications Manager: Verity Flecknall. Seated Capacity: 400 Standing capacity: 540

English National Opera The London Coliseum, St Martin's Lane, London, WC2N 4ES **t** 020 7836 0111 Gen Mgr: Nicholas Payne. Seated Capacity: 2358

The Enterprise 2 Haverstock Hill, London, NW3 2BL **e** info@camdenenterprise.com **w** camdenenterprise.com Contact: Adie Nunn, Sophie Nicolas 020 7485 2659.

Esquires 60A Bromham Road, Bedford, MK40 2QG **t** 01234 340120 **f** 01234 356630

The Event II Kingswest, West Street, Brighton, East Sussex **t** 01273 732627 **f** 01273 208996 Info Mgr: Dan Boorman. Standing capacity: 1920

Everyman Theatre 5-9 Hope Street, Liverpool, Merseyside **t** 0151 708 0338 **f** 0151 709 0398 **e** info@everymanplayhouse.com **w** everyman.merseyworld.com Contact: The General Mgr. Seated Capacity: 450

Evesham Arts Centre Victoria Avenue, Evesham, Worcestershire, WR11 4QH **t** 01386 48883 Contact: LA Griffith-Jones. Seated Capacity: 300

Exeter Corn Exchange Market St, Exeter, Devon, EX1 1BU **t** 01392 665866 **f** 01392 665940 **e** cornexchange@exeter.gov.uk **w** exeter.gov.uk/cornexchange Venue Manager: David Lewis. Seated Capacity: 500 Standing capacity: 500

Exeter Phoenix Bradninch Place, Gandy Street, Exeter, Devon, EX4 3LS **t** 01392 667056 **f** 01392 667599 The Arts Mgr: Andy Morley. Seated Capacity: 216 Standing capacity: 500

Fairfield Halls Park Lane, Croydon, Surrey, CR9 1DG **t** 020 8681 0821 **e** johnspring@fairfield.co.uk **w** fairfield.co.uk Spring: John. Seated Capacity: 1550

Falmouth Arts Centre Church Street, Falmouth, Cornwall, TR11 3EG **t** 01326 212719 **e** adrian@falmoutharts.org **w** falmoutharts.org GM: Adrian Watts. Seated Capacity: 200

Farnborough Recreation Centre 1 Westmead, Farnborough, Hampshire, GU14 7LD **t** 01252 370411 **f** 01252 372280 Standing capacity: 2100

Fat Sam's Nightclub and Live Music Venue 31 South Ward Rd, Dundee, DD1 1PU **t** 01382 226836 **f** 01382 224780 **e** gus@fatsams.co.uk **w** fatsams.co.uk MD / General Manager: Angus Robb / Colin Rattray. Seated Capacity: 480 Standing capacity: 480

Ferneham Hall, Fareham Osborn Road, Fareham, Hampshire, PO16 0TL **t** 01329 824864 **f** 01329 281486 **e** rdavies@fareham.gov.uk **w** fareham.gov.uk Head of Arts & Ents: Russell Davies. Seated Capacity: 752 Standing capacity: 800

Fez Club 5-6 Gun St, Reading, RG1 2JR **t** 01189 586 839 **f** 01189 586 796 **e** info@sakurareading.com **w** readingfez.com GM: Olly Smith. Standing capacity: 400

Fibbers Stonebow House, The Stonebow, York, YO1 7NP **t** 01904 651 250 **f** 01904 670 542 **e** fibbers@fibbers.co.uk **w** fibbers.co.uk Promoter: Tim Hornsby. Standing capacity: 200

Live: Venues

The Fibbers Group Units 8-12, Stonebow House, Stonebow, York, North Yorkshire, YO1 7NP **t** 01904 466148 **f** 01904 675315 **e** fibbers@fibbers.co.uk **w** fibbers.co.uk ✉ MD: Tim Hornsby. Seated Capacity: 200 Standing capacity: 250

The Fleece 12 St Thomas Street, Bristol, BS1 6JJ **t** 0117 927 7150 **e** fleece@gigs.demon.co.uk **w** gigs.demon.co.uk ✉ Promoter: David Brayley. Standing capacity: 400

Fort Regent Leisure Centre St Helier, Jersey, Channel Islands, JE2 4UX **t** 01534 449609 **f** 01534 449641 **e** c.stanier@gov.je **w** esc.gov.je ✉ Marketing Mgr: Colin Stanier. Seated Capacity: 1974 Standing capacity: 2500

The Forum Fonthill, The Common, Tunbridge Wells, Kent, TN4 8YU **t** 08712 777 101 **f** 08712 777 101 **e** twforum@globalnet.co.uk **w** twforum.co.uk ✉ Manager: Mark Davyd. Seated Capacity: 110 Standing capacity: 250

Forum 28 28 Duke Street, Barrow-in-Furness, Cumbria, LA14 1HH **t** 01229 820000 **f** 01229 894942 **e** nward@barrowbc.gov.uk **w** barrowbc.gov.uk ✉ Bookings Mgr: Neil Ward. Seated Capacity: 485 Standing capacity: 720

The Foundry Beak Street, Birmingham, West Midlands, B1 1LS **t** 0121 622 1894 **w** dr-p.demon.co.uk/foundry.html

The Fridge 1 Town Hall Parade, Brixton Hill, London, SW2 1RJ **t** 020 7333 2233 **e** manager@fridge.co.uk **w** fridge.co.uk ✉ Mgr: Sam Naaqib. Seated Capacity: 1100 Standing capacity: 1100

Futurist Theatre Foreshore Road, Scarborough, North Yorkshire, YO11 1NT **t** 01723 370742 **f** 01723 365456 Standing capacity: 2155

Gaiety Theatre Douglas, Isle of Man **t** 01624 620046 Seated Capacity: 800

The Garage 490 Sauchiehall St, Glasgow, G2 3LW **t** 0141 332 1120 **f** 0141 332 1130 **w** cplweb.com ✉ MD: Donald Macleod. Standing capacity: 700

The Gardner Arts Centre University Of Sussex, Falmer, Brighton, East Sussex, BN1 9RA **t** 01273 685447 **f** 01273 678551 **e** info@gardnerarts.co.uk **w** gardnerarts.co.uk ✉ Dir: Sue Webster. Seated Capacity: 476 Standing capacity: 476

Garrick Theatre Barrington Road, Altrincham, Cheshire, WA14 1HZ **t** 0161 929 8779 (mktg) ✉ Contact: 0161 928 1677 (box). Seated Capacity: 472

Gateshead International Stadium Neilson Road, Gateshead, Tyne & Wear, NE10 0EF **t** 0191 478 1687 **f** 0191 477 1315 Seated Capacity: 11000 Standing capacity: 38000

Glamorgan University Student Union, Forest Grove, Treforest, Pontypridd, Mid Glamorgan, CF37 1UF **t** 01443 408227 **f** 01443 491589 ✉ Contact: Jason Crimmins. Seated Capacity: 200 Standing capacity: 500

Glasgow Caledonian University Students Union, 70 Cowcaddens Road, Glasgow, Lanarkshire, G4 0BA **t** 0141 332 0681 **f** 0141 353 0029 **e** d.mcbride@gcal.ac.uk **w** caledonianstudent.com ✉ Venue Mgr: Denis McBride. Standing capacity: 595

Glasgow City Halls 32 Albion Street, Glasgow, Lanarkshire, G1 1QU **t** 0141 287 5005 **f** 0141 287 5533 ✉ Susan Deighan: Head of Programming. Seated Capacity: 1121 Standing capacity: 800

Glasgow Garage 490 Sauchiehall St, Glasgow, Lanarkshire, G2 3LW **t** 0141 332 1120 **f** 0141 332 1130 ✉ Contact: Donald Macleod. Standing capacity: 600

Glasgow King's Theatre Glasgow City Council, Cultural and Leisure Services, 229 George Street, Glasgow, G1 1QU **t** 0141 287 3922 **f** 0141 287 5533 ✉ Contact: Pauline Murphy. Seated Capacity: 1785

Glasgow Pavilion Theatre 121 Renfield Street, Glasgow, Lanarkshire, G2 3AX **t** 0141 332 7579 **f** 0141 331 2745 ✉ Theatre Mgr: Iain Gordon 0141 332 1846. Seated Capacity: 1449

Glasgow's Concert Halls 2 Sauchiehall St, Glasgow, G2 3NY **t** 0141 353 8080 **f** 0141 353 8006 **e** karentaylor@glasgowconcerthalls.com **w** glasgowconcerthalls.com ✉ Head of Events and Commercial Development: Karen Taylor. Seated Capacity: 2417

Glastonbury Festival 28 Northload St, Glastonbury, Somerset, BA6 9JJ **t** 01458 834596 **e** office@glastonburyfestivals.co.uk **w** glastonburyfestivals.co.uk Standing capacity: 177500

Glee Club The Arcadian Centre, Hurst St, Birmingham, West Midlands, B5 4TD **t** 07973 121958 **e** markus_sargeant@yahoo.com **w** glee.co.uk ✉ Promoter: Markus Sargeant. Seated Capacity: 400 Standing capacity: 400

The Globe Blackpool Pleasure Beach, Ocean Boulevard, Blackpool, Lancashire, FY4 1EZ **t** 01253 341033 **f** 01253 401098 ✉ Contact: Michelle Barratt. Seated Capacity: 940

Gloucester Leisure Centre Bruton Way, Gloucester, GL1 1DT **t** 01452 385310 ✉ Contact: 01452 306498. Seated Capacity: 2100 Standing capacity: 2500

Goldsmiths College Student Union Dixon Road, New Cross, London, SE14 6NW **t** 020 8692 1406 **f** 020 8694 9789 **e** gcsu@gold.ac.uk **w** gcsu.org.uk ✉ Entertainment Manager: Barrie Schooling. Seated Capacity: 350 Standing capacity: 600

The Good Ship 289 Kilburn High Rd, London, NW6 7JR **t** 07949 008253 **e** john@thegoodship.co.uk **w** thegoodship.co.uk facebook.com/goodshipkilburn myspace.com/thegoodship twitter.com/thegoodshipnw6 ✉ Manager: John McCooke. Standing capacity: 200

Live: Venues

Gordon Craig Theatre Stevenage Arts & Leisure Ctr, Lytton Way, Stevenage, Hertfordshire, SG1 1LZ **t** 01438 242642 **f** 01438 242342 **e** gordoncraig@stevenage-leisure.co.uk **w** stevenage.gov.uk/GordonCraig ☎ Bookings Mgr: Bob Bustance. Standing capacity: 500

Robert Gordon University Student Union, 60 Schoolhill, Aberdeen, Grampian, AB10 1JQ **t** 01224 262262 **f** 01224 262268 **e** rgusa@rgu.ac.uk **w** rgu.ac.uk Seated Capacity: 150 Standing capacity: 200

The Grafton West Derby Road, Liverpool, L6 9BY **t** 0151 263 2303 **f** 0151 263 4985 Seated Capacity: 1425

Grand Opera House Great Victoria Street, Belfast, Co Antrim, BT2 7HR **t** 028 9024 0411 **f** 028 9023 6842 **w** goh.co.uk ☎ Contact: Derek Nicholls. Seated Capacity: 1001

Grand Theatre Church Street, Blackpool, Lancashire, FY1 1HT **t** 01253 290111 **f** 01253 751767 **e** gm@blackpoolgrand.co.uk **w** blackpoolgrand.co.uk ☎ Contact: Stephanie Sir. Seated Capacity: 1200

Grand Theatre Wolverhampton, West Midlands **t** 01902 429212

Great Grimsby Town Hall Town Hall Square, Great Grimsby, North East Lincolnshire, DN31 1HX **t** 01472 324109 **f** 01472 324108 ☎ Contact: John Callison. Seated Capacity: 350 Standing capacity: 400

Grimsby Auditorium Cromwell Road, Grimsby, South Humberside, DN31 2BH **t** 01472 323100 **f** 01472 323102 ☎ Contact: Mr Morris. Seated Capacity: 1200 Standing capacity: 2000

Group Theatre Bedford Street, Belfast, Co Antrim, BT2 7FF **t** 028 9032 3900 **f** 028 9024 7199 ☎ Contact: Pat Falls. Seated Capacity: 221

Guildhall Lancaster Road, Preston, Lancashire, PR1 1HT **t** 01772 203456 Seated Capacity: 780

Guildhall 23 Eastgate Street, Gloucester, GL1 1QR **t** 01452 505089 Seated Capacity: 250 Standing capacity: 150

Hackney Empire Ltd. 291 Mare St, London, E8 1EJ **t** 020 8510 4500 **f** 020 8510 4530 **e** frank.sweeney@hackneyempire.co.uk **w** hackneyempire.co.uk ☎ Programmer: Frank Sweeney. Seated Capacity: 1300 Standing capacity: 1500

Halfmoon, Putney 93 Lower Richmond Rd, London, SW15 1EU **t** 020 8780 9383 **f** 020 8789 7863 **e** gigguide@halfmoon.co.uk **w** halfmoon.co.uk ☎ Bookings/Promotions Mgr: Kirk Barclay. Seated Capacity: 150 Standing capacity: 200

Hare And Hounds High Street, King's Heath, Birmingham, B14 7JZ **t** 0121 444 2081 ☎ Contact: The Manager 0121 444 3578. Seated Capacity: 140

Harlow Bandstand Harlow Council Leisure Service, Latton Bush Centre, Southern Way, Harlow, Essex, CM18 7BL **t** 01279 446404 **f** 01279 446431 ☎ Contact: Recreation Services Officer. Standing capacity: 5000

Harlow Playhouse Playhouse Sq, Harlow, Essex, CM20 1LS **t** 01279 446760 **f** 01279 424391 **e** scott.ramsay@harlow.gov.uk **w** playhouseharlow.com ☎ General Manager: Scott Ramsay 01279 446740. Seated Capacity: 419

Harlow Showground Harlow Council Leisure Service, Latton Bush Centre, Southern Way, Harlow, Essex, CM18 7BL **t** 01279 446404 **f** 01279 446431 ☎ Contact: Recreation Services Officer. Standing capacity: 15000

Harrogate International Centre Kings Road, Harrogate, North Yorkshire, HG1 5LA **t** 01423 500 500 **f** 01423 537 270 **e** sales@harrogateinternationalcentre.co.uk **w** harrogateinternationalcentre.co.uk ☎ Director: Stuart Quin. Seated Capacity: 2009 Standing capacity: 1431

Hawick Town Hall 44 High Street, Hawick, TD9 9EF **t** 01450 364743 Seated Capacity: 600 Standing capacity: 900

The Hawth, Crawley Hawth Avenue, Crawley, West Sussex, RH10 6YZ **t** 01293 552941 **f** 01293 533362 **e** info@hawth.co.uk **w** hawth.co.uk ☎ Head Of Arts: Kevin Eason. Seated Capacity: 850 Standing capacity: 950

Haymarket Theatre 1 Belgrave Gate, Garrick Walk, Leicester, LE1 3YQ **t** 0116 253 0021 **f** 0116 251 3310 Seated Capacity: 888

Hazlitt Theatre Earl Street, Maidstone, Kent, ME14 1PL **t** 01622 602178 **f** 01622 602194 **e** mandyhare@maidstone.gov.uk ☎ Manager: Mandy Hare. Seated Capacity: 381 Standing capacity: 400

Heriot-Watt University Students Union Students Association, The Union, Riccarton Campus, Edinburgh, EH14 4AS **t** 0131 451 5333 **f** 0131 451 5344 **e** K.Easton@hw.ac.uk **w** hwusa.org ☎ Venue & Commercial Manager: Keith Easton. Seated Capacity: 250 Standing capacity: 450

University of Hertfordshire Student Union, College Lane, Hatfield, Hertfordshire, AL10 9AB **t** 01707 285008 **f** 01707 286151 **e** uhsu@herts.ac.uk **w** uhsu.herts.ac.uk ☎ Contact: Venue Mgr 01707 285000. Seated Capacity: 450 Standing capacity: 1300

Hexagon Queen's Walk, Reading, Berkshire, RG1 7UA **t** 0118 939 0123 **f** 0118 939 0028 **e** boxoffice@readingarts.com **w** readingarts.com ☎ Prog Co-ordinator: Charity Gordon. Seated Capacity: 1484 Standing capacity: 1686

Hippodrome Leicester Square, London, WC2 7JH **t** 020 7437 4311 **f** 020 7434 4225 **w** londonhippodrome.com ☎ Contact: Annette Morris. Seated Capacity: 700 Standing capacity: 1945

His Majesty's Theatre Rosemount Viaduct, Aberdeen, AB25 1GL **t** 01224 637788 **f** 01224 632519 **e** venues@arts-rec.aberdeen.net.uk **w** aberdeencity.gov.uk/venues ☎ GM: Duncan Hendry. Seated Capacity: 1446

Live: Venues

The Hive, Glasgow University Glasgow University, 32 University Avenue, Glasgow, G12 8LX **t** 0141 339 8697 **f** 0141 339 8931 **e** libraries@guu.co.uk **w** guu.co.uk ☏ Contact: The Porter's Box. Standing capacity: 1000

HMV Forum 9-17 Highgate Rd, London, NW5 1JY **t** 020 7428 4099 **f** 020 7485 5604 **e** info@kentishtownforum.com **w** kentishtownforum.com ☏ Contact: Lucy Roiter. Seated Capacity: 1400 Standing capacity: 2110

HMV Hammersmith Apollo Queen Caroline St, London, W6 9QH **t** 020 8563 3800 **f** 0870 749 0851 **e** info@hammersmithapollo.net **w** hammersmithapollo.net ☏ GM: Jan Chadwick. Seated Capacity: 3632 Standing capacity: 5025

The Horn UK Live Music Venue of the Year 2008 & 2009 The Horn, Victoria St, St Albans, Herts, AL1 3TE **t** 01727 853143 **e** info@thehorn.co.uk **w** thehorn.co.uk
◾ facebook.com/group.php?gid=78970836486&ref=search&sid=507417968.1719924662...1
☏ myspace.com/thehornvenue ☏ twitter.com/hornvenue ☏ Bookings: Adrian Bell / Hansi Koppe 01727 844627. Standing capacity: 350

The Horns 1 Hempstead Road, Watford, Herts., WD17 3RL **t** 01923 225 020 **f** 01923 233 048 **e** info@thehornswatford.co.uk **w** thehornswatford.co.uk ☏ Bookings: Denis Cook. Standing capacity: 200

Horsham Arts Centre North Street, Horsham, West Sussex, RH12 1RL **t** 01403 259708 **f** 01403 211502 ☏ Mgr: Michael Gattrell 01403 268689. Seated Capacity: 438

Hove Centre @ Hove Town Hall Norton Road, Hove, East Sussex, BN3 4AH **t** 01273 292902 **f** 01273 292936 **e** venuehire@brighton-hove.gov.uk ☏ Admins Officer: Amanda-Jane Stone. Seated Capacity: 1000 Standing capacity: 1000

HUB 2 Goulston St, Aldgate, London, E1 7TP **t** 020 7133 4243 **f** 020 7133 2127 **e** pete.williams@londonmet.ac.uk
◾ facebook.com/home.php#/profile.php?id=100000273794389&ref=profile ☏ myspace.com/hubeastlondon ☏ Venue Booker: Pete Williams. Seated Capacity: 150 Standing capacity: 300

Huddersfield Town Hall (also Batley, Dewsbury) Cultural Services HQ, Red Doles Lane, Huddersfield, West Yorkshire, HD2 1YF **t** 01484 226300 **f** 01484 221541 **e** julia.robinson@kirkleesmc.gov.uk ☏ Town Halls Manager: Julia Robinson. Seated Capacity: 1200 Standing capacity: 700

Huddersfield University Student Union, Queensgate, Huddersfield, HD1 3DH **t** 01484 538156 **f** 01484 432333 **e** k.j.stead@hud.ac.uk **w** huddersfieldstudent.com ☏ Ents Co-ordinator: Kerry Stead. Seated Capacity: 250 Standing capacity: 300

Hull Arena Kingston Street, Hull, East Yorkshire, HU1 2DZ **t** 01482 325252 **f** 01482 216066 **w** hullarena.co.uk ☏ Contact: Linda Parker. Seated Capacity: 3250 Standing capacity: 3750

Hull City Hall Victoria Square, Hull, East Yorkshire, HU1 3NA **t** 01482 613880 **f** 01482 613961 ☏ Programming Mgr: Mike Lister. Seated Capacity: 1400 Standing capacity: 1800

Hull New Theatre Kingston Square, Kingston Upon Hull, East Yorkshire, HU1 3HF **t** 01482 613880 **f** 01482 613961 ☏ Programming Mgr: Michael Lister. Seated Capacity: 1189

Hull University University House, Cottingham Road, Hull, East Yorkshire, HU2 9BT **t** 01482 466253 **f** 01482 466280 **e** j.a.brooks@hull.ac.uk **w** hull.ac.uk ☏ Ents Co-ordinator: James Brooks. Standing capacity: 1500

ICA The Mall, London, SW1Y 5AH **t** 020 7930 0493 **e** jamie.eastman@ica.org.uk **w** ica.org.uk ☏ Director of Music: Jamie Eastman 020 7766 1444. Seated Capacity: 167 Standing capacity: 350

Imperial College Union, Beit Quad, Prince Consort Road, London, SW7 2BB **t** 020 7594 8068 **f** 020 7594 8065 **e** ents@ic.ac.uk **w** union.ic.ac.uk ☏ Ents Manager: Ham Al-Rubaie. Seated Capacity: 300 Standing capacity: 450

IndigO2 at the O2 Peninsula Sq, Greenwich, London, SE10 0DX **t** 020 8463 2000 **e** bookings@theindigo2.com **w** theindigo2.co.uk ☏ Bookers: Laurie Pegg & Leo Green.

INDIGO2 AT THE O2

indigO₂ at The **O₂**

The O2, Peninsula Sq, London, SE10 0JF **t** 020 8463 2000 **e** lpegg@theindigo2.com **w** theo2.co.uk/indigo2 ☏ twitter.com/indigo2atthe2 ☏ Senior Booker: Laurie Pegg 020 8463 2707. Senior Booker: Laurie Pegg. General Manager: Sally Davies. Marketing: Emma Reynolds.

Inverurie Town Hall Market Place, Inverurie, Aberdeenshire **t** 01467 621610 Seated Capacity: 400

ION 161-165 Ladbroke Grove, London, W10 6HJ **t** 020 8960 1702 **w** meanfiddler.com

Ipswich Corn Exchange King Street, Ipswich, Suffolk, IP1 1DH **t** 01473 433 133 **f** 01473 433 450 **e** firstname.lastname@ipswich.gov.uk **w** ipswichcornexchange.com ☏ Operations & Events Mgr: Craig Oldfield. Seated Capacity: 900 Standing capacity: 1000

Ipswich Regent Theatre 3 St Helens St, Ipswich, Suffolk, IP4 1HE **t** 01473 433 555 **f** 01473 433 727 **e** firstname.lastname@ipswich.gov.uk **w** ipswichregent.com ☏ Manager: Hazel Clover. Seated Capacity: 1781 Standing capacity: 1781

Irish Centre York Road, Leeds, West Yorkshire, LS9 9NT **t** 0113 248 0613

Isha Lounge Bar 43 Richmond Road, Kingston Upon Thames, Surrey, KT2 5BW **t** 020 8546 0099 **e** ishalounge@hotmail.com **w** ishalounge.com 🖂 Contact: Titch Deegun. Standing capacity: 200

The Jaffa Cake 28 Kings Stables Road, Edinburgh, Lothian, EH1 2JY **t** 0131 229 9438

JAGZ At the Station, Station Hill, Ascot, Berks, SL5 9EG **t** 01344 878 100 **e** music@jagz.co.uk **w** jagz.co.uk 🖂 Promotions Manager: Miles Gripton. Seated Capacity: 100 Standing capacity: 150

Jazz Cafe 5 Parkway, Camden Town, London, NW1 7PG **t** 020 7485 6834 **f** 020 7267 9219 **e** info@jazzcafe.co.uk **w** jazzcafe.co.uk 🖪 facebook.com/pages/london.united.kingdom/jazz-cafe/50097478644 🖂 General Business Manager: Lisa Auger. Seated Capacity: 250 Standing capacity: 400

Jersey Opera House Gloucester Street, St Hellier, Jersey, Channel Islands, JE2 3QL **t** 01534 617521 **f** 01534 610624 🖂 Contact: Ian Stephens. Seated Capacity: 680

The Joiners 141 St Mary St, Southampton, Hampshire, SO14 1NS **t** 0238 022 5612 **f** 01962 878812 **e** dave@joinerslive.co.uk, chris@joinerslive.co.uk, glenn@joinerslive.co.uk **w** joinerslive.co.uk 🖪 facebook.com/group.php?gid=18151233324 🖪 myspace.com/joinerspromotions 🖂 Head Booker, Head of Promotions, Owner (respectively): Dave Rowett, Chris Stemp, Glenn Lovell 023 8022 5612. Standing capacity: 250

Jug Of Ale 43 Alcester Road, Moseley, Birmingham, West Midlands, B13 8AA **t** 0121 449 1082

The Junction CDC ltd Clifton Way, Cambridge, CB1 7GX **t** 01223 578000 **e** tickets@junction.co.uk **w** junction.co.uk 🖂 Commercial Prog Mgr: Rob Tinkler. Seated Capacity: 278 Standing capacity: 850

Kartouche Princes Street, Ipswich, Suffolk, IP2 9TD **t** 01473 230666 **f** 01473 232579 **e** info@kartouche.net **w** kartouche.net 🖂 Manager: Georgie Smith. Standing capacity: 1450

KCLSU King's College London Students Union, Macadam Bldg, Surrey Street, London, WC2R 2NS **t** 020 7848 1588 **f** 020 7379 9833 **e** firstname.lastname@kclsu.org **w** kclsu.org 🖂 Venues Duty Manager (Stage & Events): Rob Hampton. Standing capacity: 600

Keele University Student Union, Keele, Newcastle-under-Lyme, Staffs, ST5 5BJ **t** 01782 583700 **f** 01782 712671 **e** r.chamberlain@keele.ac.uk; ents@keele.ac.uk **w** kusu.net 🖂 Ents Mgr: Rob Chamberlain. Seated Capacity: 400 Standing capacity: 1100

Kef 9 Belmont St, Aberdeen, AB10 1JR **t** 01224 645328 **f** 01224 644737 **e** angela_stirling@hotmail.com 🖂 Promoter: Paul Stewart 01224 648000. Seated Capacity: 120 Standing capacity: 250

Kendal Town Hall Highgate, Kendal, Cumbria, LA9 4DL **t** 01539 725758 **f** 01539 734457 🖂 Bookings: Debbie Mckee. Seated Capacity: 400 Standing capacity: 400

Town Hall, Kensington Royal Borough Kensington, & Chelsea, Horton Street, London, W8 7NX **t** 020 7361 2220 **f** 020 7361 3442 **e** hall-let@rbkc.gov.uk **w** rbkc.gov.uk 🖂 Conference/Events Office: Maxine Howitt. Seated Capacity: 860 Standing capacity: 900

Kettering Arena Thurston Drive, Kettering, Northamptonshire, NN15 6PB **t** 01536 414141 **f** 01536 414334 🖂 Contact: Tony Remington. Seated Capacity: 2000 Standing capacity: 3000

Kidderminster Town Hall Vicar Street, Kidderminster, Worcestershire, DY10 2BL **t** 01562 732158 **f** 01562 750708 🖂 Contact: The Mgr. Seated Capacity: 450

Kilmarnock Palace Theatre 9 Green Street, Kilmarnock, KA1 3BN **t** 01563 537710 **f** 01563 573047 🖂 Asst Theatre & Ents Mgr: Laura Brown 01563 523590. Standing capacity: 1100

King Tut's Wah Wah Hut 272A St Vincent Street, Glasgow, G2 5RL **t** 0141 248 5158 **f** 0141 248 5202 **e** kingtuts@dfconcerts.co.uk **w** kingtuts.co.uk 🖂 Promoter/Venue Mgr: Dave McGeachan. Standing capacity: 300

King's Hall Exhibition & Conference Centre Balmoral, Belfast, Co Antrim, BT9 6GW **t** 028 9066 5225 **f** 028 9066 1264 **e** info@kingshall.co.uk **w** kingshall.co.uk Seated Capacity: 5000 Standing capacity: 8000

Kingston University Guild Of Students Penrhyn Road, Kingston upon Thames, Surrey, KT1 2EE **t** 020 8547 2000 **f** 020 8255 0032 **w** kingston.ac.uk Standing capacity: 700

KoKo (formerly known as The Camden Palace) 1A Camden High St, London, NW1 7JE **t** 0870 432 5527 **f** 020 7388 3883 **e** daveid@koko.uk.com **w** koko.uk.com 🖂 Head of Music: Daveid Phillips. Standing capacity: 2434

Komedia 44-47 Gardner St, Brighton, East Sussex, BN1 1KN **t** 01273 647100 **f** 01273 647102 **e** admin@komedia.co.uk **w** komedia.co.uk 🖂 Programmer: Marina Kobler 01273 647101. Seated Capacity: 210

University of Wales - Lampeter Student Union, Ty Ceredig, Lampeter, Ceredigion, SA48 7ED **t** 01570 422 619 **f** 01570 422 480 **e** ents@lamp.ac.uk **w** lamp.ac.uk 🖂 Ents Officer: Philip Birch.

Lancaster University (The Sugar House) Student Union, Slaidburn House, Lancaster, LA1 4YT **t** 01524 63508 **f** 01524 846732 **e** a.m.davies@lancaster.ac.uk **w** thesugarhouse.co.uk 🖂 Venue Manager: Louise Davies. Standing capacity: 1200

The Landmark Seafront, Wilder Road, Ilfracombe, Devon, EX34 9BZ **t** 01271 865655 **f** 01271 867707 **e** info@northdevontheatres.org.uk **w** northdevontheatres.org.uk 🖂 Programming Dir: Karen Turner. Seated Capacity: 483

Larkfield Leisure Centre New Hythe Lane, Larkfield, Aylesford, Kent, ME20 6RH **t** 01622 719345 **f** 01622 710822 🖂 Contact: Operations Mgr. Seated Capacity: 600

Live: Venues

The Leadmill 6 Leadmill Rd, Sheffield, Yorkshire, S1 4SE
t 0114 221 2828 **e** rebecca@leadmill.co.uk **w** leadmill.co.uk
🔲 myspace.com/theleadmill 🔲 Live Promoter: Rebecca
Walker 0114 221 2861. Seated Capacity: 500 Standing
capacity: 900

Leas Cliff Hall The Leas, Folkestone, Kent, CT20 2DZ
t 01303 228600 **f** 01303 221175 **e** mail@leascliffhall.co.uk
w leascliffhall.co.uk 🔲 GM: Stephen Levine. Seated
Capacity: 1000 Standing capacity: 1500

Leeds Civic Theatre Cookridge Street, Leeds,
West Yorkshire, LS2 8BH **t** 0113 245 6343 **f** 0113 246 5906
w leeds.gov.uk/tourinfo/theatre Seated Capacity: 521

Leeds Grand Theatre & Opera House
46 New Briggate, Leeds, West Yorkshire, LS1 6NZ
t 0113 245 6014 **f** 0113 246 5906
w leeds.gov.uk/GrandTheatre 🔲 General Mgr: Warren Smith.
Seated Capacity: 1550

Leeds Metropolitan University Student Union,
Calverley Street, Leeds, West Yorkshire, LS1 3HE
t 0113 209 8416 **f** 0113 234 2973 **e** events@lmusu.org.uk
w lmusu.org.uk Seated Capacity: 500 Standing capacity:
1050

Leeds University PO Box 157, Leeds, West Yorkshire,
LS1 1UH **t** 0113 380 1334 **f** 0113 380 1336
e s.w.keeble@leeds.ac.uk **w** leedstickets.com 🔲 Venues
Mgr: Steve Keeble. Standing capacity: 1750

Leicester University Student Union, University Road,
Leicester, LE1 7RH **t** 0116 223 1169 **f** 0116 223 1207
e jk69@le.ac.uk **w** le.ac.uk/su 🔲 Bars & Ents Manager: Jo
Kenning 0116 223 1122. Seated Capacity: 500 Standing
capacity: 1300

Life Cafe 23 Peter St, Manchester, M2 5QR
t 0161 833 3000 **f** 0161 839 4000 **e** Lifecafe-
manchester@luminar.co.uk **w** lifecafe.info
🔲 Promoter: David Potts. Seated Capacity: 950

Lighthouse Pooles' Centre for the Arts, Kingland Rd,
Poole, Dorset, BH15 1UG **t** 01202 665 334
f 01202 670 016 **e** jamesg@lighthousepoole.co.uk
w lighthousepoole.co.uk 🔲 Programmer: James Greenwood.
Seated Capacity: 1463 Standing capacity: 2459

Limelight 17 Ormeau Aveue, Belfast, Co Antrim, BT2 8HD
t 028 9032 5942 **f** 028 9031 3131 **e** info@cdcleisure.com
w thelimelightbelfast.com 🔲 Manager: David Neeley.
Standing capacity: 500

Limelight Theatre Queens Park Centre, Queens Park,
Aylesbury, Buckinghamshire, HP21 7RT **t** 01296 431272
f 01296 337363 **e** qpc@ukonline.co.uk **w** qpc.org 🔲 Artistic
Dir: Amanda Eels 01296 424332. Seated Capacity: 120
Standing capacity: 120

The Little Civic North Street, Wolverhampton,
West Midlands, WV1 1RQ **t** 01902 552122 **f** 01902 713665
Standing capacity: 140

Live At The Suite Ltd Utopia Village, 7 Chalcot Road,
London, NW1 8LH **t** 020 7813 7964 **f** 020 7209 4092
e ladyb@thesuite.sh **w** liveatthesuite.com
🔲 Contact: Andrew, Lady B.

Liverpool Empire Theatre Lime Street, Liverpool,
Merseyside, L1 1JE **t** 0151 708 3200 **f** 0151 709 6757
e firstname.lastname@livenation.co.uk **w** liverpool-
empire.co.uk 🔲 Gen Mgr: Hannah Collins. Seated Capacity:
2370

Liverpool Guild of Students 160 Mount Pleasant,
Liverpool, L3 5TR **t** 0151 794 4143 **f** 0151 794 4174
e firstname.lastname@liv.ac.uk **w** lgos.org 🔲 Venue
Programme Manager: Adam Aggas. Seated Capacity: 700
Standing capacity: 1530

Liverpool Students Union 160 Mount Pleasant,
Liverpool, L69 7BR **t** 0151 794 4116 **f** 0151 794 4174
e guild@liv.ac.uk **w** liverpoolguild.org.uk 🔲 Ents Mgr: Carl
Bathgate 0151 794 4143. Standing capacity: 700

Logan Hall Institute of Education, 20 Bedford Way,
London, WC1H 0AL **t** 020 7612 6401 **f** 020 7612 6402
e s.nazim@ioe.ac.uk **w** ioe.ac.uk 🔲 Conference Office
Mgr: Sittika Nazim. Seated Capacity: 933

London Palladium Argyll Street, London, W1A 3AB
t 020 7494 5020 **f** 020 7437 4010 🔲 Contact: Gareth
Parnell 020 7734 6846. Seated Capacity: 2291

Loose PO Box 67, Runcorn, Cheshire, WA7 4NL
t 01928 566261 **e** jaki.florek@virgin.net 🔲 Manager: Jaki
Florek.

Loreburn Hall Newall Terrace, Dumfries, DG1 1LN
t 01387 260243 **f** 01387 2672255 🔲 Area Mgr, East: John
MacMillan. Seated Capacity: 800 Standing capacity: 1400

Loughborough Student Union, Ashby Road,
Loughborough, Leicestershire, LE11 3TT **t** 01509 632020
f 01509 235593 **e** davehowes@lborosu.org.uk **w** lufbra.net
🔲 Ents Mgr: Dave Howes. Seated Capacity: 400 Standing
capacity: 2500

The Louisiana Bathurst Parade, Wapping Rd, Bristol,
BS1 6UA **t** 0117 926 5978 **w** thelouisiana.net
🔲 Promoter: Michele Schillaci 0117 966 3388. Standing
capacity: 170

The Lowry Pier 8, Salford Quays, Manchester, M50 3AZ
t 0161 876 2020 **f** 0161 876 2021 **e** info@thelowry.com
w thelowry.com Seated Capacity: 218

LSE SU Entertainments LSE SU East Building,
East Building, Houghton Street, London, WC2A 2AE
t 020 7955 7136 **f** 020 7955 6789 **e** su.ents@lse.ac.uk
w lse.ac.uk/union 🔲 Ents Officer: George Ioannou. Seated
Capacity: 440 Standing capacity: 550

LSO St Luke's 161 Old St, London, EC1V 9NG
t 020 7490 3939 **f** 020 7566 2881 **e** lsostlukes@lso.co.uk
w lso.co.uk/lsostlukes 🔲 Centre Director: Simon Wales.
Seated Capacity: 370

The Luminaire 311 Kilburn High Rd, London, NW6 7JR
t 020 7372 7123 **e** andy@theluminaire.co.uk
w theluminaire.co.uk 🔲 Director: Andy Inglis. Standing
capacity: 250

University of Luton Student Union
Europa House, Vicarage Street, Luton, Bedfordshire,
LU1 3JU t 01582 743272 f 01582 457187
e su.entsofficer@luton.ac.uk w ulsu.co.uk ✉ Venue &
Events Manager: Darren Reed. Seated Capacity: 1000
Standing capacity: 1000

Lyric Theatre, Hammersmith King Street, London,
W6 0QL t 020 8741 0824 f 020 8741 7694
e foh@lyric.co.uk w lyric.co.uk ✉ Theatre Mgr: Howard
Meaden. Seated Capacity: 560

Magnum Theatre & Concert Hall
Magnum Leisure Centre, Harbourside, Irvine, North Ayrshire,
KA12 8PP t 01294 316463 f 01294 273172
e tduff@kaleisure.com w kaleisure.com ✉ Duty
Manager: Thomas Duff 01294 317409. Seated Capacity:
1164 Standing capacity: 1700

Manchester Academy & University
Student Union, Oxford Road, Manchester, M13 9PR
t 0161 275 2930 f 0161 275 2936
e maximum@umu.man.ac.uk w umu.man.ac.uk ✉ Events
Manager: Sean Morgan. Standing capacity: 1800

Manchester Apollo Stockport Rd, Ardwick Green,
Manchester, M12 6AP t 0161 273 6921 f 0870 749 0779
e manchester.apollo@livenation.co.uk w LiveNation.co.uk
◼ facebook.com/pages/Manchester/Manchester-
Apollo/36573911309 ◼ twitter.com/mancapollo
◼ youtube.com/ManchesterApollo ✉ GM: Phil Rogers.
Seated Capacity: 2693 Standing capacity: 3500

Manchester Evening News Arena
Victoria Station, Manchester, M3 1AR t 0161 950 5000
f 0161 950 5558 e event.marketing@men-arena.com
w men-arena.com ✉ General Manager: John Knight. Seated
Capacity: 19500

Manchester Met Students' Union
99 Oxford Road, Manchester, M1 7EL t 0161 247 6468
f 0161 247 6314 e s.u.ents@mmu.ac.uk w mmsu.com
✉ Ents Mgr: Ben Casasola. Seated Capacity: 950 Standing
capacity: 1100

Manchester Opera House Quay St, Manchester,
M3 3HP t 0161 828 1700 f 0161 834 5243
e stewart.dornford-may@livenation.co.uk
w palaceandoperahouse.org.uk
◼ facebook.com/PalaceAndOperaHouseManchester
◼ twitter.com/PalaceandOpera
◼ youtube.com/user/PalaceAndOperaHouse ✉ General
Manager: Stewart Dornford-May. Seated Capacity: 1909

Manchester Palace Theatre Oxford Street,
Manchester, M1 6FT t 0161 228 6255 f 0161 237 5746
w manchestertheatres.co.uk ✉ Contact: Rachel Miller.
Seated Capacity: 1996

Mansfield Leisure Centre Chesterfield Road South,
Mansfield, Nottinghamshire, NG19 7BQ t 01623 463800
f 01623 463912 ✉ Mgr: M Darnell. Seated Capacity: 1100
Standing capacity: 1500

Marco's An Aird Fort William, PH33 6AN
t 01397 700707 f 01397 700708 Seated Capacity: 1500
Standing capacity: 2100

Marcus Garvey Centre Lenton Boulevard,
Nottingham, NG7 2BY t 0115 942 0297 f 0115 942 0297
✉ Contact: Mr T Brown.

Margate Winter Gardens Fort Crescent, Margate,
Kent, CT9 1HX t 01843 296111 f 01843 295180 ✉ Ops
Mgr: Mr S Davis. Seated Capacity: 1400 Standing capacity:
1900

Marina Theatre The Marina, Lowestoft, Suffolk,
NR32 1HH t 01502 533200 (Box) f 01502 538179
e info@marinatheatre.co.uk w marinatheatre.co.uk
✉ Venues Mgr: Martin Halliday 01502 533203. Seated
Capacity: 751

Marlowe Theatre The Friars, Canterbury, Kent, CT1 2AS
t 01227 763262 f 01227 781802
e mark.everett@canterbury.gov.uk w marlowetheatre.com
✉ Theatre Dir: Mark Everett. Seated Capacity: 993

Maryport Civic Hall Lower Church Street, Maryport,
Cumbria t 01900 812652 ✉ Mgr: Margaret Craig. Seated
Capacity: 400 Standing capacity: 600

Mayfield Leisure Centre 10 Mayfield Place, Mayfield,
Dalkeith, Midlothian, EH22 5JG t 0131 663 2219
f 0131 660 9539 ✉ Contact: Area Leisure Mgr. Seated
Capacity: 400 Standing capacity: 600

The Mayflower Commercial Road, Southampton,
Hampshire, S015 1GE t 023 8071 1800 f 023 8071 1801
e Dennis.hall@mayflower.org.uk w the-mayflower.com
✉ Chief Executive: Dennis Hall. Seated Capacity: 2406

Medina Theatre Mountbatten Centre, Fairlee Road,
Newport, Isle of Wight, PO30 2DX t 01983 527020
f 01983 822821 ✉ Contact: Paul Broome. Seated Capacity:
425

Mercury Theatre Balkerne Gate, Colchester, Essex,
CO1 1PT t 01206 577 006 f 01206 769 607
e info@mercurytheatre.co.uk w mercurytheatre.co.uk
✉ Administration Services Manager: Tom Lagden. Seated
Capacity: 496

The Met Arts Centre Market St, Bury, Lancashire,
BL9 0BW t 0161 761 7107 e post@themet.biz
w themet.biz ✉ Dir: David Agnew. Seated Capacity: 230
Standing capacity: 300

Metro Radio Arena Arena Way, Newcastle upon Tyne,
NE4 7NA t 0844 493 4567 w metroradioarena.co.uk
◼ twitter.com/ArenaNewcastle Seated Capacity: 9700
Standing capacity: 11321

The Metropole Galleries The Metropole Galleries,
The Leas, Folkestone, Kent, CT20 2LS t 01303 255070
f 01303 851353 e info@metropole.org.uk
w mertopole.org.uk ✉ Dir: Nick Ewbank. Seated Capacity:
140 Standing capacity: 200

Middlesbrough Town Hall PO Box 69, Albert Road,
Middlesbrough, Cleveland, TS1 1EL t 01642 263848
f 01642 221866 ✉ Bookings Mgr: Jean Hewitt 01642
263850. Seated Capacity: 1190 Standing capacity: 1352

indigO₂ The entertainment venue at The O₂ www.theo2.co.uk/indigo2
BOOKINGS ENQUIRIES: Laurie Pegg 020 8463 2707 | lpegg@theindigo2.com

Middlesex University Student Union, Bramley Road, London, N14 4YZ **t** 020 8411 6450 **f** 020 8440 5944 **e** d.medawar@mdx.ac.uk **w** musu.mdx.ac.uk 🖃 VP Ents: David Medawar. Seated Capacity: 400 Standing capacity: 850

Middleton Civic Hall Fountain Street, Middleton, Manchester, M24 1AF **t** 0161 643 2470 **f** 0161 654 0221 🖃 Contact: 0161 643 2389. Seated Capacity: 565 Standing capacity: 750

Milton Keynes College Chaffron Way, Leadenhall, Milton Keynes, MK6 5LP **t** 01908 230797 **f** 01908 684399 Standing capacity: 250

Ministry of Sound 103 Gaunt Street, London, SE1 6DP **t** 020 7378 6528 **f** 020 7403 5348 **e** arnie@ministryofsound.com **w** ministryofsound.com 🖃 General Manager: Gary Smart. Standing capacity: 1500

Mitchell Theatre Exchange House, 229 George Street, Glasgow, Lanarkshire, G1 1QU **t** 0141 287 4855 **f** 0141 221 0695 Seated Capacity: 418

Moles Club 14 George Street, Bath, BA1 2EN **t** 01225 404445 **f** 01225 404447 **e** kath@moles.co.uk **w** moles.co.uk 🖃 Bookings Mgr: Kath O'Connor. Standing capacity: 200

The Monarch 40-42 Chalk Farm Rd, London, NW1 8BG **e** info@monarchbar.com **w** monarchbar.com 🖃 Contact: Adie Nunn, Jeremy Ledlin 020 7482 2054.

Monroes Bar Carnegie Theatre, Finkle St, Workington, Cumbria, CA14 2BD **t** 01900 602122 **e** paul.sherwin@allerdale.gov.uk **w** monroesbar.co.uk 🖃 Mgr: Paul Sherwin. Standing capacity: 200

Morfa Stadium Upper Bank, Pentrechwyth, Swansea, SA1 7DF **t** 01792 476578 **f** 01792 467995

Mote Hall Maidstone Leisure Centre, Mote Park, Maidstone, Kent, ME15 7RN **t** 01622 220234 **f** 01622 672462 🖃 Events Mgr: Barry Reynolds. Seated Capacity: 1200 Standing capacity: 1080

Motherwell Concert Hall & Theatre PO Box 14, Civic Centre, Motherwell, Lanarkshire, ML1 1TW **t** 01698 267515 **f** 01698 268806 🖃 Contact: Theatre Mgr. Seated Capacity: 883 Standing capacity: 1800

Motherwell Theatre, Civic Centre PO Box 14, Motherwell, North Lanarkshire, ML1 1TW **t** 01698 267515 **f** 01698 268806 🖃 Theatre Mgr: Lynn McDougal. Seated Capacity: 395

The Musician Clyde Street, Leicester, LE1 2DE **t** 0116 251 0080 **f** 0116 251 0474 **e** rideout@stayfree.co.uk **w** themusicianpub.co.uk 🖃 Booker/Mgr: Darren Nockles. Seated Capacity: 120 Standing capacity: 220

Napier Student Association 12 Merchiston Place, Edinburgh, EH10 4NR **t** 0131 229 8791 **f** 0131 228 3462 **e** e.reynolds@napier.ac.uk **w** napierstudents.com 🖃 Contact: Ents Officer. Standing capacity: 100

The National Bowl at Milton Keynes c/o BS Group plc, Abbey Stadium, Lady Lane, Swindon, Wiltshire, SW2 4DW **t** 0117 952 0600 **f** 0117 952 5500 🖃 Contact: Gordon Cockhill. Standing capacity: 65000

National Club 234 Kilburn High Road, London, NW6 4JR **t** 020 7625 4444 🖃 Contact: PJ Carey 020 7328 3141. Standing capacity: 1200

The National Indoor Arena King Edward's Rd, Birmingham, West Midlands, B1 2AA **t** 0121 780 4141 **e** nia-sales@necgroup.co.uk **w** necgroup.co.uk 🖃 MD, Arenas: Phil Mead. Seated Capacity: 8000 Standing capacity: 12000

NEC Arena The NEC, Birmingham, West Midlands, B40 1NT **t** 0121 767 3981 **e** phil.mead@necgroup.co.uk **w** necgroup.co.uk 🖃 MD: Phil Mead. Seated Capacity: 16000

The Nerve Centre 7-8 Magazine St, Londonderry, BT48 6HJ **t** 028 7126 0562 **f** 028 7137 1738 **e** info@nerve-create.org.uk **w** nerve-create.org.uk 🖃 Promoter: Tony Doherty. Standing capacity: 600

New Roadmender 1 Ladys Lane, Northampton, Northamptonshire, NN1 3AH **t** 01604 230638 **w** newroadmender.com Seated Capacity: 300 Standing capacity: 900

New Theatre George St, Oxford, OX1 2AG **t** 01865 320760 **f** 08707 490836 **e** jamie.baskeyfield@livenation.co.uk **w** newtheatreoxford.org.uk 🔲 facebook.com/oxfordtheatres 🔲 twitter.com/oxfordtheatres 🔲 youtube.com/newtheatreoxford 🖃 Theatre Manager: Jamie Baskeyfield. Seated Capacity: 1826

New Theatre Royal Guildhall Walk, Portsmouth, Hampshire, PO1 2DD **t** 01705 646477 **f** 01705 646488 🖃 Contact: Fiona Cole 01705 649000. Seated Capacity: 320 Standing capacity: 450

New Theatre, Cardiff Park Place, Cardiff, CF10 3LN **t** 029 2087 8787 **f** 029 2087 8788 🖃 Contact: Giles Ballisat 029 2087 8889. Seated Capacity: 1156

New Victoria Theatre Woking, Surrey **t** 01483 761144

New Wimbledon Theatre 93 The Broadway, London, SW19 1QG **t** 020 8545 7900 **f** 020 8543 6637 **e** sambain@theambassadors.com **w** ambassadortickets.com/wimbledon 🖃 Administration & Events Manager: Sam Bain. Seated Capacity: 1700

Newcastle City Hall Northumberland Road, Newcastle upon Tyne, Tyne and Wear, NE1 8SF **t** 0191 222 1778 **f** 0191 261 8102 🖃 Mgr: Peter Brennan 0191 261 2606. Seated Capacity: 2133

Newcastle University Union Student Union, Kings Walk, Newcastle upon Tyne, Tyne & Wear, NE1 8QB **t** 0191 239 3926 **f** 0191 222 1876 **e** union-entertainments@ncl.ac.uk **w** unionsociety.co.uk/ents 🖃 Entertainments Manager: Davey Bruce. Standing capacity: 1200

Newham Leisure Centre 281 Prince Regent Lane, London, E13 8SD **t** 020 7511 4477 **f** 020 7511 6463

Live: Venues

Newman College Of Education Student Union, Genners Lane, Bartley Green, Birmingham, B32 3NT **t** 0121 475 6714 **f** 0121 475 6714 **e** ncsu@newman.ac.uk ☏ Contact: Louise Beasley. Seated Capacity: 160 Standing capacity: 300

Newport Centre Kingsway, Newport, Gwent, NP20 1UH **t** 01633 662663 **f** 01633 662675 ☏ Events Mgr: Roger Broome. Seated Capacity: 2000 Standing capacity: 1600

Nice 'n' Sleazy 421 Sauchiehall Street, Glasgow, Lanarkshire, G2 3LG **t** 0141 333 9637 **f** 0141 333 0900 **e** sleazys@hotmail.com **w** nicensleazy.com ☏ Promoter: Mig 0141 333 0900. Standing capacity: 200

Night & Day Cafe 26 Oldham St, Northern Quarter, Manchester, M1 1JN **t** 0161 236 4597 **f** 0161 236 1822 **e** ben@nightnday.org **w** nightnday.org ☏ Promoter/Manager: Ben Taylor. Standing capacity: 250

North Devon Theatres Queen's Theatre, Boutport St, Barnstaple, Devon, EX31 1SY **t** 01271 327357 **f** 01271 326412 **e** info@northdevontheatres.org.uk **w** northdevontheatres.org.uk ☏ Colin May: Programming Director 01271 865655. Seated Capacity: 688

North Wales Theatre And Conference Centre The Promenade, Llandudno, Conwy, LL30 1BB **t** 01492 872000 **e** admin@nwtheatre.co.uk **w** nwtheatre.co.uk ☏ GM: Sarah Ecob. Seated Capacity: 1500 Standing capacity: 1100

North Worcestershire College Student Union, Burcot Lane, Bromsgrove, Worcestershire, B60 1PQ **t** 01527 570020 **f** 01527 572900

Northgate Arena Victoria Road, Chester, CH2 2AU **t** 01244 377086 **f** 01244 381693 **e** cadsart@compuserve.com **w** northgatearena.com ☏ Business Development Mgr: Jon Kelly. Seated Capacity: 800 Standing capacity: 1800

Northumbria University Union Building, 2 Sandyford Road, Newcastle upon Tyne, NE1 8SB **t** 0191 227 3791 **f** 0191 227 3776 **e** s.collier@unn.ac.uk ☏ Ents Mgr: Sue Collier. Standing capacity: 1680

Norwich Arts Centre Reeves Yard, St Benedicts, Norfolk, NR2 4PG **t** 01603 660387 **f** 01603 660352 ☏ Centre Mgr: Pam Reekie. Seated Capacity: 120 Standing capacity: 250

Norwich City Hall St Peters Street, Norwich, Norfolk, NR2 1NH **t** 01603 622233 **f** 01603 213000

Notting Hill Arts Club 21 Notting Hill Gate, London, W11 3JQ **t** 020 7460 4459 **e** david@nottinghillartsclub.com Standing capacity: 218

Nottingham Albert Hall North Circus Street, Off Derby Road, Nottinghamshire, NG1 5AA **t** 0115 950 0411 **f** 0115 947 6512 ☏ Events Mgr: Sarah Robinson. Seated Capacity: 900

Nottingham Arena At the National Ice Centre, Bolero Sq, The Lace Market, Nottingham, NG1 1LA **t** 0115 853 3011 **f** 0115 853 3066 **e** firstname.lastname@nottingham-arena.com **w** trentfmarenanottingham.com Seated Capacity: 10000

Nottingham Trent University Student Union, Byron House, Shakespeare Street, Nottingham, NG1 4GH **t** 0115 848 6209 **f** 0115 848 6201 **e** ents@su.ntu.ac.uk **w** trentstudents.org ☏ Ents Manager: Rebecca Ebbs. Standing capacity: 640

University of Nottingham Student Union, Portland Building, University Park, Nottingham, NG7 2RD **t** 0115 935 1100 ☏ Social Sec: Tanya Nathan. Seated Capacity: 200

Number10 10 Golborne Road, London, W10 5PE **t** 020 8969 8922 **f** 020 8969 8933 **e** tris@number10london.com **w** number10london.com ☏ Events Co-ordinator: Tris Dickin.

The O2 Arena Peninsula Square, London, SE10 0DX **t** 020 8463 2000 **e** sales@theo2.co.uk **w** theo2.co.uk ☏ Head of Sales - The O2: Caroline McNamara. Seated Capacity: 20000

O2 ABC Glasgow 300 Sauchiehall Street, Glasgow, G2 3JA **t** 0141 332 2232 **e** mig@abcglasgow.com or mig@o2abcglasgow.co.uk **w** o2abcglasgow.co.uk 🇫 facebook.com/o2abcglasgow 🇹 twitter.com/O2ABC ☏ Promotions Manager: Mig 0141 352 4569. Standing capacity: 1550

O2 Academy Islington N1 Centre, 16 Parkfield St, London, N1 0PS **t** 020 7288 4400 **f** 020 7288 4401 **e** pernilla@o2academyislington.co.uk **w** o2academyislington.co.uk 🇫 facebook.com/o2academyislington?ref=mf ☏ General Manager: Pernilla Holl. Standing capacity: 250

O2 Academy Bournemouth 570 Christchurch Rd, Bournemouth, Dorset, BH1 4BH **t** 01202 399 922 **f** 01202 646 519 **e** Ester@o2academybournemouth.co.uk **w** o2academybournemouth.co.uk ☏ GM: Ester Gill 01202 399922. Seated Capacity: 1925

O2 Academy Bristol Frogmore St, Bristol, BS1 5NA **t** 0117 927 9227 **f** 0117 927 9295 **w** o2academybristol.co.uk 🇫 facebook.com/o2academybristol 🇹 twitter.com/o2academybristo Standing capacity: 350

O2 Academy Brixton 211 Stockwell Rd, Brixton, London, SW9 9SL **t** 020 7771 3000 **f** 020 7738 4427 **e** mail@o2academybrixton.co.uk **w** O2academybrixton.co.uk ☏ Gen Mgr: Nigel Downs. Standing capacity: 4921

O2 Academy Liverpool 11-13 Hotham St, Liverpool, L3 5UF **t** 0151 707 3200 **f** 0151 707 3201 **w** o2academyliverpool.co.uk 🇫 facebook.com/o2academyliverpool 🇹 http://twitter.com/o2academylpool Seated Capacity: 250 Standing capacity: 500

O2 Academy Newcastle Westgate Rd, Newcastle,
NE1 1SW t 0191 260 2020 f 0191 260 4650
e mail@o2academynewcastle.co.uk
w o2academynewcastle.co.uk ✉ GM: Paul Twynham.
Standing capacity: 397

O2 Academy Oxford 190 Cowley Road, Oxford,
OX4 1UE t 01895 420042 f 01895 420045
w o2academyoxford.co.uk
🅵 facebook.com/o2academyoxford
🅃 twitter.com/O2AcademyOxford Standing capacity: 1350

O2 Shepherd's Bush Empire
Shepherds Bush Green, London, W12 8TT t 020 8354 3300
f 020 8743 3218 e mail@O2shepherdsbushempire.co.uk
w O2shepherdsbushempire.co.uk
🅵 facebook.com/o2shepherdsbushempire
🅃 twitter.com/o2sbe ✉ GM: Bill Marshall. Seated Capacity:
1278 Standing capacity: 2000

The O2, Dublin East Link Bridge, Dublin 1, Ireland
t 00 353 1 819 8888 w theo2.ie ✉ Gen Mgr: Cormac
Rennick. Seated Capacity: 6500 Standing capacity: 8500

Oakengates Theatre Lines Walk, Oakengates, Telford,
Shropshire, TF2 6EP t 01952 619020 f 01552 610164
e oakthea@telford.gov.uk w oakengates.ws ✉ Theatre
Mgr: Psyche Hudson. Seated Capacity: 650 Standing
capacity: 780

Ocean 270 Mare St, Hackney, London, E8 1HE
t 020 8986 2327 e brian.comcannon@hackney.gov.uk
✉ Venue Manager: Brian Comcannon. Seated Capacity:
2100 Standing capacity: 900

Octagon Theatre Howell Croft South, Bolton,
Lancashire, BL1 1SB t 01204 529407 f 01204 380110
✉ Contact: The Administrator 01204 520661. Seated
Capacity: 420

Odyssey Arena 2 Queen's Quay, Belfast, BT3 9QQ
t 028 9076 6000 f 028 9076 6111
e info@odysseyarena.com w odysseyarena.com ✉ Chief
Executive: Nicky Dunn 028 90766000. Seated Capacity:
9500 Standing capacity: 10000

The Old Institute 9 The Strand, Derby, DE1 1BJ
t 01332 381770 f 01332 381745
e paulneedham7@btopenworld.com ✉ GM/Promoter: Paul
Needham. Standing capacity: 500

The Old Market Upper Market St, Hove, E. Sussex,
BN3 1AS t 01273 736 222 f 01273 329 636
e carolinebrown@theoldmarket.co.uk w theoldmarket.co.uk
✉ Artistic Dir: Caroline Brown. Seated Capacity: 300
Standing capacity: 500

The Old Town Hall High St, Old Town,
Hemel Hempstead, Herts, HP1 3AE t 01442 228098
f 01442 234072 e barbara.cunningham@dacorum.gov.uk
w oldtownhall.co.uk ✉ Marketing & Publicity
Officer: Barbara Cunningham. Seated Capacity: 120

The Orchard Theatre Home Gardens, Dartford, Kent,
DA1 1ED t 01322 220099 f 01322 227122
e vanessa.hart@dartford.gov.uk w orchardtheatre.co.uk
✉ Theate Mgr: Vanessa Hart. Seated Capacity: 950

Ormond Multi Media Centre
14 Lower Ormond Quay, Dublin 1, Ireland t +353 1 872 3500
f +353 1 872 3348

The Overdraft 300-310 High Road, Ilford, Essex,
IG1 1QW t 020 8514 4400

Oxford University Student Union
New Barnet House, Little Clarendon Street, Oxford,
OX1 2HU t 01865 270777 f 01865 270776
e president@ousu.org w ousu.org ✉ President: Ruth Hunt
01865 270769.

Paisley Arts Centre New Street, Paisley, Renfrewshire,
PA1 1EZ t 0141 887 1010 f 0141 887 6300
e artsinfo@renfrewshire.gov.uk ✉ Principle Arts
Officer: John Harding. Seated Capacity: 158

University of Paisley - Ayr Campus
Student Association, Beech Grove, Ayr, KA8 0SR
t 01292 886330 office f 01292 886271
e dpa@upsa.org.uk ✉ Deputy President: Kim Macintyre
01292 886362 union. Seated Capacity: 100 Standing
capacity: 200

Paradise Bar 460 New Cross Road, London, SE14 6TJ
t 020 8692 1530 f 020 8691 0445 w paradisebar.co.uk
✉ Contact: David Roberts. Standing capacity: 300

The Paradise Room Blackpool Pleasure Peach,
Ocean Boulevard, Blackpool, Lancashire, FY4 1EZ
t 01253 341033 f 01253 407609
e debbie.hawksey@bpbltd.com w bpbltd.com
✉ Contact: Debbie Hawksey. Seated Capacity: 600
Standing capacity: 750

Parr Hall Palmyra Square South, Warrington, Cheshire,
WA1 1BL t 01925 442345 f 01925 443228
e parrhall@warrington.gov.uk w parrhall.co.uk ✉ Arts &
Project Mgr: John Perry. Seated Capacity: 1000 Standing
capacity: 1100

Pavilion Argyle Street, Rothesay, Isle Of Bute
t 01546 602127 f 01700 504225 ✉ Contact: 01700
504250 mgr. Seated Capacity: 4100 Standing capacity:
5250

Pavilion Theatre Marine Parade, Worthing,
West Sussex, BN11 3PX t 01903 231799 f 01903 215337
e theatres@worthing.gov.uk w worthingtheatres.co.uk
✉ Theatres Manager: Peter Bailey. Seated Capacity: 867
Standing capacity: 1100

Peacock Arts And Entertainment Centre
Victoria Way, Woking, Surrey, GU21 1GQ t 01483 747422
f 01483 770477 Standing capacity: 500

The Penny 30-31 Northgate, Canterbury, Kent, CT1 1BL
t 01227 450333 f 01227 450333 ✉ Contact: Ian Mills
01227 470512. Seated Capacity: 100 Standing capacity:
200

Philharmonic Hall Liverpool Philharmonic Hall, Hope St, Liverpool, Merseyside, L1 9BP **t** 0151 709 3789 **f** 0151 210 2902 **e** hall@liverpoolphil.com **w** liverpoolphil.com ⓕ facebook.com/profile.php?id=560691598&ref=name#/liverpoolphil 🅜 myspace.com/philharmonichall 🅣 twitter.com/liverpoolphil 🅨 youtube.com/user/LiverpoolPhilHall 🅑 Executive Director: Simon Glinn 0151 210 2895. Seated Capacity: 1682

The Platform Old Station Buildings, Central Promenade, Morecambe, Lancashire, LA4 4DB **t** 01524 582801 **f** 01524 831704 **e** Jharris@lancaster.gov.uk **w** lancaster.gov.uk 🅑 Head of Arts and Events: Jon Harris. Seated Capacity: 350 Standing capacity: 1000

Playhouse Theatre High St, Weston-Super-Mare, Somerset, BS23 1HP **t** 01934 645544 (Box Office) **e** firstname.lastname@n-somerset.gov.uk **w** theplayhouse.co.uk 🅑 Promotions & Publicity: Paul Travers 01934 427277 / 427209 (Admin). Seated Capacity: 664

The Plug 14-16 Matilda St, Sheffield, South Yorkshire, S1 4QD **t** 0114 241 3040 **f** 0114 272 9879 **e** info@the-plug.com **w** the-plug.com 🅑 Bookings: Matt Hammond. Standing capacity: 1200

Plymouth College Of Art & Design Student Union, Tavistock Place, Plymouth, Devon, PL4 8AT **t** 01752 203434 **f** 01752 203444

Plymouth Pavilions Millbay Rd, Plymouth, Devon, PL1 3LF **t** 0845 146 1460 **f** 01752 262226 **e** enquiries@plymouthpavilions.com **w** plymouthpavilions.com 🅑 Marketing/Press Officer: Robert Maltby 01752 522212. Seated Capacity: 2400 Standing capacity: 4000

Plymouth University Student Union, Drake Circus, Plymouth, Devon, PL4 8AA **t** 01752 663337 **f** 01752 251669 🅑 Contact: Mark Witherall. Standing capacity: 600

The Point The Plain, Oxford, OX4 1EA **t** 01865 798794 **f** 01865 798794 **e** mac@thepoint.oxfordmusic.net **w** thepoint.oxfordmusic.net 🅑 Promoter: Mac. Seated Capacity: 220 Standing capacity: 220

The Pop Factory Welsh Hills Works, Jenkin St, Porth, CF39 9PP **t** 01443 688500 **f** 01443 688501 **e** info@thepopfactory.com **w** thepopfactory.com 🅑 Contact: Mair Afan Davies 01443 688504. Standing capacity: 300

The Porter Cellar Bar 15 George St, Bath, BA1 2QS **t** 01225 424104 **f** 01225 404447 **e** steve@moles.co.uk **w** moles.co.uk 🅑 Booker: Steve Wheadon. Seated Capacity: 150 Standing capacity: 150

Portobello Town Hall 147 Portobello High Street, Edinburgh, Lothian, EH15 1AF **t** 0131 669 5800 **f** 0131 669 5800 🅑 Hall Keeper: Andrew Crazy. Seated Capacity: 771

Portsmouth Guildhall Guildhall Square, Portsmouth, Hampshire, PO1 2AB **t** 01705 834146 **f** 01705 834177 🅑 Gen Mgr: Martin Dodd. Seated Capacity: 2017 Standing capacity: 2228

Portsmouth University The Student Centre, Cambridge Rd, Portsmouth, Hampshire, PO1 2EF **t** 02392 843640 **f** 02392 843667 **e** janet.hillier@port.ac.uk **w** upsu.net 🅑 Trad Op's Exec: Janet Hillier. Standing capacity: 450

Pressure Point 33 Richmond Place, Brighton, BN2 9NA **t** 01273 684 501 **e** gareth@pressurepoint.me.uk **w** pressurepoint.me.uk 🅑 Bookings Mgr: Simon Parker. Standing capacity: 210

Prince of Wales Theatre Coventry Street, London, W1V 8AS **t** 020 7930 9901 **f** 020 7976 1336 🅑 Contact: George Biggs. Seated Capacity: 1100 Standing capacity: 100

Princes Hall Princes Way, Aldershot, Hampshire, GU11 1NX **t** 01252 327671 **f** 01252 320269 **w** rushmoor.gov.uk/princes/index.htm 🅑 Gen Mgr: Steven Pugh. Seated Capacity: 700 Standing capacity: 700

Princes Theatre Station Road, Clacton-on-Sea, Essex, CO15 1SE **t** 01255 253208 **f** 01255 253200 **e** rfoster@tendringdc.gov.uk **w** tendringdc.gov.uk 🅑 Ents Officer: Bob Foster. Seated Capacity: 820 Standing capacity: 800

Princess Pavilion Theatre & Gyllyndune Gardens 41 Melvill Road, Falmouth, Cornwall, TR11 4AR **t** 01326 311277 **f** 01326 315382 🅑 Contact: Mr RHD Phipps 01326 211222. Seated Capacity: 400 Standing capacity: 400

Princess Theatre Torbay Road, Torquay, Devon, TQ2 5EZ **t** 01803 290288 **f** 01803 290170 🅑 Gen Mgr: Wendy Bennett 01803 290290 (BO). Seated Capacity: 1487

Purcell Room Queen Elizabeth Hall, South Bank Centre, Belvedere Rd, London, SE1 8XX **t** 020 7960 4200 **e** customer@southbankcentre.co.uk **w** southbankcentre.co.uk 🅑 Contact: Switch Board. Seated Capacity: 367

Purple Turtle 9 Gunn Street, Reading, Berkshire, RG1 2JR **t** 0118 959 7196 **f** 0118 958 3142 **e** andy@purpleturtlebar.com **w** purpleturtlebar.com 🅑 Bookings Manager: Andy Churchill. Standing capacity: 470

Q Magazine Mappin House, 4 Winsley St, London, W1W 8HF **t** 020 7182 8482 **f** 020 7182 8547 **e** firstname.lastname@qthemusic.com **w** qthemusic.com 🅑 Editor in chief: Paul Rees.

Quay Arts Centre Sea Street, Newport Harbour, Isle Of Wight, PO30 5BD **t** 01983 822490 **f** 01938 526606 **e** info@quayarts.org **w** quayarts.org 🅑 Dir/Programming: Stephen Munn. Seated Capacity: 134

Queen Elizabeth Hall Belvedere Rd, London, SE1 8XX
t 020 7960 4200
e firstname.lastname@southbankcentre.co.uk
w southbankcentre.co.uk
f facebook.com/southbankcentre
t twitter.com/Southbankcentre 🎫 Hd of Hall
Program'g: Pam Chowhan. Seated Capacity: 902

Queen Elizabeth Hall West Street, Oldham,
Lancashire, OL1 1UT **t** 0161 911 4071 **f** 0161 911 3094
🎫 Admin Mgr: Shelagh Malley. Seated Capacity: 1300
Standing capacity: 2000

*The Students' Union Queen Margaret
University, Edinburgh* The Student's Union,
Queen Margaret University Drive, Edinburgh, EH21 6UU
t 0131 474 0000 **f** 0131 474 0001 **e** union@qmu.ac.uk
w qmusu.org.uk **t** twitter.com/qmusu 🎫 Membership
Services Coordinator: Ed Blackburn. Seated Capacity: 300
Standing capacity: 400

Queen's Hall Arts Centre Beaumont Street,
Hexham, Northumberland, NE46 3LS **t** 01434 606787
f 01434 606043 🎫 Arts Mgr: Geoff Keys 01434 607272.
Seated Capacity: 399

The Queens Hall Edinburgh Clerk Street, Edinburgh,
Lothian, EH8 9JG **t** 0131 668 3456 **f** 0131 668 2656 🎫 Hall
Mgr: Iain McQueen. Seated Capacity: 868 Standing capacity:
900

Queens University Students Union, 79-
81 University Road, Belfast, Co Antrim, BT7 1PE
t 028 9032 4803 **f** 028 9023 6900 **e** info@qubsu-ents.com
w qubsu-ents.com Standing capacity: 800

Queensway Hall Vernon Place, Dunstable,
Bedfordshire, LU5 4EU **t** 01582 603326 **f** 01582 471190
🎫 Gen Mgr: Yvonne Mullens. Seated Capacity: 900 Standing
capacity: 1200

Reading University PO Box 230, Whiteknights,
Reading, Berkshire, RG6 2AZ **t** 0118 986 0222
f 0118 975 5283 Standing capacity: 1400

The Red Brick Theatre Aqueduct Road, Blackburn,
Lancashire, BB2 4HT **t** 01254 698859 **f** 01254 265640
🎫 Contact: Miss C Kay 01254 265566. Seated Capacity:
380

Redditch Palace Theatre Alcester Street, Redditch,
Worcestershire, B98 8AE **t** 01527 61544 **f** 01527 60243
🎫 Bookings Mgr: Michael Dyer 01527 65203. Seated
Capacity: 399

Relentless Garage 20-22 Highbury Corner, London,
N5 1RD **t** 020 7619 6727 and 020 7619 6728
e boxoffice@relentlessgarage.co.uk **w** thegarage.co.uk
f facebook.com/pages/London-United-
Kingdom/Relentless-Garage/105978362370
t twitter.com/GarageLondon Standing capacity: 500

The Rex 361 Stratford High Street, London, E15 4QZ
t 020 8215 6003 **f** 020 8215 6004 **w** meanfiddler.com

The Rhythm Station Station House, Station Court,
Newhallhey Road, Rawtenstall, Rossendale, Lancashire,
BB4 6AJ **t** 01706 214039 Standing capacity: 800

Richmond Theatre The Green, Richmond, Surrey,
TW9 1QJ **t** 020 8940 0220 **f** 020 8948 3601 🎫 Theatre
Dir: Karin Gartzke. Seated Capacity: 840

The Richmond 10 Fisher Street, Carlisle, Cumbria,
CA3 8R **t** 01228 512220 **f** 01228 534168
e Rvenue@aol.com **w** jnightclub.co.uk
🎫 Promoter/Owner: David Jackson. Standing capacity: 325

Rio's Leeds The Grand Arcade, 9 Merrion Street, Leeds,
LS1 6PQ **t** 0844 414 2182 **f** 0844 414 2183 **e** steve@rios-
leeds.com **w** rios-leeds.com 🎫 Events Manager: Steve
Hawthorn. Standing capacity: 1000

The Ritz Ballroom Whitworth Street West,
Manchester, M1 5NQ **t** 0161 236 4355 **f** 0161 236 7515
e eddieritz@hotmail.com 🎫 GM: Eddie Challiner. Standing
capacity: 1500

Riverside Studios Crisp Road, Hammersmith, London,
W6 9RL **t** 020 8237 1000 **f** 020 8237 1011
e jonfawcett@riversidestudios.co.uk
w riversidestudios.co.uk 🎫 Hires Mgr: Jon Fawcett. Seated
Capacity: 500 Standing capacity: 500

The Roadhouse 8 Newton St, Piccadilly, Manchester,
M1 2AN **t** 0161 237 9789 **f** 0161 236 9289
e kris@theroadhouselive.co.uk **w** theroadhouselive.co.uk
🎫 Promoters: Jon Green/Lucy Hunt 0161 228 1789.
Standing capacity: 350

The Robin 2 26-28 Mount Pleasant, Bilston,
Wolverhampton, West Midlands, WV14 7LJ
t 01902 405 511 **f** 01902 401 418 **e** music@therobin.co.uk
w therobin.co.uk 🎫 Director: Mike Hamblett 01902 401
211. Standing capacity: 700

Rock City 8 Talbot St, Nottingham, NG1 5GG
t 0871 3100 000 **f** 0115 9418 438 **e** boxoffice@rock-
city.co.uk **w** rock-city.co.uk
f facebook.com/group.php?gid=15923779162
🟦 myspace.com/nottinghamrockcity
t twitter.com/Rock_City_Notts Standing capacity: 2450

The Rock Garden/Gardening Club
Bedford Chambers, The Piazza, Covent Garden, London,
WC2E 8HA **t** 07779 582 927 **f** 020 7379 4793
e info@platformmusic.net **w** rockgarden.co.uk 🎫 Platform
Promoter: Lisa Cowan. Standing capacity: 250

The Rocket Complex 166-220 Holloway Rd, London,
N7 8DB **t** 020 7133 2238 **e** info.rocket@londonmet.ac.uk
w rocket-complex.net 🎫 Event Mgr: Geoff Barnett.
Standing capacity: 1200

Ronnie Scott's 47 Frith St, London, W1D 4HT
t 020 7439 0747 **f** 020 7437 5081
e ronniescotts@ronniescotts.co.uk **w** ronniescotts.co.uk
🎫 Marketing Director: Caroline Bolland. Seated Capacity:
300 Standing capacity: 100

Rotherham Civic Theatre Catherine Street,
Rotherham, South Yorkshire, S65 1EB **t** 01709 823640
f 01709 823638 Seated Capacity: 357

Rothes Halls The Kingdom Centre, Glenrothes, Fife, KY7 5NX **t** 01592 612121 **f** 01592 612220 **e** admin@rotheshalls.org.uk **w** rotheshalls.org.uk 📧 Halls Mgr: Frank Chinn 01592 611101 (box). Seated Capacity: 616 Standing capacity: 1400

Roundhouse Chalk Farm Rd, London, NW1 8EH **t** 020 7424 9991 **f** 020 7424 9992 **e** info@roundhouse.org.uk **w** roundhouse.org.uk 📧 Marketing and PR Officer: Nadia Syed. Standing capacity: 3000

Royal Albert Hall Kensington Gore, London, SW7 2AP **t** 020 7589 3203 **f** 020 7823 7725 **e** jsilvester@royalalberthall.com **w** royalalberthall.com 📘 facebook.com/home.php?#/pages/London-United-Kingdom/Royal-Albert-Hall/36132613726?ref=nf 📧 Marketing Manager: Jessica Silvester. Seated Capacity: 5266

Royal Centre Theatre Sq, Nottingham, NG1 5ND **t** 0115 989 5500 **f** 0115 947 4218 **e** enquiry@royalcentre-nottingham.co.uk **w** royalcentre-nottingham.co.uk 📘 facebook.com/business/dashboard/#/pages/Nottingham-United-Kingdom/The-Royal-Centre/87350812002?v=wall 📧 MD: Robert Sanderson 0115 9895500. Seated Capacity: 2499

Royal Court Theatre 1 Roe Street, Liverpool, Merseyside, L1 1HL **t** 0151 709 1808 **f** 0151 709 7611 **e** Richard.Maides@iclway.co.uk **w** royalcourttheatre.net 📧 Theatre Manager: Richard Maides 0151 709 4321. Seated Capacity: 1525 Standing capacity: 1796

Royal Court Theatre Sloane Sq, London, SW1W 8AS **t** 020 7565 5050 **f** 020 7565 5001 **e** info@royalcourttheatre.com **w** royalcourttheatre.com 📧 Theatre Manager: Bobbie Stokes. Seated Capacity: 396

Royal Exchange Theatre St Ann's Square, Manchester, M2 7DH **t** 0161 833 9333 **f** 0161 832 0881 **e** functions@royalexchange.co.uk **w** royalexchange.co.uk Seated Capacity: 700

Royal Festival Hall Belvedere Rd, London, SE1 8XX **t** 020 7960 4200 **e** lastname.firstname@southbankcentre.co.uk **w** southbankcentre.co.uk 📘 facebook.com/southbankcentre 🐦 twitter.com/Southbankcentre 📧 Head of Music: Marshall Marcus. Seated Capacity: 2900

Royal Highland Centre Ingliston, Edinburgh, EH28 8NF **t** 0131 335 6200 **f** 0131 333 5236 **e** info@rhass.org.uk **w** royalhighlandcentre.com 📧 Dir: Grant Knight.

Royal Lyceum Theatre Grindlay Street, Edinburgh, EH3 9AX **t** 0131 248 4800 **f** 0131 228 3955 **e** info@lyceum.org.uk **w** lyceum.org.uk 📧 Admin Mgr: Ruth Butterworth 0131 248 4848. Seated Capacity: 658

Royal Spa Centre Newbold Terrace, Leamington Spa, Warwickshire, CV32 4HN **t** 01926 334418 **f** 01926 832054 📧 Gen Mgr: Peter Nicholson. Seated Capacity: 800 Standing capacity: 800

Royal Victoria Hall London Road, Southborough, Tunbridge Wells, Kent, TN4 0ND **t** 01892 529176 **f** 01892 541402 Seated Capacity: 322

The Royal Pall Mall, Hanley, Stoke On Trent, Staffordshire, ST1 1EE **t** 01782 206000 **f** 01782 204955 **w** webfactory.co.uk/theroyal 📧 Dir: Mike Lloyd 01782 207777 box off. Seated Capacity: 1451 Standing capacity: 1900

The Sage Gateshead St Mary's Sq, Gateshead Quays, Gateshead, NE8 2JR **t** 0191 443 4666 **f** 0191 443 4550 **e** john.nassau@thesagegateshead.org **w** thesagegateshead.org 📧 Contact: John Nassau. Seated Capacity: 1600

St David's Hall The Hayes, Cardiff, CF10 1SH **t** 029 2087 8500 **f** 029 2087 8599 📧 Head Arts & Cultural Serv: Judi Richards. Seated Capacity: 1956

St George's Concert Hall Bridge Street, Bradford, W. Yorks, BD1 1JT **t** 01274 432 186 **f** 01274 720 736 **e** christine.raby@bradford.gov.uk **w** bradford-theatres.co.uk 📧 Programme & Bookings Mgr: Christine Raby. Seated Capacity: 1574 Standing capacity: 1872

St James Concert & Assembly Hall College Street, St Peter Port, Guernsey, Channel Islands, GY1 2NZ **t** 01481 711360 **f** 01481 711364 📧 Contact: Miss KR Simon. Seated Capacity: 480 Standing capacity: 350

St John's Tavern 91 Junction Road, London, N19 5QU **t** 020 7272 1587 **f** 020 7371 8797 📧 Contact: Nick Sharpe.

St Mary's College Student Union, Waldergrave Road, Strawberry Hill, Twickenham, Middlesex, TW1 4SX **t** 020 8240 4314 **f** 020 8744 1700 📧 Contact: Kieran Renihan. Seated Capacity: 300 Standing capacity: 600

Salford University Student Union, University House, The Crescent, Salford, Greater Manchester, M5 4WT **t** 0161 736 7811 **f** 0161 737 1633 **e** Entsorg-ussu@salford.ac.uk **w** salfordstudents.com

Salisbury Arts Centre Bedwin St, Salisbury, Wiltshire, SP1 3UT **t** 01722 343020 **f** 01722 343030 **e** sophie@salisburyarts.co.uk **w** salisburyartscentre.co.uk 📧 Marketing & Development Manager: Sophie Dubber. Seated Capacity: 300 Standing capacity: 400

Salisbury City Hall Malthouse Lane, Salisbury, Wiltshire, SP2 7TU **t** 01722 334432 **f** 01722 337059 **e** gpettifer@salisbury.gov.uk 📧 Sales & Marketing Mgr: Gail Pettifer. Seated Capacity: 953 Standing capacity: 1116

The Sands Centre, Carlisle The Sands Centre, Carlisle, Cumbria, CA1 1JQ **t** 01228 625222 **f** 01228 625666 **e** jonathan.higgins@carlisleleisure.com **w** thesandscentre.co.uk 📧 Arts & Events Programme Manager: Jonathan Higgins 01228 625208. Seated Capacity: 1350 Standing capacity: 1750

Scala 275 Pentonville Rd, Kingscross, London, N1 9NL **t** 020 7833 2022 **f** 020 7520 0045 **e** tina@scala-london.co.uk **w** scala-london.co.uk 📧 Events Assistant: Tina Barton. Standing capacity: 1145

indigO₂   The entertainment venue at The O₂ www.theo2.co.uk/indigo2
BOOKINGS ENQUIRIES: Laurie Pegg 020 8463 2707 | lpegg@theindigo2.com

Scarborough Univerity College Student Union,
Filey Road, Scarborough, North Yorkshire, YO11 3AZ
t 01723 362392 **f** 01723 370815 ☎ Contact: Nick Evans.
Standing capacity: 250

Scottish Exhibition & Conference Centre
Glasgow, Lanarkshire, G3 8YW **t** 0141 248 3000
f 0141 226 3423 ☎ Acct Mgr, Concerts: Susan Verlaque.
Seated Capacity: 9300 Standing capacity: 10000

Shanklin Theatre Prospect Road, Shanklin,
Isle of Wight, PO37 6AJ **t** 01983 862739 **f** 01983 867682
☎ Contact: David Redston. Seated Capacity: 472

Sheffield City Hall Barkers Pool, Sheffield,
South Yorkshire, S1 2JA **t** 0114 223 3701
e c.procter@sheffieldcityhall.co.uk **w** sheffieldcityhall.com
◼ facebook.com/group.php?gid=12577763454&ref=ts
◲ twitter.com/sheffcityhall ◼ youtube.com/user/SIVltd
☎ Bookings: Carol Procter. Seated Capacity: 2346

Sheffield Hallam University Student's Union,
Nelson Mandela Building, Pond Street, Sheffield,
South Yorksire, S1 2BW **t** 0114 225 4122 **f** 0114 225 4140
e a.sewell@shu.ac.uk **w** shu.ac.uk/su ☎ Ents Co-
ordinator: Alice Sewell. Seated Capacity: 250 Standing
capacity: 900

Sheffield University Union of Students
Western Bank, Sheffield, South Yorkshire, S10 2TG
t 0114 222 8556 **f** 0114 222 8574
e c.white@sheffield.ac.uk **w** sheffieldunion.com ☎ Head of
Entertainments and Events: Chris White. Seated Capacity:
1000 Standing capacity: 1500

Showsec Head Office,, Regent House, 16 West Walk,
Leicester, LE1 7NA **t** 01162 043333 **f** 01162 043303
e mark.harding@showsec.co.uk **w** showsec.co.uk
☎ MD: Mark Harding.

Snape Maltings Concert Hall High Street,
Aldeburgh, Suffolk, IP15 5AX **t** 01728 687100
f 01728 687120 **e** enquiries@aldeburghfestivals.org
w aldeburgh.co.uk ☎ Concert Mgr: Sharon Godard. Seated
Capacity: 830

Sound Swiss Centre, 10 Wardour Street, London,
W1V 3HG **t** 020 7287 1010 **f** 020 7437 1029
e info@soundlondon.com **w** soundlondon.com ☎ Head of
Corporate: Phil Bridges. Seated Capacity: 300 Standing
capacity: 1335

South Bank University Student Union,
Keyworth Street, London, SE1 6NG **t** 020 7815 6060
f 020 7815 6061 ☎ Ents Mgr: Tom Dinnis. Seated Capacity:
400 Standing capacity: 800

South Hill Park Arts Centre Ringmead, Birch Hill,
Bracknell, Berkshire, RG12 7PA **t** 01344 484858
f 01344 411427 **e** music@southhillpark.org.uk
w southhillpark.org.uk
◼ facebook.com/music.events.southhillpark
◲ myspace.com/shpmusic
◼ youtube.com/watch?v=kTE1KQc6eu4&feature=related
☎ Head of Music & Programmer for Big Day Out Festival of
Music & Performing Arts: William Trevelyan 01344 416 260.
Seated Capacity: 330 Standing capacity: 600

South Holland Centre 23 Market Place, Spalding,
Lincolnshire, PE11 1SS **t** 01775 725031

South Street 21 South Street, Reading, Berkshire,
RG1 4QU **t** 0118 901 5234 **f** 0118 901 5235
e 21southstreet@reading.gov.uk **w** readingarts.com
☎ Venue Mgr: John Luther. Seated Capacity: 125 Standing
capacity: 200

Southampton Guildhall Civic Centre, Southampton,
Hampshire, SO14 7LP **t** 023 8083 2453 **f** 0870 749 2354
e mandy.fields@livenation.co.uk
w livenation.co.uk/southampton
◼ facebook.com/southamptonguildhall
◲ myspace.com/southamptonguildhall
◲ twitter.com/sguildhall
◼ youtube.com/SouthamptonGuildhall ☎ Venue
Manager: Mandy Fields. Seated Capacity: 1350 Standing
capacity: 1700

Southampton University Student Union,
Highfield Campus, University Road, Southampton, SO17 1BJ
t 023 8059 5213 **f** 023 8059 5245 **e** em@susu.org
w susu.org ☎ Entertainments Manager: Melissa Taylor 023
8059 5221. Standing capacity: 800

Southport Arts Centre Lord Street, Southport,
Merseyside, PR8 1DB **t** 0151 934 2134 **f** 0151 934 2126
e jake.roney@leisure.sefton.gov.uk **w** seftonarts.co.uk
☎ Programme Mgr: Jake Roney. Seated Capacity: 472

Southport Theatre & Floral Hall Promenade,
Southport, Merseyside, PR9 0DZ **t** 01704 540454
f 01704 536841 ☎ Contact: Lisa Chu. Seated Capacity:
1631

Spa Pavilion Theatre Seafront, Felixstowe, Suffolk,
IP11 8AQ **t** 01394 282126 **f** 01394 278978 Seated
Capacity: 892

The Square Fourth Avenue, Harlow, Essex, CM20 1DW
t 01279 305000 **f** 01279 866151
e promotion@harlowsquare.com **w** harlowsquare.com
☎ Music Promoter: Tom Hawkins. Standing capacity: 325

St Andrews University - Venue 1, Venue 2
Student Union, St Mary's Place, St Andrews, KY16 9UZ
t 01334 462700 **f** 01334 462740 **e** doserv@st-and.ac.uk
w yourunion.net ☎ Building Supervisor: Bruce Turner.
Seated Capacity: 450 Standing capacity: 1000

St George's Bristol Great George Street,
(off Park Street), Bristol, BS1 5RR **t** 0117 929 4929
f 0117 927 6537 **e** administration@stgeorgesbristol.co.uk
w stgeorgesbristol.co.uk ☎ Director: Suzanne Rolt.

The St Helens Citadel Waterloo Street, St Helens,
Merseyside, WA10 1PX **t** 01744 735436 **f** 01744 20836
☎ Contact: Jake Roney. Seated Capacity: 172 Standing
capacity: 300

Live: Venues

The Stables The Yukon Bar, 11 Dominick St, Mullingar, Co. Westmeath, Ireland **t** +353 44 934 0251 **e** info@stableslive.com **w** stableslive.com
facebook.com/business/dashboard/?ref=sb#/pages/The-Stables-Music-Venue/50579378961
myspace.com/stableslive twitter.com/stableslive bebo.com/stableslive Bookings: David McLynn +353 87 773 3565.

Stables Theatre Stockwell Lane, Wavendon, Milton Keynes, Buckinghamshire, MK17 8LU **t** 01908 280814 **f** 01908 280827 **e** stables@stables.org **w** stables.org Programmer: Penny Griffiths. Seated Capacity: 396

Stafford Gatehouse Eastgate Street, Stafford, ST16 2LT **t** 01785 253595 **f** 01785 225622 Mgr: Daniel Shaw. Seated Capacity: 564

Staffordshire University, Legends Nightclub Student Union, Beaconside, Stafford, Staffordshire, ST18 0AD **t** 01782 294582 **f** 01785 353599 **e** b.clements@staffs.ac.uk **w** staffs.ac.uk Ents & Venues Manager: Ben Clements. Standing capacity: 500

Staffordshire University, Stoke On Trent Student Union, College Road, Stoke On Trent, Staffordshire, ST4 2DE **t** 01782 294582 **f** 01782 295736 **e** b.clements@staffs.ac.uk **w** staffsunion.com Ents & Venues Manager: Ben Clements.

The Standard Music Venue 1 Blackhorse Lane, London, E17 6DS **t** 020 8503 2523 **f** 020 8527 1944 **e** thestandard@btinternet.com **w** standardmusicvenue.co.uk Contact: Nigel Henson 020 8527 1966. Standing capacity: 400

Stantonbury Leisure Centre Purbeck, Stantonbury, Milton Keynes, Buckinghamshire, MK14 6BN **t** 01908 314466 **f** 01908 318754 Mgr: Matthew Partridge. Seated Capacity: 1000 Standing capacity: 1000

Stirling University Students Association Student Union, The Robbins Centre, Stirling University, Stirling, FK9 4LA **t** 01786 467189 **f** 01786 467190 **e** susa-services@stir.ac.uk **w** susaonline.org.uk VP Services: Robert Hudd. Seated Capacity: 1100

Stour Centre Tannery Lane, Ashford, Kent, TN23 1PL **t** 01233 625801 **f** 01233 645654 Seated Capacity: 1500 Standing capacity: 1800

Stourbridge Town Hall Crown Centre, Stourbridge, West Midlands, DY8 1YE **t** 01384 812948 **f** 01384 812963 Contact: Laurence Hanna 01384 812960. Seated Capacity: 300 Standing capacity: 650

University of Strathcylde Students Association, 90 John Street, Glasgow, Lanarkshire, G1 1JH **t** 0141 567 5023 **f** 0141 567 5033 **e** a.j.mawn@strath.ac.uk Seated Capacity: 300 Standing capacity: 700

The Studio Tower Street, Hartlepool, TS24 7HQ **t** 01429 424440 **f** 01429 424441 **e** studiohartlepool@btconnect.com **w** studiohartlepool.com Studio Manager: Liz Carter.

Sub Zero Music 20-22 Mount Pleasant, Bilston, Wolverhampton, West Midlands, WV14 7LJ **t** 01902 405511 **f** 01902 401418 **e** music@therobin.co.uk **w** subzeromusic.com Dir: Mike Hamblett.

Sunderland University Student Union, Manor Quay, Charles Street, Sunderland, SR6 0AN **t** 0191 515 3583 **f** 0191 515 2499 **e** andy.fitzpatrick@sunderland.ac.uk **w** mq@sunderland.co.uk Contact: A Fitzpatrick. Seated Capacity: 1200 Standing capacity: 1200

The Superdome Ocean Boulevard, Blackpool, Lancashire, FY4 1EZ **t** 01253 341033 **f** 01253 401098 Seated Capacity: 1000

University of Surrey Union Club Union House, University of Surrey, Guildford, Surrey, GU2 7XH **t** 01483 689983 **e** ents@ussu.co.uk **w** ussu.co.uk Events Mgr: Alan Roy. Standing capacity: 1600

Sussex University Student Union, Falmer House, Falmer, Brighton, BN1 9QF **t** 01273 678555 **f** 01273 678875 Contact: Entertainments Dept.

The Swan 215 Clapham Rd, London, SW9 9BE **t** 020 7978 9778 **f** 020 7738 6722 **e** info@theswanstockwell.co.uk **w** theswanstockwell.co.uk
I love the swan stockwell Entertainment manager: Claire Jeanjean. Seated Capacity: 300 Standing capacity: 500

The Swan Abbey Barn Road, High Wycombe, Buckinghamshire, HP11 1RS **t** 01494 539482

University of Wales - Swansea Student Union, Fulton House, Singleton Park, Swansea, SA2 8PP **t** 01792 295485 **f** 01792 513006 **e** suents@swansea.ac.uk **w** swansea-union.co.uk/ents Seated Capacity: 800 Standing capacity: 800

Symphony Hall International Convention Ctr, Broad Street, Birmingham, B1 2EA **t** 0121 200 2000 **f** 0121 212 1982 **e** feedback@symphonyhall.co.uk **w** symphonyhall.co.uk MD: Andrew Jowett. Seated Capacity: 2260

Tait Hall Edenside Road, Kelso, Roxburgh, TD5 7BS **t** 01573 224233 Seated Capacity: 700

Tameside Hippodrome Oldham Road, Ashton-under-Lyne, Tameside, OL6 7SE **t** 0161 330 2095 **f** 0161 343 5839 **e** stuart.dornford-May@clearchannel.co.uk **w** getlive.co.uk Theatre Manager: Stuart Dornford-May. Seated Capacity: 1262

Teesside University University of Teesside Union, Southfield Road, Middlesbrough, Cleveland, TS1 3BA **t** 01642 342234 **f** 01642 342241 **e** L.Stretton@utsu.org.uk **w** utsu.org.uk Ent & Promotions Mgr: Luke Stretton. Seated Capacity: 450 Standing capacity: 1000

Telford Ice Rink Telford Town Centre, Telford, Shropshire, TF3 4JQ **t** 01952 291511 **f** 01952 291543 Mgr: Robert Fountain. Seated Capacity: 3300 Standing capacity: 4000

Thames Valley University Students Union, St Mary's Road, London, W5 5RF **t** 020 8231 2531 **f** 020 8231 2589

Live: Venues

Theatre Royal Corporation Street, St Helens, Merseyside, WA10 1LQ **t** 01744 756333 admin **f** 01744 756777 ✉ Gen Mgr: Basil Soper 01744 756000 bo. Seated Capacity: 698

Theatre Royal Royal Parade, Plymouth, Devon, PL1 2TR **t** 01752 668282 **f** 01752 671179 **e** info@theatreroyal.com **w** theatreroyal.com ✉ Chief Exec: Adrian Vinken 01752 267222. Seated Capacity: 1296

Theatre Royal Grey Street, Newcastle upon Tyne, Tyne and Wear, NE1 6BR **t** 0191 232 0997 **f** 0191 261 1906 ✉ Contact: Peter Sarah. Seated Capacity: 1294

Theatre Royal Theatre Sq, Nottingham, NG1 5ND **t** 0115 989 5500 **f** 0115 947 4218 **e** enquiry@royalcentre.co.uk **w** royalcentre-nottingham.co.uk ✉ MD: Mr Robert Sanderson. Seated Capacity: 1135

Theatre Royal 282 Hope Street, Glasgow, G2 3QA **t** 0141 332 3321 admin **f** 0141 332 4477 **w** theatreroyalglasgow.com ✉ Theatre Mgr: Martin Ritchie 0141 332 9000 box. Seated Capacity: 1555

Theatre Severn Frankwell Quay, Shrewsbury, Shropshire, SY3 8FT **t** 01743 281281 **f** 01743 281283 **e** j.edmondson@theatresevern.co.uk **w** theatresevern.co.uk ✉ Marketing Manager: Jan Edmondson 01743 256566. Seated Capacity: 384 Standing capacity: 500

Time Club Bangor Student Union, Deiniol Road, Bangor, Gwynedd, LL57 2TH **t** 01248 388033 **f** 01248 388031 **e** adami@undeb.bangor.ac.uk **w** undeb.bangor.ac.uk ✉ Ents Mgr: Adam Isbell. Standing capacity: 700

Tiverton New Hall Barrington Street, Tiverton, Devon, Exeter, EX16 6QP **t** 01884 253404 **f** 01884 243677 ✉ Town Clerk: B Lough. Seated Capacity: 222 Standing capacity: 300

TJ's Disco 16-18 Clarence Place, Newport, South Wales, NP19 0AE **t** 01633 216608 **e** sam@tjs-newport.demon.co.uk **w** tjs-newport.demon.co.uk ✉ Manager: John Sicolo. Seated Capacity: 500

The Top of Reilly's 10 Thurland Street, Nottingham, NG1 3DR **t** 0115 941 7709 **f** 0115 941 5604 Standing capacity: 450

Torbay Leisure Centre Clennon Valley, Penwill Way, Paignton, Devon, TQ4 5JR **t** 01803 522240 **w** torbay.gov.uk Seated Capacity: 2000 Standing capacity: 3400

The Tower Ballroom Reservoir Road, Edgbaston, Birmingham, West Midlands, B16 9EE **t** 0121 454 0107 **f** 0121 455 9313 **e** tower@zanzibar.co.uk **w** zanzibar.co.uk ✉ MD: Susan Prince. Seated Capacity: 1000 Standing capacity: 1200

The Tower Ballroom Blackpool Tower, Promenade, Blackpool, Lancashire, FY1 4BJ **t** 01253 629600 **f** 01253 629700 **e** firstname+lastname@leisure-parcs.co.uk **w** blackpooltower.co.uk ✉ Entertainments Co-ord: Donna Molyneaux. Seated Capacity: 1650 Standing capacity: 1700

Town Hall Birmingham Victoria Sq, Birmingham, B3 3DQ **t** 0121 644 6157 **f** 0121 212 1982 **e** simon.wales@thsh.co.uk **w** thsh.co.uk ✉ GM: Simon Wales. Seated Capacity: 1100

Tramway 25 Albert Drive, Pollockshields, Glasgow, Lanarkshire, G41 2PE **t** 0141 276 0950 **f** 0141 276 0954 **e** info@tramway.org **w** tramway.org ✉ Administrator: Margaret Dalzell. Seated Capacity: 1000 Standing capacity: 1500

Trinity & All Saints College The Base, Brownberrie Lane, Horsforth, Leeds, West Yorkshire, LS18 5HD **t** 0113 283 7241 **f** 0113 283 7283 **e** president@tasc.ac.uk **w** tasc.ac.uk Standing capacity: 600

The Trinity Centre Trinity Rd, Bristol, BS2 0NW **t** 01179 351200 **e** info@3ca.org.uk **w** 3ca.org.uk ✉ Centre Manager: Emma Harvey. Seated Capacity: 225 Standing capacity: 500

Truro Hall for Cornwall Back Quay, Truro, Cornwall, TR1 2LL **t** 01872 262465 **f** 01872 260246 **e** admin@hallforcornwall.org.uk **w** hallforcornwall.co.uk Seated Capacity: 950 Standing capacity: 1700

Tufnells 162, Tufnell Park Road, London, N7 0EE **t** 020 7272 2078 **f** 020 8546 3689 **e** tufnellsclub@yahoo.co.uk ✉ Bookings: Chris Larsen. Standing capacity: 500

The Tunnels Carnegie's Brae, Aberdeen, AB10 1BF **t** 01224 211 121 **e** info@thetunnels.co.uk **w** thetunnels.co.uk ✉ Bookings Mgr: Hen Beverly. Standing capacity: 300

University of Ulster Cromore Road, Coleraine, Co Antrim, BT52 1SA **t** 028 9036 5121 **f** 028 9036 6817

Ulster Hall Bedford Street, Belfast, Co Antrim, BT2 7FF **t** 028 9032 3900 **f** 028 9024 7199 **e** ulsterhall@belfastcity.gov.uk **w** ulsterhall.co.uk ✉ Manager: Pat Falls. Seated Capacity: 1000 Standing capacity: 1800

Ulster University Students' Association, York Street, Belfast, Co Antrim, BT15 1ED **t** 028 9032 8515 **f** 028 9026 7351 **e** info@uusu.org **w** uusu.org Standing capacity: 450

ULU (University of London Union) Malet St, London, WC1E 7HY **t** 020 7664 2011 **f** 020 7436 4604 **w** ulu.co.uk Seated Capacity: 320 Standing capacity: 828

UMIST Union PO Box 88, Sackville Street, Manchester, M60 1QD **t** 0161 275 2959 **f** 0161 200 3268 **e** sean.morgan@su.umist.ac.uk **w** umsu.manchester.ac.uk ✉ Contact: Sean Morgan. Seated Capacity: 350 Standing capacity: 600

The Underworld 174 Camden High St, London, NW1 0NE **t** 020 7267 3939 **f** 020 7482 1955 **e** contact@theunderworldcamden.co.uk **w** theunderworldcamden.co.uk ✉ Bookings Mgr: Jon Vyner. Seated Capacity: 500 Standing capacity: 500

Live: Venues

Unex Towerlands Arena Panfield Road, Braintree, Essex, CM7 5BJ **t** 01376 326802 **f** 01376 552487 **e** info@unextowerlands.com **w** unextowerlands.com ⊠ Mktg Mgr: Holly Gredley. Seated Capacity: 3600 Standing capacity: 4000

Union Chapel Compton Avenue, London, N1 2XD **t** 020 7226 3750 **f** 020 7354 8343 **e** events@unionchapel.org.uk **w** unionchapel.org.uk ⊠ Venue Mgr: Pete Stapleton. Seated Capacity: 500

Union of UEA Students Students Union, University Plain, Norwich, Norfolk, NR4 7TJ **t** 01603 505401 **f** 01603 593465 **e** ents@uea.ac.uk **w** ueaticketbookings.co.uk ⊠ Ents Mgr: Nick Rayns 01603 593460. Seated Capacity: 780 Standing capacity: 1470

Unit 113 St Marys Rd, Southampton, Hampshire, SO14 0AN **t** 0238 022 5612 **e** chris@joinerslive.co.uk, neil@joinerslive.co.uk, glenn@joinerslive.co.uk **w** joinerslive.co.uk ⊠ Head of Promotions, General Manager, Owner: Chris Stemp, Neil Downton, Glenn Lovell 023 8022 5612.

University College Of St Martin Student Union, Rydal Road, Ambleside, Cumbria, LA22 9BB **t** 01539 430216 **f** 01539 430309

University of Chester - Warrington Campus Student Union, Crab Lane, Warrington, Cheshire, WA2 0DB **t** 01925 534375 **f** 01925 534267 **e** csuw.ents@chester.ac.uk **w** chestersu.com ⊠ Entertainments Officer: David Cowell. Seated Capacity: 400 Standing capacity: 500

University of Essex Students' Union Students' Union, Uni of Essex, Colchester, Essex, CO4 3SQ **t** 01206 863211 **f** 01206 870915 **e** ents@essex.ac.uk **w** essexventsonline.com ⊠ Ents & Venues Mgr: Lee Pugh. Seated Capacity: 400 Standing capacity: 1000

University of Gloucestershire Students' Union Student Union, PO Box 220, The Park, Cheltenham, GL52 2EH **t** 01242 532848 **f** 01242 361381 **e** union@ugsu.org **w** ugsu.org ⊠ VP Communications: John Webb. Seated Capacity: 600 Standing capacity: 1200

University of Greenwich Student Union, Bathway, Woolwich, London, SE18 6QX **t** 020 8331 8268 **f** 020 8331 8591

University of the Arts London Student Union, 2-6 Catton St, Holborn, London, WC1R 4AA **t** 020 7514 6270 **f** 020 7514 7838 **e** a.lukes@su.arts.ac.uk **w** thestudentsunion.info ⊠ Ents Manager: Adrian Lukes.

Usher Hall Lothian Rd, Edinburgh, EH1 2EA **t** 0131 228 8616 **f** 0131 228 8848 **w** usherhall.co.uk ⊠ General Manager: Karl Chapman. Seated Capacity: 2200 Standing capacity: 2800

The Venue at Kent University Kent Student Union, Mandela Building, Canterbury, Kent, CT2 7NW **t** 01227 824 245 **f** 01227 824 207 **e** g.newlands@kent.ac.uk **w** kentunion.co.uk ⊠ Venue & Entertainments Manager: Graham Newlands. Seated Capacity: 1500 Standing capacity: 1500

Vibe Bar 91-95 Brick Lane, London, E1 6QL **t** 020 7247 3479 **f** 020 7426 0641 **e** jon@vibe-bar.co.uk **w** vibe-bar.co.uk ⊠ Events Manager: Jon Wright. Standing capacity: 300

Victoria Community Centre Oakley Building, West Street, Crewe, Cheshire, CW1 2PZ **t** 01270 211422 **f** 01270 537960 ⊠ Centre Mgr: Mrs E McFahn. Seated Capacity: 550 Standing capacity: 1000

The Victoria Hall Bagnall Street, Hanley, Stoke-on-Trent, Staffordshire, ST1 3AD **t** 01782 213808 **f** 01782 214 738 **e** Firstname+lastname@theambassadors.com **w** victoria-hall.info ⊠ GM: Mike Keane. Seated Capacity: 1700 Standing capacity: 637

Victoria Hall Akeman Street, Tring, Hertfordshire, HP23 6AA **t** 01442 228951 Seated Capacity: 250 Standing capacity: 250

The Victoria Inn 12 Midland Place, Derby, DE1 2RR **t** 01332 740 091 **e** info@thevicinn.co.uk **w** thevicinn.co.uk ⊠ Promoters: Micky Sheehan, Andy Sewell. Standing capacity: 150

Victoria Theatre Wards End, Halifax, West Yorkshire, HX1 1BU **t** 01422 351156 **f** 01422 320552 **e** victoriatheatre@calderdale.gov.uk **w** calderdale.gov.uk/tourism/victoriatheatre ⊠ Contact: George Candler 01422 351158. Seated Capacity: 1585 Standing capacity: 1585

Vortex Jazz Unit E1, 3 Bradbury St, London, N16 8JN **t** 020 7254 4097 **e** info@vortexjazz.co.uk **w** vortexjazz.co.uk ◻ vortexjazz ◻ myspace.com/vortexjazz ⊠ Manager: Todd Wills.

The Vortex Jazz Club 11 Gillett Street, London, N16 8JH **t** 020 7254 4097 **e** info@vortexjazz.co.uk **w** vortexjazz.co.uk ⊠ Venue Manager: Will Gresford. Standing capacity: 100

Wakefield Theatre Royal & Opera House Drury Lane, Wakefield, West Yorks, WF1 2TE **t** 01924 211 311 **f** 01924 215 525 **e** marketing@theatreroyalwakefield.co.uk **w** theatreroyalwakefield.co.uk ⊠ Gen Mgr: Murray Edwards. Seated Capacity: 509 Standing capacity: 509

Warwick Arts Centre University Of Warwick, Coventry, West Midlands, CV4 7AL **t** 024 7652 4524 **f** 024 4652 4777 **e** box.office@warwick.ac.uk **w** warwickartscentre.co.uk ⊠ Dir: Alan Rivett. Seated Capacity: 1462 Standing capacity: 1462

Warwick University Student Union, Gibbet Hill Road, Coventry, West Midlands, CV4 7AL **t** 024 7657 3056 **f** 024 7657 3070 **e** dwalter@sunion.warwick.ac.uk **w** sunion.warwick.ac.uk/ents ⊠ Entertainments Manager: Darren Walter. Standing capacity: 2700

The Waterfront 139 King St, Norwich, Norfolk, NR1 1QH **t** 01603 632717 **f** 01603 615463 **e** p.ingleby@uea.ac.uk **w** ueaticketbookings.co.uk ⊠ Programmer: Paul Ingleby. Standing capacity: 700

Live: Venues

Watermans Arts Centre 40 High Street, Brentford,
Middlesex, TW8 0DS **t** 020 8847 5651 **f** 020 8569 8592
☑ Contact: Lorna O'Leary. Standing capacity: 500

Watford Colosseum Rickmansworth Road, Watford,
Hertfordshire, WD1 7JN **t** 01923 445300 **f** 01923 445225
☑ Contact: John Wallace. Seated Capacity: 298 Standing
capacity: 1200

The Wedgewood Rooms 147B Albert Road,
Southsea, Portsmouth, Hampshire, PO4 0JW
t 023 9286 3911 **f** 023 9285 1326 **e** tickets@wedgewood-
rooms.co.uk **w** wedgewood-rooms.co.uk ☑ GM: Geoff
Priestley. Seated Capacity: 300 Standing capacity: 400

The Welly Club 105-107 Beverley Rd, Hull, HU3 1TS
t 01482 221 113 **f** 01482 221 676
e info@thewelly.karoo.co.uk **w** giveitsomewelly.com
☑ GM: Mark Hall. Standing capacity: 885

Wembley Arena Arena Sq, Engineers Way, Wembley,
London, HA9 0DH **t** 020 8782 5622
e emma.bownes@livenation.co.uk **w** wembleyarena.co.uk
☑ Bookings Manager: Emma Bownes. Seated Capacity:
12000 Standing capacity: 12500

Wembley Stadium PO Box 1966, London, SW1P 9EQ
t 0844 980 8001 **e** jim.frayling@wembleystadium.com
w wembleystadium.com ☑ Head of Music & New
Events: Jim Frayling 020 8795 9618. Seated Capacity:
90000

West End Centre Queens Road, Aldershot, Hampshire,
GU11 3JD **t** 01252 408 040 **f** 01252 408 041
e westendcentre@hants.gov.uk **w** westendcentre.co.uk
☑ Centre Dir: Barney Jeavons. Seated Capacity: 150
Standing capacity: 200

University of West England Student Union,
Coldharbour Lane, Frenchay, Bristol, B16 1QY
t 0117 965 6261 x 2580 **f** 0117 976 3909
e union@uwe.ac.uk
w gate.uwe.ac.uk:8000/union/ents/index.html
☑ Contact: Programming Asst. Seated Capacity: 400
Standing capacity: 1500

University of Westminster Student Union,
32 Wells Street, London, W1T 3UW **t** 020 7911 5000 x 2306
f 020 7911 5848 **e** edfrith@hotmail.com ☑ Events Mgr: Ed
Frith. Seated Capacity: 150 Standing capacity: 630

Westpoint Arena Clyst St Mary, Exeter, Devon, EX5 1DJ
t 01392 446 000 **f** 01392 445 843 **e** info@westpoint-
devonshow.co.uk **w** westpoint-devonshow.co.uk ☑ Events
Mgr: Emily Egan. Seated Capacity: 6000 Standing capacity:
7500

Weymouth Pavilion The Esplanade, Weymouth,
Dorset, DT4 8ED **t** 01305 765218 **f** 01305 789922 ☑ Arts
& Entertainments Mgr: Stephen Young 01305 765214.
Seated Capacity: 1000

The Wheatsheaf Live Music Venue
Church Street, Stoke On Trent, Staffordshire, ST4 1BU
t 01782 844438 **f** 01782 410340 ☑ Contact: Anne Riddle.
Standing capacity: 400

White Rock Theatre White Rock, Hastings,
East Sussex, TN34 1JX **t** 01424 781010 **f** 01424 781170
☑ Contact: Andy Mould 01424 781000. Seated Capacity:
1165 Standing capacity: 1500

Whitehaven Civic Hall Lowther St, Whitehaven,
Cumbria, CA28 7SH **t** 01946 852 821
e civichalls@copelandbc.gov.uk **w** copelandbc.gov.uk
☑ Marketing Officer: Paul Tomlinson. Standing capacity: 600

Whitley Bay Ice Rink Hillheads Road, Whitley Bay,
Tyne and Wear, NE25 8HP **t** 0191 291 1000
f 0191 291 1001 ☑ Contact: Francis Smith. Seated
Capacity: 6000 Standing capacity: 6000

Winchester Guildhall Broadway, High St, Winchester,
Hampshire, SO23 9GH **t** 01962 840820 **f** 01962 878458
e guildhall@winchester.gov.uk **w** winchesterguildhall.co.uk
☑ GM: Ian Folger. Seated Capacity: 600 Standing capacity:
800

Winchester School Of Art Student Union,
Park Avenue, Winchester, Hampshire, SO23 8DL
t 01962 840772 **f** 01962 840772
e cvasudev@hotmail.com **w** soton.ac.uk/~wsasu
☑ President: Chetan. Seated Capacity: 250 Standing
capacity: 250

Windmill Brixton 22 Blenheim Gardens,
(off Brixton Hill), London, SW2 5BZ **t** 020 8674 0055
e windmillbrixton@yahoo.co.uk **w** windmillbrixton.co.uk
⬛ facebook.com/pages/London-United-
Kingdom/Windmill-Brixton/58502258990?ref=search&sid=
712682025.487038565..1
⬛ myspace.com/windmillbrixton
⬛ twitter.com/WindmillBrixton ☑ Booker: Tim Perry 07931
351971. Standing capacity: 130

Windsor Arts Centre St Leonard's Road, Windsor,
Berkshire, SL4 3BL **t** 01753 859421 **f** 01753 621527
☑ Contact: Debbie Stubbs 01753 859336. Seated
Capacity: 179 Standing capacity: 100

**The Winter Gardens - Opera House, Empress
Ballroom** Church St, Blackpool, FY1 3PL **t** 01253 625 252
f 01253 751 203 **e** events@leisure-parcs.co.uk
w wintergardensblackpool.co.uk ☑ Contact: Events Team.

The Winter Gardens Pavilion Royal Parade, Weston-
super-Mare, Somerset, BS23 1AJ **t** 01934 417117
f 01934 612323 **e** Peter.Undery@n-somerset.gov.uk
w thewintergardens.com ☑ GM: Peter Undery. Seated
Capacity: 500 Standing capacity: 550

Wolverhampton Civic Halls North St,
Wolverhampton, West Midlands, WV1 1RQ **t** 01902 552122
f 01902 552123 **e** markblackstock@wolvescivic.co.uk
w wolvescivic.co.uk ☑ Gen Mgr: Mark Blackstock. Seated
Capacity: 2200 Standing capacity: 3000

Wolverhampton University Students Union,
Wulfruna Street, Wolverhampton, West Midlands, WV1 1LY
t 01902 322021 **f** 01902 322020 **w** wlv.ac.uk Seated
Capacity: 200 Standing capacity: 600

Woodville Halls Theatre Woodville Pl, Gravesend, Kent, DA12 1DD **t** 01474 337611 **f** 01474 337458 **e** woodville.halls@gravesham.gov.uk **w** woodvillehalls.com **f** Woodville Halls **t** twitter.com/woodvillehalls **youtube** youtube.com/gravesham **✉** Venue Manager: Graham Long. Seated Capacity: 814 Standing capacity: 1000

Wyvern Theatre Theatre Square, Swindon, Wiltshire, SN1 1QN **t** 01793 535 534 **f** 01793 480 278 **e** admin@wyverntheatre.org.uk **w** wyverntheatre.org.uk **✉** Theatre Dir: Andrew Hill. Seated Capacity: 615

Yeovil Octagon Theatre Hendford, Yeovil, Somerset, BA20 1UX **t** 01935 422836 **f** 01935 475281 **✉** Gen Mgr: John G White 01935 422720. Seated Capacity: 625

York Barbican Centre Barbican Road, York, North Yorkshire, Y010 4NT **t** 01904 628991 **f** 01904 628227 **e** craig.smart@york.gov.uk **w** fibbers.co.uk/barbican **✉** Contact: Craig Smart 01904 621477. Seated Capacity: 1500 Standing capacity: 1860

York University Students Union, Goodricke College, Heslington, York, North Yorkshire, YO1 5DD **t** 01904 433724 **f** 01904 434664 **e** ents@york.ac.uk **w** york.ac.uk/student/su/index.shtml **✉** Andrew Windsor: Entertainments Officer. Seated Capacity: 300 Standing capacity: 540

Zanzibar 43 Seel Street, Liverpool, Merseyside, L1 4AZ **t** 0151 707 0633 **f** 0151 707 0633

Festivals

Americana International The Heartbeat Of The USA In The UK Americana Promotions Ltd, Jacksonville, 1 Middle Orchard St, Stapleford, Nottinghamshire, NG9 8DD **t** 01159 390595 **f** 01159 490856 **e** silvereagleuk@ntlworld.com **w** americana-international.co.uk **✉** myspace.com/americanajack **✉** Directors: Chris R & Bev J Jackson 0870 863 2100.

Beautiful Days **e** info@beautifuldays.org

Belladrum Festival Phoineas, By Beauly, Inverness-shire, IV4 7BA **e** info@tartanheartfestival.co.uk **✉** Contact: General Enquiries 01463 741366.

Bestival Ltd 3rd Floor, 25 Denmark St, London, WC2H 8NJ **e** hello@bestival.net **w** bestival.net **✉** Contact: 020 7379 3133.

Big Chill Festival see Festival Republic

Birmingham International Jazz Festival PO Box 944, Birmingham, B16 8UT **t** 0121 454 7020 **f** 0121 454 9996 **e** jim@bigbearmusic.com **w** bigbearmusic.com **✉** Festival Director: Jim Simpson.

Bloodstock Amust4music Ltd, 54 Arundel Drive, Derby, DE21 7QW **t** 01332 666370 **f** 01332 675099 **e** paul@bloodstock.uk.com **✉** Contact: Paul Gregory.

Brecon Jazz c/o The Drill Hall, 25 Lion St, Hay-on-Wye, HR3 5AD **t** 01497 822620 **f** 01497 821066 **e** sarah@breconjazz.org **w** breconjazz.org **✉** Producer: Sarah Dennehy.

Cambridge Folk Festival **e** admin.cornex@cambridge.gov.uk **w** cambridgefolkfestival.co.uk

Cornbury Festival 4b Ledbury Mews, London, W11 2AF **e** mail@cornburyfestival.com **✉** Contact: Organisers 020 7229 2219.

Creamfields Cream Office, Wolstenholme Sq, 1-3 Parr St, Liverpool, L1 4JJ **e** gill@cream.co.uk **✉** Press Contact: Gill Nightingale 0151 707 1309.

Download Festival Live Nation (Music) UK Ltd, 2nd Floor, Regent Arcade House, 19-25 Argyll St, London, W1F 7TS **e** info@livenation.co.uk **✉** Contact: Live nation press office.

Festival Republic 35 Bow St, London, WC2E 7AU **t** 020 7009 3000 **e** info@festivalrepublic.com **w** festivalrepublic.com **✉** MD: Melvyn Benn.

Glade Festival Aldermaston, Berkshire **e** info@gladefestival.com **w** gladefestival.com **✉** myspace.com/gladefestival

Glastonbury Festival Glastonbury Festival Office, 28 Northload St, Glastonbury, Somerset, BA6 9JJ **e** office@glastonburyfestivals.co.uk **w** glastonburyfestivals.co.uk **✉** Contact: Press Office 01458 834596.

Global Gathering Angel Music Group Ltd, The Old Stables, Newhouse Farm, Langley Rd, Warwick **e** vicky@angelmusicgroup.com **✉** Press Officer: Vicky Beercock 0845 009 8885.

Guilfest 54 Haydon Pl, Guildford, Surrey **t** 01483 454159 **w** guilfest.co.uk

Hop Farm Festival The Hop Farm, Paddock Wood, Kent, TN12 6PT **t** 0871 220 0260 **w** hopfarmfestival.com **✉** Press Contact: Ian Roberts 020 7836 1122.

Hope Street Feast 13 Hope St, Liverpool, Merseyside, L1 9BH **t** 0151 708 7441 **f** 0151 709 3515 **e** info@hopestreetfeast.com **w** hopestreetfeast.com **✉** Director: Simon Glinn.

Isle of Wight Festival **w** isleofwightfestival.com

Larmer Tree Festival PO Box 1790, Salisbury, Wiltshire, SP5 5WA **t** 01725 552300 **e** info@larmertreefestival.co.uk **w** larmertreefestival.co.uk

Leeds Festival Festival Republic Ltd, 2nd Floor, Regent Arcade House, 19-25 Argyll St, London, W1F 7TS **e** info@festivalrepublic.com **✉** Contact: General Enquiries 020 7009 3001.

Loopallu Ullapool, Wester Ross, Highlands **w** loopallu.co.uk **✉** Contact: Robert Hicks.

Lovebox Weekender London **e** press@loveboxlondon.com

North By Northeast Music & Film Festival 189 Church St, Toronto, Ontario, M5B 1Y7, Canada **t** +1 416 863 6963 **f** +1 416 863 0828 **e** info@nxne.com **w** nxne.com **f** tinyurl.com/ydcuzh5 **✉** myspace.com/nxne **t** twitter.com/nxnefest **✉** Projects Manager: Gillian Zulauf.

Contacts   Facebook   MySpace   Twitter   YouTube

Live: Festivals, Ticketing Services, Touring & Stage Services

onedotzero Unit 212C, Curtain House, 134-146 Curtain Rd, London, EC2A 3AR **t** 020 7729 0072 **f** 020 7729 0057 **e** info@onedotzero.com **w** onedotzero.com ✉ Director / Senior Producer & Curator: Shane Walter / Claire Cook.

Oxegen Festival Dublin, Ireland **w** oxegen.ie

Reading Festival Festival Republic Ltd, 2nd Floor, Regent Arcade House, 19-25 Argyll St, London, W1F 7TS **e** info@festivalrepublic.com ✉ Contact: General Enquiries 020 7009 3001.

Rockness e david.frossman@aeglive.co.uk ✉ Press Contact: David Frossman 020 7536 1618.

Sensoria Music & Film Festival PO Box 4454, Sheffield, S8 2FX **e** info@sensoria.org.uk **w** sensoria.org.uk ✉ Contact: Jo Wingate 0114 2558431.

Sonisphere Festival w sonispherefestivals.com

V Festival PO Box 34286, London, NW5 2XQ **e** hello@vfestival.com ✉ Contact: General Enquiries.

Wakestock e bex@wakestock.co.uk ✉ Press Contact: Rebecca Tappin 01758 714002.

Wicker Man Festival 10 Quay St, Ullapool, Wester Ross, IV26 2UE **e** carolinemccleary@yahoo.co.uk ✉ PR/Press Officer: Caroline McCleary 01671 404143.

WOMAD Festival Box Mill, Mill Lane, Box, Wiltshire **t** 01225 743188 **f** 01225 744369 **w** womad.com

Ticketing Services

Aloud.com Bauer, Endeavour House, 189 Shaftesbury Ave, London, WC2H 8JG **t** 020 7295 5000 **e** wendy.shaw@bauermedia.co.uk **w** aloud.com ✉ Strategic Partnerships: Wendy Shaw.

Crash Records 35 The Headrow, Leeds, West Yorkshire, LS1 6PU **t** 0113 243 6743 **f** 0113 234 0421 **e** store@crashrecords.co.uk **w** crashrecords.co.uk ✉ Prop: Ian De-Whytell.

CrowdSurge 175-185 Grays Inn Rd, London, WC1X 8UE **t** 0207 812 0688 **f** 0207 812 0650 **e** greg.delaney@crowdsurge.com **w** crowdsurge.com ✉ Contact: Greg Delaney.

eTickets.to (self service eticketing) 60, Maltings Place, London, SW6 2BX **t** 0845 644 4184 **f** 020 7168 3868 **e** hello@etickets.to **w** etickets.to ✉ MD: Matt McNeill.

Mobiqa 111 George St, Edinburgh, EH2 4JN **t** 0131 225 3141 **f** 0131 220 5353 **e** info@mobiqa.com **w** mobiqa.com ✉ CEO: Iain McCready.

Needtickets.com 17 Lloyd Villas, Brockley, London, SE4 1US **t** 07779 594012 **e** simon.harper@needtickets.com **w** Needtickets.com ✉ twitter.com/Needticketsguru ✉ Managing Director: Simon Harper.

SEE Tickets Manor House, 21 Soho Sq, London, W1D 3QP **t** 020 7087 7800 **w** seetickets.com ✉ Contact: Nick Blackburn.

Ticket Zone Unit 3, Barum Gate, Whiddon Valley, Barnstaple, Devon, EX32 8QD **t** 01271 323355 **f** 01271 375902 **e** customerservices@ticketzone.co.uk **w** ticketzone.co.uk ✉ Contact: Domingo Tjornelund or Bob Cotton.

Ticketmaster UK 48 Leicester Sq, London, WC2H 7LR **t** 020 7344 4000 **f** 020 7915 0411 **e** sales@ticketmaster.co.uk **w** ticketmaster.co.uk ✉ Sales Director: Andrew Parsons.

TicketWeb UK 48 Leicester Sq, London, WC2H 7LR **t** 020 7344 4000 **f** 020 7915 0411 **e** clients@ticketweb.co.uk **w** ticketweb.co.uk ✉ Operations Director: Janine Douglas-Hall.

WeGotTickets.com 9 Park End St, Oxford, OX1 1HH **t** 01865 798797 **f** 01865 798792 **e** info@wegottickets.com **w** WeGotTickets.com ✉ Marketing Dir: Laura Kramer.

Touring & Stage Services

23 Management **t** 07785 228000 **f** 0870 130 5365 **e** ifan@23management.com **w** 23management.com ✉ Tour Manager: Ifan Thomas +61 415 498 955.

5 Star Cases Broad End Industrial Estate, Broad End Rd, Walsoken, Wisbech, Cambridgeshire, PE14 7BQ **t** 01945 427000 **f** 01945 427015 **e** info@5star-cases.com **w** 5star-cases.com ✉ MD: Keith Sykes.

Arc Sound Ltd Unit A, 443 New Cross Rd, London, SE14 6TA **t** 020 8691 8161 **f** 020 7183 6997 **e** info@arcsound.co.uk **w** arcsound.co.uk ✉ myspace.com/arcsound ✉ Director: James Dougill 07760 217906.

Backline For Bands 42 Woodstock Rd East, Begbroke, Oxford, OX5 1RG **t** 01865 842840 **e** info@backlineforbands.com **w** backlineforbands.com ✉ MD: Tarrant Anderson 07950 293530.

Band Pass Ltd 1st Floor, 20 Sunnydown, Witley, Surrey, GU8 5RP **t** 01428 684 926 **f** 01428 683 501 **e** maxine@band-pass.co.uk **w** band-pass.co.uk ✉ Director: Maxine Gale.

Beat The Street UK (Tour Coaches) Unit 103, Cariocca Business Park, Hellidon Close, Ardwick, Manchester, M12 4AH **t** 0161 273 5984 **f** 0161 272 7772 **e** beatthestreetuk@aol.com **w** beatthestreet.net ✉ Manager: Paul Collis.

Bennett Audio 41 Sherriff Rd, London, NW6 2AS **t** 07748 705 067 **e** bennettaudio1@f2s.com **w** bennettaudio.co.uk ✉ Dir. and Audio Engineer: Clem Bennett 020 7372 1077.

Blackout Ltd 280 Western Road, London, SW19 2QA **t** 020 8687 8400 **f** 020 8687 8500 **e** sales@blackout-ltd.com **w** blackout-ltd.com ✉ Contact: Sales.

Contacts   Facebook   MySpace   Twitter   YouTube

Capes UK Security Services Ltd Unit 1, West Street Business Park, Stamford, Lincolnshire, PE9 2PR **t** 01780 480712 **f** 01780 480824

Chameleon Pro Audio & Lighting Scotland Industrial Estate, London Rd, Coalville, Leicestershire, LE67 3JJ **t** 01530 831337 **f** 01530 838319 **e** info@chameleon-pa.co.uk **w** chameleon-pa.co.uk Managing Director: Stewart Duckworth.

Clearwater Special Projects Ltd (Threat Management & Security) Netley Hall, Shrewsbury, Shropshire, SY5 7JZ **t** 01743 719 109 **f** 01743 719 170 **e** i.dewsnip@clearwaterprojects.com **w** clearwaterprojects.com Operations Manager: Ian Dewsnip.

David Lawrence Tour Mgmt & Security Solutions Suite 358, 78 Marylebone High St, London, W1U 5AP **t** 0800 043 0932 **e** info@david-lawrence.co.uk **w** david-lawrence.co.uk MD: Lawrence Levy.

DiGiCo Unit 10, Silverglade Buisness Pk, Leatherhead Rd, Chessington, Surrey, KT18 7LX **t** 01372 845600 **f** 01372 845656 **e** info@digiconsoles.com **w** digico.org Managing Director: James Gordon.

The Distribution Company TDC Ltd Unit 208 Buspace Studios, Conlan Street, London, W10 1TB **t** 020 8969 9771 **f** 020 8969 9772 **e** sales@thedistributionco.co.uk Senior Account Mgr: Claire Gibson.

Eat Your Hearts Out Basement, 108A Elgin Avenue, London, W9 2HD **t** 020 7289 9446 **f** 020 7266 3160 **e** eyho@dial.pipex.com MD: Kim Davenport.

ES Group Ltd Bell Lane, North Woolwich Rd, London, E16 2AB **t** 020 7055 7200 **f** 020 7055 7201 **e** jeffb@ess-uk.com **w** esgroup-uk.com Director: Jeff Burke.

Extreme Music Production - Tour Management 4-7 Forewoods Common, Holt, Wiltshire, BA14 6PJ **t** 01225 782 984 **e** george@empspace.com **w** empspace.com Tour Manager: George Allen 01225 782984.

Fineline Lighting Hire Unit 3, Hither Green Trading Estate, Clevedon, Bristol, BS21 6XT **t** 01275 871800 **f** 01275 875200 **e** rob@fineline.uk.com **w** fineline.uk.com Hire Manager: Rob Sangwell.

Fruit Pie Music Productions Ltd The Shop, 443 Streatham High Road, London, SW16 3PH **t** 020 8679 9289 **f** 020 8679 9775 **e** info@fruitpiemusic.com **w** fruitpiemusic.com MD: Kumar Kamalagharan.

Futurist Sound and Light LTD Unit 15, Pickering St, Leeds, West Yorkshire, LS12 2QG **t** 0113 279 0033 **f** 0113 279 0066 **e** info@futurist.co.uk **w** futurist.co.uk Director: James Hudson.

GWH Backline Rental GWH, Pegasus House, 550 Newark Rd North Hykeham, Lincoln, LN6 9NG **t** 01522 501814 **e** gary@gwhmusic.com **w** gwhmusic.com Director: Gary Weight.

Hello Currency Ltd 2nd Floor, 145-157 St.John Street, London, EC1V 4PY **t** 020 7788 7765 **f** 0845 280 1549 **e** ngoddard@hellocurrency.com **w** hellocurrency.com MD: Noel Goddard.

ICP Group (Threat Management & Security) 2 Old Brompton Rd, London, SW1 3DQ **t** 020 7031 4440 **e** info@icpgroup.ltd.uk **w** icpgroup.ltd.uk MD: Will Geddes.

LarMac Live Unit 232, Great Guildford Business Sq, 30 Great Guildford St, London, SE1 0HS **t** 0207 401 0480 **f** 07092 840 701 **e** ian@larmaclive.com **w** larmaclive.com Director: Ian Greenway.

LXco Unit G, Brocks Business Centre, Homefield Rd, Haverhill, CB9 8QP **t** 0870 861 1456 **f** 0870 861 1457 **e** info@lxco.co.uk **w** lxco.co.uk Director: James Cobb.

Malvern Theatres Grange Rd, Malvern, Worcestershire, WR14 3HB **t** 01684 892277 **f** 01684 893300 **e** post@malvern-theatres.co.uk **w** malvern-theaters.co.uk Chief Exec: Nicolas Lloyd. Seated Capacity: 850

Matt Snowball Music Ltd Unit 2, 3-9 Brewery Rd, London, N7 9QJ **t** 020 7700 6555 **f** 020 7700 6990 **e** enquiries@mattsnowball.com **w** mattsnowball.com Hire/Sales: Kent Jolly.

Midland Custom Cases 24 Proctor St, Birmingham, B7 4EE **t** 0121 333 7711 **f** 0121 333 7799 **e** admin@cloudone.net **w** cloudone.net MD: Paul Stratford.

Millsea Production Services 2A Rotherwood Mansion, 78 Madeira Rd, Streatham, London, SW16 2DE **t** 020 8677 2370 **f** 020 8677 8690 **e** millsea@aol.com Tour Manager: Caron Malcolm 07770 428 096.

Music & Arts Security Ltd 13 Grove Mews, Hammersmith, London, W6 7HS **t** 020 8563 9444 **f** 020 8563 9555 **e** sales@musicartssecurity.co.uk **w** music-and-arts-security.co.uk MD: Jerry Judge.

NPB Group (Instrument Repair & Servicing) Electron House 2, Landmere Close, Ilkeston, Derbyshire, DE7 9HQ **t** 01159 321447 **f** 01159 321447 **e** npbelectronics@btinternet.com **w** npbgroup.net Contact: Pauline Barker.

PRG Lighting The Hoover Building, Western Avenue, Perivale, London, UB6 8DW **t** 0845 470 6400 **f** 0845 470 6401 **e** prglighting@prg.com **w** prglighting.co.uk CEO: Martin Locket.

Prism Lighting Unit 5A, Hampton Industrial Estate, Malpas, Cheshire, SY14 8LU **t** 01948 820201 **f** 01948 820480 **e** mail@prismlighting.co.uk **w** prismlighting.co.uk Project Manager: Ian Tobin.

The Production Office Ltd 18 Fleet Street, Beaminster, Dorset, DT8 3EF **t** 01308 861 374 **f** 01308 861 375 **e** Theproductionoffice@mac.com Directors: Chris Vaughan, Keely Myers.

Saucery Catering Watchcott, Nordan, Leominster, Herefordshire, HR6 0AJ **t** 01568 614221 **f** 01568 610256 **e** saucery@aol.com MD: Alison Taylor.

Contacts Facebook 🟦 MySpace 🅃 Twitter ▶ YouTube

School Touring 216 Buspace Studios, Conlan St, London, W10 5AP **t** 020 8962 1275
e steverandrews@btinternet.com 📇 MD: Steve Andrews.

Sensible Music (Ireland) Unit 53, Parkwest Enterprise Centre, Lavery Avenue, Nangor Rd, Dublin 12, Ireland **t** +353 1 620 8321 **f** +353 1 620 8322
e info@sensiblemusic.ie **w** sensiblemusic.ie 📇 Dir: John Munnis.

Shell Shock Firework Ltd Furze Hill Farm, Knossington, Oakham, Leicestershire, LE15 8LX
t 01664 454994 **f** 01664 454995 **e** zoe@shell-shock.co.uk
w shellshockfireworks.co.uk 📇 Dir: Zoe Gibson.

Skylight Cinema 3 Jubilee Wharf, Commercial Rd, Penryn, Cornwall, TR10 8FG **t** 01326 377738
e tim@metronome.co.uk **w** skylightcinema.co.uk
📇 Managing Director: Tim Smithies.

SSE Audio Group Burnt Meadow House, Burnt Meadow Rd, North Moons Moat, Redditch, B98 9PA
t 01527 528 822 **f** 01527 528 840
e enquiries@sseaudio.com **w** sseaudiogroup.com
📇 Managing Director: John Penn.

Stage Light Design 3 Palace Gate House, Hampton Court Rd, East Molesey, London, SW19 2PT
t 020 8397 8691 **f** 020 8020 1435
e mw@stagelightdesign.com **w** stagelightdesign.com
📇 MD: John Rinaldi.

System Sound (UK) Ltd 1 Liddall Way, Horton Rd, West Drayton, Middlesex, UB7 8PG **t** 01895 432995
f 01895 432976 **e** simon@systemsound.com
w systemsound.com 📇 Director: Simon Biddulph.

Tiger Production c/o 6 Elizabeth Court, Higher Lane, Plymouth, PL1 2AN **t** 07785 228511 **f** 07053 441299
e jim@tigerproduction.co.uk **w** tigerproduction.co.uk
📇 Owner: Jim Parsons.

Tour Concepts - Tour Management
14 Wakefield Rd, London, N15 4NL **t** 020 8808 8115
f 0870 1265960 **e** mail@tourconcepts.com
w tourconcepts.com 📇 Owner: Andy Reynolds.

Tour Logistics t 07733 431 200
e hamish@tourlogistics.co.uk **w** tourlogistics.co.uk
📇 Production Manager: Hamish Duff.

TourHouse Productions 5 Knoll Road, Sidcup, Kent, DA14 4QT **t** 020 8308 9363 **f** 020 8308 9364
e steve@tourhouse.org 📇 Tour Manager / Production Manager: Steve Martin.

Vans For Bands Ltd 42 Woodstock Rd East, Begbroke, Oxford, OX5 1RG **t** 01865 842840
e info@vansforbands.co.uk **w** vansforbands.co.uk
📇 MD: Tarrant Anderson.

Violation Tour Production Eastcourt, 39 Eastgate, Sleaford, Lincs, NG34 7DU **t** 07768 667076
f 0870 831 3726 **e** dickmeredith@mac.com
📇 Manager: Dick Meredith.

The Vocal Zone - Vocal Coach PO Box 25269, London, N12 9ZT **t** 07970 924 190
e info@thevocalzone.co.uk **w** thevocalzone.co.uk
📇 Contact: Kenny Thomas.

Travel & Transport Services

Aeromega Ltd Stapleford Tawney Aerodrome, Stapleford Tawney, Essex, RM4 1SJ **t** 01708 688 361
f 01708 688 566 **e** abere@aeromega.com
w aeromega.com 📇 GM: James White.

Air Brokers International Charity Farm, Fulborough Road, Parham, Sussex, RH20 4HP
t 01903 740 200 **f** 01903 740 102 **e** bugle@instoneair.com
📇 Contact: Mike Bugle.

Air Charter Service plc Charter House, 45C High Street, Hampton Wick, Kingston upon Thames, Surrey, KT1 4DG **t** 020 8614 6299 **f** 020 8943 1062
e catherine.skaggs@aircharter.co.uk **w** aircharter.co.uk
📇 Passenger Charter Analyst: Catherine Skaggs.

Air Partner Platinum House, Gatwick Rd, Crawley, West Sussex, RH10 9RP **t** 01293 844 855 **f** 01293 844 859
e travel@airpartner.com **w** airpartner.com 📇 Contact: Sarah Jamieson.

Air Partner plc Platinum House, Gatwick Rd, Crawley, West Sussex, RH10 9RP **t** 01293 844812 **f** 01293 844859
e arts@airpartner.com **w** airpartner.com 📇 Senior Analyst: Ian Browne.

Anglo Pacific International Units 1 & 2, Bush Industrial Estate, Standard Road, London, NW10 6DF
t 020 8965 1234 **f** 020 8965 4954
e info@anglopacific.co.uk **w** anglopacific.co.uk 📇 MD: Steve Perry.

Beat The Street UK (Tour Coaches) Unit 103, Cariocca Business Park, Hellidon Close, Ardwick, Manchester, M12 4AH **t** 0161 273 5984 **f** 0161 272 7772
e beatthestreetuk@aol.com **w** beatthestreet.net
📇 Manager: Paul Collis.

Chapman Freeborn Airchartering Limited
Astral Towers, 6th Floor, Betts Way, Crawley, West Sussex, RH10 9UY **t** 01293 572872 **f** 01293 572873
e vipteam@chapman-freeborn.com **w** chapman-freeborn.com 📇 VIP Charters Manager: Claudette Gharbi 01293 572829.

Civilised Car Hire Company Ltd.
50 Parsons Green Lane, London, SW6 4HU **t** 020 7703 3737
f 020 7384 3366 **e** mail@londoncarhire.com
w londoncarhire.com 📇 MD: Toby Hobson 020 7384 1133.

The Concert Travel Company Unit 3, Barum Gate, Widdon Valley, Barnstaple, Devon, EX32 8QD
t 01271 323 355 **f** 01271 375 902
e sales@ticketzone.co.uk **w** ticketzone.co.uk
📇 Contact: Robert Cotton.

Live: Travel & Transport Services

Detonate Music & Entertainment Travel Services 104-105 High Street, Eton, Windsor, Berks, SL4 6AF t 01753 801 200 f 01753 672 710 e Detonate@eton-travel.co.uk w detonatetravel.com

DJB Passports & Visas 1st Floor, 16-20 Kingsland Road, Shoreditch, London, E2 8DA t 020 7684 6242 f 020 7739 5244 e info@djbvisas.com w djbvisas.com ◼ Accounts Manager: James Cox.

Dunn-Line Travel Dunn-Line Holdings, Beechdale Road, Nottingham, Nottinghamshire, NG8 3EU t 0870 012 1212 f 0115 900 7051 e enquiries@dunn-line.com w dunn-line.com ◼ MD: Scott Dunn.

EST Ltd Bell Lane, North Woolwich Rd, London, E16 2AB t 020 7055 7200 f 020 7055 7201 e delr@est-uk.com w yourock-weroll.co.uk ◼ Director: Del Roll.

ET Travel 35 Britannia Row, Islington, London, N1 8QH t 020 7359 7161 f 020 7354 3270 e info@ettravel.co.uk w ettravel.co.uk ◼ Manager: Clare Rolston.

EXECUTOURS

Tour Management / Ground Transport & Logistics t 07774 137910 e info@executours.co.uk w executours.co.uk ◼ Contact: Guy Anderson. **Company profile: (UK) 07774 137 910 (US) +1 973 262 5068 (AUS) + 61 423 193866**

Fineminster Europe Worth Corner, Pound Hill, Crawley, West Sussex, RH10 7SL t 01293 885888 f 01293 883238 e charter@fineminster.com w fineminster.com ◼ MD: Graham Plunkett as above.

Genesis Adoration Ltd Redwood House, Hurstwood Grange, Hurstwood Lane, Haywards Heath, W. Sussex, RH17 7QX t 01444 476 120 f 01444 476 101 e lorna.milner@genesisadoration.com w genesisadoration.com ◼ Events Manager: Lorna Milner.

GWH Backline Rental GWH, Pegasus House, 550 Newark Rd North Hykeham, Lincoln, LN6 9NG t 01522 501814 e gary@gwhmusic.com w gwhmusic.com ◼ Director: Gary Weight.

K West Hotel & Spa Richmond Way, London, W14 0AX t 020 8008 6640 f 020 8008 6696 e cj@k-west.co.uk w k-west.co.uk ◼ facebook.com/pages/London-United-Kingdom/K-West-Hotel-Spa/103287936008 ◼ twitter.com/kwesthotel ◼ Senior Sales Manager - Music & Entertainment: Carla Judge.

Marken Time Critical Express Unit 2, Metro Centre, St Johns Road, Isleworth, Middlesex, TW7 6NJ t 020 8388 8555 f 020 8388 8666 e info@marken.com w marken.com ◼ Bus Devel Mgr: Rob Paterson.

Millennium Concert Travel 1a Dickson Road, Blackpool, Lancashire, FY1 2AX t 01253 299 266 f 01253 299 454 e sales@mct-online.com w mct-online.com ◼ Contact: Julian Murray.

Movin' Music Ltd (London) Suite 1, 52 Highfield Road, Purley, Surrey, CRB 2JG t 020 8763 0767 f 020 8668 2214 e info@movinmusic.net w movinmusic.net ◼ Dir: Brenda Lillywhite.

Movin' Music Ltd (Manchester) Studio 2, 33 Albany Rd, Chorlton, Manchester, M21 0BH t 0161 881 9227 f 0161 881 9089 e info@movinmusic.net w movinmusic.net ◼ Dir: Nick Robinson.

Moving Space Rentals Ltd Unit C4 Connaught business center, Hyde Estate Rd Hendon, London, NW9 6JP t 020 8205 2503 e charlene@movingspacetours.com w movingspacetours.com ◼ Manager: Nick Yeatman, Charlene Bukowska.

Music By Appointment (MBA) - Tour Travel Agents The Linen House, 253 Kilburn Lane, London, W10 4BQ t 020 8960 1600 f 020 8960 1255 e caroline.mccann@appointmentgroup.com w musicbyappointment.com ◼ Supervisor: Caroline McCann 020 8962 6751.

Nightsky Travel Ltd Starcloth Way, Mullacott Ind. Est, Ilfracombe, Devon, EX34 8AY t 01271 855 138 f 01271 867 120 e info@nightskytravel.com w nightskytravel.com ◼ Director: Danny Hudson.

Nova Travel 20 Old Lydd Rd, Camber, East Sussex, TN31 7RH t 08452 300039 e Info@Novabussing.co.uk w Novabussing.com ◼ Contact: Peter Davie.

Pinnacle Chauffeur Transport London North 14 Lucerne Close, London, N13 4QJ t 0800 783 4107 e info@yourchauffeur.co.uk w yourchauffeur.co.uk ◼ Director: Alan D Pinner.

Premier Aviation UK Ltd 2 Newhouse Business Centre, Old Crawley Rd, Horsham, West Sussex, RH12 4RU t 01293 852688 f 01293 852699 e operations@premieraviation.com w premieraviation.com ◼ MD: Adrian Whitmarsh.

Rima Travel 10 Angel Gate, City Rd, London, EC1V 2PT t 020 7833 5071 f 020 7278 4700 e ernie.garcia@rima-travel.co.uk w rimatravel.co.uk ◼ MD: Ernie Garcia.

Screen And Music Travel Ltd Colne House, High St, Colnebrook, SL3 0LX t 01753 764 050 f 01753 764 051 e groups@screenandmusictravel.com w screenandmusic.travel ◼ facebook.com/pages/screen-and-music-travel/23237181745 ◼ Special Project Manager: Colin Doran.

Sound Moves (UK) Ltd Abbeygate House, Challenge Rd, Ashford, Middx, TW15 1AX t 01784 424470 f 01784 424490 e london@soundmoves.com w soundmoves.com ◼ MD: Martin Corr.

Stardes Ashes Buildings, Old Lane, Holbrook Industrial Estate, Halfway, Sheffield, S20 3GZ t 0114 251 0051 f 0114 251 0555 e info@stardes.co.uk w stardes.co.uk ◼ Contact: David Harvey-Steinberg.

Contacts | Facebook | MySpace | Twitter | YouTube

Studio Moves 54a Coningham Rd, London, W12 8BH
t 07970 518217 **f** 020 8746 9329
e info@studiomoves.co.uk **w** studiomoves.co.uk
studiomoves Contact: Peter Stewart 07970 518 217.

The Tour Company 1st Floor, 5 Eagle St, Glasgow,
G4 9XA **t** 0141 353 8800 **f** 0141 353 8801
e admin@thetourcompany.co.uk **w** thetourcompany.co.uk
facebook.com/home.php#/thetourcompany?ref=ts
MD: Tina Waters.

Tour Logistics t 07733 431 200
e hamish@tourlogistics.co.uk **w** tourlogistics.co.uk
Production Manager: Hamish Duff.

Tourpro Suite 136, Viglen House, Alperton Lane, HA0 1HD
t 0845 116 1300 **e** bookings@tourpro.co.uk
w tourpro.co.uk Operations Manager: Michele Conroy.

Travel4Tours Ashbourne Way, Woodthorpe, York,
North Yorkshire, YO24 2SW **t** 01904 777217
f 01904 777172 **e** info@travel4tours.com
w travel4tours.com travel4tours

Tour Miscellaneous

5 Star Cases lTD Broad End Industrial Estate,
Broad End Rd, Walsoken, Wisbech, Cambs, PE14 7BQ
t 01945 427000 **f** 01945 427015 **e** info@5star-
cases.com **w** 5star-cases.com MD: Keith Sykes.

BCS Multi Media (Computer Visuals)
Grantham House, Macclesfield, Cheshire, SK10 3NP
t 01625 615 379 **f** 01625 429 667
e dpl@bcsmm.fsnet.co.uk **w** bcsmm.fsnet.co.uk
Director: Duncan Latham.

Calma - Complementary Therapies
PO Box 49669, London, N8 4YU **t** 07973 887520
e caroline@calma.biz **w** calma.biz Therapist: Caroline
Dapre.

Complete Tours Wayside, Magna Mile, Ludford,
Market Rasen, LN8 6AD **t** 07879 073488 **f** 01652 654243
e info@completetours.co.uk **w** completetours.co.uk
Mgr: Nathan Clark.

**Crawfords of London Executive Chauffeur
hire UK & International** 8 Concord Business Centre,
Concord Rd, London, W3 0TJ **t** 020 8896 3030
f 020 8896 3300 **e** crawfords@cdsgroup.co.uk
w crawfordsoflondon.com Operational Director: Dave
Roberts.

Crisp Productions Tour Mgmt & Support Services,
21 Stupton Rd, Sheffield, S9 1BQ **t** 0114 261 1649
f 0114 261 1649 **e** dc@cprod.win-uk.net MD: Darren
Crisp.

The Departure Lounge 29 Kingdon Road, London,
NW6 1PJ **t** 020 7431 2070 **f** 020 7431 2070
Contact: Susan Ransom.

**Detonate Music & Entertainment Travel
Services** 104-105 High Street, Eton, Windsor, Berks,
SL4 6AF **t** 01753 801 200 **f** 01753 672 710
e Detonate@eton-travel.co.uk **w** detonatetravel.com

Eat To The Beat Studio 4-5, Garnet Close,
Greycaine Rd, Watford, Herts, WD2 4JN **t** 01923 211702
f 01923 211704 **e** catering@eattothebeat.com
w globalinfusiongroup.com Operations Director: Mary
Shelley-Smith.

Front Of House Productions 81 Harriet Street,
Trecynon, Aberdare, Rhondda Cynon Taff, CF44 8PL
t 01685 881006 **f** 01685 881006
e info@fohproductions.co.uk **w** fohproductions.co.uk
Production Mgr: Jules Jones.

Fruition Chestnut Farm, Frodsham, Cheshire
t 01928 734422 **f** 01928 734433
e mtasker@fruition.co.uk **w** fruition.co.uk
Contact: Mark Tasker 020 7430 0700.

Grand Tours 93b Scrubs Lane, London, NW10 6QU
t 020 8968 7798 **f** 020 8968 3377
e johndawkins@granduniongroup.com **w** grand-tours.net
Manager: John Dawkins.

Health & Safety Advice PO Box 32295, London,
W5 1WD **t** 0870 066 0272 **f** 0870 066 0273
e info@health-safetyadvice.co.uk **w** health-
safetyadvice.co.uk Dir: Jan Goodwin.

John Henry's 16-24 Brewery Road, London, N7 9NH
t 020 7609 9181 **f** 020 7700 7040
e johnh@johnhenrys.com **w** johnhenrys.com MD: John
Henry.

Key Cargo International
7 Millbrook Business Centre, Floats Rd, Roundthorn,
Manchester, M23 9YJ **t** 0161 283 2471 **f** 0161 283 2472
e info@keycargo.net Operations Director: Steve Plant.

Knights Guitar Electronics and Flight Cases
28 Hill Grove, Romford, Essex, RM1 4JP **t** 07788 740793
f 07092 231176 **e** kge@freeuk.com **w** welcome.to/kge
MD: Ron Knights.

MEDIA TRAVEL LTD

mediatravel ★
travel management for the entertainment industry

Studio G2, Battersea Studios, 80 Silverthorne Rd, London,
SW8 3HE **t** 020 7627 2200 **f** 020 7627 2221
e fran@mediatravel.com **w** mediatravel.com MD: Fran
Green.

Midnight Costume Design & Wardrobe London,
SW3 **t** 07722 882 847
e Midnight_wardrobe@hotmail.com
w midnightwardrobe.com Wardrobe
Specialist/Stylist/Designer: Midnight.

Movin' Music Ltd (London) Suite 1,
52 Highfield Road, Purley, Surrey, CRB 2JG
t 020 8763 0767 **f** 020 8668 2214
e info@movinmusic.net **w** movinmusic.net Dir: Brenda
Lillywhite.

Live: Travel & Transport Services, Tour Miscellaneous

Live: Tour Miscellaneous

Movin' Music Ltd (Manchester) Studio 2, 33 Albany Rd, Chorlton, Manchester, M21 0BH **t** 0161 881 9227 **f** 0161 881 9089 **e** info@movinmusic.net **w** movinmusic.net 🔲 Dir: Nick Robinson.

MTFX Velt House, Velt House Lane, Elmore, Gloucester, GL2 3NY **t** 01452 729903 **f** 01452 729904 **e** info@mtfx.com **w** mtfx.com 🔲 MD: Mark Turner.

Pa-Boom Phenomenal Fireworks Ltd 49 Carters Close, Sherington, Buckinghamshire, MK16 9NW **t** 01908 612 593 **f** 01908 216 400 **e** pa@boom.demon.co.uk **w** pa-boom.com 🔲 Contact: Neil Canham 0860 439 380.

Packhorse Case Co 9 Stapledon Road, Orton Southgate, Peterborough, Cambs, PE2 6TB **t** 01733 232440 **f** 01733 232556 🔲 Contact: Sam Robinson.

Personality Artistes Ltd PO Box 1, Blackpool, Lancashire, FY6 7WS **t** 01253 899 988 **f** 01253 899 333 **e** info@personalityartistes.com **w** personalityartistes.com 🔲 MD: Mal Ford 07860 479 092.

Pod Bluman 65 Coppetts Road, London, N10 1JH **t** 020 8374 8400 **f** 020 8374 2982 **e** pod.projects@blueyonder.co.uk

Pyramid Productions & Promotions Cadillac Ranch, Pencraig Uchaf, Cwm Bach, Whitland, Carms., SA34 0DT **t** 01994 484466 **f** 01994 484294 **e** cadillacranch@telco4u.net 🔲 Dir: Weepy Moyer.

So Touring Services PO Box 20750, London, E3 2YU **t** 020 8573 6652 **f** 020 8573 6784 **e** sotouring@aol.com 🔲 Contact: Sean O'Neill.

Sonic Movement Flat 2, 110 Chepstow Rd, London, W2 5QS **t** 020 7229 0196 **f** 020 7691 7276 **e** JOwens666@btinternet.com 🔲 Tour Manager: Jamie Owens.

SPA Catering Services 44 Oak Hill Road, London, SW15 2QR **t** 020 7563 2550 **f** 020 8871 4579 **e** spacatering@hotmail.com 🔲 MD: Simon Peter 07788 785 493.

Taurus Self Drive Ltd 55 Wyverne Road, Chorlton, Manchester, M21 0ZW **t** 0161 434 9823 **f** 0161 434 9823 🔲 Contact: Sean Shannon 020 7434 9823.

TCP International Ltd 101 Shepherds Bush Rd, London, W6 7LP **t** 020 7602 8822 **f** 020 7603 2352 🔲 Live Manager/Event Prod: John Fairs.

TM International 4 Badby Rd, Newnham, Daventry, Northamptonshire, NN11 3HE **t** 01327 705032 **e** hotel.india@virgin.net 🔲 Tour Manager: Harry Isles 07785 267751.

The Tough Enough Touring Company Tour Mngmt & Splitter Van Hire, 88 Calvert Rd, Greenwich, London, SE10 0DF **t** 020 8333 9447 **e** sam.towers@ganzmanagement.com 🔲 Contact: Sam Towers 07985 142 193.

Tour Logistics t 07733 431 200 **e** hamish@tourlogistics.co.uk **w** tourlogistics.co.uk 🔲 Production Manager: Hamish Duff.

Tour Supply Ltd Ground Floor Unit 1, Apollo Business Centre, Apsley Grove, Ardwick, Manchester, M12 6AW **t** 08454 238687 **f** 0161 272 7772 **e** paul@toursupply.com **w** toursupply.co.uk 🔲 Managing Director: Paul Collis 07976 265042.

Len Wright Band Services 9 Elton Way, Watford, Hertfordshire, WD2 8HH **t** 01923 238611 **f** 01923 230134 **e** lwbs1@aol.com 🔲 Contact: Les Collins 07831 811201.

METROPOLIS

STUDIOS
MASTERING
DIGITAL MEDIA

WWW.METROPOLIS-GROUP.CO.UK
+44 (0)20 8742 1111

KATY SAMWELL
STUDIO MANAGER
KATY.SAMWELL@METROPOLIS-GROUP.CO.UK

YVONNE ZIMMERLING
MASTERING MANAGER
YVONNE.ZIMMERLING@METROPOLIS-GROUP.CO.UK

RICH OSBORN
HEAD OF DIGITAL MEDIA
RICH@METROPOLIS-GROUP.CO.UK

The Power House
70 Chiswick High Road
W4 1SY
hello@metropolis-group.co.uk

THE **MUSIC PRODUCERS GUILD AWARDS 2010**

▶ the music producers guild awards

The Music Producers Guild Awards take place on February 11th 2010 to celebrate the creative talent and technical ability of the UK's music producers, engineers, mixers and re-mixers.

Visit www.mpgawards.co.uk
to find out more.

For information about sponsorship opportunities for the 2011 event please contact Natalie Besbrode: natalie@bubblesqueak.co.uk

For press releases, information and/or comments from the MPG board of directors, contact Sue Silitoe: sue@whitenoisepr.co.uk

headline sponsors

PPL *Prism Sound* SADiE 6

Contacts Facebook MySpace Twitter  YouTube

Recording Studios & Services

Recording Studios

128 Studios (The Next Room) 5B Oakleigh Mews, Oakleigh Rd North, Whetstone, North London, N20 9HE **t** 020 8343 9971 **e** studio@thenextroom.com **w** thenextroom.com **f** facebook.com/pages/The-Next-Room-Productions/42890293937 🅜 myspace.com/thenextroom 🅑 Producers, Writers and Remixers: Rich and Bob 07930 180989.

2KHz Studios 145c Crouch Hill Rd, Crouch End, London, UK, N8 9QH **t** 07775 723996 **e** ian.grimble@virgin.net **w** 2khzstudios.com 🅜 myspace.com/2khz 🅑 Producer/Mixer: Ian Grimble.

3kyoti Studio Flat 2/1, 91 Oban Drive, Glasgow, G20 6AB **t** 0141 533 1837 **e** info@markfreegard.com **w** markfreegard.com 🅑 recording engineer/producer: Mark Freegard 07977 101081.

45 RPM Imex House, VIP Trading Estate, Anchor & Hope Lane, London, SE7 7TE **t** 020 8269 0352 **f** 020 8269 0353 **e** suzanne@quixoticrecords.com 🅑 Contact: Suzanne Hunt, Glenn Tilbrook.

80 Hertz Studios 39 Queen St, Manchester, M3 7DQ **t** 07714 145880 **e** george@80hertz.com **w** 80hertz.com **f** facebook.com/group.php?gid=4674293619&ref=ts 🅜 myspace.com/80_hertz_studios 🅣 twitter.com/80hertz 🅨 youtube.com/user/80Hertz 🅑 Dir & Producer: George Atkins.

Abbey Road Studios 3 Abbey Rd, London, NW8 9AY **t** 020 7266 7000 **f** 020 7266 7250 **e** bookings@abbeyroad.com **w** abbeyroad.com 🅑 Studio Manager: Colette Barber.

AGM Studios 1927 Building. 2 Michael Rd, London, SW6 2AD **t** 020 7371 0234 **e** contacts@agmstudios.com **w** agmstudios.com 🅑 Producer/Writer: Alex Golding.

Air Studios Lyndhurst Hall, Lyndhurst Road, Hampstead, London, NW3 5NG **t** 020 7794 0660 **f** 020 7794 8518 **e** info@airstudios.com **w** airstudios.com 🅑 Studio Mgr: Alison Burton.

Air-Edel Recording Studios 18 Rodmarton St, London, W1U 8BJ **t** 020 7486 6466 **f** 020 7224 0344 **e** bethan.barron@air-edel.co.uk **w** air-edel.co.uk 🅑 Studio Manager: Bethan Barron.

Airtight Productions Unit 16, Albany Rd Trading Estate, Chorlton, Manchester, M21 0AZ **t** 0161 881 5157 **e** info@airtightproductions.co.uk **w** airtightproductions.co.uk 🅑 Dir: Anthony Davey.

Alaska Studio 127-129 Alaska St, London, SE1 8XE **t** 020 7928 7440 **f** 020 7928 8070 **e** blodge_uk@yahoo.com **w** alaskastudio.co.uk 🅜 myspace.com/alaskastudio 🅣 alaskastudio 🅑 Studio Mgr: Beverley Lodge 07737395296.

Albert Studios Unit 29, Cygnus Business Centre, Dalmeyer Road, London, NW10 2XA **t** 020 8830 0330 **f** 020 8830 0220 **e** info@alberts.co.uk **w** albertmusic.co.uk 🅑 Studio Manager: Will Maya.

All of Music PO Box 2361, Romford, Essex, RM2 6EZ **t** 01708 688 088 **f** 020 7691 9508 **e** michelle@allofmusic.co.uk **w** allofmusic.co.uk 🅑 MD: Danielle Barnett.

ALPHA CENTAURI RECORDING

1 Maybury Gardens, Willesden Green, London, NW10 2NB **t** 020 3239 5880 **f** 020 7000 1253 **e** bookings@alpha.uk.com **w** alpha.uk.com **Possibly the UK's best equipped SSL room in a very stylish setting.**

Angel Recording Studios Ltd 311 Upper St, London, N1 2TU **t** 020 7354 2525 **f** 020 7226 9624 **e** angel@angelstudios.co.uk **w** angelstudios.co.uk 🅑 Studio Manager: Lucy Jones.

Arclite Productions The Grove Music Studios, Unit 10.Latimer Ind. Est, Latimer Rd, London, W10 6RQ **t** 020 8964 9047 **e** info@arcliteproductions.com **w** arcliteproductions.com 🅑 Producer: Alan Bleay 02089649047.

Ariwa Sounds 34 Whitehorse Lane, London, SE25 6RE **t** 020 8653 7744 **f** 020 8771 1911 **e** info@ariwa.com **w** ariwa.com 🅑 Studio Mgr: Joseph Fraser 020 8771 1470.

Ariwa Studios 34 Whitehorse Lane, South Norwood, London, SE25 6RE **t** 020 8653 7744 **f** 020 8771 1911 **e** ariwastudios@aol.com **w** ariwa.com 🅑 Sound engineer: Joseph Fraser 02086537744.

Arriba Studios 256-258 Gray's Inn Road, London, WC1X 8ED **t** 020 7713 0998 **e** info@arriba-records.com **w** arriba-records.com 🅑 Contact: SJ/Baby Doc.

Artisan Audio 46a Woodbridge Road, Moseley, Birmingham, B13 8EJ **t** 0121 249 0598 **f** 0709 214 8920 **e** enquiries@artisanaudio.com **w** artisanaudio.com 🅑 Owner: Jon Cotton.

Contacts   Facebook   MySpace   Twitter   YouTube

The Audio Workshop 217 Askew Rd, London,
W12 9AZ **t** 020 8742 9242 **f** 020 8743 4231
e info@theaudioworkshop.co.uk
w theaudioworkshop.co.uk MD: Martin Cook.

Band On The Wall Studio 25 Swan Street,
Northern Quarter, Manchester, M4 5JZ **t** 0161 834 1786
f 0161 834 2559 **w** bandonthewall.org
Promotions: Gavin Sharp.

Bandwagon Studios Westfield Folkhouse,
Westfield Lane, Mansfield, Notts, NG18 1TL
t 01623 422962 **f** 01623 633449
e info@bandwagonstudios.co.uk
w bandwagonstudios.co.uk Studio Mgr: Andy Dawson.

Bark Studio 1A Blenheim Rd, London, E17 6HS
t 020 8523 0110 **f** 020 8523 0110
e Brian@barkstudio.co.uk **w** barkstudio.co.uk Studio
Manager: Brian O'Shaughnessy.

BBC Resources (London) Maida Vale Music Studios,
Delaware Road, London, W9 2LH **t** 020 7765 3374
f 020 7765 3203 **e** adam.askew@bbc.co.uk
Ops Mgr: Adam Askew.

Berlin Recording Studios Caxton House,
Caxton Avenue, Blackpool, Lancashire, FY2 9AP
t 01253 591 169 **f** 01253 508 670
e info@berlinstudios.co.uk **w** berlinstudios.co.uk
MD: Ron Sharples.

Berry Street Studio 1 Berry St, London, EC1V 0AA
t 020 7253 5885 **e** kp@berrystreetstudio.com
w berrystreetstudio.com
myspace.com/berrystreetstudio berryststudio
MD: Kevin Poree.

Big Noise Recordings 12 Gregory Street,
Northampton, NN1 1TA **t** 01604 634 455
e bignoisestudios@hotmail.co.uk
w myspace.com/bignoisestudio
Studio Mgr: Kim Gordelier.

Blakamix International Garvey House,
42 Margetts Road, Bedford, MK42 8DS **t** 01234 856 164
f 01234 854 344 **e** info@blakamix.co.uk **w** blakamix.co.uk
MD: Dennis Bedeau.

Blossom Studio Station Rd, Blaina, Gwent, NP13 3PW
t 01495 290 960 **e** info@blossomstudio.co.uk
w blossomstudio.co.uk Proprietor & Engineer: Noel
Watson 07932 377 109.

BLUE PRO STUDIOS

Unit 11, 407-409 Hornsey Rd, London, N19 4DX
t +44 (0)207 272 0358 **e** info@blueprostudios.com
w blueprostudios.com myspace.com/blueprostudios
twitter.com/blueprogroup
youtube.com/blueprostudios Director: Alexander
Balfour. Engineer: John Webber. Engineer: Charles
Westropp. Engineer: Paul Borg. Engineer: Gavin Cheung
(Nookie). Engineer: Jerome Schmitt.

Blueprint Studios Elizabeth House, 39 Queen St,
Salford, Manchester, Greater Manchester, M3 7DQ
t 0161 817 2524 **f** 0161 834 9184 **e** tim@blueprint-
studios.com **w** blueprint-studios.com
myspace.com/blueprintstudiosuk
twitter.com/blueprintstudio Studio Manager: Tim
Thomas 0161 817 2520.

BonaFideStudio Burbage House, 83-85 Curtain Rd,
London, EC2A 3BS **t** 020 7684 5350
e info@bonafidestudio.co.uk **w** bonafidestudio.co.uk
myspace.com/recordingbonafidestudio Studio
Director: Deanna Gardner 020 7684 5350; 020 7684
5351.

Boomtown (ProTools) Studio Valetta Rd, London,
W3 7TG **t** 020 8723 9548 **e** info@boomtownstudio.co.uk
w boomtownstudio.co.uk Contact: Simon Wilkinson.

Born To Dance Studios
Unit 34, DRCA Business Centre, Charlotte Despard Ave,
Battersea, London, SW11 5JH **t** 01273 301555
f 01273 305266 **e** studio@borntodance.com
w borntodance.com Studio Mgr: Gavin McCall.

The Bridge Facilities Ltd 55-
57 Great Marlborough St, London, W1F 7JX
t 020 7434 9861 **f** 020 7494 4658
e bookings@thebridge.co.uk **w** thebridge.co.uk
Facilities Mgr: Dionne James.

Brighton Electric Tramway House, 43-
45 Coombe Terrace, Brighton, East Sussex, BN2 4AD
t 01273 819617 **e** enquiries@brightonelectric.co.uk
w brightonelectric.co.uk
myspace.com/brightonelectric Studio
Manager: James Stringfellow.

Britannia Row Studios 3 Bridge Studios, 318-
326 Wandsworth Bridge Rd, Fulham, London, SW6 2TZ
t 020 7371 5872 **f** 020 7384 3706
e jamie@britanniarowstudios.co.uk
w britanniarowstudios.co.uk Studio Manager:
Jamie Lane.

British Grove Studios 20 British Grove, Chiswick, London, W4 2NL **t** 020 8741 8941 **f** 020 8748 1038 **e** info@britishgrovestudios.com **w** britishgrovestudios.com 📇 Studio Manager: David Stewart.

Bryn Derwen Studio Coed Y Parc, Bethesda, Gwynedd, LL57 4YW **t** 07760 105773 **f** 01248 600234 **e** L.Gane@btinternet.com **w** brynderwen.co.uk 📇 Manager: Laurie Gane.

The Building 37 Rowley Street, Stafford, Staffs, ST16 2RH **t** 01785 245649 **e** info@thebuilding.co.uk **w** thebuilding.co.uk 📇 Studio Mgr: Tim Simmons 07866 718010.

Ca Va Sound - Ca Va Soundmobile 30 Bentinck St, Kelvingrove, Glasgow, Strathclyde, G3 7TT **t** 0141 334 5099 **f** 0141 339 0271 **e** cavasound@mac.com **w** cavasound.com 📇 cavasoundglasgow 📇 Studio Mgr: Brian Young.

Cabin Studios 82 London Rd, Coventry, West Midlands, CV1 2JT **t** 02476 220749 **e** office@sonar-records.demon.co.uk **w** cabinstudio.co.uk 📇 Studio Mgr: Jon Lord.

Cadillac Ranch Recording Studio Cadillac Ranch, Pencraig Uchaf, Cwmbach, Whitland, Carms., SA34 0DT **t** 01994 484466 **f** 01994 48446 **e** cadillacranch@telco4u.net **w** nikturner.com 📇 Dir: Moose Magoon.

Castlesound Studios The Old School, Park View, Pencaitland, East Lothian, EH34 5DW **t** 0131 666 1024 **f** 0131 666 1024 **w** castlesound.co.uk 📇 Studio & Bookings Mgr: Freeland Barbour.

The Cave Studio 155 Acton Lane, Park Royal, London, NW10 7NJ **t** 020 8961 5818 **f** 020 8965 7008 **e** danny@jetstar.co.uk 📇 Studio Manager: Danny Ray.

Chamber Recording Studio 120A West Granton Rd, Edinburgh, Midlothian, EH5 1PF **t** 0131 551 6632 **f** 0131 551 6632 **e** mail@humancondition.co.uk **w** chamberstudio.co.uk 📇 Studio Mgr: Jamie Watson.

Chem19 Recording Studios Unit 51B, South Avenue, Blantyre Industrial Estate, Blantyre, G72 0XB **t** 01698 324 246 **f** 01698 327 979 **e** jim@chemikal.co.uk **w** chem19studios.co.uk 📇 Dir: Jim Savage.

Chestnut Studios 17 Barons Court Rd, West Kensington, London, W14 9DP **t** 020 7384 5960 **e** info@chestnutstudios.com **w** chestnutstudios.com 📇 myspace.com/chestnutstudios 📇 Studio Manager: Chris Young.

The Church Road Recording Company 197-201 Church Rd, Hove, East Sussex, BN3 2AH **t** 07803 173003 **e** info@churchroad.net **w** churchroad.net 📇 myspace.com/churchroadrecordingco 📇 Producer/Engineer: Julian Tardo 07803 173 003.

Classic Sound 5 Falcon Pk, Neasden Lane, London, NW10 1RZ **t** 020 8208 8100 **f** 020 8208 8111 **e** info@classicsound.net **w** classicsound.net 📇 Director: Neil Hutchinson.

The Classical Recording Co.Ltd 16-17 Wolsey Mews, Kentish Town, London, NW5 2DX **t** 020 7482 2303 **f** 020 7482 2302 **e** info@classicalrecording.com **w** classicalrecording.com 📇 Snr Producer: Simon Weir.

CMS Studios The Millennium Centre, 11-13 Clearwell Drive, London, W9 2JZ **t** 020 7641 3679 **e** john@miller9878.fsnet.co.uk 📇 Contact: John Miller 07747 451 704.

Conversion Studios Woolfields, Milton On Stour, Gillingham, Dorset, SP8 5PX **t** 01747 824729 **e** info@conversionstudios.co.uk **w** conversionstudios.co.uk 📇 myspace.com/conversionstudios 📇 Director: Owen Thomas.

Cordella Music Alhambra, High St, Shirrell Heath, Southampton, Hants, SO32 2JH **t** 08450 616 616 **f** 01329 833 433 **e** barry@cordellamusic.co.uk **w** cordellamusic.co.uk 📇 MD: Barry Upton.

Cottage Recording Studios 2 Gawsworth Rd, Macclesfield, Cheshire, SK11 8UE **t** 01625 420163 **f** 01625 420168 **e** rogerboden@cottagegroup.co.uk **w** cottagegroup.co.uk 📇 myspace.com/cottagestudios 📇 MD: Roger Boden.

Courtyard Recording Studios Gorsey Mount Street, Waterloo Road, Stockport, Cheshire, SK1 3BU **t** 0161 477 6531 **e** courtyardrecording@mac.com **w** iWav.co.uk 📇 Studio Mgr: Tim Woodward.

Courtyard Studio 21 The Nursery, Sutton Courtenay, Oxon, OX14 4UA **t** 01622 880 990 **f** 0870 051 0183 **e** pippa@cyard.com 📇 Studio Mgr: Pippa Mole.

The Cutting Rooms Abraham Moss Centre, Crescent Road, Manchester, M8 5UF **t** 0161 740 9438 **f** 0161 740 9438 **e** cuttingrooms@hotmail.com **w** citycol.com/cuttingrooms 📇 Studio Mgr: Andrew Harris.

Dada Studios 157A Hubert Grove, Stockwell, London, SW9 9NZ **t** 07956 945417 **f** 020 7501 9216 **e** dadastudios@mac.com **w** dadastudios.co.uk 📇 Studio Manager: George Holt 07956 945 417.

The Dairy 43-45 Tunstall Rd, London, SW9 8BZ **t** 020 7738 7777 **f** 020 7738 7007 **e** info@thedairy.co.uk **w** thedairy.co.uk 📇 Contact: Mary Evans.

The Dairy Studios 43-45 Tunstall Rd, London, SW9 8BZ **t** 020 7387 7777 **f** 020 7738 7007 **e** info@thedairy.co.uk 📇 Studio Manager: Mary Evans 020 7738 7777.

Dean St. Studios 59 Dean Street, Soho, London, W1D 6AN **t** 020 7734 8009 **e** info@deanst.com **w** deanst.com 📇 Studio Manager: Jasmin Lee.

Recording Studios & Services: Recording Studios

Contacts **Facebook** **MySpace** **Twitter** **YouTube**

deBrett Studios 42 Wood Vale, Muswell Hill, London, N10 3DP **t** 020 8372 6179
e jwest@debrett41.freeserve.co.uk
Proprietor: Jon West 07814 267 792.

Deep Blue Recording Studio 38 Looe St, Plymouth, Devon, PL4 0EB **t** 01752 210801
e dbs@deepbluesound.co.uk. **w** deepbluestudio.co.uk
myspace.com/deepbluestudiouk Studio Manager: Matt Bernard 01752 210801 ext130.

Deep Recording Co Po Box 38134, London, W10 6XL **t** 020 8964 8256 **f** Email Only Please
e mark@deeprecordingstudios.com
w deeprecordingstudios.com Manager: Mark Rose.

Deep Recording Studios 187 Freston Rd, London, W10 6TH **t** 020 8964 8256 **f** email only please
e bookings@deeprecordingstudios.com
w deeprecordingstudios.com
myspace.com/deeprecordingstudios
Studio Manager/Producer/Engineer: Mark Rose.

Delta Recording Studios Deanery Farm, Bolts Hill, Chatham, Kent, CT4 7LD **t** 01227 732140
f 01227 732140 **e** deltastudios@btconnect.com
w deltastudios.co.uk Contact: Julian Whitfield.

DeQoY Productions 6 Pound Lane, Marlow, Bucks, SL7 2AQ **t** 07551 343333 **f** 01628 478217
e info@deqoy.com **w** DeQoY.com deqoy
myspace.com/deqoy deqoy youtube.com/deqoy
Senior Director: Tarek Karaman 07793 140156.

Dreamhouse Studio (Right Bank Music UK)
Home Park House, Hampton Court Road,
Kingston Upon Thames, Surrey, KT1 4AE **t** 020 8977 0666
f 020 8977 0660
e rightbankmusicuk@rightbankmusicuk.com
w rightbankmusic.com VP: Ian Mack.

Dubrek Studios 97C Monk St, Derby, DE22 3QE
t 07595 158654 **e** dubrek@tiscali.co.uk **w** dubrek.co.uk
myspace.com/dubrek Owner/Chief Engineer: Justin Dean.

Earth Productions 163 Gerrard Street, Birmingham, West Midlands, B19 2AP **t** 0121 554 7424
f 0121 551 9250 **e** info@earthproductions.co.uk
w earthproductions.co.uk Studio Mgr: Lorna Williams.

Eastcote Studios Ltd 249 Kensal Road, London, W10 5DB **t** 020 8969 3739 **f** 020 8960 1836
e peggy@eastcotestudios.co.uk **w** eastcotestudios.co.uk
Studio Mgr: Peggy Fussell.

Ebony & Ivory Productions 11 Varley Parade, Edgware Road, Colindale, London, NW9 6RR
t 020 8200 7090 **e** SVLProds@aol.com Studio Manager: Alan Bradshaw.

Echo Studios Park Manor Industries, Moreton Rd, Buckingham, Bucks, MK18 1PP **t** 01280 823158
e info@echostudios.org.uk **w** echostudios.org.uk
myspace.com/echorecordingstudios Studio Manager: Jamie Masters.

Elevator Studios 23-27 Cheapside, Liverpool, L2 2DY **t** 0151 255 0195 **f** 0151 255 0195
e harriet@elevatorstudios.com Contact: Harriet.

Emglow Records Norton Cottage, Colchester Rd, Wivenhoe, Essex, CO7 9HT **t** 01206 826342
e emglorecs@aspects.net Contact: Marcel Glover 07974 677532.

EMS Audio Ltd 12 Balloo Avenue, Bangor, Co Down, BT19 7QT **t** 028 9127 4411 **f** 028 9127 4412
e info@musicshop.to **w** musicshop.to Director: William Thompson.

Fairlight Mews Studios Fairlight Mews,
15 St. Johns Rd, Kingston upon Thames, Surrey, KT1 4AN **t** 0208 977 0632 **f** 0870 770 8669
e info@missionlimited.com **w** missionlimited.com
Twitter.com/missionlimited MD: Sir Harry.

Fairview Studio Cavewood Grange Farm,
Common Lane, North Cave, Brough, East Yorks, HU15 2PE **t** 0800 0181 482 **f** 01430 425 547
e info@fairviewstudios.co.uk **w** fairviewrecording.co.uk
Studio Manager: Andy Newlove 01430 425 546.

Floating Earth Ltd Unit 14, 21 Wadsworth Rd, Perivale, Middlesex, UB6 7JD **t** 020 8997 4000
f 020 8998 5767 **e** record@floatingearth.com
w floatingearth.com Director: Steve Long.

Foel Studio Foel Studio, Llanfair Caereinion,
Nr Welshpool, Powys, SY21 0DS **t** 01938 810758
f 01938 810758 **e** foel.studio@dial.pipex.com
w foelstudio.co.uk facebook.com/pages/Foel-Studio/141053547513?v=info&ref=search
twitter.com/foelstudio MD: Dave Anderson.

Forum Music Village Piazza Euclide 34, Rome, 00197, Italy **t** +39 06 808 4259 **f** +39 06 807 4947
e m.patrignani@forummusicvillage.com
w forummusicvillage.com MD: Marco Patrignani.

Freak'n See Music Ltd 19c Heathmans Rd, London, SW6 4TJ **t** 020 7384 2429 **f** 020 7384 2429
e firstname@freaknsee.com **w** freaknsee.com
MD: Jimmy Mikaoui.

The Funky Bunker Recording Studios Unit 5, 10 Acklam Road, London, W10 5QZ **t** 020 8968 2222
f 020 8968 2220 **e** info@ice-pr.com **w** ice-pr.com
Contact: Jason Price.

Gargleblast Records 8 Dornoch Court, Bellshill, Lanarkshire, ML4 1HN **t** 01698 842899
e info@gargleblastrecords.com **w** gargleblastrecords.com
myspace.com/gargleblaststudio gargleblast studio
Label Manager: Shaun Tallamy 07716 167979.

Giginabox 444 Shoreham St, Sheffield, S2 4FD
t 0114 221 6283 **e** davecarrick@googlemail.com **w** none at present. coming. coming. Contact: Dave Carrick 07960 510889.

The Granary Studio Bewlbridge Farm, Lamberhurst, Kent, TN3 8JJ **t** 01892 891 128
e granarystudio@btconnect.com
w thegranarystudio.co.uk Studio Mgr: Guy Denning.

📇 Contacts   📘 Facebook   🟦 MySpace   🟦 Twitter   ▶️ YouTube

Grand Central Studios 51-53 Gt Marlborough St, London, W1F 7TJ **t** 020 7306 5600 **f** 020 7306 5616 **e** info@grand-central-studios.com **w** grand-central-studios.com 📇 Bookings Manager: Chris Lagden.

Grapevine Studios 190 Old Station Rd, Hampton-in-Arden, Solihull, Birmingham, B92 0HQ **t** 03300 881663 **f** 03300 881664 **e** info@grapevinestudios.co.uk **w** grapevinestudios.co.uk 📇 Engineer: Tim Reid.

Gravity Shack Studio Unit 3, Rear of 328 Balham High Rd, London, SW17 7AA **t** 020 8767 1125 **e** jessica@gubbinsproductions.co.uk **w** gravityshackstudios.com 🟦 myspace.com/gravityshackstudios 📇 Producer/Engineer: Jessica Corcoran.

Green Room Productions The Laurels, New Park Rd, Harefield, Middlesex, UB9 6EQ **t** 01895 822771 **e** tony@greenroomproductions.biz **w** greenroomproductions.biz 📇 Rec Engineer: Tony Faulkner.

Greystoke Studios Ealing, London, W5 1JL **t** 07850 735591 **e** andy@greystokeproductions.co.uk **w** andywhitmore.com 📇 Record Producer: Andy Whitmore.

Groovestyle Recording Studio 33 Upper Holt St, Earls Colne, Colchester, Essex, CO6 2PG **t** 01787 220326 **e** info@groovewithus.com **w** groovewithus.com 📇 Owner: Graham Game.

Grouse Lodge Residential Studios Rosemount, Moate, Westmeath, Ireland **t** +353 906 436 175 **f** +353 906 436 131 **e** info@grouselodge.com **w** grouselodge.com 📘 facebook.com/people/Grouse-Lodge/100000108387274 📇 Bookings Mgr: Tracy Bolger +353 (0) 87 6614394.

H2O Enterprises Sphere Studios, 2 Shuttleworth Rd, Battersea, London, SW11 3EA **t** 020 7326 9460 **f** 020 7326 9499 **e** simonb@h2o.co.uk **w** h2o.co.uk 📇 Bkngs/Studio Mgr: Simon Bohannon.

Harewood Farm Studios Harewood Farm Studios, Little Harewood Farm, Clamgoose Lane, Kingsley, Staffs, ST10 2EG **t** 07973 157 920 **f** 01538 755 735 **e** kristian@harewoodfarmstudios.com **w** harewoodfarmstudios.com 📇 Producer: Kristian Gilroy.

Hatch Farm Studios Chertsey Rd, Addlestone, Surrey, KT15 2EH **t** 01932 828715 **f** 01932 828717 **e** brian.adams@dial.pipex.com 📇 MD: Brian Adams.

HD1 Studios St Peters Chambers, St Peters St, Huddersfield, West Yorkshire, HD1 1RA **t** 01484 452013 **f** 01484 435861 **e** samroberts@hd1studios.co.uk **w** hd1studios.co.uk 📇 Studio Mgr: Sam Roberts.

HD1 Studios St Peter's Chambers, St Peter's St, Huddersfield, West Yorkshire, HD1 1RA **t** 01484 452013 **f** 01484 435861 **e** samroberts@hd1studios.co.uk **w** hd1studios.co.uk 🟦 myspace.com/hd1studios 📇 Studio Manager: Sam Roberts.

Hear No Evil 6 Lillie Yard, London, SW6 1UB **t** 020 7385 8244 **f** 020 7385 0700 **e** info@hearnoevil.net **w** hearnoevil.net 📇 MD: Steve Parr 07886 380175.

Heartbeat Recording Studio Guildie House Farm, North Middleton, North Middleton, Mid Lothian, EH23 4QP **t** 01875 821102 **e** info@heartbeatstudio.co.uk **w** info@heartbeatstudio.co.uk 📇 Engineer/Prod: David L Valentine 07855 428074.

High Barn Studio The Bardfield Centre, Great Bardfield, Braintree, Essex, CM7 4SL **t** 01371 811 291 **f** 01371 811 404 **e** info@high-barn.com **w** highbarnstudio.com 📇 Studio Manager: Simon Allen.

The Hospital Group 24 Endell St, London, WC2H 9HQ **t** 020 7170 9110 **f** 020 7170 9102 **e** studio@thehospitalclub.com **w** thehospitalclub.com 📇 Studio Sales Manager: Anne Marie Phelan.

ICC Studios 4 Regency Mews, Silverdale Road, Eastbourne, East Sussex, BN20 7AB **t** 01323 643341 **f** 01323 649240 **e** info@iccstudios.co.uk **w** iccstudios.co.uk 📇 Studio & Bookings Mgr: Neil Costello.

The ICE Group 3 St Andrews St, Lincoln, Lincolnshire, LN5 7NE **t** 01522 539883 **f** 01522 528964 **e** steve.hawkins@easynet.co.uk **w** icegroup.co.uk 📇 MD: Steve Hawkins.

Iguana Studios Unit 1, 88a Acre Lane, London, SW2 5QN **t** 020 7924 0496 **e** info@iguanastudio.co.uk **w** iguanastudio.co.uk 📇 MD: Andrea Terrano.

Impulse Studio 71 High Street East, Wallsend, Tyne and Wear, NE28 7RJ **t** 0191 262 4999 **f** 0191 263 7082 📇 MD: David Wood.

INFX Recording Studios High Wycombe Campus, Queen Alexandra Rd, High Wycombe, Bucks, HP11 2JZ **t** 01494 522141 ex 4020 **e** fmacke01@bucks.ac.uk 📇 Studio Manager: Frazer Mackenzie.

Instant Music 14 Moorend Crescent, Cheltenham, Gloucestershire, GL53 0EL **t** 01242 523 304 **f** 01242 523 304 **e** info@instantmusic.co.uk **w** instantmusic.co.uk 📇 MD: Martin Mitchell 07957 355 630.

Intercom Recordings 48 Peddars Lane, Beccles, Suffolk, NR34 9UE **t** 01502 715449 **f** 01502 715449 **e** inter.comrecordings@virgin.net **w** myspace.com/ezrollers 📇 Label Manager: Jay Hurren.

Intimate Recording Studios The Smokehouse, 120 Pennington St, London, E1W 9BB **t** 07860 109612 **e** p.madden47@ntlworld.com **w** intimatestudios.com 📇 Contact: Paul Madden 020 7702 0789.

Jutland Studios 33 Parkgate Rd, London, SW11 4NP **t** 020 7801 0093 **e** jay@jutlandavestudios.com **w** jutlandavestudios.com 📇 Studio manager: Jay K A.

KD's Studio see Saturn Music Group.

Keynote Studios Burghfield Bridge, Green Lane, Burghfield, Reading, RG30 3XN **t** 01189 599 944 **f** 01189 596 442 **e** tom@keynotestudios.com **w** keynotestudios.com 📇 Studio Mgr: Tom Languish.

Contacts  Facebook MySpace Twitter ▶️ YouTube

Komodo Studios 79 Magheraconluce Rd, Hillsborough, Co. Down, BT26 6PR **t** 02892 688 285 **e** info@komodorecordings.com **w** myspace.com/komodostudios ☑ Studio Engineer: Alwyn Walker.

Konk Studios 84-86 Tottenham Lane, London, N8 7EE **t** 020 8340 4757 **f** 020 8348 3952 **e** linda@konkstudio.com ☑ Studio Mgr: Sarah Lockwood 020 8340 7873.

The Lab Music Studio Unit J, Blackhorse Mews, off Blackhorse Lane, London, E17 6SL **t** 020 8527 7300 **e** info@thelabmusicstudio.com **w** thelabmusicstudio.com ☑ Studio Manager: Mikee Hughes.

Bob Lamb's Recording Studio 122A Highbury Road, Kings Heath, Birmingham, West Midlands, B14 7QP **t** 0121 443 2186 **e** boblamb@recklessltd.com ☑ Studio Mgr/Prop: Bob Lamb.

CTS Lansdowne Recording Studios Rickmansworth Road, Watford, WD17 3JN **t** 020 8846 9444 **f** 05601 155 009 **e** info@cts-lansdowne.co.uk **w** cts-lansdowne.co.uk ☑ Bookings Enquiries: Sharon Rose.

LBS Manchester 11-13 Bamford St, Stockport, Cheshire, SK1 3NZ **t** 0161 477 2710 **f** 0161 480 9497 **e** info@lbs.co.uk **w** lbs.co.uk ☑ Producer: Adders.

Leeders Farm School Lane, Spooner Row, Norfolk, NR18 9JP **t** 01953 604 951 **w** leedersfarm.com ☑ Studio Manager: Producer/engineer: Nick Brine info@leedersfarm.com.

The Leisure Factory Ltd 20-22 Mount Pleasant, Bilston, Wolverhampton, West Midlands, WV14 7LJ **t** 01902 405511 **f** 01902 401418 **e** Music@therobin.co.uk **w** theleisurefactory.com ☑ Director: Mike Hamblett.

leloftmusic t 01995 601 880 **e** alan@leloftmusic.com **w** leloftmusic.com ☑ Owner: Alan Richard Olive.

Lime Street Sound 3 Lime Court, Lime Street, Dublin 2, Ireland **t** +353 1 671 7271 **f** +353 1 670 7639 **e** limesound@eircom.net **w** limesound.com ☑ Dir: Steve McGrath.

Linden Studio The Granary, Coatflatt, Tebay, Cumbria, CA10 3SZ **t** 01539 624827 **e** guy@lindenstudio.co.uk **w** lindenstudio.co.uk ☑ Producer/Engineer: Guy Forrester.

The Live Room 2 Firbank Rd, London, SE15 2DD **t** 020 7732 2889 **e** tim@kickhorns.com **w** kickhorns.com ▶️ myspace.com/tjnsanders ☑ Studio Manager: Tim Sanders 07931 776155.

Livingston Recording Studios Brook Road, off Mayes Road, London, N22 6TR **t** 020 8889 6558 **f** 020 8888 2698 **e** mail@livingstonstudios.co.uk **w** livingstonstudios.co.uk ☑ Bkings/Studio Mgrs: Lise Regan & Verity Boys.

The Lodge 23 Abington Square, Northampton, NN1 4AE **t** 01604 475399 **f** 01604 516999 **e** studio@lodgstud.demon.co.uk **w** demon.co.uk/lodgstud ☑ Snr Engineer/Owner: Max Read.

London Recording Studios 9-13 Osborn Street, London, E1 6TD **t** 020 7247 5862 **e** info@thelondonrecordingstudios.com **w** thelondonrecordingstudios.com ☑ Studio Manager: Jasmin Lee.

Loose Ingledene, 94, Holloway, Runcorn, Cheshire, WA7 4TJ **t** 01928 566261 **e** william.leach1@virgin.net ☑ Studio Manager: Bill Leach.

Lost Boys Studio Hillgreen Farm, Bourne End, Cranfield, Bedfordshire, MK43 0AX **t** 01234 750 730 **f** 01234 751 277 **e** lostboysstudio@onetel.com **w** lostboysstudio.com ☑ Studio Mgr: Rupert Cook.

LUMEN STUDIO

lumenstudio

103 Islingword Rd, Brighton, East Sussex, BN2 9SG **t** 01273 690149 **f** 01273 690149 **e** info@lumenstudio.co.uk **w** lumenstudio.co.uk ☑ MD: Mark Williams. Chief Engineer: Tristan Learmonth.

MA Music Studios PO Box 106, Potton, Beds, SG19 2ZS **t** 01767 262 040 **e** info@mamusicstudios.co.uk **w** mamusicstudios.co.uk ☑ Studio Mgr: Noel Rafferty.

MACH 2 412 Beersbridge Rd, Belfast, BT5 5EB **t** 028 9065 4450 **e** michael@machtwo.co.uk **w** machtwo.co.uk ☑ Director: Michael Taylor.

Map Music Ltd 46 Grafton Rd, London, NW5 3DU **t** 020 7916 0544 **e** info@mapmusic.net **w** mapmusic.net ▶️ myspace.com/mapmusic1 ☑ MD: Chris Townsend 020 7916 0545.

Martian Studio East Nethercott, Whitstone, Bude, Cornwall, EX22 6LD **t** 01288 341 400 **f** 01288 341 707 **e** mail@martianengineering.com **w** martianengineering.com ☑ Owner: Mark Hawley.

Mayfair Recording Studios 11A Sharpleshall Street, London, NW1 8YN **t** 020 7586 7746 **f** 020 7586 9721 **e** bookings@mayfair-studios.co.uk **w** mayfair-studios.co.uk ☑ Bkings/Studio Mgr: Daniel Mills.

Recording Studios & Services: Recording Studios

Metropolis Studios The Power House,
70 Chiswick High Rd, London, W4 1SY **t** 020 8742 1111
f 020 8742 2626 **e** studios@metropolis-group.co.uk
w metropolisstudios.co.uk
⨍ facebook.com/metropolisstudios
☒ myspace.com/metropolisstudios
☒ twitter.com/metropolisgroup
▶ youtube.com/user/MetropolisStudios
☒ Studio Manager: Katy Samwell.

Mex One Recordings The Basement, 3 Eaton Pl,
Brighton, East Sussex, BN2 1EH **t** 01273 572090
e info@mexonerecordings.co.uk
w mexonerecordings.co.uk ⨍ facebook.com/paul.mex
☒ myspace.com/mexonerecordings
☒ twitter.com/mexonerecording
▶ youtube.com/user/mexonerecordings ☒ Music
Producer & Proprietor: Paul Mex.

Mighty Atom Studios 43d Bryn Rd, Swansea,
SA2 0AP **t** 07771 546772
e info@mightyatomstudios.co.uk
w mightyatomstudios.co.uk
☒ myspacemusic/mightyatomstudios
☒ Producer: Joe Gibb.

Mill Hill Recording Company Ltd
Unit 7, Bunns Lane Works, Bunns Lane, Mill Hill, London,
NW7 2AJ **t** 020 8906 5038 **f** 020 8906 9991
e enquiries@millhillmusic.co.uk **w** millhillmusic.co.uk
☒ MD: Roger Tichborne.

Miloco Studios 36 Leroy St, London, SE1 4SP
t 020 7232 0008 **f** 020 7237 6109 **e** info@miloco.co.uk
w miloco.co.uk ☒ Studio Manager: Vicki Dempsey.

MIX Records Studio North Lodge, Auchineden,
Blanefield, Glasgow, G63 9AX
t 01360 771 069 or 07968 240 958
e andy@mixrecords.com **w** mixrecords.com ☒ Studio
Manager: Andy Malkin.

Mixing Rooms 222-226 West Regent Street, Glasgow,
G2 4DQ **t** 0141 221 7795 **f** 0141 847 0495
e chris_h@mixingrooms.co.uk **w** mixingrooms.co.uk
☒ Assistant Studio Manager: Chris Hely.

Modern World Studios
Unit 3, Tetbury Industrial Estate, Cirencester Rd, Tetbury,
Gloucs, GL8 8EZ **t** 01666 504 300
e nick@modernworldstudios.co.uk
w modernworldstudios.co.uk ☒ Owner: Nick Cowan.

Moles Studio 14 George St, Bath, BA1 2EN
t 01225 404446 **f** 01225 404447 **e** nick@moles.co.uk
w moles.co.uk ☒ Studio Mgr: Nick Jopling.

Monkey Puzzle House: Residential Studio
Monkey Puzzle House, Heath Rd, Woolpit,
Bury St Edmunds, Suffolk, IP30 9RJ **t** 01359 245050
f 01359 245060 **e** studio@monkeypuzzlehouse.com
w monkeypuzzlehouse.com ☒ Studio Owner: Rupert
Matthews.

Monnow Valley Studio Old Mill House, Rockfield,
Monmouth, NP25 5QE **t** 01600 712761 **f** 01600 715039
e enquiries@monnowvalleystudio.com
w monnowvalleystudio.com ☒ Bookings Mgr: Jo Hunt
07770 988503.

Mother Digital Avon House, Glenalmond Rd, Sheffield,
S11 7GW **t** 07767 622567
e studio@motherdigitalstudio.com
w motherdigitalstudio.com ☒ Owner: Justin Morey.

The Motor Museum Studios 1 Hesketh Street,
Aigburth, Liverpool, Merseyside, L17 8XJ **t** 0151 726 9808
f 0151 222 0190 **e** office@themotormuseum.co.uk
w themotormuseum.co.uk ☒ Studio Manager: Julia Jeory.

Music 4 Studios 41-42 Berners St, London, W1T 3NB
t 020 7016 2000 **e** sarah@music4.com **w** music4.com
☒ Facilities Manager: Sarah Davis.

The Music Barn PO Box 92, Gloucester, GL4 8HW
t 01452 814321 **f** 01452 812106
e vic_coppersmith@hotmail.com ☒ MD: Vic Coppersmith-
Heaven.

The Music Complex Ltd 20 Tanners Hill, Deptford,
London, SE8 4PJ **t** 020 8691 6666 **f** 020 8692 9999
e info@musiccomplex.co.uk **w** musiccomplex.co.uk
☒ Mgrs: Myles Bradley and Chris Raw.

The Music Factory Hawthorne House,
Fitzwilliam Street, Parkgate, Rotherham, South Yorkshire,
S62 6EP **t** 01709 710022 **f** 01709 523141
e info@musicfactory.co.uk **w** mfeg.co.uk ☒ CEO: Andy
Pickles.

MVD Studios Unit 4, Rampart Business Pk,
Greenbank Ind, Estate, Newry, Co Down, BT34 2QU
t 028 3026 2926 **f** 028 3026 2671 **e** mail@wren.ie
w soundsirish.com ☒ Studio Manager: Jim McGirr.

MySoundRules Croydon Hse, 1 Peall Road, Croydon,
Surrey, CR0 3EX **t** 07985 733 177
e mysoundrules@yahoo.co.uk
w myspace.com/mysoundrules ☒ Contact: Mike Sogga
07737 143 181.

Natural Grooves Studio 3 Tannsfeld, London,
SE26 5DQ **t** 020 8488 3677 **f** 020 8333 2572
e jon@naturalgrooves.co.uk **w** naturalgrooves.co.uk
☒ Studio Manager: Jonathan Sharif.

Nucool Studio 34 Beaumont Rd, London, W4 5AP
t 020 8248 2157 **e** richard@richardniles.com
w richardniles.com ☒ Producer: Richard Niles.

Old Smithy Recording Studio 1 Post Office Lane,
Kempsey, Worcestershire, WR5 3NS **t** 01905 820659
f 01905 820015 **e** muffmurfin@btconnect.com
☒ Bookings Mgr: Janet Allsopp.

Online Studios Ltd Unit 18-19 Croydon House,
1 Peall Rd, Croydon, Surrey, CR0 3EX **t** 020 8287 8585
f 020 8287 0220 **e** info@onlinestudios.co.uk
w onlinestudios.co.uk ☒ myspace.com/onlinestudios
☒ twitter.com/onlinestudiosuk
▶ youtube.com/onlinestudiosuk ☒ MD: Rob Pearson.

Contacts   Facebook   MySpace   Twitter   YouTube

Panther Recording Studios 5 Doods Rd, Reigate, Surrey, RH2 0NT **t** 01737 210 848 **f** 01737 210 848 **e** studios@dial.pipex.com **w** ds.dial.pipex.com/sema/panther.htm Studio Manager: Richard Coppen.

Park Lane 974 Pollokshaws Road, Glasgow, Strathclyde, G41 2HA **t** 0141 636 1218 **f** 0141 649 0042 **e** info@parklanerecordingstudios.com **w** parklanerecordingstudios.com Studio Mgr: Paul McGeechan.

Parkbench Studios 12a Albert Mansions, Albert Bridge Rd, Battersea, London, SW11 4QB **t** 07770 918078 **e** info@parkbenchstudios.co.uk **w** parkbenchstudios.co.uk MD: Ben Adams.

Parr Street Studios 33-45 Parr Street, Liverpool, L1 4JN **t** 0151 707 1050 **f** 0151 709 4090 **e** info@parrstreetstudios.com **w** parrstreetstudios.com Bookings: Pete or Peasy.

Phoenix Sound Pinewood Studios, Pinewood Road, Iver Heath, Bucks, SL0 0NH **t** 01753 785 495 **f** 01753 656 153 **e** info@phoenixsound.net **w** phoenixsound.net Studio Mgr: Pete Fielder.

Planet Audio Studios 33 Bournehall Avenue, Bushey, Herts, WD23 3AU **t** 08707 605365 **f** 020 8950 1294 **e** mix@planetaudiostudios.com **w** planetaudiostudios.com GM: Helen Gammons.

Pluto Studios - Pluto Music Hulgrave Hall, Tiverton, Tarporley, Cheshire, CW6 9UQ **t** 01829 732427 **f** 01829 733802 **e** info@plutomusic.com **w** plutomusic.com Studio Mgr: Keith Hopwood.

PM Muzik Studio 226 Seven Sisters Rd, London, N4 3GG. **t** 020 7372 6806 **f** 020 7372 0969 **e** info@pmmuzik.com **w** pmmuzik.com Bookings: Mikey Campbell.

Point Blank 23-28 Penn St, Hoxton, London, N1 5DL **t** 020 7729 4884 **f** 020 7729 8789 **e** studio@pointblanklondon.com **w** pointblanklondon.com CEO: Rob Cowan.

Pollen Studios 97 Main Street, Bishop Wilton, York, North Yorkshire, YO42 1SQ **t** 01759 368223 **e** sales@pollenstudio.co.uk **w** pollenstudio.co.uk Prop: Dick Sefton.

The Pop Factory Welsh Hills Works, Jenkin St, Porth, CF39 9PP **t** 01443 688500 **f** 01443 688501 **e** info@thepopfactory.com **w** thepopfactory.com Contact: Emyr Afan Davies.

Power Recording Studios Unit 11, Impress House, Mansell Rd, London, W3 7QH **t** 020 8932 3033 **f** 0870 139 3608 **e** Keith@power.co.uk **w** power.co.uk Studio Mgr: Keith Neill.

The Premises Studios Ltd 201-205 Hackney Road, Shoreditch, London, E2 8JL **t** 020 7729 7593 **f** 020 7739 5600 **e** info@premises.demon.co.uk **w** premises.demon.co.uk CEO: Viv Broughton.

Presshouse Recording Studios PO Box 6, Colyton, Devon, EX24 6YS **t** 01297 553 508 **f** 01297 553 709 **e** presshouse@zetnet.co.uk Studio Mgr: Mark Tucker.

Priory Recording Studios 3 The Priory, London Rd, Canwell, Sutton Coldfield, West Midlands, B75 5SH **t** 0121 323 3332 **f** 0121 308 8815 **e** greg@prioryrecordingstudios.co.uk **w** prioryrecordingstudios.co.uk Studio Mgr: Greg Chandler.

The Propagation House Studios East Lodge, Ogbeare, North Tamerton, Holsworthy, Devon, EX22 6SE **t** 01409 271111 **f** 01409 271111 **e** office@propagationhouse.com **w** http://www.propagationhouse.com Studio Mgr: Mark Ellis.

Pulse Recording Studios 67 Pleasants Place, Dublin 8, Ireland **t** +353 1 478 4045 **f** +353 1 475 8730 **e** pulserecording@pulserecording.com **w** pulserecording.com Dir: Tony Perrey.

Q10 Studios Kings Court, 7 Osborne St, Glasgow, G1 5QN **t** 0141 552 6677 **f** 0141 552 1354 **e** q10studios@aol.com **w** myspace.com/q10studios Co-Dirs: Alan Walsh, Martin McQuillan.

Qton Studios Unit 105, 326 Kensal Road, London, W10 5BZ **t** 0208 960 8909 **e** enquiries@qtonstudios.com **w** qtonstudios.com Business Manager: Charlotte Hersh.

Quince 62a Balcombe St, Marylebone, London, NW1 6NE **t** 07810 752765 **f** 020 7723 1010 **e** info@quincestudios.co.uk **w** quincestudios.co.uk myspace.com/quincestudios Dir: Matt Walters 07810 752 765.

Raezor Studio 25 Frogmore, London, SW18 1JA **t** 020 8870 4036 **f** 020 8874 4133 Studio Mgr: Ian Wilkinson.

Rainmaker Music Music Bank, Building D, Tower Bridge Business Complex, 100 Clements Rd, London, SE16 4DG **t** 020 7252 0001 **f** 020 7231 3002 **e** rainmakermusic@aol.com **w** rain-makermusic.com MD: Chris Tsangarides 07980 607 808.

RAK Recording Studios 42-48 Charlbert Street, London, NW8 7BU **t** 020 7586 2012 **f** 020 7722 5823 **e** trisha@rakstudios.co.uk **w** rakstudios.co.uk Bookings Mgr: Trisha Wegg.

RCM Studios Royal College of Music (London), Prince Consort Rd, London, SW7 2BS **t** 020 7591 4384 **f** 020 7591 4382 **e** studio@rcm.ac.uk **w** rcm.ac.uk/studios Studio Manager: Jonathan Rule 020 7591 4789.

Real World Studios Box Mill, Mill Lane, Box, Corsham, Wiltshire, SN13 8PL **t** 01225 740600 **f** 0845 146 1724 **e** eleanor.household@realworld.co.uk **w** realworldstudios.com Studio Mgr: Eleanor Household 01225 740 600.

Red Bus Recording & TV Studios 34 Salisbury St, London, NW8 8QE **t** 020 7402 9111 **f** 020 7723 3064 **e** eliot@redbusstudios.com **w** redbusstudios.com MD: Eliot M Cohen.

Recording Studios & Services: Recording Studios

Contacts   Facebook   MySpace   Twitter   YouTube

Red Fort Studios & Keda Records
Keda Records & Red Fort Studios, Global Sound Village,
Priory Way, Southall, Middlesex, UB2 5EB **t** 020 8843 1546
e kuljit@kuljitbhamra.com **w** info@globalsoundvillage.com
Owner: Kuljit Bhamra MBE.

Red Kite Studio Cwmargenau, Llanwrda, Carms,
SA19 8AP **t** 01550 722000 **f** 01550 722022
e andy@redkitestudio.co.uk **w** redkitestudio.co.uk
myspace.com/redkitestudio
twitter.com/redkitestudio
Studio & Bookings Manager: Andy Thomas.

Red Rhythm Productions 2 Longlane, Staines,
Middlesex, TW19 7AA **t** 01784 255629
e cliffrandall@telco4u.net Studio Mgr: Cliff Randall.

Red Triangle Productions PO Box 7268, Wimborne,
Dorset, BH21 9FE **t** 01725 517204
e studio@redtriangleproductions.co.uk
w redtriangleproductions.co.uk
myspace.com/redtrianglepro
twitter.com/redtrianglepro
Studio Manager: George Tizzard.

Reeltime Music
c/o Newarthill Community and Education Centre,
50 High Street, Newarthill, Motherwell, ML1 5JU
t 01698 862 860 **f** 01698 862 860
e info@reeltimemusic.net **w** reeltimemusic.net
Marketing & Evaluation Officer: Carol McEntegart.

Revolution Studios 11 Church Road, Cheadle Hulme,
Cheadle, Cheshire, SK8 6LS **t** 0161 485 8942
f 0161 485 8942 **e** revolution@wahtup.com
Prop: Andrew MacPherson 0161 486 6903.

Ride Studio 9 Coach Ride, Marlow, Bucks, SL7 3BN
t 07734 975 576 **e** info@ridestudio.co.uk
w ridestudio.co.uk Studio Manager: Pete Hutchins.

RL-2 - RL2 Music 15 Boulevard Aristide Briand,
Pouzolles, 34480, France **t** 020 8123 7669 **e** info9@rl-
2.com **w** rl-2.com GM: Paul Lilly.

RMS Studios 43-45 Clifton Rd, London, SE25 6PX
t 020 8653 4965 **e** rmsstudioslondon@googlemail.com
w rms-studios.co.uk Bookings Mgr: Alan Jones.

Rockbarn Studio Sarn, Nr. Newtown, Powys, SY16 4EJ
t 07805 747806 **e** john@rockbarn.net
myspace.com/johnhardman Owner: John Hardman.

Rockfield Studios Amberley Court, Rockfield Rd,
Monmouth, Monmouthshire, NP25 5ST **t** 01600 712449
f 01600 714421 **e** lisaward@rockfieldstudios.com
w rockfieldstudios.com Studio Manager: Lisa Ward.

Rockrooms Studio Unit 1, Standingford House,
26 Cave St, Oxford, OX4 1BA **t** 07884 173891
e ops@rockrooms.co.uk **w** rockrooms.co.uk
Manager: Joe Deller.

Rogue Studios RA 4 Bermondsey Trading Estate,
Rotherhithe New Road, London, SE16 3LL
t 020 7231 3257 **f** 020 7231 7358
e info@RogueStudios.co.uk **w** roguestudios.co.uk
Contact: Jon Paul Harper/Jim Down.

Rollover Studios 29 Beethoven St, London, W10 4LJ
t 020 8969 0299 **f** 0871 714 2605
e music.studios@rollover.co.uk **w** rollover.co.uk
myspace.com/rollovermusic
twitter.com/rollovermusic Studio Mgr: Bruin Housley.

Roundhouse Recording Studios 91 Saffron Hill,
Clerkenwell, London, EC1N 8PT **t** 020 7404 3333
f 020 7404 2947 **e** roundhouse@stardiamond.com
w stardiamond.com/roundhouse Studio Managers: Lisa
Gunther & Maddy Clarke.

Sahara Sound Unit 18a/b, Farm Lane Trading Estate,
101 Farm Lane, London, SW6 1QJ **t** 020 7386 2400
f 020 7386 2401 **e** info@saharasound.com
w saharasound.com Contact: Cath Cloherty, Javier
Weyler.

Sain Canolfan Sain, Llandwrog, Caernarfon, Gwynedd,
LL54 5TG **t** 01286 831111 **f** 01286 831497
e studio@sain.wales.com **w** sain.wales.com Studio
Mgr: Eryl Davies.

Sarm Hook End Hook End Manor, Checkendon,
Nr Reading, Berks, RG8 0UE **t** 01491 681000
f 01491 681926 **e** markcollins@hookendstudio.com
w hookendstudio.com Studio Mgr: Mark Collins.

Sarm West The Blue Building, 8-10 Basing St, London,
W11 1ET **t** 020 7229 1229 **f** 020 7221 9247
e julie@spz.com **w** sarmstudios.com Studio Mgr: Julie
Bateman.

Saturn Music Group Unit 1-133 Clarence Rd, London,
E5 8EE **t** 020 8533 1067 **f** 020 8533 1067 **e** info@saturn-
web.co.uk Contact: Chris Harraway 07904 773 908.

Sawmills Studio Golant, Fowey, Cornwall, PL23 1LW
t 01726 833338 **f** 01726 832015 **e** ruth@sawmills.co.uk
w sawmills.co.uk Studio Mgr: Ruth Taylor 01726
833752.

Sensible Music Studios 90-96 Brewery Rd, London,
N7 9NT **t** 020 7700 9900 **f** 020 7700 4802
e studio@sensible-music.co.uk **w** sensible-music.co.uk
Studio Manager: Pat Tate.

shushstudio Rockville, 10 Plaines Close,
Cippenham Meadows, Slough, Berkshire, SL1 5TY
t 01753 537206 **e** studio@shushstudio.com
w shushstudio.com
myspace.com/shushstudiodannydematos
twitter.com/danny_de_matos producer: danny de
matos 07956 816243.

Silk Sound Ltd 13 Berwick Street, London, W1F 0PW
t 020 7434 3461 **f** 020 7494 1748 **e** bookings@silk.co.uk
w silk.co.uk Studio Mgr: Paula Ryman.

Silk Studios 23 New Mount St, Manchester, M4 4DE
t 0161 953 4045 **f** 0161 953 4001
e leestanley@silkstudios.co.uk Dir: Lee Stanley 07887
564 485.

SJTMusic 51 Rosemullion Avenue, Tattenhoe,
Milton Keynes, Bucks, MK4 3AH **t** 07968 795 503
e sjtmusic@mac.com **w** sjtmusic.co.uk
Dir: Simon Turner.

Soho Recording Studios The Heals Building, 22-24 Torrington Place, London, WC2E 7AJ **t** 020 7419 2444 **f** 020 7419 2333 **e** dominic@sohostudios.co.uk **w** sohostudios.co.uk 🖼 Bkngs/Studio Mgr: Dominic Sanders 020 7419 2555.

Solitaire Residential Recording Studio 3 The Collops, Kingscourt, Co. Cavan, Ireland **t** +353 42 966 8793 **e** info@solitairestudio.com **w** solitairestudio.com 🖼 MD: Alan Whelan +353 (0)872611655.

Sonar Records Limited 82 London Rd, Coventry, West Midlands, CV1 2JT **t** 024 7622 0749 **e** office@sonar-records.demon.co.uk **w** cabinstudio.co.uk 🖼 GM: Jon Lord.

Songmaker Ltd Suite 296, 2 Lansdowne Row, London, W1J 6HL **t** 0871 750 5555 **f** 0871 226 4256 **e** michelle@songmaker.co.uk **w** songmaker.co.uk 🖼 PA to Director: Michelle Parsons.

Songwriting & Musical Productions Sovereign House, 12 Trewartha Rd. Praa Sands, Penzance, Cornwall, TR20 9ST **t** 01736 762826 **f** 01736 763328 **e** panamus@aol.com **w** songwriters-guild.co.uk 🅼 myspace.com/guildofsongwriters 🖼 MD: Colin Eade.

Sound Recording Technology Audio House, Edison Road, St Ives, Cambs, PE27 3LF **t** 01480 461 880 **f** 01480 496 100 **e** sales@soundrecordingtechnology.co.uk **w** soundrecordingtechnology.co.uk 🖼 Dirs: Sarah Pownall, Karen Kenney.

Soundlab Studios Unit 22, Oakwood Hill Industrial Estate, Loughton, Essex, IG10 3TZ **t** 020 8508 2726 **e** mail@soundlabstudios.co.uk **w** soundlabstudios.co.uk 🖼 Studio Manager: James Horwood.

Southern Studios 10 Myddleton Rd, London, N22 8NS **t** 020 8888 8949 **e** studio@southern.com **w** southern.com/studio 🅼 myspace.com/harveybirrell 🖼 Studio Manager/Engineer: Harvey Birrell +44 (0)7802 259156.

Southside Studios Ltd 8 Southside, Clapham Common, London, SW4 7AA **t** 020 7627 2086 **e** pbarraclough@claranet.co.uk **w** southsidestudios.eu 🖼 Director/Studio Manager: Peter Barraclough 07939 564 832.

Space Eko Recording Studio Unit 42, 72 Farm Lane, London, SW6 1QA **t** 020 7381 0059 **e** alex@thefutureshapeofsound.com **w** thefutureshapeofsound.com 🖼 Contact: Alex McGowan.

Spatial Audio c/o The Soundhouse Ltd, Unit 11 Goldhawk Industrial Estate, 2a Brackenbury Rd, London, W6 0BA **t** 07802 657258 **f** 020 8932 3465 **e** gerry@spatial-audio.co.uk **w** spatial-audio.co.uk 🅼 myspace.com/spatial_audio 🖼 Sound Engineer: Gerry O'Riordan.

Sphere Studios 2 Shuttleworth Rd, London, SW11 3EA **t** 020 7326 9450 **f** 020 7326 9499 **e** inform@spherestudios.com **w** spherestudios.com 🖼 Studio Mgr: Simon Bohannon.

SPM Studios 9 Lichfield Way, South Croydon, Surrey, CR2 8SD **t** 020 8657 8363 **f** 020 8657 8380 **e** steve@spmstudios.co.uk **w** spmstudios.co.uk 🖼 Prop: Steve Parkes 07970 646 166.

Sprint Music - Sprint Studios High Jarmany Farm, Jarmany Hill, Barton St David, Somerton, Somerset, TA11 6DA **t** 01458 851187 **f** 01458 851187 **e** info@sprintmusic.co.uk **w** sprintmusic.co.uk 🖼 Industry Consultant, Producer, Writer: John Ratcliff.

The Stables Recording Studio 5 Stables Lane, Eastbourne, East Sussex, BN21 4RE **t** 01323 720784 **f** 01323 720784 **e** doug.sturrock@btconnect.com **w** thestablesstudo.com 🖼 Owner: Douglas Sturrock 07889 160147.

The Stables Studio The Stables, 3 Stables Lane, Eastbourne, BN21 4RE **t** 01323 720784 **e** not supplied **w** myspace.co.uk/thestables

State Of The Ark Studios Rear Building, 144 Sheen Rd, Richmond, Surrey, TW9 1UU **t** 07979 651000 **e** danbritten@hotmail.co.uk 🖼 Studio Manager: Dan Britten.

Steelworks Studio Unit D, 3 Brown St, Sheffield, S1 2BS **t** 0114 272 0300 **f** 0114 272 0303 **e** steelworksmu@aol.com **w** steelworks-studios.com 🖼 Studio Mgr: Dan Panton.

Street Level Studios 1st Floor, 17 Bowater Road, Westminster Industrial Estate, Woolwich, London, SE18 5TF **t** 07886 260 686 **e** ceo@streetlevelenterprises.co.uk **w** streetlevelenterprises.com 🖼 MD: Sam Crawford.

Strongroom 120-124 Curtain Rd, London, EC2A 3SQ **t** 020 7426 5100 **f** 020 7426 5102 **e** mix@strongroom.com **w** strongroom.com 🅼 myspace.com/strongroom 🅣 twitter.com/strongroom 🖼 Bookings Co-ordinator: Charlie Mines.

Studio 17 17 David's Road, London, SE23 3EP **t** 020 8291 6253 **f** 020 8291 1097 **e** chris@dubvendor.co.uk 🖼 Dir: Chris Lane.

Studio Sonic Enterprise Studios, 1-6 Denmark Place, London, WC2H 8NL **t** 020 7379 1155 **e** info@studio-sonic.co.uk **w** studio-sonic.co.uk 🖼 Studio Manager: Andy Brook 020 7379 1166.

The Studio Tower Street, Hartlepool, TS24 7HQ **t** 01429 424440 **f** 01429 424441 **e** studiohartlepool@btconnect.com **w** studiohartlepool.com 🖼 Studio Manager: Liz Carter.

Subside Records SNC Via Vecchia Fiuggi 382, 03015-Fiuggi, FR, Italy **t** +39 0775 515122 **f** +39 0775 514218 **e** info@subsiderec.com **w** subsiderec.com 🖼 CEO: Vanni Giorgilli.

Recording Studios & Services: Recording Studios

The Suite - Suite Music Ltd Utopia Village, Chalcot Rd, London, NW1 8LH **t** 020 7813 7964 **f** 020 7209 5384 **e** music@thesuite.sh **w** liveatthesuite.com ■ myspace.com/atthesuite ■ thesuite ■ MD: Andrew Maurice.

Sun Studios - 1 & 2 8 Crow Street, Dublin 2, Ireland **t** +353 1 677 7255 **f** +353 1 679 1968 **e** apollo@templelanestudios.com **w** templelanestudios.com ■ Studio Mgr: John Hanley.

TEMPLE LANE RECORDING STUDIOS

8 Crow St, Temple Bar, Dublin 2, Ireland **t** +353 1 677 7255 **f** +353 1 670 9042 **e** templelanestudios@gmail.com ■ templelanestudios.com ■ Studio Mgr: John Hanley 00 353 1 6777255.

Temple Music Studio 48 The Ridgway, Sutton, Surrey, SM2 5JU **t** 07802 822006 **f** 020 8642 8692 **e** jh@temple-music.com **w** temple-music-studio.com ■ Producer/Engineer: Jon Hiseman.

Temple Studios 97A Kenilworth Rd, Edgware, Middlesex, HA8 8XB **t** 020 8958 4332 **f** 020 8958 4332 **e** contact@templestudios.co.uk **w** templestudios.co.uk ■ Producer: Howard Temple 07956 510620.

Ten21 Little Milgate, Otham Lane, Bearsted, Maidstone, Kent, ME15 8SJ **t** 01622 735200 **f** 01622 735200 **e** info@ten21.biz **w** ten21.biz ■ Owner: Sean Kenny.

Tin Pan Alley Studio 22 Denmark St, London, WC2H 8NG **t** 020 7240 0816 **e** info@tinpanalleystudio.com **w** tinpanalleystudio.com ■ Studio Mgr: Alexandra Fry.

Tinman Creative Sound Recording Studios Quinta da Figueirinha, Silves, Algarve, 8300-028, Portugal **t** +351 28 244 0702 **e** webmaster@tinman-creative.com **w** tinman-creative.com ■ Executive Producer: Mike Myers.

Toast Recordings Bridgewater Mill Studios, Legh St, Eccles, Manchester, M30 0UT **t** 07964 957458 **e** chris@toastrecordings.com **w** toastrecordings.com ■ Studio Mgr: Chris Hamilton.

Toerag Studios 166A Glyn Rd, London, E5 0JE **t** 020 8985 8862 **e** toeragstudios1@hotmail.com **w** toeragstudios.com ■ MD: Liam Watson.

Touchwood Audio Productions 6 Hyde Park Terrace, Leeds, W. Yorks, LS6 1BJ **t** 0113 278 7180 **e** bruce@touchwoodaudio.com **w** touchwoodaudio.com ■ Dir: Bruce Wood 07745 377 772.

Tribal Tree Studios 66c Chalk Farm Road, Camden, London, NW1 8AN **t** 020 7482 6945 **e** info@triangle-records.co.uk **w** tribaltreestudios.co.uk ■ Studio Manager: Chris Lock.

Twin Peaks Studio Ty Neuadd, Torpantau, Brecon Beacons, Mid Glamorgan, CF48 2UT **t** 01685 359932 **e** twinpeaksstudio@btconnect.com **w** TwinPeaksStudio.com ■ Director: Adele Nozedar.

Unit Q Studio Unit Q The Maltings, Station Rd, Sawbridgeworth, Herts, CM21 9JX **t** 01279 600078 **e** unitq@orgyrecords.com **w** orgyrecords.com ■ Partner: Darren Bazzoni.

Univibe Audio Unit 6, Lawford Close, Birmingham, West Midlands, B7 4HJ **t** 01922 709152 **e** info@univibeaudio.co.uk **w** univibeaudio.co.uk ■ Owner: Joel Spencer 07734 151589.

Vertical Rooms 5-6 Road Farm, Ermine Way, Arrington, Herts, SG8 0AA **t** 01223 207 007 **f** 01223 207 007 **e** info@verticalrooms.com **w** verticalrooms.com ■ Dir: Pete Brazier.

Vital Spark Studios 1 Waterloo, Breakish, Isle Of Skye, IV42 8QE **t** 01471 822 484 **e** chris@vitalsparkmusic.demon.co.uk **w** vitalsparkmusic.co.uk ■ Owner/manager: Chris Harley (aka Chris Rainbow) 07768 031 060.

The Vocal Booth Toxteth TV, 37-45 Windsor St, Liverpool, L8 1XE **t** 0151 707 2833 **f** 0151 707 2833 **e** mike.moran@thevocalbooth.com **w** thevocalbooth.com ■ myspace.com/thevocalbooth ■ Producer: Mike Moran 07800 993192.

Warehouse Studios 60 Sandford Lane, Kennington, Oxford, OX1 5RW **t** 01865 736 411 **e** info@warehousestudios.com **w** warehousestudios.com ■ Studio Mgr: Steve Watkins.

Warwick Hall of Sound Warwick Hall, off Banastre Avenue, Heath, Cardiff, CF14 3NR **t** 029 2069 4455 **f** 029 2069 4455 **e** adamstangroom@btconnect.com **w** myspace.com/cardiffswarwickhallrecordingstudio ■ Dirs: Martin Bowen, Adam Stangroom 029 2069 4450.

Welsh Media Music Gorwelion, Llanfynydd, Carmarthen, Dyfed, SA32 7TG **t** 01558 668525 **e** dpierce@fsmail.net **w** bluelagoonrock.com ■ MD: Dafydd Pierce 07774 100430.

West Orange Unit 1, 16B Pechell St, Ashton, Preston, Lancashire, PR2 2RN **t** 01772 722626 **f** 01772 722626 **e** westorange@btclick.com ■ Studio Mgr: Alan Gregson.

Westland Studios 5-6 Lombard Street East, Dublin, 2, Ireland **t** +353 87 282 0273 **f** +353 1 671 0421 **e** westland@indigo.ie **w** westlandstudios.ie ■ MySpace.com/westlandstudios ■ youtube.com/WestlandStudios ■ General Manager: Deirdre Costello.

Westpoint Studio Unit GA, 39-40 Westpoint, Warple Way, London, W3 0RG **t** 020 8740 1616 **f** 020 8740 4488 **e** info@westpointstudio.co.uk **w** westpointstudio.co.uk ■ Studio Manager: Ian Sherwin.

White's Farm Studios Whites Farm, Wilton Lane, Kenyon Culcheth, WA3 4BA **t** 0161 790 4830 **f** 0161 703 8521 **e** whitesfarmstudio@aol.com **w** whitesfarmstudios.com ■ Dir: Gary Hastings.

Contacts   **Facebook**   **MySpace**   **Twitter**   **YouTube**

Windmill Lane Recording Studios
20 Ringsend Rd, Dublin 4, Dublin, Ireland
t +353 1 668 5567 **f** +353 1 668 5352 **e** info@windmill.ie
w windmill.ie facebook.com/pages/Dublin/Windmill-
Lane-Recording-Studios/76908637654 House
Engineer: Niall McMonagle.

Wired Studios Ltd 26-28 Silver Street, Reading,
Berkshire, RG1 2ST **t** 0118 986 0973
e office@wiredstudios.demon.co.uk
w wiredstudios.demon.co.uk Manager: Chris Britton.

Wise Buddah Creative 74 Great Titchfield St,
London, W1W 7QP **t** 020 7307 1600 **f** 020 7307 1601
e neil@wisebuddah.com **w** wisebuddah.com Client
Services Manager: Neil Wease.

Wizard Sound Studios Prospect House,
Lower Caldecote, Biggleswade, Beds, SG18 9UH
t 01767 601398 **e** davysmyth@wizardsoundstudios.com
w wizardsoundstudios.com Owner Producer: Davy
Smyth.

Wolf Studios 83 Brixton Water Lane, London, SW2 1PH
t 020 7733 8088 **f** 020 7326 4016 **e** brethes@mac.com
w wolfstudios.co.uk Director: Dominique Brethes.

Woodbine Street Recording Studio
1 St Mary's Crescent, Leamington Spa, Warwickshire,
CV31 1JL **t** 01926 338971 **e** jony2r@ntlworld.com
w woodbinestreet.com MD/Studio Mgr: John A Rivers.

Woodside Studio Woodside, Eason's Green,
Framfield, Nr. Uckfield, East Sussex, TN22 5RE
t 01825 841484 **f** 01825 880019
e woodsidestudios@btconnect.com
w woodsidestudios.com Studio Manager: Terri Myles.

Yellow Arch Studios 30-36 Burton Road, Neepsend,
Sheffield, S3 8BX **t** 0114 273 0800 **e** jon@yellowarch.com
w yellowarch.com Studio Manager: Jon Dean.

Zoo Studios 145 Wardour Street, London, W1F 8WB
t 020 7734 2000 **f** 020 7734 2200
e bookings@thejunglegroup.co.uk
w thejunglegroup.co.uk Bookings Manager: Charlotte
Martin.

Mobile Studios

Abbey Road Mobiles 3 Abbey Rd, London, NW8 9AY
t 020 7266 7000 **f** 020 7266 7250
e bookings@abbeyroad.com **w** abbeyroad.com Studio
Manager: Colette Barber.

As The Crow Flies The Retreat, Pidney,
Hazlebury Bryan, Dorset, DT10 2EB **t** 01258 817214
f 01258 817207 **e** PeteFreshney@compuserve.com
w petefreshney.co.uk Contact: Pete Freshney 07971
686961.

BBC Radio Outside Broadcasts (London)
Brock House, 19 Langham St, London, W1A 1AA
t 020 7765 4888 **f** 020 7765 5504
e will.garnett@bbc.co.uk Operations Mgr: Will Garnett.

Circle Sound Services Circle House,
14 Waveney Close, Bicester, Oxfordshire, OX26 2GP
t 01869 240051 **f** 0870 705 9679
e sound@circlesound.net **w** circlesound.net
 Owner: John Willett.

The Classical Recording Company Ltd. 16-
17 Wolsey Mews, Kentish Town, London, NW5 2DX
t 020 7482 2303 **f** 020 7482 2302
e info@classicalrecording.com **w** classicalrecording.com
 Senior Producer: Simon Weir.

Doyen Recordings Ltd The Doyen Centre,
Vulcan Street, Oldham, Lancashire, OL1 4EP
t 0161 628 3799 **f** 0161 628 0177 **e** sales@doyen-
recordings.co.uk **w** doyen-recordings.co.uk
 MD: Nicholas J Childs.

K&A Productions 5 Wyllyotts Place, Potters Bar,
Hertfordshire, EN6 2HN **t** 01707 661200 **f** 01707 661400
e info@kaproductions.co.uk **w** kaproductions.co.uk
 MD: Andrew Walton.

Komodo Recordings 79 Magheraconluce Rd,
Hillsborough, Co. Down, BT26 6PR **t** 02892 688 285
e info@komodorecordings.com **w** komodorecordings.com
 Mobile Recording Engineer: Darrell 07803 627 595.

Leapfrog Audiovisual 1 Currievale Farm Cottages,
Currie, Midlothian, EH14 4AA **t** 0131 449 5808
e claudeharper@supanet.com Prop: Claude Harper
07941 346813.

Make Some Noise Recording & Mastering
PO Box 792, Maidstone, Kent, ME14 5LG **t** 01622 691 106
f 01622 691 106 **e** info@makesomenoiserecords.com
w makesomenoiserecords.com Manager: Clive Austen.

Manor Mobiles Denham Media Park,
North Orbital Road, Denham, Bucks, UB9 5HQ
t 08700 771 071 **f** 08700 771 068
e tim.s@fleetwoodmobiles.com **w** fleetwoodmobiles.com
 Dir: Tim Summerhayes.

Ninth Wave Audio 46 Elizabeth Rd, Moseley,
Birmingham, West Midlands, B13 8QJ **t** 0121 442 2276
e Tgw@ninthwaveaudio.com **w** ninthwaveaudio.com
 Studio Mgr: Tony Wass 07770 364464.

**OFFSLIP - Live Band Recordings As They're
Meant To Be** London **e** danfeel@offslip.co.uk Live
Recording Engineer: Dan Feel 07912 091979.

Professional Audio Company Ltd Unit 19,
Jubilee Trade Centre, Jubilee Rd, Letchworth Garden City,
Hertfordshire, SG6 1SP **t** 07971 612060
e martin@professionalaudiocompany.co.uk
w professionalaudiocompany.co.uk
 myspace.com/professionalaudiocompany
 twitter.com/proaudioco Director: Martin Knight
07971 612 060.

The Real Stereo Recording Company
14 Moorend Crescent, Cheltenham, Gloucestershire,
GL53 0EL **t** 01242 523304 **f** 01242 523304
e martin@instantmusic.co.uk **w** instantmusic.co.uk
 Prod Mgr: Martin Mitchell 07957 355630.

Red TX Ltd Admin 102, Pinewood Studios, Pinewood Rd, Iver Heath, Bucks, SL0 0NH **t** 020 7183 2266 **e** conrad@red-tx.com **w** red-tx.com ☑ Dir: Conrad Fletcher.

Remote Live Recordings 36 Shrewsbury Rd, Carshalton, Surrey, SM5 1LZ **t** 07968 100 557 **e** info@remoteliverecordings.co.uk **w** remoteliverecordings.co.uk ☑ Proprietor: Mike Knight.

Silk Recordings 65 High Street, Kings Langley, Herts., WD4 9HU **t** 01923 270 852 **e** info@silkrecordings.com **w** silkrecordings.com ☑ MD: Bob Whitney 07812 602 535.

SJTMusic 51 Rosemullion Avenue, Tattenhoe, Milton Keynes, Bucks, MK4 3AH **t** 07968 795 503 **e** sjtmusic@mac.com **w** sjtmusic.co.uk ☑ Dir: Simon Turner.

Sound Moves The Oaks, Cross Lane, Smallfield, Horley, Surrey, RH6 9SA **t** 01342 844 190 **f** 01342 844 290 **e** steve@sound-moves.com **w** sound-moves.com ☑ Proprietor: Steve Williams.

Tenth Egg Productions 47 Stanley Avenue, Beckenham, Kent, BR3 6PU **t** 020 7193 9603 **e** info@tenthegg.co.uk **w** tenthegg.co.uk ☑ Head Engineer: Nick Barron.

Producers & Producer Management

140dB Management The Chapel, Everwood Court, Maybury Gardens, London, NW10 2AF **t** 020 8208 5660 **f** 020 8459 3789 **e** firstname@140db.co.uk **w** 140db.co.uk ☑ Managers: Ros Earls, Justin Pritchard and Jen Greenwood.

19 Management 33 Ransomes Dock, 35-37 Parkgate Road, London, SW11 4NP **t** 020 7801 1919 **f** 020 7801 1920 **e** reception@19.co.uk **w** 19.co.uk ☑ MD: Simon Fuller.

24 Management Westfield Cottage, Scragged Oak Rd, Maidstone, Kent, ME143HA **t** 01622 632 634 **f** 01622 632 634 **e** info@24twentyfour.com ☑ MD: Andy Rutherford.

2am Productions Contact: The Lemon Group

3 Wise Men Contact: Ambush Management

365 Artists Ltd Unit 4, 9 Thorpe Close, London, W10 5XL **t** 020 8968 2071 **f** 020 8960 1588 **e** info@365artists.com **w** 365artists.com ☑ Creative Director: Paul Smith.

3D Media Services Seton Lodge, 26 Sutton Avenue, Seaford, East Sussex, BN25 4UJ **t** 01323 892 303 **e** talk2us@3dmediaservices.com **w** 3dmediaservices.com ☑ MDs: Anthony Duke, Kim Duke.

3kHz 54 Pentney Rd, London, SW12 0NY **t** 020 8772 0108 **f** 020 8675 1636 **e** threekhz@hotmail.com ☑ Manager: Jessica Norbury.

A Side Productions Contact: XL Talent

Jim Abbiss Contact: This Much Talent

Absolute Contact: Native Management

Rich Adlam Contact: 365 Artists Ltd

Advanced Alternative Media Ltd 36 Forsyth Gardens, London, SE17 3NE **e** chrisw@aaminc.com **w** aaminc.com ☑ Manager: Chris Woo.

Afreex Contact: Stephen Budd Management

AIR Management Lyndhurst Hall, Lyndhurst Rd, Hampstead, London, NW3 5NG **t** 020 7426 5131 or 020 7426 5132 **f** 020 7426 5102 **e** coral@airstudios.com **w** air-management.co.uk ⓕ facebook.com/pages/AIR-Management ☑ Dirs: Coral Worman or Lucy Matthews 020 7426 5132.

Matt Aitken Contact: Menace Management

Akira The Don Contact: Paul Brown Management

Alan Cowderoy Management 2 Devonport Mews, London, W12 8NG **t** 020 8743 9336 **f** 020 8743 9809 **e** alan@producermanagement.co.uk **w** producermanagement.co.uk ☑ MD: Alan Cowderoy.

The All Seeing I Contact: Menace Management

Chris Allison c/o Sonic360, 33 Riding House St, London, W1W 7DZ **t** 020 7636 3939 **f** 020 7636 0033 **e** info@sonic360.com ☑ Contact: Chris Allison.

Ambush Management 32 Ransome's Dock, 35-37 Parkgate Road, London, SW11 4NP **t** 020 7801 1919 **f** 020 7738 1819 **e** alambush.native@19.co.uk **w** ambushgroup.co.uk ☑ MD: Alister Jamieson.

Andy Whitmore Productions 39 Greystoke Park Terrace, London, W5 1JL **t** 020 8998 5529 **e** andy@andywhitmore.com **w** andywhitmore.com ☑ Producer: Andy Whitmore 07850 735591.

ArchangelUK 5A Invicta Parade, Sidcup High St, Sidcup, DA16 5ER **t** 020 8300 0094 **e** info@archangeluk.co.uk **w** archangeluk.co.uk ☑ A&R: Bruce Elliott-Smith.

Animal Farm Contact: SJP/Dodgy Productions

Anu Pillai Contact: Illicit Entertainment

Apollo 440 Contact: XL Talent

Arclite Productions The Grove Music Studios, Unit 10.Latimer Ind. Est, Latimer Rd, London, W10 6RQ **t** 020 8964 9047 **e** info@arcliteproductions.com **w** arcliteproductions.com ☑ Producer: Alan Bleay/Laurie Jenkins.

Peter Arnold Contact: Panama Productions

Artfield 5 Grosvenor Square, London, W1K 4AF **t** 020 7499 9941 **f** 020 7499 5519 **e** info@artfieldmusic.com **w** bbcooper.com ☑ MD: BB Cooper.

Artist, Music & Talent International PO Box 43, Manchester, M8 0BB **t** 0161 795 7717 **f** 0161 795 7717 **e** amti@btconnect.com ✉ MD: Peter Lewyckyj 07905 001 687.

Jon Astley Contact: Pachuco Management

Atlas Realisations Music Trendalls Cottage, Beacons Bottom, Bucks, HP14 3XF **t** 01494 483121 **f** 01494 484303 **e** craig@craigleon.com **w** craigleon.com ✉ Producer: Craig Leon.

Audio Authority Management 1, Sherwood Oaks, Frensham Rd, Kenley, Surrey, CR8 5NS **t** 020 7101 2880 **e** tim.hole@audioauthority.co.uk **w** audioauthority.co.uk ✉ Contact: Tim Hole.

Audio-Freaks t 07843 006461 **e** matt@audio-freaks.com **w** audio-freaks.com ✉ Managing Director: Matt Meyers.

AudioJunkie Sovereign House, 12 Trewartha Rd, Praa Sands, Penzance, Cornwall, TR20 9ST **t** 01736 762826 **f** 01736 763328 **e** panamus@aol.com **w** panamamusic.co.uk ✉ myspace.com/digimixrecords ✉ MD: Roderick Jones.

Dan Austin Contact: 140dB Management

David Ayers and Felix Tod Contact: Giles Stanley Management

Baby Ash Contact: This Much Talent

Bacon & Quarmby Contact: Alan Cowderoy Management

Jon Bailey Contact: AIR Management

Lee Baker Contact: Giles Stanley Management

Arthur Baker Contact: Stephen Budd Management

Fred Ball Contact: Native Management

James Banbury Contact: Giles Stanley Management

Barny Contact: This Much Talent

Dave Bascombe Contact: Alan Cowderoy Management

Beatguru The Lansdowne Suite, Lansdowne House, Lansdowne Rd, London, W11 3LP **t** 020 7727 4214 **e** lesley@beatguru.com ✉ Contact: Magnus Fiennes 07880 865 754.

Sam Bell Contact: Smoothside Organisation

Joe Belmaati Contact: XL Talent

Haydn Bendall Contact: Duncan Management

Vito Benito Contact: Ambush Management

Gary Benson Contact: Menace Management

Biffco Management
t 01273 607 484 or +353 87 278 0233 **e** Ejbiffco@mac.com **w** biffco.net ✉ Contact: Emma Jane Lennon.

Big George and Sons PO Box 7094, Kiln Farm, MK11 1LL **t** 01908 566 453 **e** big.george@btinternet.com **w** biggeorge.co.uk ✉ Manager: Big George Webley.

BIG LIFE MANAGEMENT

«**biglife**»

67-69 Chalton St, London, NW1 1HY **t** 020 7554 2100 **f** 020 7554 2101 **e** jill@biglifemanagement.com **w** biglifeproducers.com ✉ Producer Management: Jill Hollywood & Tim Parry.

Ned Bigham Contact: Ocean Bloem Productions

Peter Biker Contact: 365 Artists Ltd

Henry Binns Contact: Solar Management Ltd

Björn Again PO Box 63564, London, N6 9AN **t** 020 8341 4900 **e** rod@bjornagain.com **w** bjornagain.com ✉ Creator: Rod Stephen.

Black Man Jack Productions
The Garage Workshop Ltd, 1st Floor Office Suit, 122 Montague St, Worthing, West Sussex, BN11 3HG **t** 01903 606 513 **e** Owen.thegarageworkshop@gmail.com **w** thegarageworkshop.com ✉ Producer: Owen A Smith 07861 232 006.

Bobfalola Music Production 628 Old Kent Road, London, SE15 1JB **t** 07989 471263 **e** bobfalola@aol.com ✉ Dir: Bob Falola.

Roger Boden Contact: The Cottage Group - Amco Music Productions

Phil Bodger 69 Freshfield Rd, Brighton, BN2 0BL **t** 07855 944 640 **e** phil@coastaudio.net **w** coastaudio.net ✉ Producer/Remixer: Phil Bodger.

Bodyrockers Contact: 24 Management

Jason Boshoff Contact: Audio Authority Management

Andy Bradfield Contact: 365 Artists Ltd

Michael Brauer Contact: Erik Eger Entertainment, Inc.

Pete Briquette Contact: Pachuco Management

Ian Broudie Contact: Alan Cowderoy Management

Chris Brown Contact: SJP/Dodgy Productions

Lukas Burton Contact: XL Talent

Steve Bush Contact: Paul Brown Management

Adrian Bushby Contact: This Much Talent

Buzz-erk Music Studio Two, Chocolate Factory 2, 4 Coburg Road, London, N22 6UJ **e** info@buzz-erk.com **w** buzz-erk.com ✉ Director: Niraj Chag.

C A Management PO Box 379, Lymington, Hampshire, SO41 1AU **e** adam@camanagement.co.uk **w** camanagement.co.uk ✉ MD: Adam Sharp.

Colin Campsie Contact: WG Stonebridge Producer Management

«biglife»

PRODUCER MANAGEMENT
Jill Hollywood / jill@biglifemanagement.com
0207 554 2105 / biglifeproducers.com

Cargogold Productions 39 Clitterhouse Crescent, Cricklewood, London, NW2 1DB **t** 020 8458 1020 **e** mike@mikecarr.co.uk **w** mikecarr.co.uk **MD:** Mike Carr.

Nick Carpenter PO Box 22626, London, N15 3WW **t** 020 8211 0272 **f** 020 8211 0272

Guy Chambers Contact: Sleeper Music

Change of Weather Productions 29 Gladwell Road, London, N8 9AA **t** 020 8245 2136 **e** pcarmichael@changeofweather.com **w** changeofweather.com ✉ MD: Paul Carmichael 07974 070 880.

DJ Chaos Contact: Panama Productions

Jon Collyer Contact: AIR Management

Con Fitzpatrick Productions Big Guitar Recording Studio, Gravity Shack, Unit 3, Rear of 328 Balham High Rd, London, SW17 7AA **t** 020 8672 4772 **e** con.fitzpatrick@btinternet.com ✉ Contact: Con Fitzpatrick.

Cordella Music Alhambra, High St, Shirrell Heath, Southampton, Hants, SO32 2JH **t** 08450 616 616 **f** 01329 833 433 **e** barry@cordellamusic.co.uk **w** cordellamusic.co.uk ✉ MD: Barry Upton.

Rich Costey Contact: 140dB Management

The Cottage Group - Amco Music Productions 2 Gawsworth Rd, Macclesfield, Cheshire, SK11 8UE **t** 01625 420163 **f** 01625 420168 **e** info@amcomusic.co.uk **w** amcomusic.co.uk ▶ myspace.com/amcomusicpublishing ▶ youtube.com/amcomusic ✉ MD: Roger Boden.

Rupert Coulson Contact: AIR Management

Courtyard Productions Ltd 22 The Nursery, Sutton Courtenay, Oxon, OX14 4UA **t** 01622 880 990 **f** 0845 127 4663 **e** kate@cyard.com ✉ Dir: Chris Hufford & Bryce Edge.

Covert Music Management 5 Parr Court, Revere Way, West Ewell, Surrey, KT19 9RJ **t** 07958 958541 **f** 0871 264 1322 **e** simon@covertmusic.co.uk **w** covertmusic.co.uk ✉ MD: Simon King.

Stewart Coxhead Munro House, High Close, Rawdon, Leeds, West Yorkshire, LS19 6HF **t** 0113 250 3338 **f** 0113 250 7343 **e** stewart@stewartcoxhead.com **w** acoustic-alchemy.net ✉ MD: Stewart Coxhead.

Pete Craigie Contact: Z Management

Creative Productions (UK) Ltd 1 Roundtown, Aynho, Oxfordshire, OX17 3BG **t** 01869 810956 **e** guy@creativeproductionsuk.com ✉ Contact: Guy Stanway, Gary Stevenson.

Stuart Crichton Contact: Z Management

Crocodile Music 431 Linen Hall, 162-168 Regent St, London, W1B 5TE **t** 020 7580 0080 **f** 020 7637 0097 **e** music@crocodilemusic.com **w** crocodilemusic.com ✉ Contact: Malcolm Ironton, Ray Tattle.

Mike Crossey Contact: Alan Cowderoy Management

Phil Culbertson 5-6 Road Farm, Ermine Way, Arrington, Herts, SG8 0AA **t** 01223 207 007 **f** 01223 207 007 **e** info@verticalrooms.com **w** verticalrooms.com ✉ Dir: Pete Brazier.

Ross Cullum Contact: FKM

Ian Curnow Contact: Z Management

Cutfather Contact: XL Talent

The Cutting Room Abraham Moss Centre, Crescent Centre, Manchester, M8 5UF **t** 0161 740 9438 **f** 0161 740 0583

Graham Philip D'Ancey Chez Couilaud, Chatain, 86250, France **t** +33 (0) 549 874 062 **e** graham.dancey@wanadoo.fr **w** gpdmusic.com

Dan O'Sullivan and Antti Uusimaki Contact: Paul Brown Management

Danny D Contact: 19 Management

Darah Music - Q Zone Ltd 21C Heathmans Rd, Parsons Green, London, SW6 4TJ **t** 020 7731 9313 **f** 020 7731 9314 **e** mail@darah.co.uk ✉ MD: David Howells.

David Beard Producers and Producer Management 176 Sandbed Lane, Belper, Derbyshire, DE56 0SN **t** 01773 824 340 **e** info@davidbeardmusic.com **w** davidbeardmusic.com ✉ MD: David Beard 07815 573 121.

David Jaymes Associates Ltd Hope House, 40 St Peters Rd, London, W6 9BN **t** 020 8741 6020 **e** info@spiritmm.com **w** irl.org.uk ▶ myspace.com/spiritmusicmedia ✉ Directors: David Jaymes, Tom Haxell.

Pete Davis Contact: Native Management

Charlotte Day Contact: The Cottage Group - Amco Music Productions

Edward de Bono Contact: Wingfoot Productions

John de Bono Contact: Wingfoot Productions

Marius De Vries Contact: Native Management

Dead Stereo Contact: Ambush Management

Deep Production Company 187 Freston Rd, London, W10 6TH **t** 020 8964 8256 **e** mark@deeprecordingstudios.com **w** deeprecordingstudios.com ✉ Manager: Mark Rose.

DeepFrost Studios AS Vestre Rosten 78, Tiller, N-7075, Norway **t** +47 7288 5923 **e** office@deepfrost.no **w** deepfrost.no ✉ Manager / producer / writer: Thomas Heyerdahl.

Georgie Dennis Contact: 365 Artists Ltd

Digimix Music Productions Sovereign House, 12 Trewartha Road, Praa Sands, Penzance, Cornwall, TR20 9ST **t** 01736 762 826 **f** 01736 763 328 **e** panamis@aol.com **w** panamamusic.co.uk ✉ MD: Roderick Jones. Contact: Panama Productions

Sam Dixon Contact: EMI Music Publishing Management

«*biglife*»

PRODUCER MANAGEMENT
Jill Hollywood / jill@biglifemanagement.com
0207 554 2105 / biglifeproducers.com

DJ Stylus Sovereign House, 12 Trewartha Rd, Praa Sands, Penzance, Cornwall, TR20 9ST
t 01736 762826 **f** 01736 763328 **e** panamus@aol.com **w** panamamusic.co.uk
◩ myspace.com/scampmusicpublishing ✉ MD: Roderick Jones.

Craigie Dodds Contact: Native Management

Graham Dominy Contact: Innocent Management

Double Jointed Productions
(address witheld by request) **t** 020 7836 7553
e djp@musicard.co.uk ✉ Production Mgr: David Newell.

Johnny Douglas Contact: Twenty Four Seven Music Management

Dr. Luke Contact: Advanced Alternative Media Ltd

Dreamscape Music 36 Eastcastle Street, London, W1W 8DP **t** 020 7631 1799 **f** 020 7631 1720
e lester@lesterbarnes.com **w** lesterbarnes.com
✉ Composer: Lester Barnes 07767 771 157.

Duffnote Productions Ltd Vine Cottage, North Road, Bosham, W. Sussex, PO18 8NL
t 01243 774606 or 575110 **e** info@duffnote.com **w** duffnote.com ✉ Dirs: Danny Jones, Richard Earnshaw.

Duncan Management Unit 59 Canalot Studios, 222 Kensal Rd, London, W10 5BN **t** 07990 550 001
e rebecca@duncanmanagement.com
w duncanmanagement.com ✉ MD: Rebecca Duncan 07990 550001.

The Dust Brothers Contact: Advanced Alternative Media Ltd

Colin Eade Sovereign House, 12 Trewartha Rd, Praa Sands, Penzance, Cornwall, TR20 9ST
t 01736 762826 **f** 01736 763328 **e** panamus@aol.com **w** panamamusic.co.uk
◩ myspace.com/scampmusicpublishing ✉ MD: Roderick Jones.

Steve Edwards Contact: Menace Management

Finn Eiles Contact: Interface

Bruno Ellingham Contact: Illicit Entertainment

Colin Elliot Contact: 365 Artists Ltd

Jorgen Elofsson Contact: XL Talent

EMI Music Publishing Management
27 Wrights Lane, Kensington, London, W8 5SW
t 020 3059 3085 **e** initial+lastname@emimusicpub.com
✉ GM: Anna Carpenter.

Colin Emmanuel (C Swing) Contact: Stephen Budd Management

Erik Eger Entertainment, Inc.
17 West 20th St, Suite 5E, New York, NY, 10011, United States **t** +1 212 684 9242 **f** +1 212 488 2054
e info@erikegerentertainment.com
w erikegerentertainment.com
�f facebook.com/erikegerentertainment
✉ President: Erik Eger.

Dave Eringa Contact: Solar Management Ltd

Steve Evans Contact: Positive Management

The Fern Organisation Fern Studios, 5 Low Road, Conisbrough, Doncaster, South Yorkshire, DN12 3AB
t 01709 868511 **f** 01709 867274 ✉ Contact: Howard Johnson.

Pedro Ferreira Contact: AIR Management

Debbie Ffrench Contact: 365 Artists Ltd

Jerry Finn Contact: Advanced Alternative Media Ltd

Firebird Studios - Firebird.com Ltd
Kyrle House Studios, Edde Cross St, Ross-on-Wye, Herefordshire, HR9 7BZ **t** 01989 762269
e info@firebird.com **w** firebird.com
�f facebook.com/pages/Phoenix-J/77298323726
◩ myspace.com/phoenixjmusic ✆ twitter.com/phoenix_j
✉ CEO: Peter Martin.

Stephen Fitzmaurice Contact: Native Management

FKM PO Box 242, Haslemere, Surrey, GU26 6ZT
t 01428 608 149 **e** fken10353@aol.com
✉ Chairman: Fraser Kennedy.

FLAM 8 boulevard de Ménilmontant, Paris, 75020, France
t +33 143 484 444 **f** +33 143 480 044 **e** carlito@flam.biz
w flammusic.com ✉ International / Asst. Man: Charles Vallette Viallard (aka Carlito).

Andrew Flintham Productions PO box 1255, Newton Flotman, Norwich, Norfolk, NR151WH
t 01508 471 485 **e** andrew@overthrillrecords.com
w overthrillrecords.com ✉ Producer/Record Company Owner: Andrew Flintham.

Flood Contact: 140dB Management

John Fortis Contact: XL Talent

Matt Foster Contact: Interface

Geoff Foster Contact: AIR Management

Charlie Francis Contact: Paul Brown Management

Nick Franglen Contact: Big Life Management

Freak'n See Music Ltd 19c Heathmans Rd, London, SW6 4TJ **t** 020 7384 2429 **f** 020 7384 2429
e firstname@freaknsee.com **w** freaknsee.com
✉ MD: Jimmy Mikaoui.

Freeform Five Contact: Illicit Entertainment

Freelance Hellraiser Contact: Big Life Management

Mark Frith Contact: Positive Management

Full Phatt Productions Contact: Twenty Four Seven Music Management

Fume Productions 30 Kilburn Lane, Kensal Green, London, W10 4AH **t** 020 8969 2909 **f** 020 8969 3825
e info@fume.co.uk **w** fume.co.uk ✉ MD: Seamus Morley.

Fundamental Music 64 Manor Rd, Wheathampstead, Hertfordshire, AL4 8JD **t** 01582 622757
e karen@fundamentalmusic.co.uk ✉ Manager: Karen Ciccone 07815 898488.

«biglife»

PRODUCER MANAGEMENT
Jill Hollywood / jill@biglifemanagement.com
0207 554 2105 / biglifeproducers.com

Pascal Gabriel Contact: This Much Talent

Pete Gage Production 47 Prout Grove, London, NW10 1PU **t** 020 8450 5789 **f** 020 8450 0150 ✉ MD: Pete Gage.

Galaxy P Contact: Jamdown Ltd

Rod Gammons c/o G2 Music, 33 Bournehall Avenue, Bushey, Herts, WD23 3AU **t** 020 8950 1485 **f** 020 8950 1294 **e** sales@planetaudiosystems.co.uk **w** g2-music.com ✉ Contact: Rod Gammons.

Gaudi Contact: The Lemon Group

Sean Genockey Contact: Solar Management Ltd

Serban Ghenea Contact: Advanced Alternative Media Ltd

Brad Gilderman Contact: Pachuco Management

Giles Stanley Management Fruit Tree, Otterbourne Rd, Winchester, Hants, SO21 2RT **t** 07718 653218 **e** info@gs-music.com **w** gs-music.com ✉ MD: Giles Stanley.

Andy Gill Contact: Big Life Management

Kristian Gilroy Harewood Farm Studios, Little Harewood Farm, Clamgoose Lane, Kingsley, Staffs, ST10 2EG **t** 07973 157 920 **f** 01538 755 735 **e** kristian@harewoodfarmstudios.com **w** harewoodfarmstudios.com ✉ Producer: Kristian Gilroy.

Mick Glossop Contact: Giles Stanley Management

Go Crazy Music The Studio, Penybryn, Tydcombe Rd, Warlingham, Surrey, CR6 9LU **t** 01883 626859 **e** gocrazymusic@aol.com ✉ GM: Sara Watts.

Clive Goddard Contact: Big Life Management

Goetz B Contact: 365 Artists Ltd

Simon Gogerly Contact: Stephen Budd Management

Goldman Associates 16 Red Hill Lane, Great Shelford, Cambridge, CB2 5JR **t** 01223 840436 **f** 01223 840436 **e** dox@goldman.co.uk **w** goldman.co.uk ✉ Contact: Martin Goldman.

Nigel Godrich Contact: Solar Management Ltd

Tim Gordine Contact: This Much Talent

Graphite 133 Kew Rd, Richmond, Surrey, TW9 2PN **t** 020 8948 5446 **e** info@graphitemedia.net **w** graphitemedia.net ✉ Director: Ben Turner.

Jon Gray Contact: Big Life Management

Howard Gray Contact: XL Talent

Andy Green Contact: Giles Stanley Management

Green Sky Mixes 56 Cole Park Rd, Twickenham, TW1 1HS **t** 020 8891 3333 **f** 020 8891 3222 **e** julian@redshadow.co.uk ✉ Director: Julian Spear 07939 118015.

Drew Griffiths Contact: Duncan Management

Ian Grimble Contact: Stephen Budd Management

Raj Gupta Contact: Solar Management Ltd

Stephen Hague Contact: Stephen Budd Management

Hamm & Bertoni Contact: Big Life Management

Hannah Management Fulham Palace, Bishops Avenue, London, SW6 6EA **t** 020 7758 1494 **e** mel@hannahmanagement.co.uk **w** hannahmanagement.co.uk ✉ myspace.com/barberahannah ✉ Contact: Hugh Gadsdon, Mel Stephenson, Gareth White.

Happybeat 101 Greenway Rd, Higher Tranmere, Merseyside, CH42 0NE **t** 0151 653 3463 **e** happybeatstudios@yahoo.co.uk **w** happybeat.net ✉ myspace.com/happybeat ✉ Contact: Fran Ashcroft.

Ed Harcourt Contact: Native Management

Phil Harding Contact: P.J. Music

Martin Harrington Contact: Native Management

Paul Harris Contact: EMI Music Publishing Management

Mads Hauge Contact: WG Stonebridge Producer Management

Greg Haver Contact: Stephen Budd Management

Head Contact: Paul Brown Management

Heavy Duty Productions 162 Springfield Road, Brighton, BN1 6DG **t** 01273 906 908 **e** info@heavydutyproductions.co.uk **w** heavydutyproductions.co.uk ✉ Dir: Stewart Crackett.

Mike Hedges Contact: 3kHz

Sally Herbert Contact: Solar Management Ltd

Thomas J. Heyerdahl Contact: DeepFrost Studios AS

Max Heyes Contact: Z Management

Paul Hicks Contact: 3kHz

Ben Hillier Contact: 140dB Management

Steve Hilton Contact: Stephen Budd Management

Joe Hirst Contact: Interface

Pete Hofmann Contact: Interface

Jimmy Hogarth Contact: Native Management

Emma Holland Contact: 365 Artists Ltd

Tim Holmes Contact: AIR Management

Holyrood Recording & Film Productions 86 Causewayside, Edinburgh, EH9 1PY **t** 0131 668 3366 **f** 0131 662 4463 **e** neil@holyroodproductions.com ✉ MD: Neil Ross.

Dean Honer Contact: Menace Management

Trevor Horn Contact: Sarm Management

Hot Source Productions Island Cottage, Rod Eyot, Wargrave Rd, Henley-on-Thames, Oxon, RG9 3JD **t** 01491 412 946 **e** Jay-F@hotsourceproductions.com ✉ Contact: Jay-F.

Liam Howe Contact: This Much Talent

«biglife» **PRODUCER MANAGEMENT**
Jill Hollywood / jill@biglifemanagement.com
0207 554 2105 / biglifeproducers.com

Howie B Contact: Native Management

Hoxton Whores Contact: 24 Management

Chris Hughes Contact: Positive Management

Matt Hyde Contact: Interface

I Monster Contact: Menace Management

Illicit Entertainment PO Box 51871, London, NW2 9BR **t** 020 8830 7831 **f** 020 8830 7859 **e** ian@illicit.tv **w** illicit.tv ✉ MD: Ian Clifford.

Independent Music Group Ltd - Memory Lane Music 3 York House, Langston Rd, Loughton, Essex, IG10 3TQ **t** 0845 371 1113 **f** 0845 371 1114 **e** erich@independentmusicgroup.com **w** independentmusicgroup.com ✉ CEO: Ellis Rich.

Innocent Management 45 Sylvan Avenue, London, N22 5JA **t** 07896 428 861 **e** info@innocentmanangement.com **w** innocentmanangement.com ✉ Contact: Lise Regan.

The Insects Contact: Paul Brown Management

Interface 36 Leroy St, London, SE1 4SP **t** 020 7232 0008 **f** 020 7237 6109 **e** jo@interfaceyourmusic.com **w** interfaceyourmusic.com ✉ Producer Manager: Jo Beckett.

Jacknife Lee Contact: Big Life Management

Jon Jacobs Contact: Giles Stanley Management

Jamdown Ltd Stanley House Studios, 39 Stanley Gardens, London, W3 7SY **t** 020 8735 0280 **f** 020 8930 1073 **e** othman@jamdown-music.com **w** jamdown-music.com ✉ MD: Othman Mukhlis.

JamDVD London **t** 07976 820 774 **f** 07092 003 937 **e** jamdvd@macunlimited.net **w** jamdvd.com ✉ Producer: Julie Gardner.

Eliot James Contact: Audio Authority Management

Jeff Jarratt Hotrock Music, Forestdene, Barnet, Hertfordshire, EN5 4PP **t** 020 8449 0830 **f** 020 8447 1210 **e** jeff@abbeyroadcafe.com ✉ MD: Jeff Jarratt.

JAY Productions 107 Kentish Town Rd, London, NW1 8PD **t** 020 7485 9593 **f** 020 7485 2282 **e** john@jayrecords.com **w** jayrecords.com ✉ Producer: John Yap.

Jazz UK Magazine First Floor, 132 Southwark St, London, SE1 0SW **t** 020 7928 9089 **f** 020 7401 6870 **e** listings@jazzservices.org.uk **w** jazzservices.org.uk ✉ Listings Editor: Yots.

Jazzwad Contact: Jamdown Ltd

Martin Jenkins Contact: Interface

Jimmy Thomas PO Box 38805, London, W12 7XL **t** 020 8740 8898 **e** jimmythomas@osceolarecords.com **w** osceolarecords.com

Joe Brown Productions Ltd PO Box 272, London, N20 0BY **t** 020 8368 0340 **f** 020 8361 3370 **e** john@jt-management.demon.co.uk ✉ MD: John Taylor.

Tore Johansson Contact: Stephen Budd Management

Wessley Johnson Contact: 365 Artists Ltd

Roderick Jones Sovereign House, 12 Trewartha Rd, Praa Sands, Penzance, Cornwall, TR20 9ST **t** 01736 762826 **f** 01736 763328 **e** panamus@aol.com **w** panamamusic.co.uk ✉ myspace.com/scampmusicpublishing ✉ MD: Roderick Jones.

Charlie Jones Contact: Positive Management

Cliff Jones Contact: Audio Authority Management

Hugh Jones Contact: Alan Cowderoy Management

Steve 'Dub' Jones Contact: Interface

DC Joseph Contact: Big Life Management

Jump Off TV **t** 020 7253 7766 **f** 020 7681 1007 **e** harry@jumpoff.tv **w** jumpoff.tv ✉ CEO: Harold Anthony.

Junk Scientist Contact: Giles Stanley Management

K-Klass The Bunker Recording Studio, Borras Road, Borras, Wrexham, LL13 9TW **t** 01978 263295 **f** 01978 263295 **e** kklass@btconnect.com **w** k-klass.com ✉ Contact: Andrew Willimas/Carl Thomas.

David Kahne Contact: Advanced Alternative Media Ltd

Jon Kelly Contact: Stephen Budd Management

Dave Kelly Contact: EMI Music Publishing Management

Kenisha Contact: Stephen Budd Management

Kick Production The Carriage House, 26B Dunstable Rd, Richmond upon Thames, Surrey, TW9 1UH **t** 020 8332 7525 **f** 020 8332 7527 **e** firstname@kickproduction.co.uk **w** kickproduction.com ✉ Contact: Terry J Neale.

Chris Kimsey Contact: Giles Stanley Management

King Unique Contact: 24 Management

Rob Kirwan Contact: 140dB Management

KK Contact: Stephen Budd Management

Kookie Contact: XL Talent

Jagz Kooner Contact: Big Life Management

Carsten Kroeyer Contact: Stephen Budd Management

Bob Lamb 122A Highbury Road, Kings Heath, Birmingham, West Midlands, B14 7QP **t** 0121 443 2186 **e** boblamb@recklessltd.com ✉ Studio Mgr/Prop: Bob Lamb.

Clive Langer Contact: Hannah Management

Larry Hibbitt Contact: Paul Brown Management

Laurie Latham Contact: SJP/Dodgy Productions

Simon Law & Lee Hamblin Contact: Z Management

Peter Lawlor c/o Water Music Productions, 1st Floor, Block 2, 6 Erskine Road, London, NW3 3AJ **t** 020 7722 3478 **f** 020 7722 6605 ✉ Contact: Tessa Sturridge.

Matt Lawrence Contact: Audio Authority Management

Graham Le Fevre 59 Park View Road, London, NW10 1AJ **t** 020 8450 5154 **f** 020 8452 0187 **e** rubiconrecords@btopenworld.com **w** rubiconrecords.co.uk ✉ Founder: Graham Le Fevre.

Leafman 31 Belsize Park, London, NW3 4DX **t** 07767 405 056 **e** liam@leafsongs.com ✉ MD: Liam Teeling.

John Leckie Contact: SJP/Dodgy Productions

Damian LeGassick Contact: AIR Management

The Lemon Group 1st Floor, 17 Bowater Road, Westminster Industrial Estate, Woolwich, London, SE18 5TF **t** 07989 340 593 **e** brian@thelemongroup.com **w** thelemongroup.com ✉ MD: Brian Allen.

Lester Barnes Contact: Dreamscape Music

James Lewis Contact: Stephen Budd Management

The Liaison and Promotion Company 124 Great Portland St, London, W1W 6PP **t** 020 7636 2345 **f** 020 7580 0045 **e** garydavison@fmware.com ✉ Dir: Gary Davison.

Liberty City Music PO Box 451, Macclesfield, Cheshire, SK10 3FR **t** 07921 626 900 **e** darren@libertycity.biz **w** libertycity.biz ✉ MD: Darren Eager.

Jan "Janski" Lindvaag Contact: DeepFrost Studios AS

Linus Loves Contact: Illicit Entertainment

Stephen Lipson Contact: Native Management

Steve Lironi Contact: Stephen Budd Management

Long Island Studios Long Island House, 1-4 Warple Way, London, W3 0RG **t** 020 8954 7144 **e** info@longislandstudios.com **w** longislandstudios.com ✉ Contact: Leanne Myers.

Steve Lyon Contact: Stephen Budd Management

Steve Mac Contact: Darah Music - Q Zone Ltd

Macwell Contact: Smac Music

Per Magnusson & David Kreuger Contact: XL Talent

Makis G Contact: The Lemon Group

Richard Manwaring 25 Waldeck Road, London, W13 8LY **t** 020 8991 0495

Pete 'Boxsta' Martin Contact: 365 Artists Ltd

Sir George Martin Contact: C A Management

Giles Martin Contact: C A Management

Guy Massey Contact: 140dB Management

Matpro Ltd Cary Point, Babbacombe Downs, Torquay, Devon, TQ1 3LU **t** 01803 322 233 **f** 01803 322 244 **e** mail@matpro-show.biz **w** babbacombe-theatre.com ✉ MD: Colin Matthews.

The Matrix Contact: Advanced Alternative Media Ltd

Gareth Matthews C/O Deep Recording Studios

Maximum Music Ltd 9 Heathmans Rd, Parsons Green, London, SW6 4TJ **t** 020 7731 1112 **e** nicky.graham@maximummusic.co.uk **w** nickygraham.com ✉ MD: Nicky Graham, Deni Lew.

Dave McCracken Contact: 140dB Management

Reg McLean RMO Music, 37 Philip Close, carshalton, Surrey, SM5 2FE **t** 020 8646 3378 **f** 020 8646 3376

Neil McLellan Contact: This Much Talent

James McMillan Contact: Giles Stanley Management

Richard McNamara Contact: Big Life Management

Dave Meegan Contact: Z Management

Menace Management 2 Park Rd, Radlett, Hertfordshire, WD7 8EQ **t** 01923 853789 **f** 01923 853318 **e** menacemusicmanagement@btopenworld.com ✉ MD: Dennis Collopy.

Messy Productions Studio 2, Soho Recording Studios, 22-24 Torrington Place, London, WC1E 7HJ **t** 020 7813 7202 **f** 020 7419 2333 **e** info@messypro.com **w** messypro.com ✉ MD: Zak Vracelli.

Miami Calling Contact: Ambush Management

Midi Mafia Contact: XL Talent

Teo Miller Contact: Stephen Budd Management

Grant Mitchell Contact: Sarm Management

Martin Mitchell Commercial Music Productions 14 Moorend Crescent, Cheltenham, Gloucestershire, GL53 0EL **t** 01242 523304 **f** 01242 523304 **e** mmitchell@hrpl.u-net.com ✉ MD: Martin Mitchell.

The Mob Film Company 10-11 Great Russell St, London, WC1B 3NH **t** 020 7580 8142 **f** 020 7255 1721 **e** mail@mobfilm.com **w** mobfilm.com ✉ Producer: John Brocklehurst.

Mobb Rule Productions PO Box 26335, London, N8 9ZA **t** 020 8340 8050 **e** info@mobbrule.com **w** mobbrule.com ✉ MD: Stewart Pettey.

Mo'Betta Musiq Utopia Village, Studio One, 7, Chalcot Road, London, Primrose Hill, NW1 8LH **t** 020 7586 9899 **e** enquiries@mobettamusiq.com **w** mobettamusiq.com ✉ Contact: Monty Joseph.

Gavin Monaghan Contact: Smoothside Organisation

Moneypenny The Stables, Westwood House, Main Street, North Dalton, Driffield, East Yorkshire, YO25 9XA **t** 01377 217815 **f** 01377 217754 **e** nigel@adastey.demon.co.uk ✉ MD: Nigel Morton.

Paul Mooney Suite 16, 7 Abingdon Rd, Middlesbrough, TS1 2DP **t** 01642 806795 **f** 01642 351962
e info@millbrand.com **w** millbrand.com
facebook.com/millbrand myspace.com/millbrand
Contact: Paul Mooney 07724 051117.

Owen Morris Contact: Nomadic Music

Ian Morrow Contact: Sarm Management

Motive Music Management 93b Scrubs Lane, London, NW10 6QU **t** 07808 939 919
e nathan@motivemusic.co.uk Contact: Nathan Leeks.

Alan Moulder Contact: Fundamental Music

Muirhead Management 202 Fulham Rd, Chelsea, London, SW10 9PJ **t** 020 7460 4668
e dennis@muirheadmanagement.co.uk
w muirheadmanagement.co.uk CEO: Dennis Muirhead 07785 226542.

Murlyn Music Group Box 7013, Solna, 170 07, Sweden **t** +46 (0)8 444 99 50 **f** +46 (0)8 444 99 69
e mail@murlyn.se **w** murlyn.se

Music Factory Entertainment Group
Hawthorne House, Fitzwilliam Street, Parkgate, Rotherham, South Yorkshire, S62 6EP **t** 01709 710 022
f 01709 523 141 **e** info@musicfactory.co.uk
w musicfactory.co.uk Contact: Andy Pickles.

Music Masters Ltd Orchard End, Upper Oddington, Moreton-in-Marsh, Gloucestershire, GL56 0XH
t 01451 812288 **f** 01451 870702 **e** info@music-masters.co.uk **w** music-masters.co.uk MD: Nick John.

The Music Sculptors 32-34 Rathbone Place, London, W1P 1AD **t** 020 7636 1001 **f** 020 7636 1506

Native Management Unit 32, Ransomes Dock, 35-37 Parkgate Rd, London, SW11 4NP **t** 020 7801 1919
f 020 7738 1819 **e** marie.native@19.co.uk
w nativemanagement.com MD: Peter Evans.

Christopher Neil The Hoods, High Street, Wethersfield, nr Braintree, CM7 4BY **t** 01371 850 238
e stpierre.roger@dsl.pipex.uk MD: Roger St Pierre. Contact: Worlds End (America) Inc

Ken Nelson Contact: Oxygen Music Management

Alan Nglish Contact: EMI Music Publishing Management

Mike Nielsen Contact: AIR Management

Nightmoves Contact: Illicit Entertainment

Niles Productions Ltd. 34 Beaumont Rd, London, W4 5AP **t** 020 8248 2157 **e** r.niles@richardniles.com
w richardniles.com Dir: Dr. Richard Niles.

Richard Niles Contact: Niles Productions Ltd.

Adam Noble Contact: AIR Management

Noko Contact: XL Talent

Nomadic Music Unit 18, Farm Lane Trading Estate, 101 Farm Lane, London, SW6 1QJ **t** 020 7386 6800
f 020 7386 2401 **e** info@nomadicmusic.net
w nomadicmusic.net Label Head: Paul Flanagan 07779 257 577.

Chuck Norman Contact: Solar Management Ltd

Rick Nowels Contact: Stephen Budd Management

Nuff Productions 139 Whitfield St, London, W1T 5EN
t 020 7380 1000 **f** 020 7380 1000 **e** neil@nuff.co.uk
w nuff.co.uk Contact: Neil 'Nuff' Stainton, Vito Benito 07768 242 057.

Paul Staveley O'Duffy Contact: 365 Artists Ltd

Ocean Bloem Productions Unit 127, Canalot Production Studios, 222 Kensal Rd, London, W10 5BN **t** 020 8960 3888 **e** ned@oceanbloem.com
w oceanbloem.com Producer: Ned Bigham.

OD Hunte Contact: Treasure Hunte Productions

Tim Oliver Contact: Positive Management

William Orbit Contact: Advanced Alternative Media Ltd

Steve Orchard Contact: AIR Management

Steve Osborne Contact: 140dB Management

Out Of Office Contact: Ambush Management

The Outfit Productions Sherwood Plaza, 530a Mansfield Road, Sherwood, Nottingham, NG5 2FR
t 07798 902 749 **e** info@theoutfitproductions.com
w theoutfitproductions.com Producer: James Hancock.

Gorwel Owen Ein Hoff Le, Llanfaelog, Ty Croes, Ynys Mon, LL63 5TN **t** 01407 810 742 **f** 01407 810 742
e gorwel@rhwng.com Contact: 07987 672 824.

Oxbridge Records (Classical, Choral & Organ only) 1 Abbey Street, Eynsham, Oxford, OX8 1HR
t 01865 880240 **f** 01865 880240 MD: HF Mudd.

Oxygen Music Management 33-45 Parr St, Liverpool, Merseyside, L1 4JN **t** 0151 707 1050
f 0151 709 4090 **e** oxygenmusic@btinternet.com
MD: Pete Byrne.

P.J. Music Willow Barn, Wrenshall Farm, Walsham-Le-Willows, Bury St Edmunds, Suffolk, IP31 3AS
t 01359 258686 **f** 01359 258686
e phil.harding@virgin.net **w** philharding.co.uk
myspace.com/philthepowerharding MD: Phil Harding.

Pachuco Management Old Fold Manor, Old Fold Lane, Hadley Green, Herts, EN5 5NQ
t 07968 369805 **e** grahamcarpenter@hotmail.com
MD: Graham Carpenter.

Hugh Padgham Contact: Giles Stanley Management

Panama Productions Sovereign House, 12 Trewartha Rd, Praa Sands, Penzance, Cornwall, TR20 9ST **t** 01736 762826 **f** 01736 763328
e panamus@aol.com **w** panamamusic.co.uk
myspace.com/scampmusicpublishing MD: Roderick Jones 01736 762 826.

P+E Music Contact: P.J. Music

Gareth Parton Contact: Big Life Management

Andy Paterson C/O Deep Recording Studios

Nick Patrick Contact: Giles Stanley Management

Paul Brown Management 81 Vespan Rd, London, London W12 9QG **t** 020 8740 4455 **e** paulb@pbmanagement.co.uk **w** pbmanagement.co.uk MD: Paul Brown 07715 541 676.

Paul Lani Contact: Paul Brown Management

Kevin Paul Contact: Audio Authority Management

Ewan Pearson Contact: Illicit Entertainment

Mike Pela Contact: Giles Stanley Management

Mike Pelanconi Contact: Motive Music Management

Pete Kirtley Chestnut Tree Cottage, Brick Hill, Chobham, Surrey, GU24 8TL **t** 07767 607907 **e** pete@jiant.co.uk myspace.com/petekirtley Producer: Pete Kirtley.

Ferg Peterkin Contact: Interface

PHAB High Notes, Sheerwater Avenue, Woodham, Surrey, KT15 3DS **t** 019323 48174 **f** 019323 40921 MD: Philip HA Bailey.

Phatrax Productions **e** phatraxproductions.googlemail.com **w** phatraxproductions.googlepages.com Contact: Mark Mills.

Mark Phythian Contact: Innocent Management

Pierce c/o Pierce Ent., Pierce House, Hammersmith Apollo, Queen Caroline Street, London, W6 9QH **t** 020 8563 1234 **f** 020 8563 1337 Contact: Deborah Cable.

Pivotal Music Management 4 Heathgate Place, 75-83 Agincourt Rd, London, NW3 2NU **t** 020 7424 8688 **f** 020 7424 8699 **e** info@pivotalmusic.co.uk Contact: Björn Hall.

Platinum Tones Productions Ltd PO Box 5935, Towcester, Northants, NN12 7ZL **t** 01327 811618 **e** tp@platinumtones.com **w** platinumtones.com myspace.com/platinumtone twitter.com/platinumtone Recording Engineer & Producer: Tony Platt.

Tony Platt Contact: Platinum Tones Productions Ltd

Poet Name Life Contact: Audio Authority Management

Point4 Productions 16 Talina Centre, Bagleys Lane, Fulham, London, SW6 2BW **t** 07788 420315 **e** info@point4music.com **w** point4music.com Dirs: Paul Newton, Peter Day.

Point4 Records 7 Queens Road, Brixham, Devon, TQ5 BGG **e** info@point4music.com **w** point4music.com Dirs: Paul Newton, Peter Day.

Karen Poole Contact: EMI Music Publishing Management

John Porter Contact: Advanced Alternative Media Ltd

Poseidon Music 46a Woodbridge Road, Moseley, Birmingham, B13 8EJ **t** 0121 249 0598 **f** 0709 214 8920 **e** enquiries@poseidonmusic.com **w** poseidonmusic.com MD: Jon Cotton.

Positive Management 4th Floor Studio, 16 Abbey Churchyard, Bath, BA1 1LY **t** 01225 311 661 **f** 01225 482 013 **e** info@positiveproducermanager.com **w** positiveproducermanagement.com Mgr: Carole Davies 07968 354 878.

Chris Potter Contact: Z Management

Steve Power Contact: Zomba Management

Ade Pressly Contact: AIR Management

Matt Prime Contact: Native Management

Principle Management 30-32 Sir John Rogersons Quay, Dublin 2, Ireland **t** +353 1 677 7330 **f** +353 1 677 7276 **e** Candida@numb.ie Dir: Paul McGuinness.

Prohibition Management Fulham Palace, Bishops Avenue, London, SW6 6EA **t** 020 7384 7372 **f** 020 7371 7940 **e** Caroline@prohibitiondj.com **w** prohibitiondj.com MD: Caroline Prothero 07967 610 877.

Project G Contact: The Cottage Group - Amco Music Productions

Q-Zone 21c Heathmans Rd, Parsons Green, London, SW6 4TJ **t** 020 7731 9313 **f** 020 7731 9314 **e** mail@darah.co.uk Contact: Nicki L'Amy.

QD Music 72A Lilyville Rd, London, SW6 5DW **t** 07779 653930 **e** drewtodd@qdmusic.co.uk **w** reverbnation.com/drewtodd facebook.com/pages/Drew-Todd/6007473492 MD: Drew Todd.

Quiz & Larossi Contact: XL Talent

Peter Raeburn Contact: Soundtree Music

Mark Rankin Contact: Interface

Louis Read Contact: Alan Cowderoy Management

Red Fort Studios The Sight And Sound Centre, Priory Way, Southall, Middlesex, UB2 5EB **t** 020 8843 1546 **f** 020 8574 4243 Contact: Kuljit Bhamra.

Red Jam Productions 24A Mellifont Avenue, Dun Laoghaire, Co Dublin, Ireland **t** +353 1 2300 118 **f** +353 1 2300 349 **e** firstname@redjamproductions.com **w** redjamproductions.com Producers: Mary McCarthy, Debbie Byrne.

Red Rhythm Productions Red Rhythm Towers, 2 Longlane, Stains, Middlesex, TW19 7AA **t** 01784 255629 **e** cliffrandall@telco4u.net Ace Production Team: Cliff Randall.

Red Triangle Productions Pinetree Farm, Cranborne, Dorset, BH21 5RR **t** 01725 517204 **f** 01725 517801 **e** studio@redtriangleproductions.co.uk **w** redtriangleproductions.co.uk 🔲 myspace.com/redtrianglepro 🔳 twitter.com/redtrianglepro ✉ Producers: Rick Parkhouse & George Tizzard.

Salaam Remi Contact: EMI Music Publishing Management

Fiona Renshaw Contact: 365 Artists Ltd

Jay Reynolds Contact: Long Island Studios

Rhythm of Life Ltd Lazonby, Penrith, CA10 1BG **t** 01768 898888 **f** 01768 898809 **e** events@rhythm.co.uk **w** rhythm.co.uk ✉ MD: Andrew Lennie.

Richard Lightman Productions 111 Sheen Rd, Richmond upon Thames, Surrey, TW9 1YJ **t** 07976 654643 **e** richard@lightman.demon.co.uk **w** richardlightman.com ✉ Producer: Richard Lightman.

Richard Rainey Contact: Duncan Management

Richard Robson Contact: Stephen Budd Management

Neil Richmond 12 Fairwall House, Peckham Road, London, SE5 8QW **t** 020 7703 4668 **f** 020 7703 4668 ✉ Contact: 0799 0932850.

Max Richter Contact: Stephen Budd Management

Right Bank Music Productions Home Park House, Hampton Court Rd, Kingston upon Thames, Surrey, KT1 4AE **t** 020 8977 0666 **f** 020 8977 0660 **e** rightbankmusicuk@rightbankmusicuk.com **w** rightbankmusicuk.com ✉ VP: Ian Mack.

Ro-lo Productions 35 Dillotford Avenue, Coventry, West Midlands, CV3 5DR **t** 024 7641 0388 **e** rog@rogerlomas.com **w** rogerlomas.com ✉ Record Producer: Roger Lomas 07711 817475.

Iain Roberton Contact: Sarm Management

Hannah Robinson Contact: Native Management

Robot Club Contact: Smoothside Organisation

Jony Rockstar Contact: Z Management

Emma Rohan Contact: 365 Artists Ltd

Christopher Rojas Contact: Advanced Alternative Media Ltd

Roll Over Productions 29 Beethoven Street, London, W10 4LJ **t** 020 8968 0299 **f** 020 8968 1047 **w** rollover.co.uk ✉ Contact: Phil Jacobs.

Mark Ronson Contact: Advanced Alternative Media Ltd

Mike Rose Contact: Native Management

Rose Rouge International AWS House, Trinity Square, St Peter Port, Guernsey, GY1 1LX **t** 01481 728 283 **f** 01481 714 118 **e** roserouge@cwgsy.net ✉ Director/Producer/Composer: Steve Free.

Mark Rose C/O Deep Recording Studios

Matt Rowe Contact: Native Management

RPM Management Ltd Pierce House, London Apollo Complex, Queen Caroline Street, London, W6 9QU **t** 020 8741 5557 **f** 020 8741 5888 **e** marlene-rpm@pierce-entertainment.com **w** pierce-entertainment.com ✉ MD: Marlene Gaynor.

Rumour Music Management PO Box 54127, London, W5 9BE **t** 020 8997 7893 **f** 020 8997 7901 **e** post@rumour.demon.co.uk ✉ Managing Director: Anne Plaxton.

Russ Russell Contact: Audio Authority Management

Ron Saint Germain Contact: SJP/Dodgy Productions

James Sanger Contact: Z Management

Sarm Management The Blue Building, 8-10 Basing St, London, W11 1ET **t** 020 7229 1229 **f** 020 7221 9247 **e** mel@spz.com **w** sarmstudios.com ✉ Contact: Mel Hoven.

Rob Schnapf Contact: Advanced Alternative Media Ltd

Segs Contact: Interface

Sentinel Management 60 Sellons Avenue, London, NW10 4HH **t** 020 8961 6992 **e** sentinel7@hotmail.com ✉ Dirs: Sandra Scott 07932 737 547.

Shanelle Sovereign House, 12 Trewartha Rd, Praa Sands, Penzance, Cornwall, TR20 9ST **t** 01736 762826 **f** 01736 763328 **e** panamus@aol.com **w** panamamusic.co.uk 🔲 myspace.com/digimixrecords ✉ MD: Roderick Jones.

Chris Sheldon Contact: Alan Cowderoy Management

George Shilling Contact: SJP/Dodgy Productions

Kevin Shirley Contact: Duncan Management

Valgeir Sigurdsson Contact: Stephen Budd Management

Silver Lion Productions 10 Oakwood Road, London, NW11 6QX **t** 07937 345368 ✉ Contact: Tony Wilson.

Craig Silvey Contact: Smoothside Organisation

Julian Simmons Contact: Smoothside Organisation

Will Simms Contact: Big Life Management

Rik Simpson Contact: Stephen Budd Management

SJP/Dodgy Productions 263 Putney Bridge Rd, London, SW15 2PU **t** 020 8780 3311 **f** 020 8785 9894 **e** info@sjpdodgy.co.uk **w** sjpdodgy.co.uk ✉ Managing Director: Safta Jaffery.

SJTMusic 51 Rosemullion Avenue, Tattenhoe, Milton Keynes, Bucks, MK4 3AH **t** 07968 795 503 **e** sjtmusic@mac.com **w** sjtmusic.co.uk ✉ Dir: Simon Turner.

Skatta Cordel Burrell Contact: Jamdown Ltd

Skylark Contact: 24 Management

«**biglife**»

Sleeper Music Block 2, 6 Erskine Road, Primrose Hill, London, NW3 3AJ **t** 020 7580 3995 **f** 020 7900 6244 **e** info@sleepermusic.co.uk **w** guychambers.com **✉** Contact: Dylan Chambers, Louise Jeremy.

Smac Music The Studio, 1 Tanworth Close, Northwood, Middx, HA6 2GF **t** 01923 450 928 **e** macwell@smacmusic.com **w** smacmusic.com **✉** Contact: Stuart Macwell 07904 546 729.

Alexis Smith Contact: 365 Artists Ltd

John Smith Contact: AIR Management

Smoothside Organisation Stoke House, South Green, Kirtlington, Oxford, OX5 3HJ **t** 01869 351268 **e** barbara@smoothside.co.uk **w** smoothside.com **✉** MD: Barbara Jeffries.

Sniffy Dog 26 Harcourt St, London, W1H 4HW **t** 020 7724 9700 **f** 020 7724 2598 **e** info@coochie-hart.com **w** sniffy-dog.com **✉** Contact: Michael Blainey.

Solar Management Ltd 13 Rosemont Rd, London, NW3 6NG **t** 020 7794 3388 **f** 020 7794 5588 **e** info@solarmanagement.co.uk **w** solarmanagement.co.uk **✉** MD: Carol Crabtree.

The SongStore 15 Kangerong Rd, Box Hill, Melbourne, Australia, 3128, Australia **t** +61 417 098 226 **e** barb@songstore.com.au **w** songstore.com.au **✉** barb@songstore.com.au **✉** Contact: Adrian Hannan & Barbara Hannan.

Sonic Music Production Building 348a, Westcott Venture Park, Westcott, Aylesbury, Bucks, HP18 0XB **t** 01296 655 880 **e** reception@sonic.uk.com **w** sonic.uk.com **✉** MD: Adrienne Aiken.

Sonny Contact: Innocent Management

Soul Mekanik Contact: Illicit Entertainment

Soundcakes 14A Hornsey Rise, London, N19 3SB **t** 020 7281 0018 **f** 020 7272 9609 **✉** Gen Mgr: Kris Hoffmann.

Soundtree Music 1st Floor Fenton House, 55 - 57 Great Marlborough St, London, W1F 7JX **t** 020 7478 1730 **f** 020 7287 0365 **e** jay@soundtree.co.uk **w** soundtree.co.uk **✉** MD: Jay James.

Soundz Of Muzik Ltd The Courtyard, 42 Colwith Road, London, W6 9EY **t** 020 8741 1419 **f** 020 8741 3289 **e** firstname@evolverecords.co.uk **✉** Director: Trevor Porter.

John Spence - Freelance Engineer/Producer 20 Churchside, Appleby, North Lincs, DN15 0AJ **t** 01724 732 062 **e** john@spence252.wanadoo.co.uk **w** fairviewrecording.co.uk **✉** Contact: 07718 061 297.

Jim Spencer Contact: Paul Brown Management

Mike Spencer Contact: EMI Music Publishing Management

Jack Splash Contact: EMI Music Publishing Management

John Springate 61 Lansdowne Lane, London, SE7 8TN **t** 020 8853 0728 **f** 020 8853 0728 **e** handbagmusic@cwcom.net **w** starguitar.mcmail.com/johnspring.html

SRB Music - Beat Factory Productions PO Box 189, Hastings, TN34 2WE **t** 01424 435 693 **f** 01424 461 058 **e** jimsrbmusic@aol.com **w** myspace.com/jimbeadle **✉** Dir: Jim Beadle 07889 279040.

Stab Productions Ltd 223b Victoria Park Road, London, E9 7HD **t** 020 8985 1115 **f** 020 8985 1113 **e** info@stabgroup.com **w** stabgroup.com **✉** Dirs: Bradley & Stewart James.

Jeremy Stacey Contact: Sarm Management

Neil "Nuff" Stainton Contact: Ambush Management

Stan Green Management PO Box 4, Dartmouth, Devon, TQ6 0YD **t** 01803 770046 **f** 01803 770075 **e** tv@stangreen.co.uk **w** stangreen.co.uk **✉** MD: Stan Green.

Ian Stanley Contact: Alan Cowderoy Management

Richard "Biff" Stannard Contact: Biffco Management

Paul Statham Contact: This Much Talent

Ali Staton Contact: Giles Stanley Management

Billy Steinberg Contact: Stephen Budd Management

Mark 'Spike' Stent Contact: TLS Music Management

Stephen Budd Management 56-59 Worship St, London, EC2A 2DU **t** 020 7688 8995 **f** 020 7688 8999 **e** info@record-producers.com **w** record-producers.com **✉** MD: Stephen Budd.

Steve Christian Contact: Paul Brown Management

Steve Cooper - Production/Engineering/Sound Design **t** 07989 301910 **e** steve@radiotone.co.uk **w** radiotone.co.uk **✉** MD: Steve Cooper.

Steve Smith 167, Ringwood Rd, St. Leonards, Ringwood, Hants, BH24 2NP **t** 01425 473 432 **f** 01425 473 432 **e** info@rwav.co.uk **w** rwav.co.uk

Graeme Stewart Contact: Solar Management Ltd

Rufus Stone 11a Newburgh St, London, W1F 7RW **t** 020 7287 9601 **f** 020 7287 9602 **e** rufus@sister-pr.com **✉** Singer, Songwriter, Producer: Rufus Stone.

Al Stone Contact: Smoothside Organisation

Vegard Strand Contact: DeepFrost Studios AS

Street Level Contact: Street Level Management Ltd

Street Level Management Ltd 1st Floor, 17 Bowater Road, Westminster Industrial Estate, Woolwich, London, SE18 5TF **t** 07886 260 686 **e** ceo@streetlevelenterprises.co.uk **w** streetlevelenterprises.com **✉** MD: Sam Crawford.

Streetfeat Management 26 Bradmore Park Road, London, W6 0DT **t** 020 8846 9984

«biglife»

PRODUCER MANAGEMENT
Jill Hollywood / jill@biglifemanagement.com
0207 554 2105 / biglifeproducers.com

Suli n' Stef Productions Ltd. 56 Fraser Road, Perivale, Middlesex, UB6 7AL **t** 020 8723 6158 **f** 020 7738 1764 **e** suli.hirani@btinternet.com 🕿 Producer: Suli.

Sunship Contact: Jamdown Ltd

Danton Supple Contact: 140dB Management

Martin Sutton Contact: WG Stonebridge Producer Management

Dan Swift Contact: Z Management

Brio Taliaferro Contact: 365 Artists Ltd

Shel Talmy Productions 14 Raynham Road, London, W6 0HY **t** 020 8846 9912 **f** 020 8748 6683 🕿 Contact: Judy Lipson.

Ted de Bono 41A Cavendish Rd, London, NW6 7XR **t** 020 8459 2833 **e** edwarddebono@f2s.com 🕿 Producer and Surround Sound Consultant: Ted de Bono 07958 521099.

Ben Thackeray Contact: Interface

This Much Talent The Chapel, Everwood Court, Maybury Gardens, London, NW10 2AF **t** 020 8208 5660 **e** contact@thismuchtalent.co.uk **w** thismuchtalent.co.uk 🕿 MD: Sandy Dworniak.

Ken Thomas Contact: AIR Management

Rod Thompson Music 73 Bromfelde Road, London, SW4 6PP **t** 020 7720 0866 **f** 020 7720 0866

Ali Thomson Contact: Sarm Management

Phil Thornalley Contact: WG Stonebridge Producer Management

Darrell Thorp Contact: Solar Management Ltd

TidyTrax Contact: Music Factory Entertainment Group

Dimitri Tikovoi Contact: 140dB Management

Paul Tipler Contact: Motive Music Management

TLS Music Management London **t** 07785 706 565 **e** tracy@tlsmanagement.com 🕿 Contact: Tracey Slater.

TMC Records PO Box 150, Chesterfield, Derbyshire, S40 0YT **t** 01246 236667 **f** 01246 236667 🕿 Contact: 07711 774369.

Cenzo Townshend Contact: Alan Cowderoy Management

Toy Productions see Principle Management

Treasure Hunte Productions London **t** 07774 265211 **f** 0207 8068147 **e** odhunte@thp-online.com **w** odhunte.com 🗗 facebook.com/odhunte 🔲 myspace.com/odhunte 🔳 twitter.com/odhunte 🔳 youtube.com/odhunte 🕿 Music Producer: OD Hunte 07774 265 211.

Triple M Productions The Vocal Booth, 31-45 Windsor St, Liverpool, L8 1XE **t** 0151 707 2833 **e** triplem@thevocalbooth.com **w** song-tank.com/triplem 🔲 myspace.com/triplemliverpool 🕿 Producer/Composer: Mike Moran 07800 993192.

Tropical Fish Music 351 Long Lane, London, N2 8JW **t** 0870 444 5468 **f** 0870 132 3318 **e** info@tropicalfishmusic.com **w** tropicalfishmusic.com 🕿 MD: Grishma Jashapara 07973 386 279.

Chris Tsangarides Contact: Audio Authority Management

Twenty Four Seven Music Management PO Box 2470, The Studio, Chobham, Surrey, GU24 8ZD **t** 01276 855247 **f** 01276 856897 **e** info@24-7musicmanagement.com **w** 24-7musicmanagement.com 🕿 MD: Craig Logan.

Two Twiggs Xperiment 80 Coleridge Sq, Ealing, London, W13 0JX **t** 07954 135842 **e** greg@twotwiggs.com **w** twotwiggs.com 🗗 facebook.com/group.php?gid=5159687354 🔳 myspace.com/twotwiggs 🕿 Dir: Greg Viljoen.

Ty Contact: Sentinel Management

U-Freqs 20 Athol Court, 13 Pine Grove, London, N4 3GU **t** 07831 770 394 **f** 0870 131 0432 **e** info@u-freqs.com **w** u-freqs.com 🕿 Partner: Stevino.

The Umbrella Group Send email for details **t** 07802 535 696 **f** 020 7603 9930 **e** Tommy@Umbrella-Group.com **w** Umbrella-Group.com 🕿 Dir: Tommy Manzi.

UMU Productions 144 Princes Avenue, London, W3 8LT **t** 020 8992 7351 **f** 020 8400 4931 **e** promo@ciscoeurope.co.uk 🕿 MD: Mimi Kobayashi.

Barry Upton Contact: Cordella Music

Utopia Records Utopia Village, 7 Chalcot Rd, London, NW1 8LH **t** 020 7586 3434 **f** 020 7586 3438 **e** utopiarec@aol.com 🕿 MD: Phil Wainman.

Martijn Ten Velden Contact: Stephen Budd Management

Peter-John Vettese Contact: FKM

Dan Vickers Contact: Sarm Management

Phil Vinall Contact: AIR Management

Tony Visconti Tony Visconte Productions Inc, PO Box 314, Pomona, NY, USA, 10970 **t** 001 845 362 8876 **f** 001 845 362 9190 **w** tonyvisconti.com 🕿 Contact: May Pang.

Vision Discs PO Box 92, Gloucester, GL4 8HW **t** 01452 814321 **f** 01452 812106 **e** vic_coppersmith@hotmail.com **w** visiondiscs.com 🕿 MD: Vic Coppersmith-Heaven.

VocalTuning.com 9 Woodmancote Vale, Cheltenham, Glocs, GL52 9RJ **t** 01242 676 672 **e** enquiries@vocaltuning.com **w** vocaltuning.com 🕿 Sound engineer: James Kinnear.

Alwyn Walker 79 Magheraconluce Rd, Hillsborough, Co. Down, BT26 6PR **t** 02892 688 285 **e** info@komodorecordings.com **w** myspace.com/alwynwalker 🕿 Producer: Alwyn Walker.

Andy Wallace Contact: Advanced Alternative Media Ltd

«biglife»

Mark Wallis Contact: Stephen Budd Management

Greg Walsh Contact: The Liaison and Promotion Company

Peter Walsh Contact: Paul Brown Management

Rik Walton Giffords Oasthouse, Battle Rd, Dallington, E Sussex, TN21 9LH **t** 01424 838148 **f** 01424 838148 **e** rik.walton@virgin.net ✉ Producer/Engineer: Rik Walton 07808 453 321.

Ward 21 Contact: Jamdown Ltd

Liam Watson Contact: Smoothside Organisation

WG Stonebridge Producer Management PO Box 49155, London, SW20 0YL **t** 020 8946 7242 **f** 020 8946 7242 **e** w.stonebridge@btinternet.com ✉ Contact: Bill Stonebridge.

Jeremy Wheatley Contact: 365 Artists Ltd

David White Contact: The Liaison and Promotion Company

Allister Whitehead Contact: Ambush Management

Mark Williams Contact: 140dB Management

Sam Williams Contact: Alan Cowderoy Management

Tim Wills Contact: Z Management

Kasper Winding Contact: 365 Artists Ltd

Wingfoot Productions 15 Flower Lane, London, NW7 2JA **t** 020 8180 8074 **f** 020 8959 5913 **e** info@wingfoot.co.uk **w** wingfoot.co.uk ✉ MD: John de Bono.

Alan Winstanley Contact: Hannah Management

Nick Wollage Contact: AIR Management

Nina Woodford Contact: Twenty Four Seven Music Management

Worlds End (America) Inc 183 N.Martel Avenue, Suite 270, Los Angeles, CA, 90036, United States **t** +1 323 965 1540 **f** +1 323 965 1547 **e** Sandy@worldsend.com **w** worldsend.com ✉ Contact: Sandy Robertson.

XL Talent Reverb House, Bennett St, London, W4 2AH **t** 020 8747 0660 **f** 020 8747 0880 **e** management@reverbxl.com **w** reverbxl.com ✉ Contact: Julian Palmer.

Yazuka Productions 30 West Block, Rosebery Square, London, EC1A 4PT **t** 020 7916 9205 ✉ Contact: Brett Hunter.

Youth Contact: Big Life Management

Z Management The Palm House, PO Box 19734, London, SW15 2WU **t** 020 8874 3337 **f** 020 8874 3599 **e** office@zman.co.uk **w** zman.co.uk ✉ MD: Zita Wadwa-McQ.

Zomba Management 20 Fulham Broadway, London, SW6 1AH **t** 020 7835 5260 **f** 020 7835 5261 **e** firstname.lastname@zomba.com ✉ GM: Tim Smith.

Rehearsal Studios

3 Mills Studios Three Mill Lane, London, E3 3DU **t** 020 7363 3336 **f** 020 8215 3349 **e** info@3mills.com **w** 3mills.com ✉ Bookings Manager: Melanie Faulkner.

Achieve Fitness New Islington Mill, Regent Trading Estate, Oldfield Road, Manchester, M5 7DE **t** 0161 832 9310 **f** 0161 832 9310 ✉ Prop: Glenn Ashton.

All of Music PO Box 2361, Romford, Essex, RM2 6EZ **t** 01708 688 088 **f** 020 7691 9508 **e** michelle@allofmusic.co.uk **w** allofmusic.co.uk ✉ MD: Danielle Barnett.

Backstreet Rehearsal Studios 313 Holloway Road, London, N7 9SU **t** 020 7609 1313 **f** 020 7609 5229 **e** backstreet.studios@virgin.net **w** backstreet.co.uk ✉ Prop: John Dalligan.

Bally Studios 16-18 Millmead Business Centre, Millmead Road, Tottenham Hale, London, N17 9QU **t** 020 8808 0472 **e** info@ballystudios.co.uk **w** ballystudios.co.uk ✉ Studio Manager: Jimmy Mulvihill.

Banana Row Rehearsal Studios 47 Eyre Place, Edinburgh, EH3 5EY **t** 0131 557 2088 **f** 0131 558 9848 **e** info@bananarow.com **w** bananarow.com ✉ MD: Craig Hunter.

Beechpark Studios Kilteel Rd, Rathcoole, Co Dublin, Ireland **t** +353 1 458 8500 **f** +353 1 458 8577 **e** info@beechpark.com **w** beechpark.com ✉ Studio Manager: Dara Winston +353 86 389 9722.

Berkeley 2 54 Washington Street, Glasgow, G3 8AZ **t** 0141 248 7290 **f** 0141 204 1138 **w** berkeley2.co.uk ✉ Prop: Steve Cheyne.

Big City Studios (Dance only) 159-161 Balls Pond Road, London, N1 4BG **t** 020 7241 6655 **f** 020 7241 3006 **e** pineapple.agency@btinternet.com **w** pineapple-agency.com ✉ Prop: Rebecca Paton.

Big Noise 12 Gregory Street, Northampton, NN1 1TA **t** 01604 634 455 **e** bignoisestudios@hotmail.co.uk **w** myspace.com/bignoisestudio ✉ Studio Mgr: Kim Gordelier.

Chem19 Rehearsal Studios Unit 5C, Peacock Cross Trading Estate, Burnbank Road, Hamilton, ML3 9AY **t** 01698 286 882 **f** 01698 327 979 **e** jim@chemikal.co.uk **w** chem19studios.co.uk ✉ Dir: Jim Savage.

Crash Rehearsal Studios Imperial Warehouse, 11 Davies Street, Liverpool, Merseyside, L1 6HB **t** 0151 236 0989 **f** 0151 236 0989 ✉ Directors: John White, Mark Davies.

Downs Sounds Studio Units 3-4 New Southgate Industrial Estate, Lower Park Rd, London, N11 1QD **t** 020 8211 3656 **e** info@downssounds.co.uk **w** downssounds.co.uk ✉ Proprietor: Adam Downs.

Earthworks Music Studios 62 The Rear,
Barnet High St, Barnet, Herts, EN5 5SJ **t** 020 8449 2258
e info@earthworksstudio.co.uk **w** earthworksstudio.co.uk
🔳 myspace.com/earthworksstudio 🔲 Head
Engineer: Leigh Darlow 07863 185264.

Elevator Studios 23-27 Cheapside, Liverpool, L2 2DY
t 0151 255 0195 **f** 0151 255 0195
e harriet@elevatorstudios.com 🔲 Contact: Harriet.

Gracelands East Acton Lane, London, W3 7HD
t 020 8740 8922 **f** 020 8740 8922 🔲 Prop: Paul Burrows.

Groovestyle Recording Studio 33 Upper Holt St,
Earls Colne, Colchester, Essex, CO6 2PG **t** 01787 220326
e info@groovewithus.com **w** groovewithus.com
🔲 Owner: Graham Game.

The Grove Music Studios
10 Latimer Industrial Estate, Latimer Road, London,
W10 6RQ **t** 020 8960 9601 **f** 020 8960 9606
e info@musicspace.co.uk **w** musicspace.co.uk
🔲 Dir: Alistair R. Fincham.

House of Mook Studios Unit 1, Authorpe Works,
Authorpe Rd, Leeds, LS6 4JB **t** 0113 230 4008
e mail@mookhouse.ndo.co.uk **w** mookhouse.ndo.co.uk
🔳 houseofmook 🔵 PhilMook 🔲 Studio Mgr: Phil Mayne.

Islington Arts Factory 2 Parkhurst Road, Holloway,
London, N7 0SF **t** 020 7607 0561 **f** 020 7700 7229
e IAF@islingtonartsfactory.fsnet.co.uk
w islingtonartsfactory.org.uk 🔲 Music Technician: Daniel
Taylor-Lind.

JJM Studios 20 Pool St, Walsall, West Midlands,
WS1 2EN **t** 01922 629 700 **e** info@jjmstudios.com
w jjmstudios.com 🔲 Contact: Jay Mitchell.

John Henry's 16-24 Brewery Road, London, N7 9NH
t 020 7609 9181 **f** 020 7700 7040
e johnh@johnhenrys.com **w** johnhenrys.com 🔲 MD: John
Henry.

MGMH Sound Station D-
72 Okhla Industrial Area Phase 1, New Delhi, 110020, India
t +91 11 4652 5992 **e** soundstation@mgmh.net
w mgmh.net
🔳 facebook.com/group.php?gid=113973267921&ref=ts
🔳 myspace.com/soundstation 🔲 Owner: Ritnika Nayan
+91 98 1007 8890.

The Music Box Stevenson College Edinburgh,
Bankhead Avenue, Edinburgh, EH11 4DE **t** 0131 535 4757
f 0131 535 4666 **e** themusicbox@stevenson.ac.uk
w stevenson.ac.uk/music-box.html 🔲 Contact: Elaine
Indoo.

The Music Complex Ltd 20 Tanners Hill, Deptford,
London, SE8 4PJ **t** 020 8691 6666 **f** 020 8692 9999
e info@musiccomplex.co.uk **w** musiccomplex.co.uk
🔲 Mgrs: Myles Bradley and Chris Raw.

OTR Studios Ltd 143 Mare St, Hackney, London,
E8 3RH **t** 020 8985 9880
e info@otrstudios.wanadoo.co.uk **w** otrstudios.co.uk
🔳 myspace.com/otrstudios143 🔲 Director: Paul Lewis
07956 450607.

14 Trading Estate Rd, Park Royal, London, NW10 7LU
t 020 8961 9540 / 020 8965 1122
e mroberts.drums@virgin.net **w** panic-music.co.uk
🔲 Director: Mark Roberts 020 8965 1122. Director: Mark
Roberts.

The Premises Studios 201-205 Hackney Road,
Shoreditch, London, E2 8JL **t** 020 7729 7593
f 020 7739 5600 **e** info@premises.demon.co.uk
w premises.demon.co.uk 🔲 CEO: Viv Broughton.

Q10 Studios Kings Court, 7 Osborne St, Glasgow,
G1 5QN **t** 0141 552 6677 **f** 0141 552 1354
e q10studios@aol.com **w** myspace.com/q10studios
🔲 Co-Dirs: Alan Walsh, Martin McQuillan.

Quo Vadis Recording and Rehearsal Studios
Unit 1 Morrison Yard, 551A High Rd, London, N17 6SB
t 020 8365 1999 **e** info@quovadisstudios.net
w quovadisstudios.net 🔲 Studio Mgr: Don MacKenzie.

Red Onion Rehearsal Studios 26-
28 Hatherley Mews, Walthamstow, London, E17 4QP
t 020 8520 3975 **f** 020 8521 6646
e info@redonion.uk.com **w** redonion.uk.com 🔲 MD: Dee
Curtis.

Reeltime Music
c/o Newarthill Community and Education Centre,
50 High Street, Newarthill, Motherwell, ML1 5JU
t 01698 862 860 **f** 01698 862 860
e info@reeltimemusic.net **w** reeltimemusic.net
🔲 Marketing & Evaluation Officer: Carol McEntegart.

Rich Bitch 505 Bristol Road, Selly Oak, Birmingham,
West Midlands, B29 6AU **t** 0121 471 1339
f 0121 471 2070 **e** richbitchstudios@aol.com **w** rich-
bitch.co.uk 🔲 Owner: Rob Bruce.

Ritz Studios - Peter Webber Hire 110-
112 Disraeli Rd, Putney, London, SW15 2DX
t 020 8870 1335 **f** 020 8877 1036
e firstname@peterwebberhire.com
w peterwebberhire.com 🔲 Director: Lee or Ben Webber
02088701335.

Rogue Studios RA 4, Bermondsey Trading Estate,
Rotherhithe New Road, London, SE16 3LL
t 020 7231 3257 **f** 020 7231 7358
e info@roguestudios.co.uk **w** roguestudios.co.uk
🔲 Contact: Jon-Paul Harper/Jim Down.

The Rooms Rehearsal Studios Lynchford Lane,
North Camp, Farnborough, Hants, GU14 6JD
t 01252 371 177 **e** minister.g@ntlworld.com
🔲 Directors: Gerry Bryant, Shaun Streams.

Rooz Studios 2A Corsham Street, London, N1 6DP
t 020 7490 1919 🔲 Studio Mgr: Graham Clarke.

Rotator Studios / Interzone Management 74-77 Magdalen Road, Oxford, OX4 1RE **t** 01865 715705 **e** info@rotator.co.uk **w** rotator.co.uk **MD:** Richard Cotton.

Sound Station D-72 Okhla Industrial Area Phase 1, 110020, India **t** +91 11 4652 5992 **e** soundstation@mgmh.net **w** mgmh.net 📇 Contact: Ritnika Nayan +91 9810078890.

Soundbite Studios Unit 32, 17 Cumberland Business Park, Cumberland Avenue, London, NW10 7RG **t** 020 8961 8509 **f** 020 8961 8994 📇 Owner: Ranj Kumar.

The Studio Tower Street, Hartlepool, TS24 7HQ **t** 01429 424440 **f** 01429 424441 **e** studiohartlepool@btconnect.com **w** studiohartlepool.com 📇 Studio Manager: Liz Carter.

Survival Studios Unit B18, Acton Business Centre, School Road, London, NW10 6TD **t** 020 8961 1977 📇 Mgr: Simon Elson.

Terminal Studios 4-10 Lamb Walk, London Bridge, London, SE1 3TT **t** 020 7403 3050 **f** 020 7407 6123 **e** info@terminal.co.uk **w** terminal.co.uk 📇 Prop: Charlie Barrett.

Tweeters Unit C1, Business Park 7, Brookway, Kingston Rd, Leatherhead, Surrey, KT22 7NA **t** 01372 386592 **e** info@tweeters.ltd.uk **w** tweeters.ltd.uk 🅼 myspace.com/tweeters.studios 📇 Studio Manager: Nigel Read.

Unit 25 - Mill Hill Music Complex Bunns Lane Works, Bunns Lane, London, NW7 2AJ **t** 020 8906 9991 **f** 020 8906 9991 **e** enquiries@millhillmusic.co.uk **w** millhillmusic.co.uk 📇 Dir: Roger Tichbourne.

Warehouse Studios 60 Sandford Lane, Kennington, Oxford, OX1 5RW **t** 01865 736 411 **e** info@warehousestudios.com **w** warehousestudios.com 📇 Studio Mgr: Steve Watkins.

Warwick Hall of Sound Warwick Hall, off Banastre Avenue, Heath, Cardiff, CF14 3NR **t** 029 2069 4455 **f** 029 2069 4455 **e** adamstangroom@btconnect.com **w** myspace.com/cardiffswarwickhallrecordingstudio 📇 Dirs: Martin Bowen, Adam Stangroom 029 2069 4450.

Waterloo Sunset Tower Bridge Business Complex, 100 Clements Road, London, SE16 4DG **t** 020 7252 0001 **f** 020 7231 3002 **e** nunu@musicbank.org **w** musicbank.org/waterloo.html 📇 Studio Mgr: Dave Whiting.

WaterRat Music Studios Unit 2 Monument Way East, Woking, Surrey, GU21 5LY **t** 01483 764 444 **e** jayne@waterrat.co.uk **w** waterrat.co.uk 📇 Prop: Jayne Wallis.

Westbourne Rehearsal Studios The Rear Basement, 92-98 Bourne Terrace, Little Venice, London, W2 5TH **t** 020 7289 8142 **f** 020 7289 8142 **w** myspace.com/westbournerehearsals 📇 Studio Mgr: Chris Thomas.

White Rooms Rehearsal Studios Roden House, Alfred St South, Nottingham, NG3 1JH **t** 0115 932 2802 **e** whiterooms@btinternet.com **w** npbgroup.net 📇 Prop: Pauline Barker.

Session Fixers

AKlass Entertainment PO Box 42371, London, N12 0WS **t** 020 8368 7760 **e** info@aklass.biz **w** aklassentertainment.com 📇 Director: Patsy McKay.

The Helen Astrid Singing Academy 61 Bollo Bridge Road, London, W3 8AX **t** 07710 245 904 **f** 0870 774 0486 **e** helen@thehelenastridsingingacademy.com **w** thehelenastridsingingacademy.com 📇 Vocal Coach: Helen Astrid (R.A.M.) plus associates.

B&H Management PO Box 1162, Bovingdon, Herts., HP1 9DE **t** 01442 832010 **f** 01442 834910 **e** simon@bandhmanagement.demon.co.uk **w** sessionmusicians.co.uk 🅼 myspace.com/bandhmanagement 📇 MD: Simon Harrison.

Citizen K Gospel Choir Hilton Grove Business Centre, Hatherley Mews, London, E17 4QP **t** 020 8520 3975 **e** info@redonion.uk.com **w** citizenk.co.uk 📇 MD: Dee Curtis.

Eclipse-PJM (Vocalists) PO Box 3059, South Croydon, Surrey, CR2 8TL **t** 020 8657 2627 **f** 020 8657 2627 **e** Eclipsepjm@btinternet.com 📇 Mgr & PA: Paul Johnson & Iris Sutherland 07798 651691.

Face Music 13 Elvendon Rd, London, N13 4SJ **t** 020 8889 3969 **f** 020 8889 3969 **e** facemusic@btinternet.com 📇 MD: Sue Carling.

Isobel Griffiths t 020 7351 7383 **f** 020 7376 3034 **e** isobel@isobelgriffiths.co.uk 📇 MD: Isobel Griffiths.

Kick Horns 158 Upland Rd, London, SE22 0DQ **t** 020 8693 5991 **e** info@kickhorns.com **w** kickhorns.com 🅼 myspace.com/kickhorns 📇 Director: Simon Clarke 07941 054219.

Lager Productions 10 Barley Rise, Baldock, Herts, SG7 6RT **t** 01462 636799 **f** 01462 636799 **e** dan@Lockupmusic.co.uk 📇 Dir: Steve Knight.

London Musicians Ltd Cedar House, Vine Lane, Hillingdon, Middlesex, UB10 0BX **t** 01895 252 555 **f** 01872 863 557 **e** mail@londonmuscians.co.uk 📇 MD: David White.

London Symphony Orchestra Barbican Centre, Silk Street, London, EC2Y 8DS **t** 020 7588 1116 **f** 020 7374 0127 **e** smallet@lso.co.uk **w** lso.co.uk 📇 Director of Planning: Sue Mallet.

More Music PO Box 306, Harrow, Middx, HA2 0XL **t** 020 8423 1078 **f** 020 8423 1078 **e** info@moremusicagency.com 📇 Contact: Debra Williams 07721 623 171.

Recording Studios & Services: Session Fixers, Studio Equipment Hire & Sales

Red Onion Productions 26-28 Hatherley Mews, Walthamstow, London, E17 4QP **t** 020 8520 3975 **f** 020 8521 6646 **e** info@redonion.uk.com **w** redonion.uk.com 🔲 MD: Dee Curtis.

Rhythm & Bookings Ltd Townhouse Studios, 150 Goldhawk Rd, London, W12 8HH **t** 020 8354 1726 **f** 020 8354 1719 **e** randb@pennies.demon.co.uk **w** rhythmandbookings.com 🔲 Booker/Contractor: Graeme Perkins.

Royal Philharmonic Orchestra 16 Clerkenwell Green, London, EC1R 0QT **t** 020 7608 8800 **f** 020 7608 8801 **e** info@rpo.co.uk **w** rpo.co.uk 🔲 MD: Ian Maclay.

SD Creative 113b Leander Road, London, SW2 2NB **t** 020 7652 9676 **e** office@sdcreative.co.uk 🔲 Session Coordinator: Suzann Douglas.

Sense of Sound Training Parr Street Studios, 33-45 Parr St, Liverpool, L1 4JN **t** 0151 707 1050 **f** 0151 709 8612 **e** info@senseofsound.net **w** senseofsound.net 🔲 Artistic Director: Jennifer John.

Session Connection PO Box 46307, London, SW17 0WS **t** 07801 070362 **e** sessionconnection@mac.com **w** thesessionconnection.com 🔲 MD: Tina Hamilton.

Solomon Productions 25a Chesterfield Road, Chiswick, London, W4 3HQ **t** 07949 507 018 **e** mail@solomonproductions.com 🔲 Dir: Sue Ballingall.

Tuff The Session Agency Ltd Unit 15, Millmead Business Centre, Millmead Road, London, N17 9QU **t** 0870 8030 672 **f** 0870 8030 692 **e** info@tuffsessions.com **w** tuffsessions.com 🔲 Business Manager: Joanne Costello.

Wired Strings 12 Rosemont Rd, Hampstead, London, NW3 6NE **t** 07976 157277 **f** 020 7794 1997 **e** rosie@wiredstrings.com **w** wiredstrings.com 🔲 Director: Rosie Danvers.

The Wrecking Crew 15 Westmeads Rd, Whitstable, Kent, CT5 1LP **t** 07957 686 152 **f** 01227 264 966 **e** sophie.sirota@onetel.com **w** thewreckingcrew.co.uk 🔲 Bookings: Sophie Sirota.

Studio Equipment Hire & Sales

Absolute Music Solutions (Audio Sales) 58 Nuffield Rd, Poole, Dorset, BH17 0RT **t** 0845 025 55 55 **f** 01202 684900 **e** shop@absolutemusic.co.uk **w** absolutemusic.co.uk 🔲 Pro Audio Sales: Andy Legg.

Advanced Sounds Ltd Admin address on request. **t** 01305 757088 **f** 01305 268947 **e** advancedsoundsltd@btinternet.com **w** advancedsounds.co.uk 🔲 Hire, Sales & Repairs: Mike Moreton.

Audiohire The Old Dairy, 133-137 Kilburn Lane, London, W10 4AN **t** 020 8960 4466 **f** 020 8964 0343 **e** admin@audiohire.co.uk **w** audiohire.co.uk 🔲 MD: Jerry Evans.

Autograph Sales Ltd. Unit 6, Bush Industrial Estate, Station Rd, London, N19 5UN **t** 0207 281 7574 **f** 0207 281 3042 **e** sales@autograph.co.uk **w** autograph.co.uk 🔲 General Manager: Debbie Lovelock.

Batmink Beckery Rd, Glastonbury, Somerset, BA6 9NX **t** 01458 833186 **f** 01458 835320 **e** info@batmink.co.uk **w** batmink.co.uk 🔲 Director: D Churches.

Delta Concert Systems Unit 4, Springside, Trinity, Jersey, Channel Islands, JE3 5DG **t** 01534 865885 **f** 01534 863759 **e** hire@delta-av.com **w** delta-av.com 🔲 Director: Cristin Bouchet.

Enlightened Lighting Ltd Unit 12, The Maltings Industrial Estate, Brassmill Lane, Bath, Somerset, BA1 3JL **t** 01225 311964 **f** 01225 445454 **e** enq@enlightenedlighting.co.uk **w** enlightenedlighting.co.uk 🔲 Director: Simon Marcus.

FX Rentals 38-40 Telford Way, London, W3 7XS **t** 020 8746 2121 **f** 020 8746 4100 **e** info@fxrentals.co.uk **w** fxgroup.net 🔲 Operations Director: Peter Brooks.

GB Audio Unit D, 51 Brunswick Rd, Edinburgh, EH7 5PD **t** 0131 661 0022 **e** info@gbaudio.co.uk **w** gbaudio.co.uk 🔲 Contact: G Bodenham.

Harris Hire 49 Hayes Way, Park Langley, Beckenham, Kent, BR3 6RR **t** 020 8663 1807 **f** 020 8658 2803 **e** philharris335@aol.com **w** harris-hire.co.uk 🔲 MD: Phil Harris.

HHB Communications 73-75 Scrubs Lane, London, NW10 6QU **t** 020 8962 5000 **f** 020 8962 5050 **e** sales@hhb.co.uk **w** hhb.co.uk 🔲 Sales & Marketing Dir.: Steve Angel.

John Henry's 16-24 Brewery Road, London, N7 9NH **t** 020 7609 9181 **f** 020 7700 7040 **e** johnh@johnhenrys.com **w** johnhenrys.com 🔲 MD: John Henry.

The M Corporation (Audio Sales) 58 Nuffield Rd, Poole, Dorset, BH17 0RT **t** 0845 025 5555 **f** 01202 684900 **e** sales@absolute.ms **w** absolutemusic.co.uk 🔲 Pro Audio Sales: Andy Legg.

Midnight Electronics Off Quay Building, Foundry Lane, Newcastle upon Tyne, Tyne and Wear, NE6 1LH **t** 0191 224 0088 **f** 0191 224 0080 **e** info@midnightelectronics.co.uk **w** midnightelectronics.co.uk 🔲 Manager: Dave Cross.

The Music Complex Ltd 20 Tanners Hill, Deptford, London, SE8 4PJ **t** 020 8691 6666 **f** 020 8692 9999 **e** info@musiccomplex.co.uk **w** musiccomplex.co.uk 📇 Mgrs: Myles Bradley and Chris Raw.

PA Music Unit 4, The Old Print Works, Tapsr Street, Barnet, North London, EN5 5TH **t** 020 8440 8008 **e** mail@pamusic.net **w** pamusic.net 📇 Prop: Mr MW Lowe.

Sensible Rentals 88 Brewery Road, London, N7 9NT **t** 020 7700 6655 **f** 020 7609 9478 **e** johnnyh@sensiblerentals.com **w** sensiblerentals.com 📇 Hire Mgr: Johnny Henry.

Strong Hire 120-124 Curtain Rd, London, EC2A 3SQ **t** 020 7426 5150 **f** 020 7426 5102 **e** hire@stronghire.com **w** stronghire.com 📇 Bookings: Alex Green 07973 828449.

Studiocare Professional Audio Unit 9 Century Building, Brunswick Business Pk, Summers Rd, Liverpool, L3 4BL **t** 0845 345 8910 **f** 0845 345 8911 **e** hire@studiocare.com **w** studiocare.com 📇 Hire Department Manager: Andrew Culshaw.

Studiohire 8 Daleham Mews, London, NW3 5DB **t** 020 7431 0212 **f** 020 7431 1134 **e** mail@studiohire.net **w** studiohire.net 💬 Studiohire London 📇 GM: Sam Thomas.

Studiospares Ltd 964 North Circular Rd, London, NW2 7JR **t** 0844 375 5000 **f** 020 8450 4390 **e** sales@studiospares.com **w** studiospares.com 📇 Mgrs: Richard Venables/Mike Dowsett.

Tickle Music Hire Ltd The Old Dairy, 133-137 Kilburn Lane, London, W10 4AN **t** 020 8964 3399 **f** 020 8964 0343 **e** hire@ticklemusichire.com **w** ticklemusichire.com 📇 Director: Jerry Evans.

Vintage and Rare Guitars Ltd 6 Denmark St, London, WC2 8LX **t** 020 7240 7500 **f** 020 7240 8900 **e** enquiries@vintageandrareguitars.com **w** vintageandrareguitars.com 📇 Mgr: Adam Newman.

Volume Audio 6 All Saints Crescent, Garston, Watford, Hertfordshire, WD25 0LU **t** 01923 673027 **f** 01923 893733 **e** david@finn.com 📇 Dir: David Finn.

Studio Equipment Manufacture & Distribution

AES Pro Audio North Lodge, Stonehill Road, Ottershaw, Surrey, KT16 0AQ **t** 01932 872672 **f** 01932 874364 **e** aesaudio@intonet.co.uk **w** aesproaudio.com 📇 Dir: Mike Stockdale.

Allen & Heath Ltd Kernick Industrial Estate, Penryn, Cornwall, TR10 9LU **t** 01326 372070 **f** 01326 377097 **e** sales@allen-heath.com **w** allen-heath.com 📇 Sales Dir: Bob Goleniowski.

AMG Electronics 2 High Street, Haslemere, Surrey, GU27 2LR **t** 01428 658775 **f** 01428 658438 **e** amg@c-ducer.com **w** c-ducer.com 📇 Proprietor: AW French.

AMS Neve plc Billington Road, Burnley, Lancs, BB11 5UB **t** 01282 457 011 **f** 01282 417 282 **e** info@ams-neve.com **w** ams-neve.com 📇 Dir of Commercial Oper.: Greg Cluskey.

APT Codecs 729 Springfield Rd, Belfast, Co Antrim, BT12 7FP **t** 028 9067 7200 **f** 028 9067 7201 **e** kcampbell@aptcodecs.com **w** aptcodecs.com 📇 Sales Director: Kevin Campbell.

Audio & Design Reading Ltd 51 Padick Drive, Lower Earley, Reading, Berkshire, RG6 4HF **t** 0118 324 0046 **f** 0118 324 0048 **e** sales@adrl.co.uk **w** adrl.co.uk 📇 Sales Manager: Ian Harley.

Audio Agency PO Box 4601, Kiln Farm, Milton Keynes, Bucks, MK19 7ZN **t** 01908 510123 **f** 01908 511123 **w** audioagency.co.uk 📇 Sales Mgr: Paul Eastwood.

Audio Developments Ltd Hall Lane, Walsall Wood, Walsall, West Midlands, WS9 9AU **t** 01543 375351 **f** 01543 361051 **e** sales@audio.co.uk **w** audio.co.uk 📇 Sales Director: Antony Levesley.

Audio-Technica Technica House, Royal London Industrial Estate, Old Lane, Leeds, LS11 8AG **t** 0113 277 1441 **f** 0113 270 4836 **e** marketing@audio-technica.co.uk **w** audio-technica.com 📇 Senior Marketing Manager: Harvey Roberts.

BBM Electronics Group Ltd Kestrel House, Garth Road, Morden, Surrey, SM4 4LP **t** 020 8330 3111 **f** 020 8330 3222 **e** sales@trantec.co.uk **w** trantec.co.uk 📇 Dir: Steve Baker.

Canford Audio plc Crowther Industrial Estate, Crowther Rd, Washington, Tyne and Wear, NE38 0BW **t** 0191 418 1122 **f** 0191 418 1123 **e** sales@canford.co.uk **w** canford.co.uk 📇 Director of Sales & Marketing: David Holloway.

Cunnings Recording Associates Brodrick Hall, Brodrick Road, London, SW17 7DY **t** 0870 90 66 44 0 **f** 020 8767 8525 **e** info@cunnings.co.uk **w** cunnings.co.uk 📇 Proprietor: Malcolm J Cunnings.

Recording Studios & Services: Studio Equipment Manufacture & Distribution

📧 Contacts   📘 Facebook   🅜 MySpace   🇹 Twitter   ▶️ YouTube

D&M Professional Chiltern Hill, Chalfont St Peter, Buckinghamshire, SL9 9UG **t** 01753 888447 **f** 01753 880109 **e** info@d-mpro.eu.com **w** d-mpro.eu.com 📧 Sales & Marketing Mgr: Simon Curtis.

DEM Manufacturing Deltron Emcon House, Hargreaves Way,, Scunthorpe, N. Lincs, DN15 8RF **t** 01724 273200 **f** 01724 280353 **e** sales@dem-uk.com **w** dem-uk.com 📧 Mktng Co-ord: Diane Kilminster.

Digidesign UK Westside Complex, Pinewood Studios, Pinewood Rd, Iver Heath, Bucks, SL0 0NH **t** 01753 658496 **e** sales-uk@digidesign.com **w** digidesign.com/uk 📘 facebook.com/AvidProTools 🅜 myspace.com/digizine 🇹 twitter.com/digidesign ▶️ youtube.com/user/digidesign 📧 UK Sales Specialist: Simon Caton.

Direct Distribution Unit 6 Belfont Trading Estate, Mucklow Hill, Halesowen, West Midlands, B62 8DR **t** 0121 550 2777 **f** 0121 585 8003 **e** info@directdistribution.uk.com **w** directdistribution.uk.com 📧 UK Manager: Andrew Scott.

Drawmer Distribution Ltd Charlotte St Business Centre, Charlotte Street, Wakefield, West Yorkshire, WF1 1UH **t** 01924 378669 **f** 01924 290460 **e** sales@drawmer.com **w** drawmer.com 📧 MD: Ken Giles.

EA Sowter Ltd The Boatyard, Cullingham Rd, Suffolk, IP1 2EL **t** 01473 252794 **f** 01473 236188 **e** sales@sowter.co.uk **w** sowter.co.uk 📧 MD: Brian W Last.

EAW 2 Blenheim Court, Hurricane Way, Wickford, Essex, SS11 8YT **t** 01268 571 212 **f** 01268 570 809 **e** firstname.lastname@mackie.com **w** mackie.com 📧 UK Sales Manager: John Kaukis.

Euphonix Europe Ltd Newport Rd, Hayes, UB4 8JX **t** 020 8561 2566 **f** 020 8589 0766 **e** mhosking@euphonix.com **w** euphonix.com 📧 Director of Sales: Mark Hosking.

Focusrite Audio Engineering Windsor House, Turnpike Rd, High Wycombe, Bucks, HP12 3FX **t** 01494 462246 **f** 01494 459920 **e** sales@focusrite.com **w** focusrite.com 📧 Artist & Media Relations: Chris Mayes-wright.

Fuzion PLC 9 Lyon Rd, Walton On Thames, Surrey, KT12 3PU **t** 01932 882222 **f** 01932 882244 **e** info@fuzion.co.uk **w** fuzion.co.uk 📧 MD: Tony Oates.

Harbeth Audio Ltd Unit 3, Enterprise Park, Lindfield, W Sussex, RH16 2LH **t** 0870 803 4788 **f** 05600 756 442 **e** sound@harbeth.co.uk **w** harbeth.com 📧 MD: Alan Shaw.

Junger Audio Invicta Works, Elliott Road, Bromley, Kent, BR2 9NT **t** 020 8460 7299 **f** 020 8460 0499 **e** sales@michael-stevens.com **w** michael-stevens.com 📧 UL Sales Mgr: Simon Adamson.

Klark Teknik Telex Communications (UK) Ltd, Klark Teknik Building, Walter Nash Rd, Kidderminster, Worcestershire, DY11 7HJ **t** 01562 741515 **f** 01562 745371 **e** firstname.lastname@uk.telex.com **w** klarkteknik.com 📧 Marketing Manager: James Godbehear.

Logic System Pro Audio Ltd Unit 46, Corringham Road Industrial Est, Gainsborough, Lincolnshire, DN21 1QB **t** 01427 611791 **f** 01427 677008 **e** sales@logic-system.co.uk **w** logic-system.co.uk 📧 MD: Chris Scott.

MC2 Audio Ltd Units 6 & 7 Kingsgate, Heathpark Industrial Estate, Honiton, Devon, EX14 1YG **t** 01404 44633 **f** 01404 44660 **e** mc2@mc2-audio.co.uk **w** mc2-audio.co.uk 📧 MD: Ian McCarthy.

MJQ Ltd (Studio Consultants) Swillett House, 52 Heronsgate Road, Chorleywood, Herts, WD3 5BB **t** 01923 285 266 **f** 01923 285 168 **e** sales@mjq.co.uk **w** mjq.co.uk 📧 MD: Malcolm Jackson.

MTR Ltd Ford House, 58 Cross Rd, Bushey, Hertfordshire, WD19 4DQ **t** 01923 234050 **f** 01923 255746 **e** support@mtraudio.com **w** mtraudio.com 📧 MD: Tony Reeves 01923-234050.

Mutronics Unit 12 Impress House, Mansell Rd, London, W3 7QH **t** 020 8735 0042 **f** 020 8735 0041 **e** james@mutronics.co.uk **w** mutronics.co.uk 📧 Dir: James Dunbar.

Ohm (UK) Ltd Wellington Close, Parkgate, Knutsford, Cheshire, WA16 8XL **t** 01565 654641 **f** 01565 755641 **e** clive@ohm.co.uk **w** ohm.co.uk 📧 Sales Manager: Clive Kinton.

Peavey Electronics Great Folds Rd, Oakley Hay, Corby, Northants, NN18 9ET **t** 01536 461234 **f** 01536 747222 **e** sales@peavey-eu.com **w** peavey-eu.com 📧 Contact: Ken Achard.

Penny & Giles Controls Ltd Nine Mile Point Ind Estate, Cwmfelinfach, Gwent, NP11 7HZ **t** 01495 202000 **f** 01495 202006 **e** sales@pennyandgiles.com **w** pennyandgiles.com 📧 Product Manager - Controllers: Andrew Clarke.

Planet Audio Systems 33 Bournehall Ave, Bushey, Herts, WD23 3AU **t** 08707 605 365 **f** 020 8950 1294 **e** proaudiosales@planetaudiosystems.com **w** planetaudiosystems.com 📧 MD: Rod Gammons.

Polar Audio 17 Albert Drive, Burgess Hill, West Sussex, RH15 9TN **t** 01444 258258 **f** 01444 258444 **e** sales@beyerdynamic.co.uk **w** beyerdynamic.co.uk 📧 MD: John Midgley.

PRECO (Broadcast Systems) Ltd 3 Four Seasons Crescent, Kimpton Road, Sutton, Surrey, SM3 9QR **t** 020 8644 4447 **f** 020 8644 0474 **e** sales@preco.co.uk **w** preco.co.uk 📧 MD: Tony Costello.

Quested Monitoring Systems Ltd Units 6&7 Kingsgate, Heathpark Industrial Estate, Honiton, Devon, EX14 1YG **t** (0)1404 41500 **f** (0)1404 44660 **e** sales@quested.com **w** quested.com 📧 MD: Ian McCarthy.

Ridge Farm Industries Rusper Rd, Capel, Surrey, RH5 5HG **t** 01306 711202 **e** info@ridgefarmstudio.com **w** ridgefarmindustries.com 📧 MD: Frank Andrews.

Recording Studios & Services: Studio Equipment Manufacture & Distribution

Contacts **Facebook** **MySpace** **Twitter** **YouTube**

River Pro Audio Unit 6a, Juno Way, London, SE14 5RW
t 020 3183 0000 **f** 020 3183 0006
e sales@riverproaudio.co.uk **w** riverproaudio.com
 Contact: Joel Monger.

RMPA & Rauch Amplification 42 Lower Ferry Lane,
Callow End, Worcester, WR2 4UN **t** 01905 831877
f 01905 830906 **e** rmpaworcester@aol.com
w rmpa.co.uk Owner: Richard Bailey 07836 617158.

Rock Solid Sound Systems Limited
The Old Barn, Rosier Business Pk, Coneyhurst Rd,
Billingshurst, West Sussex, RH14 9DE **t** 01403 782221
e info@rocksolidsounds.co.uk **w** rocksolidsounds.co.uk
 M D: Ray Rowles 07950 274224.

Roland (UK) Ltd Atlantic Close,
Swansea Enterprise Park, Swansea, West Glamorgan,
SA7 9FJ **t** 01792 515 020 **f** 01792 515 048
e customers@roland.co.uk **w** roland.co.uk

SADiE UK The Old School, Stretham, Ely,
Cambridgeshire, CB6 3LD **t** 01353 648 888
f 01353 648 867 **e** sales@sadie.com **w** sadie.com
 Sales & Mkt Mgr: Geoff Calver.

SCV London 40 Chigwell Lane,
Oakwood Hill Ind. Estate, Loughton, Essex, IG10 3NY
t 020 8418 0778 **f** 020 8418 0624
e marketing@scvlondon.co.uk **w** scvlondon.co.uk Sales
and Marketing Director: Andrew Stirling 020 8418 1470.

Sennheiser UK 3 Century Point, Halifax Road,
High Wycombe, Buckinghamshire, HP12 3SL
t 01494 551 551 **f** 01494 551 550
e info@sennheiser.co.uk **w** sennheiser.co.uk Director of
Marketing: John Steven.

Shep Associates Long Barn, North End, Meldrith,
Royston, Herts, SG8 6NT **t** 01763 261 686
f 01763 262 154 **e** info@shep.co.uk **w** shep.co.uk
 MD: Derek Stoddart.

Shuttlesound 4 The Willows Centre, Willow Lane,
Mitcham, Surrey, CR4 4NX **t** 020 8254 5660
f 020 8254 5666 **e** shuttlesound.info@uk.telex.com
w shuttlesound.com MD: Paul Barretta.

Solid State Logic Spring Hill Road, Oxford, OX5 1RU
t 01865 842300 **f** 01865 842118 **e** info@solid-state-
logic.com **w** solid-state-logic.com Sales Dir: Niall
Feldman.

Sound and Video Services UK Ltd
Shentonfield Rd, Sharston Industrial Estate, Manchester,
M22 4RW **t** 0161 491 6660 **f** 0161 491 6669
e sales@svsmedia.com **w** svsmedia.com Sales
Director: John Cooper.

Sound Control 61 Jamaica Street, Glasgow, G1 4NN
t 0141 204 2774 **f** 0141 204 0614
e sales@soundcontrol.co.uk **w** soundcontrol.co.uk
 GM: Kenny Graham 0141 204 0322.

Sound Technology plc 17 Letchworth Point,
Letchworth, Hertfordshire, SG6 1ND **t** 01462 480000
f 01462 480800 **e** info@soundtech.co.uk
w soundtech.co.uk Sales Office Manager: Colin Haines.

Soundcraft/Studer Cranborne House,
Cranborne Road, Potters Bar, Hertfordshire, EN6 3JN
t 01707 665 000 **f** 01707 660 482
e info@harmanpro.com **w** soundcraft.com VP,
Sales: Adrian Curtis.

Speed Music PLC 195 Caerleon Road, Newport,
NP19 7HA **t** 01633 215 577 **f** 01633 213 214
e info@speedmusic.co.uk **w** speedmusic.co.uk
 Director: Nick Fowler.

Straight Edge Manufacturing Ltd
Bladewater Marina, The Esplanade, Mayland, Chelmsford,
Essex, CM3 6FD **t** 01621 742000 **f** 01621 742222
e info@straight-edge.co.uk **w** straight-edge.co.uk
 MD: Ian Wilson.

Tannoy Rosehall Industrial Estate, Coatbridge,
North Lanarkshire, ML5 4TF **t** 01236 420199
f 01236 428230 **e** pr@tannoy.co.uk **w** tannoy.com
 facebook.com/pages/Tannoy/58636265737
 twitter.com/TannoyPro PR & Communications: Mark
Flanagan.

TDK UK Ltd TDK House, 5-7 Queensway, Redhill, Surrey,
RH1 1YB **t** 01737 773773 **f** 01737 773809 **w** tdk-
europe.com Brand Dev Mgr: Donna de Souza.

TEAC UK Limited (TASCAM) Marlin House,
The Croxley Centre, Watford, Hertfordshire, WD18 8TE
t 01923 438880 **f** 01923 236290 **e** info@teac.co.uk
w teac.co.uk Sales Mgr: Neil Wells.

Thurlby Thandar Instruments Ltd Glebe Road,
Huntingdon, Cambridgeshire, PE29 7DR **t** 01480 412451
f 01480 450409 **e** sales@tti-test.com **w** tti-test.com
 Dir: John Cornwell.

TL Audio Sonic Touch, ICENI Court, Icknield Way,
Letchworth, Hertfordshire, SG6 1TN **t** 01462 492090
f 01462 492097 **e** sales@tlaudio.co.uk **w** tlaudio.co.uk
 facebook.com/pages/TL-Audio-Ltd/54847133607
 twitter.com/TLAudio
 youtube.com/user/TLAudioLtdEngland Managing
Director: Tony Larking 01462 492 090.

TL Commerce Ltd / Trading As Larking's List
Unit 2 Iceni Court, Icknield Way, Letchworth, SG6 1TN
t 01234 772244 **f** 01462 492097
e info@tlcommerce.co.uk **w** tlcommerce.co.uk
 MD: Tony Larking 01462 492090.

Turbosound Star Road, Partridge Green, West Sussex,
RH13 8RY **t** 01403 711 447 **f** 01403 710 155
e sales@turbosound.com **w** turbosound.com Sales
Dir: Rik Kirby.

Volt Loudspeakers Ltd Manor Farm, High St,
Burton Bradstock, Dorchester, Dorset, DT6 4QA
t 01308 898763 **f** 01308 898593
e info@voltloudspeakers.co.uk **w** voltloudspeakers.co.uk
 MD: David Lyth.

Wharfedale Professional Ltd
IAG House, Sovereign Court, Ermine Business Park, Huntingdon, Cambridgeshire, PE29 6XU **t** 01480 447709 **f** 01480 431767 **e** marketing@wharfedale.co.uk **w** wharfedalepro.com Int'l Marketing Manager: Lisa Fletcher.

Yamaha-Kemble Music (UK) Sherbourne Drive,
Tilbrook, Milton Keynes, Buckinghamshire, MK7 8BL **t** 01908 366700 **f** 01908 368872 **w** yamaha-music.co.uk MD: Andrew Kemble.

Studio Design & Construction

Acoustics Design Group 30 Pewley Hill, Guildford,
Surrey, GU1 3SN **t** 01483 503681 **f** 01483 303217 **e** acousticsdesign@aol.com Prop: John Flynn.

Asadul Ltd Hophouse, Colchester Road, West Bergholt,
Colchester, Essex, CO6 3TJ **t** 01206 241 600 **e** officeasadul@copperstream.co.uk Dir: Phil Gambling, Andy Raison.

AVD (FM) Ltd 342 St Leonards Rd, Windsor, Berks,
SL4 3DX **t** 01753 622666 **f** 01753 622666 **e** advltd@btinternet.com **w** avdco.com Director: Alan Stewart 07973 820090.

Black Box Ltd (UK) 1 Greenwich Quay, London,
SE8 3EY **t** 020 8858 6883 **f** 020 8692 6957 **e** info@blackbox-design.com **w** blackbox-design.com Director: Hugh Flynn.

Cablesystems 8 Woodend, London, SE19 3NU
t 020 8653 5451 **e** cablesystems@yahoo.com Owner: Alan Maskall 07771 755 339.

Eastlake Audio (UK) PO Box 160, Tonbridge, Kent,
TN12 8BX **t** 01892 722164 **f** 01892 722128 **e** info@eastlake-audio.co.uk **w** eastlake-audio.co.uk Director: David Hawkins.

IAC IAC House, Moorside Road, Winchester, Hampshire,
SO23 7US **t** 01962 873000 **f** 01962 873111 **e** info@iacl.co.uk **w** iacl.co.uk Sales Manager: Ian Rich.

Munro Acoustics Unit 3G1, The Leather Market, 11-
13 Weston St, London, SE1 3ER **t** 020 7403 3808 **f** 020 7403 0957 **e** andymunro@munro.co.uk **w** munro.co.uk Director: Andy Munro.

PG Stage Electrical Studio House,
Tameside Work Centre, Ryecroft St, Ashton under Lyne, UK, OL7 0BY **t** 0161 830 0303 **f** 0161 830 0302 **e** sales@pgstage.co.uk **w** pgstage.co.uk Managing Director: Paul Holt.

Recording Architecture Ltd (UK)
1 Greenwich Quay, Greenwich, London, SE8 3EY **t** 020 8692 6992 **e** ra@aaa-design.com **w** aaa-design.com MD: Roger D'Arcy.

Sound Workshop (Sound System Design/Installation) 19-21 Queens Road, Halifax,
W. Yorks, HX1 3NS **t** 01422 345 021 **f** 01422 363 440 **e** enquiries@thesoundworkshop.com **w** thesoundworkshop.com MD: David Mitchell.

The Studio Wizard Organisation Sawmill Cottage,
Melton Pk, Melton Constable, Norfolk, NR24 2NJ **t** 07092 123666 **f** 07092 123666 **e** info@studiowizard.com **w** studiowizard.com MD: Howard Turner 01263 862999.

Veale Associates 16 North Rd, Stevenage,
Hertfordshire, SG1 4AL **t** 01438 747666 **f** 01438 742500 **e** info@vealea.com **w** vealea.com MD: Edward Veale.

Nick Whitaker Electroacoustics
33 Occupation Lane, Shooters Hill, London, SE18 3JQ **t** 020 8319 2423 **e** nickwhitaker@homechoice.co.uk **w** nickwhitaker.homechoice.co.uk Designer: Nick Whitaker 07718 632 165.

Studio Miscellaneous

Audio Transfers @ Inflight Studios
15 Stukeley St, Covent Garden, London, WC2B 5LT **t** 020 7400 8569 **e** alex.tomlin@inflightstudios.com **w** ifsaudiotransfers.com Chief Engineer: Alex Tomlin 020 7400 8570.

GTek The Barley Mow Centre, 10, Barley Mow Passage,
Chiswick, London, W4 4PH **t** 020 8994 6477 x3069 **e** gtek@jgtek.demon.co.uk Prop: Jon Griffin.

John Henry's 16-24 Brewery Road, London, N7 9NH
t 020 7609 9181 **f** 020 7700 7040 **e** johnh@johnhenrys.com **w** johnhenrys.com MD: John Henry.

The LMS (Ronnie Lane Mobile Studio)
C/O The Smokehouse, 120 Pennington St, London, E1W 2BB **t** 020 7702 0789 **e** info@lmsmobilestudio.com **w** lmsmobile.com Contact: Paul Madden 07860 109612.

Madrigal Production Co Guy Hall, Awre,
Gloucestershire, GL14 1EL **t** 01594 510512 **e** artists@madrigalmusic.co.uk **w** madrigalmusic.co.uk myspace.com/madrigalmusicmanagement MD: Nick Ford.

Smokehouse Studios 120 Pennington St, London,
EW1 2BB **t** 0207 702 0789 **e** hello@smokehousestudios.com **w** smokehousestudios.com Contact: Paul Madden 07860 109612.

Speed Music PLC 195 Caerleon Road, Newport,
NP19 7HA **t** 01633 215 577 **f** 01633 213 214 **e** info@speedmusic.co.uk **w** speedmusic.co.uk Director: Nick Fowler.

Advertisers' Index

Advertisers

PPL — Inside front cover

Publishers
SongLink International — Divider
Publishers & Affiliates
First Music Control — 61

Design, Pressing & Distribution
Pressers & Duplicators
Clear Sound And Vision Ltd — 123
Sound Performance — 125
Blue Pro Media — 121
Mastering & Post Production
Blue Pro Mastering — 127
Printers & Packaging
The Box Set Company — 130
London Fancy Box Co Ltd — 131
Senol Printing — 133

Business Services
Web Sheriff — Divider
PPL (Phonographic Performance Ltd) — Divider
Accountants
Breckman & Company — 154
Legal
DWFM Beckman — 159
Music Royalty Investigations — 163

Press & Promotion
Music House Group — Divider
Promoters & Pluggers
Fleming Associates PR — 243
Lander PR Ltd — 245
Public City PR — 247
Stay Tuned — 248
PR Companies
A Star PR — 250
Stephen Anderson Publicity — 262

Live
John Henry's — Divider

Recording Studios & Services
Metropolis Group — Divider

BMI — Outside back cover

Sponsorship Advertisers

Design, Pressing & Distribution
Pressers & Duplicators
Sound Performance — 121-124
Mastering & Post Production
Blue Pro Mastering — 125-129
Printers & Packaging
The Box Set Company — 130-133
Distributors
Absolute Marketing & Distribution Ltd — 140-148

Business Services
Accountants
Bevis & Co — 153-158
Legal
Web Sheriff — 159-165
Artist Management
Web Sheriff — 166-190

Press & Promotion
PR Companies
Fifth Element PR — 249-264

Live
Venues
Indigo2 at the O2 — 283-309

Recording Studios & Services
Producers & Producer Management
Big Life Management — 331-343